Approaching Literature

Reading, Thinking, Writing

D0160981

Fourth Edition

Approaching Literature

Reading, Thinking, Writing

Peter Schakel
Hope College

Jack Ridl
Hope College

bedford/st.martin's
Macmillan Learning

Boston | New York

For Bedford/St. Martin's

Vice President, Editorial, Macmillan Learning Humanities: Edwin Hill
Editorial Director, English: Karen S. Henry
Senior Executive Editor: Stephen A. Scipione
Executive Editor for Literature: Vivian Garcia
Executive Development Manager: Maura Shea
Editorial Assistant: Julia Domenicucci
Senior Media Producer: Allison Hart
Publishing Services Manager: Andrea Cava
Production Supervisor: Robert Cherry
Marketing Manager: Sophia Latorre-Zengierski
Project Management: Jouve
Photo Editor: Angela Boehler
Permissions Editor: Arthur Johnson
Senior Art Director: Anna Palchik
Text Design: Jouve
Cover Design: John Callahan
Cover Image: Posing in Old San Juan, 2008, Laura James/Private Collection/Bridgeman Images
Composition: Jouve
Printing and Binding: Edwards Brothers Malloy, Inc.

Copyright © 2017, 2012, 2008, 2005 by Bedford/St. Martin's.

All rights reserved. No part of this book may be reproduced, stored in a retrieval system, or transmitted in any form or by any means, electronic, mechanical, photocopying, recording, or otherwise, except as may be expressly permitted by the applicable copyright statutes or in writing by the Publisher.

Manufactured in the United States of America.
1   0   9   8   7   6
f   e   d   c   b   a

For information, write: Bedford/St. Martin's, 75 Arlington Street, Boston, MA 02116
(617-399-4000)

ISBN 978-1-4576-8803-4

Acknowledgments

Text acknowledgments and copyrights appear at the back of the book on pages 1151–1157, which constitute an extension of the copyright page. Art acknowledgments and copyrights appear on the same page as the art selections they cover.

Preface for Instructors

In the fourth edition of *Approaching Literature: Reading, Thinking, Writing*, we have sought not only to include a diverse array of fresh literary works but also to streamline our own instructional text in order to make the pedagogy as accessible as possible. When students are required to take literature courses, it is not uncommon that their previous experience with literature is minimal. As teachers, we do not see ourselves as guardians of literature's stronghold but as its ambassadors and guides, reaching out to invite students to enjoy literature's beauty and be moved by its power, wisdom, and relevance. This has been our guiding principle in preparing *Approaching Literature*.

We're sure our students are not the only ones who have asked for a choice of literature that speaks to them, to their wide interests, varied cultures, and unique circumstances. Therefore, we have tried to shape the contents of this book to reflect the extraordinary diversity of contemporary literature while drawing on important writers and works of the past so that students may come to see how timeless great literature can be and affirm its continued resonance. Throughout, *Approaching Literature* mingles, juxtaposes, and connects recent and diverse writing with works from the traditional canon, often using the one as a gateway to the other.

We want students to understand that any literary work concerns itself with a multiplicity of ideas, not a single topic, theme, or view that readers must identify through some seemingly mysterious and esoteric method. Our approach, which teaches reading and writing as processes, affirms students' own experiences and cultural backgrounds as it enlarges their ways of perceiving and understanding. By reading Megan Foss's essay "Love Letters," for example, by identifying what she learned through writing and reading, by comparing her "lesson" with similar lessons from their own lives, students are empowered to see that reading literature and writing about it involves an exploration of *all* that can be discovered in a work and that such exploration can start from wherever they are, whatever their background.

We introduce writing sequentially, starting with observations that students write in the margins of books as they read and progressing by sensible, gradual steps to notes, journal writing, short critical papers, and longer research papers. We show how active reading can lead directly to student writing. The comments that students scribble in the margins of Alice Walker's "The Flowers" may culminate in a paper that analyzes the moment when a character's childhood innocence ends. We also emphasize that each strategy and form of writing, while valuable in itself, is part of an overall repertoire of skills that apply in many other reading–writing situations beyond a literature course.

In brief, our intention in *Approaching Literature* is to invite students in, to create an accessible introduction to fiction, poetry, and drama for all students, whatever their previous exposure to literature. The general principles outlined here guided us in all of our work developing this book. This will become clearer in a more detailed look at how these principles have influenced and shaped specific elements in our text.

Features of *Approaching Literature*

A Common Ground for Exploring Contemporary and Classic Literature

Lucille Clifton has said, "In this polyglot we call America, literature *has* to include all voices. Nothing else makes sense." This anthology, of course, does not include all voices (what anthology could?), but it does include, juxtapose, and connect an uncommon number of fresh, contemporary works with some of the most frequently taught texts from the traditional canon. It uses current voices to help students recognize the relevance of older works, and older works to see the depth and significance of newer works.

Classic and contemporary works are grouped in chapters that focus on the literary elements to facilitate understanding of that element. For example, in Chapter 9, students can study how tone, style, and irony work in Kate Chopin's nineteenth-century work "The Story of an Hour," along with Amy Tan's story "Two Kinds" and Daniel Orozco's "Orientation," written in the late 1980s and early 1990s, respectively. While chapters are focused on elements and forms, thematic connections can also be made throughout the selections in the book, especially through use of the new Contents by Theme.

Clusters of Short-Short Works

Our students delight in discovering that even the briefest literary works, when read closely, reveal startling and satisfying complexities. Thus, we offer a collection of very short literary works at the beginning of each genre's anthology; works such as Jamaica Kincaid's "Girl," Denise Levertov's "Leaving Forever," and Deanna Alisa Ableser's *Black Coffee* can be read quickly but examined deeply. Brief introductions to these sections explain how these forms—flash fiction, very short poems, and ten-minute plays—relate to the larger framework of the main genres.

A Student-Friendly Approach to Literature

We need hardly tell you that students enter introductory literature courses with varied levels of education and experience. *Approaching Literature* attempts to bridge those levels by addressing students in a way that does not presuppose prior knowledge of or experience with literature. We present information concisely, in step-by-step fashion, avoiding overly technical vocabulary. We pause frequently to summarize and remind; for example, every chapter ends with boxed checklists that serve as memory refreshers and quick references. Also, each chapter treating the literary elements begins with a very short story, poem, or play that sets an accessible and engaging tone for the chapter and provides illustrations for discussing the topic at hand. We include pictures of the students whose papers we reprint, along with their comments about writing those papers at each stage of the process, in the expectation that your students will discover that their concerns are shared and their experiences are reflected in the book.

A Focus on Active Reading

Right from the start, *Approaching Literature* invites students to become active readers. Our discussion of the reading process in Chapter 1 is built around a personal essay by Sherman Alexie and a creative nonfiction essay by Megan Foss, both of whom testify to how reading and writing saved their lives. Seeing how these writers participate fully with a work, connecting with it intellectually, emotionally, and imaginatively, reveals reading as a vital part of one's life and serves as an inspiration and a model for students' own active reading. Throughout the book, "Approaching the Reading" prompts precede the selections and provide students with context and ways to engage with the work holistically. "Reflecting on What You've Read" prompts follow the stories, poems, and plays; they give students ways to think critically about the work and to reflect on and apply the techniques of reading they have learned. By placing emphasis on what literary techniques and elements *do* and what readers do *with* them, we try to help students interact more deeply with literature and realize how enjoyable and meaningful stories, poems, and plays can be.

An Emphasis on Critical Thinking

Another central aim of this book is to foster habits and skills of critical thinking. By critical thinking, we mean two things: a set of skills for examining information and a developed ability to use those skills to guide one's responses. Critical thinking contrasts with passively taking in information and confining the reasons for remembering it only to comprehension. It is not just possessing a set of skills; it always involves using those skills in active, practical ways.

Thus, Chapter 1 stresses how students can develop habits of mind to engage fully with the texts they read—not simply to track what is going on in texts but to enter them imaginatively, to ask questions of them, and to resist settling for trite or simple answers. Chapter 2 helps students see themselves as makers of knowledge as they read with pens or pencils in hand, participate in discussions, analyze questions and topics, and construct argumentative theses and papers. Subsequent chapters on the elements of fiction, poetry, and drama discuss how to connect in personally important ways with literary texts, how to understand them on a level that goes beyond merely comprehending what is going on, how to interrogate, analyze, and value them—critical skills reinforced throughout the book by the reading prompts and writing assignments.

Practical Explanation of the Writing Process

Chapters 2, 3, 11, 20, and 25 lead students in a unified, cumulative, step-by-step way through the writing process. We begin with how to find possible topics to write about and how to shape these into successful topics by using critical thinking skills. We show how to turn the organization and development of ideas into convincing, well-supported arguments. Each stage of the writing process is accompanied by real student comments that address individual writing experiences, and the book provides five complete student papers, two of which are accompanied by rough drafts so students can see revision in action. Our aim is to offer the students who use the book models to follow that will give them confidence that they can do the work described in the chapters. In addition, the book provides sample marginal annotations, journal entries, and exam answers to clarify the different forms of writing.

Clear, Sensible Guidance on Using Sources and Research

The new edition is particularly attentive to twenty-first-century research challenges and includes specific coverage of the benefits and pitfalls involved in using electronic resources. Chapter 3 guides students step by step through the literary research process, from finding material, to reading it, evaluating it, incorporating it effectively, citing it accurately, and avoiding plagiarism. Each step of writing instruction is accompanied by a first-person account of how a student writer moved from conception to completion. It offers thorough, detailed, easy-to-use information about parenthetical citations and bibliography form and an annotated sample paper that provides a clear, helpful model for handling various situations students may encounter.

A unique feature of this book is its appendix on reading critical essays, which provides practical instruction on how to approach and read the academic essay, a genre that, in itself, is unfamiliar to many students and that students may be asked to use as sources in their own writing.

New to the Fourth Edition

Streamlined Instructional Chapters Designed to Be Taught in One Class Session

We have broken up our treatment of the literary elements and forms into shorter, more singularly focused chapters that can be taught easily in a single class period. For instance, in Part 3, Approaching Poetry, Chapter 16 now focuses solely on sound, with three short poems woven into the instructional apparatus, and four more poems offered as options for further reading. Our goal is to make the instructional chapters as accessible and readable as possible, even for today's busy students.

Continued Emphasis on Inclusiveness in Almost Forty-Five New Selections

We've continued to look for the most engaging, contemporary, and diverse literature while also bringing in canonical selections that have stood the test of time. Specifically, we have selected one new essay, fifteen new stories, twenty-five new poems, and four new plays for this edition, including:

- new examples of contemporary fiction by Daniel Orozco, George Saunders, Chimamanda Ngozi Adichie, Marjane Satrapi (graphic fiction), Edwidge Danticat, Lydia Davis, and Xu Xi; contemporary poetry by Janice Mirikitani, Ray A. Young Bear, Anna Maria Hong, Ted Kooser, Rita Dove, Honorée Fanonne Jeffers, and Billy Collins; and contemporary drama by Deanna Alisa Ablesera and Suzanne Bradbeer.

- new selections from canonical writers such as Ray Bradbury, Margaret Atwood, James Thurber, William Wordsworth, William Butler Yeats, Sophocles, and William Shakespeare.

More Ways to Teach and Connect the Works within the Anthology

Following the regular table of contents is a **new thematic table of contents** with shaded corners for easy access and suggests ways to teach and think about works across genre and form. Fruitful themes include coming of age, cultural clashes, earth and the environment, food, and identity. Our students delight in discovering the connections between works.

Up-to-Date and More Accessible Treatment of the Research Process

The discussion of writing a literary research paper in Chapter 3 has been fully updated to reflect current sources, citation models, and practices (based on the eighth edition [2016] of the *MLA Handbook*). A new student writer's research process is fully documented and annotated along with her final paper on Robert Frost's poem "After Apple-Picking." It provides students with a practical, current example of the research process in action.

Acknowledgments

We want to express again our appreciation to many colleagues at Hope College for their generous assistance and encouragement as we worked on this and earlier editions of *Approaching Literature*: Ion Agheana, Susanna Childress, John Cox, Jane Currie, Miguel De La Torre, Natalie Dykstra, Curtis Gruenler, Stephen Hemenway, Charles Huttar, Rhoda Janzen, Robert Kenagy, David Klooster, Marla Lunderberg, William Pannapacker, Pablo Peschiera, William Reynolds, Heather Sellers, Carla Vissers, and Jennifer Young—and especially to Jesus Montaño for his generous help in each edition. We want to thank Julie

Ridl and Elizabeth Trembley for their help in selecting and discussing graphic literature for this edition. Sarah Baar, office manager for the English department at Hope College, assisted us with research, use of computers, and preparation of manuscript copy. Special thanks to Deja Ruddick for her meticulous and imaginative revisions to and updating of Chapter 3.

We are grateful also to our students at Hope College, from whom we learn as they learn, and especially to Alicia Abood, Kortney DeVito, Julian Hinson, Sunkyo Hong, Kristina Martinez, Marisela Meraz, and Annie Otto for allowing us to include their writing in this book.

We appreciate also the assistance and feedback given by colleagues elsewhere to shape this fourth edition, especially Stephen Ahern, Acadia University; Douglas Barrett, Western Nevada College; Nancy Barta-Smith, Slippery Rock University; Tom Birol, Valencia College; Marilyn Boutwell, LIU Brooklyn; Mike Bove, Southern Maine Community College; Merlyn Brito, Valencia College; Allison Carpenter, Northampton Community College; Ernest Cole, Hope College; Christina Crossgrove, Barry University; Lynda Dekens, Lethbridge College; Bonnie Dowd, Montclair State University; Carolyn Fargnoli, Syracuse University; Barbara Goldstein, Hillsborough Community College; Ken Kerr, Frederick Community College; Cindy King, University of North Texas at Dallas; Albert LaFarge, Massachusetts College of Art & Design; Sharon Levy, Northampton Community College; Gerrie Logan, Montclair State University; Jordine Logan, Montclair State University; Jesus Montaño, Hope College; Stephanie Satie, California State University, Northridge; Peter Scheponik, Montgomery County Community College; John Steinbrink, University of Tampa; Kevin Sweeney, Southern Maine Community College; John VanDyke, Hillsborough Community College; Christa Verem, Montclair State University; and Ken Winkler, Santa Monica College.

Finally, we want to thank those at Bedford/St. Martin's who made this book possible and worked hard on it. We are grateful to Edwin Hill, Karen Henry, Vivian Garcia, and Steve Scipione for their support of the project and their vision for what the book should be. And we are grateful to those who helped develop the current edition in a number of ways: to Andrea Cava at Bedford/St. Martin's and John Shannon and Susan McNally at Jouve for guiding the book expertly through the production process; to Marianne L'Abbate for her attentive and knowledgeable copy editing; to Arthur Johnson for his careful and alert work on permissions; and Julia Domenicucci for her tireless assistance with research, manuscript preparation, and other details of revision. Finally, we want to express our gratitude to our editor, Maura Shea, for her amazingly helpful guidance and counsel as we worked on streamlining the book for its fourth edition. Because of her wide knowledge of literature; her experience in publishing; her intelligence, judgment, creativity, patience, and understanding, she seemed more like our coauthor than our editor. It was a great pleasure to work with her, and we are deeply indebted to her.

And we are profoundly grateful for the support of our wives, Julie Ridl and the late Karen Schakel.

Get the Most Out of Your Course with *Approaching Literature*'s Additional Resources for Teaching and Learning

Download Your Instructor's Manual.   Available online, the manual supports every selection in *Approaching Literature* with entry points, suggestions for opening discussions, provocative pairings for each selection, and useful teaching tips. Download the Instructor's Manual at **macmillanlearning .com/approachinglit/catalog**.

Join Our Community.   The Macmillan English Community is home to Bedford/St. Martin's professional resources, featuring content to support the teaching of literature — including our popular blog, *LitBits*, as well as articles, research studies, and testimonials on the importance of literature in our classrooms and in our lives. Community members may also review projects and ideas in the pipeline. Join at **community.macmillan.com**.

Package One of Our Best-Selling Brief Handbooks at a Discount.   Do you need a pocket-sized handbook for your course? Package *EasyWriter* by Andrea Lunsford or *A Pocket Style Manual* by Diana Hacker and Nancy Sommers with this text at a 20 percent discount. For more information, go to **macmillanlearning.com/easywriter/catalog** or **macmillanlearning .com/pocket/catalog**.

Teach Longer Works at a Nice Price.   Volumes from our Literary Reprint series — the Case Studies in Contemporary Criticism series, the Bedford Cultural Editions series, the Bedford Shakespeare series, and the Bedford College Editions — can be shrinkwrapped with *Approaching Literature* at a discount. For a complete list of available titles, visit **macmillanlearning .com/literaryreprints/catalog**.

Trade Up and Save 50 Percent.   Add more value and choice to your students' learning experiences by packaging their Macmillan textbook with one of a thousand titles from our sister publishers, including Farrar, Straus & Giroux and St. Martin's Press — at a discount of 50 percent off the regular prices. Visit **macmillanhighered/tradeup** for details.

LaunchPad Solo
macmillan learning

Pairing *Approaching Literature* with *LaunchPad Solo for Literature* helps students succeed.

Available for free when packaged with *Approaching Literature*, LaunchPad Solo for Literature gets to the heart of close reading. It offers a set of online materials that help beginning literature students learn and practice close reading and critical thinking skills in an interactive environment.

To package *LaunchPad Solo for Literature*, use ISBN 978-1-319-08498-1.

How can *LaunchPad Solo for Literature* enhance your course?

It helps students come prepared to class. Assign one of almost 500 reading comprehension quizzes on commonly taught stories, poems, plays, and essays to ensure that your students complete and understand their reading. For homework assignments, have students work through close reading modules that will prepare them for lively, informed classroom discussions.

It gives students hands-on practice in close reading. Easy-to-use and easy-to-assign modules based on widely taught literary selections guide students through three common assignment types:

- **Respond to a Reading**
  Marginal questions that refer to specific passages in a publisher-provided literary work prompt students to read carefully and think critically about key issues raised by the text.

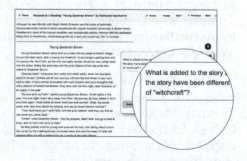

- **Draw Connections**
  Students read and compare two or more publisher-provided texts that illuminate each other. Students can download these texts, which have been annotated to highlight key moments and contextual information, and respond in writing to a series of questions that highlight important similarities and differences between and among the texts.

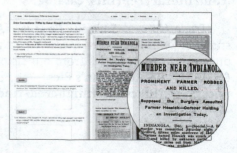

To explore *LaunchPad Solo for Literature*, visit **macmillanhighered.com/launchpadsolo/literature**.

- **Collaborate on a Reading**
  Instructors can upload their favorite text or choose from over 200 publisher-provided texts to create a customized lesson on close reading. Using the highlighting tools and notes feature in LaunchPad, the instructor can post notes or questions about specific passages or issues in a text, prompting students to respond with their own comments, questions, or observations. Students can also respond to each other, further collaborating and deepening their understanding of a text.

It lets you create multimedia assignments about literature. *LaunchPad Solo for Literature* enables you to embed videos, including favorite selections from YouTube, directly into your digital course. Whether you want students to analyze a Shakespearean scene, listen to W. B. Yeats reading his poems, or compare *The Great Gatsby* in print and on film, the tools are at your fingertips. You can annotate these videos for your students, or ask them to leave their own comments directly on the video content itself. Consider some of these assignment suggestions:

- **Create a Dialogue around an Assignment**
  Some projects are complicated because they involve many choices and stages. Record yourself explaining the project, and upload the video to the Video Assignment tool. Require students to comment by asking a question or by proposing a topic.

- **Critique a Video as a Group**
  Embed a video from YouTube or from another source. In your assignment instructions, provide discussion questions. Require students to add 2-3 comments on the video that respond to the prompt. You may grade this assignment with a rubric.

- **Collaborate on Acting out a Scene from a Play**
  Although students most often study plays as written texts, it can be fun and informative to have them act out scenes for their classmates. Assign small groups of students to record themselves acting out their favorite scene from a play and upload the video for the class to watch. You can add your feedback and comments directly on the video.

- **Compare and Share Poems Your Students Read Aloud**
  Sound is essential in poetry, and how a poem is read can be as important to understanding as the words themselves. Invite students to record themselves — either using video, or audio only — and share the results with the class. Consider giving each student a "mood" for their reading, so that the class can hear how different tones and interpretations affect their response to the poem.

Brief Contents

Contents

8   Setting
Meeting Meaning in Places   196

9   Tone, Style, and Irony
Attending to Expression and Attitude   221

10 Symbol and Theme
Being Open to Insights   247

11 Writing about Fiction
Applying What You've Learned   285

12 A Collection of Stories
Investigating Various Vistas   296

16 Sound

Hearing How Sense Is Said   502

PART 4   Approaching DRAMA   661

22 Reading Drama
Participating in Serious Play   663

23 Character, Conflict, and Dramatic Action
Thinking about Who Does What to Whom and Why   669

> "It's become stale to say something is NEW. What's the new new?
> We need the new NEW."

Contents by Theme

PLAY

THE ARTS

STORIES

POEMS

PLAY

ATHLETICS

STORIES

POEMS

PLAY

BIRTH

POEMS

THE CITY

STORIES

POEMS

PLAYS

CULTURAL CLASHES

STORIES

POEMS

PLAY

DEATH

STORIES

POEMS

PLAYS

EARTH AND THE ENVIRONMENT

POEMS

ECONOMICS

STORIES

NONFICTION

POEMS

PLAY

FAMILY

STORIES

NONFICTION

POEMS

PLAYS

FOOD

STORIES

HOME/GOING HOME

STORIES

NONFICTION

POEMS

PLAYS

IDENTITY
STORIES

LOSS

STORIES

POEMS

PLAYS

LOVE

STORIES

NONFICTION

POEMS

PLAYS

MEMORY

STORIES

NONFICTION

POEMS

PLAYS

NATURE

STORY

POEMS

PARENT-CHILD RELATIONSHIPS

STORIES

NONFICTION

POEMS

PLAYS

POVERTY

STORIES

POEMS

PLAY

PROGRESS/CHANGE

STORIES

POEMS

PLAYS

RACE

STORIES

NONFICTION

POEMS

PLAY

RELATIONSHIPS

STORIES

NONFICTION

PLAYS

RELIGION/GOD
STORIES

POEMS

SEASONS
POEMS

VIOLENCE
STORIES

POEMS

WOMEN'S ISSUES

STORIES

NONFICTION

POEMS

PLAYS

WORK

STORIES

Using This Book

- Terms that are **boldface** in the text are defined in the Glossary of Literary Terms at the end of the book.
- The dates provided for stories indicate their earliest publication; dates for poems give the first publication in a book; dates for plays are for their initial performance. For some poems, when publication was delayed, the probable date of composition is given as well, in *italics*.
- A rule (——) indicates a space break (in a story) or a stanza break (in a poem) that falls at the bottom or top of a page and otherwise might be undetectable.
- For untitled poems, the first line is often used as a convenient form of reference, although it should not be thought of as a title and thus does not follow the capitalization rules for titles.

Approaching Literature

Reading, Thinking, Writing

Approaching LITERATURE

Photo: Bernard Gotfryd/Getty Images

Overleaf: Alice Walker in the 1970s, around the time she wrote her second novel, Meridien *(1976), a semiautobiographical work about civil rights activists in the South of the 1960s. Alice Walker is known as a writer and an activist. As in her fiction, where characters often confront racism, sexism, and violence, in life Alice Walker travels the world speaking out and standing with the oppressed and impoverished. (See p. 1083 for a short biography.)*

I read because it takes me out of myself, it enlarges me. **Kathleen Norris**

(American Poet and Nonfiction Writer)

Reading Literature

CHAPTER **1**

Taking Part in a Process

Why read? Why take the time and possibly even the effort that a story, poem, or play requires when we have movies, television, DVDs, and the Internet? Maybe you already love to read and you know why. Maybe you used to read a lot, but something turned you away. Or maybe you never did like to read. If that's the case, we hope that you will consider what so many have discovered: that through reading they learned that they are not alone in what they've experienced. They have had their minds and their worlds opened to include new people and situations different from their own. They have found that the intimate experience of being engaged in reading a book can be personally meaningful and that this form of escape can be an entrance to something richly rewarding. They have found, as they read, that they learn, feel, and think; that they can pause to wonder or reflect; that they feel an inexplicable sense of being alive.

Reading to Connect with Others Although reading may seem at first like an individual act, it is by its nature shared and communal. We read what others have written. Reading is not only a source of ideas, challenges, and meanings but it is also an invitation to understanding, empathy, sympathy, judgment, and compassion. Reading enables us to connect with others, to enter the thoughts, feelings, and experiences of those both similar to and different from ourselves. Reading fills a deep yet often unrecognized need, assisting us to become more fully human and more fully humane.

3

APPROACHING THE READING

The following is a personal essay written by Sherman Alexie. An *essay* is a brief discussion, usually in prose, of a limited topic or idea; a *personal essay* deals with a particular part of its author's life and experience. Alexie grew up on the Spokane Indian Reservation in Wellpinit, Washington, where — surprisingly, he says — he found that first reading and then writing became essential to his very being. As you read the essay, pay attention to the way Alexie began reading — not at all a passive taking in, but an active engagement with the work before him. Notice also what goes on as you read the essay, how it requires you also to involve yourself actively in the process.

Sherman Alexie   b. 1966

Superman and Me   [1997]

I learned to read with a *Superman* comic book. Simple enough, I suppose. I cannot recall which particular *Superman* comic book I read, nor can I remember which villain he fought in that issue. I cannot remember the plot, nor the means by which I obtained the comic book. What I can remember is this: I was three years old, a Spokane Indian boy living with his family on the Spokane Indian Reservation in eastern Washington state. We were poor by most standards, but one of my parents usually managed to find some minimum-wage job or another, which made us middle class by reservation standards. I had a brother and three sisters. We lived on a combination of irregular paychecks, hope, fear, and government-surplus food.

> **APPROACHING THE AUTHOR**
>
> **Sherman Alexie** planned to be a doctor and enrolled in premed courses at Washington State University, but after fainting numerous times in human anatomy class, he realized he needed to change his career path.
>
> For more about him, see page 1053.

My father, who is one of the few Indians who went to Catholic school on purpose, was an avid reader of westerns, spy thrillers, murder mysteries, gangster epics, basketball-player biographies, and anything else he could find. He bought his books by the pound at Dutch's Pawn Shop, Goodwill, Salvation Army, and Value Village. When he had extra money, he bought new novels at supermarkets, convenience stores, and hospital gift shops. Our house was filled with books. They were stacked in crazy piles in the bathroom, bedrooms, and living room. In a fit of unemployment-inspired creative energy, my father built a set of bookshelves and soon filled them with a random assortment of books about the Kennedy assassination, Watergate, the Vietnam War, and the entire twenty-three-book series of the Apache westerns. My father loved books, and since I loved my father with an aching devotion, I decided to love books as well.

I can remember picking up my father's books before I could read. The words themselves were mostly foreign, but I still remember the exact moment when I first understood, with a sudden clarity, the purpose of a paragraph. I didn't have the vocabulary to say "paragraph," but I realized that a paragraph was a fence that held words. The words inside a paragraph worked together for a common purpose. They had some specific reason for being inside the same fence. This knowledge delighted me. I began to think of everything in terms of paragraphs. Our reservation was a small paragraph within the United States. My family's house was a paragraph, distinct from the other paragraphs of the LeBrets to the north, the Fords to our south, and the Tribal School to the west. Inside our house, each family member existed as a separate paragraph, but still had genetics and common experiences to link us. Now, using this logic, I can see my changed family as an essay of seven paragraphs: mother, father, older brother, the deceased sister, my younger twin sisters, and our adopted little brother.

At the same time I was seeing the world in paragraphs, I also picked up that *Superman* comic book. Each panel, complete with picture, dialogue, and narrative, was a three-dimensional paragraph. In one panel, Superman breaks through a door. His suit is red, blue, and yellow. The brown door shatters into many pieces. I look at the narrative above the picture. I cannot read the words, but I assume it tells me that Superman is breaking down the door. Aloud, I pretend to read the words and say "Superman is breaking down the door." Words, dialogue, also float out of Superman's mouth. Because he is breaking down the door, I assume he says, "I am breaking down the door." Once again, I pretend to read the words and say aloud, "I am breaking down the door." In this way, I learned to read.

This might be an interesting story all by itself. A little Indian boy teaches   5
himself to read at an early age and advances quickly. He reads *Grapes of Wrath* in kindergarten when other children are struggling through Dick and Jane. If he'd been anything but an Indian boy living on the reservation, he might have been called a prodigy. But he is an Indian boy living on the reservation, and is simply an oddity. He grows into a man who often speaks of his childhood in the third-person, as if it will somehow dull the pain and make him sound more modest about his talents.

A smart Indian is a dangerous person, widely feared and ridiculed by Indians and non-Indians alike. I fought with my classmates on a daily basis. They wanted me to stay quiet when the non-Indian teacher asked for answers, for volunteers, for help. We were Indian children who were expected to be stupid. Most lived up to those expectations inside the classroom, but subverted them on the outside. They struggled with basic reading in school, but could remember how to sing a few dozen powwow songs. They were monosyllabic in front of their non-Indian teachers, but could tell complicated stories and jokes at the dinner table. They submissively ducked their heads when confronted by a non-Indian adult, but would slug it out with the Indian bully who was ten years older. As Indian children, we were expected to fail in the non-Indian world. Those who failed were ceremonially accepted by other Indians and appropriately pitied by non-Indians.

I refused to fail. I was smart. I was arrogant. I was lucky. I read books late into the night, until I could barely keep my eyes open. I read books at recess, then during lunch, and in the few minutes left after I had finished my classroom assignments. I read books in the car when my family traveled to powwows or basketball games. In shopping malls, I ran to the bookstores and read bits and pieces of as many books as I could. I read the books my father brought home from the pawnshops and secondhand stores. I read the books I borrowed from the library. I read the backs of cereal boxes. I read the newspaper. I read the bulletins posted on the walls of the school, the clinic, the tribal offices, the post office. I read junk mail. I read auto-repair manuals. I read magazines. I read anything that had words and paragraphs. I read with equal parts joy and desperation. I loved those books, but I also knew that love had only one purpose. I was trying to save my life.

Despite all the books I read, I am still surprised I became a writer. I was going to be a pediatrician. These days, I write novels, short stories, and poems. I visit schools and teach creative writing to Indian kids. In all my years in the reservation school system, I was never taught how to write poetry, short stories, or novels. I was certainly never taught that Indians wrote poetry, short stories, and novels. Writing was something beyond Indians. I cannot recall a single time that a guest teacher visited the reservation. There must have been visiting teachers. Who were they? Where are they now? Do they exist? I visit the schools as often as possible. The Indian kids crowd the classroom. Many are writing their own poems, short stories, and novels. They have read my books. They have read many other books. They look at me with bright eyes and arrogant wonder. They are trying to save their lives. Then there are the sullen and already defeated Indian kids who sit in the back rows and ignore me with theatrical precision. The pages of their notebooks are empty. They carry neither pencil nor pen. They stare out the window. They refuse and resist. "Books," I say to them. "Books," I say. I throw my weight against their locked doors. The door holds. I am smart. I am arrogant. I am lucky. I am trying to save our lives.

REFLECTING ON WHAT YOU'VE READ

1. This chapter opens by giving some reasons people need to read. Which of those reasons do you think apply to Alexie? Why does he need to read?

2. List some things in Alexie's life that made love of reading difficult to sustain, that worked against his learning and growth. Think briefly about your own life. Do you love to read the way Alexie does? If not, are there factors that work against reading, that make it difficult to do or love?

3. Think about what is involved in the process of reading. How do ideas, feelings, and descriptions get from Alexie's heart and mind to your heart and mind? In what sense are you essential for the communication process to be complete?

Reading to Live   Alexie says he read to save his life. He doesn't mean surviving physically, of course. Rather, he realized that his mind and heart and imagination required regular nourishment, which he found could come from books. Without this nourishment, parts of himself, parts essential to his very identity that make him who he really is, would weaken and perhaps eventually starve. If you don't feel that way yourself, we hope this course and this book will lead you to the real value of making reading and writing a vital part of your life, perhaps even change your life. We hope that you will give reading a new chance, will put into reading the attentiveness and receptivity it requires and deserves. If it doesn't *save* your life, at least it certainly will *enrich* it.

THE NATURE OF READING

What Is Reading?   If reading is so important, it only makes sense to look more closely at it. Let's start with some very fundamental questions. What *is* reading? What goes on when we read? How do we "read well"? Reading is not just taking in the words on a page and extracting their meaning. That may be the first step for most people as they learn to read, as it was for Sherman Alexie, but reading has to go beyond that. We are not decoding machines like a radio receiving signals and emitting sounds. We are humans engaged in a fairly complex process that involves our whole beings. So, what actually happens when we read?

Reading as Sense-Making   Most reading specialists agree that reading is a sense-*making* activity. It is an interactive encounter between an author, a work, and a reader within a cultural context. The author takes ideas, details, and experiences and puts them into words (often called a "text"). The reader takes in the writer's words, processes them, relates them to what she or he already knows, and constructs pictures, feelings, and meanings. The writer depends on the reader to complete the process, to lift the words off the page and fill them with life and meaning. The way Alexie made sense of paragraphs and related them to his family and tribe is an example of how that process works.

Interacting Personally   Reading as a sense-making activity is inevitably personal and individual. What is written does not convey the same thing to every reader. That doesn't mean, of course, that a text means anything a reader says it means. "It is going to snow" cannot mean "An elephant is doing math," no matter what a particular reader asserts. There *is* a text; there *are* words and sentences on the page that we must look at, take in, and respond to. But *we* both discern what the words mean and fill the words with personal meaning.

ACTIVE READING

Completing What the Author Started The stories, poems, and plays in this book are not objects, not just words on a page; rather, they are potential works that are *completed in the reader's mind.* Texts (the words of the writer) are similar to musical scores: The notes on paper are only potential music until a musician brings them to life by performing them. So, too, the reader "performs" a story, poem, or play by bringing it to life in her or his mind through the method of active reading. There can be a text without a reader, but there can't be a living literary work (a story, poem, or play) without a reader (or listener) to complete what the writer began.

Responding Individually *Meaning,* then, is the result of an interaction between a piece of writing and an individual reader. Since no two people have the same personality and the same experiences, the story, poem, or play they actualize out of the same text, though perhaps similar, will not be identical. The rooms filled with books that you see in your mind's eye as you read "Superman and Me" may be similar to those someone else imagines, but they won't be the same; we shouldn't gloss over the difference by saying that it is only what they have in common that really matters.

Responding Holistically Your whole being—including your intellect, imagination, emotions, and values—can and should be involved in the reading process. Reading is not a spectator sport: We do not observe words passively from the sidelines. To be good readers, we need to participate, to be actively involved at every moment, with every word. As we read, we draw on our memories and our own understanding of definitions; we create pictures that make sense of the words and phrases we encounter; we anticipate what may be ahead; we revise our earlier anticipation in light of what we find later; we make judgments about what is said and done; and sometimes we need to revise those judgments to come to a satisfactory conclusion.

Responding Literarily All reading is not the same. Actively reading a chemistry book takes different skills from those you use in actively reading a novel; reading an Internet site differs from reading a newspaper. Active reading of literary texts asks you to imagine characters, form mental images, visualize locations and series of actions, and listen for sounds and rhythms. Actively reading literature requires you to pay attention not only to *what* is said but also to *how* it is said, to the techniques a writer uses to develop a work. This book is designed to help you do these things: Its chapters introduce features and techniques that will enrich your reading experience; develop your skills for reading fiction, poetry, and drama; and expand and strengthen your skills in writing about literature.

Responding Interactively   Active reading also involves asking questions, wondering "Why? Why? Why?" It includes talking with other readers, talking back to the author or text, underlining words and phrases, jotting notes in the margins, and perhaps writing an outline to clarify the organization of a work. (More is said about these particular reading strategies in Chapter 2.) Active reading is a challenging and an exciting skill, one that leads you to feel dynamically engaged with the work you are reading. You are no longer merely a passive recipient. You are an active participant. We believe this book will encourage you to develop this ability, leading you to find greater and greater pleasure and enrichment from reading literature and from writing about the works you read.

☑ CHECKLIST on Active Reading

❑ Read attentively and alertly—don't put off reading until the last thing at night when it's hard to concentrate.

❑ Adjust to the kind of material you are reading—when reading a chemistry textbook, your mind must be principally involved in studying the material; literary works, in addition to demanding your intellect, also require the involvement of your emotions and imagination.

❑ Respond to literature with your whole being—empathize with characters and situations, and let yourself feel a rich complex of emotions when the work calls for it.

❑ Use a pen or pencil—mark up the text if you own and plan to keep the book; take notes if you don't. Jotting things down helps you to concentrate and to remember.

❑ Interrogate the text—ask questions as you read, such as why some things are omitted, why other things are included, why a certain approach or technique is used, and what difference looking at things from another perspective would make.

APPROACHING THE READING

Why would someone write love letters, and keep writing them, but not put them in the mail? You'll find out a unique and very interesting answer in the following work.

"Love Letters" is an example of "creative nonfiction," a type of literature that tells about true things—this is Megan Foss's real story—but it uses techniques generally used in novels or short stories to make the writing more vivid and interesting. Thus, "Love Letters" describes people in detail, as if they were characters in a story, and it creates scenes in which the action pauses and the characters talk to each other in dialogue, as characters do in fiction. The dialogue does not necessarily reproduce, word for word, what the people involved actually said — the "creative" part of "creative nonfiction" allows for shaping events into scenes and for giving characters words similar to what those involved originally said.

As you read "Love Letters," watch for the way it is organized and the way it has passages describing events and scenes and passages of dialogue between characters. Think about whether the story would be less interesting and effective to read if the whole work was narrated the way the first five paragraphs are.

Megan Foss   b. 1957

Love Letters   [1998]

I

The first time my old man went to prison I wrote him letters. I wrote Darryl long rambling letters that went on for 10 or 11 pages.

I didn't have a home and I had maybe one change of clothes. Our car got confiscated when he got popped, along with everything I owned in the world except for what I was carrying in my backpack when it happened. So I didn't even have shoes at the beginning of that summer but I always had tablets of yellow paper and something to write with. I could fit that in my bag along with my hairbrush and bits and pieces of makeup and a prescription bottle fulla water and the leather cigarette case that held my syringes and cotton and twisted spoons.

> **APPROACHING THE AUTHOR**
>
> **Megan Foss** dropped out of high school after eighth grade. She resumed her formal education twenty years later and went on to earn two degrees at Western Washington University.

I wrote him letters and them tablets of paper got to be as critical for survival as black tape and crazy glue and bolt-cutters. And I can't think of anything much more suspicious in that community than a hooker who spent her spare time recording things on paper. I think I got away with it because it was the first thing I did after Darryl went away. I bought paper and wrote and folks who mighta otherwise found my behavior strange to the point of being problematic knew why I was writing. They knew I was Darryl Masters' old lady and he'd just gotten busted and if what made me happy was to sit and scribble it didn't disrupt anything critical in the life cycle. Sometimes people would watch me while I was writing with their eyes kinda narrowed studying me like I mighta been half-crazy and ask me why I was doing it. And I really didn't have an answer because although I wrote Darryl all them letters, I never mailed a single one.

The tablets would fill up with details about business and weather reports and stories about who was getting busted and who was getting sick. I remember sitting on the hood of a car in the parking lot at Marg's bar in my cutoffs with my legs crossed and dangling over the hood of the car and catching dates with that tablet on my lap. And I remember more than a couple sheriffs stopping to see what I was doing and scratching their heads and kinda chuckling at me. And even that didn't really seem to spook anybody. I suppose it shoulda occurred to me that sitting there with that tablet on my lap and a CoCo County Sheriff chatting me up wasn't the brightest thing I coulda done.

But I never thought about what I was putting in them tablets as informa-   5
tion. Never thought of it as secrets. That wasn't the purpose in writing. Darryl had been a constant presence in my life—we'd been together as close to 24/7 as two people could be. We shared the same pillow and the same air and the same food and the same dope and the same syringes. In all the months and years we were together I probably never said as many words out loud as I poured into a single one of them 10-page letters. And as long as I kept writing them I could pretend he was still there.

For a while I saved the tablets as they filled up but after I had three or four of them in my pack it started getting crowded and uncomfortable. Stuff would shift around inside and the hard cardboard corners would jab me in the back. So I started another ritual. As a new one would fill up I'd take the oldest and tear all the pages into tiny pieces and throw them away. Until I started doing that, people actually thought I was mailing the letters but Billy Jay Meckles caught me sitting in the 24-hour laundromat one night tearing up them pages and asked me what the hell I was doing. I started to shove the tablet I had half torn up back in my pack but he snatched it outa my hand. He didn't read anything on it—just held it there between us.

"They're just letters," I told him. Billy Jay was huge and probably had the potential to be one mean motherfucka after four years in the joint but he was one of the best-natured junkies I ever knew. He was always finding something to laugh at and the one or two girls working the streets who had kids always left their kids with Billy Jay when they worked. He kept himself fixed that way. The kids never lasted long. Social Services always ended up taking them away but while they were there, he was kinda like the community daycare. It was partly cause he always had a place to live—his mom had left him a small house that he managed to hang onto in between visits to the pen—but it had more to do with knowing kids were safe with Billy Jay. Their mothers could go to work and not have to worry about them and when they picked them up they always dropped off a piece of dope. Billy Jay probably had the cleanest hustle on the stroll.

His eyebrows arched over his round bright blue eyes and he tossed a long blonde curl off his shoulder. "Why aren't ya mailing them?"

"I will. That was just a kinda practice letter. Didn't really say what I wanted to say." The zipper was open on my pack and you couldn't help but see the other two tablets covered with ink and pages curling up at the corners.

"How long ya been trying to find the right thing to say?" he asked and 10
pointed at my pack.

"I don't know. What difference does it make?" I liked Billy Jay but he was
getting into shit that he couldn't possibly understand.

"It makes a difference if Darryl ain't gettin any of them letters."

"He does—he will."

"Ya mean in all this time ya ain't mailed a single one? Shit Mickey, he's
been gone almost three months."

I cringed when he said it. I'd let people think we were in pretty close 15
contact.

If anybody had actually thought beyond the words I said, they woulda realized how unlikely that was. Where could he write to me at? But people with
habits don't have time to waste analyzing shit like that so when I told folks he
was doing good and I couldn't wait to see him, they just accepted it. And maybe
after a while I convinced myself that somehow we were still in contact. That just
writing the letters kept us together.

But Billy Jay had done time and he knew what them letters meant and he
wasn't letting it go. "Why aren't ya mailing them? He's probably goin outa his
mind, Mickey."

I didn't answer. Didn't have an answer. At least not one I wanted to share
with him. He'd think I was crazy and I wasn't entirely sure he woulda been
wrong in his assessment. As long as writing had a purpose—a reason—it made
sense. Writing to communicate was logical. Just wandering around scribbling
thoughts and observations down for no apparent reason pointed to one of two
things. A rat or a nut. I knew it wasn't the former and that left only the crazi-
ness as an option. And if I told Billy Jay the real reason I wasn't mailing the
letters, I knew he'd confirm my diagnosis.

He sat down beside me on the wood slat bench. "What's up with ya, girl?
Why ya writing all this shit down if ya don't plan on sending it to him?"

"I do. I am gonna send them." I paused and then latched onto what seemed 20
like a reasonable excuse only because of the pressure I felt to come up with one.
"I don't got any stamps or envelopes."

"Ya make two or three-hundred bucks a night—what's a fuckin stamp
cost?" It wasn't how much they cost. It was acquiring them that was the real
problem. You could buy postage stamps in some of the grocery stores, but I
hadn't been in a regular grocery store in over a couple years. I'd got so accustomed to getting thrown outa places of business in Bella Vista that I stopped
going anywhere but Dave's liquor store—and Dave didn't sell stamps. And in
the beginning when Darryl first went away, I'd intended to mail them letters
and I'd even got as far as the parking lot of the Thrifty Foods intending to go in
and buy stamps and an envelope. But I'd stood outside with the sun so hot on
my shoulders I could smell the heat rising off my skin and changed my mind.
Even if I'd had shoes I don't think I coulda forced myself to go in there. We
owned the streets in Bella Vista but the square folks owned the grocery stores
and the restaurants and gas stations. When they had to go out on the streets,

they drove with their windows rolled up and the doors locked and their eyes aimed anywhere but at the working girls and I knew if I went in that store the same thing would happen. I'd walk up to the cash register with a small box of envelopes and ask for a sheet of stamps and no one would respond. Their eyes would go over my head and they'd wait on the person ahead of me and behind me but they'd refuse to see me. And if I made them see me, they'd have me thrown out.

And the post office was absolutely outa the question—all them people in uniforms. So that day in fronta the store I told myself I'd come back at night. And when I went back at night I told myself the next time I had a little extra cash I'd get a pair of shoes and then go back to get my stamps. And after a while I stopped bothering to make excuses to myself. After a while I found that I liked writing the letters better because I knew I'd never mail them. But it was a long time until I understood why and saying something like that to Billy Jay without a good why to back it up wouldn't fly.

"Girl I'm gonna buy some fuckin stamps and envelopes and we're gonna mail some of them letters. Homeboy's gotta be tweakin hard about this by now." I hated hearing him talk about Darryl being in prison. I hated hearing anybody talk specifically about it. When people asked about him they didn't say, So how's Darryl doing in the joint? They just asked how he was and I could say fine like he was just waiting for me out in the car.

"Ya know what, Billy? You're gonna think I'm fuckin spun—but it's like—as long as I don't mail them letters I don't gotta think about him bein gone."

"Huh?"

25

"It's like I'm just savin stuff up to tell him when he gets back at night. And then at night I know he's not coming back—at least not for a long time—and I can't stand thinkin about it so I just shove it all outa my mind. I tell myself he just went off to cop or take care of some business and he'll be here when I wake up in the mornin."

It was only half a lie. It was my habit more than anything else that kept me from mailing the letters. I learned in those first few months when Darryl was gone and I not only had to earn the money but had to take care of business too, that even something as minimal as mailing a letter required more energy units than I had to spare if I was gonna stay fixed and on toppa my hustle. It's hard to conceive that such a tiny task coulda been so entirely overwhelming but it was. And I knew within the first couple weeks that I'd probably never mail a single one. And on those rare occasions when I allowed myself to remember that Darryl was in prison and not waiting for me at the motel or in the car out by the river—I did know that we was suffering for my inability to get it together. I did know that he'd be sitting up in his cell late at night wondering if I'd stopped loving him. The girl before me did him like that.

He'd loved Bridget like a kid loves the first time, only he was almost 30 when he loved her. And when he went to the joint she hooked up with a heroin-dealer named Fernando and as hard as them guys in the joint are—shit like that rocks their world.

And he'd thought when he went in that I was gonna get clean and when he got out we were gonna do the square thing and have a place to live with walls and rooms instead of back seats and front seats. That had been his insurance against losing me while he was down. Clean — he thought I'd wait for him. Hooked — he thought I'd pull a Bridget on him. Not having heard a single word from me since they transferred him to Vacaville from the county lock-up in Martinez — he musta spent endless empty hours working out scenarios of betrayal in his mind. But I hadn't done any time then so even my worst imaginings didn't come close to understanding such an experience.

II

I mailed him the letters I wrote the first time I went to jail. The first time I 30 went and stayed. I didn't fill up tablets fulla letters but the ones I wrote did get mailed. The county gave us unlimited access to paper and pencils and envelopes. You could get five pages and an envelope mailed for a single stamp and they even gave us two free stamps a week. You didn't wanna go over the five-page limit cause that would take both your stamps.

Years later he'd claim he never got the letters but I mailed them to his sister's house and they never got returned to me at the jail, so I know they went somewhere. They were very different letters. No long wandering descriptions of how the leaves on the tree branches hanging over the river made shadows that looked like lace in the moonlight. No convoluted explanations about what it was like to fall in love with someone else while he sat in the joint pumping iron and occasionally reading about my latest bust in the paper. No spiraling logic that attempted to claim it wasn't really the same thing as what Bridget did because I'd fallen in love with a girl and it didn't take anything away from him or mean that I loved him any less. There weren't any of them things to write about in jail. And we'd been separated since he got outa the joint that last time so I couldn't even write to him about what it was like being separated from him because it was Charley I hurt for and reached for in the night. But writing was one of the few officially sanctioned ways to pass the time and Darryl was the only person I knew who had a place he could collect mail from so I wrote letters to him.

And because paper and pencils were the only things we had access to without having money on our books — writing was the most normal thing in the world to do. Reading and writing. The library cart came around once a week. The first few weeks I kicked too hard to care about living or dying much less communicating with the free world or tuning into the completely familiar paranoia in Robert Ludlum novels. And at first when I started to feel better all I wanted to do was sit in fronta the TV. I hadn't seen TV for months and I hadn't seen it through clear eyes for years. I missed the Reagan years almost in their entirety and watching the news fascinated me. Movies and MTV and soap operas were fun to watch but the news was the first real look I'd had at the straight world since getting strung out.

I mean—I'd seen the news and TV from time to time. The nights we had motels we always had the TV on—but them people on the news then had been them and we'd been us and it was very different tuning in when I'd been clean for a few weeks because I was no longer sure where the boundary was.

That's what I wrote to Darryl about while I was in jail and that's why I mailed them letters. I wrote to him about how it would be when I was back on the streets. I wrote to him in order to establish where my future would happen. I wrote to try to document that boundary line and my position relative to it. And my world would undoubtedly be a very different place today if he'd answered my letters. If he'd confirmed my vision. But he didn't. He never got the letters and what he might have done if he had is a question we prefer to leave unanswered between us. And after a month passed and I didn't get a single response, I stopped writing the letters with the intention of mailing them.

I lucked out when I did my time. I don't know how county jails in other 35 jurisdictions work but in the winter of '88 the powers that be at the CoCo County jail seemed to be of the opinion that rehabilitation did serve some purpose. I had access to psychologists and spiritual advisers and books and excellent public defense and people whose whole jobs were about helping people like me make some kinda life plan against the day when the door locked behind instead of in fronta them. And I had access to an English teacher.

I had no idea how much time I was gonna do. It took almost 40 days to get all the charges straightened out. For the most part they were misdemeanors but there were a couple potential felonies that coulda pulled a couple years. One thing I did know for certain was that less was better than more and when I found out I could get time off my eventual sentence by attending classes I jumped on it.

They had art classes and English classes and I signed up for both. I had almost no interest in art but that was another one of them things you could do with the free paper and pencils so I was willing to give it a shot—along with everybody else. We had so many people doing art that they had to use the big visiting room to hold class and twice a week we earned a half-day off our sentences sitting down and listening to a short young blonde woman talk to us about art.

We had mostly men in the art class and it was kinda comical to watch the tiny and clearly uncomfortable young teacher trying to be the leader amongst that group of hard-core gangsters. She'd hold her books up and point to something and talk about DaVinci and her finger would be visibly shaking when she pointed at the text. I realize now that she was trying to teach theory but she didn't have any kinda art-theory that spoke to them guys. They kept pointing to the tattoos on their arms as art. Smoking guns and reapers and leaping panthers with huge and clearly articulated musculature and it was obvious that nothing in her education had prepared her to theorize on that particular form. She kept insisting that it wasn't art but she couldn't explain why. And we knew enough about theorizing to be able to poke holes in everything she said after that.

Half the guys on the unit went to art class but there were only two of us who went to the English class and we were both female. The English teacher wasn't particularly young or even remotely nervous. She woulda been far better prepared to handle the homeboys who were always cracking on the art teacher but art wasn't her calling. Letters were her thing.

She was tall and had long cinnamon-colored hair with random strands of silver growing everywhere and she stood at least 5' 9" in her flats. Because there were just the three of us we didn't need a larger room. We didn't use a room at all. We sat at one of the tables they used at chow time to serve up and on the first day the first thing she had us do was take a spelling test. Shelley was the other girl in the class. She had the cell next to me and we kinda chuckled when the teacher told us we were having a spelling test because we spent a bunch of our spare time playing Scrabble. "Maybe this will improve my game," Shelley said.

That made it seem a little less childish and I raised my eyebrows and said, "Ya never know."

I don't remember any of the words on that test except the single one I missed. Dessert. The teacher used it in a sentence so I knew she was talking about cake and pie and shit like that but I spelled it "desert." And she gave me one of them cheesy tips for remembering how to spell words like that—words that have two different meanings depending on how you spell them.

"When you're trying to remember whether it's one s or two, tell yourself that you like two helpings of dessert," she said. If I've spelled that word wrong since then, it was a typo.

We sat there after the test and talked about English for a while. And it's almost impossible to imagine now—but at the time I didn't have enough knowledge about what English was to know that it was about writing and how to use words until the teacher explained it that way. Shelley got bored shortly after the spelling test when the teacher started talking about reasons for writing but I kept listening. It was much like the conversations I'd had with myself when I was carrying around them notebooks fulla words that weren't ever gonna get read by anybody but me. And then when the two hours were over, I had an idea.

"Could I—like do some kinda homework and get time-credit for it?"

She studied me for a second. "Maybe. What do you have in mind?"

I didn't quite know how to say I wanted to write. It felt embarrassing. When I didn't say anything she said, "I can't give you time-credit for just reading. Everybody in here reads. If I gave time-credit for everybody in here reading books, we could have everybody released by Easter."

"No," I told her. "I wasn't thinkin about readin. I was thinkin about writin. I been doing a lot of writin."

"What kind of writing?" She seemed honestly interested and it made me comfortable talking about it. For the most part I'd gotten used to people thinking I was strange for writing—strange for wanting to write. But this woman seemed to value the act.

"Well—they started out bein letters—," I paused and she interrupted me.   50
"Everybody in here writes letters too," she said.
"Well they're not really letters. They started out bein that way but I never mailed them and they kinda turned into—well I'm not sure what you'd call them. Stories maybe."
"Have you been doing that ever since you got here?"
"Shit—I been doin it for a few years now."
"Really?" She said it like she really wasn't expecting an answer. She finished   55
gathering up her books and materials and then stood there with it all piled up in her arms staring at me and I started being sorry I'd mentioned it. Suddenly it seemed like the quintessential arrogance to think I had anything to say that might qualify as a story. And she was looking at me like she couldn't decide whether or not to take me seriously—whether or not I wanted to write or just wanted to get outa jail faster.
"Tell you what I'll do. You bring something you've already written to the next class and I'll read it. Then we'll talk about time-credit. OK?"
I nodded and said, "OK," trying to think of what I had already written up in my room that I could show her.
Later that night in my cell I looked through the stack of papers on my little wooden writing table. I didn't know what she'd be expecting or what she'd be looking for. Mostly what I had in my cell didn't add up to more than a diary of the time I'd been there. Anecdotes and details about the people I shared that space with but not really stories and I told her I wrote stories.
The journals probably woulda served my purpose but somewhere between thinking that I might be able to get time off my sentence in exchange for my scribbling and sitting at my desk trying to decide what to show her my purpose changed a tiny bit. I cared about what she thought for what it could gain me but I also started caring what she thought simply for the sake of the story.
I went back in my mind looking for stories and finally decided I'd write a few   60
pages about Charley. I spent the next four days reconstructing a moment from our relationship and whatever the teacher had been looking for musta been there cause after she read it she agreed that for every two pages I wrote she'd give me credit for one class session. The first independent study project of my education.
And I spent hours sitting at that desk after that. During the day I still hung out on the unit and watched Madonna on MTV and played Scrabble with Shelley but I took to staying up half the night with pencil and paper. I wrote so much my pencils always went dull before I'd quit and go to sleep. The last thing I did before lock-down was sharpen all my pencils and by morning, the points were always all rubbed down to smooth black nubs.

Darryl never wrote but he came to see me twice. Charley ended up in the hospital with endocarditis that winter and so she couldn't come but Darryl did manage to show up two different times.
I'd been there almost two months when he finally showed up. I don't suppose I really had any right to expect anything more from him because we'd been

separated for a while when I got popped—but I did. I'd taken care of him for years and I'd expected him—at least while I was at County—to do the same. To make sure I had money for cigarettes and candy bars from the canteen. To buy a bag of Taffy Creme cookies. Life's little luxuries.

By the time he showed up, I'd begun to think about options other than returning to the back seats and the spoon and the grasping hands on my body. I'd begun writing a different kinda letter. With my world on the streets completely cut off I turned—for the first time in years—towards the people I'd spent the first years of my life with. My family. Initially those letters were just to make contact—to re-establish connections that had been stretched and frayed and miswired and all but irreparably severed over the years. When my sentence and my charges were being negotiated, the court sent one of them people who specialize in rehabilitation plans to see me and the first thing the man told me to do was try to make family contact. "One of the things they're going to consider when they look at your time is what your odds are for becoming a productive member of society. You're looking at some serious felonies but the courts have been known to reduce those to misdemeanors in those cases when the defendant has a workable plan for being mainstreamed," he told me.

"Mainstreamed?"

"Becoming a part of mainstream society. Things like having a home and learning how to find a job and take care of yourself."

In the back of our minds we all knew that was what kept us from getting straight. Being hooked on heroin didn't keep us in the spoon so much as our lack of knowledge about the world outside of it. We didn't know how to "mainstream" and in those opaque shadow moments of solitude when we allowed ourselves to think about what existed beyond our borders, we didn't know how they did it—the people in the mainstream. When they needed a place to live we didn't know how they found one. Did they just walk up to apartment buildings and say, I need one of these? We knew that when they needed jobs they used their experience to get them—but we didn't have any experience. And we couldn't even get most businesses to let us in when we had money. How could we ever have gotten them to pay us to be there? But the county had them people who specialized in teaching people like me how to do just exactly that.

And the first parta that process had to do with what the man called "creating a community." He told me that sometimes religious organizations sponsored people like me but for the most part, our families were our last chance to avoid the pen. The words came strained and passive at first—but I wrote them letters and they were the first contact I had with the outside world in years. The doctors and the teachers and the advisors in jail all belonged to that outside world—but I was their job. We were their jobs. Those first tentative letters were an attempt to make contact with a world that had no obligation to acknowledge me. A peace treaty after living for years as one half of a them-against-us equation. And initially my plan was to make that contact and convince my parents to agree to participate in planning my rehabilitation. I didn't plan on going through with it but at the time I needed them involved to turn those

65

felonies into misdemeanors. Like the English classes—the letters I wrote my parents had the potential to cut my time.

If Darryl had come to see me sooner that's probably the only purpose the letters ever woulda served. But somewhere in that second month—between the letters on the Scrabble board and the letters in the spelling tests and the letters to and from my parents—the words became the girders in the formation of a straight identity. I would write about a future absent of drugs and sleeping in cars and working in cars and living and loving on street corners in random moments stolen from the larger narrative of addiction. They were non-specific words because I didn't know any of those specifics. I could only think of the future in terms of the past. It held no meaning beyond what it was not. But as non-specific as the words were, they were the only familiar territory that existed in that limbo. Words were the same on either side of the equation. Later I would discover how many different things a single word could mean—but then I latched onto the idea that language was the same on both sides of the bars. They might not let me go in their restaurants or pay me money to do a job—but if I used the words right there was no way to tell that I was any different from any one of them. And initially I recognized words as tools to perpetuate a scam. I could use them to con people. And if Darryl hadn't waited so long to put in an appearance, I probably never woulda understood how much more letters and words could be than a means to an end.

But he waited and by the time he showed up the words I was writing had 70 shifted in purpose. I was by no means sure that I wanted to change my life. To leave the only home and the only family I'd known for years—to go play at being normal. But I had stopped believing that I couldn't. I believed that in the language I'd found a way out—I just hadn't definitively decided to take it. And now in my letters and in my stories I was writing to discover. To come to the decision.

The second and last time Darryl came, I still hadn't decided. I'd made all the plans. My parents had written letters agreeing to provide me with a home and supervision should the court choose to release me into their custody. I'd had lengthy discussions with counselors about rehabilitation—about AA and NA and CA and all them other alphabet groups. I'd gone to my classes and been a model prisoner and convinced my public defender that—oh yeah—I was that one in a thousand you could put your faith in. I convinced them all. Using words.

I just hadn't convinced myself. It all sounded good in theory. But the theories had all been developed by people with big fancy degrees and I could tell by the way they talked that they didn't have much grounding in practice. My visions of their world lacked the specifics to make it truly conceivable. And their theories had specifics but they were irrelevant enough to make the reality of my life almost inconceivable to them. Their specifics came from books and those books were written by people who got their information from books—ad infinitum. And when the man from the courthouse talked to me about things like finding jobs, I doubted if any of the words he knew coulda helped me where I needed it most. He could talk to me about appearance and the kinda questions I'd get asked on applications. He could even—with the assistance of some tests—tell me what I'd probably be best at. But he couldn't tell me how—after my almost 15 years of prostitution and all that accompanies that—to deal with men on any other level. He couldn't tell me how to keep myself from flinching if a man moved quickly in my presence. Couldn't tell me how to believe that they looked at me and saw anything but sex. I had some understanding of their side of the equation because I'd lived those first years of my life there. But they didn't know anything concrete about the place they were trying to pull me away from and so as great as their theories sounded—I kept finding holes in them. As much as I found myself drawn to the future those theories promised—it was still a blind date and I wasn't sure I wanted to go.

Until Darryl came to see me that last time. He sat on his side of the glass and I sat on mine and there wasn't anything specific in his words or his appearance that made me decide to go. He'd been outa the pen for almost seven months on that run and it was starting to tell. He'd gotten thin and his normally deep-set brown eyes looked sunk almost into the back of his skull with the dark purple shadows beneath them. His hair had grown down to his shoulders and was dull where the street dust stuck to the grease because he had nowhere to wash it. And while seeing that after two months being clean mighta convinced some people that they never wanted to live that way again, it just reminded me that if I left I'd be leaving half my life behind. A lifetime of living dirty on the streets—but it was my lifetime and all I had.

Nothing he said or did made up my mind. There was never any one deciding factor. But sitting there looking at him through the glass I caught myself trying to memorize the details of his appearance. The way his eyebrows grew together and the front tooth that was broken. The tiny mole beside his mouth that disappeared in a wrinkle when he smiled. The smooth satin drawl of his voice when he tipped his head and said "Aw Mickey—don't go" like he had a hundred times before. Only when he said it at the jail that day I snatched the words and ironed them into memory. Tone by tone. And then I realized I'd never see him again. Never hear him say them words again. I was going home.

I wrote one more story. Once I decided to leave, the hardest part became 75 shoving away the thoughts of everything and everyone that would stay behind. And there were a thousand places and things and people I'd miss but they all massed in my mind as Darryl. He'd been the single longest presence in my life. In my mind he became the embodiment of the specifics of memory. When I cried for all things lost, the picture in my mind was of Darryl sleeping in the backseat of the Oldsmobile. Or Darryl standing at the payphone calling for dope. Or Darryl reminding me to wear shoes because it was getting to be cold again. And during the day with access to the support system I had developed, it seemed entirely doable. But at night I would tell myself I'd never be able to pull it off. Never be able to leave him and go on into that alien place where my parents lived almost a thousand miles away.

So I wrote that last story and attempted to envision a future without Darryl and all that he'd represented in the past. And I didn't start out planning to kill him off but that's how it worked out. It took 30 handwritten pages and in the end I lived and he died and once I put the last word on the last sheet of paper—it was over. He was dead and so there was no longer anything to grieve about leaving. He was already gone.

Of course I knew it wasn't true. But just like never mailing him the letters I wrote the first time he went away allowed me to pretend he wasn't gone until such time as my mind could handle the reality—writing that story helped me to bury the past until it was safe to resurrect it.

III

I didn't go to jail and read "Native Son" and suddenly come to some blinding insight about how my own experience hooked up with the larger narratives of society. Didn't discover the power of voice in the words of others. Years later I read Richard Wright and found myself incredibly drawn to Bigger Thomas—to the many similarities in our experience. But in jail I wouldn't have had the knowledge base to appreciate them similarities. I didn't know anything about power structures or dominant classes and I wouldn't have had the ability to appreciate Bigger's position relative to those things anymore than I could have appreciated my own.

I went to jail and I wrote because the writing had value. It was a commodity and I could trade it for freedom. It had a purpose I could identify. In the process I discovered the myriad other purposes and value inherent in the act and I ended up writing in jail for the same reasons I wrote them letters I never mailed. I wrote to discover and I wrote to heal and I wrote to decide. I wrote to make meaning in a world that held none.

And the first thing I bought with the first paycheck I earned on the outside 80 was a typewriter. In those first few years when I understood nothing—I wrote to make sense outa the things I observed around me. Once I got to Washington and had them thousand miles to cross if I really wanted to go back, I allowed myself to remember that Darryl was alive and I started writing long rambling letters again. I wrote long commentaries on what it felt like to come into the straight world. I wrote about how nice it was to keep my body private and untouched. What it was like to have a home of my own with a door that I could lock. I wrote about how long it took me to stop instinctively thinking I needed to run when I saw a cop and about what it felt like to go shopping—to pay for things and carry them outa stores in bags instead of my pockets. About gaining the ability to move amongst the public without being picked off—without looking like an other. I wrote about what it felt like to pass. But I still didn't mail the letters. Not yet. I was still in a state of becoming and didn't yet know who or what I would become.

But one thing I learned early on was that people are judged by their use of language—that how they spoke could define them as trailer-park trash or it could define them as being potentially suitable for admittance to the country club. I knew that my successful reinvention would depend on how facile I could become with words. I read constantly—trying to teach myself all the things I'd never had instruction in. I learned how to imitate the precise conventional language that marked people as educated so well that when I took entrance exams at the local community college, I placed directly into freshman English without any prep classes. And for the next two years I was trained in formal academic prose until I could spit out papers on anything from the development of the atomic bomb to Henry VIII's obsession with having a son.

But I missed my language. The ungrammatical non-standard English that in its broken rhythms seemed to define the broken rhythms of our lives on the streets. And for a while I prided myself on speaking two languages. I told myself that I was socially bilingual—that it was a gift because I could walk in two worlds. That's what I told myself but I couldn't avoid knowing that the other language was useless because nobody in my here and now spoke it. So I poured it all into the letters that I kept writing to Darryl but even that was hollow because I had nowhere to mail them.

By the time I transferred to the university I was an English major thoroughly indoctrinated in how to speak and compose according to arbitrary conventions created by people who'd been dead for centuries and whose lives bore no resemblance to my own. I had masked and altered and realigned my voice until even I wasn't sure that I'd ever spoken any other way—that there'd ever been a girl who called herself Mickey Masters who wrote down the lives she'd encountered selling her body on Willow Pass Road all those years ago.

And then I found Darryl. It amazed me—while I was on the phone with the California Department of Corrections and the Parole Board—how if I spoke with authority and big words, they'd give me the information I wanted. How language was the biggest con of all. I thought of the thousand ways I coulda exploited that knowledge if I'd only had it back then. You could tell virtually any lie and if you spoke properly, people didn't pause to question. In the other language it didn't matter what I said because nobody ever looked beyond what my voice said about my social circumstances to try to make out my words.

Darryl was at San Quentin doing a parole violation when I found him and finally—almost 10 years after I wrote the first one—I mailed him letters. The past had become so distant that the first one I mailed began "you might not remember me. . . ." But once we started writing and reliving memories, the lazy cadence and the singular vocabulary of the streets took over my writing. 85

And some of it spilled over into my schoolwork. It seemed to me like the creative part of creative writing would allow me to use my own voice but I got told that using words like "hermeneutics" and "gonna" in the same sentence just wouldn't fly. That no one would buy such a voice. The gentle elderly professor of my nonfiction class told me that he'd be more comfortable if I'd present my prose as fiction. Perhaps then such a voice would be acceptable. In real life no one would ever believe that a $20 hooker with an eighth-grade education would know what hermeneutics meant. And when I tried to tell him that he was wrong—that I had known what the word meant—he told me it didn't matter. No one would believe it. I could never tell it true because the truth was somehow too disturbing. And it wasn't the $20 blow jobs or the self-mutilation of my veins that disturbed him as much as it was the apparent conflict between language and experience. I think I understand what's at the core of that discomfort. I think I understand that to accept that the drug-addicted hooker that I was could have possessed intelligence and critical thinking skills somehow speaks to a societal failure as well as my own. And so rather than forcing the world to question its own assumptions—rather than challenging the status quo—I was told to present my life as a lie—as a piece of fiction.

I probably never woulda told the stories—never woulda written them down anywhere except in the letters if it hadn't been for the intervention of another professor. I did an independent study with Suzanne and she liked the stories I wrote—was intrigued by my memories of Charley and Darryl. But the voice was still a problem. She called me "Miss Passive Voice" and told me to write it the way I spoke it. To whittle away the academese and the moderated tone. And I couldn't do it. I'd write the word "ain't" and it would feel like I was crossing a bigger line than it felt the first time I sold my body.

But some combination of her Bajan heritage and a childhood spent in New Jersey with a cemetery for a backyard allowed her to understand the strange nature of my experiences. We were the same age and sometimes when I looked at her I thought that I coulda been like her if I hadn't stopped along the way to be Mickey—and I trusted her.

She kept encouraging me to talk—to say it the way it happened even if I couldn't make myself write it that way. And I was sitting at my computer one night writing to Darryl and I realized staring at the words on the screen that I had maintained the other voice—the other language. I showed them letters to Suzanne and she said, "Yeah—that's it. That's a natural voice."

I struggled with it at first. I'd use an expression like "spun" or "rig" and spend the next five sentences trying to define the word in the context of the streets. And Suzanne would tell me not to—that the meaning was embedded in the story itself. Language had been my disguise through every step of my education and it was easier to spell out the details of being raped by a trick than it was to deviate from standard English.

There was less at stake with the rape. That was in the past. That happened to Mickey—not to Megan.

But I found—as I worked through the combining of the voices—that I was healing. Losing my fear of the straight world because it wasn't a con anymore. I wasn't disguising my version of the truth in words and structures designed to make it palatable to the rest of the world. As long as it had been a con, I had to live with the possibility that I might get found out. That someone might discover that although I could imitate the language of the masters I didn't understand its substructures and component parts. That the theories behind it all seemed like nothing more than job security for the academic elite and that I couldn't make heads or tails of it. It didn't matter anymore if the whole world found out that I was trailer park trash because I'd discovered something. I can say "gonna" and "hermeneutics" in the same sentence and if it doesn't sound authentic, the problem is with the way the world listens and not the way I speak.

During my second year of grad school I ran across a composition theorist who claimed while working with remedial readers and writers that, "Slowly something has been shifting in my perception: the errors—the weird commas and the missing letters, the fragments and irregular punctuation—they are ceasing to be slips of the hand and brain. They are becoming part of the stories themselves. They are the only fitting way, it seems, to render dislocation—shacks and field labor and children lost to the inner city. . . ."[1] And I realized that it isn't the broken language and the twisted syntax of the dispossessed that bothers the world. It is the stories they render. It is the fear that beneath the ain'ts and the sentence fragments are bright beautiful minds that would condemn the world for their alienation and exclusion if they ever got the chance to be heard.

Reclaiming my language—proving that being trailer park trash doesn't preclude intelligence—has gone a long way towards bringing me comfort in my new world. I've been allowed to keep my memories whole and intact and the letters have made Mickey and Megan a single being.

And yet every quarter when I look out at the 24 new faces in the freshman 95 composition class that I teach—I remember that I spent half my life as a heroin-addicted hooker and I wonder what their parents would say if they knew. I wonder how they've been educated and if they'll notice that I talk differently than they do. That I pay no attention to speaking standard English. That my words run together and my sentences are punctuated by the kinda slang their high school English teachers woulda rapped their knuckles for using. And just for a moment I remember standing on my corner negotiating to do blowjobs for men who coulda been their fathers and I ponder on the magic that could have delivered me from the one place to the other. The wordplay and the letters that saved us both—Mickey and Megan.

REFLECTING ON WHAT YOU'VE READ

1. Consider your experience of reading "Love Letters." What things did you especially like? What things didn't you like? Did the work help you expand your horizons, enter other people's lives, go places you couldn't go in other ways, consider things you hadn't before? If so, where in the text did it happen? Talk about the way or ways you were affected.

2. Did you connect with "Love Letters" imaginatively and emotionally as well as intellectually? Talk about some specific places in the narrative where you made those connections, why you made them, and how the author facilitated them. How do you picture the characters, places, and actions? What

---

[1]Mike Rose, *Lives on the Boundary* (New York: Penguin, 1990), 214.

emotions did the author inspire you to feel? At what point were they evoked? When did you start to care about the main character, to like her (or dislike her)? Explain some of those feelings and how the writing draws them out.

3. Find several reasons why Mickey began to write and continued writing. Reflect on why those reasons were important to her, why writing was necessary to her life and to finding her real self.

4. Mickey/Megan says, "I prided myself on speaking two languages," the academic language she learned in college and the ungrammatical, nonstandard English she used on the streets. Look closely at the first few paragraphs, or another paragraph chosen at random, and point out examples of how she combines the two languages, thus achieving what she calls on page 22 her "voice."

5. As Mickey tells her own story, she mentions writing "one more story" (p. 20), in which she ends up killing Darryl. Why does she feel the need to write such a story? What does it say about the power of writing? About the power of story?

E. M. Forster

(English Novelist, Short Story Writer, Essayist)

CHAPTER 2 Writing in Response to Literature

Entering the Conversation

Responding to literature is like participating in a great, ongoing conversation. It's a lot like posting comments on the most popular Facebook page the world has ever known, one that has postings from the distant past as well as the present and all times in between. Some of this conversation is personal, some public, and the subjects cover an endlessly wide range. Authors read other authors and respond. Scholars and critics publish their ideas and others respond to them. We readers talk about what we're reading with our friends. We talk to ourselves. We find ourselves saying things like, "I really relate to this story" or "Why do we have to read this poem?" Your conversation might go all the way back to your childhood, if when someone read to you, you kept interrupting to say, "I'm scared of him" or "I love the part where the bear goes in the back door. Read it again!"

In a sense, writing about literature is simply putting your thoughtful responses to a work on paper. You are taking part in the continuing conversation, adding your own two cents' worth to the table talk. Think of this kind of writing as something that will be listened to, considered, and added to by others who love this kind of discussion. This chapter can help you develop confidence in your ability to participate in literary conversations. Learning to do so thoughtfully and skillfully is no different—except in its means for doing so—from being able to talk about any subject—such as basketball, hip-hop, fashion, or cars.

This chapter traces the range of writing about literature through a series of increasingly complex forms:

- Writing in the margins of a book
- Journal writing
- Writing exam essays
- Writing short papers

Another, even more complex form, writing research papers, will be covered in the next chapter.

A basic assumption of this book is that writing is a process: Good writing does not happen in one last-minute, two-hour stage, during which you crank out a first/final draft to turn in to a teacher. Good writing involves a series of stages, from reading to thinking, jotting, outlining, drafting, revising, and checking. This chapter walks you through those steps, to show how they are manageable. Learning to go through the stages attentively is at the heart of what it means to be a writer.

APPROACHING THE READING

Throughout this chapter, we draw illustrations from a very short story by African American author Alice Walker, best known for her novel *The Color Purple*. The story shows how a seemingly small event on an ordinary day can turn out to be a life-changing occurrence. Read it twice: once to get a feel for it and a second time to feel more at home with the story and alert to specifics in it.

Alice Walker   b. 1944

The Flowers   [1973]

It seemed to Myop as she skipped lightly from hen house to pigpen to smokehouse that the days had never been as beautiful as these. The air held a keenness that made her nose twitch. The harvesting of the corn and cotton, peanuts and squash, made each day a golden surprise that caused excited little tremors to run up her jaws.

Myop carried a short, knobby stick. She struck out at random at chickens she liked, and worked out the beat of a song on the fence around the pigpen. She felt light and good in the warm sun. She was ten, and nothing existed for her but her song, the stick clutched in her dark brown hand, and the tat-de-ta-ta-ta of accompaniment.

Turning her back on the rusty boards of her family's sharecropper cabin, Myop walked along the fence till it ran into the stream made by the spring. Around

APPROACHING THE AUTHOR

Alice Walker's parents were sharecroppers who made about $300 a year. Walker would have grown up helping out in the fields, but when she was four years old a schoolteacher noticed her, got her new clothes, and made sure she went to school every day.

For more about her, see page 1083.

the spring, where the family got drinking water, silver ferns and wildflowers grew. Along the shallow banks pigs rooted. Myop watched the tiny white bubbles disrupt the thin black scale of soil and the water that silently rose and slid away down the stream.

She had explored the woods behind the house many times. Often, in late autumn, her mother took her to gather nuts among the fallen leaves. Today she made her own path, bouncing this way and that way, vaguely keeping an eye out for snakes. She found, in addition to various common but pretty ferns and leaves, an armful of strange blue flowers with velvety ridges and a sweetsuds bush full of the brown, fragrant buds.

By twelve o'clock, her arms laden with sprigs of her findings, she was a mile   5 or more from home. She had often been as far before, but the strangeness of the land made it not as pleasant as her usual haunts. It seemed gloomy in the little cove in which she found herself. The air was damp, the silence close and deep.

Myop began to circle back to the house, back to the peacefulness of the morning. It was then she stepped smack into his eyes. Her heel became lodged in the broken ridge between brow and nose, and she reached down quickly, unafraid, to free herself. It was only when she saw his naked grin that she gave a little yelp of surprise.

He had been a tall man. From feet to neck covered a long space. His head lay beside him. When she pushed back the leaves and layers of earth and debris Myop saw that he'd had large white teeth, all of them cracked or broken, long fingers, and very big bones. All his clothes had rotted away except some threads of blue denim from his overalls. The buckles of the overalls had turned green.

Myop gazed around the spot with interest. Very near where she'd stepped into the head was a wild pink rose. As she picked it to add to her bundle she noticed a raised mound, a ring, around the rose's root. It was the rotted remains of a noose, a bit of shredding plowline, now blending benignly into the soil. Around an overhanging limb of a great spreading oak clung another piece. Frayed, rotted, bleached, and frazzled—barely there—but spinning restlessly in the breeze. Myop laid down her flowers.

And the summer was over.

WRITING IN THE MARGINS

Chapter 1 describes reading as an interactive process: The text speaks to the reader, and the reader responds to the text. Your reading should never feel like a one-way "lecture," with you merely taking in the work passively. You, as an active reader, can talk back to the work, agreeing with it, interrogating it, connecting with it, challenging it. One way of doing this is to read with a pencil in hand and jot down your side of the conversation.

Marking Up the Work   If you own the work you are reading, you can jot notes in and around the text itself. If you don't own the work, have paper available, maybe as a bookmark, and use it for keeping notes.

- **Underline or Highlight Key Parts** Underline sentences or phrases that you really like or that strike you as especially important. But don't underline or highlight *everything*—then nothing stands out. Circle words you find particularly noteworthy.
- **Flag Key Sentences in the Text** Put a star, a question mark, or an exclamation point, especially during a first reading, next to passages you might want to return to later to figure out or to think about in light of more information.
- **Talk Back to the Text** Write comments in the margins as you move through a work: "What does this mean?" "Big point!" "Stupid idea!" "Tone shifts."
- **Talk to Yourself about the Text** Jot down thoughts that occur to you as you read—things that remind you of other books you've read, for example, or that connect with a movie or song you like or with something you learned in a biology, history, psychology, or religion course.
- **Write Notes about the Text** Write out definitions and explanations of words and details you had to look up.

This form of "engaged reading," writing in a book, is an ancient and honored tradition. Reading the marginal notes (or *marginalia*) that people centuries ago or very recently wrote in their books can let us know a great deal about the tastes, values, and judgments of some interesting and important people.

Making the Work Yours   Personally annotating a work is a way to make it "yours." It now contains your ideas and inquiries as well as the author's. Try it in this book. You might find it interesting to revisit this book years from now, to reread stories, poems, and plays you liked especially and to look again at the notes you wrote about them. You may wonder who that person was who wrote those notes; you might reacquaint yourself with who you were then; or you might discover how much you have added to your experience with literature (and life) since then.

To illustrate what we mean (not to prescribe how it should be done), here in the margins of "The Flowers" is some writing by one of our students, Kortney DeVito (pictured at right). She later used these notes to write a journal entry on the story (see p. 32) and then used the journal entry as the starting point for a paper (see p. 52).

Courtesy of Kortney DeVito.

Sample Student Annotations

Alice Walker

The Flowers

interesting name It seemed to (Myop) as she skipped lightly from hen house to pigpen to smokehouse that the days had never been as beautiful as these. The air held a keenness that made her nose twitch. <u>The harvesting of the corn and cotton, peanuts and squash, made</u>

Great imagery! <u>each day a golden surprise that caused excited little tremors to run up her jaws.</u>

Myop carried a short, knobby stick. She struck out at random at chickens she liked, and worked out the beat of a song on the fence around the pigpen. She felt light and good in the warm sun. She was ten, and nothing existed for her but her song, the

I can nearly hear her sing. stick clutched in her dark brown hand, and the <u>tat-de-ta-ta-ta of accompaniment.</u>

Turning her back on the rusty boards of her family's sharecropper cabin, Myop walked along the fence till it ran into the

I adore this description. stream made by the spring. Around the spring, where the family got drinking water, silver ferns and wildflowers grew. Along the

Does Myop see the stream the same way as the narrator? shallow banks pigs rooted. <u>Myop watched the tiny white bubbles disrupt the thin black scale of soil and the water that silently rose and slid away down the stream.</u>

She had explored the woods behind the house many times.

growing older, independent Often, in late autumn, her mother took her to gather nuts among the fallen leaves. Today she made (her own path) bouncing this way and that way, vaguely keeping an eye out for snakes. She found, in addition to various common but pretty ferns and leaves, an armful of strange blue flowers with velvety ridges and a sweetsuds bush full of the brown, fragrant buds.

By twelve o'clock, her arms laden with sprigs of her findings, she was a mile or more from home. She had often been as far before, but the strangeness of the land made it not as pleasant as

Uh-oh, foreshadowing— sounds creepy. her usual haunts. <u>It seemed gloomy in the little cove in which she found herself. The air was damp, the silence close and deep.</u>

Myop began to circle back to the house, back to the peacefulness of the morning. It was then she stepped smack into his eyes.
Her heel became lodged in the broken ridge between brow and nose,   *Yuck!*
and she reached down quickly, unafraid, to free herself. It was only
when she saw his naked grin that she gave a little yelp of surprise.

He had been a tall man. From feet to neck covered a long   *Past tense!*
space. His head lay beside him. When she pushed back the leaves
and layers of earth and debris Myop saw that he'd had large   *He had been*
white teeth, all of them cracked or broken, long fingers, and very   *there for a*
big bones. All his clothes had rotted away except some threads of   *while.*
blue denim from his overalls. The buckles of the overalls had   *Most 10-year-*
turned green.   *olds would have*
     run away!

Myop gazed around the spot with interest. Very near where
she'd stepped into the head was a wild pink rose. As she picked it   *Gross!!!*
to add to her bundle she noticed a raised mound, a ring, around   *Beautiful!*
the rose's root. It was the rotted remains of a noose, a bit of
shredding plowline, now blending benignly into the soil. Around   *Details*
an overhanging limb of a great spreading oak clung another piece.
Frayed, rotted, bleached, and frazzled—barely there—but spin-   *For the dead*
ning restlessly in the breeze. Myop laid down her flowers.   *man or her*
And the summer was over.   *childhood and*
     innocence?

JOURNAL WRITING

Journal writing enables you to take the brief notes you jotted in the margins or on paper and extend them into longer responses in which you develop your reactions, insights, and ideas in greater detail. Think of a journal,
whether assigned or something you do on your own, as halfway between a
diary and a class notebook. It's not intimate or confessional as diaries often
are, nor is it as objective, remote, and impersonal as the notebook. A journal
is a good place to store information, like characters' names; lines you want
to remember; things you were drawn to or put off by. You could regard your
journal as a place to reorganize the notes you took in class, perhaps, and to
clarify and expand on them (which can be a great help for reviewing later).
A journal also provides a place where you can express ideas or emotions
stimulated by what you read or by your conversations with other people.

Getting Started   If a journal is assigned for your course or if keeping a
journal simply appeals to you, buy a notebook or create a document in Word
or on Google Docs and begin entering responses to literary works, to chapters

of this book, or to discussions and assignments connected with this course. The suggestions for writing at the ends of chapters may stimulate some ideas; your teacher will bring up some; you will think of others yourself. Try to be specific and precise (include brief quotations and page numbers), and date each entry. Keeping journals can help you trace your own development and growth in taste, judgment, and attitudes. As mentioned before, it can be surprising, interesting, and helpful one day to look back at them.

After the Tips box, there is a page from Kortney's journal on "The Flowers." Notice the places where she carries over ideas from her marginal notations and elaborates on or changes them.

> ## TIPS for Effective Journal Writing
>
> - **Choose the right format.** Decide what format (such as notebook, note cards, or computer files) will be most effective, most readily available to you, and most convenient—that is, one that you will actually use and keep up.
> - **Don't put it off.** Jot down your notes and reactions directly after you've read the piece, while your thoughts are fresh. Later, add further reflections to what you wrote first.
> - **Be honest.** Express your genuine responses and opinions, not what you think a teacher wants you to say or think. Include quotations or page references that support your responses and opinions.
> - **Make quotations apparent.** Including quotations helps you remember favorite passages and key points and saves you from needing to go back to the work to find them. Be careful to make clear what is quoted and what is summarized or paraphrased (you don't want a paraphrase to appear as if it's a direct quote, or vice versa).
> - **Include page references.** Check to be sure you include titles and page numbers so you can find the passages you wrote about or quoted. This too can save you valuable time later.

Sample Student Journal Entry

Alice Walker, "The Flowers"

Why the need for a story such as this? Why combine such a beautiful beginning with such a hauntingly grotesque ending? It conveys that throughout life there is death — not just of others but of ourselves. Not one person can stay in one season of his/her life forever. Each season of our lives teaches something special, but at the same time each season becomes obsolete and passes away.

Myop was going through the season known as childhood at the begin-
ning of the story. She thought there was nothing but beauty in the world;
each day was a "golden surprise." When she encountered the head of the
decaying man, she began to realize the harsh reality that life can possess.
It was almost as if she was Eve eating from the Tree of Knowledge in the
Garden of Eden — she began to see the horrible truths life is capable of
delivering — not just death, but the evil of death by lynching. At the end of
the story Myop "laid down her flowers." A question is: where and for whom?
Some may say it was to the man whose life was cut short. I believe Myop
laid the flowers down for her childhood — the innocence she once possessed
was now dead to her.

WRITING EXAM ESSAYS

Teachers often include essay topics on examinations to see if you are
developing your skill to think through a problem. The prompt and the response become a sort of conversation between you and your teacher. Think
of it as an opportunity to talk to your teacher one-on-one, to have your
teacher's undivided attention for what you want to get across. The object is
not just to find out *what* you know but also what you can *do with* what you
know — synthesize it, apply it, see it in relation to other things, and respond
to its challenges. Here are a few tips for writing essay exams.

READ THE PROMPT CAREFULLY

Read the prompt several times and make sure you understand what it
asks you to do. It is crucial to understand what the prompt is focusing on.
Look for two things: a *subject* (the work or character or kind of images or
whatever else it asks you to write about) and an *approach* (what it asks you
to *do with* that subject, such as explain, compare, contrast, compare and
contrast, or discuss).

Explain [APPROACH] what the final sentence [SUBJECT] of "The Flowers"
indicates about the long-term effect of this experience on Myop [SUBJECT].

Compare and contrast [APPROACH] Myop's experience in "The Flowers" with
that of the speaker as a young boy in Countee Cullen's "Incident" [SUBJECT].

ASK FOR CLARIFICATION IF NEEDED

If you need clarification of the subject or approach, ask your teacher for
it rather than risk going at the essay incorrectly. If it's an open-book exam

(one during which you are allowed to use your book in class), double-check whether and how you may use notes or the marginalia you've jotted in your book.

ORGANIZE YOUR THOUGHTS

Don't plunge right in. You will actually use your time more effectively if you pause to plan and organize before beginning to write. Reflect on how the approach relates to the material (why was that approach selected for exploring this subject?), and think about what details you need to support what you want to say about the subject.

MAKE A POINT

Your essay should not be a summary of the work or a list of things you noticed or a few comparisons and contrasts; what you say should add up to something, make a claim. Jot that claim down as your "thesis" and make sure that you state it clearly in your essay—at the beginning, at the end, or both. Sketch an outline of points that will clarify what you mean and will support and illustrate its validity.

START WRITING

The most efficient way to get moving is to state your central claim in the first sentence of the essay. As you do, repeat words from the prompt to indicate that you are addressing it directly, meeting it head-on.

INCORPORATE NEW INSIGHTS

Keep your outline in mind but don't stick to it slavishly. In the process of writing an exam essay, you may get insights and ideas you didn't expect when you began. These often take off in new directions and may even be opposite to what you originally intended to say. There's no time to revise and incorporate such discoveries in a unified way. So, should you ignore the new insight and stick to your outline or should you include it? We think it's better to include it, but you should explain that you're changing directions ("That's the way it looked to me at first, but as I examine the work more closely I see something different in it"). Don't leave the teacher thinking you don't realize that what you are saying now doesn't fit with the way you started.

DIVIDE YOUR ESSAY INTO PARAGRAPHS

Start a new paragraph when you move to a new subpoint, or insert paragraph symbols (¶) to indicate paragraph breaks. This makes the essay clearer and easier for your teacher to read and follow.

WRITE CLEARLY

Whatever you do, don't write so fast that your handwriting becomes illegible—the best ideas in the world are useless if your teacher can't read them.

PROOFREAD YOUR ANSWER

Courtesy of Annie Otto.

Try to leave yourself a couple of minutes to read through your essay. Be sure you have offered support (explanations, details, quotations) for each subpoint. Check spelling and grammar.

The best way to learn how to write better exam essays is to look at examples of ineffective and effective ones. The second of these essays (the effective one) is by Annie Otto (pictured at right). In the first one, we rewrote Annie's essay to make it less effective.

SAMPLE STUDENT EXAM ESSAYS, MORE AND LESS EFFECTIVE

Less Effective Example   Assignment: Explain the difference in effect if Alice Walker's story had been titled "The Corpse" instead of "The Flowers." (30 minutes)

Titles have a large influence on a reader. When one reads a title, one expects to read about things that relate to it. When I first saw "The Flowers" I thought of feelings and ideas. I imagined sunshine, fields, joy, beauty. As I started reading Alice Walker's short story, I got everything I expected.

Opening too broad—not closely related to topic.

If Alice Walker's story had been titled "The Corpse," I would not have been so surprised when Myop ran into the corpse, but as it was, I was shocked. When Myop first started picking the flowers, I expected her to skip back to her family's cabin to put them in a jar for display. I had no idea that they would be used for mourning a man's death.

Doesn't respond directly to topic.

Myop is ten years old. She feels the sun shining warm rays down to her and she has her very own song to sing. She feels as though she needs to go for a walk and pick wild flowers. Walker includes specific pictures of sunshine, fields, joy, beauty, and a peaceful scene. Then Myop steps into the rotten corpse of a man who was hanged long ago. Whatever my expectations were for Myop, they were not for her to push the debris around to uncover the face of the corpse. Nor did I think that she would "gaze around the spot with interest." Why? Why would a little girl be interested in that?

Not outlined as clearly as it should be.

Includes specific details, but they're not connected to "effect."

 The cove that Myop found the corpse in gave me a cold feeling, an uncomfortable feeling. When Myop picked that wild pink rose that grew in the center of the rotted noose and added it to her bundle of flowers to lay down by the remains, she paid her respects to the man that used to be. That day she lost her childish innocence.

Never actually addresses assigned topic.

 The title of a piece of literature prepares readers for specific images. When the story twists so rapidly on us, it is quite unexpected. "The Flowers" ended entirely opposite of what I anticipated.

More Effective Example Assignment: Explain the difference in effect if Alice Walker's story had been titled "The Corpse" instead of "The Flowers." (30 minutes)

Clear statement of central claim in opening sentence; repeats words from topic.

 The main difference in effect when "The Corpse" is substituted for "The Flowers" in Walker's story is that it wipes out the surprising twist built into the plot construction and lessens the sense of horror the reader experiences.

Focuses well on "effect."

 The title "The Flowers" puts an initial expectation into the reader's mind. Walker tells us of a little girl, Myop, skipping around her yard and enjoying the warm sun's rays. She goes for a walk to pick wildflowers. There is so much life in the story and the descriptions pull the reader into the scene. Walker includes specific pictures of sunshine, fields, joy, beauty, and harmony as seen through the eyes of a child.

Clear, logical outline throughout.

 As I continued to read, I noticed words like "haunts" and "gloomy." I wondered why the author had added some darkness to the story. Myop wanted to turn back to the "peacefulness of the morning," which to me meant that there was a whisper of unrest.

Good example of "effect."

 Then there came a scream of surprise, shock, and horror. That scream was not from the ten-year-old, Myop. It was from me, the twenty-year-old reader. Myop had stepped into the rotten corpse of a man who was hanged long ago. The shock effect was huge, intensified by the contrast between the beauty of nature (the flowers) and the ugliness of a decayed body. I suppose that I tend to react extremely when I get startled as I did when reading this story. I expected that Myop would react similarly and run home screaming, not that she would "gaze around the spot with interest." Why? Why would a little girl be interested in that?

Good use of specific supporting details.

 The realization of a person's death is a difficult thing for a child to handle, and death by lynching is an action full of hate. When Myop picked that wild pink rose that grew in the center of the rotted noose and added it to her bundle of flowers to lay down by the remains, she paid her respects to the man that used to be. That day she lost her childish innocence.

If the story had been titled "The Corpse," I would have expected a corpse to appear and would not have been so surprised at what Myop found. As it was, I was shocked, and that shock intensified the horror I felt not only at Myop's finding a corpse, but also at the horrible way the man had met his end.

Clear contrast to actual title; wraps up discussion nicely.

WRITING SHORT PAPERS

Writing papers in college can (perhaps idealistically) be viewed as an opportunity rather than as an obligation. Like exam essays, papers give you a chance to communicate directly with your teacher, to have your teacher's undivided attention for what you want to get across. They also give you the opportunity to think through a topic carefully, develop an idea or a position about it, and express it for others to hear. When writing papers on stories, poems, and plays, you will need to handle topics and supporting material differently; thus, specific suggestions for writing papers on each genre, and sample papers for each genre, are given in Chapters 11, 20, and 25. In this chapter we offer suggestions that apply to literature papers of all kinds.

Steps in the Writing Process   We said earlier that writing is a process. Most writers proceed through a series of stages that take them from beginning to think about a subject to printing the final draft. As we discuss the process of writing short papers, we will view it in three stages, which we will break down into smaller steps:

- Prewriting
  - finding a topic
  - narrowing that topic
  - deciding on an approach
  - framing a thesis and preparing an outline
- Writing (developing and supporting the thesis)
- Revising, proofreading, and formatting

It's important to realize that writing is an individual act: Everyone does it differently. You as a writer may not follow these steps in this order or may not need to do all of them every time, though you'll need to achieve the result they are aimed at. Also, the steps overlap, so you may be working on more than one at the same time.

In the rest of the chapter, we follow Kortney DeVito as she returns to the marginal notes and journal entry we read earlier (pp. 30–33) and uses them as she moves through the remaining steps toward completing a short paper on "The Flowers."

STEP 1. PREWRITING: FINDING A TOPIC

Getting Started   If you are given a topic, read the assignment carefully several times to make sure you understand the terms being used and what idea the topic is getting at. And keep in mind that, although you are being given a topic, you still need to find a thesis that develops a central claim about the topic (see p. 42). If you can choose your own topic, look through your class notes, marginal jottings, and journal entries for works or subjects that got your attention — ones that intrigued you; puzzled you; or opened up new perceptions, insights, or ideas. And check the topics suggested at the end of chapters in this book, in case one might be right for you.

Courtesy of Kortney DeVito.

Kortney DeVito, on finding a topic: Before starting to write a paper on 'The Flowers,' I needed to find a topic. Rather than write on a whim, I decided to reread the story and then reread my journal entry on the story to see if I had any 'profound' ideas that might have a foundation for writing a paper. I looked for ideas or sentences that stuck out to me and could be the catalyst for a thesis. At this point, I was trying to get my ideas down on paper — I knew I would probably not have a polished thesis at this point. I had plenty of opportunity for that in the other writing steps.

Generating Ideas   To get ideas flowing, you might start by reading or rereading the work two or three times so you get a solid feel for it, underlining and annotating as you read. Look for an intriguing theme or issue in the work or an unusual technique or approach or a difficulty you struggled with while you read. Any of these might turn into a worthwhile topic. Look for connections, patterns, focuses, questions, or problems.

Asking Questions   The most important strategy for generating ideas and getting into a subject is to ask questions. Begin by asking *why:* Why is the speaker's tone this way? Why did the character make that decision? Why does the work end this way? Why was that word used to describe this character? Why does the author bring up that idea? Consider alternatives: Ask how the work's effect would change if it had used a different speaker or different metaphors, been arranged in a different order, or been written in third person instead of first.

Freewriting and Clustering   If ideas don't start coming, try *freewriting* — writing anything that comes to mind about the topic in five minutes, in any order, without stopping, editing, or changing anything. Or try *clustering:* Write down your main point and circle it. Then write points related to the topic in a ring around the main point, circle them, and use lines to connect them to the first circle. For each circle in the ring, write any ideas, examples, facts, and details you think of and use lines to connect them to the points with which they are associated. Below is some clustering that Annie

Otto did to pull together her thinking about "The Flowers." Clustering can be very useful for grasping relationships among the various parts of a topic and clarifying what materials are available or needed for developing subtopics.

STEP 2. PREWRITING: NARROWING THE TOPIC

The process we just described will enable you to generate ideas, which could lead you to an interesting subject area to work with. But it's important to remember that a key aspect of planning a paper involves narrowing and focusing that broad subject area to a clearly defined topic that you can explore in detail within the assigned length. Too large a topic for the length ("Gender and Sexuality in the Novels of Alice Walker") for a five-page paper will prove ineffective because it will skim rather than cover. Too limited a topic ("Lynching in Alice Walker's 'The Flowers'") can leave you without enough to say to fill the needed pages.

Focusing on a Key Issue   Questions are very useful in narrowing your topic as well as for generating ideas. Try phrasing your topic initially as a question, as Kortney did: "Could Alice Walker have chosen to include contrasting ideas of youth, innocence, and beauty vs. death, decay, and grotesqueness to strengthen the piece and highlight the differences between the lightness of childhood and dark reality of adulthood?" The paper then would be your attempt to answer the question. (Later you will need to convert the question into a statement; your final thesis should not be phrased as a question.)

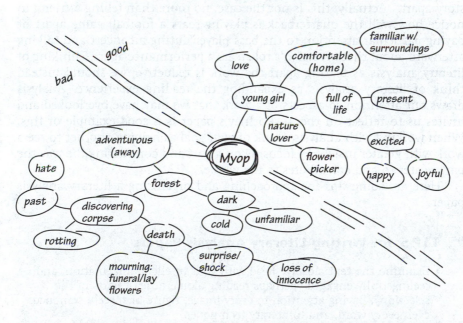

Annie Otto's brainstorm clustering for "The Flowers"

Limiting the Scope   You may need to concentrate on one aspect of the issue or make just one point instead of covering everything about it. Limiting the topic in this way enables you to go into depth and achieve some fresh insights about a small slice of the topic. If you attempt to touch on everything at a surface level, both the paper and you will come across as shallow or superficial.

STEP 3. PREWRITING: DECIDING ON AN APPROACH

You've decided on a topic and narrowed it to a manageable size. But before you start drafting your paper, take some time to consider the kind of topic you've decided on and how that will affect the way you approach its development.

Three Kinds of Topic   For papers about literature, topics can be grouped roughly into three categories: those that focus on what goes on *inside* the story, poem, or play (literary analysis); those that focus on what *connects* to the work (comparison-contrast); and those that focus on what infuses the work but also *surrounds* the work (social and cultural criticism). The kind of topic you choose affects the way you frame and carry out your discussion of it.

Literary Analysis Papers   One way of writing about literature is to look closely at a work and discuss things going on within it that you find particularly interesting. You might analyze a character, an episode, a theme or an idea, or a technique. Some people feel that literary analysis "tears a story apart." Actually, this is not the case, no more than telling a friend to notice how well the quarterback is playing tears a football game apart or paying particular attention to the bass player during a concert and talking afterward about that musician's role tears a performance apart. Thinking of literary analysis as tearing apart the work is reductive; we should instead think of literary analysis as expanding the reading experience. Analysis draws our attention to aspects of a work that we may have overlooked and invites us to reflect on them—Kortney's paper is a good example of this. When working with analysis, think of your goal as helping another to see a work with greater insight by focusing on a part and considering the way the part relates to and contributes to the whole.

Here are some tips for approaching and organizing a literary analysis paper:

> ### ▶ TIPS for Writing Literary Analysis Papers
>
> • **Examine the text closely.** Read with your intellect, imagination, and feelings fully engaged (perhaps reading aloud, at least parts of the selection), paying attention to every image, figure of speech, sentence, even every word, and to literary techniques.

- **Take on a challenge.** Look for something unusual, subtle, or particularly thought-provoking or difficult to discover initially, or look for what makes the work particularly effective. What you choose to write about does not have to be what is most central or important to the work: Very strong and interesting papers often focus on the handling of a small detail or minor character.

- **Narrow your scope.** Limit yourself to one or two elements or to one section of the story; don't try to cover too much.

- **Provide ample illustrations.** Back up your analysis with specific examples (including quotations). This grounds and substantiates your conclusions: It shows that you have been attentive to the work and that you can use the work itself to back up your conclusion.

- **Avoid summary.** Retelling a story or summarizing a poem is not literary analysis. Your emphasis needs to be on clarification and explanation. You should work with the *how* and *why* of your subject.

- **Organize topically.** An effective way to guard against putting in too much summary is to avoid using the work itself as the outline for your paper. It's better to organize the paper instead by topics or ideas, a series of techniques, or a series of points about your central idea.

Comparison-Contrast Papers Another way of writing about literature is to compare and contrast things within a work or to compare and contrast a work with another work. To *compare* things is to point out similarities between or among them; to *contrast* things is to focus on their differences. Often a thoughtful paper does both. For your paper to be effective, the things that you choose to compare and contrast must have a good deal in common or share one especially important feature, such as two stories containing characters who are trying to find a first job or who grow up in a difficult family situation. The fact that two poems contain personifications or that two different characters in a play have sisters is in itself probably not significant enough to build a comparison-contrast paper around. These same principles apply to a contrast paper: If two things are totally different, with nothing in common, there's little value in pointing out the differences. It would be as useful as comparing apples with San Diego.

Here are some tips for approaching and organizing a comparison-contrast paper:

TIPS for Writing Comparison-Contrast Papers

- **Watch for meaningful pairings.** As you read, watch for things that pair up: a plot, scene, character, setting, symbol, or technique that reminds you of another in the same work or another work. Especially be alert for comparisons that come from unlikely pairings.

(continued)

- **Outline similarities and differences.** Make lists and then group related items and select two or three topics to focus on.
- **Spell out comparisons and contrasts.** Don't just list and describe the things you are comparing and contrasting; explain why you think there is a connection and why you think it has significance.
- **Organize effectively.** A paper comparing and contrasting two works, or two aspects of the same work, may use the first half to discuss one work and the second half to bring out similar points about the second. A risk in using this approach is that the paper may come across as two separate minipapers on the same topic. A wise alternative is to discuss first the one work and then the other for each point you want to compare and contrast. It is not necessary to give equal space to comparing and to contrasting, nor do you need to give equal time to both items you are discussing.
- **Develop a thesis.** Your paper must not be merely a list of similarities and differences. To be an effective paper, the comparisons and contrasts must add up to something: They need to assert and support a central claim that brings out the significance of the comparisons and contrasts being made.

Social and Cultural Criticism Papers   In addition to literary analysis topics and comparison-contrast topics, papers can examine a work's relation to the cultural and social context that infuses it but that also ties the story to real-world issues that surround us. Such topics involve the use of social and cultural criticism. Usually such papers deal with what a story reveals about social attitudes and relations generally and, more specifically, with issues regarding such factors as social background, gender, class, ethnicity, power, and privilege. Authors write works at a specific time, surrounded by specific circumstances and attitudes. Even if the work does not refer directly to events or attitudes contemporary to the writing, those events and attitudes influence the writer and the work, consciously or unconsciously, whether she or he accepts and reflects prevailing attitudes or ignores, rejects, or challenges them. Cultural critics direct our attention to such issues and clarify the relationship between the author and the work and the cultural context in which they exist.

Here are some tips for approaching and organizing a social and cultural criticism paper.

▶ **TIPS for Writing Social and Cultural Criticism Papers**

- **Read expansively.** Social and cultural critics concentrate on the way the events, ideas, or attitudes in a work are influenced by the economic conditions, political situations, or social conventions that existed when it was written. They can also explore the way that a work is part of a culture and can influence, and perhaps change, the economic conditions, political situations, or social conventions of its time or later times.

- **Plan on doing research.** Social criticism and cultural criticism usually involve information beyond what is found in the text or in common knowledge; they often deal with background information you'll find only by further investigation.
- **Connections are crucial.** Social criticism and cultural criticism usually involve making connections of various kinds: between issues within and outside the text, for example, or between a text and historical or cultural events contemporary with it or between a text and a theoretical text. Social criticism and cultural criticism may, but don't have to, use the comparison-contrast method.
- **Make a point.** Simply describing cultural connections is not enough. A paper has to make a significant, coherent central claim and develop it with supporting claims and with explanations of their relevance and their implications.
- **Organize topically.** Social criticism and cultural criticism are analytical. Papers using these approaches, much like literary analysis papers, need to be organized stepwise in the development of the topics or ideas being dealt with.

STEP 4. PREWRITING: FRAMING A THESIS AND PREPARING AN OUTLINE

Once you've narrowed the topic, you need to sharpen what you want to say about that topic. You need to do more than merely summarize or describe the story or poem or play you're dealing with—that's seldom interesting or valuable for you or your reader. Readers can read the work for themselves. And your teacher certainly has. They can follow the outline and pick out images. But what they can't know in any other way are *your* explanations, interpretations, observations, perceptions, and connections. That's what you need to get across, in as clear, inviting, and accessible a way as possible. What you say needs to be centered in a claim that has some insight, interest, and significance. Your job is to persuade readers that your views are sound and convincing.

Topic Versus Thesis   Literary papers are usually expected to be argumentative, not in the sense of annoyingly contentious but in the sense of making a claim about a topic and backing up the claim with logical thinking and specific evidence. The central claim (or *thesis*) is usually placed at or near the end of the first paragraph.

It's important to notice the difference between a topic and a thesis. A *topic* just names a subject area: "The loss of childhood innocence in 'The Flowers.'"

It states a fact. A *thesis*, on the other hand, adds a *comment* about the subject and turns it into something requiring persuasive support, as in Kortney's unifying claim: "I believe Myop laid the flowers down to symbolize the loss of her childhood; the innocence she once possessed is now dead to her." A thesis states an idea that readers may disagree with or reject and that needs to be made convincing by supportive explanations and details (including quotations) from the text.

Working Thesis   As you think about your topic and what to say about it, you might start by framing a working *thesis*, a tentative statement of the main claim you think you will make in the paper. Kortney was able to use the last sentence of her journal entry as her working thesis: That's one of the reasons for taking notes and recording them in a journal. The working thesis often changes or develops as you write—that's natural. But beginning with a tentative point, even if you know it will not be your final version, helps you organize the rest of the paper.

Assessing the Thesis   To develop a convincing paper, you should first examine the thesis to determine what parts of it need to be explained and supported. Kortney revised her working thesis only slightly. Her final thesis, quoted two paragraphs above, implies a series of steps that will develop her ideas. Here is how she analyzed her thesis to identify the points she would need to work on.

> After revising the working thesis, I reread "The Flowers" looking for examples from the text that support my argument. I looked for examples that support the <u>childhood</u> component of my paper, and for places where Myop is <u>transitioning from childhood to maturity</u>, and for examples of where Myop experiences the <u>death of her childhood</u>. Specifically, I focused particularly on her actions and feelings.

She had here a potential outline for the body of the paper: a three-part or three-paragraph development. Carefully analyzing the thesis often yields an outline for the paper as well as a better understanding of what it is asserting.

Preparing an Outline   Many writers, like Kortney, find it helpful to have an outline—a plan, an advance sketch of the steps that the paper will take the reader through.

Kortney DeVito, on preparing an outline: Before starting to write, I often use an outline as a way to organize my thoughts. It is a wonderful way to help guide where I am going with my paper and helps to ensure I won't leave out any of my ideas. My final paper often looks different from the outline I created. I may decide that ideas need rearranging to fit well together. All I want is a road map for guiding me in getting my rough draft down on paper. I can reorganize things later as needed.

Some students write out a detailed, formal outline with roman numerals, letters, and arabic numerals as headings (as Kortney did). Others jot down a list of subtopics. Still others have a clear plan in their heads and don't write it down. Some even write an outline mirroring the finished draft to see if it follows a clear, logical organizational pattern. People work in different ways; you need to find what works best for you.

Kortney's Outline

I. Introduction/Question I am answering: Who does Myop lay the flowers for?
   A. Describe Myop briefly
   B. Touch on the dead man Myop encountered
   C. Thesis: I believe Myop laid the flowers down to symbolize the loss of her childhood; the innocence she once possessed as a child is now dead to her.
II. Childhood — Supporting that Myop is a child at the beginning of the story
   A. Actions
      1. Skipping lightly (para. 1)
      2. Picking up stick (para. 2)
         a. To hit chickens
         b. To make music — "tat-de-ta-ta-ta"
      3. Bouncing (para. 4)
      4. Collecting an armful of flowers (para. 5)
   B. Thoughts
      1. Each day is a "golden surprise" (para. 1)
      2. All that exists is the present (para. 2)
      3. No responsibility — she doesn't have to go out to gather nuts like her mother (para. 4)
III. Transition from childhood to maturity
   A. Exploring by herself — no mother or adult around (para. 4)
      1. A mile away from home (para. 5)
   B. "Making her own path" (para. 4)
   C. Feeling uncomfortable with the strange new surroundings (para. 5)
   D. Wants to head back to the peacefulness of morning (para. 6)
IV. Maturity
   A. Suddenly steps into the eyes of the dead man (para. 6)
      1. Heel becomes lodged between nose and brow (para. 6)
   B. Myop notices the noose from the lynching while picking up a rose (para. 8)
      1. Realizes the harsh reality of life. No longer will the childhood innocence protect her.
   C. Myop laying the flowers for her childhood as soon as she puts together the events of the man's death.

V. Conclusion — Myop loses her childhood innocence
   A. Remind audience of her childish actions at the beginning of the story.
   B. Discuss the horror Myop sees and how it causes her to grow up quickly.

STEP 5. WRITING: DEVELOPING AND SUPPORTING THE THESIS

After all that prewriting, at last you're ready to start writing. But getting started isn't always easy. It's not uncommon for someone to waste an hour or more staring at a blank computer screen, searching for the right words to appear. Don't do that. The key to getting started is to *start*. Waiting to be "in the right mood" doesn't work. Start writing and, more often than not, you will find yourself getting caught up in your subject. And don't start by spending all evening coming up with a brilliant introduction. The first paragraph you write often gets discarded anyhow. Many writers actually compose the introduction after writing the body of the paper because it's often easier to decide on the most effective opening after all the ideas have been articulated.

Some people find that it works best to write a first draft rapidly, getting their ideas down without worrying about neatness, grammar, or spelling. Others need to work more slowly, getting each sentence and each paragraph right before moving on to the next one. There is no single "right" process; find and use the one that suits you best.

Start with Idea Sentences   The way you start the paragraphs in the body of a paper is very important. Just as the thesis of your paper must state an idea, not just a fact, so too should the first sentence — or "topic sentence" — of each paragraph. The opening sentence of a paragraph is a minithesis: It should state briefly the supporting claim to be developed in that paragraph. If a paragraph starts with a statement of a fact rather than a statement of an idea, the rest of the paragraph is likely to consist of summary and more factual statements, not to explore an idea or develop an argument.

The second sentence of the paragraph should expand on the point or idea stated in the topic sentence, bringing out its significance and implications, and the rest of the paragraph must develop and support the point or idea. The final draft of Kortney's paper has effective topic sentences (compare them to her rough draft, in which the opening sentences are less effective).

Illustrate and Explain   As you write paragraphs developing the points in your outline, you need to include two things: (1) details from the story and (2) your explanations of them. The two need to go together. Details by themselves do not prove anything. Your explanations are needed to indicate what is important about the details and to tie them in to the whole fabric you are weaving in the paper. Likewise, explanations without supporting details are not specific enough and do not anchor themselves to the work. The key to a successful paper lies in its development and illustration of its ideas: It needs to explain ideas so readers understand them readily and to support ideas with specific details so readers have confidence that the points are well-grounded and worth considering.

Include Quotations   In any literary paper, some of the supporting evidence must be quotations. Quotations connect your explanations and interpretations directly to the work(s) and show that they are firmly based. Be careful that the phrases or sentences you quote convey what they mean in their context. The way words are selected for quotation must never distort the way they are used in the original text. The final draft of Kortney's paper illustrates effective use of quotations (pp. 53–57).

Focus on Key Passages   When you write about literature, you may be tempted to start at the beginning of the literary work and follow it through to the end. Unfortunately, that often leads to summarizing it rather than examining and discussing it. Instead, it's better to organize the paper by topics or ideas—a series of techniques or a series of points about your central idea. One way to be specific and detailed without lapsing into summary is to focus on what teacher and literary critic Benjamin De Mott calls *"key passages."* As we listen to and look at a story, poem, or play, we try to take the whole work into consideration as we seek to grasp its essence. In doing so, we usually find that a particular section—a sentence, a few sentences, a paragraph, a particular scene—seems to shed light on all the other parts of the story.

Key passages are not something writers insert deliberately into a work, as clues to readers; they are simply parts of the work that appear particularly meaningful to an individual reader, in relation to that reader's interpretation. So, instead of trying futilely to discuss every part of a work, you can focus on a key passage in depth, or perhaps two or three key passages, and use it or them to represent, connect with, and illuminate what is occurring in the work as a whole.

Write with Readers in Mind   All writers need to be aware of the audience they are addressing. A paper for a literature course should include a larger audience than your teacher alone. In practice, only your teacher may read it, but ideally other people would read it too. And that is how your teacher will read your paper, as if she or he is part of this larger audience.

In some classes, students read each other's papers to learn from one another, to help each other, to stimulate discussion, and to create a sense that they are writing for the larger conversation we mentioned at the beginning of this chapter.

Blending Quotations into Your Writing

Handling quotations effectively requires you to blend them into your writing smoothly and coherently. Here are some suggestions:

- Avoid long quotations whenever possible. Often the best approach is to combine quotations with summary and to slip quoted extracts into your prose style gracefully, as Kortney does in her paper:

  > Myop wanted to experience the feelings of independence so in paragraph four we learn "she made her own path." She left the "rusty boards of her family's sharecropper cabin" to explore her surroundings on a summer morning.

- In some cases, however, it is most effective to introduce a quotation formally, with your sentence coming to a full stop, followed by a colon.

  > At the end of paragraph five the once pleasant scenery changes: "It seemed gloomy in the little cove in which she found herself. The air was damp, the silence close and deep." This is a harsh disparity from the summer gaiety Myop experienced at the beginning of the story.

- Quotations can be shortened also by the omission of words or phrases or even sentences. Such omissions must be signaled by the use of ellipses (. . .). For guidelines on handling ellipses, see page 60.
- Don't automatically put commas before and after a quotation: They are needed only if the same words would require commas even if they were not a quotation.
- You should not start a paragraph with a quotation. The paragraph needs an opening topic sentence, setting up the point you want to develop, stated in your own words.
- Don't automatically start a new paragraph after a quotation. Usually each quotation should be followed by an explanation or a comment in your words on the point being illustrated, tying it in to the point the paragraph is developing.

And remember that quotations also require proper punctuation and formatting. For guidelines, see pages 59–60.

Avoid Summary   When you write a paper for a literature course, address the same group you talk to in class. Visualize your fellow students as well as your teacher as readers. Assume that your audience has read the stories, poems, or plays you are writing about. Thus, you don't need to retell or summarize the work. Take for granted that your audience knows the plot or subject matter, but assume that readers would benefit from help in understanding the work more fully or in seeing all the implications you see. Think of your paper as part of the continuing conversation, helping interested readers by talking clearly about things they would like to think more about.

Use the "Literary Present" When describing, discussing, or introducing specific passages or events from works of literature, use the present tense, even if the work was written in ancient times and even if the work itself uses the past tense. This is referred to as the *literary present* — that is, the action within a literary work continues to happen even if the telling about it looks back from a later point. Thus, if you are writing about Myop's character in Alice Walker's "The Flowers" (p. 27), the story says, "She *was* ten, and nothing *existed* for her but her song," but you should say, "Myop *is* a ten-year-old whose happy songs *demonstrate* the innocent, carefree life she *leads* before encountering the skeleton."

Although you should use the present tense when writing about characters and events in literary works, you should use past tense to relate actual historical facts that are outside the work itself, as, for example,

Alice Walker's "The Flowers" was first published in 1973.

Introductions Many people find writing introductions and conclusions difficult. There is no easy and sure-fire method we can give you. The opening of a paper should entice a reader to keep reading. It needs to capture your reader's attention immediately, from the first sentence. It can do that by raising an important thought about the subject or by being imaginative in style and wording. It's an opportunity for creativity or wit or a personal touch. As we mentioned before, many writers compose the introduction last. In some cases, the last paragraph you write, the one you planned as the conclusion, can be turned into a good introduction. The final draft of Kortney's paper uses a standard technique by starting with a universal idea about the subject, then narrowing down to the specific case of Myop in "The Flowers."

Conclusions Your final paragraph should round out the paper and give your readers a sense of finality and resolution. A good conclusion summarizes the central points of the paper, preferably in fresh wording, like Kortney does in her final draft, and doesn't just repeat the way things were said before. Conclusions often refer back to introductions, giving papers a sense of symmetry and unity by commenting further on something said there or answering a question raised there. Good conclusions are usually brief; don't let yours go on and on.

Selecting a Title Your paper needs a title. Make sure you create a *title* that indicates the subject of or an idea about your paper (for instance, "Point of View in Alice Walker's 'The Flowers'") and not a *heading* that is vague (as, for example, "Point of View"). Don't use the title of the literary work as the label for your paper: "The Flowers" is Walker's title; it can't be yours. A title that uses alliteration or wit, one that is catchy or strikingly worded, helps capture the reader's interest and suggests that the rest of the paper will be well written and appealing. Kortney's title, "The Death of Myop's Childhood," is effective because of its personification of childhood: It leads her readers to want to know how a childhood could die and why Myop's does.

Your own title at the top of the paper should not be put in quotation marks (see the sample paper on p. 53).

STEP 6. REVISING, PROOFREADING, AND FORMATTING

Once you finish a draft of the paper, the next steps are to revise and then proofread it. Notice that these are separate steps. Revising doesn't mean correcting spelling and grammar errors: That's proofreading, the final step. Revising comes first. The word *revision* derives from the Latin words for *look* and *again*: Revising means examining closely what you've written, thinking through it again, and trying to find ways to improve its content, organization, and expression. The notes in the margins of Kortney's paper show how she looked again at the content, development, and organization of her paper and made changes to improve them.

Reasons for Revising   Revision is crucial to effective writing: Making your paper the strongest possible usually requires several drafts. You may be able to write one draft and get a C or even a B, but the writing simply won't be as thoughtful and engaging as it would be if you revised. And revision is one of the best ways to learn even more about writing.

 CHECKLIST for Revising

❑ Content:
  • Are your ideas explained and developed fully? Have you included enough solid support so that the points you make are convincing?
  • Have you supplied enough details and examples to show that your points are well-grounded in the work?

❑ Organization:
  • Are your paragraphs in the most effective order? Do they build from one to the next? Would it be more effective to rearrange them?
  • Are the transitions between paragraphs clear and easy to follow?

❑ Expression:
  • Is your tone serious but not pretentious, warm but not cute or breezy?
  • Is there variety in the length and structure of your sentences? Do they read easily, with fluid, appealing rhythms?
  • Do the words sound good together? Are there places where a combination of words is too hard to say together or where an unintentional rhyme is distracting? (TIP: Reading a paper aloud is a helpful way to test its style.)

Gaining Some Distance   It's hard to get a fresh look right after you finish writing. You are usually still too close to your writing to come up with different ways to explain, arrange, and express. Revision often works best if you can lay your paper aside for a day or two—or even longer—before thinking about changes. It also may help to have someone else read the paper, someone whose intelligence will enable her or him to check if the ideas and organization are clear and adequately supported.

Checking for Errors   After revising your paper, proofread and edit it carefully to check for errors in spelling and grammar, for inconsistencies, and for any awkward expressions. If you write your paper on a computer, use its programs to check spelling and grammar. There's no excuse for simple typos when spending a few minutes spell-checking would catch them.

A computer check, of course, doesn't free you from the need to read closely as well. The computer can tell you that it doesn't recognize *thier* and ask if you intended to write *their*, but it won't notice if you wrote *their* when you should have used *there*. Again, distance (coming back after a couple of days) can be helpful because you may have become so familiar with your essay that it is hard to see what should be different. Some writers proofread by starting at the end and reading backward as a way of looking at the words instead of getting caught up in the meaning. Again, having someone read your essay is often useful—if she or he is a good speller and an attentive reader.

Even if you revise and proofread initially on a computer screen, we recommend at least one revision (and the final proofreading and editing) be done from a printed copy. It is helpful to see the sentences and paragraphs the way they will look on paper in the finished product.

Formatting   Papers should be typed (keyboarded), double-spaced throughout, with one-inch margins all around, and printed in an easy-to-read, 12-point font (e.g., Times New Roman) on 8½ × 11 inch white paper. Use a paper clip to hold pages together, unless your instructor asks that they be stapled. Use Tab to indent the first line of each paragraph a half inch. Left-align the text.

Identification and Title   Modern Language Association (MLA) style does not require a title page. Instead, at the top of the first page, against the left margin, on separate double-spaced lines, place your name, your instructor's name, the course number, and the date. Then, double-space and center your title. (See p. 53 for a sample first page.) If your instructor requires a title page, ask for guidelines on formatting it.

Pagination   Place the page number (in arabic numerals) preceded by your last name in the upper right-hand corner of each page, a half inch below the top edge (see the sample paper on pp. 53–57).

SAMPLE STUDENT SHORT PAPER

To allow you to see more of Kortney's writing process, we've printed the rough draft of her paper on the left-hand pages, and the final draft with her comments on the right-hand pages.

Kortney DeVito's Rough Draft

─────────────── ROUGH DRAFT ───────────────

DeVito 1

Kortney DeVito
Professor Schakel
ENGL 248
7 May 2015

Who did Myop lay the flowers for in Alice Walker's "The Flowers." Was is for the lynched man who lay decaying in the ground next to a wild pink rose? No, I believe Myop laid the flowers down to symbolize the loss of her childhood. There are many seasons we experience throughout our lives; we cannot stay in the same season forever. I believe Myop was forced to grow up very quickly because of her realization.

At the beginning of the story, the reader is meets a curious and energetic ten-year-old girl. Rather than walk, Myop skipped around the farm. Also, Myop carried a stick to tease chickens make a song to carry her along a carefree day. She looked at the beautiful day as a "golden surprise". Through her actions you can tell Myop is a child.

You can tell Myop wanted to experience the feelings of independence when she takes out on an adventure on her own on a summer afternoon. Although she desires to be alone and grown-up on her journey more than a mile away from home, she still exhibits the actions of a child: collecting an armful of wildflowers with no purpose and "bouncing this way and that way". She wants to be grown-up but still acts like a child.

Kortney DeVito's Final Draft with Her Notes

─────── **FINAL DRAFT** ───────

DeVito 1

Kortney DeVito
Professor Schakel
ENGL 248
20 May 2015

The Death of Myop's Childhood

Childhood is one of the many seasons we experience throughout life. It is a time filled with wonderment and exploration, merriment and magic, innocence and discovery. Unfortunately, we cannot stay in this season forever. Sometimes we transition through these seasons on our own volition; other times it is because of circumstances we encounter. In Alice Walker's "The Flowers," we are introduced to a young girl named Myop whose childhood departs swiftly because of an awful discovery. After encountering the remains of a lynched man, Myop lays her flowers down. Some say the flowers are for the lynched man. I believe Myop lays the flowers down to symbolize the loss of her childhood — the innocence she once possessed is now dead to her.

At the beginning of the story, the narrator introduces an innocent, energetic, and curious ten-year-old girl. Her actions exude childlike whimsy. Rather than walking idly in paragraph one, Myop "skipped lightly" around the farm in a youthful fashion. In paragraph two, Myop "carried a short, knobby stick" selecting chickens to tease and creating a rhythmic song "tat-de-ta-ta-ta" to carry her along a carefree day — she is in her own world: "nothing existed for her but her song." She looks at the beautiful day as a "golden surprise," savoring the succulent smells of the farm's harvest. The appreciation of simple things and the actions of Myop paint a picture of a young girl delighting in the wonders of her childhood.

However charming the morning is, the confines of the farm become too restricting for Myop; perhaps, the confines of her childhood were becoming restraining as well. Myop wants to experience the feelings of independence, so in paragraph four we learn "she made her own path." She left the "rusty boards of her family's share-

My introduction didn't grab the audience's attention, so I reworked the conclusion of my rough draft to use it as the new introduction.

My thesis needed to be stronger, so I added to it.

I needed more support to paint a picture of Myop's childish actions and perceptions. I used my notes and referenced the text to flesh out this paragraph.

---- ROUGH DRAFT ----

DeVito 2

At the end of paragraph five, the once pleasant scenery changes: "It seemed gloomy in the little cove in which she found herself. The air was damp, the silence close and deep." This is very different from the beginning of the story. Myop's heel suddenly becomes lodged in between the ridge of a man's brow and nose. The only fear she shows is a "yelp of surprise" when she sees the man's grin. She takes note of his characteristics. Such a haunting situation paired with the bizarre inquisitiveness of the character causes the reader to think Myop still possess a piece of her childhood. That little piece soon vanishes when Myop realizes that the man she discovered did not die by accident. She pieces the execution together. At first, she measures him, looks at his decapitated body. Then she stumbles upon the "rotted remains of the noose" in the soil. Still, there is no sign of fear or revulsion from Myop. However, when Myop discovers the other half of the rope on the limb of an oak tree "spinning restlessly in the breeze" she reacts. Myop realizes that this day is no longer "a golden surprise" and that life can be cruel. As suddenly as she stepped in the eyes of the man, Myop lost the gift of innocence childhood provides. "Myop laid down her flowers" to mourn her loss.

cropper cabin" to explore her surroundings on a summer morning. Although she desires to be alone and grown-up on her journey more than a mile away from home, she still exhibits the actions of a child: collecting an armful of wildflowers with no purpose and "bouncing this way and that way." It appears Myop is bordering the great divide of childhood and maturity; in a seemingly juvenile man-ner, Myop creates a new path for herself in unchartered territory.

To engage the reader, I incor-porated more sentence variety and lengthened this paragraph. I wrote a more gripping topic sentence and added quotations as support.

The land along Myop's "own path" exhibits an unpleasant-ness and "strangeness" in its unfamiliarity. At the end of paragraph five the once pleasant scenery changes: "It seemed gloomy in the little cove in which she found herself. The air was damp, the silence close and deep." This is a harsh disparity from the summer gaiety Myop experiences at the beginning of the story. To magnify this disparity, a grotesque event unexpectedly occurs when "she stepped smack into his eyes." Myop's heel suddenly becomes lodged in between the ridge of his brow and nose. Surprisingly, the curiosity and boldness of her childlike nature allow her to reach down to free her foot. The only fear she shows is a "yelp of surprise" when she sees the man's grin; oddly, however, she continues to investigate the corpse. She takes note of his characteristics: his height, the details of his teeth, the largeness of his bones, even the condition of his clothes. Such a haunting situation paired with the bizarre inquisitiveness of the character cause the reader to think Myop still possesses a piece of her childhood.

I wrote a stronger topic sentence.

I needed to split my original paragraph into two parts: 1. Discuss time before Myop realizes how the man had died, when a part of her childhood still exists.

That little piece soon vanishes when Myop realizes that the man she discovers did not die by accident. She pieces the execution together. At first, she measures him "from feet to neck" and sees his head lying beside his body. Then, when reaching down to pick a wild pink rose, she stumbles upon the "rotted remains of the noose" in the soil. Still, there is no sign of fear or revulsion from Myop. However, when Myop discovers the other half of the rope on the limb of an oak tree "spinning restlessly in the breeze," she reacts. I believe the innocence of the morning is sto-len as soon as she pieces together the evidence surrounding her. Myop realizes that this day is no longer "a golden surprise" and that life can be cruel. Gone is the childish innocence of thinking that

2. Discuss when she sees the noose—at which point her child-hood is gone.

—————————— **ROUGH DRAFT** ——————————

DeVito 3

    Childhood is one of the many seasons we experience throughout life. It is a time filled with wonderment and exploration, innocence. Unfortunately, we cannot stay in this season forever. Sometimes we transition through these seasons on our own; other times it is because of circumstances. In Alice Walker's "The Flowers," we are introduced to a young girl named Myop whose childhood departs swiftly. After encountering the remains of a lynched man, Myop laid her flowers down. Some say the flowers are for the lynched man. I believe Myop laid the flowers down to symbolize the loss of her childhood; the innocence she once possessed is now dead to her.

FINAL DRAFT

DeVito 3

life will last forever and there is only goodness in humanity—she discovers that the hatred and ugliness humanity possesses murdered this man. As suddenly as she stepped in the eyes of the man, Myop lost the gift of innocence childhood provides. "Myop laid down her flowers" to mourn her loss.

Within moments during a late summer afternoon, Myop lost something very dear. No longer skipping, bouncing, and making music with a stick, Myop suddenly loses the innocence of childhood—something we all cherish—because of a single encounter. Myop realizes there are more than the sweet smells of harvest, the songs she creates, or the beauty of a flower; there are also hatred, death, and wretchedness. The haunting reality of the world's malice leads Myop to lay the flowers on the forest floor where the lynched man rests. She says goodbye to her season of childhood.

I wanted to answer two questions in this paragraph: What causes Myop to lay the flowers down? And why is the loss of her childhood sad?

For my new conclusion, I wanted brief highlights of each paragraph and I wanted my last sentence to be simple, to illustrate the solemnity of the story.

 TIPS for Writing a Successful Short Paper

The following are five characteristics of a successful short paper.

- **Significant topic.** A successful paper grows out of asking a probing question; it focuses on a central claim and explores it in some depth.
- **Appropriate approach.** It develops an idea, or an angle, about the problem, selecting an insightful approach to it.
- **Solid preparation.** It shows evidence of careful, perceptive reading and clear critical thinking.
- **Strong development.** It avoids broad generalizations and plot summary but provides precise, pointed explanations and uses details and brief quotations as support and expansion of the idea or interpretation.
- **Good writing.** It is unified and organized coherently and is written in clear, polished prose with correct grammar, spelling, and punctuation.

A CLOSER LOOK AT
Handling Titles

1. Titles of books or long poems (the names of any long work published independently, with its name on the title page) and the names of plays, movies, and TV shows are italicized.

2. Titles of short works (poems, short stories, essays), ones that name a part of a book rather than the whole, are placed within quotation marks.

   "The Flowers" is found in Alice Walker's book *In Love and Trouble: Stories of Black Women*.

   Quotation marks are also used around chapter titles in a book or titles of individual episodes of a TV series.

   The final episode of *Baywatch* in 2001 was entitled "Rescue Me."

3. When a normally italicized title (as in 1 above) appears within another italicized title, the title within is neither italicized nor enclosed in quotation marks; it is in roman.

   Lister, Rachel. *Alice Walker,* The Color Purple: *A Reader's Guide to Essential Criticism*. Palgrave Macmillan, 2010. Reader's Guides to Essential Criticism.

A CLOSER LOOK AT

Punctuating and
Formatting Quotations

Handling quotations well requires proper punctuation and formatting. Firmly fix the guidelines below in your mind so you get them right automatically, without needing to think about them.

1. Place quotation marks outside commas and periods (.” or ,”) but inside semicolons and colons (”; or ”:). U.S. punctuation conventions never put the period or comma outside quotation marks.

2. Always use double quotation marks (”), except for a quotation within a quotation, which is indicated by single marks (’). However, if an entire quotation consists of dialogue by one speaker and is so introduced, it is not necessary to use the extra single quotation marks.

3. Treat longer passages (more than three lines of poetry or more than four lines of a prose passage) as block quotations, set off from the rest of the text by starting a new line and indenting the passage one-half inch—sometimes more for poetry—from the left margin. Block quotations should be double-spaced. See Marisela Meraz paper on page 80 for an example.

4. Treating a passage as a block quotation is the same as putting quotation marks around it. Use quotation marks around an indented passage only if it has quotation marks around it in the source. If, however, the entire quotation consists of dialogue by one speaker and is so introduced, quotation marks are not necessary.

5. The end punctuation of a quotation may be (often should be) dropped and replaced by punctuation appropriate to your sentence; thus, a period ending a quotation may be replaced with a comma if your sentence goes on (you should never have .”, or ,”. in a paper) or it can be omitted if a parenthetical citation follows: ” (**source**). The period or comma is placed *after* a parenthetical citation (as at the end of the previous sentence), not before it. The parenthesis should not be left unattached between two sentences.

6. In all other respects, quotations must be precisely accurate, including original spelling, capitalization, and punctuation. The initial letter of a line of poetry must be capitalized if it is capitalized in the original, even

if the quotation is not indented. Always double-check quotations to make sure they are correct.

7. If you need to insert a word into a quotation (adding a verb to integrate the quotation into your sentence, for example, or changing a pronoun to a noun for clarity), place the inserted word in square brackets [ ], not in parentheses.

8. In some cases, you will want to omit words or punctuation marks to shorten quotations and to make them fit your sentence construction more effectively. Ellipsis points (three periods with a space before and after each: . . .) must be used whenever you omit something from *within* a quotation.

9. Ellipsis points are not used at the beginning or the end of a quotation if what is quoted coincides with the beginning or end of the original sentence or if it is obvious that what is quoted is not a complete sentence in the original (for example, if you quote a brief fragment).

10. If the passage being quoted has ellipsis points in it, square brackets should be placed around your ellipsis to clarify that yours have been added: [. . .].

11. Four dots (a period plus the three ellipsis dots) are needed if you omit (1) the last part of a quoted sentence, (2) the first part of the following sentence, (3) a whole sentence or more, or (4) a whole paragraph or more. If a sentence ends with a question mark or an exclamation point in the original, that punctuation is used instead of the first or fourth period. What precedes and follows the four dots should be grammatically complete sentences, either as quoted or as connected to the text surrounding it.

12. The use of an ellipsis mark must not distort the meaning of the passage being quoted.

The *MLA Handbook*, 8th edition (Modern Language Association of America, 2016), includes sections providing guidelines on matters of style and punctuation, as does *The Chicago Manual of Style*, 16th edition (University of Chicago Press, 2010). Or you can consult the MLA Web site or a college writing handbook, such as Diana Hacker and Nancy Sommers's *A Writer's Reference*, 8th edition (Boston: Bedford/St. Martin's, 2015).

When you're writing, you're trying to find out something that you don't know.

James Baldwin

(American Fiction Writer and Playwright; see pp. 324 and 1055)

Writing a Literary Research Paper

CHAPTER 3

Entering the Larger Conversation

If you have a smartphone or access to the Internet, you probably do research all of the time—though you may not think of it as research. When you see a movie and want to know what else the star has acted in, you look it up. When you want to buy the best laptop you can afford, you read reviews and ask experts for advice. In a way, our almost universally easy access to the Internet means that we live in a culture of research—the margin of time between when we have a question and when it's answered continues to shrink.

When it comes to conducting literary research, this aspect of contemporary culture will work both for and against you. The benefit is that you're in the habit of asking a question and finding your own answer. But you may not be used to research that takes the amount of time and level of careful thinking appropriate to academic, literary study. It won't be enough to Google a search term and assume that the first thing you see is accurate and will fit your needs. The process is more rigorous—and more rewarding.

Once you've decided which literary work you want to focus on, this chapter will walk you through locating background information about authors, works, and eras as well as commentary and analysis from well-informed literary critics about the work you're writing on. You'll learn how to start with your ideas, gather the ideas of others, and develop a paper that not only becomes part of your own conversation with literature but also contributes in some way to the centuries-old, continuous conversation about literature in the world at large.

The Larger Conversation   In Chapter 2, we said that responding to literature is like entering a huge, ongoing conversation. It starts with reading as "listening" to a work and "talking" to it by writing notes in the margins and journaling, and it expands when you discuss the work within the community of your class. The conversation expands even more when you access the work of literary scholars who publish their critical insights about a particular work or era or theme and add those insights to your own.

It can be valuable for you, as a student of literature, to enter that larger conversation in order to magnify your understanding and deepen your insights about what you read. While you might do more casual research about any author or work you're interested in, our main concern here is to help you improve the way you write research papers for college courses, and to increase your confidence and skills in doing so.

This chapter traces how one writer, Marisela Meraz, a student probably a lot like you, moved through the research process—

- finding materials;
- evaluating sources;
- keeping track of what she read

—and through the steps in writing a research paper:

- finding a topic;
- developing ideas;
- incorporating sources;
- documenting sources;
- revising, proofreading, and double-checking.

THE RESEARCH PROCESS

THE NATURE OF LITERARY RESEARCH

Before we begin following Marisela's progress, we should pause to clarify three main types of literary research: factual, primary, and secondary. All three yield different kinds of information, so it's important to recognize each type and to consider which will be most applicable in different situations.

- **Factual research**, the first level of research, involves finding the basic facts you don't know about the text. You might look up definitions of words, the meaning of details mentioned that you don't understand, the source of allusions, and the biographical and historical context in which the work was written. This kind of research is really an extension of reading, a way of making sure you understand what's on the page.
- **Primary research** seeks out what we call primary sources, which are any kind of text (written, graphic, or oral) contemporary with or earlier

than the one you're focused on. Primary sources include letters, diaries, journals, memoirs, newspapers, or even music and works of art, and they are used to acquire firsthand information about an author's life, times, or culture and to understand literary or artistic influences and traditions that affected an author or helped shape a work. If your subject involves very recent literature, this may be the only kind of research you can do. (For more on this, see page 69.)

- **Secondary research** refers to the search for anything scholars have written about literary texts and about the biographical, literary, social, or cultural context of an author or a work. Such works are called *secondary* because they aren't firsthand works written *by* an author or her or his contemporaries, but secondhand ones written *about* an author or her or his works or era. Secondary sources include critical books or essays about a work or group of works; biographies of an author; and books discussing the events, culture, and ideas of the author's time.

To write a literary research paper, you'll need to do some secondary research, but before you reach for commentary by other writers, make sure you've arrived at some of your own conclusions about what you've read and begun jotting down ideas for possible topics. Otherwise, your own thoughts might become lost in the conclusions you read from others.

WARNING! A word of caution about one other kind of source. You're probably aware of various types of "study guides," online and in print, for many literary authors and works. They typically offer plot summaries, analyses of characters and themes, and commentaries about key passages. *We recommend that you don't use these.* Here are a few reasons why:

- They're rarely written by established literary scholars, so they can't actually be trusted. Errors of fact are very common.
- They often simplify a work in order to provide a list of themes (for example, these are *the* themes to find in *Hamlet*) and therefore reduce the actual complexity and richness of literature. This can mislead unwary readers into thinking the work is not as challenging as it actually is.
- They are a poor and unnecessary substitute for your own careful, attentive reading of the text, and your search for sources from qualified and dedicated scholars.

If you do use them, be sure to do so with great care, making sure of their validity. You may want to check with your teacher concerning them. Your teacher will likely explain that, if you decide to read one as preparation for writing a paper, *its use must be acknowledged in the bibliography, even if you do not cite it in the paper.* The truth is, as tempting as it may seem to read all of the "answers" spread out in front of you, these are not sources that will enhance the quality of your paper.

FINDING MATERIALS

When it comes to research materials, there used to be hard and fast divisions between online and print sources. Before the Internet, research sources were objects you held in your hands: books or copies of articles. Research, in general, was more physical. Once online sources arrived, they existed in the wild, intangible world of the Internet, and because it's easy for anyone to post online, Web sources were generally untrustworthy routes to literary study.

Now those divisions have blurred somewhat. Millions of books are available digitally. More literary scholars have learned how to harness the Internet's power to present their work and to collect the work of other scholars. Many (if not most) professional journals make their publications available through databases, and you can use several databases of high quality to find what you're looking for online.

When you begin searching for sources, chances are good that you'll start by turning on a computer, and you're more than right to begin there. But before you turn on your laptop, and before we present our best tips for conducting quality research, we'd like to make a plea: Use the softening of these divisions between online and print sources as wisely as you can. Don't avoid physical books because they require you to take the stairs and learn call numbers—the pleasure and luck of finding an even more perfect book nestled beside the one you were looking for can't be reproduced digitally. Try blending technology with pre-Internet ways: If an article you want isn't available full-text, learn how to find the physical copy, take pictures of its pages, and email them to yourself. If an article or book isn't available through your library, ask about your school's interlibrary loan program and try getting it from another. The world of literary research is your oyster; don't limit yourself by settling for what you can access from your glowing screen. Instead, to continue the metaphor, use your screen and any other means possible to pry open the oyster.

Marisela Meraz on searching for scholarly books: My main resource for finding books was my school's online library catalog. I was searching for any books that included "After Apple-Picking" and analyses or critical essays on the poem. Through the catalog, I found two books that I thought would be helpful for me in my research. I was also able to find and access an e-book that I could read online and that was helpful in giving me more information on potential themes of the poem.

Courtesy of
Marisela Meraz.

DOING LIBRARY SEARCHES—FOR BOOKS

Using an Online Catalog   The basic tool for finding library books is your school's online catalog. It may have a unique, perhaps catchy tag (the college where we teach calls it HopeCAT), and the layouts vary, but what is on the page is basically standard. You will be given a choice of several ways to search, and often you can select whether to search a specific collection within the library, the entire collection, or the collections of all libraries linked through a particular system.

If you already know about a book you'd like to check out, use the search page to find the call number and location of the book. You can also use the online catalog as a search engine to find books you don't yet know about. Thus, Marisela could look for other works by Frost by doing an *author search*, she could look for biographical works and critical studies of Frost by doing a *subject search*, or she could look for works about nature poetry by doing a *keyword search*. If the number and variety of items called up is overwhelming, it may help to limit your search: Look on the catalog page for the Advanced Search option or a Help link — or ask a librarian for guidance. Librarians are generally eager to help, and they are very good at doing so.

Using Reference Books   Your library's reference section can provide good background and bibliographical information about many authors and texts, and these can be good places to build the groundwork of your research. Many libraries duplicate or supplement their reference holdings with online sources, so it's worth asking about the best way to find reference materials at your library.

Here's a brief list of significant literary reference works to get you started. A company called Gale publishes several comprehensive series of books on literary topics, and Gale's reference resources are now available as searchable databases as well: Try perusing the *Dictionary of Literary Biography*, *Short Story Criticism*, or *Poetry Criticism*, choosing which one you look at according to which genre (poetry, story) you're writing on. You can also try the *Columbia Literary History of the United States*, published by Columbia University Press, or *The Princeton Encyclopedia of Poetry and Poetics*. If you're writing about something in British literature, turn to *The Oxford History of English Literature*, published by Oxford University Press.

Note that reference books are a great place to start your research, but they should never be the place you stop. And you should never use them as the main sources in a paper.

DOING LIBRARY SEARCHES — FOR ARTICLES

Many of the most valuable studies of particular literary works appear as articles (or essays) in literary journals or in books of collected essays. In most cases, such articles do not show up in searches of library catalogs, so locating them requires you to access additional databases.

Finding Articles in Journals   Essays about literary topics are usually published as articles in magazines or journals (commonly referred to as *periodicals* because they are published periodically, at regular intervals — weekly, monthly, or quarterly — rather than once, like a book). For the most part, your search should concentrate on literary journals because they are written by literary scholars and peer reviewed (see p. 70) and are therefore more likely to provide the kind of material you'll need than are general magazines. The articles Marisela found in *The Explicator* and *American Literature*, for example, would be more appropriate for her project than articles in *People* or *Newsweek* would be. You might find personal information, such as interviews with an author, in a general magazine, but not the more thorough critical studies of the kind you need in a college research paper.

> **Marisela Meraz on searching for periodicals:** After looking for books, I mainly used the *MLA Bibliography* and *JSTOR* to find journal articles relating to the poem. I also found other useful sources by examining each article's bibliography or works cited page and looking up the sources that seemed promising so I could read those, too.

Using Literary Databases   The most comprehensive resource for finding articles about authors and literary topics is the *MLA International Bibliography of Books and Articles in the Modern Languages and Literature*. Look for a link to the *MLA Bibliography* on your library's Web site and experiment with ways to focus and restrict your searches: A keyword search for Robert Frost in the *MLA Bibliography* yields around eighteen hundred hits; adding "After Apple-Picking" to the search reduces the hits to seventeen. Though eighteen hundred seems like an exciting number, seventeen is much more manageable: You'll never make your way through hundreds of source entries to pick the best ones, but you'll certainly make it through less than twenty. You can try doing a variety of searches, using different terms related to your topic, and you can focus your searches by using connector words (*and, or, not*). Ask a librarian for other ways to sharpen your approach.

In many cases, the full texts of journal articles are now available online, especially through databases like *JSTOR* and *Project MUSE*. Both are great resources, and they are good places to land after you've looked at *MLA*. Linking immediately to a full-text article is an undeniably convenient feature, and you may be tempted to start with sources that automatically provide it. But remember that the *MLA Bibliography* is the most comprehensive, so don't skip it if you'd like the best range of articles to choose from, and you do. You can always check for the full text in other databases once you've found what you're looking for—some library Web sites have a one-click feature that makes this very simple. In the pursuit of convenience, it would be a shame to miss an article that contains just the insight you need to write a truly excellent paper.

Finding Articles in Books   Scholarly articles are sometimes published in books of collected essays focused on an author or a topic. The contents may be articles previously published in journals and gathered into a book

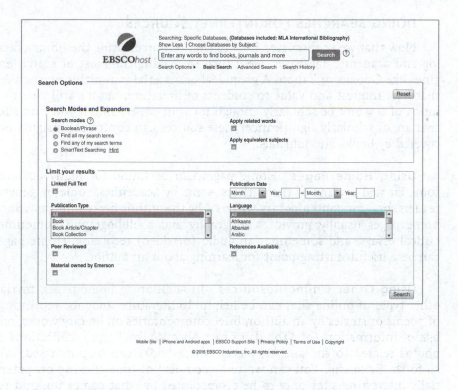

MLA Bibliography. EBSCOhost offers access to a broad range of online academic and bibliographic databases, including the MLA Bibliography.

by an editor to make them more accessible. Or the book may be made up of essays written especially for the collection and published for the first time in it (for example, *Frost: Centennial Essays II*, edited by Jac Tharpe, cited in Marisela's paper). The books can be found by searching a library's online catalog, but the essays in the books are indexed in the *MLA Bibliography* among journal articles. This means you can either find the book in the library catalog and scan the table of contents, or be prepared to locate some of the articles in a book once you've found it in the database.

Using Other Bibliographic Databases   If your topic requires doing a broader search to include other academic disciplines, seek out databases that bring in other subjects. There are plenty to choose from. Two of the best-known examples are Gale's *General OneFile* and the Online Computer Library Center's (OCLC) *FirstSearch* databases. These databases cover the humanities, the social sciences, and the sciences. Ask a librarian for the name of particular databases of this type to which your library subscribes (for example, *EBSCOhost*, *ProQuest Research Library*, *Academic Search Premier*, and *Humanities Abstracts*).

DOING SEARCHES FOR INTERNET SOURCES

Now that we've discussed how to find resources using the library catalog and academic databases, we'll turn to making the most of search engines like Google, or Yahoo! A great deal of material is available on the Web that is of interest and value to students of literature, but it's still true that much of it won't be scholarly enough for your paper. Still, if you find sites that are of scholarly significance, these sources can contribute insights not covered by books and journals.

Using Home Pages Home pages can be found for many authors, some created by fans of the authors, some by academics, some by general readers, or — for contemporary writers — by the author her- or himself. Such home pages usually provide a biography and a bibliography, sometimes critical essays, and sometimes an audio (or video) recording. Home pages can be a useful starting point for learning about an author.

Using Other Online Resources In addition to home pages, myriad other types of online sites can be helpful to literature students: reprintings of poems or stories by an author, brief commentaries on literary works, odd bits of information (of "The day I met Alice Walker" type), collections of photos related to the author, places where books can be purchased, and so forth. *Be careful.* You can waste a good deal of time clicking on potentially interesting sites only to be disappointed by what comes up, and remember that the majority of what you find won't be appropriate for your paper.

If you identify advanced search options to narrow your results, your Internet research will prove more useful. In other words, rather than simply typing in "Robert Frost" and then trying to sift your way to something useful through millions of results, try restricting your search in ways similar to those described above for databases.

Using Lists of Recommended Web Sites To bypass Google's millions of hits and the hours you could spend clicking through them, seek out a vetted list of respected Web sites. The English departments at many colleges and universities have assembled lists of sites they regard as well organized, reliable, and trustworthy. Such sites are usually linked to their department's or library's home page and are easy to find and access. Or try one of these two highly regarded Web sites: Jack Lynch's *Literary Resources on the Net* and Alan Liu's *Voice of the Shuttle*, both of which were created and are maintained by faculty members at major universities.

For college-level literary research, however, the most useful material is found in sources that at least began in print, so plan to look for books and articles (or e-books and full-text articles), and use true Internet sources sparingly and carefully.

RESEARCH ON CONTEMPORARY LITERATURE

If your topic involves very recent literature, doing a research paper will probably present some different challenges and opportunities. For contemporary authors, there often are no published studies to go back to. Therefore, you will need to do the kind of research scholars do, locating background and contextual information, applying it to the author's works, and doing original critical studies of them. You might start by looking for biographical information and interviews. If you find that the author has said that certain writers and works have been influential, you could study and draw from them. Search for newspapers, magazines, movies, art, television, advertising, reputable online works, or whatever else might clarify the sources of and influences on the writer's ideas and artistry. For some current authors, published book reviews may be available, and these may fill a role similar to that of critical essays.

When published reviews aren't available, look at the unsolicited reviews or comments posted on sites like Amazon.com or Barnesandnoble.com; remember that these sources must be used with care, but in many cases they are thoughtful and judicious, and they reflect quite accurately how some other readers are responding to a work. Look also at the publishers' summaries and publicity blurbs on those sites; they aren't meant to be objective criticism, but they can provide starting points for getting into a work. For contemporary authors, however, you will often need to concentrate on primary sources and what they contribute to a deeper understanding of the authors and works you want to study.

EVALUATING SOURCES

Using the Best Sources   A very important principle of research, in any field, is that "all sources are not equal." It follows that research that uses stronger sources is regarded more highly than research that uses weaker sources. One way of assessing a student paper or a book of literary criticism is to look at its bibliography. A bibliography that lists mostly popular magazines, Internet sources, or books and articles from the 1960s won't be as strong as a bibliography that lists scholarly articles and includes books written during the past ten to fifteen years. From the beginning of your research project, *be selective* about the sources you decide to consider further.

> **Marisela Meraz on evaluating sources:** Before I printed out each of the articles I found, I quickly read through them and took out the ones that were published too long ago, those with invalid sources, and those with topics that weren't relevant to the theme of my essay. I also did a short online search of each author's credentials, just to make sure the author was who he or she claimed to be.

Assessing Carefully   As you consider which potential sources to include in your working bibliography, *assess each one carefully*. When you read books, articles, and Internet material, your first job is to get an accurate grasp of what is being said. Only then can you decide how valid and valuable the point might be to your work. Books and essays are not "good" just because they're in print or posted on the Web: Don't use just any source you happen to find. Evaluating the worth of a source is crucial. The quality of your sources affects, even determines, the quality of your paper. To help you evaluate sources, here are five questions to ask.

1. *Who is the author and what are her or his qualifications?* As in any other field of study, those who devote their careers to a subject are most qualified to offer commentary, so you want to look for authors who have credentials (degrees, academic positions, awards, or other publications) in the field. Marisela followed good steps by checking out authors before adopting them into her Works Cited. It can sometimes be difficult to track down authors for online articles: an organization name will work in some cases, but if an article appears to be truly anonymous, it's generally best not to use it.

2. *Where was the work published?* Articles submitted to scholarly journals, and books submitted to well-established presses are carefully screened by experts; this process is known as "peer review." Only works that peer experts regard as accurate and important are accepted for publication. The fact that an article appears in a highly regarded journal or that a book is published by a highly reputable press in most cases can give you confidence in its quality, though you still have to assess it on its own merits. For material on the Internet, check who hosts the site. Items posted by academic institutions (.edu) are generally more promising than items on commercial sites (.com), though that isn't a perfect rule. In some cases, the host organization is identified at the bottom of the initial page. Try to find out more about the organization and what it has at stake before entirely trusting what you read.

3. *Is the source or its author cited by other scholars?* One way to measure acceptance by other scholars is to note how frequently a scholar's works are favorably commented on or referred to by other scholars or included in their bibliographies. If other scholars rely on a source, you can be fairly sure that its author is respected in the field. Some databases can provide you with information on how often an article has been cited.

4. *What is the date of publication?* In some fields (especially the sciences and social sciences), research more than a decade or two old may be outdated. That tends to be less so in the humanities, but it is still true to some extent. Recent scholarship builds on earlier work, adding to earlier studies and correcting their mistakes, and it draws on current ideas and theoretical approaches. It's acceptable to have some older studies in your bibliography, but in most cases your sources should also include recent, up-to-date research.

5. *How relevant is it to your topic and argument?* Avoid the temptation to add items to your bibliography or to slip quotations into your paper just because they are written by a leading expert or published by a major press. A source helps your paper only if it fits your topic or relates to your argument and is something you actually can use. Readers are not impressed when your bibliography lists books by several widely known experts but all the citations in your text are to unscholarly Web sites.

KEEPING TRACK OF WHAT YOU'VE READ

Using Technology   While there are several tried-and-true ways to keep track of your research that don't rely on technology at all (and we'll get to those in a moment), it will probably come naturally to use your computer and other electronic devices. When you find an online source using your computer, you can highlight and/or copy and paste quotations and ideas into a document, or you can create a document for each source and collect them in a file. If you're attached to a smartphone, you might take pictures of article pages, list your sources and ideas in a "notes" app, or record an audio file as you talk through your sources and ideas.

From there, it's possible to get just about as sophisticated and complicated as you'd like to be when it comes to digital tools. Several applications help organize sources for research, and more are developed constantly, so it might be worth the time spent finding your best option—one that connects with the way you think and can carry you through your years in school. Applications like OneNote allow you to "clip" Web pages, scan handwritten notes, integrate photos, and share your notes across all your devices and with collaborators. If you tend to think and organize thoughts visually, look for mind-mapping software like XMind: This system allows you to create digital versions of brainstorming clusters, including images and links to articles, and you can easily represent hierarchies and divisions using graphics, color, font, and text size. Systems like Dropbox and Google Docs allow you to store and back up your research files, access your work from any computer, and share files with others. Many students appreciate software like Zotero, which bills itself as a "personal research assistant" and will automatically index the content of all your files so they are easy to search. Whatever digital system you use, make sure you stay organized, keep track of all your sources, and avoid getting so distracted by the technological bells and whistles that you forget your real task is to write an excellent paper.

Handwritten Notes   In the old days, scholars took notes on 3 × 5 or 4 × 6 inch cards (or, earlier, on slips of paper), using one set for bibliographical information and another for summary notes and quotations, cross-referenced to the corresponding bibliography card. This produced excellent results for centuries and is still a good system, so don't discount it entirely. Note cards are easy to keep with you, they don't crash or get viruses, and the organization is physical and therefore perhaps less likely to get complicated.

You may also find it's worth printing out copies of articles or making photocopies[1] from books and periodicals (as Marisela did), and highlighting the old-fashioned way. There's absolute freedom when you have your own copy of a research source in hand: You can add notes in the margins, draw arrows between related ideas, and use the back of the page to scribble out the progression of your argument. (Note that it's decidedly inappropriate and crass to do these things to the library's copy.) Consider what may be more convenient for you to do by hand. The world will go on inventing new ways to keep track of ideas, but when it comes down to it, it's hard to improve upon the simple technology of pen and paper.

> **Marisela Meraz on organizing her research:** Most of the articles I found were not long in length, so I read through them on my computer. However, I still found it important to print them out because I like to highlight any important quotations to include in my essay as well as take notes. I used a binder to hold all of my articles to make it easier for me to find each one when I started writing. Because I knew I would be using all of the articles in my research, I also began my Works Cited page right away.

Some Guidelines for Keeping Track   No matter what system you use, some principles are the same.

- *Check for completeness.* Be sure to include the author's name and all the information needed for finding the source:
  - For print sources: published by whom, where, when; page numbers for articles. Put down call numbers for books and articles; they aren't needed in your paper, but having them is convenient in case you have to go back to these sources later.
  - For Web sources: title of Web site, author's name, names of editors and sponsoring organization, database used, date the site was accessed. Keep a record of the DOI, permalink, or URL; you will need it for your Works Cited page and it may prove valuable if you have to return to the source later.
  - Review your notes before moving on to be sure that you have everything down. You certainly don't want to discover (especially the night before a paper is due!) that you forgot to include a date or page number and must go back to the library (assuming it's not closed for the night) to find it.

---

[1]Copyright protection allows photocopying of articles and selected pages from a book when used for personal research but forbids photocopying an entire book or even most of one.

TIP: You will save time later if, as you take notes, you begin preparing the actual Works Cited page for your paper instead of leaving it to the end, when you're weary and perhaps pressed for time. It is most convenient to create a separate Works Cited file in your computer as you compile your list and to add the list to the end of your paper when it's nearly finished, so the pages will be paginated consecutively with the body of the paper. If you use a database or some other online tool to help you build your Works Cited page, make sure you check it against MLA guidelines and correct any errors—students who use these online tools often turn their papers in with citation mistakes. These tools are convenient, but they are far from perfect.

- *Check for accuracy.* After you write or type a direct quotation, check that every word and punctuation mark is accurate before you move on. If you leave out a word, phrase, or sentence, be sure you indicate that with ellipsis marks (see p. 60). Make sure your in-text citations are accurate.

- *Check for clarity.* However you keep track of notes, be sure to indicate clearly what is quoted and what is summary. It's a good idea to write or tag each point with "quote" or "summary" to make sure you won't mistake one for the other, something that can lead to charges of plagiarism. Also, add a label indicating what point in your paper the notes apply to. That will make it much easier for you to find and organize your notes when you get ready to use them.

WRITING A RESEARCH PAPER

In nature and form, a research paper is very similar to the papers discussed in Chapter 2, but it is usually longer and broader in scope and goes into more depth. Because the basic steps for writing research papers are pretty much the same as those given for writing shorter essays in Chapter 2, we will not repeat them here. Instead we will focus on what is different for research projects.

FINDING A TOPIC

The suggestions on pages 38–39 for finding a topic apply to deciding on a research paper too. It could be helpful to review those suggestions. The difference for a research paper is that there has to be something in the topic that needs to be investigated, something you can do research on.

Don't Approach Your Paper as a Report   Perhaps the most helpful thing to remember as you think about a topic is that *a literary research paper*

Marisela Meraz on finding a topic and writing a thesis: This process was one of trial and error. Each time I found a potential topic, I would see if there was enough scholarly research addressing that general theme. Eventually, I settled on the topic of self-discovery in the poem because I felt like the speaker was beginning to realize not only how "tired" he is of his work, but how his work is not fulfilling him in any way. So, though it eventually changed, I wrote my first potential thesis for my essay: "The speaker's weariness addresses the idea that our labor most often does not give us a feeling of self-satisfaction after our work is done." I still had a long way to go, but it felt good to have a beginning.

is not a report. A report gives an account of something, and its nature is objective: The writer usually does not interject opinions or interpretations. A research paper sometimes takes the form of a report. For example, for a paper on climate and crops in Papua New Guinea, a student might search for information on the subject and piece together an account of the climatic conditions, how they affect what can be grown, and how that contributes to the degree of poverty in the country. Often such a paper turns out to be a long string of quotations and paraphrases, with transitional sentences connecting and holding them together. Writing that type of paper is not what this chapter is teaching you to do.

Use an Approach That Focuses on a Thesis   A report is not what college professors mean by a literary research paper. Like other literary essays, a research paper is unified around a thesis, a central claim that takes a position to be discussed and supported. The most important part of a research paper is what *you* say in it, the development of *your* approach and ideas and interpretations, so your topic needs to be one that invites such an approach.

Aim for Originality   Use an approach that focuses on a thesis, and remember that the thesis should reflect your own thinking. As you carry out your research, however, you may find that someone else has already explored the topic you were planning to focus on, perhaps even argued for the same thesis you had tentatively decided on. It may feel discouraging, but it shouldn't actually be a problem. For a student paper, originality isn't saying something that never has been said before. Recycling a thesis you find in a critical essay is an acceptable way to form the topic for an undergraduate research paper as long as you acknowledge your source and find different ways to develop and support the argument.

You might bring in your own explanations and examples, ones different from those used before. Or you might approach an issue in a different way. Or you might combine ideas from different fields. Students are in an ideal situation to do this: Try using concepts from your philosophy, sociology, psychology, or political science courses to illuminate works you study in your literature course. Remember, it is essential that the paper embody your own thinking and approach. Don't let it turn into a report on or paraphrase of the earlier article.

As you look for and read sources, it can be tempting to keep only those that agree with your ideas and ignore those that don't. Resist that temptation. Reading different opinions can help sharpen your conclusions and strengthen your arguments, and bringing opposing views into your paper and refuting them can lead to a more thoughtful and thought-provoking paper.

Marisela Meraz on focusing her thesis: While doing my research, I came across a quotation from Robert Frost on what poetry should do, and it stuck with me. What Frost said eventually helped me clarify what I was trying to say, and I used a piece of that quotation in my introduction and thesis.

DEVELOPING IDEAS

After deciding on a topic and tentative thesis, you need to think out several subpoints that explore the central point, decide on an outline that organizes the subpoints effectively, and start writing. As you write, amplify the ideas by supplying details and illustrations that support the points you make and by explaining how the ideas and examples support each other in a convincing way. You might want to review the more detailed discussion of these steps on pages 38–51.

Marisela Meraz on developing an outline: My outline for this essay was pretty general, but I found that simply writing what each paragraph was going to be about helped me start the writing process. Because I already had my sources and my main points highlighted and annotated, having an outline to connect annotations made the process go a lot faster.

The main difference from the papers discussed in Chapter 2 is that, as you shape and develop and support your ideas, an additional resource is available to you: the information and ideas found in the sources you've consulted. These can be used as supporting evidence for points you make or as ideas you think need to be expanded or corrected.

INCORPORATING SOURCES

Once you've found quality sources and identified passages that support your ideas, you'll need to make decisions about how to incorporate those sources. You can incorporate outside materials into your paper using any of the following four methods:

- citation,
- summary,
- paraphrase, and
- quotation.

We illustrate these methods below with examples taken from Marisela's paper (pp. 80–85).

> **Marisela Meraz on supporting her ideas:** For the most part, I wanted to high-light my sources by choosing quotations that would back up or clarify my own ideas. I made sure not to overload my essay with too many quotes because I wanted it to be a representation of my own interpretations, enhanced but not bulldozed by other ideas.

Citation   In some cases you may want to mention a source that makes a point related to one you are making, though you do not summarize or paraphrase it in developing your ideas. You can do so by making a passing reference to it, or *citing* it, without saying more about it. Take a look at how Marisela uses this technique:

> The poem starts out like a realistic description of rural life and the hard work that farmers do for a living, a "farm poem" that many readers think of as typical of Frost (Doyle 26).

Citations can also be used to supply additional examples from other sources that you want your reader to be aware of, but you don't feel it's important to explain more than one in greater detail.

Summary   In many cases, you will bring sources into your paper by summarizing some information, a key idea, or an overall argument you find valuable. The summary should be a brief restatement of the author's point put in your own words. To avoid accidentally using the author's exact words, summarize from memory, without looking back at the text (close the book or clear the computer screen). In this example, Marisela summa-rizes the first part of Frost's point, and then quotes directly from what comes after in Frost's essay.

> Frost himself said that poetry should do more than *describe* life and work; rather, good poetry leads to "a clarification of life," what Frost said all poems should attain — "not necessarily a great clarification . . . but a momentary stay against confusion" ("Figure" 18).

What you incorporate does not have to summarize the whole book, chapter, or article but may summarize one section or simply one paragraph or point.

Summary is often used as a way to bring primary texts usefully and ef-ficiently into a paper. Marisela does this in the first sentence of her paper to introduce the poem and the focus of her analysis immediately:

> In Robert Frost's "After Apple-Picking," the speaker describes the fatigue he feels after a long day of picking apples in the orchard.

Paraphrase   A paraphrase, like a summary, is a restatement of an author's point in your own words, but at greater length — usually approximately equal in length to the original passage.

Marisela didn't find occasion for paraphrase in her paper, but it's a good idea to use this approach instead of summary when the details of a scholar's argument are important. You might use it, for example, in order to call specific attention to each step in an argument because you want to dispute it step by step. Quoting the passage in such a case might not work as well because a paraphrase allows you to enumerate each point even if the author didn't do so.

Quotation   When asked to write a research paper, you'll need to use quotations from secondary sources as well as quotations from primary texts. The best guideline is to quote when you encounter passages written so effectively that paraphrasing them wouldn't be the same as using the original wording. Be careful, however, not to load your paper with too many, turning it into a "collage of quotations." You might be worried about finding enough quotations, but the greater danger is handing your paper over to them entirely by using too many or by using several lengthy ones. Quotations must not carry the argument of a paper but must support and illustrate the argument you are presenting in your own words.

The best approach is to combine quotations with summary and to blend brief quoted extracts into your prose style as gracefully as possible. Marisela's paper does this well, as illustrated here.

> Perhaps the "woodchuck could 'say' whether his sleep resembles the speaker's," but the woodchuck is gone (Owens 35). It could be an ordinary night's rest. But, as Fagan points out, the speaker's reference to a long sleep "seems suggestive of the long sleep of death" (25), and that long sleep could be like the woodchuck's hibernation, or it could be unending. The speaker can't tell, and the poem doesn't provide an answer to the reader.

PLAGIARISM ALERT

Plagiarism is the presentation of the work of others as if it were one's own. This is a serious offense. Treating another person's effort and ideas as if they are your own is dishonest. It violates the expectations of trust and honesty in an academic community. In addition, it undercuts the basic purposes of higher education by short-circuiting the processes of inquiry, reflection, and communication that lead to learning.

For examples of plagiarism and ways to avoid it, see "A Closer Look at Avoiding Plagiarism" on pages 86–88.

The guidelines in Chapter 2 for handling quotations effectively are even more important to follow when writing research papers than when writing short papers. You might want to review them, too (pp. 59–60).

DOCUMENTING SOURCES

The method of citing sources for papers on literature preferred by most teachers is the MLA style, described in detail in the *MLA Handbook*, 8th ed. (Modern Language Association of America, 2016) and on the *MLA Style Center* website.[2] It is a simple, convenient, two-step system that uses parenthetical citations in the text, which match an alphabetical list of works at the end of the paper. In the sentence below from Marisela's paper, the name in the parentheses identifies the source being used. To find information about where the source can be found, you would look in the Cs of the Works Cited list for the name "Conder":

> **Marisela Meraz on documenting her sources:** What is really helpful about finding sources on *JSTOR* (or in any other database) is that it provides all of the information you need to cite your source in your Works Cited. From there, you can fit the information to the proper formatting for MLA citation. I started on my Works Cited as I began writing my paper to make it easier for me at the end of my writing process.

In-Text Citation

Here's an example of how Marisela includes in-text citations in her paper:

> Critics have shown that the farm poem stereotype of Frost's poetry isn't accurate — "the literal meaning of such poems is far from the full meaning . . ." (Conder 171).

Note that there isn't a comma after the author's last name, and that you don't need "p." or "page" before the page number. You should also take a close look at how the closing punctuation is handled: the quotation mark comes before the opening parenthesis and the period of the entire sentence comes after the closing parenthesis.

In many cases it works well to use an introductory phrase in your sentence leading into your summary, paraphrase, or quotation, giving the source's name and, if significant, a word or phrase indicating the source's qualifications.

---

[2]Other methods are preferred in other fields of study: APA (American Psychological Association) style is used in the social sciences; CBE (Council of Biology Editors) style is used in the sciences; and *Chicago* style (*Chicago Manual of Style*) is generally used for history. Each style focuses on the kind of information considered most useful in that discipline and on the format regarded as most convenient.

The ladder points, as Brooks and Warren explain, "not toward the
sky or even the heavens, words that carry merely a literal meaning, . . .
but toward *heaven*, the place of man's rewards . . ." (365).

If you include the name of the source in your sentence, you do not need to
repeat it in the parenthetical citation.

For more details and examples of in-text citations, see page 89.

Entry in the List of Works Cited

Conder, John J. "'After Apple-Picking': Frost's Troubled Sleep." *Frost:
Centennial Essays*, UP of Mississippi, 1973, pp. 171–81.

The entry you see above may or may not look complicated to you, but it follows a very specific pattern dictated by MLA format. We won't pause here to
explain that pattern, or explain how to put a Works Cited page together, but
we go into essential detail in the section beginning on page 89.

REVISING, PROOFREADING, AND DOUBLE-CHECKING

Everything we said about revising and proofreading in Chapter 2 applies
equally here. Review pages 50–51 and go through the same steps as the final
stage in working on your research paper. Add to that list what Marisela talks
about: Double-check that your quotations and your Works Cited entries are
completely accurate.

> **Marisela Meraz on revising and proofreading:** When I finish writing a paper, I
> first go through to make sure there aren't any spelling or grammatical errors,
> then I read to make sure I didn't overuse certain words. I like to print out a copy
> of the paper and use that as I go through this process. I use a pen or highlighter,
> and read what I wrote out loud, marking on the printed copy as I go. Then I enter
> the changes I marked in my Word document.
>
> To make sure all my sources are used correctly, I use the Works Cited list I
> start early in my writing process and put a check mark by each item that I actu-
> ally used in the paper. I check each quotation and citation for accuracy and delete
> the ones I didn't use.

SAMPLE STUDENT RESEARCH PAPER

Here is the final draft of Marisela's paper.

Marisela Meraz
Professor Schakel
ENGL 248
20 April 2016

Sleeping and Dreaming in Robert Frost's "After Apple-Picking"

In Robert Frost's "After Apple-Picking," the speaker describes the fatigue he feels after a long day of picking apples in the
orchard. The poem starts out like a realistic description of rural life
and the hard work that farmers do for a living, a "'farm' poem" that
many readers think of as typical of Frost (Doyle 26). But critics
have shown that the farm poem stereotype of Frost's poetry isn't
accurate — "the literal meaning of such poems is far from the full
meaning . . ." (Conder 171). Frost himself said that poetry should
do more than *describe* life and work; rather, good poetry leads to "a
clarification of life," what Frost said all poems should attain — "not
necessarily a great clarification . . . but . . . a momentary stay
against confusion" (Frost, "Figure" 18). "After Apple-Picking" consists of a series of momentary confusions between reality and
dream. By working out a "stay" against that confusion in the lines
of the poem, Frost shows how attention to sleep and dreaming can
result in a valuable clarification of the life we live while awake.

The beginning of the poem informs the reader of the hard
day's work the speaker has been doing in the orchard:

My long two-pointed ladder's sticking through a tree
Toward heaven still,
And there's a barrel that I didn't fill
Beside it, and there may be two or three
Apples I didn't pick upon some bough. (1-5)

*Title included in
citation because
two works by
Frost appear in
Works Cited.*

*Thesis sentence
states central
idea.*

*Extended block
quotation sets
up discussion of
the poem. This
technique is
used throughout
the essay.*

On the surface, these lines merely say that his work for the day is
done. Images of "ladder," "tree," "barrel," and "two or three /
Apples" seem part of the realistic scene, but the word "heaven"
complicates the images. The ladder points, as Brooks and Warren
explain, "not toward the sky or even the heavens, words that
carry merely a literal meaning, . . . but toward *heaven*, the place
of man's rewards . . ." (365). The following line, "But I am done
with apple-picking now" (6), conveys a sense of finality, too
strong to refer only to the end of a day's work, and that tone
continues throughout the rest of the poem. Line 7 introduces the
motif of sleep: "Essence of winter sleep is on the night." Again
an adjective complicates the meaning: "winter sleep" suggests
not an ordinary night's sleep, but perhaps "a sleep similar to
nature's" (Conder 174), the way nature quiets and rests through
the winter.

     In line 8, the speaker is "drowsing off," and from sleep it
seems a natural step to dreams. The following lines create a
dreamy effect:

     I cannot rub the strangeness from my sight
     I got from looking through a pane of glass
     I skimmed this morning from the drinking trough
     And held against the world of hoary grass.
     It melted, and I let it fall and break. (9-13)

Here, the speaker's depiction of remembering the way he saw
through the thin piece of ice from the trough becomes blurred
and creates uncertainty about what he is really imagining. Deirdre
Fagan describes it this way: as if looking through "Alice's looking
glass, . . . the world described here is as worn, tired, and old as
the speaker feels, and a world brighter and more magical can be
seen only as a mirage, momentarily held before it melts" (24). In
this passage, the dream and literal worlds begin to overlap more
closely as the speaker recalls looking through a makeshift lens
that made his ordinary vision stranger.

*A mix of
primary and
secondary source
quotations
builds a strong,
well-supported
point.*

The dreaminess turns to actual dream: "And I could tell / What form my dreaming was about to take" (16-17) — that is, "the kind of dream we all experience after working at anything too hard and too long . . ." (Borroff 27):

Primary text quoted to back up assertion.

> Magnified apples appear and disappear,
> Stem end and blossom end,
> And every fleck of russet showing clear.
> My instep arch not only keeps the ache,
> It keeps the pressure of a ladder-round. (18-22)

Secondary source quoted to expand point.

As Priscilla Paton puts it, because "of his day's absorption in work and his consequent weariness, he confuses tenses and his sense of time and place" (49). It becomes clear to the reader that this wearied life the speaker is living in not only consumes his everyday life, but also his sleep, which should be the time for the speaker to finally rest. It's clear he's talking about more than just one day, but an entire life of work that hasn't let him truly rest.

Clear topic sentences are used throughout the paper.

Dreams can embody ideals, or they can be nightmares. The speaker's dreams could be either — there is the ideal of an abundant harvest ("ten thousand thousand fruit" — 30), but there is also the nightmare that the amount of work involved with such a harvest can seem unending. "Magnified apples" (18) can suggest the magnitude of abundance, or the "extravagance" of oversupply. "The rumbling sound / Of load on load of apples coming in" (25-26) can convey the richness of harvest, or the weight of the labor involved. That weight leads the speaker to say: "For I have had too much / Of apple-picking: I am overtired" (27-29).

Quick but clear quoting of several parts of the poem build several pieces of evidence at once.

Perhaps the speaker's statement merely states the obvious: that after a long day and rich harvest he is tired and needs a good night's sleep. But the tone and the sense of finality within the line itself could point further, that the speaker is physically and mentally weary from a lifetime of great harvests, as Paton concludes: the "pains and exhaustion from committed labor,"

Secondary source quoted to advance argument, with signal phrase naming author.

Meraz 4

which once were manageable, have now become an exhaustible
burden (50).

> The last lines of the poem return to sleep:
> One can see what will trouble
> This sleep of mine, whatever sleep it is.
> Were he not gone,
> The woodchuck could say whether it's like his
> Long sleep, as I describe its coming on,
> Or just some human sleep. (37-42)

The question of what kind of sleep he will have remains unclear.
Perhaps the "woodchuck could 'say' whether his sleep resembles
the speaker's," but the woodchuck is gone (Owens 35). It could be
an ordinary night's rest. But, as Fagan points out, the speaker's
reference to a long sleep "seems metaphorically suggestive of the
long sleep of death" (25), and that long sleep could be like the
woodchuck's hibernation, or it could be unending. The speaker
can't tell, and the poem doesn't provide an answer to the reader.
As Conder says,

> He is only falling asleep in this poem, and he does not
> yet know which sleep his will be. Its duration will deter-
> mine its nature. It is his uncertainty as to when (or
> whether) he will awaken which will be carried into his
> sleep, troubling it. Ironically enough, only when he
> awakens will he know what sleep it is — or, rather,
> was. (180)

Block quotation from secondary source supports what's come before and sets up rest of the paper.

Doyle adds, "Man has always wanted to know what follows after
the last breath, but as long as he is man he cannot know" (31).
And that is where Frost leaves us, "search[ing] for meaning in the
modern world . . ." ("Robert Frost"). We've received our "momentary stay against confusion" and the poem releases us back into
our lives.

No page number for Web source.

Much of what is written in "After Apple Picking," from
the images of the apples to the descriptions of the arduous labor
that the speaker must complete each day, comes together to form

Conclusion circles back to the introduction without feeling repetitive.

a picture of the tired life of the speaker — a life that seems to be troubled with not just the preoccupations of his day-to-day job but also the uncertainty of what might be beyond. His longing to rest signifies the only way to escape his hardships and his fatigue; in his sleep and his dreams he finds rest from his tiring day and his wearied life.

Meraz 6

Works Cited

Borroff, Marie. "Robert Frost: 'To Earthward.'" *Frost: Centennial Essays II*,
    edited by Jac Tharpe, UP of Mississippi, 1976, pp. 21-39.

Brooks, Cleanth, and Robert Penn Warren. *Understanding Poetry*. Holt,
    Rinehart and Winston, 1938.

Conder, John J. "'After Apple-Picking': Frost's Troubled Sleep." *Frost:
    Centennial Essays*, UP of Mississippi, 1973, pp. 171-81.

Doyle, John Robert, Jr. *The Poetry of Robert Frost: An Analysis*. Hafner
    Press, 1962.

Fagan, Deirdre J. *Critical Companion to Robert Frost: A Literary Reference
    to His Life and Work*. Facts on File, 2007.

Frost, Robert. "After Apple-Picking." 1914. *Approaching Literature:
    Reading + Thinking + Writing*, edited by Peter Schakel and Jack Ridl,
    4th ed., Bedford/St. Martin's, 2017, pp. 803-4.

---. "The Figure a Poem Makes." *Selected Prose of Robert Frost*, edited
    by Hyde Cox and Edward Connery Lathem, Holt, Rinehart and
    Winston, 1966, pp. 17-20.

Owens, Clarke W. "Robert Frost's 'After Apple-Picking'." *The Explicator,*
    vol. 71, no. 1, Mar. 2013, pp. 35-37. *JSTOR,* doi:
    10.1080/00144940.2012.758619.

Paton, Priscilla M. "Robert Frost: 'The Fact Is the Sweetest Dream That
    Labor Knows.'" *American Literature,* vol. 53, no. 1, Mar. 1981,
    pp. 43-55. *JSTOR,* doi: 10.2307/2926193.

"Robert Frost." *Poems and Poets*. The Poetry Foundation, www
    .poetryfoundation.org/bio/robert-frost. Accessed 18 Mar. 2016.

A CLOSER LOOK AT

Avoiding Plagiarism

WHAT PLAGIARISM IS

The *Oxford English Dictionary* defines *plagiarism* as "The action or practice of taking someone else's work, idea, etc., and passing it off as one's own; literary theft." The word comes from a Latin verb that means "to kidnap." Plagiarism is wrongfully taking someone else's ideas or words and turning them in or publishing them as if they were your own. It is dishonest because your reader or instructor has a right to believe that you did the work yourself unless you acknowledge that you received help drawn from someone else's words, sentences, or ideas. It is shortsighted as well because only the process of doing work yourself has educational value, not the act of turning in work drawn from the efforts of others.

EXAMPLES OF PLAGIARISM

More specific examples of plagiarism clarify that broad description:

- Buying a paper from a commercial source and submitting it as your own, or doing so with a paper from a classmate, friend, fraternity or sorority file, or using parts of such a paper—even if you change the introduction or alter some of the wording
- Cutting and pasting material from the Internet into your paper without indicating where it came from
- Using the exact words of another writer in your paper without indicating that they are quoted and providing proper citations for them
- Paraphrasing or summarizing the words of another writer without providing citations that indicate they are rewordings
- Taking important ideas from sources and including them in your paper as if you thought them up, even if the wording is not the same as in the original
- Letting someone else (a friend, classmate, parent, etc.) write parts of your paper for you or correct or edit a paper so extensively that it no longer accurately reflects your work
- Submitting a drawing, painting, musical composition, computer program, or any other kind of material created originally by someone else and claiming or implying that you created it yourself

REUSING A PAPER

One final example of plagiarism often surprises students: Turning in the same paper in different courses is plagiarism, even though all the material is yours. Instructors expect papers to be work done specifically during and for the course for which they were assigned; it's not fair if other students take the time to write a new paper and you just reuse one you wrote in high school or in an earlier college course.

In some cases, you may want to do a research project that involves two courses you are taking at the same time—literature and psychology, for example. In that case, talk to both instructors. They will probably encourage you because making connections between disciplines is a valuable way of learning. But they may require you to do separate papers for each course or allow you to submit the same paper for both courses but require it to be longer than those done by other students.

UNINTENTIONAL PLAGIARISM

Some of the examples above are deliberate cheating. Everyone knows it is unacceptable to buy a paper and turn it in as your own work. Those who do it deserve the severe penalties most instructors and institutions impose. In some cases, however, students stumble into inadvertent plagiarism by not knowing the rules for citation. They may believe, for example, that only direct quotations need to be acknowledged; therefore, they assume that if they totally rephrase a passage and avoid using any words from the original, they don't need to cite a source for it. Not so. You need to give credit to the person who came up with the idea or who did the work of tracing a historical allusion or detail or who thought out the interpretation of a story or poem, even though your phrasing of the material is different. *You are responsible for knowing what plagiarism is and how to avoid it*: Ignorance is not an adequate excuse.

AVOIDING PLAGIARISM

Here are a few guidelines for avoiding plagiarism:

- Put quotation marks around any groups of words (phrases or whole sentences) taken directly from a source.
- Document every direct quotation except phrases that are so common that most people would recognize the source without being told ("Four score and seven years ago," for example).

- Document any idea or information that you attained through your research, except for information that is widely available from many different sources (even if you looked up the place and date of Alice Walker's birth, you don't need to give a source because that information is readily available in many places).
- Keep in mind that you are taking part in a time-honored tradition: the extension of the ongoing conversation about a literary work of art. Respecting the work of others by acknowledging their contributions is a matter of personal integrity and a standard by which you are welcomed into the community of both established and beginning scholars.

A CLOSER LOOK AT

In-Text Citations and Preparing a Works Cited Page

STEP 1. IN-TEXT CITATIONS

The MLA system begins with brief in-text citations. After a quotation or a sentence that borrows words, facts, or opinions from a specific source, one inserts parentheses with, ordinarily, the last name of the author and the page or pages on which the information is found, as shown in this sentence from Marisela's paper:

> Critics have shown that the farm poem stereotype of Frost's poetry isn't accurate — "the literal meaning of such poems is far from the full meaning . . ." (Conder 171).

This is the most basic form of in-text citation. Notice three formatting conventions followed in it:

1. There is no comma after the author's name and no "page" or "p." preceding the number.
2. The quotation marks come before the parenthetical citation. This is because the in-text citation identifies the source of the quotation but is not part of the quotation.
3. The punctuation mark closing the sentence follows the parenthetical citation so that the citation is included in the sentence, not left floating unattached between sentences. (An exception is in the case of block quotations, where the period precedes the parenthetical citation.)

MLA In-Text Citations: Variations on the Basic Form

- If the author is named in the text leading up to the quotation (and this is good practice), the name is not repeated in parentheses:

> The ladder points, as Brooks and Warren explain, "not toward the sky or even the heavens, words that carry merely a literal meaning, . . . but toward *heaven*, the place of man's rewards" (365).

(continued)

- If you borrow from two or more works by the same author, your parenthetical citations should include a short title after the author's name.

    Frost himself said that poetry should do more than *describe* life and work; rather, good poetry leads to "a clarification of life," what Frost said all poems should attain — "not necessarily a great clarification . . . but . . . a momentary stay against confusion" (Frost, "Figure" 18).

- If the author of the material being cited is unknown, use the title or a shortened form of the title in parentheses, where the author's name would have been. Titles of books and plays should be italicized; titles of stories, poems, and essays should be placed within quotation marks.
- If the work does not have page numbers, omit them from your citation. This is frequently the case for Web sources, except for stable sources such as PDF files, in which case page numbers should be cited. For electronic sources that number their paragraphs, give those numbers.
- If you borrow from two authors with the same last name, include an initial in your parenthetical citation, unless the author's full name is given in the text leading up to the quotation.
- If you borrow from a work you found in an anthology, use the name of the author of the work, not that of the anthology's editor: (Frost 803–4), not (Schakel and Ridl 803–4).
- If you want to quote something you found quoted by someone else in an essay or a book, the best procedure is to find the original source (that's one of the values of having bibliographical information provided in a work), quote from it directly, and cite it as the source. If your library does not have the original work or it's checked out, it's okay to copy the quote from the secondary source and use the abbreviation "qtd. in" to indicate that you are doing so.
- If you want to cite two or more sources at once to indicate that they say much the same thing about a point you are making, you can list them together parenthetically.

STEP 2. WORKS CITED PAGE

The other key part of the MLA system is the bibliography. The *MLA Handbook*, 8th Edition, recommends that it be a list of Works Cited — that is, a list containing only works referred to within the paper. In some cases, for a student paper, a bibliography of works *consulted* might be preferred over one of works cited to indicate the range of research, if noncited works are an important part of the context of the paper. Check with your teacher if you think that might apply to your paper.

To find additional advice for preparing a Works Cited page, refer to a handbook or an online resource such as Writer's Help (Bedford/St. Martin's) at writershelp.com.

BASIC GUIDELINES

Here are some basic details about formatting a Works Cited page:

1. Begin on a new page. Continue the pagination begun in the earlier parts of the paper.
2. Center the heading "Works Cited" at the top of the page. Use capitals and lowercase letters; do not use bold or italic type.
3. Make the first line of each entry flush with the left margin, with subsequent lines, if any, indented a half inch (learn how to use a "hanging indent," if you don't know already).
4. Double-space the entire list, without extra spaces between entries.
5. Arrange your list alphabetically, by the last names of the authors or, for anonymous works, by the first significant word in the title (ignoring an initial *A*, *An*, or *The*). If two authors have the same last name, alphabetize first by their last names, then by their first names.
6. To list two or more books by the same author, give the name only in the first entry. For the other entries, substitute three hyphens followed by a period for the author's name. If the person edited or translated one or more of the books, place a comma after the three hyphens, then the appropriate role ("editor" or "translator"), then the title. The titles should be in alphabetical order.

> Frost, Robert. "After Apple-Picking." 1914. *Approaching Literature: Reading + Thinking + Writing*, edited by Peter Schakel and Jack Ridl, 4th ed., Bedford/St. Martin's, 2017, pp. 803-4.
>
> ---. "The Figure a Poem Makes." *Selected Prose of Robert Frost*, edited by Hyde Cox and Edward Connery Lathem, Holt, Rinehart and Winston, 1966, pp. 17-20.

For an example of a properly formatted Works Cited page, see page 85.

The rest of this chapter provides explanations and examples of the information and forms used in the MLA system for Works Cited entries for works you are most likely to encounter:

- Books used as sources (pp. 92–94)
- Books used as containers (pp. 94–96)
- Sources contained in scholarly journals, magazines, and newspapers (pp. 96–98)
- Articles accessed electronically (pp. 98–99)
- Book reviews, interviews, letters, and e-mail messages (pp. 99–100)
- Web sources (pp. 100–102)

BOOKS USED AS SOURCES

The books you use in your research project will often be written by a single author and used by you as sources of information and opinions. The basic Works Cited entries for such books have three parts:

Author's name. *Title of the Book*. Publication information.

This is the way such an entry looks on Marisela's Works Cited page:

Doyle, John Robert, Jr. *The Poetry of Robert Frost: An Analysis*. Hafner Press, 1962.

Here are some guidelines that clarify these basic parts:

- **Name of the author**, last name first, followed by a period. If the name ends with an initial, only one period is needed.
- **Title of the book**, italicized, followed by a period. If the book has a subtitle, include it as well, preceded by a colon. For guidelines on handling titles, see page 58.
- **Name of the publisher**. Include the full publisher name as printed on the title page of the work, followed by a comma. Retain terms such as *Books* and *Publisher* but shorten terms such as *Inc*. ("Macmillan Publishing Company, Inc." not "Macmillan"). Use abbreviations such as "UP" for "University Press." The city of publication is not included.
- **For pre-1900 sources only: give the city of publication**, followed by a comma, instead of the publisher's name. If more than one city is listed on the title page of the book, give only the first. Give the name of the city only, not the state.
- **Year of publication**, followed by a period. If the date of publication is not given on the title page, look for it on the following page (the copyright page). If more than one date is given there, use the date of the edition you are using; usually that will be the last date in the list.

Often those basic parts are all that you'll need for listing books. But some books you use may require additional information:

- **Name of the editor, translator,** or **compiler,** for a book that has one in addition to an author. Place it after the title and edition used (if other than the first), preceded by the specific role ("Edited by" or "Translated by" or "Compiled by"), followed by a comma.
- **Edition used,** if other than the first, abbreviation followed by a comma ("3rd ed.,").
- **Volume used,** for a work that has more than one volume, followed by a comma ("vol. 5").

- **Date of original publication,** for republished books. (See 1d below.)
- **Series name,** and number (if any), not italicized or enclosed within quotation marks and followed by a period. (See 1c below.)

Here are explanations and examples to clarify some of those items and to clarify how to list works published in books.

1a. A Book by Two or More Authors

To cite a book by two authors, list the author's names in the order they appear on the title page; reverse the first author's name, followed by a comma, and list the second author's name in normal order.

> Brooks, Cleanth, and Robert Penn Warren. *Understanding Poetry*. Holt,
> Rinehart and Winston, 1938.

For three or more authors, give just the first author, followed by "et al." (the abbreviation for the Latin *et alii* or *et aliae*, "and others").

1b. A Book in a Series

If the book is part of a series (as indicated on the title page or on the copyright page that follows), include the series name (not italicized or in quotation marks) and number, if any. Follow it with a period.

> Defusco, Andrea, editor. *Readings on Robert Frost*. Greenhaven, 1999.
> Literary Companion Series.

1c. A Republished Book

To cite a republished book—for example, a paperback reprint of a hardcover book—give the original date of publication (optional), followed by a period, and the publication information for the book you are using.

> Kendall, Tim. *The Art of Robert Frost*. 2012. Yale UP, 2013.

1d. An Edited Collection

To cite as a single source a book made up of chapters by different authors, use the same form as for a book attributed in its entirety to one or more authors, with "editor" or "editors" added after the name(s) of the editor(s), preceded by a comma.

> Faggen, Robert, editor. *The Cambridge Companion to Robert Frost*.
> Cambridge UP, 2001.

To cite a specific chapter from such a collection, see 2c below.

1e. An Edited Edition

To cite a work prepared for publication by someone other than the author—by an editor—provide the information you would provide for a republished book, with the name of the editor inserted before the publication information, preceded by "Edited by."

> Frost, Robert. *The Collected Poems, Complete and Unabridged*. Edited by
>   Edward Connery Lathem, Henry Holt, 1969.

Note that, although the title page reads *The Poetry of Robert Frost: The Collected Poems, Complete and Unabridged*, repetition can be avoided to make it fit conventional citation form. The following example is not a reprint but the first printing of a collected edition of stories that were originally published separately in several books.

> Hughes, Langston. *The Return of Simple*. Edited by Akiba Sullivan
>   Harper, Hill, 1994.

1f. A Multivolume Work

To cite two or more volumes of a multivolume work, give the total number of volumes in the set after the publication information, using an arabic numeral followed by the abbreviation "vols." Parenthetical references in the text will require volume number plus page numbers ("2: 145–47"). For a work in which volumes were published separately, in different years, give the first and last dates.

> Martin, Wendy. *All Things Dickinson: An Encyclopedia of Emily Dickinson's
>   World*. Greenwood, 2014. 2 vols.

When you use only one volume of a multivolume work, give its volume number after the title, followed by a comma. In this case, only the page numbers are needed in parenthetical references in the text.

> Martin, Wendy. *All Things Dickinson: An Encyclopedia of Emily Dickinson's
>   World*. Vol. 2. Greenwood, 2014. 2 vols.

BOOKS USED AS CONTAINERS

Often sources you use will be items found in books. In such cases books are treated as containers instead of sources. The three basic Works Cited entry parts stay the same, but other information needs to added.

2a. A Work in a Collection of Stories or Poems

When you borrow from a work contained in a collection of stories or poems by a single author, insert the title of the story or poem, in quotation marks, between the name of the author and the title of the book, and give the first and last pages on which it appears after the date of publication, preceded by a comma.

Frost, Robert. "After Apple-Picking." *The Poetry of Robert Frost,* edited
    by. Edward Connery Latham, Holt, Rinehart and Winston, 1969,
    pp. 68–69.

If you borrow form additional works in the same collection, see 2b for cross referencing.

2b. A Work in an Anthology

When citing a work published in an anthology, give the author's name, the title of the work (in quotation marks for a story, a poem, or an essay; italicized for a play or screenplay), the title of the anthology, the editors, the publication information, and the first and last page numbers on which the work appears. If you want to include the original year of publication for clarity, insert it directly after the title.

Frost, Robert. "After Apple-Picking." 1914. *Approaching Literature:*
    Reading + Thinking + Writing, edited by Peter Schakel and Jack Ridl,
    4th ed., Bedford/St. Martin's, 2017, pp. 803-4.

If you borrow from several works in the same anthology, unnecessary repetition can be avoided by creating a main entry for the anthology and cross-referencing individual works to it.

Ríos, Alberto. "Nani." 1982. Schakel and Ridl, pp. 857-58.
Schakel, Peter, and Jack Ridl, editors. *Approaching Literature: Reading +*
    Thinking + Writing, 4th ed., Bedford/St. Martin's, 2017.
Walker, Alice. "The Flowers." 1973. Schakel and Ridl, pp. 20-21.

2c. A Scholarly Essay Published in a Collection of Essays

The information needed and the structure are the same as in 2b above.

Borroff, Marie. "Robert Frost: 'To Earthward.'" *Frost: Centennial Essays II,*
    edited by Jac Tharpe, UP of Mississippi, 1976, pp. 21-39.

2d. An Entry from an Encyclopedia or Dictionary

The citation for an encyclopedia article or dictionary entry follows the pattern for an essay in a collection (see 2c above). When the work has multiple editors, their names usually are not included. If the article or entry is signed, start with the author (sometimes articles in reference books are signed with initials identified elsewhere in the book); if it is anonymous, start with the title of the entry. If entries are arranged alphabetically in the encyclopedia or dictionary, volume and page numbers may be omitted.

> Richardson, Mark. "'After Apple-Picking'" *The Robert Frost Encyclopedia*,
>   edited by Nancy Lewis Tuten and John Zubizarreta, Greenwood
>   Press, 2001.

If you accessed the encyclopedia or dictionary entry online, include the URL (without http://). When available, DOIs and permalinks are preferable to URLs. Date of access is optional. Use it for Web sources that do not have a publication date.

> Durante, Amy M. "Finn Mac Cumhail." *Encyclopedia Mythica*, 17 Apr.
>   2011, www.pantheon.org/articles/f/finn_mac_cumhail.html.

SOURCES CONTAINED IN SCHOLARLY JOURNALS, MAGAZINES, AND NEWSPAPERS

3a. An Article Published in a Scholarly Journal

Although some scholarly articles are contained in books, more often they are contained in scholarly journals (often called "periodicals" because they are published periodically—usually once or twice or four times a year). Each year is designated as a volume, and pages are usually numbered continuously throughout the volume. Works Cited entries for journal articles include four basic parts:

> Author's name. "Title of Source [Article]." *Title of Container [Journal]*,
>   Publication information.

Here are some guidelines that clarify these basic parts:

- **Name of the author,** last name first, followed by a period.
- **Title of the article,** enclosed in quotation marks, followed by a period (inside the quotation mark), unless the title ends with a question mark or an exclamation point.

- **Title of the journal,** italicized, with comma following it.
- **Volume number of the journal** preceded by the abbreviation "vol." and using arabic numerals even if roman numerals are used in the journal, followed by a comma.
- **Issue number** (if available), preceded by the abbreviation "no." followed by a comma. For journals that number issues without using volume numbers, give the issue number alone: for example, "*Victorian Newsletter*, no. 118,".
- **Season or month and year of publication,** following the issue number and followed by a comma. Months are abbreviated except for May, June, and July.
- **Page numbers** (first and last), preceded by abbreviation "pp." and followed by a period.

Here is an example:

> Paton, Priscilla M. "Robert Frost: 'The Fact is the Sweetest Dream that Labor Knows.'" *American Literature,* vol. 53, no. 1, Mar. 1981, pp. 43-55.

3b. An Article Published in a Magazine

Magazines are usually printed more frequently than scholarly journals (often weekly, biweekly, monthly, or bimonthly) and pages are numbered separately in each issue. Magazines have volume numbers, but they are not important for locating an issue and are usually left out of Works Cited entries. Works Cited entries for magazine articles use the same four parts and punctuation as journal article entries:

> Author's name. "Title of Source [Article]." *Title of Container [Magazine],* Publication information.

But the publication information is handled differently. Here are some guidelines to follow:

- **Date of publication** Day, month (abbreviated, except for May, June, and July), and year (in that order) are given for weekly or biweekly magazines; only month or months and year are given for magazines published monthly or bimonthly. A comma follows, in either case.
- **Page numbers** If the article is longer than one page, give its first and last pages, not just the ones you used, followed by a period. If pagination is not consecutive (for example, the article begins on page 4 and continues on page 8), write only the first page number and a plus sign (4+), with no space between them.

Marisela did not use any magazine articles in her paper, but here is what a Works Cited entry for one would look like:

Kirsch, Adam. "Extracting the Woodchuck: Robert Frost's 'Doubleness' Revealed in His Letters — And Poems." *Harvard Magazine*, Jan.-Feb. 2014, pp. 44-48.

3c. An Article Published in a Newspaper

The format for citing an article in a newspaper is exactly the same as for a weekly magazine, unless the newspaper is published in varied editions (late edition, suburban edition); in that case, the edition is included after the date, separated by a comma. If a newspaper is divided into sections, include the section letter or section number with the page number. If the article is on nonconsecutive pages, give the first page number followed by a plus sign, with no space between them. The title of the newspaper should be given the way it appears on the masthead, but introductory articles should be omitted (*New York Times*, not *The New York Times*).

Kinzie, Susan. "Unknown Frost Poem Comes Out From Hiding at U-Va." *Washington Post,* 19 Sep. 2006, Metro sec., pp. B1+.

ARTICLES ACCESSED ELECTRONICALLY

Before the electronic era, a Works Cited list needed only to describe how to locate the printed volumes articles were contained in. Now such articles usually are accessed electronically, and electronic containers need to be described as well. For Works Cited entries involving the full text of a journal or magazine article accessed through a database such as *JSTOR*, *Project MUSE*, or *InfoTrac*, you must provide information about its original publication as well as the information a reader needs to access the source electronically. The basic pattern for such an entry has four parts:

Name of the author. "Title of Source [Article]." Information about print publication [Container 1]. Information about electronic posting [Container 2].

When the source does not provide all of that information, give as much as you can, following or adapting the following guidelines:

- **Name of the author,** last name first and followed by a period.
- **Title of the article,** enclosed in quotation marks, followed by a period, unless the title ends with a question mark or an exclamation point.

- **As much information about its publication in a journal or magazine as the database makes available,** following the guidelines above for journals and magazines. If no information about print publication is provided, proceed to the next step.
- **Information about where you accessed the article:** Give the name of the database you used (italicized), followed by a comma; if the DOI (digital object identifier) number or a permalink is available include that followed by a period. If not, include the complete URL for a database that has a stable URL or a truncated URL for library subscription databases such as EBSCO.

This is the way such an entry looks on Marisela's Works Cited page:

Paton, Priscilla M. "Robert Frost: 'The Fact Is the Sweetest Dream That Labor Knows.'" *American Literature,* vol. 53, no. 1, Mar. 1981, pp. 43-55. *JSTOR,* doi: 10.2307/2926193.

BOOK REVIEWS, INTERVIEWS, LETTERS, AND E-MAIL MESSAGES

The following pages provide instructions for and examples of many other—but not all—types of entries. If you can't find the help you need here, go to the *Writer's Help* (Bedford/St. Martin's) at writershelp.com.

4a. A Review

For a review, include the title and author of the work being reviewed after the review title and before the periodical title.

Della Subin, Anna. "It Has Burned My Heart." Review of *The Lives of Muhammad,* by Kecia Ali, *London Review of Books,* 22 Oct. 2015, www.lrb.co.uk/v37/n20/anna-della-subin/it-has-burned-my-heart.

4b. A Previously Published Journal Article Reprinted in a Collection

For a previously published scholarly article reprinted in a collection, give the complete data for the earlier publication and then add "Rpt. in" (for "Reprinted in"), the title of the collection, and its publication data.

Vendler, Helen. "Wallace Stevens: Memory, Dead and Alive." *The Wallace Stevens Journal,* vol. 28, no. 2, Sept. 2004, pp. 247-60. Rpt. in *The Ocean, the Bird, and the Scholar: Essays on Poets and Poetry.* Harvard UP, 2015, pp. 289-303.

4c. An Interview

For an interview, first give the name of the person being interviewed. If the interview has been published, provide the title (if it has one), in quotation marks, followed by a period and "Interview by," without quotation marks or italics. Add the name of the interviewer if known, and pertinent bibliographic information.

> Frost, Robert. "The Art of Poetry No. 2." Interview by Richard Poirier, *The Paris Review*, no. 24, Summer-Fall 1960, pp. 97-103.

For an interview you conducted personally, give the name of the person interviewed, the kind of interview ("Personal interview," "Telephone interview," "E-mail interview"), and the date or dates, such as the following (which we wish had really taken place):

> Nye, Naomi Shihab. Personal interview. 7 Sept. 2014.
> Nye, Naomi Shihab. E-mail interview. 13-15 Oct. 2014.

4d. A Personal Letter or an E-mail

For a personal written communication that you received, give the name of the sender, the type of communication, and its date

> Nye, Naomi Shihab. Letter to the author. 21 Oct. 2014.
> Nye, Naomi Shihab. E-mail to the author. 28 Oct. 2014.

WEB SOURCES

5a. A Work in an Online Scholarly Journal

In contrast to 2a above, some scholarly journals exist only in electronic form on the Web, not in print. They are periodicals, appearing on a regular schedule. Thus, to enter a work from such a journal in a Works Cited list, follow the guidelines in 3a as closely as possible, but end with the following items:

- The DOI (digital object identifier) or permalink if available. If not available, include the URL.
- Date of Access only for Web sources that do not have a publication date. Include the day, month, and year after the URL:
  [. . .] www.npr/org/. Accessed 3 Mar. 2016.

Amao, Olumuyiwa Babatunde, and Ufo Okeke-Uzodike. "Nigeria, Afrocentrism, and Conflict Resolution: After Five Decades — How Far, How Well?" *African Studies Quarterly*, vol. 15, no. 4, Sept. 2015, pp. 1–23, asq.africa.ufl.edu/files/Volume-15-Issue-4-OLUMUYIWA-BABATUNDE-AMAO.pdf.

5b. A Work in an Online Magazine

In contrast to 2b above, some magazines appear, on a regular schedule, only on the Web, not in print. To enter such a work in a Works Cited list, follow the guidelines in 2b as closely as possible, but end with the following items:

- The DOI (digital object identifier) or permalink if available. If not available, include the URL.
- Date of Access only for Web sources that do not have a publication date. Include the day, month, and year after the URL:

Leonard, Andrew. "The Surveillance State High School." *Salon*, 27 Nov. 2012, www.salon.com/2012/11/27/the_surveillance_state_high_school/.

5c. Information in a Web Page

Most Web sites are not periodicals. They are not updated on a regular basis, only as needed or as time permits. Some remain online but are neglected after a promising start, thus possibly reducing their freshness or reliability. Varying amounts and kinds of information are supplied, which makes doing Works Cited entries more challenging. Entries for such sources should contain as much of the following as possible:

- **Name of the author(s) or editor(s)** of the site, if available, followed by a period. If not available, start with the title.
- **Title of the work,** followed by a period. Italicize if this is the title of the entire site; enclose it in quotation marks if the work is part of a larger work.
- **Title of the overall Web site** (italicized, followed by a comma if different from the title of the work being used).
- **The name of the sponsoring organization or institution,** followed by a comma (if available).
- **Date of publication or posting** (day, month, and year, as available), followed by a comma. If no date is indicated, include your date of access after the URL. Abbreviate all months except May, June, and July.
- **URL** (without http://).

Here are some examples:

Railton, Stephen. *Mark Twain in His Times*. Stephen Railton / U of Virginia Library, 2012, twain.lib.virginia.edu/.

"Robert Frost." *Poems and Poets*. The Poetry Foundation, www.poetry foundation.org/bio/robert-frost. Accessed 18 Mar. 2016.

Transparency International. *Transparency International: The Global Coalition against Corruption*. 2015, www.transparency.org/.

For guidance on handling Works Cited entries for other electronic resources and nonprint media—such as television or radio broadcasts, sound recordings, performances, visual art, and others—see the *MLA Handbook*, 8th ed. (Modern Language Association of America, 2016) in the *MLA Style Center* website.

TIPS for Handling Online Sources

MLA style now requires the DOI (digital object identifier), permalink, or URL at which you found the document. DOIs and permalinks are generally more stable and reliable than URLs, so include these instead of a URL when available. It is always a good idea to check with your instructor on her or his preferences. Some instructors ask that URLs always be included, to make it easier to verify sources.

Because Internet sites sometimes disappear or move and can't be located again, it is a good idea to print out a copy of the material used for your paper. That way you can still verify information in case the site becomes inaccessible.

Approaching
FICTION

Photo: © Bettmann/Corbis

Overleaf: The author *James* Baldwin in a *relaxed* portrait of a writer at work, photographed in his New York apartment in 1963. Not yet forty years old when this photograph was taken, Baldwin was already established as a major literary presence with the publication of his semiautobiographical first novel, Go Tell It on the Mountain *(1953),* the essay collection Notes of a Native Son *(1955), and his second novel,* Giovanni's Room *(1956), among other works. Baldwin's work explores what it meant to be an African American in the twentieth century, and he was a lifelong and fierce defender of racial justice and equality. The responsibility of the writer, Baldwin told an interviewer, "is to excavate the experience of the people who produced him." (See p. 1055 for a short biography.)*

*F*iction is the lie that tells the truth.

Neil Gaiman

(English Fiction Writer and Graphic Novelist)

Reading Fiction CHAPTER 4
Responding to the
Real World of Stories

What are your own stories? What books and movies do you love? What television shows do you follow? The stories that you own, that you love, may incline toward realism or science fiction or romance—each of us is different, with individual tastes. But almost all of us are drawn toward stories of some sort. What is it about stories that draws you into their world, that makes you keep reading the book, watch every episode of the show, and watch the movie a third and fourth time?

We know that what we are reading or watching is not factual: These are made-up characters doing imaginary things. Yet we become deeply invested in their lives: We begin to think about the characters as if they are real, and we care about what happens to them. Why do we begin to sympathize deeply with a grieving mother or delight in the achievements of a college sophomore, neither of whom actually exists? The answer to these questions must start with the impressive power of imagination—with the way our imaginations respond to the imaginative creations of excellent writers. In the chapters to come, we look closely at such imaginative creations and at the way we use our own imaginations to enter, enjoy, and appreciate them.

WHAT IS FICTION?

Story Before we start that closer look, we need to clarify what it is we're talking about. *Story*, considered broadly, is any account of a related series of events in sequential order, usually chronological order (the order in which they happened). Stories did not start as something to be read: Long before people read stories or watched them being acted out in plays, they listened to stories being told or sung. From the time ancient peoples gathered around fires in the evening for warmth and safety, they told stories to each other. And although we no longer need campfires for warmth and protection, the storytelling tradition of "stories around the campfire" continues wherever people gather for companionship. Generations of children around the world have said to parents, "Tell me a story."

Story, in this broad sense, includes events that are true or made up — an account of the invading of Normandy in World War II, the planning for the prom during your junior year in high school, or the landing of three-headed cyborgs in an Iowa cornfield. The account can be narrated (told by a storyteller) or dramatized (acted out in drama). It can be told in prose or verse. Chapters 5 to 10 deal only with narrated stories, only with stories in prose, and only with stories that are fictional.

Fiction   *Fiction* refers to narrated stories that are drawn from the imagination or are an imaginative reworking of actual experiences. Incidents and details in a work of fiction can originate in fact, history, or everyday life, but the characters and events as a whole are primarily invented, or altered, in the author's imagination. Imaginative fiction (like movies) varies widely in types, from fast-paced adventures that focus on action to stories that examine characters and ideas in depth; they can be told at great length (*novels* or *epics*) or more briefly (*novellas* or short stories).

Short Stories   The works of fiction included in this book are *short stories*, relatively brief fictional narratives in prose that often focus on the essential aspects of a character (instead of showing character development over time, the way a novel can) and on a single event or episode — often a life-changing circumstance. They are characterized by careful, deliberate craftsmanship (in handling of plot, characterization, and point of view).

The short stories included in this book explore the complexities of life and people; they lead us to interact imaginatively with significant human issues; they offer us an opportunity to expand our understanding of ourselves, others, and the multiple cultures we find ourselves living with and within. They are widely respected by other writers, scholars, and general readers for the way they handle the techniques of fiction (the techniques discussed in Chapters 5 to 10) and for their insights into people, their values, their experiences, and their cultures.

WHY READ FICTION?

Entering Other Lives   What is the value of reading such stories? Most important, perhaps, is the way they can take us outside ourselves and, through our imaginations, enable us to enter other lives; other selves; other times, places, and cultures; other feelings and experiences. All of us live limited lives. We want to see more, expand our range of experiences, meet people whose lives are different from our own. That's why many people like to travel and why many students want to go away to college. A story enables us, without leaving our chairs, to escape our boundaries and broaden our understanding and vision. Think again of Sherman Alexie (see p. 4) and what reading stories did to "save his life."

Enlargement of Being   Author and literary critic C. S. Lewis explained the appeal of story this way: "We seek an enlargement of our being. We want to be more than ourselves. . . . We want to see with other eyes, to imagine with other imaginations, to feel with other hearts, as well as with our own" (*An Experiment in Criticism* [Cambridge University Press, 1961], 137). Fiction can do that. A story can mirror our own world, take us to a world that is not part of our daily experience, or create a world entirely new to us. To read fiction is to enter a place where you both disappear and find yourself—a place where, when you put the book down and look up, you feel even more yourself than you did before reading.

The Truth of Fiction   You have likely heard someone say, "Fiction? I don't read fiction. I want to read what's true." Fiction is not fact. It may contain facts, but it is still fiction. A literary scholar and a historian who were on a panel together were asked the difference between the two disciplines. The historian spoke about how important it was to get the facts correct in his work. The literary scholar then replied, "Yes. You deal with facts. I deal with truth." What was the literary scholar implying? Not that the historian wasn't searching for the truth within the facts, but that fiction is the embodiment of truth, at times factual truth, but always—if it is a fine work of fiction—the kind of truth that exists within, around, or beyond fact. This is a different kind of truth, the kind of truth that needs story to contain it, the truth of what it is like to live the facts, the kind of truth that exists and comes to life through what the writer "makes up." It is the truth of Captain Ahab's obsession with a white whale, Jane Eyre's dreams, Sherman Alexie's Superman. We need this truth. We need our stories.

ACTIVE READING: Fiction

The more you read, and the more widely you read, the more confident you will become in your ability to follow a story and appreciate what goes on in it. The purpose of Chapters 5 to 10 is to help you become a more skilled reader of fiction—more alert to the richness of a work of fiction, to the fascinating variety of good things it has to offer. Most of the things covered in those chapters, however, should not concern you the first time you read a short story or novel. Here are some suggestions for the first time you go through a story with an active imagination.

- *Give the work a fair chance.* Writers generally try to catch a reader's interest immediately, but some short stories and novels start slowly. Don't quit reading after a few paragraphs or pages. Give yourself enough time to get involved in the action and with the characters.

- *Keep going.* Even if some things aren't completely clear, later events probably will clarify them.

- *Watch for what's happening.* As in movies, some stories are filled with action and excitement. Others, often ones that deal with inner struggles, move more deliberately and with less external action.

- *Watch for who it is happening to.* Pay attention to the characters—their appearances, personalities, values, attitudes, struggles, weaknesses, strengths, and so forth.

- *Watch for "why"—why do the story's events happen as they do?* What happens that leads to the situations and actions? What causes the action? What motivates the characters?

REREADING: Fiction

Experiencing a story fully requires reading it more than once. The first time through, you concentrate primarily on what's going on. The second and third times through, you begin paying attention to other things—to easily overlooked details and nuances concerning plot and character and to the way the piece is written, the subtlety of techniques the author used.

You probably already do this with movies and music you love. Good movies, ones you really like, you watch twice, or many times, and you listen to favorite CDs over and over. We enjoy experiencing again the things we liked at first, of course; but our follow-up experience is different, richer, because we notice what we didn't notice before. It's the same for reading. Once you get into it, you'll enjoy rereading books or stories for the same reasons you like watching films or listening to music again. Here are some suggestions for rereading.

- *Slow down.* Let yourself absorb the flavor and style; roll the sentences and rhythms around on your tongue; reread paragraphs that aren't fully clear or that you find especially well written and enjoyable; go back to earlier parts to check on details that tie in with later ones.

- *Pay attention to the title.* Often it's significant and revealing, though its significance may not be evident during the first reading. In such cases, as you reread, it's worth reflecting on possible ways the title links to the actions and characters.

- *Look up things that aren't familiar.* Check unfamiliar words in a dictionary. The context often clarifies new words, but in other cases it doesn't, and you can miss something. Do some research on people from history, other literature, or historical events mentioned in the story. Look at a map when real places are used.

- *Pay attention to the first sentence and the first paragraph, especially for short stories.* Authors often embed within them a lot of important indicators about tone, style, setting, and subject. For the same reasons, pay close attention to the last paragraph and last sentence.

- *Pay attention to things that do not seem needed.* What appears insignificant may actually be a subtlety. Reflecting on its part in the whole can open up a deeper understanding of the characters or events.

If a true artist were born in a pigpen and raised in a sty, he would still find plenty of information for his work.

Willa Cather

(American Novelist)

CHAPTER **5** **Plot**

Watching What Happens

We hear and tell stories every day. "I heard your car broke down before you got to Sante Fe. What happened after that?" "Tell me about your first day at college when you have a few minutes to spare." Some people can all but mesmerize you with their portrayal of an event—they keep your attention focused on the subject, they include lots of specific details, they build momentum toward the important points. They never say, "Uh, where was I?" And others send you off daydreaming and hoping the end is coming soon. This chapter focuses on plot—on what happens in a story and how effective storytellers structure it in engaging ways that maintain interest and move readers to emotion, reflection, connection, empathy, realization, and more. We start here because plot is what most readers notice first. Without a good plot, most readers lose interest quickly.

APPROACHING THE READING

Read the following short story, about an unexpected encounter between a young man and a young woman on a street in Los Angeles. After getting a sense of the story from a first reading, read it again. This time see what more you notice in it, especially about the description of what happens and the way the two characters are depicted. Give some thought to how you feel about what happens and how you react to the characters.

Dagoberto Gilb   b. 1950

Love in L.A.   [1993]

Jake slouched in a clot of near motionless traffic, in the peculiar gray of concrete, smog, and early morning beneath the overpass of the Hollywood Freeway on Alvarado Street. He didn't really mind because he knew how much worse it could be trying to make a left onto the onramp. He certainly didn't do that every day of his life, and he'd assure anyone who'd ask that he never would either. A steady occupation had its advantages and he couldn't deny thinking about that too. He needed an FM radio in something better than this '58 Buick he drove. It would have crushed velvet interior with electric controls for the L.A. summer, a nice warm heater and defroster for the winter drives at the beach, a cruise control for those longer trips, mellow speakers front and rear of course, windows that hum closed, snuffing out that nasty exterior noise of freeways. The fact was that he'd probably have to change his whole style. Exotic colognes, plush, dark nightclubs, maitais and daquiris, necklaced ladies in satin gowns, misty and sexy like in a tequila ad. Jake could imagine lots of possibilities when he let himself, but none that ended up with him pressed onto a stalled freeway.

Jake was thinking about this freedom of his so much that when he glimpsed its green light he just went ahead and stared bye bye to the steadily employed. When he turned his head the same direction his windshield faced, it was maybe one second too late. He pounced the brake pedal and steered the front wheels away from the tiny brakelights but the smack was unavoidable. Just one second sooner and it would only have been close. One second more and he'd be crawling up the Toyota's trunk. As it was, it seemed like only a harmless smack, much less solid than the one against his back bumper.

APPROACHING THE AUTHOR

Dagoberto Gilb says that his most popular story, "Look on the Bright Side," was rejected 125 times before being accepted for publication.

For more about him, see page 1063.

Jake considered driving past the Toyota but was afraid the traffic ahead would make it too difficult. As he pulled up against the curb a few carlengths ahead, it occurred to him that the traffic might have helped him get away too. He slammed the car door twice to make sure it was closed fully and to give himself another second more, then toured front and rear of his Buick for damage on or near the bumpers. Not an impressionable scratch even in the chrome. He perked up. Though the car's beauty was secondary to its ability to start and move, the body and paint were clean except for a few minor dings. This stood out as one of his few clearcut accomplishments over the years.

Before he spoke to the driver of the Toyota, whose looks he could see might present him with an added complication, he signaled to the driver of the car that hit him, still in his car and stopped behind the Toyota, and waved his hands and shook his head to let the man know there was no problem as far as he was concerned. The driver waved back and started his engine.

"It didn't even scratch my paint," Jake told her in that way of his. "So how you doin? Any damage to the car? I'm kinda hoping so, just so it takes a little more time and we can talk some. Or else you can give me your phone number now and I won't have to lay my regular b.s. on you to get it later."

He took her smile as a good sign and relaxed. He inhaled her scent like it was clean air and straightened out his less than new but not unhip clothes.

"You've got Florida plates. You look like you must be Cuban."

"My parents are from Venezuela."

"My name's Jake." He held out his hand.

"Mariana."

They shook hands like she'd never done it before in her life.

"I really am sorry about hitting you like that." He sounded genuine. He fondled the wide dimple near the cracked taillight. "It's amazing how easy it is to put a dent in these new cars. They're so soft they might replace waterbeds soon." Jake was confused about how to proceed with this. So much seemed so unlikely, but there was always possibility. "So maybe we should go out to breakfast somewhere and talk it over."

"I don't eat breakfast."

"Some coffee then."

"Thanks, but I really can't."

"You're not married, are you? Not that that would matter that much to me. I'm an openminded kinda guy."

She was smiling. "I have to get to work."

"That sounds boring."

"I better get your driver's license," she said.

Jake nodded, disappointed. "One little problem," he said. "I didn't bring it. I just forgot it this morning. I'm a musician," he exaggerated greatly, "and, well, I dunno, I left my wallet in the pants I was wearing last night. If you have some paper and a pen I'll give my address and all that."

He followed her to the glove compartment side of her car.

"What if we don't report it to the insurance companies? I'll just get it fixed for you."

"I don't think my dad would let me do that."

"Your dad? It's not your car?"

"He bought it for me. And I live at home."

"Right." She was slipping away from him. He went back around to the back of her new Toyota and looked over the damage again. There was the trunk lid, the bumper, a rear panel, a taillight.

"You do have insurance?" she asked, suspicious, as she came around the back of the car.

"Oh yeah," he lied.

"I guess you better write the name of that down too."

He made up a last name and address and wrote down the name of an insurance company an old girlfriend once belonged to. He considered giving a real phone number but went against that idea and made one up.

"I act too," he lied to enhance the effect more. "Been in a couple of movies."

She smiled like a fan.

"So how about your phone number?" He was rebounding maturely.

She gave it to him.

"Mariana, you are beautiful," he said in his most sincere voice.   35

"Call me," she said timidly.

Jake beamed. "We'll see you, Mariana," he said holding out his hand. Her hand felt so warm and soft he felt like he'd been kissed.

Back in his car he took a moment or two to feel both proud and sad about his performance. Then he watched the rear view mirror as Mariana pulled up behind him. She was writing down the license plate numbers on his Buick, ones that he'd taken off a junk because the ones that belonged to his had expired so long ago. He turned the ignition key and revved the big engine and clicked into drive. His sense of freedom swelled as he drove into the now moving street traffic, though he couldn't stop the thought about that FM stereo radio and crushed velvet interior and the new car smell that would even make it better.

REFLECTING ON WHAT YOU'VE READ

1. Try sketching out the story, what happens in the order it happens. Reflect on the organization of the plot: Why does it start where it does? How would the effect be different if it had started at a different point? Why does it linger on certain sections and go into great detail? Why does it stop where it does and not follow through to the consequences of what happens here?

2. Now think about what is left out and what is emphasized in plotting the story. Why is what Jake is thinking before his car hits Mariana's important to the basic story? If you think it isn't important, explain why the author might have included it. What about the exact words that Jake and Mariana use makes them crucial to the story's impact? Why are they included?

3. Think about what both characters are like. What do you feel about each? Do your feelings about either change as the story proceeds? In what way or ways?

4. What significance or implications arise out of the decisions about what to include, what not to include, and how these details are organized in the story? Pick out several specific details and think about their relation to the point of the story.

READING FOR PLOT

Story and Plot   *Plot*, in a literary sense, is the action in a story and the way events are selected and arranged to present them most effectively to the reader. Comparing *plot* with *story* can help clarify that. *Story*, as we use the word in Chapter 4, is a straightforward account of everything that happens, in the order it happens. A story is what you would hear if you saw Mariana that evening and she said, "Let me tell you about my day." Story provides the materials (the events, the characters, the outcome) from which a plot is constructed.

Plot as Structure   As an author constructs a story into a plot, she or he decides what to include and what to leave out (things that aren't essential for the effect and emphasis desired) and in what order to tell about what happens (whether to start at the beginning—as "Love in L.A." does—or in the middle or near the end). The author also needs to establish causal connections between the key events. Plot provides the *structure* of a work of fiction, that is, the arrangement of material in it, the ordering of its parts, the design used to draw out and convey its significance.

STARTING THE ACTION

Where to Start   A plot usually starts at a point that relates directly and significantly to the series of events being recorded: "Love in L.A." starts at the beginning of the sequence of events the author wanted to focus on, with Jake in his car caught in a traffic jam. But works of fiction don't need to start at the beginning of a sequence of events. Sometimes the first events in the sequence, though necessary to the story, are not the best place to start. "Love in L.A." could have begun in the middle, with Jake's car bumping Mariana's, and then gone back to explain what Jake was daydreaming about instead of paying attention to his driving. If Dagoberto Gilb had wanted to emphasize the accident itself, as a highly dramatic moment, he might have started in the middle. But because he wants readers to focus more on Jake's character than on the accident, he starts with what is going on in Jake's head before the fender bender occurs.

ORGANIZING THE ACTION

Strategies of Organization   Decisions about how to arrange events follow from the decision of where to start. Because "Love in L.A." starts at the sequence's beginning, it is organized in *chronological order*, the order in which the events occur. Stories that don't start at the beginning need different organizational strategies. This way of starting has been used for thousands of years—the Latin phrase *in medias res*, meaning "into the middle of things," is used to describe it. Earlier background events are usually filled in through *flashback* (in which earlier events are presented as an inserted narrative or a scene, perhaps with a character *remembering* what happened earlier) or through *exposition* (a nondramatized explanation, often a speech by a character or the narrator, *explaining* what occurred before the initial action of a story or play).

Developing a Conflict Organizing how the story is told includes incorporating techniques for increasing intensity and holding interest. A crucial technique is to create some kind of *conflict*, some struggle or confrontation between opposing characters or a character and opposing forces. In most cases, at least one side of the struggle involves the main character. Conflict arises in three main forms:

- **Physical conflict.** One basic kind of conflict occurs as a physical struggle or confrontation between a character or group of characters and another character or group of characters: the showdown between a sheriff's posse and a gang of outlaws in an old Western, for example, or a fistfight between two rivals at a high school prom. Physical conflict can also involve humans struggling against nature: a group of sailors, perhaps led by an inexperienced captain, attempting to survive a fierce storm. "Love in L.A." has no physical conflict, but it's easy to imagine how the events could have turned into a road-rage story with physical conflict at its center.

- **Social conflict.** A second type of conflict involves differences regarding personal or societal relationships or values. This is a common motif in modern fiction. Examples could include a teenager challenging her or his parents, or an activist confronting a social injustice. Part of the conflict in "Love in L.A." is the way Jake's lifestyle runs counter to social norms: Society expects drivers to have insurance and accept responsibility for any damage they cause to other people's property; it requires people to carry their driver's licenses and have accurate license plates on their cars. The story gives you as reader the options of identifying with Jake and enjoying the way he flouts social expectations or dismissing him as irresponsible or, perhaps, feeling caught between accepting Jake's laid-back charm and rejecting what he does as illegal and immoral. This is a good example of how conflict can be reflected back to us when we read actively, causing us to internalize the conflict, to reenact the story internally.

- **Internal or psychological conflict.** Another variety of conflict deals with struggles within a character, as she or he wrestles with competing moral claims or a difficult decision. This has always been a central issue for literature. Numerous stories in this book show characters engaged in such inner struggles, often at crucial moments in the characters' lives. For example:
  - an identity crisis, when an event forces a character to a new or deeper sense of self-knowledge or self-awareness, often a moment of maturation, like Myop's in "The Flowers" (p. 27)
  - facing the moment of death, as the grandmother does in "A Good Man Is Hard to Find" (p. 159)
  - a belief crisis, when something causes a character to reexamine the foundation of what she or he puts faith or trust in, as in "Young Goodman Brown" (p. 359)

- a values crisis, when something forces a character to make a moral or an ethical decision, such as Sammy's in "A & P" (p. 188), or sometimes to adhere to standards she or he has held to — or should have adhered to — in the past.

A lack of inner conflict can be equally significant: One of the most revealing things about Jake in "Love in L.A." is his lack of any internal struggle, despite doing some things that would trouble most readers' consciences at least somewhat.

> **TIP:** Focusing on a conflict can be a helpful way to "get into" a story. Usually when you identify a story's conflict or conflicts, you are getting to the center of what's important in the story. That can lead to a valuable discussion about why the conflict is worth taking seriously and how the conflict may serve as a unifying factor in the work.

Developmental Techniques   In addition to the use of conflict for organizing the action in stories, authors rely on several other techniques that you can enjoy discovering. Be alert to the following, at least when you are rereading:

- **Suspense.** To hold readers' interest, a plot often creates some degree of *suspense*, some uncertainty and concern about how things will turn out, who did what, what the effects on the characters or events will be, or if or when disaster will fall or a rescue occur. The word *suspense* might feel too strong for "Love in L.A.," but the story does make us curious, at least, to find out if Jake gets away with all that he's trying to.
- **Foreshadowing.** The beginning and middle of a story often contain *foreshadowings*, anticipations of things that will happen later. In "The Flowers," for example, the words "It seemed gloomy in the little cove" and "the air was damp, the silence close and deep" (p. 27) sound ominous and foreshadow that this beautiful scene is not going to stay peaceful and beautiful.
- **Repetition.** Repeating a word or an image or a detail can draw attention to especially important aspects of a story. The repetition of "that FM stereo radio and crushed velvet interior" in "Love in L.A." (para. 1, 38) signals what is most important in Jake's value system, and the repeated references to death in Flannery O'Connor's "A Good Man Is Hard to Find" (p. 159) foreshadow what happens at the end of the story.
- **Climax.** The development of a plot holds readers' attention by becoming more complex and more intense (sometimes referred to as *rising action* or *complication*), until it reaches a crisis of some sort, often called the *climax*. It's important to remember that identifying a climax is not the same as understanding a work of fiction, nor is it a definite feature all readers

identify the same way. There can be differences of opinion about what a story's climax is or even about whether a given story has one. If "Love in L.A." has a climax, it might well come in the next-to-last paragraph when Jake seems not only to have avoided responsibility for the accident but also to have won Mariana's interest in him: "'Call me,' she said timidly" (para. 36). But she has not been totally taken in by his "performance" (para. 38) — she also writes down his illegal license plate number.

- **Epiphany.** One particular type of climax is called an *epiphany*, a moment when a character experiences a sudden moment of illumination or revelation, especially as the result of perceiving a commonplace object in a new way or through a new context. Esperanza in "The House on Mango Street" (p. 145) might be said to experience an epiphany when the nun points to her third-floor apartment and says, "You live *there*?" (para. 9). Suddenly she realizes how other people regard her house, what the house says about her and her family, how much she needs to have a "real house" to improve her sense of self-worth and identity.

- **Gaps.** A literary work can't (and shouldn't) include everything that happens during the series of events it is relating — whatever is not significant to the action typically is left out. In "Love in L.A." we hear only about a few minutes in Jake's day. The rest is left out: what time he got up, whether he had breakfast, where he is going. These details may be important in Jake's larger life, but because they are not relevant to his encounter with Mariana, they do not concern readers. For fiction writers, decisions about what to leave out are important to the story's structure, as important as decisions about what to include.

  - Some intentional gaps are omissions of insignificant details and occur only to avoid cluttering the story with irrelevancies. We aren't told what Jake had for breakfast that morning because what he ate had nothing to do with what happened later.
  - Some intentional gaps omit significant details and are used as a way of getting readers actively involved. Mystery and detective stories always create gaps (Who did it? Why?) within their structure. Part of the enjoyment of reading stories is using our imaginations to supply missing details or connecting links, anticipating what may be ahead, and revising our earlier anticipations in light of what we find out later.
  - Some intentional gaps omit details that could distract us from what is more important.
  - Some gaps, however, are unintentional — for example, not including women in a particular story or relegating them to minor roles. Such gaps are significant nonetheless. What the author does *not* think about is part of her or his idea framework as much as what she or he consciously does think about. Paying attention not just to what is there but also to what is not there requires alert, active involvement in a *process*. Reading this way can feel demanding, but the rewards are well worth the effort.

CONCLUDING THE ACTION

Ending a Story   A story must end, of course—it can't go on forever. But it also can't just stop. The difference between just stopping and an effective ending is that the latter gives a sense of wholeness and leaves the reader satisfied or satisfyingly unsatisfied. One of the big differences between fiction and real life is that life carries on after a "big event," while the series of events in a fictional plot reach a terminal point, the conflicts around which it was shaped are resolved (or shown to be unresolvable), and the story ends.

The last paragraph of "Love in L.A.," for example, has a feeling of finality: The lives of Jake and Mariana do not end, but nothing that could follow would be relevant to the story of their encounter under the Alvarado Street overpass. You, as an active reader, might imagine Mariana's pained and disappointed reaction and her father's furious response when they find out that all the information Jake gave her was false, which might then form an important part of how you feel about Jake's actions in the final analysis. Jake and Mariana's personal encounter could have touched Jake and made a difference in his life, but the last sentence shows that it didn't. The end takes us back to the beginning and the daydreams he chooses over reality. (The French term *dénouement* is often used in discussing conclusions.)

 CHECKLIST on Reading for Plot

❏ Notice the structuring of plot:
  - its strategies for starting, developing, and ending the action
  - its handling of suspense, foreshadowing, repetition, climax, and in some cases epiphany
  - its decisions about what to include and what to leave out (gaps)

❏ Look for conflicts—physical, social, internal—and use them as a way to get into the story and to explore its complexity.

❏ Try outlining the story as a way of seeing its organizational structure.

FURTHER READING

APPROACHING THE READING

The following story is about two brothers, Lyman and Henry, and a car that comes to epitomize their love for each other. It was written by Louise Erdrich, who grew up near the Turtle Mountain Reservation and is a member of the Turtle Mountain Band of Chippewa. Many of the place names in the story can be found on maps of North and South Dakota.

Pay attention to how the story handles plot—which details the author includes, how these details are arranged, and how they relate to each other and work together to convey a unified effect.

Louise Erdrich b. 1954

The Red Convertible [1984]

I was the first one to drive a convertible on my reservation. And of course it was red, a red Olds. I owned that car along with my brother Henry Junior. We owned it together until his boots filled with water on a windy night and he bought out my share. Now Henry owns the whole car, and his younger brother Lyman (that's myself), Lyman walks everywhere he goes.

How did I earn enough money to buy my share in the first place? My one talent was I could always make money. I had a touch for it, unusual in a Chippewa. From the first I was different that way, and everyone recognized it. I was the only kid they let in the American Legion Hall to shine shoes, for example, and one Christmas I sold spiritual bouquets for the mission door to door. The nuns let me keep a percentage. Once I started, it seemed the more money I made the easier the money came. Everyone encouraged it. When I was fifteen I got a job washing dishes at the Joliet Café, and that was where my first big break happened.

APPROACHING THE AUTHOR

Louise Erdrich held jobs as a lifeguard, waitress, poetry teacher at prisons, truck weigher on the interstate, and construction-flag signaler before she became an editor for *The Circle*, a Boston Indian Council newspaper.

Ulf Andersen/Getty Images

For more about her, see page 1062.

It wasn't long before I was promoted to busing tables, and then the short-order cook quit and I was hired to take her place. No sooner than you know it I was managing the Joliet. The rest is history. I went on managing. I soon became part owner, and of course there was no stopping me then. It wasn't long before the whole thing was mine.

After I'd owned the Joliet for one year, it blew over in the worst tornado ever seen around here. The whole operation was smashed to bits. A total loss. The fryalator was up in a tree, the grill torn in half like it was paper. I was only sixteen. I had it all in my mother's name, and I lost it quick, but before I lost it I had every one of my relatives, and their relatives, to dinner, and I also bought that red Olds I mentioned, along with Henry.

The first time we saw it! I'll tell you when we first saw it. We had gotten a ride up to Winnipeg, and both of us had money. Don't ask me why, because we never mentioned a car or anything, we just had all our money. Mine was cash, a big bankroll from the Joliet's insurance. Henry had two checks—a week's extra pay for being laid off, and his regular check from the Jewel Bearing Plant.

We were walking down Portage anyway, seeing the sights, when we saw it. There it was, parked, large as life. Really as *if* it was alive. I thought of the word *repose*, because the car wasn't simply stopped, parked, or whatever. That car reposed, calm and gleaming, a FOR SALE sign in its left front window. Then, before we had thought it over at all, the car belonged to us and our pockets were empty. We had just enough money for gas back home.

We went places in that car, me and Henry. We took off driving all one whole summer. We started off toward the Little Knife River and Mandaree in Fort Berthold and then we found ourselves down in Wakpala somehow, and then suddenly we were over in Montana on the Rocky Boy, and yet the summer was not even half over. Some people hang on to details when they travel, but we didn't let them bother us and just lived our everyday lives here to there.

I do remember this one place with willows. I remember I laid under those trees and it was comfortable. So comfortable. The branches bent down all around me like a tent or a stable. And quiet, it was quiet, even though there was a powwow close enough so I could see it going on. The air was not too still, not too windy either. When the dust rises up and hangs in the air around the dancers like that, I feel good. Henry was asleep with his arms thrown wide. Later on, he woke up and we started driving again. We were somewhere in Montana, or maybe on the Blood Reserve—it could have been anywhere. Anyway it was where we met the girl.

All her hair was in buns around her ears, that's the first thing I noticed about her. She was posed alongside the road with her arm out, so we stopped. That girl was short, so short her lumber shirt looked comical on her, like a nightgown. She had jeans on and fancy moccasins and she carried a little suitcase.

"Hop on in," says Henry. So she climbs in between us.   10

"We'll take you home," I says. "Where do you live?"

"Chicken," she says.

"Where the hell's that?" I ask her.

"Alaska."

"Okay," says Henry, and we drive.   15

We got up there and never wanted to leave. The sun doesn't truly set there in summer, and the night is more a soft dusk. You might doze off, sometimes, but before you know it you're up again, like an animal in nature. You never feel like you have to sleep hard or put away the world. And things would grow up there. One day just dirt or moss, the next day flowers and long grass. The girl's name was Susy. Her family really took to us. They fed us and put us up. We had our own tent to live in by their house, and the kids would be in and out of there all day and night. They couldn't get over me and Henry being brothers, we looked so different. We told them we knew we had the same mother, anyway.

One night Susy came in to visit us. We sat around in the tent talking of this and that. The season was changing. It was getting darker by that time, and the cold was even getting just a little mean. I told her it was time for us to go. She stood up on a chair.

"You never seen my hair," Susy said.

That was true. She was standing on a chair, but still, when she unclipped her buns the hair reached all the way to the ground. Our eyes opened. You couldn't tell how much hair she had when it was rolled up so neatly. Then my brother Henry did something funny. He went up to the chair and said, "Jump on my shoulders." So she did that, and her hair reached down past his waist, and he started twirling, this way and that, so her hair was flung out from side to side.

"I always wondered what it was like to have long pretty hair," Henry says. Well we laughed. It was a funny sight, the way he did it. The next morning we got up and took leave of those people.

On to greener pastures, as they say. It was down through Spokane and across Idaho then Montana and very soon we were racing the weather right along under the Canadian border through Columbus, Des Lacs, and then we were in Bottineau County and soon home. We'd made most of the trip, that summer, without putting up the car hood at all. We got home just in time, it turned out, for the army to remember Henry had signed up to join it.

I don't wonder that the army was so glad to get my brother that they turned him into a Marine. He was built like a brick outhouse anyway. We liked to tease him that they really wanted him for his Indian nose. He had a nose big and sharp as a hatchet, like the nose on Red Tomahawk, the Indian who killed Sitting Bull, whose profile is on signs all along the North Dakota highways. Henry went off to training camp, came home once during Christmas, then the next thing you know we got an overseas letter from him. It was 1970, and he said he was stationed up in the northern hill country. Whereabouts I did not know. He wasn't such a hot letter writer, and only got off two before the enemy caught him. I could never keep it straight, which direction those good Vietnam soldiers were from.

I wrote him back several times, even though I didn't know if those letters would get through. I kept him informed all about the car. Most of the time I had it up on blocks in the yard or half taken apart, because that long trip did a hard job on it under the hood.

I always had good luck with numbers, and never worried about the draft myself. I never even had to think about what my number was.° But Henry was never lucky in the same way as me. It was at least three years before Henry came

---

what my number was: A lottery system based on birthdays was used for the military draft from 1970 until 1973. Capsules containing the 365 days of the year were prepared and the days listed in the order drawn. Men like Henry, with birthdays drawn early (approximately the upper third), were certain to be called up for service, while those whose birthdays came in the bottom third (presumably like Lyman) were likely not to be needed. In 1973, the draft ended and the United States converted to an all-volunteer military.

home. By then I guess the whole war was solved in the government's mind, but for him it would keep on going. In those years I'd put his car into almost perfect shape. I always thought of it as his car while he was gone, even though when he left he said, "Now it's yours," and threw me his key.

"Thanks for the extra key," I'd said. "I'll put it up in your drawer just in case 25 I need it." He laughed.

When he came home, though, Henry was very different, and I'll say this: the change was no good. You could hardly expect him to change for the better, I know. But he was quiet, so quiet, and never comfortable sitting still anywhere but always up and moving around. I thought back to times we'd sat still for whole afternoons, never moving a muscle, just shifting our weight along the ground, talking to whoever sat with us, watching things. He'd always had a joke, then, too, and now you couldn't get him to laugh, or when he did it was more the sound of a man choking, a sound that stopped up the throats of other people around him. They got to leaving him alone most of the time, and I didn't blame them. It was a fact: Henry was jumpy and mean.

I'd bought a color TV set for my mom and the rest of us while Henry was away. Money still came very easy. I was sorry I'd ever bought it though, because of Henry. I was also sorry I'd bought color, because with black-and-white the pictures seem older and farther away. But what are you going to do? He sat in front of it, watching it, and that was the only time he was completely still. But it was the kind of stillness that you see in a rabbit when it freezes and before it will bolt. He was not easy. He sat in his chair gripping the armrests with all his might, as if the chair itself was moving at a high speed and if he let go at all he would rocket forward and maybe crash right through the set.

Once I was in the room watching TV with Henry and I heard his teeth click at something. I looked over, and he'd bitten through his lip. Blood was going down his chin. I tell you right then I wanted to smash that tube to pieces. I went over to it but Henry must have known what I was up to. He rushed from his chair and shoved me out of the way, against the wall. I told myself he didn't know what he was doing.

My mom came in, turned the set off real quiet, and told us she had made something for supper. So we went and sat down. There was still blood going down Henry's chin, but he didn't notice it and no one said anything, even though every time he took a bite of his bread his blood fell onto it until he was eating his own blood mixed in with the food.

While Henry was not around we talked about what was going to happen to 30 him. There were no Indian doctors on the reservation, and my mom couldn't come around to trusting the old man, Moses Pillager, because he courted her long ago and was jealous of her husbands. He might take revenge through her son. We were afraid that if we brought Henry to a regular hospital they would keep him.

"They don't fix them in those places," Mom said; "they just give them drugs."

"We wouldn't get him there in the first place," I agreed, "so let's just forget about it."

Then I thought about the car.

Henry had not even looked at the car since he'd gotten home, though like I said, it was in tip-top condition and ready to drive. I thought the car might bring the old Henry back somehow. So I bided my time and waited for my chance to interest him in the vehicle.

One night Henry was off somewhere. I took myself a hammer. I went out   35 to that car and I did a number on its underside. Whacked it up. Bent the tail pipe double. Ripped the muffler loose. By the time I was done with the car it looked worse than any typical Indian car that has been driven all its life on reservation roads, which they always say are like government promises — full of holes. It just about hurt me, I'll tell you that! I threw dirt in the carburetor and I ripped all the electric tape off the seats. I made it look just as beat up as I could. Then I sat back and waited for Henry to find it.

Still, it took him over a month. That was all right, because it was just getting warm enough, not melting, but warm enough to work outside.

"Lyman," he says, walking in one day, "that red car looks like shit."

"Well it's old," I says. "You got to expect that."

"No way!" says Henry. "That car's a classic! But you went and ran the piss right out of it, Lyman, and you know it don't deserve that. I kept that car in A-one shape. You don't remember. You're too young. But when I left, that car was running like a watch. Now I don't even know if I can get it to start again, let alone get it anywhere near its old condition."

"Well you try," I said, like I was getting mad, "but I say it's a piece of junk."   40

Then I walked out before he could realize I knew he'd strung together more than six words at once.

After that I thought he'd freeze himself to death working on that car. He was out there all day, and at night he rigged up a little lamp, ran a cord out the window, and had himself some light to see by while he worked. He was better than he had been before, but that's still not saying much. It was easier for him to do the things the rest of us did. He ate more slowly and didn't jump up and down during the meal to get this or that or look out the window. I put my hand in the back of the TV set, I admit, and fiddled around with it good, so that it was almost impossible now to get a clear picture. He didn't look at it very often anyway. He was always out with that car or going off to get parts for it. By the time it was really melting outside, he had it fixed.

I had been feeling down in the dumps about Henry around this time. We had always been together before. Henry and Lyman. But he was such a loner now that I didn't know how to take it. So I jumped at the chance one day when Henry seemed friendly. It's not that he smiled or anything. He just said, "Let's take that old shitbox for a spin." Just the way he said it made me think he could be coming around.

We went out to the car. It was spring. The sun was shining very bright. My only sister, Bonita, who was just eleven years old, came out and made us stand together for a picture. Henry leaned his elbow on the red car's windshield, and he took his other arm and put it over my shoulder, very carefully, as though it was heavy for him to lift and he didn't want to bring the weight down all at once.

"Smile," Bonita said, and he did.   45

That picture. I never look at it anymore. A few months ago, I don't know why, I got his picture out and tacked it on the wall. I felt good about Henry at the time, close to him. I felt good having his picture on the wall, until one night when I was looking at television. I was a little drunk and stoned. I looked up at the wall and Henry was staring at me. I don't know what it was, but his smile had changed, or maybe it was gone. All I know is I couldn't stay in the same room with that picture. I was shaking. I got up, closed the door, and went into the kitchen. A little later my friend Ray came over and we both went back into that room. We put the picture in a brown bag, folded the bag over and over tightly, then put it way back in a closet.

I still see that picture now, as if it tugs at me, whenever I pass that closet door. The picture is very clear in my mind. It was so sunny that day Henry had to squint against the glare. Or maybe the camera Bonita held flashed like a mirror, blinding him, before she snapped the picture. My face is right out in the sun, big and round. But he might have drawn back, because the shadows on his face are deep as holes. There are two shadows curved like little hooks around the ends of his smile, as if to frame it and try to keep it there—that one, first smile that looked like it might have hurt his face. He has his field jacket on and the worn-in clothes he'd come back in and kept wearing ever since. After Bonita took the picture, she went into the house and we got into the car. There was a full cooler in the trunk. We started off, east, toward Pembina and the Red River because Henry said he wanted to see the high water.

The trip over there was beautiful. When everything starts changing, drying up, clearing off, you feel like your whole life is starting. Henry felt it, too. The top was down and the car hummed like a top. He'd really put it back in shape, even the tape on the seats was very carefully put down and glued back in layers. It's not that he smiled again or even joked, but his face looked to me as if it was clear, more peaceful. It looked as though he wasn't thinking of anything in particular except the bare fields and windbreaks and houses we were passing.

The river was high and full of winter trash when we got there. The sun was still out, but it was colder by the river. There were still little clumps of dirty snow here and there on the banks. The water hadn't gone over the banks yet, but it would, you could tell. It was just at its limit, hard swollen, glossy like an old gray scar. We made ourselves a fire, and we sat down and watched the current go. As I watched it I felt something squeezing inside me and tightening and trying to let go all at the same time. I knew I was not just feeling it myself; I knew I was feeling what Henry was going through at that moment. Except that I couldn't stand it, the closing and opening. I jumped to my feet. I took Henry by the shoulders and I started shaking him. "Wake up," I says, "wake up, wake up, wake up!" I didn't know what had come over me. I sat down beside him again.

His face was totally white and hard. Then it broke, like stones break all of 50 a sudden when water boils up inside them.

"I know it," he says. "I know it. I can't help it. It's no use."

We start talking. He said he knew what I'd done with the car. It was obvious it had been whacked out of shape and not just neglected. He said he wanted to give the car to me for good now, it was no use. He said he'd fixed it just to give it back and I should take it.

"No way," I says. "I don't want it."

"That's okay," he says, "you take it."

"I don't want it, though," I says back to him, and then to emphasize, just 55 to emphasize, you understand, I touch his shoulder. He slaps my hand off.

"Take that car," he says.

"No," I say. "Make me," I say, and then he grabs my jacket and rips the arm loose. That jacket is a class act, suede with tags and zippers. I push Henry backwards, off the log. He jumps up and bowls me over. We go down in a clinch and come up swinging hard, for all we're worth, with our fists. He socks my jaw so hard I feel like it swings loose. Then I'm at his rib cage and land a good one under his chin so his head snaps back. He's dazzled. He looks at me and I look at him and then his eyes are full of tears and blood and at first I think he's crying. But no, he's laughing. "Ha! Ha!" he says. "Ha! Ha! Take good care of it."

"Okay," I says. "Okay, no problem. Ha! Ha!"

I can't help it, and I start laughing, too. My face feels fat and strange, and after a while I get a beer from the cooler in the trunk, and when I hand it to Henry he takes his shirt and wipes my germs off. "Hoof-and-mouth disease," he says. For some reason this cracks me up, and so we're really laughing for a while, and then we drink all the rest of the beers one by one and throw them in the river and see how far, how fast, the current takes them before they fill up and sink.

"You want to go on back?" I ask after a while. "Maybe we could snag a 60 couple nice Kashpaw girls."

He says nothing. But I can tell his mood is turning again.

"They're all crazy, the girls up here, every damn one of them."

"You're crazy too," I say, to jolly him up. "Crazy Lamartine boys!"

He looks as though he will take this wrong at first. His face twists, then clears, and he jumps up on his feet. "That's right!" he says. "Crazier 'n hell. Crazy Indians!"

I think it's the old Henry again. He throws off his jacket and starts spring- 65
ing his legs up from the knees like a fancy dancer.° He's down doing something
between a grass dance and a bunny hop, no kind of dance I ever saw before, but
neither has anyone else on all this green growing earth. He's wild. He wants to
pitch whoopee! He's up and at me and all over. All this time I'm laughing so
hard, so hard my belly is getting tied up in a knot.

"Got to cool me off!" he shouts all of a sudden. Then he runs over to the
river and jumps in.

There's boards and other things in the current. It's so high. No sound
comes from the river after the splash he makes, so I run right over. I look
around. It's getting dark. I see he's halfway across the water already, and I know
he didn't swim there but the current took him. It's far. I hear his voice, though,
very clearly across it.

"My boots are filling," he says.

He says this in a normal voice, like he just noticed and he doesn't know
what to think of it. Then he's gone. A branch comes by. Another branch. And I
go in.

By the time I get out of the river, off the snag I pulled myself onto, the 70
sun is down. I walk back to the car, turn on the high beams, and drive it up
the bank. I put it in first gear and then I take my foot off the clutch. I get out, close
the door, and watch it plow softly into the water. The headlights reach in as they
go down, searching, still lighted even after the water swirls over the back end. I
wait. The wires short out. It is all finally dark. And then there is only the water,
the sound of it going and running and going and running and running.

REFLECTING ON WHAT YOU'VE READ

1. Outline the plot of "The Red Convertible." Then comment on the way
   it starts, the way it builds in the middle (what kinds of conflicts appear,
   how the material is arranged), and the way it ends. What effects are
   achieved through the way the plot is organized and developed?

2. Think about what is left out and what is added or emphasized in plotting
   the story. What gaps are left in the story? How do they force you to become
   actively involved as a reader? What does the inclusion of the episodes about
   Henry and Lyman's travels — the place under the willows where they rested
   and taking Susy home to Alaska — contribute to the story? What would be
   lost if those details were not there?

---

fancy dancer: A person performing (often in contests) a style of Native American dance based
on traditional and grass dances but done in brilliant costumes, at rapid speeds, with fancy
footwork, acrobatic steps, and varied body movements.

3. Describe what Lyman and Henry are like. How much of what we know about Henry depends on what we know about Lyman, and what difference does that make?

4. Why does Henry jump into the river? Does he intend to drown, or is it accidental? In what ways does he change in the story, and what things cause him to change? Why does Lyman roll the car into the river?

APPROACHING THE READING

Here is another story about cars and young people, but in a very different style and tone (more like a psychological thriller). It was written by Joyce Carol Oates, whose work has explored the nature of violence in America extensively. Like "The Red Convertible," it is a carefully constructed story. As you read or reread it, pay close attention to its plot: what is included, what is left out, the way it is arranged, and the way it builds to a very tense climax.

Joyce Carol Oates   b. 1938

Where Are You Going, Where Have You Been?   [1966]
For Bob Dylan

Her name was Connie. She was fifteen and she had a quick, nervous giggling habit of craning her neck to glance into mirrors or checking other people's faces to make sure her own was all right. Her mother, who noticed everything and knew everything and who hadn't much reason any longer to look at her own face, always scolded Connie about it. "Stop gawking at yourself. Who are you? You think you're so pretty?" she would say. Connie would raise her eyebrows at these familiar old complaints and look right through her mother, into a shadowy vision of herself as she was right at that moment: she knew she was pretty and that was everything. Her mother had been pretty once too, if you could believe those old snapshots in the album, but now her looks were gone and that was why she was always after Connie.

> **APPROACHING THE AUTHOR**
>
> **Joyce Carol Oates** went to the same one-room schoolhouse her mother attended. Oates was the first member of her family to earn a high-school diploma.
>
> For more about her, see page 1074.

"Why don't you keep your room clean like your sister? How've you got your hair fixed—what the hell stinks? Hair spray? You don't see your sister using that junk."

Her sister June was twenty-four and still lived at home. She was a secretary in the high school Connie attended, and if that wasn't bad enough—with her in the same building — she was so plain and chunky and steady that Connie had to hear her praised all the time by her mother and her mother's sisters. June did this, June did that, she saved money and helped clean the house and cooked and Connie couldn't do a thing, her mind was all filled with trashy daydreams. Their father was away at work most of the time and when he came home he wanted supper and he read the newspaper at supper and after supper he went to bed. He didn't bother talking much to them, but around his bent head Connie's mother kept picking at her until Connie wished her mother was dead and she herself was dead and it was all over. "She makes me want to throw up sometimes," she complained to her friends. She had a high, breathless, amused voice that made everything she said sound a little forced, whether it was sincere or not.

There was one good thing: June went places with girl friends of hers, girls who were just as plain and steady as she, and so when Connie wanted to do that her mother had no objections. The father of Connie's best girl friend drove the girls the three miles to town and left them at a shopping plaza so they could walk through the stores or go to a movie, and when he came to pick them up again at eleven he never bothered to ask what they had done.

They must have been familiar sights, walking around the shopping plaza in their shorts and flat ballerina slippers that always scuffed the sidewalk, with charm bracelets jingling on their thin wrists; they would lean together to whisper and laugh secretly if someone passed who amused or interested them. Connie had long dark blond hair that drew anyone's eye to it, and she wore part of it pulled up on her head and puffed out and the rest of it she let fall down her back. She wore a pullover jersey blouse that looked one way when she was at home and another way when she was away from home. Everything about her had two sides to it, one for home and one for anywhere that was not home: her walk, which could be childlike and bobbing, or languid enough to make anyone think she was hearing music in her head; her mouth, which was pale and smirking most of the time, but bright and pink on these evenings out; her laugh, which was cynical and drawling at home — "Ha, ha, very funny" — but high-pitched and nervous anywhere else, like the jingling of the charms on her bracelet.

Sometimes they did go shopping or to a movie, but sometimes they went across the highway, ducking fast across the busy road, to a drive-in restaurant where older kids hung out. The restaurant was shaped like a big bottle, though squatter than a real bottle, and on its cap was a revolving figure of a grinning boy holding a hamburger aloft. One night in midsummer they ran across, breathless with daring, and right away someone leaned out a car window and invited them over, but it was just a boy from high school they didn't like. It made them feel good to be able to ignore him. They went up through the maze of parked and cruising cars to the bright-lit, fly-infested restaurant, their faces pleased and expectant as if they were entering a sacred building that loomed up out of the night to give them what haven and blessing they yearned for. They sat at the counter and crossed their legs at the ankles, their thin shoulders rigid with excitement, and listened to the music that made everything so good: the

5

music was always in the background, like music at a church service; it was something to depend upon.

A boy named Eddie came in to talk with them. He sat backwards on his stool, turning himself jerkily around in semicircles and then stopping and turning back again, and after a while he asked Connie if she would like something to eat. She said she would and so she tapped her friend's arm on her way out—her friend pulled her face up into a brave, droll look—and Connie said she would meet her at eleven, across the way. "I just hate to leave her like that," Connie said earnestly, but the boy said that she wouldn't be alone for long. So they went out to his car, and on the way Connie couldn't help but let her eyes wander over the windshields and faces all around her, her face gleaming with a joy that had nothing to do with Eddie or even this place; it might have been the music. She drew her shoulders up and sucked in her breath with the pure pleasure of being alive, and just at that moment she happened to glance at a face just a few feet from hers. It was a boy with shaggy black hair, in a convertible jalopy painted gold. He stared at her and then his lips widened into a grin. Connie slit her eyes at him and turned away, but she couldn't help glancing back and there he was, still watching her. He wagged a finger and laughed and said, "Gonna get you, baby," and Connie turned away again without Eddie noticing anything.

She spent three hours with him, at the restaurant where they ate hamburgers and drank Cokes in wax cups that were always sweating, and then down an alley a mile or so away, and when he left her off at five to eleven only the movie house was still open at the plaza. Her girl friend was there, talking with a boy. When Connie came up, the two girls smiled at each other and Connie said, "How was the movie?" and the girl said, "*You* should know." They rode off with the girl's father, sleepy and pleased, and Connie couldn't help but look back at the darkened shopping plaza with its big empty parking lot and its signs that were faded and ghostly now, and over at the drive-in restaurant where cars were still circling tirelessly. She couldn't hear the music at this distance.

Next morning June asked her how the movie was and Connie said, "So-so."

She and that girl and occasionally another girl went out several times a 10 week, and the rest of the time Connie spent around the house—it was summer vacation—getting in her mother's way and thinking, dreaming about the boys she met. But all the boys fell back and dissolved into a single face that was not even a face but an idea, a feeling, mixed up with the urgent insistent pounding of the music and the humid night of July. Connie's mother kept dragging her back to the daylight by finding things for her to do or saying suddenly, "What's this about the Pettinger girl?"

And Connie would say nervously, "Oh, her. That dope." She always drew thick clear lines between herself and such girls, and her mother was simple and kind enough to believe it. Her mother was so simple, Connie thought, that it was maybe cruel to fool her so much. Her mother went scuffling around the house in old bedroom slippers and complained over the telephone to one sister about the other, then the other called up and the two of them complained about the third one. If June's name was mentioned her mother's tone was approving, and if Connie's name was mentioned it was disapproving. This did not really mean she disliked Connie, and actually Connie thought that her mother preferred her to June just because she was prettier, but the two of them kept up a pretense of exasperation, a sense that they were tugging and struggling over something of little value to either of them. Sometimes, over coffee, they were almost friends, but something would come up—some vexation that was like a fly buzzing suddenly around their heads—and their faces went hard with contempt.

One Sunday Connie got up at eleven—none of them bothered with church—and washed her hair so that it could dry all day long in the sun. Her parents and sister were going to a barbecue at an aunt's house and Connie said no, she wasn't interested, rolling her eyes to let her mother know just what she thought of it. "Stay home alone then," her mother said sharply. Connie sat out back in a lawn chair and watched them drive away, her father quiet and bald, hunched around so that he could back the car out, her mother with a look that was still angry and not at all softened through the windshield, and in the back seat poor old June, all dressed up as if she didn't know what a barbecue was, with all the running yelling kids and the flies. Connie sat with her eyes closed in the sun, dreaming and dazed with the warmth about her as if this were a kind of love, the caresses of love, and her mind slipped over onto thoughts of the boy she had been with the night before and how nice he had been, how sweet it always was, not the way someone like June would suppose but sweet, gentle, the way it was in movies and promised in songs; and when she opened her eyes she hardly knew where she was, the back yard ran off into weeds and a fence-like line of trees and behind it the sky was perfectly blue and still. The asbestos "ranch house" that was now three years old startled her—it looked small. She shook her head as if to get awake.

It was too hot. She went inside the house and turned on the radio to drown out the quiet. She sat on the edge of her bed, barefoot, and listened for an hour and a half to a program called XYZ Sunday Jamboree, record after record of hard, fast, shrieking songs she sang along with, interspersed by exclamations from "Bobby King": "An' look here, you girls at Napoleon's—Son and Charley want you to pay real close attention to this song coming up!"

And Connie paid close attention herself, bathed in a glow of slow-pulsed joy that seemed to rise mysteriously out of the music itself and lay languidly about the airless little room, breathed in and breathed out with each gentle rise and fall of her chest.

After a while she heard a car coming up the drive. She sat up at once, 15 startled, because it couldn't be her father so soon. The gravel kept crunching all the way in from the road—the driveway was long—and Connie ran to the window. It was a car she didn't know. It was an open jalopy, painted a bright gold that caught the sunlight opaquely. Her heart began to pound and her fingers snatched at her hair, checking it, and she whispered, "Christ, Christ," wondering how bad she looked. The car came to a stop at the side door and the horn sounded four short taps, as if this were a signal Connie knew.

She went into the kitchen and approached the door slowly, then hung out the screen door, her bare toes curling down off the step. There were two boys in the car and now she recognized the driver: he had shaggy, shabby black hair that looked crazy as a wig and he was grinning at her.

"I ain't late, am I?" he said.

"Who the hell do you think you are?" Connie said.

"Toldja I'd be out, didn't I?"

"I don't even know who you are." 20

She spoke sullenly, careful to show no interest or pleasure, and he spoke in a fast, bright monotone. Connie looked past him to the other boy, taking her time. He had fair brown hair, with a lock that fell onto his forehead. His sideburns gave him a fierce, embarrassed look, but so far he hadn't even bothered to glance at her. Both boys wore sunglasses. The driver's glasses were metallic and mirrored everything in miniature.

"You wanta come for a ride?" he said.

Connie smirked and let her hair fall loose over one shoulder.

"Don'tcha like my car? New paint job," he said. "Hey."

"What?" 25

"You're cute."

She pretended to fidget, chasing flies away from the door.

"Don'tcha believe me, or what?" he said.

"Look, I don't even know who you are," Connie said in disgust.

"Hey, Ellie's got a radio, see. Mine broke down." He lifted his friend's arm 30 and showed her the little transistor radio the boy was holding, and now Connie began to hear the music. It was the same program that was playing inside the house.

"Bobby King?" she said.

"I listen to him all the time. I think he's great."

"He's kind of great," Connie said reluctantly.

"Listen, that guy's *great*. He knows where the action is."

Connie blushed a little, because the glasses made it impossible for her to 35 see just what this boy was looking at. She couldn't decide if she liked him or if he was just a jerk, and so she dawdled in the doorway and wouldn't come down or go back inside. She said, "What's all that stuff painted on your car?"

"Can'tcha read it?" He opened the door very carefully, as if he were afraid it might fall off. He slid out just as carefully, planting his feet firmly on the ground, the tiny metallic world in his glasses slowing down like gelatine hardening, and in the midst of it Connie's bright green blouse. "This here is my name, to begin with," he said. ARNOLD FRIEND was written in tarlike black letters on the side, with a drawing of a round, grinning face that reminded Connie of a pumpkin, except it wore sunglasses. "I wanta introduce myself, I'm Arnold Friend and that's my real name and I'm gonna be your friend, honey, and inside the car's Ellie Oscar, he's kinda shy." Ellie brought his transistor radio up to his shoulder and balanced it there. "Now, these numbers are a secret code, honey," Arnold Friend explained. He read off the numbers 33, 19, 17 and raised his eyebrows at her to see what she thought of that, but she didn't think much of it. The left rear fender had been smashed and around it was written, on the gleaming gold background: DONE BY CRAZY WOMAN DRIVER. Connie had to laugh at that. Arnold Friend was pleased at her laughter and looked up at her. "Around the other side's a lot more—you wanta come and see them?"

"No."

"Why not?"

"Why should I?"

"Don'tcha wanta see what's on the car? Don'tcha wanta go for a ride?"   40

"I don't know."

"Why not?"

"I got things to do."

"Like what?"

"Things."   45

He laughed as if she had said something funny. He slapped his thighs. He was standing in a strange way, leaning back against the car as if he were balancing himself. He wasn't tall, only an inch or so taller than she would be if she came down to him. Connie liked the way he was dressed, which was the way all of them dressed: tight faded jeans stuffed into black, scuffed boots, a belt that pulled his waist in and showed how lean he was, and a white pullover shirt that was a little soiled and showed the hard small muscles of his arms and shoulders. He looked as if he probably did hard work, lifting and carrying things. Even his neck looked muscular. And his face was a familiar face, somehow: the jaw and chin and cheeks slightly darkened because he hadn't shaved for a day or two, and the nose long and hawklike, sniffing as if she were a treat he was going to gobble up and it was all a joke.

"Connie, you ain't telling the truth. This is your day set aside for a ride with me and you know it," he said, still laughing. The way he straightened and recovered from his fit of laughing showed that it had been all fake.

"How do you know what my name is?" she said suspiciously.

"It's Connie."

"Maybe and maybe not."   50

"I know my Connie," he said, wagging his finger. Now she remembered him even better, back at the restaurant, and her cheeks warmed at the thought of how she had sucked in her breath just at the moment she passed him—how she must have looked to him. And he had remembered her. "Ellie and I come out here especially for you," he said. "Ellie can sit in back. How about it?"

"Where?"

"Where what?"

"Where're we going?"

He looked at her. He took off the sunglasses and she saw how pale the skin   55 around his eyes was, like holes that were not in shadow but instead in light. His eyes were like chips of broken glass that catch the light in an amiable way. He smiled. It was as if the idea of going for a ride somewhere, to someplace, was a new idea to him.

"Just for a ride, Connie sweetheart."

"I never said my name was Connie," she said.

"But I know what it is. I know your name and all about you, lots of things," Arnold Friend said. He had not moved yet but stood still leaning back against the side of his jalopy. "I took a special interest in you, such a pretty girl, and found out all about you—like I know your parents and sister are gone somewheres and I know where and how long they're going to be gone, and I know who you were with last night, and your best girl friend's name is Betty. Right?"

He spoke in a simple lilting voice, exactly as if he were reciting the words to a song. His smile assured her that everything was fine. In the car Ellie turned up the volume on his radio and did not bother to look around at them.

"Ellie can sit in the back seat," Arnold Friend said. He indicated his friend with a casual jerk of his chin, as if Ellie did not count and she should not bother with him.   60

"How'd you find out all that stuff?" Connie said.

"Listen: Betty Schultz and Tony Fitch and Jimmy Pettinger and Nancy Pettinger," he said in a chant. "Raymond Stanley and Bob Hutter—"

"Do you know all those kids?"

"I know everybody."

"Look, you're kidding. You're not from around here."   65

"Sure."

"But—how come we never saw you before?"

"Sure you saw me before," he said. He looked down at his boots, as if he were a little offended. "You just don't remember."

"I guess I'd remember you," Connie said.

"Yeah?" He looked up at this, beaming. He was pleased. He began to mark   70 time with the music from Ellie's radio, tapping his fists lightly together. Connie looked away from his smile to the car, which was painted so bright it almost hurt her eyes to look at it. She looked at that name, ARNOLD FRIEND. And up at the front fender was an expression that was familiar—MAN THE FLYING SAUCERS. It was an expression kids had used the year before but didn't use this year. She looked at it for a while as if the words meant something to her that she did not yet know.

"What're you thinking about? Huh?" Arnold Friend demanded. "Not worried about your hair blowing around in the car, are you?"

"No."

"Think I maybe can't drive good?"

"How do I know?"

"You're a hard girl to handle. How come?" he said. "Don't you know I'm   75 your friend? Didn't you see me put my sign in the air when you walked by?"

"What sign?"

"My sign." And he drew an X in the air, leaning out toward her. They were maybe ten feet apart. After his hand fell back to his side the X was still in the air, almost visible. Connie let the screen door close and stood perfectly still inside it, listening to the music from her radio and the boy's blend together. She stared at Arnold Friend. He stood there so stiffly relaxed, pretending to be relaxed, with one hand idly on the door handle as if he were keeping himself up that way and had no intention of ever moving again. She recognized most things about him, the tight jeans that showed his thighs and buttocks and the greasy leather boots and the tight shirt, and even that slippery friendly smile of his, that sleepy dreamy smile that all the boys used to get across ideas they didn't want to put into words. She recognized all this and also the singsong way he talked, slightly mocking, kidding, but serious and a little melancholy, and she recognized the way he tapped one fist against the other in homage to the perpetual music behind him. But all these things did not come together.

She said suddenly, "Hey, how old are you?"

His smile faded. She could see then that he wasn't a kid, he was much older — thirty, maybe more. At this knowledge her heart began to pound faster.

"That's a crazy thing to ask. Can'tcha see I'm your own age?"   80

"Like hell you are."

"Or maybe a coupla years older. I'm eighteen."

"Eighteen?" she said doubtfully.

He grinned to reassure her and lines appeared at the corners of his mouth. His teeth were big and white. He grinned so broadly his eyes became slits and she saw how thick the lashes were, thick and black as if painted with a black tarlike material. Then, abruptly, he seemed to become embarrassed and looked over his shoulder at Ellie. "*Him*, he's crazy," he said. "Ain't he a riot? He's a nut, a real character." Ellie was still listening to the music. His sunglasses told nothing about what he was thinking. He wore a bright orange shirt unbuttoned halfway to show his chest, which was a pale, bluish chest and not muscular like Arnold Friend's. His shirt collar was turned up all around and the very tips of the collar pointed out past his chin as if they were protecting him. He was pressing the transistor radio up against his ear and sat there in a kind of daze, right in the sun.

"He's kinda strange," Connie said.   85

"Hey, she says you're kinda strange! Kinda strange!" Arnold Friend cried. He pounded on the car to get Ellie's attention. Ellie turned for the first time and Connie saw with shock that he wasn't a kid either — he had a fair, hairless face, cheeks reddened slightly as if the veins grew too close to the surface of his skin, the face of a forty-year-old baby. Connie felt a wave of dizziness rise in her at this sight and she stared at him as if waiting for something to change the shock of the moment, make it all right again. Ellie's lips kept shaping words, mumbling along with the words blasting in his ear.

"Maybe you two better go away," Connie said faintly.

"What? How come?" Arnold Friend cried. "We come out here to take you for a ride. It's Sunday." He had the voice of the man on the radio now. It was the same voice, Connie thought. "Don'tcha know it's Sunday all day? And honey, no matter who you were with last night, today you're with Arnold Friend and don't you forget it! Maybe you better step out here," he said, and this last was in a different voice. It was a little flatter, as if the heat was finally getting to him.

"No. I got things to do."

"Hey."   90

"You two better leave."

"We ain't leaving until you come with us."

"Like hell I am—"

"Connie, don't fool around with me. I mean—I mean, don't fool *around*,"
he said, shaking his head. He laughed incredulously. He placed his sunglasses
on top of his head, carefully, as if he were indeed wearing a wig, and brought
the stems down behind his ears. Connie stared at him, another wave of dizziness and fear rising in her so that for a moment he wasn't even in focus but
was just a blur standing there against his gold car, and she had the idea that he
had driven up the driveway all right but had come from nowhere before that
and belonged nowhere and that everything about him and even about the music
that was so familiar to her was only half real.

"If my father comes and sees you—"   95

"He ain't coming. He's at a barbecue."

"How do you know that?"

"Aunt Tillie's. Right now they're—uh—they're drinking. Sitting around,"
he said vaguely, squinting as if he were staring all the way to town and over to
Aunt Tillie's back yard. Then the vision seemed to get clear and he nodded energetically. "Yeah. Sitting around. There's your sister in a blue dress, huh? And
high heels, the poor sad bitch—nothing like you, sweetheart! And your mother's helping some fat woman with the corn, they're cleaning the corn—husking
the corn—"

"What fat woman?" Connie cried.

"How do I know what fat woman, I don't know every goddamn fat woman   100
in the world!" Arnold Friend laughed.

"Oh, that's Mrs. Hornsby. . . . Who invited her?" Connie said. She felt a
little lightheaded. Her breath was coming quickly.

"She's too fat. I don't like them fat. I like them the way you are, honey," he
said, smiling sleepily at her. They stared at each other for a while through the
screen door. He said softly, "Now, what you're going to do is this: you're going
to come out that door. You're going to sit up front with me and Ellie's going to
sit in the back, the hell with Ellie, right? This isn't Ellie's date. You're my date.
I'm your lover, honey."

"What? You're crazy—"

"Yes, I'm your lover. You don't know what that is but you will," he said. "I
know that too. I know all about you. But look: it's real nice and you couldn't
ask for nobody better than me, or more polite. I always keep my word. I'll tell
you how it is, I'm always nice at first, the first time. I'll hold you so tight you
won't think you have to try to get away or pretend anything because you'll know
you can't. And I'll come inside you where it's all secret and you'll give in to me
and you'll love me—"

"Shut up! You're crazy!" Connie said. She backed away from the door. She   105
put her hands up against her ears as if she'd heard something terrible, something

not meant for her. "People don't talk like that, you're crazy," she muttered. Her heart was almost too big now for her chest and its pumping made sweat break out all over her. She looked out to see Arnold Friend pause and then take a step toward the porch, lurching. He almost fell. But, like a clever drunken man, he managed to catch his balance. He wobbled in his high boots and grabbed hold of one of the porch posts.

"Honey?" he said. "You still listening?"

"Get the hell out of here!"

"Be nice, honey. Listen."

"I'm going to call the police—"

He wobbled again and out of the side of his mouth came a fast spat curse, an aside not meant for her to hear. But even this "Christ!" sounded forced. Then he began to smile again. She watched this smile come, awkward as if he were smiling from inside a mask. His whole face was a mask, she thought wildly, tanned down to his throat but then running out as if he had plastered makeup on his face but had forgotten about his throat.

"Honey—? Listen, here's how it is. I always tell the truth and I promise you this: I ain't coming in that house after you."

"You better not! I'm going to call the police if you—if you don't—"

"Honey," he said, talking right through her voice, "honey, I'm not coming in there but you are coming out here. You know why?"

She was panting. The kitchen looked like a place she had never seen before, some room she had run inside but that wasn't good enough, wasn't going to help her. The kitchen window had never had a curtain, after three years, and there were dishes in the sink for her to do—probably—and if you ran your hand across the table you'd probably feel something sticky there.

"You listening, honey? Hey?"

"—going to call the police—"

"Soon as you touch the phone I don't need to keep my promise and can come inside. You won't want that."

She rushed forward and tried to lock the door. Her fingers were shaking. "But why lock it," Arnold Friend said gently, talking right into her face. "It's just a screen door. It's just nothing." One of his boots was at a strange angle, as if his foot wasn't in it. It pointed out to the left, bent at the ankle. "I mean, anybody can break through a screen door and glass and wood and iron or anything else if he needs to, anybody at all, and specially Arnold Friend. If the place got lit up with a fire, honey, you'd come runnin' out into my arms, right into my arms an' safe at home—like you knew I was your lover and'd stopped fooling around." Part of those words were spoken with a slight rhythmic lilt, and Connie somehow recognized them—the echo of a song from last year, about a girl rushing into her boy friend's arms and coming home again—

Connie stood barefoot on the linoleum floor, staring at him. "What do you want?" she whispered.

"I want you," he said.

"What?"

"Seen you that night and thought, that's the one, yes sir. I never needed to look anymore."

"But my father's coming back. He's coming to get me. I had to wash my hair first—" She spoke in a dry, rapid voice, hardly raising it for him to hear.

"No, your daddy is not coming and yes, you had to wash your hair and you washed it for me. It's nice and shining and all for me. I thank you sweetheart," he said with a mock bow, but again he almost lost his balance. He had to bend and adjust his boots. Evidently his feet did not go all the way down; the boots must have been stuffed with something so that he would seem taller. Connie stared out at him and behind him at Ellie in the car, who seemed to be looking off toward Connie's right, into nothing. This Ellie said, pulling the words out of the air one after another as if he were just discovering them, "You want me to pull out the phone?"

"Shut your mouth and keep it shut," Arnold Friend said, his face red from 125 bending over or maybe from embarrassment because Connie had seen his boots. "This ain't none of your business."

"What—what are you doing? What do you want?" Connie said. "If I call the police they'll get you, they'll arrest you—"

"Promise was not to come in unless you touch that phone, and I'll keep that promise," he said. He resumed his erect position and tried to force his shoulders back. He sounded like a hero in a movie, declaring something important. But he spoke too loudly and it was as if he were speaking to someone behind Connie. "I ain't made plans for coming in that house where I don't belong but just for you to come out to me, the way you should. Don't you know who I am?"

"You're crazy," she whispered. She backed away from the door but did not want to go into another part of the house, as if this would give him permission to come through the door. "What do you . . . you're crazy, you. . . ."

"Huh? What're you saying, honey?"

Her eyes darted everywhere in the kitchen. She could not remember what 130 it was, this room.

"This is how it is, honey: you come out and we'll drive away, have a nice ride. But if you don't come out we're gonna wait till your people come home and then they're all going to get it."

"You want that telephone pulled out?" Ellie said. He held the radio away from his ear and grimaced, as if without the radio the air was too much for him.

"I toldja shut up, Ellie," Arnold Friend said, "you're deaf, get a hearing aid, right? Fix yourself up. This little girl's no trouble and's gonna be nice to me, so Ellie keep to yourself, this ain't your date—right? Don't hem in on me, don't hog, don't crush, don't bird dog, don't trail me," he said in a rapid, meaningless voice, as if he were running through all the expressions he'd learned but was no longer sure which of them was in style, then rushing on to new ones, making them up with his eyes closed. "Don't crawl under my fence, don't squeeze in my chipmunk hole, don't sniff my glue, suck my popsicle, keep your own greasy fingers on yourself!" He shaded his eyes and peered in at Connie, who was backed against the kitchen table. "Don't mind him, honey, he's just a creep. He's a dope. Right? I'm the boy for you and like I said, you come out here nice like a lady and give me your hand, and nobody else gets hurt, I mean, your nice old bald-headed daddy and your mummy and your sister in her high heels. Because listen: why bring them in this?"

"Leave me alone," Connie whispered.

"Hey, you know that old woman down the road, the one with the chickens 135
and stuff—you know her?"

"She's dead!"

"Dead? What? You know her?" Arnold Friend said.

"She's dead—"

"Don't you like her?"

"She's dead—she's—she isn't here any more—" 140

"But don't you like her, I mean, you got something against her? Some grudge or something?" Then his voice dipped as if he were conscious of a rudeness. He touched the sunglasses perched up on top of his head as if to make sure they were still there. "Now, you be a good girl."

"What are you going to do?"

"Just two things, or maybe three," Arnold Friend said. "But I promise it won't last long and you'll like me the way you get to like people you're close to. You will. It's all over for you here, so come on out. You don't want your people in any trouble, do you?"

She turned and bumped against a chair or something, hurting her leg, but she ran into the back room and picked up the telephone. Something roared in her ear, a tiny roaring, and she was so sick with fear that she could do nothing but listen to it—the telephone was clammy and very heavy and her fingers groped down to the dial but were too weak to touch it. She began to scream into the phone, into the roaring. She cried out, she cried for her mother, she felt her breath start jerking back and forth in her lungs as if it were something Arnold Friend was stabbing her with again and again with no tenderness. A noisy sorrowful wailing rose all about her and she was locked inside it the way she was locked inside this house.

After a while she could hear again. She was sitting on the floor with her wet 145
back against the wall.

Arnold Friend was saying from the door, "That's a good girl. Put the phone back."

She kicked the phone away from her.

"No, honey. Pick it up. Put it back right."

She picked it up and put it back. The dial tone stopped.

"That's a good girl. Now, you come outside." 150

She was hollow with what had been fear but what was now just an emptiness. All that screaming had blasted it out of her. She sat, one leg cramped under her, and deep inside her brain was something like a pinpoint of light that kept going and would not let her relax. She thought, I'm not going to see my mother again. She thought, I'm not going to sleep in my bed again. Her bright green blouse was all wet.

Arnold Friend said, in a gentle-loud voice that was like a stage voice, "The place where you came from ain't there any more, and where you had in mind to go is cancelled out. This place you are now—inside your daddy's house—is nothing but a cardboard box I can knock down any time. You know that and always did know it. You hear me?"

She thought, I have got to think. I have got to know what to do.

"We'll go out to a nice field, out in the country here where it smells so nice and it's sunny," Arnold Friend said. "I'll have my arms tight around you so you won't need to try to get away and I'll show you what love is like, what it does. The hell with this house! It looks solid all right," he said. He ran a fingernail down the screen and the noise did not make Connie shiver, as it would have the day before. "Now, put your hand on your heart, honey. Feel that? That feels solid too but we know better. Be nice to me, be sweet like you can because what else is there for a girl like you but to be sweet and pretty and give in?—and get away before her people come back?"

She felt her pounding heart. Her hand seemed to enclose it. She thought for the first time in her life that it was nothing that was hers, that belonged to her, but just a pounding, living thing inside this body that wasn't really hers either.   155

"You don't want them to get hurt," Arnold Friend went on. "Now, get up, honey. Get up all by yourself."

She stood.

"Now, turn this way. That's right. Come over here to me.—Ellie, put that away, didn't I tell you? You dope. You miserable creepy dope," Arnold Friend said. His words were not angry but only part of an incantation. The incantation was kindly. "Now, come out through the kitchen to me, honey, and let's see a smile, try it, you're a brave, sweet little girl and now they're eating corn and hot dogs cooked to bursting over an outdoor fire, and they don't know one thing about you and never did and honey, you're better than them because not a one of them would have done this for you."

Connie felt the linoleum under her feet; it was cool. She brushed her hair back out of her eyes. Arnold Friend let go of the post tentatively and opened his arms for her, his elbows pointing in toward each other and his wrists limp, to show that this was an embarrassed embrace and a little mocking, he didn't want to make her self-conscious.

She put out her hand against the screen. She watched herself push the door slowly open as if she were back safe somewhere in the other doorway, watching this body and this head of long hair moving out into the sunlight where Arnold Friend waited.   160

"My sweet little blue-eyed girl," he said in a half-sung sigh that had nothing to do with her brown eyes but was taken up just the same by the vast sunlit reaches of the land behind him and on all sides of him—so much land that Connie had never seen before and did not recognize except to know that she was going to it.

REFLECTING ON WHAT YOU'VE READ

1. Look closely at the way the story begins — at the first sentence and the first paragraph, for example. What effect do they have on you?

2. Pick out the steps in the story's development — try outlining the plot. Why do you think the story includes the paragraphs about June, about trips to the mall, about evenings with Eddie and other friends? In what paragraph does the plot change direction and pick up momentum? Notice the way the encounter with Arnold Friend is organized to make it build in intensity and suspense.

3. Oates says the story grew out of reading about an actual serial rapist and murderer in Arizona. The story ends with Connie going out the door to join Arnold Friend. What do you assume would have happened next, if the story hadn't ended there? Why do you think the author chose not to continue the story further? In what ways might stopping where it does indicate what is of greatest interest or importance for the story, and what is not of central interest or importance?

4. The story is dedicated to singer and composer Bob Dylan. References to music appear frequently in the story. Consider what these references say and what they contribute to the story's effect. If you aren't familiar with Bob Dylan's music, listen to some and do some research on him. Is his music the kind that "made everything so good" for Connie? Does the Dylan reference seem to relate to the story, or is it simply an honorific dedication?

5. Suggest two or three ways the title could relate to the story.

RESPONDING THROUGH Writing

WRITING ABOUT PLOT

Journal Entries

1. The first paragraph of this chapter (p. 110) talks about how some people describe things that happen to them in more interesting and engaging ways than others can. Write a journal entry reflecting on how elements of plot help account for that difference and how understanding this can help you understand plot in fiction more fully.

2. Experiment with the basic principles of plot construction by writing a plot analysis of a TV show or a movie: its beginning, its handling of gaps, its use of flashbacks, its rising action or development (look for conflict, suspense, foreshadowing, and repetitions), and its ending. Write a journal entry summarizing the result and discussing whether, how, and why basic aspects of plot are universal.

3. Choose a crucial event from your past. In a journal entry, outline it as a plot. Consider what you need to include and what you can leave out, what order would be most effective for presenting it, and so on. Add a few sentences pointing out the techniques you bring in and discussing what you learn about plot construction.

Literary Analysis Papers

4. Write a paper on the importance and handling of gaps in the plotting of Louise Erdrich's "The Red Convertible" (p. 119).

5. Write a paper examining the relation of plot construction to title in James Baldwin's "Sonny's Blues" (p. 324), James Joyce's "Araby" (p. 389), or Xu Xi's "Famine" (p. 446).

6. Write a paper examining the plot construction of Margaret Atwood's "Happy Endings" (p. 321) and what the story says or implies about constructing a story effectively.

Comparison-Contrast Papers

7. Write a paper comparing the inside view of the Vietnam War presented by the plot of Tim O'Brien's "The Things They Carried" (p. 257) with the outside view found in Louise Erdrich's "The Red Convertible" (p. 119). (You could focus on the handling of gaps in both stories.)

8. Write a paper that analyzes the use of comparison and contrast as a structural technique in Megan Foss's "Love Letters" (p. 10); for example, you can compare and contrast Darryl being in jail in section 1 and Mickey being in jail in section 2.

> ## TIPS for Writing about Plot
>
> - **Explain techniques.** In writing about plot, be sure to *explain* the selection and arrangement of events; don't just summarize what happens in the story.
>
> - **Limit your scope.** In writing about plot, focus on an aspect — or perhaps two or three — that are unique or particularly significant; don't try to deal with everything covered in this chapter.
>
> - **Start with conflicts.** As you select a topic related to plot, look for the key conflict or conflicts in the story, then at how the plot structure makes the conflict stand out. Notice if the story includes an epiphany. If it does, notice how the epiphany is set up. That can often turn into a valuable topic.
>
> - **Connect to theme.** An analysis of plot is of most interest as it relates to and brings out theme in the story (see p. 255 for an explanation of theme); try to connect your discussion of plot to the overall effect of the story.

WRITING ABOUT CONNECTIONS

One of the most important skills for you to develop is how to make connections between the great variety of things you are learning, things that may at first appear to be unrelated: for example, between things dealt with early in a course and those that come later, and between what you have learned in one course or discipline and what you have covered in others. Making connections is also crucial in understanding literature. Throughout this book, this skill is emphasized by connecting chapters and topics to other chapters and topics.

It's also valuable and interesting for you to make connections between different works that you read. Doing so can enhance your reading experience and reveal important insights. The connections can be between similar (or contrasting) plots or other techniques and can be thematic. To give you practice and encouragement making connections, each chapter includes "Writing about Connections" prompts. The pairings suggested usually are for works of the same genre, though equally appropriate pairings could be made across genres. We have selected connections, often between contemporary works and earlier works from the literary canon, that we hope you will find thought-provoking and challenging. Here are three such suggestions, which are intended to provide you with a model for coming up with others on your own.

1. "Love and the City": Reaching for Relationships in Dagoberto Gilb's "Love in L.A." (p. 111) and Lydia Davis's "Blind Date" (p. 357)

2. "My Brother's Keeper": Supporting Siblings in Louise Erdrich's "The Red Convertible" (p. 119) and James Baldwin's "Sonny's Blues" (p. 324)

3. "Good Men Are Hard to Find": Encounters with Evil in Joyce Carol Oates's "Where Are You Going, Where Have You Been?" (p. 127) and Flannery O'Connor's "A Good Man Is Hard to Find" (p. 159)

WRITING RESEARCH PAPERS

1. In the United States and many other societies, cars carry cultural importance. Research the role that cars play in American culture and write a paper on the significance of cars in Dagoberto Gilb's "Love in L.A." (p. 111), Louise Erdrich's "The Red Convertible" (p. 119), Joyce Carol Oates's "Where Are You Going, Where Have You Been?" (p. 127), and your own experience. Consider what types of cars carry various meanings for different cultures. How do cars embody distinctions, and at times conflicts, between cultures? Consider the ironies that you find in this "car culture."

2. Henry's experiences leaving the reservation to enter basic training and then going to Vietnam for active service are not covered in Louise Erdrich's "The Red Convertible" (p. 119) because of the narrator's limited point of view. But they remain very much a part of the story. Research what Native Americans often encounter when they leave reservations and what military action in Vietnam was like. Then write a paper describing what Henry's experiences probably were like and why he was a changed man when he returned.

I do not ask the wounded person how he feels, I myself become the wounded person.

Walt Whitman

(American Poet; see pp. 657 and 1083)

CHAPTER 6 Narration and Point of View

Being Alert to Angles

This book is about *reading* literature, specifically reading in the interactive manner described in Chapter 1. As we say there, reading literature differs from most other reading: It is often more like listening to someone, more like hearing a voice, than what we usually think of as reading. You've probably heard the phrase "seeing with the mind's eye"; you can also hear with the mind's ear. Responding fully to literature requires training the ear so you can enjoy and benefit from listening to the voices in the story, starting with the voice of the narrator. As an author constructs a story into a plot, she or he has to make a decision about who will tell about what happens, and from what perspective or perspectives (what point or points of view) it will be told. Your experience while reading will be richer and more personal if you're alert to and aware of such perspectives. It's fascinating to take it into account as you figure out what and whom to believe.

APPROACHING THE READING

Using your "mind's ear," listen to the following story as if it were being spoken directly to you. It is the first in a series of forty-six connected stories told by a young girl, Esperanza Cordero, growing up in a Latino section of Chicago and seeking both to escape that world and to find herself. Consider what she is like as a narrator and why it is important to hear the story from her point of view.

Sandra Cisneros   b. 1954

The House on Mango Street   [1983]

We didn't always live on Mango Street. Before that we lived on Loomis on the third floor, and before that we lived on Keeler. Before Keeler it was Paulina, and before that I can't remember. But what I remember most is moving a lot. Each time it seemed there'd be one more of us. By the time we got to Mango Street we were six—Mama, Papa, Carlos, Kiki, my sister Nenny, and me.

The house on Mango Street is ours, and we don't have to pay rent to anybody, or share the yard with the people downstairs, or be careful not to make too much noise, and there isn't a landlord banging on the ceiling with a broom. But even so, it's not the house we'd thought we'd get.

We had to leave the flat on Loomis quick. The water pipes broke and the landlord wouldn't fix them because the house was too old. We had to leave fast. We were using the washroom next door and carrying water over in empty milk gallons. That's why Mama and Papa looked for a house, and that's why we moved into the house on Mango Street, far away, on the other side of town.

They always told us that one day we would move into a house, a real house that would be ours for always so we wouldn't have to move each year. And our house would have running water and pipes that worked. And inside it would have real stairs, not hallway stairs, but stairs inside like the houses on TV. And we'd have a basement and at least three washrooms so when we took a bath we wouldn't have to tell everybody. Our house would be white with trees around it, a great big yard, and grass growing without a fence. This was the house Papa talked about when he held a lottery ticket and this was the house Mama dreamed up in the stories she told us before we went to bed.

But the house on Mango Street is not the way they told it at all. It's small   5 and red with tight steps in front and windows so small you'd think they were holding their breath. Bricks are crumbling in places, and the front door is so swollen you have to push hard to get in. There is no front yard, only four little elms the city planted by the curb. Out back is a small garage for the car we don't own yet and a small yard that looks smaller between the two buildings on either side. There are stairs in our house, but they're ordinary hallway stairs, and the house has only one washroom. Everybody has to share a bedroom—Mama and Papa, Carlos and Kiki, me and Nenny.

APPROACHING THE AUTHOR

Sandra Cisneros was in the news in Texas for two years because of the color of her house. She lives in a historic district of San Antonio and when she painted

Ulf Andersen/Getty Images

her house a very brilliant purple the city board objected. The dispute went on, until the paint faded to a shade of lavender, which the city deemed "historically appropriate."

For more about her, see page 1059.

Once when we were living on Loomis, a nun from my school passed by and saw me playing out front. The laundromat downstairs had been boarded up because it had been robbed two days before and the owner had painted on the wood YES WE'RE OPEN so as not to lose business.

Where do you live? she asked.

There, I said pointing up to the third floor.

You live *there*?

There. I had to look to where she pointed—the third floor, the paint peeling,   10 wooden bars Papa had nailed on the windows so we wouldn't fall out. You live *there*? The way she said it made me feel like nothing. *There*. I lived *there*. I nodded.

I knew then I had to have a house. A real house. One I could point to. But this isn't it. The house on Mango Street isn't it. For the time being, Mama says. Temporary, says Papa. But I know how those things go.

REFLECTING ON WHAT YOU'VE READ

1. Describe the voice you hear in "The House on Mango Street." How old do you imagine the speaker is? What makes you think that? What else can you tell about her from the way she sounds as you listen to her?

2. What is the effect of having the voice and perspective be those of Esperanza? How do you think the story would differ if it were told by Esperanza's mother? Her father? One of her brothers?

3. Considering the story as a whole, what emotions does it create as you read it? Does it lead you to empathize with Esperanza and her family?

READING FOR POINT OF VIEW

As you read a work of fiction, one of the first things to pay attention to is who is telling, or "narrating," the story, whose voice you are listening to as you read. Compare the two short stories that open Chapters 5 and 6. The different techniques used in them reflect differences in the way you view the action in each. "The House on Mango Street" is told by a character who is involved in the story and views the events from the inside. Esperanza uses *I* (the first person) as she tells her story. "Love in L.A." is told by an unnamed, unidentified storyteller (or *narrator*) who is not involved in the story but views it from the outside. The storyteller does not use *I* but refers to characters in the third person ("she" or "he"). The kind of narrator and the way the narrator looks at the events that occur in the story are called the *point of view*. This chapter deals with two questions it is helpful to ask as you read or reflect on a story: Who tells the story? And, how much does she or he know? Answering those questions can be very helpful in developing your confidence in being able to talk and write about this often-overlooked aspect.

FIRST-PERSON NARRATION

When a story is told by a narrator using the first-person pronoun *I*, the story is said to be using a ***first-person point of view***. The use of first-person narration can make the story seem more up close and personal, as if the author is relating events from her or his own life. The *I* in any story, however, should *not* be assumed to be the author: The narrator in a work of fiction is always a *narrative construct*, an imagined speaker created by the writer.

It is true that in "The House on Mango Street" many details about Esperanza's life parallel the author's: Cisneros was born in Chicago; was part of a large family (six brothers, no sisters); moved often during her childhood, between Chicago and Mexico, where her father was born; and shared Esperanza's sense of dislocation and a lack of permanence.

However, Cisneros did not write an autobiographical essay, the way Sherman Alexie did in "Superman and Me" (p. 4). She clearly drew on her own experiences as she wrote, but she used her imagination to alter the facts of her own life and to invent new ones. She constructed a character for the narrator, one who takes part in, as well as relates, the story. The story's power depends on hearing it from a child's perspective. We, as readers older than Esperanza is, can recognize implications in her story that she is not aware of yet, about poverty, class distinctions, housing patterns, and the power of landlords.

Picking out this point of view is generally straightforward: Just watch for a narrator using *I*. (Occasionally an author uses the first-person plural, *we*, as in "A Rose for Emily," which appears on page 205.) But don't stop there. Once again, alert, active reading is essential. Follow up by asking how much the narrator knows as she or he tells the story. First-person narrators can tell only about what they experience, observe, or are told. They cannot look into other characters' minds or feelings, and they may not understand fully the implications of what they see, hear, or experience. Three labels are most often used to indicate the different categories, or different degrees of knowledge, that first-person narrators generally fall into.

Naïve Narrator The first is *naïve narrator*, a narrator too young or too inexperienced to understand fully the implications of what she or he is talking about. In such cases, active reading is even more important than usual, as you—who understand more than the narrator—must fill in implications the narrator cannot grasp. Such is the case in "The House on Mango Street": Esperanza knows what the family's dream house would be like, and she knows that their present house falls far short of their dreams. But she doesn't understand, until the day the nun sees her playing out front, what the house they live in says about their social situation, and she doesn't realize the kind of economic realities her family is up against. Much of the power of the story comes from our ability, as readers who are older than Esperanza is, to understand the reasons behind her pains and disappointments.

Unreliable Narrator   Esperanza's knowledge is limited by her youth and inexperience. Older narrators may have limited knowledge as well or may not reveal all that they know, for various reasons. Similar to a naïve narrator is a narrator who does not have the mental capacity to provide a coherent account of events or a narrator who has prejudices (against a race or class or against a particular individual in the story) or a restricted range of experience that the reader perceives even though the narrator is unaware of it. In such cases they are at least partially **unreliable narrators**. We cannot accept in an unquestioning way what they tell us about people and events.

That is the case with Lyman in Louise Erdrich's "The Red Convertible" (p. 119). He is not naïve, like Esperanza, and he tells us the truth, as far as he understands it. But the limited range of his experience prevents him from understanding as much as we as readers of the story do. We pick up clues from things that he says, like "I could never keep it straight, which direction those good Vietnam soldiers were from" (para. 22). However, it is important to recognize that it is often the case that we only realize the narrator's limitations at the end of the story. It's probably not until our second reading of "The Red Convertible" that we grasp how Lyman is groping toward an understanding of what we grasp more fully than he is able to.

There are also cases when we can't trust everything the narrator says. The narrator may not tell the whole truth or may distort some things, perhaps deliberately to make them look better or unintentionally because they are too painful to face. In many cases an unreliable narrator's account of what happens is accurate, as in Edgar Allan Poe's "The Cask of Amontillado" (p. 427); but we find that we cannot trust what the narrator tells us about her or his motivation or interpretation of the events. Here, too, you may not realize this until you think back on the story. Sometimes you may start picking up clues earlier, from the tone or style in which the narrator speaks or details the narrator lets slip out. If you think you've picked up such a clue, you'll want to start figuring out what you can take straightforwardly and where you need to make allowances for or corrections in what you are being told.

Reliable Narrator   First-person narrators often do tell their stories accurately and honestly (as far as they and we can tell). In that case the story is said to have a *reliable narrator*: We can believe or rely on what she or he says, as we do with the narrator in Edwidge Danticat's "New York Day Women" (p. 353) and Katherine Min's "Courting a Monk" (p. 394). In those stories the narrators give us no reason to doubt or question what

> **NOTE:** A first-person narrator who seems to speak directly for the author is often referred to as a *persona*: the "character" projected by the author, the *I* of a narrative poem or novel or the speaker whose voice is heard in a lyric poem. Even if a first-person narrator seems to speak directly for the author or is given the author's name, the speaker created by the words of the story or poem is not identical to the real-life author who writes the words.

they are saying. They don't know everything about everything, of course. But they have a convincing degree of understanding about themselves and what is happening to them, and we feel that, as we read, we can trust and rely on both their accounts of events and their understandings of what occurred.

THIRD-PERSON NARRATION

Stories told by anonymous or identified outside observers who do not refer to themselves using the pronouns *I* or *we* are said to use *third-person point of view*. "Love in L.A." (p. 111) is such a story. It is told by someone who observes and tells about what happened that morning in L.A. from the outside. We are not told who the narrator is. We might assume that, because Dagoberto Gilb is writing the story, he is also its narrator, and in this case that would not be misleading. The narrator and the author do seem very close. But that assumption is not always valid. In some cases a narrator conveys values or positions quite different from the author's. It is well to keep in mind that any narrator, even one who seems very similar to the author, is an imaginative construct, fashioned by the author as a vehicle for telling the story. When you answer the question of who is telling a story, it is safer to refer to the storyteller as a "narrator" instead of as "the author."

The question "What does the narrator know?" applies to third-person point of view as well as to first-person, but the categories for describing the various answers are different. Here are the most important possibilities:

Third-Person Omniscient Point of View   When a story is told by an external narrator who relates actions and conversations but also describes the thoughts or feelings of more than one character, the point of view is referred to as third-person *omniscient* (that is, "having unlimited knowledge"). It's important to keep in mind that omniscient point of view doesn't mean the narrator has to tell the reader everything about a sequence of events or a set of characters; no story can tell everything. Not disclosing everything doesn't mean the narrator is not omniscient. And the fact that the narrator *can see* into every character doesn't mean she or he *will* do so. In Zora Neale Hurston's "Sweat" (p. 372) the third-person narrator shows the flexibility available to an omniscient narrator. The story is told primarily from Delia Jones's perspective, but occasionally the perspective shifts to the men sitting in front of the village store or to Sykes, the husband who abuses Delia. Sometimes the narrator tells what Delia is thinking or feeling (para. 3), and sometimes tells us what her husband is feeling (para. 24) or experiencing (para. 98).

Third-Person Objective Point of View A third-person *objective point of view*, like third-person omniscient, takes an outside view and relates the actions and dialogue; but the narrator is "objective" in the sense of not commenting on what happens and not including inner, personal thoughts or feelings of any of the characters. By describing events only from the outside and not looking into the minds or feelings of characters or explaining why any of the characters do what they do, the narrator leaves it to the reader to draw conclusions from the details and dialogue provided.

The invisible narrator in Ernest Hemingway's "Hills Like White Elephants" (p. 197), for example, simply describes where two characters are and what they do and relates what they say to each other, never looking into their thoughts or commenting on or explaining what is going on between them. However, and this is often misunderstood, for a story to be narrated objectively does not necessarily mean that the story is totally objective. The author can convey an attitude or judgment by the way a character is depicted or the choice of words the author uses, as may be the case in "Hills Like White Elephants."

Third-Person Limited Point of View A third-person limited narrator can look into the mind or feelings of only one character, in contrast to an omniscient narrator, who can see into the minds or feelings of more than one character or all characters. Such a point of view is referred to as *limited omniscient* (that is, partially omniscient). Because the narrator focuses on and follows one character, the narrator generally knows everything that affects that character but does not know about things that occur when that character is not present or about things going on inside other characters.

In Flannery O'Connor's "A Good Man Is Hard to Find" (p. 159), for example, the narrator limits description of the actions and dialogue to what is seen and heard by the grandmother, except for the last six paragraphs, when she is dead, and with minor exceptions describes only the thoughts and feelings of the grandmother. The limited point of view is most evident in that we are never taken into the mind or feelings of The Misfit. We know about him only through dialogue and what he does.

If a story is told entirely through the consciousness (the experiences, thoughts, feelings, and memories) of one character, the approach can be called *center of consciousness*. This is where "Love in L.A." (p. 111) fits best. We are in Jake's car when the story opens and enter his mind in the second sentence. From there on we experience everything through Jake's perspective.

Even all that we know about Mariana comes through his interactions with and impressions of her. The character that the author centers on may be the main character or a minor character; the author may give some third-person description or background information, but it will be a limited amount. See also the Glossary entries for *interior monologue* (p. 1139) and *stream of consciousness* (p. 1148).

 CHECKLIST for Reading about Point of View

❑ Pay attention to who is telling the story (the narrator) and how much the narrator knows:

- *First-person:* a partially knowing *I* or *we*, sometimes reliable, sometimes naïve or unreliable
- *Third-person omniscient:* an all-knowing, often anonymous, reporter of words and actions and the thoughts of more than one character
- *Third-person objective:* a reporter of words and actions, not thoughts or motives
- *Third-person limited:* an observer or participant with partial knowledge
  - Center of consciousness — seeing a story through the consciousness of a particular character
  - Interior monologue — direct presentation of a character's thoughts and memories, without intervention by a narrator
  - Stream of consciousness — the seemingly unstructured perceptions, images, and reflections flowing through a mind

FURTHER READING

APPROACHING THE READING

The following is another story by Alice Walker, who also wrote "The Flowers" (p. 27), which you read in Chapter 2. This one takes us back to the 1960s, when African Americans began turning to Africa in search of their roots and identity, when the adoption of African-influenced clothing, hairstyles, and names in an attempt to connect with one's heritage was new and startling (especially in the old world of the rural South). As you read the story, pay attention to the voice you hear and to the handling of point of view and perspective. Think about the extent to which the way that the story "works," the way it achieves its effects, depends on the voice and personality of the narrator.

Alice Walker   b. 1944

Everyday Use   [1973]

for your grandmama

I will wait for her in the yard that Maggie and I made so clean and wavy yesterday afternoon. A yard like this is more comfortable than most people know. It is not just a yard. It is like an extended living room. When the hard clay is swept clean as a floor and the fine sand around the edges lined with tiny, irregular grooves, anyone can come and sit and look up into the elm tree and wait for the breezes that never come inside the house.

APPROACHING THE AUTHOR

One of **Alice Walker**'s brothers accidentally shot her in the eye with a BB gun while playing cowboys and Indians when she was eight years old. She went blind in her right eye. That unfortunate event may have led to her being able to attend college, as she was granted a rehabilitation scholarship from the state of Georgia.

For more about her, see page 1083.

Maggie will be nervous until after her sister goes: she will stand hopelessly in corners, homely and ashamed of the burn scars down her arms and legs, eyeing her sister with a mixture of envy and awe. She thinks her sister has held life always in the palm of one hand, that "no" is a word the world never learned to say to her.

You've no doubt seen those TV shows where the child who has "made it" is confronted, as a surprise, by her own mother and father, tottering in weakly from backstage. (A pleasant surprise, of course: What would they do if parent and child came on the show only to curse out and insult each other?) On TV mother and child embrace and smile into each other's faces. Sometimes the mother and father weep, the child wraps them in her arms and leans across the table to tell how she would not have made it without their help. I have seen these programs.

Sometimes I dream a dream in which Dee and I are suddenly brought together on a TV program of this sort. Out of a dark and soft-seated limousine I am ushered into a bright room filled with many people. There I meet a smiling, gray, sporty man like Johnny Carson° who shakes my hand and tells me what a fine girl I have. Then we are on the stage and Dee is embracing me with tears in her eyes. She pins on my dress a large orchid, even though she has told me once that she thinks orchids are tacky flowers.

In real life I am a large, big-boned woman with rough, man-working hands.   5 In the winter I wear flannel nightgowns to bed and overalls during the day. I can kill and clean a hog as mercilessly as a man. My fat keeps me hot in zero weather. I can work outside all day, breaking ice to get water for washing; I can

---

Johnny Carson: (1925–2005) U.S. comedian and host of *The Tonight Show Starring Johnny Carson* from 1962 to 1992.

eat pork liver cooked over the open fire minutes after it comes steaming from the hog. One winter I knocked a bull calf straight in the brain between the eyes with a sledge hammer and had the meat hung up to chill before nightfall. But of course all this does not show on television. I am the way my daughter would want me to be: a hundred pounds lighter, my skin like an uncooked barley pancake. My hair glistens in the hot bright lights. Johnny Carson has much to do to keep up with my quick and witty tongue.

But that is a mistake. I know even before I wake up. Who ever knew a Johnson with a quick tongue? Who can even imagine me looking a strange white man in the eye? It seems to me I have talked to them always with one foot raised in flight, with my head turned in whichever way is farthest from them. Dee, though. She would always look anyone in the eye. Hesitation was no part of her nature.

"How do I look, Mama?" Maggie says, showing just enough of her thin body enveloped in pink skirt and red blouse for me to know she's there, almost hidden by the door.

"Come out into the yard," I say.

Have you ever seen a lame animal, perhaps a dog run over by some careless person rich enough to own a car, sidle up to someone who is ignorant enough to be kind to him? That is the way my Maggie walks. She has been like this, chin on chest, eyes on ground, feet in shuffle, ever since the fire that burned the other house to the ground.

Dee is lighter than Maggie, with nicer hair and a fuller figure. She's a 10 woman now, though sometimes I forget. How long ago was it that the other house burned? Ten, twelve years? Sometimes I can still hear the flames and feel Maggie's arms sticking to me, her hair smoking and her dress falling off her in little black papery flakes. Her eyes seemed stretched open, blazed open by the flames reflected in them. And Dee. I see her standing off under the sweet gum tree she used to dig gum out of; a look of concentration on her face as she watched the last dingy gray board of the house fall in toward the red-hot brick chimney. Why don't you do a dance around the ashes? I'd wanted to ask her. She had hated the house that much.

I used to think she hated Maggie, too. But that was before we raised the money, the church and me, to send her to Augusta to school. She used to read to us without pity; forcing words, lies, other folks' habits, whole lives upon us two, sitting trapped and ignorant underneath her voice. She washed us in a river of make-believe, burned us with a lot of knowledge we didn't necessarily need to know. Pressed us to her with the serious way she read, to shove us away at just the moment, like dimwits, we seemed about to understand.

Dee wanted nice things. A yellow organdy dress to wear to her graduation from high school; black pumps to match a green suit she'd made from an old suit somebody gave me. She was determined to stare down any disaster in her efforts. Her eyelids would not flicker for minutes at a time. Often I fought off the temptation to shake her. At sixteen she had a style of her own: and knew what style was.

I never had an education myself. After second grade the school was closed down. Don't ask me why: in 1927 colored asked fewer questions than they do now. Sometimes Maggie reads to me. She stumbles along good-naturedly but can't see well. She knows she is not bright. Like good looks and money, quickness passed her by. She will marry John Thomas (who has mossy teeth in an earnest face) and then I'll be free to sit here and I guess just sing church songs to myself. Although I never was a good singer. Never could carry a tune. I was always better at a man's job. I used to love to milk till I was hooked in the side in '49. Cows are soothing and slow and don't bother you, unless you try to milk them the wrong way.

I have deliberately turned my back on the house. It is three rooms, just like the one that burned, except the roof is tin; they don't make shingle roofs any more. There are no real windows, just some holes cut in the sides, like the portholes in a ship, but not round and not square, with rawhide holding the shutters up on the outside. This house is in a pasture, too, like the other one. No doubt when Dee sees it she will want to tear it down. She wrote me once that no matter where we "choose" to live, she will manage to come see us. But she will never bring her friends. Maggie and I thought about this and Maggie asked me, "Mama, when did Dee ever *have* any friends?"

She had a few. Furtive boys in pink shirts hanging about on washday after 15 school. Nervous girls who never laughed. Impressed with her they worshiped the well-turned phrase, the cute shape, the scalding humor that erupted like bubbles in lye. She read to them.

When she was courting Jimmy T she didn't have much time to pay to us, but turned all her faultfinding power on him. He *flew* to marry a cheap city girl from a family of ignorant flashy people. She hardly had time to recompose herself.

When she comes I will meet—but there they are!

Maggie attempts to make a dash for the house, in her shuffling way, but I stay her with my hand. "Come back here," I say. And she stops and tries to dig a well in the sand with her toe.

It is hard to see them clearly through the strong sun. But even the first glimpse of leg out of the car tells me it is Dee. Her feet were always neat-looking, as if God himself had shaped them with a certain style. From the other side of the car comes a short, stocky man. Hair is all over his head a foot long and hanging from his chin like a kinky mule tail. I hear Maggie suck in her breath. "Uhnnnh," is what it sounds like. Like when you see the wriggling end of a snake just in front of your foot on the road. "Uhnnnh."

Dee next. A dress down to the ground, in this hot weather. A dress so loud 20 it hurts my eyes. There are yellows and oranges enough to throw back the light of the sun. I feel my whole face warming from the heat waves it throws out.

Earrings gold, too, and hanging down to her shoulders. Bracelets dangling and making noises when she moves her arm up to shake the folds of the dress out of her armpits. The dress is loose and flows, and as she walks closer, I like it. I hear Maggie go "Uhnnnh" again. It is her sister's hair. It stands straight up like the wool on a sheep. It is black as night and around the edges are two long pigtails that rope about like small lizards disappearing behind her ears.

"Wa-su-zo-Tean-o!" she says, coming on in that gliding way the dress makes her move. The short stocky fellow with the hair to his navel is all grinning and he follows up with "Asalamalakim, my mother and sister!" He moves to hug Maggie but she falls back, right up against the back of my chair. I feel her trembling there and when I look up I see the perspiration falling off her chin.

"Don't get up," says Dee. Since I am stout it takes something of a push. You can see me trying to move a second or two before I make it. She turns, showing white heels through her sandals, and goes back to the car. Out she peeks next with a Polaroid. She stoops down quickly and lines up picture after picture of me sitting there in front of the house with Maggie cowering behind me. She never takes a shot without making sure the house is included. When a cow comes nibbling around the edge of the yard she snaps it and me and Maggie *and* the house. Then she puts the Polaroid in the back seat of the car, and comes up and kisses me on the forehead.

Meanwhile Asalamalakim is going through motions with Maggie's hand. Maggie's hand is as limp as a fish, and probably as cold, despite the sweat, and she keeps trying to pull it back. It looks like Asalamalakim wants to shake hands but wants to do it fancy. Or maybe he don't know how people shake hands. Anyhow, he soon gives up on Maggie.

"Well," I say. "Dee."

"No, Mama," she says. "Not 'Dee,' Wangero Leewanika Kemanjo!"   25

"What happened to 'Dee'?" I wanted to know.

"She's dead," Wangero said. "I couldn't bear it any longer, being named after the people who oppress me."

"You know as well as me you was named after your aunt Dicie," I said. Dicie is my sister. She named Dee. We called her "Big Dee" after Dee was born.

"But who was *she* named after?" asked Wangero.

"I guess after Grandma Dee," I said.   30

"And who was she named after?" asked Wangero.

"Her mother," I said, and saw Wangero was getting tired. "That's about as far back as I can trace it," I said. Though, in fact, I probably could have carried it back beyond the Civil War through the branches.

"Well," said Asalamalakim, "there you are."

"Uhnnnh," I heard Maggie say.

"There I was not," I said, "before 'Dicie' cropped up in our family, so why   35 should I try to trace it that far back?"

He just stood there grinning, looking down on me like somebody inspecting a Model A car. Every once in a while he and Wangero sent eye signals over my head.

"How do you pronounce this name?" I asked.

"You don't have to call me by it if you don't want to," said Wangero.

"Why shouldn't I?" I asked. "If that's what you want us to call you, we'll call you."

"I know it might sound awkward at first," said Wangero.   40

"I'll get used to it," I said. "Ream it out again."

Well, soon we got the name out of the way. Asalamalakim had a name twice as long and three times as hard. After I tripped over it two or three times he told me to just call him Hakim-a-barber. I wanted to ask him was he a barber, but I didn't really think he was, so I didn't ask.

"You must belong to those beef-cattle peoples down the road," I said. They said "Asalamalakim" when they met you, too, but they didn't shake hands. Always too busy: feeding the cattle, fixing the fences, putting up salt-lick shelters, throwing down hay. When the white folks poisoned some of the herd the men stayed up all night with rifles in their hands. I walked a mile and a half just to see the sight.

Hakim-a-barber said, "I accept some of their doctrines, but farming and raising cattle is not my style." (They didn't tell me, and I didn't ask, whether Wangero (Dee) had really gone and married him.)

We sat down to eat and right away he said he didn't eat collards and pork 45 was unclean. Wangero, though, went on through the chitlins and corn bread, the greens and everything else. She talked a blue streak over the sweet potatoes. Everything delighted her. Even the fact that we still used the benches her daddy made for the table when we couldn't afford to buy chairs.

"Oh, Mama!" she cried. Then turned to Hakim-a-barber. "I never knew how lovely these benches are. You can feel the rump prints," she said, running her hands underneath her and along the bench. Then she gave a sigh and her hand closed over Grandma Dee's butter dish. "That's it!" she said. "I knew there was something I wanted to ask you if I could have." She jumped up from the table and went over in the corner where the churn stood, the milk in it clabber by now. She looked at the churn and looked at it.

"This churn top is what I need," she said. "Didn't Uncle Buddy whittle it out of a tree you all used to have?"

"Yes," I said.

"Uh huh," she said happily. "And I want the dasher, too."

"Uncle Buddy whittle that, too?" asked the barber.   50

Dee (Wangero) looked up at me.

"Aunt Dee's first husband whittled the dash," said Maggie so low you almost couldn't hear her. "His name was Henry, but they called him Stash."

"Maggie's brain is like an elephant's," Wangero said, laughing. "I can use the churn top as a centerpiece for the alcove table," she said, sliding a plate over the churn, "and I'll think of something artistic to do with the dasher."

When she finished wrapping the dasher the handle stuck out. I took it for a moment in my hands. You didn't even have to look close to see where hands pushing the dasher up and down to make butter had left a kind of sink in the wood. In fact, there were a lot of small sinks; you could see where thumbs and fingers had sunk into the wood. It was beautiful light yellow wood, from a tree that grew in the yard where Big Dee and Stash had lived.

After dinner Dee (Wangero) went to the trunk at the foot of my bed 55 and started rifling through it. Maggie hung back in the kitchen over the dishpan. Out came Wangero with two quilts. They had been pieced by Grandma Dee and then Big Dee and me had hung them on the quilt frames on the front porch and quilted them. One was in the Lone Star pattern. The other was Walk Around the Mountain. In both of them were scraps of dresses Grandma Dee had worn fifty and more years ago. Bits and pieces of Grandpa Jarrell's Paisley shirts. And one teeny faded blue piece, about the size of a penny matchbox, that was from Great Grandpa Ezra's uniform that he wore in the Civil War.

"Mama," Wangero said sweet as a bird. "Can I have these old quilts?"

I heard something fall in the kitchen, and a minute later the kitchen door slammed.

"Why don't you take one or two of the others?" I asked. "These old things was just done by me and Big Dee from some tops your grandma pieced before she died."

"No," said Wangero. "I don't want those. They are stitched around the borders by machine."

"That'll make them last better," I said. 60

"That's not the point," said Wangero. "These are all pieces of dresses Grandma used to wear. She did all this stitching by hand. Imagine!" She held the quilts securely in her arms, stroking them.

"Some of the pieces, like those lavender ones, come from old clothes her mother handed down to her," I said, moving up to touch the quilts. Dee (Wangero) moved back just enough so that I couldn't reach the quilts. They already belonged to her.

"Imagine!" she breathed again, clutching them closely to her bosom.

"The truth is," I said, "I promised to give them quilts to Maggie, for when she marries John Thomas."

She gasped like a bee had stung her. 65

"Maggie can't appreciate these quilts!" she said. "She'd probably be backward enough to put them to everyday use."

"I reckon she would," I said. "God knows I been saving 'em for long enough with nobody using 'em. I hope she will!" I didn't want to bring up how I had offered Dee (Wangero) a quilt when she went away to college. Then she had told me they were old-fashioned, out of style.

"But they're *priceless*!" she was saying now, furiously; for she has a temper. "Maggie would put them on the bed and in five years they'd be in rags. Less than that!"

"She can always make some more," I said. "Maggie knows how to quilt."

Dee (Wangero) looked at me with hatred. "You just will not understand. 70
The point is these quilts, *these* quilts!"

"Well," I said, stumped. "What would *you* do with them?"

"Hang them," she said. As if that was the only thing you *could* do with
quilts.

Maggie by now was standing in the door. I could almost hear the sound her
feet made as they scraped over each other.

"She can have them, Mama," she said, like somebody used to never winning anything, or having anything reserved for her. "I can 'member Grandma
Dee without the quilts."

I looked at her hard. She had filled her bottom lip with checkerberry snuff 75
and it gave her face a kind of dopey, hangdog look. It was Grandma Dee and
Big Dee who taught her how to quilt herself. She stood there with her scarred
hands hidden in the folds of her skirt. She looked at her sister with something
like fear but she wasn't mad at her. This was Maggie's portion. This was the way
she knew God to work.

When I looked at her like that something hit me in the top of my head and
ran down to the soles of my feet. Just like when I'm in church and the spirit of
God touches me and I get happy and shout. I did something I never had done
before: hugged Maggie to me, then dragged her on into the room, snatched the
quilts out of Miss Wangero's hands and dumped them into Maggie's lap.
Maggie just sat there on my bed with her mouth open.

"Take one or two of the others," I said to Dee.

But she turned without a word and went out to Hakim-a-barber.

"You just don't understand," she said, as Maggie and I came out to the car.

"What don't I understand?" I wanted to know. 80

"Your heritage," she said. And then she turned to Maggie, kissed her, and
said, "You ought to try to make something of yourself, too, Maggie. It's really a
new day for us. But from the way you and Mama still live you'd never know it."

She put on some sunglasses that hid everything above the tip of her nose
and her chin.

Maggie smiled; maybe at the sunglasses. But a real smile, not scared. After
we watched the car dust settle I asked Maggie to bring me a dip of snuff. And
then the two of us sat there just enjoying, until it was time to go in the house
and go to bed.

REFLECTING ON WHAT YOU'VE READ

1. Describe the voice you hear in "Everyday Use." What can you tell about the
   narrator from the way she sounds as you listen to her? What kind of personality comes through in what she says and the way she says it?

2. Identify the point of view used in the story. What is the particular effect of
   having the narrator address the reader as *you*? In what ways does the effect
   of the story depend on its voice and perspective?

3. Think about the narrator and decide whether she is totally reliable, partially reliable, or generally unreliable. Explain how you made your decision and be sure to refer to specific places in the story that support your choice.

4. Look carefully at the final paragraph of the story. Does it fit well with what you said about voice? Is it an effective and satisfying ending? If so, how and why? If you find it unsatisfying, explain why.

APPROACHING THE READING

Here is another story about the South, but it's a story very different in style and tone from those of "Everyday Use." Flannery O'Connor lived in Georgia and wrote about the South. Her short stories are carefully crafted, with crisp humor. They often focus on unappealing characters who are redeemed by grace, reflecting the influence of her Catholic faith. The first time you read the story, let your emotions get fully involved with what happens. O'Connor is going to take you on an emotional roller coaster.

Flannery O'Connor   1925–1964

A Good Man Is Hard to Find   [1955]

The grandmother didn't want to go to Florida. She wanted to visit some of her connections in east Tennessee and she was seizing at every chance to change Bailey's mind. Bailey was the son she lived with, her only boy. He was sitting on the edge of his chair at the table, bent over the orange sports section of the *Journal*. "Now look here, Bailey," she said, "see here, read this," and she stood with one hand on her thin hip and the other rattling the newspaper at his bald head. "Here this fellow that calls himself The Misfit is aloose from the Federal Pen and headed toward Florida and you read here what it says he did to these people. Just you read it. I wouldn't take my children in any direction with a criminal like that aloose in it. I couldn't answer to my conscience if I did."

Bailey didn't look up from his reading so she wheeled around then and faced the children's mother, a young woman in slacks, whose face was as broad and innocent as a cabbage and was tied around with a green head-kerchief that

APPROACHING THE AUTHOR

When **Flannery O'Connor** was five years old, she taught her pet chicken to walk backward. The Pathe Newsreel Company filmed O'Connor and her

APIC/Getty Images

chicken and played the reel in movie theaters across the country in 1932.

For more about her, see page 1074.

had two points on the top like rabbit's ears. She was sitting on the sofa, feeding the baby his apricots out of a jar. "The children have been to Florida before," the old lady said. "You all ought to take them somewhere else for a change so they would see different parts of the world and be broad. They never have been to east Tennessee."

The children's mother didn't seem to hear her but the eight-year-old boy, John Wesley, a stocky child with glasses, said, "If you don't want to go to Florida, why dontcha stay at home?" He and the little girl, June Star, were reading the funny papers on the floor.

"She wouldn't stay at home to be queen for a day,"° June Star said without raising her yellow head.

"Yes and what would you do if this fellow, The Misfit, caught you?" the   5
grandmother asked.

"I'd smack his face," John Wesley said.

"She wouldn't stay at home for a million bucks," June Star said. "Afraid she'd miss something. She has to go everywhere we go."

"All right, Miss," the grandmother said. "Just remember that the next time you want me to curl your hair."

June Star said her hair was naturally curly.

The next morning the grandmother was the first one in the car, ready to   10
go. She had her big black valise that looked like the head of a hippopotamus in one corner, and underneath it she was hiding a basket with Pitty Sing, the cat, in it. She didn't intend for the cat to be left alone in the house for three days because he would miss her too much and she was afraid he might brush against one of the gas burners and accidentally asphyxiate himself. Her son, Bailey, didn't like to arrive at a motel with a cat.

She sat in the middle of the back seat with John Wesley and June Star on either side of her. Bailey and the children's mother and the baby sat in front and they left Atlanta at eight forty-five with the mileage on the car at 55890. The grandmother wrote this down because she thought it would be interesting to say how many miles they had been when they got back. It took them twenty minutes to reach the outskirts of the city.

The old lady settled herself comfortably, removing her white cotton gloves and putting them up with her purse on the shelf in front of the back window. The children's mother still had on slacks and still had her head tied up in a green kerchief, but the grandmother had on a navy blue straw sailor hat with a bunch of white violets on the brim and a navy blue dress with a small white dot in the print. Her collars and cuffs were white organdy trimmed with lace and at her neckline she had pinned a purple spray of cloth violets containing a sachet. In case of an accident, anyone seeing her dead on the highway would know at once that she was a lady.

Queen for a day: Alluding to the American radio (1945–1957) and television (1956–1964, 1969–1970) show on which several women experiencing difficult circumstances competed, by telling their stories winsomely, to be treated like royalty for a day.

She said she thought it was going to be a good day for driving, neither too hot nor too cold, and she cautioned Bailey that the speed limit was fifty-five miles an hour and that the patrolmen hid themselves behind billboards and small clumps of trees and sped out after you before you had a chance to slow down. She pointed out interesting details of the scenery: Stone Mountain; the blue granite that in some places came up to both sides of the highway; the brilliant red clay banks slightly streaked with purple; and the various crops that made rows of green lace-work on the ground. The trees were full of silver-white sunlight and the meanest of them sparkled. The children were reading comic magazines and their mother had gone back to sleep.

"Let's go through Georgia fast so we won't have to look at it much," John Wesley said.

"If I were a little boy," said the grandmother, "I wouldn't talk about my 15 native state that way. Tennessee has the mountains and Georgia has the hills."

"Tennessee is just a hillbilly dumping ground," John Wesley said, "and Georgia is a lousy state too."

"You said it," June Star said.

"In my time," said the grandmother, folding her thin veined fingers, "children were more respectful of their native states and their parents and everything else. People did right then. Oh look at the cute little pickaninny!" she said and pointed to a Negro child standing in the door of a shack. "Wouldn't that make a picture, now?" she asked and they all turned and looked at the little Negro out of the back window. He waved.

"He didn't have any britches on," June Star said.

"He probably didn't have any," the grandmother explained. "Little niggers 20 in the country don't have things like we do. If I could paint, I'd paint that picture," she said.

The children exchanged comic books.

The grandmother offered to hold the baby and the children's mother passed him over the front seat to her. She set him on her knee and bounced him and told him about the things they were passing. She rolled her eyes and screwed up her mouth and stuck her leathery thin face into his smooth bland one. Occasionally he gave her a faraway smile. They passed a large cotton field with five or six graves fenced in the middle of it, like a small island. "Look at the graveyard!" the grandmother said, pointing it out. "That was the old family burying ground. That belonged to the plantation."

"Where's the plantation?" John Wesley asked.

"Gone With the Wind,"° said the grandmother. "Ha. Ha."

When the children finished all the comic books they had brought, they 25 opened the lunch and ate it. The grandmother ate a peanut butter sandwich and an olive and would not let the children throw the box and the paper napkins

---

Gone With the Wind: The title of the best-selling 1936 novel by Margaret Mitchell dealing with the period of the American Civil War and the Reconstruction, made into an Academy Award–winning film in 1939.

out the window. When there was nothing else to do they played a game by choosing a cloud and making the other two guess what shape it suggested. John Wesley took one the shape of a cow and June Star guessed a cow and John Wesley said, no, an automobile, and June Star said he didn't play fair, and they began to slap each other over the grandmother.

The grandmother said she would tell them a story if they would keep quiet. When she told a story, she rolled her eyes and waved her head and was very dramatic. She said once when she was a maiden lady she had been courted by a Mr. Edgar Atkins Teagarden from Jasper, Georgia. She said he was a very good-looking man and a gentleman and that he brought her a watermelon every Saturday afternoon with his initials cut in it, E. A. T. Well, one Saturday, she said, Mr. Teagarden brought the watermelon and there was nobody at home and he left it on the front porch and returned in his buggy to Jasper, but she never got the watermelon, she said, because a nigger boy ate it when he saw the initials, E. A. T.! This story tickled John Wesley's funny bone and he giggled and giggled but June Star didn't think it was any good. She said she wouldn't marry a man that just brought her a watermelon on Saturday. The grandmother said she would have done well to marry Mr. Teagarden because he was a gentleman and had bought Coca-Cola stock when it first came out and that he had died only a few years ago, a very wealthy man.

They stopped at The Tower for barbecued sandwiches. The Tower was a part stucco and part wood filling station and dance hall set in a clearing outside of Timothy. A fat man named Red Sammy Butts ran it and there were signs stuck here and there on the building and for miles up and down the highway saying, TRY RED SAMMY'S FAMOUS BARBECUE. NONE LIKE FAMOUS RED SAMMY'S! RED SAM! THE FAT BOY WITH THE HAPPY LAUGH. A VETERAN! RED SAMMY'S YOUR MAN!

Red Sammy was lying on the bare ground outside The Tower with his head under a truck while a gray monkey about a foot high, chained to a small chinaberry tree, chattered nearby. The monkey sprang back into the tree and got on the highest limb as soon as he saw the children jump out of the car and run toward him.

Inside, The Tower was a long dark room with a counter at one end and tables at the other and dancing space in the middle. They all sat down at a board table next to the nickelodeon and Red Sam's wife, a tall burnt-brown woman with hair and eyes lighter than her skin, came and took their order. The children's mother put a dime in the machine and played "The Tennessee Waltz," and the grandmother said that tune always made her want to dance. She asked Bailey if he would like to dance but he only glared at her. He didn't have a naturally sunny disposition like she did and trips made him nervous. The grandmother's brown eyes were very bright. She swayed her head from side to side and pretended she was dancing in her chair. June Star said play something she could tap to so the children's mother put in another dime and played a fast number and June Star stepped out onto the dance floor and did her tap routine.

"Ain't she cute?" Red Sam's wife said, leaning over the counter. "Would you 30
like to come be my little girl?"

"No I certainly wouldn't," June Star said. "I wouldn't live in a broken-down place like this for a million bucks!" and she ran back to the table.

"Ain't she cute?" the woman repeated, stretching her mouth politely.

"Aren't you ashamed?" hissed the grandmother.

Red Sam came in and told his wife to quit lounging on the counter and hurry up with these people's order. His khaki trousers reached just to his hip bones and his stomach hung over them like a sack of meal swaying under his shirt. He came over and sat down at a table nearby and let out a combination sigh and yodel. "You can't win," he said. "You can't win," and he wiped his sweating red face off with a gray handkerchief. "These days you don't know who to trust," he said. "Ain't that the truth?"

"People are certainly not nice like they used to be," said the grandmother. 35

"Two fellers come in here last week," Red Sammy said, "driving a Chrysler. It was a old beat-up car but it was a good one and these boys looked all right to me. Said they worked at the mill and you know I let them fellers charge the gas they bought? Now why did I do that?"

"Because you're a good man!" the grandmother said at once.

"Yes'm, I suppose so," Red Sam said as if he were struck with this answer.

His wife brought the orders, carrying the five plates all at once without a tray, two in each hand and one balanced on her arm. "It isn't a soul in this green world of God's that you can trust," she said. "And I don't count nobody out of that, not nobody," she repeated, looking at Red Sammy.

"Did you read about that criminal, The Misfit, that's escaped?" asked the 40 grandmother.

"I wouldn't be a bit surprised if he didn't attact this place right here," said the woman. "If he hears about it being here, I wouldn't be none surprised to see him. If he hears it's two cent in the cash register, I wouldn't be a tall surprised if he . . ."

"That'll do," Red Sam said. "Go bring these people their Co'-Colas," and the woman went off to get the rest of the order.

"A good man is hard to find," Red Sammy said. "Everything is getting terrible. I remember the day you could go off and leave your screen door unlatched. Not no more."

He and the grandmother discussed better times. The old lady said that in her opinion Europe was entirely to blame for the way things were now. She said the way Europe acted you would think we were made of money and Red Sam said it was no use talking about it, she was exactly right. The children ran outside into the white sunlight and looked at the monkey in the lacy chinaberry tree. He was busy catching fleas on himself and biting each one carefully between his teeth as if it were a delicacy.

They drove off again into the hot afternoon. The grandmother took cat 45 naps and woke up every few minutes with her own snoring. Outside of Toombsboro she woke up and recalled an old plantation that she had visited in this neighborhood once when she was a young lady. She said the house had six white columns across the front and that there was an avenue of oaks leading up to it and two little wooden trellis arbors on either side in front where you sat down with your suitor after a stroll in the garden. She recalled exactly which road to turn off to get to it. She knew that Bailey would not be willing to lose any time looking at an old house, but the more she talked about it, the more she wanted to see it once again and find out if the little twin arbors were still standing. "There was a secret panel in this house," she said craftily, not telling the truth but wishing that she were, "and the story went that all the family silver was hidden in it when Sherman came through° but it was never found . . ."

"Hey!" John Wesley said. "Let's go see it! We'll find it! We'll poke all the woodwork and find it! Who lives there? Where do you turn off at? Hey Pop, can't we turn off there?"

"We never have seen a house with a secret panel!" June Star shrieked. "Let's go to the house with the secret panel! Hey Pop, can't we go see the house with the secret panel!"

"It's not far from here, I know," the grandmother said. "It wouldn't take over twenty minutes."

Bailey was looking straight ahead. His jaw was as rigid as a horseshoe. "No," he said.

The children began to yell and scream that they wanted to see the house   50 with the secret panel. John Wesley kicked the back of the front seat and June Star hung over her mother's shoulder and whined desperately into her ear that they never had any fun even on their vacation, that they could never do what THEY wanted to do. The baby began to scream and John Wesley kicked the back of the seat so hard that his father could feel the blows in his kidney.

"All right!" he shouted and drew the car to a stop at the side of the road. "Will you all shut up? Will you all just shut up for one second? If you don't shut up, we won't go anywhere."

"It would be very educational for them," the grandmother murmured.

"All right," Bailey said, "but get this: this is the only time we're going to stop for anything like this. This is the one and only time."

"The dirt road that you have to turn down is about a mile back," the grand-mother directed. "I marked it when we passed."

"A dirt road," Bailey groaned.   55

After they had turned around and were headed toward the dirt road, the grandmother recalled other points about the house, the beautiful glass over the front doorway and the candle-lamp in the hall. John Wesley said that the secret panel was probably in the fireplace.

"You can't go inside this house," Bailey said. "You don't know who lives there."

Sherman came through: In November and December 1864, General William Tecumseh Sherman marched with over 60,000 Union soldiers from Atlanta to the Atlantic coast, pillaging and burning towns and farms along the way.

"While you all talk to the people in front, I'll run around behind and get in a window," John Wesley suggested.

"We'll all stay in the car," his mother said.

They turned onto the dirt road and the car raced roughly along in a swirl of pink dust. The grandmother recalled the times when there were no paved roads and thirty miles was a day's journey. The dirt road was hilly and there were sudden washes in it and sharp curves on dangerous embankments. All at once they would be on a hill, looking down over the blue tops of trees for miles around, then the next minute, they would be in a red depression with the dust-coated trees looking down on them.

"This place had better turn up in a minute," Bailey said, "or I'm going to turn around."

The road looked as if no one had traveled on it in months.

"It's not much farther," the grandmother said and just as she said it, a horrible thought came to her. The thought was so embarrassing that she turned red in the face and her eyes dilated and her feet jumped up, upsetting her valise in the corner. The instant the valise moved, the newspaper top she had over the basket under it rose with a snarl and Pitty Sing, the cat, sprang onto Bailey's shoulder.

The children were thrown to the floor and their mother, clutching the baby, was thrown out the door onto the ground; the old lady was thrown into the front seat. The car turned over once and landed right-side-up in a gulch off the side of the road. Bailey remained in the driver's seat with the cat—gray-striped with a broad white face and an orange nose—clinging to his neck like a caterpillar.

As soon as the children saw they could move their arms and legs, they scrambled out of the car, shouting, "We've had an ACCIDENT!" The grandmother was curled up under the dashboard, hoping she was injured so that Bailey's wrath would not come down on her all at once. The horrible thought she had had before the accident was that the house she had remembered so vividly was not in Georgia but in Tennessee.

Bailey removed the cat from his neck with both hands and flung it out the window against the side of a pine tree. Then he got out of the car and started looking for the children's mother. She was sitting against the side of the red gutted ditch, holding the screaming baby, but she only had a cut down her face and a broken shoulder. "We've had an ACCIDENT!" the children screamed in a frenzy of delight.

"But nobody's killed," June Star said with disappointment as the grandmother limped out of the car, her hat still pinned to her head but the broken front brim standing up at a jaunty angle and the violet spray hanging off the side. They all sat down in the ditch, except the children, to recover from the shock. They were all shaking.

"Maybe a car will come along," said the children's mother hoarsely.

"I believe I have injured an organ," said the grandmother, pressing her side, but no one answered her. Bailey's teeth were clattering. He had on a yellow sport shirt with bright blue parrots designed in it and his face was as yellow as the shirt. The grandmother decided that she would not mention that the house was in Tennessee.

The road was about ten feet above and they could see only the tops of the 70 trees on the other side of it. Behind the ditch they were sitting in there were more woods, tall and dark and deep. In a few minutes they saw a car some distance away on top of a hill, coming slowly as if the occupants were watching them. The grandmother stood up and waved both arms dramatically to attract their attention. The car continued to come on slowly, disappeared around a bend and appeared again, moving even slower, on top of the hill they had gone over. It was a big black battered hearse-like automobile. There were three men in it.

It came to a stop just over them and for some minutes, the driver looked down with a steady expressionless gaze to where they were sitting, and didn't speak. Then he turned his head and muttered something to the other two and they got out. One was a fat boy in black trousers and a red sweat shirt with a silver stallion embossed on the front of it. He moved around on the right side of them and stood staring, his mouth partly open in a kind of loose grin. The other had on khaki pants and a blue striped coat and a gray hat pulled down very low, hiding most of his face. He came around slowly on the left side. Neither spoke.

The driver got out of the car and stood by the side of it, looking down at them. He was an older man than the other two. His hair was just beginning to gray and he wore silver-rimmed spectacles that gave him a scholarly look. He had a long creased face and didn't have on any shirt or undershirt. He had on blue jeans that were too tight for him and was holding a black hat and a gun. The two boys also had guns.

"We've had an ACCIDENT!" the children screamed.

The grandmother had the peculiar feeling that the bespectacled man was someone she knew. His face was as familiar to her as if she had known him all her life but she could not recall who he was. He moved away from the car and began to come down the embankment, placing his feet carefully so that he wouldn't slip. He had on tan and white shoes and no socks, and his ankles were red and thin. "Good afternoon," he said. "I see you all had you a little spill."

"We turned over twice!" said the grandmother.   75

"Oncet," he corrected. "We seen it happen. Try their car and see will it run, Hiram," he said quietly to the boy with the gray hat.

"What you got that gun for?" John Wesley asked. "Whatcha gonna do with that gun?"

"Lady," the man said to the children's mother, "would you mind calling them children to sit down by you? Children make me nervous. I want all you all to sit down right together there where you're at."

"What are you telling US what to do for?" June Star asked.

Behind them the line of woods gaped like a dark open mouth. "Come 80 here," said their mother.

"Look here now," Bailey began suddenly, "we're in a predicament! We're in . . ."

The grandmother shrieked. She scrambled to her feet and stood staring. "You're The Misfit!" she said. "I recognized you at once!"

"Yes'm," the man said, smiling slightly as if he were pleased in spite of himself to be known, "but it would have been better for all of you, lady, if you hadn't of reckernized me."

Bailey turned his head sharply and said something to his mother that shocked even the children. The old lady began to cry and The Misfit reddened.

"Lady," he said, "don't you get upset. Sometimes a man says things he don't 85 mean. I don't reckon he meant to talk to you thataway."

"You wouldn't shoot a lady, would you?" the grandmother said and removed a clean handkerchief from her cuff and began to slap at her eyes with it.

The Misfit pointed the toe of his shoe into the ground and made a little hole and then covered it up again. "I would hate to have to," he said.

"Listen," the grandmother almost screamed, "I know you're a good man. You don't look a bit like you have common blood. I know you must come from nice people!"

"Yes mam," he said, "finest people in the world." When he smiled he showed a row of strong white teeth. "God never made a finer woman than my mother and my daddy's heart was pure gold," he said. The boy with the red sweat shirt had come around behind them and was standing with his gun at his hip. The Misfit squatted down on the ground. "Watch them children, Bobby Lee," he said. "You know they make me nervous." He looked at the six of them huddled together in front of him and he seemed to be embarrassed as if he couldn't think of anything to say. "Ain't a cloud in the sky," he remarked, looking up at it. "Don't see no sun but don't see no cloud neither."

"Yes, it's a beautiful day," said the grandmother. "Listen," she said, "you 90 shouldn't call yourself The Misfit because I know you're a good man at heart. I can just look at you and tell."

"Hush!" Bailey yelled. "Hush! Everybody shut up and let me handle this!" He was squatting in the position of a runner about to sprint forward but he didn't move.

"I pre-chate that, lady," The Misfit said and drew a little circle in the ground with the butt of his gun.

"It'll take a half a hour to fix this here car," Hiram called, looking over the raised hood of it.

"Well, first you and Bobby Lee get him and that little boy to step over yonder with you," The Misfit said, pointing to Bailey and John Wesley. "The boys want to ast you something," he said to Bailey. "Would you mind stepping back in them woods there with them?"

"Listen," Bailey began, "we're in a terrible predicament! Nobody realizes 95 what this is," and his voice cracked. His eyes were as blue and intense as the parrots in his shirt and he remained perfectly still.

The grandmother reached up to adjust her hat brim as if she were going to the woods with him but it came off in her hand. She stood staring at it and after a second she let it fall on the ground. Hiram pulled Bailey up by the arm as if he were assisting an old man. John Wesley caught hold of his father's hand and Bobby Lee followed. They went off toward the woods and just as they reached the dark edge, Bailey turned and supporting himself against a gray naked pine trunk, he shouted, "I'll be back in a minute, Mamma, wait on me!"

"Come back this instant!" his mother shrilled but they all disappeared into the woods.

"Bailey Boy!" the grandmother called in a tragic voice but she found she was looking at The Misfit squatting on the ground in front of her. "I just know you're a good man," she said desperately. "You're not a bit common!"

"Nome, I ain't a good man," The Misfit said after a second as if he had considered her statement carefully, "but I ain't the worst in the world neither. My daddy said I was a different breed of dog from my brothers and sisters. 'You know,' Daddy said, 'it's some that can live their whole life out without asking about it and it's others has to know why it is, and this boy is one of the latters. He's going to be into everything!'" He put on his black hat and looked up suddenly and then away deep into the woods as if he were embarrassed again. "I'm sorry I don't have on a shirt before you ladies," he said, hunching his shoulders slightly. "We buried our clothes that we had on when we escaped and we're just making do until we can get better. We borrowed these from some folks we met," he explained.

"That's perfectly all right," the grandmother said. "Maybe Bailey has an   100 extra shirt in his suitcase."

"I'll look and see terrectly," The Misfit said.

"Where are they taking him?" the children's mother screamed.

"Daddy was a card himself," The Misfit said. "You couldn't put anything over on him. He never got in trouble with the Authorities though. Just had the knack of handling them."

"You could be honest too if you'd only try," said the grandmother. "Think how wonderful it would be to settle down and live a comfortable life and not have to think about somebody chasing you all the time."

The Misfit kept scratching in the ground with the butt of his gun as if he   105 were thinking about it. "Yes'm, somebody is always after you," he murmured.

The grandmother noticed how thin his shoulder blades were just behind his hat because she was standing up looking down on him. "Do you ever pray?" she asked.

He shook his head. All she saw was the black hat wiggle between his shoulder blades. "Nome," he said.

There was a pistol shot from the woods, followed closely by another. Then silence. The old lady's head jerked around. She could hear the wind move through the tree tops like a long satisfied insuck of breath. "Bailey Boy!" she called.

"I was a gospel singer for a while," The Misfit said. "I been most everything. Been in the arm service, both land and sea, at home and abroad, been twice married, been an undertaker, been with the railroads, plowed Mother Earth, been in a tornado, seen a man burnt alive oncet," and he looked up at the children's mother and the little girl who were sitting close together, their faces white and their eyes glassy; "I even seen a woman flogged," he said.

"Pray, pray," the grandmother began, "pray, pray . . ." 110

"I never was a bad boy that I remember of," The Misfit said in an almost dreamy voice, "but somewheres along the line I done something wrong and got sent to the penitentiary. I was buried alive," and he looked up and held her attention to him by a steady stare.

"That's when you should have started to pray," she said. "What did you do to get sent to the penitentiary that first time?"

"Turn to the right, it was a wall," The Misfit said, looking up again at the cloudless sky. "Turn to the left, it was a wall. Look up it was a ceiling, look down it was a floor. I forget what I done, lady. I set there and set there, trying to remember what it was I done and I ain't recalled it to this day. Oncet in a while, I would think it was coming to me, but it never come."

"Maybe they put you in by mistake," the old lady said vaguely.

"Nome," he said. "It wasn't no mistake. They had the papers on me." 115

"You must have stolen something," she said.

The Misfit sneered slightly. "Nobody had nothing I wanted," he said. "It was a head-doctor at the penitentiary said what I had done was kill my daddy but I known that for a lie. My daddy died in nineteen ought nineteen of the epidemic flu° and I never had a thing to do with it. He was buried in the Mount Hopewell Baptist churchyard and you can go there and see for yourself."

"If you would pray," the old lady said, "Jesus would help you."

"That's right," The Misfit said.

"Well then, why don't you pray?" she asked trembling with delight 120 suddenly.

"I don't want no hep," he said. "I'm doing all right by myself."

Bobby Lee and Hiram came ambling back from the woods. Bobby Lee was dragging a yellow shirt with bright blue parrots in it.

"Thow me that shirt, Bobby Lee," The Misfit said. The shirt came flying at him and landed on his shoulder and he put it on. The grandmother couldn't name what the shirt reminded her of. "No, lady," The Misfit said while he was buttoning it up, "I found out the crime don't matter. You can do one thing or you can do another, kill a man or take a tire off his car, because sooner or later you're going to forget what it was you done and just be punished for it."

The children's mother had begun to make heaving noises as if she couldn't get her breath. "Lady," he asked, "would you and that little girl like to step off yonder with Bobby Lee and Hiram and join your husband?"

---

epidemic flu: An influenza epidemic in 1918–1919 killed twenty to forty million people worldwide.

"Yes, thank you," the mother said faintly. Her left arm dangled helplessly 125
and she was holding the baby, who had gone to sleep, in the other. "Hep that
lady up, Hiram," The Misfit said as she struggled to climb out of the ditch, "and
Bobby Lee, you hold onto that little girl's hand."

"I don't want to hold hands with him," June Star said. "He reminds me of
a pig."

The fat boy blushed and laughed and caught her by the arm and pulled her
off into the woods after Hiram and her mother.

Alone with The Misfit, the grandmother found that she had lost her voice.
There was not a cloud in the sky nor any sun. There was nothing around her
but woods. She wanted to tell him that he must pray. She opened and closed her
mouth several times before anything came out. Finally she found herself saying,
"Jesus. Jesus," meaning, Jesus will help you, but the way she was saying it, it
sounded as if she might be cursing.

"Yes'm," The Misfit said as if he agreed. "Jesus thown everything off balance. It was the same case with Him as with me except He hadn't committed
any crime and they could prove I had committed one because they had the
papers on me. Of course," he said, "they never shown me my papers. That's why
I sign myself now. I said long ago, you get you a signature and sign everything
you do and keep a copy of it. Then you'll know what you done and you can hold
up the crime to the punishment and see do they match and in the end you'll
have something to prove you ain't been treated right. I call myself The Misfit,"
he said, "because I can't make what all I done wrong fit what all I gone through
in punishment."

There was a piercing scream from the woods, followed closely by a pistol 130
report. "Does it seem right to you, lady, that one is punished a heap and
another ain't punished at all?"

"Jesus!" the old lady cried. "You've got good blood! I know you wouldn't
shoot a lady! I know you come from nice people! Pray! Jesus, you ought not to
shoot a lady. I'll give you all the money I've got!"

"Lady," The Misfit said, looking beyond her far into the woods, "there never
was a body that give the undertaker a tip."

There were two more pistol reports and the grandmother raised her head
like a parched old turkey hen crying for water and called, "Bailey Boy, Bailey
Boy!" as if her heart would break.

"Jesus was the only One that ever raised the dead," The Misfit continued,
"and He shouldn't have done it. He thrown everything off balance. If He did
what He said, then it's nothing for you to do but throw away everything and
follow Him, and if He didn't, then it's nothing for you to do but enjoy the few
minutes you got left the best way you can—by killing somebody or burning
down his house or doing some other meanness to him. No pleasure but meanness," he said and his voice had become almost a snarl.

"Maybe He didn't raise the dead," the old lady mumbled, not knowing what 135
she was saying and feeling so dizzy that she sank down in the ditch with her legs
twisted under her.

"I wasn't there so I can't say He didn't," The Misfit said. "I wisht I had of been there," he said, hitting the ground with his fist. "It ain't right I wasn't there because if I had of been there I would of known. Listen lady," he said in a high voice, "if I had of been there I would of known and I wouldn't be like I am now." His voice seemed about to crack and the grandmother's head cleared for an instant. She saw the man's face twisted close to her own as if he were going to cry and she murmured, "Why you're one of my babies. You're one of my own children!" She reached out and touched him on the shoulder. The Misfit sprang back as if a snake had bitten him and shot her three times through the chest. Then he put his gun down on the ground and took off his glasses and began to clean them.

Hiram and Bobby Lee returned from the woods and stood over the ditch, looking down at the grandmother who half sat and half lay in a puddle of blood with her legs crossed under her like a child's and her face smiling up at the cloudless sky.

Without his glasses, The Misfit's eyes were red-rimmed and pale and defenseless-looking. "Take her off and thow her where you thown the others," he said, picking up the cat that was rubbing itself against his leg.

"She was a talker, wasn't she?" Bobby Lee said, sliding down the ditch with a yodel.

"She would of been a good woman," The Misfit said, "if it had been some- 140 body there to shoot her every minute of her life."

"Some fun!" Bobby Lee said.

"Shut up, Bobby Lee," The Misfit said. "It's no real pleasure in life."

REFLECTING ON WHAT YOU'VE READ

1. Be ready to talk about what you experienced emotionally as you read the story the first time. What did you feel about the characters (minor as well as major characters), and what did you feel about what occurs, especially what happens in the last four or five pages?

2. As you reread or review the story, identify its point of view and perspective, and be ready to explain and support your answer. Why is that point of view a good choice for this story?

3. This story is very carefully organized. Review it and make a brief outline. How does that help you see its structure? Pick out parallels and contrasts in the plot. Look for examples of repetition and foreshadowing. Think about what they contribute to the effect of the story.

4. The "Approaching the Reading" on page 159 explains that O'Connor's stories usually have religious themes, often involving unappealing characters who are unexpectedly offered a "moment of grace," as she put it. Where do you see that happening in this story? Who has a life-changing experience and how does it occur?

RESPONDING THROUGH **Writing**

WRITING ABOUT NARRATION AND POINT OF VIEW

Journal Entries

1. As a way of grasping point of view in fiction, pay attention to point of view in several TV shows or movies. Notice the perspective from which each is presented: Does it stick to one character or group of characters, or does it switch back and forth between two (or more) characters or groups of characters? Watch the use of the camera as an "eye": From what perspective does it let you see what's happening—only from "outside" and at a distance? Does it ever show just what one character is seeing? Write a journal entry summarizing what you observe and discussing how what you observed might apply to or clarify point of view in fiction.

2. In your journal, rewrite part of a story using a different point of view—Sandra Cisneros's "The House on Mango Street" (p. 145) or John Updike's "A&P" (p. 188) as a third-person instead of first-person narrative, for example.

3. In your journal, rewrite part of a story from a different perspective, for example, from the perspective of the mother in Sandra Cisneros's "The House on Mango Street" (p. 145).

Literary Analysis Papers

4. Write a paper in which you examine how the handling of point of view and time contribute to theme in Marjane Satrapi's "The Veil" (p. 305).

5. Discussions of point of view usually center on the question of how appropriate and effective the point of view is in terms of the best way to present the action and characters and to develop the story's theme. Write a paper discussing the appropriateness and effectiveness of point of view to presentation and theme in one of the following stories:

   • first-person unreliable in Alice Walker's "Everyday Use" (p. 152)
   • first-person reliable in John Updike's "A&P" (p. 188)
   • third-person omniscient in Zora Neale Hurston's "Sweat" (p. 372)
   • third-person limited in James Thurber's "The Catbird Seat" (p. 429)
   • third-person limited and stream of consciousness in Katherine Anne Porter's "The Jilting of Granny Weatherall" (p. 432)
   • interior monologue in Tillie Olsen's "I Stand Here Ironing" (p. 405)

6. Write a paper discussing the title of "Everyday Use" (p. 152). Include a consideration of the title as it applies to Dee (Wangero) and to her mother and sister. Consider what Dee means by, "You just don't understand" (para. 79). What does *Dee* not understand?

Comparison-Contrast Papers

7. Stories about "outsiders" look different depending on the point of view from which they are told. Does a character feel, or is she or he made to feel, like an outsider? Does one character look at another as an outsider? Compare and contrast both perspectives in a story dealing with an outsider—Esperanza in Sandra Cisneros's "The House on Mango Street" (p. 145) or Henry in Louise Erdrich's "The Red Convertible" (p. 119) or Arnold in Joyce Carol Oates's "Where Are You Going, Where Have You Been?" (p. 127) or the narrator in Ralph Ellison's "Battle Royal" (p. 271).

TIPS for Writing about Narration and Point of View

- **Point out point of view.** Almost every paper about a work of fiction should identify its point of view, usually through a passing reference.

- **Analyze if unusual.** Point of view should be a central focus in a paper only if it is unusual or complex or crucial to the way the story works.

- **Be thorough.** When a paper focuses on point of view, clarify both the person and the perspective precisely, using quotations to illustrate and support what you say. Then explain, with supporting evidence, what is important about how they are handled in the story.

8. Write a paper that compares and contrasts the handling of parent-child conflict in two of the following stories: Alice Walker's "Everyday Use" (p. 152), Tillie Olsen's "I Stand Here Ironing" (p. 405), or Amy Tan's "Two Kinds" (p. 235).

WRITING ABOUT CONNECTIONS

Points of view, by the way they work in a story, connect us with the complexities, both joyful and disappointing, of our own and others' lives. Such connections often yield even richer and more nuanced experiences and insights when stories are paired with each other, especially when two stories from different cultures or different time periods are brought together. Here are just a few examples to consider:

1. "Staring Out Front Windows": Seeking Escape in Sandra Cisneros's "The House on Mango Street" (p. 145) and James Joyce's "Araby" (p. 389)

2. "Can You Come Home Again?": The Difficulty of Returning in Alice Walker's "Everyday Use" (p. 152) and James Baldwin's "Sonny's Blues" (p. 324)

3. "Tales of Entrapment": Lives Lacking Fulfillment in Marjane Satrapi's "The Veil" (p. 305) and Ha Jin's "Saboteur" (p. 381)

WRITING RESEARCH PAPERS

1. Conduct research into the cultural meaning of houses—of owning one's own place, of the type of house one owns, and its location. In what ways does the house one lives in affect one's self and life, have power, and lead to acceptance or conflict or rejection? Write a paper on this topic, focusing on Sandra Cisneros's "The House on Mango Street" (p. 145) and Alice Walker's "Everyday Use" (p. 152) as starting points.

2. Explore the importance of quilts as cultural artifacts. In what ways are they important beyond providing warmth? What do they reveal about the people who make them and the society that values them? Write a paper applying what you find to Alice Walker's "Everyday Use" (p. 152), showing how a deeper knowledge of quilts adds more meaning to the story.

We are a species that needs and wants to understand who we are. Sheep lice do not seem to share this longing, which is one reason they write so little.

Anne Lamott

(American Novelist and Nonfiction Writer)

Character

Watching What Happens to Whom

As you read a story for the first time, what interests you most is likely to be the plot—you want to know what is happening. But as you find out what is happening, you probably start to be interested in the characters who are involved in what happens. Plot and characters are at the heart of fiction. We relate to, and connect with, plot and characters—they're so basic to life. We care about people: family, friends, enemies, the famous and influential, the overlooked. What goes on in their lives affects our lives. In literature, much the same thing happens: Characters relate to and connect with each other, and we follow their interactions with interest and can be deeply moved by what happens to them—they are imaginative constructs, and yet they are real. That's part of the magical power of the imagination. This chapter focuses on the ways writers create characters, "bring them to life," and make us care about them and about what happens to them.

APPROACHING THE READING

In the following story, a woman describes an incident that she remembers as being highly significant earlier in her life. As you read, pay attention to what happened and notice the various reasons why that particular day was so important. After finishing the story, think about the perspective from which it is told and why perspective is important to understanding the story and the main character in it.

Alison Townsend   b. 1953

The Barbie Birthday   [2003]

Girls learn how to be women not from their dolls but from the women around them.

—Yona Zeldis McDonough

APPROACHING THE AUTHOR

Alison Townsend's most recent book reinvents the ancient Greek myth of Demeter and Persephone as seen from the modern woman's perspective.

For more about her, see page 1082.

The first gift my father's girlfriend gave me was the Barbie I wanted. Not the original—blonde, pony-tailed Barbie in her zebra-striped swimsuit and matching cat-eye shades—but a bubble-cut brunette, her hair a color the box described as "Titian," a brownish-orange I've never seen since. But I didn't care. My hair was brown too. And Barbie was Barbie, the same impossible body when you stripped off her suit, peeling it down over those breasts without nipples, then pulling it back up again. Which was the whole point, of course.

There must have been a cake. And ten candles. And singing. But what I remember is how my future stepmother stepped from the car and into the house, her auburn curls bouncing in the early May light, her suit of fuchsia wool blooming like some exotic flower. Just that, then Barbie—whom I crept away with afterwards, stealing upstairs to play beneath a sunny window in what had been my parents' bedroom.

She likes me, she really likes me, I thought, recalling Shirley's smile when I opened the package. As I lifted the lid of Barbie's narrow, coffin-like box, she stared up at me, sloe-eyed, lids bruised blue, lashes caked thick with mascara, her mouth stuck in a pout both seductive and sullen. Alone, I turned her over and over in my hands, marveling at her stiff, shiny body—the torpedo breasts, the wasp waist, the tall-drink-of-water legs that didn't bend, and the feet on perpetual tiptoe, their arches crimped to fit her spike-heeled mules as she strutted across the sunny windowsill.

All Barbie had to do was glance back once and I followed, casting my lot with every girl on every block in America, signing on for life. She was who I wanted to be, though I couldn't have said that then, anymore than I could have said that Barbie was sex without sex. I don't think my stepmother-to-be knew that either, just that she wanted to please me, the eldest daughter who remembered too much and who had been too shy to visit. My mother had been dead five months, both her breasts cut off like raw meat. But I yearned for the doll she'd forbidden, as if Barbie could tell me what everything meant—how to be a woman when I was a girl with no mother, how to dress and talk, how to thank Shirley for the hard, plastic body that grew warm when I touched it, leading me back to the world.

REFLECTING ON WHAT YOU'VE READ

1. A lot of difficult things were occurring in the narrator's life at the time of the story. Jot down a list of things that were affecting her. How would you describe the narrator? What in the story leads to your characterization? In what way does the Barbie doll reveal things about her?

2. A change comes over the narrator because of the doll as a gift and because of the doll itself. How would you describe the changes? Why was the doll so important to her?

3. The narrator says Barbie was "who I wanted to be, though I wouldn't have said that then." What do you think that means and how does it relate to the narrator?

4. Why do you think the narrator is so startlingly graphic as she speaks of her mother's breasts? Is there a connection to Barbie's breasts? If so, what is it?

5. The story is told from the perspective of the narrator as an older person. Think about what difference it would make if the perspective were that of the narrator as a ten-year-old. What difference would it make if the story were told from the perspective of the narrator's father, or of the father's girlfriend?

6. Where did you notice the narrator's feelings shift? What explanation would you give for that change?

7. The story opens with an epigraph, a quotation from Yona Zeldis McDonough's book *The Barbie Chronicles*. The quotation becomes more meaningful after you have read the story. What explanation would you give to it? Did it influence your reading? In what way?

READING FOR CHARACTER

Important as the events in a story are, they cannot be separated from the people involved in the events who carry out the actions. *Characters*, the created persons who appear or are referred to in narratives and dramas (and at times in poems), are in many cases the aspect that is of greatest appeal and interest in the work. Literature offers us the opportunity to learn about, and even imaginatively to enter, the lives of people we would otherwise never get close to, at least not close enough to understand their lives and situations to a significant extent and to sympathize, or even empathize, with them.

When we meet such people in literature, we want to know what they are like, what makes them tick, how they deal with the situations and relationships they encounter. *Characterization* refers to the methods and techniques an author uses to represent people and to enable us to know and relate to them. As we read a work of fiction, we understand characters more fully and accurately if we pay attention to the means by which we attain our knowledge, to the kind of techniques through which they are brought to life in the story.

TECHNIQUES OF CHARACTERIZATION

Here are some of the most important means of characterization to pay attention to. They can appear individually or in a variety of combinations.

Telling   In the most direct method of characterization, we are simply told what the characters are like, all at once as they are first introduced or bit by bit as they reappear in the story. A good example of this is Joyce Carol Oates's story "Where Are You Going, Where Have You Been?" (p. 127). The narrator begins by giving us information right from the start that we need to know about the main character: "Her name was Connie. She was fifteen and she had a quick, nervous giggling habit of craning her neck to glance into mirrors or checking other people's faces to make sure her own was all right."

Showing   What a character is like can come out through the character's actions, which may be presented without interpretive comment, leaving the reader to draw her or his own conclusions. What Jake does in response to hitting Mariana's car shows the kind of person he is. Aside from suggesting through word choice some reservations about Jake, the narrator does not explicitly evaluate his behavior. We—as active readers— are left to figure out what he is like and decide what we think and feel about him.

Dialogue   A great deal can be revealed about a character by what she or he says: *Dialogue* (conversation between characters) is an important characterization technique. We gain valuable insights into Jake when he says, "You're not married, are you? Not that that would matter that much to me. I'm an openminded kinda guy" (para. 16) and "I left my wallet in the pants I was wearing last night" (20) and that he'd "[b]een in a couple of movies" (31). What a character is like can also be brought out by having other characters say things about her or him. However, it's important to keep in mind that what characters say depends on how they relate to the characters they are talking about. What is said may need to be taken with a grain or a pound of salt because of a character's bias for or against the character being discussed.

Entering a Character's Mind   What a character is like can be revealed through her or his thoughts and feelings. The author takes us into a character's mind using techniques such as a partially or wholly omniscient narrator (used in "Love in L.A." to show what goes on in Jake's mind through daydreams, thoughts, and observations).

Naming   In some cases, the names of characters reveal aspects of what they are like. Henry Fielding, one of the first English novelists, names one of his characters Squire Allworthy to reveal how admirable he is in every respect. In other cases, Fielding uses *allusions* to the Bible in naming a character: Parson Abraham Adams, for example, is a man of great faith (like the biblical Abraham) but is also a person as innocent and trusting as the Adam of Genesis Chapters 2–3. In many cases, however, names are simply names, yet somehow they invariably sound right (think of David Copperfield or Huckleberry Finn) and fit the character.

CATEGORIES OF CHARACTERIZATION

Our understanding and appreciation of characters in a story are enhanced when we are alert to the varying degrees of their complexity and importance. This analysis is often intricate and difficult but it can be very rewarding and can lead to an effective paper if you are asked to write one. Here are some of the ways those varying degrees of character complexity are indicated, along with the terminology widely used for discussing them.

Round/Flat   The novelist E. M. Forster used the terms *flat* and *round* to illustrate differences in complexity.

- **Round characters** are complex and sometimes even challenging to understand. We are offered many sides and facets of their lives and personalities and we may need to reconcile what seem to be incompatible ideas or behaviors. Round characters often are *dynamic*, shown as changing and growing because of what happens to them. But they also can be *static*, not shown as changing, though they may be described in such rich detail that we have a clear sense of how they would, or will, change, even though we don't see it happening. We are shown enough about Henry in "The Red Convertible" (p. 119) for his character to be rounded out; the story shows the changes in him before he goes to Vietnam and after he returns, even though we do not see the changes actually taking place.
- **Flat Characters** are generally developed less fully than round, or dynamic, characters. Usually they are static and are represented through only one or two main features or aspects. Unlike round characters, they often can be summed up in a sentence or two. If these one or two traits

are developed in considerable detail, the characters may be very interesting. But we can't come to know them as thoroughly and in as much depth as characters who are depicted with more complexity or who are developed more fully and shown as ones who change and grow throughout the story. Jake and Mariana in "Love in L.A." are flat characters, who do not change or grow. That's all they need to be and all that could be expected in such a short, short story.

Major/Minor   Most major characters in a story or play are round characters, while minor characters are usually flat. Minor characters are at times *stock characters*, stereotypes easily recognized by readers or audiences because of their frequent use, such as the absent-minded professor, the evil stepmother, the nerdy computer geek, or the smart but quiet detective or police sergeant. Use of flat characters is not necessarily "bad writing." Some excellent fiction writers create central characters who are flat but are described in such rich detail that they come fully to life. There isn't time in most short stories to develop more than one character in a rounded way, perhaps not even one. Even in a novel or play, the reader might find it too much to handle if every character were rounded out fully.

Protagonist/Antagonist   The terms *protagonist* and *antagonist* are often used to define relationships between characters. The **protagonist** is the central character in a work (the older term **hero** seems less useful because the central character doesn't have to be "heroic"). The **antagonist** is the character, force, or collected forces opposed to the protagonist that give rise to the central conflict of the work—the rival, opponent, or enemy of the protagonist (the older term *villain* works less well because the antagonist isn't always evil and isn't always a person). In the stories included in previous chapters, the grandmother is the protagonist of "A Good Man Is Hard to Find"; The Misfit is the antagonist. Henry is the protagonist of "The Red Convertible"; white society and the world outside the reservation are the antagonists.

QUALITIES OF CHARACTERIZATION

Motivated   After you know what the characters are like, you will want to understand why they do the things they do, why they make the kinds of decisions and choices they do. This important aspect of characterization involves *motivation*, conveying the reasons, explanations, or justifications behind a character's behavior. Motivation in fiction usually grows out of a sense of what a character deeply wants or desires and how that leads the character to react in a specific situation. For example, Jake clearly finds Mariana attractive, but his desire to avoid paying the costs of the accident is a stronger motivation than his desire to pursue a relationship with her.

Consistent   A great deal is revealed about characters also by the *way* they handle situations — especially difficult, problematic, or tragic situations or relationships. For characters to be plausible, there must be consistency between their motivations and their actions and consistency in the way they deal with circumstances. If they respond to a situation one way at one time and differently at another, there should be clear reasons for the difference (their inconsistency must be understandable and believable). The fact that Jake has license plates from a junker is consistent with his giving Mariana false information about insurance, and together they reveal a great deal about him as a character.

☑ CHECKLIST on Reading for Character

❑ Be attentive to the methods of characterization: Notice what you are told and shown; listen to what characters say and to what other characters say about them; watch what goes on in characters' minds; and consider the way they are named.

❑ Consider how fully characters are developed: whether they are round or flat, whether they change or stay pretty much the same.

APPROACHING THE READING

In the following story, characterization plays a very important role. Sylvia, a young African American girl growing up in Harlem, goes on a field trip to Midtown Manhattan to visit F.A.O. Schwarz, one of the most famous (and expensive) toy stores in the world. The experience expands her horizons in several dynamic ways. After your first reading, notice and reflect on the point of view, what Sylvia is like, and how you get to know her. Then read the story again, this time asking yourself where in the story Sylvia changes and how setting contributes to her development.

Toni Cade Bambara   1939–1995

The Lesson   [1972]

Back in the days when everyone was old and stupid or young and foolish and me and Sugar were the only ones just right, this lady moved on our block with nappy hair and proper speech and no makeup. And quite naturally we laughed at her, laughed the way we did at the junk man who went about his business like he was some big-time president and his sorry-ass horse his secretary. And we kinda

APPROACHING THE AUTHOR

Toni Cade Bambara was born Miltona Mirkin Cade and changed her name to Toni Cade while in kindergarten. In 1970 she adopted the name Bambara, which she discovered as a signature on a sketchbook in her great-grandmother's trunk.

© Susan J. Ross

For more about her, see page 1055.

hated her too, hated the way we did the winos who cluttered up our parks and pissed on our handball walls and stank up our hallways and stairs so you couldn't halfway play hide-and-seek without a goddamn gas mask. Miss Moore was her name. The only woman on the block with no first name. And she was black as hell, cept for her feet, which were fish-white and spooky. And she was always planning these boring-ass things for us to do, us being my cousin, mostly, who lived on the block cause we all moved North the same time and to the same apartment then spread out gradual to breathe. And our parents would yank our heads into some kinda shape and crisp up our clothes so we'd be presentable for travel with Miss Moore, who always looked like she was going to church, though she never did. Which is just one of the things the grownups talked about when they talked behind her back like a dog. But when she came calling with some sachet she'd sewed up or some gingerbread she'd made or some book, why then they'd all be too embarrassed to turn her down and we'd get handed over all spruced up. She'd been to college and said it was only right that she should take responsibility for the young ones' education, and she not even related by marriage or blood. So they'd go for it. Specially Aunt Gretchen. She was the main gofer in the family. You got some ole dumb shit foolishness you want somebody to go for, you send for Aunt Gretchen. She been screwed into the go-along for so long, it's a blood-deep natural thing with her. Which is how she got saddled with me and Sugar and Junior in the first place while our mothers were in a la-de-da apartment up the block having a good ole time.

So this one day Miss Moore rounds us all up at the mailbox and it's puredee hot and she's knockin herself out about arithmetic. And school suppose to let up in summer I heard, but she don't never let up. And the starch in my pinafore scratching the shit outta me and I'm really hating this nappy-head bitch and her goddamn college degree. I'd much rather go to the pool or to the show where it's cool. So me and Sugar leaning on the mailbox being surly, which is a Miss Moore word. And Flyboy checking out what everybody brought for lunch. And Fat Butt already wasting his peanut-butter-and-jelly sandwich like the pig he is. And Junebug punchin on Q.T.'s arm for potato chips. And Rosie Giraffe shifting from one hip to the other waiting for somebody to step on her foot or ask her if she from Georgia so she can kick ass, preferably Mercedes'. And Miss Moore asking us do we know what money is, like we a bunch of retards. I mean real money, she say, like it's only poker chips or monopoly papers we lay on the grocer. So right away I'm tired of this and say so. And would much rather snatch Sugar and go to the Sunset and terrorize the West Indian kids and take their hair ribbons and their money too. And Miss Moore files that remark away for next week's lesson on brotherhood, I can tell. And finally I say we oughta get to the subway cause it's cooler and besides we might meet some cute boys. Sugar done swiped her mama's lipstick, so we ready.

So we heading down the street and she's boring us silly about what things cost and what our parents make and how much goes for rent and how money ain't divided up right in this country. And then she gets to the part about we all poor and live in the slums, which I don't feature. And I'm ready to speak on that, but she steps out in the street and hails two cabs just like that. Then she hustles half the crew in with her and hands me a five-dollar bill and tells me to calculate 10 percent tip for the driver. And we're off. Me and Sugar and Junebug and Flyboy hangin out the window and hollering to everybody, putting lipstick on each other cause Flyboy a faggot anyway, and making farts with our sweaty armpits. But I'm mostly trying to figure how to spend this money. But they all fascinated with the meter ticking and Junebug starts laying bets as to how much it'll read when Flyboy can't hold his breath no more. Then Sugar lays bets as to how much it'll be when we get there. So I'm stuck. Don't nobody want to go for my plan, which is to jump out at the next light and run off to the first bar-b-que we can find. Then the driver tells us to get the hell out cause we there already. And the meter reads eighty-five cents. And I'm stalling to figure out the tip and Sugar say give him a dime. And I decide he don't need it bad as I do, so later for him. But then he tries to take off with Junebug foot still in the door so we talk about his mama something ferocious. Then we check out that we on Fifth Avenue and everybody dressed up in stockings. One lady in a fur coat, hot as it is. White folks crazy.

"This is the place," Miss Moore say, presenting it to us in the voice she uses at the museum. "Let's look in the windows before we go in."

"Can we steal?" Sugar asks very serious like she's getting the ground rules   5 squared away before she plays. "I beg your pardon," say Miss Moore, and we fall out. So she leads us around the windows of the toy store and me and Sugar screamin, "This is mine, that's mine, I gotta have that, that was made for me, I was born for that," till Big Butt drowns us out.

"Hey, I'm goin to buy that there."

"That there? You don't even know what it is, stupid."

"I do so," he say punchin on Rosie Giraffe. "It's a microscope."

"Whatcha gonna do with a microscope, fool?"

"Look at things."   10

"Like what, Ronald?" ask Miss Moore. And Big Butt ain't got the first notion. So here go Miss Moore gabbing about the thousands of bacteria in a drop of water and the somethinorother in a speck of blood and the million and one living things in the air around us is invisible to the naked eye. And what she say that for? Junebug go to town on that "naked" and we rolling. Then Miss Moore ask what it cost. So we all jam into the window smudgin it up and the price tag say $300. So then she ask how long'd take for Big Butt and Junebug to save up their allowances. "Too long," I say. "Yeh," adds Sugar, "outgrown it by that time." And Miss Moore say no, you never outgrow learning instruments. "Why, even medical students and interns and," blah, blah, blah. And we ready to choke Big Butt for bringing it up in the first damn place.

"This here costs four hundred eighty dollars," say Rosie Giraffe. So we pile up all over her to see what she pointin out. My eyes tell me it's a chunk of glass cracked with something heavy, and different-color inks dripped into the splits, then the whole thing put into a oven or something. But for $480 it don't make sense.

"That's a paperweight made of semi-precious stones fused together under tremendous pressure," she explains slowly, with her hands doing the mining and all the factory work.

"So what's a paperweight?" asks Rosie Giraffe.

"To weigh paper with, dumbbell," say Flyboy, the wise man from the East.   15

"Not exactly," say Miss Moore, which is what she say when you warm or way off too. "It's to weigh paper down so it won't scatter and make your desk untidy." So right away me and Sugar curtsy to each other and then to Mercedes who is more the tidy type.

"We don't keep paper on top of the desk in my class," say Junebug, figuring Miss Moore crazy or lyin one.

"At home, then," she say. "Don't you have a calendar and a pencil case and a blotter and a letter-opener on your desk at home where you do your home-work?" And she know damn well what our homes look like cause she nosys around in them every chance she gets.

"I don't even have a desk," say Junebug. "Do we?"

"No. And I don't get no homework neither," say Big Butt.   20

"And I don't even have a home," say Flyboy like he do at school to keep the white folks off his back and sorry for him. Send this poor kid to camp posters, is his specialty.

"I do," says Mercedes. "I have a box of stationery on my desk and a picture of my cat. My godmother bought the stationery and the desk. There's a big rose on each sheet and the envelopes smell like roses."

"Who wants to know about your smelly-ass stationery," say Rosie Giraffe fore I can get my two cents in.

"It's important to have a work area all your own so that . . ."

"Will you look at this sailboat, please," say Flyboy, cuttin her off and poin-   25 tin to the thing like it was his. So once again we tumble all over each other to gaze at this magnificent thing in the toy store which is just big enough to maybe sail two kittens across the pond if you strap them to the posts tight. We all start reciting the price tag like we in assembly. "Handcrafted sailboat of fiberglass at one thousand one hundred ninety-five dollars."

"Unbelievable," I hear myself say and am really stunned. I read it again for myself just in case the group recitation put me in a trance. Same thing. For some reason this pisses me off. We look at Miss Moore and she lookin at us, waiting for I dunno what.

"Who'd pay all that when you can buy a sailboat set for a quarter at Pop's, a tube of glue for a dime, and a ball of string for eight cents? It must have a motor and a whole lot else besides," I say. "My sailboat cost me about fifty cents."

"But will it take water?" say Mercedes with her smart ass.

"Took mine to Alley Pond Park once," say Flyboy. "String broke. Lost it. Pity."

"Sailed mine in Central Park and it keeled over and sank. Had to ask my 30 father for another dollar."

"And you got the strap," laugh Big Butt. "The jerk didn't even have a string on it. My old man wailed on his behind."

Little Q.T. was staring hard at the sailboat and you could see he wanted it bad. But he too little and somebody'd just take it from him. So what the hell. "This boat for kids, Miss Moore?"

"Parents silly to buy something like that just to get all broke up," say Rosie Giraffe.

"That much money it should last forever," I figure.

"My father'd buy it for me if I wanted it." 35

"Your father, my ass," say Rosie Giraffe getting a chance to finally push Mercedes.

"Must be rich people shop here," say Q.T.

"You are a very bright boy," say Flyboy. "What was your first clue?" And he rap him on the head with the back of his knuckles, since Q.T. the only one he could get away with. Though Q.T. liable to come up behind you years later and get his licks in when you half expect it.

"What I want to know is," I says to Miss Moore though I never talk to her, I wouldn't give the bitch that satisfaction, "is how much a real boat costs? I figure a thousand'd get you a yacht any day."

"Why don't you check that out," she says, "and report back to the group?" 40 Which really pains my ass. If you gonna mess up a perfectly good swim day least you could do is have some answers. "Let's go in," she say like she got something up her sleeve. Only she don't lead the way. So me and Sugar turn the corner to where the entrance is, but when we get there I kinda hang back. Not that I'm scared, what's there to be afraid of, just a toy store. But I feel funny, shame. But what I got to be shamed about? Got as much right to go in as anybody. But somehow I can't seem to get hold of the door, so I step away for Sugar to lead. But she hangs back too. And I look at her and she looks at me and this is ridiculous. I mean, damn, I have never ever been shy about doing nothing or going nowhere. But then Mercedes steps up and then Rosie Giraffe and Big Butt crowd in behind and shove, and next thing we all stuffed into the doorway with only Mercedes squeezing past us, smoothing out her jumper and walking right down the aisle. Then the rest of us tumble in like a glued-together jigsaw done all wrong. And people lookin at us. And it's like the time me and Sugar crashed into the Catholic church on a dare. But once we got in there and everything so hushed and holy and the candles and the bowin and the handkerchiefs on all the drooping heads, I just couldn't go through with the plan. Which was for me to run up to the altar and do a tap dance while Sugar played the nose flute and messed around in the holy water. And Sugar kept givin me the elbow. Then later teased me so bad I tied her up in the shower and turned it on and locked her in. And she'd be there till this day if Aunt Gretchen hadn't finally figured I was lyin about the boarder takin a shower.

Same thing in the store. We all walkin on tiptoe and hardly touchin the games and puzzles and things. And I watched Miss Moore who is steady watchin us like she waitin for a sign. Like Mama Drewery watches the sky and sniffs the air and takes note of just how much slant is in the bird formation. Then me and Sugar bump smack into each other, so busy gazing at the toys, 'specially the sailboat. But we don't laugh and go into our fat-lady bump-stomach routine. We just stare at that price tag. Then Sugar run a finger over the whole boat. And I'm jealous and want to hit her. Maybe not her, but I sure want to punch somebody in the mouth.

"Watcha bring us here for, Miss Moore?"

"You sound angry, Sylvia. Are you mad about something?" Givin me one of them grins like she tellin a grown-up joke that never turns out to be funny. And she's lookin very closely at me like maybe she plannin to do my portrait from memory. I'm mad, but I won't give her that satisfaction. So I slouch around the store bein very bored and say, "Let's go."

Me and Sugar at the back of the train watchin the tracks whizzin by large then small then gettin gobbled up in the dark. I'm thinkin about this tricky toy I saw in the store. A clown that somersaults on a bar then does chin-ups just cause you yank lightly at his leg. Cost $35. I could see me askin my mother for a $35 birthday clown. "You wanna who that costs what?" she'd say, cocking her head to the side to get a better view of the hole in my head. Thirty-five dollars could buy new bunk beds for Junior and Gretchen's boy. Thirty-five dollars and the whole household could go visit Granddaddy Nelson in the country. Thirty-five dollars would pay for the rent and the piano bill too. Who are these people that spend that much for performing clowns and $1,000 for toy sailboats? What kinda work they do and how they live and how come we ain't in on it? Where we are is who we are, Miss Moore always pointin out. But it don't necessarily have to be that way, she always adds then waits for somebody to say that poor people have to wake up and demand their share of the pie and don't none of us know what kind of pie she talkin about in the first damn place. But she ain't so smart cause I still got her four dollars from the taxi and she sure ain't gettin it. Messin up my day with this shit. Sugar nudges me in my pocket and winks.

Miss Moore lines us up in front of the mailbox where we started from, seem 45
like years ago, and I got a headache for thinkin so hard. And we lean all over each other so we can hold up under the draggy-ass lecture she always finishes us off with at the end before we thank her for borin us to tears. But she just looks at us like she readin tea leaves. Finally she say, "Well, what did you think of F.A.O. Schwarz?"

Rosie Giraffe mumbles, "White folks crazy."

"I'd like to go there again when I get my birthday money," says Mercedes, and we shove her out the pack so she has to lean on the mailbox by herself.

"I'd like a shower. Tiring day," say Flyboy.

Then Sugar surprises me by sayin, "You know, Miss Moore, I don't think all of us here put together eat in a year what that sailboat costs." And Miss Moore lights up like somebody goosed her. "And?" she say, urging Sugar on. Only I'm standin on her foot so she don't continue.

"Imagine for a minute what kind of society it is in which some people can ₅₀
spend on a toy what it would cost to feed a family of six or seven. What do you
think?"

"I think," say Sugar pushing me off her feet like she never done before,
cause I whip her ass in a minute, "that this is not much of a democracy if you
ask me. Equal chance to pursue happiness means an equal crack at the dough,
don't it?" Miss Moore is besides herself and I am disgusted with Sugar's treachery. So I stand on her foot one more time to see if she'll shove me. She shuts
up, and Miss Moore looks at me, sorrowfully I'm thinkin. And somethin weird
is goin on, I can feel it in my chest.

"Anybody else learn anything today?" lookin dead at me. I walk away and
Sugar has to run to catch up and don't even seem to notice when I shrug her
arm off my shoulder.

"Well, we got four dollars anyway," she says.

"Uh hunh."

"We could go to Hascombs and get half a chocolate layer and then go to ₅₅
the Sunset and still have plenty money for potato chips and ice-cream sodas."

"Uh hunh."

"Race you to Hascombs," she say.

We start down the block and she gets ahead which is O.K. by me cause I'm
goin to the West End and then over to the Drive to think this day through. She
can run if she want to and even run faster. But ain't nobody gonna beat me at
nuthin.

REFLECTING ON WHAT YOU'VE READ

1. If you're not familiar with New York City and the F.A.O. Schwarz store there,
   do some research that will help bring the setting to life for you. Go online or
   to the library to find a map of New York City. Locate Harlem, find some
   photographs of it, and then read about its distinctive culture both in the past
   and present. Then use the map to pick out Fifth Avenue at West 58th Street,
   where F.A.O. Schwarz was located until July 2015 and look at Web sites that
   describe and include photos of the New York F.A.O. Schwarz store.

2. Be ready to discuss the attitude Sylvia has toward Miss Moore, the other
   children, white people, and the world in general. How does where she lives
   help shape her attitude? Describe the ways Sylvia's horizons are expanded.

3. What is Sylvia, the narrator of the story, like? Try sketching her character.
   In what ways does the "voice" you hear as she tells the story help develop
   her character? How did you feel about her on your first reading of the story?
   While rereading the story, or as you thought back over it, did your feelings
   about her change or become more complex? Do you notice specific evidence that Sylvia herself changes? If so, point out the particular things that
   in your eyes both reveal and lead to a change.

4. In what ways is the point of view important to the effect of the story? How would the story change if it had a different point of view? How would you describe the author's attitude toward Sylvia? What is it about the use of the first-person point of view that enables this attitude to come through?

5. Does Miss Moore have a teaching plan? What lessons do the children learn that day? In what ways do you think those lessons are or are not the ones Miss Moore intended them to learn? Why do you think so? It seems clear that Sugar is affected by what she experiences. Do you think that Sylvia is similarly affected, or do you think that she successfully resists? Try describing the kind of person you predict Sylvia will be when she reaches college age, if the story were to follow her life further.

APPROACHING THE READING

In the following story, a young man faces a life crisis in a most unlikely place: the checkout line of the grocery store in which he works. As you read and reflect on the story, focus on his character and what we learn about him — from his job and where he is in life; what he says and the way he says it; what he feels; and what he does, especially in the surprising turn of events near the end.

John Updike   1932–2009

A&P°   [1961]

In walks these three girls in nothing but bathing suits. I'm in the third checkout slot, with my back to the door, so I don't see them until they're over by the bread. The one that caught my eye first was the one in the plaid green two-piece. She was a chunky kid, with a good tan and a sweet broad soft-looking can with those two crescents of white just under it, where the sun never seems to hit, at the top of the backs of her legs. I stood there with my hand on a box of HiHo crackers trying to remember if I rang it up or not. I ring it up again and the customer starts giving me hell. She's one of these cash-register-watchers, a witch about fifty with rouge on her cheekbones and no eyebrows, and I know it made her day to trip me up. She'd been watching cash registers for fifty years and probably never seen a mistake before.

APPROACHING THE AUTHOR

John Updike is one of only three authors to win the Pulitzer Prize for Fiction more than once (the others were Booth Tarkington and William Faulkner).

For more about him, see page 1083.

A&P: Grocery stores operated by the Great Atlantic & Pacific Tea Company, which was founded in New York City in 1859 and is currently headquartered in Montvale, New Jersey.

By the time I got her feathers smoothed and her goodies into a bag — she gives me a little snort in passing, if she'd been born at the right time they would have burned her over in Salem — by the time I get her on her way the girls had circled around the bread and were coming back, without a pushcart, back my way along the counters, in the aisle between the checkouts and the Special bins. They didn't even have shoes on. There was this chunky one, with the two-piece — it was bright green and the seams on the bra were still sharp and her belly was still pretty pale so I guessed she just got it (the suit) — there was this one, with one of those chubby berry-faces, the lips all bunched together under her nose, this one, and a tall one, with black hair that hadn't quite frizzed right, and one of these sunburns right across under the eyes, and a chin that was too long — you know, the kind of girl other girls think is very "striking" and "attractive" but never quite makes it, as they very well know, which is why they like her so much — and then the third one, that wasn't quite so tall. She was the queen. She kind of led them, the other two peeking around and making their shoulders round. She didn't look around, not this queen, she just walked straight on slowly, on these long white prima-donna legs. She came down a little hard on her heels, as if she didn't walk in her bare feet that much, putting down her heels and then letting the weight move along to her toes as if she was testing the floor with every step, putting a little deliberate extra action into it. You never know for sure how girls' minds work (do you really think it's a mind in there or just a little buzz like a bee in a glass jar?) but you got the idea she had talked the other two into coming in here with her, and now she was showing them how to do it, walk slow and hold yourself straight.

She had on a kind of dirty-pink — beige maybe, I don't know — bathing suit with a little nubble all over it and, what got me, the straps were down. They were off her shoulders looped loose around the cool tops of her arms, and I guess as a result the suit had slipped a little on her, so all around the top of the cloth there was this shining rim. If it hadn't been there you wouldn't have known there could have been anything whiter than those shoulders. With the straps pushed off, there was nothing between the top of the suit and the top of her head except just *her*, this clean bare plane of the top of her chest down from the shoulder bones like a dented sheet of metal tilted in the light. I mean, it was more than pretty.

She had sort of oaky hair that the sun and salt had bleached, done up in a bun that was unravelling, and a kind of prim face. Walking into the A & P with your straps down, I suppose it's the only kind of face you *can* have. She held her head so high her neck, coming up out of those white shoulders, looked kind of stretched, but I didn't mind. The longer her neck was, the more of her there was.

She must have felt in the corner of her eye me and over my shoulder 5 Stokesie in the second slot watching, but she didn't tip. Not this queen. She kept her eyes moving across the racks, and stopped, and turned so slow it made my stomach rub the inside of my apron, and buzzed to the other two, who kind of huddled against her for relief, and then they all three of them went up the cat-and-dog-food-breakfast-cereal-macaroni-rice-raisins-seasonings-spreads-spaghetti-soft-drinks-crackers-and-cookies aisle. From the third slot I look straight up this aisle to the meat counter, and I watched them all the way. The fat one with the tan sort of fumbled with the cookies, but on second thought she put the package back. The sheep pushing their carts down the aisle—the girls were walking against the usual traffic (not that we have one-way signs or anything)—were pretty hilarious. You could see them, when Queenie's white shoulders dawned on them, kind of jerk, or hop, or hiccup, but their eyes snapped back to their own baskets and on they pushed. I bet you could set off dynamite in an A & P and the people would by and large keep reaching and checking oatmeal off their lists and muttering "Let me see, there was a third thing, began with A, asparagus, no, ah, yes, applesauce!" or whatever it is they do mutter. But there was no doubt, this jiggled them. A few houseslaves in pin curlers even looked around after pushing their carts past to make sure what they had seen was correct.

You know, it's one thing to have a girl in a bathing suit down on the beach, where what with the glare nobody can look at each other much anyway, and another thing in the cool of the A & P, under the fluorescent lights, against all those stacked packages, with her feet paddling along naked over our checkerboard green-and-cream rubber-tile floor.

"Oh Daddy," Stokesie said beside me. "I feel so faint."

"Darling," I said. "Hold me tight." Stokesie's married, with two babies chalked up on his fuselage already, but as far as I can tell that's the only difference. He's twenty-two, and I was nineteen this April.

"Is it done?" he asks, the responsible married man finding his voice. I forgot to say he thinks he's going to be manager some sunny day, maybe in 1990 when it's called the Great Alexandrov and Petrooshki Tea Company or something.

What he meant was, our town is five miles from a beach, with a big summer 10 colony out on the Point, but we're right in the middle of town, and the women generally put on a shirt or shorts or something before they get out of the car into the street. And anyway these are usually women with six children and varicose veins mapping their legs and nobody, including them, could care less. As I say, we're right in the middle of town, and if you stand at our front doors you can see two banks and the Congregational church and the newspaper store and three real-estate offices and about twenty-seven old freeloaders tearing up Central Street because the sewer broke again. It's not as if we're on the Cape; we're north of Boston and there's people in this town haven't seen the ocean for twenty years.

The girls had reached the meat counter and were asking McMahon something. He pointed, they pointed, and they shuffled out of sight behind a pyramid of Diet Delight peaches. All that was left for us to see was old McMahon patting his mouth and looking after them sizing up their joints. Poor kids, I began to feel sorry for them, they couldn't help it.

Now here comes the sad part of the story, at least my family says it's sad, but I don't think it's so sad myself. The store's pretty empty, it being Thursday afternoon, so there was nothing much to do except lean on the register and wait for the girls to show up again. The whole store was like a pinball machine and I didn't know which tunnel they'd come out of. After a while they come around out of the far aisle, around the light bulbs, records at discount of the Caribbean Six or Tony Martin Sings or some such gunk you wonder they waste the wax on, sixpacks of candy bars, and plastic toys done up in cellophane that fall apart when a kid looks at them anyway. Around they come, Queenie still leading the way, and holding a little gray jar in her hand. Slots Three through Seven are unmanned and I could see her wondering between Stokes and me, but Stokesie with his usual luck draws an old party in baggy gray pants who stumbles up with four giant cans of pineapple juice (what do these bums *do* with all that pineapple juice? I've often asked myself) so the girls come to me. Queenie puts down the jar and I take it into my fingers icy cold. Kingfish Fancy Herring Snacks in Pure Sour Cream: 49¢. Now her hands are empty, not a ring or a bracelet, bare as God made them, and I wonder where the money's coming from. Still with that prim look she lifts a folded dollar bill out of the hollow at the center of her nubbled pink top. The jar went heavy in my hand. Really, I thought that was so cute.

Then everybody's luck begins to run out. Lengel comes in from haggling with a truck full of cabbages on the lot and is about to scuttle into that door marked MANAGER behind which he hides all day when the girls touch his eye. Lengel's pretty dreary, teaches Sunday school and the rest, but he doesn't miss that much. He comes over and says, "Girls, this isn't the beach."

Queenie blushes, though maybe it's just a brush of sunburn I was noticing for the first time, now that she was so close. "My mother asked me to pick up a jar of herring snacks." Her voice kind of startled me, the way voices do when you see the people first, coming out so flat and dumb yet kind of tony, too, the way it ticked over "pick up" and "snacks." All of a sudden I slid right down her voice into her living room. Her father and the other men were standing around in ice-cream coats and bow ties and the women were in sandals picking up herring snacks on toothpicks off a big glass plate and they were all holding drinks the color of water with olives and sprigs of mint in them. When my parents have somebody over they get lemonade and if it's a real racy affair Schlitz in tall glasses with "They'll Do It Every Time" cartoons stencilled on.

"That's all right," Lengel said. "But this isn't the beach." His repeating this 15 struck me as funny, as if it had just occurred to him, and he had been thinking all these years the A & P was a great big dune and he was the head lifeguard. He didn't like my smiling — as I say he doesn't miss much — but he concentrates on giving the girls that sad Sunday-school-superintendent stare.

Queenie's blush is no sunburn now, and the plump one in plaid, that I liked better from the back — a really sweet can — pipes up, "We weren't doing any shopping. We just came in for the one thing."

"That makes no difference," Lengel tells her, and I could see from the way his eyes went that he hadn't noticed she was wearing a two-piece before. "We want you decently dressed when you come in here."

"We *are* decent," Queenie says suddenly, her lower lip pushing, getting sore now that she remembers her place, a place from which the crowd that runs the A & P must look pretty crummy. Fancy Herring Snacks flashed in her very blue eyes.

"Girls, I don't want to argue with you. After this come in here with your shoulders covered. It's our policy." He turns his back. That's policy for you. Policy is what the kingpins want. What the others want is juvenile delinquency.

All this while, the customers had been showing up with their carts but, you 20 know, sheep, seeing a scene, they had all bunched up on Stokesie, who shook open a paper bag as gently as peeling a peach, not wanting to miss a word. I could feel in the silence everybody getting nervous, most of all Lengel, who asks me, "Sammy, have you rung up their purchase?"

I thought and said "No" but it wasn't about that I was thinking. I go through the punches, 4, 9, GROC, TOT—it's more complicated than you think, and after you do it often enough, it begins to make a little song, that you hear words to, in my case "Hello (*bing*) there, you (*gung*) hap-py *pee*-pul (*splat*)!"— the *splat* being the drawer flying out. I uncrease the bill, tenderly as you may imagine, it just having come from between the two smoothest scoops of vanilla I had ever known were there, and pass a half and a penny into her narrow pink palm, and nestle the herrings in a bag and twist its neck and hand it over, all the time thinking.

The girls, and who'd blame them, are in a hurry to get out, so I say "I quit" to Lengel quick enough for them to hear, hoping they'll stop and watch me, their unsuspected hero. They keep right on going, into the electric eye; the door flies open and they flicker across the lot to their car, Queenie and Plaid and Big Tall Goony-Goony (not that as raw material she was so bad), leaving me with Lengel and a kink in his eyebrow.

"Did you say something, Sammy?"

"I said I quit."

"I thought you did." 25

"You didn't have to embarrass them."

"It was they who were embarrassing us."

I started to say something that came out "Fiddle-de-doo." It's a saying of my grandmother's, and I know she would have been pleased.

"I don't think you know what you're saying," Lengel said.

"I know you don't," I said. "But I do." I pull the bow at the back of my 30 apron and start shrugging it off my shoulders. A couple customers that had been heading for my slot begin to knock against each other, like scared pigs in a chute.

Lengel sighs and begins to look very patient and old and gray. He's been a friend of my parents for years. "Sammy, you don't want to do this to your Mom and Dad," he tells me. It's true, I don't. But it seems to me that once you begin a gesture it's fatal not to go through with it. I fold the apron, "Sammy" stitched in red on the pocket, and put it on the counter, and drop the bow tie on top of it. The bow tie is theirs, if you've ever wondered. "You'll feel this for the rest of your life," Lengel says, and I know that's true, too, but remembering how he made that pretty girl blush makes me so scrunchy inside I punch the No Sale tab and the machine whirs "pee-pul" and the drawer splats out. One advantage to this scene taking place in summer, I can follow this up with a clean exit, there's no fumbling around getting your coat and galoshes, I just saunter into the electric eye in my white shirt that my mother ironed the night before, and the door heaves itself open, and outside the sunshine is skating around on the asphalt.

I look around for my girls, but they're gone, of course. There wasn't anybody but some young married screaming with her children about some candy they didn't get by the door of a powder-blue Falcon station wagon. Looking back in the big windows, over the bags of peat moss and aluminum lawn furniture stacked on the pavement, I could see Lengel in my place in the slot, checking the sheep through. His face was dark gray and his back stiff, as if he'd just had an injection of iron, and my stomach kind of fell as I felt how hard the world was going to be to me hereafter.

REFLECTING ON WHAT YOU'VE READ

1. Be ready to discuss Sammy's character, all the things (admirable and otherwise) we learn from what he tells us directly and what we can infer indirectly. Be sure to pay attention to the breezy, "hip" way he talks and to the many details he brings into his description of the episode.

2. Consider what other characters contribute, directly and indirectly, through similarities and through ways in which they contrast to him. Consider the extent to which the three girls are a contrast to Sammy.

3. Consider how location (the town Sammy lives in and the store he works in) affects or contributes to the story. Does the story seem particularly to reflect attitudes of the early 1960s, when it was written, or isn't the time setting important to the story's effect?

4. Identify several conflicts (minor and major) in the story and their cumulative effect on Sammy. Do you think Sammy changes as a result of these conflicts, or stays pretty much the same? Why?

5. Why does Sammy quit his job? How would you describe what he does as heroic? As a foolish, mistaken impulse, or empty gesture? As a failed attempt at heroism? Or as something else or a mixture of some of these?

6. Prepare to discuss the last line: "[M]y stomach kind of fell as I felt how hard the world was going to be to me hereafter" (p. 193). Is it an indication of a genuine change from who Sammy was in the opening paragraph? Why or why not?

RESPONDING THROUGH Writing

WRITING ABOUT CHARACTER

Journal Entries

1. Write an analysis of characterization techniques in a TV show or movie: Look for how telling, showing, dialoguing, conveying a character's thoughts, and naming choices are used to reveal character. Consider which characters are round and which are flat. Write a journal entry summarizing the result and discussing whether, how, and why basic aspects of characterization are similar across different genres.

2. Think about someone from your past and write a journal entry describing her or his character. Add a few sentences pointing out the techniques you use and discussing what you learn about characterization.

3. Read Alison Townsend's short story "The Barbie Birthday" (p. 176) and Denise Duhamel's poem "One Afternoon When Barbie Wanted to Join the Military" (p. 622). Write a journal entry discussing the differences and similarities between them, as each relates to character.

Literary Analysis Papers

4. Write a paper on the importance and handling of gaps in the development of characters in Louise Erdrich's "The Red Convertible" (p. 119).

5. Write a paper examining the relation of the title to character development in James Baldwin's "Sonny's Blues" (p. 324), James Joyce's "Araby" (p. 389), or Zora Neale Hurston's "Sweat" (p. 372).

6. Write a paper discussing characterization techniques in Chimamanda Ngozi Adichie's "The Thing Around Your Neck" (p. 314) or Katherine Anne Porter's "The Jilting of Granny Weatherall" (p. 432).

Comparison-Contrast Papers

7. Write a paper comparing and contrasting Arnold Friend in Joyce Carol Oates's "Where Are You Going, Where Have You Been?" (p. 127) and The Misfit in Flannery O'Connor's "A Good Man Is Hard to Find" (p. 159).

8. Write a paper exploring the similarities and differences between Sammy in John Updike's "A&P" (p. 188) and the narrator in Sherman Alexie's "The Lone Ranger and Tonto Fistfight in Heaven" (p. 213) as each tries to fit into society.

> **TIPS for Writing about Character**
>
> - **Focus on methods.** In writing about character, it's usually best to focus on methods of characterization: Show how aspects of the character are revealed; don't just describe what the character is like. Watch especially for juxtapositions—comparisons and contrasts between characters—in addition to the specific techniques covered in this chapter. Juxtapositions often provide a useful way to organize a paper.
> - **Connect to theme.** Character development is most interesting as it relates to theme in the story; try to connect your discussion of plot or character to the overall effect of the story.

WRITING ABOUT CONNECTIONS

It's often interesting to discover connections among characters in the same story or in several stories. We do this with those we know: "They both have quick tempers"; "All four grew up in single-parent homes"; "You guys have a lot in common." Making such connections between characters can lead to interesting literary analyses and paper topics. Here are a few possibilities.

1. "Sticking Together": Relationship Tensions in Etgar Keret's "Crazy Glue" (p. 393) and Michael Oppenheimer's "The Paring Knife" (p. 300)

2. "Life Lessons Learned, or Not": Growing Up in Toni Cade Bambara's "The Lesson" (p. 181), Amy Tan's "Two Kinds" (p. 235), and/or Langston Hughes's "Thank You, M'am" (p. 369)

3. "Mothering Through Difficult Times": The Challenges Faced by the Central Characters in Tillie Olsen's "I Stand Here Ironing" (p. 405) and Katherine Anne Porter's "The Jilting of Granny Weatherall" (p. 432)

WRITING RESEARCH PAPERS

1. Many studies have been done on Barbie dolls and the adverse effect they may have on society's views about women. Conduct research in this area and relate what you find to Alison Townsend's "The Barbie Birthday" (p. 176) and/or Denise Duhamel's "One Afternoon When Barbie Wanted to Join the Military" (p. 622), and perhaps to other stories and poems about Barbie dolls.

2. Do some research into Flannery O'Connor's religious faith and write a paper exploring how it influences her character development. The paper could focus just on "A Good Man Is Hard to Find" (p. 159), or it could include one or more of her other stories.

Remember in your story that setting is the other character. It is as important to your story as the people in it.

Rob Parnell

(Author of The Easy Way to Write a Novel)

8 Setting

Meeting Meaning in Places

Of all the memories we look back on, those involving places often carry particularly important emotional weight. We may have special memories of a grandmother's house or a good friend's apartment, a street corner or a park down the street, or a gymnasium or playground across town. Maybe we have even nightmarish memories of an abandoned house in the country, a cemetery, or a back alley. Reflect for a moment on some significant places in your own life. What specific details come back to mind?

Place (or setting) is also very important in stories: as the area and context in which the characters live and where the events occur. Place may be the key locale of a story, or in addition it may convey symbolic meaning, taking on an expanding significance beyond that of the location of the action. This chapter explores setting to help you realize more fully what it contributes to a story.

APPROACHING THE READING

The *setting* of a story, poem, or play is its overall context — where, when, and in what circumstances the action occurs. In the following story, the setting plays an important role. Two characters, a young woman named Jig and her male companion, are waiting for a train. As you read about them, listen for a major conflict in their relationship and what their discussion of it reveals about their characters. Focus also on where they are (the country, the part of the country, the specific building and its surroundings) and on how the place is described. Look for connections between where they are and what they are talking about.

Ernest Hemingway   1899–1961

Hills Like White Elephants   [1927]

The hills across the valley of the Ebro were long and white. On this side there was no shade and no trees and the station was between two lines of rails in the sun. Close against the side of the station there was the warm shadow of the building and a curtain, made of strings of bamboo beads, hung across the open door into the bar, to keep out flies. The American and the girl with him sat at a table in the shade, outside the building. It was very hot and the express from Barcelona would come in forty minutes. It stopped at this junction for two minutes and went on to Madrid.

"What should we drink?" the girl asked. She had taken off her hat and put it on the table.

"It's pretty hot," the man said.

"Let's drink beer."

"Dos cervezas,"° the man said into the curtain.   5

"Big ones?" a woman asked from the doorway.

"Yes. Two big ones."

The woman brought two glasses of beer and two felt pads. She put the felt pads and the beer glasses on the table and looked at the man and the girl. The girl was looking off at the line of hills. They were white in the sun and the country was brown and dry.

"They look like white elephants," she said.

"I've never seen one," the man drank his beer.   10

"No, you wouldn't have."

"I might have," the man said. "Just because you say I wouldn't have doesn't prove anything."

The girl looked at the bead curtain. "They've painted something on it," she said. "What does it say?"

"Anis del Toro. It's a drink."

"Could we try it?"   15

The man called "Listen" through the curtain. The woman came out from the bar.

"Four reales."

"We want two Anis del Toro."

"With water?"

APPROACHING THE AUTHOR

A sea captain once gave **Ernest Hemingway** a six-toed cat. Today you can visit his former home (now a museum) in Key West, Florida, which houses sixty cats; many of them are descendants of that original cat and have extra toes.

For more about him, see page 1065.

© AS400 DB/Corbis

Dos cervezas: Two beers (Spanish).

"Do you want it with water?"   20

"I don't know," the girl said. "Is it good with water?"

"It's all right."

"You want them with water?" asked the woman.

"Yes, with water."

"It tastes like licorice," the girl said and put the glass down.   25

"That's the way with everything."

"Yes," said the girl. "Everything tastes of licorice. Especially all the things you've waited so long for, like absinthe."

"Oh, cut it out."

"You started it," the girl said. "I was being amused. I was having a fine time."

"Well, let's try and have a fine time."   30

"All right. I was trying. I said the mountains looked like white elephants. Wasn't that bright?"

"That was bright."

"I wanted to try this new drink. That's all we do, isn't it—look at things and try new drinks?"

"I guess so."

The girl looked across at the hills.   35

"They're lovely hills," she said. "They don't really look like white elephants. I just meant the coloring of their skin through the trees."

"Should we have another drink?"

"All right."

The warm wind blew the bead curtain against the table.

"The beer's nice and cool," the man said.   40

"It's lovely," the girl said.

"It's really an awfully simple operation, Jig," the man said. "It's not really an operation at all."

The girl looked at the ground the table legs rested on.

"I know you wouldn't mind it, Jig. It's really not anything. It's just to let the air in."

The girl did not say anything.   45

"I'll go with you and I'll stay with you all the time. They just let the air in and then it's all perfectly natural."

"Then what will we do afterward?"

"We'll be fine afterward. Just like we were before."

"What makes you think so?"

"That's the only thing that bothers us. It's the only thing that's made us   50
unhappy."

The girl looked at the bead curtain, put her hand out and took hold of two of the strings of beads.

"And you think then we'll be all right and be happy."

"I know we will. You don't have to be afraid. I've known lots of people that have done it."

"So have I," said the girl. "And afterward they were all so happy."

"Well," the man said, "if you don't want to you don't have to. I wouldn't 55 have you do it if you didn't want to. But I know it's perfectly simple."

"And you really want to?"

"I think it's the best thing to do. But I don't want you to do it if you don't really want to."

"And if I do it you'll be happy and things will be like they were and you'll love me?"

"I love you now. You know I love you."

"I know. But if I do it, then it will be nice again if I say things are like white 60 elephants, and you'll like it?"

"I'll love it. I love it now but I just can't think about it. You know how I get when I worry."

"If I do it you won't ever worry?"

"I won't worry about that because it's perfectly simple."

"Then I'll do it. Because I don't care about me."

"What do you mean?"   65

"I don't care about me."

"Well, I care about you."

"Oh, yes. But I don't care about me. And I'll do it and then everything will be fine."

"I don't want you to do it if you feel that way."

The girl stood up and walked to the end of the station. Across, on the other 70 side, were fields of grain and trees along the banks of the Ebro. Far away, beyond the river, were mountains. The shadow of a cloud moved across the field of grain and she saw the river through the trees.

"And we could have all this," she said. "And we could have everything and every day we make it more impossible."

"What did you say?"

"I said we could have everything."

"We can have everything."

"No, we can't."   75

"We can have the whole world."

"No, we can't."

"We can go everywhere."

"No, we can't. It isn't ours any more."

"It's ours."   80

"No, it isn't. And once they take it away, you never get it back."

"But they haven't taken it away."

"We'll wait and see."

"Come on back in the shade," he said. "You mustn't feel that way."

"I don't feel any way," the girl said. "I just know things."   85

"I don't want you to do anything that you don't want to do—"

"Nor that isn't good for me," she said. "I know. Could we have another beer?"

"All right. But you've got to realize—"

"I realize," the girl said. "Can't we maybe stop talking?"

They sat down at the table and the girl looked across at the hills on the dry 90
side of the valley and the man looked at her and at the table.

"You've got to realize," he said, "that I don't want you to do it if you don't
want to. I'm perfectly willing to go through with it if it means anything to you."

"Doesn't it mean anything to you? We could get along."

"Of course it does. But I don't want anybody but you. I don't want any one
else. And I know it's perfectly simple."

"Yes, you know it's perfectly simple."

"It's all right for you to say that, but I do know it."   95

"Would you do something for me now?"

"I'd do anything for you."

"Would you please please please please please please please stop talking?"

He did not say anything but looked at the bags against the wall of the station. There were labels on them from all the hotels where they had spent nights.

"But I don't want you to," he said, "I don't care anything about it."   100

"I'll scream," the girl said.

The woman came out through the curtains with two glasses of beer and put
them down on the damp felt pads. "The train comes in five minutes," she said.

"What did she say?" asked the girl.

"That the train is coming in five minutes."

The girl smiled brightly at the woman, to thank her.   105

"I'd better take the bags over to the other side of the station," the man said.
She smiled at him.

"All right. Then come back and we'll finish the beer."

He picked up the two heavy bags and carried them around the station to
the other tracks. He looked up the tracks but could not see the train. Coming
back, he walked through the barroom, where people waiting for the train were
drinking. He drank an Anis at the bar and looked at the people. They were all
waiting reasonably for the train. He went out through the bead curtain. She was
sitting at the table and smiled at him.

"Do you feel better?" he asked.

"I feel fine," she said. "There's nothing wrong with me. I feel fine."   110

REFLECTING ON WHAT YOU'VE READ

1. Think first about what you saw as you read the story. References to
   Barcelona, Madrid, and the Ebro broadly identify the place where the scene
   happens as Spain. You might look at a map to identify where these places
   are and some images of that area so you can visualize the scene more precisely. How does it affect you to have the story occur in Europe? How might
   the effect differ if it had occurred in the United States?

2. Think about the immediate location — a train junction out in the middle of
   nowhere. What is the effect of the rural train junction? How would it be

different if the American and Jig were in a big train station in Madrid? Sitting in a coffee shop in Paris or New York or a small town in the United States?

3. White elephants are mentioned in the title and several times in the story. Jig says she is referring to elephants that are white. Could there be more to the words than that? Look up "white elephant" in a dictionary or Google it and apply what you find to the story.

4. Consider possible connections between white elephants and the conflict, or conflicts, between the main characters. What do you think is the operation the man is urging on Jig? What details from the story support your answer? Is the operation their only conflict?

5. "We'll be fine afterward. Just like we were before," the American says to Jig (para. 48). This line opens an enormous gap—their future—for you to fill in. Where do you think they would go if the story continued? What would happen? How does ending where it does indicate what is important in the story? How do you respond to Jig's concluding lines?

READING FOR SETTING

SETTING AS PLACE

Indicating Place   Basic to a story's context is place, or locale—the physical environment. We need to know the locale in a broad sense: Where does the action take place? What country? What city or region of that country? We also need to know the locale in a specific, narrower sense: What kind of place—downtown, suburban neighborhood, rural area, or highway? What specific street, house, farm, or junction? Physical setting—whether an apartment, a factory, a train station, or a prison camp—can be presented through vibrant, specific details, or it can be sketched broadly with a few, quick strokes. The setting of "Hills Like White Elephants" is indicated in the first paragraph: the broad setting—eastern Spain, about a third of the way from Barcelona to Madrid—and the specific setting—a hot day at a rural train station, a junction where two lines meet in the middle of nowhere.

Significance of Place   The description of a setting often evokes its significance, what it conveys and suggests. Reflect, for example, on the significance of the principal setting in "The Red Convertible" (p. 119) being a reservation. Ask yourself how the story would be different if Lyman and Henry lived in Chicago. Think about the locale of "Hills Like White Elephants," how by creating a sense of isolation, the story focuses our attention on the two people and their problem. There are other people in the bar, but we see no one else except the waitress—the other people are just there, like the chairs and tables.

The location includes only a railway junction: No town or city is indicated, which increases the sense of isolation. There is no community to support or affect the American and Jig in what they face or decide (especially in what Jig faces and must decide) — just two individuals, making an individual decision as if it affects no one but themselves (at least that's how the man views it). Using a train station as locale also creates a sense of transience — no roots, no home, no ties. And placing the story at a junction suggests that the characters are facing a decision about the direction in which they should go.

SETTING AS TIME

Setting also includes the time in which events occur, time in all its dimensions: the century, the year, the season, the day, the hour, maybe even the exact second. In some cases, a specific time is not indicated: The events are universal and could have occurred a minute or a millennium ago. Often, however, a specific or approximate time is either assumed (the time may seem the same as when the story was written or published) or indicated — perhaps by giving a date in the story; by mentioning historical events that were going on at the time the story was written; or by describing the way people talk, act, or dress. In those cases, the specific time may be significant, and knowing something about that time period may help you understand what is going on or the significance of what occurs.

Historical Events   Assessing the significance of a specific time may require asking questions and then doing some investigating — in an encyclopedia, or on the Internet, or through more specialized books, depending on the time period involved and the way the story uses its setting.

Consider, for example, "Hills Like White Elephants." The action is probably contemporaneous with when it was written, in the mid-1920s. To decide if that time setting is significant to the story, ask what was going on at that time, what was significant or noteworthy. You might check a time line of world or European historical events. You'll notice that the story takes place less than ten years after the end of World War I (1914–1918).

To gain the full impact of the story's setting in time, you might need to do some reading about the war and its aftermath (an encyclopedia entry on the war probably would suffice). The war caused immense loss of life, physical suffering, and psychological and emotional damage from trench warfare and the use of nerve gas. It is estimated that 8.5 million military personnel died (a high percentage of a whole generation's young men), along with 10 million civilians. Although the corresponding numbers in World War II were much greater, at the time the number of deaths and amount of devastation were unprecedented. It was called the Great War with good reason.

Social Milieu   Your investigation might include the social environment of the era, especially the social changes that took place during and after the war. Information from an encyclopedia, books, or Internet articles might help clarify what was going on in the background of "Hills Like White Elephants," if you find yourself interested enough to explore at another level. (The more you dig, the more you'll find and the richer your reading of the story will become.) In broad terms, the war shattered the optimistic outlook held by much of the population in Western Europe and the United States. After the war ended, many people reacted by deciding to enjoy life fully in the present because the war showed that life can end so quickly, and by rejecting older values (including prevailing sexual mores) and traditional roles (especially for women). The war led to changes in gender roles: With young men away in the military, women had to work in factories instead of in homes, schools, or offices.

The war also led to changes in family and community life. Having seen large cities and other countries, young people found it difficult to return to the sheltered, conservative communities in which they grew up. A large number of writers, artists, and socialites — Ernest Hemingway among them — moved from the United States to Europe, which they considered more sophisticated. The American man in "Hills Like White Elephants" seems to be one of them and to reflect the sense of restlessness and desire to see new places and have new experiences. "That's all we do, isn't it," Jig says, "look at things and try new drinks?" (para. 33).

SETTING AS CULTURAL CONTEXT

Social Circumstances   Setting also involves the social circumstances of the time and place. Here too, active reading may require some research. Beyond the historical events at the time, try to find what attitudes people held about what was going on. What social and political problems were people facing? How were people below the poverty line treated, and what were the attitudes of the economically secure? What kinds of social change were occurring?

Such social and cultural contexts are closely related to the kind of historical events we discussed above — actually, all aspects of setting are interrelated and inseparable. So, for example, to understand "The Red Convertible" fully it helps to know something about the Vietnam War and attitudes toward it. Notice also how it involves transplanting a young Native American from his familiar, traditional culture to a strikingly different military culture and then to a strange foreign culture.

Cultural Transplantation   Like "The Red Convertible," "Hills Like White Elephants" involves cultural transplantation: an American writer, Ernest Hemingway, living in Paris, writing in English (thus mainly for an American audience), about an American traveling in Spain (a conservative, predominantly Catholic country) with a companion (to whom he does not seem to be married) from an unspecified country. The fact that he is called "the American" suggests that Jig is not American; she apparently is not from Spain because she cannot converse with the waitress (we are supposed to assume the man is talking to the waitress in Spanish, even though his words and hers are written in English). Such details convey economically and efficiently a mixture of cultures and values, as well as a cosmopolitan outlook.

THE EFFECTS OF SETTING

Thus, setting provides a world for a story to take place in, a location and a background for the events. But as you pay even closer attention to setting, you'll see that it usually does more. Again, you need to ask questions, especially about further implications of when and where the events happen. Ask yourself what the setting reveals about characters. What is suggested by where a person lives (the kind of house and furniture) or the place in which we encounter her or him (a bar, a gym, a library, the woods)? Does the setting help clarify what she or he is like?

SETTING AND ATMOSPHERE

Ask yourself also how setting affects the way you feel about the characters and events. Setting can be important in evoking *atmosphere*—that is, the mood or emotional quality that surrounds and permeates a literary work. Part of the effect in the *gothic* story "A Rose for Emily" (p. 205) is created by the eerie atmosphere of the house in which Miss Emily secludes herself for much of her life. In other stories the emotional aura may be less dramatic, but it is always there and affects how you respond to the work as a whole.

CHECKLIST on Reading for Setting

❑ Be attentive to setting in a literary work:
- setting in terms of place, in its broad sense and in its sense of narrower, individual places
- setting in time
- setting as historical, social, and cultural context

❑ Be aware of different effects that setting can have in a work—revealing character, conveying atmosphere, reinforcing meaning, serving as a symbol or occasionally almost as a character.

FURTHER READING

APPROACHING THE READING

Like Alice Walker's "Everyday Use" (p. 152) and Flannery O'Connor's "A Good Man Is Hard to Find" (p. 159), the following story takes place in the South, and setting (in all aspects—location, time, cultural context) is very important. This one, however, takes place earlier in the century in a white community. It tells of a reclusive elderly woman who seems a mystery to the other residents of her small town, especially the younger people with their contemporary attitudes and changing ways of doing things that marginalize her all the more. It is a story that depends heavily on the point of view and perspective from which it is told. Notice both as you read and reflect.

William Faulkner   1897–1962

A Rose for Emily   [1931]

I

When Miss Emily Grierson died, our whole town went to her funeral: the men through a sort of respectful affection for a fallen monument, the women mostly out of curiosity to see the inside of her house, which no one save an old manservant—a combined gardener and cook—had seen in at least ten years.

x

It was a big, squarish frame house that had once been white, decorated with cupolas and spires and scrolled balconies in the heavily lightsome style of the seventies, set on what had once been our most select street. But garages and cotton gins had

APPROACHING THE AUTHOR

William Faulkner was campus postmaster for two years at the University of Mississippi but was fired because he spent his time reading and working on a novel and people couldn't rely on him to distribute or forward the mail.

For more about him, see page 1063.

Carl Mydans/Getty

encroached and obliterated even the august names of that neighborhood; only Miss Emily's house was left, lifting its stubborn and coquettish decay above the cotton wagons and the gasoline pumps—an eyesore among eyesores. And now Miss Emily had gone to join the representatives of those august names where they lay in the cedar-bemused cemetery among the ranked and anonymous graves of Union and Confederate soldiers who fell at the battle of Jefferson.

Alive, Miss Emily had been a tradition, a duty, and a care; a sort of hereditary obligation upon the town, dating from that day in 1894 when Colonel Sartoris, the mayor—he who fathered the edict that no Negro woman should appear on the streets without an apron—remitted her taxes, the dispensation dating from the death of her father on into perpetuity. Not that Miss Emily would have accepted charity. Colonel Sartoris invented an involved tale to the effect that Miss Emily's father had loaned money to the town, which the town, as a matter of business, preferred this way of repaying. Only a man of Colonel Sartoris' generation and thought could have invented it, and only a woman could have believed it.

When the next generation, with its more modern ideas, became mayors and aldermen, this arrangement created some little dissatisfaction. On the first of the year they mailed her a tax notice. February came, and there was no reply. They wrote her a formal letter, asking her to call at the sheriff's office at her convenience. A week later the mayor wrote her himself, offering to call or to send his car for her, and received in reply a note on paper of an archaic shape, in a thin, flowing calligraphy in faded ink, to the effect that she no longer went out at all. The tax notice was also enclosed, without comment.

They called a special meeting of the Board of Aldermen. A deputation 5 waited upon her, knocked at the door through which no visitor had passed since she ceased giving china-painting lessons eight or ten years earlier. They were admitted by the old Negro into a dim hall from which a stairway mounted into still more shadow. It smelled of dust and disuse—a close, dank smell. The Negro led them into the parlor. It was furnished in heavy, leather-covered furniture. When the Negro opened the blinds of one window, they could see that the leather was cracked; and when they sat down, a faint dust rose sluggishly about their thighs, spinning with slow motes in the single sun-ray. On a tarnished gilt easel before the fireplace stood a crayon portrait of Miss Emily's father.

They rose when she entered—a small, fat woman in black, with a thin gold chain descending to her waist and vanishing into her belt, leaning on an ebony cane with a tarnished gold head. Her skeleton was small and spare; perhaps that was why what would have been merely plumpness in another was obesity in her. She looked bloated, like a body long submerged in motionless water, and of that pallid hue. Her eyes, lost in the fatty ridges of her face, looked like two small pieces of coal pressed into a lump of dough as they moved from one face to another while the visitors stated their errand.

She did not ask them to sit. She just stood in the door and listened quietly until the spokesman came to a stumbling halt. Then they could hear the invisible watch ticking at the end of the gold chain.

Her voice was dry and cold. "I have no taxes in Jefferson. Colonel Sartoris explained it to me. Perhaps one of you can gain access to the city records and satisfy yourselves."

"But we have. We are the city authorities, Miss Emily. Didn't you get a notice from the sheriff, signed by him?"

"I received a paper, yes," Miss Emily said. "Perhaps he considers himself the 10 sheriff . . . I have no taxes in Jefferson."

"But there is nothing on the books to show that, you see. We must go by the—"

"See Colonel Sartoris. I have no taxes in Jefferson."

"But, Miss Emily—"

"See Colonel Sartoris." (Colonel Sartoris had been dead almost ten years.) "I have no taxes in Jefferson. Tobe!" The Negro appeared. "Show these gentlemen out."

II

So she vanquished them, horse and foot, just as she had vanquished their 15 fathers thirty years before about the smell. That was two years after her father's death and a short time after her sweetheart—the one we believed would marry her—had deserted her. After her father's death she went out very little; after her sweetheart went away, people hardly saw her at all. A few of the ladies had the temerity to call, but were not received, and the only sign of life about the place was the Negro man—a young man then—going in and out with a market basket.

"Just as if a man—any man—could keep a kitchen properly," the ladies said; so they were not surprised when the smell developed. It was another link between the gross, teeming world and the high and mighty Griersons.

A neighbor, a woman, complained to the mayor, Judge Stevens, eighty years old.

"But what will you have me do about it, madam?" he said.

"Why, send her word to stop it," the woman said. "Isn't there a law?"

"I'm sure that won't be necessary," Judge Stevens said. "It's probably just a 20 snake or a rat that nigger of hers killed in the yard. I'll speak to him about it."

The next day he received two more complaints, one from a man who came in diffident deprecation. "We really must do something about it, Judge. I'd be the last one in the world to bother Miss Emily, but we've got to do something." That night the Board of Aldermen met—three graybeards and one younger man, a member of the rising generation.

"It's simple enough," he said. "Send her word to have her place cleaned up. Give her a certain time to do it in, and if she don't . . ."

"Dammit, sir," Judge Stevens said, "will you accuse a lady to her face of smelling bad?"

So the next night, after midnight, four men crossed Miss Emily's lawn and slunk about the house like burglars, sniffing along the base of the brickwork and at the cellar openings while one of them performed a regular sowing motion with his hand out of a sack slung from his shoulder. They broke open the cellar door and sprinkled lime there, and in all the outbuildings. As they recrossed the lawn, a window that had been dark was lighted and Miss Emily sat in it, the light behind her, and her upright torso motionless as that of an idol. They crept quietly across the lawn and into the shadow of the locusts that lined the street. After a week or two the smell went away.

That was when people had begun to feel really sorry for her. People in our 25 town, remembering how old lady Wyatt, her great-aunt, had gone completely crazy at last, believed that the Griersons held themselves a little too high for what they really were. None of the young men were quite good enough for Miss Emily and such. We had long thought of them as a tableau,° Miss Emily a slender figure in white in the background, her father a spraddled silhouette in the foreground, his back to her and clutching a horsewhip, the two of them framed by the back-flung front door. So when she got to be thirty and was still single, we were not pleased exactly, but vindicated; even with insanity in the family she wouldn't have turned down all of her chances if they had really materialized.

When her father died, it got about that the house was all that was left to her; and in a way, people were glad. At last they could pity Miss Emily. Being left alone, and a pauper, she had become humanized. Now she too would know the old thrill and the old despair of a penny more or less.

The day after his death all the ladies prepared to call at the house and offer condolence and aid, as is our custom. Miss Emily met them at the door, dressed as usual and with no trace of grief on her face. She told them that her father was not dead. She did that for three days, with the ministers calling on her, and the doctors, trying to persuade her to let them dispose of the body. Just as they were about to resort to law and force, she broke down, and they buried her father quickly.

We did not say she was crazy then. We believed she had to do that. We remembered all the young men her father had driven away, and we knew that with nothing left, she would have to cling to that which had robbed her, as people will.

III

She was sick for a long time. When we saw her again, her hair was cut short, making her look like a girl, with a vague resemblance to those angels in colored church windows—sort of tragic and serene.

The town had just let the contracts for paving the sidewalks, and in the   30
summer after her father's death they began the work. The construction company came with niggers and mules and machinery, and a foreman named Homer Barron, a Yankee—a big, dark, ready man, with a big voice and eyes lighter than his face. The little boys would follow in groups to hear him cuss the niggers, and the niggers singing in time to the rise and fall of picks. Pretty soon he knew everybody in town. Whenever you heard a lot of laughing anywhere about the square, Homer Barron would be in the center of the group. Presently we began to see him and Miss Emily on Sunday afternoons driving in the yellow-wheeled buggy and the matched team of bays from the livery stable.

---

tableau: short for *tableau vivant* (French), "living painting"; a depiction of a scene or picture by a person or group in costume, posing silently without moving.

At first we were glad that Miss Emily would have an interest, because the ladies all said, "Of course a Grierson would not think seriously of a Northerner, a day laborer." But there were still others, older people, who said that even grief could not cause a real lady to forget *noblesse oblige*° — without calling it *noblesse oblige*. They just said, "Poor Emily. Her kinsfolk should come to her." She had some kin in Alabama; but years ago her father had fallen out with them over the estate of old lady Wyatt, the crazy woman, and there was no communication between the two families. They had not even been represented at the funeral.

And as soon as the old people said, "Poor Emily," the whispering began. "Do you suppose it's really so?" they said to one another. "Of course it is. What else could . . ." This behind their hands; rustling of craned silk and satin behind jalousies closed upon the sun of Sunday afternoon as the thin, swift clop-clop-clop of the matched team passed: "Poor Emily."

She carried her head high enough — even when we believed that she was fallen. It was as if she demanded more than ever the recognition of her dignity as the last Grierson; as if it had wanted that touch of earthiness to reaffirm her imperviousness. Like when she bought the rat poison, the arsenic. That was over a year after they had begun to say "Poor Emily," and while the two female cousins were visiting her.

"I want some poison," she said to the druggist. She was over thirty then, still a slight woman, though thinner than usual, with cold, haughty black eyes in a face the flesh of which was strained across the temples and about the eye-sockets as you imagine a lighthouse-keeper's face ought to look. "I want some poison," she said.

"Yes, Miss Emily. What kind? For rats and such? I'd recom—"   35

"I want the best you have. I don't care what kind."

The druggist named several. "They'll kill anything up to an elephant. But what you want is—"

"Arsenic," Miss Emily said. "Is that a good one?"

"Is . . . arsenic? Yes, ma'am. But what you want—"

"I want arsenic."   40

The druggist looked down at her. She looked back at him, erect, her face like a strained flag. "Why, of course," the druggist said. "If that's what you want. But the law requires you to tell what you are going to use it for."

Miss Emily just stared at him, her head tilted back in order to look him eye for eye, until he looked away and went and got the arsenic and wrapped it up. The Negro delivery boy brought her the package; the druggist didn't come back. When she opened the package at home there was written on the box, under the skull and bones: "For rats."

---

noblesse oblige: French for "nobility obligates," the inferred obligation of people of high rank or social position to behave nobly, generously, and kindly toward others.

IV

So the next day we all said, "She will kill herself"; and we said it would be the best thing. When she had first begun to be seen with Homer Barron, we had said, "She will marry him." Then we said, "She will persuade him yet," because Homer himself had remarked—he liked men, and it was known that he drank with the younger men in the Elks' Club—that he was not a marrying man. Later we said, "Poor Emily" behind the jalousies as they passed on Sunday afternoon in the glittering buggy, Miss Emily with her head high and Homer Barron with his hat cocked and a cigar in his teeth, reins and whip in a yellow glove.

Then some of the ladies began to say that it was a disgrace to the town and a bad example to the young people. The men did not want to interfere, but at last the ladies forced the Baptist minister—Miss Emily's people were Episcopal—to call upon her. He would never divulge what happened during that interview, but he refused to go back again. The next Sunday they again drove about the streets, and the following day the minister's wife wrote to Miss Emily's relations in Alabama.

So she had blood-kin under her roof again and we sat back to watch devel-   45
opments. At first nothing happened. Then we were sure that they were to be married. We learned that Miss Emily had been to the jeweler's and ordered a man's toilet set in silver, with the letters H. B. on each piece. Two days later we learned that she had bought a complete outfit of men's clothing, including a nightshirt, and we said, "They are married." We were really glad. We were glad because the two female cousins were even more Grierson than Miss Emily had ever been.

So we were not surprised when Homer Barron—the streets had been finished some time since—was gone. We were a little disappointed that there was not a public blowing-off, but we believed that he had gone on to prepare for Miss Emily's coming, or to give her a chance to get rid of the cousins. (By that time it was a cabal, and we were all Miss Emily's allies to help circumvent the cousins.) Sure enough, after another week they departed. And, as we had expected all along, within three days Homer Barron was back in town. A neighbor saw the Negro man admit him at the kitchen door at dusk one evening.

And that was the last we saw of Homer Barron. And of Miss Emily for some time. The Negro man went in and out with the market basket, but the front door remained closed. Now and then we would see her at a window for a moment, as the men did that night when they sprinkled the lime, but for almost six months she did not appear on the streets. Then we knew that this was to be expected too; as if that quality of her father which had thwarted her woman's life so many times had been too virulent and too furious to die.

When we next saw Miss Emily, she had grown fat and her hair was turning gray. During the next few years it grew grayer and grayer until it attained an even pepper-and-salt iron-gray, when it ceased turning. Up to the day of her death at seventy-four it was still that vigorous iron-gray, like the hair of an active man.

From that time on her front door remained closed, save for a period of six or seven years, when she was about forty, during which she gave lessons in china-painting. She fitted up a studio in one of the downstairs rooms, where the daughters and granddaughters of Colonel Sartoris' contemporaries were sent to her with the same regularity and in the same spirit that they were sent to church on Sundays with a twenty-five-cent piece for the collection plate. Meanwhile her taxes had been remitted.

Then the newer generation became the backbone and the spirit of the town, 50 and the painting pupils grew up and fell away and did not send their children to her with boxes of color and tedious brushes and pictures cut from the ladies' magazines. The front door closed upon the last one and remained closed for good. When the town got free postal delivery, Miss Emily alone refused to let them fasten the metal numbers above her door and attach a mailbox to it. She would not listen to them.

Daily, monthly, yearly we watched the Negro grow grayer and more stooped, going in and out with the market basket. Each December we sent her a tax notice, which would be returned by the post office a week later, unclaimed. Now and then we would see her in one of the downstairs windows — she had evidently shut up the top floor of the house — like the carven torso of an idol in a niche, looking or not looking at us, we could never tell which. Thus she passed from generation to generation — dear, inescapable, impervious, tranquil, and perverse.

And so she died. Fell ill in the house filled with dust and shadows, with only a doddering Negro man to wait on her. We did not even know she was sick; we had long since given up trying to get any information from the Negro. He talked to no one, probably not even to her, for his voice had grown harsh and rusty, as if from disuse.

She died in one of the downstairs rooms, in a heavy walnut bed with a curtain, her gray head propped on a pillow yellow and moldy with age and lack of sunlight.

V

The Negro met the first of the ladies at the front door and let them in, with their hushed, sibilant voices and their quick, curious glances, and then he disappeared. He walked right through the house and out the back and was not seen again.

The two female cousins came at once. They held the funeral on the second 55 day, with the town coming to look at Miss Emily beneath a mass of bought flowers, with the crayon face of her father musing profoundly above the bier and the ladies sibilant and macabre; and the very old men — some in their brushed Confederate uniforms — on the porch and the lawn, talking of Miss Emily as if she had been a contemporary of theirs, believing that they had danced with her and courted her perhaps, confusing time with its mathematical progression, as the old do, to whom all the past is not a diminishing road but, instead, a huge meadow which no winter ever quite touches, divided from them now by the narrow bottle-neck of the most recent decade of years.

Already we knew that there was one room in that region above stairs which no one had seen in forty years, and which would have to be forced. They waited until Miss Emily was decently in the ground before they opened it.

The violence of breaking down the door seemed to fill this room with pervading dust. A thin, acrid pall as of the tomb seemed to lie everywhere upon this room decked and furnished as for a bridal: upon the valance curtains of faded rose color, upon the rose-shaded lights, upon the dressing table, upon the delicate array of crystal and the man's toilet things backed with tarnished silver, silver so tarnished that the monogram was obscured. Among them lay a collar and tie, as if they had just been removed, which, lifted, left upon the surface a pale crescent in the dust. Upon a chair hung the suit, carefully folded; beneath it the two mute shoes and the discarded socks.

The man himself lay in the bed.

For a long while we just stood there, looking down at the profound and fleshless grin. The body had apparently once lain in the attitude of an embrace, but now the long sleep that outlasts love, that conquers even the grimace of love, had cuckolded him. What was left of him, rotted beneath what was left of the nightshirt, had become inextricable from the bed in which he lay; and upon him and upon the pillow beside him lay that even coating of the patient and biding dust.

Then we noticed that in the second pillow was the indentation of a head. 60 One of us lifted something from it, and leaning forward, that faint and invisible dust dry and acrid in the nostrils, we saw a long strand of iron-gray hair.

REFLECTING ON WHAT YOU'VE READ

1. Think through what you would say in a discussion of the significance of setting in "A Rose for Emily"—the importance of the South, a small town, the early twentieth century, an old mansion in what was but no longer is the town's most prestigious neighborhood.

2. Telling a story from a first-person plural point of view is unusual. Who is the narrator? How much does the narrator know? What is the advantage in using the plural? How does the choice of first-person plural relate to the setting? Consider how the effect would be different if in each case "our" was changed to "my" and "we" changed to "I."

3. Do you think the story could have been told effectively from a third-person omniscient point of view? Why? Why not? Describe ways in which the story would be different, and how this would alter its effect.

4. Try outlining the story. This can help you see its very careful, deliberate plot structure more clearly. Point out examples of foreshadowing.

5. How would you summarize Miss Emily's character? How does the point of view affect and shape what you know about her? Do you empathize with her? Feel sorry for her? Why or why not?

6. In what ways does the title fit, or relate to, what the story is about?

APPROACHING THE READING

In the following story, a young Native American man encounters how difficult it is to be an outsider in American culture. From the very first line, setting is important: the Third Avenue 7-11, his apartment, Seattle, the state of Washington, the reservation. While you read and then reflect on the story, notice too how place influences everything that happens.

Sherman Alexie   b. 1966

The Lone Ranger and Tonto Fistfight in Heaven   [1993]

Too hot to sleep so I walked down to the Third Avenue 7-11 for a Creamsicle° and the company of a graveyard-shift cashier. I know that game. I worked graveyard for a Seattle 7-11 and got robbed once too often. The last time the bastard locked me in the cooler. He even took my money and basketball shoes.

The graveyard-shift worker in the Third Avenue 7-11 looked like they all do. Acne scars and a bad haircut, work pants that showed off his white socks, and those cheap black shoes that have no support. My arches still ache from my year at the Seattle 7-11.

> **APPROACHING THE AUTHOR**
>
> Sherman Alexie made his debut as a stand-up comedian at the Foolproof Northwest Comedy Festival in Seattle in April 1999. For more about him, see page 1053.

"Hello," he asked when I walked into his store. "How you doing?"

I gave him a half-wave as I headed back to the freezer. He looked me over so he could describe me to the police later. I knew the look. One of my old girlfriends said I started to look at her that way, too. She left me not long after that. No, I left her and don't blame her for anything. That's how it happened. When one person starts to look at another like a criminal, then the love is over. It's logical.

"I don't trust you," she said to me. "You get too angry."   5

She was white and I lived with her in Seattle. Some nights we fought so bad that I would just get in my car and drive all night, only stop to fill up on gas. In fact, I worked the graveyard shift to spend as much time away from her as possible. But I learned all about Seattle that way, driving its back ways and dirty alleys.

Creamsicle: A frozen dessert bar with a vanilla ice cream center covered by a layer of fruit-flavored ice.

Sometimes, though, I would forget where I was and get lost. I'd drive for hours, searching for something familiar. Seems like I'd spent my whole life that way, looking for anything I recognized. Once, I ended up in a nice residential neighborhood and somebody must have been worried because the police showed up and pulled me over.

"What are you doing out here?" the police officer asked me, as he looked over my license and registration.

"I'm lost."

"Well, where are you supposed to be?" he asked me, and I knew there were 10 plenty of places I wanted to be, but none where I was supposed to be.

"I got in a fight with my girlfriend," I said. "I was just driving around, blowing off steam, you know?"

"Well, you should be more careful where you drive," the officer said. "You're making people nervous. You don't fit the profile of the neighborhood."

I wanted to tell him that I didn't really fit the profile of the country but I knew it would just get me into trouble.

"Can I help you?" the 7-11 clerk asked me loudly, searching for some response that would reassure him that I wasn't an armed robber. He knew this dark skin and long, black hair of mine was dangerous. I had potential.

"Just getting a Creamsicle," I said after a long interval. It was a sick twist to 15 pull on the guy, but it was late and I was bored. I grabbed my Creamsicle and walked back to the counter slowly, scanned the aisles for effect. I wanted to whistle low and menacingly but I never learned to whistle.

"Pretty hot out tonight?" he asked, that old rhetorical weather bullshit question designed to put us both at ease.

"Hot enough to make you go crazy," I said and smiled. He swallowed hard like a white man does in those situations. I looked him over. Same old green, red, and white 7-11 jacket and thick glasses. But he wasn't ugly, just misplaced and marked by loneliness. If he wasn't working there that night, he'd be at home alone, flipping through channels and wishing he could afford HBO or Showtime.

"Will this be all?" he asked me, in that company effort to make me do some impulse shopping. Like adding a clause onto a treaty. *We'll take Washington and Oregon and you get six pine trees and a brand-new Chrysler Cordoba.* I knew how to make and break promises.

"No," I said and paused. "Give me a Cherry Slushie, too."

"What size?" he asked, relieved.   20

"Large," I said, and he turned his back to me to make the drink. He realized his mistake but it was too late. He stiffened, ready for the gunshot or the blow behind the ear. When it didn't come, he turned back to me.

"I'm sorry," he said. "What size did you say?"

"Small," I said and changed the story.

"But I thought you said large."

"If you knew I wanted a large, then why did you ask me again?" I asked him 25 and laughed. He looked at me, couldn't decide if I was giving him serious shit or just goofing. There was something about him I liked, even if it was three in the morning and he was white.

"Hey," I said. "Forget the Slushie. What I want to know is if you know all the words to the theme from 'The Brady Bunch'?"

He looked at me, confused at first, then laughed.

"Shit," he said. "I was hoping you weren't crazy. You were scaring me."

"Well, I'm going to get crazy if you don't know the words."

He laughed loudly then, told me to take the Creamsicle for free. He was the   30 graveyard-shift manager and those little demonstrations of power tickled him. All seventy-five cents of it. I knew how much everything cost.

"Thanks," I said to him and walked out the door. I took my time walking home, let the heat of the night melt the Creamsicle all over my hand. At three in the morning I could act just as young as I wanted to act. There was no one around to ask me to grow up.

In Seattle, I broke lamps. She and I would argue and I'd break a lamp, just pick it up and throw it down. At first she'd buy replacement lamps, expensive and beautiful. But after a while she'd buy lamps from Goodwill or garage sales. Then she just gave up the idea entirely and we'd argue in the dark.

"You're just like your brother," she'd yell. "Drunk all the time and stupid."

"My brother don't drink that much."

She and I never tried to hurt each other physically. I did love her, after all,   35 and she loved me. But those arguments were just as damaging as a fist. Words can be like that, you know? Whenever I get into arguments now, I remember her and I also remember Muhammad Ali. He knew the power of his fists but, more importantly, he knew the power of his words, too. Even though he only had an IQ of 80 or so, Ali was a genius. And she was a genius, too. She knew exactly what to say to cause me the most pain.

But don't get me wrong. I walked through that relationship with an executioner's hood. Or more appropriately, with war paint and sharp arrows. She was a kindergarten teacher and I continually insulted her for that.

"Hey, schoolmarm," I asked. "Did your kids teach you anything new today?"

And I always had crazy dreams. I always have had them, but it seemed they became nightmares more often in Seattle.

In one dream, she was a missionary's wife and I was a minor war chief. We fell in love and tried to keep it secret. But the missionary caught us fucking in the barn and shot me. As I lay dying, my tribe learned of the shooting and attacked the whites all across the reservation. I died and my soul drifted above the reservation.

Disembodied, I could see everything that was happening. Whites killing   40 Indians and Indians killing whites. At first it was small, just my tribe and the few whites who lived there. But my dream grew, intensified. Other tribes arrived on horseback to continue the slaughter of whites, and the United States Cavalry rode into battle.

The most vivid image of that dream stays with me. Three mounted soldiers played polo with a dead Indian woman's head. When I first dreamed it, I thought it was just a product of my anger and imagination. But since then, I've read similar accounts of that kind of evil in the old West. Even more terrifying, though, is the fact that those kinds of brutal things are happening today in places like El Salvador.

All I know for sure, though, is that I woke from that dream in terror, packed up all my possessions, and left Seattle in the middle of the night.

"I love you," she said as I left her. "And don't ever come back."

I drove through the night, over the Cascades, down into the plains of central Washington, and back home to the Spokane Indian Reservation.

When I finished the Creamsicle that the 7-11 clerk gave me, I held the 45 wooden stick up into the air and shouted out very loudly. A couple lights flashed on in windows and a police car cruised by me a few minutes later. I waved to the men in blue and they waved back accidentally. When I got home it was still too hot to sleep so I picked up a week-old newspaper from the floor and read.

There was another civil war, another terrorist bomb exploded, and one more plane crashed and all aboard were presumed dead. The crime rate was rising in every city with populations larger than 100,000, and a farmer in Iowa shot his banker after foreclosure on his 1,000 acres.

A kid from Spokane won the local spelling bee by spelling the word *rhinoceros*.

When I got back to the reservation, my family wasn't surprised to see me. They'd been expecting me back since the day I left for Seattle. There's an old Indian poet who said that Indians can reside in the city, but they can never live there. That's as close to truth as any of us can get.

Mostly I watched television. For weeks I flipped through channels, searched for answers in the game shows and soap operas. My mother would circle the want ads in red and hand the paper to me.

"What are you going to do with the rest of your life?" she asked.   50

"Don't know," I said, and normally, for almost any other Indian in the country, that would have been a perfectly fine answer. But I was special, a former college student, a smart kid. I was one of those Indians who was supposed to make it, to rise above the rest of the reservation like a fucking eagle or something. I was the new kind of warrior.

For a few months I didn't even look at the want ads my mother circled, just left the newspaper where she had set it down. After a while, though, I got tired of television and started to play basketball again. I'd been a good player in high school, nearly great, and almost played at the college I attended for a couple years. But I'd been too out of shape from drinking and sadness to ever be good again. Still, I liked the way the ball felt in my hands and the way my feet felt inside my shoes.

At first I just shot baskets by myself. It was selfish, and I also wanted to learn the game again before I played against anybody else. Since I had been good before and embarrassed fellow tribal members, I knew they would want to take revenge on me. Forget about the cowboys versus Indians business. The most intense competition on any reservation is Indians versus Indians.

But on the night I was ready to play for real, there was this white guy at the gym, playing with all the Indians.

"Who is that?" I asked Jimmy Seyler.   55

"He's the new BIA° chief's kid."

"Can he play?"

"Oh, yeah."

And he could play. He played Indian ball, fast and loose, better than all the Indians there.

"How long's he been playing here?" I asked.   60

"Long enough."

I stretched my muscles, and everybody watched me. All these Indians watched one of their old and dusty heroes. Even though I had played most of my ball at the white high school I went to, I was still all Indian, you know? I was Indian when it counted, and this BIA kid needed to be beaten by an Indian, any Indian.

I jumped into the game and played well for a little while. It felt good. I hit a few shots, grabbed a rebound or two, played enough defense to keep the other team honest. Then that white kid took over the game. He was too good. Later, he'd play college ball back East and would nearly make the Knicks team a couple years on. But we didn't know any of that would happen. We just knew he was better that day and every other day.

The next morning I woke up tired and hungry, so I grabbed the want ads, found a job I wanted, and drove to Spokane to get it. I've been working at the high school exchange program ever since, typing and answering phones. Sometimes I wonder if the people on the other end of the line know that I'm Indian and if their voices would change if they did know.

One day I picked up the phone and it was her, calling from Seattle.   65

"I got your number from your mom," she said. "I'm glad you're working."

"Yeah, nothing like a regular paycheck."

"Are you drinking?"

"No, I've been on the wagon for almost a year."

"Good."   70

The connection was good. I could hear her breathing in the spaces between our words. How do you talk to the real person whose ghost has haunted you? How do you tell the difference between the two?

"Listen," I said. "I'm sorry for everything."

"Me, too."

"What's going to happen to us?" I asked her and wished I had the answer for myself.

"I don't know," she said. "I want to change the world."   75

―――――――

BIA: Bureau of Indian Affairs.

These days, living alone in Spokane, I wish I lived closer to the river, to the falls where ghosts of salmon jump. I wish I could sleep. I put down my paper or book and turn off all the lights, lie quietly in the dark. It may take hours, even years, for me to sleep again. There's nothing surprising or disappointing in that. I know how all my dreams end anyway.

REFLECTING ON WHAT YOU'VE READ

1. What would you focus on in a discussion about how the various settings in the story influence and affect the narrator's search for a "place" in American society?

2. How would you talk about the narrator as a character? What is he like? What is he searching for? Be ready to point out particular sentences that comment on identity. Consider particularly how a variety of conflicts bring out the complex aspects of his character.

3. Reflect on the narrator's dreams. How do they relate to his life and character?

4. What has basketball to do with the narrator's character and the larger issue of the conflicts between white culture and Indian culture?

5. Reread the last two paragraphs. Think about what they mean, how they relate to the rest of the story, and what you would bring to a discussion of them.

6. Look up the Lone Ranger and Tonto. Be ready to discuss how the title relates to the narrator and to the story as a whole?

RESPONDING THROUGH Writing

WRITING ABOUT SETTING

Journal Entries

1. Focus on the way settings are handled in two or three TV shows or movies. Pay attention to what was discussed in this chapter: setting as place broadly and specifically, setting in time, setting in social and cultural context. Consider uses and effects of setting: for plot, characterization, and atmosphere. Then write a journal entry discussing how what you discovered can enhance your grasp of setting in literature.

2. Read Tim O'Brien's "The Things They Carried" (p. 257) and find ways to deepen your visual sense of what being a soldier in Vietnam was like for the characters. Find a book of photographs on the Vietnam War and/or watch films such as *Platoon*; *Good Morning, Vietnam*; or *Apocalypse Now*. Write a

journal entry in which you describe how these visual texts affect the way you imagine the setting and action of the story. Does it make a significant difference? Think about why it does or does not in light of the power of literary description.

3. Write a journal entry discussing the importance of setting in Chrystos's "Traditional Style Indian Garage" (p. 351).

Literary Analysis Papers

4. Write a paper discussing the importance of the setting in Flannery O'Connor's "A Good Man Is Hard to Find" (p. 159), John Updike's "A&P" (p. 188), or another story of your choice.

5. Write a paper discussing the relationship between setting and character in Ralph Ellison's "Battle Royal" (p. 271), James Baldwin's "Sonny's Blues" (p. 324), or another story of your choice.

6. Write a paper on the importance of setting to plot and character in Megan Foss's "Love Letters" (p. 10).

Comparison-Contrast Papers

7. Compare and contrast the use and significance of setting in Alice Walker's "Everyday Use" (p. 152) and ZZ Packer's "Brownies" (p. 411).

> ### ▶ TIPS for Writing about Setting
>
> - **Include setting when it's important.** Setting ordinarily is brought into a paper only if it stands out or has special significance. Discuss its effect in the story precisely and specifically.
> - **Cover setting completely.** When writing about setting, be sure to cover place in whatever dimension is important (a room, a building, a city, a country, another planet or world) and to treat time and social milieu, when relevant.

8. Write a paper on the significance and effect of the contrasting settings in paragraphs 1–59 and paragraphs 60–142 of Flannery O'Connor's "A Good Man is Hard to Find" (p. 159).

WRITING ABOUT CONNECTIONS

Setting is deeply involved with connections. We connect with people by being in the same place and time as they are. Thus, any paper you write on setting will inevitably deal with connections. Stories with setting connections and thematic connections often can lead to interesting and illuminating papers. Here are a few possibilities:

1. "Secrets of the Heart": Keeping Hope Alive in Ernest Hemingway's "Hills Like White Elephants" (p. 197) and Edwidge Danticat's "New York Day Women" (p. 353)

2. "Office Politics": Relationships and Tensions at Work in Daniel Orozco's "Orientation" (p. 230) and James Thurber's "The Catbird Seat" (p. 439)

3. "For Better or for Worse": Men as Mates in William Faulkner's "A Rose for Emily" (p. 205) and Zora Neale Hurston's "Sweat" (p. 372).

WRITING RESEARCH PAPERS

1. Find and read several stories about the war in Vietnam by authors other than Tim O'Brien, and do research on the climate and topography of the country. Write a research paper exploring the way O'Brien, in "The Things They Carried" (p. 257), and two or three other writers depict the setting and use it in a meaningful way in their stories.

2. Do some research into Yoknapatawpha County, the imaginary county in Mississippi in which most of William Faulkner's stories take place. Using "A Rose for Emily" (p. 205) and perhaps other stories by Faulkner, write a paper exploring how the locale he created becomes as real and meaningful a setting for his stories as an actual one.

I like short sentences. They are forceful and can get you out of big trouble.

Annie Dillard

(American Nonfiction Writer, Novelist, and Poet)

Tone, Style, and Irony

CHAPTER **9**

Attending to Expression and Attitude

The way things are said, their tone and style, matters—a lot. The way you phrase what you say and the tone of voice you use to express yourself can affect the meaning of your words and decidedly alter the message. "Nice shirt!" can mean you love it or you hate it, depending on how you say it. This chapter focuses on some of the key elements that create tone and style, and attends specifically to the tone of irony, in order to give you confidence as you encounter these elements in literary works.

APPROACHING THE READING

As you read the following short story the first time, you'll probably focus more on what's happening than on the tone and style. Most of us pay attention to such techniques on a second reading. So the second time, pay close attention to the way things are expressed—to particular word choices, for example, and to the way sentences are constructed. Recognize that using different words and sentence constructions would definitely alter the effect of what's said. Think about why the style seems appropriate and effective in conveying what happens to the central character and the feelings she experiences on hearing that her husband has died.

Kate Chopin   1851–1904

The Story of an Hour   [1894]

Knowing that Mrs. Mallard was afflicted with a heart trouble, great care was taken to break to her as gently as possible the news of her husband's death.

It was her sister Josephine who told her, in broken sentences; veiled hints that revealed in half concealing. Her husband's friend Richards was there, too, near her. It was he who had been in the newspaper office when intelligence of the railroad disaster was received, with Brently Mallard's name leading the list of "killed." He had only taken the time to assure himself of its truth by a second telegram, and had hastened to forestall any less careful, less tender friend in bearing the sad message.

APPROACHING THE AUTHOR

Kate Chopin was notorious for her unconventional manner of dress, especially her horseback-riding apparel, which was described as a "close fitting habit of blue

The Granger Collection, NYC

cloth, the train fastened up at the side to disclose an embroidered skirt, and the little feet encased in pretty boots with high heels."

For more about her, see page 1058.

She did not hear the story as many women have heard the same, with a paralyzed inability to accept its significance. She wept at once, with sudden, wild abandonment, in her sister's arms. When the storm of grief had spent itself she went away to her room alone. She would have no one follow her.

There stood, facing the open window, a comfortable, roomy armchair. Into this she sank, pressed down by a physical exhaustion that haunted her body and seemed to reach into her soul.

She could see in the open square before her house the tops of trees that were all aquiver with the new spring life. The delicious breath of rain was in the air. In the street below a peddler was crying his wares. The notes of a distant song which some one was singing reached her faintly, and countless sparrows were twittering in the eaves.

There were patches of blue sky showing here and there through the clouds that had met and piled one above the other in the west facing her window.

She sat with her head thrown back upon the cushion of the chair, quite motionless, except when a sob came up into her throat and shook her, as a child who has cried itself to sleep continues to sob in its dreams.

She was young, with a fair, calm face, whose lines bespoke repression and even a certain strength. But now there was a dull stare in her eyes, whose gaze was fixed away off yonder on one of those patches of blue sky. It was not a glance of reflection, but rather indicated a suspension of intelligent thought.

There was something coming to her and she was waiting for it, fearfully. What was it? She did not know; it was too subtle and elusive to name. But she felt it, creeping out of the sky, reaching toward her through the sounds, the scents, the color that filled the air.

Now her bosom rose and fell tumultuously. She was beginning to recognize 10 this thing that was approaching to possess her, and she was striving to beat it back with her will—as powerless as her two white slender hands would have been.

When she abandoned herself a little whispered word escaped her slightly parted lips. She said it over and over under her breath: "free, free, free!" The vacant stare and the look of terror that had followed it went from her eyes. They stayed keen and bright. Her pulses beat fast, and the coursing blood warmed and relaxed every inch of her body.

She did not stop to ask if it were or were not a monstrous joy that held her. A clear and exalted perception enabled her to dismiss the suggestion as trivial.

She knew that she would weep again when she saw the kind, tender hands folded in death; the face that had never looked save with love upon her, fixed and gray and dead. But she saw beyond that bitter moment a long procession of years to come that would belong to her absolutely. And she opened and spread her arms out to them in welcome.

There would be no one to live for her during those coming years; she would live for herself. There would be no powerful will bending hers in that blind persistence with which men and women believe they have a right to impose a private will upon a fellow-creature. A kind intention or a cruel intention made the act seem no less a crime as she looked upon it in that brief moment of illumination.

And yet she had loved him—sometimes. Often she had not. What did it 15 matter! What could love, the unsolved mystery, count for in face of this possession of self-assertion which she suddenly recognized as the strongest impulse of her being!

"Free! Body and soul free!" she kept whispering.

Josephine was kneeling before the closed door with her lips to the keyhole, imploring for admission. "Louise, open the door! I beg; open the door—you will make yourself ill. What are you doing, Louise? For heaven's sake open the door."

"Go away. I am not making myself ill." No; she was drinking in a very elixir of life through that open window.

Her fancy was running riot along those days ahead of her. Spring days, and summer days, and all sorts of days that would be her own. She breathed a quick prayer that life might be long. It was only yesterday she had thought with a shudder that life might be long.

She arose at length and opened the door to her sister's importunities. There 20 was a feverish triumph in her eyes, and she carried herself unwittingly like a goddess of Victory. She clasped her sister's waist, and together they descended the stairs. Richards stood waiting for them at the bottom.

Some one was opening the front door with a latchkey. It was Brently Mallard who entered, a little travel-stained, composedly carrying his grip-sack and umbrella. He had been far from the scene of accident, and did not even know there had been one. He stood amazed at Josephine's piercing cry; at Richards' quick motion to screen him from the view of his wife.

But Richards was too late.

When the doctors came they said she had died of heart disease—of joy that kills.

REFLECTING ON WHAT YOU'VE READ

1. A story about the tragic death of a husband would of course be serious in the "tone of voice" in which it is narrated. Consider how the tone is established in the first few paragraphs by the style the narrator uses in telling it. Consider the effect of the long sentences and short paragraphs, as well as the effect of word choice. The narrator's language may sound a bit formal. Even in the 1890s, words such as *afflicted, intelligence, forestall, bespoke,* and *fancy,* although part of an educated person's vocabulary, were seldom used in everyday speech. How would the depiction of Mrs. Mallard's situation feel different if the words and sentences seemed more conversational, like those in Alice Walker's "Everyday Use" (p. 152)?

2. Reflect on the character of Mrs. Mallard. What is she like? In what ways does the style suit or contribute to her character and the way we respond to her?

3. Do your feelings about her change as she begins to consider how her life will be different? How does the narrator's tone lead you to sympathize with her? Where do you find dramatic irony in the story? Do you think it is effective?

4. Consider the two single-sentence paragraphs at the end. Ask yourself what would be different if the two sentences were combined into a single paragraph. What is the effect of the very short next-to-last paragraph?

READING FOR TONE

Tone (that is, "tone of voice") is a significant aspect of all communication: It can add to, modify, or even invert the meaning of the words expressed. If someone says, "Please close the door behind you," it makes a big difference if the words are spoken as a simple reminder or as an angry demand. Therefore, when you listen to a story, it's important to pay attention to its tone. Tone in a literary work gets in, around, and behind the words to indicate the attitude the work takes toward the characters, setting, subject, or issues or the attitude a character reveals toward an issue, situation, setting, or another character.

Tone in Prose Writing   When we talk, our own tone is conveyed by the inflections in our voice. For a writer, spoken inflections, obviously, are not available, so tone must usually be created through style: Word choice, ways of phrasing, and kinds of comparisons all can convey an attitude (serious, sober, solemn, playful, excited, impassioned, and a host of other possibilities) toward what is being described or discussed. For example, as the mother in "Everyday Use" describes the way Dee used to read to her and

Maggie (p. 153), the word choice creates a tone that is not objective or positive, but rather bitter, almost angry: "She used to read to us *without pity*; *forcing* words, *lies*, other folks' habits, whole lives upon us two, sitting *trapped* and *ignorant* underneath her voice" [italics added] (p. 153; para. 11).

Complexity in Tone   A work can have a single tone, but more often it is mixed, with two or more tones juxtaposed or mingled or played off each other. And tone, especially when it is complex, can be challenging to determine. When Jig in "Hills Like White Elephants" says, "Everything tastes of licorice. Especially all the things you've waited so long for" (p. 198; para. 27), the tone is difficult to assess: Is it wistful? Angry? Bitter? Tone rarely can be summed up in a word or two. It needs to be described and discussed in a way that does justice to its full complexity.

Tone and Effect   How tone is handled can make a significant difference in the effect or meaning of a story. In "The Story of an Hour," our sympathy for Mrs. Mallard is aroused through the tone of the first two paragraphs, as she receives news of the sudden death of her husband. That tone and our sympathy continue in the following paragraphs, where she appears devastated by what she has heard. Then comes the twist: She isn't devastated, she's elated. At that point the story risks losing our sympathy. If the unexpectedness of her line "free, free, free!" would cause readers to laugh or even smile, the effect of the story would be destroyed. But the formal, dignified style prevents us from laughing and makes us sustain our serious response to her husband's death.

Responding Actively to Tone   "The Story of an Hour" goes on to say that, kind and loving though her husband had been toward her, his personality dominated their relationship, and she felt trapped. Instead of looking forward to her future, she dreaded what lay ahead. Our sympathy, thus, can turn to being happy for her when she spreads out her arms to welcome the "long procession of years to come that would belong to her absolutely." Readers who respond actively to the tone, as it changes along the way, will experience the full effect of the surprise ending: sadness and regret that she doesn't get to enjoy the new life she briefly glimpses.

READING FOR STYLE

An important ingredient in tone is *style*, the way the author handles words and sentences. Attention to style is valuable in analyzing literary works, but it is also helpful for you as a writer, as you seek to improve your writing style.

WORD CHOICE

Central to style is an author's *diction*, or word choice. A writer can employ any of several types of diction, and the kind selected by a published author, or by you as a student writer, affects the feel and impact of the writing. Style is the *way* the work presents its subject, which always needs to be appropriate to the occasion in which it is being used.

Formal Diction   The most striking thing about the diction in "The Story of an Hour" is its formality, the use of words such as *afflicted* in the first sentence and "had *hastened* to *forestall* any less careful, less tender friend in *bearing* the sad message" in the second paragraph. Try substituting more casual and common words and you'll feel the difference: "*hurried* to *get there first before* any less careful, less tender friend *brings* the sad message." The subject announced in the first sentence, "her husband's death," must be treated seriously, so a formal style is appropriate. The fact that the narrator refers to her as Mrs. Mallard rather than as Louise maintains a sense of dignity and respect—but perhaps a bit of stiffness as well, which seems to fit her traits as a character.

Other Kinds of Diction   Another type of diction can be characterized by its use of *concrete, everyday words*, like the diction in the first sentence of "Everyday Use": "I will wait for her in the yard that Maggie and I made so clean and wavy yesterday afternoon" (p. 152). Everyday language usually names things you can see and touch, such as "the *hard clay* is *swept* clean as a *floor* and the *fine sand* around the *edges* lined with *tiny, irregular grooves*" [italics added] ("Everyday Use," para. 1). Concrete language is essential for vivid descriptions (words that attend to particulars are often referred to as *images*). In contrast is **abstract language**, words that convey concepts rather than things. Note Dee's parting words of advice in "Everyday Use": "You just don't understand . . . Your *heritage* . . . make *something* of yourself . . . *a new day*" [italics added] (paras. 79–81). Words like *something* and *a new day* are vague, as if Dee can't express what they mean specifically. They suggest that it is she, not her mother or sister, who lacks the deeper understanding. Kinds of diction range much further, from the technical terminology used by experts in many fields all the way to slang and informal colloquialisms (*mighta, kinda,* "Love Letters," p. 10; para. 3). Be alert for various levels of language and to the different effects they create.

SENTENCE STRUCTURE

The way phrases and sentences are put together is crucial in creating an effective style. Writers can work with sentences of various lengths. They can craft them tightly or structure them in a loose, ambling way. They can use formal sentences or casual sentences. Here, too, appropriateness is key:

suitability to the speakers—both the narrator and the characters in dialogue—and to the occasion and the impact of events, settings, and moments.

Rhythm   An important ingredient of prose style is *rhythm*, the pattern and cadences in the flow and movement of sentences created by the arrangement of words and phrases. Thus we say that the rhythms in a piece of prose are, for example, fast, slow, syncopated, disjointed, smooth, halting, graceful, rough, deliberate, and so on. Listen for the smooth, graceful, almost wavelike rhythm in the following sentence from the opening paragraph of "Sonny's Blues": "I stared at it in the swinging lights of the subway car, and in the faces and bodies of the people, and in my own face, trapped in the darkness which roared outside" (p. 324). Notice the difference between that rhythm and the edgy, staccato rhythm of this sentence from the first paragraph of "Where Are You Going, Where Have You Been?": "Her mother, who noticed everything and knew everything and who hadn't much reason any longer to look at her own face, always scolded Connie about it" (p. 127).

Contrasting Sentence Styles   Paying attention to differences in language and sentence structure helps you develop your ear, enabling you to hear and feel on another level as you read, sensing what is often called the musicality of fine writing. Listen first to a sentence from William Faulkner's "A Rose for Emily" (p. 205) as an example of writing that is formal in its diction and *syntax* (sentence style):

> Alive, Miss Emily had been a tradition, a duty, and a care; a sort of hereditary obligation upon the town, dating from that day in 1894 when Colonel Sartoris, the mayor—he who fathered the edict that no Negro woman should appear on the streets without an apron—remitted her taxes, the dispensation dating from the death of her father on into perpetuity. (pp. 205–206; para. 3)

Writers' stylistic features are recognizable to readers who know their works well. Several things in the sentence above are typical of Faulkner's writing: the educated, exact diction; the long, languid sentences; phrases interjected into sentences; and the use of extra words ("a tradition, a duty, and a care") to get a point or feeling or image exactly right.

Contrast Faulkner's style with that of Ernest Hemingway, as in the opening paragraph of "Hills Like White Elephants":

> The hills across the valley of the Ebro were long and white. On this side there was no shade and no trees and the station was between two lines of rails in the sun. Close against the side of the station there was the warm shadow of the building and a curtain, made of strings of bamboo beads, hung across the open door into the bar, to keep out flies. The American and the girl with him sat at a table in the shade, outside the building. It was very hot and the express from Barcelona would come in forty minutes. It stopped at this junction for two minutes and went on to Madrid. (p. 197)

This passage is typical of Hemingway, with its ordinary, largely concrete, diction and its combinations of short, concise, tightly knit sentences, with cumulative longer sentences made up of short phrases connected by *and* or a comma.

Appropriateness   Appropriateness is key with sentence construction because it pertains to suitability of language to the speaker and the occasion. As with word choice, the sentences used in the narrative parts of a story must suit the narrator, and those used in dialogue must be appropriate for the characters using them and the contexts.

READING FOR IRONY

Style is particularly important for the more complex tone of *irony*: expression in which the writer or speaker creates a discrepancy or incongruity between what seems to be (appearance) and what is (reality). Because words used ironically don't mean what they literally say, readers have to be active in recognizing the difference between what is said and what is meant, and they need stylistic signals as a guide. Irony appears in a variety of forms. The paragraphs that follow describe the most important types of irony and indicate what to listen for to discern each type.

Verbal Irony   To notice *verbal irony*, be alert for when what is said is the opposite of what is meant ("Beautiful day!" when the weather is miserable). In "Where Are You Going, Where Have You Been?" (p. 127), the name *Arnold Friend* is an example. Arnold is anything but a friend to Connie. Verbal irony needs stylistic indicators that what is said is not to be taken in a straightforward way—listen for exaggerated and contradictory word choice, for example, or the sheer absurdity of what is said (it can't be straightforwardly true) or the cutting tone in which a word or phrase seems intended to be spoken.

Sarcasm   *Sarcasm* is an especially harsh, bitter, often hurtful form of irony. ("Oh, no, these eggs are fine. I *prefer* them black and fused to the plate.") Most sarcasm is like verbal irony in that the words say the opposite of what is meant; but not all verbal irony is sarcasm. Much verbal irony is more humorous, less personal and cutting than sarcasm is. The narrator's put-down of Sonny's friend, in "Sonny's Blues," "And how about you? You're pretty goddamn smart, I bet" (p. 326; para. 22), is sarcastic. If we miss such signals, we risk misreading the work.

Dramatic Irony   To notice dramatic irony, watch for when a character says or does something that a reader or audience realizes has a meaning opposite to what the character intends. You can detect dramatic irony by watching for when characters don't realize the full implications of what they are saying or of what happens to them and you see and understand more about it than they do. The last line of "The Story of an Hour" (p. 222) depends on dramatic irony: We know the doctors are wrong — Mrs. Mallard isn't killed by joy at seeing her husband alive and well but dies from shock and disappointment.

Situational Irony   To notice *situational irony*, watch for when a result or situation turns out very differently from what was expected or hoped for. Look for reversals — when something changes from what it used to be, what was expected, what was desired. In many cases, such a reversal is not only ironic in itself but also has ironic implications. In "Everyday Use," for example, as Dee insists on being given the quilts her grandmother made, Mama recalls how she "offered Dee (Wangero) a quilt when she went away to college. Then she had told me they were old-fashioned, out of style" (p. 152; para 67). Irony arises out of the altered situation, the change in Dee's attitude toward her heritage. And it's ironic when Dee accuses Mama of not appreciating her heritage when the situation clearly implies that it's Dee who lacks such understanding.

☑ CHECKLIST on Reading for Tone, Style, and Irony

❑ Listen for tone, the attitude toward the subject implied in a literary work, the "tone of voice" that indicates how what is said should be taken — seriously, ironically, sympathetically, condescendingly, and so on. Does the tone convey humor, affection, anger, frustration, horror, grief, concern, scorn, bitterness (to name only a few possibilities)?

❑ Be especially attentive to style — word selection, sentence construction, sentence rhythms — for its own sake and its effect on tone.

❑ Consider the effectiveness (appropriateness) of a story's narrative style and the style used in characters' dialogue and thoughts. When applicable, think about how style differs in various parts of a story.

❑ Be alert for irony, an expression involving a discrepancy between appearance and reality, between what is said and what is intended. Identify the kind of irony being employed:

• *Verbal irony:* a discrepancy between what is said and what is intended; saying the opposite of what is actually meant.

• *Dramatic irony:* a discrepancy between what a reader or audience knows and what is known by a speaker or character; usually the reader or audience knows more than the speaker or character or recognizes implications that the speaker or character is not aware of.

(continued)

> • *Situational irony:* a discrepancy between what is expected or what should be and what actually occurs; with situational irony, a result or situation turns out very differently from what was anticipated or hoped for.

FURTHER READING

APPROACHING THE READING

The following story is a prose adaptation of a poetic form known as *dramatic monologue* (see p. 489). As a monologue, it has one speaker, whom we overhear at a revealing moment. It is dramatic because the speaker addresses another character or characters, who do not speak (or whose responses are reported by the speaker, as here in para. 3). The speaker's words indicate what is going on in the scene and reveal insights into the speaker's character. In this story, the speaker is showing a new employee around the office, explaining where things are and how the office works. The monologue starts out very factual and ordinary, but gradually some things slip in that don't seem unusual to the speaker, but probably do to you. As you read, try keeping track of how the story makes you feel about the speaker and the office; after you finish reading, reflect on what attitude the author seems to have about the speaker and, by implication, about offices in general.

> **APPROACHING THE AUTHOR**
>
> **Daniel Orozco** says, as a writer, he always thinks in terms of pictures. The story is always in his head being blocked out precisely. Part of the precision and the concrete detail comes from that tendency to be visual.
>
> For more about him, see page 1075.

Daniel Orozco   b. 1958

Orientation   [1994]

Those are the offices and these are the cubicles. That's my cubicle there, and this is your cubicle. This is your phone. Never answer your phone. Let the Voicemail System answer it. This is your Voicemail System Manual. There are no personal phone calls allowed. We do, however, allow for emergencies. If you must make an emergency phone call, ask your supervisor first. If you can't find your supervisor, ask Phillip Spiers, who sits over there. He'll check with Clarissa Nicks, who sits over there. If you make an emergency phone call without asking, you may be let go.

These are your IN and OUT boxes. All the forms in your IN box must be logged in by the date shown in the upper left-hand corner, initialed by you in the upper right-hand corner, and distributed to the Processing Analyst whose name is numerically coded in the lower left-hand corner. The lower right-hand corner is left blank. Here's your Processing Analyst Numerical Code Index. And here's your Forms Processing Procedures Manual.

You must pace your work. What do I mean? I'm glad you asked that. We pace our work according to the eight-hour workday. If you have twelve hours of work in your IN box, for example, you must compress that work into the eight-hour day. If you have one hour of work in your IN box, you must expand that work to fill the eight-hour day. That was a good question. Feel free to ask questions. Ask too many questions, however, and you may be let go.

That is our receptionist. She is a temp. We go through receptionists here. They quit with alarming frequency. Be polite and civil to the temps. Learn their names, and invite them to lunch occasionally. But don't get close to them, as it only makes it more difficult when they leave. And they always leave. You can be sure of that.

The men's room is over there. The women's room is over there. John   5
LaFountaine, who sits over there, uses the women's room occasionally. He says it is accidental. We know better, but we let it pass. John LaFountaine is harmless, his forays into the forbidden territory of the women's room simply a benign thrill, a faint blip on the dull flat line of his life.

Russell Nash, who sits in the cubicle to your left, is in love with Amanda Pierce, who sits in the cubicle to your right. They ride the same bus together after work. For Amanda Pierce, it is just a tedious bus ride made less tedious by the idle nattering of Russell Nash. But for Russell Nash, it is the highlight of his day. It is the highlight of his life. Russell Nash has put on forty pounds, and grows fatter with each passing month, nibbling on chips and cookies while peeking glumly over the partitions at Amanda Pierce, and gorging himself at home on cold pizza and ice cream while watching adult videos on TV.

Amanda Pierce, in the cubicle to your right, has a six-year-old son named Jamie, who is autistic. Her cubicle is plastered from top to bottom with the boy's crayon artwork—sheet after sheet of precisely drawn concentric circles and ellipses, in black and yellow. She rotates them every other Friday. Be sure to comment on them. Amanda Pierce also has a husband, who is a lawyer. He subjects her to an escalating array of painful and humiliating sex games, to which Amanda Pierce reluctantly submits. She comes to work exhausted and freshly wounded every morning, wincing from the abrasions on her breasts, or the bruises on her abdomen, or the second-degree burns on the backs of her thighs.

But we're not supposed to know any of this. Do not let on. If you let on, you may be let go.

Amanda Pierce, who tolerates Russell Nash, is in love with Albert Bosch, whose office is over there. Albert Bosch, who only dimly registers Amanda Pierce's existence, has eyes only for Ellie Tapper, who sits over there. Ellie Tapper, who hates Albert Bosch, would walk through fire for Curtis Lance. But Curtis Lance hates Ellie Tapper. Isn't the world a funny place? Not in the haha sense, of course.

Anika Bloom sits in that cubicle. Last year, while reviewing quarterly reports 10
in a meeting with Barry Hacker, Anika Bloom's left palm began to bleed. She
fell into a trance, stared into her hand, and told Barry Hacker when and how
his wife would die. We laughed it off. She was, after all, a new employee. But
Barry Hacker's wife is dead. So unless you want to know exactly when and how
you'll die, never talk to Anika Bloom.

Colin Heavey sits in that cubicle over there. He was new once, just like you.
We warned him about Anika Bloom. But at last year's Christmas Potluck, he
felt sorry for her when he saw that no one was talking to her. Colin Heavey
brought her a drink. He hasn't been himself since. Colin Heavey is doomed.
There's nothing he can do about it, and we are powerless to help him. Stay away
from Colin Heavey. Never give any of your work to him. If he asks to do something, tell him you have to check with me. If he asks again, tell him I haven't
gotten back to you.

This is the Fire Exit. There are several on this floor, and they are marked
accordingly. We have a Floor Evacuation Review every three months, and an
Escape Route Quiz once a month. We have our Biannual Fire Drill twice a year,
and our Annual Earthquake Drill once a year. These are precautions only. These
things never happen.

For your information, we have a comprehensive health plan. Any cata-
strophic illness, any unforeseen tragedy is completely covered. All dependents
are completely covered. Larry Bagdikian, who sits over there, has six daughters.
If anything were to happen to any of his girls, or to all of them, if all six were
to simultaneously fall victim to illness or injury—stricken with a hideous
degenerative muscle disease or some rare toxic blood disorder, sprayed with
semiautomatic gunfire while on a class field trip, or attacked in their bunk beds
by some prowling nocturnal lunatic—if any of this were to pass, Larry's girls
would all be taken care of. Larry Bagdikian would not have to pay one dime. He
would have nothing to worry about.

We also have a generous vacation and sick leave policy. We have an excellent disability insurance plan. We have a stable and profitable pension fund. We
get group discounts for the symphony, and block seating at the ballpark. We get
commuter ticket books for the bridge. We have Direct Deposit. We are all members of Costco.

This is our kitchenette. And this, this is our Mr. Coffee. We have a coffee 15
pool, into which we each pay two dollars a week for coffee, filters, sugar, and
CoffeeMate. If you prefer Cremora or half-and-half to CoffeeMate, there is a
special pool for three dollars a week. If you prefer Sweet'n Low to sugar, there
is a special pool for two-fifty a week. We do not do decaf. You are allowed to
join the coffee pool of your choice, but you are not allowed to touch the
Mr. Coffee.

This is the microwave oven. You are allowed to *heat* food in the microwave
oven. You are not, however, allowed to *cook* food in the microwave oven.

We get one hour for lunch. We also get one fifteen-minute break in the
morning, and one fifteen-minute break in the afternoon. Always take your

breaks. If you skip a break, it is gone forever. For your information, your break is a privilege, not a right. If you abuse the break policy, we are authorized to rescind your breaks. Lunch, however, is a right, not a privilege. If you abuse the lunch policy, our hands will be tied, and we will be forced to look the other way. We will not enjoy that.

This is the refrigerator. You may put your lunch in it. Barry Hacker, who sits over there, steals food from this refrigerator. His petty theft is an outlet for his grief. Last New Year's Eve, while kissing his wife, a blood vessel burst in her brain. Barry Hacker's wife was two months pregnant at the time, and lingered in a coma for a half a year before dying. It was a tragic loss for Barry Hacker. He hasn't been himself since. Barry Hacker's wife was a beautiful woman. She was also completely covered. Barry Hacker did not have to pay one dime. But his dead wife haunts him. She haunts all of us. We have seen her, reflected in the monitors of our computers, moving past our cubicles. We have seen the dim shadow of her face in our photocopies. She pencils herself in the receptionist's appointment book, with the notation: To see Barry Hacker. She has left messages in the receptionist's Voicemail box, messages garbled by the electronic chirrups and buzzes in the phone line, her voice echoing from an immense distance within the ambient hum. But the voice is hers. And beneath her voice, beneath the tidal *whoosh* of static and hiss, the gurgling and crying of a baby can be heard.

In any case, if you bring a lunch, put a little something extra in the bag for Barry Hacker. We have four Barrys in this office. Isn't that a coincidence?

This is Matthew Payne's office. He is our Unit Manager, and his door is always closed. We have never seen him, and you will never see him. But he is here. You can be sure of that. He is all around us.

This is the Custodian's Closet. You have no business in the Custodian's Closet.

And this, this is our Supplies Cabinet. If you need supplies, see Curtis Lance. He will log you in on the Supplies Cabinet Authorization Log, then give you a Supplies Authorization Slip. Present your pink copy of the Supplies Authorization Slip to Ellie Tapper. She will log you in on the Supplies Cabinet Key Log, then give you the key. Because the Supplies Cabinet is located outside the Unit Manager's office, you must be very quiet. Gather your supplies quietly. The Supplies Cabinet is divided into four sections. Section One contains letterhead stationery, blank paper and envelopes, memo and note pads, and so on. Section Two contains pens and pencils and typewriter and printer ribbons, and the like. In Section Three we have erasers, correction fluids, transparent tapes, glue sticks, et cetera. And in Section Four we have paper clips and push pins and scissors and razor blades. And here are the spare blades for the shredder. Do not touch the shredder, which is located over there. The shredder is of no concern to you.

Gwendolyn Stich sits in that office there. She is crazy about penguins, and collects penguin knickknacks: penguin posters and coffee mugs and stationery, penguin stuffed animals, penguin jewelry, penguin sweaters and T-shirts and socks. She has a pair of penguin fuzzy slippers she wears when working late at

20

the office. She has a tape cassette of penguin sounds which she listens to for relaxation. Her favorite colors are black and white. She has personalized license plates that read PEN GWEN. Every morning, she passes through all the cubicles to wish each of us a *good* morning. She brings Danish on Wednesdays for Hump Day morning break, and doughnuts on Fridays for TGIF afternoon break. She organizes the Annual Christmas Potluck, and is in charge of the Birthday List. Gwendolyn Stich's door is always open to all of us. She will always lend an ear, and put in a good word for you; she will always give you a hand, or the shirt off her back, or a shoulder to cry on. Because her door is always open, she hides and cries in a stall in the women's room. And John LaFountaine—who, enthralled when a woman enters, sits quietly in his stall with his knees to his chest—John LaFountaine has heard her vomiting in there. We have come upon Gwendolyn Stich huddled in the stairwell, shivering in the updraft, sipping a Diet Mr. Pibb and hugging her knees. She does not let any of this interfere with her work. If it interfered with her work, she might have to be let go.

Kevin Howard sits in that cubicle over there. He is a serial killer, the one they call the Carpet Cutter, responsible for the mutilations across town. We're not supposed to know that, so do not let on. Don't worry. His compulsion inflicts itself on strangers only, and the routine established is elaborate and unwavering. The victim must be a white male, a young adult no older than thirty, heavyset, with dark hair and eyes, and the like. The victim must be chosen at random, before sunset, from a public place; the victim is followed home, and must put up a struggle; et cetera. The carnage inflicted is precise: the angle and direction of the incisions; the layering of skin and muscle tissue; the rearrangement of the visceral organs; and so on. Kevin Howard does not let any of this interfere with his work. He is, in fact, our fastest typist. He types as if he were on fire. He has a secret crush on Gwendolyn Stich, and leaves a red-foil-wrapped Hershey's Kiss on her desk every afternoon. But he hates Anika Bloom, and keeps well away from her. In his presence, she has uncontrollable fits of shaking and trembling. Her left palm does not stop bleeding.

In any case, when Kevin Howard gets caught, act surprised. Say that he   25 seemed like a nice person, a bit of a loner, perhaps, but always quiet and polite.

This is the photocopier room. And this, this is our view. It faces southwest. West is down there, toward the water. North is back there. Because we are on the seventeenth floor, we are afforded a magnificent view. Isn't it beautiful? It overlooks the park, where the tops of those trees are. You can see a segment of the bay between those two buildings there. You can see the sun set in the gap between those two buildings over there. You can see this building reflected in the glass panels of that building across the way. There. See? That's you, waving. And look there. There's Anika Bloom in the kitchenette, waving back.

Enjoy this view while photocopying. If you have problems with the photocopier, see Russell Nash. If you have any questions, ask your supervisor. If you can't find your supervisor, ask Phillip Spiers. He sits over there. He'll check with Clarissa Nicks. She sits over there. If you can't find them, feel free to ask me. That's my cubicle. I sit in there.

REFLECTING ON WHAT YOU'VE READ

1. What is this speaker like? How you feel about the speaker? What do you make of the choice of monologue as the story's form? What is it about the monologue that contributes to the speaker's character?

2. The speaker is talking to "you," another character who is present though we know nothing about her or him. Do you think the use of "you" ever creates the impression that the speaker could be addressing the reader? If so, try to point out specific places where that happens. Why do you think that could or could not be part of the intended effect of the story?

3. Clearly the setting is important. But why? Consider whether the story is mainly about this one office, or if it could also be about the corporate culture of offices more generally.

4. The speaker's tone is matter-of-fact and sincere, but the story's tone is more complex. What kinds of tone do you find: Humor? Sadness? Irony? A mix? Other? Support your answer by pointing out specific examples and the way they contribute to the story's effect.

APPROACHING THE READING

The following story, like Toni Cade Bambara's "The Lesson" (p. 181), is about lessons an adult wants a young girl to learn and the young girl's resistance to them. In it too the style and tone are those of a girl with a definite "attitude." As you reread or review the story, focus on word choice, sentence constructions, and rhythms, and listen for tone — again, both the attitude of the speaker (toward her mother and the rest of the world) and the attitude of the story toward the speaker. Think about whether the girl ends up more or less like (and likeable than) Sylvia in "The Lesson."

Amy Tan   b. 1952

Two Kinds   [1989]

My mother believed you could be anything you wanted to be in America. You could open a restaurant. You could work for the government and get good retirement. You could buy a house with almost no money down. You could become rich. You could become instantly famous.

"Of course you can be prodigy, too," my mother told me when I was nine. "You can be best anything. What does Auntie Lindo know? Her daughter, she is only best tricky."

America was where all my mother's hopes lay. She had come here in 1949 after losing everything in China: her mother and father, her family home, her

APPROACHING THE AUTHOR

When **Amy Tan** began her career by writing business manuals and speeches for executives,

Mark Mainz/Getty

she felt pressured to write under an American-sounding pseudonym, so she chose "May Brown" — she rearranged *Amy* to get *May*, and *Brown* is a synonym for *Tan*.

For more about her, see page 1081.

first husband, and two daughters, twin baby girls. But she never looked back with regret. There were so many ways for things to get better.

We didn't immediately pick the right kind of prodigy. At first my mother thought I could be a Chinese Shirley Temple.° We'd watch Shirley's old movies on TV as though they were training films. My mother would poke my arm and say, *"Ni kan"* — You watch. And I would see Shirley tapping her feet, or singing a sailor song, or pursing her lips into a very round O while saying, "Oh my goodness."

"Ni kan," said my mother as Shirley's eyes flooded with tears. "You already   5 know how. Don't need talent for crying!"

Soon after my mother got this idea about Shirley Temple, she took me to a beauty training school in the Mission district and put me in the hands of a student who could barely hold the scissors without shaking. Instead of getting big fat curls, I emerged with an uneven mass of crinkly black fuzz. My mother dragged me off to the bathroom and tried to wet down my hair.

"You look like Negro Chinese," she lamented, as if I had done this on purpose.

The instructor of the beauty training school had to lop off these soggy clumps to make my hair even again. "Peter Pan is very popular these days," the instructor assured my mother. I now had hair the length of a boy's, with straight-across bangs that hung at a slant two inches above my eyebrows. I liked the haircut and it made me actually look forward to my future fame.

In fact, in the beginning, I was just as excited as my mother, maybe even more so. I pictured this prodigy part of me as many different images, trying each one on for size. I was a dainty ballerina girl standing by the curtains, waiting to hear the right music that would send me floating on my tiptoes. I was like the Christ child lifted out of the straw manger, crying with holy indignity. I was Cinderella stepping from her pumpkin carriage with sparkly cartoon music filling the air.

In all of my imaginings, I was filled with a sense that I would soon become   10 *perfect*. My mother and father would adore me. I would be beyond reproach. I would never feel the need to sulk for anything.

But sometimes the prodigy in me became impatient. "If you don't hurry up and get me out of here, I'm disappearing for good," it warned. "And then you'll always be nothing."

Shirley Temple: American actress, singer, and dancer (1928–2014), most famous as a child film star, "America's Little Darling."

Every night after dinner, my mother and I would sit at the Formica kitchen table. She would present new tests, taking her examples from stories of amazing children she had read in *Ripley's Believe It or Not*, or *Good Housekeeping*, *Reader's Digest*, and a dozen other magazines she kept in a pile in our bathroom. My mother got these magazines from people whose houses she cleaned. And since she cleaned many houses each week, we had a great assortment. She would look through them all, searching for stories about remarkable children.

The first night she brought out a story about a three-year-old boy who knew the capitals of all the states and even most of the European countries. A teacher was quoted as saying the little boy could also pronounce the names of the foreign cities correctly.

"What's the capital of Finland?" my mother asked me, looking at the magazine story.

All I knew was the capital of California, because Sacramento was the name 15 of the street we lived on in Chinatown. "Nairobi!" I guessed, saying the most foreign word I could think of. She checked to see if that was possibly one way to pronounce "Helsinki" before showing me the answer.

The tests got harder—multiplying numbers in my head, finding the queen of hearts in a deck of cards, trying to stand on my head without using my hands, predicting the daily temperatures in Los Angeles, New York, and London.

One night I had to look at a page from the Bible for three minutes and then report everything I could remember. "Now Jehoshaphat had riches and honor in abundance and . . . that's all I remember, Ma," I said.

And after seeing my mother's disappointed face once again, something inside of me began to die. I hated the tests, the raised hopes and failed expectations. Before going to bed that night, I looked in the mirror above the bathroom sink and when I saw only my face staring back—and that it would always be this ordinary face—I began to cry. Such a sad, ugly girl! I made high-pitched noises like a crazed animal, trying to scratch out the face in the mirror.

And then I saw what seemed to be the prodigy side of me—because I had never seen that face before. I looked at my reflection, blinking so I could see more clearly. The girl staring back at me was angry, powerful. This girl and I were the same. I had new thoughts, willful thoughts, or rather thoughts filled with lots of won'ts. I won't let her change me, I promised myself. I won't be what I'm not.

So now on nights when my mother presented her tests, I performed list- 20 lessly, my head propped on one arm. I pretended to be bored. And I was. I got so bored I started counting the bellows of the foghorns out on the bay while my mother drilled me in other areas. The sound was comforting and reminded me of the cow jumping over the moon. And the next day, I played a game with myself, seeing if my mother would give up on me before eight bellows. After a while I usually counted only one, maybe two bellows at most. At last she was beginning to give up hope.

Two or three months had gone by without any mention of my being a prodigy again. And then one day my mother was watching *The Ed Sullivan Show* on TV. The TV was old and the sound kept shorting out. Every time my mother got halfway up from the sofa to adjust the set, the sound would go back on and Ed would be talking. As soon as she sat down, Ed would go silent again. She got up, the TV broke into loud piano music. She sat down. Silence. Up and down, back and forth, quiet and loud. It was like a stiff embraceless dance between her and the TV set. Finally she stood by the set with her hand on the sound dial.

She seemed entranced by the music, a little frenzied piano piece with this mesmerizing quality, sort of quick passages and then teasing lilting ones before it returned to the quick playful parts.

"*Ni kan,*" my mother said, calling me over with hurried hand gestures, "Look here."

I could see why my mother was fascinated by the music. It was being pounded out by a little Chinese girl, about nine years old, with a Peter Pan haircut. The girl had the sauciness of a Shirley Temple. She was proudly modest like a proper Chinese child. And she also did this fancy sweep of a curtsy, so that the fluffy skirt of her white dress cascaded slowly to the floor like the petals of a large carnation.

In spite of these warning signs, I wasn't worried. Our family had no piano 25 and we couldn't afford to buy one, let alone reams of sheet music and piano lessons. So I could be generous in my comments when my mother bad-mouthed the little girl on TV.

"Play note right, but doesn't sound good! No singing sound," complained my mother.

"What are you picking on her for?" I said carelessly. "She's pretty good. Maybe she's not the best, but she's trying hard." I knew almost immediately I would be sorry I said that.

"Just like you," she said. "Not the best. Because you not trying." She gave a little huff as she let go of the sound dial and sat down on the sofa.

The little Chinese girl sat down also to play an encore of "Anitra's Dance" by Grieg. I remember the song, because later on I had to learn how to play it.

Three days after watching *The Ed Sullivan Show*, my mother told me what 30 my schedule would be for piano lessons and piano practice. She had talked to Mr. Chong, who lived on the first floor of our apartment building. Mr. Chong was a retired piano teacher and my mother had traded housecleaning services for weekly lessons and a piano for me to practice on every day, two hours a day, from four until six.

When my mother told me this, I felt as though I had been sent to hell. I whined and then kicked my foot a little when I couldn't stand it anymore.

"Why don't you like me the way I am? I'm *not* a genius! I can't play the piano. And even if I could, I wouldn't go on TV if you paid me a million dollars!" I cried.

My mother slapped me. "Who ask you be genius?" she shouted. "Only ask you be your best. For you sake. You think I want you be genius? Hnnh! What for! Who ask you!"

"So ungrateful," I heard her mutter in Chinese. "If she had as much talent as she has temper, she would be famous now."

Mr. Chong, whom I secretly nicknamed Old Chong, was very strange, al- 35
ways tapping his fingers to the silent music of an invisible orchestra. He looked
ancient in my eyes. He had lost most of the hair on top of his head and he wore
thick glasses and had eyes that always looked tired and sleepy. But he must have
been younger than I thought, since he lived with his mother and was not yet
married.

I met Old Lady Chong once and that was enough. She had this peculiar
smell like a baby that had done something in its pants. And her fingers felt like
a dead person's, like an old peach I once found in the back of the refrigerator;
the skin just slid off the meat when I picked it up.

I soon found out why Old Chong had retired from teaching piano. He was
deaf. "Like Beethoven!" he shouted to me. "We're both listening only in our
head!" And he would start to conduct his frantic silent sonatas.

Our lessons went like this. He would open the book and point to different
things, explaining their purpose: "Key! Treble! Bass! No sharps or flats! So this
is C major! Listen now and play after me!"

And then he would play the C scale a few times, a simple chord, and then, as
if inspired by an old, unreachable itch, he gradually added more notes and running
trills and a pounding bass until the music was really something quite grand.

I would play after him, the simple scale, the simple chord, and then I just 40
played some nonsense that sounded like a cat running up and down on top of
garbage cans. Old Chong smiled and applauded and then said, "Very good! But
now you must learn to keep time!"

So that's how I discovered that Old Chong's eyes were too slow to keep up
with the wrong notes I was playing. He went through the motions in half-time.
To help me keep rhythm, he stood behind me, pushing down on my right shoulder for every beat. He balanced pennies on top of my wrists so I would keep
them still as I slowly played scales and arpeggios. He had me curve my hand
around an apple and keep that shape when playing chords. He marched stiffly
to show me how to make each finger dance up and down, staccato like an obedient little soldier.

He taught me all these things, and that was how I also learned I could be
lazy and get away with mistakes, lots of mistakes. If I hit the wrong notes because I hadn't practiced enough, I never corrected myself. I just kept playing in
rhythm. And Old Chong kept conducting his own private reverie.

So maybe I never really gave myself a fair chance. I did pick up the basics
pretty quickly, and I might have become a good pianist at that young age. But I
was so determined not to try, not to be anybody different that I learned to play
only the most ear-splitting preludes, the most discordant hymns.

Over the next year, I practiced like this, dutifully in my own way. And then
one day I heard my mother and her friend Lindo Jong both talking in a loud brag-
ging tone of voice so others could hear. It was after church, and I was leaning
against the brick wall wearing a dress with stiff white petticoats. Auntie Lindo's
daughter, Waverly, who was about my age, was standing farther down the wall
about five feet away. We had grown up together and shared all the closeness of two
sisters squabbling over crayons and dolls. In other words, for the most part, we

hated each other. I thought she was snotty. Waverly Jong had gained a certain amount of fame as "Chinatown's Littlest Chinese Chess Champion."

"She bring home too many trophy," lamented Auntie Lindo that Sunday. 45 "All day she play chess. All day I have no time do nothing but dust off her winnings." She threw a scolding look at Waverly, who pretended not to see her.

"You lucky you don't have this problem," said Auntie Lindo with a sigh to my mother.

And my mother squared her shoulders and bragged: "Our problem worser than yours. If we ask Jing-mei wash dish, she hear nothing but music. It's like you can't stop this natural talent."

And right then, I was determined to put a stop to her foolish pride.

A few weeks later, Old Chong and my mother conspired to have me play in a talent show which would be held in the church hall. By then, my parents had saved up enough to buy me a secondhand piano, a black Wurlitzer spinet with a scarred bench. It was the showpiece of our living room.

For the talent show, I was to play a piece called "Pleading Child" from 50 Schumann's *Scenes from Childhood*. It was a simple, moody piece that sounded more difficult than it was. I was supposed to memorize the whole thing, playing the repeat parts twice to make the piece sound longer. But I dawdled over it, playing a few bars and then cheating, looking up to see what notes followed. I never really listened to what I was playing. I daydreamed about being somewhere else, about being someone else.

The part I liked to practice best was the fancy curtsy: right foot out, touch the rose on the carpet with a pointed foot, sweep to the side, left leg bends, look up and smile.

My parents invited all the couples from the Joy Luck Club to witness my debut. Auntie Lindo and Uncle Tin were there. Waverly and her two older brothers had also come. The first two rows were filled with children both younger and older than I was. The littlest ones got to go first. They recited simple nursery rhymes, squawked out tunes on miniature violins, twirled Hula Hoops, pranced in pink ballet tutus, and when they bowed or curtsied, the audience would sigh in unison, "Awww," and then clap enthusiastically.

When my turn came, I was very confident. I remember my childish excitement. It was as if I knew, without a doubt, that the prodigy side of me really did exist. I had no fear whatsoever, no nervousness. I remember thinking to myself, This is it! This is it! I looked out over the audience, at my mother's blank face, my father's yawn, Auntie Lindo's stiff-lipped smile, Waverly's sulky expression. I had on a white dress layered with sheets of lace, and a pink bow in my Peter Pan haircut. As I sat down I envisioned people jumping to their feet and Ed Sullivan rushing up to introduce me to everyone on TV.

And I started to play. It was so beautiful. I was so caught up in how lovely I looked that at first I didn't worry how I would sound. So it was a surprise to me when I hit the first wrong note and I realized something didn't sound quite right. And then I hit another and another followed that. A chill started at the top of my head and began to trickle down. Yet I couldn't stop playing, as though my hands were bewitched. I kept thinking my fingers would adjust themselves back, like a train switching to the right track. I played this strange jumble through two repeats, the sour notes staying with me all the way to the end.

When I stood up, I discovered my legs were shaking. Maybe I had just been 55 nervous and the audience, like Old Chong, had seen me go through the right motions and had not heard anything wrong at all. I swept my right foot out, went down on my knee, looked up and smiled. The room was quiet, except for Old Chong, who was beaming and shouting, "Bravo! Bravo! Well done!" But then I saw my mother's face, her stricken face. The audience clapped weakly, and as I walked back to my chair, with my whole face quivering as I tried not to cry, I heard a little boy whisper loudly to his mother, "That was awful," and the mother whispered back, "Well, she certainly tried."

And now I realized how many people were in the audience, the whole world it seemed. I was aware of eyes burning into my back. I felt the shame of my mother and father as they sat stiffly throughout the rest of the show.

We could have escaped during intermission. Pride and some strange sense of honor must have anchored my parents to their chairs. And so we watched it all: the eighteen-year-old boy with a fake mustache who did a magic show and juggled flaming hoops while riding a unicycle. The breasted girl with white makeup who sang from *Madama Butterfly* and got honorable mention. And the eleven-year-old boy who won first prize playing a tricky violin song that sounded like a busy bee.

After the show, the Hsus, the Jongs, and the St. Clairs from the Joy Luck Club came up to my mother and father.

"Lots of talented kids," Auntie Lindo said vaguely, smiling broadly.

"That was somethin' else," said my father, and I wondered if he was refer- 60 ring to me in a humorous way, or whether he even remembered what I had done.

Waverly looked at me and shrugged her shoulders. "You aren't a genius like me," she said matter-of-factly. And if I hadn't felt so bad, I would have pulled her braids and punched her stomach.

But my mother's expression was what devastated me: a quiet, blank look that said she had lost everything. I felt the same way, and it seemed as if everybody were now coming up, like gawkers at the scene of an accident, to see what parts were actually missing. When we got on the bus to go home, my father was humming the busy-bee tune and my mother was silent. I kept thinking she wanted to wait until we got home before shouting at me. But when my father unlocked the door to our apartment, my mother walked in and then went to the back, into the bedroom. No accusations. No blame. And in a way, I felt disappointed. I had been waiting for her to start shouting, so I could shout back and cry and blame her for all my misery.

I assumed my talent-show fiasco meant I never had to play the piano again. But two days later, after school, my mother came out of the kitchen and saw me watching TV.

"Four clock," she reminded me as if it were any other day. I was stunned, as though she were asking me to go through the talent-show torture again. I wedged myself more tightly in front of the TV.

"Turn off TV," she called from the kitchen five minutes later. 65

I didn't budge. And then I decided. I didn't have to do what my mother said anymore. I wasn't her slave. This wasn't China. I had listened to her before and look what happened. She was the stupid one.

She came out from the kitchen and stood in the arched entryway of the living room. "Four clock," she said once again, louder.

"I'm not going to play anymore," I said nonchalantly. "Why should I? I'm not a genius."

She walked over and stood in front of the TV. I saw her chest was heaving up and down in an angry way.

"No!" I said, and I now felt stronger, as if my true self had finally emerged. 70 So this was what had been inside me all along.

"No! I won't!" I screamed.

She yanked me by the arm, pulled me off the floor, snapped off the TV. She was frighteningly strong, half pulling, half carrying me toward the piano as I kicked the throw rugs under my feet. She lifted me up and onto the hard bench. I was sobbing by now, looking at her bitterly. Her chest was heaving even more and her mouth was open, smiling crazily as if she were pleased I was crying.

"You want me to be someone that I'm not!" I sobbed. "I'll never be the kind of daughter you want me to be!"

"Only two kinds of daughters," she shouted in Chinese. "Those who are obedient and those who follow their own mind! Only one kind of daughter can live in this house. Obedient daughter!"

"Then I wish I wasn't your daughter. I wish you weren't my mother," 75 I shouted. As I said these things I got scared. It felt like worms and toads and slimy things crawling out of my chest, but it also felt good, as if this awful side of me had surfaced, at last.

"Too late change this," said my mother shrilly.

And I could sense her anger rising to its breaking point. I wanted to see it spill over. And that's when I remembered the babies she had lost in China, the ones we never talked about. "Then I wish I'd never been born!" I shouted. "I wish I were dead! Like them."

It was as if I had said the magic words. Alakazam! — and her face went blank, her mouth closed, her arms went slack, and she backed out of the room, stunned, as if she were blowing away like a small brown leaf, thin, brittle, lifeless.

It was not the only disappointment my mother felt in me. In the years that followed, I failed her so many times, each time asserting my own will, my right to fall short of expectations. I didn't get straight As. I didn't become class president. I didn't get into Stanford. I dropped out of college.

For unlike my mother, I did not believe I could be anything I wanted to be. 80 I could only be me.

And for all those years, we never talked about the disaster at the recital or my terrible accusations afterward at the piano bench. All that remained unchecked, like a betrayal that was now unspeakable. So I never found a way to ask her why she had hoped for something so large that failure was inevitable.

And even worse, I never asked her what frightened me the most: Why had she given up hope?

For after our struggle at the piano, she never mentioned my playing again. The lessons stopped. The lid to the piano was closed, shutting out the dust, my misery, and her dreams.

So she surprised me. A few years ago, she offered to give me the piano, for my thirtieth birthday. I had not played in all those years. I saw the offer as a sign of forgiveness, a tremendous burden removed.

"Are you sure?" I asked shyly. "I mean, won't you and Dad miss it?"   85

"No, this your piano," she said firmly. "Always your piano. You only one can play."

"Well, I probably can't play anymore," I said. "It's been years."

"You pick up fast," said my mother, as if she knew this was certain. "You have natural talent. You could been genius if you want to."

"No I couldn't."

"You just not trying," said my mother. And she was neither angry nor   90 sad. She said it as if to announce a fact that could never be disproved. "Take it," she said.

But I didn't at first. It was enough that she had offered it to me. And after that, every time I saw it in my parents' living room, standing in front of the bay windows, it made me feel proud, as if it were a shiny trophy I had won back.

Last week I sent a tuner over to my parents' apartment and had the piano reconditioned, for purely sentimental reasons. My mother had died a few months before and I had been getting things in order for my father, a little bit at a time. I put the jewelry in special silk pouches. The sweaters she had knitted in yellow, pink, bright orange—all the colors I hated—I put those in moth-proof boxes. I found some old Chinese silk dresses, the kind with little slits up the sides. I rubbed the old silk against my skin, then wrapped them in tissue and decided to take them home with me.

After I had the piano tuned, I opened the lid and touched the keys. It sounded even richer than I remembered. Really, it was a very good piano. Inside the bench were the same exercise notes with handwritten scales, the same secondhand music books with their covers held together with yellow tape.

I opened up the Schumann book to the dark little piece I had played at the recital. It was on the left-hand side of the page, "Pleading Child." It looked more difficult than I remembered. I played a few bars, surprised at how easily the notes came back to me.

And for the first time, or so it seemed, I noticed the piece on the right-hand   95 side. It was called "Perfectly Contented." I tried to play this one as well. It had a lighter melody but the same flowing rhythm and turned out to be quite easy. "Pleading Child" was shorter but slower; "Perfectly Contented" was longer, but faster. And after I played them both a few times, I realized they were two halves of the same song.

REFLECTING ON WHAT YOU'VE READ

1. Describe Tan's style in "Two Kinds." Look closely at the style of the narrative passages, such as paragraphs 1, 9, and 19–20. Notice the word choices, sentence structures, rhythm. Think about how the narrator's style contributes to characterization—of her as a young girl and of her as a woman looking back at the events. Consider the style used for the mother. How does her broken English and incorporation of occasional Chinese phrases contribute to her characterization and to the effect of the story?

2. Consider the importance of various tones in the story. How is the attitude of the young girl toward her mother revealed? How does the attitude of the narrator toward her mother, on looking back at her, differ from her earlier attitude, and how is it brought out? Pick out examples of irony and of humor in the story. What do they contribute to its tone and overall effect?

3. Do you think the use of Shirley Temple in the story is effective or appropriate? What ironies can you think of in using her? What issues are involved in holding up a figure from one culture as a model for a person from another?

4. "And then you'll always be nothing," warns the prodigy side of the speaker (para. 11). What is ironic in this warning? How do this fear of failure and the often required "make something of yourself" play out in this story? What are the cultural implications of these ideas? In what ways do they conflict with other ideas embedded in your or any culture?

5. Reflect on and be ready to comment on style and tone in the final paragraph. Why, for you, is the ending satisfying or unsatisfying, effective or ineffective?

RESPONDING THROUGH Writing

WRITING ABOUT TONE, STYLE, AND IRONY

Journal Entries

1. Keep a list of the various tones of voice you hear people use during a day. Write a journal entry on what you learn about the importance of tone in communication.

2. In the course of a day, listen and watch for the word *style* in regard to anything—music, clothes, sports, and so on. Pay attention to radio voices, TV shows, advertisements, what you say, and what you overhear other people saying. Write a journal entry describing several styles you discover. How can the ways in which words are used elsewhere help clarify their uses in literature?

3. In your journal, list instances of irony that you notice during a day. Discuss how and why verbal irony in particular was used and how it affected the people at whom it was directed.

Literary Analysis Papers

4. Write a paper examining the related effect of humor and handling of style in James Thurber's "The Catbird Seat" (p. 439).

5. Write a paper analyzing the relation of style, tone, and theme in Jamaica Kincaid's "Girl" (p. 298), Ralph Ellison's "Battle Royal" (p. 271), or Ha Jin's "Saboteur" (p. 381).

6. Write a paper discussing the importance of irony in Flannery O'Connor's "A Good Man Is Hard to Find" (p. 159), Joyce Carol Oates's "Where Are You Going, Where Have You Been?" (p. 127), or ZZ Packer's "Brownies" (p. 411).

Comparison-Contrast Papers

7. Write a paper exploring how Katherine Min's use of comparisons and contrasts in "Courting a Monk" (p. 394) — between Gina and her father, for example, or Micah and Gina's father, or Gina and Micah — contribute to its richness of tone and theme.

8. Write a paper in which you compare and contrast style, tone, and theme in Margaret Atwood's "Happy Endings" (p. 321) and Edwidge Danticat's "New York Day Women" (p. 353).

▶ **TIPS for Writing about Tone, Style, and Irony**

- **Concentrating on tone.** Tone can be the central topic of a paper if it is a crucial element in achieving the effect of a story or novel. The outline for such an analysis might include two or three aspects or techniques used to create tone(s) or two or three points about how tone alters or shifts in significant ways in the work.

- **Including style.** Prose style is one of the most challenging and rewarding topics to write about, requiring close, careful analysis and precise, detailed explanations. Include it in a paper only when the style is unusual or important, perhaps bringing it up in passing or treating it in one paragraph, as an aspect contributing to a broader analysis of the story. Be sure to discuss its effect in the story and its connections to other elements.

- **Centering on style.** In some cases, when style is unusually complex or distinctive, it can be the subject of an entire paper. In that case, three or four stylistic features become the outline of the paper.

(continued)

- **Pointing out irony.** When irony plays an important role in a story, it is essential at least to point it out in a paper and explain its role in creating the story's effect.

- **Focusing on irony.** If irony plays a major part in a story's approach and effect, analyzing the techniques through which it is established or the way it shapes meaning can form the topic for a whole paper. Be sure to ground your discussion in specific details and examples.

WRITING ABOUT CONNECTIONS

Tone, style, and irony are used by writers not only for the story itself but also to connect with readers, to help shape the effect a story has on people as they read it. Looking at the way tone, style, and/or irony are handled in two stories, and the ways they can connect the two stories' themes, can be an interesting and valuable paper topic. The results can be especially revealing when the stories come from different eras or cultures. Here are a few possibilities:

1. "Getting Away with Murder": Planning the Perfect Crime in Edgar Allen Poe's "The Cask of Amontillado" (p. 427) and James Thurber's "The Catbird Seat" (p. 439).

2. "Tales of Survival": Coping with Life in Katherine Anne Porter's "The Jilting of Granny Weatherall" (p. 432) and Chimamanda Kgozi Adichie's "The Thing around Your Neck" (p. 314).

3. "Tales of Terror": The Handling of Tone in Joyce Carol Oates's "Where Are You Going, Where Have You Been?" (p. 127), Zora Neale Hurston's "Sweat" (p. 372), and/or Edgar Allan Poe's "The Cask of Amontillado" (p. 427).

WRITING RESEARCH PAPERS

1. A full understanding of and appreciation for Katherine Min's "Courting a Monk" (p. 394) requires some knowledge of Buddhism. Research Buddhism and write a research paper in which you clarify and illuminate parts of the text that could benefit from such explanation and explicate the reversal of roles at the end of the story.

2. The idea of achieving the American dream has had a profound impact on many people. This concept distinctively affected many minorities. Do some research into that idea—what it means, how it arose, how realistic its attainment has been and can be. Write a research paper using what you learn as you compare and contrast ways that theme is embodied (and the tone in which it is handled) in Katherine Min's "Courting a Monk" (p. 394) and James Baldwin's "Sonny's Blues" (p. 324).

In symbol there is concealment and yet revelation.

Thomas Carlyle

(Scottish Philosopher and Historian)

Symbol and Theme

CHAPTER **10**

Being Open to Insights

After five chapters focusing on elements of fiction (plot, point of view, character, setting, and tone), you may be ready to say, "Okay, these things are important. I get it. But when I read, what I really want to know is what a work *means*." Fair enough. Let's think further about that. Some readers try to find meaning by looking for symbols, others by allegorizing the work. Reading this way relies mostly on the intellect, instead of responding to imaginative writings in an imaginative way. This chapter might surprise you because it will ask if searching for meaning is actually the most valuable thing to do. Perhaps it would be more helpful to experience stories and poems and plays holistically by getting involved with them personally, emotionally, and imaginatively as well as intellectually.

APPROACHING THE READING

The following story is set in the future—perhaps in 2061, though the characters aren't sure about that. Many readers find such stories interesting for the ways in which the world then compares to our world today. How has it changed? What caused the changes? As you read, notice details that indicate what has changed and watch for explanations of why things are different. You may be surprised by the nature of that day's festival and by what the title refers to.

Ray Bradbury 1920–2012

The Smile   [1952]

In the town square the queue had formed at five in the morning while cocks were crowing far out in the rimed country and there were no fires. All about, among the ruined buildings, bits of mist had clung at first, but now with the new light of seven o'clock it was beginning to disperse. Down the road, in twos and threes, more people were gathering in for the day of marketing, the day of festival.

The small boy stood immediately behind two men who had been talking loudly in the clear air, and all of the sounds they made seemed twice as loud because of the cold. The small boy stomped his feet and blew on his red, chapped hands, and looked up at the soiled gunny sack clothing of the men and down the long line of men and women ahead.

APPROACHING THE AUTHOR

Ray Bradbury first earned money as a writer at the age of fourteen, when comedian George Burns hired him to write for the *Burns and Allen* radio show.
For more about him, see page 1056.

"Here, boy, what're you doing out so early?" said the man behind him.

"Got my place in line, I have," said the boy.

"Whyn't you run off, give your place to someone who appreciates?"   5

"Leave the boy alone," said the man ahead, suddenly turning.

"I was joking." The man behind put his hand on the boy's head. The boy shook it away coldly. "I just thought it strange, a boy out of bed so early."

"This boy's an appreciator of arts, I'll have you know," said the boy's defender, a man named Grigsby. "What's your name, lad?"

"Tom."

"Tom here is going to spit clean and true, right, Tom?"   10

"I sure am!"

Laughter passed down the line.

A man was selling cracked cups of hot coffee up ahead. Tom looked and saw the little hot fire and the brew bubbling in a rusty pan. It wasn't really coffee. It was made from some berry that grew on the meadowlands beyond town, and it sold a penny a cup to warm their stomachs; but not many were buying, not many had the wealth.

Tom stared ahead to the place where the line ended, beyond a bombed-out stone wall.

"They say she *smiles*," said the boy.   15

"Aye, she does," said Grigsby.

"They say she's made of oil and canvas."

"True. And that's what makes me think she's not the original one. The original, now, I've heard, was painted on wood a long time ago."

"They say she's four centuries old."

"Maybe more. No one knows what year this is, to be sure."   20
"It's 2061!"
"That's what they say, boy, yes. Liars. Could be 3000 or 5000, for all we know. Things were in a fearful mess there for a while. All we got now is bits and pieces."

They shuffled along the cold stones of the street.

"How much longer before we see her?" asked Tom uneasily.

"Just a few more minutes. They got her set up with four brass poles and   25 velvet rope, all fancy, to keep folks back. Now mind, no rocks, Tom; they don't allow rocks thrown at her."

"Yes, sir."

The sun rose higher in the heavens, bringing heat which made the men shed their grimy coats and greasy hats.

"Why're we all here in line?" asked Tom at last. "Why're we all here to spit?"

Grigsby did not glance down at him, but judged the sun. "Well, Tom, there's lots of reasons." He reached absently for a pocket that was long gone, for a cigarette that wasn't there. Tom had seen the gesture a million times. "Tom, it has to do with hate. Hate for everything in the past. I ask you, Tom, how did we get in such a state, cities all junk, roads like jigsaws from bombs, and half the cornfields glowing with radioactivity at night? Ain't that a lousy stew, I ask you?"

"Yes, sir, I guess so."   30

"It's this way, Tom. You hate whatever it was that got you all knocked down and ruined. That's human nature. Unthinking, maybe, but human nature anyway."

"There's hardly nobody or nothing we don't hate," said Tom.

"Right! The whole blooming kaboodle of them people in the past who run the world. So here we are on a Thursday morning with our guts plastered to our spines, cold, live in caves and such, don't smoke, don't drink, don't nothing except have our festivals, Tom, our festivals."

And Tom thought of the festivals in the past few years. The year they tore up all the books in the square and burned them and everyone was drunk and laughing. And the festival of science a month ago when they dragged in the last motorcar and picked lots and each lucky man who won was allowed one smash of a sledgehammer at the car.

"Do I remember *that*, Tom? Do I *remember*? Why, I got to smash the front   35 window, the window, you hear? My Lord, it made a lovely sound! *Crash!*"

Tom could hear the glass fall in glittering heaps.

"And Bill Henderson, he got to bash the engine. Oh, he did a smart job of it, with great efficiency. Wham!"

"But best of all," recalled Grigsby, "there was the time they smashed a factory that was still trying to turn out airplanes.

"Lord, did we feel good blowing it up!" said Grigsby. "And then we found that newspaper plant and the munitions depot and exploded them together. Do you understand, Tom?"

Tom puzzled over it. "I guess."   40

It was high noon. Now the odors of the ruined city stank on the hot air and things crawled among the tumbled buildings.

"Won't it ever come back, mister?"

"What, civilization? Nobody wants it. Not me!"

"I could stand a bit of it," said the man behind another man. "There were a few spots of beauty in it."

"Don't worry your heads," shouted Grigsby. "There's no room for that, either."   45

"Ah," said the man behind the man. "Someone'll come along someday with imagination and patch it up. Mark my words. Someone with a heart."

"No," said Grigsby.

"I say yes. Someone with a soul for pretty things. Might give us back a kind of *limited* sort of civilization, the kind we could live in in peace."

"First thing you know there's war!"

"But maybe next time it'd be different."   50

At last they stood in the main square. A man on horseback was riding from the distance into the town. He had a piece of paper in his hand. In the center of the square was the roped-off area. Tom, Grigsby, and the others were collecting their spittle and moving forward — moving forward prepared and ready, eyes wide. Tom felt his heart beating very strongly and excitedly, and the earth was hot under his bare feet.

"Here we go, Tom, let fly!"

Four policemen stood at the corners of the roped area, four men with bits of yellow twine on their wrists to show their authority over other men. They were there to prevent rocks being hurled.

"This way," said Grigsby at the last moment, "everyone feels he's had his chance at her, you see, Tom? Go on, now!"

Tom stood before the painting and looked at it for a long time.   55

"Tom, spit!"

His mouth was dry.

"Get on, Tom! Move!"

"But," said Tom, slowly, "she's *beautiful!*"

"Here, I'll spit for you!" Grigsby spat and the missile flew in the sunlight.   60
The woman in the portrait smiled serenely, secretly, at Tom, and he looked back at her, his heart beating, a kind of music in his ears.

"She's beautiful," he said.

"Now get on, before the police — "

"Attention!"

The line fell silent. One moment they were berating Tom for not moving forward, now they were turning to the man on horseback.

"What do they call it, sir?" asked Tom, quietly.   65

"The picture? *Mona Lisa,* Tom, I think. Yes, the *Mona Lisa.*"

"I have an announcement," said the man on horseback. "The authorities have decreed that as of high noon today the portrait in the square is to be given over into the hands of the populace there, so they may participate in the destruction of — "

Tom hadn't even time to scream before the crowd bore him, shouting and pummeling about, stampeding toward the portrait. There was a sharp ripping sound. The police ran to escape. The crowd was in full cry, their hands like so many hungry birds pecking away at the portrait. Tom felt himself thrust almost through the broken thing. Reaching out in blind imitation of the others, he snatched a scrap of oily canvas, yanked, felt the canvas give, then fell, was kicked, sent rolling to the outer rim of the mob. Bloody, his clothing torn, he watched old women chew pieces of canvas, men break the frame, kick the ragged cloth, and rip it into confetti.

Only Tom stood apart, silent in the moving square. He looked down at his hand. It clutched the piece of canvas close to his chest, hidden.

"Hey there, Tom!" cried Grigsby.   70

Without a word, sobbing, Tom ran. He ran out and down the bomb-pitted road, into a field, across a shallow stream, not looking back, his hand clenched tightly, tucked under his coat.

At sunset he reached the small village and passed on through. By nine o'clock he came to the ruined farm dwelling. Around back, in the half silo, in the part that still remained upright, tented over, he heard the sounds of sleeping, the family — his mother, father, and brother. He slipped quickly, silently, through the small door and lay down, panting.

"Tom?" called his mother in the dark.

"Yes."

"Where've you been?" snapped his father. "I'll beat you in the morning."   75

Someone kicked him. His brother, who had been left behind to work their little patch of ground.

"Go to sleep," cried his mother, faintly.

Another kick.

Tom lay getting his breath. All was quiet. His hand was pushed to his chest, tight, tight. He lay for half an hour this way, eyes closed.

Then he felt something, and it was a cold white light. The moon rose very   80 high and the little square of light moved in the silo and crept slowly over Tom's body. Then, and only then, did his hand relax. Slowly, carefully, listening to those who slept about him, Tom drew his hand forth. He hesitated, sucked in his breath, and then, waiting, opened his hand and uncrumpled the tiny fragment of painted canvas.

All the world was asleep in the moonlight.

And there on his hand was the Smile.

He looked at it in the white illumination from the midnight sky. And he thought, over and over to himself, quietly, *the Smile, the lovely Smile.*

An hour later he could still see it, even after he had folded it carefully and hidden it. He shut his eyes and the Smile was there in the darkness. And it was still there, warm and gentle, when he went to sleep and the world was silent and the moon sailed up and then down the cold sky toward morning.

REFLECTING ON WHAT YOU'VE READ

1. Be ready to discuss how the setting is important in some ways and unimportant in others. Why do you think the specific location is not identified more precisely than it is?

2. Describe the two main characters (Tom and Grigsby), as fully as the story permits. What traits are important in each?

3. A key image in the story is the *Mona Lisa*, painted by Leonardo da Vinci in the early 1500s. If you aren't already familiar with the painting and why it is famous, look at a photo of it and do some reading about its background. Be ready to discuss why it was a meaningful and appropriate painting to use in this story.

4. Read the section below, Reading for Symbols. Based on what it says, do you think Mona Lisa's smile is a symbol as well as an image? If so, explain why and what meaning or meanings it embodies. Do you think there are other symbols in the story? If so, point them out and be ready to talk about why you think so and what they mean and contribute to the story.

READING FOR SYMBOLS

Works of literature can help us to see things in fresh and meaningful ways. One way they do so is through symbolism. Noticing symbols can be a useful way to realize fully what a story is about, but only if it is done with a clear understanding of what symbols are and how they work.

A *symbol* in literature is an object, an event, or a person that suggests more than its literal meaning. Every day you encounter symbols. You send flowers to someone important to you. The flowers are an object, something that can be touched and smelled. But of course you hope that the recipient will recognize them as more than just objects, that she or he will know the flowers suggest your love, concern, and support and therefore will respond to their *symbolic* implications.

Note that *implications* in the previous sentence is plural. Symbols usually convey a cluster of possible meanings; they are rich, suggestive, and evocative. It's crucial that we never reduce them to a single, definite meaning: The verb *suggests* may be safer to use than the verb *symbolizes* because it conveys better a sense of a symbol's openness, inclusivity, and plurality, as in our sentence about the flowers above.

RECOGNIZING SYMBOLS

Even though almost anything can take on symbolic significance, not every object, character, or act in a literary work should be labeled a symbol. Symbols draw their power from standing out, and they don't stand out if we call everything a symbol. A wise way to proceed is to assume that objects, characters, and actions are always themselves and are not meant to be taken as symbols *unless* a further sense of meaning forces itself on us. If you miss something others regard as a symbol, don't worry. Symbols add to a work's meaning, but a work usually doesn't depend on your recognizing them. It's better to miss a symbolic meaning than to impose one and reduce a work to a string of abstractions.

Prominence or Weightiness   How, then, do you recognize a symbol? The key signal is *prominence*: Objects that are mentioned repeatedly, described in detail, or appear in noticeable or strategic positions (at the beginning or end, in the title, at a crucial moment, in the climactic lines) may point toward a meaning beyond themselves. The red convertible in Louise Erdrich's story (p. 119) certainly meets all these criteria. Signals, however, are not always structural. Another signal can be a sense of *weightiness* or *significance*: Sometimes you may notice that an image, character, or action differs from others, that it is beginning to embody an idea related to an area of major concern in the work. In such a case, it might be a symbol.

Image Comes First   Be careful, however, not to undermine the use of concrete details by dismissing their crucial part in the work because you see them as symbols. Their literal role always comes first. A symbol is first an image, and its representation of an actual thing plays a key role in a work even if it also becomes a symbol. The quilts in "Everyday Use" (p. 152) come to symbolize the Johnson family's culture and heritage, but first and foremost they are actual quilts. At the end of the story, the narrator gives Maggie coverings she can put on a bed, not some abstract "heritage" (though the bed coverings carry that sense of heritage with them). To separate the symbolic meaning from the literal diminishes the richness of both. The warmth of the Johnsons' heritage comes alive in the warmth provided by the quilts.

The red convertible is a real object in Erdrich's story: Lyman and Henry buy a car, fix it up, and drive around in it. But beyond being an object the brothers own, the car also represents their friendship and the bond they share. It suggests youth, freedom, and spontaneity (think of the difference if the car was a tan minivan); perhaps it even reflects Henry's life and soul. When Lyman rolls the car into the river, the red convertible becomes part of a symbolic act. He isn't just getting rid of the car; he is giving it to Henry, evidence of his love for and close connection to his brother.

Similarly, the scrap of canvas with Mona Lisa's smile painted on it is first an image in Bradbury's story, an object Tom sees, tears off, and carries away with him. In the painting, the smile is an image, not a symbol, though art critics have always wondered what the smile means: Why is she smiling? At whom is she smiling? What kind of smile is it? The story doesn't raise such issues. But the scrap of canvas with the smile does have the prominence and weightiness to justify calling it a symbol. The smile is in the title, and the whole plot focuses on it, right to the end. What does the smile symbolize? It becomes the embodiment of the culture that Grigsby and others have rejected and are aiming to destroy, a culture they blame for the wars that have ruined their lives. It symbolizes love and gentleness. Both have all but disappeared from the postwar world. Notice that there is no love in Tom's home and family; we see only hatred and suspicion and brutality. The fact that Tom appreciates the beauty of the painting and the smile, that he clutches the scrap of canvas to his heart, creates a spark of hope that civilization will stay alive in hearts like his.

Be careful not to turn an abstraction into a symbol. A rose can be a symbol of love, but love (an abstraction) can never be a symbol of something else. And be sure that the symbolic meaning seems plausible: Its connection to the image, character, or action must seem likely and convincing within the context of the story. To claim that the red convertible is a symbol of Lyman's Marxist leanings (because red was associated with communism during the Cold War) has no relevance to the context of the story.

READING FOR ALLEGORY

Another way readers try to recognize meaning in a story is to read it allegorically. That is appropriate and helpful, but only if the story is allegorical. *Allegory* is a form or manner, usually narrative, in which objects, persons, and actions literally present in a story are equated in a sustained, obvious, one-to-one way with meanings that lie outside the story, usually indicated by names or characteristics ascribed to them. Those meanings, in allegory, often seem or are of more importance to the work than the literal story. A classic example of allegory is John Bunyan's *Pilgrim's Progress* (1678), an allegorical dream vision in which a character named Christian undertakes a journey through the wilderness of this world, passing through such places as the Slough (swamp) of Despair and a carnival called Vanity Fair on his way to the Celestial City (heaven).

A Caution about Reading Allegorically   Be careful not to impose an allegorical reading (looking for representational meaning everywhere) on works that are not allegorical. This happens especially when readers are taught to search for "deeper meanings" in literary works and to ask, for almost every character, object, and event, "What does it stand for?" That may appear to be active reading, but it's not. Active readers wisely refrain from trying to find meanings everywhere, "hidden" below the surface. Rather, they seek to engage actively with what is right there on the surface. It is vitally important to get to know characters, actions, and objects as themselves, to understand them as thoroughly as possible — which in some cases includes their representational significance but in most cases does not.

READING FOR THEME

How can you recognize "meaning" or "theme"? *Theme* (or themes) in a literary work refers to what it is *about* in the sense of "what it all adds up to," one or more central ideas or concepts conveyed in the work. The *all* in "what it all adds up to" is important—theme must take everything into account, all the different techniques used in telling the story (everything discussed in Chapters 5–10) and all the things that happen to all the characters.

Stating a Theme   A statement of theme should be expressed in two parts: a *subject* and a *predicate* (something about the subject). The subject of "The House on Mango Street," for example, could be said to be a poor immigrant family's search for adequate housing. To turn that into a statement of theme, we would need to add a predicate, perhaps something about how adequate housing involves more than just having a warm, dry place to live. Putting these together—subject and predicate—we might say that the need for adequate housing goes beyond comfort and convenience. It also involves giving a poor immigrant family a sense of respect and self-worth.

Limits of Theme   Theme can never encompass the work as a whole; it is always less than the experience of reading the work itself, and even if you are told the theme, knowing it is never an adequate substitute for reading the whole work. Extracting a statement of theme runs the risk of reducing your reading from a holistic and personally rewarding experience, involving the emotions and imagination as well as the intellect, to an intellectual exercise only. It is never an enriching experience to read simply for theme. Articulating a theme is one of the many ways of saying something about a work, but it is never a substitute for fully experiencing the theme itself, let alone the whole work.

Validity of Theme   Theme is always at least somewhat subjective. Works often have more than one theme and rarely have a single "right" theme that all readers find and express in the same way. Each of us may find different themes in a rich work of literature, and we may express them in different ways. However, that does not mean that every interpretation is equally valid, or even valid at all. If someone says the theme of "The House on Mango Street" is the importance of mothers in holding families together through difficult circumstances, there would be good reason to object that such an interpretation is not grounded in the story, that it is more an effort to extract a lesson from the story than to draw together what it all adds up to.

Statements of theme must grow out of details in the story, not out of ideas, experiences, or values *we bring to* the story. Stating a theme should not be thought of as finding a moral or lesson in the work; there may be a lesson, but often a literary work is more interested in depicting human behavior than in judging it or drawing lessons from it. We do not need to agree with characters' beliefs or approve of their actions to enjoy and appreciate the work in which they appear.

> ### ☑ CHECKLIST for Reading for Symbol and Theme
>
> ❏ Be able to explain the difference between an image or an action or a character that is only itself and one used as a symbol (an image or an action or a character that also embodies an idea).
>
> ❏ Know the formal devices commonly used for indicating that an image, an action, or a character may be a symbol: repetition, description, prominent placement (title, beginning, ending, climactic scene), or a sense of weightiness or significance beyond the literal function in the work. Be able to use those signals to perceive when a work is using symbols.
>
> ❏ Be alert to the ways that symbols can enrich the meaning and effect of a literary work.
>
> ❏ Be able to recognize allegory (a sustained equating of objects, persons, or actions in a story with a pattern of abstract meaning outside the story, which is often more important than the literal story), and be able to differentiate that from symbol.
>
> ❏ Be comfortable with allowing details to be details.
>
> ❏ Pay attention to a story's theme or themes, the central ideas or concepts conveyed in the story:
>   - Make sure that your theme statement is complete, that it includes what the story adds up to.
>   - Make sure that your statement is firmly grounded in the story.
>   - Make sure that you have specific details to support the adequacy and importance of your statement of theme.
>   - Make sure you have found a statement of theme, not just a moral or lesson that can be imposed on the story.

FURTHER READING

APPROACHING THE READING

Setting and symbol figure significantly in the following story about a platoon of soldiers on patrol during the Vietnam War. Through the things they carried, we come to know a lot about them and about war. We learn that the things the men carried in their hearts are just as important as the things they carried on their backs. The story is packed with objects that are images, but watch for some that may seem also to carry symbolic significance. Be ready to discuss the way a theme or several themes develop through the interaction of plot, characters, setting, images, and symbols.

Tim O'Brien b. 1946

The Things They Carried   [1986]

First Lieutenant Jimmy Cross carried letters from a girl named Martha, a junior at Mount Sebastian College in New Jersey. They were not love letters, but Lieutenant Cross was hoping, so he kept them folded in plastic at the bottom of his rucksack. In the late afternoon, after a day's march, he would dig his foxhole, wash his hands under a canteen, unwrap the letters, hold them with the tips of his fingers, and spend the last hour of light pretending. He would imagine romantic camping trips into the White Mountains in New Hampshire. He would sometimes taste the envelope flaps, knowing her tongue had been there. More than anything, he wanted Martha to love him as he loved her, but the letters were mostly chatty, elusive on the matter of love. She was a virgin, he was almost sure. She was an English major at Mount Sebastian, and she wrote beautifully about her professors and roommates and midterm exams, about her respect for Chaucer and her great affection for Virginia Woolf. She often quoted lines of poetry; she never mentioned the war, except to say, Jimmy, take care of yourself. The letters weighed 10 ounces. They were signed Love, Martha, but Lieutenant Cross understood that Love was only a way of signing and did not mean what he sometimes pretended it meant. At dusk, he would carefully return the letters to his rucksack. Slowly, a bit distracted, he would get up and move among his men, checking the perimeter, then at full dark he would return to his hole and watch the night and wonder if Martha was a virgin.

> **APPROACHING THE AUTHOR**
>
> **Tim O'Brien** says, "I didn't get into writing to make money or get famous or any of that. I got into it to hit hearts."
>
> For more about him, see page 1074.

The things they carried were largely determined by necessity. Among the necessities or near-necessities were P-38 can openers, pocket knives, heat tabs, wristwatches, dog tags, mosquito repellent, chewing gum, candy, cigarettes, salt tablets, packets of Kool-Aid, lighters, matches, sewing kits, Military Payment Certificates, C rations, and two or three canteens of water. Together, these items weighed between 15 and 20 pounds, depending upon a man's habits or rate of metabolism. Henry Dobbins, who was a big man, carried extra rations; he was especially fond of canned peaches in heavy syrup over pound cake. Dave Jensen, who practiced field hygiene, carried a toothbrush, dental floss, and several hotel-sized bars of soap he'd stolen on R&R° in Sydney, Australia. Ted Lavender, who was scared, carried tranquilizers until he was shot in the head outside the village of Than Khe in mid-April. By necessity, and because it was SOP,° they all

---

R&R: Rest and recreation; a brief getaway from active service.
SOP: Standard operating procedure.

carried steel helmets that weighed 5 pounds including the liner and camouflage cover. They carried the standard fatigue jackets and trousers. Very few carried underwear. On their feet they carried jungle boots—2.1 pounds—and Dave Jensen carried three pairs of socks and a can of Dr. Scholl's foot powder as a precaution against trench foot. Until he was shot, Ted Lavender carried six or seven ounces of premium dope, which for him was a necessity. Mitchell Sanders, the RTO,° carried condoms. Norman Bowker carried a diary. Rat Kiley carried comic books. Kiowa, a devout Baptist, carried an illustrated New Testament that had been presented to him by his father, who taught Sunday school in Oklahoma City, Oklahoma. As a hedge against bad times, however, Kiowa also carried his grandmother's distrust of the white man, his grandfather's old hunting hatchet. Necessity dictated. Because the land was mined and booby-trapped, it was SOP for each man to carry a steel-centered, nylon-covered flak jacket, which weighed 6.7 pounds, but which on hot days seemed much heavier. Because you could die so quickly, each man carried at least one large compress bandage, usually in the helmet band for easy access. Because the nights were cold, and because the monsoons were wet, each carried a green plastic poncho that could be used as a raincoat or groundsheet or makeshift tent. With its quilted liner, the poncho weighed almost two pounds, but it was worth every ounce. In April, for instance, when Ted Lavender was shot, they used his poncho to wrap him up, then to carry him across the paddy, then to lift him into the chopper that took him away.

They were called legs or grunts.

To carry something was to hump it, as when Lieutenant Jimmy Cross humped his love for Martha up the hills and through the swamps. In its intransitive form, to hump meant to walk, or to march, but it implied burdens far beyond the intransitive.

Almost everyone humped photographs. In his wallet, Lieutenant Cross carried two photographs of Martha. The first was a Kodacolor snapshot signed Love, though he knew better. She stood against a brick wall. Her eyes were gray and neutral, her lips slightly open as she stared straight-on at the camera. At night, sometimes, Lieutenant Cross wondered who had taken the picture, because he knew she had boyfriends, because he loved her so much, and because he could see the shadow of the picture-taker spreading out against the brick wall. The second photograph had been clipped from the 1968 Mount Sebastian yearbook. It was an action shot—women's volleyball—and Martha was bent horizontal to the floor, reaching, the palms of her hands in sharp focus, the tongue taut, the expression frank and competitive. There was no visible sweat. She wore white gym shorts. Her legs, he thought, were almost certainly the legs of a virgin, dry and without hair, the left knee cocked and carrying her entire weight, which was just over one hundred pounds. Lieutenant Cross remembered

5

RTO: Radio and telephone operator.

touching that left knee. A dark theater, he remembered, and the movie was *Bonnie and Clyde*, and Martha wore a tweed skirt, and during the final scene, when he touched her knee, she turned and looked at him in a sad, sober way that made him pull his hand back, but he would always remember the feel of the tweed skirt and the knee beneath it and the sound of the gunfire that killed Bonnie and Clyde, how embarrassing it was, how slow and oppressive. He remembered kissing her good night at the dorm door. Right then, he thought, he should've done something brave. He should've carried her up the stairs to her room and tied her to the bed and touched that left knee all night long. He should've risked it. Whenever he looked at the photographs, he thought of new things he should've done.

What they carried was partly a function of rank, partly of field specialty.

As a first lieutenant and platoon leader, Jimmy Cross carried a compass, maps, code books, binoculars, and a .45-caliber pistol that weighed 2.9 pounds fully loaded. He carried a strobe light and the responsibility for the lives of his men.

As an RTO, Mitchell Sanders carried the PRC-25 radio, a killer, 26 pounds with its battery.

As a medic, Rat Kiley carried a canvas satchel filled with morphine and plasma and malaria tablets and surgical tape and comic books and all the things a medic must carry, including M&M's° for especially bad wounds, for a total weight of nearly 20 pounds.

As a big man, therefore a machine gunner, Henry Dobbins carried the 10 M-60, which weighed 23 pounds unloaded, but which was almost always loaded. In addition, Dobbins carried between 10 and 15 pounds of ammunition draped in belts across his chest and shoulders.

As PFCs or Spec 4s, most of them were common grunts and carried the standard M-16 gas-operated assault rifle. The weapon weighed 7.5 pounds unloaded, 8.2 pounds with its full 20-round magazine. Depending on numerous factors, such as topography and psychology, the riflemen carried anywhere from 12 to 20 magazines, usually in cloth bandoliers, adding on another 8.4 pounds at minimum, 14 pounds at maximum. When it was available, they also carried M-16 maintenance gear—rods and steel brushes and swabs and tubes of LSA oil—all of which weighed about a pound. Among the grunts, some carried the M-79 grenade launcher, 5.9 pounds unloaded, a reasonably light weapon except for the ammunition, which was heavy. A single round weighed 10 ounces. The typical load was 25 rounds. But Ted Lavender, who was scared, carried 34 rounds when he was shot and killed outside Than Khe, and he went down under an exceptional burden, more than 20 pounds of ammunition, plus the flak jacket and helmet and rations and water and toilet paper and tranquilizers and all the rest, plus the unweighed fear. He was dead weight. There was no twitching or flopping. Kiowa, who saw it happen, said it was like watching

---

M&M's: Medical supplies.

a rock fall, or a big sandbag or something—just boom, then down—not like the movies where the dead guy rolls around and does fancy spins and goes ass over teakettle—not like that, Kiowa said, the poor bastard just flat-fuck fell. Boom. Down. Nothing else. It was a bright morning in mid-April. Lieutenant Cross felt the pain. He blamed himself. They stripped off Lavender's canteens and ammo, all the heavy things, and Rat Kiley said the obvious, the guy's dead, and Mitchell Sanders used his radio to report one U.S. KIA° and to request a chopper. Then they wrapped Lavender in his poncho. They carried him out to a dry paddy, established security, and sat smoking the dead man's dope until the chopper came. Lieutenant Cross kept to himself. He pictured Martha's smooth young face, thinking he loved her more than anything, more than his men, and now Ted Lavender was dead because he loved her so much and could not stop thinking about her. When the dustoff arrived, they carried Lavender aboard. Afterward they burned Than Khe. They marched until dusk, then dug their holes, and that night Kiowa kept explaining how you had to be there, how fast it was, how the poor guy just dropped like so much concrete. Boom-down, he said. Like cement.

In addition to the three standard weapons—the M-60, M-16, and M-79—they carried whatever presented itself, or whatever seemed appropriate as a means of killing or staying alive. They carried catch-as-catch-can. At various times, in various situations, they carried M-14s and CAR-15s and Swedish Ks and grease guns and captured AK-47s and Chi-Coms and RPGs and Simonov carbines and black market Uzis and .38-caliber Smith & Wesson handguns and 66 mm LAWs and shotguns and silencers and blackjacks and bayonets and C-4 plastic explosives. Lee Strunk carried a slingshot; a weapon of last resort, he called it. Mitchell Sanders carried brass knuckles. Kiowa carried his grandfather's feathered hatchet. Every third or fourth man carried a Claymore antipersonnel mine—3.5 pounds with its firing device. They all carried fragmentation grenades—14 ounces each. They all carried at least one M-18 colored smoke grenade—24 ounces. Some carried CS or tear gas grenades. Some carried white phosphorus grenades. They carried all they could bear, and then some, including a silent awe for the terrible power of the things they carried.

In the first week of April, before Lavender died, Lieutenant Jimmy Cross received a good-luck charm from Martha. It was a simple pebble, an ounce at most. Smooth to the touch, it was a milky white color with flecks of orange and violet, oval-shaped, like a miniature egg. In the accompanying letter, Martha wrote that she had found the pebble on the Jersey shoreline, precisely where the land touched water at high tide, where things came together but also separated. It was this separate-but-together quality, she wrote, that had inspired her to pick up the pebble and to carry it in her breast pocket for several

---

KIA: Killed in action.

days, where it seemed weightless, and then to send it through the mail, by air, as a token of her truest feelings for him. Lieutenant Cross found this romantic. But he wondered what her truest feelings were, exactly, and what she meant by separate-but-together. He wondered how the tides and waves had come into play on that afternoon along the Jersey shoreline when Martha saw the pebble and bent down to rescue it from geology. He imagined bare feet. Martha was a poet, with the poet's sensibilities, and her feet would be brown and bare, the toenails unpainted, the eyes chilly and somber like the ocean in March, and though it was painful, he wondered who had been with her that afternoon. He imagined a pair of shadows moving along the strip of sand where things came together but also separated. It was phantom jealousy, he knew, but he couldn't help himself. He loved her so much. On the march, through the hot days of early April, he carried the pebble in his mouth, turning it with his tongue, tasting sea salt and moisture. His mind wandered. He had difficulty keeping his attention on the war. On occasion he would yell at his men to spread out the column, to keep their eyes open, but then he would slip away into daydreams, just pretending, walking barefoot along the Jersey shore, with Martha, carrying nothing. He would feel himself rising. Sun and waves and gentle winds, all love and lightness.

What they carried varied by mission.

When a mission took them to the mountains, they carried mosquito net- 15 ting, machetes, canvas tarps, and extra bug juice.

If a mission seemed especially hazardous, or if it involved a place they knew to be bad, they carried everything they could. In certain heavily mined AOs,° where the land was dense with Toe Poppers and Bouncing Betties, they took turns humping a 28-pound mine detector. With its headphones and big sensing plate, the equipment was a stress on the lower back and shoulders, awkward to handle, often useless because of the shrapnel in the earth, but they carried it anyway, partly for safety, partly for the illusion of safety.

On ambush, or other night missions, they carried peculiar little odds and ends. Kiowa always took along his New Testament and a pair of moccasins for silence. Dave Jensen carried night-sight vitamins high in carotene. Lee Strunk carried his slingshot; ammo, he claimed, would never be a problem. Rat Kiley carried brandy and M&M's candy. Until he was shot, Ted Lavender carried the starlight scope, which weighed 6.3 pounds with its aluminum carrying case. Henry Dobbins carried his girlfriend's pantyhose wrapped around his neck as a comforter. They all carried ghosts. When dark came, they would move out single file across the meadows and paddies to their ambush coordinates, where they would quietly set up the Claymores and lie down and spend the night waiting.

_____

AOs: Areas of operations.

Other missions were more complicated and required special equipment. In mid-April, it was their mission to search out and destroy the elaborate tunnel complexes in the Than Khe area south of Chu Lai. To blow the tunnels, they carried one-pound blocks of pentrite high explosives, four blocks to a man, 68 pounds in all. They carried wiring, detonators, and battery-powered clackers. Dave Jensen carried earplugs. Most often, before blowing the tunnels, they were ordered by higher command to search them, which was considered bad news, but by and large they just shrugged and carried out orders. Because he was a big man, Henry Dobbins was excused from tunnel duty. The others would draw numbers. Before Lavender died there were 17 men in the platoon, and whoever drew the number 17 would strip off his gear and crawl in headfirst with a flashlight and Lieutenant Cross's .45-caliber pistol. The rest of them would fan out as security. They would sit down or kneel, not facing the hole, listening to the ground beneath them, imagining cobwebs and ghosts, whatever was down there — the tunnel walls squeezing in — how the flashlight seemed impossibly heavy in the hand and how it was tunnel vision in the very strictest sense, compression in all ways, even time, and how you had to wiggle in — ass and elbows — a swallowed-up feeling — and how you found yourself worrying about odd things: Will your flashlight go dead? Do rats carry rabies? If you screamed, how far would the sound carry? Would your buddies hear it? Would they have the courage to drag you out? In some respects, though not many, the waiting was worse than the tunnel itself. Imagination was a killer.

On April 16, when Lee Strunk drew the number 17, he laughed and muttered something and went down quickly. The morning was hot and very still. Not good, Kiowa said. He looked at the tunnel opening, then out across a dry paddy toward the village of Than Khe. Nothing moved. No clouds or birds or people. As they waited, the men smoked and drank Kool-Aid, not talking much, feeling sympathy for Lee Strunk but also feeling the luck of the draw. You win some, you lose some, said Mitchell Sanders, and sometimes you settle for a rain check. It was a tired line and no one laughed.

Henry Dobbins ate a tropical chocolate bar. Ted Lavender popped a tran- 20 quilizer and went off to pee.

After five minutes, Lieutenant Jimmy Cross moved to the tunnel, leaned down, and examined the darkness. Trouble, he thought — a cave-in maybe. And then suddenly, without willing it, he was thinking about Martha. The stresses and fractures, the quick collapse, the two of them buried alive under all that weight. Dense, crushing love. Kneeling, watching the hole, he tried to concentrate on Lee Strunk and the war, all the dangers, but his love was too much for him, he felt paralyzed, he wanted to sleep inside her lungs and breathe her blood and be smothered. He wanted her to be a virgin and not a virgin, all at once. He wanted to know her. Intimate secrets: Why poetry? Why so sad? Why that grayness in her eyes? Why so alone? Not lonely, just alone — riding her bike across campus or sitting off by herself in the cafeteria — even dancing, she danced alone — and it was the aloneness that filled him with love. He remembered telling her that one evening. How she nodded and looked away. And how, later, when he kissed her, she received the kiss without returning it, her eyes wide open, not afraid, not a virgin's eyes, just flat and uninvolved.

Lieutenant Cross gazed at the tunnel. But he was not there. He was buried with Martha under the white sand at the Jersey shore. They were pressed together, and the pebble in his mouth was her tongue. He was smiling. Vaguely, he was aware of how quiet the day was, the sullen paddies, yet he could not bring himself to worry about matters of security. He was beyond that. He was just a kid at war, in love. He was twenty-four years old. He couldn't help it.

A few moments later Lee Strunk crawled out of the tunnel. He came up grinning, filthy but alive. Lieutenant Cross nodded and closed his eyes while the others clapped Strunk on the back and made jokes about rising from the dead.

Worms, Rat Kiley said. Right out of the grave. Fuckin' zombie.

The men laughed. They all felt great relief.   25

Spook city, said Mitchell Sanders.

Lee Strunk made a funny ghost sound, a kind of moaning, yet very happy, and right then, when Strunk made that high happy moaning sound, when he went *Ahhooooo*, right then Ted Lavender was shot in the head on his way back from peeing. He lay with his mouth open. The teeth were broken. There was a swollen black bruise under his left eye. The cheekbone was gone. Oh shit, Rat Kiley said, the guy's dead. The guy's dead, he kept saying, which seemed profound — the guy's dead. I mean really.

The things they carried were determined to some extent by superstition. Lieutenant Cross carried his good-luck pebble. Dave Jensen carried a rabbit's foot. Norman Bowker, otherwise a very gentle person, carried a thumb that had been presented to him as a gift by Mitchell Sanders. The thumb was dark brown, rubbery to the touch, and weighed four ounces at most. It had been cut from a VC corpse, a boy of fifteen or sixteen. They'd found him at the bottom of an irrigation ditch, badly burned, flies in his mouth and eyes. The boy wore black shorts and sandals. At the time of his death he had been carrying a pouch of rice, a rifle, and three magazines of ammunition.

You want my opinion, Mitchell Sanders said, there's a definite moral here.

He put his hand on the dead boy's wrist. He was quiet for a time, as if 30 counting a pulse, then he patted the stomach, almost affectionately, and used Kiowa's hunting hatchet to remove the thumb.

Henry Dobbins asked what the moral was.

Moral?

You know. *Moral.*

Sanders wrapped the thumb in toilet paper and handed it across to Norman Bowker. There was no blood. Smiling, he kicked the boy's head, watched the flies scatter, and said, It's like with that old TV show — Paladin. Have gun, will travel.

Henry Dobbins thought about it.   35
Yeah, well, he finally said. I don't see no moral.
There it *is*, man.
Fuck off.

They carried USO° stationery and pencils and pens. They carried Sterno, safety pins, trip flares, signal flares, spools of wire, razor blades, chewing tobacco, liberated joss sticks and statuettes of the smiling Buddha, candles, grease pencils, *The Stars and Stripes*, fingernail clippers, Psy Ops° leaflets, bush hats, bolos, and much more. Twice a week, when the resupply choppers came in, they carried hot chow in green mermite cans and large canvas bags filled with iced beer and soda pop. They carried plastic water containers, each with a two-gallon capacity. Mitchell Sanders carried a set of starched tiger fatigues for special occasions. Henry Dobbins carried Black Flag insecticide. Dave Jensen carried empty sandbags that could be filled at night for added protection. Lee Strunk carried tanning lotion. Some things they carried in common. Taking turns, they carried the big PRC-77 scrambler radio, which weighed 30 pounds with its battery. They shared the weight of memory. They took up what others could no longer bear. Often, they carried each other, the wounded or weak. They carried infections. They carried chess sets, basketballs, Vietnamese-English dictionaries, insignia of rank, Bronze Stars and Purple Hearts, plastic cards imprinted with the Code of Conduct. They carried diseases, among them malaria and dysentery. They carried lice and ringworm and leeches and paddy algae and various rots and molds. They carried the land itself — Vietnam, the place, the soil — a powdery orange-red dust that covered their boots and fatigues and faces. They carried the sky. The whole atmosphere, they carried it, the humidity, the monsoons, the stink of fungus and decay, all of it, they carried gravity. They moved like mules. By daylight they took sniper fire, at night they were mortared, but it was not battle, it was just the endless march, village to village, without purpose, nothing won or lost. They marched for the sake of the march. They plodded along slowly, dumbly, leaning forward against the heat, unthinking, all blood and bone, simple grunts, soldiering with their legs, toiling up the hills and down into the paddies and across the rivers and up again and down, just humping, one step and then the next and then another, but no voli-tion, no will, because it was automatic, it was anatomy, and the war was entirely a matter of posture and carriage, the hump was everything, a kind of inertia, a kind of emptiness, a dullness of desire and intellect and conscience and hope and human sensibility. Their principles were in their feet. Their calculations were biological. They had no sense of strategy or mission. They searched the villages without knowing what to look for, not caring, kicking over jars of rice, frisking children and old men, blowing tunnels, sometimes setting fires and sometimes not, then forming up and moving on to the next village, then other

---

USO: United Service Organization.
Psy Ops: Psychological operations.

villages, where it would always be the same. They carried their own lives. The pressures were enormous. In the heat of early afternoon, they would remove their helmets and flak jackets, walking bare, which was dangerous but which helped ease the strain. They would often discard things along the route of march. Purely for comfort, they would throw away rations, blow their Claymores and grenades, no matter because by nightfall the resupply choppers would arrive with more of the same, then a day or two later still more, fresh watermelons and crates of ammunition and sunglasses and woolen sweaters — the resources were stunning — sparklers for the Fourth of July, colored eggs for Easter — it was the great American war chest — the fruits of science, the smokestacks, the canneries, the arsenals at Hartford, the Minnesota forests, the machine shops, the vast fields of corn and wheat — they carried like freight trains; they carried it on their backs and shoulders — and for all the ambiguities of Vietnam, all the mysteries and unknowns, there was at least the single abiding certainty that they would never be at a loss for things to carry.

After the chopper took Lavender away, Lieutenant Jimmy Cross led his men 40 into the village of Than Khe. They burned everything. They shot chickens and dogs, they trashed the village well, they called in artillery and watched the wreckage, then they marched for several hours through the hot afternoon, and then at dusk, while Kiowa explained how Lavender died, Lieutenant Cross found himself trembling.

He tried not to cry. With his entrenching tool, which weighed five pounds, he began digging a hole in the earth.

He felt shame. He hated himself. He had loved Martha more than his men, and as a consequence Lavender was now dead, and this was something he would have to carry like a stone in his stomach for the rest of the war.

All he could do was dig. He used his entrenching tool like an ax, slashing, feeling both love and hate, and then later, when it was full dark, he sat at the bottom of his foxhole and wept. It went on for a long while. In part, he was grieving for Ted Lavender, but mostly it was for Martha, and for himself, because she belonged to another world, which was not quite real, and because she was a junior at Mount Sebastian College in New Jersey, a poet and a virgin and uninvolved, and because he realized she did not love him and never would.

Like cement, Kiowa whispered in the dark. I swear to God — boom, down. Not a word.

I've heard this, said Norman Bowker.   45

A pisser, you know? Still zipping himself up. Zapped while zipping.

All right, fine. That's enough.

Yeah, but you had to see it, the guy just —

I *heard*, man. Cement. So why not shut the fuck *up*?

Kiowa shook his head sadly and glanced over at the hole where Lieutenant 50 Jimmy Cross sat watching the night. The air was thick and wet. A warm dense fog had settled over the paddies and there was the stillness that precedes rain.

After a time Kiowa sighed.

One thing for sure, he said. The lieutenant's in some deep hurt. I mean that crying jag—the way he was carrying on—it wasn't fake or anything, it was real heavy-duty hurt. The man cares.

Sure, Norman Bowker said.

Say what you want, the man does care.

We all got problems.   55

Not Lavender.

No, I guess not, Bowker said. Do me a favor, though.

Shut up?

That's a smart Indian. Shut up.

Shrugging, Kiowa pulled off his boots. He wanted to say more, just to   60
lighten up his sleep, but instead he opened his New Testament and arranged it beneath his head as a pillow. The fog made things seem hollow and unattached. He tried not to think about Ted Lavender, but then he was thinking how fast it was, no drama, down and dead, and how it was hard to feel anything except surprise. It seemed unchristian. He wished he could find some great sadness, or even anger, but the emotion wasn't there and he couldn't make it happen. Mostly he felt pleased to be alive. He liked the smell of the New Testament under his cheek, the leather and ink and paper and glue, whatever the chemicals were. He liked hearing the sounds of night. Even his fatigue, it felt fine, the stiff muscles and the prickly awareness of his own body, a floating feeling. He enjoyed not being dead. Lying there, Kiowa admired Lieutenant Jimmy Cross's capacity for grief. He wanted to share the man's pain, he wanted to care as Jimmy Cross cared. And yet when he closed his eyes, all he could think was Boom-down, and all he could feel was the pleasure of having his boots off and the fog curling in around him and the damp soil and the Bible smells and the plush comfort of night.

After a moment Norman Bowker sat up in the dark.

What the hell, he said. You want to talk, *talk*. Tell it to me.

Forget it.

No, man, go on. One thing I hate, it's a silent Indian.

For the most part they carried themselves with poise, a kind of dignity. Now   65
and then, however, there were times of panic, when they squealed or wanted to squeal but couldn't, when they twitched and made moaning sounds and covered their heads and said Dear Jesus and flopped around on the earth and fired their weapons blindly and cringed and sobbed and begged for the noise to stop and went wild and made stupid promises to themselves and to God and to their mothers and fathers, hoping not to die. In different ways, it happened to all of them. Afterward, when the firing ended, they would blink and peek up. They would touch their bodies, feeling shame, then quickly hiding it. They would force themselves to stand. As if in slow motion, frame by frame, the world would take on the old logic—absolute silence, then the wind, then sunlight, then voices. It was the burden of being alive. Awkwardly, the men would reassemble

themselves, first in private, then in groups, becoming soldiers again. They would repair the leaks in their eyes. They would check for casualties, call in dustoffs, light cigarettes, try to smile, clear their throats and spit and begin cleaning their weapons. After a time someone would shake his head and say, No lie, I almost shit my pants, and someone else would laugh, which meant it was bad, yes, but the guy had obviously not shit his pants, it wasn't that bad, and in any case nobody would ever do such a thing and then go ahead and talk about it. They would squint into the dense, oppressive sunlight. For a few moments, perhaps, they would fall silent, lighting a joint and tracking its passage from man to man, inhaling, holding in the humiliation. Scary stuff, one of them might say. But then someone else would grin or flick his eyebrows and say, Roger-dodger, almost cut me a new asshole, *almost.*

There were numerous such poses. Some carried themselves with a sort of wistful resignation, others with pride or stiff soldierly discipline or good humor or macho zeal. They were afraid of dying but they were even more afraid to show it.

They found jokes to tell.

They used a hard vocabulary to contain the terrible softness. *Greased* they'd say. *Offed, lit up, zapped while zipping.* It wasn't cruelty, just stage presence. They were actors. When someone died, it wasn't quite dying, because in a curious way it seemed scripted, and because they had their lines mostly memorized, irony mixed with tragedy, and because they called it by other names, as if to encyst and destroy the reality of death itself. They kicked corpses. They cut off thumbs. They talked grunt lingo. They told stories about Ted Lavender's supply of tranquilizers, how the poor guy didn't feel a thing, how incredibly tranquil he was.

There's a moral here, said Mitchell Sanders.

They were waiting for Lavender's chopper, smoking the dead man's dope.   70

The moral's pretty obvious, Sanders said, and winked. Stay away from drugs. No joke, they'll ruin your day every time.

Cute, said Henry Dobbins.

Mind blower, get it? Talk about wiggy. Nothing left, just blood and brains.

They made themselves laugh.

There it is, they'd say. Over and over—there it is, my friend, there it is—as   75
if the repetition itself were an act of poise, a balance between crazy and almost crazy, knowing without going, there it is, which meant be cool, let it ride, because Oh yeah, man, you can't change what can't be changed, there it is, there it absolutely and positively and fucking well *is.*

They were tough.

They carried all the emotional baggage of men who might die. Grief, terror, love, longing—these were intangibles, but the intangibles had their own mass and specific gravity, they had tangible weight. They carried shameful memories. They carried the common secret of cowardice barely restrained, the instinct to run or freeze or hide, and in many respects this was the heaviest burden of all, for it could never be put down, it required perfect balance and perfect posture.

They carried their reputations. They carried the soldier's greatest fear, which was the fear of blushing. Men killed, and died, because they were embarrassed not to. It was what had brought them to the war in the first place, nothing positive, no dreams of glory or honor, just to avoid the blush of dishonor. They died so as not to die of embarrassment. They crawled into tunnels and walked point and advanced under fire. Each morning, despite the unknowns, they made their legs move. They endured. They kept humping. They did not submit to the obvious alternative, which was simply to close the eyes and fall. So easy, really. Go limp and tumble to the ground and let the muscles unwind and not speak and not budge until your buddies picked you up and lifted you into the chopper that would roar and dip its nose and carry you off to the world. A mere matter of falling, yet no one ever fell. It was not courage, exactly; the object was not valor. Rather, they were too frightened to be cowards.

By and large they carried these things inside, maintaining the masks of composure. They sneered at sick call. They spoke bitterly about guys who had found release by shooting off their own toes or fingers. Pussies, they'd say. Candy-asses. It was fierce, mocking talk, with only a trace of envy or awe, but even so the image played itself out behind their eyes.

They imagined the muzzle against flesh. So easy: squeeze the trigger and blow away a toe. They imagined it. They imagined the quick, sweet pain, then the evacuation to Japan, then a hospital with warm beds and cute geisha nurses.

And they dreamed of freedom birds.   80

At night, on guard, staring into the dark, they were carried away by jumbo jets. They felt the rush of takeoff. *Gone!* they yelled. And then velocity — wings and engines — a smiling stewardess — but it was more than a plane, it was a real bird, a big sleek silver bird with feathers and talons and high screeching. They were flying. The weights fell off; there was nothing to bear. They laughed and held on tight, feeling the cold slap of wind and altitude, soaring, thinking *It's over, I'm gone!* — they were naked, they were light and free — it was all lightness, bright and fast and buoyant, light as light, a helium buzz in the brain, a giddy bubbling in the lungs as they were taken up over the clouds and the war, beyond duty, beyond gravity and mortification and global entanglements — *Sin loi!*° they yelled. *I'm sorry, motherfuckers, but I'm out of it, I'm goofed, I'm on a space cruise, I'm gone!* — and it was a restful, unencumbered sensation, just riding the light waves, sailing that big silver freedom bird over the mountains and oceans, over America, over the farms and great sleeping cities and cemeteries and high-ways and the golden arches of McDonald's, it was flight, a kind of fleeing, a kind of falling, falling higher and higher, spinning off the edge of the earth and beyond the sun and through the vast, silent vacuum where there were no bur-dens and where everything weighed exactly nothing — *Gone!* they screamed. *I'm sorry but I'm gone!* — and so at night, not quite dreaming, they gave themselves over to lightness, they were carried, they were purely borne.

Sin loi: Vietnamese for "sorry."

On the morning after Ted Lavender died, First Lieutenant Jimmy Cross crouched at the bottom of his foxhole and burned Martha's letters. Then he burned the two photographs. There was a steady rain falling, which made it difficult, but he used heat tabs and Sterno to build a small fire, screening it with his body, holding the photographs over the tight blue flame with the tips of his fingers.

He realized it was only a gesture. Stupid, he thought. Sentimental, too, but mostly just stupid.

Lavender was dead. You couldn't burn the blame.

Besides, the letters were in his head. And even now, without photographs, 85 Lieutenant Cross could see Martha playing volleyball in her white gym shorts and yellow T-shirt. He could see her moving in the rain.

When the fire died out, Lieutenant Cross pulled his poncho over his shoulders and ate breakfast from a can.

There was no great mystery, he decided.

In those burned letters Martha had never mentioned the war, except to say, Jimmy, take care of yourself. She wasn't involved. She signed the letters Love, but it wasn't love, and all the fine lines and technicalities did not matter. Virginity was no longer an issue. He hated her. Yes, he did. He hated her. Love, too, but it was a hard, hating kind of love.

The morning came up wet and blurry. Everything seemed part of everything else, the fog and Martha and the deepening rain.

He was a soldier, after all.   90

Half smiling, Lieutenant Jimmy Cross took out his maps. He shook his head hard, as if to clear it, then bent forward and began planning the day's march. In ten minutes, or maybe twenty, he would rouse the men and they would pack up and head west, where the maps showed the country to be green and inviting. They would do what they had always done. The rain might add some weight, but otherwise it would be one more day layered upon all the other days.

He was realistic about it. There was that new hardness in his stomach. He loved her but he hated her.

No more fantasies, he told himself.

Henceforth, when he thought about Martha, it would be only to think that she belonged elsewhere. He would shut down the daydreams. This was not Mount Sebastian, it was another world, where there were no pretty poems or mid-term exams, a place where men died because of carelessness and gross stupidity. Kiowa was right. Boom-down, and you were dead, never partly dead.

Briefly, in the rain, Lieutenant Cross saw Martha's gray eyes gazing back at him. 95

He understood.

It was very sad, he thought. The things men carried inside. The things men did or felt they had to do.

He almost nodded at her, but didn't.

Instead he went back to his maps. He was now determined to perform his duties firmly and without negligence. It wouldn't help Lavender, he knew that, but from this point on he would comport himself as an officer. He would dispose of his good-luck pebble. Swallow it, maybe, or use Lee Strunk's slingshot, or just drop it along the trail. On the march he would impose strict field discipline. He would be careful to send out flank security, to prevent straggling or bunching up, to keep his troops moving at the proper pace and at the proper interval. He would insist on clean weapons. He would confiscate the remainder of Lavender's dope. Later in the day, perhaps, he would call the men together and speak to them plainly. He would accept the blame for what had happened to Ted Lavender. He would be a man about it. He would look them in the eyes, keeping his chin level, and he would issue the new SOPs in a calm, impersonal tone of voice, a lieutenant's voice, leaving no room for argument or discussion. Commencing immediately, he'd tell them, they would no longer abandon equipment along the route of march. They would police up their acts. They would get their shit together, and keep it together, and maintain it neatly and in good working order.

He would not tolerate laxity. He would show strength, distancing himself.   100

Among the men there would be grumbling, of course, and maybe worse, because their days would seem longer and their loads heavier, but Lieutenant Jimmy Cross reminded himself that his obligation was not to be loved but to lead. He would dispense with love; it was not now a factor. And if anyone quarreled or complained, he would simply tighten his lips and arrange his shoulders in the correct command posture. He might give a curt little nod. Or he might not. He might just shrug and say, Carry on, then they would saddle up and form into a column and move out toward the villages west of Than Khe.

REFLECTING ON WHAT YOU'VE READ

1. Setting (Vietnam during the Vietnam War) is very important to the story. If you are not familiar with this conflict, do some research on it. Perhaps you know people in your family or a friend's family who were in the war. If they are willing to talk about their experience, ask them about it, especially what it was like living in that terrain.

2. What role does the setting itself play in the story? Think about how an environment affects us. How does this setting/environment affect those in the story? In what ways do you think the characters would appear to be different in a different environment? In what ways does this setting force them to struggle to maintain their identities? In what ways does the setting press them to change?

3. Notice the contrasting subjects of the first two paragraphs. Follow such alternation throughout the story and discuss how that contributes to the overall meaning (theme) of the story.

4. Pay attention to the story's organization. The way topics come up may seem random, but consider whether they might actually be carefully planned and arranged.

5. Sum up the total effect of the story.

APPROACHING THE READING

In the following story, a young African American high school graduate tries to both find his identity in the adult world and figure out how he can succeed in the still segregated South of the mid-1900s. He thinks he has found the answers when he is invited to speak to a gathering of his town's leading white citizens — it seems that he has earned the big opportunity to demonstrate his accomplishments and potential by giving there the oration he delivered on his graduation day. But his experience at the gathering proves to be very different from what he expects, and it ends up being a turning point in his life.

Ralph Ellison   1914–1994

Battle Royal   [1952]

It goes a long way back, some twenty years. All my life I had been looking for something, and everywhere I turned someone tried to tell me what it was. I accepted their answers too, though they were often in contradiction and even self-contradictory. I was naïve. I was looking for myself and asking everyone except myself questions which I, and only I, could answer. It took me a long time and much painful boomeranging of my expectations to achieve a realization everyone else appears to have been born with: That I am nobody but myself. But first I had to discover that I am an invisible man!

And yet I am no freak of nature, nor of history. I was in the cards, other things having been equal (or unequal) eighty-five years ago. I am not ashamed of my grandparents for having been slaves. I am only ashamed of myself for having at one time been ashamed. About eighty-five years ago they were told that they were free, united with others of our country in everything pertaining to the common good, and, in everything social, separate like the fingers of the hand. And they believed it. They exulted in it. They stayed in their place, worked hard, and brought up my father to do the same. But my grandfather is the one. He was an odd old guy, my grandfather, and I am told I take after him. It was he who caused the trouble. On his deathbed he called my father to him and said, "Son, after I'm gone I want you to keep up the good fight. I never told you, but our life is a war and I have been a traitor all my born

APPROACHING THE AUTHOR

Ralph Ellison was expert at fishing, hunting, repairing car engines, and assembling radios and stereo systems. One friend said Ellison "knew more about textiles than anyone I've ever met" and another called Ellison a "thoroughgoing expert on the raising of African violets."

Bernard Gotfryd/Getty Images

For more about him, see page 1062.

days, a spy in the enemy's country ever since I give up my gun back in the Reconstruction. Live with your head in the lion's mouth. I want you to overcome 'em with yeses, undermine 'em with grins, agree 'em to death and destruction, let 'em swoller you till they vomit or bust wide open." They thought the old man had gone out of his mind. He had been the meekest of men. The younger children were rushed from the room, the shades drawn and the flame of the lamp turned so low that it sputtered on the wick like the old man's breathing. "Learn it to the younguns," he whispered fiercely; then he died.

But my folks were more alarmed over his last words than over his dying. It was as though he had not died at all, his words caused so much anxiety. I was warned emphatically to forget what he had said and, indeed, this is the first time it has been mentioned outside the family circle. It had a tremendous effect upon me, however. I could never be sure of what he meant. Grandfather had been a quiet old man who never made any trouble, yet on his deathbed he had called himself a traitor and a spy, and he had spoken of his meekness as a dangerous activity. It became a constant puzzle which lay unanswered in the back of my mind. And whenever things went well for me I remembered my grandfather and felt guilty and uncomfortable. It was as though I was carrying out his advice in spite of myself. And to make it worse, everyone loved me for it. I was praised by the most lily-white men of the town. I was considered an example of desirable conduct—just as my grandfather had been. And what puzzled me was that the old man had defined it as *treachery*. When I was praised for my conduct I felt a guilt that in some way I was doing something that was really against the wishes of the white folks, that if they had understood they would have desired me to act just the opposite, that I should have been sulky and mean, and that that really would have been what they wanted, even though they were fooled and thought they wanted me to act as I did. It made me afraid that some day they would look upon me as a traitor and I would be lost. Still I was more afraid to act any other way because they didn't like that at all. The old man's words were like a curse. On my graduation day I delivered an oration in which I showed that humility was the secret, indeed, the very essence of progress. (Not that I believed this—how could I, remembering my grandfather?—I only believed that it worked.) It was a great success. Everyone praised me and I was invited to give the speech at a gathering of the town's leading white citizens. It was a triumph for our whole community.

It was in the main ballroom of the leading hotel. When I got there I discovered that it was on the occasion of a smoker, and I was told that since I was to be there anyway I might as well take part in the battle royal to be fought by some of my schoolmates as part of the entertainment. The battle royal came first.

All of the town's big shots were there in their tuxedoes, wolfing down the buffet foods, drinking beer and whiskey and smoking black cigars. It was a large room with a high ceiling. Chairs were arranged in neat rows around three sides of a portable boxing ring. The fourth side was clear, revealing a gleaming space of polished floor. I had some misgivings over the battle royal, by the way. Not from a distaste for fighting, but because I didn't care too much for the other   5 fellows who were to take part. They were tough guys who seemed to have no grandfather's curse worrying their minds. No one could mistake their toughness. And besides, I suspected that fighting a battle royal might detract from the dignity of my speech. In those pre-invisible days I visualized myself as a potential Booker T. Washington.° But the other fellows didn't care too much for me either, and there were nine of them. I felt superior to them in my way, and I didn't like the manner in which we were all crowded together into the servants' elevator. Nor did they like my being there. In fact, as the warmly lighted floors flashed past the elevator we had words over the fact that I, by taking part in the fight, had knocked one of their friends out of a night's work.

We were led out of the elevator through a rococo hall into an anteroom and told to get into our fighting togs. Each of us was issued a pair of boxing gloves and ushered out into the big mirrored hall, which we entered looking cautiously about us and whispering, lest we might accidentally be heard above the noise of the room. It was foggy with cigar smoke. And already the whiskey was taking effect. I was shocked to see some of the most important men of the town quite tipsy. They were all there—bankers, lawyers, judges, doctors, fire chiefs, teachers, merchants. Even one of the more fashionable pastors. Something we could not see was going on up front. A clarinet was vibrating sensuously and the men were standing up and moving eagerly forward. We were a small tight group, clustered together, our bare upper bodies touching and shining with anticipatory sweat; while up front the big shots were becoming increasingly excited over something we still could not see. Suddenly I heard the school superintendent, who had told me to come, yell, "Bring up the shines, gentlemen! Bring up the little shines!"

We were rushed up to the front of the ballroom, where it smelled even more strongly of tobacco and whiskey. Then we were pushed into place. I almost wet my pants. A sea of faces, some hostile, some amused, ringed around us, and in the center, facing us, stood a magnificent blonde—stark naked. There was dead silence. I felt a blast of cold air chill me. I tried to back away, but they were behind me and around me. Some of the boys stood with lowered heads, trembling. I felt a wave of irrational guilt and fear. My teeth chattered, my skin turned to goose flesh, my knees knocked. Yet I was strongly attracted and looked in spite of myself. Had the price of looking been blindness, I would have looked. The hair was yellow like that of a circus kewpie doll, the face heavily powdered and rouged, as though to form an abstract mask, the eyes hollow and smeared a cool blue, the color of a baboon's butt. I felt a desire to spit upon her as my eyes brushed slowly over her body. Her breasts were firm and round as the domes of East Indian temples, and I stood so close as to see the fine skin texture and beads of pearly perspiration glistening like dew around the pink and erected

---

Booker T. Washington: (1856–1915), African American educator, author, orator, and political leader; he advocated working with supportive whites, instead of taking a confrontational approach toward whites.

buds of her nipples. I wanted at one and the same time to run from the room, to sink through the floor, or go to her and cover her from my eyes and the eyes of the others with my body; to feel the soft thighs, to caress her and destroy her, to love her and murder her, to hide from her, and yet to stroke where below the small American flag tattooed upon her belly her thighs formed a capital V. I had a notion that of all in the room she saw only me with her impersonal eyes.

And then she began to dance, a slow sensuous movement; the smoke of a hundred cigars clinging to her like the thinnest of veils. She seemed like a fair bird-girl girdled in veils calling to me from the angry surface of some gray and threatening sea. I was transported. Then I became aware of the clarinet playing and the big shots yelling at us. Some threatened us if we looked and others if we did not. On my right I saw one boy faint. And now a man grabbed a silver pitcher from a table and stepped close as he dashed ice water upon him and stood him up and forced two of us to support him as his head hung and moans issued from his thick bluish lips. Another boy began to plead to go home. He was the largest of the group, wearing dark red fighting trunks much too small to conceal the erection which projected from him as though in answer to the insinuating low-registered moaning of the clarinet. He tried to hide himself with his boxing gloves.

And all the while the blonde continued dancing, smiling faintly at the big shots who watched her with fascination, and faintly smiling at our fear. I noticed a certain merchant who followed her hungrily, his lips loose and drooling. He was a large man who wore diamond studs in a shirtfront which swelled with the ample paunch underneath, and each time the blonde swayed her undulating hips he ran his hand through the thin hair of his bald head and, with his arms upheld, his posture clumsy like that of an intoxicated panda, wound his belly in a slow and obscene grind. This creature was completely hypnotized. The music had quickened. As the dancer flung herself about with a detached expression on her face, the men began reaching out to touch her. I could see their beefy fingers sink into the soft flesh. Some of the others tried to stop them and she began to move around the floor in graceful circles, as they gave chase, slipping and sliding over the polished floor. It was mad. Chairs went crashing, drinks were spilt, as they ran laughing and howling after her. They caught her just as she reached a door, raised her from the floor, and tossed her as college boys are tossed at a hazing, and above her red, fixed-smiling lips I saw the terror and disgust in her eyes, almost like my own terror and that which I saw in some of the other boys. As I watched, they tossed her twice and her soft breasts seemed to flatten against the air and her legs flung wildly as she spun. Some of the more sober ones helped her to escape. And I started off the floor, heading for the anteroom with the rest of the boys.

Some were still crying and in hysteria. But as we tried to leave we were 10 stopped and ordered to get into the ring. There was nothing to do but what we were told. All ten of us climbed under the ropes and allowed ourselves to be blindfolded with broad bands of white cloth. One of the men seemed to feel a bit sympathetic and tried to cheer us up as we stood with our backs against the ropes. Some of us tried to grin. "See that boy over there?" one of the men said. "I want you to run across at the bell and give it to him right in the belly. If you don't get him, I'm going to get you. I don't like his looks." Each of us was told the same. The blindfolds were put on. Yet even then I had been going over my speech. In my mind each word was as bright as flame. I felt the cloth pressed into place, and frowned so that it would be loosened when I relaxed.

But now I felt a sudden fit of blind terror. I was unused to darkness. It was as though I had suddenly found myself in a dark room filled with poisonous cottonmouths. I could hear the bleary voices yelling insistently for the battle royal to begin.

"Get going in there!"

"Let me at that big nigger!"

I strained to pick up the school superintendent's voice, as though to squeeze some security out of that slightly more familiar sound.

"Let me at those black sonsabitches!" someone yelled.   15

"No, Jackson, no!" another voice yelled. "Here, somebody, help me hold Jack."

"I want to get at that ginger-colored nigger. Tear him limb from limb," the first voice yelled.

I stood against the ropes trembling. For in those days I was what they called ginger-colored, and he sounded as though he might crunch me between his teeth like a crisp ginger cookie.

Quite a struggle was going on. Chairs were being kicked about and I could hear voices grunting as with a terrific effort. I wanted to see, to see more desperately than ever before. But the blindfold was tight as a thick skin-puckering scab and when I raised my gloved hands to push the layers of white aside a voice yelled, "Oh, no you don't, black bastard! Leave that alone!"

"Ring the bell before Jackson kills him a coon!" someone boomed in the   20 sudden silence. And I heard the bell clang and the sound of the feet scuffling forward.

A glove smacked against my head. I pivoted, striking out stiffly as someone went past, and felt the jar ripple along the length of my arm to my shoulder. Then it seemed as though all nine of the boys had turned upon me at once. Blows pounded me from all sides while I struck out as best I could. So many blows landed upon me that I wondered if I were not the only blindfolded fighter in the ring, or if the man called Jackson hadn't succeeded in getting me after all.

Blindfolded, I could no longer control my motions. I had no dignity. I stumbled about like a baby or a drunken man. The smoke had become thicker and with each new blow it seemed to sear and further restrict my lungs. My saliva became like hot bitter glue. A glove connected with my head, filling my mouth with warm blood. It was everywhere. I could not tell if the moisture I felt upon my body was sweat or blood. A blow landed hard against the nape of my neck. I felt myself going over, my head hitting the floor. Streaks of blue light filled the black world behind the blindfold. I lay prone, pretending that I was knocked out, but felt myself seized by hands and yanked to my feet. "Get going, black boy! Mix it up!" My arms were like lead, my head smarting from blows. I managed to feel my way to the ropes and held on, trying to catch my breath. A glove landed in my mid-section and I went over again, feeling as though the smoke had become a knife jabbed into my guts. Pushed this way and that by the legs milling around me, I finally pulled erect and discovered that I could see the black, sweat-washed forms weaving in the smoky-blue atmosphere like drunken dancers weaving to the rapid drum-like thuds of blows.

Everyone fought hysterically. It was complete anarchy. Everybody fought everybody else. No group fought together for long. Two, three, four, fought one, then turned to fight each other, were themselves attacked. Blows landed below the belt and in the kidney, with the gloves open as well as closed, and with my eye partly opened now there was not so much terror. I moved carefully, avoiding blows, although not too many to attract attention, fighting from group to group. The boys groped about like blind, cautious crabs crouching to protect their mid-sections, their heads pulled in short against their shoulders, their arms stretched nervously before them, with their fists testing the smoke-filled air like the knobbed feelers of hyper-sensitive snails. In one corner I glimpsed a boy violently punching the air and heard him scream in pain as he smashed his hand against a ring post. For a second I saw him bent over holding his hand, then going down as a blow caught his unprotected head. I played one group against the other, slipping in and throwing a punch then stepping out of range while pushing the others into the melee to take the blows blindly aimed at me. The smoke was agonizing and there were no rounds, no bells at three minute intervals to relieve our exhaustion. The room spun round me, a swirl of lights, smoke, sweating bodies surrounded by tense white faces. I bled from both nose and mouth, the blood spattering upon my chest.

The men kept yelling, "Slug him, black boy! Knock his guts out!"

"Uppercut him! Kill him! Kill that big boy!"   25

Taking a fake fall, I saw a boy going down heavily beside me as though we were felled by a single blow, saw a sneaker-clad foot shoot into his groin as the two who had knocked him down stumbled upon him. I rolled out of range, feeling a twinge of nausea.

The harder we fought the more threatening the men became. And yet, I had begun to worry about my speech again. How would it go? Would they recognize my ability? What would they give me?

I was fighting automatically when suddenly I noticed that one after another of the boys was leaving the ring. I was surprised, filled with panic, as though I had been left alone with an unknown danger. Then I understood. The boys had arranged it among themselves. It was the custom for the two men left in the ring to slug it out for the winner's prize. I discovered this too late. When the bell sounded two men in tuxedoes leaped into the ring and removed the blind-fold. I found myself facing Tatlock, the biggest of the gang. I felt sick at my stomach. Hardly had the bell stopped ringing in my ears than it clanged again and I saw him moving swiftly toward me. Thinking of nothing else to do I hit him smash on the nose. He kept coming, bringing the rank sharp violence of stale sweat. His face was a black blank of a face, only his eyes alive—with hate of me and aglow with a feverish terror from what had happened to us all. I became anxious. I wanted to deliver my speech and he came at me as though he meant to beat it out of me. I smashed him again and again, taking his blows as they came. Then on a sudden impulse I struck him lightly and as we clinched, I whispered, "Fake like I knocked you out, you can have the prize."

"I'll break your behind," he whispered hoarsely.

"For *them?*"

"For *me*, sonofabitch!"

They were yelling for us to break it up and Tatlock spun me half around with a blow, and as a joggled camera sweeps in a reeling scene, I saw the howling red faces crouching tense beneath the cloud of blue-gray smoke. For a moment the world wavered, unraveled, flowed, then my head cleared and Tatlock bounced before me. That fluttering shadow before my eyes was his jabbing left hand. Then falling forward, my head against his damp shoulder, I whispered,

"I'll make it five dollars more."

"Go to hell!"

But his muscles relaxed a trifle beneath my pressure and I breathed, "Seven?"

"Give it to your ma," he said, ripping me beneath the heart.

And while I still held him I butted him and moved away. I felt myself bombarded with punches. I fought back with hopeless desperation. I wanted to deliver my speech more than anything else in the world, because I felt that only these men could judge truly my ability, and now this stupid clown was ruining my chances. I began fighting carefully now, moving in to punch him and out again with my greater speed. A lucky blow to his chin and I had him going too—until I heard a loud voice yell, "I got my money on the big boy."

Hearing this, I almost dropped my guard. I was confused: Should I try to win against the voice out there? Would not this go against my speech, and was not this a moment for humility, for nonresistance? A blow to my head as I danced about sent my right eye popping like a jack-in-the-box and settled my dilemma. The room went red as I fell. It was a dream fall, my body languid and fastidious as to where to land, until the floor became impatient and smashed up to meet me. A moment later I came to. An hypnotic voice said FIVE emphatically. And I lay there, hazily watching a dark red spot of my own blood shaping itself into a butterfly, glistening and soaking into the soiled gray world of the canvas.

When the voice drawled TEN I was lifted up and dragged to a chair. I sat dazed. My eye pained and swelled with each throb of my pounding heart and I wondered if now I would be allowed to speak. I was wringing wet, my mouth still bleeding. We were grouped along the wall now. The other boys ignored me as they congratulated Tatlock and speculated as to how much they would be paid. One boy whimpered over his smashed hand. Looking up front, I saw attendants in white jackets rolling the portable ring away and placing a small

30

35

square rug in the vacant space surrounded by chairs. Perhaps, I thought, I will stand on the rug to deliver my speech.

Then the M.C. called to us, "Come on up here boys and get your money."   40

We ran forward to where the men laughed and talked in their chairs, waiting. Everyone seemed friendly now.

"There it is on the rug," the man said. I saw the rug covered with coins of all dimensions and a few crumpled bills. But what excited me, scattered here and there, were the gold pieces.

"Boys, it's all yours," the man said. "You get all you grab."

"That's right, Sambo," a blond man said, winking at me confidentially.

I trembled with excitement, forgetting my pain. I would get the gold and   45 the bills, I thought. I would use both hands. I would throw my body against the boys nearest me to block them from the gold.

"Get down around the rug now," the man commanded, "and don't anyone touch it until I give the signal."

"This ought to be good," I heard.

As told, we got around the square rug on our knees. Slowly the man raised his freckled hand as we followed it upward with our eyes.

I heard, "These niggers look like they're about to pray!"

Then, "Ready," the man said. "Go!"   50

I lunged for a yellow coin lying on the blue design of the carpet, touching it and sending a surprised shriek to join those rising around me. I tried frantically to remove my hand but could not let go. A hot, violent force tore through my body, shaking me like a wet rat. The rug was electrified. The hair bristled up on my head as I shook myself free. My muscles jumped, my nerves jangled, writhed. But I saw that this was not stopping the other boys. Laughing in fear and embarrassment, some were holding back and scooping up the coins knocked off by the painful contortions of the others. The men roared above us as we struggled.

"Pick it up, goddamnit, pick it up!" someone called like a bass-voiced parrot. "Go on, get it!"

I crawled rapidly around the floor, picking up the coins, trying to avoid the coppers and to get greenbacks and the gold. Ignoring the shock by laughing, as I brushed the coins off quickly, I discovered that I could contain the electricity — a contradiction, but it works. Then the men began to push us onto the rug. Laughing embarrassedly, we struggled out of their hands and kept after the coins. We were all wet and slippery and hard to hold. Suddenly I saw a boy lifted into the air, glistening with sweat like a circus seal, and dropped, his wet back landing flush upon the charged rug, heard him yell and saw him literally dance upon his back, his elbows beating a frenzied tattoo upon the floor, his muscles twitching like the flesh of a horse stung by many flies. When he finally rolled off, his face was gray and no one stopped him when he ran from the floor amid booming laughter.

"Get the money," the M.C. called. "That's good hard American cash!"

And we snatched and grabbed, snatched and grabbed. I was careful not to 55
come too close to the rug now, and when I felt the hot whiskey breath descend
upon me like a cloud of foul air I reached out and grabbed the leg of a chair. It
was occupied and I held on desperately.

"Leggo, nigger! Leggo!"

The huge face wavered down to mine as he tried to push me free. But my
body was slippery and he was too drunk. It was Mr. Colcord, who owned a
chain of movie houses and "entertainment palaces." Each time he grabbed me
I slipped out of his hands. It became a real struggle. I feared the rug more than
I did the drunk, so I held on, surprising myself for a moment by trying to topple
him upon the rug. It was such an enormous idea that I found myself actually
carrying it out. I tried not to be obvious, yet when I grabbed his leg, trying to
tumble him out of the chair, he raised up roaring with laughter, and, looking
at me with soberness dead in the eye, kicked me viciously in the chest. The chair
leg flew out of my hand and I felt myself going and rolled. It was as though I
had rolled through a bed of hot coals. It seemed a whole century would pass
before I would roll free, a century in which I was seared through the deepest
levels of my body to the fearful breath within me and the breath seared and
heated to the point of explosion. It'll all be over in a flash, I thought as I rolled
clear. It'll all be over in a flash.

But not yet, the men on the other side were waiting, red faces swollen as
though from apoplexy as they bent forward in their chairs. Seeing their fingers
coming toward me I rolled away as a fumbled football rolls off the receiver's
fingertips, back into the coals. That time I luckily sent the rug sliding out of
place and heard the coins ringing against the floor and the boys scuffling to
pick them up and the M.C. calling, "All right, boys, that's all. Go get dressed
and get your money."

I was limp as a dish rag. My back felt as though it had been beaten with
wires.

When we had dressed the M.C. came in and gave us each five dollars, 60
except Tatlock, who got ten for being last in the ring. Then he told us to leave.
I was not to get a chance to deliver my speech, I thought. I was going out into
the dim alley in despair when I was stopped and told to go back. I returned to
the ballroom, where the men were pushing back their chairs and gathering in
groups to talk.

The M.C. knocked on a table for quiet. "Gentlemen," he said, "we almost
forgot an important part of the program. A most serious part, gentlemen. This
boy was brought here to deliver a speech which he made at his graduation
yesterday . . ."

"Bravo!"

"I'm told that he is the smartest boy we've got out there in Greenwood. I'm
told that he knows more big words than a pocket-sized dictionary."

Much applause and laughter.

"So now, gentlemen, I want you to give him your attention." 65

There was still laughter as I faced them, my mouth dry, my eye throbbing. I began slowly, but evidently my throat was tense, because they began shouting, "Louder! Louder!"

"We of the younger generation extol the wisdom of that great leader and educator," I shouted, "who first spoke these flaming words of wisdom: 'A ship lost at sea for many days suddenly sighted a friendly vessel. From the mast of the unfortunate vessel was seen a signal: "Water, water; we die of thirst!" The answer from the friendly vessel came back: "Cast down your bucket where you are." The captain of the distressed vessel, at last heeding the injunction, cast down his bucket, and it came up full of fresh sparkling water from the mouth of the Amazon River.' And like him I say, and in his words, 'To those of my race who depend upon bettering their condition in a foreign land, or who underestimate the importance of cultivating friendly relations with the Southern white man, who is his next-door neighbor, I would say: "Cast down your bucket where you are"—cast it down in making friends in every manly way of the people of all races by whom we are surrounded . . .'"

I spoke automatically and with such fervor that I did not realize that the men were still talking and laughing until my dry mouth, filling up with blood from the cut, almost strangled me. I coughed, wanting to stop and go to one of the tall brass, sand-filled spittoons to relieve myself, but a few of the men, especially the superintendent, were listening and I was afraid. So I gulped it down, blood, saliva and all, and continued. (What powers of endurance I had during those days! What enthusiasm! What a belief in the rightness of things!) I spoke even louder in spite of the pain. But still they talked and still they laughed, as though deaf with cotton in dirty ears. So I spoke with greater emotional emphasis. I closed my ears and swallowed blood until I was nauseated. The speech seemed a hundred times as long as before, but I could not leave out a single word. All had to be said, each memorized nuance considered, rendered. Nor was that all. Whenever I uttered a word of three or more syllables a group of voices would yell for me to repeat it. I used the phrase "social responsibility" and they yelled:

"What's that word you say, boy?"

"Social responsibility," I said.   70

"What?"

"Social . . ."

"Louder."

". . . responsibility."

"More!"   75

"Respon—"

"Repeat!"

"—sibility."

The room filled with the uproar of laughter until, no doubt distracted by having to gulp down my blood, I made a mistake and yelled a phrase I had often seen denounced in newspaper editorials, heard debated in private.

"Social . . ."   80

"What?" they yelled.

". . . equality—"

The laughter hung smokelike in the sudden stillness. I opened my eyes, puzzled. Sounds of displeasure filled the room. The M.C. rushed forward. They shouted hostile phrases at me. But I did not understand.

A small dry mustached man in the front row blared out, "Say that slowly, son!"

"What, sir?" 85

"What you just said!"

"Social responsibility, sir," I said.

"You weren't being smart, were you, boy?" he said, not unkindly.

"No, sir!"

"You sure that about 'equality' was a mistake?" 90

"Oh, yes, sir," I said. "I was swallowing blood."

"Well, you had better speak more slowly so we can understand. We mean to do right by you, but you've got to know your place at all times. All right, now, go on with your speech."

I was afraid. I wanted to leave but I wanted also to speak and I was afraid they'd snatch me down.

"Thank you, sir," I said, beginning where I had left off, and having them ignore me as before.

Yet when I finished there was a thunderous applause. I was surprised to see 95 the superintendent come forth with a package wrapped in white tissue paper, and, gesturing for quiet, address the men.

"Gentlemen, you see that I did not overpraise this boy. He makes a good speech and some day he'll lead his people in the proper paths. And I don't have to tell you that that is important in these days and times. This is a good, smart boy, and so to encourage him in the right direction, in the name of the Board of Education I wish to present him a prize in the form of this . . ."

He paused, removing the tissue paper and revealing a gleaming calfskin brief case.

" . . . in the form of this first-class article from Shad Whitmore's shop."

"Boy," he said, addressing me, "take this prize and keep it well. Consider it a badge of office. Prize it. Keep developing as you are and some day it will be filled with important papers that will help shape the destiny of your people."

I was so moved that I could hardly express my thanks. A rope of bloody 100 saliva forming a shape like an undiscovered continent drooled upon the leather and I wiped it quickly away. I felt an importance that I had never dreamed.

"Open it and see what's inside," I was told.

My fingers a-tremble, I complied, smelling the fresh leather and finding an official-looking document inside. It was a scholarship to the state college for Negroes. My eyes filled with tears and I ran awkwardly off the floor.

I was overjoyed; I did not even mind when I discovered that the gold pieces I had scrambled for were brass pocket tokens advertising a certain make of automobile.

When I reached home everyone was excited. Next day the neighbors came to congratulate me. I even felt safe from grandfather, whose deathbed curse usually spoiled my triumphs. I stood beneath his photograph with my brief case in hand and smiled triumphantly into his stolid black peasant's face. It was a face that fascinated me. The eyes seemed to follow everywhere I went.

That night I dreamed I was at a circus with him and that he refused to laugh 105 at the clowns no matter what they did. Then later he told me to open my brief case and read what was inside and I did, finding an official envelope stamped with the state seal; and inside the envelope I found another and another, end-lessly, and I thought I would fall of weariness. "Them's years," he said. "Now open that one." And I did and in it I found an engraved document containing a short message in letters of gold. "Read it," my grandfather said. "Out loud!"

"To Whom It May Concern," I intoned. "Keep This Nigger-Boy Running."

I awoke with the old man's laughter ringing in my ears.

(It was a dream I was to remember and dream again for many years after. But at that time I had no insight into its meaning. First I had to attend college.)

REFLECTING ON WHAT YOU'VE READ

1. After you finish the story, reread the first paragraph. How does it sum up the conflicts the narrator encounters?

2. Also reread the second and third paragraphs. Summarize what they say about the way the narrator's grandparents and parents had fit themselves into Southern society, and the way the narrator tries to rise higher in that very same society. What is so upsetting about what the grandfather says on his deathbed? What does he mean when he says "I want you to overcome 'em with yeses, undermine 'em with grins, agree 'em to death and destruction"?

3. The naked dancer is not only an image in the story; she is symbolic as well. What is her significance? Why do the town's leading white citizens bring the boys in to have a close-up view of her?

4. What symbolic meanings do you find in the battle royal itself and in the scramble for money following it? The leading citizens apparently enjoy watching the brawl. But that is not the only reason they make the battle part of the evening's entertainment. What does the brawl suggest about the social situation African Americans faced—and that many continue to face?

5. Summarize the theme of the narrator's oration. Would his grandfather have approved of it? What is shown by the attitude of the leading citizens as the narrator delivers the speech? What is significant about the only part they actually pay attention to?

6. Describe the narrator's dream at the end and explain its significance.

7. The narrator is recounting the events about twenty years later. How has his outlook changed? What's his purpose in telling the story? How would you state the story's theme?

RESPONDING THROUGH **Writing**

WRITING ABOUT SYMBOLS AND THEMES

Journal Entries

1. Write a journal entry discussing whether the knife in Michael Oppenheimer's "The Paring Knife" (p. 300) should be regarded as a symbol and what difference that makes in the effect of the story.

2. Write a journal entry on the use of details in Tim O'Brien's "The Things They Carried" (p. 257). Pick out several details that you think are images and some that you think are symbols. Explain what it is about them that led you to put them in the groups you did.

3. Write a journal entry discussing theme in Margaret Atwood's "Happy Endings" (p. 321). What does it "all add up to," including the title?

Literary Analysis Papers

4. Write a paper on the literal and symbolic uses of music in Joyce Carol Oates's "Where Are You Going, Where Have You Been?" (p. 127) or James Baldwin's "Sonny's Blues" (p. 324).

5. Write a paper on symbols and themes in Chimamanda Ngozi Adichie's "The Thing Around Your Neck" (p. 314).

6. Write a paper exploring the confrontation of cultures as a theme in Katherine Min's "Courting a Monk" (p. 394).

Comparison-Contrast Papers

7. Compare and contrast the use of nature as setting and symbol in Nathaniel Hawthorne's "Young Goodman Brown" (p. 359) and Katherine Anne Porter's "The Jilting of Granny Weatherall" (p. 432).

> ### TIPS for Writing about Symbols and Themes
>
> - **Show; don't just say, "It's a symbol."** When you write about a symbol, be sure to explain the features that justify calling it so (as we do, for example, on pp. 252–54); don't assume your reader will agree automatically that the item is symbolic.
>
> - **Look for meanings, not *a* meaning.** Remember that a rich symbol does not usually have one definite meaning that you must find, but rather it is the focal point of a central aspect in the story.

(continued)

- **Avoid using the word** *symbolize*. In discussing symbols, it is preferable to use a verb like *suggests* or *conveys*, rather than *symbolizes* or *means*.

- **Refer to theme regularly.** Because theme is what a story "all adds up to," most papers discussing a story should at least mention its theme and explain how other elements relate to or bring out that theme.

- **Explore complex themes in depth.** When a story is particularly complex or unusual, a paper can be an in-depth exploration of the story's meaning and implications. Be sure that you do more than summarize what the story is about or restate what is obvious in it.

8. Compare and contrast the use of darkness as a symbol in James Baldwin's "Sonny's Blues" (p. 324) and Ralph Ellison's "Battle Royal" (p. 271).

WRITING ABOUT CONNECTIONS

Symbols, by their very nature, are all about meaningfully connecting an image with an abstract quality closely associated with it. Thus, any paper you write dealing with symbols will inevitably deal with connections. Connecting symbols in two or more works on related themes can be especially fruitful and enjoyable. Here are a few possibilities:

1. "'Gather Ye Rosebuds'": Looking for Love in William Faulkner's "A Rose for Emily" (p. 205) and Katherine Min's "Courting a Monk" (p. 394)

2. "What's in a Name?": The Significance of Names on the Meaning and Effect of Nathaniel Hawthorne's "Young Goodman Brown" (p. 359) and Katherine Anne Porter's "The Jilting of Granny Weatherall" (p. 432)

3. "'Trying to Save Their Lives'": The Importance of Reading and Writing in Sherman Alexie's "Superman and Me" (p. 4) and Megan Foss's "Love Letters" (p. 10).

WRITING RESEARCH PAPERS

1. Research the history of the Lone Ranger and Tonto from their beginnings on the radio in the 1930s, and write a paper exploring reasons for their popularity and their cultural significance. Relate what you find to Sherman Alexie's "The Lone Ranger and Tonto Fistfight in Heaven" (p. 213), and clarify the relationship of the title to the story.

2. Initially Ralph Ellison's "Battle Royal" was published as a short story. Later it became the first chapter of Ellison's novel *Invisible Man*. Read the novel and conduct research on Ellison's life and works, focusing particularly on the theme of invisibility.

When you write you invite a reader to look in through a window on everything.

William Stafford
(American Poet; see pp. 534 and 1080)

Writing about Fiction
CHAPTER 11

Applying What You've Learned

Writing papers about fiction is one way of participating in the ongoing conversation about literature described in Chapter 2. There's a natural progression from asking a friend or classmate about what happened in a story (Did the narrator really bury Fortunato alive? Did I get that right?) to discussing the story in class (What sort of person could do that, could have that attitude about revenge?), to writing a paper on the disturbed personality of the narrator in Edgar Allan Poe's "The Cask of Amontillado" (p. 427).

The information in Chapters 5–10 helps equip you to read fiction actively and confidently. At the same time, it prepares you to write about fiction effectively and with assurance. The section "Writing Short Papers" in Chapter 2 (pp. 37–57) provides you with general guidance for writing short literary papers. This chapter focuses on writing specifically about fiction.

We asked students in one of our introduction to literature classes to write an analytical paper on Dagoberto Gilb's "Love in L.A." (p. 111). The assignment was as follows: "Write a two- to three-page paper analyzing the way one of the techniques for fiction covered in Chapters 5–10 is handled in 'Love in L.A.'" This chapter will follow one of our students, Alicia Abood, through the writing process in completing that assignment, using her own words as she retraces her steps.

STEP 1. PREWRITING: FINDING A TOPIC

You'll write best about a story you enjoy, so start there. When you've found a story you like, read it two or three times. In the second or third reading, notice what catches your interest: techniques the author uses well (or not very well), themes or ideas the author explores, or perhaps the social or cultural context of the author or the story. Keep asking questions: Why? How? What if? Alicia asked these questions as she looked for a topic she wanted to write about.

In reading "Love in L.A.," I felt very challenged by the main character, Jake. Even after reading the story a handful of times, I felt like I still hadn't figured Jake out. He made me feel unsettled, in less than three pages! This made me think Jake's character might work for my essay. Perhaps exploring my questions about his character would allow me to feel more confident with my thoughts on this complex individual.

Courtesy of Alicia Abood.

If you have difficulty finding a topic, you might look again at the suggestions we included at the end of Chapters 5–10 (pp. 140, 172, 194, 218, 244, and 283).

STEP 2. PREWRITING: NARROWING THE TOPIC

You can't write about everything in a story. Even a story as short as "Love in L.A." is too complex for that. You need to narrow your focus to what is especially pertinent to or valuable for the topic you're interested in. To pick out parts you'll want to focus on, look for what Benjamin De Mott calls "key passages" (p. 47), then check if some of them connect with each other. That could point you toward a way of limiting the topic. Here's how Alicia carried out this important step:

Once I decided that I wanted to write a character analysis on Jake, I did a "free-writing" journal entry of sorts. I basically "thought aloud" on paper so that I could get everything I was thinking down in one place. Since I was having a difficult time pinpointing exactly how I'd examine Jake's character in an articulate manner, this was very helpful. I even wrote down questions about Jake, such as "Is Jake the jerk we're led to believe that he is?" or "Why hasn't he been able to achieve any of his dreams?" or "What does Gilb want us to think about Jake?" Though these questions sound sort of obvious, it was helpful for me to write the questions down on paper, so that they were staring back at me — asking me to process my thoughts more clearly.

STEP 3. PREWRITING: DECIDING ON AN APPROACH

Chapter 2 points out several approaches that can be used in a paper about literature: literary analysis, comparison-contrast, social and cultural analysis, or a combination of these (see pp. 40–43). Sometimes, of course, the topic you select has an approach built in, but other times the process involves figuring out what approach the topic requires—whether it focuses on what goes on *inside* the story (literary analysis), on *connections* within the story or between your story and another one (comparison-contrast), or on what infuses the work but also *surrounds* the work (social and cultural criticism). Alicia explains here how she found the approach she should decided to use:

As I considered my options on how to formally respond to "Love in L.A.," I tried to focus on what spoke to me most in the reading and rereading process. I knew pretty early on that Jake's character was one of the greatest complexities—at least in my mind—of this short story, but I still had a lot of questions about why I couldn't put my finger on what type of person Jake was and decided to do an in-depth discussion. Although I explore some of the social implications surrounding Jake's character, I chose to do a literary analysis because I wanted to examine how Jake's character is portrayed through the inner workings of the story.

STEP 4. PREWRITING: FRAMING A THESIS

Chapter 2 explains that an effective paper on literature needs a thesis, a central idea that the paper argues for and supports in a convincing way (pp. 43–50). In writing about fiction, some students slip into writing a plot summary. If a story is challenging and a student struggles to figure out the plot, she or he may feel that writing a summary is sufficient because it demonstrates success in understanding the story. But grasping what happens in a story is only the first step. A literary paper must go further. It must illuminate or clarify the story in some way, presenting ideas with convincing support, not just as statements of fact. Alicia's comment illustrates the careful consideration that framing a thesis requires.

I had a difficult time coming up with a thesis statement that I found challenging enough—my thoughts on Jake felt very straightforward, like "Jake isn't necessarily the jerk we all think he is at first." This led me to think about first impressions and society, and from there I tried coming up with something that had more meat to it. Also, I didn't want to sound *too* assuming in my thesis. Though I was able to find some sympathy for Jake's character, I didn't want to argue too strongly for this because he obviously has some serious character flaws. Between the working draft and the final draft, I was able to state my central idea in a way that felt right.

STEP 5. WRITING: DEVELOPING AND SUPPORTING THE THESIS

Chapter 2 described several ways to develop and support ideas in a paper, including "Illustrate and Explain," "Include Quotations," and "Write with Readers in Mind" (see pp. 46–47). The section "Use the 'Literary Present'" (p. 49) is especially relevant in writing about fiction. The development and support of your arguments is the heart of your paper: The most amazing ideas in the world are of little value if they are not supported convincingly. Alicia shows awareness of that in what she says about development and support:

> In the journal entry I wrote, I had included a couple of the quotes that stood out to me the most on my final readings, including the quote in which Jake tells Mariana that he is a musician. I figured that the quotes that still stood out to me in my final readings would be some of the most valuable to work with.
>
> When I began writing the actual essay, I used my journal notes to develop a very bare-bones outline so that I had a basic understanding of the body of the essay. Whenever I felt stuck during the writing process, I would reread the story again or look through the notes to help trigger more thoughts. I was able to focus my thoughts and get ideas for filling out points from writing the journal prompt. For the first draft, I started by working to get at least some form of a workable essay down on paper. I wrote the introduction and body paragraphs in one sitting—incorporating only a couple of quotes. I wrote the conclusion, added and deleted some quotes, and continued to tweak the introduction as I revised the first draft.

STEP 6. REVISING, PROOFREADING, AND FORMATTING

Careful revision and editing (proofreading) is a very important step in writing. Tips for doing it well can be found on pages 50–51 if you need a reminder. Alicia comments on how she goes about it:

> In the early stages of revision I gave my paper to a friend, and she generously looked it over. While she mainly made editing notes, she also helped the paper to become more succinct. She asked me to take out some unnecessary lines (which I did) and asked me to clarify on moments that were unclear. In looking at an earlier draft of my paper compared to the final draft, I can definitely appreciate the revision process. Having concrete feedback from one of my peers allowed me to notice errors and brought attention to added fluff that really interfered with the clarity that I wanted to achieve in the paper. After I made some editing changes that my friend provided, I took a break from the paper before going back and making more significant content changes. Since I spend a lot of time at the computer, my brain can easily turn to mush after a while, and I don't think as clearly as I need to. Furthermore, taking time *not* to think about the story allowed me to come back with a fresher and clearer perspective as I was trying to figure out what I needed to make the essay click.

Here's a demonstration of how Alicia's second paragraph changed from her first draft to the final draft (deletions are struck through; additions are in bold):

At the beginning of the story, we discover that Jake's dreams are perhaps less idealistic than most. While Jake ~~sat~~ **sits** in ~~his car,~~ **the "clot of near motionless traffic,"** he ~~dreamt of things~~ **dreams of an FM radio for his "'58 Buick" along with "crushed velvet interior," among other luxuries,** to help spruce up his current, less satisfying vehicle. His desire to make his car better appears to be a youthful, frivolous dream. Here, Gilb gives us a taste of how lost Jake is — by painting him immediately with a more superficial dream in mind. As readers, we're left to wonder about **the integrity of** Jake's dreams. Do they extend beyond improving his dumpy vehicle? An update such as an ~~f.m.~~ **FM** radio might bring Jake a temporary satisfaction, but we don't hear of anything of true substance. **Also, throughout the story, there is no mention of his family, nor external support of any kind to motivate him to do better. We're left with the sense that he is out on his own in the world — without a real driver's license or car insurance.** While we're never given an age for Jake, his dreams of a more fashionable car ask me to picture him as a teenager or young adult. We don't know where Jake ~~was~~ **is** headed when the story starts on the Hollywood ~~freeway~~ **Freeway.** Given the youthfulness of Jake's dreams, and his uncertain route, we're left to believe that Jake has yet to grow up — to discover what his dreams truly are.

SAMPLE STUDENT SHORT PAPER

Here are the rough draft and the final draft of Alicia's paper, with comments on the changes from the earlier version to the later one. To make it easier to compare them, we've printed the rough draft of her paper on the left-hand pages and the final draft on the right-hand pages, with our comments on both versions.

Alicia Abood's Rough Draft with Notes about Weaknesses

─────────────────────────── ROUGH DRAFT ───────────────────────────

Rather flat opening sentence.

For many, first impressions go a long way, but they do run the danger of being inaccurate or unfair. In Dagoberto Gilb's short story "Love in L.A.," the first impression of the main character, Jake, is a troublesome one. While at first Jake came across as egotistical and selfish, more time spent examining his actions and behaviors allow us to feel sympathy, or perhaps at least a more clarified understanding, toward him. Through examining the way Jake dreams and presents himself to the other character in the story, Mariana, the complexities of Jake's identity come to the surface. Gilb provides his audience with just enough information about Jake to force his readers to question Jake's true identity, or lack thereof.

Working thesis; will need reworking.

Weak paragraph opening: states a fact, not an idea.

While Jake sat in his car, he dreamt of things to help spruce up his current, less satisfying, vehicle. His desire to make his car better appears to be a youthful, frivolous dream. Here, Gilb indicates how lost Jake is — by painting him immediately with a more superficial dream in mind. As readers, we're left to wonder about Jake's dreams. Do they extend beyond improving his dumpy vehicle? An update such as an f.m. radio might bring Jake a temporary satisfaction, but we don't hear of anything of true substance. While we're never given an age for Jake, his dreams of a more fashionable car ask me to picture him as a teenager or young adult. We don't know where Jake was headed when the

Needs quotations to back up statements.

Alicia Abood's Final Draft with Notes about Revisions

──────────── **FINAL DRAFT** ────────────

Alicia Abood   Abood 1
Professor Schakel
English 248.02
13 April 2016

A Lost Identity: Taking a Deeper Look at Jake in "Love in L.A."

    First impressions go a long way for many people, and in Dagoberto Gilb's short story "Love in L.A.," the first impression of the main character, Jake, is a troublesome one. Gilb provides his audience with just enough information about Jake to force his readers to question Jake's true identity, or lack thereof. Through examining the way Jake dreams and presents himself to the other character in the story, Mariana, the complexities of Jake's identity come to the surface. While initially Jake comes across as egotistical and selfish, spending more time examining his actions and behaviors allows us to feel a bit of sympathy, or perhaps at least a more clarified understanding, toward him.

    At the beginning of the story, we discover that Jake's dreams are perhaps less idealistic than most. While Jake sits in the "clot of near motionless traffic," he dreams of an FM radio for his "'58 Buick" along with "crushed velvet interior," among other luxuries, to help spruce up his current, less satisfying vehicle. His desire to make his car better appears to be youthful and frivolous. Here, Gilb gives us a taste of how lost Jake is — by painting him immediately with superficial goals in mind. As readers, we're left to wonder about the integrity of Jake's dreams. Do they extend beyond improving his dumpy vehicle? An update such as an FM radio might bring Jake a temporary satisfaction, but we don't hear of anything of true substance. Also, throughout the story, there is no mention of his family or of external support of any other kind that might motivate him to do better. We're left with the sense that he is out on his own in the world — without a real driver's

Title suggests central topic.

Opening sentence more inviting than the one in the rough draft.

Thesis sentence is clearer and stronger.

Topic sentence now focuses on an idea.

Quotations blended nicely into sentences.

Improved paragraph development.

─────────── **ROUGH DRAFT** ───────────

Abood 2

story starts on the Hollywood freeway. Given the youthfulness of Jake's dreams, and his uncertain route, we're left to believe that Jake has yet to grow up — to discover what his dreams truly are.

Again, statement of fact, not of idea.

Too many short sentences together.

While Jake was daydreaming on the freeway, he hit Mariana's car. Before Jake even spoke to Mariana, he first took time to check out his vehicle and approaches her by saying "It didn't even scratch my paint" (112). This should turn us off to Jake immediately. Then he proceeds to flirt with her and tries to distract her from the situation at hand. While Jake tried to smooth talk Mariana, his naïveté becomes evident. Jake approached Mariana in a sleazy way, and he seems unashamed of the tone of his approach. Toward the end of the story, Gilb describes the interaction when Jake and Mariana shake hands: Jake's youthfulness and lack of experience is shown in the world shines through.

This paragraph needs an idea sentence.

Paragraph needs clarification and support.

When Mariana asks Jake to show her his driver's license, he makes up a lie. Gilb describes Jake's description of himself as a musician as a great exaggeration, and to the reader, Jake's lost sense of identity became even a bit heartbreaking. Jake was hiding under a mask of someone that he perhaps hopes to be, but isn't. Jake proceeds to lie — about his car insurance and his phone number, and he thinks he pulled off yet another lie. Then he looks in his rearview mirror and sees Mariana writing down his license plate numbers. We discover that even these numbers aren't real, because he pulled them off of an old vehicle after his expired.

FINAL DRAFT

Abood 2

license or car insurance. While we're never given an age for Jake, his dreams of a more fashionable car lead me to picture him as a teenager or young adult. We don't know where Jake is headed when the story starts on the Hollywood Freeway. Given the youthfulness of his dreams, and his uncertain route, we're left to believe that Jake has yet to grow up — to discover what his dreams truly are.

Jake's character is primarily shown as he interacts with Mariana — the young, innocent girl who owns the Toyota Jake hits. Before Jake even speaks to Mariana, he takes time to check out his vehicle and approaches her by saying, "It didn't even scratch my paint" (112). That his first thought is of his own car probably turns off most readers immediately. If that's not enough, he proceeds to say:

> So how you doin? Any damage to the car? I'm kinda hoping so, just so it takes a little more time and we can talk some. Or else you can give me your phone number now and I won't have to lay my regular b.s. on you to get it later. (112)

As Jake tries to smooth-talk Mariana, his naïveté becomes pressingly obvious. He approaches her in a sleazy way, and he seems unashamed — and almost unaware — of the tone of his approach. While Jake knows he is smooth-talking Mariana, he does not seem aware of the person he is becoming. Toward the end of the story, Gilb describes the interaction when Jake and Mariana shake hands: "Her hand felt so warm and soft he felt like he'd been kissed" (113). Again, Jake's lack of experience and youthfulness shine through. Jake's response to this simple handshake shows that Jake hasn't interacted with that many women before and that he still gets a thrill out of playful flirtation.

Improved transition and topic sentence.

Use of a block quotation.

Greater precision in word choice and greater fluency in sentences.

Quotation introduced formally with a colon.

──── **ROUGH DRAFT** ────

Abood 3

    Even though Jake is unsure of who he is, it also becomes clear that he is unsure of the weight of his dishonesty. It's as if he is mind is completely murky — totally unaware of his decisions. Because of his apparent youth and lack of support, Jake is able to live without a true sense of self. While Mariana seems far more innocent than Jake, his naïveté and confusion with the world still stand up against Mariana's innocence. Truthfully — Mariana's sharpness shines through at the end of the story, when she has the sense to write down Jake's license plate numbers, albeit false ones. As Mariana's apparent lack of trust is right in front of Jake's eyes, he still sits in his car and dreams of his FM radio. This lack of awareness and selfishness evokes sympathy, or at least an understanding, for Jake's character and his place in the world. While Jake's shameless actions don't give us a solid first impression of who he is, we sympathize with his character and understand him better, and hope that one day he can live up to the identity he tries to dream of for himself.

Repetition.

------- FINAL DRAFT -------

Abood 3

Most importantly, the persona that Jake presents to Mariana shows that Jake is still very uncertain of who he is. When Mariana asks Jake to show her his driver's license, he makes up a lie: "'I didn't bring it. I just forgot it this morning. I'm a musician,' he exaggerated greatly, 'and, well, I dunno, I left my wallet in the pants I was wearing last night'" (112). When Gilb points out that Jake's description of himself as a musician is a great exaggeration, Jake's lost sense of identity could seem sad for a reader. Jake is hiding under a mask of someone that he perhaps hopes to be, but isn't. Everything about him is a lie — even his car insurance and his phone number. After they say goodbye, Jake returns to his car to feel both "proud and sad about his performance" (113). All that he was doing was acting — it seems a bit sad that there apparently was nothing genuine going on at all. Then he looks in his rearview mirror and notices Mariana writing down his license plate numbers. But even these numbers aren't real — he took them "off a junk because the ones that belonged to his had expired so long ago" (113). Jake is able to move along with these lies, it seems, because he is young and the effects of such actions haven't caught up with him yet.

Even though Jake is unsure of who he is, it also becomes clear that he is unsure of the weight of his dishonesty. Because of his apparent youth and lack of support, Jake is able to live without a true sense of self. While Mariana seems far more innocent than Jake, his naïveté and confusion with the world still make an impression alongside Mariana's innocence. Mariana's sharpness is crystallized at the end of the story, when she has the sense to write down Jake's license plate numbers, albeit false ones. Although Mariana's apparent lack of trust is right in front of Jake's eyes, he still sits in his car and dreams of his FM radio. While Jake's selfishness and lack of awareness at first might initiate a disgusted response, further analysis might call on us to sympathize, or at least begin to attempt to understand his character, and hope that one day he can live up to the identity he tries to dream of for himself.

Improved transition and topic sentence.

Better development of points and precision in expression.

Improved topic sentence and expansion of the idea.

Closing summary; ties back to introduction.

CHAPTER 12 A Collection of Stories

Investigating Various Vistas

FLASH FICTION

There is a fascinating and popular fiction genre that packs an entire short story into a neatly delivered page or two, a few paragraphs, or even a smattering of sentences. Although it's known variously as flash fiction, the short-short, sudden fiction, or blaster, we use the term *flash fiction* in this book. The most famous example is attributed to Ernest Hemingway. At lunch with some other writers, Hemingway purportedly bet them ten dollars that he could write a complete story in six words. After they accepted the wager, he wrote on a napkin, "For sale: baby shoes, never worn." He passed the napkin around and won the bet.

The challenge for authors writing in this form is to plunge readers immediately into the heart of the work and propel them along to a direct ending, while allowing an interval for pausing to reflect. What is left out of such a story is often as important as what is present on the page, as is certainly the case in the example from Hemingway above. Flash fiction, though compressed, is never over before it begins. If anything, it begins after it's over.

What then is this form? How can we define it? Well, it's one that slips between the cracks of categorization. It's not a prose poem, not an anecdote, not a sketch or fragment; it's not a joke, quick take, or summary. Perhaps its only clear characteristic is its protean nature. Its very limitations of scale lead each writer to define the form by the story itself. Try defining it yourself as you read these examples.

For more information about the authors, see their Biographical Sketches on pages 000, 000, 000, and 000.

Marilyn Chin b. 1955

The True Story of Mr. and Mrs. Wong   [1996]

Mrs. Wong bore Mr. Wong four children, all girls. One after the other, they dropped out like purple plums. Years passed. One night after long hours at the restaurant and a bad gambling bout Mr. Wong came home drunk. He kicked the bedstead and shouted, "What do you get from a turtle's rotten womb but rotten turtle eggs?" So, in the next two years he quickly married three girls off to a missionary, a shell-shocked ex-Marine, and an anthropologist. The youngest ran away to Hollywood and became a successful sound specialist.

Mr. Wong said to Mrs. Wong, "Look what happened to my progeny. My ancestors in heaven are ashamed. I am a rich man now. All the Chinese restaurants in San Jose are named Wong. Yet, you couldn't offer me a healthy son. I must change my fate, buy myself a new woman. She must have fresh eggs, white and strong." So, Mr. Wong divorced Mrs. Wong, gave her a meager settlement, and sent her back to Hong Kong, where she lived to a ripe old age as the city's corpse beautician.

Two years ago, Mr. Wong became a born-again Christian. He now loves his new wife, whose name is Mrs. Fuller-Wong. At first she couldn't conceive. Then, the Good Lord performed a miracle and removed three large polyps from her womb. She would bear Mr. Wong three healthy sons who would all become corporate tax accountants.

Ray Gonzalez b. 1952

The Jalapeño Contest   [2001]

Freddy and his brother Tesoro have not seen each other in five years, and they sit at the kitchen table in Freddy's house and have a jalapeño contest. A large bowl of big green and orange jalapeño peppers sits between the two brothers. A salt shaker and two small glasses of beer accompany this feast. When Tesoro nods his head, the two men begin to eat the raw jalapeños. The contest is to see which man can eat more peppers. It is a ritual from their father, but the two brothers tried it only once, years ago. Both quit after two peppers and laughed it off. This time, things are different. They are older and have to prove a point. Freddy eats his first one more slowly than Tesoro, who takes two bites to finish his and is now on his second. Neither says anything, though a close study of each man's face would tell you that the sudden burst of jalapeño energy does not waste time in changing the eater's perception of reality. Freddy works on his second as Tesoro rips into his fourth. Freddy is already sweating from his head and is surprised to see that Tesoro's fat face has not changed its steady, consuming look. Tesoro's long black hair is neatly combed, and not one bead of sweat has popped out. He is the first to sip from the beer before hitting his fifth jalapeño. Freddy leans back as the table begins to sway in his damp vision. He coughs, and a sharp pain rips through his chest. Tesoro attempts to laugh at his brother, but Freddy sees it is something else. As Freddy finishes his third jalapeño, Tesoro begins to breathe faster upon swallowing his sixth. The contest momentarily stops as both brothers shift in their seats and the sweat pours down their faces. Freddy clutches his stomach as he reaches for a fourth delight. Tesoro has not taken his seventh, and it is clear to Freddy that his brother is suffering big-time. There is a bright blue bird sitting on Tesoro's head, and Tesoro is struggling to laugh because Freddy has a huge red spider crawling on top of his head. Freddy wipes the sweat from his eyes and finishes his fourth pepper. Tesoro sips more beer, sprinkles salt on the tip of his jalapeño, and bites it down to the stem. Freddy, who has not touched his beer, stares in amazement as two Tesoros sit in front of him. They both rise hastily, their beer guts pushing the table against Freddy, who leans back as the two Tesoros waver in the kitchen light. Freddy hears a tremendous fart erupt from his brother, who sits down again. Freddy holds his fifth jalapeño and can't breathe. Tesoro's face is purple, but the blue bird has been replaced by a burning flame of light that weaves over Tesoro's shiny head. Freddy is convinced that he is having a heart attack as he watches his brother fight for breath. Freddy bites into his fifth as Tesoro flips his eighth jalapeño into his mouth, stem and all. This is it. Freddy goes into convulsions and drops to the floor as he tries to reach for his glass of beer. He shakes on the dirty floor as the huge animal that is Tesoro pitches forward and throws up millions of jalapeño seeds all over the table. The last thing Freddy sees before he passes out is his brother's body levitating above the table as an angel, dressed in green jalapeño robes, floats into the room, extends a hand to Tesoro, and floats away with him. When Freddy wakes minutes later, he gets up and makes it to the bathroom before his body lets go through his pants. As he reaches the bathroom door, he turns and gazes upon the jalapeño plants growing healthy and large on the kitchen table, thick peppers hanging under their leaves, their branches immersed in the largest pile of yellow jalapeño seeds Freddy has ever seen.

Jamaica Kincaid   b. 1949

Girl   [1978]

Wash the white clothes on Monday and put them on the stone heap; wash the color clothes on Tuesday and put them on the clothesline to dry; don't walk barehead in the hot sun; cook pumpkin fritters in very hot sweet oil; soak your little cloths right after you take them off; when buying cotton to make yourself a nice blouse, be sure that it doesn't have gum on it, because that way it won't hold up well after a wash; soak salt fish overnight before you cook it; is it true that you sing benna° in Sunday school?; always eat your food in such a way that it won't turn someone else's stomach; on Sundays try to walk like a lady and not like the slut you are so bent on becoming; don't sing benna in Sunday school; you mustn't speak to wharf-rat boys, not even to give directions; don't eat fruits on the street—flies will follow you; *but I don't sing benna on Sundays at all and never in Sunday school*; this is how to sew on a button; this is how to make a buttonhole for the button you have just sewed on; this is how to hem a dress when you see the hem coming down and so to prevent yourself from look-ing like the slut I know you are so bent on becoming; this is how you iron your father's khaki shirt so that it doesn't have a crease; this is how you iron your father's khaki pants so that they don't have a crease; this is how you grow okra—far from the house, because okra tree harbors red ants; when you are growing dasheen,° make sure it gets plenty of water or else it makes your throat itch when you are eating it; this is how you sweep a corner; this is how you sweep a whole house; this is how you sweep a yard; this is how you smile to someone you don't like too much; this is how you smile to someone you don't like at all; this is how you smile to someone you like completely; this is how you set a table for tea; this is how you set a table for dinner; this is how you set a table for dinner with an important guest; this is how you set a table for lunch; this is how you set a table for breakfast; this is how to behave in the presence of men who don't know you very well, and this way they won't recognize imme-diately the slut I have warned you against becoming; be sure to wash every day, even if it is with your own spit; don't squat down to play marbles—you are not a boy, you know; don't pick people's flowers—you might catch something; don't throw stones at blackbirds, because it might not be a blackbird at all; this is how to make a bread pudding; this is how to make doukona;° this is how to make pepper pot;° this is how to make a good medicine for a cold; this is how to make a good medicine to throw away a child before it even becomes a child; this is how to catch a fish; this is how to throw back a fish you don't like, and that way something bad won't fall on you; this is how to bully a man; this is how a man bullies you; this is how to love a man, and if this doesn't work there are other ways, and if they don't work don't feel too bad about giving up; this is how to spit up in the air if you feel like it, and this is how to move quick so that it doesn't fall on you; this is how to make ends meet; always squeeze bread to make sure it's fresh; *but what if the baker won't let me feel the bread?*; you mean to say that after all you are really going to be the kind of woman who the baker won't let near the bread?

---

benna: Calypso music.
dasheen: Caribbean herb.
doukona: A spicy Caribbean pudding.
pepper pot: A stewed meat dish popular in the Caribbean.

Michael Oppenheimer b. 1943

The Paring Knife   [1982]

I found a knife under the refrigerator while the woman I love and I were cleaning our house. It was a small paring knife that we lost many years before and had since forgotten about. I showed the knife to the woman I love and she said, "Oh. Where did you find it?" After I told her, she put the knife on the table and then went into the next room and continued to clean. While I cleaned the kitchen floor, I remembered something that happened four years before that explained how the knife had gotten under the refrigerator.

We had eaten a large dinner and had drunk many glasses of wine. We turned all the lights out, took our clothing off, and went to bed. We thought we would make love, but something happened and we had an argument while making love. We had never experienced such a thing. We both became extremely angry. I said some very hurtful things to the woman I love. She kicked at me in bed and I got out and went into the kitchen. I fumbled for a chair and sat down. I wanted to rest my arms on the table and then rest my head in my arms, but I felt the dirty dishes on the table and they were in the way. I became incensed. I swept everything that was on the table onto the floor. The noise was tremendous, but then the room was very quiet and I suddenly felt sad. I thought I had destroyed everything. I began to cry. The woman I love came into the kitchen and asked if I was all right. I said, "Yes." She turned the light on and we looked at the kitchen floor. Nothing much was broken, but the floor was very messy. We both laughed and then went back to bed and made love. The next morning we cleaned up the mess, but obviously overlooked the knife.

I was about to ask the woman I love if she remembered that incident when she came in from the next room and without saying a word, picked up the knife from the table and slid it back under the refrigerator.

George Saunders (b. 1958)

Sticks   [1994]

Every year Thanksgiving night we flocked out behind Dad as he dragged the Santa suit to the road and draped it over a kind of crucifix he'd built out of a metal pole in the yard. Super Bowl week the pole was dressed in a jersey and Rod's helmet and Rod had to clear it with Dad if he wanted to take the helmet off. On Fourth of July the pole was Uncle Sam, on Veterans Day a soldier, on Halloween a ghost. The pole was Dad's one concession to glee. We were allowed a single Crayola from the box at a time. One Christmas Eve he shrieked at Kimmie for wasting an apple slice. He hovered over us as we poured ketchup, saying, Good enough good enough good enough. Birthday parties consisted of cupcakes, no ice cream. The first time I brought a date over she said, What's with your dad and that pole? and I sat there blinking.

We left home, married, had children of our own, found the seeds of meanness blooming also within us. Dad began dressing the pole with more complexity and less discernible logic. He draped some kind of fur over it on Groundhog Day and lugged out a floodlight to ensure a shadow. When an earthquake struck Chile he laid the pole on its side and spray-painted a rift in the earth. Mom died and he dressed the pole as Death and hung from the crossbar photos of Mom as a baby. We'd stop by and find odd talismans from his youth arranged around the base: army medals, theater tickets, old sweatshirts, tubes of Mom's makeup. One autumn he painted the pole bright yellow. He covered it with cotton swabs that winter for warmth and provided offspring by hammering in six crossed sticks around the yard. He ran lengths of string between the pole and the sticks, and taped to the string letters of apology, admissions of error, pleas for understanding, all written in a frantic hand on index cards. He painted a sign saying LOVE and hung it from the pole and another that said FORGIVE? and then he died in the hall with the radio on and we sold the house to a young couple who yanked out the pole and left it by the road on garbage day.

GRAPHIC FICTION

An Ancient Art   When you think of graphic writing, you might understandably assume that such works go back only to the mid-twentieth century, when most children were told, "Comics are not the same as good literature." And if you are familiar with or are a fan of contemporary comics, you may feel that graphic literature is a new, cutting-edge form of literary art. Actually, in one sense graphic communication goes back more than 3,000 years, in the form of pictures and signs for language on Egyptian scrolls. Graphic writing has always been a serious art form. However, in the United States, only since the 1980s has it begun to attract fine artists who are also literary storytellers. Today the range of graphic literature spans short story, essay, novel, nonfiction narrative, and memoir. The 1992 Pulitzer Prize for Nonfiction was awarded to *Maus*, a graphic memoir about the Holocaust written by Art Spiegelman (see p. 312), and over the last few years several graphic novels and memoirs have been nominated for and received the United States' major literary awards.

How Graphic Literature Works   It's important to note that *graphic literature* is not the same as a story with illustrations. In graphic work, there is a dynamic relationship between what is written and what is drawn. Both the written words and the drawings can extend the narrative. At times the words are written as dialogue; at other times, as narration. The artist/author balances the visual impact of film and painting with the intimate "listening" of reading the written word. Graphic literature, by juxtaposing pictorial and written images, invites the reader/viewer to complete the dynamic between the two. And the creation of a deliberate sequence of "panels" separated by "gutters" (both of which will be more fully explained in the paragraphs that follow) leads the reader/viewer to participate by imagining the impact that happens between each depicted moment.

Older adults, accustomed to following lines of words from left to right, then down a page, may find it difficult to read a form that requires shifting from one image to another while taking in both words and visual components. However, a generation that has grown up with television, computers, and video games is readily able to engage with and respond to graphic literature. For that group, graphic literature is an accessible window through which to view our world and to imagine others.

Vocabulary and Methods   For a close look at graphic literature, it is wise to start by understanding some vocabulary and methods unique to the form. Basic to graphic literature are *panels*, the series of individual units containing drawings and words that make up the work. Panels can fill a whole page, or several panels can be presented on the same page. Sometimes they are surrounded by a border, which frames them on the page or separates the various panels. Borders are part of the art and help channel the effect on the reader: A border turns the reader into an outside observer and can create a sense of confinement or restriction within a panel. The space between panels is called a "gutter." Sometimes panels do not have borders but "bleed" out to the edge of the page or into other panels on the same page. A panel without a border can suggest that the reader is being invited into the scene and can increase the reader's involvement; it can give a sense of openness or escape.

Reading Words and Images Simultaneously   Active reading is crucial to fully enjoying and appreciating graphic literature. This kind of reading can be compared to watching a film: You must listen to the sounds and absorb the images simultaneously, integrating the two into a single experience. Similarly, in reading graphic literature, you must read the words of the text and read the images simultaneously, as a unified experience: In the hands of the finest graphic-fiction artists, the written words and the drawings are interdependent, forming a seamless whole. They need to happen together. With a bit of practice, reading this way can become as natural as watching and listening to a film.

Dealing with Fragments and Time   Active reading is necessary also because of the fragmentary nature of graphic literature: Some words of text are placed here; a cropped image, there. The reader must be able to fill out and connect the fragments in order to understand and experience the story. And active reading is needed in order to follow the passage of time. Graphic literature presents time through the use of space: Time passes as we read words, one following another, and simultaneously we see action happening in the visual images. Arrangement on the page leads to a sense of movement in time, as our eyes move sequentially from frame to frame or are guided from one part of a large frame to another. A series of small panels seems to move rapidly; a larger panel slows down our reading and the passage of time.

Listening with Our Eyes   Through active reading we imagine sounds — we listen with our eyes. The style, size, and color of the lettering affects what we "hear" in terms of volume and emotional tone. Large or bold lettering often indicates loudness, while small letters can suggest soft speech. Wavy letters may indicate a voice expressing uneasiness or fear, while a rough style of lettering may convey a harsh attitude or cruelty. In some cases words are incorporated directly into the frame; in other cases words are enclosed in balloons that connect them to their speakers. Active reading is required in interpreting the visual aspects of the balloons and the order in which the balloons are to be read.

Plot and Character in Graphic Literature   In addition to these techniques, graphic literature makes use of the elements of fiction described in Chapters 5–10 of this book, and responding to these elements also requires active reading. Just like other fiction, the plots of graphic fiction involve beginnings, middles, endings, conflicts, foreshadowings, repetitions, gaps, and a sense of wholeness. Depiction of character in graphic fiction includes the same telling, showing, saying, and so forth, as in other fiction, but it also requires that the reader be attentive to visual features: facial expressions, gestures, poses, clothes, shading, and lighting, for example. Theme, symbol, style, tone, and irony can be employed to good effect in graphic fiction, just as in other fiction.

Point of View in Graphic Literature   Point of view (discussed in Chapter 6) is vital in graphic literature. It starts with who is telling the story (first-person or third-person narrator) and that person's relation to the story, as in traditional fiction. But in graphic fiction the panel affects viewpoint, establishing perimeters and perspective. The artist can have us look down from above in a detached way, for example, or up from below, which tends to make the reader feel small and at times fearful. Notice how similar this is to filmmaking: The artist, in choosing these frame angles, is like the director of a film. When we watch a movie, we know if we are looking through a person's eyes or not; it's the same with graphic fiction.

Setting in Graphic Literature   Setting in a graphic story involves location and time, as in any other story (see Chapter 8), but the graphic work offers visual images to supplement the imagined ones of conventional fiction. The handling of setting varies with the nature and purpose of the writing: The background can be very detailed or sketched out in broad strokes. Often an "establishing shot" is used—with lots of details about the place and the character proportionally very small, all of which will be zoomed in on in later panels. (Notice that here, too, the terminology used in discussing graphic fiction is carried over from the film world.) It can be helpful to remind yourself when reading graphic literature that, as with any visual art, the form of the drawings could take a multiplicity of alternatives. The artist has chosen a particular way of presenting the visual—for a purpose, for an effect, as something you should "read."

Reading **Graphic Literature** *Reading* has become a word that we apply to almost everything. We read faces and places and moods, for example. Graphic literature extends the idea of reading to include both the written and the visual. As an active reader, you are expected to attend to both simultaneously, using your ability to realize implications, nuances, and subtleties in the language and in the visual art. To get the fullest experience from such a work, you must "read" the pictures and the words and understand that "graphic" applies to both the visual and the written.

APPROACHING THE READINGS

The following excerpts are from two well-known graphic works. The first is from Marjane Satrapi's *Persepolis*, which deals with the cultural revolution that began in Iran in 1979 and its effects, especially on women's lives. Satrapi cowrote and codirected an animated version of the book, which debuted at the 2007 Cannes Film Festival and shared a Special Jury Prize. The second is from Art Spiegelman's *Maus*, which relates the history of the Holocaust using different kinds of animals to depict different races: Jews as mice, Germans as cats, and non-Jewish Poles as pigs. In 1992 it became the first graphic novel to win a Pulitzer Prize.

Marjane Satrapi b. 1969

"The Veil" from *Persepolis* [2003]

AND ALSO BECAUSE THE YEAR BEFORE, IN 1979, WE WERE IN A FRENCH NON-RELIGIOUS SCHOOL.

WHERE BOYS AND GIRLS WERE TOGETHER.

AND THEN SUDDENLY IN 1980...

ALL BILINGUAL SCHOOLS MUST BE CLOSED DOWN.

THEY ARE SYMBOLS OF CAPITALISM.

BRAVO!

WHAT WISDOM!

OF DECADENCE.

THIS IS CALLED A "CULTURAL REVOLUTION."

WE FOUND OURSELVES VEILED AND SEPARATED FROM OUR FRIENDS.

AND THAT WAS THAT...

EVERYWHERE IN THE STREETS THERE WERE DEMONSTRATIONS FOR AND AGAINST THE VEIL.

AT ONE OF THE DEMONSTRATIONS, A GERMAN JOURNALIST TOOK A PHOTO OF MY MOTHER.

I WAS REALLY PROUD OF HER. HER PHOTO WAS PUBLISHED IN ALL THE EUROPEAN NEWSPAPERS.

AND EVEN IN ONE MAGAZINE IN IRAN. MY MOTHER WAS REALLY SCARED.

SHE DYED HER HAIR,

AND WORE DARK GLASSES FOR A LONG TIME.

I REALLY DIDN'T KNOW WHAT TO THINK ABOUT THE VEIL. DEEP DOWN I WAS VERY RELIGIOUS BUT AS A FAMILY WE WERE VERY MODERN AND AVANT-GARDE.

I WAS BORN WITH RELIGION.

AT THE AGE OF SIX I WAS ALREADY SURE I WAS THE LAST PROPHET. THIS WAS A FEW YEARS BEFORE THE REVOLUTION.

O' Celestial light!

BEFORE ME THERE HAD BEEN A FEW OTHERS.

I AM THE LAST PROPHET.

A WOMAN?

I WANTED TO BE A PROPHET...

BECAUSE OUR MAID DID NOT EAT WITH US.

BECAUSE MY FATHER HAD A CADILLAC.

AND, ABOVE ALL, BECAUSE MY GRANDMOTHER'S KNEES ALWAYS ACHED.

COME HERE MARJI! HELP ME TO STAND UP.

DON'T WORRY, SOON YOU WON'T HAVE ANY MORE PAIN. YOU'LL SEE.

LIKE ALL MY PREDECESSORS I HAD MY HOLY BOOK.

THE FIRST THREE RULES CAME FROM ZARATHUSTRA. HE WAS THE FIRST PROPHET IN MY COUNTRY BEFORE THE ARAB INVASION.

YOU MUST BASE EVERYTHING ON THESE THREE RULES: BEHAVE WELL, SPEAK WELL, ACT WELL.

I ALSO WANTED US TO CELEBRATE THE TRADITIONAL ZARATHUSTRIAN HOLIDAYS. LIKE THE FIRE CEREMONY,

BEFORE THE PERSIAN NEW YEAR, NOROUZ, ON MARCH 21ST, THE FIRST DAY OF SPRING.

ONLY MY GRANDMOTHER KNEW ABOUT MY BOOK.

RULE NUMBER SIX: EVERY-BODY SHOULD HAVE A CAR.

RULE NUMBER SEVEN: ALL MAIDS SHOULD EAT AT THE TABLE WITH THE OTHERS.

RULE NUMBER EIGHT: NO OLD PER-SON SHOULD HAVE TO SUFFER.

IN THAT CASE, I'LL BE YOUR FIRST DISCIPLE.

REALLY?

BUT TELL ME HOW YOU'LL ARRANGE FOR OLD PEOPLE NOT TO SUFFER?

IT WILL SIMPLY BE FORBIDDEN.

EVERY NIGHT I HAD A BIG DISCUSSION WITH GOD.

GOD, GIVE ME SOME MORE TIME. I AM NOT QUITE READY YET.

YES YOU ARE, CELESTIAL LIGHT, YOU ARE MY CHOICE, MY LAST AND MY BEST CHOICE.

EXCEPT FOR MY GRANDMOTHER I WAS OBVIOUSLY THE ONLY ONE WHO BELIEVED IN MYSELF.

WHAT DO YOU WANT TO BE WHEN YOU GROW UP?

I'LL BE A PROPHET.

HAHA! HAHA! HAHA!

SHE'S CRAZY.

MY PARENTS WERE CALLED IN BY THE TEACHER.

YOUR CHILD IS DISTURBED. SHE WANTS TO BECOME A PROPHET.

WHAT ABOUT IT?

DOESN'T THIS WORRY YOU?

NO! NOT AT ALL!

NONETHELESS, MY PARENTS WERE PUZZLED.

SO TELL ME, MY CHILD, WHAT DO YOU WANT TO BE WHEN YOU GROW UP?

A PROPHET.

I WANT TO BE A DOCTOR.

THAT'S FINE MY LOVE. THAT'S FINE.

I FELT GUILTY TOWARDS GOD.

YOU WANT TO BE A DOCTOR? I THOUGHT THAT...

NO, NO, I WILL BE A PROPHET BUT THEY MUSTN'T KNOW.

I WANTED TO BE JUSTICE, LOVE AND THE WRATH OF GOD ALL IN ONE.

Art Spiegelman b. 1948

From *Maus* [1986]

STORIES FOR FURTHER READING

Chimamanda Ngozi Adichie   b. 1977

The Thing Around Your Neck   [2009]

You thought everybody in America had a car and a gun; your uncles and aunts and cousins thought so, too. Right after you won the American visa lottery, they told you: In a month, you will have a big car. Soon, a big house. But don't buy a gun like those Americans.

They trooped into the room in Lagos where you lived with your father and mother and three siblings, leaning against the unpainted walls because there weren't enough chairs to go round, to say goodbye in loud voices and tell you with lowered voices what they wanted you to send them. In comparison to the big car and house (and possibly gun), the things they wanted were minor—handbags and shoes and perfumes and clothes. You said okay, no problem.

Your uncle in America, who had put in the names of all your family members for the American visa lottery, said you could live with him until you got on your feet. He picked you up at the airport and bought you a big hot dog with yellow mustard that nauseated you. Introduction to America, he said with a laugh. He lived in a small white town in Maine, in a thirty-year-old house by a lake. He told you that the company he worked for had offered him a few thousand more than the average salary plus stock options because they were desperately trying to look diverse. They included a photo of him in every brochure, even those that had nothing to do with his unit. He laughed and said the job was good, was worth living in an all-white town even though his wife had to drive an hour to find a hair salon that did black hair. The trick was to understand America, to know that America was give-and-take. You gave up a lot but you gained a lot, too.

He showed you how to apply for a cashier job in the gas station on Main Street and he enrolled you in a community college, where the girls had thick thighs and wore bright-red nail polish, and self-tanner that made them look orange. They asked where you learned to speak English and if you had real houses back in Africa and if you'd seen a car before you came to America. They gawped at your hair. Does it stand up or fall down when you take out the braids? They wanted to know. All of it stands up? How? Why? Do you use a comb? You smiled tightly when they asked those questions. Your uncle told you to expect it; a mixture of ignorance and arrogance, he called it. Then he told you how the neighbors said, a few months after he moved into his house, that the squirrels had started to disappear. They had heard that Africans ate all kinds of wild animals.

You laughed with your uncle and you felt at home in his house; his wife called you *nwanne*, sister, and his two school-age children called you Aunty. They spoke Igbo and ate *garri* for lunch and it was like home. Until your uncle

5

came into the cramped basement where you slept with old boxes and cartons and pulled you forcefully to him, squeezing your buttocks, moaning. He wasn't really your uncle; he was actually a brother of your father's sister's husband, not related by blood. After you pushed him away, he sat on your bed—it was his house, after all—and smiled and said you were no longer a child at twenty-two. If you let him, he would do many things for you. Smart women did it all the time. How did you think those women back home in Lagos with well-paying jobs made it? Even women in New York City?

You locked yourself in the bathroom until he went back upstairs, and the next morning, you left, walking the long windy road, smelling the baby fish in the lake. You saw him drive past—he had always dropped you off at Main Street—and he didn't honk. You wondered what he would tell his wife, why you had left. And you remembered what he said, that America was give-and-take.

You ended up in Connecticut, in another little town, because it was the last stop of the Greyhound bus you got on. You walked into the restaurant with the bright, clean awning and said you would work for two dollars less than the other waitresses. The manager, Juan, had inky-black hair and smiled to show a gold tooth. He said he had never had a Nigerian employee but all immigrants worked hard. He knew, he'd been there. He'd pay you a dollar less, but under the table; he didn't like all the taxes they were making him pay.

You could not afford to go to school, because now you paid rent for the tiny room with the stained carpet. Besides, the small Connecticut town didn't have a community college and credits at the state university cost too much. So you went to the public library, you looked up course syllabi on school Web sites and read some of the books. Sometimes you sat on the lumpy mattress of your twin bed and thought about home—your aunts who hawked dried fish and plantains, cajoling customers to buy and then shouting insults when they didn't; your uncles who drank local gin and crammed their families and lives into single rooms; your friends who had come out to say goodbye before you left, to rejoice because you won the American visa lottery, to confess their envy; your parents who often held hands as they walked to church on Sunday mornings, the neighbors from the next room laughing and teasing them; your father who brought back his boss's old newspapers from work and made your brothers read them; your mother whose salary was barely enough to pay your brothers' school fees at the secondary school where teachers gave an A when someone slipped them a brown envelope.

You had never needed to pay for an A, never slipped a brown envelope to a teacher in secondary school. Still, you chose long brown envelopes to send half your month's earnings to your parents at the address of the parastatal° where your mother was a cleaner; you always used the dollar notes that Juan gave you because those were crisp, unlike the tips. Every month. You wrapped the money carefully in white paper but you didn't write a letter. There was nothing to write about.

---

parastatal: A company or agency owned or controlled by the government.

In later weeks, though, you wanted to write because you had stories to tell. 10
You wanted to write about the surprising openness of people in America, how
eagerly they told you about their mother fighting cancer, about their sister-in-
law's preemie, the kinds of things that one should hide or should reveal only to
the family members who wished them well. You wanted to write about the way
people left so much food on their plates and crumpled a few dollar bills down,
as though it was an offering, expiation for the wasted food. You wanted to write
about the child who started to cry and pull at her blond hair and push the
menus off the table and instead of the parents making her shut up, they pleaded
with her, a child of perhaps five years old, and then they all got up and left. You
wanted to write about the rich people who wore shabby clothes and tattered
sneakers, who looked like the night watchmen in front of the large compounds
in Lagos. You wanted to write that rich Americans were thin and poor
Americans were fat and that many did not have a big house and car; you still
were not sure about the guns, though, because they might have them inside
their pockets.

It wasn't just to your parents you wanted to write, it was also to your
friends, and cousins and aunts and uncles. But you could never afford enough
perfumes and clothes and handbags and shoes to go around and still pay your
rent on what you earned at the waitressing job, so you wrote nobody.

Nobody knew where you were, because you told no one. Sometimes you felt
invisible and tried to walk through your room wall into the hallway, and when
you bumped into the wall, it left bruises on your arms. Once, Juan asked if you
had a man that hit you because he would take care of him and you laughed a
mysterious laugh.

At night, something would wrap itself around your neck, something that
very nearly choked you before you fell asleep.

Many people at the restaurant asked when you had come from Jamaica,
because they thought that every black person with a foreign accent was
Jamaican. Or some who guessed that you were African told you that they loved
elephants and wanted to go on a safari.

So when he asked you, in the dimness of the restaurant after you recited 15
the daily specials, what African country you were from, you said Nigeria and
expected him to say that he had donated money to fight AIDS in Botswana. But
he asked if you were Yoruba or Igbo, because you didn't have a Fulani face. You
were surprised—you thought he must be a professor of anthropology at the
state university, a little young in his late twenties or so, but who was to say?
Igbo, you said. He asked your name and said Akunna was pretty. He did not ask
what it meant, fortunately, because you were sick of how people said, " 'Father's
Wealth'? You mean, like, your father will actually sell you to a husband?"

He told you he had been to Ghana and Uganda and Tanzania, loved the
poetry of Okot p'Bitek and the novels of Amos Tutuola and had read a lot about
sub-Saharan African countries, their histories, their complexities. You wanted
to feel disdain, to show it as you brought his order, because white people who

liked Africa too much and those who liked Africa too little were the same —
condescending. But he didn't shake his head in the superior way that Professor
Cobbledick back in the Maine community college did during a class discussion on decolonization in Africa. He didn't have that expression of Professor
Cobbledick's, that expression of a person who thought himself better than the
people he knew about. He came in the next day and sat at the same table and
when you asked if the chicken was okay, he asked if you had grown up in Lagos.
He came in the third day and began talking before he ordered, about how he
had visited Bombay and now wanted to visit Lagos, to see how real people lived,
like in the shantytowns, because he never did any of the silly tourist stuff when
he was abroad. He talked and talked and you had to tell him it was against
restaurant policy. He brushed your hand when you set the glass of water down.
The fourth day, when you saw him arrive, you told Juan you didn't want that
table anymore. After your shift that night, he was waiting outside, earphones
stuck in his ears, asking you to go out with him because your name rhymed with
hakuna matata and *The Lion King* was the only maudlin movie he'd ever liked.
You didn't know what *The Lion King* was. You looked at him in the bright light
and noticed that his eyes were the color of extra-virgin olive oil, a greenish gold.
Extra-virgin olive oil was the only thing you loved, truly loved, in America.

He was a senior at the state university. He told you how old he was and you
asked why he had not graduated yet. This was America, after all, it was not like
back home, where universities closed so often that people added three years to
their normal course of study and lecturers went on strike after strike and still
were not paid. He said he had taken a couple of years off to discover himself
and travel, mostly to Africa and Asia. You asked him where he ended up finding
himself and he laughed. You did not laugh. You did not know that people could
simply choose not to go to school, that people could dictate to life. You were
used to accepting what life gave, writing down what life dictated.

You said no the following four days to going out with him, because you were
uncomfortable with the way he looked at your face, that intense, consuming
way he looked at your face that made you say goodbye to him but also made you
reluctant to walk away. And then, the fifth night, you panicked when he was not
standing at the door after your shift. You prayed for the first time in a long time
and when he came up behind you and said hey, you said yes, you would go out
with him, even before he asked. You were scared he would not ask again.

The next day, he took you to dinner at Chang's and your fortune cookie had
two strips of paper. Both of them were blank.

You knew you had become comfortable when you told him that you 20
watched *Jeopardy* on the restaurant TV and that you rooted for the following, in
this order: women of color, black men, and white women, before, finally, white
men — which meant you never rooted for white men. He laughed and told you
he was used to not being rooted for, his mother taught women's studies.

And you knew you had become close when you told him that your father
was really not a schoolteacher in Lagos, that he was a junior driver for a

construction company. And you told him about that day in Lagos traffic in the rickety Peugeot 504 your father drove; it was raining and your seat was wet because of the rust-eaten hole in the roof. The traffic was heavy, the traffic was always heavy in Lagos, and when it rained it was chaos. The roads became muddy ponds and cars got stuck and some of your cousins went out and made some money pushing the cars out. The rain, the swampiness, you thought, made your father step on the brakes too late that day. You heard the bump before you felt it. The car your father rammed into was wide, foreign, and dark green, with golden headlights like the eyes of a leopard. Your father started to cry and beg even before he got out of the car and laid himself flat on the road, causing much blowing of horns. Sorry sir, sorry sir, he chanted. If you sell me and my family, you cannot buy even one tire on your car. Sorry sir.

The Big Man seated at the back did not come out, but his driver did, examining the damage, looking at your father's sprawled form from the corner of his eye as though the pleading was like pornography, a performance he was ashamed to admit he enjoyed. At last he let your father go. Waved him away. The other cars' horns blew and drivers cursed. When your father came back into the car, you refused to look at him because he was just like the pigs that wallowed in the marshes around the market. Your father looked like *nsi*. Shit.

After you told him this, he pursed his lips and held your hand and said he understood how you felt. You shook your hand free, suddenly annoyed, because he thought the world was, or ought to be, full of people like him. You told him there was nothing to understand, it was just the way it was.

He found the African store in the Hartford yellow pages and drove you there. Because of the way he walked around with familiarity, tilting the bottle of palm wine to see how much sediment it had, the Ghanaian store owner asked him if he was African, like the white Kenyans or South Africans, and he said yes, but he'd been in America for a long time. He looked pleased that the store owner had believed him. You cooked that evening with the things you had bought, and after he ate *garri*° and *onugbu* soup,° he threw up in your sink. You didn't mind, though, because now you would be able to cook *onugbu* soup with meat.

He didn't eat meat because he thought it was wrong the way they killed animals; he said they released fear toxins into the animals and the fear toxins made people paranoid. Back home, the meat pieces you ate, when there was meat, were the size of half your finger. But you did not tell him that. You did not tell him either that the *dawadawa*° cubes your mother cooked everything with, because curry and thyme were too expensive, had MSG, *were* MSG. He said MSG caused cancer, it was the reason he liked Chang's; Chang didn't cook with MSG.

Once, at Chang's, he told the waiter he had recently visited Shanghai, that he spoke some Mandarin. The waiter warmed up and told him what soup was

---

garri: A popular West African food made from cassava tubers.
onugbu soup: Bitter leaf soup; a traditional Nigerian dish.
dawadawa: Fermented African locust beans, used as a spice.

best and then asked him, "You have girlfriend in Shanghai now?" And he smiled and said nothing.

You lost your appetite, the region deep in your chest felt clogged. That night, you didn't moan when he was inside you, you bit your lips and pretended that you didn't come because you knew he would worry. Later you told him why you were upset, that even though you went to Chang's so often together, even though you had kissed just before the menus came, the Chinese man had assumed you could not possibly be his girlfriend, and he had smiled and said nothing. Before he apologized, he gazed at you blankly and you knew that he did not understand.

He bought you presents and when you objected about the cost, he said his grandfather in Boston had been wealthy but hastily added that the old man had given a lot away and so the trust fund he had wasn't huge. His presents mystified you. A fist-size glass ball that you shook to watch a tiny, shapely doll in pink spin around. A shiny rock whose surface took on the color of whatever touched it. An expensive scarf hand-painted in Mexico. Finally you told him, your voice stretched in irony, that in your life presents were always useful. The rock, for instance, would work if you could grind things with it. He laughed long and hard but you did not laugh. You realized that in his life, he could buy presents that were just presents and nothing else, nothing useful. When he started to buy you shoes and clothes and books, you asked him not to, you didn't want any presents at all. He bought them anyway and you kept them for your cousins and uncles and aunts, for when you would one day be able to visit home, even though you did not know how you could ever afford a ticket *and* your rent. He said he really wanted to see Nigeria and he could pay for you both to go. You did not want him to pay for you to visit home. You did not want him to go to Nigeria, to add it to the list of countries where he went to gawk at the lives of poor people who could never gawk back at *his* life. You told him this on a sunny day, when he took you to see Long Island Sound, and the two of you argued, your voices raised as you walked along the calm water. He said you were wrong to call him self-righteous. You said he was wrong to call only the poor Indians in Bombay the real Indians. Did it mean he wasn't a real American, since he was not like the poor fat people you and he had seen in Hartford? He hurried ahead of you, his upper body bare and pale, his flip-flops raising bits of sand, but then he came back and held out his hand for yours. You made up and made love and ran your hands through each other's hair, his soft and yellow like the swinging tassels of growing corn, yours dark and bouncy like the filling of a pillow. He had got too much sun and his skin turned the color of a ripe watermelon and you kissed his back before you rubbed lotion on it.

The thing that wrapped itself around your neck, that nearly choked you before you fell asleep, started to loosen, to let go.

You knew by people's reactions that you two were abnormal—the way the nasty ones were too nasty and the nice ones too nice. The old white men and women who muttered and glared at him, the black men who shook their heads at you, the black women whose pitying eyes bemoaned your lack of self-esteem, your self-loathing. Or the black women who smiled swift solidarity smiles; the black men who tried too hard to forgive you, saying a too-obvious hi to him; the white men and women who said "What a good-looking pair" too brightly, too loudly, as though to prove their own open-mindedness to themselves.

But his parents were different; they almost made you think it was all normal. His mother told you that he had never brought a girl to meet them, except for his high school prom date, and he grinned stiffly and held your hand. The tablecloth shielded your clasped hands. He squeezed your hand and you squeezed back and wondered why he was so stiff, why his extra-virgin-olive-oil-colored eyes darkened as he spoke to his parents. His mother was delighted when she asked if you'd read Nawal el Saadawi and you said yes. His father asked how similar Indian food was to Nigerian food and teased you about paying when the check came. You looked at them and felt grateful that they did not examine you like an exotic trophy, an ivory tusk.

Afterwards, he told you about his issues with his parents, how they portioned out love like a birthday cake, how they would give him a bigger slice if only he'd agree to go to law school. You wanted to sympathize. But instead you were angry.

You were angrier when he told you he had refused to go up to Canada with them for a week or two, to their summer cottage in the Quebec countryside. They had even asked him to bring you. He showed you pictures of the cottage and you wondered why it was called a cottage because the buildings that big around your neighborhood back home were banks and churches. You dropped a glass and it shattered on the hardwood of his apartment floor and he asked what was wrong and you said nothing, although you thought a lot was wrong. Later, in the shower, you started to cry. You watched the water dilute your tears and you didn't know why you were crying.

You wrote home finally. A short letter to your parents, slipped in between the crisp dollar bills, and you included your address. You got a reply only days later, by courier. Your mother wrote the letter herself; you knew from the spidery penmanship, from the misspelled words.

Your father was dead; he had slumped over the steering wheel of his 35 company car. Five months now, she wrote. They had used some of the money you sent to give him a good funeral: They killed a goat for the guests and buried him in a good coffin. You curled up in bed, pressed your knees to your chest, and tried to remember what you had been doing when your father died, what you had been doing for all the months when he was already dead. Perhaps your father died on the day your whole body had been covered in goosebumps, hard as uncooked rice, that you could not explain, Juan teasing you about taking over from the chef so that the heat in the kitchen would warm you up. Perhaps your father died on one of the days you took a drive to Mystic or watched a play in Manchester or had dinner at Chang's.

He held you while you cried, smoothed your hair, and offered to buy your ticket, to go with you to see your family. You said no, you needed to go alone.

He asked if you would come back and you reminded him that you had a green card and you would lose it if you did not come back in one year. He said you knew what he meant, would you come back, come back?

You turned away and said nothing, and when he drove you to the airport, you hugged him tight for a long, long moment, and then you let go.

Margaret Atwood   b. 1939

Happy Endings   [1983]

John and Mary meet.
What happens next?
If you want a happy ending, try A.

A

John and Mary fall in love and get married. They both have worthwhile and remunerative jobs which they find stimulating and challenging. They buy a charming house. Real estate values go up. Eventually, when they can afford live-in help, they have two children, to whom they are devoted. The children turn out well. John and Mary have a stimulating and challenging sex life and worthwhile friends. They go on fun vacations together. They retire. They both have hobbies which they find stimulating and challenging. Eventually they die. This is the end of the story.

B

Mary falls in love with John but John doesn't fall in love with Mary. He   5 merely uses her body for selfish pleasure and ego gratification of a tepid kind. He comes to her apartment twice a week and she cooks him dinner, you'll notice that he doesn't even consider her worth the price of a dinner out, and after he's eaten the dinner he fucks her and after that he falls asleep, while she does the dishes so he won't think she's untidy, having all those dirty dishes lying around, and puts on fresh lipstick so she'll look good when he wakes up, but when he wakes up he doesn't even notice, he puts on his socks and his shorts and his pants and his shirt and his tie and his shoes, the reverse order from the one in which he took them off. He doesn't take off Mary's clothes, she takes them off herself, she acts as if she's dying for it every time, not because she likes sex exactly, she doesn't, but she wants John to think she does because if they do it often enough surely he'll get used to her, he'll come to depend on her and they will get married, but John goes out the door with hardly so much as a good-night and three days later he turns up at six o'clock and they do the whole thing over again.

Mary gets run-down. Crying is bad for your face, everyone knows that and so does Mary but she can't stop. People at work notice. Her friends tell her John is a rat, a pig, a dog, he isn't good enough for her, but she can't believe it. Inside John, she thinks, is another John, who is much nicer. This other John will emerge like a butterfly from a cocoon, a Jack from a box, a pit from a prune, if the first John is only squeezed enough.

One evening John complains about the food. He has never complained about the food before. Mary is hurt.

Her friends tell her they've seen him in a restaurant with another woman, whose name is Madge. It's not even Madge that finally gets to Mary: It's the restaurant. John has never taken Mary to a restaurant. Mary collects all the sleeping pills and aspirins she can find, and takes them and a half a bottle of sherry. You can see what kind of a woman she is by the fact that it's not even whiskey. She leaves a note for John. She hopes he'll discover her and get her to the hospital in time and repent and then they can get married, but this fails to happen and she dies.

John marries Madge and everything continues as in A.

C

John, who is an older man, falls in love with Mary, and Mary, who is only 10 twenty-two, feels sorry for him because he's worried about his hair falling out. She sleeps with him even though she's not in love with him. She met him at work. She's in love with someone called James, who is twenty-two also and not yet ready to settle down.

John on the contrary settled down long ago: This is what is bothering him. John has a steady, respectable job and is getting ahead in his field, but Mary isn't impressed by him, she's impressed by James, who has a motorcycle and a fabulous record collection. But James is often away on his motorcycle, being free. Freedom isn't the same for girls, so in the meantime Mary spends Thursday evenings with John. Thursdays are the only days John can get away.

John is married to a woman called Madge and they have two children, a charming house which they bought just before the real estate values went up, and hobbies which they find stimulating and challenging, when they have the time. John tells Mary how important she is to him, but of course he can't leave his wife because a commitment is a commitment. He goes on about this more than is necessary and Mary finds it boring, but older men can keep it up longer so on the whole she has a fairly good time.

One day James breezes in on his motorcycle with some top-grade California hybrid and James and Mary get higher than you'd believe possible and they climb into bed. Everything becomes very underwater, but along comes John, who has a key to Mary's apartment. He finds them stoned and entwined. He's hardly in any position to be jealous, considering Madge, but nevertheless he's overcome with despair. Finally he's middle-aged, in two years he'll be bald as an egg and he can't stand it. He purchases a handgun, saying he needs it for target practice—this is the thin part of the plot, but it can be dealt with later—and shoots the two of them and himself.

Madge, after a suitable period of mourning, marries an understanding man called Fred and everything continues as in A, but under different names.

D

Fred and Madge have no problems. They get along exceptionally well and   15
are good at working out any little difficulties that may arise. But their charming house is by the seashore and one day a giant tidal wave approaches. Real estate values go down. The rest of the story is about what caused the tidal wave and how they escape from it. They do, though thousands drown, but Fred and Madge are virtuous and lucky. Finally on high ground they clasp each other, wet and dripping and grateful, and continue as in A.

E

Yes, but Fred has a bad heart. The rest of the story is about how kind and understanding they both are until Fred dies. Then Madge devotes herself to charity work until the end of A. If you like, it can be "Madge," "cancer," "guilty and confused," and "bird watching."

F

If you think this is all too bourgeois, make John a revolutionary and Mary a counterespionage agent and see how far that gets you. Remember, this is Canada. You'll still end up with A, though in between you may get a lustful brawling saga of passionate involvement, a chronicle of our times, sort of.

You'll have to face it, the endings are the same however you slice it. Don't be deluded by any other endings, they're all fake, either deliberately fake, with malicious intent to deceive, or just motivated by excessive optimism if not by downright sentimentality.

The only authentic ending is the one provided here:

John and Mary die. John and Mary die. John and Mary die.   20

So much for endings. Beginnings are always more fun. True connoisseurs, however, are known to favor the stretch in between, since it's the hardest to do anything with.

That's about all that can be said for plots, which anyway are just one thing after another, a what and a what and a what.

Now try How and Why.

James Baldwin   1924–1987

Sonny's Blues   [1957]

I read about it in the paper, in the subway, on my way to work. I read it, and I couldn't believe it, and I read it again. Then perhaps I just stared at it, at the newsprint spelling out his name, spelling out the story. I stared at it in the swinging lights of the subway car, and in the faces and bodies of the people, and in my own face, trapped in the darkness which roared outside.

APPROACHING THE AUTHOR

James Baldwin published his first story in a church newspaper when he was twelve and became a preacher at the small Fireside Pentecostal Church in Harlem when he was fourteen.

For more about him, see page 1055.

It was not to be believed and I kept telling myself that, as I walked from the subway station to the high school. And at the same time I couldn't doubt it. I was scared, scared for Sonny. He became real to me again. A great block of ice got settled in my belly and kept melting there slowly all day long, while I taught my classes algebra. It was a special kind of ice. It kept melting, sending trickles of ice water all up and down my veins, but it never got less. Sometimes it hardened and seemed to expand until I felt my guts were going to come spilling out or that I was going to choke or scream. This would always be at a moment when I was remembering some specific thing Sonny had once said or done.

When he was about as old as the boys in my classes his face had been bright and open, there was a lot of copper in it; and he'd had wonderfully direct brown eyes, and great gentleness and privacy. I wondered what he looked like now. He had been picked up, the evening before, in a raid on an apartment downtown, for peddling and using heroin.

I couldn't believe it: but what I mean by that is that I couldn't find any room for it anywhere inside me. I had kept it outside me for a long time. I hadn't wanted to know. I had had suspicions, but I didn't name them, I kept putting them away. I told myself that Sonny was wild, but he wasn't crazy. And he'd always been a good boy, he hadn't ever turned hard or evil or disrespectful, the way kids can, so quick, so quick, especially in Harlem. I didn't want to believe that I'd ever see my brother going down, coming to nothing, all that light in his face gone out, in the condition I'd already seen so many others. Yet it had happened and here I was, talking about algebra to a lot of boys who might, every one of them for all I knew, be popping off needles every time they went to the head. Maybe it did more for them than algebra could.

I was sure that the first time Sonny had ever had horse,° he couldn't have 5
been much older than these boys were now. These boys, now, were living as we'd
been living then, they were growing up with a rush and their heads bumped
abruptly against the low ceiling of their actual possibilities. They were filled with
rage. All they really knew were two darknesses, the darkness of their lives, which
was now closing in on them, and the darkness of the movies, which had blinded
them to that other darkness, and in which they now, vindictively, dreamed, at
once more together than they were at any other time, and more alone.

When the last bell rang, the last class ended, I let out my breath. It seemed I'd
been holding it for all that time. My clothes were wet—I may have looked as
though I'd been sitting in a steam bath, all dressed up, all afternoon. I sat alone in
the classroom a long time. I listened to the boys outside, downstairs, shouting and
cursing and laughing. Their laughter struck me for perhaps the first time. It was
not the joyous laughter which—God knows why—one associates with children. It
was mocking and insular, its intent to denigrate. It was disenchanted, and in this,
also, lay the authority of their curses. Perhaps I was listening to them because I was
thinking about my brother and in them I heard my brother. And myself.

One boy was whistling a tune, at once very complicated and very simple, it
seemed to be pouring out of him as though he were a bird, and it sounded very
cool and moving through all that harsh, bright air, only just holding its own
through all those other sounds.

I stood up and walked over to the window and looked down into the courtyard. It was the beginning of the spring and the sap was rising in the boys. A
teacher passed through them every now and again, quickly, as though he or she
couldn't wait to get out of that courtyard, to get those boys out of their sight
and off their minds. I started collecting my stuff. I thought I'd better get home
and talk to Isabel.

The courtyard was almost deserted by the time I got downstairs. I saw
this boy standing in the shadow of a doorway, looking just like Sonny. I almost
called his name. Then I saw that it wasn't Sonny, but somebody we used to
know, a boy from around our block. He'd been Sonny's friend. He'd never been
mine, having been too young for me, and, anyway, I'd never liked him. And
now, even though he was a grown-up man, he still hung around that block, still
spent hours on the street corners, was always high and raggy. I used to run into
him from time to time and he'd often work around to asking me for a quarter
or fifty cents. He always had some real good excuse, too, and I always gave it to
him, I don't know why.

But now, abruptly, I hated him. I couldn't stand the way he looked at me, 10
partly like a dog, partly like a cunning child. I wanted to ask him what the hell
he was doing in the school courtyard.

He sort of shuffled over to me, and he said, "I see you got the papers. So
you already know about it."

Horse: Heroin.

"You mean about Sonny? Yes, I already know about it. How come they didn't get you?"

He grinned. It made him repulsive and it also brought to mind what he'd looked like as a kid. "I wasn't there. I stay away from them people."

"Good for you." I offered him a cigarette and I watched him through the smoke. "You come all the way down here just to tell me about Sonny?"

"That's right." He was sort of shaking his head and his eyes looked strange,   15
as though they were about to cross. The bright sun deadened his damp dark brown skin and it made his eyes look yellow and showed up the dirt in his kinked hair. He smelled funky. I moved a little away from him and I said, "Well, thanks. But I already know about it and I got to get home."

"I'll walk you a little ways," he said. We started walking. There were a couple of kids still loitering in the courtyard and one of them said goodnight to me and looked strangely at the boy beside me.

"What're you going to do?" he asked me. "I mean, about Sonny?"

"Look. I haven't seen Sonny for over a year, I'm not sure I'm going to do anything. Anyway, what the hell *can* I do?"

"That's right," he said quickly, "ain't nothing you can do. Can't much help old Sonny no more, I guess."

It was what I was thinking and so it seemed to me he had no right to   20
say it.

"I'm surprised at Sonny, though," he went on—he had a funny way of talking, he looked straight ahead as though he were talking to himself—"I thought Sonny was a smart boy, I thought he was too smart to get hung."

"I guess he thought so too," I said sharply, "and that's how he got hung. And how about you? You're pretty goddamn smart, I bet."

Then he looked directly at me, just for a minute. "I ain't smart," he said. "If I was smart, I'd have reached for a pistol a long time ago."

"Look. Don't tell *me* your sad story, if it was up to me, I'd give you one." Then I felt guilty—guilty, probably, for never having supposed that the poor bastard *had* a story of his own, much less a sad one, and I asked, quickly, "What's going to happen to him now?"

He didn't answer this. He was off by himself some place. "Funny thing," he   25
said, and from his tone we might have been discussing the quickest way to get to Brooklyn, "when I saw the papers this morning, the first thing I asked myself was if I had anything to do with it. I felt sort of responsible."

I began to listen more carefully. The subway station was on the corner, just before us, and I stopped. He stopped, too. We were in front of a bar and he ducked lightly, peering in, but whoever he was looking for didn't seem to be there. The juke box was blasting away with something black and bouncy and I half watched the barmaid as she danced her way from the juke box to her place behind the bar. And I watched her face as she laughingly responded to something someone said to her, still keeping time to the music. When she smiled one saw the little girl, one sensed the doomed, still-struggling woman beneath the battered face of the semi-whore.

"I never *give* Sonny nothing," the boy said finally, "but a long time ago I come to school high and Sonny asked me how it felt." He paused, I couldn't bear to watch him, I watched the barmaid, and I listened to the music which seemed to be causing the pavement to shake. "I told him it felt great." The music stopped, the barmaid paused and watched the juke box until the music began again. "It did."

All this was carrying me some place I didn't want to go. I certainly didn't want to know how it felt. It filled everything, the people, the houses, the music, the dark, quicksilver barmaid, with menace; and this menace was their reality.

"What's going to happen to him now?" I asked again.

"They'll send him away some place and they'll try to cure him." He shook   30 his head. "Maybe he'll even think he's kicked the habit. Then they'll let him loose" — he gestured, throwing his cigarette into the gutter. "That's all."

"What do you mean, that's *all?*"

But I knew what he meant.

"I *mean*, that's *all.*" He turned his head and looked at me, pulling down the corners of his mouth. "Don't you know what I mean?" he asked, softly.

"How the hell *would* I know what you mean?" I almost whispered it, I don't know why.

"That's right," he said to the air, "how would *he* know what I mean?" He   35 turned toward me again, patient and calm, and yet I somehow felt him shaking, shaking as though he were going to fall apart. I felt that ice in my guts again, the dread I'd felt all afternoon; and again I watched the barmaid, moving about the bar, washing glasses, and singing. "Listen. They'll let him out and then it'll just start all over again. That's what I mean."

"You mean — they'll let him out. And then he'll just start working his way back in again. You mean he'll never kick the habit. Is that what you mean?"

"That's right," he said, cheerfully. "*You* see what I mean."

"Tell me," I said at last, "why does he want to die? He must want to die, he's killing himself, why does he want to die?"

He looked at me in surprise. He licked his lips. "He don't want to die. He wants to live. Don't nobody want to die, ever."

Then I wanted to ask him — too many things. He could not have answered,   40 or if he had, I could not have borne the answers. I started walking. "Well, I guess it's none of my business."

"It's going to be rough on old Sonny," he said. We reached the subway station. "This is your station?" he asked. I nodded. I took one step down. "Damn!" he said, suddenly. I looked up at him. He grinned again. "Damn it if I didn't leave all my money home. You ain't got a dollar on you, have you? Just for a couple of days, is all."

All at once something inside gave and threatened to come pouring out of me. I didn't hate him any more. I felt that in another moment I'd start crying like a child.

"Sure," I said. "Don't sweat." I looked in my wallet and didn't have a dollar, I only had a five. "Here," I said. "That hold you?"

He didn't look at it—he didn't want to look at it. A terrible closed look came over his face, as though he were keeping the number on the bill a secret from him and me. "Thanks," he said, and now he was dying to see me go. "Don't worry about Sonny. Maybe I'll write him or something."

"Sure," I said. "You do that. So long."   45

"Be seeing you," he said. I went on down the steps.

And I didn't write Sonny or send him anything for a long time. When I finally did, it was just after my little girl died, he wrote me back a letter which made me feel like a bastard.

Here's what he said:

> Dear brother,
> You don't know how much I needed to hear from you. I wanted to write you many a time but I dug how much I must have hurt you and so I didn't write. But now I feel like a man who's been trying to climb up out of some deep, real deep and funky hole and just saw the sun up there, outside. I got to get outside.
> I can't tell you much about how I got here. I mean I don't know how to tell you. I guess I was afraid of something or I was trying to escape from something and you know I have never been very strong in the head (smile). I'm glad Mama and Daddy are dead and can't see what's happened to their son and I swear if I'd known what I was doing I would never have hurt you so, you and a lot of other fine people who were nice to me and who believed in me.
> I don't want you to think it had anything to do with me being a musician. It's more than that. Or maybe less than that. I can't get anything straight in my head down here and I try not to think about what's going to happen to me when I get outside again. Sometime I think I'm going to flip and *never* get outside and sometime I think I'll come straight back. I tell you one thing, though, I'd rather blow my brains out than go through this again. But that's what they all say, so they tell me. If I tell you when I'm coming to New York and if you could meet me, I sure would appreciate it. Give my love to Isabel and the kids and I was sure sorry to hear about little Gracie. I wish I could be like Mama and say the Lord's will be done, but I don't know it seems to me that trouble is the one thing that never does get stopped and I don't know what good it does to blame it on the Lord. But maybe it does some good if you believe it.
>   Your brother,
>   Sonny

Then I kept in constant touch with him and I sent him whatever I could and I went to meet him when he came back to New York. When I saw him many things I thought I had forgotten came flooding back to me. This was because I had begun, finally, to wonder about Sonny, about the life that Sonny lived inside. This life, whatever it was, had made him older and thinner and it had deepened the distant stillness in which he had always moved. He looked very unlike my baby brother. Yet, when he smiled, when we shook hands, the baby brother I'd never known looked out from the depths of his private life, like an animal waiting to be coaxed into the light.

"How you been keeping?" he asked me.   50

"All right. And you?"

"Just fine." He was smiling all over his face. "It's good to see you again."

"It's good to see you."

The seven years' difference in our ages lay between us like a chasm: I wondered if these years would ever operate between us as a bridge. I was remembering, and it made it hard to catch my breath, that I had been there when he was born; and I had heard the first words he had ever spoken. When he started to walk, he walked from our mother straight to me. I caught him just before he fell when he took the first steps he ever took in this world.

"How's Isabel?"   55

"Just fine. She's dying to see you."

"And the boys?"

"They're fine, too. They're anxious to see their uncle."

"Oh, come on. You know they don't remember me."

"Are you kidding? Of course they remember you."   60

He grinned again. We got into a taxi. We had a lot to say to each other, far too much to know how to begin.

As the taxi began to move, I asked, "You still want to go to India?"

He laughed. "You still remember that. Hell, no. This place is Indian enough for me."

"It used to belong to them," I said.

And he laughed again. "They damn sure knew what they were doing when   65
they got rid of it."

Years ago, when he was around fourteen, he'd been all hipped on the idea of going to India. He read books about people sitting on rocks, naked, in all kinds of weather, but mostly bad, naturally, and walking barefoot through hot coals and arriving at wisdom. I used to say that it sounded to me as though they were getting away from wisdom as fast as they could. I think he sort of looked down on me for that.

"Do you mind," he asked, "if we have the driver drive alongside the park? On the west side — I haven't seen the city in so long."

"Of course not," I said. I was afraid that I might sound as though I were humoring him, but I hoped he wouldn't take it that way.

So we drove along, between the green of the park and the stony, lifeless elegance of hotels and apartment buildings, toward the vivid, killing streets of our childhood. These streets hadn't changed, though housing projects jutted up out of them now like rocks in the middle of a boiling sea. Most of the houses in which we had grown up had vanished, as had the stores from which we had stolen, the basements in which we had first tried sex, the rooftops from which we had hurled tin cans and bricks. But houses exactly like the houses of our past yet dominated the landscape, boys exactly like the boys we once had been found themselves smothering in these houses, came down into the streets for light and air and found themselves encircled by disaster. Some escaped the trap, most didn't. Those who got out always left something of themselves behind, as some animals amputate a leg and leave it in the trap. It might be said, perhaps, that I had escaped, after all, I was a school teacher; or that Sonny had, he hadn't lived in Harlem for years. Yet, as the cab moved uptown through streets which seemed, with a rush, to darken with dark people, and as I covertly studied Sonny's face, it came to me that what we both were seeking through our separate cab windows was that part of ourselves which had been left behind. It's always at the hour of trouble and confrontation that the missing member aches.

We hit 110th Street and started rolling up Lenox Avenue. And I'd known 70
this avenue all my life, but it seemed to me again, as it had seemed on the day I'd first heard about Sonny's trouble, filled with a hidden menace which was its very breath of life.

"We almost there," said Sonny.

"Almost." We were both too nervous to say anything more.

We live in a housing project. It hasn't been up long. A few days after it was up it seemed uninhabitably new, now, of course, it's already rundown. It looks like a parody of the good, clean, faceless life—God knows the people who live in it do their best to make it a parody. The beat-looking grass lying around isn't enough to make their lives green, the hedges will never hold out the streets, and they know it. The big windows fool no one, they aren't big enough to make space out of no space. They don't bother with the windows, they watch the TV screen instead. The playground is most popular with the children who don't play at jacks, or skip rope, or roller skate, or swing, and they can be found in it after dark. We moved in partly because it's not too far from where I teach, and partly for the kids; but it's really just like the houses in which Sonny and I grew up. The same things happen, they'll have the same things to remember. The moment Sonny and I started into the house I had the feeling that I was simply bringing him back into the danger he had almost died trying to escape.

Sonny has never been talkative. So I don't know why I was sure he'd be dying to talk to me when supper was over the first night. Everything went fine, the oldest boy remembered him, and the youngest boy liked him, and Sonny had remembered to bring something for each of them; and Isabel, who is really much nicer than I am, more open and giving, had gone to a lot of trouble about dinner and was genuinely glad to see him. And she's always been able to tease Sonny in a way that I haven't. It was nice to see her face so vivid again and to hear her laugh and watch her make Sonny laugh. She wasn't, or, anyway, she didn't seem to be, at all uneasy or embarrassed. She chatted as though there were no subject which had to be avoided and she got Sonny past his first, faint stiffness. And thank God she was there, for I was filled with that icy dread again. Everything I did seemed awkward to me, and everything I said sounded freighted with hidden meaning. I was trying to remember everything I'd heard about dope addiction and I couldn't help watching Sonny for signs. I wasn't doing it out of malice. I was trying to find out something about my brother. I was dying to hear him tell me he was safe.

"Safe!" my father grunted, whenever Mama suggested trying to move to a 75 neighborhood which might be safer for children. "Safe, hell! Ain't no place safe for kids, nor nobody."

He always went on like this, but he wasn't, ever, really as bad as he sounded, not even on weekends, when he got drunk. As a matter of fact, he was always on the lookout for "something a little better," but he died before he found it. He died suddenly, during a drunken weekend in the middle of the war, when Sonny was fifteen. He and Sonny hadn't ever got on too well. And this was partly because Sonny was the apple of his father's eye. It was because he loved Sonny so much and was frightened for him, that he was always fighting with him. It doesn't do any good to fight with Sonny. Sonny just moves back, inside himself, where he can't be reached. But the principal reason that they never hit it off is that they were so much alike. Daddy was big and rough and loud-talking, just the opposite of Sonny, but they both had—that same privacy.

Mama tried to tell me something about this, just after Daddy died. I was home on leave from the army.

This was the last time I ever saw my mother alive. Just the same, this picture gets all mixed up in my mind with pictures I had of her when she was younger. The way I always see her is the way she used to be on a Sunday afternoon, say, when the old folks were talking after the big Sunday dinner. I always see her wearing pale blue. She'd be sitting on the sofa. And my father would be sitting in the easy chair, not far from her. And the living room would be full of church folks and relatives. There they sit, in chairs all around the living room, and the night is creeping up outside, but nobody knows it yet. You can see the darkness growing against the windowpanes and you hear the street noises every now and again, or maybe the jangling beat of a tambourine from one of the churches close by, but it's real quiet in the room. For a moment nobody's talking, but every face looks darkening, like the sky outside. And my mother rocks a little from the waist, and my father's eyes are closed. Everyone is looking at something a child can't see. For a minute they've forgotten the children. Maybe a kid is lying on the rug, half asleep. Maybe somebody's got a kid in his lap and is absent-mindedly stroking the kid's head. Maybe there's a kid, quiet and big-eyed, curled up in a big chair in the corner. The silence, the darkness coming, and the darkness in the faces frightens the child obscurely. He hopes that the hand which strokes his forehead will never stop—will never die. He hopes that there will never come a time when the old folks won't be sitting around the living room, talking about where they've come from, and what they've seen, and what's happened to them and their kinfolk.

But something deep and watchful in the child knows that this is bound to end, is already ending. In a moment someone will get up and turn on the light. Then the old folks will remember the children and they won't talk any more that day. And when light fills the room, the child is filled with darkness. He knows that everytime this happens he's moved just a little closer to that darkness outside. The darkness outside is what the old folks have been talking about. It's what they've come from. It's what they endure. The child knows that they won't talk any more because if he knows too much about what's happened to *them*, he'll know too much too soon, about what's going to happen to *him*.

The last time I talked to my mother, I remember I was restless. I wanted to 80 get out and see Isabel. We weren't married then and we had a lot to straighten out between us.

There Mama sat, in black, by the window. She was humming an old church song, *Lord, you brought me from a long ways off.* Sonny was out somewhere. Mama kept watching the streets.

"I don't know," she said, "if I'll ever see you again, after you go off from here. But I hope you'll remember the things I tried to teach you."

"Don't talk like that," I said, and smiled. "You'll be here a long time yet."

She smiled, too, but she said nothing. She was quiet for a long time. And I said, "Mama, don't you worry about nothing. I'll be writing all the time, and you be getting the checks. . . ."

"I want to talk to you about your brother," she said, suddenly. "If anything 85 happens to me he ain't going to have nobody to look out for him."

"Mama," I said, "ain't nothing going to happen to you *or* Sonny. Sonny's all right. He's a good boy and he's got good sense."

"It ain't a question of his being a good boy," Mama said, "nor of his having good sense. It ain't only the bad ones, nor yet the dumb ones that gets sucked under." She stopped, looking at me. "Your Daddy once had a brother," she said, and she smiled in a way that made me feel she was in pain. "You didn't never know that, did you?"

"No," I said, "I never knew that," and I watched her face.

"Oh, yes," she said, "your Daddy had a brother." She looked out of the window again. "I know you never saw your Daddy cry. But *I* did—many a time, through all these years."

I asked her, "What happened to his brother? How come nobody's ever 90 talked about him?"

This was the first time I ever saw my mother look old.

"His brother got killed," she said, "when he was just a little younger than you are now. I knew him. He was a fine boy. He was maybe a little full of the devil, but he didn't mean nobody no harm."

Then she stopped and the room was silent, exactly as it had sometimes been on those Sunday afternoons. Mama kept looking out into the streets.

"He used to have a job in the mill," she said, "and, like all young folks, he just liked to perform on Saturday nights. Saturday nights, him and your father would drift around to different places, go to dances and things like that, or just sit around with people they knew, and your father's brother would sing, he had a fine voice, and play along with himself on his guitar. Well, this particular Saturday night, him and your father was coming home from some place, and they were both a little drunk and there was a moon that night, it was bright like day. Your father's brother was feeling kind of good, and he was whistling to himself, and he had his guitar slung over his shoulder. They was coming down a hill and beneath them was a road that turned off from the highway. Well, your father's brother, being always kind of frisky, decided to run down this hill, and he did, with that guitar banging and clanging behind him, and he ran across the road, and he was making water behind a tree. And your father was sort of amused at him and he was still coming down the hill, kind of slow. Then he heard a car motor and that same minute his brother stepped from behind the tree, into the road, in the moonlight. And he started to cross the road. And your father started to run down the hill, he says he don't know why. This car was full of white men. They was all drunk, and when they seen your father's brother they let out a great whoop and holler and they aimed the car straight at him. They was having fun, they just wanted to scare him, the way they do some-times, you know. But they was drunk. And I guess the boy, being drunk, too, and scared, kind of lost his head. By the time he jumped it was too late. Your father says he heard his brother scream when the car rolled over him, and he heard the wood of that guitar when it give, and he heard them strings go flying, and he heard them white men shouting, and the car kept on a-going and it ain't stopped till this day. And, time your father got down the hill, his brother weren't nothing but blood and pulp."

Tears were gleaming on my mother's face. There wasn't anything I could say. 95

"He never mentioned it," she said, "because I never let him mention it before you children. Your Daddy was like a crazy man that night and for many a night thereafter. He says he never in his life seen anything as dark as that road after the lights of that car had gone away. Weren't nothing, weren't nobody on that road, just your Daddy and his brother and that busted guitar. Oh, yes. Your Daddy never did really get right again. Till the day he died he weren't sure but that every white man he saw was the man that killed his brother."

She stopped and took out her handkerchief and dried her eyes and looked at me.

"I ain't telling you all this," she said, "to make you scared or bitter or to make you hate nobody. I'm telling you this because you got a brother. And the world ain't changed."

I guess I didn't want to believe this. I guess she saw this in my face. She turned away from me, toward the window again, searching those streets.

"But I praise my Redeemer," she said at last, "that He called your Daddy 100 home before me. I ain't saying it to throw no flowers at myself, but, I declare, it keeps me from feeling too cast down to know I helped your father get safely through this world. Your father always acted like he was the roughest, strongest man on earth. And everybody took him to be like that. But if he hadn't had *me* there—to see his tears!"

She was crying again. Still, I couldn't move. I said, "Lord, Lord, Mama, I didn't know it was like that."

"Oh, honey," she said, "there's a lot that you don't know. But you are going to find it out." She stood up from the window and came over to me. "You got to hold on to your brother," she said, "and don't let him fall, no matter what it looks like is happening to him and no matter how evil you gets with him. You going to be evil with him many a time. But don't you forget what I told you, you hear?"

"I won't forget," I said. "Don't you worry, I won't forget. I won't let nothing happen to Sonny."

My mother smiled as though she were amused at something she saw in my face. Then, "You may not be able to stop nothing from happening. But you got to let him know you's *there*."

Two days later I was married, and then I was gone. And I had a lot of things on my mind and I pretty well forgot my promise to Mama until I got shipped home on a special furlough for her funeral.

And, after the funeral, with just Sonny and me alone in the empty kitchen, I tried to find out something about him.

"What do you want to do?" I asked him.

"I'm going to be a musician," he said.

For he had graduated, in the time I had been away, from dancing to the juke box to finding out who was playing what, and what they were doing with it, and he had bought himself a set of drums.

"You mean, you want to be a drummer?" I somehow had the feeling that being a drummer might be all right for other people but not for my brother Sonny.

"I don't think," he said, looking at me very gravely, "that I'll ever be a good drummer. But I think I can play a piano."

I frowned. I'd never played the role of the older brother quite so seriously before, had scarcely ever, in fact, *asked* Sonny a damn thing. I sensed myself in the presence of something I didn't really know how to handle, didn't understand. So I made my frown a little deeper as I asked: "What kind of musician do you want to be?"

He grinned. "How many kinds do you think there are?"

"Be *serious*," I said.

He laughed, throwing his head back, and then looked at me. "I *am* serious."

"Well, then, for Christ's sake, stop kidding around and answer a serious question. I mean, do you want to be a concert pianist, you want to play classical music and all that, or — or what?" Long before I finished he was laughing again. "For Christ's *sake*, Sonny!"

He sobered, but with difficulty. "I'm sorry. But you sound so — scared!" and he was off again.

"Well, you may think it's funny now, baby, but it's not going to be so funny when you have to make your living at it, let me tell you *that*." I was furious because I knew he was laughing at me and I didn't know why.

"No," he said, very sober now, and afraid, perhaps, that he'd hurt me, "I don't want to be a classical pianist. That isn't what interests me. I mean" — he paused, looking hard at me, as though his eyes would help me to understand, and then gestured helplessly, as though perhaps his hand would

105

110

115

help — "I mean, I'll have a lot of studying to do, and I'll have to study *every-thing*, but, I mean, I want to play *with* — jazz musicians." He stopped. "I want to play jazz," he said.

Well, the word had never before sounded as heavy, as real, as it sounded 120 that afternoon in Sonny's mouth. I just looked at him and I was probably frowning a real frown by this time. I simply couldn't see why on earth he'd want to spend his time hanging around nightclubs, clowning around on bandstands, while people pushed each other around a dance floor. It seemed — beneath him, somehow. I had never thought about it before, had never been forced to, but I suppose I had always put jazz musicians in a class with what Daddy called "good-time people."

"Are you *serious?*"

"Hell, *yes*, I'm serious."

He looked more helpless than ever, and annoyed, and deeply hurt.

I suggested, helpfully: "You mean — like Louis Armstrong?"

His face closed as though I'd struck him. "No. I'm not talking about none 125 of that old-time, down home crap."

"Well, look, Sonny, I'm sorry, don't get mad. I just don't altogether get it, that's all. Name somebody — you know, a jazz musician you admire."

"Bird."

"Who?"

"Bird! Charlie Parker!° Don't they teach you nothing in the goddamn army?"

I lit a cigarette. I was surprised and then a little amused to discover that I 130 was trembling. "I've been out of touch," I said. "You'll have to be patient with me. Now. Who's this Parker character?"

"He's just one of the greatest jazz musicians alive," said Sonny, sullenly, his hands in his pockets, his back to me. "Maybe *the* greatest," he added, bitterly, "that's probably why you never heard of him."

"All right," I said, "I'm ignorant. I'm sorry. I'll go out and buy all the cat's records right away, all right?"

"It don't," said Sonny, with dignity, "make any difference to me. I don't care what you listen to. Don't do me no favors."

I was beginning to realize that I'd never seen him so upset before. With another part of my mind I was thinking that this would probably turn out to be one of those things kids go through and that I shouldn't make it seem impor-tant by pushing it too hard. Still, I didn't think it would do any harm to ask: "Doesn't all this take a lot of time? Can you make a living at it?"

He turned back to me and half leaned, half sat, on the kitchen table. 135 "Everything takes time," he said, "and — well, yes, sure, I can make a living at it.

Charlie Parker: Parker (1920–1955), saxophonist and composer, is widely regarded as one of the greatest jazz musicians. His original nickname "Yardbird" (of disputed origin) was later shortened to "Bird."

But what I don't seem to be able to make you understand is that it's the only thing I want to do."

"Well, Sonny," I said, gently, "you know people can't always do exactly what they *want* to do—"

"*No*, I don't know that," said Sonny, surprising me. "I think people *ought* to do what they want to do, what else are they alive for?"

"You getting to be a big boy," I said desperately, "it's time you started thinking about your future."

"I'm thinking about my future," said Sonny, grimly. "I think about it all the time."

I gave up. I decided, if he didn't change his mind, that we could always talk   140
about it later. "In the meantime," I said, "you got to finish school." We had already decided that he'd have to move in with Isabel and her folks. I knew this wasn't the ideal arrangement because Isabel's folks are inclined to be dicty° and they hadn't especially wanted Isabel to marry me. But I didn't know what else to do. "And we have to get you fixed up at Isabel's."

There was a long silence. He moved from the kitchen table to the window. "That's a terrible idea. You know it yourself."

"Do you have a *better* idea?"

He just walked up and down the kitchen for a minute. He was as tall as I was. He had started to shave. I suddenly had the feeling that I didn't know him at all.

He stopped at the kitchen table and picked up my cigarettes. Looking at me with a kind of mocking, amused defiance, he put one between his lips. "You mind?"

"You smoking already?"   145

He lit the cigarette and nodded, watching me through the smoke. "I just wanted to see if I'd have the courage to smoke in front of you." He grinned and blew a great cloud of smoke to the ceiling. "It was easy." He looked at my face. "Come on, now. I bet you was smoking at my age, tell the truth."

I didn't say anything but the truth was on my face, and he laughed. But now there was something very strained in his laugh. "Sure. And I bet that ain't all you was doing."

He was frightening me a little. "Cut the crap," I said. "We already decided that you was going to go and live at Isabel's. Now what's got into you all of a sudden?"

"*You* decided it," he pointed out. "*I* didn't decide nothing." He stopped in front of me, leaning against the stove, arms loosely folded. "Look, brother. I don't want to stay in Harlem no more, I really don't." He was very earnest. He looked at me, then over toward the kitchen window. There was something in his eyes I'd never seen before, some thoughtfulness, some worry all his own. He rubbed the muscle of one arm. "It's time I was getting out of here."

"Where do you want to *go*, Sonny?"   150

"I want to join the army. Or the navy, I don't care. If I say I'm old enough, they'll believe me."

―――――――――――――

dicty: Snobby, pretentious, self-important.

Then I got mad. It was because I was so scared. "You must be crazy. You goddamn fool, what the hell do you want to go and join the *army* for?"

"I just told you. To get out of Harlem."

"Sonny, you haven't even finished *school*. And if you really want to be a musician, how do you expect to study if you're in the *army*?"

He looked at me, trapped, and in anguish. "There's ways. I might be able to   155
work out some kind of deal. Anyway, I'll have the G.I. Bill when I come out."

"*If* you come out." We stared at each other. "Sonny, please. Be reasonable. I know the setup is far from perfect. But we got to do the best we can."

"I ain't learning nothing in school," he said. "Even when I go." He turned away from me and opened the window and threw his cigarette out into the narrow alley. I watched his back. "At least, I ain't learning nothing you'd want me to learn." He slammed the window so hard I thought the glass would fly out, and turned back to me. "And I'm sick of the stink of these garbage cans!"

"Sonny," I said, "I know how you feel. But if you don't finish school now, you're going to be sorry later that you didn't." I grabbed him by the shoulders. "And you only got another year. It ain't so bad. And I'll come back and I swear I'll help you do *whatever* you want to do. Just try to put up with it till I come back. Will you please do that? For me?"

He didn't answer and he wouldn't look at me.

"Sonny. You hear me?"   160

He pulled away. "I hear you. But you never hear anything *I* say."

I didn't know what to say to that. He looked out of the window and then back at me. "OK," he said, and sighed. "I'll try."

Then I said, trying to cheer him up a little, "They got a piano at Isabel's. You can practice on it."

And as a matter of fact, it did cheer him up for a minute. "That's right," he said to himself. "I forgot that." His face relaxed a little. But the worry, the thoughtfulness, played on it still, the way shadows play on a face which is staring into the fire.

But I thought I'd never hear the end of that piano. At first, Isabel would   165
write me, saying how nice it was that Sonny was so serious about his music and how, as soon as he came in from school, or wherever he had been when he was supposed to be at school, he went straight to that piano and stayed there until suppertime. And, after supper, he went back to that piano and stayed there until everybody went to bed. He was at the piano all day Saturday and all day Sunday. Then he bought a record player and started playing records. He'd play one record over and over again, all day long sometimes, and he'd improvise along with it on the piano. Or he'd play one section of the record, one chord, one change, one progression, then he'd do it on the piano. Then back to the record. Then back to the piano.

Well, I really don't know how they stood it. Isabel finally confessed that it wasn't like living with a person at all, it was like living with sound. And the sound didn't make any sense to her, didn't make any sense to any of them — naturally. They began, in a way, to be afflicted by this presence that was living in their home. It was as though Sonny were some sort of god, or monster. He moved in an atmosphere which wasn't like theirs at all. They fed him and he ate, he washed himself, he walked in and out of their door; he certainly wasn't nasty or unpleasant or rude, Sonny isn't any of those things; but it was as though he were all wrapped up in some cloud, some fire, some vision all his own; and there wasn't any way to reach him.

At the same time, he wasn't really a man yet, he was still a child, and they had to watch out for him in all kinds of ways. They certainly couldn't throw him out. Neither did they dare to make a great scene about that piano because even they dimly sensed, as I sensed, from so many thousands of miles away, that Sonny was at that piano playing for his life.

But he hadn't been going to school. One day a letter came from the school board and Isabel's mother got it — there had, apparently, been other letters but Sonny had torn them up. This day, when Sonny came in, Isabel's mother showed him the letter and asked where he'd been spending his time. And she finally got it out of him that he'd been down in Greenwich Village, with musicians and other characters, in a white girl's apartment. And this scared her and she started to scream at him and what came up, once she began — though she denies it to this day — was what sacrifices they were making to give Sonny a decent home and how little he appreciated it.

Sonny didn't play the piano that day. By evening, Isabel's mother had calmed down but then there was the old man to deal with, and Isabel herself. Isabel says she did her best to be calm but she broke down and started crying. She says she just watched Sonny's face. She could tell, by watching him, what was happening with him. And what was happening was that they penetrated his cloud, they had reached him. Even if their fingers had been a thousand times more gentle than human fingers ever are, he could hardly help feeling that they had stripped him naked and were spitting on that nakedness. For he also had to see that his presence, that music, which was life or death to him, had been torture for them and that they had endured it, not at all for his sake, but only for mine. And Sonny couldn't take that. He can take it a little better today than he could then but he's still not very good at it and, frankly, I don't know anybody who is.

The silence of the next few days must have been louder than the sound of 170 all the music ever played since time began. One morning, before she went to work, Isabel was in his room for something and she suddenly realized that all of his records were gone. And she knew for certain that he was gone. And he was. He went as far as the navy would carry him. He finally sent me a postcard from some place in Greece and that was the first I knew that Sonny was still alive. I didn't see him any more until we were both back in New York and the war had long been over.

He was a man by then, of course, but I wasn't willing to see it. He came by the house from time to time, but we fought almost every time we met. I didn't like the way he carried himself, loose and dreamlike all the time, and I didn't like his friends, and his music seemed to be merely an excuse for the life he led. It sounded just that weird and disordered.

Then we had a fight, a pretty awful fight, and I didn't see him for months. By and by I looked him up, where he was living, in a furnished room in the Village, and I tried to make it up. But there were lots of people in the room and Sonny just lay on his bed, and he wouldn't come downstairs with me, and he treated these other people as though they were his family and I weren't. So I got mad and then he got mad, and then I told him that he might just as well be dead as live the way he was living. Then he stood up and he told me not to worry about him any more in life, that he *was* dead as far as I was concerned. Then he pushed me to the door and the other people looked on as though nothing were happening, and he slammed the door behind me. I stood in the hallway, staring at the door. I heard somebody laugh in the room and then the tears came to my eyes. I started down the steps, whistling to keep from crying, I kept whistling to myself, *You going to need me, baby, one of these cold, rainy days.*

I read about Sonny's trouble in the spring. Little Grace died in the fall. She was a beautiful little girl. But she only lived a little over two years. She died of polio and she suffered. She had a slight fever for a couple of days, but it didn't seem like anything and we just kept her in bed. And we would certainly have called the doctor, but the fever dropped, she seemed to be all right. So we thought it had just been a cold. Then, one day, she was up, playing, Isabel was in the kitchen fixing lunch for the two boys when they'd come in from school, and she heard Grace fall down in the living room. When you have a lot of children you don't always start running when one of them falls, unless they start screaming or something. And, this time, Grace was quiet. Yet, Isabel says that when she heard that *thump* and then that silence, something happened in her to make her afraid. And she ran to the living room and there was little Grace on the floor, all twisted up, and the reason she hadn't screamed was that she couldn't get her breath. And when she did scream, it was the worst sound, Isabel says, that she'd ever heard in all her life, and she still hears it sometimes in her dreams. Isabel will sometimes wake me up with a low, moaning, strangled sound and I have to be quick to awaken her and hold her to me and where Isabel is weeping against me seems a mortal wound.

I think I may have written Sonny the very day that little Grace was buried. I was sitting in the living room in the dark, by myself, and I suddenly thought of Sonny. My trouble made his real.

One Saturday afternoon, when Sonny had been living with us, or, anyway, 175 been in our house, for nearly two weeks, I found myself wandering aimlessly about the living room, drinking from a can of beer, and trying to work up the courage to search Sonny's room. He was out, he was usually out whenever I was home, and Isabel had taken the children to see their grandparents. Suddenly I was standing still in front of the living room window, watching Seventh Avenue. The idea of searching Sonny's room made me still. I scarcely dared to admit to myself what I'd be searching for. I didn't know what I'd do if I found it. Or if I didn't.

On the sidewalk across from me, near the entrance to a barbecue joint, some people were holding an old-fashioned revival meeting. The barbecue cook, wearing a dirty white apron, his conked° hair reddish and metallic in the pale sun, and a cigarette between his lips, stood in the doorway, watching them. Kids and older people paused in their errands and stood there, along with some older men and a couple of very tough-looking women who watched everything that happened on the avenue, as though they owned it, or were maybe owned by it. Well, they were watching this, too. The revival was being carried on by three sisters in black, and a brother. All they had were their voices and their Bibles and a tambourine. The brother was testifying and while he testified two of the sisters stood together, seeming to say, amen, and the third sister walked around with the tambourine outstretched and a couple of people dropped coins into it. Then the brother's testimony ended and the sister who had been taking up the collection dumped the coins into her palm and transferred them to the pocket of her long black robe. Then she raised both hands, striking the tambourine against the air, and then against one hand, and she started to sing. And the two other sisters and the brother joined in.

It was strange, suddenly, to watch, though I had been seeing these street meetings all my life. So, of course, had everybody else down there. Yet, they paused and watched and listened and I stood still at the window. *"Tis the old ship of Zion,"* they sang, and the sister with the tambourine kept a steady, jangling beat, *"it has rescued many a thousand!"* Not a soul under the sound of their voices was hearing this song for the first time, not one of them had been rescued. Nor had they seen much in the way of rescue work being done around them. Neither did they especially believe in the holiness of the three sisters and the brother, they knew too much about them, knew where they lived, and how. The woman with the tambourine, whose voice dominated the air, whose face was bright with joy, was divided by very little from the woman who stood watching her, a cigarette between her heavy, chapped lips, her hair a cuckoo's nest, her face scarred and swollen from many beatings, and her black eyes glittering like coal. Perhaps they both knew this, which was why, when, as rarely, they addressed each other, they addressed each other as Sister. As the singing filled the air the watching, listening faces underwent a change, the eyes focusing on something within; the music seemed to soothe a poison out of them; and time seemed, nearly, to fall away from the sullen, belligerent, battered faces, as though they were fleeing back to their first condition, while dreaming of their last. The barbecue cook half shook his head and smiled, and dropped his cigarette and disappeared into his joint. A man fumbled in his pockets for change and stood holding it in his hand impatiently, as though he had just remembered a pressing appointment further up the avenue. He looked furious. Then I saw Sonny, standing on the edge of the

---

conked: Straightened by the use of chemicals.

crowd. He was carrying a wide, flat notebook with a green cover, and it made him look, from where I was standing, almost like a schoolboy. The coppery sun brought out the copper in his skin, he was very faintly smiling, standing very still. Then the singing stopped, the tambourine turned into a collection plate again. The furious man dropped in his coins and vanished, so did a couple of the women, and Sonny dropped some change in the plate, looking directly at the woman with a little smile. He started across the avenue, toward the house. He has a slow, loping walk something like the way Harlem hipsters walk, only he's imposed on this his own half-beat. I had never really noticed it before.

I stayed at the window, both relieved and apprehensive. As Sonny disappeared from my sight, they began singing again. And they were still singing when his key turned in the lock.

"Hey," he said.

"Hey, yourself. You want some beer?"   180

"No. Well, maybe." But he came up to the window and stood beside me, looking out. "What a warm voice," he said.

They were singing *If I could only hear my mother pray again!*

"Yes," I said, "and she can sure beat that tambourine."

"But what a terrible song," he said, and laughed. He dropped his notebook on the sofa and disappeared into the kitchen. "Where's Isabel and the kids?"

"I think they went to see their grandparents. You hungry?"   185

"No." He came back into the living room with his can of beer. "You want to come some place with me tonight?"

I sensed, I don't know how, that I couldn't possibly say no. "Sure. Where?"

He sat down on the sofa and picked up his notebook and started leafing through it. "I'm going to sit in with some fellows in a joint in the Village."

"You mean, you're going to play, tonight?"

"That's right." He took a swallow of his beer and moved back to the win- 190 dow. He gave me a sidelong look. "If you can stand it."

"I'll try," I said.

He smiled to himself and we both watched as the meeting across the way broke up. The three sisters and the brother, heads bowed, were singing *God be with you till we meet again.* The faces around them were very quiet. Then the song ended. The small crowd dispersed. We watched the three women and the lone man walk slowly up the avenue.

"When she was singing before," said Sonny, abruptly, "her voice reminded me for a minute of what heroin feels like sometimes — when it's in your veins. It makes you feel sort of warm and cool at the same time. And distant. And — and sure." He sipped his beer, very deliberately not looking at me. I watched his face. "It makes you feel — in control. Sometimes you've got to have that feeling."

"Do you?" I sat down slowly in the easy chair.

"Sometimes." He went to the sofa and picked up his notebook again. "Some 195 people do."

"In order," I asked, "to play?" And my voice was very ugly, full of contempt and anger.

"Well"—he looked at me with great, troubled eyes, as though, in fact, he hoped his eyes would tell me things he could never otherwise say—"they *think* so. And *if* they think so—!"

"And what do *you* think?" I asked.

He sat on the sofa and put his can of beer on the floor. "I don't know," he said, and I couldn't be sure if he were answering my question or pursuing his thoughts. His face didn't tell me. "It's not so much to *play*. It's to *stand* it, to be able to make it at all. On any level." He frowned and smiled: "In order to keep from shaking to pieces."

"But these friends of yours," I said, "they seem to shake themselves to 200 pieces pretty goddamn fast."

"Maybe." He played with the notebook. And something told me that I should curb my tongue, that Sonny was doing his best to talk, that I should listen. "But of course you only know the ones that've gone to pieces. Some don't—or at least they haven't *yet* and that's just about all *any* of us can say." He paused. "And then there are some who just live, really, in hell, and they know it and they see what's happening and they go right on. I don't know." He sighed, dropped the notebook, folded his arms. "Some guys, you can tell from the way they play, they on something *all* the time. And you can see that, well, it makes something real for them. But of course," he picked up his beer from the floor and sipped it and put the can down again, "they want to, too, you've got to see that. Even some of them that say they don't— *some*, not all."

"And what about you?" I asked—I couldn't help it. "What about you? Do *you* want to?"

He stood up and walked to the window and remained silent for a long time. Then he sighed. "Me," he said. Then: "While I was downstairs before, on my way here, listening to that woman sing, it struck me all of a sudden how much suffering she must have had to go through—to sing like that. It's *repulsive* to think you have to suffer that much."

I said: "But there's no way not to suffer—is there, Sonny?"

"I believe not," he said and smiled, "but that's never stopped anyone from 205 trying." He looked at me. "Has it?" I realized, with this mocking look, that there stood between us, forever, beyond the power of time or forgiveness, the fact that I had held silence—so long!—when he had needed human speech to help him. He turned back to the window. "No, there's no way not to suffer. But you try all kinds of ways to keep from drowning in it, to keep on top of it, and to make it seem—well, like *you*. Like you did something, all right, and now you're suffering for it. You know?" I said nothing. "Well you know," he said, impatiently, "why *do* people suffer? Maybe it's better to do something to give it a reason, *any* reason."

"But we just agreed," I said, "that there's no way not to suffer. Isn't it better, then, just to—take it?"

"But nobody just takes it," Sonny cried, "that's what I'm telling you! *Everybody* tries not to. You're just hung up on the *way* some people try—it's not *your* way!"

The hair on my face began to itch, my face felt wet. "That's not true," I said, "that's not true. I don't give a damn what other people do, I don't even care how they suffer. I just care how *you* suffer." And he looked at me. "Please believe me," I said, "I don't want to see you—die—trying not to suffer."

"I won't," he said, flatly, "die trying not to suffer. At least, not any faster than anybody else."

"But there's no need," I said, trying to laugh, "is there? in killing yourself."   210

I wanted to say more, but I couldn't. I wanted to talk about will power and how life could be—well, beautiful. I wanted to say that it was all within; but was it? or, rather, wasn't that exactly the trouble? And I wanted to promise that I would never fail him again. But it would all have sounded—empty words and lies.

So I made the promise to myself and prayed that I would keep it.

"It's terrible sometimes, inside," he said, "that's what's the trouble. You walk these streets, black and funky and cold, and there's not really a living ass to talk to, and there's nothing shaking, and there's no way of getting it out—that storm inside. You can't talk it and you can't make love with it, and when you finally try to get with it and play it, you realize *nobody's* listening. So *you've* got to listen. You got to find a way to listen."

And then he walked away from the window and sat on the sofa again, as though all the wind had suddenly been knocked out of him. "Sometimes you'll do *anything* to play, even cut your mother's throat." He laughed and looked at me. "Or your brother's." Then he sobered. "Or your own." Then: "Don't worry. I'm all right now and I think I'll *be* all right. But I can't forget—where I've been. I don't mean just the physical place I've been, I mean where I've *been*. And *what* I've been."

"What have you been, Sonny?" I asked.   215

He smiled—but sat sideways on the sofa, his elbow resting on the back his fingers playing with his mouth and chin, not looking at me. "I've been something I didn't recognize, didn't know I could be. Didn't know anybody could be." He stopped, looking inward, looking helplessly young, looking old. "I'm not talking about it now because I feel *guilty* or anything like that—maybe it would be better if I did, I don't know. Anyway, I can't really talk about it. Not to you, not to anybody," and now he turned and faced me. "Sometimes, you know, and it was actually when I was most *out* of the world, I felt that I was in it, that I was *with* it, really, and I could play or I didn't really have to *play*, it just came out of me, it was there. And I don't know how I played, thinking about it now, but I know I did awful things, those times, sometimes, to people. Or it wasn't that I *did* anything to them—it was that they weren't real." He picked up the beer can; it was empty; he rolled it between his palms: "And other times—well, I needed a fix, I needed to find a place to lean, I needed to clear a space to *listen*—and I couldn't find it, and I—went crazy, I did terrible things to *me*, I was terrible *for* me." He began pressing the beer can between his hands, I watched the metal begin to give. It glittered, as he played with it, like a knife, and I was afraid he would cut himself, but I said nothing. "Oh well. I can never tell you. I was all by myself at the bottom of something, stinking and sweating and crying and shaking, and I smelled it, you know? *my* stink, and I thought I'd die if I couldn't get away from it and yet, all the same, I knew that everything I was doing was just locking me in with it. And I didn't know," he paused, still flattening the beer can, "I didn't know, I still *don't* know, something kept telling me that maybe it was good to smell your own stink, but I didn't think that *that* was what I'd been trying to do—and—who can stand it?" and he abruptly dropped the ruined beer can, looking at me with a small, still smile, and then rose, walking to the window as though it were the lodestone rock. I watched his face, he watched the avenue. "I couldn't tell you when Mama died—but the reason I wanted to leave Harlem so bad was to get away from drugs. And then, when I ran away, that's what I was running from—really. When I came back, nothing had changed, *I* hadn't changed, I was just—older." And he stopped, drumming with his fingers on the windowpane. The sun had vanished, soon darkness would fall. I watched his face. "It can come again," he said, almost as though speaking to himself. Then he turned to me. "It can come again," he repeated. "I just want you to know that."

"All right," I said, at last. "So it can come again. All right."

He smiled, but the smile was sorrowful. "I had to try to tell you," he said.

"Yes," I said. "I understand that."

"You're my brother," he said, looking straight at me, and not smiling at all. 220

"Yes," I repeated, "yes. I understand that."

He turned back to the window, looking out. "All that hatred down there," he said, "all that hatred and misery and love. It's a wonder it doesn't blow the avenue apart."

We went to the only nightclub on a short, dark street, downtown. We squeezed through the narrow, chattering, jam-packed bar to the entrance of the big room, where the bandstand was. And we stood there for a moment, for the lights were very dim in this room and we couldn't see. Then, "Hello, boy," said a voice and an enormous black man, much older than Sonny or myself, erupted out of all that atmospheric lighting and put an arm around Sonny's shoulder. "I been sitting right here," he said, "waiting for you."

He had a big voice, too, and heads in the darkness turned toward us.

Sonny grinned and pulled a little away, and said, "Creole, this is my 225 brother. I told you about him."

Creole shook my hand. "I'm glad to meet you, son," he said, and it was clear that he was glad to meet me *there*, for Sonny's sake. And he smiled, "You got a real musician in *your* family," and he took his arm from Sonny's shoulder and slapped him, lightly, affectionately, with the back of his hand.

"Well. Now I've heard it all," said a voice behind us. This was another musician, and a friend of Sonny's, a coal-black cheerful-looking man, built close to the ground. He immediately began confiding to me, at the top of his lungs, the most terrible things about Sonny, his teeth gleaming like a lighthouse and his laugh coming up out of him like the beginning of an earthquake. And it turned out that everyone at the bar knew Sonny, or almost everyone; some were musicians, working there, or nearby, or not working, some were simply hangers-on, and some were there to hear Sonny play. I was introduced to all of them and they were all very polite to me. Yet, it was clear that, for them, I was only Sonny's brother. Here, I was in Sonny's world. Or, rather: his kingdom. Here, it was not even a question that his veins bore royal blood.

They were going to play soon and Creole installed me, by myself, at a table in a dark corner. Then I watched them, Creole, and the little black man, and Sonny, and the others, while they horsed around, standing just below the bandstand. The light from the bandstand spilled just a little short of them and, watching them laughing and gesturing and moving about, I had the feeling that they, nevertheless, were being most careful not to step into that circle of light too suddenly: that if they moved into the light too suddenly, without thinking, they would perish in flame. Then, while I watched, one of them, the small, black man, moved into the light and crossed the bandstand and started fooling around with his drums. Then—being funny and being, also, extremely ceremonious—Creole took Sonny by the arm and led him to the piano. A woman's voice called Sonny's name and a few hands started clapping. And Sonny, also being funny and being ceremonious, and so touched, I think, that he could have cried, but neither hiding it nor showing it, riding it like a man, grinned, and put both hands to his heart and bowed from the waist.

Creole then went to the bass fiddle and a lean, very bright-skinned brown man jumped up on the bandstand and picked up his horn. So there they were, and the atmosphere on the bandstand and in the room began to change and tighten. Someone stepped up to the microphone and announced them. Then there were all kinds of murmurs. Some people at the bar shushed others. The waitress ran around, frantically getting in the last orders, guys and chicks got closer to each other, and the lights on the bandstand, on the quartet, turned to a kind of indigo. Then they all looked different there. Creole looked about him for the last time, as though he were making certain that all his chickens were in the coop, and then he—jumped and struck the fiddle. And there they were.

All I know about music is that not many people ever really hear it. And even 230 then, on the rare occasions when something opens within, and the music enters, what we mainly hear, or hear corroborated, are personal, private, vanishing evocations. But the man who creates the music is hearing something else, is dealing with the roar rising from the void and imposing order on it as it hits the air. What is evoked in him, then, is of another order, more terrible because it has no words, and triumphant, too, for that same reason. And his triumph, when he triumphs, is ours. I just watched Sonny's face. His face was troubled, he was working hard, but he wasn't with it. And I had the feeling that, in a way, everyone on the bandstand was waiting for him, both waiting for him and pushing him along. But as I began to watch Creole, I realized that it was Creole who held them all back. He had them on a short rein. Up there, keeping the beat with his whole body, wailing on the fiddle, with his eyes half closed, he was listening to everything, but he was listening to Sonny. He was having a dialogue with Sonny. He wanted Sonny to leave the shoreline and strike out for the deep water. He was Sonny's witness that deep water and drowning were not the same thing—he had been there, and he knew. And he wanted Sonny to know. He was waiting for Sonny to do the things on the keys which would let Creole know that Sonny was in the water.

And, while Creole listened, Sonny moved, deep within, exactly like someone in torment. I had never before thought of how awful the relationship must be between the musician and his instrument. He has to fill it, this instrument, with the breath of life, his own. He has to make it do what he wants it to do. And a piano is just a piano. It's made out of so much wood and wires and little hammers and big ones, and ivory. While there's only so much you can do with it, the only way to find this out is to try; to try and make it do everything.

And Sonny hadn't been near a piano for over a year. And he wasn't on much better terms with his life, not the life that stretched before him now. He and the piano stammered, started one way, got scared, stopped; started another way, panicked, marked time, started again; then seemed to have found a direction, panicked again, got stuck. And the face I saw on Sonny I'd never seen before. Everything had been burned out of it, and, at the same time, things usually hidden were being burned in, by the fire and fury of the battle which was occurring in him up there.

Yet, watching Creole's face as they neared the end of the first set, I had the feeling that something had happened, something I hadn't heard. Then they finished, there was scattered applause, and then, without an instant's warning, Creole started into something else, it was almost sardonic, it was *Am I Blue*. And, as though he commanded, Sonny began to play. Something began to happen. And Creole let out the reins. The dry, low, black man said something awful on the drums, Creole answered, and the drums talked back. Then the horn insisted, sweet and high, slightly detached perhaps, and Creole listened, commenting now and then, dry, and driving, beautiful and calm and old. Then they all came together again, and Sonny was part of the family again. I could tell this from his face. He seemed to have found, right there beneath his fingers, a damn brand-new piano. It seemed that he couldn't get over it. Then, for awhile, just being happy with Sonny, they seemed to be agreeing with him that brand-new pianos certainly were a gas.

Then Creole stepped forward to remind them that what they were playing was the blues. He hit something in all of them, he hit something in me, myself, and the music tightened and deepened, apprehension began to beat the air. Creole began to tell us what the blues were all about. They were not about anything very new. He and his boys up there were keeping it new, at the risk of ruin, destruction, madness, and death, in order to find new ways to make us listen. For, while the tale of how we suffer, and how we are delighted, and how we may triumph is never new, it always must be heard. There isn't any other tale to tell, it's the only light we've got in all this darkness.

And this tale, according to that face, that body, those strong hands on those 235 strings, has another aspect in every country, and a new depth in every generation. Listen, Creole seemed to be saying, listen. Now these are Sonny's blues. He made the little black man on the drums know it, and the bright, brown man on the horn. Creole wasn't trying any longer to get Sonny in the water. He was wishing him Godspeed. Then he stepped back, very slowly, filling the air with the immense suggestion that Sonny speak for himself.

Then they all gathered around Sonny and Sonny played. Every now and again one of them seemed to say, amen. Sonny's fingers filled the air with life, his life. But that life contained so many others. And Sonny went all the way back, he really began with the spare, flat statement of the opening phrase of the song. Then he began to make it his. It was very beautiful because it wasn't hurried and it was no longer a lament. I seemed to hear with what burning he had made it his, with what burning we had yet to make it ours, how we could cease lamenting. Freedom lurked around us and I understood, at last, that he could help us to be free if we would listen, that he would never be free until we did. Yet, there was no battle in his face now. I heard what he had gone through, and would continue to go through until he came to rest in earth. He had made it his: that long line, of which we knew only Mama and Daddy. And he was giving it back, as everything must be given back, so that, passing through death, it can live forever. I saw my mother's face again, and felt, for the first time, how the stones of the road she had walked on must have bruised her feet. I saw the moonlit road where my father's brother died. And it brought something else back to me, and carried me past it. I saw my little girl again and felt Isabel's tears again, and I felt my own tears begin to rise. And I was yet aware that this was only a moment, that the world waited outside, as hungry as a tiger, and that trouble stretched above us, longer than the sky.

Then it was over. Creole and Sonny let out their breath, both soaking wet, and grinning. There was a lot of applause and some of it was real. In the dark, the girl came by and I asked her to take drinks to the bandstand. There was a long pause, while they talked up there in the indigo light and after awhile I saw the girl put a Scotch and milk on top of the piano for Sonny. He didn't seem to notice it, but just before they started playing again, he sipped from it and looked toward me, and nodded. Then he put it back on top of the piano. For me, then, as they began to play again, it glowed and shook above my brother's head like the very cup of trembling.

May-lee Chai   b. 1967

Your Grandmother, the War Criminal   [2004]

Everything begins with a square. A perfect square. Remember this. Fold it in half and then half again so that you have a smaller square. Unfold. Be careful. Don't rush so. Half of everything depends on unfolding things correctly. Now fold it diagonally into a triangle and then in half again. Now you can begin. After all that.

You have a lot of patience. More than I did when I was your age. My mother wanted to teach me so many things—Spanish boxes and jumping frogs, Daimyo gentlemen and Samurai hats. But all I had patience for was the first one, the crane. And then it was too late. I moved into the white family's house. I don't remember their name anymore, but I remember I had to change trolleys three times. *School-girl work,* we called it. After school I cleaned and cooked and did the laundry for the lady—what was her name?—and the two children. They were a lot younger, I think. Than me. At least they acted that way, with all their dolls—glass heads and curly gold hair silky like feathers—and toy ships, such sharp edges, I remember. Always lying on the floor. I had to pick them up before the man came home. He liked a neat house; that's what the lady said. It was a good job for a Japanese girl in those days. And who didn't need money?

I had my own room with a window level to the ground. I could watch legs and feet go by. I had my own bed. And seven books! Two were from school—math and a storybook, about horses, I think. Three from *Reader's Digest,* Book of the Month Club, the lady gave them to me. I wish I could remember her name. I must be senile. Yes, I've felt it coming on for years. She gave them to me, said her husband didn't like sea stories. I remember pirates, storms, waves taller than ships, and the men who swore into the raging wind.

Two books were from my mother—your *great* grandmother, that's right. She gave them to me before I left. Wrapped in colored paper with a giant, pink, department-store bow. A cooking book and *Manners for Young Ladies*. Oh, no, these were wonderful. Mother had to be practical. And she was wise. But also a lovely girl, a lady, everyone said. Always dressed just right, appropriate you know, though we never had any money. She made her own clothes. Didn't need a pattern, just looked at the picture and knew. She taught me to sew. I sewed for the white family too, a little. Missing buttons, ripped hems mostly. But I made a jumper for the little girl once. Blue with yellow buttons down the front. They had a Singer, nearly new; it felt like ice-cold butter, the smooth metal. But Mother sewed by hand. Perfectly. Didn't need a pattern, just looked at a picture in the magazine and knew.

She was the only Japanese in all the three stories of that department store,   5 did you know? The only Japanese who ever worked in sales, not hauling things or packing. That's what a lady she looked like. Before she was pregnant with me, of course. She couldn't work then.

Don't hold your paper in your hands like that. The sweat of your palms will make it soft. Sag.

Now fold the triangle in half, pushing the side edge to the crease; flatten it carefully. Now do the other side the same. Now you have the body. It's true, you're right; I've never seen a flowered crane before, but isn't the paper pretty? I always liked red.

It doesn't look like a real bird, that's true. But me, I've never seen a real crane, so I don't know. Maybe in Japan they look like this. I always thought we were folding seagulls. There were so many in the city. Even in the camp, after that. So beautiful. When we stepped off the bus, they were there to greet us, swooping in the sky like paper kites. They opened their beaks, and no sound came out, the wind was that strong. Stole their voices. The dust rose up in waves, and the seagulls bobbed up and down, but one hung perfectly still, suspended right in front of me just as I stepped off the bus. Mother was angry, "Help me down, what are you staring at? Like a retarded child, staring at the sky. This is no time to daydream." The gulls flew away. But I can never forget the sight of them on our first day in Manzanar.° So beautiful. A good sign, I thought. I was twelve.

Oh, yes, Mother could talk then and hear. It was only later she became death. *Deaf* I mean, that's right. We stepped off the bus, and don't you think some people stared? I heard voices, too: "*Ainoko.*" "Half-breed," their American-born kids kindly translating as if I couldn't tell already. My hair was yellow-brown then, like a toad. I heard the whispers, not quite whispers. I always wished I could have pretty black hair, like yours, but it's better now, half white, half gray. No more yellow-brown like a toad.

Mother used to praise my hair. Soft, she said. She liked the color. Blond-   10
brown, she called it. American hair.

I never knew my father, your great-grandfather. You are one-eighth English-Welsh, did you know? They separated before I was born. We used to have a picture of him, before I threw it away. He was standing in front of Pier Thirty-Nine in San Francisco; behind him, sea lions basked in the sun. I remember a felt hat on this thin man's head, a shadow on his face, just the tip of his nose catching the sun. He was tall like me.

Where were we? Ah, now it's getting complicated. Take the sides of one face and fold them to the center line, bend the top point over and back, make a good crease. Then unfold. Pull the points of the triangle in opposite directions until it unfolds into a diamond. That's right. Smooth it down, careful, careful. Now do the other side this way.

It was just the two of us together in Manzanar. Aunt Fukiko was sent to Topaz.° Uncle Hiro was in Montana. Just me and Mother stayed in California. But I felt like it was just me sometimes. Mother. Mother was preoccupied; no, she was *bon'yari*. There's no good English translation. Maybe you can say "vague."

The guards wanted us to speak only English, of course, but Mother insisted on Japanese. Not at first, not at first. She went to see the FBI men when they came to interview us. Are you loyal to the United States of America? Would you fight for America? Have you ever heard anyone you know talk about America in an unfriendly manner? They asked everyone the same questions. Only the men in suits and ties and hard leather shoes had names: Agent Brown, Agent Atkinson. We had numbers. Mother waited, nodding, smiling, signing all the oaths of loyalty, then she began again each time, patient as the first. "My daughter is

---

Manzanar: Manzanar War Relocation Center in California was one of ten camps where Japanese American citizens and resident Japanese aliens were interned during World War II.
Topaz: A Japanese internment camp in Utah.

American. My husband is American. Just like you. A real American. Look at her, you can tell. Look at her." The FBI men explained about resident aliens and Japanese nationals and the war. Mother explained to the men at the horse track when we lived in the stables, five of us in one stall, big enough for one Palomino. She explained to the men at the camp, "American husband, American daughter," until her American voice caught in her throat and there was nothing left but Japanese. Her ears plugged with the wind and dust, and she could hear only her family's voices from so long ago. They traveled across the ocean to visit with their little girl, she said. They hadn't talked since she'd left to join her big sister in America, too many girls for a poor family in a small village. All those secret conversations with ghosts came, again and again. How could she have talked to both them and me? And so, soon I was alone. Except for my seagulls.

They came throughout the summer, unexpectedly. An empty sky, and then   15
in an instant, a flock, mewing, circling the barracks, bringing the sea on the tips of their wings. Home didn't seem so far away. I saved scraps, hamburger, buns dipped in milk. It was a war crime to waste food, feed seagulls with government rations. So you see, I really was a war criminal. Imagine. Your grandmother! Ha.

I remember waiting for my gulls. We were folding laundry together, Mother and I, between the dusty blocks. The wind carried drops of water from the sheets and blouses flapping on the lines. *Mushi-atsukatta,* Mother said. Humid, sticky hot, though it was cool, fall approaching. She was thinking of her childhood on Honshu,° talking to her parents there. I couldn't understand. Mother giggled to herself, twisted a strand of hair around her index finger. I folded our blouses, our underwear, balled my socks.

The wind slapped my hair against my face, stinging my lips. I pulled a strand from my mouth, watched the wind roll the dried sagebrush ahead of a wave of dust and litter, crashing like waves across the desert.

And then a rifle shot. I remember the feeling in my heart, sharp, sharp. The soldier boys in the tower shot at rabbits, at sagebrush, at dust devils. Not at us, not at us, not at us, I reminded myself. I hoped. Did we ever try to escape? Did we ever have a place to go? The shot echoed like a door slam, like anger, in your bones. I jumped to my feet, but before I could run to see what had been hit, Mother grabbed hold of my skirt.

"Let go, let go," I told her, tugging at the cloth, but her grip was firm.

I scanned the horizon, back and forth, what could I see? My head spinning,   20
the wind in my ears, loud, loud like the ocean, like an earthquake. Underwear and socks flapping on the line between blocks twelve and thirteen; dust in funnels dancing in the wind; the shiny, salty rocks; the dark mountains; the barracks; the laundry; the gun tower; the barbed-wire fence; someone's white long johns flapping in the wind; the flat desert. My head was light; the light gathered into a haze before my eyes. I jumped, trying to break free, clutching at the air. I fell onto my knees in the dirt. It hurt. I remember. It hurt.

Honshu: The largest and most populous island of Japan.

Mother gasped. "*Mi-te!*" Look! She pointed. A single white feather, tipped in red, lay on our basket of fresh laundry. Splash, a drop of red fell like a raindrop. Then another and another. I looked up, but the sky was empty. Even the blue was gone; the sun so bright, the sky was the color of steel. Then I saw the seagull, caught on a corner eave, shot, its body a dark hole, its wings limp like seaweed. The wind tugged at the dead bird, but it was caught on a loose shingle, and only a few feathers took to the air. They fluttered over our heads like flower petals.

Mother. Mother flicked the feather out of the laundry basket, inspected her blouse for damage. She clicked her tongue against the roof of her mouth, held the fabric up in the light, a veil brushing her face. The feather's spines remained lightly sketched in red. Mother spit on the fabric, dabbed at the stain with her handkerchief.

My gull, I thought. But, of course, it wasn't really mine.

I never watched for the gulls after that. When winter came, the snow and the howling wind, the gulls left anyway. When they came back again with the summer, I was a big girl already; I didn't care. They were messy and noisy and scattered the garbage. That's what all the women said. Mother, too. In Japanese.

After the war, Mother went to live in the Heiwa Nursing Home in L.A., paid   25
for by the Japanese—indemnity money, friendship money, something like that. She wasn't so old, not like me now, but she couldn't work then, not anymore. I met your grandfather while visiting Mother, did I ever tell you? He worked in the city. We wrote letters—he would fold his into swans. I had that job in Salt Lake City, the city of seagulls. We couldn't see each other for months on end. Isn't it funny? I shouldn't cry. Not now. What's the matter with me?

But don't let me run on so. We're almost done. You really are so patient. Here, fold the bottom edges of the diamond toward the center, both sides. Then bend the left flap up and back. Now this is the hardest part. A pocket fold, see? This makes the neck. Take the tip and bend it back and forth, flatten, and refold it inside out. This is the head. Now pocket-fold the other end up to make the tail. Now bend the wings down and pull. You're almost done. See the hole in the bottom, where all the edges of the paper meet, the beginnings and the ends? Blow here, one puff—quick—give your crane life. And we're finished. A fat crane, and red red red! Pretty, huh? The flowered paper was a good idea after all. Ha.

Now you won't forget what I've taught, will you? You'll try to remember, practice every day, won't you? Remember, remember, that's a good girl, don't forget.

Chrystos   b. 1946

Traditional Style Indian Garage   [2006]

My old red car named PowWow Fever has a sunroof which leaks, which I've renamed a rain roof. There isn't a carport attached to my little green rental cabin, which has floors so crooked my cakes come out half-mast. My car is bigger than my kitchen, which gives you a sense of the proportionate meaning of things. Naturally, being a Menominee warrior, I'm too broke to get her roof fixed, because most of the money I make goes for repairs to keep her running, so I can get to work. This place, in common with many reservations, has no bus system. Actually, this is a genuine antique story at the moment (and my car only has two years to go in order to qualify), because she hasn't been running for five months. She's on sabbatical to write the novel about how much hell living with me is. Anyway, since we live in the Northwest, I can get a quart of cold rainwater splashed down the back of my neck when I start her up, unless I use my Traditional Style Indian Garage. This is very easy to replicate, if you are working on your Girl or Boy Scout merit badge in crafts. Scout around for a strong, extra-thick, large trash bag with no holes. Black is the preferred color, but many tribes have assimilated the dark green ones. Place this over the sun-roof, making sure to go past all the seams. Weigh this down in the four corners with logs and bricks. If you'd like, you may sing a little song to the Beaver Nation. Beadwork is not recommended for ornamentation, but the logs and bricks can be painted with sun symbols using yellow ochre clay, dug up only from approved pits. This adds some extra magic, which keeps you dry. Relatively speaking. The author will be happy to travel anywhere for green gas money and a red steak to demonstrate this method in person. Periodically check the bag and your soul for holes. This traditional garage can be stored in your trunk, an important consideration for us nomadic people. This garage has also been advertised on TV by a genuine Indian (not Latino) actor, so the historical significance cannot be overlooked. This has many outstanding features lacking in your ordinary garage. While arranging the bricks, I enjoy the stars and moon. I hear the sea lions hollering hello. Often my four cats assist by walking across it to test for air bubbles. If I'm really in luck, the transformer across the street will blow out in a blaze of glorious atomic aquamarine turquoise light. Somebody said the emanations of this event, which is the end of watching TV for a spell, cause cancer. Emanations is a mighty big word for a traditional Indian story, but I was accidentally caught in the crossfire of a few college English courses. So far, no one will give me disability for my wounds. I'm not too worried—I'm an Indian, so somebody is sure to kill me before I die an unnatural death. As for cancer, I have a list in my wallet of all my friends who have died from that, and not one of them lived near a transformer. I actually may already have cancer, but there's no way to tell without health insurance, which is why I keep thinking of migrating to Canada. Unfortunately, my people were a little too far south to claim dual borders. That is, below the lakes, not crazy. Although you could say we were crazy not to be more like the Dakota, so we could have had a car named after us. I've driven a Cherokee, but she wasn't a Jeep. I just have no respect! If you've been worried about paragraphs in this little monograph, there aren't going to be any. If you really need them, send along some money to this orphan with uncombed hair, so I can go back to college. Or, at least, buy a comb. The only possible problem with the garage is if the user forgets to remove the garage before driving away. This will cause dents in your hood or trunk and possible broken windows, so take precautions. This is the Voice of Experience. When removing your garage, stand well away, so you don't get wet. Always put the bricks or logs in your trunk first, to prevent ripping the garage. This garage is covered by Intellectual Property Rights, so a fee must be sent to the author — at least enough for a steak. If you are a vegetarian, send clean black cotton socks with no holes, which are a part of the traditional costume. For those of you without a car, this garage transforms miraculously, with a few snips, into an all-purpose rain-and-snow coat. In this case, some beadwork is allowed along the facial edge. This usage of the garage is particularly prevalent among the urban homeless tribes, who have also revived the new health trend for sleeping outside in all weather. We are conducting interviews to reveal the language-grouping from which the garage originated. Some Native scholars are of the opinion that this garage is a historical re-creation of an item found when Custer bit the mud. A government-funded convention is expected to decide the matter once and for all. Look for my free pH Skin dissertation on the Spider Web at Dot's commissary on bingo night. This is my gift to you in honor of our long and pleasant tea party here on Turtle Island. Accept no substitutes.

Edwidge Danticat   b. 1969

New York Day Women   [1995]

Today, walking down the street, I see my mother. She is strolling with a happy gait, her body thrust toward the DON'T WALK sign and the yellow taxicabs that make forty-five-degree turns on the corner of Madison and Fifty-seventh Street.

I have never seen her in this kind of neighborhood, peering into Chanel and Tiffany's and gawking at the jewels glowing in the Bulgari windows. My mother never shops outside of Brooklyn. She has never seen the advertising office where I work. She is afraid to take the subway, where you may meet those young black militant street preachers who curse black women for straightening their hair.

Yet, here she is, my mother, who I left at home that morning in her bathrobe, with pieces of newspapers twisted like rollers in her hair. My mother, who accuses me of random offenses as I dash out of the house.

Would you get up and give an old lady like me your subway seat? In this state of mind, I bet you don't even give up your seat to a pregnant lady.

My mother, who is often right about that. Sometimes I get up and give my seat. Other times, I don't. It all depends on how pregnant the woman is and whether or not she is with her boyfriend or husband and whether or not *he* is sitting down.

As my mother stands in front of Carnegie Hall, one taxi driver yells to another, "What do you think this is, a dance floor?"

My mother waits patiently for this dispute to be settled before crossing the street.

In Haiti when you get hit by a car, the owner of the car gets out and kicks you for getting blood on his bumper.

My mother who laughs when she says this and shows a large gap in her mouth where she lost three more molars to the dentist last week. My mother, who at fifty-nine, says dentures are okay.

You can take them out when they bother you. I'll like them. I'll like them 10
fine.

Will it feel empty when Papa kisses you?

Oh no, he doesn't kiss me that way anymore.

My mother, who watches the lottery drawing every night on channel 11 without ever having played the numbers.

A third of that money is all I would need. We would pay the mortgage, and your father could stop driving that taxicab all over Brooklyn.

I follow my mother, mesmerized by the many possibilities of her journey. 15
Even in a flowered dress, she is lost in a sea of pinstripes and gray suits, high heels and elegant short skirts, Reebok sneakers, dashing from building to building.

My mother, who won't go out to dinner with anyone.

If they want to eat with me, let them come to my house, even if I boil
water and give it to them.

My mother, who talks to herself when she peels the skin off poultry.

Fat, you know, and cholesterol. Fat and cholesterol killed your aunt
Hermine.

My mother, who makes jam with dried grapefruit peel and then puts in 20
cinnamon bark that I always think is cockroaches in the jam. My mother, whom I have always bought household appliances for, on her birthday. A nice rice cooker, a blender.

I trail the red orchids in her dress and the heavy faux leather bag on her shoulders. Realizing the ferocious pace of my pursuit, I stop against a wall to rest. My mother keeps on walking as though she owns the sidewalk under her feet.

As she heads toward the Plaza Hotel, a bicycle messenger swings so close to her that I want to dash forward and rescue her, but she stands dead in her tracks and lets him ride around her and then goes on.

My mother stops at a corner hot-dog stand and asks for something. The vendor hands her a can of soda that she slips into her bag. She stops by another vendor selling sundresses for seven dollars each. I can tell that she is looking at an African print dress, contemplating my size. I think to myself, Please Ma, don't buy it. It would be just another thing that I would bury in the garage or give to Goodwill.

Why should we give to Goodwill when there are so many people back home who need clothes? We save our clothes for the relatives in Haiti.

Twenty years we have been saving all kinds of things for the relatives in Haiti. I need the place in the garage for an exercise bike.

You are pretty enough to be a stewardess. Only dogs like bones.

This mother of mine, she stops at another hot-dog vendor's and buys a frankfurter that she eats on the street. I never knew that she ate frankfurters. With her blood pressure, she shouldn't eat anything with sodium. She has to be careful with her heart, this day woman.

I cannot just swallow salt. Salt is heavier than a hundred bags of shame.

She is slowing her pace, and now I am too close. If she turns around, she might see me. I let her walk into the park before I start to follow again.

My mother walks toward the sandbox in the middle of the park. There a woman is waiting with a child. The woman is wearing a leotard with biker's shorts and has small weights in her hands. The woman kisses the child good-bye and surrenders him to my mother; then she bolts off, running on the cemented stretches in the park.

The child given to my mother has frizzy blond hair. His hand slips into hers easily, like he's known her for a long time. When he raises his face to look at my mother, it is as though he is looking at the sky.

My mother gives this child the soda that she bought from the vendor on the street corner. The child's face lights up as she puts in a straw in the can for him. This seems to be a conspiracy just between the two of them.

My mother and the child sit and watch the other children play in the sandbox. The child pulls out a comic book from a knapsack with Big Bird on the back. My mother peers into his comic book. My mother, who taught herself to read as a little girl in Haiti from the books that her brothers brought home from school.

My mother, who has now lost six of her seven sisters in Ville Rose and has never had the strength to return for their funerals.

Many graves to kiss when I go back. Many graves to kiss.

She throws away the empty soda can when the child is done with it. I wait and watch from a corner until the woman in the leotard and biker's shorts returns, sweaty and breathless, an hour later. My mother gives the woman back her child and strolls farther into the park.

I turn around and start to walk out of the park before my mother can see me. My lunch hour is long since gone. I have to hurry back to work. I walk through a cluster of joggers, then race to a *Sweden Tours* bus. I stand behind the bus and take a peek at my mother in the park. She is standing in a circle, chatting with a group of women who are taking other people's children on an afternoon outing. They look like a Third World Parent-Teacher Association meeting.

I quickly jump into a cab heading back to the office. Would Ma have said hello had she been the one to see me first?

As the cab races away from the park, it occurs to me that perhaps one day I would chase an old woman down a street by mistake and that old woman would be somebody else's mother, who I would have mistaken for mine.

Day women come out when nobody expects them.   40

Tonight on the subway, I will get up and give my seat to a pregnant woman or a lady about Ma's age.

My mother, who stuffs thimbles in her mouth and then blows up her cheeks like Dizzy Gillespie while sewing yet another Raggedy Ann doll that she names Suzette after me.

I will have all these little Suzettes in case you never have any babies, which looks more and more like it is going to happen.

My mother who had me when she was thirty-three — l'âge du Christ — at the age that Christ died on the cross.

That's a blessing, believe you me, even if American doctors say by that   45
time you can make retarded babies.

My mother, who sews lace collars on my company softball T-shirts when she does my laundry.

Why, you can't you look like a lady playing softball?

My mother, who never went to any of my Parent-Teacher Association meetings when I was in school.

You're so good anyway. What are they going to tell me? I don't want to make you ashamed of this day woman. Shame is heavier than a hundred bags of salt.

Lydia Davis b. 1947

Blind Date

[1999]

"There isn't really much to tell," she said, but she would tell it if I liked. We were sitting in a midtown luncheonette. "I've only had one blind date in my life. And I didn't really have it. I can think of more interesting situations that are like a blind date — say when someone gives you a book as a present, when they fix you up with that book. I was once given a book of essays about reading, writing, book collecting. I felt it was a perfect match. I started reading it right away, in the back seat of the car. I stopped listening to the conversation in the front. I like to read about how other people read and collect books, even how they shelve their books. But by the time I was done with the book, I had taken a strong dislike to the author's personality. I won't have another date with *her*!" She laughed. Here we were interrupted by the waiter, and then a series of incidents followed that kept us from resuming our conversation that day.

The next time the subject came up, we were sitting in two Adirondack chairs looking out over a lake in, in fact, the Adirondacks. We were content to sit in silence at first. We were tired. We had been to the Adirondack Museum that day and seen many things of interest, including old guide boats and good examples of the original Adirondack chair. Now we watched the water and the edge of the woods, each thinking, I was sure, about James Fenimore Cooper. After some parties of canoers had gone by, older people in canvas boating hats, their quiet voices carrying far over the water to us, we went on talking. These were precious days of holiday together, and we were finishing many unfinished conversations.

"I was fifteen or sixteen, I guess," she said. "I was home from boarding school. Maybe it was summer. I don't know where my parents were. They were often away. They often left me alone there, sometimes for the evening, sometimes for weeks at a time. The phone rang. It was a boy I didn't know. He said he was a friend of a boy from school — I can't remember who. We talked a little and then he asked me if I wanted to have dinner with him. He sounded nice enough so I said I would, and we agreed on a day and a time and I told him where I lived.

"But after I got off the phone, I began thinking, worrying. What had this other boy said about me? What had the two of them said about me? Maybe I had some kind of a reputation. Even now I can't imagine that what they said was completely pure or innocent — for instance, that I was pretty and fun to be with. There had to be something nasty about it, two boys talking privately about a girl. The awful word that began to occur to me was *fast*. She's *fast*. I wasn't actually very fast. I was faster than some but not as fast as others. The more I imagined the two boys talking about me the worse I felt.

"I liked boys. I liked the boys I knew in a way that was much more innocent than they probably thought. I trusted them more than girls. Girls hurt my feelings, girls ganged up on me. I always had boys who were my friends, starting back when I was nine and ten and eleven. I didn't like this feeling that two boys were talking about me. 5

"Well, when the day came, I didn't want to go out to dinner with this boy. I just didn't want the difficulty of this date. It scared me—not because there was anything scary about the boy but because he was a stranger, I didn't know him. I didn't want to sit there face to face in some restaurant and start from the very beginning, knowing nothing. It didn't feel right. And there was the burden of that recommendation—'Give her a try.'

"Then again, maybe there were other reasons. Maybe I had been alone in that apartment so much by then that I had retreated into some kind of inner, unsociable space that was hard to come out of. Maybe I felt I had disappeared and I was comfortable that way and did not want to be forced back into existence, I don't know.

"At six o'clock, the buzzer rang. The boy was there, downstairs. I didn't answer it. It rang again. Still I did not answer it. I don't know how many times it rang or how long he leaned on it. I let it ring. At some point, I walked the length of the living room to the balcony. The apartment was four stories up. Across the street and down a flight of stone steps was a park. From the balcony on a clear day you could look out over the park and see all the way across town, maybe a mile, to the other river. At this point I think I ducked down or got down on my hands and knees and inched my way to the edge of the balcony. I think I looked over far enough to see him down there on the sidewalk below—looking up, as I remember it. Or he had gone across the street and was looking up. He didn't see me.

"I know that as I crouched there on the balcony or just back from it I had some impression of him being puzzled, disconcerted, disappointed, at a loss what to do now, not prepared for this—prepared for all sorts of other ways the date might go, other difficulties, but not for no date at all. Maybe he also felt angry or insulted, if it occurred to him then or later that maybe he hadn't made a mistake but that I had deliberately stood him up, and not the way I did it—alone up there in the apartment, uncomfortable and embarrassed, chickening out, hiding out—but, he would imagine, in collusion with someone else, a girlfriend or boyfriend, confiding in them, snickering over him.

"I don't know if he called me, or if I answered the phone if it rang. I could have given some excuse—I could have said I had gotten sick or had to go out suddenly. Or maybe I hung up when I heard his voice. In those days I did a lot of avoiding that I don't do now—avoiding confrontations, avoiding difficult encounters. And I did a fair amount of lying that I also don't do now.

"What was strange was how awful this felt. I was treating a person like a thing. And I was betraying not just him but something larger, some social contract. When you knew a decent person was waiting downstairs, someone you had made an appointment with, you did not just not answer the buzzer. What was even more surprising to me was what I felt about myself in that instant. I was behaving as though I had no responsibility to anyone or anything, and that made me feel as though I existed outside society, some kind of criminal, or didn't exist at all. I was annihilating myself even more than him. It was an awful violation."

She paused, thoughtful. We were sitting inside now, because it was raining. We had come inside to sit in a sort of lounge or recreation room provided for guests of that lakeside camp. The rain fell every afternoon there, sometimes for minutes, sometimes for hours. Across the water, the white pines and spruces were very still against the gray sky. The water was silver. We did not see any of the water birds we sometimes saw paddling around the edges of the lake—teals and loons. Inside, a fire burned in the fireplace. Over our heads hung a chandelier made of antlers. Between us stood a table constructed of a rough slab of wood resting on the legs of a deer, complete with hooves. On the table stood a lamp made from an old gun. She looked away from the lake and around the room. "In that book about the Adirondacks I was reading last night," she remarked, "he says this was what the Adirondacks was all about, I mean the Adirondacks style: things made from things."

A month or so later, when I was home again and she was back in the city, we were talking on the telephone and she said she had been hunting through one of the old diaries she had on her shelf there, that might say exactly what had happened—though of course, she said, she would just be filling in the details of something that did not actually happen. But she couldn't find this incident written down anywhere, which of course made her wonder if she had gotten the dates really wrong and she wasn't even in boarding school anymore by then. Maybe she was in college by then. But she decided to believe what she had told me. "But I'd forgotten how much I wrote about boys," she added. "Boys and books. What I wanted more than anything else at the age of sixteen was a great library."

Nathaniel Hawthorne   1804–1864

Young Goodman Brown   [1835]

Young Goodman° Brown came forth, at sunset, into the street of Salem village,° but put his head back, after crossing the threshold, to exchange a parting kiss with his young wife. And Faith, as the wife was aptly named, thrust her own pretty head into the street, letting the wind play with the pink ribbons of her cap, while she called to Goodman Brown.

"Dearest heart," whispered she, softly and rather sadly, when her lips were close to his ear, "pr'y thee, put off your journey until sunrise, and sleep in your own bed to-night. A lone woman is troubled with such dreams and such thoughts, that she's afeard of herself, sometimes. Pray, tarry with me this night, dear husband, of all nights in the year!"

"My love and my Faith," replied young Goodman Brown, "of all nights in the year, this one night must I tarry away from thee. My journey, as thou callest

---

Goodman: A man of ordinary status who was head of a household.
Salem village: Village in the Massachusetts Bay Colony.

APPROACHING THE AUTHOR

Nathaniel Hawthorne was born in Salem, Massachusetts, in 1804. His last name was originally Hathorne, without the *w*. Some speculate he added the *w* to dissociate himself from relatives, including John Hathorne, a judge during the Salem witchcraft trials.

For more about him, see page 1065.

it, forth and back again, must needs be done 'twixt now and sunrise. What, my sweet, pretty wife, dost thou doubt me already, and we but three months married!"

"Then, God bless you!" said Faith, with the pink ribbons, "and may you find all well when you come back."

"Amen!" cried Goodman Brown. "Say 5 thy prayers, dear Faith, and go to bed at dusk, and no harm will come to thee."

So they parted; and the young man pursued his way, until, being about to turn the corner by the meeting-house, he looked back, and saw the head of Faith still peeping after him, with a melancholy air, in spite of her pink ribbons.

"Poor little Faith!" thought he, for his heart smote him. "What a wretch am I, to leave her on such an errand! She talks of dreams, too. Methought, as she spoke, there was trouble in her face, as if a dream had warned her what work is to be done to-night. But, no, no! 'twould kill her to think it. Well; she's a blessed angel on earth; and after this one night, I'll cling to her skirts and follow her to Heaven."

With this excellent resolve for the future, Goodman Brown felt himself justified in making more haste on his present evil purpose. He had taken a dreary road, darkened by all the gloomiest trees of the forest, which barely stood aside to let the narrow path creep through, and closed immediately behind. It was all as lonely as could be; and there is this peculiarity in such a solitude, that the traveller knows not who may be concealed by the innumerable trunks and the thick boughs overhead; so that, with lonely footsteps, he may yet be passing through an unseen multitude.

"There may be a devilish Indian behind every tree," said Goodman Brown, to himself; and he glanced fearfully behind him, as he added, "What if the devil himself should be at my very elbow!"

His head being turned back, he passed a crook of the road, and looking 10 forward again, beheld the figure of a man, in grave and decent attire, seated at the foot of an old tree. He arose, at Goodman Brown's approach, and walked onward, side by side with him.

"You are late, Goodman Brown," said he. "The clock of the Old South was striking as I came through Boston; and that is full fifteen minutes agone."

"Faith kept me back awhile," replied the young man, with a tremor in his voice, caused by the sudden appearance of his companion, though not wholly unexpected.

It was now deep dusk in the forest, and deepest in that part of it where these two were journeying. As nearly as could be discerned, the second traveller was about fifty years old, apparently in the same rank of life as Goodman Brown, and bearing a considerable resemblance to him, though perhaps more in expression than features. Still, they might have been taken for father and son. And yet, though the elder person was as simply clad as the younger, and as simple in manner too, he had an indescribable air of one who knew the world, and would not have felt abashed at the governor's dinnertable, or in King William's court,° were it possible that his affairs should call him thither. But the only thing about him, that could be fixed upon as remarkable, was his staff, which bore the likeness of a great black snake, so curiously wrought, that it might almost be seen to twist and wriggle itself, like a living serpent. This, of course, must have been an ocular deception, assisted by the uncertain light.

"Come, Goodman Brown!" cried his fellow-traveller, "this is a dull pace for the beginning of a journey. Take my staff, if you are so soon weary."

"Friend," said the other, exchanging his slow pace for a full stop, "having 15 kept covenant by meeting thee here, it is my purpose now to return whence I came. I have scruples, touching the matter thou wot'st° of."

"Sayest thou so?" replied he of the serpent, smiling apart. "Let us walk on, nevertheless, reasoning as we go, and if I convince thee not, thou shalt turn back. We are but a little way in the forest, yet."

"Too far, too far!" exclaimed the goodman, unconsciously resuming his walk. "My father never went into the woods on such an errand, nor his father before him. We have been a race of honest men and good Christians, since the days of the martyrs.° And shall I be the first of the name of Brown, that ever took this path, and kept—"

"Such company, thou wouldst say," observed the elder person, interpreting his pause. "Well said, Goodman Brown! I have been as well acquainted with your family as with ever a one among the Puritans; and that's no trifle to say. I helped your grandfather, the constable, when he lashed the Quaker woman so smartly through the streets of Salem. And it was I that brought your father a pitch-pine knot, kindled at my own hearth, to set fire to an Indian village, in King Philip's war.° They were my good friends, both; and many a pleasant walk have we had along this path, and returned merrily after midnight. I would fain be friends with you, for their sake."

"If it be as thou sayest," replied Goodman Brown, "I marvel they never spoke of these matters. Or, verily, I marvel not, seeing that the least rumor of the sort would have driven them from New-England. We are a people of prayer, and good works, to boot, and abide no such wickedness."

"Wickedness or not," said the traveller with the twisted staff, "I have a very 20 general acquaintance here in New-England. The deacons of many a church

---

King William's court: William III was king of England from 1689 to 1702, ruling jointly with his wife Mary II until her death in 1694.
wot'st: Know.
days of the martyrs: Period in England during the rule of a Catholic monarch, Mary I (1553–1558), when Protestants were persecuted and many ancestors of the New England Pilgrims lost their lives for their religious faith.
King Philip's war: A bitter conflict (1675–1676) between the colonists and several New England tribes led by Metacomet, chief of the Wampanoag Indians, who was called King Philip by the colonists.

have drunk the communion wine with me; the selectmen, of divers towns, make me their chairman; and a majority of the Great and General Court° are firm supporters of my interest. The governor and I, too—but these are state-secrets."

"Can this be so!" cried Goodman Brown, with a stare of amazement at his undisturbed companion. "Howbeit, I have nothing to do with the governor and council; they have their own ways, and are no rule for a simple husbandman,° like me. But, were I to go on with thee, how should I meet the eye of that good old man, our minister, at Salem village? Oh, his voice would make me tremble, both Sabbath-day and lecture-day!"°

Thus far, the elder traveller had listened with due gravity, but now burst into a fit of irrepressible mirth, shaking himself so violently, that his snake-like staff actually seemed to wriggle in sympathy.

"Ha! ha! ha!" shouted he, again and again; then composing himself, "Well, go on, Goodman Brown, go on; but pr'y thee, don't kill me with laughing!"

"Well, then, to end the matter at once," said Goodman Brown, considerably nettled, "there is my wife, Faith. It would break her dear little heart; and I'd rather break my own!"

"Nay, if that be the case," answered the other, "e'en go thy ways, Goodman   25
Brown. I would not, for twenty old women like the one hobbling before us, that Faith should come to any harm."

As he spoke, he pointed his staff at a female figure on the path, in whom Goodman Brown recognized a very pious and exemplary dame, who had taught him his catechism, in youth, and was still his moral and spiritual adviser, jointly with the minister and Deacon Gookin.

"A marvel, truly, that Goody° Cloyse should be so far in the wilderness, at night-fall!" said he. "But, with your leave, friend, I shall take a cut through the woods, until we have left this Christian woman behind. Being a stranger to you, she might ask whom I was consorting with, and whither I was going."

"Be it so," said his fellow-traveller. "Betake you to the woods, and let me keep the path."

Accordingly, the young man turned aside, but took care to watch his companion, who advanced softly along the road, until he had come within a staff's length of the old dame. She, meanwhile, was making the best of her way, with singular speed for so aged a woman, and mumbling some indistinct words, a prayer, doubtless, as she went. The traveller put forth his staff, and touched her withered neck with what seemed the serpent's tail.

"The devil!" screamed the pious old lady.   30

Great and General Court: Colonial legislature.
husbandman: Farmer.
lecture-day: A weekday church service with a sermon.
Goody: Short for Goodwife, a married woman of ordinary status (cf. "goodman"). Goody Cloyse and Goody Cory, along with Martha Carrier, were sentenced to death at the Salem witchcraft trials of 1692, at which Hawthorne's great-grandfather was a judge.

"Then Goody Cloyse knows her old friend?" observed the traveller, confronting her, and leaning on his writhing stick.

"Ah, forsooth, and is it your worship, indeed?" cried the good dame. "Yea, truly is it, and in the very image of my old gossip,° Goodman Brown, the grandfather of the silly fellow that now is. But—would your worship believe it?—my broomstick hath strangely disappeared, stolen, as I suspect, by that unhanged witch, Goody Cory, and that, too, when I was all anointed with the juice of smallage and cinque-foil and wolf's-bane—"°

"Mingled with fine wheat and the fat of a new-born babe," said the shape of old Goodman Brown.

"Ah, your worship knows the receipt," cried the old lady, cackling aloud. "So, as I was saying, being all ready for the meeting, and no horse to ride on, I made up my mind to foot it; for they tell me, there is a nice young man to be taken into communion to-night. But now your good worship will lend me your arm, and we shall be there in a twinkling."

"That can hardly be," answered her friend. "I may not spare you my arm,   35 Goody Cloyse, but here is my staff, if you will."

So saying, he threw it down at her feet, where, perhaps, it assumed life, being one of the rods which its owner had formerly lent to the Egyptian Magi.° Of this fact, however, Goodman Brown could not take cognizance. He had cast up his eyes in astonishment, and looking down again, beheld neither Goody Cloyse nor the serpentine staff, but his fellow-traveller alone, who waited for him as calmly as if nothing had happened.

"That old woman taught me my catechism!" said the young man; and there was a world of meaning in this simple comment.

They continued to walk onward, while the elder traveller exhorted his companion to make good speed and persevere in the path, discoursing so aptly, that his arguments seemed rather to spring up in the bosom of his auditor, than to be suggested by himself. As they went, he plucked a branch of maple, to serve for a walking-stick, and began to strip it of the twigs and little boughs, which were wet with evening dew. The moment his fingers touched them, they became strangely withered and dried up, as with a week's sunshine. Thus the pair proceeded, at a good free pace, until suddenly, in a gloomy hollow of the road, Goodman Brown sat himself down on the stump of a tree, and refused to go any farther.

"Friend," said he, stubbornly, "my mind is made up. Not another step will I budge on this errand. What if a wretched old woman do choose to go to the devil, when I thought she was going to Heaven! Is that any reason why I should quit my dear Faith, and go after her?"

---

gossip: Godfather or godmother, sponsor at a baptism.
smallage . . . bane: "Smallage" is wild celery or water parsley; "cinque-foil" is a type of rose; "wolf's-bane" is aconite or monkshood. All are ingredients in a witch's brew.
Egyptian Magi: Egyptian magicians who were able, like Aaron in the biblical account, to turn rods into serpents. See Exodus 7:11–12.

"You will think better of this, by-and-by," said his acquaintance, compos- 40 edly. "Sit here and rest yourself awhile; and when you feel like moving again, there is my staff to help you along."

Without more words, he threw his companion the maple stick, and was as speedily out of sight, as if he had vanished into the deepening gloom. The young man sat a few moments, by the road-side, applauding himself greatly, and thinking with how clear a conscience he should meet the minister, in his morning-walk, nor shrink from the eye of good old Deacon Gookin. And what calm sleep would be his, that very night, which was to have been spent so wickedly, but purely and sweetly now, in the arms of Faith! Amidst these pleasant and praiseworthy meditations, Goodman Brown heard the tramp of horses along the road, and deemed it advisable to conceal himself within the verge of the forest, conscious of the guilty purpose that had brought him thither, though now so happily turned from it.

On came the hoof-tramps and the voices of the riders, two grave old voices, conversing soberly as they drew near. These mingled sounds appeared to pass along the road, within a few yards of the young man's hiding-place; but owing, doubtless, to the depth of the gloom, at that particular spot, neither the travellers nor their steeds were visible. Though their figures brushed the small boughs by the way-side, it could not be seen that they intercepted, even for a moment, the faint gleam from the strip of bright sky, athwart which they must have passed. Goodman Brown alternately crouched and stood on tip-toe, pulling aside the branches, and thrusting forth his head as far as he durst, without discerning so much as a shadow. It vexed him the more, because he could have sworn, were such a thing possible, that he recognized the voices of the minister and Deacon Gookin, jogging along quietly, as they were wont to do, when bound to some ordination or ecclesiastical council. While yet within hearing, one of the riders stopped to pluck a switch.

"Of the two, reverend Sir," said the voice like the deacon's, "I had rather miss an ordination-dinner than to-night's meeting. They tell me that some of our community are to be here from Falmouth and beyond, and others from Connecticut and Rhode-Island; besides several of the Indian powows,° who, after their fashion, know almost as much deviltry as the best of us. Moreover, there is a goodly young woman to be taken into communion."

"Mighty well, Deacon Gookin!" replied the solemn old tones of the minister. "Spur up, or we shall be late. Nothing can be done, you know, until I get on the ground."

The hoofs clattered again, and the voices, talking so strangely in the empty 45 air, passed on through the forest, where no church had ever been gathered, nor solitary Christian prayed. Whither, then, could these holy men be journeying, so deep into the heathen wilderness? Young Goodman Brown caught hold of a tree, for support, being ready to sink down on the ground, faint and overburthened

---

powows: Medicine men.

with the heavy sickness of his heart. He looked up to the sky, doubting whether there really was a Heaven above him. Yet, there was the blue arch, and the stars brightening in it.

"With Heaven above, and Faith below, I will yet stand firm against the devil!" cried Goodman Brown.

While he still gazed upward, into the deep arch of the firmament, and had lifted his hands to pray, a cloud, though no wind was stirring, hurried across the zenith, and hid the brightening stars. The blue sky was still visible, except directly overhead, where this black mass of cloud was sweeping swiftly north-ward. Aloft in the air, as if from the depths of the cloud, came a confused and doubtful sound of voices. Once, the listener fancied that he could distinguish the accents of town's-people of his own, men and women, both pious and ungodly, many of whom he had met at the communion-table, and had seen others rioting at the tavern. The next moment, so indistinct were the sounds, he doubted whether he had heard aught but the murmur of the old forest, whispering without a wind. Then came a stronger swell of those familiar tones, heard daily in the sunshine, at Salem village, but never, until now, from a cloud of night. There was one voice, of a young woman, uttering lamentations, yet with an uncertain sorrow, and entreating for some favor, which, perhaps, it would grieve her to obtain. And all the unseen multitude, both saints and sinners, seemed to encourage her onward.

"Faith!" shouted Goodman Brown, in a voice of agony and desperation; and the echoes of the forest mocked him, crying—"Faith! Faith!" as if bewildered wretches were seeking her, all through the wilderness.

The cry of grief, rage, and terror, was yet piercing the night, when the unhappy husband held his breath for a response. There was a scream, drowned immediately in a louder murmur of voices, fading into far-off laughter, as the dark cloud swept away, leaving the clear and silent sky above Goodman Brown. But something fluttered lightly down through the air, and caught on the branch of a tree. The young man seized it, and beheld a pink ribbon.

"My Faith is gone!" cried he, after one stupefied moment. "There is no good 50 on earth; and sin is but a name. Come, devil! for to thee is this world given."

And maddened with despair, so that he laughed loud and long, did Goodman Brown grasp his staff and set forth again, at such a rate, that he seemed to fly along the forest-path, rather than to walk or run. The road grew wilder and drearier, and more faintly traced, and vanished at length, leaving him in the heart of the dark wilderness, still rushing onward, with the instinct that guides mortal man to evil. The whole forest was peopled with frightful sounds; the creaking of the trees, the howling of wild beasts, and the yell of Indians; while, sometimes, the wind tolled like a distant church-bell, and some-times gave a broad roar around the traveller, as if all Nature were laughing him to scorn. But he was himself the chief horror of the scene, and shrank not from its other horrors.

"Ha! ha! ha!" roared Goodman Brown, when the wind laughed at him. "Let us hear which will laugh loudest! Think not to frighten me with your deviltry! Come witch, come wizard, come Indian powow, come devil himself! and here comes Goodman Brown. You may as well fear him as he fear you!"

In truth, all through the haunted forest, there could be nothing more frightful than the figure of Goodman Brown. On he flew, among the black pines, brandishing his staff with frenzied gestures, now giving vent to an inspiration of horrid blasphemy, and now shouting forth such laughter, as set all the echoes of the forest laughing like demons around him. The fiend in his own shape is less hideous, than when he rages in the breast of man. Thus sped the demoniac on his course, until, quivering among the trees, he saw a red light before him, as when the felled trunks and branches of a clearing have been set on fire, and throw up their lurid blaze against the sky, at the hour of midnight. He paused, in a lull of the tempest that had driven him onward, and heard the swell of what seemed a hymn, rolling solemnly from a distance, with the weight of many voices. He knew the tune; it was a familiar one in the choir of the village meetinghouse. The verse died heavily away, and was lengthened by a chorus, not of human voices, but of all the sounds of the benighted wilderness, pealing in awful harmony together. Goodman Brown cried out; and his cry was lost to his own ear, by its unison with the cry of the desert.

In the interval of silence, he stole forward, until the light glared full upon his eyes. At one extremity of an open space, hemmed in by the dark wall of the forest, arose a rock, bearing some rude, natural resemblance either to an altar or a pulpit, and surrounded by four blazing pines, their tops aflame, their stems untouched, like candles at an evening meeting. The mass of foliage, that had overgrown the summit of the rock, was all on fire, blazing high into the night, and fitfully illuminating the whole field. Each pendent twig and leafy festoon was in a blaze. As the red light arose and fell, a numerous congregation alternately shone forth, then disappeared in shadow, and again grew, as it were, out of the darkness, peopling the heart of the solitary woods at once.

"A grave and dark-clad company!" quoth Goodman Brown.   55

In truth, they were such. Among them, quivering to-and-fro, between gloom and splendor, appeared faces that would be seen, next day, at the council-board of the province, and others which, Sabbath after Sabbath, looked devoutly heavenward, and benignantly over the crowded pews, from the holiest pulpits in the land. Some affirm, that the lady of the governor was there. At least, there were high dames well known to her, and wives of honored husbands, and widows, a great multitude, and ancient maidens, all of excellent repute, and fair young girls, who trembled, lest their mothers should espy them. Either the sudden gleams of light, flashing over the obscure field, bedazzled Goodman Brown, or he recognized a score of the church-members of Salem village, famous for their especial sanctity. Good old Deacon Gookin had arrived, and waited at the skirts of that venerable saint, his revered pastor. But, irreverently consorting with these grave, reputable, and pious people, these elders of the church, these chaste dames and dewy virgins, there were men of dissolute lives and women of spotted fame, wretches given over to all mean and filthy vice, and suspected even of horrid crimes. It was strange to see, that the good shrank not from the wicked, nor were the sinners abashed by the saints. Scattered, also, among their pale-faced enemies, were the Indian priests, or powows, who had often scared their native forest with more hideous incantations than any known to English witchcraft.

"But, where is Faith?" thought Goodman Brown; and, as hope came into his heart, he trembled.

Another verse of the hymn arose, a slow and mournful strain, such as the pious love, but joined to words which expressed all that our nature can conceive of sin, and darkly hinted at far more. Unfathomable to mere mortals is the lore of fiends. Verse after verse was sung, and still the chorus of the desert swelled between, like the deepest tone of a mighty organ. And, with the final peal of that dreadful anthem, there came a sound, as if the roaring wind, the rushing streams, the howling beasts, and every other voice of the unconverted wilderness, were mingling and according with the voice of guilty man, in homage to the prince of all. The four blazing pines threw up a loftier flame, and obscurely discovered shapes and visages of horror on the smoke-wreaths, above the impious assembly. At the same moment, the fire on the rock shot redly forth, and formed a glowing arch above its base, where now appeared a figure. With reverence be it spoken, the figure bore no slight similitude, both in garb and manner, to some grave divine of the New-England churches.

"Bring forth the converts!" cried a voice, that echoed through the field and rolled into the forest.

At the word, Goodman Brown stept forth from the shadow of the trees, and 60 approached the congregation, with whom he felt a loathful brotherhood, by the sympathy of all that was wicked in his heart. He could have well nigh sworn, that the shape of his own dead father beckoned him to advance, looking downward from a smoke-wreath, while a woman, with dim features of despair, threw out her hand to warn him back. Was it his mother? But he had no power to retreat one step, nor to resist, even in thought, when the minister and good old Deacon Gookin seized his arms, and led him to the blazing rock. Thither came also the slender form of a veiled female, led between Goody Cloyse, that pious teacher of the catechism, and Martha Carrier, who had received the devil's promise to be queen of hell. A rampant hag was she! And there stood the proselytes, beneath the canopy of fire.

"Welcome, my children," said the dark figure, "to the communion of your race! Ye have found, thus young, your nature and your destiny. My children, look behind you!"

They turned; and flashing forth, as it were, in a sheet of flame, the fiend-worshippers were seen; the smile of welcome gleamed darkly on every visage.

"There," resumed the sable form, "are all whom ye have reverenced from youth. Ye deemed them holier than yourselves, and shrank from your own sin, contrasting it with their lives of righteousness, and prayerful aspirations heavenward. Yet, here are they all, in my worshipping assembly! This night it shall be granted you to know their secret deeds; how hoary-bearded elders of the church have whispered wanton words to the young maids of their households; how many a woman, eager for widow's weeds, has given her husband a drink at bed-time, and let him sleep his last sleep in her bosom; how beardless youths have made haste to inherit their fathers' wealth; and how fair damsels—blush not, sweet ones!—have dug little graves in the garden, and bidden me, the sole guest, to an infant's funeral. By the sympathy of your human hearts for sin, ye shall scent out all the places—whether in church, bed-chamber, street, field, or forest—where crime has been committed, and shall exult to behold the whole earth one stain of guilt, one mighty bloodspot. Far more than this! It shall be yours to penetrate, in every bosom, the deep mystery of sin, the fountain of all wicked arts, and which inexhaustibly supplies more evil impulses than human power—than my power, at its utmost!—can make manifest in deeds. And now, my children, look upon each other."

They did so; and, by the blaze of the hell-kindled torches, the wretched man beheld his Faith, and the wife her husband, trembling before that unhallowed altar.

"Lo! there ye stand, my children," said the figure, in a deep and solemn 65 tone, almost sad, with its despairing awfulness, as if his once angelic nature could yet mourn for our miserable race. "Depending upon one another's hearts, ye had still hoped, that virtue were not all a dream. Now are ye undeceived! Evil is the nature of mankind. Evil must be your only happiness. Welcome, again, my children, to the communion of your race!"

"Welcome!" repeated the fiend-worshippers, in one cry of despair and triumph.

And there they stood, the only pair, as it seemed, who were yet hesitating on the verge of wickedness, in this dark world. A basin was hollowed, naturally, in the rock. Did it contain water, reddened by the lurid light? or was it blood? or, perchance, a liquid flame? Herein did the Shape of Evil dip his hand, and prepare to lay the mark of baptism upon their foreheads, that they might be partakers of the mystery of sin, more conscious of the secret guilt of others, both in deed and thought, than they could now be of their own. The husband cast one look at his pale wife, and Faith at him. What polluted wretches would the next glance shew them to each other, shuddering alike at what they disclosed and what they saw!

"Faith! Faith!" cried the husband. "Look up to Heaven, and resist the Wicked One!"

Whether Faith obeyed, he knew not. Hardly had he spoken, when he found himself amid calm night and solitude, listening to a roar of the wind, which died heavily away through the forest. He staggered against the rock and felt it chill and damp, while a hanging twig, that had been all on fire, besprinkled his cheek with the coldest dew.

The next morning, young Goodman Brown came slowly into the street of 70 Salem village, staring around him like a bewildered man. The good old minister was taking a walk along the grave-yard, to get an appetite for breakfast and meditate his sermon, and bestowed a blessing, as he passed, on Goodman

Brown. He shrank from the venerable saint, as if to avoid an anathema.° Old Deacon Gookin was at domestic worship, and the holy words of his prayer were heard through the open window. "What God doth the wizard pray to?" quoth Goodman Brown. Goody Cloyse, that excellent old Christian, stood in the early sunshine, at her own lattice, catechising a little girl, who had brought her a pint of morning's milk. Goodman Brown snatched away the child, as from the grasp of the fiend himself. Turning the corner by the meeting-house, he spied the head of Faith, with the pink ribbons, gazing anxiously forth, and bursting into such joy at sight of him, that she skipt along the street, and almost kissed her husband before the whole village. But, Goodman Brown looked sternly and sadly into her face, and passed on without a greeting.

Had Goodman Brown fallen asleep in the forest, and only dreamed a wild dream of a witch-meeting?

Be it so, if you will. But, alas! it was a dream of evil omen for young Goodman Brown. A stern, a sad, a darkly meditative, a distrustful, if not a desperate man, did he become, from the night of that fearful dream. On the Sabbath-day, when the congregation were singing a holy psalm, he could not listen, because an anthem of sin rushed loudly upon his ear, and drowned all the blessed strain. When the minister spoke from the pulpit, with power and fervid eloquence, and, with his hand on the open Bible, of the sacred truths of our religion, and of saint-like lives and triumphant deaths, and of future bliss or misery unutterable, then did Goodman Brown turn pale, dreading, lest the roof should thunder down upon the gray blasphemer and his hearers. Often, awakening suddenly at midnight, he shrank from the bosom of Faith, and at morning or eventide, when the family knelt down at prayer, he scowled, and muttered to himself, and gazed sternly at his wife, and turned away. And when he had lived long, and was borne to his grave, a hoary corpse, followed by Faith, an aged woman, and children and grandchildren, a goodly procession, besides neighbors, not a few, they carved no hopeful verse upon his tomb-stone; for his dying hour was gloom.

Langston Hughes 1902–1967

Thank You, M'am   [1963]

She was a large woman with a large purse that had everything in it but a hammer and nails. It had a long strap, and she carried it slung across her shoulder. It was about eleven o'clock at night, dark, and she was walking alone, when a boy ran up behind her and tried to snatch her purse. The strap broke with the sudden single tug the boy gave it from behind. But the boy's weight and the

---

anathema: A thing accursed or consigned to damnation by an official decree of the church.

weight of the purse combined caused him to lose his balance. Instead of taking off full blast as he had hoped, the boy fell on his back on the sidewalk and his legs flew up. The large woman simply turned around and kicked him right square in his blue-jeaned sitter. Then she reached down, picked the boy up by his shirt front, and shook him until his teeth rattled.

After that the woman said, "Pick up my pocketbook, boy, and give it here."

She still held him tightly. But she bent down enough to permit him to stoop and pick up her purse. Then she said, "Now ain't you ashamed of yourself?"

Firmly gripped by his shirt front, the boy said, "Yes'm."

The woman said, "What did you want to do it for?"   5

The boy said, "I didn't aim to."

She said, "You a lie!"

By that time two or three people passed, stopped, turned to look, and some stood watching.

"If I turn you loose, will you run?" asked the woman.

"Yes'm," said the boy.   10

"Then I won't turn you loose," said the woman. She did not release him.

"Lady, I'm sorry," whispered the boy.

"Um-hum! Your face is dirty. I got a great mind to wash your face for you. Ain't you got nobody home to tell you to wash your face?"

"No'm," said the boy.

"Then it will get washed this evening," said the large woman, starting up   15
the street, dragging the frightened boy behind her.

He looked as if he were fourteen or fifteen, frail and willow-wild, in tennis shoes and blue jeans.

The woman said, "You ought to be my son. I would teach you right from wrong. Least I can do right now is to wash your face. Are you hungry?"

"No'm," said the being-dragged boy. "I just want you to turn me loose."

"Was I bothering *you* when I turned that corner?" asked the woman.

"No'm."   20

"But you put yourself in contact with *me*," said the woman. "If you think that that contact is not going to last awhile, you got another thought coming. When I get through with you, sir, you are going to remember Mrs. Luella Bates Washington Jones."

Sweat popped out on the boy's face and he began to struggle. Mrs. Jones stopped, jerked him around in front of her, put a half nelson about his neck, and continued to drag him up the street. When she got to her door, she dragged the boy inside, down a hall, and into a large kitchenette-furnished room at the rear of the house. She switched on the light and left the door open. The boy could hear other roomers laughing and talking in the large house. Some of their doors were open, too, so he knew he and the woman were not alone. The woman still had him by the neck in the middle of her room.

She said, "What is your name?"

"Roger," answered the boy.

"Then, Roger, you go to that sink and wash your face," said the woman, 25
whereupon she turned him loose—at last. Roger looked at the door—looked at
the woman—looked at the door—*and went to the sink.*

"Let the water run until it gets warm," she said. "Here's a clean towel."

"You gonna take me to jail?" asked the boy, bending over the sink.

"Not with that face, I would not take you nowhere," said the woman. "Here
I am trying to get home to cook me a bite to eat, and you snatch my pocketbook! Maybe you ain't been to your supper either, late as it be. Have you?"

"There's nobody home at my house," said the boy.

"Then we'll eat," said the woman. "I believe you're hungry—or been 30
hungry—to try to snatch my pocketbook!"

"I want a pair of blue suede shoes," said the boy.

"Well, you didn't have to snatch *my* pocketbook to get some suede shoes,"
said Mrs. Luella Bates Washington Jones. "You could've asked me."

"M'am?"

The water dripping from his face, the boy looked at her. There was a long
pause. A very long pause. After he had dried his face and not knowing what else
to do, dried it again, the boy turned around, wondering what next. The door was
open. He could make a dash for it down the hall. He could run, run, run, *run!*

The woman was sitting on the day bed. After a while she said, "I were young 35
once and I wanted things I could not get."

There was another long pause. The boy's mouth opened. Then he frowned,
not knowing he frowned.

The woman said, "Um-hum! You thought I was going to say *but,* didn't you?
You thought I was going to say, *but I didn't snatch people's pocketbooks.* Well, I
wasn't going to say that." Pause. Silence. "I have done things, too, which I would
not tell you, son—neither tell God, if He didn't already know. Everybody's got
something in common. So you set down while I fix us something to eat. You
might run that comb through your hair so you will look presentable."

In another corner of the room behind a screen was a gas plate and an icebox. Mrs. Jones got up and went behind the screen. The woman did not watch
the boy to see if he was going to run now, nor did she watch her purse, which
she left behind her on the day bed. But the boy took care to sit on the far side
of the room, away from the purse, where he thought she could easily see him
out of the corner of her eye if she wanted to. He did not trust the woman *not*
to trust him. And he did not want to be mistrusted now.

"Do you need somebody to go to the store," asked the boy, "maybe to get
some milk or something?"

"Don't believe I do," said the woman, "unless you just want sweet milk 40
yourself. I was going to make cocoa out of this canned milk I got here."

"That will be fine," said the boy.

She heated some lima beans and ham she had in the icebox, made the
cocoa, and set the table. The woman did not ask the boy anything about where
he lived, or his folks, or anything else that would embarrass him. Instead, as
they ate, she told him about her job in a hotel beauty shop that stayed open late,

what the work was like, and how all kinds of women came in and out, blondes, redheads, and Spanish. Then she cut him a half of her ten-cent cake.

"Eat some more, son," she said.

When they were finished eating, she got up and said, "Now here, take this ten dollars and buy yourself some blue suede shoes. And next time, do not make the mistake of latching onto *my* pocketbook *nor nobody else's*—because shoes got by devilish ways will burn your feet. I got to get my rest now. But from here on in, son, I hope you will behave yourself."

She led him down the hall to the front door and opened it. "Good night!   45
Behave yourself, boy!" she said, looking out into the street as he went down the steps.

The boy wanted to say something other than, "Thank you, m'am," to Mrs. Luella Bates Washington Jones, but although his lips moved, he couldn't even say that as he turned at the foot of the barren stoop and looked up at the large woman in the door. Then she shut the door.

Zora Neale Hurston   1891–1960

Sweat   [1926]

It was eleven o'clock of a Spring night in Florida. It was Sunday. Any other night, Delia Jones would have been in bed for two hours by this time. But she was a washwoman, and Monday morning meant a great deal to her. So she collected the soiled clothes on Saturday when she returned the clean things. Sunday night after church, she sorted them and put the white things to soak. It saved her almost a half day's start. A great hamper in the bedroom held the clothes that she brought home. It was so much neater than a number of bundles lying around.

She squatted on the kitchen floor beside the great pile of clothes, sorting them into small heaps according to color, and humming a song in a mournful key, but wondering through it all where Sykes, her husband, had gone with her horse and buckboard.

Just then something long, round, limp and black fell upon her shoulders and slithered to the floor beside her. A great terror took hold of her. It softened her knees and dried her mouth so that it was a full minute before she could cry out or move. Then she saw that it was the big bull whip her husband liked to carry when he drove.

She lifted her eyes to the door and saw him standing there bent over with laughter at her fright. She screamed at him.

APPROACHING THE AUTHOR

When **Zora Neale Hurston** moved to Baltimore at age twenty-six, she still hadn't finished high school. Needing to present herself as a teenager to qualify for free public schooling, she lopped ten years off her life—giving her age as sixteen and the year of her birth as 1901.

For more about her, see page 1067.

"Sykes, what you throw dat whip on me like dat? You know it would skeer 5
me—looks just like a snake, an' you knows how skeered Ah is of snakes."

"Course Ah knowed it! That's how come Ah done it." He slapped his leg
with his hand and almost rolled on the ground in his mirth. "If you such a big
fool dat you got to have a fit over a earth worm or a string, Ah don't keer how
bad Ah skeer you."

"You aint got no business doing it. Gawd knows it's a sin. Some day Ah'm
gointuh drop dead from some of yo' foolishness. 'Nother thing, where you been
wid mah rig? Ah feeds dat pony. He aint fuh you to be drivin' wid no bull whip."

"You sho is one aggravatin' nigger woman!" he declared and stepped into
the room. She resumed her work and did not answer him at once. "Ah done tole
you time and again to keep them white folks' clothes outa dis house."

He picked up the whip and glared down at her. Delia went on with her work.
She went out into the yard and returned with a galvanized tub and sat it on the
washbench. She saw that Sykes had kicked all of the clothes together again, and
now stood in her way truculently, his whole manner hoping, *praying*, for an argument. But she walked calmly around him and commenced to re-sort the things.

"Next time, Ah'm gointer kick 'em outdoors," he threatened as he struck a 10
match along the leg of his corduroy breeches.

Delia never looked up from her work, and her thin, stooped shoulders
sagged further.

"Ah aint for no fuss t'night, Sykes. Ah just come from taking sacrament at
the church house."

He snorted scornfully. "Yeah, you just come from de church house on a
Sunday night, but heah you is gone to work on them clothes. You ain't nothing
but a hypocrite. One of them amen-corner Christians—sing, whoop, and
shout, then come home and wash white folks clothes on the Sabbath."

He stepped roughly upon the whitest pile of things, kicking them helter-
skelter as he crossed the room. His wife gave a little scream of dismay, and
quickly gathered them together again.

"Sykes, you quit grindin' dirt into these clothes! How can Ah git through 15
by Sat'day if Ah don't start on Sunday?"

"Ah don't keer if you never git through. Anyhow, Ah done promised Gawd
and a couple of other men, Ah aint gointer have it in mah house. Don't gimme
no lip neither, else Ah'll throw 'em out and put mah fist up side yo' head to boot."

Delia's habitual meekness seemed to slip from her shoulders like a blown
scarf. She was on her feet; her poor little body, her bare knuckly hands bravely
defying the strapping hulk before her.

"Looka heah, Sykes, you done gone too fur. Ah been married to you fur
fifteen years, and Ah been takin' in washin' fur fifteen years. Sweat, sweat,
sweat! Work and sweat, cry and sweat, pray and sweat!"

"What's that got to do with me?" he asked brutally.

"What's it got to do with you, Sykes? Mah tub of suds is filled yo' belly with 20
vittles more times than yo' hands is filled it. Mah sweat is done paid for this
house and Ah reckon Ah kin keep on sweatin' in it."

She seized the iron skillet from the stove and struck a defensive pose, which act surprised him greatly, coming from her. It cowed him and he did not strike her as he usually did.

"Naw you won't," she panted, "that ole snaggle-toothed black woman you runnin' with aint comin' heah to pile up on *mah* sweat and blood. You aint paid for nothin' on this place, and Ah'm gointer stay right heah till Ah'm toted out foot foremost."

"Well, you better quit gittin' me riled up, else they'll be totin' you out sooner than you expect. Ah'm so tired of you Ah don't know whut to do. Gawd! how Ah hates skinny wimmen!"

A little awed by this new Delia, he sidled out of the door and slammed the back gate after him. He did not say where he had gone, but she knew too well. She knew very well that he would not return until nearly daybreak also. Her work over, she went on to bed but not to sleep at once. Things had come to a pretty pass!

She lay awake, gazing upon the debris that cluttered their matrimonial 25 trail. Not an image left standing along the way. Anything like flowers had long ago been drowned in the salty stream that had been pressed from her heart. Her tears, her sweat, her blood. She had brought love to the union and he had brought a longing after the flesh. Two months after the wedding, he had given her the first brutal beating. She had the memory of his numerous trips to Orlando with all of his wages when he had returned to her penniless, even before the first year had passed. She was young and soft then, but now she thought of her knotty, muscled limbs, her harsh knuckly hands, and drew herself up into an unhappy little ball in the middle of the big feather bed. Too late now to hope for love, even if it were not Bertha it would be someone else. This case differed from the others only in that she was bolder than the others. Too late for everything except her little home. She had built it for her old days, and planted one by one the trees and flowers there. It was lovely to her, lovely.

Somehow, before sleep came, she found herself saying aloud: "Oh well, whatever goes over the Devil's back, is got to come under his belly. Sometime or ruther, Sykes, like everybody else, is gointer reap his sowing." After that she was able to build a spiritual earthworks against her husband. His shells could no longer reach her. *Amen.* She went to sleep and slept until he announced his presence in bed by kicking her feet and rudely snatching the cover away.

"Gimme some kivah heah, an' git yo' damn foots over on yo' own side! Ah oughter mash you in yo' mouf fuh drawing dat skillet on me."

Delia went clear to the rail without answering him. A triumphant indifference to all that he was or did.

The week was as full of work for Delia as all other weeks, and Saturday found her behind her little pony, collecting and delivering clothes.

It was a hot, hot day near the end of July. The village men on Joe Clarke's 30 porch even chewed cane listlessly. They did not hurl the cane-knots as usual. They let them dribble over the edge of the porch. Even conversation had collapsed under the heat.

"Heah come Delia Jones," Jim Merchant said, as the shaggy pony came 'round the bend of the road toward them. The rusty buckboard was heaped with baskets of crisp, clean laundry.

"Yep," Joe Lindsay agreed. "Hot or col', rain or shine, jes ez reg'lar ez de weeks roll roun' Delia carries 'em an' fetches 'em on Sat'day."

"She better if she wanter eat," said Moss. "Sykes Jones aint wuth de shot an' powder hit would tek tuh kill 'em. Not to *huh* he aint."

"He sho' aint," Walter Thomas chimed in. "It's too bad, too, cause she wuz a right pritty li'l trick when he got huh. Ah'd uh mah'ied huh mahseff if he hadnter beat me to it."

Delia nodded briefly at the men as she drove past.   35

"Too much knockin' will ruin *any* 'oman. He done beat huh 'nough tuh kill three women, let 'lone change they looks," said Elijah Moseley. "How Sykes kin stommuck dat big black greasy Mogul he's layin' roun' wid, gits me. Ah swear dat eight-rock couldn't kiss a sardine can Ah done thowed out de back do' 'way las' yeah."

"Aw, she's fat, thass how come. He's allus been crazy 'bout fat women," put in Merchant. "He'd a' been tied up wid one long time ago if he could a' found one tuh have him. Did Ah tell yuh 'bout him come sidlin' roun' *mah* wife— bringin' her a basket uh pee-cans outa his yard fuh a present? Yessir, mah wife! She tol' him tuh take 'em right straight back home, cause Delia works so hard ovah dat washtub she reckon everything on de place taste lak sweat an' soap-suds. Ah jus' wisht Ah'd a' caught 'im 'roun' dere! Ah'd a' made his hips ketch on fiah down dat shell road."

"Ah know he done it, too. Ah sees 'im grinnin' at every 'oman dat passes," Walter Thomas said. "But even so, he useter eat some mighty big hunks uh humble pie tuh git dat lil' 'oman he got. She wuz ez pritty ez a speckled pup! Dat wuz fifteen yeahs ago. He useter be so skeered uh losin' huh, she could make him do some parts of a husband's duty. Dey never wuz de same in de mind."

"There oughter be a law about him," said Lindsay. "He aint fit tuh carry guts tuh a bear."

Clarke spoke for the first time. "Taint no law on earth dat kin make a man 40 be decent if it aint in 'im. There's plenty men dat takes a wife lak dey do a joint uh sugar-cane. It's round, juicy an' sweet when dey gits it. But dey squeeze an' grind, squeeze an' grind an' wring tell dey wring every drop uh pleasure dat's in 'em out. When dey's satisfied dat dey is wrung dry, dey treats 'em jes lak dey do a cane-chew. Dey thows 'em away. Dey knows whut dey is doin' while dey is at it, an' hates theirselves fuh it but they keeps on hangin' after huh tell she's empty. Den dey hates huh fuh bein' a cane-chew an' in de way."

"We oughter take Sykes an' dat stray 'oman uh his'n down in Lake Howell swamp an' lay on de rawhide till they cain't say 'Lawd a' mussy.' He allus wuz uh ovahbearin' niggah, but since dat white 'oman from up north done teached 'im how to run a automobile, he done got too biggety to live—an' we oughter kill 'im," Old Man Anderson advised.

A grunt of approval went around the porch. But the heat was melting their civic virtue and Elijah Moseley began to bait Joe Clarke.

"Come on, Joe, git a melon outa dere an' slice it up for yo' customers. We'se all sufferin' wid de heat. De bear's done got *me*!"

"Thass right, Joe, a watermelon is jes' whut Ah needs tuh cure de eppizu- dicks." Walter Thomas joined forces with Moseley. "Come on dere, Joe. We all is steady customers an' you aint set us up in a long time. Ah chooses dat long, bowlegged Floridy favorite."

"A god, an' be dough. You all gimme twenty cents and slice away," Clarke 45 retorted. "Ah needs a col' slice m'self. Heah, everybody chip in. Ah'll lend y'all mah meat knife."

The money was quickly subscribed and the huge melon brought forth. At that moment, Sykes and Bertha arrived. A determined silence fell on the porch and the melon was put away again.

Merchant snapped down the blade of his jack-knife and moved toward the store door.

"Come on in, Joe, an' gimme a slab uh sow belly an' uh pound uh coffee— almost fuhgot 'twas Sat'day. Got to git on home." Most of the men left also.

Just then Delia drove past on her way home, as Sykes was ordering mag- nificently for Bertha. It pleased him for Delia to see.

"Git whutsoever yo' heart desires, Honey. Wait a minute, Joe. Give huh two 50 bottles uh strawberry soda-water, uh quart uh parched ground-peas, an a block uh chewin' gum."

With all this they left the store, with Sykes reminding Bertha that this was his town and she could have it if she wanted it.

The men returned soon after they left, and held their watermelon feast.

"Where did Sykes Jones git dat 'oman from nohow?" Lindsay asked.

"Ovah Apopka. Guess dey musta been cleanin' out de town when she lef'. She don't look lak a thing but a hunk uh liver wid hair on it."

"Well, she sho' kin squall," Dave Carter contributed. "When she gits ready 55 tuh laff, she jes' opens huh mouf an' latches it back tuh de las' notch. No ole grandpa alligator down in Lake Bell aint got nothin' on huh."

Bertha had been in town three months now. Sykes was still paying her room rent at Della Lewis'—the only house in town that would have taken her in. Sykes took her frequently to Winter Park to "stomps." He still assured her that he was the swellest man in the state.

"Sho' you kin have dat lil' ole house soon's Ah kin git dat 'oman outa dere. Everything b'longs tuh me an' you sho' kin have it. Ah sho' 'bominates uh skinny 'oman. Lawdy, you sho' is got one portly shape on you! You kin git *anything* you wants. Dis is *mah* town an' you sho' kin have it."

Delia's work-worn knees crawled over the earth in Gethsemane° and up the rocks of Calvary many, many times during these months. She avoided the villagers and meeting places in her efforts to be blind and deaf. But Bertha nullified this to a degree, by coming to Delia's house to call Sykes out to her at the gate.

Gethsemane: The garden in which Jesus agonized and prayed (Matthew 26:36–46) before being taken prisoner and crucified on a hill called Calvary (Luke 23:33).

Delia and Sykes fought all the time now with no peaceful interludes. They slept and ate in silence. Two or three times Delia had attempted a timid friendliness, but she was repulsed each time. It was plain that the breaches must remain agape.

The sun had burned July to August. The heat streamed down like a million 60 hot arrows, smiting all things living upon the earth. Grass withered, leaves browned, snakes went blind in shedding and men and dogs went mad. Dog days!

Delia came home one day and found Sykes there before her. She wondered, but started to go on into the house without speaking, even though he was standing in the kitchen door and she must either stoop under his arm or ask him to move. He made no room for her. She noticed a soap box beside the steps, but paid no particular attention to it, knowing that he must have brought it there. As she was stooping to pass under his outstretched arm, he suddenly pushed her backward, laughingly.

"Look in de box dere Delia, Ah done brung yuh somethin'!"

She nearly fell upon the box in her stumbling, and when she saw what it held, she all but fainted outright.

"Sykes! Sykes, mah Gawd! You take dat rattlesnake 'way from heah! You *gottuh.* Oh, Jesus, have mussy!"

"Ah aint gut tuh do nuthin' uh de kin'—fact is Ah aint got tuh do nothin' 65 but die. Taint no use uh you puttin' on airs makin' out lak you skeered uh dat snake—he's gointer stay right heah tell he die. He wouldn't bite me cause Ah knows how tuh handle 'im. Nohow he wouldn't risk breakin' out his fangs 'gin yo' skinny laigs."

"Naw, now Sykes, don't keep dat thing 'roun' heah tuh skeer me tuh death. You knows Ah'm even feared uh earth worms. Thass de biggest snake Ah evah did see. Kill 'im Sykes, please."

"Doan ast me tuh do nothin' fuh yuh. Goin' 'roun' tryin' tuh be so damn astorperious.° Naw, Ah aint gonna kill it. Ah think uh damn sight mo' uh him dan you! Dat's a nice snake an' anybody doan lak 'im kin jes' hit de grit."

The village soon heard that Sykes had the snake, and came to see and ask questions.

"How de hen-fire did you ketch dat six-foot rattler, Sykes?" Thomas asked.

"He's full uh frogs so he caint hardly move, thass how Ah eased up on 'm. 70 But Ah'm a snake charmer an' knows how tuh handle 'em. Shux, dat aint nothin'. Ah could ketch one eve'y day if Ah so wanted tuh."

"Whut he needs is a heavy hick'ry club leaned real heavy on his head. Dat's de bes 'way tuh charm a rattlesnake."

"Naw, Walt, y'all jes' don't understand dese diamon' backs lak Ah do," said Sykes in a superior tone of voice.

The village agreed with Walter, but the snake stayed on. His box remained by the kitchen door with its screen wire covering. Two or three days later it had digested its meal of frogs and literally came to life. It rattled at every movement

---

astorperious: Uppity, acting like a member of the prominent Astor family.

in the kitchen or the yard. One day as Delia came down the kitchen steps she saw his chalky-white fangs curved like scimitars hung in the wire meshes. This time she did not run away with averted eyes as usual. She stood for a long time in the doorway in a red fury that grew bloodier for every second that she regarded the creature that was her torment.

That night she broached the subject as soon as Sykes sat down to the table.

"Sykes, Ah wants you tuh take dat snake 'way fum heah. You done starved   75
me an' Ah put up widcher, you done beat me an Ah took dat, but you done kilt all mah insides bringin' dat varmint heah."

Sykes poured out a saucer full of coffee and drank it deliberately before he answered her.

"A whole lot Ah keer 'bout how you feels inside uh out. Dat snake aint goin' no damn wheah till Ah gits ready fuh 'im tuh go. So fur as beatin' is concerned, yuh aint took near all dat you gointer take ef yuh stay 'roun' me."

Delia pushed back her plate and got up from the table. "Ah hates you, Sykes," she said calmly. "Ah hates you tuh de same degree dat Ah useter love yuh. Ah done took an' took till mah belly is full up tuh mah neck. Dat's de reason Ah got mah letter fum de church an' moved mah membership tuh Woodbridge—so Ah don't haftuh take no sacrament wid yuh. Ah don't wantuh see yuh 'roun' me a-tall. Lay 'roun' wid dat 'oman all yuh wants tuh, but gwan 'way fum me an' mah house. Ah hates yuh lak uh suck-egg dog."

Sykes almost let the huge wad of corn bread and collard greens he was chewing fall out of his mouth in amazement. He had a hard time whipping himself up to the proper fury to try to answer Delia.

"Well, Ah'm glad you does hate me. Ah'm sho' tiahed uh you hangin' ontuh   80
me. Ah don't want yuh. Look at yuh stringey ole neck! Yo' rawbony laigs an' arms is enough tuh cut uh man tuh death. You looks jes' lak de devvul's doll-baby tuh me. You cain't hate me no worse dan Ah hates you. Ah been hatin' you fuh years."

"Yo' ole black hide don't look lak nothin' tuh me, but uh passel uh wrinkled up rubber, wid yo' big ole yeahs flappin' on each side lak uh paih uh buzzard wings. Don't think Ah'm gointuh be run 'way fum mah house neither. Ah'm goin' tuh de white folks bout you, mah young man, de very nex' time you lay yo' han's on me. Mah cup is done run ovah." Delia said this with no signs of fear and Sykes departed from the house, threatening her, but made not the slightest move to carry out any of them.

That night he did not return at all, and the next day being Sunday, Delia was glad that she did not have to quarrel before she hitched up her pony and drove the four miles to Woodbridge.

She stayed to the night service—"love feast"—which was very warm and full of spirit. In the emotional winds her domestic trials were borne far and wide so that she sang as she drove homeward,

Jurden water, black an' col'
Chills de body, not de soul
An' Ah wantah cross Jurden in uh calm time.

She came from the barn to the kitchen door and stopped.

"Whut's de mattah, ol' satan, you aint kickin' up yo' racket?" She addressed 85
the snake's box. Complete silence. She went on into the house with a new hope
in its birth struggles. Perhaps her threat to go to the white folks had frightened
Sykes! Perhaps he was sorry! Fifteen years of misery and suppression had
brought Delia to the place where she would hope *anything* that looked towards
a way over or through her wall of inhibitions.

She felt in the match safe behind the stove at once for a match. There was
only one there.

"Dat niggah wouldn't fetch nothin' heah tuh save his rotten neck, but he
kin run thew whut Ah brings quick enough. Now he done toted off nigh on tuh
haff uh box uh matches. He done had dat 'oman heah in mah house, too."

Nobody but a woman could tell how she knew this even before she struck
the match. But she did and it put her into a new fury.

Presently she brought in the tubs to put the white things to soak. This time
she decided she need not bring the hamper out of the bedroom; she would go
in there and do the sorting. She picked up the pot-bellied lamp and went in. The
room was small and the hamper stood hard by the foot of the white iron bed.
She could sit and reach through the bedposts—resting as she worked.

"Ah wantah cross Jurden in uh calm time." She was singing again. The 90
mood of the "love feast" had returned. She threw back the lid of the basket almost gaily. Then, moved by both horror and terror, she sprung back
toward the door. *There lay the snake in the basket!* He moved sluggishly at first,
but even as she turned round and round, jumped up and down in an insanity
of fear, he began to stir vigorously. She saw him pouring his awful beauty from
the basket upon the bed, then she seized the lamp and ran as fast as she could
to the kitchen. The wind from the open door blew out the light and the darkness added to her terror. She sped to the darkness of the yard, slamming the
door after her before she thought to set down the lamp. She did not feel safe
even on the ground, so she climbed up in the hay barn.

There for an hour or more she lay sprawled upon the hay a gibbering wreck.

Finally she grew quiet, and after that, coherent thought. With this, stalked
through her a cold, bloody rage. Hours of this. A period of introspection, a space
of retrospection, then a mixture of both. Out of this an awful calm.

"Well, Ah done de bes' Ah could. If things aint right, Gawd knows taint
mah fault."

She went to sleep—a twitchy sleep—and woke up to a faint gray sky. There
was a loud hollow sound below. She peered out. Sykes was at the wood-pile,
demolishing a wire-covered box.

He hurried to the kitchen door, but hung outside there some minutes 95
before he entered, and stood some minutes more inside before he closed it
after him.

The gray in the sky was spreading. Delia descended without fear now, and
crouched beneath the low bedroom window. The drawn shade shut out the
dawn, shut in the night. But the thin walls held back no sound.

"Dat ol' scratch is woke up now!" She mused at the tremendous whirr inside, which every woodsman knows, is one of the sound illusions. The rattler is a ventriloquist. His whirr sounds to the right, to the left, straight ahead, behind, close under foot—everywhere but where it is. Woe to him who guesses wrong unless he is prepared to hold up his end of the argument! Sometimes he strikes without rattling at all.

Inside, Sykes heard nothing until he knocked a pot lid off the stove while trying to reach the match safe in the dark. He had emptied his pockets at Bertha's.

The snake seemed to wake up under the stove and Sykes made a quick leap into the bedroom. In spite of the gin he had had, his head was clearing now.

"Mah Gawd!" he chattered, "ef Ah could on'y strack uh light!"   100

The rattling ceased for a moment as he stood paralyzed. He waited. It seemed that the snake waited also.

"Oh fuh de light! Ah thought he'd be too sick"—Sykes was muttering to himself when the whirr began again, closer, right underfoot this time. Long before this, Sykes' ability to think had been flattened down to primitive instinct and he leaped—onto the bed.

Outside Delia heard a cry that might have come from a maddened chimpanzee, a stricken gorilla. All the terror, all the horror, all the rage that man possibly could express, without a recognizable human sound.

A tremendous stir inside there, another series of animal screams, the intermittent whirr of the reptile. The shade torn violently down from the window, letting in the red dawn, a huge brown hand seizing the window stick, great dull blows upon the wooden floor punctuating the gibberish of sound long after the rattle of the snake had abruptly subsided. All this Delia could see and hear from her place beneath the window, and it made her ill. She crept over to the four-o'clocks and stretched herself on the cool earth to recover.

She lay there. "Delia, Delia!" She could hear Sykes calling in a most   105 despairing tone as one who expected no answer. The sun crept on up, and he called. Delia could not move—her legs were gone flabby. She never moved, he called, and the sun kept rising.

"Mah Gawd!" she heard him moan. "Mah Gawd fum Heben!" She heard him stumbling about and got up from her flower-bed. The sun was growing warm. As she approached the door she heard him call out hopefully, "Delia, is dat you Ah heah?"

She saw him on his hands and knees as soon as she reached the door. He crept an inch or two toward her—all that he was able, and she saw his horribly swollen neck and his one open eye shining with hope. A surge of pity too strong to support bore her away from that eye that must, could not, fail to see the tubs. He would see the lamp. Orlando with its doctors was too far. She could scarcely reach the Chinaberry tree, where she waited in the growing heat while inside she knew the cold river was creeping up and up to extinguish that eye which must know by now that she knew.

Ha Jin   b. 1956

Saboteur   [2000]

Mr. Chiu and his bride were having lunch in the square before Muji Train
Station. On the table between them were two bottles of soda spewing out brown
foam and two paper boxes of rice and sautéed cucumber and pork. "Let's eat,"
he said to her, and broke the connected ends of the chopsticks. He picked up a
slice of streaky pork and put it into his mouth. As he was chewing, a few crin-
kles appeared on his thin jaw.

To his right, at another table, two railroad policemen were drinking tea and laughing; it seemed that the stout, middle-aged
man was telling a joke to his young comrade, who was tall and of athletic build. Now
and again they would steal a glance at
Mr. Chiu's table.

The air smelled of rotten melon. A few
flies kept buzzing above the couple's lunch.
Hundreds of people were rushing around to
get on the platform or to catch buses to
downtown. Food and fruit vendors were
crying for customers in lazy voices. About a

APPROACHING THE AUTHOR

Ha Jin intended to return to China after
completing his dissertation at Brandeis
University. After watching televised
coverage of the Tiananmen Square
massacre, however, he decided to stay in
the United States with his wife and young
son and be a teacher. When he couldn't
find a teaching job, he turned to writing
instead.

For more about him, see page 1068.

dozen young women, representing the local hotels, held up placards which
displayed the daily prices and words as large as a palm, like FREE MEALS, AIR-
CONDITIONING, and ON THE RIVER. In the center of the square stood a concrete
statue of Chairman Mao, at whose feet peasants were napping, their backs on
the warm granite and their faces toward the sunny sky. A flock of pigeons
perched on the Chairman's raised hand and forearm.

The rice and cucumber tasted good, and Mr. Chiu was eating unhurriedly.
His sallow face showed exhaustion. He was glad that the honeymoon was
finally over and that he and his bride were heading back for Harbin. During the
two weeks' vacation, he had been worried about his liver, because three months
ago he had suffered from acute hepatitis; he was afraid he might have a relapse.
But he had had no severe symptoms, despite his liver being still big and tender.
On the whole he was pleased with his health, which could endure even the
strain of a honeymoon; indeed, he was on the course of recovery. He looked at
his bride, who took off her wire glasses, kneading the root of her nose with her
fingertips. Beads of sweat coated her pale cheeks.

"Are you all right, sweetheart?" he asked.   5

"I have a headache. I didn't sleep well last night."

"Take an aspirin, will you?"

"It's not that serious. Tomorrow is Sunday and I can sleep in. Don't worry."

As they were talking, the stout policeman at the next table stood up and threw a bowl of tea in their direction. Both Mr. Chiu's and his bride's sandals were wet instantly.

"Hooligan!" she said in a low voice.   10

Mr. Chiu got to his feet and said out loud, "Comrade Policeman, why did you do this?" He stretched out his right foot to show the wet sandal.

"Do what?" the stout man asked huskily, glaring at Mr. Chiu while the young fellow was whistling.

"See, you dumped tea on our feet."

"You're lying. You wet your shoes yourself."

"Comrade Policeman, your duty is to keep order, but you purposely tortured 15
us common citizens. Why violate the law you are supposed to enforce?" As Mr. Chiu was speaking, dozens of people began gathering around.

With a wave of his hand, the man said to the young fellow, "Let's get hold of him!"

They grabbed Mr. Chiu and clamped handcuffs around his wrists. He cried, "You can't do this to me. This is utterly unreasonable."

"Shut up!" The man pulled out his pistol. "You can use your tongue at our headquarters."

The young fellow added, "You're a saboteur, you know that? You're disrupting public order."

The bride was too petrified to say anything coherent. She was a recent col- 20
lege graduate, had majored in fine arts, and had never seen the police make an arrest. All she could say was, "Oh, please, please!"

The policemen were pulling Mr. Chiu, but he refused to go with them, holding the corner of the table and shouting, "We have a train to catch. We already bought the tickets."

The stout man punched him in the chest. "Shut up. Let your ticket expire." With the pistol butt he chopped Mr. Chiu's hands, which at once released the table. Together the two men were dragging him away to the police station.

Realizing he had to go with them, Mr. Chiu turned his head and shouted to his bride, "Don't wait for me here. Take the train. If I'm not back by tomorrow morning, send someone over to get me out."

She nodded, covering her sobbing mouth with her palm.

After removing his belt, they locked Mr. Chiu into a cell in the back of the 25
Railroad Police Station. The single window in the room was blocked by six steel bars; it faced a spacious yard, in which stood a few pines. Beyond the trees, two swings hung from an iron frame, swaying gently in the breeze. Somewhere in the building a cleaver was chopping rhythmically. There must be a kitchen upstairs, Mr. Chiu thought.

He was too exhausted to worry about what they would do to him, so he lay down on the narrow bed and shut his eyes. He wasn't afraid. The Cultural Revolution was over already, and recently the Party had been propagating the idea that all citizens were equal before the law. The police ought to be a law-abiding model for common people. As long as he remained coolheaded and reasoned with them, they probably wouldn't harm him.

Late in the afternoon he was taken to the Interrogation Bureau on the second floor. On his way there, in the stairwell, he ran into the middle-aged policeman who had manhandled him. The man grinned, rolling his bulgy eyes and pointing his fingers at him as if firing a pistol. Egg of a tortoise! Mr. Chiu cursed mentally.

The moment he sat down in the office, he burped, his palm shielding his mouth. In front of him, across a long desk, sat the chief of the bureau and a donkey-faced man. On the glass desktop was a folder containing information on his case. He felt it bizarre that in just a matter of hours they had accumulated a small pile of writing about him. On second thought he began to wonder whether they had kept a file on him all the time. How could this have happened? He lived and worked in Harbin, more than three hundred miles away, and this was his first time in Muji City.

The chief of the bureau was a thin, bald man who looked serene and intelligent. His slim hands handled the written pages in the folder in the manner of a lecturing scholar. To Mr. Chiu's left sat a young scribe, with a clipboard on his knee and a black fountain pen in his hand.

"Your name?" the chief asked, apparently reading out the question from a form. 30

"Chiu Maguang."

"Age?"

"Thirty-four."

"Profession?"

"Lecturer." 35

"Work unit?"

"Harbin University."

"Political status?"

"Communist Party member."

The chief put down the paper and began to speak. "Your crime is sabotage, 40 although it hasn't induced serious consequences yet. Because you are a Party member, you should be punished more. You have failed to be a model for the masses and you—"

"Excuse me, sir," Mr. Chiu cut him off.

"What?"

"I didn't do anything. Your men are the saboteurs of our social order. They threw hot tea on my feet and on my wife's feet. Logically speaking, you should criticize them, if not punish them."

"That statement is groundless. You have no witness. Why should I believe you?" the chief said matter-of-factly.

"This is my evidence." He raised his right hand. "Your man hit my fingers 45 with a pistol."

"That doesn't prove how your feet got wet. Besides, you could have hurt your fingers yourself."

"But I am telling the truth!" Anger flared up in Mr. Chiu. "Your police station owes me an apology. My train ticket has expired, my new leather sandals are ruined, and I am late for a conference in the provincial capital. You must compensate me for the damage and losses. Don't mistake me for a common citizen who would tremble when you sneeze. I'm a scholar, a philosopher, and an expert in dialectical materialism. If necessary, we will argue about this in *The Northeastern Daily*, or we will go to the highest People's Court in Beijing. Tell me, what's your name?" He got carried away with his harangue, which was by no means trivial and had worked to his advantage on numerous occasions.

"Stop bluffing us," the donkey-faced man broke in. "We have seen a lot of your kind. We can easily prove you are guilty. Here are some of the statements given by eyewitnesses." He pushed a few sheets of paper toward Mr. Chiu.

Mr. Chiu was dazed to see the different handwritings, which all stated that he had shouted in the square to attract attention and refused to obey the police. One of the witnesses had identified herself as a purchasing agent from a shipyard in Shanghai. Something stirred in Mr. Chiu's stomach, a pain rising to his rib. He gave out a faint moan.

"Now you have to admit you are guilty," the chief said. "Although it's a 50 serious crime, we won't punish you severely, provided you write out a self-criticism and promise that you won't disrupt the public order again. In other words, your release will depend on your attitude toward this crime."

"You're daydreaming," Mr. Chiu cried. "I won't write a word, because I'm innocent. I demand that you provide me with a letter of apology so I can explain to my university why I'm late."

Both the interrogators smiled contemptuously. "Well, we've never done that," said the chief, taking a puff at his cigarette.

"Then make this a precedent."

"That's unnecessary. We are pretty certain that you will comply with our wishes." The chief blew a column of smoke toward Mr. Chiu's face.

At the tilt of the chief's head, two guards stepped forward and grabbed the 55 criminal by the arms. Mr. Chiu meanwhile went on saying, "I shall report you to the Provincial Administration. You'll have to pay for this! You are worse than the Japanese military police."

They dragged him out of the room.

After dinner, which consisted of a bowl of millet porridge, a corn bun, and a piece of pickled turnip, Mr. Chiu began to have a fever, shaking with a chill and sweating profusely. He knew that the fire of anger had gotten into his liver and that he was probably having a relapse. No medicine was available, because his briefcase had been left with his bride. At home it would have been time for him to sit in front of their color TV, drinking jasmine tea and watching the evening news. It was so lonesome in here. The orange bulb above the single bed was the only source of light, which enabled the guards to keep him under surveillance at night. A moment ago he had asked them for a newspaper or a magazine to read, but they turned him down.

Through the small opening on the door noises came in. It seemed that the police on duty were playing cards or chess in a nearby office; shouts and laughter could be heard now and then. Meanwhile, an accordion kept coughing from a remote corner in the building. Looking at the ballpoint and the letter paper left for him by the guards when they took him back from the Interrogation Bureau, Mr. Chiu remembered the old saying, "When a scholar runs into soldiers, the more he argues, the muddier his point becomes." How ridiculous this whole thing was. He ruffled his thick hair with his fingers.

He felt miserable, massaging his stomach continually. To tell the truth, he was more upset than frightened, because he would have to catch up with his work once he was back home—a paper that was due at the printers next week, and two dozen books he ought to read for the courses he was going to teach in the fall.

A human shadow flitted across the opening. Mr. Chiu rushed to the door 60 and shouted through the hole, "Comrade Guard, Comrade Guard!"

"What do you want?" a voice rasped.

"I want you to inform your leaders that I'm very sick. I have heart disease and hepatitis. I may die here if you keep me like this without medication."

"No leader is on duty on the weekend. You have to wait till Monday."

"What? You mean I'll stay in here tomorrow?"

"Yes." 65

"Your station will be held responsible if anything happens to me."

"We know that. Take it easy, you won't die."

It seemed illogical that Mr. Chiu slept quite well that night, though the light above his head had been on all the time and the straw mattress was hard and infested with fleas. He was afraid of ticks, mosquitoes, cockroaches—any kind of insect but fleas and bedbugs. Once, in the countryside, where his school's faculty and staff had helped the peasants harvest crops for a week, his colleagues had joked about his flesh, which they said must have tasted nonhuman to fleas. Except for him, they were all afflicted with hundreds of bites.

More amazing now, he didn't miss his bride a lot. He even enjoyed sleeping alone, perhaps because the honeymoon had tired him out and he needed more rest.

The backyard was quiet on Sunday morning. Pale sunlight streamed 70 through the pine branches. A few sparrows were jumping on the ground, catching caterpillars and ladybugs. Holding the steel bars, Mr. Chiu inhaled the morning air, which smelled meaty. There must have been an eatery or a cooked-meat stand nearby. He reminded himself that he should take this detention with ease. A sentence that Chairman Mao had written to a hospitalized friend rose in his mind: "Since you are already in here, you may as well stay and make the best of it."

His desire for peace of mind originated in his fear that his hepatitis might get worse. He tried to remain unperturbed. However, he was sure that his liver was swelling up, since the fever still persisted. For a whole day he lay in bed, thinking about his paper on the nature of contradictions. Time and again he was overwhelmed by anger, cursing aloud, "A bunch of thugs!" He swore that once he was out, he would write an article about this experience. He had better find out some of the policemen's names.

It turned out to be a restful day for the most part; he was certain that his university would send somebody to his rescue. All he should do now was remain calm and wait patiently. Sooner or later the police would have to release him, although they had no idea that he might refuse to leave unless they wrote him an apology. Damn those hoodlums, they had ordered more than they could eat!

When he woke up on Monday morning, it was already light. Somewhere a man was moaning; the sound came from the backyard. After a long yawn, and kicking off the tattered blanket, Mr. Chiu climbed out of bed and went to the window. In the middle of the yard, a young man was fastened to a pine, his wrists handcuffed around the trunk from behind. He was wriggling and swearing loudly, but there was no sight of anyone else in the yard. He looked familiar to Mr. Chiu.

Mr. Chiu squinted his eyes to see who it was. To his astonishment, he recognized the man, who was Fenjin, a recent graduate from the Law Department at Harbin University. Two years ago Mr. Chiu had taught a course in Marxist materialism, in which Fenjin had enrolled. Now, how on earth had this young devil landed here?

Then it dawned on him that Fenjin must have been sent over by his bride. 75 What a stupid woman! A bookworm, who only knew how to read foreign novels! He had expected that she would contact the school's Security Section, which would for sure send a cadre here. Fenjin held no official position; he merely worked in a private law firm that had just two lawyers; in fact, they had little business except for some detective work for men and women who suspected their spouses of having extramarital affairs. Mr. Chiu was overcome with a wave of nausea.

Should he call out to let his student know he was nearby? He decided not to, because he didn't know what had happened. Fenjin must have quarreled with the police to incur such a punishment. Yet this could never have occurred if Fenjin hadn't come to his rescue. So no matter what, Mr. Chiu had to do something. But what could he do?

It was going to be a scorcher. He could see purple steam shimmering and rising from the ground among the pines. Poor devil, he thought, as he raised a bowl of corn glue to his mouth, sipped, and took a bite of a piece of salted celery.

When a guard came to collect the bowl and the chopsticks, Mr. Chiu asked him what had happened to the man in the backyard. "He called our boss 'bandit,'" the guard said. "He claimed he was a lawyer or something. An arrogant son of a rabbit."

Now it was obvious to Mr. Chiu that he had to do something to help his rescuer. Before he could figure out a way, a scream broke out in the backyard. He rushed to the window and saw a tall policeman standing before Fenjin, an iron bucket on the ground. It was the same young fellow who had arrested

Mr. Chiu in the square two days before. The man pinched Fenjin's nose, then raised his hand, which stayed in the air for a few seconds, then slapped the lawyer across the face. As Fenjin was groaning, the man lifted up the bucket and poured water on his head.

"This will keep you from getting sunstroke, boy. I'll give you some more 80
every hour," the man said loudly.

Fenjin kept his eyes shut, yet his wry face showed that he was struggling to hold back from cursing the policeman, or, more likely, that he was sobbing in silence. He sneezed, then raised his face and shouted, "Let me go take a piss."

"Oh yeah?" the man bawled. "Pee in your pants."

Still Mr. Chiu didn't make any noise, gripping the steel bars with both hands, his fingers white. The policeman turned and glanced at the cell's window; his pistol, partly holstered, glittered in the sun. With a snort he spat his cigarette butt to the ground and stamped it into the dust.

Then the door opened and the guards motioned Mr. Chiu to come out. Again they took him upstairs to the Interrogation Bureau.

The same men were in the office, though this time the scribe was sitting 85
there empty-handed. At the sight of Mr. Chiu the chief said, "Ah, here you are. Please be seated."

After Mr. Chiu sat down, the chief waved a white silk fan and said to him, "You may have seen your lawyer. He's a young man without manners, so our director had him taught a crash course in the backyard."

"It's illegal to do that. Aren't you afraid to appear in a newspaper?"

"No, we are not, not even on TV. What else can you do? We are not afraid of any story you make up. We call it fiction. What we do care about is that you cooperate with us. That is to say, you must admit your crime."

"What if I refuse to cooperate?"

"Then your lawyer will continue his education in the sunshine." 90

A swoon swayed Mr. Chiu, and he held the arms of the chair to steady himself. A numb pain stung him in the upper stomach and nauseated him, and his head was throbbing. He was sure that the hepatitis was finally attacking him. Anger was flaming up in his chest; his throat was tight and clogged.

The chief resumed, "As a matter of fact, you don't even have to write out your self-criticism. We have your crime described clearly here. All we need is your signature."

Holding back his rage, Mr. Chiu said, "Let me look at that."

With a smirk the donkey-faced man handed him a sheet, which carried these words:

I hereby admit that on July 13 I disrupted public order at Muji Train Station, and that I refused to listen to reason when the railroad police issued their warning. Thus I myself am responsible for my arrest. After two days' detention, I have realized the reactionary nature of my crime. From now on, I shall continue to educate myself with all my effort and shall never commit this kind of crime again.

A voice started screaming in Mr. Chiu's ears, "Lie, lie!" But he shook his   95
head and forced the voice away. He asked the chief, "If I sign this, will you
release both my lawyer and me?"

"Of course, we'll do that." The chief was drumming his fingers on the blue
folder—their file on him.

Mr. Chiu signed his name and put his thumbprint under his signature.

"Now you are free to go," the chief said with a smile, and handed him a
piece of paper to wipe his thumb with.

Mr. Chiu was so sick that he couldn't stand up from the chair at first try.
Then he doubled his effort and rose to his feet. He staggered out of the building to meet his lawyer in the backyard, having forgotten to ask for his belt
back. In his chest he felt as though there were a bomb. If he were able to, he
would have razed the entire police station and eliminated all their families.
Though he knew he could do nothing like that, he made up his mind to do
something.

"I'm sorry about this torture, Fenjin," Mr. Chiu said when they met.   100

"It doesn't matter. They are savages." The lawyer brushed a patch of dirt off
his jacket with trembling fingers. Water was still dribbling from the bottoms of
his trouser legs.

"Let's go now," the teacher said.

The moment they came out of the police station, Mr. Chiu caught sight of
a tea stand. He grabbed Fenjin's arm and walked over to the old woman at the
table. "Two bowls of black tea," he said and handed her a one-yuan note.

After the first bowl, they each had another one. Then they set out for the
train station. But before they walked fifty yards, Mr. Chiu insisted on eating a
bowl of tree-ear soup at a food stand. Fenjin agreed. He told his teacher, "You
mustn't treat me like a guest."

"No, I want to eat something myself."   105

As if dying of hunger, Mr. Chiu dragged his lawyer from restaurant to restaurant near the police station, but at each place he ordered no more than two
bowls of food. Fenjin wondered why his teacher wouldn't stay at one place and
eat his fill.

Mr. Chiu bought noodles, wonton, eight-grain porridge, and chicken soup,
respectively, at four restaurants. While eating, he kept saying through his teeth,
"If only I could kill all the bastards!" At the last place he merely took a few sips
of the soup without tasting the chicken cubes and mushrooms.

Fenjin was baffled by his teacher, who looked ferocious and muttered to
himself mysteriously, and whose jaundiced face was covered with dark puckers.
For the first time Fenjin thought of Mr. Chiu as an ugly man.

Within a month over eight hundred people contracted acute hepatitis in
Muji. Six died of the disease, including two children. Nobody knew how the
epidemic had started.

James Joyce   1882–1941

Araby   [1914]

North Richmond Street, being blind, was a quiet street except at the hour when the Christian Brothers' School set the boys free. An uninhabited house of two storeys stood at the blind end, detached from its neighbors in a square ground. The other houses of the street, conscious of decent lives within them, gazed at one another with brown imperturbable faces.

The former tenant of our house, a priest, had died in the back drawing-room. Air, musty from having been long enclosed, hung in all the rooms, and the waste room behind the kitchen was littered with old useless papers. Among these I found a few paper-covered books, the pages of which were curled and damp: *The Abbot*, by Walter Scott, *The Devout Communicant*, and *The Memoirs of Vidocq*. I liked the last best because its leaves were yellow. The wild garden behind the house contained a central apple-tree and a few straggling bushes under one of which I found the late tenant's rusty bicycle-pump. He had been a very charitable priest; in his will he had left all his money to institutions and the furniture of his house to his sister.

> **APPROACHING THE AUTHOR**
>
> **James Joyce's** wife was famously apathetic toward her husband's writing. She would remark that she often told him to give up writing and take up singing.
>
> For more about him, see page 1069.

When the short days of winter came dusk fell before we had well eaten our dinners. When we met in the street the houses had grown somber. The space of sky above us was the color of ever-changing violet and towards it the lamps of the street lifted their feeble lanterns. The cold air stung us and we played till our bodies glowed. Our shouts echoed in the silent street. The career of our play brought us through the dark muddy lanes behind the houses where we ran the gauntlet of the rough tribes from the cottages, to the back doors of the dark dripping gardens where odors arose from the ashpits, to the dark odorous stables where a coachman smoothed and combed the horse or shook music from the buckled harness. When we returned to the street light from the kitchen windows had filled the areas. If my uncle was seen turning the corner we hid in the shadow until we had seen him safely housed. Or if Mangan's sister came out on the doorstep to call her brother in to his tea we watched her from our shadow peer up and down the street. We waited to see whether she would remain or go in and, if she remained, we left our shadow and walked up to Mangan's steps resignedly. She was waiting for us, her figure defined by the light from the half-opened door. Her brother always teased her before he obeyed and I stood by the railings looking at her. Her dress swung as she moved her body and the soft rope of her hair tossed from side to side.

Every morning I lay on the floor in the front parlor watching her door. The blind was pulled down to within an inch of the sash so that I could not be seen. When she came out on the doorstep my heart leaped. I ran to the hall, seized my books, and followed her. I kept her brown figure always in my eye and, when we came near the point at which our ways diverged, I quickened my pace and passed her. This happened morning after morning. I had never spoken to her, except for a few casual words, and yet her name was like a summons to all my foolish blood.

Her image accompanied me even in places the most hostile to romance. On Saturday evenings when my aunt went marketing I had to go to carry some of the parcels. We walked through the flaring streets, jostled by drunken men and bargaining women, amid the curses of laborers, the shrill litanies of shop-boys who stood on guard by the barrel of pigs' cheeks, the nasal chanting of street-singers, who sang a *come-all-you* about O'Donovan Rossa, or a ballad about the troubles in our native land. These noises converged in a single sensation of life for me: I imagined that I bore my chalice safely through a throng of foes. Her name sprang to my lips at moments in strange prayers and praises which I myself did not understand. My eyes were often full of tears (I could not tell why) and at times a flood from my heart seemed to pour itself out into my bosom. I thought little of the future. I did not know whether I would ever speak to her or not or, if I spoke to her, how I could tell her of my confused adoration. But my body was like a harp and her words and gestures were like fingers running upon the wires.

One evening I went into the back drawing-room in which the priest had died. It was a dark rainy evening and there was no sound in the house. Through one of the broken panes I heard the rain impinge upon the earth, the fine incessant needles of water playing in the sodden beds. Some distant lamp or lighted window gleamed below me. I was thankful that I could see so little. All my senses seemed to desire to veil themselves and, feeling that I was about to slip from them, I pressed the palms of my hands together until they trembled, murmuring: "*O love! O love!*" many times.

At last she spoke to me. When she addressed the first words to me I was so confused that I did not know what to answer. She asked me was I going to *Araby*. I forgot whether I answered yes or no. It would be a splendid bazaar, she said she would love to go.

"And why can't you?" I asked.

While she spoke she turned a silver bracelet round and round her wrist. She could not go, she said, because there would be a retreat that week in her convent. Her brother and two other boys were fighting for their caps and I was alone at the railings. She held one of the spikes, bowing her head towards me. The light from the lamp opposite our door caught the white curve of her neck, lit up her hair that rested there and, falling, lit up the hand upon the railing. It fell over one side of her dress and caught the white border of a petticoat, just visible as she stood at ease.

"It's well for you," she said.

"If I go," I said, "I will bring you something."

What innumerable follies laid waste my waking and sleeping thoughts after that evening! I wished to annihilate the tedious intervening days. I chafed against the work of school. At night in my bedroom and by day in the classroom her image came between me and the page I strove to read. The syllables of the word *Araby* were called to me through the silence in which my soul luxuriated and cast an Eastern enchantment over me. I asked for leave to go to the bazaar on Saturday night. My aunt was surprised and hoped it was not some Freemason affair. I answered few questions in class. I watched my master's face pass from amiability to sternness; he hoped I was not beginning to idle. I could not call my wandering thoughts together. I had hardly any patience with the serious work of life which, now that it stood between me and my desire, seemed to me child's play, ugly monotonous child's play.

On Saturday morning I reminded my uncle that I wished to go to the bazaar in the evening. He was fussing at the hallstand, looking for the hat-brush, and answered me curtly:

"Yes, boy, I know."

As he was in the hall I could not go into the front parlor and lie at the   15
window. I left the house in bad humor and walked slowly towards the school. The air was pitilessly raw and already my heart misgave me.

When I came home to dinner my uncle had not yet been home. Still it was early. I sat staring at the clock for some time and, when its ticking began to irritate me, I left the room. I mounted the staircase and gained the upper part of the house. The high cold empty gloomy rooms liberated me and I went from room to room singing. From the front window I saw my companions playing below in the street. Their cries reached me weakened and indistinct and, leaning my forehead against the cool glass, I looked over at the dark house where she lived. I may have stood there for an hour, seeing nothing but the brown-clad figure cast by my imagination, touched discreetly by the lamplight at the curved neck, at the hand upon the railings and at the border below the dress.

When I came downstairs again I found Mrs. Mercer sitting at the fire. She was an old garrulous woman, a pawnbroker's widow, who collected used stamps for some pious purpose. I had to endure the gossip of the tea-table. The meal was prolonged beyond an hour and still my uncle did not come. Mrs. Mercer stood up to go: she was sorry she couldn't wait any longer, but it was after eight o'clock and she did not like to be out late, as the night air was bad for her. When she had gone I began to walk up and down the room, clenching my fists. My aunt said:

"I'm afraid you may put off your bazaar for this night of Our Lord."

At nine o'clock I heard my uncle's latchkey in the halldoor. I heard him talking to himself and heard the hallstand rocking when it had received the weight of his overcoat. I could interpret these signs. When he was midway through his dinner I asked him to give me the money to go to the bazaar. He had forgotten.

"The people are in bed and after their first sleep now," he said.   20

I did not smile. My aunt said to him energetically:

"Can't you give him the money and let him go? You've kept him late enough as it is."

My uncle said he was very sorry he had forgotten. He said he believed in the old saying: "All work and no play makes Jack a dull boy." He asked me where I was going and, when I had told him a second time he asked me did I know *The Arab's Farewell to His Steed*. When I left the kitchen he was about to recite the opening lines of the piece to my aunt.

I held a florin° tightly in my hand as I strode down Buckingham Street towards the station. The sight of the streets thronged with buyers and glaring with gas recalled to me the purpose of my journey. I took my seat in a third-class carriage of a deserted train. After an intolerable delay the train moved out of the station slowly. It crept onward among ruinous houses and over the twinkling river. At Westland Row Station a crowd of people pressed to the carriage doors; but the porters moved them back, saying that it was a special train for the bazaar. I remained alone in the bare carriage. In a few minutes the train drew up beside an improvised wooden platform. I passed out on to the road and saw by the lighted dial of a clock that it was ten minutes to ten. In front of me was a large building which displayed the magical name.

I could not find any sixpenny entrance and, fearing that the bazaar would   25
be closed, I passed in quickly through a turnstile, handing a shilling to a weary-looking man. I found myself in a big hall girdled at half its height by a gallery. Nearly all the stalls were closed and the greater part of the hall was in darkness. I recognized a silence like that which pervades a church after a service. I walked into the center of the bazaar timidly. A few people were gathered about the stalls which were still open. Before a curtain, over which the words *Café Chantant* were written in colored lamps, two men were counting money on a salver.° I listened to the fall of the coins.

Remembering with difficulty why I had come I went over to one of the stalls and examined porcelain vases and flowered tea-sets. At the door of the stall a young lady was talking and laughing with two young gentlemen. I remarked their English accents and listened vaguely to their conversation.

"O, I never said such a thing!"

"O, but you did!"

"O, but I didn't!"

"Didn't she say that?"

"Yes. I heard her."   30

"O, there's a . . . fib!"

Observing me the young lady came over and asked me did I wish to buy anything. The tone of her voice was not encouraging; she seemed to have spoken to me out of a sense of duty. I looked humbly at the great jars that stood like eastern guards at either side of the dark entrance to the stall and murmured:

"No, thank you."

The young lady changed the position of one of the vases and went back to   35
the two young men. They began to talk of the same subject. Once or twice the young lady glanced at me over her shoulder.

---

florin: British two shilling coin, worth one tenth of a pound.
salver: A tray used for serving food or drinks.

I lingered before her stall, though I knew my stay was useless, to make my interest in her wares seem the more real. Then I turned away slowly and walked down the middle of the bazaar. I allowed the two pennies to fall against the sixpence in my pocket. I heard a voice call from one end of the gallery that the light was out. The upper part of the hall was now completely dark.

Gazing up into the darkness I saw myself as a creature driven and derided by vanity; and my eyes burned with anguish and anger.

Etgar Keret b. 1967

Crazy Glue   [2006]

She said, "Don't touch that."

"What is it?" I asked.

"It's glue," she said. "Special glue. The best kind."

"What did you buy it for?"

"Because I need it," she said. "A lot of things around here need gluing."   5

"Nothing around here needs gluing," I said. "I wish I understood why you buy all this stuff."

"For the same reason I married you," she murmured. "To help pass the time."

I didn't want to fight, so I kept quiet, and so did she.

"Is it any good, this glue?" I asked. She showed me the picture on the box, with this guy hanging upside down from the ceiling.

"No glue can really make a person stick like that," I said. "They just took the   10 picture upside down. They must have put a light fixture on the floor." I took the box from her and peered at it. "And there, look at the window. They didn't even bother to hang the blinds the other way. They're upside down, if he's really stand-ing on the ceiling. Look," I said again, pointing to the window. She didn't look.

"It's eight already," I said. "I've got to run." I picked up my briefcase and kissed her on the cheek "I'll be back pretty late. I'm working—"

"Overtime," she said. "Yes, I know."

I called Abby from the office.

"I can't make it today," I said. "I've got to get home early."

"Why?" Abby asked. "Something happen?"   15

"No . . . I mean, maybe. I think she suspects something."

There was a long silence. I could hear Abby's breathing on the other end.

"I don't see why you stay with her," she whispered. "You never do anything together. You don't even fight. I'll never understand it." There was a pause, and then she repeated, "I wish I understood." She was crying.

"I'm sorry. I'm sorry, Abby. Listen, someone just came in," I lied. "I've got to hang up. I'll come over tomorrow. I promise. We'll talk about everything then."

I got home early. I said "Hi" as I walked in, but there was no reply. I went 20 through all the rooms in the house. She wasn't in any of them. On the kitchen table I found the tube of glue, completely empty. I tried to move one of the chairs, to sit down. It didn't budge. I tried again. Not an inch. She'd glued it to the floor. The fridge wouldn't open. She'd glued it shut. I didn't understand what was happening, what would make her do such a thing. I didn't know where she was. I went into the living room to call her mother's. I couldn't lift the receiver; she'd glued that too. I kicked the table and almost broke my toe. It didn't even budge.

And then I heard her laughing. It was coming from somewhere above me. I looked up, and there she was, standing barefoot on the living room ceiling.

I stared openmouthed. When I found my voice I could only ask, "What the hell . . . are you out of your mind?"

She didn't answer, just smiled. Her smile seemed so natural, with her hanging upside down like that, as if her lips were just stretching on their own by the sheer force of gravity.

"Don't worry, I'll get you down," I said, hurrying to the shelf and grabbing the largest books. I made a tower of encyclopedia volumes and clambered on top of the pile.

"This may hurt a little," I said, trying to keep my balance. She went on 25 smiling. I pulled as hard as I could, but nothing happened. Carefully, I climbed down.

"Don't worry," I said. "I'll get the neighbors or something. I'll go next door and call for help."

"Fine," she laughed. "I'm not going anywhere."

I laughed too. She was so pretty, and so incongruous, hanging upside down from the ceiling that way. With her long hair dangling downwards, and her breasts molded like two perfect teardrops under her white T-shirt. So pretty. I climbed back up onto the pile of books and kissed her. I felt her tongue on mine. The books tumbled out from under my feet, but I stayed floating in mid-air, hanging just from her lips.

Katherine Min   b. 1959

Courting a Monk   [1996]

When I first saw my husband he was sitting cross-legged under a tree on the quad, his hair as short as peach fuzz, large blue eyes staring upward, the smile on his face so wide and undirected as to seem moronic. I went flying by him every minute or two, guarding man-to-man, or chasing down a pass, and out of the corner of my eye I would see him watching and smiling. What I noticed about him most was his tremendous capacity for stillness. His hands were like still-life objects resting on his knees; his posture was impeccable. He looked so rooted there, like some cheerful, exotic mushroom, that I began to feel awkward in my exertion. Sweat funneled into the valley of my back, cooling and sticking when I stopped, hands on knees, to regain my breath. I tried to stop my gape-mouthed panting, refashioned my ponytail, and wiped my hands on the soft front of my sweatpants.

He was still there two plays later when my team was down by one. Sully stole a pass and flipped to Graham. Graham threw me a long bomb that sailed wide and I leapt for it, sailing with the Frisbee for a moment in a parallel line — floating, flying, reaching — before coming down whap! against the ground. I groaned. I'd taken a tree root in the solar plexus. The wind was knocked out of me. I lay there, the taste of dry leaves in my mouth.

"Sorry, Gina. Lousy pass," Graham said, coming over. "You O.K.?"

"Fine," I gasped, fingering my ribs. "Just let me sit out for a while."

I sat down in the leaves, breathing carefully as I watched them play. The day   5
was growing dark and the Frisbee was hard to see. Everyone was tired and played in a sloppy rhythm of errant throws and dropped passes.

Beside me on the grass crept the guy from under the tree. I had forgotten about him. He crouched shyly next to me, leaves cracking under his feet, and, when I looked up, he whispered, "You were magnificent," and walked away smiling.

I spotted him the next day in the vegetarian dining hall. I was passing through with my plate of veal cordon bleu when I saw him sitting by himself next to the window. He took a pair of wooden chopsticks out of the breast pocket of his shirt and poked halfheartedly at his tofu and wilted mung beans. I sat down across from him and demanded his life story.

It turned out he wanted to be a monk. Not the Chaucerian kind, bald-pated and stout, with a hooded robe, ribald humor, and penchant for wine. Something even more baffling — a Buddhist. He had just returned from a semester in Nepal, studying in a monastery in the Himalayas. His hair was coming back in in soft spikes across his head and he had a watchful manner — not cautious but receptive, waiting.

He was from King of Prussia, off the Philadelphia Main Line, and this made me mistrust the depth of his beliefs. I have discovered that a fascination for the East is often a prelude to a pass, a romantic overture set in motion by an "I think Oriental girls are so beautiful," and a viselike grip on the upper thigh. But Micah was different. He understood I was not impressed by his belief, and he did not aim to impress.

"My father was raised Buddhist," I told him. "But he's a scientist now."   10

"Oh," said Micah. "So, he's not spiritual."

APPROACHING THE AUTHOR

Katherine Min says she was an incorrigible liar as a child. "And the lies I told were literally unbelievable, like that I was really Swedish but had had some sort of operation to disguise myself. From such ignoble beginnings, one has no choice but to become a fiction writer — or a felon, I suppose."

For more about her, see page 1072.

"Spirit's insubstantial," I said. "He doesn't hold with intangibility."

"Well, you can't hold atoms in your hand," Micah pointed out.

"Ah," I said, smiling, "but you can count them."

I told Micah my father was a man of science, and this was true. He was a 15
man, also, of silence. Unlike Micah, whose reticence seemed calming, so undisturbed, like a pool of light on still water, my father's silence was like the lid on
a pot, sealing off some steaming, inner pressure.

Words were not my father's medium. "Language," my father liked to say,
"is an imprecise instrument." (For though he said little, when he hit upon a
phrase he liked, he said it many times.) He was fond of Greek letters and
numerals set together in intricate equations, symbolizing a certain physical law
or experimental hypothesis. He filled yellow legal pads in a strong, vertical
hand, writing these beauties down in black, indelible felt-tip pen. I think it was
a source of tremendous irritation to him that he could not communicate with
other people in so ordered a fashion, that he could not simply draw an equals
sign after something he'd said, have them solve for x or y.

That my father's English was not fluent was only part of it. He was not a
garrulous man, even in Korean, among visiting relatives, or alone with my
mother. And with me, his only child—who could speak neither of his preferred
languages, Korean or science—my father had conspicuously little to say. "Pick
up this mess," he would tell me, returning from work in the evening.
"Homework finished?" he would inquire, raising an eyebrow over his rice bowl
as I excused myself to go watch television.

He limited himself to the imperative mood, the realm of injunction and
command; the kinds of statement that required no answer, that left no opening
for discussion or rejoinder. These communications were my father's verbal
equivalent to his neat numerical equations. They were hermetically sealed.

When I went away to college, my father's parting words constituted one of
the longest speeches I'd heard him make. Surrounded by station wagons packed
with suitcases, crates of books, and study lamps, amid the excited chattering
and calling out of students, among the adults with their nervous, parental surveillance of the scene, my father leaned awkwardly forward with his hands in
his pockets, looking at me intently. He said, "Study hard. Go to bed early. Do
not goof off. And do not let the American boys take advantages."

This was the same campus my father had set foot on twenty years before, 20
when he was a young veteran of the Korean War, with fifty dollars in his pocket
and about that many words of English. Stories of his college years constituted
family legend and, growing up, I had heard them so often they were as vivid and
dreamlike as my own memories. My father in the dorm bathroom over
Christmas, vainly trying to hard-boil an egg in a sock by running it under hot
water; his triumph in the physics lab where his ability with the new language
did not impede him, and where his maturity and keen scientific mind garnered
him highest marks and the top physics prize in his senior year—these were
events I felt I'd witnessed, like some obscure, envious ghost.

In the shadow of my father's achievements then, on the same campus where he had first bowed his head to a microscope, lost in a chalk-dust mathematical dream, I pursued words. English words. I committed myself to expertise. I studied Shakespeare and Eliot, Hardy and Conrad, Joyce and Lawrence and Hemingway and Fitzgerald. It was important to get it right, every word, every nuance, to fill in my father's immigrant silences, the gaps he had left for me.

Other gaps he'd left. Staying up late and studying little, I did things my father would have been too shocked to merely disapprove. As for American boys, I heeded my father's advice and did not let them take advantage. Instead I took advantage of them, of their proximity, their good looks, and the amiable way they would fall into bed with you if you gave them the slightest encouragement. I liked the way they moved in proud possession of their bodies, the rough feel of their unshaven cheeks, their shoulders and smooth, hairless chests, the curve of their backs like burnished wood. I liked the way I could look up at them, or down, feeling their shuddering climax like a distant earthquake; I could make it happen, moving in undulant circles from above or below, watching them, holding them, making them happy. I collected boys like baubles, like objects not particularly valued, which you stash away in the back of some drawer. It was the pleasant interchangeability of their bodies I liked. They were all white boys.

Micah refused to have sex with me. It became a matter of intellectual disagreement between us. "Sex saps the will," he said.

"Not necessarily," I argued. "Just reroutes it."

"There are higher forms of union," he said.   25

"Not with your clothes off," I replied.

"Gina," he said, looking at me with kindness, a concern that made me flush with anger. "What need do you have that sex must fill?"

"Fuck you, Micah," I said. "Be a monk, not a psychologist."

He laughed. His laughter was always a surprise to me, like a small disturbance to the universe. I wanted to seduce him, this was true. I considered Micah the only real challenge among an easy field. But more than seduction, I wanted to rattle him, to get under that sense of peace, that inward contentment. No one my age, I reasoned, had the right to such self-possession.

We went for walks in the bird sanctuary, rustling along the paths slowly,   30
discussing Emily Dickinson or maple-syrup-making, but always I brought the subject around.

"What a waste of a life," I said once. "Such indulgence. All that monkly devotion and quest for inner peace. Big deal. It's selfish. Not only is it selfish, it's a cop-out. An escape from this world and its messes."

Micah listened, a narrow smile on his lips, shaking his head regretfully. "You're so wonderfully passionate, Gina, so alive and in the world. I can't make you see. Maybe it is a cop-out, as you say, but Buddhism makes no distinction between the world outside or the world within the monastery. And historically, monks have been in the middle of political protest and persecution. Look at Tibet."

"I was thinking about, ahem, something more basic," I said.

Micah laughed. "Of course," he said. "You don't seem to understand, Gina, Buddhism is all about the renunciation of desire."

I sniffed. "What's wrong with desire? Without desire, you might as well not   35
be alive."

The truth was that I was fascinated by this idea, the renunciation of desire. My life was fueled by longing, by vast and clamorous desires; a striving toward things I did not have and, perhaps, had no hope of having. I could vaguely imagine an end, some point past desiring, of satiety, but I could not fathom the laying down of desire, walking away in full appetite.

"The desire to renounce desire," I said now, "is still desire, isn't it?"

Micah sunk his hands into his pockets and smiled. "It's not," he said, walking ahead of me. "It's a conscious choice."

We came to a pond, sun-dappled in a clearing, bordered by white birch and maples with the bright leaves of mid-autumn. A fluttering of leaves blew from the trees, landing on the water as gently as if they'd been placed. The color of the pond was a deep canvas green; glints of light snapped like sparks above the surface. There was the lyric coo of a mourning dove, the chitter-chitter of late-season insects. Micah's capacity for appreciation was vast. Whether this had anything to do with Buddhism, I didn't know, but watching him stand on the edge of the pond, his head thrown back, his eyes eagerly taking in the light, I felt his peace and also his sense of wonder. He stood motionless for a long time.

I pulled at ferns, weaved their narrow leaves in irregular samplers, braided   40
tendrils together, while Micah sat on a large rock and, taking his chopsticks from his breast pocket, began to tap them lightly against one another in a solemn rhythm.

"Every morning in the monastery," he said, "we woke to the prayer drum. Four o'clock and the sky would be dark and you'd hear the hollow wooden sound—plock, plock, plock—summoning you to meditation." He smiled dreamily. The chopsticks made a somewhat less effectual sound, a sort of ta ta ta. I imagined sunrise across a Himalayan valley—the wisps of pink-tinged cloud on a cold spring morning, the austerity of a monk's chamber.

Micah had his eyes closed, face to the sun. He continued to tap the chopsticks together slowly. He looked singular and new, sitting on that rock, like an advance scout for some new tribe, with his crest of hair and calm, and the attentiveness of his body to his surroundings.

I think it was then I fell in love with him, or, it was in that moment that my longing for him became so great that it was no longer a matter of simple gratification. I needed his response. I understood what desire was then, the disturbance of a perfect moment in anticipation of another.

"Wake-up call," I said. I peeled off my turtleneck and sweater in one clever motion and tossed them at Micah's feet. Micah opened his eyes. I pulled my pants off and my underwear and stood naked. "Plock, plock, who's there?"

Micah did not turn away. He looked at me, his chopsticks poised in the   45
air. He raised one toward me and held it, as though he were an artist with a

paintbrush raised for a proportion, or a conductor ready to lead an orchestra. He held the chopstick suspended in the space between us, and it was as though I couldn't move for as long as he held it. His eyes were fathomless blue. My nipples constricted with the cold. Around us leaves fell in shimmering lights to the water, making a soft rustling sound like the rub of stiff fabric. He brought his hand down and I was released. I turned and leapt into the water.

A few nights later I bought a bottle of cheap wine and goaded Micah into drinking it with me. We started out on the steps of the library after it had closed for the night, taking sloppy swigs from a brown paper bag. The lights of the Holyoke range blinked in the distance, across the velvet black of the freshman quad. From there we wandered the campus, sprawling on the tennis courts, bracing a stiff wind from the terrace of the science center, sedately rolling down Memorial Hill like a pair of tumbleweeds.

"J'a know what a koan is?" he asked me, when we were perched at the top of the bleachers behind home plate. We unsteadily contemplated the steep drop off the back side.

"You mean like ice cream?" I said.

"No, a ko-an. In Buddhism."

"Nope."   50

"It's a question that has no answer, sort of like a riddle. You know, like 'What is the sound of one hand clapping?' Or 'What was your face before you were born?'"

"'What was my face before it was born?' That makes no sense."

"Exactly. You're supposed to contemplate the koan until you achieve a greater awareness."

"Of what?"

"Of life, of meaning."   55

"Oh, O.K.," I said. "I've got it." I was facing backwards, the bag with the bottle in both my hands. "How 'bout, 'What's the sound of one cheek farting?'"

He laughed for a long time, then retched off the side of the bleachers. I got him home and put him to bed; his forehead was feverish, his eyes glassy with sickness.

"Sorry," I said. "I'm a bad influence." I kissed him. His lips were hot and slack.

"Don't mind," he murmured, half-asleep.

The next night we slept in the same bed together for the first time. He kept 60 his underwear on and his hands pressed firmly to his sides, like Gandhi° among his young virgins. I was determined to make it difficult for him. I kept brushing

---

Gandhi: Mahatma Gandhi (1869–1948), leader of the independence movement in India, is reputed to have slept next to naked virgins as a way of testing his vow of *brahmacharya*, or total chastity in thought and deed.

my naked body against him, draping a leg across his waist, stroking his narrow chest with my fingertips. He wiggled and pushed away, feigning sleep. When I woke in the morning, he was gone and the *Ode to Joy* was blasting from my stereo.

Graham said he missed me. We'd slept together a few times before I met Micah, enjoying the warm, healthful feeling we got from running or playing Ultimate, taking a quick sauna, and falling into bed. He was good-looking, dark and broad, with sinewy arms and a tight chest. He made love to a woman like he was lifting Nautilus, all grim purpose and timing. It was hard to believe that had ever been appealing. I told him I was seeing someone else.

"Not the guy with the crew cut?" he said. "The one who looks like a baby seal?"

I shrugged.

Graham looked at me skeptically. "He doesn't seem like your type," he said.

"No," I agreed. "But at least he's not yours." 65

Meanwhile I stepped up my attack. I asked endless questions about Buddhist teaching. Micah talked about *dukkha*; the four noble truths; the five aggregates of attachment; the noble eightfold path to enlightenment. I listened dutifully, willing to acknowledge that it all sounded nice, that the goal of perfect awareness and peace seemed worth attaining. While he talked, I stretched my feet out until my toes touched his thigh; I slid my hand along his back; or leaned way over so he could see down my loose, barely-buttoned blouse.

"Too bad you aren't Tantric,"° I said. I'd been doing research.

Micah scoffed. "Hollywood Buddhism," he said. "Heavy breathing and theatrics."

"They believe in physical desire," I said. "They have sex."

"Buddha believes in physical desire," Micah said. "It's impermanent, that's 70 all. Something to get beyond."

"To get beyond it," I said petulantly, "you have to do it."

Micah sighed. "Gina," he said, "you are beautiful, but I can't. There are a lot of guys who will."

"A lot of them do."

He smiled a bit sadly. "Well, then . . ."

I leaned down to undo his shoelaces. I tied them together in double knots. 75 "But I want you," I said.

My parents lived thirty miles from campus and my mother frequently asked me to come home for dinner. I went only once that year, and that was with Micah. My parents were not the kind of people who enjoyed the company of

---

° **Tantric:** A variant in several Indian religions that reveres the body as a temple, instead of rejecting it, and includes sexual rituals as one of its ways to seek ultimate reality.

strangers. They were insular people who did not like to socialize much or go out—or anyway, my father was that way, and my mother accommodated herself to his preferences.

My mother had set the table in the dining room with blue linen. There were crystal wine glasses and silver utensils in floral patterns. She had made some dry baked chicken with overcooked peas and carrots—the meal she reserved for when Americans came to dinner. When it came to Korean cooking, my mother was a master. She made fabulous marinated short ribs and sautèed transparent bean noodles with vegetables and beef, pork dumplings and batter-fried shrimp, and cucumber and turnip kimchis which she made herself and fermented in brown earthenware jars. But American cuisine eluded her; it bored her. I think she thought it was meant to be tasteless.

"Just make Korean," I had urged her on the phone. "He'll like that."

My mother was skeptical. "Too spicy," she said. "I know what Americans like."

"Not the chicken dish," I pleaded. "He's a vegetarian."   80

"We'll see," said my mother, conceding nothing.

Micah stared down at his plate. My mother smiled serenely. Micah nodded. He ate a forkful of vegetables, took a bite of bread. His Adam's apple seemed to be doing a lot of work. My father, too, was busy chewing, his Adam's apple moving up and down his throat like the ratchets of a tire jack. No one had said a thing since my father had uncorked the Chardonnay and read to us the description from his well-creased paperback edition of *The New York Times Guide to Wine*.

The sound of silverware scraping on ceramic plates seemed amplified. I was aware of my own prolonged chewing. My father cleared his throat. My mother looked at him expectantly. He coughed.

"Micah studied Buddhism in Nepal," I offered into the silence.

"Oh!" my mother exclaimed. She giggled.   85

My father kept eating. He swallowed exaggeratedly and looked up. "That so?" he said, sounding almost interested.

Micah nodded. "I was only there four months," he said. "Gina tells me you were brought up Buddhist."

My father grunted. "Well, of course," he said, "in Korea in those days, our families were all Buddhist. I do not consider myself a Buddhist now."

Micah and I exchanged a look.

"It's become quite fashionable, I understand," my father went on. "With   90 you American college kids. Buddhism has become fad."

I saw Micah wince.

"I think it is wonderful, Hi Joon," my mother interceded, "for Americans to learn about Asian religion and philosophy. I was a philosophy major in college, Micah. I studied Whitehead, American pragmatism."

My father leaned back in his chair and watched, frowning, while my mother and Micah talked. It was like he was trying to analyze Micah, not as a psychiatrist analyzes—my father held a dim view of psychology—but as a chemist would, breaking him down to his basic elements, the simple chemical formula that would define his makeup.

Micah was talking about the aggregates of matter, sensation, perception, mental formations, and consciousness that comprise being in Buddhist teaching. "It's a different sense of self than in Christian religions," he explained, looking at my mother.

"Nonsense," my father interrupted. "There is no self in Buddhist doctrine. . . ." 95

My mother and I watched helplessly as they launched into discussion. I was surprised that my father seemed to know so much about it, and by how much he was carrying forth. I was surprised also by Micah's deference. He seemed to have lost all his sureness, the walls of his conviction. He kept nodding and conceding to my father certain points that he had rigorously defended to me before. "I guess I don't know as much about it," he said more than once, and "Yes, I see what you mean" several times, with a sickening air of humility.

I turned from my father's glinting, pitiless intelligence, to Micah's respectfulness, his timid manner, and felt a rising irritation I could not place, anger at my father's belligerence, at Micah's backing down, at my own strange motives for having brought them together. Had I really expected them to get along? And yet, my father was concentrating on Micah with such an intensity—almost as though he were a rival—in a way in which he never focused on me.

When the dialogue lapsed, and after we had consumed as much of the food as we deemed polite, my mother took the dishes away and brought in a bowl of rice with kimchi for my father. Micah's eyes lit up. "May I have some of that, too, Mrs. Kim?"

My mother looked doubtful. "Too spicy," she said.

"Oh, I love spicy food," Micah assured her. My mother went to get him a 100 bowl.

"You can use chopsticks?" my mother said, as Micah began eating with them.

"Mom, it's no big deal," I said.

My father looked up from his bowl. Together, my parents watched while Micah ate a large piece of cabbage kimchi.

"Hah!" my father said, suddenly smiling. "Gina doesn't like kimchi," he said. He looked at me. "Gina," he said. "This boy more Korean than you."

"Doesn't take much," I said. 105

My father ignored me. "Gina always want to be American," he told Micah. "Since she was little girl, she want blue eyes, yellow hair." He stabbed a chopstick toward Micah's face. "Like yours."

"If I had hair," said Micah, grinning, rubbing a hand across his head.

My father stared into his bowl. "She doesn't want to be Korean girl. She thinks she can be 100 percent American, but she cannot. She has Korean blood—100 percent. Doesn't matter where you grow up—blood is most important. What is in the blood." He gave Micah a severe look. "You think you can become Buddhist. Same way. But it is not in your blood. You cannot know real Buddha's teaching. You should study Bible."

"God, Dad!" I said. "You sound like a Nazi!"

"Gina!" my mother warned.   110

"You're embarrassing me," I said. "Being rude to my guest. Discussing me as if I wasn't here. You can say what you want, Dad, I'm American whether you like it or not. Blood's got nothing to do with it. It's what's up here." I tapped my finger to my temple.

"It's not Nazi," my father said. "Is fact! What you have here," he pointed to his forehead, "is all from blood, from genetics. You got from me!"

"Heaven help me," I said.

"Gina!" my mother implored.

"Mr. Kim—" Micah began.   115

"You just like American girl in one thing," my father shouted. "You have no respect for father. In Korea, daughters do not talk back to their parents, is big shame!"

"In Korea, girls are supposed to be submissive doormats for fathers to wipe their feet on!" I shouted back.

"What do you know about Korea? You went there only once when you were six years old."

"It's in my blood," I said. I stood up. "I'm not going to stay here for this. Come on, Micah."

Micah looked at me uncertainly, then turned to my father.   120

My father was eating again, slowly levering rice to his mouth with his chopsticks. He paused. "She was always this way," he said, seeming to address the table. "So angry. Even as a little girl."

"Mr. Kim," Micah said, "Um, thank you very much. We're . . . I think we're heading out now."

My father chewed ruminatively. "I should never have left Korea," he said quietly, with utter conviction.

"Gina," my mother said. "Sit down. Hi Joon, please!"

"Micah," I said. "You coming?"   125

We left my father alone at the dining-room table.

"I should have sent you to live with Auntie Soo!" he called after me.

My mother followed us out to the driveway with a Tupperware container of chicken Micah hadn't eaten.

On the way home we stopped for ice cream. Koans, I told Micah. "What is the sound of Swiss chocolate almond melting?" I asked him. "What was the vanilla before it was born?"

Inside the ice-cream parlor the light was too strong, a ticking fluorescence   130
bleaching everything bone-white. Micah leaned down to survey the cardboard barrels of ice cream in their plastic cases. He looked shrunken, subdued. He ordered a scoop of mint chocolate chip and one of black cherry on a sugar cone and ate it with the long, regretful licks of a child who'd spent the last nickel of his allowance. There was a ruefulness to his movements, a sense of apology. He had lost his monklike stillness and seemed suddenly adrift.

The cold of the ice cream gave me a headache, all the blood vessels in my temples seemed strung out and tight. I shivered and the cold was like fury, spreading through me with the chill.

Micah rubbed my back.

"You're hard on your father," he said. "He's not a bad guy."

"Forget it," I said. "Let's go."

We walked from the dorm parking lot in silence. There were lights going on 135
across the quad and music spilling from the windows out into the cool air. What few stars there were seemed too distant to wage a constant light.

Back in my room, I put on the Rolling Stones at full blast. Mick Jagger's voice was taunting and cruel. I turned out the lights and lit a red candle.

"O.K., this is going to stop," I said. I felt myself trembling. I pushed Micah back on the bed. I was furious. He had ruined it for me, the lightness, the skimming quality of my life. It had seemed easy, with the boys, the glib words and feelings, the simple heat and surface pleasures. It was like the sensation of flying, leaping for the Frisbee and sailing through the air. For a moment you lose a feeling for gravity, for the consciousness of your own skin or species. For a moment you are free.

I started to dance, fast, swinging and swaying in front of the bed. I closed my eyes and twirled wildly, bouncing off the walls like a pinball, stumbling on my own stockings. I danced so hard the stereo skipped, Jagger forced to stutter in throaty monosyllables, gulping repetitions. I whirled and circled, threw my head from side to side until I could feel the baffled blood, brought my hair up off my neck and held it with both hands.

Micah watched me dance. His body made an inverted-S upon my bed, his head propped by the pillar of his own arm. The expression on his face was the same as he'd had talking with my father, that look of deference, of fawn-eyed yielding. But I could see there was something hidden.

With white-knuckled fingers, I undid the buttons of my sweater and ripped 140
my shirt lifting it off my head. I danced out of my skirt and underthings, kicking them into the corner, danced until the song was over, until I was soaked with sweat and burning—and then I jumped him.

It was like the taste of food after a day's starvation—unexpectedly strong and substantial. Micah responded to my fury, met it with his own mysterious passion; it was like a brawl, a fight, with something at stake that neither of us wanted to lose. Afterward we sat up in bed and listened to *Ode to Joy* while Micah, who had a surplus supply of chopsticks lying around the room, did his Leonard Bernstein impersonation. Later, we went out for a late-night snack to All-Star Dairy and Micah admitted to me that he was in love.

———

My father refused to attend the wedding. He liked Micah, but he did not want me to marry a Caucasian. It became a joke I would tell people. Korean custom, I said, to give the bride away four months before the ceremony.

Micah became a high-school biology teacher. I am an associate dean of students at the local college. We have two children. When Micah tells the story of our courtship, he tells it with great self-deprecation and humor. He makes it sound as though he were crazy to ever consider becoming a monk. "Think of it," he tells our kids. "Your dad."

Lately I've taken to reading books about Buddhism. Siddhartha Gotama° was thirty-five years old when he sat under the Bodhi-tree on the bank of the river Neranjara and gained Enlightenment. Sometimes, when I see my husband looking at me across the breakfast table, or walking toward me from the other side of a room, I catch a look of distress on his face, a blinking confusion, as though he cannot remember who I am. I have happened on him a few times, on a Sunday when he has disappeared from the house, sitting on a bench with the newspaper in his lap staring across the town common, so immersed in his thoughts that he is not roused by my calling of his name.

I remember the first time I saw him, that tremendous stillness he carried,   145 the contentment in his face. I remember how he looked on the rocks by that pond, like a pioneer in a new land, and I wonder if he regrets, as I do, the loss of his implausible faith. Does he miss the sound of the prayer drum, the call to an inner life without the configuration of desire? I think of my father, running a sock under heated water thousands of miles from home, as yet unaware of the daughter he will raise with the same hopeful, determined, and ultimately futile, effort. I remember the way I used to play around with koans, and I wonder, "What is the sound of a life not lived?"

Tillie Olsen   (1912–2007)

I Stand Here Ironing   [1961]

I stand here ironing, and what you asked me moves tormented back and forth with the iron.

"I wish you would manage the time to come in and talk with me about your daughter. I'm sure you can help me understand her. She's a youngster who needs help and whom I'm deeply interested in helping."

"Who needs help." . . . Even if I came, what good would it do? You think because I am her mother I have a key, or that in some way you could use me as a key? She has lived for nineteen years. There is all that life that has happened outside of me, beyond me.

APPROACHING THE AUTHOR

Tillie Olsen was determined to read all the fiction in the Omaha Public Library. She would pick up a book, read a few pages, and, if she did not like it, move on to the next.

For more about her, see page 1075.

Siddhartha Gotama: Born in India some 2,500 years ago, Siddhartha Gotama is the one to whom Theravada Buddhists generally are referring when they speak of "the Buddha."

And when is there time to remember, to sift, to weigh, to estimate, to total? I will start and there will be an interruption and I will have to gather it all together again. Or I will become engulfed with all I did or did not do, with what should have been and what cannot be helped.

She was a beautiful baby. The first and only one of our five that was beautiful   5
at birth. You do not guess how new and uneasy her tenancy in her now-loveliness. You did not know her all those years she was thought homely, or see her poring over her baby pictures, making me tell her over and over how beautiful she had been — and would be, I would tell her — and was now, to the seeing eye. But the seeing eyes were few or nonexistent. Including mine.

I nursed her. They feel that's important nowadays. I nursed all the children, but with her, with all the fierce rigidity of first motherhood, I did like the books then said. Though her cries battered me to trembling and my breasts ached with swollenness, I waited till the clock decreed.

Why do I put that first? I do not even know if it matters, or if it explains anything.

She was a beautiful baby. She blew shining bubbles of sound. She loved motion, loved light, loved color and music and textures. She would lie on the floor in her blue overalls patting the surface so hard in ecstasy her hands and feet would blur. She was a miracle to me, but when she was eight months old I had to leave her daytimes with the woman downstairs to whom she was no miracle at all, for I worked or looked for work and for Emily's father, who "could no longer endure" (he wrote in his good-bye note) "sharing want with us."

I was nineteen. It was the pre-relief, pre-WPA° world of the depression. I would start running as soon as I got off the streetcar, running up the stairs, the place smelling sour, and awake or asleep to startle awake, when she saw me she would break into a clogged weeping that could not be comforted, a weeping I can hear yet.

After a while I found a job hashing at night so I could be with her days, and   10
it was better. But it came to where I had to bring her to his family and leave her.

It took a long time to raise the money for her fare back. Then she got chicken pox and I had to wait longer. When she finally came, I hardly knew her, walking quick and nervous like her father, looking like her father, thin, and dressed in a shoddy red that yellowed her skin and glared at the pockmarks. All the baby loveliness gone.

She was two. Old enough for nursery school they said, and I did not know then what I know now — the fatigue of the long day, and the lacerations of group life in the kinds of nurseries that are only parking places for children.

Except that it would have made no difference if I had known. It was the only place there was. It was the only way we could be together, the only way I could hold a job.

WPA: The Works Progress Administration was a New Deal public works program providing jobs for the unemployed during the Great Depression in the late 1930s and early 1940s.

And even without knowing, I knew. I knew the teacher that was evil because all these years it has curdled into my memory, the little boy hunched in the corner, her rasp, "why aren't you outside, because Alvin hits you? that's no reason, go out, scaredy." I knew Emily hated it even if she did not clutch and implore "don't go Mommy" like the other children, mornings.

She always had a reason why we should stay home. Momma, you look sick. 15 Momma, I feel sick. Momma, the teachers aren't there today, they're sick. Momma, we can't go, there was a fire there last night. Momma, it's a holiday today, no school, they told me.

But never a direct protest, never rebellion. I think of our others in their three-, four-year-oldness—the explosions, the tempers, the denunciations, the demands—and I feel suddenly ill. I put the iron down. What in me demanded that goodness in her? And what was the cost to her of such goodness?

The old man living in the back once said in his gentle way: "You should smile at Emily more when you look at her." What *was* in my face when I looked at her? I loved her. There were all the acts of love.

It was only with the others I remembered what he said, and it was the face of joy, and not of care or tightness or worry I turned to them—too late for Emily. She does not smile easily, let alone almost always as her brothers and sisters do. Her face is closed and somber, but when she wants, how fluid. You must have seen it in her pantomimes, you spoke of her rare gift for comedy on the stage that rouses a laughter out of the audience so dear they applaud and applaud and do not want to let her go.

Where does it come from, that comedy? There was none of it in her when she came back to me that second time, after I had had to send her away again. She had a new daddy now to learn to love, and I think perhaps it was a better time.

Except when we left her alone nights, telling ourselves she was old enough. 20

"Can't you go some other time, Mommy, like tomorrow?" she would ask. "Will it be just a little while you'll be gone? Do you promise?"

The time we came back, the front door open, the clock on the floor in the hall. She rigid awake. "It wasn't just a little while. I didn't cry. Three times I called you, just three times, and then I ran downstairs to open the door so you could come faster. The clock talked loud. I threw it away, it scared me what it talked."

She said the clock talked loud again that night I went to the hospital to have Susan. She was delirious with the fever that comes before red measles, but she was fully conscious all the week I was gone and the week after we were home when she could not come near the new baby or me.

She did not get well. She stayed skeleton thin, not wanting to eat, and night after night she had nightmares. She would call for me, and I would rouse from exhaustion to sleepily call back: "You're all right, darling, go to sleep, it's just a dream," and if she still called, in a sterner voice, "now go to sleep, Emily, there's nothing to hurt you." Twice, only twice, when I had to get up for Susan anyhow, I went in to sit with her.

Now when it is too late (as if she would let me hold and comfort her like I 25 do the others) I get up and go to her at once at her moan or restless stirring.

"Are you awake, Emily? Can I get you something?" And the answer is always the same: "No, I'm all right, go back to sleep, Mother."

They persuaded me at the clinic to send her away to a convalescent home in the country where "she can have the kind of food and care you can't manage for her, and you'll be free to concentrate on the new baby." They still send children to that place. I see pictures on the society page of sleek young women planning affairs to raise money for it, or dancing at the affairs, or decorating Easter eggs or filling Christmas stockings for the children.

They never have a picture of the children so I do not know if the girls still wear those gigantic red bows and the ravaged looks on the every other Sunday when parents can come to visit "unless otherwise notified"—as we were notified the first six weeks.

Oh it is a handsome place, green lawns and tall trees and fluted flower beds. High up on the balconies of each cottage the children stand, the girls in their red bows and white dresses, the boys in white suits and giant red ties. The parents stand below shrieking up to be heard and the children shriek down to be heard, and between them the invisible wall "Not To Be Contaminated by Parental Germs or Physical Affection."

There was a tiny girl who always stood hand in hand with Emily. Her parents never came. One visit she was gone. "They moved her to Rose Cottage" Emily shouted in explanation. "They don't like you to love anybody here."

She wrote once a week, the labored writing of a seven-year-old. "I am fine. 30 How is the baby. If I write my leter nicly I will have a star. Love." There never was a star. We wrote every other day, letters she could never hold or keep but only hear read—once. "We simply do not have room for children to keep any personal possessions," they patiently explained when we pieced one Sunday's shrieking together to plead how much it would mean to Emily, who loved so to keep things, to be allowed to keep her letters and cards.

Each visit she looked frailer. "She isn't eating," they told us.

(They had runny eggs for breakfast or mush with lumps, Emily said later, I'd hold it in my mouth and not swallow. Nothing ever tasted good, just when they had chicken.)

It took us eight months to get her released home, and only the fact that she gained back so little of her seven lost pounds convinced the social worker.

I used to try to hold and love her after she came back, but her body would stay stiff, and after a while she'd push away. She ate little. Food sickened her, and I think much of life too. Oh she had physical lightness and brightness, twinkling by on skates, bouncing like a ball up and down up and down over the jump rope, skimming over the hill; but these were momentary.

She fretted about her appearance, thin and dark and foreign-looking at a 35 time when every little girl was supposed to look or thought she should look a chubby blonde replica of Shirley Temple.° The doorbell sometimes rang for her,

---

Shirley Temple: American actress, singer, and dancer (1928–2014), most famous as a child film star, "America's Little Darling."

but no one seemed to come and play in the house or be a best friend. Maybe because we moved so much.

There was a boy she loved painfully through two school semesters. Months later she told me how she had taken pennies from my purse to buy him candy. "Licorice was his favorite and I brought him some every day, but he still liked Jennifer better'n me. Why, Mommy?" The kind of question for which there is no answer.

School was a worry to her. She was not glib or quick in a world where glibness and quickness were easily confused with ability to learn. To her overworked and exasperated teachers she was an overconscientious "slow learner" who kept trying to catch up and was absent entirely too often.

I let her be absent, though sometimes the illness was imaginary. How different from my now-strictness about attendance with the others. I wasn't working. We had a new baby, I was home anyhow. Sometimes, after Susan grew old enough, I would keep her home from school, too, to have them all together.

Mostly Emily had asthma, and her breathing, harsh and labored, would fill the house with a curiously tranquil sound. I would bring the two old dresser mirrors and her boxes of collections to her bed. She would select beads and single earrings, bottle tops and shells, dried flowers and pebbles, old postcards and scraps, all sorts of oddments; then she and Susan would play Kingdom, setting up landscapes and furniture, peopling them with action.

Those were the only times of peaceful companionship between her and 40
Susan. I have edged away from it, that poisonous feeling between them, that terrible balancing of hurts and needs I had to do between the two, and did so badly, those earlier years.

Oh there are conflicts between the others too, each one human, needing, demanding, hurting, taking—but only between Emily and Susan, no, Emily toward Susan that corroding resentment. It seems so obvious on the surface, yet it is not obvious. Susan, the second child, Susan, golden- and curly-haired and chubby, quick and articulate and assured, everything in appearance and manner Emily was not; Susan, not able to resist Emily's precious things, losing or sometimes clumsily breaking them; Susan telling jokes and riddles to company for applause while Emily sat silent (to say to me later: that was *my* riddle, Mother, I told it to Susan); Susan, who for all the five years' difference in age was just a year behind Emily in developing physically.

I am glad for that slow physical development that widened the difference between her and her contemporaries, though she suffered over it. She was too vulnerable for that terrible world of youthful competition, of preening and parading, of constant measuring of yourself against every other, of envy, "If I had that copper hair," "If I had that skin. . . ." She tormented herself enough about not looking like the others, there was enough of the unsureness, the having to be conscious of words before you speak, the constant caring—what are they thinking of me? without having it all magnified by the merciless physical drives.

Ronnie is calling. He is wet and I change him. It is rare there is such a cry now. That time of motherhood is almost behind me when the ear is not one's own but must always be racked and listening for the child cry, the child call. We sit for a while and I hold him, looking out over the city spread in charcoal with its soft aisles of light. *"Shoogily,"* he breathes and curls closer. I carry him back to bed, asleep. *Shoogily.* A funny word, a family word, inherited from Emily, invented by her to say: *comfort.*

In this and other ways she leaves her seal, I say aloud. And startle at my saying it. What do I mean? What did I start to gather together, to try and make coherent? I was at the terrible, growing years. War years. I do not remember them well. I was working, there were four smaller ones now, there was not time for her. She had to help be a mother, and housekeeper, and shopper. She had to set her seal. Mornings of crisis and near hysteria trying to get lunches packed, hair combed, coats and shoes found, everyone to school or Child Care on time, the baby ready for transportation. And always the paper scribbled on by a smaller one, the book looked at by Susan then mislaid, the homework not done. Running out to that huge school where she was one, she was lost, she was a drop; suffering over the unpreparedness, stammering and unsure in her classes.

There was so little time left at night after the kids were bedded down. She 45 would struggle over books, always eating (it was in those years she developed her enormous appetite that is legendary in our family) and I would be ironing, or preparing food for the next day, or writing V-mail° to Bill, or tending the baby. Sometimes, to make me laugh, or out of her despair, she would imitate happenings or types at school.

I think I said once: "Why don't you do something like this in the school amateur show?" One morning she phoned me at work, hardly understandable through the weeping: "Mother, I did it. I won, I won; they gave me first prize; they clapped and clapped and wouldn't let me go."

Now suddenly she was Somebody, and as imprisoned in her difference as she had been in anonymity.

She began to be asked to perform at other high schools, even in colleges, then at city and statewide affairs. The first one we went to, I only recognized her that first moment when thin, shy, she almost drowned herself into the curtains. Then: Was this Emily? The control, the command, the convulsing and deadly clowning, the spell, then the roaring, stamping audience, unwilling to let this rare and precious laughter out of their lives.

Afterwards: You ought to do something about her with a gift like that—but without money or knowing how, what does one do? We have left it all to her, and the gift has as often eddied inside, clogged and clotted, as been used and growing.

She is coming. She runs up the stairs two at a time with her light graceful 50 step, and I know she is happy tonight. Whatever it was that occasioned your call did not happen today.

V-mail: Victory Mail, a process used during World War II for corresponding with soldiers stationed abroad.

"Aren't you ever going to finish the ironing, Mother? Whistler° painted his mother in a rocker. I'd have to paint mine standing over an ironing board." This is one of her communicative nights and she tells me everything and nothing as she fixes herself a plate of food out of the icebox.

She is so lovely. Why did you want me to come in at all? Why were you concerned? She will find her way.

She starts up the stairs to bed. "Don't get me up with the rest in the morning." "But I thought you were having midterms." "Oh, those," she comes back in, kisses me, and says quite lightly, "in a couple of years when we'll all be atom-dead they won't matter a bit."

She has said it before. She *believes* it. But because I have been dredging the past, and all that compounds a human being is so heavy and meaningful in me, I cannot endure it tonight.

I will never total it all. I will never come in to say: She was a child seldom   55 smiled at. Her father left me before she was a year old. I had to work her first six years when there was work, or I sent her home and to his relatives. There were years she had care she hated. She was dark and thin and foreign-looking in a world where the prestige went to blondeness and curly hair and dimples, she was slow where glibness was prized. She was a child of anxious, not proud, love. We were poor and could not afford for her the soil of easy growth. I was a young mother, I was a distracted mother. There were the other children pushing up, demanding. Her younger sister seemed all that she was not. There were years she did not want me to touch her. She kept too much in herself, her life was such she had to keep too much in herself. My wisdom came too late. She has much to her and probably nothing will come of it. She is a child of her age, of depression, of war, of fear.

Let her be. So all that is in her will not bloom—but in how many does it? There is still enough left to live by. Only help her to know—help make it so there is cause for her to know—that she is more than this dress on the ironing board, helpless before the iron.

ZZ Packer   b. 1973

Brownies   [2003]

By our second day at Camp Crescendo, the girls in my Brownie troop had decided to kick the asses of each and every girl in Brownie Troop 909. Troop 909 was doomed from the first day of camp; they were white girls, their complexions a blend of ice cream: strawberry, vanilla. They turtled out from their bus in

---

Whistler: James Abbott McNeill Whistler (1834–1903), American-born artist whose most famous painting, "Arrangement in Grey and Black No. 1" (1871) is commonly known as "Whistler's Mother."

pairs, their rolled-up sleeping bags chromatized with Disney characters: Sleeping Beauty, Snow White, Mickey Mouse; or the generic ones cheap parents bought: washed-out rainbows, unicorns, curly-eyelashed frogs. Some clutched Igloo coolers and still others held on to stuffed toys like pacifiers, looking all around them like tourists determined to be dazzled.

Our troop was wending its way past their bus, past the ranger station, past the colorful trail guide drawn like a treasure map, locked behind glass.

"Man, did you smell them?" Arnetta said, giving the girls a slow once-over, "They smell like Chihuahuas. *Wet* Chihuahuas." Their troop was still at the entrance, and though we had passed them by yards, Arnetta raised her nose in the air and grimaced.

Arnetta said this from the very rear of the line, far away from Mrs. Margolin, who always strung our troop behind her like a brood of obedient ducklings. Mrs. Margolin even looked like a mother duck — she had hair cropped close to a small ball of a head, almost no neck, and huge, miraculous breasts. She wore enormous belts that looked like the kind that weightlifters wear, except hers would be cheap metallic gold or rabbit fur or covered with gigantic fake sunflowers, and often these belts would become nature lessons in and of themselves. "See," Mrs. Margolin once said to us, pointing to her belt, "this one's made entirely from the feathers of baby pigeons."

The belt layered with feathers was uncanny enough, but I was more disturbed by the realization that I had never actually *seen* a baby pigeon. I searched weeks for one, in vain — scampering after pigeons whenever I was downtown with my father.

But nature lessons were not Mrs. Margolin's top priority. She saw the position of troop leader as an evangelical post. Back at the A.M.E.° church where our Brownie meetings were held, Mrs. Margolin was especially fond of imparting religious aphorisms by means of acrostics — "Satan" was the "Serpent Always Tempting and Noisome"; she'd refer to the "Bible" as "Basic Instructions Before Leaving Earth." Whenever she quizzed us on these, expecting to hear the acrostics parroted back to her, only Arnetta's correct replies soared over our vague mumblings. "Jesus?" Mrs. Margolin might ask expectantly, and Arnetta alone would dutifully answer, "Jehovah's Example, Saving Us Sinners."

Arnetta always made a point of listening to Mrs. Margolin's religious talk and giving her what she wanted to hear. Because of this, Arnetta could have blared through a megaphone that the white girls of Troop 909 were "wet Chihuahuas" without so much as a blink from Mrs. Margolin. Once, Arnetta killed the troop goldfish by feeding it a french fry covered in ketchup, and when Mrs. Margolin demanded that she explain what had happened, claimed the goldfish had been eyeing her meal for *hours,* then the fish — giving in to temptation — had leapt up and snatched a whole golden fry from her fingertips.

"*Serious* Chihuahua," Octavia added, and though neither Arnetta nor Octavia could *spell* "Chihuahua," had ever *seen* a Chihuahua, trisyllabic words had gained

5

a sort of exoticism within our fourth-grade set at Woodrow Wilson Elementary. Arnetta and Octavia would flip through the dictionary, determined to work the vulgar-sounding ones like "Djibouti" and "asinine" into conversation.

"*Caucasian* Chihuahuas," Arnetta said.

That did it. The girls in my troop turned elastic: Drema and Elise doubled 10 up on one another like inextricably entwined kites; Octavia slapped her belly; Janice jumped straight up in the air, then did it again, as if to slam-dunk her own head. They could not stop laughing. No one had laughed so hard since a boy named Martez had stuck a pencil in the electric socket and spent the whole day with a strange grin on his face.

"Girls, girls," said our parent helper, Mrs. Hedy. Mrs. Hedy was Octavia's mother, and she wagged her index finger perfunctorily, like a windshield wiper. "Stop it, now. Be good." She said this loud enough to be heard, but lazily, bereft of any feeling or indication that she meant to be obeyed, as though she could say these words again at the exact same pitch if a button somewhere on her were pressed.

But the rest of the girls didn't stop; they only laughed louder. It was the word "Caucasian" that got them all going. One day at school, about a month before the Brownie camping trip, Arnetta turned to a boy wearing impossibly high-ankled floodwater jeans and said, "What are you? *Caucasian?*" The word took off from there, and soon everything was Caucasian. If you ate too fast you ate like a Caucasian, if you ate too slow you ate like a Caucasian. The biggest feat anyone at Woodrow Wilson could do was to jump off the swing in midair, at the highest point in its arc, and if you fell (as I had, more than once) instead of landing on your feet, knees bent Olympic gymnast–style, Arnetta and Octavia were prepared to comment. They'd look at each other with the silence of passengers who'd narrowly escaped an accident, then nod their heads, whispering with solemn horror, "*Caucasian.*"

Even the only white kid in our school, Dennis, got in on the Caucasian act. That time when Martez stuck a pencil in the socket, Dennis had pointed and yelled, "That was *so* Caucasian!"

When you lived in the south suburbs of Atlanta, it was easy to forget about whites. Whites were like those baby pigeons: real and existing, but rarely seen or thought about. Everyone had been to Rich's to go clothes shopping, everyone had seen white girls and their mothers coo-cooing over dresses; everyone had gone to the downtown library and seen white businessmen swish by importantly, wrists flexed in front of them to check the time as though they would change from Clark Kent into Superman at any second. But those images were as fleeting as cards shuffled in a deck, whereas the ten white girls behind us — *invaders,* Arnetta would later call them — were instantly real and memorable, with their long, shampoo-commercial hair, straight as spaghetti from the box. This alone was reason for envy and hatred. The only black girl most of us had ever seen with hair that long was Octavia, whose hair hung past her butt like a Hawaiian hula dancer's. The sight of Octavia's mane prompted other girls to listen to her reverentially, as though whatever she had to say would somehow activate their own follicles. For example, when, on the first day of camp, Octavia made as if to speak, and everyone fell silent. "Nobody," Octavia said, "calls us niggers."

At the end of that first day, when half of our troop made their way back to 15 the cabin after tag-team restroom visits, Arnetta said she'd heard one of the Troop 909 girls call Daphne a nigger. The other half of the girls and I were helping Mrs. Margolin clean up the pots and pans from the campfire ravioli dinner. When we made our way to the restrooms to wash up and brush our teeth, we met up with Arnetta midway.

"Man, I completely heard the girl," Arnetta reported. "Right, Daphne?"

Daphne hardly ever spoke, but when she did, her voice was petite and tinkly, the voice one might expect from a shiny new earring. She'd written a poem once, for Langston Hughes Day, a poem brimming with all the teacher-winning ingredients — trees and oceans, sunsets and moons — but what cinched the poem for the grown-ups, snatching the win from Octavia's musical ode to Grandmaster Flash and the Furious Five, were Daphne's last lines:

> You are my father, the veteran
> When you cry in the dark
> It rains and rains and rains in my heart

She'd always worn clean, though faded, jumpers and dresses when Chic jeans were the fashion, but when she went up to the dais to receive her prize journal, pages trimmed in gold, she wore a new dress with a velveteen bodice and a taffeta skirt as wide as an umbrella. All the kids clapped, though none of them understood the poem. I'd read encyclopedias the way others read comics, and I didn't get it. But those last lines pricked me, they were so eerie, and as my father and I ate cereal, I'd whisper over my Froot Loops, like a mantra, *"You are my father, the veteran. You are my father, the veteran, the veteran, the veteran,"* until my father, who acted in plays as Caliban and Othello and was not a veteran, marched me up to my teacher one morning and said, "Can you tell me what's wrong with this kid?"

I thought Daphne and I might become friends, but I think she grew spooked by me whispering those lines to her, begging her to tell me what they meant, and I soon understood that two quiet people like us were better off quiet alone.

"Daphne? Didn't you hear them call you a nigger?" Arnetta asked, giving 20 Daphne a nudge.

The sun was setting behind the trees, and their leafy tops formed a canopy of black lace for the flame of the sun to pass through. Daphne shrugged her shoulders at first, then slowly nodded her head when Arnetta gave her a hard look.

Twenty minutes later, when my restroom group returned to the cabin, Arnetta was still talking about Troop 909. My restroom group had passed by some of the 909 girls. For the most part, they deferred to us, waving us into the restrooms, letting us go even though they'd gotten there first.

We'd seen them, but from afar, never within their orbit enough to see whether their faces were the way all white girls appeared on TV — ponytailed and full of energy, bubbling over with love and money. All I could see was that some of them rapidly fanned their faces with their hands, though the heat of the day had long passed. A few seemed to be lolling their heads in slow circles, half purposefully, as if exercising the muscles of their necks, half ecstactically, like Stevie Wonder.

"We can't let them get away with that," Arnetta said, dropping her voice to a laryngitic whisper. "We can't let them get away with calling us niggers. I say we teach them a lesson." She sat down cross-legged on a sleeping bag, an embittered Buddha, eyes glimmering acrylic-black. "We can't go telling Mrs. Margolin, either. Mrs. Margolin'll say something about doing unto others and the path of righteousness and all. Forget that shit." She let her eyes flutter irreverently till they half closed, as though ignoring an insult not worth returning. We could all hear Mrs. Margolin outside, gathering the last of the metal campware.

Nobody said anything for a while. Usually people were quiet after Arnetta spoke. Her tone had an upholstered confidence that was somehow both regal and vulgar at once. It demanded a few moments of silence in its wake, like the ringing of a church bell or the playing of taps. Sometimes Octavia would ditto or dissent to whatever Arnetta had said, and this was the signal that others could speak. But this time Octavia just swirled a long cord of hair into pretzel shapes.

"*Well?*" Arnetta said. She looked as if she had discerned the hidden severity of the situation and was waiting for the rest of us to catch up. Everyone looked from Arnetta to Daphne. It was, after all, Daphne who had supposedly been called the name, but Daphne sat on the bare cabin floor, flipping through the pages of the Girl Scout handbook, eyebrows arched in mock wonder, as if the handbook were a catalogue full of bright and startling foreign costumes. Janice broke the silence. She clapped her hands to broach her idea of a plan.

"They gone be sleeping," she whispered conspiratorially, "then we gone sneak into they cabin, then we'll put daddy longlegs in they sleeping bags. Then they'll wake up. Then we gone beat 'em up till they're as flat as frying pans!" She jammed her fist into the palm of her hand, then made a sizzling sound.

Janice's country accent was laughable, her looks homely, her jumpy acrobatics embarrassing to behold. Arnetta and Octavia volleyed amused, arrogant smiles whenever Janice opened her mouth, but Janice never caught the hint, spoke whenever she wanted, fluttered around Arnetta and Octavia futilely offering her opinions to their departing backs. Whenever Arnetta and Octavia shooed her away, Janice loitered until the two would finally sigh and ask, "What *is* it, Miss Caucausoid? What do you *want?*"

"Shut up, Janice," Octavia said, letting a fingered loop of hair fall to her waist as though just the sound of Janice's voice had ruined the fun of her hair twisting.

25

Janice obeyed, her mouth hung open in a loose grin, unflappable, unhurt.   30

"All right," Arnetta said, standing up. "We're going to have a secret meeting and talk about what we're going to do."

Everyone gravely nodded her head. The word "secret" had a built-in importance, the modifier form of the word carried more clout than the noun. A secret meant nothing; it was like gossip: just a bit of unpleasant knowledge about someone who happened to be someone other than yourself. A secret *meeting,* or a secret *club* was entirely different.

That was when Arnetta turned to me as though she knew that doing so was both a compliment and a charity.

"Snot, you're not going to be a bitch and tell Mrs. Margolin, are you?"

I had been called "Snot" ever since first grade, when I'd sneezed in class and   35
two long ropes of mucus had splattered a nearby girl.

"Hey," I said. "Maybe you didn't hear them right — I mean — "

"Are you gonna tell on us or not?" was all Arnetta wanted to know, and by the time the question was asked, the rest of our Brownie troop looked at me as though they'd already decided their course of action, me being the only impediment.

Camp Crescendo used to double as a high-school-band and field hockey camp until an arcing field hockey ball landed on the clasp of a girl's metal barrette, knifing a skull nerve and paralyzing the right side of her body. The camp closed down for a few years and the girl's teammates built a memorial, filling the spot on which the girl fell with hockey balls, on which they had painted — all in nail polish — get-well tidings, flowers, and hearts. The balls were still stacked there, like a shrine of ostrich eggs embedded in the ground.

On the second day of camp, Troop 909 was dancing around the mound of hockey balls, their limbs jangling awkwardly, their cries like the constant summer squeal of an amusement park. There was a stream that bordered the field hockey lawn, and the girls from my troop settled next to it, scarfing down the last of lunch: sandwiches made from salami and slices of tomato that had gotten waterlogged from the melting ice in the cooler. From the stream bank, Arnetta eyed the Troop 909 girls, scrutinizing their movements to glean inspiration for battle.

"Man," Arnetta said, "we could bumrush them right now if that damn lady   40
would *leave.*"

The 909 troop leader was a white woman with the severe pageboy hairdo of an ancient Egyptian. She lay on a picnic blanket, sphinxlike, eating a banana, sometimes holding it out in front of her like a microphone. Beside her sat a girl slowly flapping one hand like a bird with a broken wing. Occasionally, the leader would call out the names of girls who'd attempted leapfrogs and flips, or of girls who yelled too loudly or strayed far from the circle.

"I'm just glad Big Fat Mama's not following us here," Octavia said. "At least we don't have to worry about her." Mrs. Margolin, Octavia assured us, was having her Afternoon Devotional, shrouded in mosquito netting, in a clearing she'd found. Mrs. Hedy was cleaning mud from her espadrilles in the cabin.

"I handled them." Arnetta sucked on her teeth and proudly grinned. "I told her we was going to gather leaves."

"Gather leaves," Octavia said, nodding respectfully. "That's a good one. Especially since they're so mad-crazy about this camping thing." She looked from ground to sky, sky to ground. Her hair hung down her back in two braids like a squaw's. "I mean, I really don't know why it's even called *camping* — all we ever do with Nature is find some twigs and say something like, 'Wow, this fell from a tree.'" She then studied her sandwich. With two disdainful fingers, she picked out a slice of dripping tomato, the sections congealed with red slime. She pitched it into the stream embrowned with dead leaves and the murky effigies of other dead things, but in the opaque water, a group of small silver-brown fish appeared. They surrounded the tomato and nibbled.

"Look!" Janice cried. "Fishes! Fishes!" As she scrambled to the edge of the 45 stream to watch, a covey of insects threw up tantrums from the wheatgrass and nettle, a throng of tiny electric machines, all going at once. Octavia sneaked up behind Janice as if to push her in. Daphne and I exchanged terrified looks. It seemed as though only we knew that Octavia was close enough — and bold enough — to actually push Janice into the stream. Janice turned around quickly, but Octavia was already staring serenely into the still water as though she was gathering some sort of courage from it. "What's so funny?" Janice said, eyeing them all suspiciously.

Elise began humming the tune to "Karma Chameleon," all the girls joining in, their hums light and facile. Janice also began to hum, against everyone else, the high-octane opening chords of "Beat It."

"I love me some Michael Jackson," Janice said when she'd finished humming, smacking her lips as though Michael Jackson were a favorite meal. "I *will* marry Michael Jackson."

Before anyone had a chance to impress upon Janice the impossibility of this, Arnetta suddenly rose, made a sun visor of her hand, and watched Troop 909 leave the field hockey lawn.

"Dammit!" she said. "We've got to get them *alone*."

"They won't ever be alone," I said. All the rest of the girls looked at me, for 50 I usually kept quiet. If I spoke even a word, I could count on someone calling me Snot. Everyone seemed to think that we could beat up these girls; no one entertained the thought that they might fight *back*. "The only time they'll be unsupervised is in the bathroom."

"Oh shut up, Snot," Octavia said.

But Arnetta slowly nodded her head. "The bathroom," she said. "The bathroom," she said, again and again. "The bathroom! The bathroom!"

According to Octavia's watch, it took us five minutes to hike to the restrooms, which were midway between our cabin and Troop 909's. Inside, the mirrors above the sinks returned only the vaguest of reflections, as though someone had taken a scouring pad to their surfaces to obscure the shine. Pine needles, leaves, and dirty, flattened wads of chewing gum covered the floor like a mosaic. Webs of hair matted the drain in the middle of the floor. Above the sinks and below the mirrors, stacks of folded white paper towels lay on a long metal counter. Shaggy white balls of paper towels sat on the sinktops in a line like corsages on display. A thread of floss snaked from a wad of tissues dotted with the faint red-pink of blood. One of those white girls, I thought, had just lost a tooth.

Though the restroom looked almost the same as it had the night before, it somehow seemed stranger now. We hadn't noticed the wooden rafters coming together in great V's. We were, it seemed, inside a whale, viewing the ribs of the roof of its mouth.

"Wow. It's a mess," Elise said.   55

"You can say that again."

Arnetta leaned against the doorjamb of a restroom stall. "This is where they'll be again," she said. Just seeing the place, just having a plan seemed to satisfy her. "We'll go in and talk to them. You know, 'How you doing? How long'll you be here?' That sort of thing. Then Octavia and I are gonna tell them what happens when they call any one of us a nigger."

"I'm going to say something, too," Janice said.

Arnetta considered this. "Sure," she said. "Of course. Whatever you want."

Janice pointed her finger like a gun at Octavia and rehearsed the line she'd   60
thought up, "'We're gonna teach you a *lesson!*' That's what I'm going to say." She narrowed her eyes like a TV mobster. "'We're gonna teach you little girls a lesson!'"

With the back of her hand, Octavia brushed Janice's finger away. "You couldn't teach me to shit in a toilet."

"But," I said, "what if they say, 'We didn't say that? We didn't call anyone an N-I-G-G-E-R.'"

"Snot," Arnetta said, and then sighed. "Don't think. Just fight. If you even know how."

Everyone laughed except Daphne. Arnetta gently laid her hand on Daphne's shoulder. "Daphne. You don't have to fight. We're doing this for you."

Daphne walked to the counter, took a clean paper towel, and carefully   65
unfolded it like a map. With it, she began to pick up the trash all around. Everyone watched.

"C'mon," Arnetta said to everyone. "Let's beat it." We all ambled toward the doorway, where the sunshine made one large white rectangle of light. We were immediately blinded, and we shielded our eyes with our hands and our forearms.

"Daphne?" Arnetta asked. "Are you coming?"

We all looked back at the bending girl, the thin of her back hunched like the back of a custodian sweeping a stage, caught in limelight. Stray strands of her hair were lit near-transparent, thin fiber-optic threads. She did not nod yes to the question, nor did she shake her head no. She abided, bent. Then she began again, picking up leaves, wads of paper, the cotton fluff innards from a torn stuffed toy. She did it so methodically, so exquisitely, so humbly, she must have been trained. I thought of those dresses she wore, faded and old, yet so pressed and clean. I then saw the poverty in them; I then could imagine her mother, cleaning the houses of others, returning home, weary.

"I guess she's not coming."

We left her and headed back to our cabin, over pine needles and leaves, taking the path full of shade. 70

"What about our secret meeting?" Elise asked.

Arnetta enunciated her words in a way that defied contradiction: "We just had it."

It was nearing our bedtime, but the sun had not yet set.

"Hey, your mama's coming," Arnetta said to Octavia when she saw Mrs. Hedy walk toward the cabin, sniffling. When Octavia's mother wasn't giving bored, parochial orders, she sniffled continuously, mourning an imminent divorce from her husband. She might begin a sentence, "I don't know what Robert will do when Octavia and I are gone. Who'll buy him cigarettes?" and Octavia would hotly whisper, *"Mama,"* in a way that meant: Please don't talk about our problems in front of everyone. Please shut up.

But when Mrs. Hedy began talking about her husband, thinking about her 75 husband, seeing clouds shaped like the head of her husband, she couldn't be quiet, and no one could dislodge her from the comfort of her own woe. Only one thing could perk her up — Brownie songs. If the girls were quiet, and Mrs. Hedy was in her dopey, sorrowful mood, she would say, "Y'all know I like those songs, girls. Why don't you sing one?" Everyone would groan, except me and Daphne. I, for one, liked some of the songs.

"C'mon, everybody," Octavia said drearily. "She likes the Brownie song best."

We sang, loud enough to reach Mrs. Hedy:

"I've got something in my pocket;
It belongs across my face.
And I keep it very close at hand
in a most convenient place.
I'm sure you couldn't guess it
If you guessed a long, long while.
So I'll take it out and put it on —
it's a great big Brownie smile!"

The Brownie song was supposed to be sung cheerfully, as though we were elves in a workshop, singing as we merrily cobbled shoes, but everyone except me hated the song so much that they sang it like a maudlin record, played on the most sluggish of rpms.°

"That was good," Mrs. Hedy said, closing the cabin door behind her. "Wasn't that nice, Linda?"

---

rpms: Revolutions per minute. Here, phonograph playing sluggishly at 33⅓, 45, or 78 rpms.

"Praise God," Mrs. Margolin answered without raising her head from the 80
chore of counting out Popsicle sticks for the next day's craft session.

"Sing another one," Mrs. Hedy said. She said it with a sort of joyful aggression, like a drunk I'd once seen who'd refused to leave a Korean grocery.

"God, Mama, get over it," Octavia whispered in a voice meant only for
Arnetta, but Mrs. Hedy heard it and started to leave the cabin.

"Don't go," Arnetta said. She ran after Mrs. Hedy and held her by the arm.
"We haven't finished singing." She nudged us with a single look. "Let's sing the
'Friends Song.' For Mrs. Hedy."

Although I liked some of the songs, I hated this one:

> Make new friends
> But keep the o-old,
> One is silver
> And the other gold.

If most of the girls in the troop could be any type of metal, they'd be 85
bunched-up wads of tinfoil, maybe, or rusty iron nails you had to get tetanus
shots for.

"No, no, no," Mrs. Margolin said before anyone could start in on the
"Friends Song." "An uplifting song. Something to lift her up and take her mind
off all these earthly burdens."

Arnetta and Octavia rolled their eyes. Everyone knew what song
Mrs. Margolin was talking about, and no one, no one, wanted to sing it.

"Please, no," a voice called out. "Not 'The Doughnut Song.'"

"Please not 'The Doughnut Song,'" Octavia pleaded.

"I'll brush my teeth two times if I don't have to sing 'The Doughnut—'" 90

"Sing!" Mrs. Margolin demanded.

We sang:

> "Life without Jesus is like a do-ough-nut!
> Like a do-ooough-nut!
> Like a do-ooough-nut!
> Life without Jesus is like a do-ough-nut!
> There's a hole in the middle of my soul!"

There were other verses, involving other pastries, but we stopped after the
first one and cast glances toward Mrs. Margolin to see if we could gain a
reprieve. Mrs. Margolin's eyes fluttered blissfully. She was half asleep.

"Awww," Mrs. Hedy said, as though giant Mrs. Margolin were a cute baby,
"Mrs. Margolin's had a long day."

"Yes indeed," Mrs. Margolin answered. "If you don't mind, I might just go 95
to the lodge where the beds are. I haven't been the same since the operation."

I had not heard of this operation, or when it had occurred, since
Mrs. Margolin had never missed the once-a-week Brownie meetings, but I could
see from Daphne's face that she was concerned, and I could see that the other

girls had decided that Mrs. Margolin's operation must have happened long ago in some remote time unconnected to our own. Nevertheless, they put on sad faces. We had all been taught that adulthood was full of sorrow and pain, taxes and bills, dreaded work and dealings with whites, sickness and death. I tried to do what the others did. I tried to look silent.

"Go right ahead, Linda," Mrs. Hedy said. "I'll watch the girls." Mrs. Hedy seemed to forget about divorce for a moment; she looked at us with dewy eyes, as if we were mysterious, furry creatures. Meanwhile, Mrs. Margolin walked through the maze of sleeping bags until she found her own. She gathered a neat stack of clothes and pajamas slowly, as though doing so was almost painful. She took her toothbrush, her toothpaste, her pillow. "All right!" Mrs. Margolin said, addressing us all from the threshold of the cabin. "Be in bed by nine." She said it with a twinkle in her voice, letting us know she was allowing us to be naughty and stay up till nine-fifteen.

"C'mon everybody," Arnetta said after Mrs. Margolin left. "Time for us to wash up."

Everyone watched Mrs. Hedy closely, wondering whether she would insist on coming with us since it was night, making a fight with Troop 909 nearly impossible. Troop 909 would soon be in the bathroom, washing their faces, brushing their teeth—completely unsuspecting of our ambush.

"We won't be long," Arnetta said. "We're old enough to go to the restrooms 100 by ourselves."

Ms. Hedy pursed her lips at this dilemma. "Well, I guess you Brownies are almost Girl Scouts, right?"

"Right!"

"Just one more badge," Drema said.

"And about," Octavia droned, "a million more cookies to sell." Octavia looked at all of us, *Now's our chance,* her face seemed to say, but our chance to do *what,* I didn't exactly know.

Finally, Mrs. Hedy walked to the doorway where Octavia stood dutifully 105 waiting to say goodbye but looking bored doing it. Mrs. Hedy held Octavia's chin. "You'll be good?"

"Yes, Mama."

"And remember to pray for me and your father? If I'm asleep when you get back?"

"Yes, Mama."

When the other girls had finished getting their toothbrushes and wash-cloths and flashlights for the group restroom trip, I was drawing pictures of tiny birds with too many feathers. Daphne was sitting on her sleeping bag, reading.

"You're not going to come?" Octavia asked. 110

Daphne shook her head.

"I'm gonna stay, too," I said. "I'll go to the restroom when Daphne and Mrs. Hedy go."

Arnetta leaned down toward me and whispered so that Mrs. Hedy, who'd taken over Mrs. Margolin's task of counting Popsicle sticks, couldn't hear. "No, Snot. If we get in trouble, you're going to get in trouble with the rest of us."

We made our way through the darkness by flashlight. The tree branches that had shaded us just hours earlier, along the same path, now looked like arms sprouting menacing hands. The stars sprinkled the sky like spilled salt. They seemed fastened to the darkness, high up and holy, their places fixed and definite as we stirred beneath them.

Some, like me, were quiet because we were afraid of the dark; others were 115 talking like crazy for the same reason.

"Wow!" Drema said, looking up. "Why are all the stars out here? I never see stars back on Oneida Street."

"It's a camping trip, that's why," Octavia said. "You're supposed to see stars on camping trips."

Janice said, "This place smells like my mother's air freshener."

"These woods are *pine*," Elise said. "Your mother probably uses *pine* air freshener."

Janice mouthed an exaggerated "Oh," nodding her head as though she just 120 then understood one of the world's great secrets.

No one talked about fighting. Everyone was afraid enough just walking through the infinite deep of the woods. Even though I didn't fight to fight, was afraid of fighting, I felt I was part of the rest of the troop; like I was defending something. We trudged against the slight incline of the path, Arnetta leading the way.

"You know," I said, "their leader will be there. Or they won't even be there. It's dark already. Last night the sun was still in the sky. I'm sure they're already finished."

Arnetta acted as if she hadn't heard me. I followed her gaze with my flashlight, and that's when I saw the squares of light in the darkness. The bathroom was just ahead.

But the girls were there. We could hear them before we could see them.

"Octavia and I will go in first so they'll think there's just two of us, then 125 wait till I say, 'We're gonna teach you a lesson,'" Arnetta said. "Then, bust in. That'll surprise them."

"That's what I was supposed to say," Janice said.

Arnetta went inside, Octavia next to her. Janice followed, and the rest of us waited outside.

They were in there for what seemed like whole minutes, but something was wrong. Arnetta hadn't given the signal yet. I was with the girls outside when I heard one of the Troop 909 girls say, "NO. That did NOT happen!"

That was to be expected, that they'd deny the whole thing. What I hadn't expected was *the voice* in which the denial was said. The girl sounded as though her tongue were caught in her mouth. "That's a BAD word!" the girl continued. "We don't say BAD words!"

"Let's go in," Elise said. 130

"No," Drema said, "I don't want to. What if we get beat up?"

"Snot?" Elise turned to me, her flashlight blinding. It was the first time anyone had asked my opinion, though I knew they were just asking because they were afraid.

"I say we go inside, just to see what's going on."

"But Arnetta didn't give us the signal," Drema said. "She's supposed to say, 'We're gonna teach you a lesson,' and I didn't hear her say it."

"C'mon," I said. "Let's just go in." 135

We went inside. There we found the white girls — about five girls huddled up next to one big girl. I instantly knew she was the owner of the voice we'd heard. Arnetta and Octavia inched toward us as soon as we entered.

"Where's Janice?" Elise asked, then we heard a flush. "Oh."

"I think," Octavia said, whispering to Elise, "they're retarded."

"We ARE NOT retarded!" the big girl said, though it was obvious that she was. That they all were. The girls around her began to whimper.

"They're just pretending," Arnetta said, trying to convince herself. "I know 140 they are."

Octavia turned to Arnetta. "Arnetta. Let's just leave."

Janice came out of a stall, happy and relieved, then she suddenly remembered her line, pointed to the big girl, and said, "We're gonna teach you a lesson."

"Shut up, Janice," Octavia said, but her heart was not in it. Arnetta's face was set in a lost, deep scowl. Octavia turned to the big girl and said loudly, slowly, as if they were all deaf, "We're going to leave. It was nice meeting you, O.K.? You don't have to tell anyone that we were here. O.K.?"

"Why not?" said the big girl, like a taunt. When she spoke, her lips did not meet, her mouth did not close. Her tongue grazed the roof of her mouth, like a little pink fish. "You'll get in trouble. I know. *I* know."

Arnetta got back her old cunning. "If you said anything, then you'd be a 145 tattletale."

The girl looked sad for a moment, then perked up quickly. A flash of genius crossed her face. "I *like* tattletale."

"It's all right, girls. It's gonna be all right!" the 909 troop leader said. All of Troop 909 burst into tears. It was as though someone had instructed them all to cry at once. The troop leader had girls under her arm, and all the rest of the girls crowded about her. It reminded me of a hog I'd seen on a field trip, where all the little hogs gathered about the mother at feeding time, latching onto her teats. The 909 troop leader had come into the bathroom, shortly after the big girl had threatened to tell. Then the ranger came, then, once the ranger had radioed the station, Mrs. Margolin arrived with Daphne in tow.

The ranger had left the restroom area, but everyone else was huddled just outside, swatting mosquitoes.

"Oh. They *will* apologize," Mrs. Margolin said to the 909 troop leader, but she said this so angrily, I knew she was speaking more to us than to the other troop leader. "When their parents find out, every one a them will be on punishment."

"It's all right, it's all right," the 909 troop leader reassured Mrs. Margolin. 150 Her voice lilted in the same way it had when addressing the girls. She smiled the whole time she talked. She was like one of those TV-cooking-show women who talk and dice onions and smile all at the same time.

"See. It could have happened. I'm not calling your girls fibbers or anything." She shook her head ferociously from side to side, her Egyptian-style pageboy flapping against her cheeks like heavy drapes. "It *could* have happened. See. Our girls are *not* retarded. They are *delayed* learners." She said this in a syrupy instructional voice, as though our troop might be delayed learners as well. "We're from the Decatur Children's Academy. Many of them just have special needs."

"Now we won't be able to walk to the bathroom by ourselves!" the big girl said.

"Yes you will," the troop leader said, "but maybe we'll wait till we get back to Decatur—"

"I don't want to wait!" the girl said. "I want my Independence badge!"

The girls in my troop were entirely speechless. Arnetta looked stoic, as 155 though she were soon to be tortured but was determined not to appear weak. Mrs. Margolin pursed her lips solemnly and said, "Bless them, Lord. Bless them."

In contrast, the Troop 909 leader was full of words and energy. "Some of our girls are echolalic—" She smiled and happily presented one of the girls hanging onto her, but the girl widened her eyes in horror, and violently withdrew herself from the center of attention, sensing she was being sacrificed for the village sins. "Echolalic," the troop leader continued. "That means they will say whatever they hear, like an echo—that's where the word comes from. It comes from 'echo.'" She ducked her head apologetically, "I mean, not all of them have the most *progressive* of parents, so if they heard a bad word, they might have repeated it. But I guarantee it would not have been *intentional*."

Arnetta spoke. "I saw her say the word. I heard her." She pointed to a small girl, smaller than any of us, wearing an oversized T-shirt that read: "Eat Bertha's Mussels."

The troop leader shook her head and smiled, "That's impossible. She doesn't speak. She can, but she doesn't."

Arnetta furrowed her brow. "No. It wasn't her. That's right. It was *her*."

The girl Arnetta pointed to grinned as though she'd been paid a compli- 160 ment. She was the only one from either troop actually wearing a full uniform: the mocha-colored A-line shift, the orange ascot, the sash covered with badges, though all the same one—the Try-It patch. She took a few steps toward Arnetta and made a grand sweeping gesture toward the sash. "See," she said, full of self-importance, "I'm a Brownie." I had a hard time imagining this girl calling anyone a "nigger"; the girl looked perpetually delighted, as though she would have cuddled up with a grizzly if someone had let her.

On the fourth morning, we boarded the bus to go home.

The previous day had been spent building miniature churches from Popsicle sticks. We hardly left the cabin. Mrs. Margolin and Mrs. Hedy guarded us so closely, almost no one talked for the entire day.

Even on the day of departure from Camp Crescendo, all was serious and silent. The bus ride began quietly enough. Arnetta had to sit beside Mrs. Margolin; Octavia had to sit beside her mother. I sat beside Daphne, who gave me her prize journal without a word of explanation.

"You don't want it?"

She shook her head no. It was empty.   165

Then Mrs. Hedy began to weep. "Octavia," Mrs. Hedy said to her daughter without looking at her, "I'm going to sit with Mrs. Margolin. All right?"

Arnetta exchanged seats with Mrs. Hedy. With the two women up front, Elise felt it safe to speak. "Hey," she said, then she set her face into a placid, vacant stare, trying to imitate that of a Troop 909 girl. Emboldened, Arnetta made a gesture of mock pride toward an imaginary sash, the way the girl in full uniform had done. Then they all made a game of it, trying to do the most exaggerated imitations of the Troop 909 girls, all without speaking, all without laughing loud enough to catch the women's attention.

Daphne looked down at her shoes, white with sneaker polish. I opened the journal she'd given me. I looked out the window, trying to decide what to write, searching for lines, but nothing could compare with what Daphne had written, *"My father, the veteran,"* my favorite line of all time. It replayed itself in my head, and I gave up trying to write.

By then, it seemed that the rest of the troop had given up making fun of the girls in Troop 909. They were now quietly gossiping about who had passed notes to whom in school. For a moment the gossiping fell off, and all I heard was the hum of the bus as we sped down the road and the muffled sounds of Mrs. Hedy and Mrs. Margolin talking about serious things.

"You know," Octavia whispered, "why did *we* have to be stuck at a camp   170 with retarded girls? You know?"

"*You* know why," Arnetta answered. She narrowed her eyes like a cat. "My mama and I were in the mall in Buckhead, and this white lady just kept looking at us. I mean, like we were foreign or something. Like we were from China."

"What did the woman say?" Elise asked.

"Nothing," Arnetta said. "She didn't say nothing."

A few girls quietly nodded their heads.

"There was this time," I said, "when my father and I were in the mall   175 and—"

"Oh shut up, Snot," Octavia said.

I stared at Octavia, then rolled my eyes from her to the window. As I watched the trees blur, I wanted nothing more than to be through with it all: the bus ride, the troop, school—all of it. But we were going home. I'd see the same girls in school the next day. We were on a bus, and there was nowhere else to go.

"Go on, Laurel," Daphne said to me. It seemed like the first time she'd spoken the whole trip, and she'd said my name. I turned to her and smiled weakly so as not to cry, hoping she'd remember when I'd tried to be her friend, thinking maybe that her gift of the journal was an invitation of friendship. But she didn't smile back. All she said was, "What happened?"

I studied the girls, waiting for Octavia to tell me to shut up again before I even had a chance to utter another word, but everyone was amazed that Daphne had spoken. The bus was silent. I gathered my voice. "Well," I said. "My father and I were in this mall, but I was the one doing the staring." I stopped and glanced from face to face. I continued. "There were these white people dressed like Puritans or something, but they weren't Puritans. They were Mennonites. They're these people who, if you ask them to do a favor, like paint your porch or something, they have to do it. It's in their rules."

"That sucks," someone said.   180

"C'mon," Arnetta said. "You're lying."

"I am not."

"How do you know that's not just some story someone made up?" Elise asked, her head cocked full of daring. "I mean, who's gonna do whatever you ask?"

"It's not made up. I know because when I was looking at them, my father said, 'See those people? If you ask them to do something, they'll do it. Anything you want.'"

No one would call anyone's father a liar—then they'd have to fight the   185 person. But Drema parsed her words carefully. "How does your *father* know that's not just some story? Huh?"

"Because," I said, "he went up to the man and asked him would he paint our porch, and the man said yes. It's their religion."

"Man, I'm glad I'm a Baptist," Elise said, shaking her head in sympathy for the Mennonites.

"So did the guy do it?" Drema asked, scooting closer to hear if the story got juicy.

"Yeah," I said. "His whole family was with him. My dad drove them to our house. They all painted our porch. The woman and girl were in bonnets and long, long skirts with buttons up to their necks. The guy wore this weird hat and these huge suspenders."

"Why," Arnetta asked archly, as though she didn't believe a word, "would   190 someone pick a *porch*? If they'll do anything, why not make them paint the whole *house*? Why not ask for a hundred bucks?"

I thought about it, and then remembered the words my father had said about them painting our porch, though I had never seemed to think about his words after he'd said them.

"He said," I began, only then understanding the words as they uncoiled from my mouth, "it was the only time he'd have a white man on his knees doing something for a black man for free."

I now understood what he meant, and why he did it, though I didn't like it. When you've been made to feel bad for so long, you jump at the chance to do it to others. I remembered the Mennonites bending the way Daphne had bent when she was cleaning the restroom. I remembered the dark blue of their bonnets, the black of their shoes. They painted the porch as though scrubbing a floor. I was already trembling before Daphne asked quietly, "Did he thank them?"

I looked out the window. I could not tell which were the thoughts and which were the trees. "No," I said, and suddenly knew there was something mean in the world that I could not stop.

Arnetta laughed. "If I asked them to take off their long skirts and bonnets 195 and put on some jeans, would they do it?"

And Daphne's voice, quiet, steady: "Maybe they would. Just to be nice."

Edgar Allan Poe   1809–1849

The Cask of Amontillado   [1846]

The thousand injuries of Fortunato I had borne as I best could; but when he ventured upon insult, I vowed revenge. You, who so well know the nature of my soul, will not suppose, however, that I gave utterance to a threat. *At length* I would be avenged; this was a point definitively settled—but the very definitiveness with which it was resolved precluded the idea of risk. I must not only punish, but punish with impunity. A wrong is unredressed when retribution overtakes its redresser. It is equally unredressed when the avenger fails to make himself felt as such to him who has done the wrong.

It must be understood that neither by word nor deed had I given Fortunato cause to doubt my good will. I continued, as was my wont, to smile in his face, and he did not perceive that my smile *now* was at the thought of his immolation.

He had a weak point—this Fortunato—although in other regards he was a man to be respected and even feared. He prided himself on his connoisseurship in wine. Few Italians have the true virtuoso spirit. For the most part their enthusiasm is adopted to suit the time and opportunity—to practice imposture upon the British and Austrian *millionaires*. In painting and gemmary Fortunato, like his countrymen, was a quack—but in the matter of old wines he was sincere. In this respect I did not differ from him materially; I was skilful in the Italian vintages myself, and bought largely whenever I could.

It was about dusk, one evening during the supreme madness of the carnival season, that I encountered my friend. He accosted me with excessive warmth, for he had been drinking much. The man wore motley. He had on a tight-fitting parti-striped dress, and his head was surmounted by the conical cap and bells. I was so pleased to see him that I thought I should never have done wringing his hand.

I said to him—"My dear Fortunato, you are luckily met. How remarkably well you are looking to-day! But I have received a pipe° of what passes for Amontillado, and I have my doubts."

"How?" said he. "Amontillado? A pipe? Impossible! And in the middle of the carnival!"

"I have my doubts," I replied; "and I was silly enough to pay the full Amontillado price without consulting you in the matter. You were not to be found, and I was fearful of losing a bargain."

"Amontillado!"

"I have my doubts."

"Amontillado!"

"And I must satisfy them."

"Amontillado!"

"As you are engaged, I am on my way to Luchesi. If any one has a critical turn, it is he. He will tell me—"

"Luchesi cannot tell Amontillado from Sherry."

"And yet some fools will have it that his taste is a match for your own."

"Come, let us go."

"Whither?"

"To your vaults."

"My friend, no; I will not impose upon your good nature. I perceive you have an engagement. Luchesi—"

"I have no engagement;—come."

"My friend, no. It is not the engagement, but the severe cold with which I perceive you are afflicted. The vaults are insufferably damp. They are encrusted with nitre."

"Let us go, nevertheless. The cold is merely nothing. Amontillado! You have been imposed upon. And as for Luchesi, he cannot distinguish Sherry from Amontillado."

Thus speaking, Fortunato possessed himself of my arm. Putting on a mask of black silk, and drawing a *roquelaire*° closely about my person, I suffered him to hurry me to my palazzo.

There were no attendants at home; they had absconded to make merry in honor of the time. I had told them that I should not return until the morning, and had given them explicit orders not to stir from the house. These orders were sufficient, I well knew, to insure their immediate disappearance, one and all, as soon as my back was turned.

I took from their sconces two flambeaux, and giving one to Fortunato, bowed him through several suites of rooms to the archway that led into the vaults. I passed down a long and winding staircase, requesting him to be

---

pipe: A large keg or cask.
roquelaire: A short cloak.

cautious as he followed. We came at length to the foot of the descent, and stood together on the damp ground of the catacombs of the Montresors.

The gait of my friend was unsteady, and the bells upon his cap jingled as he strode.

"The pipe," said he.

"It is farther on," said I; "but observe the white web-work which gleams from these cavern walls."

He turned towards me, and looked into my eyes with two filmy orbs that distilled the rheum of intoxication.

"Nitre?" he asked, at length.   30

"Nitre," I replied. "How long have you had that cough?"

"Ugh! ugh! ugh! — ugh! ugh! ugh! — ugh! ugh! ugh! — ugh! ugh! ugh! — ugh! ugh! ugh!"

My poor friend found it impossible to reply for many minutes.

"It is nothing," he said, at last.

"Come," I said, with decision, "we will go back; your health is precious. You 35
are rich, respected, admired, beloved; you are happy, as once I was. You are a man to be missed. For me it is no matter. We will go back; you will be ill, and I cannot be responsible. Besides, there is Luchesi—"

"Enough," he said; "the cough is a mere nothing; it will not kill me. I shall not die of a cough."

"True—true," I replied; "and, indeed, I had no intention of alarming you unnecessarily—but you should use all proper caution. A draught of this Medoc will defend us from the damps."

Here I knocked off the neck of a bottle which I drew from a long row of its fellows that lay upon the mould.

"Drink," I said, presenting him the wine.

He raised it to his lips with a leer. He paused and nodded to me familiarly, 40
while his bells jingled.

"I drink," he said, "to the buried that repose around us."

"And I to your long life."

He again took my arm, and we proceeded.

"These vaults," he said, "are extensive."

"The Montresors," I replied, "were a great and numerous family."   45

"I forget your arms."

"A huge human foot d'or,° in a field azure; the foot crushes a serpent rampant whose fangs are imbedded in the heel."

"And the motto?"

"*Nemo me impune lacessit.*"°

"Good!" he said.   50

---

d'or: Of gold.

Nemo me impune lacessit: No one provokes me with impunity (Latin; the motto of the Order of the Thistle in Scotland and the national motto of Scotland).

The wine sparkled in his eyes and the bells jingled. My own fancy grew warm with the Medoc. We had passed through walls of piled bones, with casks and puncheons intermingling, into the inmost recesses of the catacombs. I paused again, and this time I made bold to seize Fortunato by an arm above the elbow.

"The nitre!" I said; "see, it increases. It hangs like moss upon the vaults. We are below the river's bed. The drops of moisture trickle among the bones. Come, we will go back ere it is too late. Your cough—"

"It is nothing," he said; "let us go on. But first, another draught of the Medoc."

I broke and reached him a flaçon of De Grâve. He emptied it at a breath. His eyes flashed with a fierce light. He laughed and threw the bottle upwards with a gesticulation I did not understand.

I looked at him in surprise. He repeated the movement—a grotesque one.   55

"You do not comprehend?" he said.

"Not I," I replied.

"Then you are not of the brotherhood."

"How?"

"You are not of the masons."   60

"Yes, yes," I said, "yes, yes."

"You? Impossible! A mason?"

"A mason," I replied.

"A sign," he said.

"It is this," I answered, producing a trowel from beneath the folds of my   65
roquelaire.

"You jest," he exclaimed, recoiling a few paces. "But let us proceed to the Amontillado."

"Be it so," I said, replacing the tool beneath the cloak, and again offering him my arm. He leaned upon it heavily. We continued our route in search of the Amontillado. We passed through a range of low arches, descended, passed on, and descending again, arrived at a deep crypt, in which the foulness of the air caused our flambeaux rather to glow than flame.

At the most remote end of the crypt there appeared another less spacious. Its walls had been lined with human remains, piled to the vault overhead, in the fashion of the great catacombs of Paris. Three sides of this interior crypt were still ornamented in this manner. From the fourth the bones had been thrown down, and lay promiscuously upon the earth, forming at one point a mound of some size. Within the wall thus exposed by the displacing of the bones, we perceived a still interior recess, in depth about four feet, in width three, in height six or seven. It seemed to have been constructed for no especial use within itself, but formed merely the interval between two of the colossal supports of the roof of the catacombs, and was backed by one of their circumscribing walls of solid granite.

It was in vain that Fortunato, uplifting his dull torch, endeavored to pry into the depth of the recess. Its termination the feeble light did not enable us to see.

"Proceed," I said; "herein is the Amontillado. As for Luchesi—" 70

"He is an ignoramus," interrupted my friend, as he stepped unsteadily forward, while I followed immediately at his heels. In an instant he had reached the extremity of the niche, and finding his progress arrested by the rock, stood stupidly bewildered. A moment more and I had fettered him to the granite. In its surface were two iron staples, distant from each other about two feet, horizontally. From one of these depended a short chain, from the other a padlock. Throwing the links about his waist, it was but the work of a few seconds to secure it. He was too much astounded to resist. Withdrawing the key I stepped back from the recess.

"Pass your hand," I said, "over the wall; you cannot help feeling the nitre. Indeed it is *very* damp. Once more let me *implore* you to return. No? Then I must positively leave you. But I must first render you all the little attentions in my power."

"The Amontillado!" ejaculated my friend, not yet recovered from his astonishment.

"True," I replied; "the Amontillado."

As I said these words I busied myself among the pile of bones of which I 75 have before spoken. Throwing them aside, I soon uncovered a quantity of building stone and mortar. With these materials and with the aid of my trowel, I began vigorously to wall up the entrance of the niche.

I had scarcely laid the first tier of the masonry when I discovered that the intoxication of Fortunato had in a great measure worn off. The earliest indication I had of this was a low moaning cry from the depth of the recess. It was *not* the cry of a drunken man. There was then a long and obstinate silence. I laid the second tier, and the third, and the fourth; and then I heard the furious vibrations of the chain. The noise lasted for several minutes, during which, that I might hearken to it with the more satisfaction, I ceased my labors and sat down upon the bones. When at last the clanking subsided, I resumed the trowel, and finished without interruption the fifth, the sixth, and the seventh tier. The wall was now nearly upon a level with my breast. I again paused, and holding the flambeaux over the mason-work, threw a few feeble rays upon the figure within.

A succession of loud and shrill screams, bursting suddenly from the throat of the chained form, seemed to thrust me violently back. For a brief moment I hesitated—I trembled. Unsheathing my rapier, I began to grope with it about the recess: but the thought of an instant reassured me. I placed my hand upon the solid fabric of the catacombs, and felt satisfied. I reapproached the wall. I replied to the yells of him who clamored. I re-echoed—I aided—I surpassed them in volume and in strength. I did this, and the clamorer grew still.

It was now midnight, and my task was drawing to a close. I had completed the eighth, the ninth, and the tenth tier. I had finished a portion of the last and the eleventh; there remained but a single stone to be fitted and plastered in. I struggled with its weight; I placed it partially in its destined position. But now there came from out the niche a low laugh that erected the hairs upon my head.

It was succeeded by a sad voice, which I had difficulty in recognizing as that of the noble Fortunato. The voice said—

"Ha! ha! ha!—he! he!—a very good joke indeed—an excellent jest. We will have many a rich laugh about it at the palazzo—he! he! he!—over our wine— he! he! he!"

"The Amontillado!" I said.   80

"He! he! he!—he! he! he!—yes, the Amontillado. But is it not getting late? Will not they be awaiting us at the palazzo, the Lady Fortunato and the rest? Let us be gone."

"Yes," I said, "let us be gone."

"For the love of God, Montresor!"

"Yes," I said, "for the love of God!"

But to these words I hearkened in vain for a reply. I grew impatient. I called 85 aloud—

"Fortunato!"

No answer. I called again—

"Fortunato!"

No answer still. I thrust a torch through the remaining aperture and let it fall within. There came forth in return only a jingling of the bells. My heart grew sick—on account of the dampness of the catacombs. I hastened to make an end of my labor. I forced the last stone into its position; I plastered it up. Against the new masonry I re-erected the old rampart of bones. For the half of a century no mortal has disturbed them. *In páce requiescat!*°

Katherine Anne Porter   1890–1980

The Jilting of Granny Weatherall   [1929]

She flicked her wrist neatly out of Doctor Harry's pudgy careful fingers and pulled the sheet up to her chin. The brat ought to be in knee breeches. Doctoring around the country with spectacles on his nose! "Get along now, take your schoolbooks and go. There's nothing wrong with me."

Doctor Harry spread a warm paw like a cushion on her forehead where the forked green vein danced and made her eyelids twitch. "Now, now, be a good girl, and we'll have you up in no time."

"That's no way to speak to a woman nearly eighty years old just because she's down. I'd have you respect your elders, young man."

"Well, Missy, excuse me." Doctor Harry patted her cheek. "But I've got to warn you, haven't I? You're a marvel, but you must be careful or you're going to be good and sorry."

In páce requiescat!: May he rest in peace!

"Don't tell me what I'm going to be. I'm on my feet now, morally speaking.   5
It's Cornelia. I had to go to bed to get rid of her."

Her bones felt loose, and floated around in her skin, and Doctor Harry
floated like a balloon around the foot of the bed. He floated and pulled down
his waistcoat and swung his glasses on a cord. "Well, stay where you are, it
certainly can't hurt you."

"Get along and doctor your sick," said Granny Weatherall. "Leave a well
woman alone. I'll call for you when I want you. . . . Where were you forty years
ago when I pulled through milk-leg° and double pneumonia? You weren't even
born. Don't let Cornelia lead you on," she shouted, because Doctor Harry
appeared to float up to the ceiling and out. "I pay my own bills, and I don't
throw my money away on nonsense!"

She meant to wave good-by, but it was too much trouble. Her eyes closed
of themselves, it was like a dark curtain drawn around the bed. The pillow rose
and floated under her, pleasant as a hammock in a light wind. She listened to
the leaves rustling outside the window. No, somebody was swishing newspapers: no, Cornelia and Doctor Harry were whispering together. She leaped broad
awake, thinking they whispered in her ear.

"She was never like this, *never* like this!" "Well, what can we expect?" "Yes,
eighty years old. . . ."

Well, and what if she was? She still had ears. It was like Cornelia to whisper   10
around doors. She always kept things secret in such a public way. She was
always being tactful and kind. Cornelia was dutiful; that was the trouble with
her. Dutiful and good: "So good and dutiful," said Granny, "that I'd like to
spank her." She saw herself spanking Cornelia and making a fine job of it.

"What'd you say, Mother?"

Granny felt her face tying up in hard knots.

"Can't a body think, I'd like to know?"

"I thought you might want something."

"I do. I want a lot of things. First off, go away and don't whisper."   15

She lay and drowsed, hoping in her sleep that the children would keep out
and let her rest a minute. It had been a long day. Not that she was tired. It was
always pleasant to snatch a minute now and then. There was always so much
to be done, let me see: tomorrow.

Tomorrow was far away and there was nothing to trouble about. Things
were finished somehow when the time came; thank God there was always a
little margin over for peace: then a person could spread out the plan of life and
tuck in the edges orderly. It was good to have everything clean and folded away,
with the hair brushes and tonic bottles sitting straight on the white embroidered
linen: the day started without fuss and the pantry shelves laid out with rows of
jelly glasses and brown jugs and white stone-china jars with blue whirligigs and

---

milk-leg: A painful swelling of the leg soon after childbirth caused by inflammation and
clotting in the veins.

words painted on them: coffee, tea, sugar, ginger, cinnamon, allspice: and the bronze clock with the lion on top nicely dusted off. The dust that lion could collect in twenty-four hours! The box in the attic with all those letters tied up, well, she'd have to go through that tomorrow. All those letters — George's letters and John's letters and her letters to them both — lying around for the children to find afterwards made her uneasy. Yes, that would be tomorrow's business. No use to let them know how silly she had been once.

While she was rummaging around she found death in her mind and it felt clammy and unfamiliar. She had spent so much time preparing for death there was no need for bringing it up again. Let it take care of itself now. When she was sixty she had felt very old, finished, and went around making farewell trips to see her children and grandchildren, with a secret in her mind: This is the very last of your mother, children! Then she made her will and came down with a long fever. That was all just a notion like a lot of other things, but it was lucky too, for she had once for all got over the idea of dying for a long time. Now she couldn't be worried. She hoped she had better sense now. Her father had lived to be one hundred and two years old and had drunk a noggin of strong hot toddy on his last birthday. He told the reporters it was his daily habit, and he owed his long life to that. He had made quite a scandal and was very pleased about it. She believed she'd just plague Cornelia a little.

"Cornelia! Cornelia!" No footsteps, but a sudden hand on her cheek. "Bless you, where have you been?"

"Here, Mother."   20

"Well, Cornelia, I want a noggin of hot toddy."

"Are you cold, darling?"

"I'm chilly, Cornelia. Lying in bed stops the circulation. I must have told you that a thousand times."

Well, she could just hear Cornelia telling her husband that Mother was getting a little childish and they'd have to humor her. The thing that most annoyed her was that Cornelia thought she was deaf, dumb, and blind. Little hasty glances and tiny gestures tossed around her and over her head saying, "Don't cross her, let her have her way, she's eighty years old," and she sitting there as if she lived in a thin glass cage. Sometimes Granny almost made up her mind to pack up and move back to her own house where nobody could remind her every minute that she was old. Wait, wait, Cornelia, till your own children whisper behind your back!

In her day she had kept a better house and had got more work done. She   25 wasn't too old yet for Lydia to be driving eighty miles for advice when one of the children jumped the track, and Jimmy still dropped in and talked things over: "Now, Mammy, you've a good business head, I want to know what you think of this? . . ." Old. Cornelia couldn't change the furniture around without asking. Little things, little things! They had been so sweet when they were little. Granny wished the old days were back again with the children young and every- thing to be done over. It had been a hard pull, but not too much for her. When she thought of all the food she had cooked, and all the clothes she had cut and sewed, and all the gardens she had made—well, the children showed it. There they were, made out of her, and they couldn't get away from that. Sometimes she wanted to see John again and point to them and say, Well, I didn't do so badly, did I? But that would have to wait. That was for tomorrow. She used to think of him as a man, but now all the children were older than their father, and he would be a child beside her if she saw him now. It seemed strange and there was something wrong in the idea. Why, he couldn't possibly recognize her. She had fenced in a hundred acres once, digging the post holes herself and clamping the wires with just a negro boy to help. That changed a woman. John would be looking for a young woman with the peaked Spanish comb in her hair and the painted fan. Digging post holes changed a woman. Riding country roads in the winter when women had their babies was another thing: sitting up nights with sick horses and sick negroes and sick children and hardly ever losing one. John, I hardly ever lost one of them! John would see that in a minute, that would be something he could understand, she wouldn't have to explain anything!

It made her feel like rolling up her sleeves and putting the whole place to rights again. No matter if Cornelia was determined to be everywhere at once, there were a great many things left undone on this place. She would start tomorrow and do them. It was good to be strong enough for everything, even if all you made melted and changed and slipped under your hands, so that by the time you finished you almost forgot what you were working for. What was it I set out to do? she asked herself intently, but she could not remember. A fog rose over the valley, she saw it marching across the creek swallowing the trees and moving up the hill like an army of ghosts. Soon it would be at the near edge of the orchard, and then it was time to go in and light the lamps. Come in, children, don't stay out in the night air.

Lighting the lamps had been beautiful. The children huddled up to her and breathed like little calves waiting at the bars in the twilight. Their eyes followed the match and watched the flame rise and settle in a blue curve, then they moved away from her. The lamp was lit, they didn't have to be scared and hang on to mother any more. Never, never, never more. God, for all my life I thank Thee. Without Thee, my God, I could never have done it. Hail, Mary, full of grace.

I want you to pick all the fruit this year and see that nothing is wasted. There's always someone who can use it. Don't let good things rot for want of using. You waste life when you waste good food. Don't let things get lost. It's bitter to lose things. Now, don't let me get to thinking, not when I am tired and taking a little nap before supper. . . .

The pillow rose about her shoulders and pressed against her heart and the memory was being squeezed out of it: oh, push down the pillow, somebody: it would smother her if she tried to hold it. Such a fresh breeze blowing and such a green day with no threats in it. But he had not come, just the same. What does a woman do when she has put on the white veil and set out the white cake for a man and he doesn't come? She tried to remember. No, I swear he never harmed me but in that. He never harmed me but in that . . . and what if he did? There was the day, the day, but a whirl of dark smoke rose and covered it, crept up and over into the bright field where everything was planted so carefully in orderly rows. That was hell, she knew hell when she saw it. For sixty years she had prayed against remembering him and against losing her soul in the deep pit of hell, and now the two things were mingled in one and the thought of him was a smoky cloud from hell that moved and crept in her head when she had just got rid of Doctor Harry and was trying to rest a minute. Wounded vanity, Ellen, said a sharp voice in the top of her mind. Don't let your wounded vanity get the upper hand of you. Plenty of girls get jilted. You were jilted, weren't you? Then stand up to it. Her eyelids wavered and let in streamers of blue-gray light like tissue paper over her eyes. She must get up and pull the shades down or she'd never sleep. She was in bed again and the shades were not down. How could that happen? Better turn over, hide from the light, sleeping in the light gave you nightmares. "Mother, how do you feel now?" and a stinging wetness on her forehead. But I don't like having my face washed in cold water!

Hapsy? George? Lydia? Jimmy? No, Cornelia, and her features were swollen   30 and full of little puddles. "They're coming, darling, they'll all be here soon." Go wash your face, child, you look funny.

Instead of obeying, Cornelia knelt down and put her head on the pillow. She seemed to be talking but there was no sound. "Well, are you tongue-tied? Whose birthday is it? Are you going to give a party?"

Cornelia's mouth moved urgently in strange shapes. "Don't do that, you bother me, daughter."

"Oh, no, Mother. Oh, no. . . ."

Nonsense. It was strange about children. They disputed your every word. "No what, Cornelia?"

"Here's Doctor Harry."   35

"I won't see that boy again. He just left five minutes ago."

"That was this morning, Mother. It's night now. Here's the nurse."

"This is Doctor Harry, Mrs. Weatherall. I never saw you look so young and happy!"

"Ah, I'll never be young again—but I'd be happy if they'd let me lie in peace and get rested."

She thought she spoke up loudly, but no one answered. A warm weight on   40 her forehead, a warm bracelet on her wrist, and a breeze went on whispering, trying to tell her something. A shuffle of leaves in the everlasting hand of God, He blew on them and they danced and rattled. "Mother, don't mind, we're going to give you a little hypodermic." "Look here, daughter, how do ants get in this bed? I saw sugar ants yesterday." Did you send for Hapsy too?

It was Hapsy she really wanted. She had to go a long way back through a great many rooms to find Hapsy standing with a baby on her arm. She seemed to herself to be Hapsy also, and the baby on Hapsy's arm was Hapsy and himself and herself, all at once, and there was no surprise in the meeting. Then Hapsy melted from within and turned flimsy as gray gauze and the baby was a gauzy shadow, and Hapsy came up close and said, "I thought you'd never come," and looked at her very searchingly and said, "You haven't changed a bit!" They leaned forward to kiss, when Cornelia began whispering from a long way off, "Oh, is there anything you want to tell me? Is there anything I can do for you?"

Yes, she had changed her mind after sixty years and she would like to see George. I want you to find George. Find him and be sure to tell him I forgot him. I want him to know I had my husband just the same and my children and my house like any other woman. A good house too and a good husband that I loved and fine children out of him. Better than I hoped for even. Tell him I was given back everything he took away and more. Oh, no, oh, God, no, there was something else besides the house and the man and the children. Oh, surely they were not all? What was it? Something not given back. . . . Her breath crowded down under her ribs and grew into a monstrous frightening shape with cutting edges; it bored up into her head, and the agony was unbelievable: Yes, John, get the Doctor now, no more talk, my time has come.

When this one was born it should be the last. The last. It should have been born first, for it was the one she had truly wanted. Everything came in good time. Nothing left out, left over. She was strong, in three days she would be as well as ever. Better. A woman needed milk in her to have her full health.

"Mother, do you hear me?"

"I've been telling you—"   45

"Mother, Father Connolly's here."

"I went to Holy Communion only last week. Tell him I'm not so sinful as all that."

"Father just wants to speak to you."

He could speak as much as he pleased. It was like him to drop in and inquire about her soul as if it were a teething baby, and then stay on for a cup of tea and a round of cards and gossip. He always had a funny story of some sort, usually about an Irishman who made his little mistakes and confessed them, and the point lay in some absurd thing he would blurt out in the confessional showing his struggles between native piety and original sin. Granny felt easy about her soul. Cornelia, where are your manners? Give Father Connolly a chair. She had her secret comfortable understanding with a few favorite saints who cleared a straight road to God for her. All as surely signed and sealed as the papers for the new Forty Acres. Forever . . . heirs and assigns forever. Since the day the wedding cake was not cut, but thrown out and wasted. The whole bottom dropped out of the world, and there she was blind and sweating with nothing under her feet and the walls falling away. His hand had caught her under the breast, she had not fallen, there was the freshly polished floor with the green rug on it, just as before. He had cursed like a sailor's parrot and said, "I'll kill him for you." Don't lay a hand on him, for my sake leave something to God. "Now, Ellen, you must believe what I tell you. . . ."

So there was nothing, nothing to worry about any more, except sometimes   50
in the night one of the children screamed in a nightmare, and they both hustled

out shaking and hunting for the matches and calling, "There, wait a minute, here we are!" John, get the doctor now, Hapsy's time has come. But there was Hapsy standing by the bed in a white cap. "Cornelia, tell Hapsy to take off her cap. I can't see her plain."

Her eyes opened very wide and the room stood out like a picture she had seen somewhere. Dark colors with the shadows rising towards the ceiling in long angles. The tall black dresser gleamed with nothing on it but John's picture, enlarged from a little one, with John's eyes very black when they should have been blue. You never saw him, so how do you know how he looked? But the man insisted the copy was perfect, it was very rich and handsome. For a picture, yes, but it's not my husband. The table by the bed had a linen cover and a candle and a crucifix. The light was blue from Cornelia's silk lampshades. No sort of light at all, just frippery. You had to live forty years with kerosene lamps to appreciate honest electricity. She felt very strong and she saw Doctor Harry with a rosy nimbus around him.

"You look like a saint, Doctor Harry, and I vow that's as near as you'll ever come to it."

"She's saying something."

"I heard you, Cornelia. What's all this carrying-on?"

"Father Connolly's saying—"   55

Cornelia's voice staggered and bumped like a cart in a bad road. It rounded corners and turned back again and arrived nowhere. Granny stepped up in the cart very lightly and reached for the reins, but a man sat beside her and she knew him by his hands, driving the cart. She did not look in his face, for she knew without seeing, but looked instead down the road where the trees leaned over and bowed to each other and a thousand birds were singing a Mass. She felt like singing too, but she put her hand in the bosom of her dress and pulled out a rosary, and Father Connolly murmured Latin in a very solemn voice and tickled her feet. My God, will you stop that nonsense? I'm a married woman. What if he did run away and leave me to face the priest by myself? I found another a whole world better. I wouldn't have exchanged my husband for anybody except St. Michael himself, and you may tell him that for me with a thank you in the bargain.

Light flashed on her closed eyelids, and a deep roaring shook her. Cornelia, is that lightning? I hear thunder. There's going to be a storm. Close all the windows. Call the children in. . . . "Mother, here we are, all of us." "Is that you, Hapsy?" "Oh, no, I'm Lydia. We drove as fast as we could." Their faces drifted above her, drifted away. The rosary fell out of her hands and Lydia put it back. Jimmy tried to help, their hands fumbled together, and Granny closed two fingers around Jimmy's thumb. Beads wouldn't do, it must be something alive. She was so amazed her thoughts ran round and round. So, my dear Lord, this is my death and I wasn't even thinking about it. My children have come to see me die. But I can't, it's not time. Oh, I always hated surprises. I wanted to give Cornelia the amethyst set—Cornelia, you're to have the amethyst set, but Hapsy's to wear it when she wants, and, Doctor Harry, do shut up. Nobody sent for you.

Oh, my dear Lord, do wait a minute. I meant to do something about the Forty Acres, Jimmy doesn't need it and Lydia will later on, with that worthless husband of hers. I meant to finish the altar cloth and send six bottles of wine to Sister Borgia for her dyspepsia. I want to send six bottles of wine to Sister Borgia, Father Connolly, now don't let me forget.

Cornelia's voice made short turns and tilted over and crashed. "Oh, Mother, oh, Mother, oh, Mother. . . ."

"I'm not going, Cornelia. I'm taken by surprise. I can't go."

You'll see Hapsy again. What about her? "I thought you'd never come." 60 Granny made a long journey outward, looking for Hapsy. What if I don't find her? What then? Her heart sank down and down, there was no bottom to death, she couldn't come to the end of it. The blue light from Cornelia's lampshade drew into a tiny point in the center of her brain, it flickered and winked like an eye, quietly it fluttered and dwindled. Granny lay curled down within herself, amazed and watchful, staring at the point of light that was herself; her body was now only a deeper mass of shadow in an endless darkness and this darkness would curl around the light and swallow it up. God, give a sign!

For the second time there was no sign. Again no bridegroom and the priest in the house. She could not remember any other sorrow because this grief wiped them all away. Oh, no, there's nothing more cruel than this—I'll never forgive it. She stretched herself with a deep breath and blew out the light.

James Thurber   1894–1961

The Catbird Seat   [1945]

Mr. Martin bought the pack of Camels on Monday night in the most crowded cigar store on Broadway. It was theater time and seven or eight men were buying cigarettes. The clerk didn't even glance at Mr. Martin, who put the pack in his overcoat pocket and went out. If any of the staff at F & S had seen him buy the cigarettes, they would have been astonished, for it was generally known that Mr. Martin did not smoke, and never had. No one saw him.

It was just a week to the day since Mr. Martin had decided to rub out Mrs. Ulgine Barrows. The term "rub out" pleased him because it suggested nothing more than the correction of an error—in this case an error of Mr. Fitweiler. Mr. Martin had spent each night of the past week working out his plan and examining it. As he walked home now he went over it again. For the hundredth time he resented the element of imprecision, the margin of guesswork that entered into the business. The project as he had worked it out was casual and bold, the risks were considerable. Something might go wrong anywhere along the line. And therein lay the cunning of his scheme. No one would ever see in it the cautious, painstaking hand of Erwin Martin, head of the filing department at F & S, of whom Mr. Fitweiler had once said, "Man is fallible but Martin isn't." No one would see his hand, that is, unless it were caught in the act.

Sitting in his apartment, drinking a glass of milk, Mr. Martin reviewed his case against Mrs. Ulgine Barrows, as he had every night for seven nights. He began at the beginning. Her quacking voice and braying laugh had first profaned the halls of F & S on March 7, 1941 (Mr. Martin had a head for dates). Old Roberts, the personnel chief, had introduced her as the newly appointed special adviser to the president of the firm, Mr. Fitweiler. The woman had appalled Mr. Martin instantly, but he hadn't shown it. He had given her his dry hand, a look of studious concentration, and a faint smile. "Well," she had said, looking at the papers on his desk, "are you lifting the oxcart out of the ditch?" As Mr. Martin recalled that moment, over his milk, he squirmed slightly. He must keep his mind on her crimes as a special adviser, not on her peccadillos as a personality. This he found difficult to do, in spite of entering an objection and sustaining it. The faults of the woman as a woman kept chattering on in his mind like an unruly witness. She had, for almost two years now, baited him. In the halls, in the elevator, even in his own office, into which she romped now and then like a circus horse, she was constantly shouting these silly questions at him. "Are you lifting the oxcart out of the ditch? Are you tearing up the pea patch? Are you hollering down the rain barrel? Are you scraping around the bottom of the pickle barrel? Are you sitting in the catbird seat?"

It was Joey Hart, one of Mr. Martin's two assistants, who had explained what the gibberish meant. "She must be a Dodger fan," he had said. "Red Barber announces the Dodger games over the radio and he uses those expressions — picked 'em up down South." Joey had gone on to explain one or two. "Tearing up the pea patch" meant going on a rampage; "sitting in the catbird seat" meant sitting pretty, like a batter with three balls and no strikes on him. Mr. Martin dismissed all this with an effort. It had been annoying, it had driven him near to distraction, but he was too solid a man to be moved to murder by anything so childish. It was fortunate, he reflected as he passed on to the important charges against Mrs. Barrows, that he had stood up under it so well. He had maintained always an outward appearance of polite tolerance. "Why, I even believe you like the woman," Miss Paird, his other assistant, had once said to him. He had simply smiled.

A gavel rapped in Mr. Martin's mind and the case proper was resumed. ⁵ Mrs. Ulgine Barrows stood charged with willful, blatant, and persistent attempts to destroy the efficiency and system of F & S. It was competent, material, and relevant to review her advent and rise to power. Mr. Martin had got the story from Miss Paird, who seemed always able to find things out. According to her, Mrs. Barrows had met Mr. Fitweiler at a party, where she had rescued him from the embraces of a powerfully built drunken man who had mistaken the president of F & S for a famous retired Middle Western football coach. She had led him to a sofa and somehow worked upon him a monstrous magic. The aging gentleman had jumped to the conclusion there and then that this was a woman of singular attainments, equipped to bring out the best in him and in the firm. A week later he had introduced her into F & S as his special adviser. On that day confusion got its foot in the door. After Miss Tyson, Mr. Brundage, and Mr. Bartlett had been fired and Mr. Munson had taken his hat and stalked out, mailing in his resignation later, old Roberts had been emboldened to speak to Mr. Fitweiler. He mentioned that Mr. Munson's department had been "a little disrupted" and hadn't they perhaps better resume the old system there? Mr. Fitweiler had said certainly not. He had the greatest faith in Mrs. Barrows' ideas. "They require a little seasoning, a little seasoning, is all," he had added. Mr. Roberts had given it up. Mr. Martin reviewed in detail all the changes wrought by Mrs. Barrows. She had begun chipping at the cornices of the firm's edifice and now she was swinging at the foundation stones with a pickaxe.

Mr. Martin came now, in his summing up, to the afternoon of Monday, November 2, 1942—just one week ago. On that day, at three P.M., Mrs. Barrows had bounced into his office. "Boo!" she had yelled. "Are you scraping around the bottom of the pickle barrel?" Mr. Martin had looked at her from under his green eyeshade, saying nothing. She had begun to wander about the office, taking it in with her great, popping eyes. "Do you really need *all* these filing cabinets?" she had demanded suddenly. Mr. Martin's heart had jumped. "Each of these files," he had said, keeping his voice even, "plays an indispensable part in the system of F & S." She had brayed at him, "Well, don't tear up the pea patch!" and gone to the door. From there she had bawled, "But you sure have got a lot of fine scrap in here!" Mr. Martin could no longer doubt that the finger was on his beloved department. Her pickaxe was on the upswing, poised for the first blow. It had not come yet; he had received no blue memo from the enchanted Mr. Fitweiler bearing nonsensical instructions deriving from the obscene woman. But there was no doubt in Mr. Martin's mind that one would be forthcoming. He must act quickly. Already a precious week had gone by. Mr. Martin stood up in his living room, still holding his milk glass. "Gentlemen of the jury," he said to himself, "I demand the death penalty for this horrible person."

The next day Mr. Martin followed his routine, as usual. He polished his glasses more often and once sharpened an already sharp pencil, but not even Miss Paird noticed. Only once did he catch sight of his victim; she swept past him in the hall with a patronizing "Hi!" At five-thirty he walked home, as usual, and had a glass of milk, as usual. He had never drunk anything stronger in his life—unless you could count ginger ale. The late Sam Schlosser, the S of F & S, had praised Mr. Martin at a staff meeting several years before for his temperate habits. "Our most efficient worker neither drinks nor smokes," he had said. "The results speak for themselves." Mr. Fitweiler had sat by, nodding approval.

Mr. Martin was still thinking about that red-letter day as he walked over to the Schrafft's on Fifth Avenue near Forty-sixth Street. He got there, as he always did, at eight o'clock. He finished his dinner and the financial page of the *Sun* at a quarter to nine, as he always did. It was his custom after dinner to take a walk. This time he walked down Fifth Avenue at a casual pace. His gloved hands felt moist and warm, his forehead cold. He transferred the Camels from his overcoat to a jacket pocket. He wondered, as he did so, if they did not represent an unnecessary note of strain. Mrs. Barrows smoked only Luckies. It was his idea to puff a few puffs on a Camel (after the rubbing-out), stub it out in the ashtray holding her lipstick-stained Luckies, and thus drag a small red herring across the trail. Perhaps it was not a good idea. It would take time. He might even choke, too loudly.

Mr. Martin had never seen the house on West Twelfth Street where Mrs. Barrows lived, but he had a clear enough picture of it. Fortunately, she had bragged to everybody about her ducky first-floor apartment in the perfectly darling three-story red-brick. There would be no doorman or other attendants; just the tenants of the second and third floors. As he walked along, Mr. Martin realized that he would get there before nine-thirty. He had considered walking north on Fifth Avenue from Schrafft's to a point from which it would take him until ten o'clock to reach the house. At that hour people were less likely to be coming in or going out. But the procedure would have made an awkward loop in the straight thread of his casualness, and he had abandoned it. It was impossible to figure when people would be entering or leaving the house, anyway. There was a great risk at any hour. If he ran into anybody, he would simply have to place the rubbing-out of Ulgine Barrows in the inactive file forever. The same thing would hold true if there were someone in her apartment. In that case he would just say that he had been passing by, recognized her charming house and thought to drop in.

It was eighteen minutes after nine when Mr. Martin turned into Twelfth 10 Street. A man passed him, and a man and a woman talking. There was no one within fifty paces when he came to the house, halfway down the block. He was up the steps and in the small vestibule in no time, pressing the bell under the card that said "Mrs. Ulgine Barrows." When the clicking in the lock started, he jumped forward against the door. He got inside fast, closing the door behind him. A bulb in a lantern hung from the hall ceiling on a chain seemed to give a monstrously bright light. There was nobody on the stair, which went up ahead of him along the left wall. A door opened down the hall in the wall on the right. He went toward it swiftly, on tiptoe.

"Well, for God's sake, look who's here!" bawled Mrs. Barrows, and her braying laugh rang out like the report of a shotgun. He rushed past her like a football tackle, bumping her. "Hey, quit shoving!" she said, closing the door behind them. They were in her living room, which seemed to Mr. Martin to be lighted by a hundred lamps. "What's after you?" she said. "You're as jumpy as a goat." He found he was unable to speak. His heart was wheezing in his throat. "I—yes," he finally brought out. She was jabbering and laughing as she started to help him off with his coat. "No, no," he said. "I'll put it here." He took it off and put it on a chair near the door. "Your hat and gloves, too," she said. "You're in a lady's house." He put his hat on top of the coat. Mrs. Barrows seemed larger than he had thought. He kept his gloves on. "I was passing by," he said. "I recognized—is there anyone here?" She laughed louder than ever. "No," she said, "we're all alone. You're as white as a sheet, you funny man. Whatever *has* come over you? I'll mix you a toddy." She started toward a door across the room. "Scotch-and-soda be all right? But say, you don't drink, do you?" She turned and gave him her amused look. Mr. Martin pulled himself together. "Scotch-and-soda will be all right," he heard himself say. He could hear her laughing in the kitchen.

Mr. Martin looked quickly around the living room for the weapon. He had counted on finding one there. There were andirons and a poker and something in a corner that looked like an Indian club. None of them would do. It couldn't be that way. He began to pace around. He came to a desk. On it lay a metal paper knife with an ornate handle. Would it be sharp enough? He reached for it and knocked over a small brass jar. Stamps spilled out of it and it fell to the floor with a clatter. "Hey," Mrs. Barrows yelled from the kitchen, "are you tearing up the pea patch?" Mr. Martin gave a strange laugh. Picking up the knife, he tried its point against his left wrist. It was blunt. It wouldn't do.

When Mrs. Barrows reappeared, carrying two highballs, Mr. Martin, standing there with his gloves on, became acutely conscious of the fantasy he had wrought. Cigarettes in his pocket, a drink prepared for him—it was all too grossly improbable. It was more than that; it was impossible. Somewhere in the back of his mind a vague idea stirred, sprouted. "For heaven's sake, take off those gloves," said Mrs. Barrows. "I always wear them in the house," said Mr. Martin. The idea began to bloom, strange and wonderful. She put the glasses on a coffee table in front of a sofa and sat on the sofa. "Come over here, you odd little man," she said. Mr. Martin went over and sat beside her. It was difficult getting a cigarette out of the pack of Camels, but he managed it. She held a match for him, laughing. "Well," she said, handing him his drink, "this is perfectly marvelous. You with a drink and a cigarette."

Mr. Martin puffed, not too awkwardly, and took a gulp of the highball. "I drink and smoke all the time," he said. He clinked his glass against hers. "Here's nuts to that old windbag, Fitweiler," he said, and gulped again. The stuff tasted awful, but he made no grimace. "Really, Mr. Martin," she said, her voice and posture changing, "you are insulting our employer." Mrs. Barrows was now all special adviser to the president. "I am preparing a bomb," said Mr. Martin, "which will blow the old goat higher than hell." He had only had a little of the drink, which was not strong. It couldn't be that. "Do you take dope or something?" Mrs. Barrows asked coldly. "Heroin," said Mr. Martin. "I'll be coked to the gills when I bump that old buzzard off." "Mr. Martin!" she shouted, getting to her feet. "That will be all of that. You must go at once." Mr. Martin took another swallow of his drink. He tapped his cigarette out in the ashtray and put the pack of Camels on the coffee table. Then he got up. She stood glaring at him. He walked over and put on his hat and coat. "Not a word about this," he said, and laid an index finger against his lips. All Mrs. Barrows could bring out was "Really!" Mr. Martin put his hand on the doorknob. "I'm sitting in the catbird seat," he said. He stuck his tongue out at her and left. Nobody saw him go.

Mr. Martin got to his apartment, walking, well before eleven. No one saw 15 him go in. He had two glasses of milk after brushing his teeth, and he felt elated. It wasn't tipsiness, because he hadn't been tipsy. Anyway, the walk had worn off all effects of the whisky. He got in bed and read a magazine for a while. He was asleep before midnight.

Mr. Martin got to the office at eight-thirty the next morning, as usual. At a quarter to nine, Ulgine Barrows, who had never before arrived at work before ten, swept into his office. "I'm reporting to Mr. Fitweiler now!" she shouted. "If he turns you over to the police, it's no more than you deserve!" Mr. Martin gave her a look of shocked surprise. "I beg your pardon?" he said. Mrs. Barrows snorted and bounced out of the room, leaving Miss Paird and Joey Hart staring after her. "What's the matter with that old devil now?" asked Miss Paird. "I have no idea," said Mr. Martin, resuming his work. The other two looked at him and then at each other. Miss Paird got up and went out. She walked slowly past the closed door of Mr. Fitweiler's office. Mrs. Barrows was yelling inside, but she was not braying. Miss Paird could not hear what the woman was saying. She went back to her desk.

Forty-five minutes later, Mrs. Barrows left the president's office and went into her own, shutting the door. It wasn't until half an hour later that Mr. Fitweiler sent for Mr. Martin. The head of the filing department, neat, quiet, attentive, stood in front of the old man's desk. Mr. Fitweiler was pale and nervous. He took his glasses off and twiddled them. He made a small, bruffing sound in his throat. "Martin," he said, "you have been with us more than twenty years." "Twenty-two, sir," said Mr. Martin. "In that time," pursued the president, "your work and your—uh—manner have been exemplary." "I trust so, sir," said Mr. Martin. "I have understood, Martin," said Mr. Fitweiler, "that you have never taken a drink or smoked." "That is correct, sir," said Mr. Martin. "Ah, yes." Mr. Fitweiler polished his glasses. "You may describe what you did after leaving the office yesterday, Martin," he said. Mr. Martin allowed less than a second for his bewildered pause. "Certainly, sir," he said. "I walked home. Then I went to Schrafft's for dinner. Afterward I walked home again. I went to bed early, sir, and read a magazine for a while. I was asleep before eleven." "Ah, yes," said Mr. Fitweiler again. He was silent for a moment, searching for the proper words to say to the head of the filing department. "Mrs. Barrows," he said finally, "Mrs. Barrows has worked hard, Martin, very hard. It grieves me to report that she has suffered a severe breakdown. It has taken the form of a persecution complex accompanied by distressing hallucinations." "I am very sorry, sir," said Mr. Martin. "Mrs. Barrows is under the delusion," continued Mr. Fitweiler, "that you visited her last evening and behaved yourself in an—uh—unseemly manner." He raised his hand to silence Mr. Martin's little pained outcry. "It is the nature of these psychological diseases," Mr. Fitweiler said, "to fix upon the least likely and most innocent party as the—uh—source of persecution. These matters are not for the lay mind to grasp, Martin. I've just had my psychiatrist, Dr. Fitch, on the phone. He would not, of course, commit himself, but he made enough generalizations to substantiate my suspicions. I suggested to Mrs. Barrows when she had completed her—uh—story to me this morning, that she visit Dr. Fitch, for I suspected a condition at once. She flew, I regret to say, into a rage, and demanded—uh—requested that I call you on the carpet. You may not know, Martin, but Mrs. Barrows had planned a reorganization of your department—subject to my approval, of course, subject to my approval. This brought you, rather than anyone else, to her mind—but again that is a phenomenon for Dr. Fitch and not for us. So, Martin, I am afraid Mrs. Barrows' usefulness here is at an end." "I am dreadfully sorry, sir," said Mr. Martin.

It was at this point that the door to the office blew open with the suddenness of a gas-main explosion and Mrs. Barrows catapulted through it. "Is the little rat denying it?" she screamed. "He can't get away with that!" Mr. Martin got up and moved discreetly to a point beside Mr. Fitweiler's chair. "You drank and smoked at my apartment," she bawled at Mr. Martin, "and you know it! You called Mr. Fitweiler an old windbag and said you were going to blow him up when you got coked to the gills on your heroin!" She stopped yelling to catch her breath and a new glint came into her popping eyes. "If you weren't such a drab, ordinary little man," she said, "I'd think you'd planned it all. Sticking your tongue out, saying you were sitting in the catbird seat, because you thought no one would believe me when I told it! My God, it's really too perfect!" She brayed loudly and hysterically, and the fury was on her again. She glared at Mr. Fitweiler. "Can't you see how he has tricked us, you old fool? Can't you see his little game?" But Mr. Fitweiler had been surreptitiously pressing all the buttons under the top of his desk and employees of F & S began pouring into the room. "Stockton," said Mr. Fitweiler, "you and Fishbein will take Mrs. Barrows to her home. Mrs. Powell, you will go with them." Stockton, who had played a little football in high school, blocked Mrs. Barrows as she made for Mr. Martin. It took him and Fishbein together to force her out of the door into the hall, crowded with stenographers and office boys. She was still screaming imprecations at Mr. Martin, tangled and contradictory imprecations. The hubbub finally died out down the corridor.

"I regret that this has happened," said Mr. Fitweiler. "I shall ask you to dismiss it from your mind, Martin." "Yes, sir," said Mr. Martin, anticipating his chief's "That will be all" by moving to the door. "I will dismiss it." He went out and shut the door, and his step was light and quick in the hall. When he entered his department he had slowed down to his customary gait, and he walked quietly across the room to the W20 file, wearing a look of studious concentration.

Xu Xi b. 1954

Famine   [2004]

I escape. I board Northwest 18 to New York, via Tokyo. The engine starts, there is no going back. Yesterday, I taught the last English class and left my job of thirty-two years. Five weeks earlier, A-Ma died of heartbreak, within days of my father's sudden death. He was ninety-five, she ninety. Unlike A-Ba, who saw the world by crewing on tankers, neither my mother nor I ever left Hong Kong.

Their deaths rid me of responsibility at last, and I could forfeit my pension and that dreary existence. I am fifty-one and an only child, unmarried.

I never expected my parents to take so long to die.

This meal is *luxurious*, better than anything I imagined.

My colleagues who fly every summer complain of the indignities of travel.   5
Cardboard food, cramped seats, long lines, and these days, too much security nonsense, they say. They fly Cathay, our "national" carrier. This makes me laugh. We have never been a nation; "national" isn't our adjective. *Semantics*, they say, dismissive, just as they dismiss what I say of debt, that it is not an inevitable state, or that children exist to be taught, not spoilt. My colleagues live in overpriced, new, mortgaged flats and indulge 1 to 2.5 children. Most of my students are uneducable.

Back, though, to this in-flight meal. Smoked salmon and cold shrimp, endive salad, strawberries and melon to clean the palate. Then, steak with mushrooms, potatoes *au gratin*, a choice between a shiraz or cabernet sauvignon. Three cheeses, white chocolate mousse, coffee, and port or a liqueur or brandy. Foods from the pages of a novel, perhaps.

My parents ate sparingly, long after we were no longer impoverished, and disdained "unhealthy" Western diets. A-Ba often said that the only thing he really discovered from travel was that the world was hungry, and that there would never be enough food for everyone. It was why, he said, he did not miss the travel when he retired.

I have no complaints of my travels so far.

My complaining colleagues do not fly business. This seat is an *island* of a bed, surrounded by air. I did not mean to fly in dignity, but having never traveled in summer, or at all, I didn't plan months ahead, long before flights filled up. I simply rang the airlines and booked Northwest, the first one that had a seat, only in business class.

Friends and former students, who do fly business when their companies   10
foot the bill, were horrified. *You* paid *full fare? No one does!* I have money, I replied, why shouldn't I? *But you've given up your "rice bowl." Think of the future.*

I hate rice, always have, even though I never left a single grain, because under my father's watchful glare, A-Ma inspected my bowl. Every meal, even after her eyes dimmed.

The Plaza Suite is nine hundred square feet, over three times the size of home. I had wanted the Vanderbilt or Ambassador and would have settled for the Louis XV, but they were all booked, by those more important than I, no doubt. Anyway, this will have to do. "Nothing unimportant" happens here at the Plaza is what their website literature claims.

The porter arrives, and wheels my bags in on a trolley.

My father bought our tiny flat in a village in Shatin with his disability settlement. When he was forty-five and I one, a falling crane crushed his left leg and groin, thus ending his sailing and procreating career. Shatin isn't very rural anymore, but our home has denied progress its due. We didn't get a phone till I was in my thirties.

I tip the porter five dollars and begin unpacking the leather luggage set. 15
There is too much space for my things.

Right about now, you're probably wondering, along with my colleagues,
former students, and friends, *What on earth does she think she's doing?* It was
what my parents shouted when I was twelve and went on my first hunger strike.

My parents were illiterate, both refugees from China's rural poverty. A-Ma
fried tofu at Shatin market. Once A-Ba recovered from his accident, he worked
there also as a cleaner, cursing his fate. They expected me to support them as
soon as possible, which should have been after six years of primary school, the
only compulsory education required by law in the sixties.

As you see, I clearly had no choice but to strike, since my exam results
proved I was smart enough for secondary school. My father beat me, threatened
to starve me. *How dare I*, when others were genuinely hungry, unlike me, the
only child of a tofu seller who always ate. *Did I want him and A-Ma to die of
hunger just to send me to school? How dare I risk their longevity and old age?*

But I was unpacking a Spanish leather suitcase when the past, that country
bumpkin's territory, so rudely interrupted.

Veronica, whom I met years ago at university while taking a literature 20
course, foisted this luggage on me. She runs her family's garment enterprise,
and is married to a banker. Between them and their three children, they own
four flats, three cars, and at least a dozen sets of luggage. Veronica invites me
out to dinner (she always pays) whenever she wants to complain about her
family. Lately, we've dined often.

"Kids," she groaned over our rice porridge, two days before my trip. "My
daughter won't use her brand-new Loewe set because, she says, that's *passé*. All
her friends at Stanford sling these canvas bags with one fat strap. Canvas, imagine. Not even leather."

"Ergonomics," I told her, annoyed at this bland and inexpensive meal. "It's
all about weight and balance." And cost, I knew, because the young overspend
to conform, just as Veronica eats rice porridge because she's overweight and no
longer complains that I'm thin.

She continued. "You're welcome to take the set if you like."

"Don't worry yourself. I can use an old school bag."

"But that's barely a cabin bag! Surely not enough to travel with." 25

In the end, I let her nag me into taking this set, which is more bag than
clothing.

Veronica sounded worried when I left her that evening. "Are you *sure* you'll
be okay?"

And would she worry, I wonder, if she could see me now, here, in this suite,
this enormous space where one night's bill would have taken my parents years,
no, *decades*, to earn and even for me, four years' pay, at least when I first started
teaching in my rural enclave (though you're thinking, of course, quite correctly,
Well, what about inflation, the thing economists cite to dismiss these longings
of an English teacher who has spent her life instructing those who care not a
whit for our "official language," the one they never speak, at least not if they
can choose, especially not now when there is, increasingly, a choice).

My unpacking is done; the past need not intrude. I draw a bath, as one does in English literature, to wash away the heat and grime of both cities in summer. *Why New York?* Veronica asked, at the end of our last evening together. Because, I told her, it will be like nothing I've ever known. For the first time since we've known each other, Veronica actually seemed to envy *me,* although perhaps it was my imagination.

The phone rings, and it's "Guest Relations" wishing to welcome me and   30 offer hospitality. The hotel must wonder, since I grace no social register. I ask for a table at Lutèce tonight. Afterwards, I tip the concierge ten dollars for successfully making the reservation. As you can see, I am no longer an ignorant bumpkin, even though I never left the schools in the New Territories, our urban countryside now that no one farms anymore. Besides, Hong Kong magazines detail lives of the rich and richer so I've read of the famous restaurant and know about the greasy palms of New Yorkers.

I order tea and scones from Room Service. It will hold me till dinner at eight.

The first time I ever tasted tea and scones was at the home of my private student. To supplement income when I enrolled in Teacher Training, I tutored Form V° students who needed to pass the School Certificate English exam. This was the compromise I agreed to with my parents before they would allow me to qualify as a teacher. Oh yes, there was a second hunger strike two years prior, before they would let me continue into Form IV. That time, I promised to keep working in the markets after school with A-Ma, which I did.

Actually, my learning English at all was a stroke of luck, since I was *hardly* at a "name school" of the elite. An American priest taught at my secondary school, so I heard a native speaker. He wasn't a very good teacher, but he paid attention to me because I was the only student who liked the subject. A little attention goes a long way.

Tea and scones! I am *supposed* to be eating, not dwelling on the ancient past. The opulence of the tray Room Service brings far surpasses what that pretentious woman served, mother of the hopeless boy, my first private student of many, who only passed his English exam because he cheated (he paid a friend to sit the exam for him), not that I'd ever tell since he's now a wealthy international businessman of some repute who can hire staff to communicate in English with the rest of the world, since he still cannot, at least not with any credibility. That scone ("from Cherikoff," she bragged) was cold and dry, hard as a rock.

Hot scones, oozing with butter. To ooze. I like the lasciviousness of that   35 word, with its excess of vowels, the way an excess of wealth allows people to waste kindness on me, as my former student still does, every lunar new year, by sending me a *laisee* packet° with a generous check which I deposit in my

---

Form V: "Form" is a British term for a class or level in school, usually ranging from first through sixth.

laisee packet: A red envelope containing a monetary gift, presented in China during holidays or special occasions.

parents' bank account, the way I surrender all my earnings, as any filial and responsible unmarried child should, or so they said.

I eat two scones oozing with butter and savor tea enriched by cream and sugar, here at this "greatest hotel in the world," to vanquish, once and for all, my parents' fear of death and opulence.

Eight does not come soon enough. In the taxi on the way to Lutèce, I ponder the question of pork.

When we were poor but not impoverished, A-Ma once dared to make pork for dinner. It was meant to be a treat, to give me a taste of meat, because I complained that tofu was bland. A-Ba became a vegetarian after his accident and prohibited meat at home; eunuchs are angry people. She dared because he was not eating with us that night, a rare event in our family (I think some sailors he used to know invited him out).

I shat a tapeworm the next morning—almost ten inches long—and she never cooked pork again.

I have since tasted properly cooked pork, naturally, since it's unavoidable in Chinese cuisine. In my twenties, I dined out with friends, despite my parents' objections. But friends marry and scatter; the truth is that there is no one but family in the end, so over time, I submitted to their way of being and seldom took meals away from home, meals my mother cooked virtually till the day she died.

I am distracted. The real question, of course, is whether or not I should order pork tonight.

I did not expect this trip to be fraught with pork!

At Lutèce, I have the distinct impression that the two couples at the next table are talking about me. Perhaps they pity me. People often pitied me my life. *Starved of affection*, they whispered, although why they felt the need to whisper what everyone could hear I failed to understand. All I desired was greater gastronomic variety, but my parents couldn't bear the idea of my eating without them. I ate our plain diet and endured their perpetual skimping because they did eventually learn to leave me alone. That much filial propriety was reasonable payment. I just didn't expect them to *stop* complaining, to fear for what little fortune they had, because somewhere someone was less fortunate than they. That fear made them cling hard to life, forcing me to suffer their fortitude, their good health, and their longevity.

I should walk over to those overdressed people and tell them how things are, about famine, I mean, the way I tried to tell my students, the way my parents dinned it into me as long as they were alive.

Famine has no menu! The waiter waits as I take too long to study the menu. He does not seem patient, making him an oxymoron in his profession. My students would no more learn the oxymoron than they would learn about famine. *Daughter, did you lecture your charges today about famine?* A-Ba would ask every night before dinner. *Yes*, I learned to lie, giving him the answer he needed. This waiter could take a lesson in patience from me.

Finally, I look up at this man who twitches, and do not order pork. *Very good,* he says, as if I should be graded for my literacy in menus. He returns shortly with a bottle of the most expensive red available, and now I *know* the people at the next table are staring. The minute he leaves, the taller of the two men from that table comes over.

"Excuse me, but I believe we met in March? At the U.S. Consulate cocktail in Hong Kong? You're Kwai-sin Ho, aren't you?" He extends his hand. "Peter Martin."

Insulted, it's my turn to stare at this total stranger. I look *nothing* like that simpering socialite who designs wildly fashionable hats that are all the rage in Asia. Hats! We don't have the weather for hats, especially not those things, which are good for neither warmth nor shelter from the sun.

Besides, what use are hats for the hungry?

I do not accept his hand. "I'm her twin sister," I lie. "Kwai-sin and I are 50 estranged."

He looks like he's about to protest, but retreats. After that, they don't stare, although I am sure they discuss me now that I've contributed new gossip for those who are nurtured by the crumbs of the rich and famous. But at least I can eat in peace.

It's my outfit, probably. Kwai-sin Ho is famous for her *cheongsams,* which is all she ever wears, the way I do. It was my idea. When we were girls together in school, I said the only thing I'd ever wear when I grew up was the *cheongsam,* the shapely dress with side slits and a neck-strangling collar. She grimaced and said they weren't fashionable, that only spinster schoolteachers and prostitutes wore them, which, back in the sixties, wasn't exactly true, but Kwai-sin was never too bright or imaginative.

That was long ago, before she became Kwai-sin in the *cheongsam* once these turned fashionable again, long before her father died and her mother became the mistress of a prominent businessman who whisked them into the strato-sphere high above mine. For a little while, she remained my friend, but then we grew up, she married one of the shipping Hos, and became the socialite who refused, albeit politely, to recognize me the one time we bumped into each other at some function in Hong Kong.

So now, vengeance is mine. I will not entertain the people who fawn over her and possess no powers of recognition.

Food is getting sidelined by memory. This is unacceptable. I cannot allow 55 all these intrusions. I must get back to the food, which is, after all, the point of famine.

This is due to a lack of diligence, as A-Ma would say, this lazy meandering from what's important, this succumbing to sloth. My mother was terrified of sloth, almost as much as she was terrified of my father.

She used to tell me an old legend about sloth.

There once was a man so lazy he wouldn't even lift food to his mouth. When he was young, his mother fed him, but as his mother aged, she couldn't. So he marries a woman who will feed him as his mother did. For a time, life is bliss.

Then one day, his wife must return to her village to visit her dying mother. "How will I eat?" he exclaims in fright. The wife conjures this plan. She bakes a gigantic cookie and hangs it on a string around his neck. All the lazy man must do is bend forward and eat. "Wonderful!" he says, and off she goes, promising to return.

On the first day, the man nibbles the edge of the cookie. Each day, he nibbles 60 further. By the fourth day, he's eaten so far down there's no more cookie unless he turns it, which his wife expected he would since he could do this with his mouth.

However, the man's so lazy he lies down instead and waits for his wife's return. As the days pass, his stomach growls and begins to eat itself. Yet the man still won't turn the cookie. By the time his wife comes home, the lazy man has starved to death.

Memory causes such unaccountable digressions! There I was in Lutèce, noticing that people pitied me. Pity made my father livid, which he took out on A-Ma and me. Anger was his one escape from timidity. He wanted no sympathy for either his dead limb or useless genitals.

Perhaps people find me odd rather than pitiful. I will describe my appearance and let you judge. I am thin but not emaciated and have strong teeth. This latter feature is most unusual for a Hong Kong person of my generation. Many years ago, a dentist courted me. He taught me well about oral hygiene, trained as he had been at an American university. Unfortunately, he was slightly rotund, which offended A-Ba. I think A-Ma wouldn't have minded the marriage, but she always sided with my father, who believed it wise to marry one's own physical type (illiteracy did not prevent him from developing philosophies, as you've already witnessed). I was then in my mid-thirties. After the dentist, there were no other men and as a result, I never left home, which is our custom for unmarried women and men, a loathsome custom but difficult to overthrow. We all must pick our battles, and my acquiring English, which my parents naturally knew not a word, was a sufficiently drastic defiance to last a lifetime, or at least till they expired.

This dinner at Lutèce has come and gone, and you haven't tasted a thing. It's what happens when we converse overmuch and do not concentrate on the food. At home, we ate in the silence of A-Ba's rage.

What a shame, but never mind, I promise to share the bounty next time. 65 This meal must have been good because the bill is in the thousands. I pay by traveler's checks because, not believing in debt, I own no credit cards.

Last night's dinner weighs badly, despite my excellent digestion, so I take a long walk late in the afternoon and end up in Chelsea. New York streets are dirtier than I imagined. Although I did not really expect pavements of gold, in my deepest fantasies, there did reign a glitter and sheen.

No one talks to me here.

The air is fetid with the day's leftover heat and odors. Under a humid, darkening sky, I almost trip over a body on the corner of Twenty-fourth and Seventh. It cannot be a corpse! Surely cadavers aren't left to rot in the streets.

A-Ma used to tell of a childhood occurrence in her village. An itinerant had stolen food from the local pig trough. The villagers caught him, beat him senseless, cut off his tongue and arms, and left him to bleed to death behind the rubbish heap. In the morning, my mother was at play, and while running, tripped over the body. She fell into a blood pool beside him. The corpse's eyes were open.

He surely didn't mean to steal, she always said in the telling, her eyes burning 70 from the memory. *Try to forget,* my father would say. My parents specialized in memory. They both remained lucid and clearheaded till they died.

But this body moves. It's a man awakening from sleep. He mumbles something. Startled, I move away. He is still speaking. I think he's saying he's hungry.

I escape. A taxi whisks me back to my hotel, where my table is reserved at the restaurant.

The ceiling at the Oak Room is roughly four times the height of an average basketball player. The ambience is not as seductive as promised by the Plaza's literature. The problem with reading the wrong kind of literature is that you are bound to be disappointed.

This is a man's restaurant, with a menu of many steaks. Hemingway and Fitzgerald used to eat here. Few of my students have heard of these two, and none of them will have read a single book by either author.

As an English teacher, especially one who was not employed at a "name 75 school" of the elite, I became increasingly marginal. Colleagues and friends converse in Cantonese, the only official language out of our three that people live as well as speak. The last time any student read an entire novel was well over twenty years ago. English literature is not on anyone's exam roster anymore; to desire it in a Chinese colony is as irresponsible as it was of me to master it in our former British one.

Teaching English is little else than a linguistic requirement. Once, it was my passion and flight away from home. Now it is merely my entrée to this former men's club.

But I must order dinner and stop thinking about literature.

The entrées make my head spin, so I turn to the desserts. There is no gooseberry tart! Ever since *David Copperfield,* I have wanted to taste a gooseberry tart (or perhaps it was another book, I don't remember). I tell the boy with the water jug this.

He says. "The magician, madam?"

"The orphan," I reply.   80

He stands, openmouthed, without pouring water. What is this imbecility of the young? They neither serve nor wait.

The waiter appears. "Can I help with the menu?"

"Why?" I snap. "It isn't heavy."

But what upsets me is the memory of my mother's story, which I'd long forgotten until this afternoon, just as I hoped to forget about the teaching of English literature, about the uselessness of the life I prepared so hard for.

The waiter hovers. "Are you feeling okay?"   85

I look up at the sound of his voice and realize my hands are shaking. Calming myself, I say, "*Au jus.* The prime rib, please, and escargots to start," and on and on I go, ordering in the manner of a man who retreats to a segregated club, who indulges in oblivion because he can, who shuts out the stirrings of the groin and the heart.

I wake to a ringing phone. Housekeeping wants to know if they may clean. It's already past noon. This must be jet lag. I tell Housekeeping, Later.

It's so *comfortable* here that I believe it is possible to forget.

I order brunch from Room Service. Five-star hotels in Hong Kong serve brunch buffets on weekends. The first time I went to one, Veronica paid. We were both students at university. She wasn't wealthy, but her parents gave her spending money, whereas my entire salary (I was already a working teacher by then) belonged to my parents. The array of food made my mouth water. *Pace yourself,* Veronica said. *It's all you can eat.* I wanted to try everything, but gluttony frightened me.

Meanwhile, A-Ba's voice. *After four or more days without food, your stomach*   90
begins to eat itself, and his laugh, dry and caustic.

But I was choosing brunch.

Mimosa. Smoked salmon. Omelet with Swiss cheese and chives. And salad, the expensive kind that's imported back home, crisp Romaine in a Caesar. Room Service asks what I'd like for dessert, so I say chocolate ice-cream sundae. Perhaps I'm more of a bumpkin than I care to admit. My colleagues, former students, and friends would consider my choices boring, unsophisticated, lacking in culinary imagination. They're right, I suppose, since everything I've eaten since coming to New York I could just as easily have obtained back home. They can't understand, though. It's not what but *how much.* How opulent. The opulence is what counts to stop the cannibalism of internal organs.

Will that be all?

I am tempted to say, Bring me an endless buffet, whatever your chef concocts, whatever your tongues desire.

How long till my money runs out, my finite account, ending this sweet   95
exile?

Guest Relations knocks, insistent. I have not let anyone in for three days. I open the door wide to show the manager that everything is fine, that their room is not wrecked, that I am not crazy even if I'm not on the social register. If you read the news, as I do, you know it's necessary to allay fears. So I do, because I do not wish to give the wrong impression. I am not a diva or an excessively famous person who trashes hotel rooms because she can.

I say, politely, that I've been a little unwell, nothing serious, and to please have Housekeeping stop in now. The "please" is significant; it shows I am not odd, that I am, in fact, cognizant of civilized language in English. The manager withdraws, relieved.

For dinner tonight, I decide on two dozen oysters, lobster, and filet mignon. I select a champagne and the wines, one white and one red. Then, it occurs to me that since this is a suite, I can order enough food for a party, so I tell Room Service that there will be a dozen guests for dinner, possibly more. *Very good,* he says, and asks how many extra bottles of champagne and wine, to which I reply, As many as needed.

My students will be my guests. They more or less were visitors during those years I tried to teach. You mustn't think I was always disillusioned, though I seem so now. To prove it to you I'll invite all my colleagues, the few friends I have, like Veronica, the dentist who courted me and his wife and two children, even Kwai-sin and my parents. I bear no grudges; I am not bitter towards them. What I'm uncertain of is whether or not they will come to my supper.

This room, this endless meal, can save me. I feel it. I am vanquishing my   100 fear of death and opulence.

There was a time we did not care about opulence and we dared to speak of death. You spoke of famine because everyone knew the stories from China were true. Now, even in this country, people more or less know. You could educate students about starvation in China or Africa or India because they knew it to be true, because they saw the hunger around them, among the beggars in our streets, and for some, even in their own homes. There was a time it was better *not* to have space, or things to put in that space, and to dream of having instead, because no one had much, except royalty and movie stars and they were *meant* to be fantasy—untouchable, unreal—somewhere in a dream of manna and celluloid.

But you can't speak of famine anymore. Anorexia's fashionable and desirably profitable on runways, so students simply *can't see the hunger.* My colleagues and friends also can't, and refuse to speak of it, changing the subject to what they prefer to see. Even our journalists can't seem to see, preferring the reality they fashion rather than the reality that is. I get angry, but then, when I'm calm, I am simply baffled. Perhaps my parents, and friends and colleagues and memory, are right, that I *am* too stubborn, perhaps even too slothful because instead of *seeing* reality, I've hidden in my parents' home, in my life as a teacher, even though the years were dreary and long, when what I truly wanted, what I desired, was to embrace the opulence, forsake the hunger, but was too lazy to turn the cookie instead.

I mustn't be angry at them, by which I mean all the "thems" I know and don't know, the big impersonal "they." Like a good English teacher I tell my students, you *must* define the "they." Students are students and continue to make the same mistakes, and all I can do is remind them that "they" are you and to please, please, try to remember because language is a root of life.

Most of the people can't be wrong all the time. Besides, whose fault is it if the dream came true? Postdream is like postmodern; no one understands it, but everyone condones its existence.

Furthermore, what you can't, or won't see, *doesn't* exist.   105

Comfort, like food, exists, *surrounds* me here.

Not wishing to let anger get the better of me, I eat. Like the Romans, I disgorge and continue. It takes hours to eat three lobsters and three steaks, plus consume five glasses of champagne and six of wine, yet still the food is not enough.

The guests arrive and more keep coming. Who would have thought all these people would show up, all these people I thought I left behind. Where do they come from? My students, colleagues, the dentist and his family, a horde of strangers. Even Kwai-sin and her silly hats, and do you know something, we *do* look a little alike, so Peter Martin wasn't completely wrong. I changed my language to change my life, but still the past throngs, bringing all these people and their Cantonese chatter. The food is not enough, the food is never enough.

Room Service obliges round the clock.

Veronica arrives and I feel a great relief, because the truth is, I no longer 110
cared for her anymore when all we ate was rice porridge. It was mean-spirited, I was ungrateful, forgetting that once she fed me my first buffet, teasing my appetite. *Come out, travel,* she urged over the years. It's not her fault I stayed at home, afraid to abandon my responsibility, traveling only in my mind.

Finally, my parents arrive. My father sits down first to the feast. His leg is whole, and sperm gushes out from between his legs. *It's not so bad here,* he says, and gestures for my mother to join him. This is good. A-Ma will eat if A-Ba does, they're like that, those two. My friends don't understand, not even Veronica. She repeats now what she often has said, that my parents are "controlling." Perhaps, I say, but that's unimportant. I'm only interested in not being responsible anymore.

The noise in the room is deafening. We can barely hear each other above the din. Cantonese is a noisy language, unlike Mandarin or English, but it is alive. This suite that was too empty is stuffed with people, all needing to be fed.

I gaze at the platters of food, piled in this space with largesse. What does it matter if there *are* too many mouths to feed? A phone call is all it takes to get more food, and more. I am fifty-one and have waited too long to eat. They're right, they're all right. If I give in, if I let go, I will vanquish my fears. *This* is bliss, truly.

A-Ma smiles at the vast quantities of food. This pleases me because she so rarely smiles. She says, *Not like lazy cookie man, hah?*

Feeling benevolent, I smile at my parents. *No, not like him,* I say. *Now, eat.* 115

PART **3**

Approaching POETRY

Photo: Paul Abdoo/Getty

Overleaf: Poet, author, and musician Joy Harjo compares writing poetry to "singing on paper." She found her own poetic voice in college in the 1970s and has published numerous volumes of award-winning poetry and prose since then. A Native American of the Muskogee Creek Nation, Joy is a native of Oklahoma, where she has fought for the rights of indigenous people. (See p. 1064 for a short biography.)

Poetry is a conversation with the world; poetry is a conversation with the words on the page in which you allow those words to speak back to you; and poetry is a conversation with yourself.

Naomi Shihab Nye

(American Poet; see pp. 645 and 1073)

Reading Poetry CHAPTER 13
Realizing the Richness in Poems

Why would a person feel suddenly compelled to write a poem? After the events of September 11, 2001, thousands of poems were written, sent, stored away, stuck in a wallet or purse, pasted in a scrapbook. Students took time out from their usual classroom studies and wrote poems. Parents sent their poems to their children away at school or gone from the nest. Poems expressed by "nonpoets" showed up on Web sites and subway walls, in newsletters, within in-house publications, and during school announcements, and in memos, letters, and e-mails. People from every walk of life wrote and expressed their reactions, what they were feeling. Very few if any of us who are not fiction writers or playwrights decide one day to sit down and write a novel or a play. And yet time and time again, people who do not consider themselves poets write poems. Why? And what might that say about the nature and value of poetry—about what poetry is and what poetry does?

WHAT IS POETRY?

We can usually tell someone what a novel, a play, or an essay is, but a poem can be baffling to explain. It can't be defined as writing that has meter: A lot of poetry is nonmetrical. It's not confined to writing that rhymes, for many poems do not use rhyme. Though most poetry is written in lines, prose poems don't have line divisions. Much poetry uses figurative language and is intense and emotional—but the same is true for powerful prose. Whatever characteristics one tries to apply are never typical of all poetry or exclusive to poetry alone. So, what is this thing we call poetry?

Those we would think ought to know usually offer personal responses: E. E. Cummings said that poetry is "dancing on your own grave." Ezra Pound purportedly said it is "what poets write." Emily Dickinson described poetry by its effect: "If I read a book [and] it makes my whole body so cold no fire ever can warm me, I know THAT is poetry. If I feel physically as if the top of my head were taken off, I know THAT is poetry. These are the only ways I know it. Is there any other way?"

WHAT DOES POETRY DO?

Poetry Says "AH-H-H"   Maybe a better way to approach the question "What is poetry?" is to ask "What does poetry do?" Poetry often comes from some deep impulse or an idea that the writer needs or wants to express; no other form of expression is sufficient under the circumstances. Lucille Clifton once said, "Poetry began when somebody walked off a savanna or out of a cave and looked up at the sky with wonder and said, 'Ah-h-h!' *That* was the first poem. The urge toward 'Ah-h-h' is very human, it's in everybody."

Poetry Crosses Boundaries   Poetry that has an emotional edge often crosses, or even eliminates, boundaries. We are all citizens in the culture of joy, pain, anger, love, fear, despair, hope. Every one of us carries the emotions of every other one of us. Our situations and stories and conflicts may differ, but the news from the heart comes to each of us. And though we can't claim "I know just how you feel," we can say with confidence, "I, too, have known that feeling."

Poetry Gives Voice   And poetry gives voice. For many of us in our day-to-day lives, voices come at us—from the news media, sales pitches, movies, and general information overload. It often seems our own voices can't be heard. Poetry offers a chance to speak, and speak from a valued part of ourselves. The words are our words, the rhythms are our rhythms, the clumsiness and sophistication of phrasings are ours, the sounds, the tones, the attempts to be artful are ours.

Poetry Is Part of Our Lives   Former poet laureate Rita Dove has stated, "[I want] to help people see that poetry is not something above them or somehow distant; it's part of their very lives. I would like to remind people that we *have* an interior life—even if we don't talk about it because it's not expedient, because it's not cool, because it's potentially embarrassing—and without that interior life, we are shells, we are nothing." Is that also why, under a sense of urgency, many feel the impulse to express themselves in poetry? Do they suddenly experience that connection to their inner lives? Do thoughts and feelings rise up and ask, even demand, to be expressed, and expressed in a person's own voice?

WHY READ POETRY?

Effects of Poetry   Poetry gives the poet a voice, but why do others read poetry? There are several reasons. Some people read poetry to hear that what they themselves are moved by and want to express is something others do too. Some read poetry to relish an artist's craftsmanship, to experience the beauty of the words and sounds and pictures through which a poem expresses emotions and ideas or tells a story. Others feel life with greater intensity through a particular poem and open themselves to wider and more inclusive experiences. Many people read poetry to be challenged, to be shaken, to be comforted.

Types of Poetry   Traditionally poetry has been classified in three major types: *narrative*, poems that follow a sequence of events; *dramatic*, plays written in verse or poems that use techniques from drama, such as rising action, climax, and dialogue; and *lyric*, usually shorter poems focusing on a specific subject and characterized by melody and intensity of feelings. A number of the poems in this book tell stories. Many of the rest are lyric poems or combine narrative with lyric.

Some poems and some kinds of poetry you will like better than others, but we hope that you give them all a chance and remain open to the variety of cultures and experiences they embody.

ACTIVE READING: Poetry

The essence of poetry is elusive. There is no one way to pin it down. Although that may be intimidating, it is also part of the appeal, part of the seductiveness of poetry. We enter the world of a poem, every poem, not really knowing what to expect. And whenever we enter something new—whether an unfamiliar city, or a new job, or a new relationship—we tend to feel uncertain. We have to look around. We have to be attentive. Here are some suggestions for reading poetry with an active imagination.

- *Read straight through.* Go straight through a poem the first time you read it. If you wonder about a word or want to savor a line, stop only briefly. Then keep going. Get a feel for the poem without worrying about what you don't know or understand.

- *Look and listen.* Be attentive to everything in and about the poem. Start with its shape, the way the poem appears on the page. Listen to its sounds—the way it sounds when it's read aloud, the rhythms, the word sounds, and the combinations of sounds. Look for what it helps you see—the mental pictures called up by some of the words.

- *Watch the words.* After noting shape and sounds, start paying attention to what the words say—not what the whole poem means, but what the words say. Don't be overly eager to figure out what a poem "means," especially some deep, "hidden" meaning. When you walk through a wood, you don't keep saying, "What does that tree mean?" or "What does that stone mean?" You accept them for what they are. So it should be with poetry: Look at the words, listen for what they say, and understand them as best you can. And if at first you don't understand all that much, don't worry—there are many things in a poem that you can experience even before you "understand" it.

- *Interact with the work.* Reading a poem differs from reading a newspaper or an e-mail message or a textbook. You usually read those to glean some information or ideas. Many poems, of course, also contain information and ideas. But they can do other things: They can lead us to feel intensely, to experience deeply, to perceive freshly, to extend our understanding of experiences different from our own, and to affirm our own ideas, feelings, and experiences.

- *Take in what is happening.* Consider what the speaker or primary character in the poem is experiencing, dealing with, going through, or feeling, much as you would with a character in a work of fiction or drama.

REREADING: Poetry

Rereading is just as important for poetry as for fiction, perhaps more so. Reread until you've internalized parts of the poem. Focus on something different each time you go back. If you're open to the poem, it will give and give. Here are some suggestions for rereading.

- *Slow down.* You have to slow down to read a poem. You can't speed-read a poem any more than you can speed-listen to your favorite recordings. So slow down and listen: Listen for, and to, the poem.

- *Read aloud.* Many poems are meant to be heard. Their sounds and rhythms need to be read aloud. In poet Robert Pinsky's phrase, you should "say the poem" so the poem comes out from within you as you vocalize the poem and feel the words, phrases, and rhythms in your mouth, the way you did as a kid when you kept saying certain words over and over just because they felt good.

- *Hear the "music."* Poems work with what is often called the musicality of language, by blending the sounds and rhythms of words and word connections. It's not unlike a song lyric together with its music, but in this case the poem is aspiring to music through the sounds and rhythms of language.

- *Focus on what catches your attention.* You might be drawn to a particular image, how it alters your usual perception of something. Maybe you like the sounds of the language or the way the rhythm shifts or remains regular in every line. Maybe the poem is funny or poignant or both. You don't have to have a masterful grasp of the whole poem to notice things within it or wonder about it or begin talking about it. Paying passionate attention to what is actually in a poem is a wise way to start.

- *Follow the sentences.* The sentences in the poem may be broken up into lines, but they are still sentences. Get their sense correct. If the order of words in a sentence is inverted, it's important to pay attention to cues that identify what is subject and what is object. If a poet uses incomplete sentences, "fragments," try to figure out the purpose behind them. After working out where sentences start and stop, focus on the lines: Begin noticing what the line divisions and line breaks add to the experience of the sentence.

- *Ask questions.* You can, of course, ask what a poem means, but you don't need to start with that question. Try instead asking questions such as, What is going on in this poem? What is this poem doing? Why am I drawn to that phrase or line? What is the poem connecting me with or challenging me about? How is the poem shifting my usual way of perceiving things and leading me to reconsider the ways I've thought and felt?

The imagery of one line exudes a sparkling fountain of energy that fills your spirit.

Jimmy Santiago Baca
(American Poet; see pp. 605 and 1055)

CHAPTER 14 Words and Images
Seizing on Sense and Sight

Perhaps you are hesitant about your ability to understand a poem or even have the feeling that a poem is in some code you have to break. Or perhaps you think that poetry can "just mean anything." With prose, we usually gain our understanding by reading whole units of focused meaning (sentences and paragraphs). But poems are often not written that way. Maybe that's a reason why we feel poems are difficult to grasp. Poems ask us to look both at and within lines and sentences, to focus our attention on particular words and particular images in them.

Poets Rely on Words   To comprehend a poem, then, requires attention to its words. That's obvious enough. But when you read poetry, you not only have to look at words but also need to pay closer attention than you usually would. *Diction*, the choice and arrangement of words, is an important aspect of style, whether in prose (see pp. 225–28) or poetry. This chapter's aim is to enable you to enjoy and appreciate poetry by developing confidence in your ability to work with the rewarding complexities of words and images.

Poets Are Fascinated by Words   Like most writers, poets are fascinated by words—their look, their sounds, their textures, the associations clustered around them, what they evoke, their power. Poets roll words around on their tongues and in their minds, experimenting with different combinations, playing with them, listening to the results. They care about their meanings, and the uses and abuses of those meanings. They look for ways to put everything into exactly the right words.

Poets Create with Words   Poets, just like fiction writers, work with words in three ways: to report ("There's a dog at the back door"), to describe ("There's a wet old dog at the back door"), and to provide a new or fresh way of perceiving ("There's a dog at the back door that looks as if it's been dragged through a car wash"). All three are found in the opening lines of Robert Hayden's "Those Winter Sundays" (p. 466). The speaker reports: "Sundays too my father got up early." He describes: "cracked hands that ached / from labor in the weekday weather." And he gives us a fresh way of perceiving: "hear the cold splintering, breaking." Watching for those uses as you continue reading poetry can help you be alert to and responsive to the ways words work.

READING FOR DENOTATION

What Words Mean   In focusing attention on words, it's important to realize that words have two dimensions, denotation and connotation. *Denotation* refers to what words mean, to their dictionary definitions, what they mean objectively and intellectually. It may seem obvious that, in reading, we need to pay attention to what the words mean, but sometimes it takes effort, and at times you will probably need to use different dictionaries. In other kinds of reading, the context may convey adequately the general meaning of an unfamiliar word, but in reading poetry, approximate meanings can lead to a misreading. And sometimes in poetry the secondary, less familiar meanings of a word may be as important as, or more important than, the first meaning.

Definitions   Denotations pose a bigger problem when you read poems from the past or from a culture different from your own. You already know you need to look up unfamiliar words. Much trickier are words that look familiar but seem unusual in the context of the poem. In some cases, often in poems written several centuries ago, word meanings have changed or previous meanings are no longer used. A desk dictionary may indicate such changes, but a better resource is the *Oxford English Dictionary*, often called the *OED*. It is a historical dictionary found in most libraries and online through many libraries. It gives you what words meant in earlier times as well as now, and it uses illustrative quotations to show when each meaning was in use and, if it is no longer current, when that usage ceased.

Consider the following lines from Shakespeare's *Julius Caesar*, where Portia asks Brutus what has been bothering him.

> Is Brutus sick? And is it physical
> To walk unbraced and suck up the humors
> Of the dank morning? (2.1.262)

Both *physical* and *humor* are familiar words, but none of our current uses seems to fit these lines. Looking in an ordinary desk dictionary won't help, but using the *OED* does. If you look up *physical* as an adjective, under definition 2b you'll find, "Beneficial to health; curative, remedial" (if this seems odd, think of the word *physician*). The line from *Julius Caesar* is quoted as an illustration of this definition. If you look up *humor* (it appears under the British spelling *humour*), the first entry fits — "Moisture; damp exhalation; vapour." The last example cited for this usage is from 1697 — this is the latest example of this usage that has been found in print. By then that meaning may already have disappeared from spoken language, or it may have lingered in speech a bit longer; in any case, it died out completely around 1700, so present-day dictionaries do not bother to include it (not even as an "archaic" usage).

APPROACHING THE READING

The following is a poem about the speaker's memory of how his father got up early every morning in the winter to warm the cold house for the rest of the family. The speaker confronts his realization that he took all that the father did for granted. The denotations of the words probably seem straightforward and clear, even from your first reading. But spend some time looking up words that you're unfamiliar with or that look important and perhaps might mean more than the context conveys (perhaps the words *banked*, *chronic*, *austere*, and *offices*; and what about *blueblack*?). Remember too that denotation involves not just the meaning of individual words but the meaning of words combined with other words: Think about the meaning of "chronic angers" and "love's austere and lonely offices."

APPROACHING THE AUTHOR

Robert Hayden had severe vision problems as a child, preventing him from participating in activities like sports. He compensated by reading voraciously and developing his talents as a writer.

For more about him, see page 1065.

Robert Hayden   1913–1980

Those Winter Sundays   [1962]

Sundays too my father got up early
and put his clothes on in the blueblack cold,
then with cracked hands that ached
from labor in the weekday weather made
banked fires blaze. No one ever thanked him.   5

I'd wake and hear the cold splintering, breaking.
When the rooms were warm, he'd call,

and slowly I would rise and dress,
fearing the chronic angers of that house,

Speaking indifferently to him,   10
who had driven out the cold
and polished my good shoes as well.
What did I know, what did I know
of love's austere and lonely offices?

REFLECTING ON WHAT YOU'VE READ

1. In addition to "important" words such as *banked, chronic, austere, offices,* and *blueblack*, pay attention to easily overlooked "little" words such as *those* in the title and *too* in line 1. Why do they matter? Discuss their effect and impact.

2. What is suggested in line 9 by the phrase "chronic angers of that house"? Why did the son speak "indifferently" to his father? What does word choice indicate about relationships in the family?

3. What do you make of the last five words of the poem? Explain why you think they are effective or ineffective as the ending of this poem.

4. What is the effect of the repetition in line 13? How is what the speaker now knows different from what he thought as a child?

One could readily argue that the success of this poem in all its elements and effects is the result of Hayden's accomplished use of diction. Notice the beautifully muted combinations of words, each of which reveals a profound intelligence quietly coming to life-changing realizations throughout the poem: "Sundays too" rather than "Even on Sunday"; "the blueblack cold"—the words and order mysteriously convey both how the cold felt to the father and how the son came to recognize the depth and continuity of the father's responsibility; "banked" starts the fifth line and rhymes with "thanked" later in the line, gently emphasizing the contrast between duty fulfilled and a lack of gratitude. "Chronic angers" (line 9) is striking in combining a technical word, *chronic*, with a common one, *angers*. The result leads us to realize and imagine the atmosphere the speaker grew up within. And the unusual combination of the word *love* with *austere, lonely,* and *offices* provokes us to reflect on and reconsider what real love is.

READING FOR CONNOTATION

What Words Imply   Of course, words are more than their dictionary definitions. Words also have **connotations**, the shared or communal implications and associations they carry subjectively in addition to their objective dictionary meanings. Two words may have almost the same denotation but very different connotations; the associations a reader connects with them could make one suitable and the other unsuitable in a certain situation. For example, in "Those Winter Sundays," "working in the weekday weather" means almost the same thing, denotatively, as "labor in the weekday weather." But Hayden uses *labor* in line 4 probably because its connotations suggest work of a harder and more fatiguing kind than *working* does, and that's what Hayden wants to say about his father.

APPROACHING THE READING

As you read the following poem about the lives of an elderly couple, pay particular attention to the words—to what the denotations of familiar and unfamiliar words and the connotations of simple, ordinary words contribute to the poem and to your experience of it.

APPROACHING THE AUTHOR

When **Gwendolyn Brooks**'s parents discovered her talent for writing poetry, they provided her with a desk and bookshelves and began excusing her from many household chores. Their support proved beneficial: By age sixteen, Brooks had published nearly seventy-five poems.

For more about her, see page 1057.

© Bettmann/CORBIS

Gwendolyn Brooks   1917–2000

The Bean Eaters   [1960]

They eat beans mostly, this old yellow pair.
Dinner is a casual affair.
Plain chipware on a plain and creaking wood,
Tin flatware.

Two who are Mostly Good.   5
Two who have lived their day,
But keep on putting on their clothes
And putting things away.

And remembering . . .
Remembering, with twinklings and twinges,   10
As they lean over the beans in their rented back room that is full of beads
    and receipts and dolls and cloths, tobacco crumbs, vases and fringes.

REFLECTING ON WHAT YOU'VE READ

1. In your own words, sum up briefly what the elderly couple and their daily lives are like. Do you know of people like them and in their situation? If so, what do they have in common with the poem's couple?

2. Look up any words whose denotations are not clear to you. What words are particularly important for their connotations?

3. Brooks chose the words she did for both denotations and connotations. Consider why they are appropriate for this couple, their daily lives, the setting, and their circumstances. Pick out some uses of diction that seem particularly striking or important and explain why you feel this way about them.

The denotations of words in "The Bean Eaters" are likely clear to you, but maybe not *flatware* (utensils, such as knives, forks, and spoons) or *chipware* (you are not likely to find it in a dictionary; it appears to be a term Brooks coined for chipped and cracked china). You can probably figure out most of the words, including *chipware*, from the context. More important are the words' connotations.

Words Carry Associations   What beans are, denotatively, is not the crucial thing; what they suggest and what we associate them with are. The feeling or association generated by a word depends to some extent on the background and experiences of the readers. Brooks probably expects that readers will associate beans with being inexpensive and ordinary. Given those connotations, it seems safe to conclude that this couple's eating beans *mostly* suggests that they are poor. *Yellow* may factually, denotatively, describe the color of their skin, but equally important are the feelings of age, health, and fragility that many people associate with the word *yellow*. The facts of what chipware and tin flatware are do not solely create their effect as words in the poem; the way we perceive them as inexpensive, utilitarian products does.

Denotatively, "rented back room" simply states that the room the couple lives in is not in the front of the building and is owned by someone else. But the connotations are meaningful. Back rooms are cheaper (and less desirable) than front rooms. Presumably, Brooks's two characters are renting a back room because they cannot afford even to rent a front room, let alone buy their own home.

Words Convey Feelings   Finally, the things listed in the last line are more important to the couple—and to us—for the feelings they evoke than for what they are in and of themselves. This old pair lives more in the past than in the present, and memories cluster with "twinklings and twinges" around the objects that fill the room. Perhaps you have more—or other—connotations for the words in the poem. Bring them into the reading of it and discuss how they differ from those we present here. Also, think about what part your background plays in your response to the poem.

READING FOR IMAGES

Our earliest knowledge of the world comes through the senses. Babies become acquainted with objects by looking at them, touching them, putting them in their mouths; everything to them is wonderfully sensate and interesting. As poet W. S. Merwin has said, "A child picks up a fallen leaf and doesn't say, what is it good for? To the child, a leaf is what it is." The senses remain crucial sources of knowledge for us as adults as well, but as we get older, we become accustomed to the things we encounter. One of the beauties of poetry is that it often reconnects us to the world of our senses and thus to a world of wonder.

Literary Images   In literature, an *image* is a word or group of words that evokes in our imagination a representation of an object or action that can be known by one or more of the senses — sight, hearing, touch, smell, taste. Poetry relies heavily on images. To comprehend and *experience* what is going on in poems, being attentive to images is vital.

APPROACHING THE READING

The sights and especially the sounds of night at a lakeshore cottage come alive in the following poem. It is rich with images that enable you to be a part of the scene. Enjoy the way your imagination converts the words into images.

APPROACHING THE AUTHOR

© Bettmann/CORBIS

Maxine Kumin and her husband lived on a two-hundred-acre farm in New Hampshire, where they bred Arabian and quarter horses. When Maxine Kumin was seventy-three, she suffered an accident while preparing a horse for competition and broke her neck. She survived and regained mobility (contrary to doctors' predictions) and went on to write about her recovery in a memoir called *Inside the Halo and Beyond* (2000).
    For more about her, see page 1070.

Maxine Kumin 1925–2014

The Sound of Night   [1961]

And now the dark comes on, all full of chitter noise.
Birds huggermugger crowd the trees,
the air thick with their vesper cries,
and bats, snub seven-pointed kites,

skitter across the lake, swing out,   5
squeak, chirp, dip, and skim on skates
of air, and the fat frogs wake and prink
wide-lipped, noisy as ducks, drunk
on the boozy black, gloating chink-chunk.

And now on the narrow beach we defend ourselves from dark.   10
The cooking done, we build our firework
bright and hot and less for outlook
than for magic, and lie in our blankets
while night nickers around us. Crickets
chorus hallelujahs; paws, quiet   15
and quick as raindrops, play on the stones
expertly soft, run past and are gone;
fish pulse in the lake; the frogs hoarsen.

Now every voice of the hour—the known, the supposed, the strange,
the mindless, the witted, the never seen—   20
sing, thrum, impinge, and rearrange
endlessly; and debarred from sleep we wait
for the birds, importantly silent,
for the crease of first eye-licking light,
for the sun, lost long ago and sweet.   25
By the lake, locked black away and tight,
we lie, day creatures, overhearing night.

REFLECTING ON WHAT YOU'VE READ

1. This poet clearly loves to explore the possibilities of language. Pick out examples of unusual uses of language and consider why they are effective. Look up words that aren't familiar. Why is each right for the place it's used?

2. Notice examples of active, energetic verbs. Consider why they are effective in creating mental images.

3. Pick out words and phrases that create mental images of the way things look, sound, and feel.

The diction of this poem aims to bring to life a scene for readers to recall or create in their imaginations. Its emphasis is not on an intellectual meaning or an abstract idea, but on evoking what you see at the lake and especially what you hear. In describing sounds, the poem emphasizes verbs, such as "skitter," "squeak," "chirp," and "prink" in the first stanza. Look for other examples in stanzas two and three. Notice also that the verbs are present tense, giving the scene immediacy. This is not a scene from the past, which is over and gone, but a scene that continues in the memory of the speaker, and now in you the reader. Having memories come to life is one of the remarkable powers of images, of imagistic language.

APPROACHING THE READING

The power of concrete detail is at the heart of William Carlos Williams's short and much-discussed poem "The Red Wheelbarrow." Focus on the mental picture that the words of the poem evoke for you. Reflect on whether creating that picture is what the poem is about or whether the poem needs to do more than just that.

APPROACHING THE AUTHOR

William Carlos Williams decided in college that he wanted to be both a physician and a writer. He went on to study pediatrics in Germany and set up private practice in his hometown of Rutherford, New Jersey, where he worked on his writing between seeing patients and after hours.

For more about him, see page 1083.

William Carlos Williams 1883–1963

The Red Wheelbarrow [1923]

so much depends
upon

a red wheel
barrow

glazed with rain   5
water

beside the white
chickens.

REFLECTING ON WHAT YOU'VE READ

1. Pick out words in the poem that help create sensory impressions in your mind (its images). How many of the words are imagistic?

2. Try sketching the scene on paper or visualizing it clearly in your mind. Consider what it would look like as a still-life painting in an art gallery. Even though this poem is highly visual, why might a sketch or painting fail to "capture" the poem?

3. What do you think is the "so much" that "depends" (line 1)? Why does it "depend"?

Some readers distrust or overlook the literal effects of Williams's images and search for "deeper meanings." The opening line of "The Red Wheelbarrow" seems to invite digging for deeper meaning—if "so much depends" on the objects mentioned, we had better figure out what they *really* mean. But the line more likely asserts the importance of images as themselves: So much depends on sensuously experiencing and respecting and realizing the value of things as themselves, on experiencing the world with our senses alert and sensitive.

Visualizing Specific Details   Writers usually work with specific details and precise images that use concrete language rather than abstract language (see p. 226). If you hear "Think of an animal," you may visualize whatever you choose. However, if you hear "Don't imagine an elephant," such is the power of images that, even though you're told not to, you can't help visualizing an elephant.

Trusting the Literal   Some people are convinced that all poetry is indirect and symbolic—even a "code." They think that reading poetry means finding hidden meanings, as if poets think of meanings and then hide them. But an image is, first and foremost, simply itself. Poems do use symbols, and much of what was said about symbols in fiction (pp. 252–54) applies as well to poetry: A symbol is initially "an image that is exactly what it is." True, an image may suggest further meanings, but it doesn't "turn into" something else. It is always itself. And it always retains its literal meaning. Because imagery is so rich a part of poetry, one starting point in reading poems is to look at—and trust—the literal, to realize, appreciate, and enjoy the images for what they are and for what they do.

☑ CHECKLIST on Reading for Words and Images

❏ Pay careful attention to denotations—the pertinent dictionary definitions of words in a poem.

❏ Use a desk dictionary and specialized dictionaries (such as the *Oxford English Dictionary*—see p. 465) for finding useful and sometimes surprising denotations.

❏ Be open to the connotations of words in poetry—the overtones or associations that become connected with a word through repeated uses.

❏ Respond with your senses, intellect, and emotions to images (words representing sensory experience or objects that can be known by one or more of the senses) and to sense images (mental representations of sensory experience) in a poem.

FURTHER READING

APPROACHING THE READING

The following poem is about a strong friendship between two young, hurting, vulnerable girls—one who is blind and the other who, missing her father, is lonely. You can imagine their relationship through a host of images, drawing on all the senses: sight, hearing, touch, smell, and taste. Watch for examples of all five, and reflect on the extent to which the images enable you to understand and empathize with both girls. We will refer back to this poem in later chapters.

APPROACHING THE AUTHOR

Anita Endrezze is an artist as well as a poet. Her paintings have been exhibited in Wales, England, Sweden, Denmark, and the United States. Several of her paintings appear on anthology covers as well as on her own books.

For more about her, see page 1062.

Anita Endrezze   b. 1952

The Girl Who Loved the Sky   [1992]

Outside the second grade room,
the jacaranda tree blossomed
into purple lanterns, the papery petals
drifted, darkening the windows.
Inside, the room smelled like glue.   5
The desks were made of yellowed wood,
the tops littered with eraser rubbings,
rulers, and big fat pencils.
Colored chalk meant special days.
The walls were covered with precise   10
bright tulips and charts with shiny stars
by certain names. There, I learned
how to make butter by shaking a jar
until the pale cream clotted
into one sweet mass. There, I learned   15
that numbers were fractious beasts
with dens like dim zeros. And there,
I met a blind girl who thought the sky

tasted like cold metal when it rained
and whose eyes were always covered   20
with the bruised petals of her lids.

She loved the formless sky, defined
only by sounds, or the cool umbrellas
of clouds. On hot, still days
we listened to the sky falling   25
like chalk dust. We heard the noon
whistle of the pig-mash factory,
smelled the sourness of home-bound men.

I had no father; she had no eyes;
we were best friends. The other girls   30
drew shaky hopscotch squares
on the dusty asphalt, talked about
pajama parties, weekend cookouts,
and parents who bought sleek-finned cars.
Alone, we sat in the canvas swings,   35
our shoes digging into the sand, then pushing,
until we flew high over their heads,
our hands streaked with red rust
from the chains that kept us safe.

I was born blind, she said, an act of nature.   40
Sure, I thought, like birds born
without wings, trees without roots.
I didn't understand. The day she moved
I saw the world clearly: the sky
backed away from me like a departing father.   45
I sat under the jacaranda, catching
the petals in my palm, enclosing them
until my fist was another lantern
hiding a small and bitter flame.

REFLECTING ON WHAT YOU'VE READ

1. This poem has an unusually rich sensory texture. Pick out examples of
   words that evoke each of the five senses — sight, hearing, smell, taste, and
   touch. Why is sensory imagery so important to the impact of this particular
   poem?

2. If you have never seen a jacaranda tree or its blossoms, look at pictures of
   them in an encyclopedia or plant book or online. How do those pictures
   help sharpen the way you visualize lines 1–4, 20–21, and 46–49?

3. We get to know the speaker and her friend partly through the poem's images, through the kinds of things they notice and experience. Describe what both girls are like, grounding your response in the poem's details.

4. Discuss the nature of the girls' friendship. What makes it solid, touching, vulnerable? How do certain images help convey that friendship?

5. Reread the final stanza of the poem on the effect of the experience on the narrator. Explain how images help get her points across. How fully did the speaker understand the experience then? What indication is there that the poet, in looking back, has a different understanding of it now?

APPROACHING THE READING

Nature is important in the following poem. When the speaker begins feeling anxiety about the world, he goes outside, where connecting with "wild things" leads him to get in touch with a different side of himself. Watch how words and images create and convey a sense of peacefulness and reveal the contrast between the worlds in which he lives.

APPROACHING THE AUTHOR

In 1965 **Wendell Berry** and his wife moved to a farm in Kentucky and began small-scale farming, using horses to work the land and employing organic methods of fertilization and pest control. Perhaps in keeping with his farming lifestyle, Berry does not use a computer.

For more about him, see page 1055.

Wendell Berry b. 1934

The Peace of Wild Things   [1968]

When despair for the world grows in me
and I wake in the night at the least sound
in fear of what my life and my children's lives may be,
I go and lie down where the wood drake
rests in his beauty on the water, and the great heron feeds.   5
I come into the peace of wild things
who do not tax their lives with forethought
of grief. I come into the presence of still water.
And I feel above me the day-blind stars
waiting with their light. For a time   10
I rest in the grace of the world, and am free.

REFLECTING ON WHAT YOU'VE READ

1. This poem is direct in what it presents through denotations. Are there any words or images that also carry connotations for you? Which ones? What are their connotations? Pick out some images, word choices, and moments that describe things you can relate to closely. Why do you think that they struck you as they did?

2. The poem is less about altering perceptions than it is about revealing how the speaker depends on the natural world. What is it about the natural world that brings renewal to the speaker? What words and images has the poet used to convey this?

3. There are some "little," "common" words and phrases in this poem that carry great importance and are used in unusual ways. Take a closer look at *for* in the phrase "for the world" (l. 1), at *in* in "the wood drake/rests in his beauty" (ll. 4–5), at *come into* in "I come into the presence of still water" (l. 8), and *with* in "the day-blind stars/waiting with their light" (ll. 9–10). How would you describe the experience these unassuming words create?

APPROACHING THE READING

Here is a poem involving a memory of nature. The speaker remembers a time during a walk in the country when he suddenly came upon a huge scene filled with daffodils. He uses vivid images to attempt to create and convey to the reader the beauty of what he saw. Think about what he says in the last stanza about the power of imagination, how it can enable us to reimagine an experience again and again, as his poem does for a reader.

APPROACHING THE AUTHOR

William Wordsworth's most famous work, *The Prelude* (1850), is considered by many to be the crowning achievement of English Romanticism.
    For more about him, see page 1084.

William Wordsworth   1770–1850

I Wandered Lonely as a Cloud   [1807]

I wandered lonely as a cloud
That floats on high o'er vales and hills,
When all at once I saw a crowd,
A host, of golden daffodils;
Beside the lake, beneath the trees,   5
Fluttering and dancing in the breeze.

Continuous as the stars that shine
And twinkle on the milky way,
They stretched in never-ending line
Along the margin of a bay: 10
Ten thousand saw I at a glance,
Tossing their heads in sprightly dance.

The waves beside them danced; but they
Outdid the sparkling waves in glee;
A poet could not but be gay,   15
In such a jocund° company;
I gazed—and gazed—but little thought
What wealth the show to me had brought:

For oft, when on my couch I lie
In vacant or in pensive mood,   20
They flash upon that inward eye
Which is the bliss of solitude;
And then my heart with pleasure fills,
And dances with the daffodils.

---

jocund: *cheerful.*

REFLECTING ON WHAT YOU'VE READ

1. Pick out visual images that help sharpen the speaker's description of what
   he saw that day. Think about how thoroughly the poem explores the sense
   of sight.

2. Pick out words that help reveal the emotions the speaker felt both that day
   and when he remembers the experience.

3. While the first three stanzas are mainly descriptive, the last stanza is reflective. This change is often called a "turn." Think about what leads the speaker's
   consciousness to shift this way.

RESPONDING THROUGH **Writing**

WRITING ABOUT WORDS AND IMAGES

Journal Entries

1. As an exercise on language, write in your journal lists of words that you notice
   during an entire day: unfamiliar words, moving words, words that sound beautiful, words that look good on the page or on the computer screen, and so on.

At the end of the day and a few days later, look back over the lists and run through the words using your memory and imagination. Jot some notes about experiences, feelings, and associations some of the words bring back to you: It may give you a new sense of the power and importance that words have.

2. Choose a nonpoetic text — a letter, an advertisement, a magazine article, or an editorial, for example — and look closely at its handling of language. Discuss in your journal how the denotations and connotations of the words are or are not manipulated.

3. Images — visual and verbal — are enormously important for the advertising industry. In your journal, list some examples of how advertisers use words and pictures to imprint images in your mind and to stimulate your imagination, to get you to notice and remember their products. Write some reflections on some ways advertisers use the same techniques as poets, though with a different purpose.

Literary Analysis Papers

4. Write a paper that examines the diction in Maxine Kumin's "The Sound of Night" (p. 470), especially how its mixing of ordinary, everyday words with

TIPS for Writing about Words and Images

- **Read words attentively.** Assume that every word that a poet chooses is used deliberately, and pay careful attention to each one. Of course you can't write about all the words, even in a short poem, so it's a good idea to focus on diction that is unusual, unexpected, striking, or especially significant.

- **Use a dictionary.** Make ample use of a good dictionary when you're writing about diction or imagery. Pay attention to etymologies as well as various definitions. Remember that a poet may want you to use more than one definition for a word, that doing so will add even more to the poem.

- **Look for patterns.** As you study a poem, watch for patterns, connections, or relationships among the words and images. Also, notice how poetic images sometimes change our usual ways of perceiving things. These often can result in insightful paper topics.

- **Avoid the general.** Don't just give lists of images or tell your reader what she or he already knows, like "The image of the stabbing was violent" or "the 'splintering cold' helps a reader feel how cold it was in the room." You might instead focus on how the word "splintering" changes our usual way of thinking about coldness.

- **Relate to effect or theme.** Whenever you write about words and images, as the topic of an entire paper or as passing comments within a larger topic, your comments need to be used to help clarify the way words or images contribute to the overall effect or theme of the poem.

evocatively lush language creates a portrait that changes our usual perceptions of the world of the country.

5. Write a paper discussing the imagery of Anita Endrezze's "The Girl Who Loved the Sky" (p. 474) or another poem by thinking of it in terms of cinematography. See the poem as film. Note where in the poem you would use crucial camera angles, shots, close-ups, pans, and so forth. Help your reader see the poem as a film. Explain why you decided to film it as you did.

6. Write a paper on the use of imagery in capturing and conveying the atmosphere of a season: autumn, for example, in T. S. Eliot's "The Love Song of J. Alfred Prufrock" (p. 624), or winter in Mary Oliver's "First Snow" (p. 538), or autumn in Robert Frost's "After Apple-Picking" (p. 628).

Comparison-Contrast Papers

7. Write a paper comparing and contrasting what two or more poems about words say about language (perhaps including the cultural implications of language) and the diction they use to communicate it. Some poems you might consider are Pat Mora's "Elena" (p. 643), Allison Joseph's "On Being Told I Don't Speak Like a Black Person" (p. 491), Gary Miranda's "Love Poem" (p. 557), and Alberto Ríos's "Nani" (p. 648).

8. Write a paper comparing and contrasting the expressions of love in Elizabeth Barrett Browning's "How do I love thee? Let me count the ways" (p. 608) and Gary Miranda's "Love Poem" (p. 557). Consider the extent to which each relies on images and how the effect of each differs.

WRITING ABOUT CONNECTIONS

Words and images are the key vehicles through which writers connect with readers, through which they convey what they hope readers will respond to. Examining a poet's choices and handling of diction and imagery in a poem can be an effective paper topic. Another way to deal with words and images in a paper is to look for thematic connections between two poems that use similar or contrasting diction and/or imagery, especially a contemporary poem and a poem from an earlier period. Here are a few examples of such topic possibilities.

1. "The Road Taken": Making Life Choices in Robert Frost's "The Road Not Taken" (p. 555) and William Stafford's "Traveling through the Dark" (p. 534)

2. "Impermanence's Permanence": Stability and Change in John Keats's "Ode on a Grecian Urn" (p. 636) and Anita Endrezze's "The Girl Who Loved the Sky" (p. 474)

3. "Hard Work If You Can Get It": Contrasting Perspectives on Work in Philip Levine's "What Work Is" (p. 638) and Natasha Trethewey's "Domestic Work 1937" (p. 655)

WRITING RESEARCH PAPERS

1. Research the way the British taught the English language in their colonies, and reflect on what might have been the effects and consequences of doing so. In what ways do your research findings compare and contrast with the issues raised by today's controversies over bilingual education? Also look into Ebonics, or black English. Use what you find to illuminate Allison Joseph's "On Being Told I Don't Speak Like a Black Person" (p. 491), especially what the poem suggests about the teaching or learning of language.

2. Select a poem of political protest, such as E. E. Cummings's "next to of course god america i" (p. 489), Luis J. Rodriguez's "Running to America" (p. 649), or Peter Blue Cloud's "Crazy Horse Monument" (p. 607). Research the historical and the social, political, and economic backgrounds of the poem. Write a paper showing how awareness of this contextual knowledge helps clarify the meaning and impact of the poem and how the poem's use of diction and images reflects the background, helping to present the situation in a powerful way.

Literary works do not endure as objects but as presences. When you read anything worth remembering, you liberate a human voice; you release into the world again a companion spirit.

Louise Glück

(Pulitzer Prize-Winning American Poet)

CHAPTER 15 Voice
Listening to Vocal Variations

In Chapter 4 we said that stories originally were not created to be read: Long before people read stories, they listened to them being told. Even today, when stories are written down, most are meant to be "heard" as you read them. The same is true of poems. In narrative poetry, you listen with your mind's ear to a storyteller, a first- or third-person narrator. In nonnarrative poetry, you hear the imagined voice of a *speaker*, of someone "speaking" the poem, either the poet directly or a character. This chapter aims to develop your ability to listen for the voice of the speaker (or narrator), to help you hear as you read.

READING FOR VOICE

You will likely need to read a poem through closely at least one time before you hear a voice. As you read, try to pick out words, images, and phrases that evoke the presence of a speaker and begin to consider what that speaker is like ("The speaker seems to be someone who . . ."). Poems are often written in the first person. The voice of the *I* speaking can be the author. But don't assume that it is. It doesn't have to be. Just as you should not assume that the *I* in a story is identical to the author (see pages 147–148), you shouldn't automatically assume that the *I* in a poem is the author.

APPROACHING THE READING

In the following poem, the speaker is reflecting on a memory. The speaker recalls his father and expresses his response to what is lost. Listen closely to the voice for indications of what the *I* is like — character traits and attitudes. What might lead you to conclude that the speaker is the poet, Li-Young Lee? How can you be or not be sure? Notice the importance of vivid images as the poem brings the speaker's experience to life in your imagination.

APPROACHING THE AUTHOR

Believing that poetry was interfering with his pursuits in activism, **Li-Young Lee** decided to stop writing. Soon after, he developed severe insomnia. Convinced his inability to sleep was the result of his having given up creating poetry, he quickly began writing again and hasn't stopped since.

For more about him, see page 1071.

Paul Elledge Photograph¥

Li-Young Lee b. 1957

Eating Alone   [1986]

I've pulled the last of the year's young onions.
The garden is bare now. The ground is cold,
brown and old. What is left of the day flames
in the maples at the corner of my
eye. I turn, a cardinal vanishes.   5
By the cellar door, I wash the onions,
then drink from the icy metal spigot.

Once, years back, I walked beside my father
among the windfall pears. I can't recall
our words. We may have strolled in silence. But   10
I still see him bend that way — left hand braced
on knee, creaky — to lift and hold to my
eye a rotten pear. In it, a hornet
spun crazily, glazed in slow, glistening juice.

It was my father I saw this morning   15
waving to me from the trees. I almost
called to him, until I came close enough

to see the shovel, leaning where I had
left it, in the flickering, deep green shade.

White rice steaming, almost done. Sweet green peas   20
fried in onions. Shrimp braised in sesame
oil and garlic. And my own loneliness.
What more could I, a young man, want.

REFLECTING ON THE READING

1. Describe the voice you heard as you listened to the poem. How would you explain the personal qualities and attributes that come through what is "said"? How does the title affect your sense of the voice of the poem?

2. The first stanza lays groundwork for the speaker's memories of the father. What in the stanza enabled you to begin to hear the voice of the poem?

3. Select five or more images in the poem that led you to hear the speaker's voice and develop a sense of what the speaker is like. Try to explain the way these images were revealing as you listened for the speaker's voice.

4. Describe how hearing the voice enriched your experience of the poem. What would be lost if you did not hear the voice?

5. What do you think is the connection of the poem's last stanza to the previous three stanzas? What do you make of the final line?

Biographical information about the author (including the biographical sketch on p. 1077) confirms basic similarities between the author and the poem. The voice we hear appears to be Li-Young Lee's voice, or perhaps we should say his voice as a poet in this poem. What we really mean when we talk about a *voice* being that of the poet is not as a biographical personality but voice as the sense conveyed by a poem of an intelligence and sensibility that has invented, arranged, and expressed the elements and ideas in a particular manner. Because the "I" in a poem never can encompass the entire personality of the author, it is usually better to refer to the "I" as "the speaker" than to use the author's name.

Conveying Voice Directly   From the beginning of "Eating Alone," the person speaking seems low-keyed, quiet, with muted emotions. He is observant, in touch with his surroundings, someone who notices the appearance of the now-barren earth, the brilliant sunset shining through the leaves of a maple tree, the flight of a cardinal. The voice in the second stanza sounds soft, sensitive, perhaps pensive, as he recalls a particular moment, years ago, with his father, who seems no longer to be living. The moment was memorable not for what they said to each other but for the particular way his father bent over to pick up a rotting pear and showed him a hornet circling drunkenly in its hollowed-out center. From his father's influence, it seems, the speaker learned the attentiveness to nature demonstrated in the first stanza.

Conveying Voice Indirectly The third stanza makes clear that the speaker felt a great deal of emotion when he thought he saw his father but then realized what he saw was actually a shovel in flickering light. But the voice we hear restrains that deep emotion, understates it, which may end up making it sound all the stronger. The understated emotion is carried over to the final stanza, in the details of an excellent meal, fit for a festive, shared occasion, in striking contrast to the speaker's "loneliness."

Complexity of Voice The word *loneliness* and the final line raise key questions about voice, questions of the kind that each reader must think through. What kind of voice says the words "my own loneliness"? Is it a depressing, isolated loneliness brought on by his feeling lost without his father? Is it an accepted loneliness, in which he misses his father's physical presence but is consoled by a sense of the father's continuing presence in his memories? Could it be a mixture of the two, or something else?

Similarly, what kind of voice says the last line, "What more could I, a young man, want"? Is the voice heavy with irony? (There's a lot more I could want, starting with having my father back!) Is the voice thoughtfully sincere, expressing genuine consolations found in good food and the flood of memories associated with the food and with other experiences? The title brings those questions about the voice into focus: Is eating alone a sad, solitary activity for the speaker? Does he feel lonely as he eats alone? When can one be alone and not be lonely? When can one not be alone and be lonely?

It is important when working with a poem to assume complexity of emotion. Our feelings are always "mixed," meaning complex, even contradictory. A poem—an effective, honest poem—is never emotionally simplistic.

Some books use the term *persona* for the first-person narrator through whom an author speaks or the speaker whose voice is heard in a lyric poem. They assume that one can never hear the author directly in a written work, even when she or he uses *I*, that the author always, inevitably talks through a mask the way actors did in Greek plays (which is where the term *persona* came from). This book does not make that assumption, though it stresses that an *I* should never automatically be equated with the author.

VOICE AND TONE

Tone is a crucially important aspect of voice. It is in fact inseparable. *Tone* was defined in Chapter 9 (p. 224) as the attitude or "stance" toward the subject and toward the reader or audience implied in a work. Tone is as important in poems as it is in stories. Poems can have a single tone, but usually the tone is complex rather than straightforward; it cannot be summed up in a word or two. More often two or more tones mix and play off or with each other.

APPROACHING THE READING

Here is another poem about a son's memories of his father. Listen carefully for its voice and tone. Pay attention to the diction, connotations, and images. Compare the father–son relationship to that of "Eating Alone."

APPROACHING THE AUTHOR

As a child, **Theodore Roethke** spent much time in the greenhouse owned by his father and uncle. His impressions of the natural world contained there would later profoundly influence the subjects and imagery of his verse.

For more about him, see page 1078.

Theodore Roethke   1908–1963

My Papa's Waltz   [1948]

The whiskey on your breath
Could make a small boy dizzy;
But I hung on like death:
Such waltzing was not easy.

We romped until the pans   5
Slid from the kitchen shelf;
My mother's countenance
Could not unfrown itself.

The hand that held my wrist
Was battered on one knuckle;   10
At every step you missed
My right ear scraped a buckle.

You beat time on my head
With a palm caked hard by dirt,
Then waltzed me off to bed   15
Still clinging to your shirt.

REFLECTING ON WHAT YOU'VE READ

1. Consider the voice in the poem. Do you think the *I* is a character narrating the episode or the voice of the poet?

2. Unlike "Eating Alone" (p. 485), which addresses the reader, this poem addresses the father as "you." How does that affect the voice of the poem? Try changing *you* and *your* to *he* and *his*. What effect does that have on the voice? How would you explain the difference?

3. Be ready to discuss the age of the speaker whose voice we hear—his age now and at the time of the event—and what you think he felt then and feels now. What difference does it make to the way you hear the voice whether the father is living or has died?

4. Discuss the effect of the word *papa* on the tone of the poem. Substitute *daddy* or *father* or *old man*. What happens?

5. Discuss the effect of the word *waltz* in the title on the tone of the poem. Substitute *drinking* or *rowdiness*. What happens?

A Dark Tone? "My Papa's Waltz" affects readers in different ways. For some, the poem describes a troubled relationship or dysfunctional home. The word *whiskey* suggests for them that the father has a drinking problem; the mother's disapproval suggests that the father and mother have a difficult relationship. *Battered* indicates that the father abuses his son and perhaps his wife. The simile "I hung on like death" in line 3 suggests a home in which fear pervades the atmosphere. For these readers, the poem has a dark tone, perhaps a tragic one, as a little boy—too young to be aware of what he's doing—puts up with his father's frightening romps because he is forced to physically and tries desperately to gain his father's love and approval.

Or a Joyful Tone? Other readers discern a different tone in the poem. For them words such as *waltz* and *romped* convey a lighter tone—a waltz is a graceful, flowing, lyrical dance that suggests joy and celebration (though, of course, the poet could be using the word ironically). The father described is a physical laborer (his hands are battered and caked with dirt) who has a couple of drinks with his buddies after work on a Friday. Feeling good, he frolics with his son, more wildly than he probably should, creating disorder in the kitchen, and more roughly than he should, thus scraping the boy's ear and tapping on his head enthusiastically. The romp is scary for the small boy ("dizzy," "like death," "clinging")—but excitingly scary. For these readers, the poem describes a speaker looking back at his childhood, recalling a happy memory, a memory that evinces his father's affection (people generally waltz with people they love) and his own positive response to his father (one can cling out of love as well as fear).

Complexity of Tone   Assessing tone is a central part of the total interpretation of a literary work. As in all interpretation, it's not simple or straightforward. Every aspect of the work can come to bear on tone. It's important always to be alert for indicators of tone. Some are the same as in fiction—word choice, ways of phrasing, repetitions, understatement, overstatement, a particular figure of speech. Others—such as the handling of sounds and rhythm, lines, and line breaks—are more particular to poetry. And as "My Papa's Waltz" makes clear, tone is not an objective detail on which all readers must agree. Readers can read tones differently, and discussions about tone often form a vital part of conversations about literature, with each side pointing to aspects that lead them to respond to the work the way that they do.

VOICE AND IRONY

Irony is as important in poetry as it is in stories. Review the discussion of irony in Chapter 9 (pp. 228-30), especially—for poetry—the sections on verbal irony and sarcasm. As you read poems, be alert for signals that what is said is not to be taken in a literal way: word choice, the sheer absurdity of what is said, the way a thought is phrased, the sounds and rhythms in which it is expressed. Recognition of irony is crucial to reading well.

APPROACHING THE READING

In the following poem, the *I* and the author are not the same. The *I* is a character delivering a speech perhaps at a patriotic celebration. Listen to his voice—to both what he says and the way he says it—and then consider the poem's tone (watch for irony). While a poem may not be in the voice of the author, the author may be making points through the speaker, and not always the same points as the speaker. Think about what points the speaker is making and what points the author is making.

APPROACHING THE AUTHOR

At the time of his death in 1962, **E. E. Cummings** was the most widely read poet in the United States, after Robert Frost.

For more about him, see page 1060.

The Granger Collection

E. E. Cummings   1894–1962

"next to of course god america i   [1926]

"next to of course god america i
love you land of the pilgrims' and so forth oh
say can you see by the dawn's early my
country 'tis of centuries come and go
and are no more what of it we should worry   5
in every language even deafanddumb
thy sons acclaim your glorious name by gorry
by jingo by gee by gosh by gum
why talk of beauty what could be more beaut-
iful than these heroic happy dead   10
who rushed like lions to the roaring slaughter
they did not stop to think they died instead
then shall the voice of liberty be mute?"
He spoke. And drank rapidly a glass of water

REFLECTING ON WHAT YOU'VE READ

1. How would you characterize the voice of the speaker and the content of his speech? Notice how the speaker casually "tosses out" one thing after another. What is the effect of that?

2. Describe the tone or tones of the poem. Where do you find irony? Be ready to talk about why tone is especially important in this poem and why it could be misunderstood.

3. Notice the punctuation of the poem. How does it influence your reading, or what is the resulting effect?

4. How would you explain the meaning and effect of the last line?

The chapters that follow go on to discuss specific techniques and elements that poets draw from when they compose a poem. As we focus on sounds, metaphors, rhythm, and form, however, it is important that you continue to listen for, and to, the voices in poems. Listen to the variety of voices, from different times, different experiences, and different backgrounds. Listen for and to the variety of things they give voice to in their poems. *Hear* the poems and *hear* what the poems are saying.

READING A DRAMATIC MONOLOGUE

One poetic form in which the *I* is definitely a character is the *dramatic monologue*. In dramatic monologues, there is only one speaker, a character overheard in a dramatic moment, usually addressing another character or characters who do not speak. The speaker's words reveal what is going on in the scene and bring out significant aspects of what the speaker is like. Therefore, you can figure out who is speaking, to whom, and on what occasion, and the substance and tone of what she or he is saying. See, for example, Robert Browning's "My Last Duchess" (p. 497). (If the character is speaking to her- or himself, the poem is using interior monologue — see the Glossary, p. 1145; that is probably the case in T. S. Eliot's "The Love Song of J. Alfred Prufrock" — p. 624.)

☑ **CHECKLIST on Reading for Voice**

❑ Listen for the voice of the speaker, determine if the speaker and poet are almost the same, or listen for the voice of the speaker and the voice of the poem if they are different. In either case, listen for the intelligence and sensibility that has invented, arranged, and expressed the elements and ideas in a particular manner.

❑ Listen for the tone: the tone of voice or attitude toward the subject or situation in the poem (playful, serious, ironic, cheerful, pessimistic, sorrowful, and so forth).

❑ Listen for irony: an expression involving a discrepancy or incongruity between appearance and reality, between what is said and what is intended. In poetry, verbal irony (saying what is nearly opposite of what is meant) is used most often, though situational irony (things turning out not as hoped or expected) is frequent as well.

FURTHER READING

APPROACHING THE READING

The following is a poem *about* voice, about people's voices sounding the way others think they should. In the poem, Allison Joseph has created a very appealing voice. As you listen, focus on the points the poem reveals and what enables you to hear its voice.

APPROACHING THE AUTHOR

As a child, **Allison Joseph** found inspiration in the poems of Gwendolyn Brooks, which she said taught her that "you don't have to write about Mount Olympus. You can write about your neighborhood — what's happening on the corner."

For more about her, see page 1069.

Allison Joseph   b. 1967

On Being Told I Don't Speak
Like a Black Person   [1999]

Emphasize the "h," you hignorant ass,
was what my mother was told
when colonial-minded teachers
slapped her open palm with a ruler
in that Jamaican schoolroom.   5
Trained in England, they tried
to force their pupils to speak
like Eliza Doolittle° after
her transformation, fancying themselves
British as Henry Higgins,°   10
despite dark, sun-ripened skin.
Mother never lost her accent,
though, the music of her voice
charming everyone, an infectious lilt
I can imitate, not duplicate.   15
No one in the States told her
to eliminate the accent,
my high school friends adoring
the way her voice would lift
when she called me to the phone—   20
A-ll-i-son, it's friend Cathy.
Why don't you sound like her,
they'd ask. I didn't sound
like anyone or anything,
no grating New Yorker nasality,   25
no fastidious British mannerisms
like the ones my father affected
when he wanted to sell someone
something. And I didn't sound
like a Black American,   30
college acquaintances observed,
sure they knew what a black person
was supposed to sound like.
Was I supposed to sound lazy,

8–10. Eliza Doolittle . . . Henry Higgins: Flower-girl with a strong Cockney (working-class) accent in George Bernard Shaw's play *Pygmalion* and the musical based on it, *My Fair Lady.* Henry Higgins, a linguistics professor, takes on the challenge of teaching her how to speak (and act and dress) like a proper British lady.

dropping syllables here and there   35
not finishing words but
slurring their final letters
so each sentence joined
the next, sliding past the listener?
Were certain words off limits,   40
too erudite for someone whose skin
came with a natural tan?
I asked them what they meant
and they stuttered, blushed,
said *you know, Black English,*   45
applying a term from that
semester's text. *Does everyone*
in your family speak alike,
I'd ask, and they'd say *don't*
take this the wrong way,   50
nothing personal.

Now I realize there's nothing
more personal than speech,
that I don't have to defend
how I speak, how any person,   55
black, white, chooses to speak.
Let us speak. Let us talk
with the sounds of our mothers
and fathers still reverberating
in our minds, wherever our mothers   60
or fathers come from:
Arkansas, Belize, Alabama,
Brazil, Aruba, Arizona.
Let us simply speak
to one another,   65
listen and prize the inflections,
never assuming how any person will sound
until his mouth opens, until her
mouth opens, greetings welcome
in any language.   70

REFLECTING ON WHAT YOU'VE READ

1. Most of the language of the poem is straightforward. Look up any words
   you aren't familiar with. Pick out a few phrases you reacted to, those with
   especially effective or interesting diction, and be prepared to explain why
   they struck you.

2. The speaker mentions that her acquaintances seemed sure they knew what a black person is supposed to sound like. What does she mean by that? Reflect on the cultural assumptions that lie behind such certainty.

3. The speaker says in lines 52–55 that "there's nothing / more personal than speech, / that I don't have to defend / how I speak." Think about your own speech. In what ways is it yours? When do you feel you have to defend your speech or even abandon or change or modify it?

4. It is interesting to think about how the lines "Let us simply speak / to one another / listen and prize the inflections" compare to what Megan Foss says about language and speech in "Love Letters" (p. 10). What would you say about the comparison?

APPROACHING THE READING

As you read the next two poems, be sure to listen for the ideas the poet is giving voice to and the way they are expressed. Both poems deal with war. In the first, a man who served in World War I recounts his memories of a gas attack and struggles with his feelings about war that the experience created.

APPROACHING THE AUTHOR

Wilfred Owen was killed in the Battle of the Sambre a week before the end of World War I. The telegram informing his mother of his death was delivered as her town's church bells were ringing in celebration of the armistice.

For more about him, see page 1075.

Wilfred Owen   1893–1918

Dulce et Decorum Est   [1920]

Bent double, like old beggars under sacks,
Knock-kneed, coughing like hags, we cursed through sludge,
Till on the haunting flares we turned our backs
And towards our distant rest began to trudge.
Men marched asleep. Many had lost their boots   5
But limped on, blood-shod. All went lame; all blind;
Drunk with fatigue; deaf even to the hoots
Of tired, outstripped Five-Nines° that dropped behind.

---

8. **Five-Nines:** 5.9-inch-caliber shells.

Gas! GAS! Quick, boys! — An ecstasy of fumbling,
Fitting the clumsy helmets just in time;   10
But someone still was yelling out and stumbling
And flound'ring like a man in fire or lime . . .
Dim, through the misty panes° and thick green light,
As under a green sea, I saw him drowning.

In all my dreams, before my helpless sight,   15
He plunges at me, guttering, choking, drowning.

If in some smothering dreams you too could pace
Behind the wagon that we flung him in,
And watch the white eyes writhing in his face,
His hanging face, like a devil's sick of sin;   20
If you could hear, at every jolt, the blood
Come gargling from the froth-corrupted lungs,
Obscene as cancer, bitter as the cud
Of vile, incurable sores on innocent tongues, —
My friend, you would not tell with such high zest   25
To children ardent for some desperate glory,
The old Lie: Dulce et decorum est
Pro patria mori.°

---

13. **misty panes:** Of a gas mask.   **27–28. Dulce . . . mori** (Latin): It is sweet and fitting / to
die for one's country (Horace, *Odes* 3.12.13).

REFLECTING ON WHAT YOU'VE READ

1. Describe the voice of and speaker in the poem. The poem uses both first-person singular (*I* and *my*) and first-person plural (*we*). Consider the effect of using both instead of only the singular.

2. The poem looks back at the incident it describes. What is the effect of having it told from a later point in time? How do you think the distance in time has affected the speaker?

3. Consider the speaker's use of the second person beginning in line 17. On the original draft of the poem, a dedication "To Jessie Pope" is scratched out and replaced with "To a certain Poetess." Jessie Pope published patriotic poems in a popular London newspaper during World War I. Neither dedication was included in published versions of "Dulce et Decorum Est." How does knowledge of the dedication affect your reading of the poem? How would your reading be affected if "you" and "My friend" were limited to Jessie Pope?

4. What particular ideas about war and military service does the poem express or give voice to (not simply "war is bad")?

5. Listen for and pay attention to the poem's use of sound. In what ways do the presence of rhymes and other repeated sounds intensify the poem and how it affects you?

APPROACHING THE READING

The speaker in this poem is looking at the Vietnam Veterans Memorial in Washington, D.C. The words and images he sees trigger fragmented memories about his own experiences in Vietnam. As you read the poem, listen to the voice as it makes nonlogical connections between images and experiences, and tries to absorb what he is looking at and make some sense of it.

APPROACHING THE AUTHOR

Yusef Komunyakaa was profoundly influenced by growing up in Bogalusa, Louisiana, which at the time was a center of Ku Klux Klan activity and later became a focal point for the civil rights movement. During the Vietnam War he served as a war correspondent, which has also influenced his poetry.

For more about him, see page 1070.

Yusef Komunyakaa   b. 1947

Facing It   [1988]

My black face fades,
hiding inside the black granite.
I said I wouldn't,
dammit: No tears.
I'm stone. I'm flesh.   5
My clouded reflection eyes me
like a bird of prey, the profile of night
slanted against morning. I turn
this way—the stone lets me go.
I turn that way—I'm inside   10
the Vietnam Veterans Memorial
again, depending on the light
to make a difference.
I go down the 58,022 names,
half-expecting to find   15
my own in letters like smoke.

I touch the name Andrew Johnson;
I see the booby trap's white flash.
Names shimmer on a woman's blouse
but when she walks away   20
the names stay on the wall.
Brushstrokes flash, a red bird's
wings cutting across my stare.
The sky. A plane in the sky.
A white vet's image floats   25
closer to me, then his pale eyes
look through mine. I'm a window.
He's lost his right arm
inside the stone. In the black mirror
a woman's trying to erase names: 30
No, she's brushing a boy's hair.

REFLECTING ON WHAT YOU'VE READ

1. Characterize the speaker of the voice you hear in the poem. What can you tell about the speaker's experiences and feelings?

2. How does the title fit the poem and the speaker? How does the last line fit?

3. Discuss the tone of the poem, and point to specific details or techniques that help shape it.

4. If you have not visited the Vietnam Veterans Memorial in Washington, D.C., look at pictures of it and read about it (you can do both on the Web or in books). Talk to someone who has seen it if you can. Reflect on how all this affects the way you visualize and experience the poem.

5. What ideas, insights, and realizations does the poem give voice to?

APPROACHING THE READING

The following poem is a dramatic monologue (p. 489) based on events that occurred in the life of Alfonso II, Duke of Ferrara in sixteenth-century northern Italy. The speaker is the duke. He is giving a guest a personal guided tour of his palace and pauses to show him a portrait of his previous wife painted by a fictitious but supposedly famous painter, Frà (that is, "brother," or monk) Pandolf. Ferrara's first wife, Lucrezia, died in 1561 at age seventeen after three years of marriage. We overhear what he says about the painting and about her. From that, we are left to determine what he is like, what she was like, who the guest is, and why the duke says what he does.

APPROACHING THE AUTHOR

Robert Browning was able to read and write by age five and by fourteen was fluent in Latin, Greek, Italian, and French. He attended University College London for one year but said later in life that "Italy was my university," for he lived there many years, and its art and atmosphere had a deep influence on him.

For more about him, see page 1057.

Robert Browning   1812–1889

My Last Duchess   [1842]

Ferrara

That's my last Duchess painted on the wall,
Looking as if she were alive. I call
That piece a wonder, now: Frà Pandolf's hands
Worked busily a day, and there she stands.
Will't please you sit and look at her? I said   5
"Frà Pandolf" by design, for never read
Strangers like you that pictured countenance,
The depth and passion of its earnest glance,
But to myself they turned (since none puts by
The curtain I have drawn for you, but I)   10
And seemed as they would ask me, if they durst,
How such a glance came there; so, not the first
Are you to turn and ask thus. Sir, 'twas not
Her husband's presence only, called that spot
Of joy into the Duchess' cheek: perhaps   15
Frà Pandolf chanced to say "Her mantle laps
Over my lady's wrist too much," or "Paint
Must never hope to reproduce the faint
Half-flush that dies along her throat": such stuff
Was courtesy, she thought, and cause enough   20
For calling up that spot of joy. She had
A heart—how shall I say?—too soon made glad,
Too easily impressed; she liked whate'er
She looked on, and her looks went everywhere.
Sir, 'twas all one! My favour at her breast,   25
The dropping of the daylight in the West,
The bough of cherries some officious fool
Broke in the orchard for her, the white mule
She rode with round the terrace—all and each

Would draw from her alike the approving speech,   30
Or blush, at least. She thanked men,—good! but thanked
Somehow—I know not how—as if she ranked
My gift of a nine-hundred-year-old name
With anybody's gift. Who'd stoop to blame
This sort of trifling? Even had you skill   35
In speech—(which I have not)—to make your will
Quite clear to such an one, and say, "Just this
Or that in you disgusts me; here you miss,
Or there exceed the mark"—and if she let
Herself be lessoned so, nor plainly set   40
Her wits to yours, forsooth, and made excuse,
—E'en then would be some stooping; and I choose
Never to stoop. Oh sir, she smiled, no doubt,
Whene'er I passed her; but who passed without
Much the same smile? This grew; I gave commands;   45
Then all smiles stopped together. There she stands
As if alive. Will't please you rise? We'll meet
The company below, then. I repeat,
The Count your master's known munificence
Is ample warrant that no just pretence   50
Of mine for dowry will be disallowed;
Though his fair daughter's self, as I avowed
At starting, is my object. Nay, we'll go
Together down, sir. Notice Neptune, though,
Taming a sea-horse, thought a rarity,   55
Which Claus of Innsbruck° cast in bronze for me!

---

56. Claus of Innsbruck: A fictional sculptor.

REFLECTING ON WHAT YOU'VE READ

1. The point of a dramatic monologue is that the speaker's voice and what it says reveal her or his character. What sort of person is the duke? Point out the details that lead you to your conclusions about him.

2. In a dramatic monologue, you listen to the voice of a character speaking in a setting and situation. What are the setting and situation in this poem? Whom is the duke talking to? Try thinking in terms of "a person who . . ."

3. What the duke says also reveals all that we can know about the duchess. What sort of person was she? What happened to her?

4. Consider tone in the poem. What is the duke's attitude toward the duchess? What is the poem's attitude toward the duke?

RESPONDING THROUGH Writing

WRITING ABOUT VOICE

Journal Entries

1. During an average day, we're bombarded with voices: from radios or TVs, at home, on the street, on a bus, in class. The list could go on and on. To some we give close attention; others we pretty much ignore. In your journal, write a list of voices you notice during a morning or even an hour. Note which ones you pay attention to and which you don't. Of the ones you do pay attention to, reflect on what matters about the quality of each voice—whether it's interesting, engaging, honest, pleasant, appealing, and so on.

2. Write a journal entry comparing the ideas about war and patriotism expressed in E. E. Cummings's "'next to of course god america i" (p. 489) and Wilfred Owen's "Dulce et Decorum Est" (p. 493). Be sure to read question 3 in Reflecting on What You've Read on page 494.

3. Take a poem and change some of the diction (words) to alter the tone. Write a journal entry describing what you did and the ways the effect of the poem now is different.

Literary Analysis Papers

4. Write a paper on the voice and tone, or shifts in them, in Robert Hayden's "Those Winter Sundays" (p. 466), Gwendolyn Brooks's "We Real Cool" (p. 564), Jack Ridl's "My Brother – A Star" (p. 647), or another poem of your choice.

5. Write a paper exploring the relation of language to cultural separation and acceptance, using poems such as Allison Joseph's "On Being Told I Don't Speak Like a Black Person" (p. 491), Marilyn Chin's "How I Got That Name" (p. 611), and Terrance Hayes's "Talk" (p. 629). Include some discussion of why poetry is an appropriate form for exploring this topic.

6. Write a paper discussing the character of the speaker in T. S. Eliot's "The Love Song of J. Alfred Prufrock" (p. 624). The poem is usually regarded as a dramatic monologue, but readers differ on whether it uses interior monologue (p. 1139). If you think it does, show how that contributes to characterization and the effect of the poem.

Comparison-Contrast Papers

7. Compare and contrast the ideas about people's voices sounding the way others think they should in Allison Joseph's "On Being Told I Don't Speak Like a Black Person" (p. 491) and Terrance Hayes's "Talk" (p. 629).

8. Compare and contrast voice and theme in two poems on the environment: William Wordsworth's "The world is too much with us" (available online) and Wendell Berry's "The Peace of Wild Things" (p. 476).

TIPS for Writing about Voice

- **Hear the poem.** Poems often are meant to be heard. As part of your preparation for writing, read the poem aloud several times, listening for its voice, tone, and sound dimensions; then listen while someone else reads it aloud to you.

- **Focus on tone.** Tone can be an interesting topic especially when the tone is unusual or complex, or one that changes or shifts in intensity as you move through the poem.

- **Illustrations and explanations.** A paper on voice must include quotations that illustrate the relevant points you are making. You also will want to explain how the effects of voice are achieved, what goes into creating those effects.

- **Relationship to effect or theme.** A crucial part in any paper on voice must be a discussion of how that element contributes to the effect, theme, or significance of the poem.

WRITING ABOUT CONNECTIONS

Although this chapter focuses particularly on poems' use of voice, those aspects can also be useful in exploring poems thematically. Interesting paper topics that lead to fresh insights can result from making connections between poems with differing voices, especially ones from different eras. Here are a few possibilities:

1. "All the Comforts of Home": Contrasting Voices of Adventure in Luis J. Rodriguez's "Running to America" (p. 649) and Alfred, Lord Tennyson's "Ulysses" (p. 653)

2. "Crumbling Statues": The contrasting voices regarding statuary in Percy Bysshe Shelley's "Ozymandias" (p. 652) and Peter Blue Cloud's "Crazy Horse Monument" (p. 607)

3. "Dancing with the Past": Movement and Memory in Theodore Roethke's "My Papa's Waltz" (p. 486), Gary Miranda's "Love Poem" (p. 557), and Billy Collins's "Nostalgia" (p. 614)

WRITING RESEARCH PAPERS

1. Research the shootings at Virginia Tech University on April 16, 2007. Compare and contrast poems written by two poets who were then Virginia Tech faculty members: Nikki Giovanni's "We Are Virginia Tech" (available online) and Bob Hicok's "In the loop" (p. 630). Consider and discuss the value of poetry as a response to such tragic events.

2. Conduct interviews with one or two war veterans, if they are willing to talk about the experiences. Listen to the way they talk about their experiences as well as to what they say. Write a paper discussing similarities and/or differences between their ways of "voicing" their experiences and that in Wilfred Owen's "Dulce et Decorum Est" (p. 493) or Yusef Komunyakaa's "Facing It" (p. 495).

"Go" does not sound like "Stop."

Mary Oliver

(American Poet, see pp. 538 and 1074)

CHAPTER **16** **Sound**

Hearing How Sense
Is Said

READING FOR SOUND

Fine writers have "good ears." They attend to sounds of words as well as combinations of sounds, listening for the way sound and rhythm work together to create the poem's "music," all of which contribute to the voice of a poem. This chapter focuses on the effects of repeating or contrasting syllable sounds, vowel sounds, and consonant sounds. (Rhythm is treated later in the book, in Chapter 18.) To gain the full experience of effective writing, a reader needs to listen not just to the words but also to the repetitions, connections, contrasts, and combinations of vowels, consonants, and syllables that form the words.

APPROACHING THE READING

The following poem is about an African American driver being stopped by a police officer. Listen for the sounds made by the words and phrases—repetitions of words, parallel constructions, felicitous phrasings, echoes of vowel and consonant sounds, and rhyming words as well as the sound of the speaker's voice. Think about the ways that the sounds help create the impact of the experience.

Sekou Sundiata   1948–2007

Blink Your Eyes   [1995]

Remembering Sterling A. Brown°

I was on my way to see my woman
but the Law said I was on my way
thru a red light red light red light
and if you saw my woman
you could understand,   5
I was just being a man
It wasn't about no light
it was about my ride
and if you saw my ride
you could dig that too, you dig?   10
Sunroof stereo radio black leather
bucket seats sit low you know,
the body's cool, but the tires are worn.
Ride when the hard time come, ride
when they're gone, in other words   15
the light was green.

I could wake up in the morning
without a warning
and my world could change:
blink your eyes.   20
All depends, all depends on the skin,
all depends on the skin you're living in.

Up to the window comes the Law
with his hand on his gun
what's up? what's happening?   25
I said I guess
that's when I really broke the law.
He said *a routine, step out the car*
a routine, assume the position.
Put your hands up in the air   30
you know the routine, like you just don't care.
License and registration.
Deep was the night and the light
from the North Star on the car door, déjà vu
we've been through this before,   35

APPROACHING THE AUTHOR

When **Sekou Sundiata** discovered there was poetry in "the language we speak," he realized we could, as he put it, make poetry out of what we say all the time. He often gave readings with a group of jazz musicians, fusing his poetry with their music.

   For more about him, see page 1081.

New York Daily News Archive.

Sterling A. Brown: Brown (1901–1989) was an African American poet and a longtime professor at Howard University.

why did you stop me?
Somebody had to stop you.
I watch the news, you always lose.
You're unreliable, that's undeniable.
This is serious, you could be dangerous.   40

I could wake up in the morning
without a warning
and my world could change:
blink your eyes.
All depends, all depends on the skin,   45
all depends on the skin you're living in.

New York City, they got laws
Can't no bruthas drive outdoors,
in certain neighborhoods, on particular streets
near and around certain types of people.   50
They got laws.
All depends, all depends on the skin,
all depends on the skin you're living in.

REFLECTING ON WHAT YOU'VE READ

1. As you listen to the *I* in this poem, does it seem like you are hearing the voice of the author directly, a character speaking for the author, or a character different from the author? What would you use to support your conclusion?

2. Is there an overall tone in the poem, or do different types of tone appear in different parts? If there is more than one, would you say that both or all are true? How would you describe the tone of the repeated phrase "all depends on the skin you're living in"?

3. Reread the first stanza of the poem aloud. Pay close attention to the sounds of the syllables, words, and phrases in those lines (not sounds they describe, but the sounds you hear as you say them aloud). Find examples of repeated consonant sounds and vowel sounds, of words repeated rhythmically, of words that rhyme. Reflect on the "feel" and tone that the sounds create.

4. Do an online search for "Sundiata Blink Your Eyes." You should be able to find video or audio of Sundiata performing the poem. As you listen, compare his reading with the one you just did, and consider if listening to him adds to your impression of the poem and to its effectiveness.

A significant portion of the effect of "Blink Your Eyes" arises from the sounds—the rhymes, the repetitions, the echoes of vowels and consonants that create an aura and reinforce the poem's ironies.

The poem describes an experience of racial profiling: Encountering such racism has the potential to change one's world in the blink of an eye. Even though the speaker voices the poem as an event in his past, he is still able to remember the innocence of his excited anticipation of driving to see his lover. We can feel that throughout the poem's opening section with its vivid picture of how "cool" his car was, as conveyed by the images, and how hip he was, as conveyed by the sounds and rhythms of the words he uses.

Then he is accused of running a red light and everything changes. He realizes there are two different worlds with two different ways of enforcing the law, that it "all depends on the skin you're living in." The subject turns more serious after line 23, but the use of rhyme, the repetition of phrases, and the echoes of vowels and consonants continue, creating a spirit of positive defiance in the face of injustice.

Close examination of techniques of sound can become technical and abstract and risks making you want to back away. Yet only by looking closely can we see exactly how the effects we appreciate are created. We ask you to focus on just four important types of sound technique—alliteration, assonance, repetition, and rhyme—with examples from "Blink Your Eyes" to illustrate them.

TIPS for Reading Poems Aloud

Because of the importance of voice and sounds, it can be helpful to read poems aloud at least once, if not several times, and to listen to someone else read them. Attending to the sounds and rhythms will bring out aspects of the poem that you otherwise might overlook. Here are some suggestions for reading aloud:

- **Don't rush.** Reading too fast distorts the rhythms and blurs the words and sounds.

- **Pay attention to punctuation.** Take a full stop at a period or semi-colon and a brief pause at a comma, both within lines and at the ends of lines.

- **Read with expression.** Your voice needs to convey what the sentences are saying, which means you need to understand the content and tone. But be careful not to overdramatize.

- **Read to communicate.** Even if you are reading to yourself, pretend that you have an audience and that you are trying hard to help them receive and appreciate the poem fully.

Reading aloud might feel uncomfortable at first, but soon you may find yourself enjoying what can happen when you do. It can also influence your silent reading, making you more attentive to your mental voice.

ALLITERATION

One kind of sound, *alliteration*, is the repetition of identical consonant sounds in words relatively near one another (in the same line or adjacent lines usually). Alliteration is most common at the beginnings of words or syllables, especially the beginnings of stressed syllables ("*green* as *grass*"), though it sometimes can occur within words and syllables as well ("*golden baggage*"). Throughout this chapter, the pronunciation is what matters, not the letters. "*Call* the *kid* in the center" does alliterate (Call / kid), but "Call" and "center" do not. Notice the alliterative *s, r, b,* and *l* sounds in these lines:

> Sunroof stereo radio black leather
> bucket seats sit low you know.

Alliteration should be used meaningfully, not just to "show off" an ability. It can call attention to words, giving them greater emphasis, linking words together to get us to connect their meanings, and making phrases more memorable. And it can evoke the feeling of an experience, can elicit emotion, and can intensify tone.

A variant on alliteration is *consonance*, the use of words whose consonant sounds are the same but whose vowels are different. In perfect examples, all the consonants are alike: *live, love; chitter, chatter; reader, rider;* or, in Romeo's words, "I'll *look* to *like,* if *looking liking* move" (*Romeo and Juliet* 1.4.98). The more usual examples of consonance are words in which the consonants following the main vowels are identical: *dive, love; swatter, chitter; sound, bond.* Line 5 of "Blink Your Eyes" (p. 503) employs consonance: "you *could* understand"; likewise, lines 7–8: "It wasn't about no light / it was about my ride."

Thus, alliteration is the repetition of *initial* consonant sounds; consonance is the repetition of *final* consonant sounds.

ASSONANCE

Another kind of sound, *assonance*, is the repetition of identical vowel sounds in words whose consonants differ. It too can be initial ("*under* the *umbrella*"), though internal is more usual ("*tree* by *leaf*," "*tree* and *treat*"). Its strongest effect is a subtle musical quality that often reinforces the tone of a poem, adds gradations to its feel, and contributes to levels of meaning by making connections and adding emphasis. Listen for the assonance in lines 14–16 from "Blink Your Eyes." Then reread them, thinking about its effects.

> Ride when the hard time come, ride
> when they're gone, in other words
> the light was green.

REPETITION

Repetition is the reuse of a word, group of words, line, or lines later in the same poem, but close enough so you remember the earlier use. You may hear the later use as an echo or as a contrast created by a shift in intensity or implication. The lines "All depends, all depends on the skin, / all depends on the skin you're living in" repeat "all depends" and "all depends on the skin" for rhythmic effect, for emphasis, and to build up to the climactic key phrase "on the skin you're living in." These two lines are repeated three times in the poem, increasing the intensity of their emphasis.

APPROACHING THE READING

The following poem is about unrequited love. Listen to how the speaker expresses his feelings and regrets. Notice the poem's unusual twist on memory poems, as it asks the "you" sometime in the future to think back on the speaker and his love. Pay attention to the poem's use of sounds and think about why they are appropriate to what the poem is saying.

APPROACHING THE AUTHOR

William Butler Yeats was tone-deaf. Ironically, in hopes of reviving the bardic tradition in Ireland, he fiercely advocated that his poems be sung or intoned while accompanied by the psaltery, a stringed instrument.

For more about him, see page 1084.

William Butler Yeats   1865–1939

When You Are Old   [1893]

When you are old and grey and full of sleep,
And nodding by the fire, take down this book,
And slowly read, and dream of the soft look
Your eyes had once, and of their shadows deep;

How many loved your moments of glad grace,   5
And loved your beauty with love false or true,
But one man loved the pilgrim soul in you,
And loved the sorrows of your changing face;

And bending down beside the glowing bars,
Murmur, a little sadly, how Love fled   10
And paced upon the mountains overhead
And hid his face amid a crowd of stars.

REFLECTING ON WHAT YOU'VE READ

1. Describe the personality behind the voice heard in the poem.
2. Pick out examples of alliteration and assonance. Consider what these contribute to the poem and how they contribute to its effectiveness.
3. Consider the repeated use of the word *and* and describe the effect its use creates.
4. What do you imagine the reactions of the "you" would be to what the speaker says? What in the poem's use of sounds might have an impact on the one spoken to?

RHYME

You are probably familiar with rhyme. Rhyme, often thought of—wrongly—as a defining characteristic of poetry, is, in fact, only one of many kinds of sound that can appear in a poem. Many poems do not use rhyme. *Rhyme* is the repetition of the final vowel sound and all following consonant sounds in two or more words that have differing consonant sounds preceding the vowel, as in the words *air* and *care* in lines 30–31 from "Blink Your Eyes":

> *Put your hands up in the* air
> *you know the routine, like you just don't* care.

Rhyme leads to various effects. In the lines above, the rhymes become a bitter comic device, used to ridicule the officer who has stopped and racially profiled the speaker. In other situations, rhyme emphasizes important words; it creates a connection or a bonding; it tightens the organization and strengthens unity; it contains meaning; it provides a sense of completion, or termination, to lines, stanzas, and whole poems; and it pleases the ear through its musicality and expectation or surprise. If well written—and well read—rhyme does not distract us from the poem itself but blends with everything else in the poem. When reading a poem aloud, make sure to say the rhyming words in a way that enables a listener to hear the rhymes as echoes of sound, without letting them "steal the show."

Rhyme is described according to several categories: exact or approximate, end or internal, single or double.

Exact or Approximate The definition given above is for *exact rhyme*, in which the vowel and the consonant sounds following the vowel are the same: br*ight* and n*ight*, *art* and h*eart*, "I watch the n*ews, you always* lose."

Approximate rhyme, or *slant rhyme*, is a form of rhyme in which words contain similar sounds but do not rhyme perfectly (usually involving assonance or, more frequently, consonance): d*eep* and f*eet*; rh*yme* and wr*ithe*; g*ate* and m*at*; *all* and st*ole*, w*ill*, or h*ale*.

End or Internal   *End rhyme* involves rhyming words that occur at the ends of lines, such as *air* and *care*:

> Put your hands up in the *air*
> you know the routine, like you just don't *care*.

In **internal rhyme**, two or more words within a line, or within lines near each other, rhyme with each other, or words within lines rhyme with words at the ends:

> I *watch* the news, you *always* lose.
> *You're* unreliable, *that's* undeniable.

Single or Double   *Single rhyme* involves only the final, stressed syllable in rhyming words: *west* and *vest*, a*way* and to*day*.

> All depends, all depends on the *skin*,
> all depends on the *skin* you're living *in*.

In **double rhyme** the accented, rhyming syllable is followed by one or more identical, unstressed syllables: *thrilling* and *killing*, *marry* and *tarry*, un*reliable* and un*deniable*.

> I could wake up in the *morning*
> without a *warning*.

Unless specified otherwise, the word *rhyme* used alone means "exact, end, single rhyme."

Single rhyme used to be called **masculine rhyme** (because it was considered "strong" and "forceful"), and double rhyme was called **feminine rhyme** (because it was regarded as "weaker" than single rhyme). These labels generally are no longer used because of their sexist overtones.

The pattern of end rhymes in a poem or stanza, that is, its recurring sequence, is called its *rhyme scheme*. The pattern is usually described by assigning a letter to each word sound, the same word sounds having the same letter. For poems in stanzas, the pattern is usually the same for each stanza. In that case, you need to mark the rhyme scheme only once. Thus the rhyme scheme of William Butler Yeats's "When You Are Old" (p. 507) is abba.

APPROACHING THE READING

The point of view in the next poem is unusual—the speaker is dead, has been for some time (for centuries), and is thinking back to when she died. Watch for the way her death is described, paying attention to the very precise choices of words and images. And notice the poem's skillful use of alliteration, assonance, and rhyme.

APPROACHING THE AUTHOR

Emily Dickinson wrote nearly eighteen hundred poems during her lifetime, but only about a dozen were published. After her death, her younger sister found forty small, carefully ordered, sewn booklets full of nearly eight hundred of her poems. It took over fifty years for all of her poems to be published in their original form.

For more about her, see page 1061.

Emily Dickinson   1830–1886

Because I could not stop for Death   [c. 1863; pub. 1890]

Because I could not stop for Death—
He kindly stopped for me—
The Carriage held but just Ourselves—
And Immortality.

We slowly drove—He knew no haste   5
And I had put away
My labor and my leisure too,
For His Civility—

We passed the School, where Children strove
At Recess—in the Ring—   10
We passed the Fields of Gazing Grain—
We passed the Setting Sun—

Or rather—He passed Us—
The Dews drew quivering and chill—
For only Gossamer, my Gown—   15
My Tippet°—only Tulle°—   *scarf/silk net*

We paused before a House that seemed
A Swelling of the Ground—
The Roof was scarcely visible—
The Cornice—in the Ground—   20

Since then — 'tis Centuries — and yet
Feels shorter than the Day
I first surmised the Horses' Heads
Were toward Eternity —

REFLECTING ON WHAT YOU'VE READ

1. Summarize the way the poem describes the speaker's passing; explain the central comparison used and the way details and images establish and amplify that comparison.

2. Discuss the implications of the first two lines. What does the speaker suggest when she says she *could* not stop for death? Why not "would not"? Why is death said to "kindly" stop for her? Is it ironic? Why "stopped for me"? Who is in control?

3. Pay attention to the tone of the poem. Do you find a tonal shift? If so, where do you see it in the poem, and what is its effect?

4. There is lots of alliteration and assonance in the poem — pick out examples, and consider what they contribute to voice and tone.

5. Label the poem's rhyme scheme. Notice that the first stanza uses perfect rhyme, but the remaining stanzas use slant rhymes. Think about what that may suggest and how that affects voice and tone.

6. Reflect on the poem as a whole. Death is no joking matter, yet there is a lightness in this poem's central comparison and its use of details. What's going on? Would you call it dark humor? Why or why not? There seems to be a serious point behind it all: If you think there is, how would you describe and discuss it?

Onomatopoeia   In some cases, sounds seem to suggest meaning. This is particularly true in *onomatopoeia*, words whose pronunciation suggests their meaning. In the eighteenth century, Samuel Johnson described it this way: "Every language has some words framed to exhibit the noises which they express, as *thump, rattle, growl, hiss*." Onomatopoeia, at its best, involves not just individual words but entire passages that carry their meaning in their sounds. Listen to these lines from "The Princess" by Alfred, Lord Tennyson: "The moan of doves in immemorial elms, / And murmuring of innumerable bees." Reread Maxine Kumin's "The Sound of Night" (p. 470) and notice her effective use of onomatopoetic language such as "chitter noise," "huggermugger crowd," "skitter across," and "squeak, chirp, dip, and skim."

Sounds Fitting Meaning   The important thing to notice is that sounds in a poem do generally seem to fit the meanings being expressed. Alexander Pope illustrated that point in his poem "An Essay on Criticism" (1711) by suggesting differences in the sounds of the words used to describe a gentle breeze and a fierce storm: "Soft is the strain when Zephyr gently blows" and "The hoarse, rough verse shou'd like the Torrent roar." For an active reader of poetry, therefore, listening attentively to the sounds of words and syllables can enrich your understanding of the meaning that those words are creating.

 CHECKLIST on Reading for Sound

❑ Listen for patterns of sound in poems and pay attention to their effects, especially alliteration (repetition of initial consonant sounds), consonance (repetition of all consonant sounds or of final consonant sounds), assonance (repetition of identical vowel sounds), rhyme (repetition of the accented vowel sound of a word and all succeeding sounds), onomatopoeia (words whose pronunciation suggests their meaning), and repetitions (of words, phrases, or lines).

❑ Practice reading poems aloud and hearing your voice. Notice the syllable sounds, vowel sounds, consonant sounds, and the repetitions and combinations of sounds, and reflect on what they contribute to the poem's effect.

❑ Listen to other people read poems aloud, paying attention particularly to the sounds and their effect.

FURTHER READING

APPROACHING THE READING

The next poem is about a mother's love for her daughter. Notice, as she sews slippers for her daughter's wedding, how the poem weaves together actions in the present with memories from the past and anticipations for the future. Listen to how sounds become part of the weaving, an unobtrusive technique helping to unify the poem's effect.

APPROACHING THE AUTHOR

David Paul Morris/ Getty.

Janice Mirikitani is the founding president of Glide Foundation, an organization dedicated to helping poor people in San Francisco.

For more about her, see page 1072.

Janice Mirikitani   b. 1942

For a Daughter Who Leaves   [2001]

*"More than gems in my comb box shaped by the God of the Sea,
I prize you, my daughter . . ."*

—Lady Otomo, 8th century, Japan

A woman weaves
her daughter's wedding
slippers that will carry
her steps into a new life.
The mother weeps alone   5
into her jeweled sewing box
slips red thread
around its spool,
the same she used to stitch
her daughter's first silk jacket   10
embroidered with turtles
that would bring luck, long life.
She remembers all the steps
taken by her daughter's
unbound quick feet: 15
dancing on the stones
of the yard among yellow
butterflies and white breasted sparrows.
And she grew, legs strong
body long, mind   20
independent.
Now she captures all eyes
with her hair combed smooth
and her hips gently
swaying like bamboo.   25
The woman
spins her thread
from the spool of her heart,
knotted to her daughter's
departing   30
wedding slippers.

REFLECTING ON WHAT YOU'VE READ

1. Try dividing the poem into sections that use luminous, culturally connected
   images to capture experiences the mother recalls. For each, reflect on what
   it is about the images that brings out the meaningfulness of the experiences.

2. Look closely at the poem's use of alliteration and assonance. Read the poem aloud, listening for those sounds. What do you think they add to the poem's effectiveness?

3. What changes in cultural ideas and conditions between the two generations are revealed in the poem? Think about how you react to these changes.

4. What does the epigraph quoting Lady Otomo add to the poem?

APPROACHING THE READING

The following is a narrative poem about an important memory. It recalls an unusual and surprising encounter from the perspective of two of those involved. Listen to the first-person voice as it describes what happens, and be especially aware of the ways that word choice, images, and sounds contribute to the poem's effect.

APPROACHING THE AUTHOR

In addition to her poetry for adults, **Marilyn Nelson** has published four collections of verse for children, including *The Cat Walked through the Casserole.*

For more about her, see page 1073.

Marilyn Nelson   b. 1946

Minor Miracle   [1997]

Which reminds me of another knock-on-wood
memory. I was cycling with a male friend,
through a small midwestern town. We came to a 4-way
stop and stopped, chatting. As we started again,
a rusty old pick-up truck, ignoring the stop sign,   5
hurricaned past scant inches from our front wheels.
My partner called, "Hey, that was a 4-way stop!"
The truck driver, stringy blond hair a long fringe
under his brand-name beer cap, looked back and yelled,
     "You fucking niggers!"   10
And sped off.
My friend and I looked at each other and shook our heads.
We remounted our bikes and headed out of town.
We were pedaling through a clear blue afternoon
between two fields of almost-ripened wheat   15

bordered by cornflowers and Queen Anne's lace
when we heard an unmuffled motor, a honk-honking.
We stopped, closed ranks, made fists.
It was the same truck. It pulled over.
A tall, very much in shape young white guy slid out: 20
greasy jeans, homemade finger tattoos, probably
a Marine Corps boot-camp footlockerful
of martial arts techniques.

"What did you say back there!" he shouted.
My friend said, "I said it was a 4-way stop.   25
You went through it."
"And what did I say?" the white guy asked.
"You said: 'You fucking niggers.'"
The afternoon froze.

"Well," said the white guy,   30
shoving his hands into his pockets
and pushing dirt around with the pointed toe of his boot,
"I just want to say I'm sorry."
He climbed back into his truck
and drove away.   35

REFLECTING ON WHAT YOU'VE READ

1. Notice the way the first sentence seems to continue a conversation, giving an informal, chatty effect to the sound of the poem. How does calling it a "knock-on-wood" memory set up the story? On a second reading, notice how it takes on more significance.

2. Consider how details are used, especially the particularly vivid images. Think about the way imagery creates contrasts that contribute to the surprising way the story ends.

3. Pick out uses of alliteration and assonance in the poem, and consider how the sound contributes to the poem's effectiveness.

4. Consider the poem's title. Why "Miracle"? Why "Minor"?

APPROACHING THE READING

The following poem is a gentle tribute to a grandmother and what made her special. As you read the poem, notice the way it divides into three sections, each beginning "if i" and focusing on a different sense—sight, touch, hearing. Surely much more could have been said about the grandmother; consider why the poem focuses on what it does and why this is enough to achieve its aim.

APPROACHING THE AUTHOR

Ray A. Young Bear first wrote poetry in his tribal language, Meskwaki, and translated it into English. He published his first poem in 1968.
  For more about him, see page 1085.

Ray A. Young Bear   b. 1950

grandmother   [1979]

if i were to see
her shape from a mile away
i'd know so quickly
that it would be her.
the purple scarf   5
and the plastic
shopping bag.
if i felt
hands on my head
i'd know that those   10
were her hands
warm and damp
with the smell
of roots.
if i heard   15
a voice
coming from
a rock
i'd know
and her words   20
would flow inside me
like the light
of someone
stirring ashes
from a sleeping fire   25
at night.

REFLECTING ON WHAT YOU'VE READ

1. After listening to the voice in the poem, think about the extent to which it reveals details about the speaker in light of what it says about the grandmother.

2. Pay attention to the alliteration, assonance, and repetitions. What does their presence contribute to the effectiveness of the poem?

3. The poem relies on straightforward statements until the last five lines, which stand out because they introduce a simile (an explicit comparison using "like" or "as"). Sum up the lines in your own words. Is ending the poem this way satisfying to you? Why? Why not?

4. The poem expresses the speaker's deep devotion to a particular grandmother. If the poem enables you to think of your own grandmother in a fresh way, describe how you now think of her.

APPROACHING THE READING

This next poem invites you to play detective. It gives you a set of clues about why the farmhouse was abandoned and leaves it to you to piece them together and understand what happened. "Something went wrong," the poem says, but it doesn't say what. Be ready to compare your answer with those of other students.

APPROACHING THE AUTHOR

In addition to his career as a poet, **Ted Kooser** worked as vice president of a life insurance company in Lincoln, Nebraska. He would write in the morning before going to work, and he'd show his secretary what he'd written. He'd ask if the poem made sense to her; if it didn't, he knew he had to keep working on it.

For more about him, see page 1070.

Ted Kooser   [b. 1939]

Abandoned Farmhouse   [1980]

He was a big man, says the size of his shoes
on a pile of broken dishes by the house;
a tall man too, says the length of the bed
in an upstairs room; and a good, God-fearing man,
says the Bible with a broken back   5
on the floor below the window, dusty with sun;
but not a man for farming, say the fields
cluttered with boulders and the leaky barn.

A woman lived with him, says the bedroom wall
papered with lilacs and the kitchen shelves   10
covered with oilcloth, and they had a child,
says the sandbox made from a tractor tire.
Money was scarce say the jars of plum preserves

and canned tomatoes sealed in the cellar hole.
And the winters cold, say the rags in the window frames.   15
It was lonely here, says the narrow country road.

Something went wrong, says the empty house
in the weed-choked yard. Stones in the fields
say he was not a farmer; the still-sealed jars
in the cellar say she left in a nervous haste.   20
And the child? Its toys are strewn in the yard
like branches after a storm—a rubber cow,
a rusty tractor with a broken plow,
a doll in overalls. Something went wrong, they say.

REFLECTING ON WHAT YOU'VE READ

1. Detectives trying to solve a case pay close attention to details, especially to little things that might reveal a clue. Explain how this poem employs a similar strategy. What do the various clues suggest about difficulties this family encountered? What do you think went wrong? Were any of the clues particularly helpful? Which ones? Why?

2. The poem includes one simile (an explicit comparison using "like" or "as"), in lines 21–22. Restate the comparison in your own words. Does it stand out or distract you because it's the only one? What might be particularly important about it?

3. The poem uses a lot of alliteration, assonance, and repetition of words. Discuss what those sounds contribute to your experiencing of the poem.

4. Consider the way the poem ends. How did its last two words strike you?

RESPONDING THROUGH Writing

WRITING ABOUT SOUND

Journal Entries

1. The same techniques for word sounds discussed in this chapter are also very important in the world of advertising. As you read or hear advertisements during a day or a few hours, keep track of techniques you notice (alliteration, assonance, repetition, rhyme, and so forth). Jot notes describing the effects that the techniques achieve.

2. Janice Mirikitani's "For a Daughter Who Leaves" (p. 513) about a mother and daughter is told from the mother's perspective. Write a journal

entry in which you retell the story from the daughter's perspective, explaining what the experiences and the cultural artifacts mean from her point of view.

3. The speaker in Marilyn Nelson's poem writes about a "minor miracle" that occurred in her life. Write a journal entry about a minor miracle that occurred in your life. Start by explaining what you mean by "miracle" and "minor."

Literary Analysis Papers

4. Write a paper discussing techniques of sound and their effect in Robert Browning's "My Last Duchess" (p. 497), Leslie Marmon Silko's "Prayer to the Pacific" (p. 575), Garrett Kaoru Hongo's "Yellow Light" (p. 632), Alberto Ríos's "Nani" (p. 648), or another poem of your choice.

5. Write a paper analyzing several effects of using rhyme in Wilfred Owen's "Dulce et Decorum Est" (p. 493).

6. Write a paper analyzing the techniques of sounds used in Emily Dickinson's "Because I could not stop for Death" (p. 510) and their contributions to the poem's meaning and overall effect.

Comparison-Contrast Papers

7. Write a paper on Wilfred Owen's "Dulce et Decorum Est" (p. 493) and Richard Lovelace's "To Lucasta, Going to the Wars" (available online). Explore what you discover about similarities and differences in what they say about war and in how they express their ideas through voice, tone, and sound.

8. Write a paper in which you compare and contrast the use of sounds in two or more poems about taste (food and eating), such as Gwendolyn Brooks's "The Bean Eaters" (p. 468), Li-Young Lee's "Eating Alone" (p. 483), Susan Atefat-Peckham's "Dates" (p. 602), Jimmy Santiago Baca's "Family Ties" (p. 605), or Alberto Ríos's "Nani" (p. 648).

▶ TIPS for Writing about Sound

- **Hear the poem.** Poems often are meant to be heard. As part of your preparation for writing, read the poem aloud several times, listening for its voice and sound dimensions; then listen while someone else reads it aloud to you.

- **Sounds' effects.** The use of sounds (alliteration, assonance, repetition, rhyme) can be a challenging paper topic, especially for poems that make prominent use of such devices—but even their absence can be worth attention as a topic or subtopic in a paper. In addition to describing what devices are used, your paper should consider how they are used, to what degree, and in what contexts, and you should discuss in what ways they are appropriate for what the poem is dealing with.

(continued)

> • **Illustrations and explanations.** A paper on sound must include quotations that illustrate the relevant points you are making. You also will want to explain how the effects of sound are achieved, what goes into creating those effects.
>
> • **Relationship to effect or theme.** A crucial part in any paper on sound must be a discussion of how that element contributes to the effect, theme, or significance of the poem.

WRITING ABOUT CONNECTIONS

Although this chapter focuses particularly on the way sounds interconnect in poems, attention to sounds can also be useful in exploring poems thematically. Focusing on the connections between poems rich in sounds, especially poems from different eras, can lead to a topic that will be interesting to work on and will lead to fresh insights. Here are a few possibilities:

1. "Honoring Grandmothers": Cultural Similarities and Differences in poems about grandmothers, such as Ray A. Young Bear's "grandmother" (p. 516), Judith Ortiz Cofer's "Cold as Heaven" (p. 539), and Alberto Ríos's "Nani" (p. 648)

2. "Writing about Art": How Poems Explore Other Arts in W. H. Auden's "Musée des Beaux Arts" (p. 603), Peter Blue Cloud's "Crazy Horse Monument" (p. 607), John Keats's "Ode on a Grecian Urn" (p. 636), and Kevin Young's "Blues" (p. 660)

3. "Poetry and the Environment": Caring about the Natural World in Wendell Berry's "The Peace of Wild Things" (p. 476), William Stafford's "Traveling through the Dark" (p. 534), and Gerard Manley Hopkins's "God's Grandeur" (p. 572)

WRITING RESEARCH PAPERS

1. Research racial profiling and, if possible, talk to people who have experienced it. Write a paper discussing Sekou Sundiata's "Blink Your Eyes" (p. 503) in light of what you discover.

2. Conduct research into the origins and history of the blues as a musical tradition, and into ways that the blues play a significant roles in literary works, such as Kevin Young's "Blues" (p. 660), James Baldwin's "Sonny's Blues" (p. 324), Honorée Jeffers's "Cotton Field Sestina" (p. 635), and at least six others you find online.

Metaphor has interested me more as a way of knowledge, a way of grasping something. I like to . . . use the metaphor as a way to discover something about the nature of reality.

Charles Simic

(Pulitzer Prize-Winning American Poet)

Figurative Language

CHAPTER 17

Wondering What This Has to Do with That

When Romeo says, "But, soft, what light through yonder window breaks? / It is the east, and Juliet is the sun," the hearer or reader of Shakespeare's *Romeo and Juliet* knows perfectly well that Romeo doesn't think Juliet actually is the sun. He may be lovesick, but he's not loony. The ability almost all of us have to process language lets us understand, almost instantaneously, that Romeo is comparing Juliet to, or identifying her with, the sun. Romeo is making imaginative, not logical, sense. He is using a *figure of speech* or *figurative language*, that is, a shift from standard or customary usage of words to achieve a special effect or particular meaning. He is trying to pack lots of meaning into a few words: that Juliet's beauty dazzles like the sun, that Juliet is the center of his life the way the sun is central to all life and growth. An important part of comprehending poetry is being able to recognize when language is to be taken "figuratively" instead of at face value and what its figurativeness conveys.

From the dozens of specific types of figurative language available to writers, it is valuable for you to know and recognize only five. Some people grimace when asked to learn the particular vocabulary of poetry. But think about it. When you are talking about a sound system, you might use the terms *bass* or *amplifier*. If you can assume that your listener understands these terms, you don't need to take the time to explain them. Similarly, knowing the names of figures provides a useful, shared shorthand when talking about a poem. Equally or even more important than using the correct label, however, is being able to describe what the figure creates in the poem and how it affects your reading. That is the focus in this chapter.

READING FOR SIMILE

To help someone understand something—how you felt on the first day of the new school year, for example—you might use a *comparison*: "When I walked into my first class, my mind seemed as blank as the paper in my notebook." You would be using **simile**, an expression of a direct similarity, using words such as *like*, *as*, or *than*, between two things that would ordinarily be regarded as dissimilar.

Such figurative (that is, unexpected and imaginative) comparisons occur when we discover that two things we assumed were entirely dissimilar actually have attributes in common or when the comparison leads us to a new way of perceiving or considering something. The comparison stretches our ideas about perception and about experiences of the things compared ("I've never thought about or seen it that way before"). The following poem may do this for you.

APPROACHING THE AUTHOR

Martín Espada worked as a salesperson, clerk, telephone solicitor, gas station attendant, bouncer, bartender, printing plant bindery worker, tenant lawyer, and supervisor of a legal services program before becoming a professor of creative writing.

For more about him, see page 1063.

Martín Espada   b. 1957

Latin Night at the Pawnshop   [1990]

Chelsea, Massachusetts,
Christmas, 1987

The apparition of a salsa band
gleaming in the Liberty Loan
pawnshop window:

Golden trumpet,
silver trombone,
congas, maracas, tambourine,   5

all with price tags dangling
like the city morgue ticket
on a dead man's toe.

REFLECTING ON WHAT YOU'VE READ

1. Consider the simile in the last three lines. What makes it such a surprise in this poem? After thinking about the simile and its relation to the rest of the poem, talk about its effect and what makes it, surprising as it is, appropriate. What does it suggest?

2. The simile at the very end of the poem affects all that comes before and makes us reread the poem in a new light. Discuss how that final simile affected your perceptions of and feelings about what came prior to it. Describe the difference in effect if the simile had come at the start of the poem.

3. Discuss the role of the title and why it is an integral part of the poem.

At first the poem can be seen as a vivid description of a collection of instruments in a pawnshop window. But when we encounter the word *apparition*, we realize that the instruments are a ghostly appearance of the band in which they were played. And then we notice the surprising simile that turns the instruments into corpses of unidentified victims in the city morgue. The simile brings out another layer of meaning: In desperation the musicians sold their instruments, leading to the death of the music they loved and, perhaps, to the death of their dreams.

Figures Stretch Our Imaginations   Reread Anita Endrezze's poem "The Girl Who Loved the Sky" (p. 474). Endrezze uses comparisons to get across how a blind girl experiences the world, especially how she conceives the sky she cannot see: "I met a blind girl who thought the sky / tasted like cold metal when it rained." What is the taste of cold metal? Is its taste different in the rain? How can the sky have taste at all? The blind girl uses her imagination to grasp what the sky is like because she can't see it. Endrezze helps us experience that imaginative process by giving us language that stretches our imaginations to a point where our rational minds can't grasp or put into logical terms what the words are expressing. And yet we intuitively understand it.

Figures in Everyday Language   Actually, figurative language isn't limited to literary writers. All of us use it all the time: "I worked like a dog," "tough as nails." In fact, much of language by its very nature is figurative. Almost all of the words we use, except ones that identify concrete objects or actions such as *cup* or *kick*, involve figures. We don't even notice or react to most of the figures we use in everyday language. Some originally inventive figures (a river bed, a table leg) have been absorbed into the language to such an extent that, though they still are figures, we seldom think of them as figurative. And yet even these, when you look at them as figures, may surprise you.

Direct, Surprising Comparisons   Direct comparisons, or similes, are usually the easiest figures to notice because they carry the signal word with them. But only surprising, unexpected comparisons are similes. The comparison discussed above from Anita Endrezze's "The Girl Who Loved the Sky" was a simile. So is this, a few lines further: "On hot, still days / we listened to the sky falling / like chalk dust." The comparison is surprising: It would take keen hearing to catch the sound of chalk dust falling; one would have to be even more alert to hear the sound of the sky falling. Similes appear again later in the poem:

> I was born blind, she said, an act of nature.
> Sure, I thought, like birds born
> without wings, trees without roots.

Here the speaker's comparisons bring out her anger at her friend's fate, but also her failure to understand that her friend, though she cannot see physically, is not rendered helpless the way a bird without wings would be. Also,

> The day she moved
> I saw the world clearly: the sky
> backed away from me like a departing father.

The simile connects two great losses in the speaker's world — her father's absence and her friend's departure — and those losses, at this point anyhow, come to define the way she views her world.

Nonfigurative Comparisons   On the other hand, Endrezze's line "the room smells like glue" is not a simile: It is not surprising and not imaginative (the room smells the way glue smells or smells of glue because glue is used in the room). Comparisons between similar things (squid tastes like chicken; his eyes are like his father's) are straightforward analogies, not similes and not figurative.

APPROACHING THE READING

The following poem uses a series of six comparisons to suggest the effect of having the attainment of one's hopes and aspirations delayed indefinitely. Watch for them as you read, and notice how the sixth is different from the first five.

APPROACHING THE AUTHOR

Langston Hughes thought attending Columbia University would allow him to jump-start his career in poetry, but he actually got his first big break after dropping out and working odd jobs. It was while Hughes was working as a busboy at a hotel in Washington, D.C., that the famous poet Vachel Lindsay, a guest there, discovered Hughes's poems and publicized them. For more about him, see page 1067.

Fred Stein Archive/Getty.

Langston Hughes 1902–1967

Harlem [1951]

What happens to a dream deferred?

Does it dry up
like a raisin in the sun?
Or fester like a sore —
And then run?   5
Does it stink like rotten meat?
Or crust and sugar over —
like a syrupy sweet?

Maybe it just sags
like a heavy load.   10

Or does it explode?

REFLECTING ON WHAT YOU'VE READ

1. How would you explain why each of the comparisons is effective and meaningful?

2. How is the comparison in the final line different from the other five? How does that difference increase its power as well as the impact of the whole poem?

3. The poem refers to any dreams, but especially to the "American dream." If you are not familiar with the term, look it up. Relate it to the title of the poem and consider the bitter ironies that reading evokes.

In response to the question raised in the opening line, Hughes's poem poses further questions, suggesting a number of possible answers. These follow-up questions rely on similes to intensify their points. Read the lines without the similes and notice what happens: "What happens to a dream deferred? Does it dry up or fester? Does it stink, or crust and sugar over? Maybe it just sags." The points make sense. Dreams can dry up if their fulfillment keeps getting put off and the dreamer loses hope of ever achieving or receiving what she or he dreams about. But the points by themselves lack emotional intensity and they certainly aren't memorable.

READING FOR METAPHOR

"All the world is like a stage." "All the world is a stage." Sense the difference? The former is a simile; the latter is a **metaphor,** a figure of speech in which two things usually thought to be dissimilar are treated as if they were the same, the same because they have characteristics in common. The word *metaphor* is derived from the Greek *metaphora,* "carry (*phor*) across (*meta*)." In a metaphor, characteristics of one thing are "carried across" to another, from the thing used to illustrate ("stage") to the subject being illustrated ("world").

Not "Like" But "The Same As"   Metaphors are basic to poetry and are widely used in fiction and drama as well. Shakespeare's character Jaques asserts, "All the world's a stage," in the comedy *As You Like It.* Without even thinking about it, we may treat this as a comparison ("the world is *like* a stage," with people playing roles, making entrances and exits, and so on). The line does not say, however, that the world is *like* a stage but that it *is* a stage. Common sense and logic, of course, claim that the world is not part of a theater. But the figure says it is. Here metaphor opens our minds, enabling us to see what we may not have seen before.

Not Explicit But Implied   Metaphors are easiest to recognize when the comparison is explicit, when *is* or *are* or some other linking word is present, as in "All the world is a stage." More difficult to recognize and explain are *implied metaphors*, in which the *to be* verb is omitted and the comparison may be implied, or "buried," rather than stated directly. "A car thief is a dirty dog" is direct metaphor. "Some dirty dog stole my car" contains an implied metaphor: The key term ("car thief") is implied, and you must supply it to complete the equation involved. Look again at "Harlem." Notice how it relies on a shift from similes in lines 2–10 to the implied metaphor of line 11: "*Or does it explode?*" The reader must supply the object that describes the ultimate effect of having dreams deferred: the possibility of frustration exploding into riot? defeat? revolution? despair? The fact that the poem doesn't use the word it refers to but has the reader think of it makes the conclusion more interactive and its impact all the stronger.

Emotive As Well As Informative   In "The Girl Who Loved the Sky" (p. 474), Endrezze uses both explicit and implied metaphors. "I learned / that numbers were fractious beasts" is an explicit metaphor: Math is equated with a threateningly wild beast. The comparison conveys her feelings vividly. "The bruised petals of her lids" is an implied, or buried, metaphor: The blind girl's eyelids apparently are dark, and this line compares them, even equates them, to the purple petals of the jacaranda tree outside the classroom. Similarly, the final lines of the poem also use metaphor: "until my fist was another lantern / hiding a small and bitter flame." Her fist is not a lantern, but the figure equates it with one; and her fist, like her heart, holds not a literal flame but petals and memories that remind her how the world takes those she loves from her, leaving her lonely and angry.

APPROACHING THE READING

Read the following poem in which the speaker reflects on a southern African city at night and expresses his affection for it, despite its many problems. The poem is rich with figurative language, especially similes and implied metaphors. Watch for the way the figures pack the poem with meaning, beyond what literal equivalents could convey.

APPROACHING THE AUTHOR

Dennis Brutus led the fight to use sports as a weapon against the apartheid policies of South Africa. As a result, he was exiled, shot in the back, and imprisoned in a cell next to Nelson Mandela's on Robben Island, the notorious prison colony.

For more about him, see page 1057.

Dennis Brutus   1924–2009

Nightsong: City   [1963]

Sleep well, my love, sleep well:
the harbour lights glaze over restless docks,
police cars cockroach through the tunnel streets;

from the shanties creaking iron-sheets
violence like a bug-infested rag is tossed   5
and fear is immanent as sound in the wind-swung bell;

the long day's anger pants from sand and rocks;
but for this breathing night at least,
my land, my love, sleep well.

REFLECTING ON WHAT YOU'VE READ

1. The poem starts off as if it were a love poem addressed to a person. At what point do you realize that line 1 is figurative and the "love" it refers to is the city the speaker calls home? What leads you to that realization?

2. In line 3, the author uses a noun (*cockroach*) as a verb and turns it into a vivid metaphor. Explain how it works figuratively and why you think it is effective.

3. Line 4 takes us to a shantytown and helps us see houses with sheet-metal walls and roofs, and hear the sounds as they creak in the wind. The following two lines use similes to convey the violence and fear that pervade the area. Explain the comparisons and discuss their effectiveness.

4. Pick out the metaphors in lines 7 and 8 and, after reading the next section, the personification in line 9. Explain what each contributes to the poem.

The poem starts out with "Sleep well, my love." The title might suggest that a city is the setting for a night song to someone. It might be only after reading it a second time or looking back from the end of the poem that you realize that "my love" is the city that the speaker loves. Saying that a city can sleep compares it to, or identifies it with, a living creature—an animal (metaphor) or a human being (see the next section on personification). The latter seems to fit best: The words of the first line sound like ones the speaker would offer at night to someone cherished. It may come as a surprise that the words are spoken to a city, but of course that shows how much he cares about it.

In this poem, the figurative comparisons add distinctness and vivid immediacy to the appearance of the city at night (harbor lights make the docks look shiny, the way a glaze does when applied to pottery or china; police cars dart around between rows of buildings with the quickness and agility of cockroaches). And they intensify the emotional impact of the descriptions of life in the city: Violence pervades the shantytowns the way bugs infest a rag, fear is as present through the city as the sound of a bell, and the anger that fills the days "pants" everywhere like a fierce animal. But, for the moment, the speaker wants to forget all that. For this one living, "breathing" night, he hopes his beloved city rests quietly and sleeps well.

READING FOR PERSONIFICATION

Personification is a figure of speech in which something nonhuman is given attributes of a person, is treated as if it has human characteristics, or takes human actions. Sometimes abstract qualities are treated as if they are human: In the line "Death, be not proud," from a sonnet by John Donne (p. 620), for example, death is treated as if it is human and could have the human attribute of pride. In other cases, concrete things are given human characteristics: In the lines "the sky / backed away from me like a departing father," from "The Girl Who Loved the Sky" (p. 474), the sky is made human for a moment, able to walk away from the speaker the way her father did.

Personification is sometimes defined incorrectly as treating something not living in terms of just being alive rather than specifically being human. For example, in Shakespeare's *Romeo and Juliet*, Juliet, fearful of being drugged and buried in a vault, expresses fear of the tomb's "foul mouth [that] no healthsome air breathes in" (4.3.34). "Mouth" here is metaphor, not personification, because animals as well as humans have mouths and breathe through them.

A particular type of personification is *apostrophe*, that is, addressing someone not present or something ordinarily not spoken to as if present or capable of understanding, as when Macbeth says "Time, thou anticipatest my dread exploits" (4.1.144). Dennis Brutus uses apostrophe as well when his speaker in "Nightsong: City" talks to the city as if it could hear and understand.

APPROACHING THE READING

The following poem uses figurative language in describing a scene in nature. Watch for places where a nonliving thing is spoken of as if it were living. Then decide which of these exemplify personification and consider what such personifications contribute to the effect of the poem.

APPROACHING THE AUTHOR

Angelina Weld Grimké wrote her three-act play *Rachel* to protest lynching and other racial violence. First performed in Washington, D.C., in 1916 by an all-black cast, it was a response to the highly controversial 1915 silent film *The Birth of a Nation*, which depicts the Ku Klux Klan as heroes and southern blacks as villains.

For more about her, see page 1064.

Angelina Weld Grimké   1880–1958

A Winter Twilight   [1923]

A silence slipping around like death,
Yet chased by a whisper, a sigh, a breath;
One group of trees, lean, naked and cold,
Inking their crest 'gainst a sky green-gold;
One path that knows where the corn flowers were;   5
Lonely, apart, unyielding, one fir;
And over it softly leaning down,
One star that I loved ere the fields went brown.

REFLECTING ON WHAT YOU'VE READ

1. What examples do you find of nonliving things treated as if alive? Point out ones that are personification—where the living attributes apply only to humans—and ones that are metaphors—where the connection could also apply to animals.

2. Consider the effect of personifications in the poem. What do they contribute that a comparison to something nonhuman wouldn't?

You may have heard someone speak of how a painting "brings a scene to life." That could be said of "A Winter Twilight" as well. The poem creates a picture, almost a verbal landscape painting. And, as with a painting, it slows everything to a stop, arrests this one moment, suspending it in time so that we can experience it more deeply. Actual life experiences go by so fast that we can't experience them fully. We need the arts to give us the chance to stop and really take in what otherwise goes by and is lost.

This poet wants not only to see the scene—she also wants to bring alive its feeling and aura. She does so through metaphors and personifications comparing landscape features to living things. That this is a quiet scene is evoked by the way silence "slips around" in it, as an animal or a person would, and the way it is "chased by a whisper." For the trees to be "naked" treats them as living beings, specifically as persons, because that word generally is applied only to humans. Similarly, the path comes alive through personification (since it "knows" where the corn flowers are), as does the "lonely" fir tree (a word usually reserved for a human conscious reaction to feeling cut off from what matters).

A winter scene can seem dead and lifeless, and the poem is acutely aware of death, mentioning it in the opening line; but that very awareness heightens the way the figures of speech bring out the life present even in a "barren" landscape. The poem closes with a sense of the intimacy of life and death: The star is given the living attribute of "leaning down," but this is a star the speaker loved (past tense—does she or he no longer love it?) before the fields "went brown" (died? lost their appeal and desirability?).

READING FOR METONYMY AND SYNECDOCHE

Substituting Something Closely Associated Another figure of speech that, like metaphor, talks about one thing in terms of another is *metonymy*, a figure of speech in which the name of one thing is substituted for that of something closely associated with it. Like similes and metaphors, metonymies are used every day. When you hear a news reporter say, "The White House announced today . . . ," you've encountered a metonymy: "White House" invites you to visualize a familiar image closely associated with the president that substitutes for the staff members who issued the announcement. When the speaker in "The Girl Who Loved the Sky" (p. 474) says her friend "had no eyes," she does not mean that the girl's eye sockets were empty; she substitutes "eyes" for what is closely associated with eyes, "sight," because the word *eyes* is more concrete and vivid than the abstract word *sight*.

Substituting a Part for the Whole   A subset of metonymy is *synecdoche*, a special kind of metonymy in which part of a thing is substituted for the whole of which it is a part. When someone says to you, "Give me a hand," she or he actually wants help not just from your hands but also from the rest of you. Likewise, the familiar phrases "many mouths to feed" or "let's count noses" use synecdoche. When the two girls in "The Girl Who Loved the Sky" (p. 474) are swinging and flying (note the metaphor—riding in a swing is something like flying) high over the other girls' heads, "heads" is synecdoche, a part substituted for the whole because it is the highest part of the other girls' bodies.

The Importance of Little Things   Recognizing metonymies and synecdoches helps you appreciate the way little things can have greater importance than they seem to at first. Robert Frost said, "If I must be classified as a poet, I might be called a Synecdochist, for I prefer the synecdoche in poetry," that figure of speech in which "a little thing touches a larger thing." Instead of starting with huge, complex themes and issues, Frost often uses local, everyday experiences as subjects, trusting our minds will be led to "a larger thing."

APPROACHING THE READING

The following poem is about a wealthy man whose lifestyle everyone envies. Watch in it for examples of nonliteral expression, figures of various sorts, including metonymy and synecdoche. Consider how the figures work (what is compared to what or what is substituted for what), and why the use of figures is effective and contributes to the poem's overall effect.

APPROACHING THE AUTHOR

Because **Edwin Arlington Robinson**'s parents wanted a girl, they hadn't decided on a boy's name before he was born. When they visited a holiday resort with their still-unnamed six-month-old, the other vacationers decided that he should have a name. They selected a man from Arlington, Massachusetts, to draw one out of a hat.

For more about him, see page 1078.

Edwin Arlington Robinson   1869–1935

Richard Cory   [1897]

Whenever Richard Cory went down town,
We people on the pavement looked at him:
He was a gentleman from sole to crown,
Clean favored, and imperially slim.

And he was always quietly arrayed,   5
And he was always human when he talked;
But still he fluttered pulses when he said,
"Good-morning," and he glittered when he walked.

And he was rich—yes, richer than a king—
And admirably schooled in every grace: 10
In fine, we thought that he was everything
To make us wish that we were in his place.

So on we worked, and waited for the light,
And went without the meat, and cursed the bread;
And Richard Cory, one calm summer night,   15
Went home and put a bullet through his head.

REFLECTING ON WHAT YOU'VE READ

1. Pick out examples of metonymy and synecdoche and explain how they
   work (what is being substituted for what). What do they contribute to the
   effect of the poem?

Here are three other figures of speech that you will frequently encounter:

- *Paradox*: A figure of speech in which a statement initially seeming
  self-contradictory or absurd turns out to make good sense when
  seen in another light. In Shakespeare's *Much Ado about Nothing*, for
  example, when the Friar says to Hero, "Come, lady, die to live"
  (4.1.252), he is using paradox. By pretending to die, she may
  regain the reputation she has lost through false slander. A subset of
  paradox is *oxymoron*, a self-contradictory combination of words or
  phrases, such as "O brawling love! O loving hate! . . . Feather of lead,
  bright smoke, cold fire, sick health!" in Shakespeare's *Romeo and
  Juliet* (1.1).
- *Hyperbole*: Exaggeration, or overstatement; a figure of speech in which
  something is stated more strongly than is warranted. Hyperbole is
  often used to make a point emphatically, as when Hamlet protests

that he loved Ophelia much more than her brother did: "Forty thousand brothers / Could not with all their quantity of love / Make up my sum" (5.1.272–74).

- *Understatement*: A figure of speech that expresses something in an unexpectedly restrained way. Paradoxically, to de-emphasize through understatement can be a way of emphasizing, of making people react with "there must be more to it than that." When Mercutio in *Romeo and Juliet*, after being stabbed by Tybalt, calls his wound "a scratch, a scratch" (3.1.92), he is understating, for the wound is serious. He calls for a doctor in the next line and dies a few minutes later.

2. Describe the speaker. What is the effect of using *we* for the speaker instead of *I*? Could one say that "We people on the pavement" is a kind of synecdoche? Explain.

3. Pick out examples of other figures of speech. Explain how they work and what they bring to the poem. Also point out examples of irony (see p. 488). Consider how both figures and irony bring out the "point" of the poem.

Robinson's poem seems a good example of Frost's point about being a synecdochist: The poem has lots of little things that touch larger things. One person speaks the poem but uses the pronoun *we*, thus attempting to suggest that what he felt was true for the whole population of the town. The poem focuses on "little" details—the way Richard Cory dresses, walks, and talks (even the way he says so little a thing as "Good-morning" makes hearts beat faster). The townspeople long for any little thing to improve their lives, "light" substituting for "better days" because they see only dark despair around them and get by on almost nothing ("bread" substituted for "bare essentials") because they can't afford anything more ("meat" substituted for luxuries of any sort). Robinson could have told the story without figures of speech, but the use of synecdoches especially, with their emphasis on parts and small aspects, seems right for a poem that contrasts having a lot and having very little.

TWO OTHER OBSERVATIONS ABOUT FIGURES

No sharp lines divide figures of speech from one another. Read the following poem about a driver coming upon a deer that an earlier driver had struck and killed. Watch for the way it relies on images and figures for its effect and for the way some figures could be labeled and explained in different ways.

APPROACHING THE AUTHOR

William Stafford began publishing his poetry late in life, his first major
collection appearing when he was forty-eight years old. He kept a daily
journal for fifty years and composed nearly 22,000 poems, of which
roughly 3,000 were published.
  For more about him, see page 1080.

William Stafford   1914–1993

Traveling through the Dark   [1962]

Traveling through the dark I found a deer
dead on the edge of the Wilson River road.
It is usually best to roll them into the canyon:
that road is narrow; to swerve might make more dead.

By glow of the tail-light I stumbled back of the car   5
and stood by the heap, a doe, a recent killing;
she had stiffened already, almost cold.
I dragged her off; she was large in the belly.

My fingers touching her side brought me the reason—
her side was warm; her fawn lay there waiting,   10
alive, still, never to be born.
Beside that mountain road I hesitated.

The car aimed ahead its lowered parking lights;
under the hood purred the steady engine.
I stood in the glare of the warm exhaust turning red;   15
around our group I could hear the wilderness listen.

I thought hard for us all—my only swerving—
hithen pushed her over the edge into the river.

REFLECTING ON WHAT YOU'VE READ

1. Pick out several figures of speech, identify them, and explain how they
   work. Which ones could be labeled as more than one type of figure? Explain
   why or how. Consider why images seem appropriate in the first twelve lines
   and figures in the last six.

2. The figures supply a large part of the poetic impact of the poem. However,
   there are other poetic aspects that come through the use of alliteration and
   assonance, along with some slant rhyme (see p. 509). Mark examples of such
   sound techniques. Think about how they cooperate with the figurative language to develop the theme of the poem.

The first twelve lines of the poem are narrative, describing what happened. They rely on images, without any figures. Lines 13–18 reflect on the experience and use a good deal of figurative language, such as bringing the car to life by having it purr like a harmless cat (though ironically it was a similar car that killed the deer) and making the wilderness not just a living thing but one that listens and presumably understands. And the word *swerve*, which is used in a literal sense in line 4, comes back in a figurative sense in line 17 as the speaker momentarily avoids doing what he must before proceeding to do it.

ALTERNATIVE WAYS OF EXPLAINING FIGURES

The poem illustrates two important characteristics of figurative language. First, a figure often fits into more than one category. "I could hear the wilderness listen," for example, stands either as metonymy ("wilderness" being substituted for the creatures and the natural habitat in it) or as personification ("wilderness" given the humanlike ability to understand, not just hear). In this and most cases, applying labels to figures is a means to an end: It alerts you to their presence, helps you talk and write about them, and helps clarify the nature of the imaginative action you experience as you read them.

In addition to being aware that figures overlap with each other, keep in mind that figures of speech occur *within* poems, not *as* poems. Some people attempt to treat entire poems as figures of speech. After reading "Traveling through the Dark," they may say, "On the surface it's about a man finding a deer on the road, but what it's *really* about is our journey through life and the difficult decisions we face along the way." They substitute an abstract "meaning" for the concrete images of the poem. The poem is *really* about a deer on the road, though it may *also* (as opposed to *really*) be about life's journey. This book discusses images before figures because of the importance of grounding the experience in images and of letting the action or description be first and always itself.

 CHECKLIST on Reading for Figurative Language

❑ Notice any figurative language and the way it works imaginatively, especially these five types:

- Simile: the expression of a direct similarity, using words such as *like*, *as*, or *than*, between two things usually regarded as dissimilar
- Metaphor: treating two things usually thought to be dissimilar as if they are the same and have characteristics in common

(continued)

- Personification: treating something nonhuman as if it has human characteristics or takes human actions
- Metonymy: substituting the name of one thing for that of something closely associated with it
- Synecdoche: substituting a part of something for the whole of it

❑ Consider how the choice of a figure affects the concept being developed.

FURTHER READING

APPROACHING THE READING

In the following poem the speaker thinks back to her boarding school days, recalling her excitement on parental visitation days. She eagerly anticipates the arrival of her mother, whom she idolizes as all but perfect in appearance and self-confidence. As you read and then reread the poem, think about the way it uses similes and metaphors to clarify and amplify the speaker's emotions then and later.

APPROACHING THE AUTHOR

Chris Felver/Getty.

Sharon Olds developed a program at Goldwater Hospital (a hospital in New York City for the severely disabled) that enables residents to create poems.

For more about her, see page 1074.

Sharon Olds   b. 1942

Parents' Day   [1995]

I breathed shallow as I looked for her
in the crowd of oncoming parents, I strained
forward, like a gazehound held back on a leash,
then I raced toward her. I remember her being
much bigger than I, her smile of the highest   5

wattage, a little stiff, sparkling
with consciousness of her prettiness—I
pitied the other girls for having mothers
who looked like mothers, who did not blush.
Sometimes she would have braids around her head like a   10
goddess or an advertisement for California raisins—
I worshipped her cleanliness, her transfixing
irises, sometimes I thought she could
sense a few genes of hers
dotted here and there in my body   15
like bits of undissolved sugar
in a recipe that did not quite work out.
For years, when I thought of her, I thought
of the long souring of her life, but on Parents' Day
my heart would bang and my lungs swell so I could   20
feel the tucks and puckers of embroidered
smocking on my chest press into my ribs,
my washboard front vibrate like scraped
tin to see that woman arriving
and to know she was mine.   25

REFLECTING ON WHAT YOU'VE READ

1. Consider what the speaker's voice expresses beyond what the words explicitly say.

2. Pick out similes and metaphors and be attentive to what they reveal about the mother and daughter. In what ways do they add to the poem's impact?

3. The speaker's present feelings about her mother are not the same as the ones she remembers. Describe the difference, and point out specific places where the difference appears. Why do you think it was important for the speaker to express her feelings about her memories of Parents' Day?

4. What is suggested by the final line—what is significant enough about it to give it that emphatic position?

APPROACHING THE READING

The following poem creates an uncommon way of experiencing and reflecting on a snowstorm. On a second reading, consider how its depiction of snow is achieved through its images and figures of speech. Notice how the poem leads you to visualize the snowfall and invites you to consider some deep and lasting human questions.

APPROACHING THE AUTHOR

Mary Oliver draws much of her poetry from the natural landscape of
Cape Cod where she lives. She once found herself lost in the woods and
deeply inspired, but without pen and paper. She soon returned and hid
pencils in the trees so she would never find herself in the same situation
again.

For more about her, see page 1074.

Mary Oliver   b. 1935

First Snow   [1983]

The snow
began here
this morning and all day
continued, its white
rhetoric everywhere   5
calling us back to *why, how,*
whence such beauty and *what*
the meaning; such
an oracular fever! flowing
past windows, an energy it seemed   10
would never ebb, never settle
less than lovely! and only now,
deep into night,
it has finally ended.
The silence   15
is immense,
and the heavens still hold
a million candles; nowhere
the familiar things:
stars, the moon,   20
the darkness we expect
and nightly turn from. Trees
glitter like castles
of ribbons, the broad fields
smolder with light, a passing   25
creekbed lies
heaped with shining hills;
and though the questions
that have assailed us all day
remain—not a single   30
answer has been found—

walking out now
into the silence and the light
under the trees,
and through the fields,   35
feels like one.

REFLECTING ON WHAT YOU'VE READ

1. The poem begins with a narrative account of the snow falling all day, using several figures that invite readers to reflect and wonder. For a couple of them, you may need to look up words ("white *rhetoric*," "*oracular* fever"); be ready to explain them, as well as the use of *flowing* and *ebb*.

2. About halfway through, the figures turn visual. Pick out several examples and be able to describe the effect of that change. How do the images and figures in the first half relate to those in the second half?

3. What do you think "the questions / that have assailed us all day" are? How would you explain the lines in the context of the poem?

4. What do you think the speaker implies by saying that walking out into the snowfall feels like an "answer"?

APPROACHING THE READING

The next poem, like the previous one, is about snow — but this one takes a different perspective. The speaker is trying to explain snow to her dying grandmother who has lived her entire life in the Caribbean and who thinks of heaven as cool and refreshing. Watch for the speaker's use of strikingly imaginative figures of speech to describe what experiencing snow is like.

APPROACHING THE AUTHOR

Of her career, **Judith Ortiz Cofer** says, "All I know is that I'm a writer, period, writing about the one thing that defines me as a human being — my biculturalism."
   For more about her, see page 1059.

Judith Ortiz Cofer   b. 1952

Cold as Heaven   [1995]

Before there is a breeze again
before the cooling days of Lent, she may be gone.
My grandmother asks me to tell her
again about the snow.
We sit on her white bed   5

in this white room, while outside
the Caribbean sun winds up the world
like an old alarm clock. I tell her
about the enveloping blizzard I lived through
that made everything and everyone the same;   10
how we lost ourselves in drifts so tall
we fell through our own footprints;
how wrapped like mummies in layers of wool
that almost immobilized us, we could only
take hesitant steps like toddlers   15
toward food, warmth, shelter.
I talk winter real for her,
as she would once conjure for me to dream
at sweltering siesta time,
cool stone castles in lands far north.   20
Her eyes wander to the window,
to the teeming scene of children
pouring out of a yellow bus, then to the bottle
dripping minutes through a tube
into her veins. When her eyes return to me,   25
I can see she's waiting to hear more
about the purifying nature of ice,
how snow makes way for a body,
how you can make yourself an angel
by just lying down and waving your arms   30
as you do when you say
good-bye.

REFLECTING ON WHAT YOU'VE READ

1. Consider weather in the poem. How does literal weather fit in the poem?
   In what ways is weather metaphorical? Why are both essential for the poem
   to have the deepest impact?

2. Pick out uses of simile, metaphor, metonymy, and synecdoche. What do
   they add to the poem's meaning and effect?

3. Discuss the relationship between the granddaughter and grandmother.
   How would you describe the tone (attitude of the speaker toward her
   grandmother's death and toward herself)? Point out figures that express
   what both are feeling.

4. How would you explain the implications of the simile in the poem's title?
   Consider the contrasts between cold and heat throughout the poem. What
   does snow convey in the poem? What do you think the speaker means in
   line 17 by saying, "I talk winter real for her"?

RESPONDING THROUGH **Writing**

WRITING ABOUT FIGURATIVE LANGUAGE

Journal Entries

1. Look for similes as you read your favorite magazine; look at advertisements in magazines, online, or on billboards; or watch commercials on TV. List several examples in your journal, and comment on why advertisement writers often use similes.

2. As a journal entry, finish this line: "Waiting for you is like _____." Come up with three different similes, each having the effect of "stretching your reader's perception." Try to push each one further than the one before. For example:

   like waiting for summer
   like listening to a scratched CD
   like Thursday

   Then, choose a subject and write several different figures for it, for example:

   Love is like _____.
   Love is _____.
   Love _____.

   Write a paragraph in which you discuss the varied effects that the different figures create.

3. Watch and/or listen to several comedians. Write a journal entry discussing their uses of paradox, overstatement, and understatement.

Literary Analysis Papers

4. Write an explication focused on the role of personification and metaphor in Emily Dickinson's "Because I could not stop for Death" (p. 510).

5. Go back to one of the poems in Chapters 14–16 that relies heavily on figurative language, such as Robert Hayden's "Those Winter Sundays" (p. 466), Li-Young Lee's "Eating Alone" (p. 483), or Wilfred Owen's "Dulce et Decorum Est" (p. 493). Write a paper discussing the effect of figurative language in the poem.

6. Write a paper discussing the use of figures (see pp. 521–535) and archetypes (see pp 112–113) in A. E. Housman's "To an Athlete Dying Young" (p. 633). Consider how the poem's ideas relate to the present-day emphasis on superstar athletes and athletics.

Comparison-Contrast Papers

7. Write a paper comparing and contrasting the attempts to escape difficult economic situations in Orlando Ricardo Menes's "Courtyard of Clotheslines, Angel Hill" (p. 641) and Luis Rodriguez's "Running to America" (p. 649).

8. Write a paper comparing and contrasting these two poems about sports and death: A. E. Housman's "To an Athlete Dying Young" (p. 633) and Jack Ridl's "My Brother—A Star" (p. 647).

TIPS for Writing about Figurative Language

- **Main topic or subtopic** As with most elements of poetry, you can concentrate on figurative language as the main subject of a paper or include it as a subtopic in a paper that concentrates on other aspects of the poem.

- **How it works and what it achieves** When writing about figurative language, you should both explain how the figure works (what is compared to what or equated with what or substituted for what) and discuss the effect, role, or meaning that the imaginative language contributes to the poem.

- **Focusing on altered perceptions** Figurative language often alters the ways we perceive things. For example, it may lead readers to see an image in a fresh, unusual, even challenging way. Explaining in detail how that occurs can turn into an engaging topic for a paper or a section of a paper.

- **Focusing on figurative patterns** A discussion of the imagery of a poem or group of poems, in the sense of a related pattern of imaginative comparisons and allusions running through an entire literary work or a portion of one (see p. 1139), can be an illuminating topic for a paper.

- **Using correct labels** For a paper dealing specifically with figurative language, it is wise to use the traditional terminology (*simile, metaphor, implied metaphor, personification, metonymy, synecdoche,* and *paradox*) and to use it precisely.

WRITING ABOUT CONNECTIONS

Figures of speech, by their nature, make connections, and many of the topics suggested above involve discussions of the surprising and meaningful comparisons, equations, and substitutions that establish such imaginative connections. The same kind of imaginative thinking can be used in noticing surprising and meaningful thematic connections between poems and turning them into interesting paper topics. Here are a few possibilities to illustrate:

1. "Let me count the ways": Contrasting Approaches to Love Poetry in Elizabeth Barrett Browning's "How do I love thee?" (p. 608) and Gary Miranda's "Love Poem" (p. 557)

2. "A Joyful Melancholy": Nature and Beauty in Mary Oliver's "First Snow" (p. 538) and Angelina Weld Grimké's "A Winter Twilight" (p. 529)

3. "A Peaceful Passing": Metaphors of Death in Robert Frost's "After Apple-Picking" (p. 628) and Jane Kenyon's "Let Evening Come" (p. 638)

WRITING RESEARCH PAPERS

1. Research the history and controversies surrounding the Crazy Horse Memorial in the Black Hills of South Dakota and use what you find to illuminate Peter Blue Cloud's poem "Crazy Horse Monument" (p. 607).

2. Conduct research into the problem of spouse or partner abuse and into poems related to the subject, such as Jo Carson's "I Cannot Remember All the Times" (available online) or poems in Mary Marecek's book *Breaking Free from Partner Abuse; Voices of Battered Women Caught in the Cycle of Domestic Violence* (1993) or another similar book. Write a paper on how poetry has been and can be used as a way of dealing with the problem or communicating to others about the problem.

There's poetry in the language I speak. There's poetry,
therefore, in my culture, and in this place.

Sekou Sundiata

(American Poet; see pp. 503 and 1081)

CHAPTER **18 Rhythm and Meter**

Feeling the Beat, the Flux, and the Flow

Our lives are rich with rhythms: the regular rhythms of sunrise and
sunset, the change of seasons, the waves on the shore, the beats of our heart,
even the routines in our lives—holidays, trash days, final exam week, income
tax time. Life also has irregular rhythms that are, paradoxically, rhythmical:
the syncopations of the city, the stutter step of a basketball player, the anxious cadence of our speech under stress and uncertainty, people dropping by,
and the infamous pop quiz. We need rhythms and live by them, regardless
of whether we are aware of them. The same can be said of poetry: Every
poem has rhythm, and experiencing a poem fully requires being attentive to
its rhythms. This chapter focuses on the ways rhythms, regular and irregular,
contribute to a poem's impact and meanings and on ways to help you hear
and feel these rhythms more accurately and more intensely.

READING FOR RHYTHM

All dynamic writing has **rhythm**, the patterned "movement" created by
words and their arrangement. Poetry in particular emphasizes it. Rhythm is
somewhat difficult to describe. Because no set of precise descriptive labels is
available, we turn to metaphorical language. We say that rhythm is, for example, fast, slow, syncopated, disjointed, smooth, halting, graceful, rough,
deliberate, frenzied, or a mixture of any of these. The differing rhythms result
from different ways of handling a variety of formal structures in the poems.

LINE LENGTH

Short lines can have one effect, long lines another, though the effect varies from poem to poem. Usually short lines create a faster rhythm and longer lines create a slower rhythm, but that's not always the case. Compare the rapid rhythms in the short lines of Maya Angelou's "Africa" (p. 602) with the slower ones of Lucille Clifton's "at the cemetery, walnut grove plantation, south carolina" (p. 554), and the fairly rapid, long lines of David Mura's "Grandfather-in-Law" (p. 643) with the slower ones of Gerard Manley Hopkins's "God's Grandeur" (p. 572).

PHRASINGS

The combinations of short and longer groups of words into phrases affect a poem's rhythm, creating cadences, especially the regularity or irregularity of movement across and down the page. See, for example, how phrasings contribute to Leslie Marmon Silko's "Prayer to the Pacific" (p. 575).

LINE ENDINGS

Lines without end punctuation are said to "run on" into the next line (**run-on lines**; also called **enjambment**), which tends toward a faster, smoother pace from line to line. Lines with end punctuation, especially periods and semicolons (**end-stopped lines**), often slow the reader down. Notice the difference in rhythm between lines 1–2 (end-stopped) and lines 3–4 (run-on) of the third stanza of Edwin Arlington Robinson's, "Richard Cory" (p. 532):

> And he was rich—yes, richer than a king—
> And admirably schooled in every grace:
> In fine, we thought that he was everything
> To make us wish that we were in his place.

Lines broken at unexpected or irregular places create a jolt and break up the rhythmic flow; line breaks at expected or "natural" places create a gentle shift that carries the rhythm along gracefully.

PAUSES

Pauses (or lack of them) within lines can affect their pace and smoothness. A *pause*, called a *caesura* and usually indicated by punctuation, tends to break up the flow of a line, slow it down a bit, sometimes even make it "jagged" or "halting." Compare the first three lines, broken by pauses, with the unbroken last line of the final stanza of "Richard Cory" (p. 532):

So on we worked, and waited for the light,
And went without the meat, and cursed the bread;
And Richard Cory, one calm summer night,
Went home and put a bullet through his head.

How would placing a comma after "home" in the last line change the effect?

SPACES

Leaving gaps within, at the beginning or end of, or between lines can slow the movement, even stop it altogether, or indicate which words to group together; crowding things together can speed up a rhythm. (Note the various uses of spacing in "Buffalo Bill 's" on the next page.)

WORD CHOICE AND COMBINATIONS OF SOUNDS

Words that are easy to say together can create a steady, smooth, harmonious pace in a line; those hard to say can make it "jagged" or "harsh" or "tired" or simply slow and deliberate. Notice the difference between the way sounds slide into each other and are easy to say in the line "And he was always human when he talked," from the second stanza of "Richard Cory," and the way the words in the last line, "Went home and put a bullet through his head," force us to enunciate each separately and distinctly. The sounds don't flow together but come from different parts of the mouth, which takes longer to get them out.

It is important to realize that different rhythms may be appropriate for the same experience. For example, a frantic or a calm rhythm may be appropriate for a poem about a traffic accident, depending on what the poet wants you to experience.

APPROACHING THE READING

The following poem celebrates a hero of the old American West. As you read it, notice the effects of line lengths, line endings, pauses within lines (or lack of them), spaces, word choices, and combinations of sounds.

APPROACHING THE AUTHOR

E. E. Cummings wrote his first of some eventual 2,900 poems when he was only three years old. It read, "Oh, the pretty birdie, O; / with his little toe, toe, toe!"

For more about him, see page 1060.

E. E. Cummings 1894–1962

Buffalo Bill 's   [1923]

Buffalo Bill 's
defunct
             who used to
             ride a watersmooth-silver
                                      stallion   5
and break onetwothreefourfive pigeonsjustlikethat
                                         Jesus
he was a handsome man
                      and what i want to know is
how do you like your blueeyed boy   10
Mister Death

REFLECTING ON WHAT YOU'VE READ

1. Try reading the poem aloud, respecting line divisions by pausing briefly at
   the ends of lines (but without letting your voice drop the way it does at the
   end of a sentence) and reading "onetwothreefourfive" as nearly like one
   word as possible. Listen for how all this affects pace and rhythm.

2. Then read for meaning. What is the effect on meaning to put individual
   words on separate lines, to break lines and situate words at unexpected
   places, and to jam several words together? Write a brief statement of your
   interpretation of the poem's theme.

To help focus on the effect of gaps, spaces, line divisions, and line
groupings, listen to the poem the way it could have been written—in six
lines, using conventional punctuation, and a fairly regular beat:

Buffalo Bill's defunct, who used to ride
A water-smooth silver stallion and break
One, two, three, four, five pigeons, just like that.
Jesus, he was a handsome man.
And what I want to know is,
How do you like your blue-eyed boy, Mister Death?

Notice how Cummings's form of the poem creates a rhythm entirely different from this version written in six conventional lines. The rhythm definitely affects the meaning.

• A line break invites you to pause briefly after "Buffalo Bill 's," to linger
  on the name and give it emphasis as well as creating a moment of

anticipation. Without the line break, the emphasis would fall on "defunct," instead of each line receiving emphasis.

- The pause in the middle of the infinitive "to ride" shifts meaning from "used to *ride*" to "who *used to*," which reinforces the meaning of "defunct" (used to but does so no more). This break simultaneously sets up anticipation and emphasizes the loss.
- Emphasis falls next on "a watersmooth-silver" and on "stallion," a single-word line emphatic in both rhythm and meaning.
- Jamming the words "onetwothreefourfive" and "pigeonsjustlikethat" together creates a quick staccato rhythm that echoes the rapid firing of a revolver.
- The rhythm slows with "Jesus" set off in a line of its own far to the right: Its position far to the right requires a pause, not unlike the exhaled sigh one expresses when saying "Jesus" in this manner, but so does the extra space between it and the next line of text.
- The next three phrases also are slower and more reflective. Their similarity in length (six, seven, and eight syllables) creates a rhythmical similarity that makes the short, abrupt last line surprising in rhythm as well as in meaning and tone.

After saying all this about rhythmic strategies in "Buffalo Bill 's," it is important to emphasize that rhythm is not fixed. Your involvement as a reader is crucial. How long a word is to be "held," how much stress is to be put on a syllable, how short a short line is and how long a long line is, and how much pause there is in a pause are effects you create or decide on.

READING FOR METER

As part of their rhythm, poems can have a regular "beat." You're already familiar with beat: When you listen to certain types of music, you are probably struck by or react to the beat. You may say or hear someone else say, "I love the beat of that song."

Stressed and Unstressed Syllables   A beat in poetry arises from the contrast of emphasized (stressed or accented) and muted (unstressed or unaccented) syllables. Poetry with a steady beat, or measured pulse, is said to have *meter*, a regularized beat created by a repeating pattern of accents or syllables or both. The most widely used type of meter in English (called *accentual-syllabic*) takes into account both the number of stresses and the number of syllables per line. If you're unsure about syllables and accents for a particular word, check a dictionary: It divides each word into syllables and indicates where the stress falls as you pronounce it.

The process of picking out a poem's meter by marking stressed and un-stressed syllables is called *scansion*. For a fuller and more technical discussion of meter and scansion, see the appendix on scansion (p. 1086).

Poetic Feet   The basis of accentual-syllabic meter is the repetition of metrical "feet." A *foot* is a two- or three-syllable metrical unit made up (usually) of one stressed and one or two unstressed syllables. As these combinations of unstressed plus stressed syllables (*da DA*, or *da da DA*) are repeated, a regular pattern or beat (*da DA da DA da DA*, or *da da DA da da DA*) becomes established in your ear; you unconsciously expect to continue to hear it, and you notice variations from the "norm."

Iambic Meter   There are terms, or names, for these feet. The *da DA* feet, called *iambs*, create iambic meter. Listen for it in this line:

i AM bic ME ter GOES like THIS.

Now listen for it in the opening lines of Alfred, Lord Tennyson's "Ulysses" (p. 653):

it LITtle PROfits THAT an I-dle KING
by THIS STILL HEARTH, aMONG these BARren CRAGS,
MATCHED with an A-ged WIFE, i METE and DOLE
unEqual LAWS unTO a SAvage RACE,
that HOARD, and SLEEP, and FEED, and KNOW not ME

Iambic is by far the most frequently used foot. The other feet are often used for variation in mostly iambic poems, though sometimes they are found as the dominant foot in an entire poem.

Trochaic Meter   The inversion of the iambic foot is the *trochee* (*DA da*), which forms a trochaic meter (again, listen for it):

TRO chees PUT the AC cent FIRST.

In the third line quoted above from "Ulysses," "MATCHED with" is a trochaic foot, used as a *substitution* (a different kind of foot put in place of the one normally demanded by the meter). Substitutions add variety, emphasize the dominant foot by contrasting with it, and often coincide with a switch in meaning. Here the substitution makes "MATCHED with" more emphatic and foregrounds its meaning.

Listen for trochaic feet in this stanza from the introduction to William Blake's (mostly cheerful) *Songs of Innocence*:

> PIPing DOWN the VALleys WILD,
> PIPing SONGS of PLEASant GLEE,
> ON a CLOUD i SAW a CHILD,
> AND he LAUGHing SAID to ME:
>
> "PIPE a SONG aBOUT a LAMB."
> SO i PIPED with MERry CHEER.

Stresses are never equally strong; this lack of equality is one way of attaining rhythmic variety even in lines that are metrically regular. Thus, in the third line, CLOUD and CHILD get more stress than ON and SAW. Some syllables (AND in line 4, SO in line 6) are given a light stress mainly because we expect, from the pattern established, that they *should* be stressed. You may have noticed that these lines have four stressed syllables but only three unstressed syllables; the fourth trochee in each line is incomplete, lacking its unstressed syllable, which is replaced by a mandatory pause: All the lines are end-stopped. This is another way to do something unusual with, and add variety to, a metrical poem.

Anapestic and Dactylic Meters   Two other feet add an unstressed syllable to the feet described above: an *anapest* adds one to an iamb (*da da DA*), and a *dactyl* adds one to a trochee (*DA da da*). Whole poems in these meters are unusual; they are typically used for substitutions in predominantly iambic or trochaic poems. Here, however, are the final lines from a poem mostly in anapestic meter, also by William Blake, "The Chimney Sweeper" (available online), which appeared in his more pessimistic *Songs of Experience*. The poem describes the awful lives of small boys forced to climb up chimneys and clean out the soot. The lilting anapests create a sharply ironic contrast with the content, as Tom receives comfort from a dream about heaven he had the night before:

> Though the MORNing was COLD, Tom was HAPpy and WARM;
> So if ALL do their DUty, they NEED not fear HARM.

Spondee   One other important foot, the *spondee*, has two stressed syllables (*DA DA*), with no unstressed syllables, as in GOOD NIGHT and RAGE, RAGE in these lines from a poem by Dylan Thomas pleading to his father not to accept death passively and quietly (p. 584):

> Do NOT go GENtle INto THAT GOOD NIGHT.
> RAGE, RAGE aGAINST the DYing OF the LIGHT.

Many other feet have been given names, but knowing these five (iamb, trochee, anapest, dactyl, spondee) will enable you to describe the basic meter and variations from it in most poems—and describing them will help you hear them more clearly.

Line Lengths The other thing to notice in poems in traditional meters involves the length of the lines. Line lengths are measured by the number of feet in each line and are labeled with names derived from Greek roots; for example,

monometer = a line with one foot

dimeter = a line with two feet

trimeter = a line with three feet

tetrameter = a line with four feet

pentameter = a line with five feet

hexameter = a line with six feet (and so on)

The line we used above ("iAMbic MEter GOES like THIS") is *iambic tetrameter*. The description identifies the predominant foot (here, iamb) and the predominant line length (four feet) in a poem—that is, the ones used the majority of the time.

APPROACHING THE READING

The following poem by a late-nineteenth-century African American poet expresses the conflict experienced by persons of color forced to conform to societal expectations of behavior and attitude. Wearing a mask serves as a powerful metaphor for keeping their true feelings hidden. Try picking out the meter in the poem by noting the syllables stressed in each line.

APPROACHING THE AUTHOR

Although he excelled in school, **Paul Laurence Dunbar** was forced to take a job as an elevator operator because of his race. He frequently wrote poetry during slow hours, earning him the moniker "elevator boy poet."

For more about him, see page 1062.

Paul Laurence Dunbar   1872–1906

We Wear the Mask   [1896]

We wear the mask that grins and lies,
It hides our cheeks and shades our eyes,—
This debt we pay to human guile;
With torn and bleeding hearts we smile,
And mouth with myriad subtleties.   5

Why should the world be over-wise,
In counting all our tears and sighs?
Nay, let them only see us, while
    We wear the mask.

We smile, but, O great Christ, our cries   10
To thee from tortured souls arise.
We sing, but oh the clay is vile
Beneath our feet, and long the mile;
But let the world dream otherwise,
    We wear the mask!   15

REFLECTING ON WHAT YOU'VE READ

1. Hearing a regular beat in the first few lines should be fairly easy: All the words have one syllable, and important words alternate with less important ones. Label the predominant meter and the predominant line length. Do you find any variations (substitutions) from the predominant feet? If so, point them out.

2. Label the metrical feet and length of lines 9 and 15. What is the effect of changing from the longer lines to which our ears have become accustomed to a shorter line?

3. Notice the interplay between rhythmic devices and meter. The meter provides a very regular beat, but pauses and variance in line endings break up the rhythm and keep the beat from dominating the poem. Point out examples, especially from lines 8–15.

4. In what sense could writing a poem on this topic in a traditional meter be thought of as an example of wearing a mask?

In this poem, the meter stands out; it is almost glaringly regular. Here and there a spondee may be substituted for one of the predominant iambs, depending on where a reader decides to place particular emphasis. "We" might well be stressed equally with the verb following it in lines 1, 9, 10, 12, and 15, in order to emphasize the *people* who are forced to present a false image to others while hiding their authentic self: "WE WEAR," "WE SMILE," "WE SING." A poem that calls attention to the mask also lifts it off, enabling us to realize that it is a mask, that it is a lie (line 1), and, ironically, that it is a form of resistance at the same time it is a mark of servitude.

One could even ask, in that regard, if the use of meter in Dunbar's poem serves also as a mask. In the late nineteenth century, meter was still expected in poetry. Only a few poets, such as Walt Whitman, wrote nonmetrical poems, and Whitman was regarded warily as a radical. An African American poet had to use meter to have her or his work be read widely and not be dismissed as unskilled. But it must have created some tension to write in the cadences of white educated society instead of the cadences and rhythms sung by workers in the fields or when they gathered in the evenings. So

Dunbar wrote in meter, probably to have his verse accepted but also perhaps because its strict, almost excessive regularity might suggest that the metrical form is a mask, a lie, a form not freely chosen but forced on him.

What does paying attention to meter gain you? It can help you hear more clearly a central rhythmic feature in a metrical poem: its regular beat and the irregular alterations in that beat. Poems written in meter usually have a dominant foot, that is, one used the majority of the time. Once you get accustomed to the meter, your ear becomes attuned to that foot, begins to expect it, and notices when a different foot is substituted and alters the "sameness." Such substitution is an important means of controlling emphasis as well as adding variety.

> ☑ **CHECKLIST on Reading for Rhythm and Meter**
>
> ❑ Listen for and respond to the rhythms of poems.
>
> ❑ Note formal structures that affect rhythm (such as line length, line endings, pauses, word choice, combinations of sound).
>
> ❑ Listen for the difference between poems with metrical verse (written in meter with a regular beat, such as "Richard Cory" — p. 532) and nonmetrical verse (such as "Cold as Heaven" — p. 539).
>
> ❑ Listen for the recurring beat in metrical poems and be able to identify the most important traditional metrical feet: iamb (*da DA*), trochee (*DA da*), anapest (*da da DA*), dactyl (*DA da da*), and spondee (*DA DA*).

FURTHER READING

APPROACHING THE READING

In the following poem, the speaker recalls and reflects on a visit to a plantation and what the tour guide does and does not point out. The guide says nothing about the slaves who worked there. It is as if they never lived. Listen to the poem's rhythms — how the lines, line endings and groupings, combinations of words and sounds and pauses all lead you to speed up, slow down, pause, and adjust your timing, and thus contribute significantly to the poem's impact.

APPROACHING THE AUTHOR

Lucille Clifton traced her family's roots back to the West African kingdom of Dahomey, which is now the Republic of Benin. Caroline, the captured Dahomey woman who founded Clifton's family in America, recurs throughout Clifton's poetry as a motif of strength and endurance.

For more about her, see page 1059.

AP Photo/Mark Lennihan.

Lucille Clifton   1936–2010

at the cemetery, walnut grove plantation,
south carolina, 1989   [1991]

among the rocks
at walnut grove
your silence drumming
in my bones,
tell me your names.   5

nobody mentioned slaves
and yet the curious tools
shine with your fingerprints.
nobody mentioned slaves
but somebody did this work   10
who had no guide, no stone,
who moulders under rock.

tell me your names,
tell me your bashful names
and i will testify.   15

the inventory lists ten slaves
but only men were recognized.

among the rocks
at walnut grove
some of these honored dead   20
were dark
some of these dark
were slaves
some of these slaves
were women   25
some of them did this
honored work.
tell me your names
foremothers, brothers,
tell me your dishonored names.   30
here lies
here lies
here lies
here lies
hear   35

REFLECTING ON WHAT YOU'VE READ

1. This poem begins as a poem of address. Consider how the rhythms of the poem fit the way that the speaker addresses the dead slaves.

2. Select groups of two or three lines anywhere in the poem and mark the stressed syllables (see the appendix on scansion [p. 1086] for the traditional method of doing so). Is there a regular beat all the time, or some of the time, or never? If there is a regular beat at all, comment on how it contributes to the rhythm and effect of the poem.

3. Describe the rhythm of the last five lines. What makes it effective? What is the effect of the serious pun as the last line?

4. "[T]ell me your names," the speaker says, "and i will testify" (ll. 13, 15). What does "testify" denote and connote here? In what sense is the poem itself a testimony? In what sense does it have the rhythms of testimony? Why can the speaker testify even though she receives no response to her request in line 13?

APPROACHING THE READING

The following poem is also a memory poem: The speaker thinks back on a decision, a turning point she or he will long remember and reflect on. Unlike the previous poem, this one is metrical throughout. Read the poem, emphasizing the meter. Then reread it, concentrating on words and expression, feeling the meter as you would a bass guitar behind a rhythm guitar. Think about how meter contributes in significant ways to the poem's rhythm.

APPROACHING THE AUTHOR
Robert Frost never worked at a desk or in a designated writing room. He preferred sitting in an armless chair with a writing board. "I use all sorts of things," he once said. "Write on the sole of my shoe."

Lofman/Getty.

For more about him, see page 1063.

Robert Frost   1874–1963

The Road Not Taken   [1916]

Two roads diverged in a yellow wood,
And sorry I could not travel both
And be one traveler, long I stood
And looked down one as far as I could
To where it bent in the undergrowth;   5

Then took the other, as just as fair,
And having perhaps the better claim,
Because it was grassy and wanted wear;
Though as for that, the passing there
Had worn them really about the same,   10

And both that morning equally lay
In leaves no step had trodden black.
Oh, I kept the first for another day!
Yet knowing how way leads on to way,
I doubted if I should ever come back.   15

I shall be telling this with a sigh
Somewhere ages and ages hence:
Two roads diverged in a wood, and I—
I took the one less traveled by,
And that has made all the difference.   20

REFLECTING ON WHAT YOU'VE READ

1. This poem is often read as a poem about not conforming to the majority, taking the road that most do *not* take. However, Robert Frost was hesitant about advocating that reading. What other reading or readings could you give to the poem? Think about a choice you made in your life and what you found yourself thinking about it afterward.

2. Frost called himself a "Synecdochist" because he preferred poetry in which "a little thing touches a larger thing" (see p. 531 for the quote and p. 531 for *synecdoche*). What does this suggest about the choice that the speaker made and about the poem as a whole? What does it suggest about details in the poem? Consider the little word *by* in line 19. What different ways can you read that line based on the meanings of the word?

3. Frost commented that his poems often say one thing in order to mean another. Where do you see possible instances of that in this poem? For example, what do you make of the word *sigh* (l. 16)? Think about some of its connotations.

4. Mark the stressed and unstressed syllables in the poem, and try dividing them into poetic feet. What foot is predominant? Label it and the line length. Note instances that vary from the predominant foot, and consider how such variations affect the way you read the poem.

5. Describe the poem's rhythm, and point out techniques that shape the rhythm. Be ready to comment on how meter contributes to the overall rhythm.

6. Why would a poet as intelligent and crafty as Frost end this famous poem with a cliché, with something so trite?

APPROACHING THE READING

The following poem, like the two previous ones, is a memory poem, or at least culminates as a memory poem. Unlike the others, it is a love poem, albeit an unusual one because it approaches its subject indirectly. Notice rhythms as you read and reread it: The poem talks about rhythm ("slow motion," music, dancing) as well as employs it. Reflect on how the poem's rhythm fits with and contributes to its meaning and effect.

> **APPROACHING THE AUTHOR**
>
> **Gary Miranda** stopped writing poetry when he became a father, feeling that he couldn't do justice to both callings. He turned to writing screenplays instead and has completed six so far.
>   For more about him, see page 1072.

Gary Miranda   b. 1938

Love Poem   [1978]

A kind of slant: the way a ball will glance
off the end of a bat when you swing for the fence
and miss — that is, if you could watch that once,
up close and in slow motion; or the chance
meanings, not even remotely intended, that dance   5
at the edge of words, like sparks. Bats bounce
just so off the edges of the dark at a moment's
notice, as swallows do off sunlight. Slants

like these have something to do with why *angle*
is one of my favorite words, whenever it chances   10
to be a verb; and with why the music I single
out tonight — eighteenth-century dances —
made me think just now of you untangling
blueberries, carefully, from their dense branches.

REFLECTING ON WHAT YOU'VE READ

1. Miranda brings together a group of things that one would not expect to go together, let alone in a love poem: a foul ball when the batter swings for a home run, the music of eighteenth-century dances, untangling blueberry branches, his love of the word *angle* when used as a verb, bats and swallows, dense branches. What do you make of this combination, and what do you think these things have to do with love?

2. Notice as you read how the rhythms of the lines fit what the poem is saying. Think about how you would describe that.

3. Look for where there is a regular beat (a metrical beat) and where you find that breaking down or becoming more of a syncopated rhythm. Consider what makes this appropriate, effective for what the poem is working with.

4. How would you describe the speaker and the speaker's attitude toward love?

APPROACHING THE READING

Each of the following three poems deals with the theme of identity. Decide which of them is / are written in meter and which is / are nonmetrical. Watch for how their handling of rhythm, metrical or nonmetrical, contributes to the effect and meaning of each poem.

Emily Dickinson   1830–1886

I'm Nobody! Who are you?   [c. *1861*; pub. 1891]

I'm Nobody! Who are you?
Are you—Nobody—Too?
Then there's a pair of us?
Don't tell! they'd advertise—you know!

How dreary—to be—Somebody!   5
How public—like a Frog—
To tell one's name—the livelong June—
To an admiring Bog!

Sylvia Plath   1932–1963

Metaphors   [1960]

I'm a riddle in nine syllables,
An elephant, a ponderous house,
A melon strolling on two tendrils.
O red fruit, ivory, fine timbers!
This loaf's big with its yeasty rising.   5
Money's new-minted in this fat purse.
I'm a means, a stage, a cow in calf.
I've eaten a bag of green apples,
Boarded the train there's no getting off.

Georgia Douglas Johnson · 1880–1966

Wishes   [1927]

I'm tired of pacing the petty round of the ring of the thing I know—
I want to stand on the daylight's edge and see where the sunsets go.

I want to sail on a swallow's tail and peep through the sky's blue glass.
I want to see if the dreams in me shall perish or come to pass.

I want to look through the moon's pale crook and gaze on the moon-man's
    face.   5
I want to keep all the tears I weep and sail to some unknown place.

REFLECTING ON WHAT YOU'VE READ

1. Read each poem aloud. Listen for a regular beat or look for a regular pattern; if you find a regular beat and/or pattern, mark syllables in several lines to help you decide if the poem is metrical.

2. If the lines are metrical, label the metrical form and listen for how the meter interacts with and becomes part of the rhythm. Consider how the meter shapes or contributes to intensity, emphasis, meaning, and implications.

3. If the lines are not metrical, consider how the rhythm seems appropriate to and helps develop the subject, tone, and theme.

4. For each poem, write a brief statement of theme and a brief explanation of how rhythm contributes to the way the poem deals with its themes.

RESPONDING THROUGH Writing

WRITING ABOUT RHYTHM AND METER

Journal Entries

1. Review the discussion of prose rhythms in Chapter 9 (p. 227). Then read a poem written in long, prose-like lines, such as Joanne Diaz's "Pride and Prejudice" (p. 619), David Mura's "Grandfather-in-Law" (p. 643), or Walt Whitman's "Song of Myself" (p. 657). In your journal, discuss ways that rhythms in prose and rhythms in poetry are similar and different (and are created in similar and different ways).

2. Fill in the following sentence: I got up this morning and _____, then I _____, and then I _____. Now break it into rhythmic units,

writing each unit as a line of poetry. Try dividing it in other places. In your journal, discuss how rhythm and emphasis change as a result of different breaks, and reflect on the kinds of aesthetic decisions a writer has to make about where to divide lines.

3. Nursery rhymes and children's poetry are often written in meter. Choose two or three examples, write a few lines of each in your journal, mark the stressed syllables, and label the metric foot and line length. Then write a journal entry examining the handling of meter in a nursery rhyme or children's poem—or more than one of them—and discussing why meter is an effective technique in verse for children.

Literary Analysis Papers

4. Write a paper on the effect of sound and rhythm on the characterization of the speaker and the development of theme in T. S. Eliot's "The Love Song of J. Alfred Prufrock" (p. 624).

5. Write a paper discussing the interaction of meter and rhythm in Wilfred Owen's "Dulce et Decorum Est" (p. 495), Andrew Marvell's "To His Coy Mistress" (p. 640), Dudley Randall's "Ballad of Birmingham" (p. 646), or Dylan Thomas's "Do not go gentle into that good night" (p. 584).

6. Write an analysis of rhythm in Quincy Troupe's "A Poem for 'Magic'" (p. 656). As you closely study the poem, watch for ways that the rhythms of basketball become part of the rhythms of the poem.

Comparison-Contrast Papers

7. Write a paper discussing similarities and differences in tone, technique, and theme in Lucille Clifton's "at the cemetery, walnut grove plantation, south carolina, 1989" (p. 554) and Thomas Gray's "Elegy Written in a Country Churchyard" (published 1751 and available online).

8. Rhythm is important in poems about dance, often for theme as well as technique. Write a paper comparing and contrasting the presence of rhythm in two or more of the following poems: Theodore Roethke's "My Papa's Waltz" (p. 486), Gary Miranda's "Love Poem" (p. 557), Lucille Clifton's "homage to my hips" (p. 613), and Billy Collins's "Nostalgia" (p. 614), and Natasha Trethewey's "Domestic Work, 1937."

▶ **TIPS for Writing about Rhythm and Meter**

- **Deciding about rhythm and meter.** If rhythm and meter are integral to the discussion of your topic, it is essential to include them, at least as a subtopic. Be sure to use specific examples (including quotations) and thorough explanations. Otherwise, making them part of your

(continued)

paper is seldom crucial in the way it might be for diction, tone, or figurative language. However, finding a way to refer to them could enrich your paper and add more sophistication to it.

- **Focusing on rhythm.** When working with a poem's rhythm as the main subject of a paper, it is important to make sure that you choose a poem or poems in which the rhythm plays a key role, is distinctive, carries meaning and / or feeling, creates an impact, or is handled in an otherwise especially subtle or distinctive way. Such a paper will need to include a careful analysis of the techniques used to achieve the poem's rhythmic effects and of the way they contribute to its theme or significance.

- **Focusing on appropriateness.** An interesting approach to a paper about rhythm can be one in which you examine how the rhythm of a poem is appropriate for the speaker or the speaker's tone and voice in dealing with the poem's subject or some combination thereof.

- **Focusing on form and rhythm in free verse.** For free verse, writing about the relationship between form and rhythm, especially how form often results from decisions about rhythm, can be a fruitful topic for a paper or a subtopic in a paper focusing on other aspects of the poem.

- **Focusing on meter.** For an example of how to write a paper focused on meter and its effect on rhythm, see the appendix on scansion (p. 1086). Working with such a topic turns out best when an author uses meter in especially meaningful, integrated, or unusual ways. A metrical poem that is almost entirely regular and predictable won't give you much to talk about unless there is particular significance, accomplishment, or irony in its regularity.

WRITING ABOUT CONNECTIONS

There is a tendency to think in terms of relating metrical poems to other metrical poems and nonmetrical poems to nonmetrical ones, but that overlooks other significant linkages. Valuable thematic connections can occur from pairing poems that have similar subjects but that handle rhythm quite differently. Here are some possibilities:

1. "On the Road Again": The Search for Self in Lorna Dee Cervantes's "Freeway 280" (p. 610) and Alfred, Lord Tennyson's "Ulysses" (p. 653)

2. "Seeing the World Clearly": The Theme of Abandonment in Anita Endrezze's "The Girl Who Loved the Sky" (p. 474) and Ted Kooser's "Abandoned Farmhouse" (p. 517)

3. "Grief beyond Grief": Dealing with Death in two or more of the following: Emily Dickinson's "Because I could not stop for Death" (p. 510), Judith Ortiz Cofer's "Cold as Heaven" (p. 539), Susan Atefat-Peckham's "Dates" (p. 602), John Donne's "Death, be not proud" (p. 620), A. E. Housman's "To an Athlete Dying Young" (p. 633), Jane Kenyon's "Let Evening Come" (p. 638), and Jack Ridl's "My Brother—A Star" (p. 647)

WRITING RESEARCH PAPERS

1. Conduct research on Walt Whitman (1819–1892) as an innovator in American poetry, especially in his use of rhythms. Start with the biographical sketch on page 1083 and the excerpts from "Song of Myself" on page 657. Go on from there to read more of his poetry and more about his life, works, and influence.

2. Write a paper on William Blake's critique of the social and / or economic situation in early nineteenth-century England, especially the neglect and exploitation of children. Do research on the topic, and read several poems by Blake that deal with the subject, including "The Chimney Sweeper" and others from Blake's *Songs of Experience*, such as "Holy Thursday" and "London" (they are available online). As part of your analysis, consider the appropriateness of Blake's use of form, meter, rhythm, and rhyme in developing his themes.

That's something which is not always recognized, the freeing effect of a lot of traditional techniques.

Richard Wilbur
(Pulitzer Prize-Winning American Poet)

Form and Type
Delighting in Design

Think of the effect when a well-designed Internet site appears on the screen—how it can catch your eye, grab your attention, and make you want to explore the site further. We notice such effective uses of shape or layout every day all around us. The impact of visual design, along with internal design, is often part of poetry's appeal. *Form* can refer to external structure, the way the poem looks on the page—which may relate to the type of poem it is (its "genre") and to what the poem is dealing with. It can refer also to the inner structure that arranges, organizes, or connects the various elements in a work. Every poem has form, in both senses. This chapter will help you appreciate the formal constructs of poems. It will discuss the role of form and of poetic types, as well as what form can mean, embody, express, or reveal.

In some cases, poets start out with an external form in mind. It may be an "inherited" stanza form like ballad stanza or blank verse, or an inherited poetic type—perhaps a haiku or a sonnet or a villanelle. In other cases, instead of starting with a form in mind, poets begin with an image, feeling, experience, or idea, or with a few words or lines. The writing itself leads to or creates the form, both the inner arrangement and the external shape. The form is a result, therefore, of working with the other elements of poetry.

READING FOR LINES

Most poems are written in *lines*, and each line normally focuses our attention and holds something of significance to the whole poem. In prose, the layout on the page is controlled by margins. Poets, however, control the beginnings and ends of lines, giving them additional opportunities for added attention, anticipation, and emphasis. Each line also creates a rhythm, what Ezra Pound called "the musical phrase."

Lines can also become units of rhythm discovered or decided on within a sentence. As you read line by line, feel the musicality with each. At the same time you need to read "past" the lines to follow the meaning of the sentences. This superimposing of lines on sentences can also direct our attention to words that might otherwise get passed over. Watch for this in the following poem.

APPROACHING THE AUTHOR

In 1950, **Gwendolyn Brooks** became the first African American to win a Pulitzer Prize.

For more about her, see page 1057.

Gwendolyn Brooks   1917–2000

We Real Cool   [1960]

The Pool Players.
Seven at the Golden Shovel.

We real cool. We
Left school. We

Lurk late. We
Strike straight. We

Sing sin. We
Thin gin.° We

Jazz June.° We   5
Die soon.

REFLECTING ON WHAT YOU'VE READ

1. Read the poem aloud, pausing at the end of each line by emphasizing the *We.* Don't let your voice drop because the sentence continues in the next line.

2. What is the effect of dividing the sentences into two lines?

---

thin gin: drink diluted gin.
Jazz June: Brooks, in a PBS NewsHour interview, said, "I used the month of June as a symbol, an establishment symbol. Whereas the rest of us love and respect June, and wait for it to come so we can enjoy it, they would jazz June, derange it, scratch in it; do anything that would annoy the establishment."

3. What is the effect of starting each new sentence at the end of each line?

4. Notice the cumulative effect of the various things the pool players at the Golden Shovel boast about doing. What poetic devices are used to unify and build the intensity of the lines?

5. What is the effect of having a deliberate rhyme scheme (see p. 509), even a typical end-rhyme format? How is it affected by the addition of the repeated *We* at the line's end?

6. Notice the last line, lacking the *We* and the third beat. What effect does this create?

Not all poems are separated into lines: *Prose poems* are a notable exception. The prose poem works with all the elements of poetry except line. It is often written in common paragraph form. It is a hybrid form, drawing together some of the best aspects of both prose and poetry, thus creating new possibilities out of the challenges presented by the way it fuses the two forms. For an example of a prose poem, see Atsuro Riley's "Drill" (p. 581).

The unusual line breaks create anticipation and a jazzlike rhythm, they place emphasis on both the subjects and predicates of the sentences, and they lead to the isolated and unsettling last line. Test the effect of the poem's line breaks and the importance of its form by reading it this way:

We real cool.
We left school.

We lurk late.
We strike straight.

We sing sin.
We thin gin.

We jazz June.
We die soon.

The words are the same, but it is not the same poem. Changing the form of a poem gives it a different effect and makes it a different work.

Part of the pleasure for us as readers is that we can respond to the rhythms of lines, can notice and feel how certain words get emphasized by their position in the line, can appreciate the interplay between line and sentence, and can recognize and experience the role of each line in the life of a poem. Notice and feel the rhythms and emphases in the lines as they are used in varying ways throughout the rest of this chapter.

READING FOR STANZAS

The word *stanza* derives from the Italian word for "room," so one could say that stanzas are "rooms" into which some poems are divided. A **stanza** is a grouping of poetic lines into a section, set off by a space, either according to a given form—each section having the same number of lines and the same arrangement of line lengths, meter, and rhyme—or according to shifts in thought, moment, setting, effect, voice, time, and so on.

Invented Stanza Forms   Stanza shapes can be *invented*, that is, individually created, and thus be unique to a particular poem. The poet may plan such a stanza form before beginning to write or may create it in the process of writing. Look again at "We Real Cool" (p. 564). Probably no other poem in existence has stanzas just like these. Perhaps the first stanza found its own form, without conscious attention to it; perhaps Brooks initially wrote

> We real cool.
> We left school.

and then realized the powerful effect of ending the lines with *We*. If so, at that point Brooks began consciously thinking about the form and making the other stanzas fit the form she had "found" for the first one.

Inherited Stanza Forms   Many stanza patterns, however, are not invented but *inherited*: handed down through the centuries, from one generation of poets to another, often with a prescribed meter and sometimes a set rhyme scheme. The most frequently used inherited stanza forms, in the past and today, are four-line stanzas called **quatrains**. One variety of quatrain, the **ballad stanza**, has a long history and was used in traditional ballads for many centuries. The ballad stanza is a simple but easily adaptable form—four-line stanzas rhyming *abcb* with eight syllables in the first and third lines, six in the second and fourth. Perhaps it is easier to visualize in diagram form (each square equals one syllable):

							a
						b	
							c
						b	

Look for that structure in the following poem, about a young boy's first encounter with racism and the lasting impression that experience had on him (in some of its lines, you will find an extra syllable—that's typical of the form).

Countee Cullen   1903–1946

Incident   [1925]

for Eric Walrond°

Once riding in old Baltimore,
   Heart-filled, head-filled with glee,
I saw a Baltimorean
   Keep looking straight at me.

Now I was eight and very small,   5
   And he was no whit bigger,
And so I smiled, but he poked out
   His tongue, and called me, "Nigger."

I saw the whole of Baltimore
   From May until December;   10
Of all the things that happened there
   That's all that I remember.

APPROACHING THE AUTHOR

Countee Cullen was born 30 March 1903, but scholars don't know where (Louisville? Baltimore? New York City?) nor with whom he spent the earliest years of his childhood.
   For more about him, see page 1060.

REFLECTING ON WHAT YOU'VE READ

1. Notice that each stanza is made up of one sentence. What is the effect of the spaces after lines 4 and 8 that divide the poem into three stanzas? How would the poem read differently if it were a single unit of twelve lines, without stanza breaks? Explain.

2. Each sentence is divided into four lines. On the one hand, we need to read past the lines and grasp the meaning of the sentence as a whole. But we also should give attention to the lines as units. What is the effect of the division into lines? What is lost when you read straight through without such divisions?

Traditionally, ballad stanzas were used for narrative poems, often tragic stories with a melancholy tone. Cullen's use of the form seems appropriate:

Eric Walrond: Walrond (1898–1966) was a writer and activist in the New York literary community from the early 1920s.

Like the early folk ballads, it tells a sad story, with a distinctly melancholy tone. A great deal of the poem's emotional power is generated by its form. The stanzas divide the incident into three distinct segments, each building to a climax. The lines help control the rhythm, leading us to pause after each line and focus on each statement individually, letting its point sink in. And the words at the end of the second and fourth lines in each stanza receive strong emphasis, from their position in the stanzas and from the rhyme. The poem opens with an "old world" sense of decorum conveying the child's natural excitement, void of any apprehension. Then comes the "incident" and we move to the speaker's later realization: that no matter how much positive experience he accumulates, it is cruelty's impact that he remembers. The word *incident* sometimes carries a connotation of inconsequence. The irony of Cullen's title is certainly bitter.

> Other stanza forms are used less frequently. Some well-known inherited examples are described in the glossary (pp. 1131–50). Look, for example, at *Chaucerian stanza, ottava rima, Spenserian stanza,* and *terza rima.*

Inherited Poetic Types   In addition to inherited stanza forms are inherited poetic types. A poet may start out planning to write a poem as a preset type, such as a sestina or a sonnet, because its traditional form feels right for the subject. Or the poet may use an inherited type to participate in a centuries-old poetic tradition, or to meet the imaginative challenge of working within specified formal requirements.

Or the poet may think about an inherited form while writing — may start with a subject or images but no particular form in mind, and then discover that an effective way the poem can develop is as a sonnet, as a sestina, as couplets, or as a variation on a particular form. In such cases, the poet discovers that the poem "needs" or perhaps even "demands" that form, or the poet may realize that the form may be the perfect "fit" for that poem.

READING SONNETS

The inherited form you are likely to encounter most often is the *sonnet*. These fourteen-line poems originally were lyrical love poems, but they came to be used also for meditations on death and nature. Poets now use the sonnet form for all subjects. In English, they are usually written in iambic pentameter (see p. 551). You can visualize a typical sonnet as a grid of 140 squares in fourteen rows, each row containing ten squares. The poet must fit one syllable into each square, with those in the even-numbered squares usually being stressed, those in the odd-numbered ones unstressed, and the final syllables fitting a given rhyme scheme. Sonnets in English typically fall into two types, differentiated by the structure of their development and their rhyme schemes.

ENGLISH (OR SHAKESPEAREAN) SONNET

The *English sonnet* is formed of three quatrains (four-line units, typically rhyming *abab cdcd efef*) and a couplet (two rhyming lines), as in the following diagram:

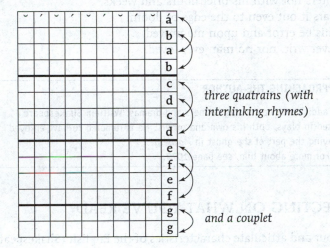

three quatrains (with interlinking rhymes)

and a couplet

Usually the subject is introduced in the first quatrain, expanded or restated in different terms in the second, and expanded further or restated again in the third; the couplet adds a logical, sometimes pithy conclusion or a surprising twist.

APPROACHING THE READING

The following sonnet can be read as a definition, proclaiming that true love remains devoted regardless of what affects it. It explains by saying what true love is and what it is not. That alternating pattern clarifies and reinforces the meaning. Watch for how Shakespeare uses figurative language to both structure the poem and amplify its meaning.

William Shakespeare   1564–1616

Let me not to the marriage of true minds   [1609]

Let me not to the marriage of true minds
Admit impediments. Love is not love
Which alters when it alteration finds,
Or bends with the remover to remove.
Oh, no, it is an ever-fixèd mark   5

That looks on tempests and is never shaken;
It is the star to every wand'ring bark,
Whose worth's unknown, although his height be taken.
Love's not Time's fool, though rosy lips and cheeks
Within his bending sickle's compass come;   10
Love alters not with his brief hours and weeks,
But bears it out even to the edge of doom.
  If this be error and upon me proved,
  I never writ, nor no man ever loved.

APPROACHING THE AUTHOR

In addition to composing sonnets and dramas, **William Shakespeare**
acted in plays, both his own and others'. He is rumored to have enjoyed
playing the part of the ghost in *Macbeth*.
  For more about him, see page 1079.

REFLECTING ON WHAT YOU'VE READ

1. Point out and articulate characteristics of the English (Shakespearean) sonnet in this poem.

2. Outline the poem by summarizing the ideas developed in each quatrain and the concluding couplet. Watch for and experience how the sonnet's meaning builds step by step.

3. Explain the relationship between lines 1–12 and lines 13–14.

4. How would you explain why the subject matter is appropriate for the traditional uses of the sonnet form?

This sonnet is one of Shakespeare's most famous because its theme resonates with so many people. It illustrates well the typical way Shakespeare structures his sonnets with three quatrains and a couplet. In lines 1 and 2, he introduces his theme: Let nothing stand in the way of true love. To paraphrase the lines, "Let me not acknowledge or concede as valid any obstacle to the union of those who love truly." Lines 2–4 begin clarifying what true love is by stating what it is and implying what it is not.

By using metaphors related to ships and the sea, the second quatrain further clarifies what true love *is*. It is permanent and reliable (ever-fixed, stable), the way a seamark (an object that indicates direction or position, such as a lighthouse), even if buffeted by fierce storms, is always the same and trustworthy. The third quatrain returns to affirmation of true love's permanence and stability by affirming that not even constantly moving, constantly changing time can alter it. In lines 9 and 10, time is personified as the grim reaper (death), whose figurative sickle can mow down youthful appearance—no true lover is foolish enough to think that such external changes signal a change in the inner essence of true love. Time's rapid passing in short hours and weeks does not change love, if it is true.

The last two lines provide the typical "turn," the pithy twist or practical application, typical of Shakespearean sonnets. In this case, the conclusion plays with logic: If what the poem has said about true love is wrong and can be proved to be erroneous, Shakespeare says he has never written a poem and no one has ever loved truly—but this poem exists and men and women have loved truly: The existence of the poem itself becomes a pleasantly humorous proof of the poem's argument.

ITALIAN (OR PETRARCHAN) SONNET

The *Italian sonnet* is composed of an *octave* (an eight-line unit), rhyming *abbaabba*, and a *sestet* (a six-line unit), often rhyming *cdecde* or *cdcdcd*, though variations are frequent. The octave usually develops an idea or question or problem, then the poem pauses or "turns," and the sestet completes the idea, answers the question, or resolves the difficulty. See, for example, Gary Miranda's "Love Poem" (p. 557) and the following poem.

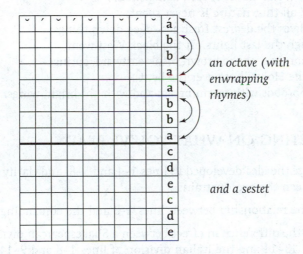

an octave (with enwrapping rhymes)

and a sestet

APPROACHING THE READING

In 1877, Gerard Manley Hopkins was ordained a Catholic priest. Almost all of the poetry he wrote after becoming a Catholic was deeply religious, though seldom dogmatic. The octave of "God's Grandeur" declares that the beauty of the world is a reflection of God's glory and expresses profound concern that humankind has not respected and taken adequate care of that world. The sestet then affirms that, despite such neglect, God continues to love and nurture it.

APPROACHING THE AUTHOR

After his conversion to Roman Catholicism, **Gerard Manley Hopkins**
burned all the poetry he had written up to that point and did not write
poems again until his superiors in the church encouraged him to do so
seven years later.
   For more about him, see page 1067.

Gerard Manley Hopkins   1844–1889

God's Grandeur   [*1877*; pub. 1918]

The world is charged with the grandeur of God.	
It will flame out, like shining from shook foil;°	*shaken gold foil*
It gathers to a greatness, like the ooze of oil°	*from olives*
Crushed. Why do men then now not reck° his rod?°	*recognize; discipline*
Generations have trod, have trod, have trod;	5
And all is seared with trade; bleared, smeared with toil;	
And wears man's smudge and shares man's smell: the soil	
Is bare now, nor can foot feel, being shod.	
And, for° all this, nature is never spent;	*despite*
There lives the dearest freshness deep down things;	10
And though the last lights off the black West went	
Oh, morning, at the brown brink eastward, springs—	
Because the Holy Ghost over the bent	
World broods with warm breast and with ah! bright wings.	

REFLECTING ON WHAT YOU'VE READ

1. Summarize the idea developed in lines 1–4 and 5–8, and clarify the connection between the two quatrains.

2. Explain the relationship between lines 1–8 and the concluding sestet.

3. Consider the difference in effect between a Shakespearean division of lines
   1–12 and 13–14 and the Italian division of lines 1–8 and 9–14.

The opening quatrain affirms that the natural world, in its great beauty,
is filled with—loaded to capacity with—God's glory. It should be unmissable—
it should flash in our eyes the way sunlight shines off a piece of gold foil; it
collects around us the way olive oil emerges as olives are crushed. Yet people
ignore God by neglecting their responsibility to the world that God created.
The second quatrain creates an image of that neglect: For generations people
have focused on trade, industry, and self-advancement. That they are out of
touch with nature is signaled by shoes: No longer do we feel the soil and thus
care about its condition.

The sestet is set off by a space, as if the speaker pauses to draw a big breath and then give vent to an outburst of praise and affirmation: No matter what human beings do to the earth, they will never eliminate God from it. Even if they destroy all human life, put out the "last lights," and leave the planet in darkness, God's presence will be there still, arising as the light of a new day. The poem concludes by comparing God's constant, caring presence to a mother bird brooding over her newborn chicks, but with the bright wings of an angel.

The tight, orderly traditional form of the sonnet seems fitting for a poem conveying a sense of orderliness—that God has a plan for the world itself that humans should not violate. The rhythms and sounds are intensified by their confinement in a compressed space: The energy of the poem seems to burst out as the reader opens the poem.

There are many other inherited types of poem. Here are two illustrated in this book:

- *Sestina* A lyric poem consisting of six six-line stanzas and a three-line concluding stanza (or "envoy"). The six end-words of the first stanza must be used as the end-words of the other five stanzas, in a prescribed pattern. Read Elizabeth Bishop's "Sestina" (p. 606) or Honorée Fanonne Jeffers's "Cotton Field Sestina" (p. 635) and try to pick out the pattern on your own; then check the results by looking in the glossary (p. 1131).
- *Villanelle* A nineteen-line lyric poem divided into five tercets and a final four-line stanza, with a prescribed rhyme scheme and some lines repeated in a set pattern. Try to pick out the formal patterns in Dylan Thomas's "Do not go gentle into that good night" (p. 584), or Rafael Campo's "The Enemy" (p. 609)—then look up the term in the glossary (p. 1131).

Some other well-known types are described in the glossary (p. 1131). Look, for example, at *epic*, *ballad*, *epigram*, and *haiku*.

There are also inherited patterns for nonstanzaic verse. Two important ones are:

- *Blank verse* Lines of unrhymed iambic pentameter. This is the most widely used verse form in English poetry, the one found in many Shakespearean plays, John Milton's *Paradise Lost* and *Paradise Regained*, William Wordsworth's *Prelude*, and countless other long poems. For an example in this book, see Alfred, Lord Tennyson's "Ulysses" (p. 653).
- *Couplet* A unit consisting of two consecutive lines of poetry with the same end rhyme. Couplets can be grouped into stanzas (as in A. E. Housman's "To an Athlete Dying Young," p. 633), but more often they are strung out in extended, nonstanzaic poems or passages: See, for example, Robert Browning's "My Last Duchess" (p. 497) and Gwendolyn Brooks's "We Real Cool" (p. 564).

READING FREE VERSE

Many modern and contemporary poets do not use inherited or pre-planned forms, preferring to work without a blueprint for a poem's form. They allow the entire poem to "find" its own shape. The poem may emerge from the poet's imagination and skillful intuition in the form that it needs, or the form may develop in the process of writing and revising. In either case, the poet's attention is focused primarily on other things — on images, sounds, rhythms — and the poet allows the form to develop, either consciously shaping it as it is discovered or letting it result from attention to line, line break, rhythm, and so forth.

Such poems traditionally have been called *free verse* because they are free of predetermined metrical and stanzaic patterns. The term *free verse* is misleading, however, if it is interpreted to mean "anything goes" or that form and the other elements don't matter. Some books use the term **open form** to avoid such misunderstanding. Either term is usually acceptable. Just remember that, no matter how "free" a poem appears, it *does have form*. Every poem does.

Unlike metrical or stanzaic poetry, free verse does not rely on organized structural repetition (like those of meter, rhyme, stanza, or identical syllable counts) to achieve form and coherence. Instead, it relies on connected images and sounds, and parallelism in phrasing and in the handling of lines, spaces, rhythms, indentations, gaps, and timing. For the beginning poet, writing in open form may look easier than writing in inherited forms. However, each approach requires an ability to work with the elements of poetry. Each is challenging when one is aware of the complexities of writing any poem well. Each is easy only if done carelessly.

APPROACHING THE READING

In the following poem, the speaker stands at the shore of the Pacific and offers thanks to the ocean for carrying her people to this land and for continuing to provide them with the gift of rain. Obviously, the poem is not written in traditional Anglo-European meter and stanza patterns; however, it is certainly influenced by tradition and an understanding of form. Reflect on how its form contributes to the effect of what it is saying.

APPROACHING THE AUTHOR

Leslie Marmon Silko grew up in a prominent mixed-blood family on the Laguna Pueblo reservation and struggled to be fully accepted by both the Laguna tribe and whites. Nonetheless, she eventually learned to identify with her tribal culture and says that she considers herself first and foremost Laguna.

For more about her, see page 1080.

Leslie Marmon Silko   b. 1948

Prayer to the Pacific   [1981]

I traveled to the ocean
    distant
        from my southwest land of sandrock
        to the moving blue water
     Big as the myth of origin.   5

Pale
pale water in the yellow-white light of
     sun   floating west
        to China
     where ocean herself was born.   10
Clouds that blow across the sand are wet.

Squat in the wet sand and speak to the Ocean:
    I return to you   turquoise   the red coral you sent us,
       sister spirit of Earth.
Four round stones in my pocket   I carry back the ocean   15
      to suck and to taste.

Thirty thousand years ago
      Indians came riding across the ocean
     carried by giant sea turtles.

Waves were high that day   20
    great sea turtles waded   slowly out
      from the gray sundown sea.

Grandfather Turtle rolled in the sand   four times
    and disappeared
       swimming into the sun.   25

And so   from that time
    immemorial,
      as the old people say,
rain clouds drift from the west
      gift from the ocean.   30

Green leaves in the wind
Wet earth on my feet
   swallowing raindrops
     clear from China.

REFLECTING ON WHAT YOU'VE READ

1. Examine the form of the poem carefully, focusing on its visual appearance. Consider how the structure affects your reading of the poem, how the lines' placement creates a kind of choreography of movement for your eyes. How is this structure essential to the timing, energy, and rhythm within the poem?

2. Follow the way sentences run through several lines. Discuss what the juxtaposition of lines with sentences adds to the effect of the poem.

3. In what ways is the form appropriate to the speaker and to the prayer being offered?

A striking formal feature of this poem is the attractiveness of its layout on the page. To look at the poem is like observing a work of visual art, with its clear attention to composition, design, and proportion. There is a kinetic sense to Silko's poem. As we follow the movement of the lines, we can feel in our bodies the energy, oceanic rhythm, and "flow" of the poem.

Along with such visual appeal, the poem's division into lines and its arrangement on the page indicate how it should be read—which lines go together, where pauses amplify its impact, what particular words should be emphasized. The poem describes the speaker's journey to the seaside to offer a prayer to the ocean—by dropping four round stones into its waters. It is a prayer of gratitude for the gift in the past of the ocean carrying the speaker's ancestors to these shores on giant turtles and for the gift in the present of carrying clouds with much-needed rain across the waters to the land that the speaker inhabits.

The use of open, seemingly organic form to evoke a trust in the natural world feels appropriate to the Native American stories it recounts, certainly more appropriate than using an inherited verse form from another culture, such as those discussed earlier in this chapter.

READING FOR INTERNAL FORM

In addition to shape, or external form, a poem also has an *internal form*, the inner arrangement or organization of its parts and content. The variety of techniques and arrangements used by poets is extensive; we list here some of the most important ones.

PARALLELISM

Parallelism can be considered in two ways. (1) The first is when elements of equal weight within phrases, sentences, or paragraphs are expressed in a similar grammatical order and structure. It can appear within a line or pair of lines: "And he was always quietly arrayed, / And he was always human when he talked"—Edwin Arlington Robinson's "Richard Cory"

(p. 532); or, more noticeably, it can appear as a series of parallel items, as in Langston Hughes's "Harlem" (p. 525). (2) The second is when two consecutive lines in open form are related by the second line's repeating, expanding on, or contrasting with the idea of the first, as, for example, in the poetry of Walt Whitman (p. 651).

JUXTAPOSITION

Juxtaposition is the placement of things (often very different things) side by side or close together for comparison or contrast or to create something new from the union, without necessarily making them grammatically parallel. See, for example, how Victor Hernández Cruz's "Problems with Hurricanes" (p. 615) juxtaposes the seriousness of death during a hurricane (drowning or being hurled by the wind against a mountain) with the ludicrous danger of dying from being smashed by a mango, banana, or plantain.

NARRATIVE

One of the most basic approaches to structure is *narrative*, a poet recounting an event as a sequence of actions and details, as in Marilyn Nelson's "Minor Miracle" (p. 514) or Jimmy Santiago Baca's "Family Ties" (p. 605). There are also *long* narrative poems, stories cast in poetic form, from Homer down to present-day authors.

LOGICAL PATTERN

Material can be arranged in a logical pattern of development. This could be in the form of a logical argument, like the three-part attempt at persuasion in Andrew Marvell's "To His Coy Mistress" (p. 640), or of logical explanation, as in Marilyn Chin's "How I Got That Name" (p. 611).

QUESTION-ANSWER

Poems can raise a question (explicitly or implicitly) and work toward an answer (which also can be stated or implied). Emily Dickinson's "I'm Nobody! Who are you?" (p. 558) raises and explores a deep, perennial question. Langston Hughes's "Harlem" (p. 525) is a series of questions with an implied answer phrased as a final question.

MEDITATIVE MOVEMENT

Some poems are arranged as meditations, often moving from a reflection on a physical place or object or a scene to personal or spiritual perceptions, as in Lucille Clifton's "at the cemetery, walnut grove plantation, south carolina, 1989" (p. 554).

LISTS (OR CATALOGS) AND LITANIES

Lists and litanies are a common use of form (we all construct them). Lists can create range, rhythm, intensity, and texture. A poem structured as a litany uses a series of invocations and repeated responses—see, for example, Joy Harjo's "She Had Some Horses" (p. 579). Catalogs also can structure parts of a poem, as in the last line of Gwendolyn Brooks's "The Bean Eaters" (p. 468).

> ☑ **CHECKLIST on Reading for Form and Type**
>
> ❑ Notice the role that form plays in a poem and the effect it has on your experience of reading the poem.
>
> ❑ Watch for the handlings of lines, and consider the various ways they affect a poem's appearance, rhythm, and emphasis, and the way they interact with sentences.
>
> ❑ Be aware of both a poem's external form (the way the poem looks on the page) and its inner form (the artistic design or structure that arranges, organizes, or connects the various elements).
>
> ❑ For poems in stanzas, consider the effectiveness and appropriateness of the form selected for the poem. If the poet introduces a variation in the form that has been established, consider what the changes convey in meaning, tone, and effect.
>
> ❑ Watch for inherited types (such as the English sonnet, the Italian sonnet, couplets, and blank verse) and consider the kind of creativity and imaginativeness that writing such poetry entails.
>
> ❑ Watch for poetry written as free verse (lacking repeated features such as rhyme, meter, or stanza but using unity of pattern, such as visual structures, parallelism, or rhythm), and consider the kind of creativity and craft that writing such poetry requires.

FURTHER READING

APPROACHING THE READING

The next poem is composed in one of the oldest of forms, the litany. A litany is a repetitive or incantatory recital traditionally used in religious ceremonies for prayers of adoration or supplication. This poem is a contemporary litany. Read it aloud. Listen to the rhythms of its lines and inner arrangement, and feel the impact created by the chanting sound and repeated phrases.

APPROACHING THE AUTHOR

Joy Harjo performs her poetry and plays saxophone with her band, Poetic Justice. You can hear some of her music on her Web site.

For more about her, see page 1064.

Paul Abdoo/MPI/Getty
Images.

Joy Harjo   b. 1951

She Had Some Horses   [1983]

She had some horses.

She had horses who were bodies of sand.
She had horses who were maps drawn of blood.
She had horses who were skins of ocean water.
She had horses who were the blue air of sky.   5
She had horses who were fur and teeth.
She had horses who were clay and would break.
She had horses who were splintered red cliff.

She had some horses.

She had horses with long, pointed breasts.   10
She had horses with full, brown thighs.
She had horses who laughed too much.
She had horses who threw rocks at glass houses.
She had horses who licked razor blades.

She had some horses.   15
She had horses who danced in their mothers' arms.
She had horses who thought they were the sun and their
bodies shone and burned like stars.
She had horses who waltzed nightly on the moon.
She had horses who were much too shy, and kept quiet   20
in stalls of their own making.

She had some horses.

She had horses who liked Creek Stomp Dance songs.
She had horses who cried in their beer.
She had horses who spit at male queens who made   25
them afraid of themselves.
She had horses who said they weren't afraid.

She had horses who lied.
She had horses who told the truth, who were stripped
bare of their tongues.   30

She had some horses.

She had horses who called themselves, "horse."
She had horses who called themselves, "spirit," and kept
their voices secret and to themselves.
She had horses who had no names.   35
She had horses who had books of names.

She had some horses.

She had horses who whispered in the dark, who were afraid to speak.
She had horses who screamed out of fear of the silence, who
carried knives to protect themselves from ghosts.   40
She had horses who waited for destruction.
She had horses who waited for resurrection.

She had some horses.

She had horses who got down on their knees for any savior.
She had horses who thought their high price had saved them.   45
She had horses who tried to save her, who climbed in her
bed at night and prayed as they raped her.

She had some horses.

She had some horses she loved.
She had some horses she hated.   50

These were the same horses.

REFLECTING ON WHAT YOU'VE READ

1. When have you experienced nonpoetry examples of the use of litany, such
   as cheers at sports events or in music you enjoy? Why do you think litany
   is used? What makes it appealing and powerful?

2. What is it about the litany form that gives such power to "She Had Some
   Horses"? How would you describe that power? Is it a prayer? Is it an affirmation of belief? Is it an assertion of being and presence? What do you think the
   poem is meant to do? Did you have a different response when you reread it?

3. In the first line and the refrain, the horses seem to be simply horses. But in
   other lines, they become metaphors or are personified. Look closely at specific lines that are about people (such as lines 38–42 and 44–47). What
   would you say is the difference in effect of expressing the points through
   horses instead of stating them directly? Try substituting a word for "horses" —
   she had some *friends* or *classmates* or *fellow human beings* who . . . . Does it
   work? What is better about using "horses"?

4. Who do you think is the "she"? Try substituting "he." In what ways does that change the impact?

5. How can the horses in the last three lines be the same horses?

6. Harjo has said that she has been asked the most about this poem and has the least to say about it. Speculate on why you think each is the case.

APPROACHING THE READING

The following is a prose poem: Rather than being divided through pre-determined line breaks, its lines wrap at the right margin. The speaker describes his mother's last-minute rush to get her homemade products to the fair, where she hopes to win blue ribbons. As you read, watch for the ways you can experience it the same ways you do with poetry written in lines, even though this poem is composed in prose. Reflect on what you have learned in Chapters 13–19 about what makes for an effective poem.

APPROACHING THE AUTHOR

Atsuro Riley grew up in South Carolina. His poems often include images connected to living in the rural South.

For more about him, see page 1077.

Atsuro Riley   b. 1960

Drill   [2010]

Mama talks in this one.

Here's us, backing down our driveway's maze of red-dirt dog-legs, her at the wheel (with a fresh-forged license), me turned around navigating, the yard black-dark but flushed now (and now) and now with brake-lights, her Kool-tip flaring on every hard in-breath, river-reek and oil-scorch and marsh-gas mingling, our under-chassis (and rear axle, eyeteeth) chuttering due to roots and rain-ruts, our rust-crusting Rambler swerving and fishtailing and near-missing trees.

At the mailbox, gears knock, gnaw, grind, find Forward eventually: we're missile-heading straight (more or less) for the Low Country fairgrounds; here's us, late, loud, breaknecking her blue-ribbon hoard to the Fair.

Everything is home-made.

Not just our back-seat freight of gem-flame jelly-jars (slip-skin grape, beet,   5
black- and blueberry, brunt-apple, seed-splacked fig) and payload of pressure-torqued pickle-jars (wrick-kinked banana-peppers, lethal hot-hat peppers, (green) tear-tomatoes, hairy okra, baby-dills in brine), but also the crazy-quilt safe-swaddling them, the gummed saliva-labels neat-naming them, my mama's name—hieroglyphical, grease-penciled, "KAY" (KAZUE) HUTTO—branding lids.

Do you reckon tomorrow they'll put my picture in the paper?
Will somebody do a write-up when I win?

REFLECTING ON WHAT YOU'VE READ

1. "Drill," as we indicated above, is a prose poem. What do you think makes it prose *poetry*, not just prose? Point out some poetic characteristics that appear in it. How do they intensify the impact?

2. "Drill" was published in a related sequence of poems narrated by a boy, Romey, who is recording and trying to give order to his childhood world alongside a river in the Low Country of South Carolina. The first line links to the previous poem, and foreshadows the mother's words in the last two lines. In what way is prose poetry an appropriate form for the poem?

3. Notice the lists of images. What is it about the use of sound that especially enlivens them?

4. Reflect on the last two lines. Is this where "mama talks in this one" (line 1)? Or is it Romey knowing and expressing what she would say or be thinking? Or is it something else?

APPROACHING THE READING

Most traditional sonnets have been serious reflections on serious topics such as love, death, and nature. Some modern poets experiment with the form, however, using it playfully to juxtapose the assumed seriousness of traditional form with comic takes on content. Examples of this include E. E. Cummings's "next to of course god america i" (p. 489), Gary Miranda's "Love Poem" (p. 557), and Mary Jo Salter's "Half a Double Sonnet" (p. 652), as well as the following fanciful retelling of the fairytale of the Frog-Prince.

> **APPROACHING THE AUTHOR**
>
> **Anna Maria Hong** enjoys experimenting with how far the rigorous shape of the sonnet can be pushed and still be recognized as a sonnet.
> For more about her, see page 1066.

Anna Maria Hong

The Frog-Prince   [2013]

"You're just like every toad I've ever met,"
said the Princess to her smooth companion.
"Except maybe more persistent," she thought
quietly. "I'm still not sure why a person

like me should bother with a totally slimy,   5
webfooted *thing*, when I'm so perfectly
content with my ball and myself." "I see,"
said the frog laconically. "Perfectly

content." Something about his tone—half-burp,
so sure—instantly enraged the Princess, who   10
then grabbed the frog's slick carapace and threw

it at the wall, which broke the beast into
his handsome, manly origins. "How warped,"
said the plussed Princess. "Now what do I do?"

REFLECTING ON WHAT YOU'VE READ

1. If you don't know the fairy tale about the frog prince, find and read it.
   Notice how the poet plays with the old tale in creating a new one.
2. Watch as the poem follows the usual formal structure of a sonnet, and
   notice the ways it toys with the form. What does the sonnet form add to
   the subject and tone?
3. The poem not only plays with form, but it also is playful with language. Pick
   out places where the poet has used words in surprising ways or has made
   up words. Look up "laconically," "carapace," warped," and "plussed" if you
   are unfamiliar with them and consider the effect of using them.
4. Think about what comes to mind when you come across the term *traditional sonnet*. As you read this sonnet, note the way the common assumptions are changed.
5. In what ways does the poem expand your understanding of the relationship
   between traditional form and language?

APPROACHING THE READING

The villanelle is one of the strictest of poetic forms: nineteen lines divided
into five tercets and a final four-line stanza, rhyming *aba aba aba aba aba
abaa*. Line 1 is repeated to form lines 6, 12, and 18; line 3 is repeated to
form lines 9, 15, and 19. Watch for those formal characteristics in the
following poem in which the speaker pleads with his father to resist his
approaching death and hold onto life and light. Think about how the form
fits and reinforces what the speaker is urging.

APPROACHING THE AUTHOR

Dylan Thomas suffered from bronchitis and
asthma throughout his life and was considered
too frail to fight in World War II. He instead
served the United Kingdom by writing scripts for
the government.
  For more about him, see page 1081.

G.D. Hackett / Getty Images.

Dylan Thomas   1914–1953

Do not go gentle into that good night   [1952]

Do not go gentle into that good night,
Old age should burn and rave at close of day;
Rage, rage against the dying of the light.

Though wise men at their end know dark is right,
Because their words had forked no lightning they   5
Do not go gentle into that good night.

Good men, the last wave by, crying how bright
Their frail deeds might have danced in a green bay,
Rage, rage against the dying of the light.

Wild men who caught and sang the sun in flight,   10
And learn, too late, they grieved it on its way,
Do not go gentle into that good night.

Grave men, near death, who see with blinding sight
Blind eyes could blaze like meteors and be gay,
Rage, rage against the dying of the light.   15

And you, my father, there on the sad height,
Curse, bless, me now with your fierce tears, I pray.
Do not go gentle into that good night.
Rage, rage against the dying of the light.

REFLECTING ON WHAT YOU'VE READ

1. Consider the relationship between the father and the speaker. Start with the speaker: What is he feeling? What is his tone? What are his attitudes toward his father, toward what is happening, and toward himself? What does the speaker want from his father? Why does he want him not to "go gentle into that good night."

2. Notice the different types of men alluded to in lines 4–15. Discuss why the poet chooses these and what their role is in the poem. What might they represent? Why does he use these in relation to his father?

3. After reading the poem, reflect on how the villanelle form adds to the meaning and the effect of the poem. Notice what happens to the impact or tone or meaning of the repeated lines when they appear in a new context.

4. Discuss the use of paradox in the poem. For example, talk about the speaker saying in the last stanza "Curse, bless, me now," or about uncommon modifiers such as "blinding sight," "sad height," and "fierce tears" and their effect in the poem.

5. Read Rafael Campo's villanelle "The Enemy" (p. 609). Reading two vil-lanelles together may help clarify how the form works. If doing so helps you, explain what the form adds to the poems.

RESPONDING THROUGH Writing

WRITING ABOUT FORM AND TYPE

Journal Entries

1. Choose a poem and change the way it is divided into lines. Then write in your journal about what you discovered from these changes.

2. Be on the lookout for *found poetry*, that is, prose found in newspapers, magazines, advertisements, textbooks, or elsewhere in everyday life that contains elements of poetry, such as effective rhythm, phrasings that can be divided into lines, meter, imaginative uses of language and sound, and so on. Collect several examples for your journal, dividing them carefully into poetic lines. Comment briefly on what this reveals to you about the choices that poets make about line divisions and about their effect.

3. In your journal, describe and discuss briefly the inner arrangements for two of the following poems: Joanne Diaz's "Pride and Prejudice" (p. 619), Denise Duhamel's "One Afternoon when Barbie Wanted to Join the Military" (p. 622), Jack Ridl's "My Brother—A Star" (p. 647), Luis Rodriguez's "Running to America" (p. 649), or Natasha Trethewey's "Domestic Work, 1937" (p. 655).

Literary Analysis Papers

4. For one of the following poems, write a paper describing its form and discuss-ing the effectiveness and appropriateness of its distinctive handling of lines: W. H. Auden's "Musée des Beaux Arts" (p. 603), Lorna Dee Cervantes's "Freeway 280" (p. 610), Garrett Kaoru Hongo's "Yellow Light" (p. 632), David Mura's "Grandfather-in-Law" (p. 643), Luis Rodriguez's "Running to America" (p. 649), or Walt Whitman's "Song of Myself" (p. 657).

5. Write an analysis of the effect of Dudley Randall's "Ballad of Birmingham" (p. 646) as it follows and adapts the ballad tradition.

6. Write a paper explicating a sonnet and placing emphasis on the way its structure fits and brings out its subject and theme. Use a traditional sonnet such as William Shakespeare's "Let me not to the marriage of true minds" (p. 569), Gerard Manley Hopkins's "God's Grandeur" (p. 572), Claude McKay's "If we must die" (p. 639), Elizabeth Barrett Browning's "How do I love thee? Let me count the ways" (p. 608), or Percy Bysshe Shelley's "Ozymandias" (p. 652), or an innovative use of sonnet form, such

as E. E. Cummings's "next to of course god america i" (p. 489), Gary Miranda's "Love Poem" (p. 557), Anna Maria Hong's "The Frog-Prince" (p. 582), or Mary Jo Salter's "Half a Double Sonnet" (p. 652).

Comparison-Contrast Papers

7. There is a long tradition of poets writing poems about poetry, about what poetry is and does, as for example Marianne Moore's "Poetry" (p. 601) and its earlier, longer version, "Poetry" (available online). Do an online search for "poems about poetry" and read a dozen or two. Choose two that you like, and compare and contrast their ideas and the way form and type contribute to what they say and do.

8. Write a paper comparing the free verse form used in two of the following poems and discussing for each how the invented form fits and accentuates the poem's subject and theme: Quincy Troupe's "A Poem for Magic" (p. 656), Leslie Marmon Silko's "Prayer to the Pacific" (p. 575), Linda Hogan's "Crow's Law" (p. 631), Jack Ridl's "My Brother—A Star" (p. 647), Luis Rodriguez's "Running to America" (p. 649), or Walt Whitman's "Song of Myself" (p. 657).

TIPS for Writing about Form and Type

- **Look for the unusual.** When a poem's form is quite unusual or when it contributes in a significant way to effect or meaning, it can make a revealing topic for a paper. Handling it successfully requires describing the form in detail and explaining carefully how and why it creates the effects that it does. But even when you are writing about other elements in a poem, it can be helpful to include a brief description of the poem's form or type (for example, mentioning that it's in blank verse or a variation on the Italian sonnet or free verse).

- **Look for juxtapositions.** Even when writing about other elements, it is wise to watch for juxtapositions. They can highlight the importance of particular images or the speaker's vision or point of view, or how a poem takes a common way of seeing and turns it into a fresh point of view. An example could be an important structural feature, often emphasizing how things that ordinarily are not associated with one another create a dynamic experience when placed together. A single juxtaposition can sometimes make an entire poem cohere.

- **Consider what to cover.** A paper dealing with form doesn't have to cover all aspects. Good papers can result from focusing on one aspect, such as handling of line breaks, line lengths, meter, stanza structures, collage, or shape.

- **Consider form in free verse.** Form can lead to a perceptive paper (or part of a topic) on free-verse poetry, especially when the form is strikingly apt for the poem's subject. Such a paper must go beyond describing the form and include discussion of the form's appropriateness, its effects, its possible meaningfulness, and the ways it embodies the artistry of the poem as a whole.

- **Consider the effect of using a traditional type.** For poems written in traditional types (such as sonnet, sestina, or villanelle), you might discuss why the choice of type is fitting and why it is effective. This can make for a whole paper or a segment of a broader one.

WRITING ABOUT CONNECTIONS

Obviously connections occur between poems using the same inherited form or type. For example, topic 6 above involves looking at how two or more poets handle sonnets. One can also find connections between free-verse poems through formal strategies or techniques. In addition to formal connections, thematic connections can be found between poems in the same type and across types, between poets writing in the same century or different centuries. Here are a few topic possibilities:

1. "Amazing Grace": Being Blessed from Within and from Without in Mary Oliver's "First Snow" (p. 538) and Gerard Manley Hopkins's "God's Grandeur" (p. 572)

2. "'Which thou must leave ere long'": Confronting Separation in Elizabeth Bishop's "Sestina" (p. 606) and William Shakespeare's "That time of year thou mayst in me behold" (available online)

3. "The Solace of Solitude": Place and Peace in Wendell Berry's "The Peace of Wild Things" (p. 476) and Maxine Kumin's "The Sound of Night" (p. 470)

WRITING RESEARCH PAPERS

1. Research the significance of turtles (especially Grandfather Turtle) in Native American legends and use what you find to illuminate the Father Turtle story in Leslie Marmon Silko's "Prayer to the Pacific" (p. 575).

2. Research the history, use, and development of the villanelle as a type, and write a paper in which you discuss how a villanelle "works" (how it affects and appeals to poets and to readers). Illustrate your paper with examples from at least two villanelles, perhaps the ones in this book — Dylan Thomas's "Do not go gentle into that good night" (p. 584) and Rafael Campo's "The Enemy" (p. 609).

In the writing process, the more a thing cooks the better.
Doris Lessing
(English Novelist)

CHAPTER 20 Writing about Poetry

Applying What You've Learned

We write about poetry for the same reasons we write about fiction — to participate in an ongoing conversation about things that interest, provoke, excite, or puzzle us about the literary works we read. As Chapters 13–19 helped prepare you to read poetry with increasing sensitivity, alertness and confidence, they were also preparing you to write about poetry. Each chapter provides ways to move into a poem and to enlarge your experience of the variety of things happening in it: in terms of subject matter, formal elements, range of effects, and techniques through which effects are achieved. Chapter 2 provides you with general guidance for writing essays on literature. This chapter examines the particular challenges posed by writing about poetry.

We gave students in one of our introduction to literature classes the following assignment: Write a two- to three-page paper discussing how one of the following poems explores an author's experience with nature — Wendell Barry's "The Peace of Wild Things" (p. 476), William Stafford's "Traveling through the Dark" (p. 534), or Mary Oliver's "First Snow" (p. 538). One of our students, Sunkyo Hong, chose to write on "First Snow." This chapter follows Sunkyo through the steps in the writing process as he completed that assignment, using his own words as he retraces his steps.

STEP 1. PREWRITING: FINDING A TOPIC

Look first for a poem you enjoy reading and thinking about: You will always write best when you deal with a work you enjoy. It's wise to spread a dozen or more readings of the poem over at least a week. Coming back to a poem every day leads you to see things that reading it several times in one sitting won't.

Sometimes read the poem aloud; sometimes—if you can arrange it—listen to someone else read it. Each time you read the poem, focus on a different aspect—one time on techniques the poet uses (the handling of speaker and voice, images, figurative language, rhythm, symbols, and so on), another time on ideas explored in the poem, yet another on the poem's social or cultural context if it influences the poem significantly.

Photocopy the poem and mark it up; jot notes that you can come back to later. When you do this, the poem becomes part of you (to the point that you'll probably even be able to recite parts or all of it from memory). To generate ideas, keep asking questions: What is the poem revealing? What is the poem doing? Why is this or that handled the way it is? What is the effect or impact of the poet's use of particular elements? What if it were done differently?

Sunkyo got started by getting a clear understanding of the assignment and then deciding to do an analytic paper on themes and techniques in "First Snow":

When I was given the assignment, I read the three poems several times each, looking for possible meanings, alternative interpretations, and structural clues. I liked all of the choices, but I was drawn to "First Snow": I felt I could relate to it because I like snow and because the poem does a great job of conveying wonder with pictures and comparisons. Having decided on a poem, I had my topic: the author's experience with nature in Mary Oliver's "First Snow."

Photograph courtesy of Sunkyo Hong.

If you're still looking for a topic, you might consider again the suggestions made at the end of Chapters 14–19 (pp. 478, 499, 518, 541, 559, and 585).

STEP 2. PREWRITING: NARROWING THE TOPIC

Although most poems are shorter than most stories and plays, you can't write about everything in them. There's simply too much going on in terms of techniques and themes. You need to focus on what interests you and is particularly significant or valuable to your topic. For discussing poems as well as stories and plays, Benjamin De Mott's technique of focusing on "key passages" (see p. 47) often works well. Reread the poem, marking it up further and jotting more notes to yourself. Then look for connections between what you've marked or jotted. Such connections will likely point you toward a way of limiting the topic. Here's how Sunkyo narrowed his topic:

> Limiting my topic came about mostly through taking notes as I worked through the poem intensively. I started outlining the main topics dealt with in the poem: It snows all day, it stops snowing at night, the speaker walks out in the snow, the speaker describes not just the snow but the way the snow makes her feel. I decided to try focusing my topic on wonder, in two of its senses, as a noun (a sense of amazement or admiration) and as a verb (to be curious about, to question).

STEP 3. PREWRITING: DECIDING ON AN APPROACH

Chapter 2 described four major approaches to writing about literature: literary analysis, comparison-contrast, social and cultural analysis, or a combination of these (see pp. 40–43). Sometimes, of course, the topic you select or the assignment you are given tells you the approach to take. But other times, part of the process of focusing your topic and preparing to frame a thesis, and then deciding how to develop it, involves figuring out what approach the topic needs. If you do need to figure out what approach to take, the best way to start is to notice whether the topic focuses on what goes on *inside* the poem, in theme or technique (literary analysis), focuses on *connections* between your poem and another one (comparison-contrast), or focuses on what infuses the poem but also *surrounds* the poem (social and cultural criticism). Sunkyo explains his decisions about his approach this way:

> The assignment pretty much prescribed the approach for my paper. When the assignment says, "Discuss how one of the following poems explores an author's experience with nature," it is telling me to do an analysis, to look closely at and into the poem. My challenge is not deciding on an approach but deciding on what kind of analysis, of themes or techniques or both. I decided on both.

Explicating A Poem   One kind of literary analysis is particularly well suited to writing about poetry: *explication*. Explication involves looking closely at a poem, opening it up line by line, clarifying how diction, images, figurative language, symbols, sounds, rhythm, form, and allusions contribute to shaping what the poem says or depicts or reveals and how they contribute to the poem's effect. Such analysis should never isolate a single feature from the rest of the work; instead, it must always look closely at how the feature contributes to seeing the entire poem more clearly and fully. Explication often focuses on ambiguities, complexities, gaps, and the interrelationships within a text. It requires you to be especially attentive to specific words and phrases, considering their effects, discussing the impact and implications of ambiguities and subtleties, and explaining how these elements work together toward a particular purpose or theme. For longer poems, you may need to explicate only a key passage and relate it to the whole poem.

Organizing An Explication   An explication paper can be organized by going through the poem from beginning to end, line by line (or section by section), clarifying how techniques and features in the lines create their meaning or effect. An explication paper also can be organized topically. That is, one paragraph might discuss the poem's use of images; another its use of figures; and others its tone, use of sound techniques, and rhythm. Each paragraph should include examples from different parts of the poem, chosen so that somewhere in the paper nearly every line or combination of lines is discussed (though not necessarily in the order they appear in the poem). Each paragraph needs to explain how the element it covers contributes to building the total effect of the poem. An advantage of this approach is that it usually runs less risk of sliding into a mere summary of the poem than the line-by-line approach does.

STEP 4. PREWRITING: FRAMING A THESIS

Chapter 2 explains that an effective paper on literature needs an argumentative thesis, a central claim that is developed and supported. Your job as a writer is to convince your readers that your claim is sound and helpful, worth considering seriously. Reviewing pages 43–46 on ways of making sure you have an idea-based thesis might be helpful. This is what Sunkyo said about framing his thesis:

I started with this as an elaboration of my topic: "Mary Oliver's poem 'First Snow' is about a time when it snowed and what the experience was like for the author. The author found the snow wonderful and beautiful. When she stepped out into the snow, she felt that an 'answer [had] been found' (line 31)." I then worked further on the poem to gain a thorough in-depth knowledge of it. I looked up words, for example, *rhetoric* (with its phrase "white rhetoric") and *oracular*. Then I focused on the questions raised by the speaker in the poem: "its white / rhetoric everywhere / calling us back to *why, how, / whence* such beauty and *what* / the meaning." I spent a lot of time pondering those lines and rereading the poem to see how they fit in, how they relate to "oracular." What kind of divinely inspired pronouncement was the snow making? Eventually I came up with the following as a tentative thesis: "Watching the snow from inside, the author had felt wonder at the sight. Now being in it, she feels a part of it. It might be that questions cannot continue to be uttered in the profound silence, and the light feels enlightening, so in a way, the author has found the answer to her questions through experiencing the snow."

STEP 5. WRITING: DEVELOPING AND SUPPORTING THE THESIS

The methods of developing and supporting the ideas in a paper on poetry include explaining clearly, illustrating fully, using quotations, focusing on key passages, and avoiding summary (see pp. 46–50). The development and support of the arguments you advance will be the heart of your paper. The most brilliant insights are of little value if they can't be supported convincingly. Here's what Sunkyo said about developing and supporting his thesis:

> Once I had a working thesis, the first challenge in developing it was deciding how to organize the steps in my discussion of the poem, how to divide it up. I decided to go through the poem from beginning to end, dividing it into three sections: lines 1–12, on the speaker looking back on how the snow fell all day; lines 12–27, that night as the speaker shifts to present tense and reflects on how everything looks and feels different now; and lines 28–36, which shift from description to participation, as the speaker goes out into the snow and seems to find answers to the questions asked in section one. Each section has a crux to deal with — a group of lines that I needed to study carefully, looking up words and figuring out what was going on in them. For each section I chose lines to quote and discuss in detail, trying as I did so to unify the paper by relating parts to each other. With all this sketched out, I just started writing a first draft.

TIPS for Quoting Poetry

Because of the line divisions in poetry, some conventions for dealing with quotations are unique to poetry. Here are four tips on handling poetry quotations:

- **Fewer than four lines of poetry.** Blend them into your sentence, using a slash, with a space before and after, to indicate line divisions:

  My favorite part of Gary Miranda's "Love Poem" is, "or the chance / meanings, not even remotely intended, that dance / at the edge of words, like sparks" (lines 4–6).

- **Four or more lines of poetry.** Type them into the paper as a block quotation with each line on a separate line. Indent the passage an inch and a half or two inches from the left. The passage should look the same way it looks in the source, with the same indentations and spacing. If you begin the quotation in the middle of a poetic line, place the first word approximately where it occurs in the line, not at the left-hand margin. (See, for example, Sunkyo Hong's paper, p. 597.)

- **Citations.** Put line numbers in parentheses at the end of the passage for lines quoted or cited. For the first reference, include the word "line" (not abbreviated); for later references, give the numbers alone. Page numbers will be included on the Works Cited page.

- **Omissions.** If you omit words, indicate that by including an ellipsis (see p. 60). If you omit a complete line or more than one line, indicate this by a row of spaced periods as long as a line of the poem.

Read Synkyo's first draft on pages 594, 596, and 598. Then go on to Step 6.

STEP 6. REVISING, PROOFREADING, AND FORMATTING

Good writing always requires careful revision and editing (proofreading). Here's the way Sunkyo went about revising and editing his first draft.

I don't like working with technically clumsy drafts, so I like to make technical corrections and adjustments before I revise content and structure. For example, I deleted the word *line* from all the citations in parentheses following quotations except the first one, to follow MLA practice—that the rest also refer to line numbers can be inferred. I put *oracular* and *fever* in italics in the third paragraph of the draft because that is the convention when looking at words as words. And I caught a few mistakes in punctuation. I changed the quotation in draft paragraph 4 to an indented quotation because in the final paper it is more than three lines long.

In regard to content, there were four major things I felt I should work on:

(1) I needed a better title, one that was not just a heading but that reflected the central idea in the paper.

(2) I needed a better opening paragraph. The original one is short and thin, only vaguely touching on what the paper will discuss. I want the beginning to be more appealing and inviting, and I want to give readers help in following the movement of the paper. After experimenting with a couple of openings, I decided to preface the essay with a personal anecdote because the experience described in the poem is personal.

(3) The fourth paragraph needs refocusing: Elsewhere I describe the author's experiences; here I get caught up in what the candles are and are not. I can get to focusing on the experience by putting the word pictures back into the context of the grand scene because the choice of words used to describe a scene reveals how the writer experiences that scene.

(4) The ending needs to be improved. It feels a bit abrupt and somehow doesn't seem to convey a satisfying conclusive touch. I had to do a lot of experimenting to find a solution that felt right to me.

SAMPLE SHORT PAPER

Here is the first draft of Sunkyo's paper. To allow you to see more of Sunkyo's writing process, we've printed the rough draft of his paper on the left-hand pages, and the final draft on the right-hand pages.

ROUGH DRAFT

Hong 1

Mary Oliver's "First Snow"

Mary Oliver's poem "First Snow" is about a time when it snowed, and what that experience was like for the author. In the poem, the author finds snow wonderful and beautiful. When she steps out into the snow, she feels that an "answer has been found" (line 31).

The poem begins with the author describing how the snow began: "The snow / began here / this morning" (lines 1–3). With this opening, the author gives the reader a natural starting place. This opening is similar to the common story opening, i.e., "Once upon a time in such and such a place."

The poem then proceeds to say that the snow kept falling throughout the day (lines 3–4) and describes how the snow fell and what it seemed like. The snow falling had "white / rhetoric every-where" (lines 4–5). Rhetoric is persuasive speaking or writing. The next lines say what the snow's white rhetoric was doing: "calling us back to *why, how, / whence* such beauty and *what /* the meaning" (lines 6–8). The rhetoric was persuading the author to wonder, in the literal sense, about the beauty and meaning of the snow and wonder at it in the sense of amazement also. The questions of "why, how, whence such beauty" and "what the meaning" indicate that

---

Here is the revised, final draft of Sunkyo's paper.

──────────── **FINAL DRAFT** ────────────

Hong 1

Sunkyo Hong
Professor Ridl
English 248
15 May 2016

Experiencing "First Snow"

   I had seen snow before coming to college in Michigan,
but never like this. I woke up one December morning to find yesterday's green lawns a continuous, smooth, white expanse. The indifferent ground of the day before now noticed my shoe soles and
kept their shape as I took a few experimental steps outside the
doorway. Another time, as I walked through the pine grove in the
center of campus during a large-flaked snowfall, I could not see a
single campus building or a single person. I felt that I had somehow stepped into a gentle winter world without time. It was calming how the falling of a million flaky water-drops could transform
a landscape and absorb my attention.
   Mary Oliver's poem "First Snow" recalls a similar
experience. In the poem, Oliver describes the snowfall, from the
morning, when it began, to the night, when it ended. Her
chronological tracing of the event allows us to experience the
same wonder and admiration she feels in watching the snow and
its effects.
   The poem begins with the author describing how the
snow began: "The snow / began here / this morning" (lines 1–3).
With this opening, the author gives the reader a natural starting
place. The opening is similar to the common story opening, that
is, "Once upon a time in such and such a place."
   The poem continues with Oliver describing how the snow
fell throughout the day and what it was like. The snow falling had
"white / rhetoric everywhere" (4–5). Rhetoric is persuasive speaking or writing. The next lines say what the snow's "white rhetoric"

---- **ROUGH DRAFT** ----

the author is dumbfounded. Her sense of amazement continues into the next line, where she exclaims "such / an oracular fever!" (lines 8–9). "Oracular" means of an oracle, and therefore inspired, authoritative, or sent from above. "Fever" can mean having a high body temperature or a state of excitement or activity. Since there is no indication in the poem that the author is ill, "fever" describes how the snow is moving and the excitement the author is feeling. Thus, the oracular fever is both the swirling flurry of snow the author sees and the inspired, giddy feeling she gets from watching it.

Until now, the poem has been about how the snow has fallen throughout the day and has been told in the past tense. For the rest of the poem, the author focuses on the present, describing how the scene is now, blanketed by snow. By line 13, it is night, and the snow has stopped falling. The author can feel the silence because it is "immense" (lines 15–16). And although it is night, the sky still brims with light as if lit by "a million candles" (line 18). At first, it seems like the million candles are stars, but lines 18–20 show that there are no stars: "nowhere / the familiar things: / stars." Whatever the candles are is not obvious, but it is clear that they convey the sense of brightness, which is further developed by the details of smoldering fields (lines 24–25), "shining hills" (line 27), and "light / under the trees" (lines 33–34). Light is there in abundance and changes the appearance of things. It obscures the stars, the moon, and the darkness (lines 20–21). It allows the trees to "glitter like castles / of ribbons" (lines 22–24).

---- **FINAL DRAFT** ----

Hong 2

was doing: "calling us back to *why, how, / whence* such beauty
and *what /* the meaning" (6–8). The rhetoric was persuading the
author to wonder, in the literal sense, about the beauty and
meaning of the snow and wonder at it in the sense of amazement
also. The questions of *"why, how, / whence* such beauty" and
"what / the meaning" indicate that the author is dumbfounded.
Her sense of amazement continues into the next line, where she
exclaims "such / an oracular fever!" (8–9). *Oracular* means pertaining to an oracle, thus a prophetic utterance, often enigmatic
or mysterious. Since there is no indication of illness in the poem,
fever describes how the snow is moving and the excitement the
author is feeling. Thus, the "oracular fever" is both the swirling
flurry of snow the author sees and the inspired feeling of awe and
mystery she gets from watching it. We share her marvel as we witness the snow-white energy "[flow] / past [the] windows" (9–10)
and show no sign of waning or becoming "less than lovely" (12).

Until now, the poem has been about how the snow has
fallen throughout the day, and it has been told in the past tense.
For the rest of the poem, Oliver focuses on the present, describing
how the scene is now blanketed by snow. By line 13 it is night,
and the snow has stopped falling. The author can feel the silence
because it is "immense" (15–16). Although it is night, the sky
still brims with light as if lit by "a million candles" (18). At first,
it seems as if the million candles are stars, but lines 18–22 show
that the skyscape has been transformed so much because of the
snow that the stars are not visible:

> nowhere
> the familiar things:
> stars, the moon,
> the darkness we expect
> and nightly turn from.

—— **ROUGH DRAFT** ——

In the final part of the poem, the author steps out into the snow. She has observed the snow falling all day, so the questions that have "assailed" (line 29) her are none other than *"why, how / whence* such beauty and *what /* the meaning" (lines 6–8) in the snowfall. The author says in the final line that walking out into the snow — "into the silence and the light / under the trees, / and through the fields" (lines 33–35) — "feels like" an answer (line 36). Watching the snow from inside, the author had felt wonder at the sight. Now being in it, she feels a part of it. It might be that questions cannot continue to be uttered in the profound silence and the light feels enlightening, so in a way, the author has found the answer to her questions in experiencing the snow.

─────── **FINAL DRAFT** ───────

The heavens are bright, with "broad fields / smolder[ing] with light" (24–25) and "a passing / creekbed . . . / heaped with shining hills" (25–27). There is "light / under the trees" (33–34). The "broad fields" and "shining hills" indicate that the landscape has also changed. In this burning landscape, trees glitter with frost "like castles / of ribbons" (22–24), reminding us of some romantic fantasyland.

The final section of the poem shifts from a description of the snow-covered scene to participation in it. Oliver and her companions — let us imagine we are they — walk out into the snow and feel that an answer has been found: "[T]he questions / that have assailed us all day / remain" (28–30) — "why, how, / whence such beauty and what / the meaning" (6–8) — and "not a single / answer has been found" (30–31). We had been wondering at the sight all day. Now, trooping "into the silence and the light / under the trees, / and through the fields" (33–35) — in short, immersing ourselves in the snow that made us wonder — "feels like [an answer]" (36). This is because walking out into the snow places us in the wonder itself, and that experience somehow satisfies our wonder without diminishing it. Thus, the answer is the experience.

"First Snow" presents an impressionistic account of a snowfall. The poem unfolds chronologically, and this ordering enables us to follow Oliver's experience vicariously with ease. The author witnesses the seemingly infinite falling of the snow throughout the day, observes the transformed landscape after the snow has stopped falling, and feels the immense silence when walking out into the snow. We share her wonder at each step, and at the end of the poem we share the answer of stepping out into the snow with our imaginations. This experiential answer is what makes every snowfall a "first snow."

CHAPTER 21 A Collection of Poems

Valuing Various Voices

SOME VERY SHORT POEMS

For pedagogical purposes, the majority of poems selected for this book are not very long. There are, of course, many significant, long poems, from the book-length verses of Dante's *The Divine Comedy*, John Milton's *Paradise Lost*, and William Wordsworth's *The Prelude* to myriad others that are several pages in length and composed by equally accomplished writers. So what then is poetry's version of "short short" or "sudden fiction"? Of the one-act or "ten-minute" play of drama? Is it a poem that can be read in ten seconds?

Time, of course, is not the issue: Many short poems create an experience outside those parameters measured by a clock. Instead, the "short short poem" has to have an impact with very little, if any, buildup. It must "hit home" soon after the first line or the first few lines, creating a kind of whip-crack of sudden realization, of an arresting moment, of blinding insight, or of a shift in attention or a change in perception. There is no time for the poet to lead up to the situation, to create an extended description of setting or context, to give a thorough background; there is no time to build to a conclusion, resolution, or surprise in a gradually unfolding manner. It's hit or miss. See how the following poems hit or miss you.

For additional information on these authors, see "Biographical Sketches," pages 1053–1085.

Denise Levertov   1923–1997

Leaving Forever   [1964]

He says the waves in the ship's wake
are like stones rolling away.
I don't see it that way.
But I see the mountain turning,
turning away its face as the ship   5
takes us away.

Marianne Moore   1887–1972

Poetry   [1967]

I, too, dislike it.
    Reading it, however, with a perfect contempt for it, one discovers in it,
    after all, a place for the genuine.

Ezra Pound   1885–1972

In a Station of the Metro   [1916]

The apparition of these faces in the crowd;
Petals on a wet, black bough.

Carl Sandburg   1878–1967

Fog   [1916]

The fog comes
on little cat feet.

It sits looking
over harbor and city
on silent haunches   5
and then moves on.

POEMS FOR FURTHER READING

For additional information about the poets included in this chapter, see "Biographical Sketches" pages 1053–1085.

Maya Angelou   1928–2014

Africa   [1975]

Thus she had lain
sugar cane sweet
deserts her hair
golden her feet
mountains her breasts   5
two Niles her tears
Thus she has lain
Black through the years.

Over the white seas
rime white and cold   10
brigands ungentled
icicle bold
took her young daughters
sold her strong sons
churched her with Jesus   15
bled her with guns.
Thus she has lain.

Now she is rising
remember her pain
remember the losses   20
her screams loud and vain
remember her riches
her history slain
now she is striding
although she had lain.   25

Susan Atefat-Peckham   1970–2004

Dates   [2001]

Three days and they wrapped
his washed body in muslin,
no lumbering sounds of coffins
carried, only the white ripple

of cloth. I sat back where all   5
women sat, staring from behind
a wooden net, carved and set
aside. The others swayed
as if crows under the mirrored
dome of the mosque webbed   10
in their chadors, breathing cloth
in and out of their wailing,
in and out. Their black heads
bobbed against the carved light
of the wooden boundary, the roar   15
and echo of men beating themselves
downstairs, pounding their chests
tightly, fists on flesh, to the rhythm
of a prayer for the dead.

A woman stood and held a tray,   20
the edges of her chador clenched
in her teeth and wrapped so tightly
around her face that it cut angles
into her cheeks. She offered us
a silver tray of fruit as chanting   25
grew, beating grew, that fleshy
rhythm. And the woman
with dates walked the aisles
offering the shriveled skin
and its sweet stench on a silver tray,   30
making her way from one woman
to the next. Somewhere under
Iranian earth, seamless cloth lay
on its side, a turned face frozen
under a concrete canopy, legs bent   35
toward Mecca. She lowered the tray.
I reached for a date, and my mouth
watered to taste its sugar.

W. H. Auden   1907–1973

Musée des Beaux Arts°   [1940]

About suffering they were never wrong,
The Old Masters: how well they understood
Its human position; how it takes place

Musée des Beaux Arts: The painting *Landscape with the Fall of Icarus* (p. 604), on which
the poem is based, is in the Musées Royaux des Beaux-Arts in Brussels.

While someone else is eating or opening a window or just
    walking dully along;
How, when the aged are reverently, passionately waiting   5
For the miraculous birth, there always must be
Children who did not specially want it to happen, skating
On a pond at the edge of the wood:
They never forgot
That even the dreadful martyrdom must run its course   10
Anyhow in a corner, some untidy spot
Where the dogs go on with their doggy life and the torturer's horse
Scratches its innocent behind on a tree.

In Breughel's *Icarus*, for instance: how everything turns away
Quite leisurely from the disaster; the ploughman may   15
Have heard the splash, the forsaken cry,
But for him it was not an important failure; the sun shone
As it had to on the white legs disappearing into the green
Water; and the expensive delicate ship that must have seen
Something amazing, a boy falling out of the sky,   20
Had somewhere to get to and sailed calmly on.

Pieter Brueghel the Elder (c. 1525–1569), *Landscape with the Fall
of Icarus, 1558*.
Scala/Art Resource, NY.

APPROACHING THE AUTHOR

Jimmy Santiago Baca taught himself to read and write and fashioned himself a poet while in prison. It was a fellow inmate who encouraged him to submit his work to *Mother Jones,* a move that would prove pivotal to launching his literary career.

For more about him, see page 1055.

Jimmy Santiago Baca   b. 1952

Family Ties   [1989]

Mountain barbecue.
They arrive, young cousins singly,
older aunts and uncles in twos and threes,
like trees. I play with a new generation
of children, my hands in streambed silt   5
of their lives, a scuba diver's hands, dusting
surface sand for buried treasure.
Freshly shaved and powdered faces
of uncles and aunts surround taco
and tamale tables. Mounted elk head on wall,   10
brass rearing horse cowboy clock
on fireplace mantle. Sons and daughters
converse round beer and whiskey table.
Tempers ignite on land grant issues.
Children scurry round my legs.   15
Old bow-legged men toss horseshoes on lawn,
other farmhands from Mexico sit on a bench,
broken lives repaired for this occasion.
I feel no love or family tie here. I rise
to go hiking, to find abandoned rock cabins   20
in the mountains. We come to a grass clearing,
my wife rolls her jeans up past ankles,
wades ice cold stream, and I barefooted,
carry a son in each arm and follow.
We cannot afford a place like this.   25
At the party again, I eat bean and chile
burrito, and after my third glass of rum,
we climb in the car and my wife drives
us home. My sons sleep in the back,
dream of the open clearing,   30

they are chasing each other with cattails
in the sunlit pasture, giggling,
as I stare out the window
at no trespassing signs white flashing past.

Jim Barnes   b. 1933

Return to La Plata, Missouri   [1982]

The warping bandstand reminds you of the hard rage
you felt in the heart of the town the day you said goodbye
to the park, silver jet, and cicadas dead in the sage.

The town is basic red, although it browns. A cry
of murder, rape, or wrong will always bend the night   5
hard into the broken grass. You listen close for sighs

of lovers on the ground. The darkness gathers light
and throws it down: something glows that you cannot name,
something fierce, abstract, given time and space you might

on a journey leave behind, a stone to carve your fame   10
on, or a simple word like *love*. The sun is down
or always going down in La Plata, the same

sun. Same too the child's cry that turns the mother's frown
brittle as chalk or the town's face against the moon.
Same too the moan of dog and diesel circling the town   15

in an air so heavy with cloud that there is little room
for breath or moon. Strange: in a town so country, so
foreign, you never hear a song nor see a loom

pattern dark threads into a history you would know
and would not know. You think you see one silver star.   20
But the town offers only itself, and you must go.

Elizabeth Bishop   1911–1979

Sestina   [1965]

September rain falls on the house.
In the failing light, the old grandmother
sits in the kitchen with the child
beside the Little Marvel Stove,
reading the jokes from the almanac,   5
laughing and talking to hide her tears.

She thinks that her equinoctial tears
and the rain that beats on the roof of the house
were both foretold by the almanac,
but only known to a grandmother.   10
The iron kettle sings on the stove.
She cuts some bread and says to the child,

It's time for tea now; but the child
is watching the teakettle's small hard tears
dance like mad on the hot black stove,   15
the way the rain must dance on the house.
Tidying up, the old grandmother
hangs up the clever almanac

on its string. Birdlike, the almanac
hovers half open above the child,   20
hovers above the old grandmother
and her teacup full of dark brown tears.
She shivers and says she thinks the house
feels chilly, and puts more wood in the stove.

It was to be, says the Marvel Stove.   25
I know what I know, says the almanac.
With crayons the child draws a rigid house
and a winding pathway. Then the child
puts in a man with buttons like tears
and shows it proudly to the grandmother.   30

But secretly, while the grandmother
busies herself about the stove,
the little moons fall down like tears
from between the pages of the almanac
into the flower bed the child   35
has carefully placed in the front of the house.

Time to plant tears, says the almanac.
The grandmother sings to the marvellous stove
and the child draws another inscrutable house.

Peter Blue Cloud   1935–2011

Crazy Horse Monument   [1995]

Hailstones falling like sharp blue sky chips
howling winds the brown grass bends, while
buffalo paw and stamp and blow billowing steam,
and prairie wolves chorus the moon in moaning.

The spotted snake of a village on the move   5
a silent file of horses rounding hills,
in a robe of grey, the sky chief clutches thunder
and winter seeks to find the strongest men.

   Crazy Horse rides the circle of his people's sleep,
       from Little Big Horn to Wounded Knee,   10
   Black Hills, their shadows are his only robe
       dark breast feathers of a future storm.

Those of broken bodies piled in death,
of frozen blood upon the white of snow,
yours is now the sky chant of spirit making,   15
pacing the rhythm of Crazy Horse's mount.

And he would cry in anger of a single death,
and dare the guns of mounted soldiers blue,
for his was the blood and pulse of rivers,
and mountains and plains taken in sacred trust.   20

   Crazy Horse rides the circle of his people's sleep,
       from Little Big Horn to Wounded Knee,
   Black Hills, their shadows are his only robe
       dark breast feathers of a future storm.

And what would he think of the cold steel chisel,   25
and of dynamite blasting mountain's face,
what value the crumbled glories of Greece and Rome,
to a people made cold and hungry?
To capture in stone the essence of a man's spirit,
to portray the love and respect of children and elders,   30
fashion instead the point of a hunting arrow sharp,
and leave to the elements the wearing-down of time.

   Crazy Horse rides the circle of his people's sleep,
       from Little Big Horn to Wounded Knee,
   Black Hills, their shadows are his only robe   35
       dark breast feathers of a future storm.

Elizabeth Barrett Browning   1806–1861

How do I love thee? Let me count the ways   [1850]

How do I love thee? Let me count the ways.
I love thee to the depth and breadth and height
My soul can reach, when feeling out of sight
For the ends of Being and ideal Grace.

I love thee to the level of every day's   5
Most quiet need, by sun and candlelight.
I love thee freely, as men strive for Right;
I love thee purely, as they turn from Praise.
I love thee with the passion put to use
In my old griefs, and with my childhood's faith.   10
I love thee with a love I seemed to lose
With my lost saints — I love thee with the breath,
Smiles, tears, of all my life! — and, if God choose,
I shall but love thee better after death.

Rafael Campo   b. 1964

The Enemy   [2007]

The buildings' wounds are what I can't forget;
though nothing could absorb my sense of loss
I stared into their blackness, what was not

supposed to be there, billowing of soot
and ragged maw of splintered steel, glass.   5
The buildings' wounds are what I can't forget,

the people dropping past them, fleeting spots
approaching death as if concerned with grace.
I stared into the blackness, what was not

inhuman, since by men's hands they were wrought;   10
reflected on the TV's screen, my face
upon the buildings' wounds. I can't forget

this rage, I don't know what to do with it —
it's in my nightmares, towers, plumes of dust,
a staring in the blackness. What was not   15

conceivable is now our every thought:
We fear the enemy is all of us.
The buildings' wounds are what I can't forget.
I stared into their blackness, what was not.

APPROACHING THE AUTHOR

Lorna Dee Cervantes's parents allowed her and her brother to speak only English at home, to avoid the racism present in her community at that time. The resulting inability to identify fully with her heritage fueled her later poetry.

For more about her, see page 1058.

Lorna Dee Cervantes   b. 1954

Freeway 280   [1981]

Las casitas° near the gray cannery,   *little houses*
nestled amid wild abrazos° of climbing roses   *hugs*
and man-high red geraniums
are gone now. The freeway conceals it
all beneath a raised scar.   5

But under the fake windsounds of the open lanes,
in the abandoned lots below, new grasses sprout,
wild mustard remembers, old gardens
come back stronger than they were,
trees have been left standing in their yards.   10
Albaricoqueros, cerezos, nogales° . . .   *apricot, cherry, walnut trees*
Viejitas° come here with paper bags to gather greens.   *old women*
Espinaca, verdolagas, yerbabuena° . . .   *spinach, purslane, mint*

I scramble over the wire fence
that would have kept me out.   15
Once, I wanted out, wanted the rigid lanes
to take me to a place without sun,
without the smell of tomatoes burning
on swing shift in the greasy summer air.

Maybe it's here   20
en los campos extraños de esta ciudad°   *in the strange fields of this city*
where I'll find it, that part of me
mown under
like a corpse
or a loose seed.   25

Marilyn Chin   b. 1955

How I Got That Name   [1994]
an essay on assimilation

I am Marilyn Mei Ling Chin.
Oh, how I love the resoluteness
of that first person singular
followed by that stalwart indicative
of "be," without the uncertain i-n-g   5
of "becoming." Of course,
the name had been changed
somewhere between Angel Island° and the sea,
when my father the paperson°
in the late 1950s   10
obsessed with a bombshell blonde
transliterated "Mei Ling" to "Marilyn."
And nobody dared question
his initial impulse — for we all know
lust drove men to greatness,   15
not goodness, not decency.
And there I was, a wayward pink baby,
named after some tragic white woman
swollen with gin and Nembutal.°
My mother couldn't pronounce the "r."   20
She dubbed me "Numba one female offshoot"
for brevity: henceforth, she will live and die
in sublime ignorance, flanked
by loving children and the "kitchen deity."
While my father dithers,   25
a tomcat in Hong Kong trash —
a gambler, a petty thug,
who bought a chain of chopsuey joints
in Piss River, Oregon,
with bootlegged Gucci cash.   30
Nobody dared question his integrity given
his nice, devout daughters
and his bright, industrious sons
as if filial piety were the standard

---

8. **Angel Island:** An island in San Francisco Bay, site of the Angel Island Immigration Station that processed approximately 1 million Asian immigrants between 1910 and 1940.   9. **paperson:** A "paper son" is a term used for young Chinese males entering the United States who claimed to be sons of U.S. citizens but were, in fact, sons on paper only.   19. **Nembutal:** A short-acting barbituate (Pentobarbital) prescribed as a sedative but also used as an intoxicant.

by which all earthly men were measured.   35
Oh, how trustworthy our daughters,
how thrifty our sons!
How we've managed to fool the experts
in education, statistics and demography —
We're not very creative but not adverse to rote-learning.   40
Indeed, they can *use* us.
But the "Model Minority" is a tease.
We know you are watching now,
so we refuse to give you any!
Oh, bamboo shoots, bamboo shoots!   45
The further west we go, we'll hit east;
the deeper down we dig, we'll find China.
History has turned its stomach
on a black polluted beach —
where life doesn't hinge   50
on that red, red wheelbarrow,°
but whether or not our new lover
in the final episode of "Santa Barbara"°
will lean over a scented candle
and call us a "bitch."   55
Oh God, where have we gone wrong?
We have no inner resources!

Then, one redolent spring morning
the Great Patriarch Chin
peered down from his kiosk in heaven   60
and saw that his descendants were ugly.
One had a squarish head and a nose without a bridge.
Another's profile — long and knobbed as a gourd.
A third, the sad, brutish one
may never, never marry.   65
And I, his least favorite —
"not quite boiled, not quite cooked,"
a plump pomfret simmering in my juices —
too listless to fight for my people's destiny.
"To kill without resistance is not slaughter"   70
says the proverb. So, I wait for imminent death.
The fact that this death is also metaphorical
is testament to my lethargy.

---

51. **red wheelbarrow:** See the poem by William Carlos Williams on page 472.
53. **"Santa Barbara":** American television soap opera, 1984–1993, that focused
on the lives of the wealthy Capwell family of Santa Barbara, California.

So here lies Marilyn Mei Ling Chin,
married once, twice to so-and-so, a Lee and a Wong,   75
granddaughter of Jack "the patriarch"
and the brooding Suilin Fong,
daughter of the virtuous Yuet Kuen Wong
and G. G. Chin the infamous,
sister of a dozen, cousin of a million,   80
survived by everybody and forgotten by all.
She was neither black nor white,
neither cherished nor vanquished,
just another squatter in her own bamboo grove
minding her poetry—   85
when one day heaven was unmerciful,
and a chasm opened where she stood.
Like the jowls of a mighty white whale,°
or the jaws of a metaphysical Godzilla,°
it swallowed her whole.   90
She did not flinch nor writhe,
nor fret about the afterlife,
but stayed! Solid as wood, happily
a little gnawed, tattered, mesmerized
by all that was lavished upon her   95
and all that was taken away!

---

88. mighty white whale: The whale in Herman Melville's 1851 novel *Moby Dick*.
89. Godzilla: A monster which appeared first in Ishirō Honda's 1954 film *Godzilla* and became a pop culture icon in twenty-eight additional films.

Lucille Clifton   1936–2010

homage to my hips   [1980]

these hips are big hips
they need space to
move around in.
they don't fit into little
petty places. these hips   5
are free hips.
they don't like to be held back.
these hips have never been enslaved,
they go where they want to go
they do what they want to do.   10
these hips are mighty hips.

these hips are magic hips.
i have known them
to put a spell on a man and
spin him like a top!   15

APPROACHING THE AUTHOR

Lynn Goldsmith/CORBIS.

When **Billy Collins** served as poet laureate of the
United States, he created a poetry channel for Delta
Airlines so people can listen to recited poetry while
they fly, and he developed Poetry 180, a program
for high schools that encourages a poem be read
each day with the morning announcements. His
strong belief in presenting poetry in unexpected
places stems from the example set by his mother,
who would often recite lines of poetry at random
during his childhood.

For more about him, see page 1059.

Billy Collins   b. 1941

Nostalgia   [1991]

Remember the 1340s? We were doing a dance called the Catapult.
You always wore brown, the color craze of the decade,
and I was draped in one of those capes that were popular,
the ones with unicorns and pomegranates in needlework.
Everyone would pause for beer and onions in the afternoon,   5
and at night we would play a game called "Find the Cow."
Everything was hand-lettered then, not like today.

Where has the summer of 1572 gone? Brocade and sonnet
marathons were the rage. We used to dress up in the flags
of rival baronies and conquer one another in cold rooms of stone.   10
Out on the dance floor we were all doing the Struggle
while your sister practiced the Daphne all alone in her room.
We borrowed the jargon of farriers for our slang.
These days language seems transparent, a badly broken code.

The 1790s will never come again. Childhood was big.   15
People would take walks to the very tops of hills
and write down what they saw in their journals without speaking.
Our collars were high and our hats were extremely soft.

We would surprise each other with alphabets made of twigs.
It was a wonderful time to be alive, or even dead.   20

I am very fond of the period between 1815 and 1821.
Europe trembled while we sat still for our portraits.
And I would love to return to 1901 if only for a moment,
time enough to wind up a music box and do a few dance steps,
or shoot me back to 1922 or 1941, or at least let me   25
recapture the serenity of last month when we picked
berries and glided through afternoons in a canoe.

Even this morning would be an improvement over the present.
I was in the garden then, surrounded by the hum of bees
and the Latin names of flowers, watching the early light   30
flash off the slanted windows of the greenhouse
and silver the limbs on the rows of dark hemlocks.

As usual, I was thinking about the moments of the past,
letting my memory rush over them like water
rushing over the stones on the bottom of a stream.   35
I was even thinking a little about the future, that place
where people are doing a dance we cannot imagine,
a dance whose name we can only guess.

APPROACHING THE AUTHOR

Victor Hernández Cruz's homeland is Puerto Rico, but he grew up near the Avenue D housing project on Manhattan's Lower East Side, where the population was primarily African American and Puerto Rican. "There was a constant blend of these cultures on the street. So I naturally combine *all* these influences."
   For more about him, see page 1059.

Victor Hernández Cruz   b. 1949

Problems with Hurricanes   [1991]

A campesino looked at the air
And told me:
With hurricanes it's not the wind
or the noise or the water.

I'll tell you he said: 5
it's the mangoes, avocados
Green plantains and bananas
flying into town like projectiles.

How would your family
feel if they had to tell   10
The generations that you
got killed by a flying
Banana.

Death by drowning has honor
If the wind picked you up   15
and slammed you
Against a mountain boulder
This would not carry shame
But
to suffer a mango smashing   20
Your skull
or a plantain hitting your
Temple at 70 miles per hour
is the ultimate disgrace.

The campesino takes off his hat—   25
As a sign of respect
towards the fury of the wind
And says:
Don't worry about the noise
Don't worry about the water   30
Don't worry about the wind—
If you are going out
beware of mangoes
And all such beautiful
sweet things.   35

Toi Derricotte   b. 1941

A Note on My Son's Face   [1989]

I

Tonight, I look, thunderstruck
at the gold head of my grandchild.
Almost asleep, he buries his feet
between my thighs;
his little straw eyes   5
close in the near dark.
I smell the warmth of his raw
slightly foul breath, the new death

waiting to rot inside him.
Our breaths equalize our heartbeats;   10
every muscle of the chest uncoils,
the arm bones loosen in the nest
of nerves. I think of the peace
of walking through the house,
pointing to the name of this, the name of that,   15
an educator of a new man.

Mother. Grandmother. Wise
Snake-woman who will show the way;
Spider-woman whose black tentacles
hold him precious. Or will tear off his head,   20
her teeth over the little husband,
the small fist clotted in trust at her breast.

This morning, looking at the face of his father,
I remembered how, an infant, his face was too dark,
nose too broad, mouth too wide.   25
I did not look in that mirror
and see the face that could save me
from my own darkness.
Did he, looking in my eye, see
what I turned from: 30
my own dark grandmother
bending over gladioli in the field,
her shaking black hand defenseless
at the shining cock of flower?

I wanted that face to die,   35
to be reborn in the face of a white child.

I wanted the soul to stay the same,
for I loved to death,
to damnation and God-death,
the soul that broke out of me.   40
I crowed: My Son! My Beautiful!
But when I peeked in the basket,
I saw the face of a black man.

Did I bend over his nose
and straighten it with my fingers   45
like a vine growing the wrong way?
Did he feel my hand in malice?

Generations we prayed and fucked
for this light child,
the shining god of the second coming;   50

we bow down in shame
and carry the children of the past
in our wallets, begging forgiveness.

II

A picture in a book,
a lynching   55
The bland faces of men who watch
a Christ go up in flames, smiling,
as if he were a hooked
fish, a felled antelope, some
wild thing tied to boards and burned.   60
His charring body
gives off light—a halo
burns out of him.
His face scorched featureless;
the hair matted to the scalp   65
like feathers.
One man stands with his hand on his hip,
another with his arm
slung over the shoulder of a friend,
as if this moment were large enough   70
to hold affection.

III

How can we wake
from a dream
we are born into,
that shines around us,   75
the terrible bright air?

Having awakened,
having seen our own bloody hands,
how can we ask forgiveness,
bring before our children the real   80
monster of their nightmares?

The worst is true.
Everything you did not want to know.

Joanne Diaz   b. 1972

Pride and Prejudice   [2014]

Reader, if someday the heiress of a major American department store
calls and asks you to lead a discussion of *Pride and Prejudice*,

just remember that it is never a good idea to accept the invitation
if you harbor suspicions of the wealthy that could sully the discussion

of what is otherwise one of the most perfect novels ever written.   5
And if you do decide to take the job, don't, in the midst

of a conversation about the finances of Darcy and the Bennetts,
remind the women that their own worth is just as easy to find

on Google as the newest You Tube clip; don't listen to the women
begrudge the importance of money as they sip their tea; and don't   10

be surprised when they offer you no food and you find yourself
swooning, partly from midmorning hypoglycemia, partly

from the thought of what your mother laid out for the measliest
of events, your mother in her modest kitchen of linoleum

and Formica and petaled wallpaper and the overhead light   15
that turned even the cannolis a little blue. Above all,

don't be too disappointed when, after all the lively talk of women
"marrying up" and the urgent debate over why Jane Austen

is still a classic, the check that you receive for your services
is just big enough to buy a box of plastic ornaments   20

at the major American department store owned by the woman
who called you in the first place. Because, in the end, you are merely

an ornament, a bell tinkling on the giant tree of capitalism.
Remember this when, after seeing the amount on your check

and walking down the driveway full of Mercedes, you realize   25
that you have to use the toilet after all, and that when you knock

on the glass and they squint as if they have never seen you before,
it is because they see a strand of tinsel, a silvery nothing, waiting to
   drift back in.

John Donne   1572–1631

Death, be not proud   [1633]

Death, be not proud, though some have callèd thee
Mighty and dreadful, for thou art not so;
For those whom thou think'st thou dost overthrow
Die not, poor Death, nor yet canst thou kill me.
From rest and sleep, which but thy pictures be,   5
Much pleasure; then from thee much more must flow,
And soonest our best men with thee do go,
Rest of their bones, and soul's delivery.
Thou art slave to fate, chance, kings, and desperate men,
And dost with poison, war, and sickness dwell,   10
And poppy° or charms can make us sleep as well   *opium*
And better than thy stroke; why swell'st° thou then?   *(with pride)*
One short sleep past, we wake eternally
And death shall be no more; Death, thou shalt die.

Mark Doty   b. 1953

Tiara   [1991]

Peter died in a paper tiara
cut from a book of princess paper dolls;
he loved royalty, sashes

and jewels. *I don't know,*
he said, when he woke in the hospice,   5
I was watching the Bette Davis film festival

on Channel 57 and then—
At the wake, the tension broke
when someone guessed

the casket closed because   10
he was *in there in a big wig*
and heels, and someone said,

You know he's always late,
he probably isn't here yet—
he's still fixing his makeup.   15

And someone said he asked for it.
Asked for it—
when all he did was go down

into the salt tide
of wanting as much as he wanted,   20
giving himself over so drunk

or stoned it almost didn't matter who,
though they were beautiful,
stampeding into him in the simple,

ravishing music of their hurry.   25
I think heaven is perfect stasis
poised over the realms of desire,

where dreaming and waking men lie
on the grass while wet horses
roam among them, huge fragments   30

of the music we die into
in the body's paradise.
Sometimes we wake not knowing

how we came to lie here,
or who has crowned us with these temporary,   35
precious stones. And given

the world's perfectly turned shoulders,
the deep hollows blued by longing,
given the irreplaceable silk

of horses rippling in orchards,   40
fruit thundering and chiming down,
given the ordinary marvels of form

and gravity, what could he do,
what could any of us ever do
but ask for it?   45

APPROACHING THE AUTHOR

Rita Dove played the cello in her youth and later wrote song cycles for works by a variety of composers, one of which was performed by the revered Boston Symphony Orchestra. When not writing, she studies classical voice and practices the viola da gamba, a seventeenth-century forerunner of the modern cello.

© Christopher Felver/ CORBIS.

For more about her, see page 1061.

Rita Dove b. 1952

Horse and Tree   [1989]

Everybody who's anybody longs to be a tree —
or ride one, hair blown to froth.
That's why horses were invented, and saddles
tooled with singular stars.

This is why we braid their harsh manes   5
as if they were children, why children
might fear a carousel at first for the way
it insists that life is round. No,

we reply, there is music and then it stops;
the beautiful is always rising and falling.   10
We call and the children sing back *one more time*.
In the tree the luminous sap ascends.

Denise Duhamel b. 1961

One Afternoon When Barbie Wanted
to Join the Military   [1997]

It was a crazy idea, she admits now,
but camouflage was one costume she still hadn't tried.
Barbie'd gone mod with go-go boots° during Vietnam.
Throughout Panama° she was busy playing with a Frisbee
the size of a Coke bottle cap. And while troops   5
were fighting in the Gulf,°
she wore a gown inspired by Ivana Trump.°
When Mattel told her, hell no — she couldn't go,
Barbie borrowed GI Joe's° fatigues,
safety pinning his pants's big waist   10
to better fit her own.

---

3. go-go boots: Low-heeled, knee-length women's fashion boots. **4. Panama:** U.S. invasion of Panama on 20 December 1989 in order to remove military dictator Manuel Noriega. **6. Gulf:** War in the Persian Gulf region (August 1990-January 1991) in which United States-led coalition forces defeated Iraq. **7. Ivana Trump:** A former Czechoslovakian Olympic skier and fashion model (b. 1949) who was married to magnate Donald Trump from 1977 to 1991. **9. GI Joe:** An American soldier. *G. I.* is an abbreviation for *government issue,* used for equipment designed or provided for members of the U.S. armed forces. The poem refers to the G.I. Joe toy action figure.

She settled on his olive tank.
But Barbie thought it was boring.
"Why don't you try running over something small?"
coaxed GI Joe, who sat naked behind the leg   15
of a human's living room chair.
Barbie saw imaginary bunnies
hopping through the shag carpet.
"I can't," she said.
GI Joe suggested she gun down the enemy,   20
who was sneaking up behind her.
Barbie couldn't muster up the rage
for killing, even if it was only play.
Maybe if someone tried to take her parking space
or scratched her red Trans Am.   25
Maybe if someone had called her a derogatory name.
But what had this soldier from the other side done?
GI Joe, seeing their plan was a mistake,
asked her to return his clothes,
making Barbie promise not to tell anyone.   30
As she slipped back into her classic baby blue
one-piece swimsuit, she realized
this would be her second secret.
She couldn't tell about the time
she posed nude for *Hustler.*°   35
A young photographer who lived in the house
dipped her legs in a full bottle of Johnson's Baby Oil,
then swabbed some more on her torso.
Barbie lounged on the red satin lining
of the kid's Sunday jacket. He dimmed   40
the lights and lit a candle
to create a glossy centerfold mood.
"Lick your lips," he kept saying,
forgetting Barbie didn't have a tongue.
She couldn't pout. She couldn't even bite   45
the maraschino cherry he dangled in front of her mouth.
Luckily there was no film in his sister's camera,
so the boy's pictures never came out.
Luckily GI Joe wasn't in the real Army
or he said he would risk being court-martialed—   50
he wasn't supposed to lend his uniform
to anyone, especially a girl.

---

35. *Hustler:* a monthly pornographic magazine, first published in the United States
in 1974.

Just then a human hand deposited Ken from the sky.
Somewhere along the way he'd lost his sandals.
"What have you two been up to?" he asked.   55
Barbie didn't have the kind of eyes that could shift away
so she lost herself in the memory of a joke
made by her favorite comedian Sandra Bernhard,°
who said she liked her dates to be androgynous
because if she was going to be with a man   60
she didn't want to have to face that fact.
Barbie was grateful for Ken's plastic flat feet
and plastic flat crotch. No military
would ever take him, even if there was a draft.
As GI Joe bullied Ken into a headlock,   65
Barbie told the boys to cut it out. She threatened
that if he kept it up, GI Joe would
never get that honorable discharge.

---

58. **Sandra Bernhard:** American comedian and actress (b. 1955).

T. S. Eliot   1888–1965

The Love Song of J. Alfred Prufrock   [1917]

S'io credesse che mia risposta fosse
A persona che mai tornasse al mondo,
Questa fiamma staria senza piu scosse.
Ma perciocche giammai di questo fondo
Non torno vivo alcun, s'i'odo il vero,
Senza tema d'infamia ti rispondo.°

Let us go then, you and I,
When the evening is spread out against the sky
Like a patient etherized upon a table;
Let us go, through certain half-deserted streets,

Epigraph: "If I thought that my answer were being made to someone who would ever
return to earth, this flame would remain without further movement; but since no one
has ever returned alive from this depth, if what I hear is true, I answer you without fear
of infamy" (Dante, *Inferno* 27.61–66). Dante encounters Guido de Montefeltro in the
eighth circle of hell, where souls are trapped within flames (tongues of fire) as punishment for giving evil counsel. Guido tells Dante details about his evil life only because he
assumes that Dante is on his way to an even deeper circle in hell and will never return to
earth and thus be able to repeat what he has heard.

The muttering retreats   5
Of restless nights in one-night cheap hotels
And sawdust restaurants with oyster-shells:
Streets that follow like a tedious argument
Of insidious intent
To lead you to an overwhelming question . . .   10
Oh, do not ask, "What is it?"
Let us go and make our visit.

    In the room the women come and go
Talking of Michelangelo.

    The yellow fog that rubs its back upon the window-panes,   15
The yellow smoke that rubs its muzzle on the window-panes
Licked its tongue into the corners of the evening,
Lingered upon the pools that stand in drains,
Let fall upon its back the soot that falls from chimneys,
Slipped by the terrace, made a sudden leap,   20
And seeing that it was a soft October night,
Curled once about the house, and fell asleep.

    And indeed there will be time
For the yellow smoke that slides along the street,
Rubbing its back upon the window-panes;   25
There will be time, there will be time
To prepare a face to meet the faces that you meet;
There will be time to murder and create,
And time for all the works and days° of hands
That lift and drop a question on your plate;   30
Time for you and time for me,
And time yet for a hundred indecisions,
And for a hundred visions and revisions,
Before the taking of a toast and tea.

    In the room the women come and go   35
Talking of Michelangelo.

    And indeed there will be time
To wonder, "Do I dare?" and, "Do I dare?"
Time to turn back and descend the stair,
With a bald spot in the middle of my hair —   40
(They will say: "How his hair is growing thin!")

---

29. works and days: *Works and Days* is the title of a didactic poem about farming by the
Greek poet Hesiod (eighth century B.C.E.) that includes instruction about doing each task
at the proper time.

My morning coat, my collar mounting firmly to the chin,
My necktie rich and modest, but asserted by a simple pin —
(They will say: "But how his arms and legs are thin!")
Do I dare   45
Disturb the universe?
In a minute there is time
For decisions and revisions which a minute will reverse.

    For I have known them all already, known them all: —
Have known the evenings, mornings, afternoons,   50
I have measured out my life with coffee spoons;
I know the voices dying with a dying fall°
Beneath the music from a farther room.
    So how should I presume?

    And I have known the eyes already, known them all —   55
The eyes that fix you in a formulated phrase,
And when I am formulated, sprawling on a pin,
When I am pinned and wriggling on the wall,
Then how should I begin
To spit out all the butt-ends of my days and ways?   60
    And how should I presume?

    And I have known the arms already, known them all —
Arms that are braceleted and white and bare
  (But in the lamplight, downed with light brown hair!)
Is it perfume from a dress   65
That makes me so digress?
Arms that lie along a table, or wrap about a shawl.
    And should I then presume?
    And how should I begin?

               ———————

Shall I say, I have gone at dusk through narrow streets   70
And watched the smoke that rises from the pipes
Of lonely men in shirt-sleeves, leaning out of windows? . . .

    I should have been a pair of ragged claws
Scuttling across the floors of silent seas.

               ———————

And the afternoon, the evening, sleeps so peacefully!   75
Smoothed by long fingers,
Asleep . . . tired . . . or it malingers,

———————

52. a dying fall: An allusion to Shakespeare's *Twelfth Night* (1.1.4): "That strain
[of music] again! It had a dying fall" (a cadence that falls away).

Stretched on the floor, here beside you and me.
Should I, after tea and cakes and ices,
Have the strength to force the moment to its crisis?   80
But though I have wept and fasted, wept and prayed,
Though I have seen my head (grown slightly bald) brought in upon a
    platter,°
I am no prophet—and here's no great matter;
I have seen the moment of my greatness flicker,
And I have seen the eternal Footman hold my coat, and snicker,   85
And in short, I was afraid.

    And would it have been worth it, after all,
After the cups, the marmalade, the tea,
Among the porcelain, among some talk of you and me,
Would it have been worth while,   90
To have bitten off the matter with a smile,
To have squeezed the universe into a ball
To roll it toward some overwhelming question,
To say: "I am Lazarus,° come from the dead,
Come back to tell you all, I shall tell you all"—   95
If one, settling a pillow by her head,
    Should say: "That is not what I meant at all.
    That is not it, at all."

    And would it have been worth it, after all,
Would it have been worth while,   100
After the sunsets and the dooryards and the sprinkled streets,
After the novels, after the teacups, after the skirts that trail along
    the floor—
And this, and so much more?—
It is impossible to say just what I mean!
But as if a magic lantern threw the nerves in patterns on a screen: 105
Would it have been worth while
If one, settling a pillow or throwing off a shawl,
And turning toward the window, should say:
    "That is not it at all,
    That is not what I meant, at all."   110

No! I am not Prince Hamlet, nor was meant to be;
Am an attendant lord, one that will do
To swell a progress,° start a scene or two,

---

82. head . . . platter: As a reward for dancing before King Herod, Salome, his step-
daughter, asked for the head of John the Baptist to be presented to her on a platter
(Matthew 14:1-12; Mark 6:17-28). **94. Lazarus:** Either the beggar Lazarus, who in
Luke 16:19-31 did not return from the dead, or Jesus' friend Lazarus, who did (John
11:1-44). **113. progress:** Ceremonial journey made by a royal court.

Advise the prince; no doubt, an easy tool,
Deferential, glad to be of use,   115
Politic, cautious, and meticulous;
Full of high sentence,° but a bit obtuse;   *sententiousness*
At times, indeed, almost ridiculous —
Almost, at times, the Fool.

   I grow old . . . I grow old . . .   120
I shall wear the bottoms of my trousers rolled.°   *turned up, with cuffs*

   Shall I part my hair behind? Do I dare to eat a peach?
I shall wear white flannel trousers, and walk upon the beach.
I have heard the mermaids singing, each to each.

   I do not think that they will sing to me.   125

   I have seen them riding seaward on the waves
Combing the white hair of the waves blown back
When the wind blows the water white and black.

   We have lingered in the chambers of the sea
By sea-girls wreathed with seaweed red and brown   130
Till human voices wake us, and we drown.

Robert Frost   1874–1963

After Apple-Picking   [1914]

My long two-pointed ladder's sticking through a tree
Toward heaven still,
And there's a barrel that I didn't fill
Beside it, and there may be two or three
Apples I didn't pick upon some bough.   5
But I am done with apple-picking now.
Essence of winter sleep is on the night,
The scent of apples: I am drowsing off.
I cannot rub the strangeness from my sight
I got from looking through a pane of glass   10
I skimmed this morning from the drinking trough
And held against the world of hoary grass.
It melted, and I let it fall and break.
But I was well
Upon my way to sleep before it fell,   15
And I could tell
What form my dreaming was about to take.

Magnified apples appear and disappear,
Stem end and blossom end,
And every fleck of russet showing clear.   20
My instep arch not only keeps the ache,
It keeps the pressure of a ladder-round.
I feel the ladder sway as the boughs bend.
And I keep hearing from the cellar bin
The rumbling sound   25
Of load on load of apples coming in.
For I have had too much
Of apple-picking: I am overtired
Of the great harvest I myself desired.
There were ten thousand thousand fruit to touch,   30
Cherish in hand, lift down, and not let fall.
For all
That struck the earth,
No matter if not bruised or spiked with stubble,
Went surely to the cider-apple heap   35
As of no worth.
One can see what will trouble
This sleep of mine, whatever sleep it is.
Were he not gone,
The woodchuck could say whether it's like his   40
Long sleep, as I describe its coming on,
Or just some human sleep.

Terrance Hayes   b. 1971

Talk   [2006]

like a nigger now, my white friend, M, said
after my M.L.K. and Ronald Reagan impersonations,
the two of us alone and shirtless in the locker room,

and if you're thinking my knuckles knocked
a few times against his jaw or my fingers knotted   5
at his throat, you're wrong because I pretended

I didn't hear him, and when he didn't ask it again,
we slipped into our middle school uniforms
since it was November, the beginning

of basketball season, and jogged out   10
onto the court to play together
in that vision all Americans wish for

their children, and the point is we slipped
into our uniform harmony, and spit out *Go Team!*,
our hands stacked on and beneath the hands   15

of our teammates and that was as close
as I have come to passing for one
of the members of The Dream, my white friend

thinking I was so far from that word
that he could say it to me, which I guess   20
he could since I didn't let him taste the salt

and iron in the blood, I didn't teach him
what it's like to squint through a black eye,
and if I had I wonder if he would have grown

up to be the kind of white man who believes   25
all blacks are thugs or if he would have learned
to bite his tongue or let his belly be filled

by shame, but more importantly, would I be
the kind of black man who believes silence
is worth more than talk or that it can be   30

a kind of grace, though I'm not sure
that's the kind of black man I've become,
and in any case, M, wherever you are,

I'd just like to say I heard it, but let it go
because I was afraid to lose our friendship   35
or afraid we'd lose the game—which we did anyway.

APPROACHING THE AUTHOR

Before he published his first book of poetry in his mid-thirties, **Bob Hicok** was an automotive die designer who owned his own company. For more about him, see page 1066.

Bob Hicok   b. 1960

In the loop   [2010]

I heard from people after the shootings.° People
I knew well or barely or not at all. Largely
the same message: how horrible it was, how little

---

the shootings: 32 people killed, 17 wounded, at Virginia Tech. University in 2007.

there was to say about how horrible it was.
People wrote, called, mostly e-mailed   5
to say, there's nothing to say. Eventually
I answered these messages: there's nothing
to say back except of course there's nothing
to say, thank you for your willingness to say it.
Because this was about nothing. A boy who felt   10
that he was nothing, who erased and entered
that erasure, and guns that are good for nothing,
and talk of guns that is good for nothing,
and spring that is good for flowers, and Jesus
for some, and scotch for others, and "and"   15
for me in this poem, "and" that is good
for sewing the minutes together, which otherwise
go about going away, bereft of us and us
of them, like a scarf left on a train
and nothing like a scarf left on a train,   20
like the train, empty of everything but a scarf,
and still it opens its doors at every stop,
because this is what a train does,
this is what a man does with his hand on a lever,
because otherwise why the lever, why the hand,   25
and then it was over, and then it had just begun.

Linda Hogan   b. 1947

Crow Law   [1993]

The temple where crow worships
walks forward in tall, black grass.
Betrayal is crow's way of saying grace
to the wolf
so it can eat   5
what is left
when blood is on the ground,
until what remains of moose
is crow
walking out   10
the sacred temple of ribs
in a dance of leaving
the red tracks of scarce and private gods.
It is the oldest war
where moose becomes wolf and crow,   15

where the road ceases
to become the old forest
where crow is calling,
where we are still afraid.

APPROACHING THE AUTHOR

Garrett Kaoru Hongo began writing poetry to create awareness of the
Japanese internments in the United States during World War II, a subject
he found overlooked in school curricula. He believes that he has a moral
responsibility to tell the repressed story of this earlier generation of
Japanese Americans.

For more about him, see page 1066.

Garrett Kaoru Hongo   b. 1951

Yellow Light   [1982]

One arm hooked around the frayed strap
of a tar-black patent-leather purse,
the other cradling something for dinner:
fresh bunches of spinach from a J-Town *yaoya*,°
sides of a split Spanish mackerel from Alviso's,   5
maybe a loaf of Langendorf;° she steps
off the hissing bus at Olympic and Fig,
begins the three-block climb up the hill,
passing gangs of schoolboys playing war,
Japs against Japs, Chicanas chalking sidewalks   10
with the holy double-yoked crosses of hopscotch,
and the Korean grocer's wife out for a stroll
around this neighborhood of Hawaiian apartments
just starting to steam with cooking
and the anger of young couples coming home   15
from work, yelling at kids, flicking on
TV sets for the Wednesday Night Fights.

If it were May, hydrangeas and jacaranda
flowers in the streetside trees would be
blooming through the smog of late spring.   20
Wisteria in Masuda's front yard would be

---

4. **J-Town *yaoya***: A vegetable shop or stand in Japan-Town.   6. **a loaf of Langendorf**:
Bread from a well-known California bakery.

shaking out the long tresses of its purple hair.
Maybe mosquitoes, moths, a few orange butterflies
settling on the lattice of monkey flowers
tangled in chain-link fences by the trash.   25

But this is October, and Los Angeles
seethes like a billboard under twilight.
From used-car lots and the movie houses uptown,
long silver sticks of light probe the sky.
From the Miracle Mile, whole freeways away,   30
a brilliant fluorescence breaks out
and makes war with the dim squares
of yellow kitchen light winking on
in all the side streets of the Barrio.

She climbs up the two flights of flagstone   35
stairs to 201-B, the spikes of her high heels
clicking like kitchen knives on a cutting board,
props the groceries against the door,
fishes through memo pads, a compact,
empty packs of chewing gum, and finds her keys.   40

The moon then, cruising from behind
a screen of eucalyptus across the street,
covers everything, everything in sight,
in a heavy light like yellow onions.

A. E. Housman   1859–1936

To an Athlete Dying Young   [1896]

The time you won your town the race
We chaired you through the market-place;
Man and boy stood cheering by,
And home we brought you shoulder-high.

To-day, the road all runners come,   5
Shoulder-high we bring you home,
And set you at your threshold down,
Townsman of a stiller town.

Smart lad, to slip betimes away
From fields where glory does not stay   10
And early though the laurel grows
It withers quicker than the rose.

Eyes the shady night has shut
Cannot see the record cut,°   *broken*
And silence sounds no worse than cheers   15
After earth has stopped the ears:

Now you will not swell the rout
Of lads that wore their honours out,
Runners whom renown outran
And the name died before the man.   20

So set, before its echoes fade,
The fleet foot on the sill of shade,
And hold to the low lintel up
The still-defended challenge-cup.

And round that early-laurelled head   25
Will flock to gaze the strengthless dead,
And find unwithered on its curls
The garland briefer than a girl's.

Langston Hughes   1902–1967

The Negro Speaks of Rivers   [1926]

I've known rivers:
I've known rivers ancient as the world and older than the flow of
    human blood in human veins.

My soul has grown deep like the rivers.

I bathed in the Euphrates when dawns were young.
I built my hut near the Congo and it lulled me to sleep.   5
I looked upon the Nile and raised the pyramids above it.
I heard the singing of the Mississippi when Abe Lincoln went down
    to New Orleans, and I've seen its muddy bosom turn all golden
    in the sunset.

I've known rivers:
Ancient, dusky rivers.

My soul has grown deep like the rivers.   10

Honorée Fanonne Jeffers   b. 1967

Cotton Field Sestina   [2007]

The bolls by the side of the road —
at first this picture of startling cream lies
to the senses — maybe snow? — but the blues
rises up, the heat rises up, the sweat — so much water
down my neck. At last I see the dusty   5
flecks are cotton, what I should know in my gut.

On the radio, the song plucked on a gut
string reminds me this is a hard road
I tried to leave behind haloed by dust,
along with the poetics of lies.   10
I think of ancestry: copper folk gone, salt water
Africans bent over the land, original blues.

Come back home, girl. Isn't my blues
about reconciliation, not escape? What my gut
hollers, thus speaks the guilty water   15
chattering down my face? This road
is my lonely path cut through trees, lying
like a frog-fed snake in the dust.

I remember: feet caked with red dust,
tongues coated with loud blues.   20
I remember: old men telling them lies
and their good deep laughter in the gut —
what waits for me down this road
if I could cross the big water

of my fear, of my guilt, drink the water   25
thirsty in the women's veins, shake the dust
from my clothes and whisper the road,
hear the country voices raised in drylongso° blues.
First, I have to crawl through my mother's gut
past the long braid of her lies.   30

My mother, my mama, she calls me a liar,
she denies me her waters,
turns me out of her sweet gut
if I don't shake loose my fist of grave dust,
if I don't stop writing down my blues,   35
if I don't trot behind her on her smooth road.

---

28. **drylongso:** everyday; ordinary.

Come back home, girl to what lies in Georgia dust:
no love in truth's water, no birdsong blues,
no home in my gut — cotton by the roadside.

John Keats   1795–1821

Ode on a Grecian Urn   [1820]

1

Thou still unravished bride of quietness,
   Thou foster child of silence and slow time,
Sylvan historian, who canst thus express
   A flowery tale more sweetly than our rhyme:
What leaf-fringed legend haunts about thy shape   5
   Of deities or mortals, or of both,
      In Tempe or the dales of Arcady?°
   What men or gods are these? What maidens loath?
What mad pursuit? What struggle to escape?
   What pipes and timbrels? What wild ecstasy?   10

2

Heard melodies are sweet, but those unheard
   Are sweeter; therefore, ye soft pipes, play on;
Not to the sensual ear,° but, more endeared,
   Pipe to the spirit ditties of no tone:
Fair youth, beneath the trees, thou canst not leave   15
   Thy song, nor ever can those trees be bare;
      Bold lover, never, never canst thou kiss,
Though winning near the goal — yet, do not grieve;
   She cannot fade, though thou hast not thy bliss,
Forever wilt thou love, and she be fair!   20

3

Ah, happy, happy boughs! that cannot shed
   Your leaves, nor ever bid the spring adieu;

---

7. **Tempe, Arcady:** Tempe, a valley in Greece, and Arcadia ("Arcady"), a region of ancient Greece, represent ideal pastoral landscapes. **13. Not . . . ear:** Not to the ear of the senses but to the imagination.

And, happy melodist, unwearièd,
    Forever piping songs forever new;
More happy love! more happy, happy love!   25
    Forever warm and still to be enjoyed,
        Forever panting, and forever young;
All breathing human passion far above,
    That leaves a heart high-sorrowful and cloyed,
        A burning forehead, and a parching tongue.   30

4

Who are these coming to the sacrifice?
    To what green altar, O mysterious priest,
Lead'st thou that heifer lowing at the skies,
    And all her silken flanks with garlands dressed?
What little town by river or sea shore,   35
    Or mountain-built with peaceful citadel,
        Is emptied of this folk, this pious morn?
And, little town, thy streets forevermore
    Will silent be; and not a soul to tell
        Why thou art desolate, can e'er return.   40

5

O Attic° shape! Fair attitude! with brede°
    Of marble men and maidens overwrought,
With forest branches and the trodden weed;
    Thou, silent form, dost tease us out of thought
As doth eternity: Cold Pastoral!   45
    When old age shall this generation waste,
        Thou shalt remain, in midst of other woe
Than ours, a friend to man, to whom thou say'st,
"Beauty is truth, truth beauty,"° —that is all
    Ye know on earth, and all ye need to know.   50

---

41. Attic: Greek, specifically Athenian; **brede:** Interwoven pattern. **49. "Beauty . . . beauty":** The quotation marks around this phrase were found in its earliest printing, an 1820 volume of poetry by Keats, but not in a printing later that year or in written transcripts. This discrepancy has led to considerable critical controversy concerning the last two lines. Critics disagree whether "Beauty is truth, truth beauty" is spoken by the urn (and thus perhaps expressing a limited perspective not to be taken at face value) or by the speaker in the poem, or whether the last two lines in their entirety are said by the urn (some recent editors enclose both lines in quotation marks to make this explicit) or by the speaker.

Jane Kenyon   1947–1995

Let Evening Come   [1996]

Let the light of late afternoon
shine through chinks in the barn, moving
up the bales as the sun moves down.

Let the cricket take up chafing
as a woman takes up her needles   5
and her yarn. Let evening come.

Let dew collect on the hoe abandoned
in long grass. Let the stars appear
and the moon disclose her silver horn.

Let the fox go back to its sandy den.   10
Let the wind die down. Let the shed
go black inside. Let evening come.

To the bottle in the ditch, to the scoop
in the oats, to air in the lung
let evening come.   15

Let it come, as it will, and don't
be afraid. God does not leave us
comfortless, so let evening come.

Philip Levine   1928–2015

What Work Is   [1991]

We stand in the rain in a long line
waiting at Ford Highland Park. For work.
You know what work is—if you're
old enough to read this you know what
work is, although you may not do it.   5
Forget you. This is about waiting,
shifting from one foot to another.
Feeling the light rain falling like mist
into your hair, blurring your vision
until you think you see your own brother   10
ahead of you, maybe ten places.
You rub your glasses with your fingers,
and of course it's someone else's brother,

narrower across the shoulders than
yours but with the same sad slouch, the grin   15
that does not hide the stubbornness,
the sad refusal to give in to
rain, to the hours wasted waiting,
to the knowledge that somewhere ahead
a man is waiting who will say, "No,   20
we're not hiring today," for any
reason he wants. You love your brother,
now suddenly you can hardly stand
the love flooding you for your brother,
who's not beside you or behind or   25
ahead because he's home trying to
sleep off a miserable night shift
at Cadillac so he can get up
before noon to study his German.
Works eight hours a night so he can sing   30
Wagner, the opera you hate most,
the worst music ever invented.
How long has it been since you told him
you loved him, held his wide shoulders,
opened your eyes wide and said those words,   35
and maybe kissed his cheek? You've never
done something so simple, so obvious,
not because you're too young or too dumb,
not because you're jealous or even mean
or incapable of crying in   40
the presence of another man, no,
just because you don't know what work is.

APPROACHING THE AUTHOR

Claude McKay was attracted to communism in his early life, but after
a visit to the Soviet Union, he decided that communism was too
disciplined and confining.

For more about him, see page 1071.

Claude McKay 1890–1948

If we must die   [1919]

If we must die, let it not be like hogs
Hunted and penned in an inglorious spot,
While round us bark the mad and hungry dogs,

Making their mock at our accursed lot.
If we must die, O let us nobly die,   5
So that our precious blood may not be shed
In vain; then even the monsters we defy
Shall be constrained to honor us though dead!
O kinsmen! we must meet the common foe!
Though far outnumbered let us show us brave,   10
And for their thousand blows deal one deathblow!
What though before us lies the open grave?
Like men we'll face the murderous, cowardly pack,
Pressed to the wall, dying, but fighting back!

Andrew Marvell   1621–1678

To His Coy° Mistress   [c. 1650; pub. 1681]

Had we but world enough, and time,
This coyness, lady, were no crime.
We would sit down, and think which way
To walk, and pass our long love's day.
Thou by the Indian Ganges' side   5
Shouldst rubies find; I by the tide
Of Humber would complain.° I would
Love you ten years before the Flood,
And you should, if you please, refuse
Till the conversion of the Jews.°   10
My vegetable° love should grow   *living and growing*
Vaster than empires, and more slow;
An hundred years should go to praise
Thine eyes, and on thy forehead gaze;
Two hundred to adore each breast,   15
But thirty thousand to the rest;
An age at least to every part,
And the last age should show your heart.
For, lady, you deserve this state,°   *dignity*
Nor would I love at lower rate.   20
But at my back I always hear

Coy: In the seventeenth century, *coy* could carry its older meaning, "shy," or its modern
sense of "coquettish." **5–7. Indian Ganges', Humber:** The Ganges River in India, with its
distant, romantic associations, contrasts with the Humber River, running through Hull
in northeast England, Marvell's hometown.   **10. conversion . . . Jews:** An occurrence
foretold, in some traditions, as one of the concluding events of human history.

Time's wingèd chariot hurrying near;
And yonder all before us lie
Deserts of vast eternity.
Thy beauty shall no more be found,   25
Nor, in thy marble vault, shall sound
My echoing song; then worms shall try
That long-preserved virginity,
And your quaint honor turn to dust,
And into ashes all my lust: 30
The grave's a fine and private place,
But none, I think, do there embrace.
    Now therefore, while the youthful hue
Sits on thy skin like morning dew,
And while thy willing soul transpires°   *breathes forth* 35
At every pore with instant fires,°   *urgent passion*
Now let us sport us while we may,
And now, like amorous birds of prey,
Rather at once our time devour
Than languish in his slow-chapped° power.   40
Let us roll all our strength and all
Our sweetness up into one ball,
And tear our pleasures with rough strife
Thorough° the iron gates of life;   *through*
Thus, though we cannot make our sun   45
Stand still,° yet we will make him run.

---

40. **slow-chapped:** Slow-jawed, devouring slowly. **45–46. make our sun Stand still:** An allusion to Joshua 10:12. In answer to Joshua's prayer, God made the sun stand still, to prolong the day and give the Israelites more time to defeat the Amorites.

Orlando Ricardo Menes   b. 1958

Courtyard of Clotheslines, Angel Hill   [2013]

Though dark clouds hint the kind of rain
that strafes a city, the long drought has made
fresh water scarce as milk or gasoline.
Sand like raw sugar blows from Gabon,°
burying creek and aqueduct alike,   5
even agaves° wither in tin-can gardens,

---

4. Gabon: Country in central west Africa. **6. agaves:** Plants having spiny-margined leaves and flowers in tall spreading panicles; some are cultivated for their fiber or sap or for ornament.

and the women of Angel Hill make do
with shortages more numerous than bristles
on a pig. No meat today? They grind
plantain peels or pickle mop rags. No soap?   10
They churn clothes in boiled seawater,
rig sisal lines° to iron balconies that crisscross
the stone courtyard like a cat's cradle,°
and because Havana Bay is so close,
wayward gusts wreck the frazzled rope—   15
a darned diaper or threadbare blouse
tossed like some injured bird astray
in cumuli° that scud° Caribbean shores.
While clothes can be replaced by barter
or theft, those kin lost at sea are grieved   20
in shrines of patched photos, wild flowers,
the clay and cowrie-eyed Eleggua,° "way opener,"
mollified by rum-soaked tobacco,
these desperate men and women, called *escoria*,
scum, by the government, who take   25
to the Florida Straits on rafts stitched
from boards, wire mesh, inner tubes,
whose hasty provisions fall overboard
in the high swells, who clamor to María°
or Yemayá° for sweet water, calm seas,   30
dry land, then plunge into the waves
when angels whisper from the brine.

---

12. **sisal lines:** Clotheslines made out of sisal, a hemp fiber. 13. **cat's cradle:** A series
of string figures created between two (or more) people as a game. 18. **cumuli:** Cumulus
clouds; **scud:** Move briskly. 22. **cowrie-eyed Eleggua:** In Santería, the Yoruba religion
of Cuba, Eleggua is the trickster spirit who rules over the crossroads. His representation
consists of a conical head usually made of cement with cowrie shells for the eyes and the
mouth. 29. **María:** The Virgin Mary. 30. **Yemayá:** The great mother, in the Yoruba
religion, who rules over the sea.

APPROACHING THE AUTHOR

Pat Mora's grandparents moved to the United States during the Mexican
Revolution. They settled in El Paso, Texas, where Mora's mother grew up
in a Spanish-speaking household while attending a school where English
was spoken. Her mother often played translator between these two
worlds. One generation later, Mora grew up in a bilingual home and
attended a school where English was spoken.
For more about Pat Mora, see page 1072.

Pat Mora   b. 1942

Elena   [2000]

My Spanish isn't enough.
I remember how I'd smile
listening to my little ones,
understanding every word they'd say,
their jokes, their songs, their plots.   5
    Vamos a pedirle dulces a mamá. Vamos.°
But that was in Mexico.
Now my children go to American high schools.
They speak English. At night they sit around
the kitchen table, laugh with one another.   10
I stand by the stove and feel dumb, alone.
I bought a book to learn English.
My husband frowned, drank more beer.
My oldest said, "Mamá, he doesn't want you
to be smarter than he is." I'm forty,   15
embarrassed at mispronouncing words,
embarrassed at the laughter of my children,
the grocer, the mailman. Sometimes I take
my English book and lock myself in the bathroom,
say the thick words softly,   20
for if I stop trying, I will be deaf
when my children need my help.

---

6. *Vamos . . . Vamos:* Let's go ask Mother for some candy.

> **APPROACHING THE AUTHOR**
>
> In addition to his poetry, **David Mura** creates performance and theater
> pieces and is founder of the Asian-American Renaissance, an arts organi-
> zation in Minneapolis.
>
> For more about him, see page 1073.

David Mura   b. 1952

Grandfather-in-Law   [1989]

It's nothing really, and really, it could have been worse, and of course,
    he's now several years dead,
and his widow, well, if oftentimes she's somewhat distracted, overly
    cautious when we visit—

after all, Boston isn't New York — she seems, for some reason, enormously
    proud that there's now a writer in the family,
and periodically, sends me clippings about the poet laureate, Thoreau,
    Anne Sexton's daughter, Lowell, New England literary lore —
in which I fit, if I fit at all, simply because I write in English — as if
    color of skin didn't matter anymore.   5
Still, years ago, during my first visit to Boston, when we were all asleep,
he, who used to require that my wife memorize lines of Longfellow or Poe
    and recite them on the phone,
so that, every time he called, she ran outdoors and had to be coaxed back,
    sometimes with threats, to talk to Pops
(though she remembers too his sly imitations of Lincoln, ice cream at
    Brighams, burgers and fries, all the usual grandfatherly treats),
he, who for some reason was prejudiced against Albanians — where on
    earth did he find them I wondered —   10
who, in the thirties, would vanish to New York, catch a show, buy a suit,
    while up north,
the gas and water bills pounded the front door (his spendthrift ways
    startled me with my grandfather's resemblance),
who for over forty years came down each morning, "How's the old goat?"
    with a tie only his wife could knot circling his neck,
he slipped into my wife's room — we were unmarried at the time — and
    whispered so softly she thought
he almost believed she was really asleep, and was saying this like a wish
    or spell, some bohunk° miscalculated Boston sense of duty: 15
"Don't make a mistake with your life, Susie. Don't make a mistake . . ."
Well. The thing that gets me now, despite the dangling rantings I've let
    go, is that, at least at that time,
he was right: There was, inside me, some pressing, raw unpeeled persistence,
    some libidinous desire for dominance
that, in the scribbled first drafts of my life, seemed to mark me as wastrel
    and rageful, bound to be unfaithful,
to destroy, in some powerful, nuclear need, fissioned both by childhood
    and racism, whatever came near —   20
And I can't help but feel, forgiving him now, that if she had listened, if
    she had been awake,
if this flourishing solace, this muscled-for-happiness, shared by us now,
    had never awakened,

---

15. bohunk: A disparaging term for a person from east-central Europe, especially a
manual laborer.

he would have become for me a symbol of my rage and self-destruction,
  another raw, never healing wound,
and not this silenced grandfatherly presence, a crank and scoundrel, red-
  necked Yankee who created the delicate seed of my wife, my child.

APPROACHING THE AUTHOR

Naomi Shihab Nye has traveled widely and lived in multiple countries, but she says that she finds much of her inspiration in the local, drawing her poetry from the day-to-day goings-on and street conversations of her neighbors in San Antonio, Texas.

For more about her, see page 1073.

Roberto Ricciuti/Getty.

Naomi Shihab Nye   b. 1952

Kindness   [1980]

Before you know what kindness really is
you must lose things,
feel the future dissolve in a moment
like salt in a weakened broth.
What you held in your hand,   5
what you counted and carefully saved,
all this must go so you know
how desolate the landscape can be
between the regions of kindness.
How you ride and ride   10
thinking the bus will never stop,
the passengers eating maize and chicken
will stare out the window forever.

Before you learn the tender gravity of kindness,
you must travel where the Indian in a white poncho   15
lies dead by the side of the road.
You must see how this could be you,
how he too was someone
who journeyed through the night with plans
and the simple breath that kept him alive.   20

Before you know kindness as the deepest thing inside,
you must know sorrow as the other deepest thing.
You must wake up with sorrow.
You must speak to it till your voice
catches the thread of all sorrows   25
and you see the size of the cloth.

Then it is only kindness that makes sense anymore,
only kindness that ties your shoes
and sends you out into the day to mail letters and purchase bread,
only kindness that raises its head   30
from the crowd of the world to say
It is I you have been looking for,
and then goes with you everywhere
like a shadow or a friend.

Columbia

Dudley Randall   1914–2000

Ballad of Birmingham   [1969]
On the bombing of a church in Birmingham, Alabama, 1963

"Mother dear, may I go downtown
Instead of out to play,
And march the streets of Birmingham
In a Freedom March today?"

"No, baby, no, you may not go,   5
For the dogs are fierce and wild,
And clubs and hoses, guns and jails
Aren't good for a little child."

"But, mother, I won't be alone.
Other children will go with me,   10
And march the streets of Birmingham
To make our country free."

"No, baby, no, you may not go,
For I fear those guns will fire.
But you may go to church instead   15
And sing in the children's choir."

She has combed and brushed her night-dark hair,
And bathed rose petal sweet,
And drawn white gloves on her small brown hands,
And white shoes on her feet.   20

The mother smiled to know her child
Was in the sacred place,
But that smile was the last smile
To come upon her face.

For when she heard the explosion,   25
Her eyes grew wet and wild.
She raced through the streets of Birmingham
Calling for her child.

She clawed through bits of glass and brick,
Then lifted out a shoe.   30
"Oh, here's the shoe my baby wore,
But, baby, where are you?"

Jack Ridl b. 1944

My Brother—A Star   [1988]

My mother was pregnant through the first
nine games of the season. We were 7–2.
I waited for a brother. My father
kept to the hard schedule. Waking
the morning of the tenth game, I thought   5
of skipping school and shooting hoops.
My cornflakes were ready, soggy. There
was a note: "The baby may come today.
Get your haircut." We were into January,
and the long December snow had turned   10
to slush. The wind was mean. My father
was gone. I looked in on my mother still
asleep and hoped she'd be OK.
I watched her, dreamed her dream: John
at forward, me at guard. He'd   15
learn fast. At noon, my father
picked me up at the playground. My team
was ahead by six.
We drove toward the gym.
"Mom's OK," he said and tapped his fist   20
against my leg. The Plymouth ship that rode
the hood pulled us down the street.
"The baby died," he said. I felt my feet press hard
against the floorboard. I put my elbow on the door handle,
my head on my hand, and watched the town: 25

Kenner's Five and Ten, Walker's Hardware,
Jarret's Bakery, Shaffer's Barber Shop, the bank.
Dick Green and Carl Stacey waved. "It was
a boy."

We drove back to school. "You gonna   30
coach tonight?" "Yes." "Mom's OK?"
"Yes. She's fine. Sad. But fine. She said
for you to grab a sandwich after school. I'll see you
at the game. Don't forget about your hair." I
got out, walked in late to class.   35
"We're doing geography," Mrs. Wilson said. "Page
ninety-seven. The prairie."

That night in bed
I watched this kid firing in jump shots
from everywhere on the court. He'd cut left,
I'd feed him a fine pass, he'd hit.   40
I'd dribble down the side, spot him in the corner, thread
the ball through a crowd to his soft hands, and he'd
loft a star up into the lights where it would pause
then gently drop, fall through the cheers and through the net.
The game never ended. I fell into sleep. My hair
was short. We were 8 and 2.   45

for my mother and my father

Alberto Ríos   b. 1952

Nani°   [1982]

Sitting at her table, she serves
the sopa de arroz° to me   *rice soup*
instinctively, and I watch her,
the absolute *mamá*, and eat words
I might have had to say more   5
out of embarrassment. To speak,
now-foreign words I used to speak,
too, dribble down her mouth as she serves
me albondigas.° No more   *meatballs*
than a third are easy to me.   10
By the stove she does something with words
and looks at me only with her
back. I am full. I tell her
I taste the mint, and watch her speak

Nani: Diminutive for "grandmother."

smiles at the stove. All my words   15
make her smile. Nani never serves
herself, she only watches me
with her skin, her hair. I ask for more.

I watch the *mamá* warming more
tortillas for me. I watch her   20
fingers in the flame for me.
Near her mouth, I see a wrinkle speak
of a man whose body serves
the ants like she serves me, then more words
from more wrinkles about children, words   25
about this and that, flowing more
easily from these other mouths. Each serves
as a tremendous string around her,
holding her together. They speak
nani was this and that to me   30
and I wonder just how much of me
will die with her, what were the words
I could have been, was. Her insides speak
through a hundred wrinkles, now, more
than she can bear, steel around her,   35
shouting, then, What is this thing she serves?

She asks me if I want more.
I own no words to stop her.
Even before I speak, she serves.

Luis J. Rodriguez   b. 1954

Running to America   [1989]

For Alfonso and María Estela; immigrants.

They are night shadows
violating borders;
fingers curled through chain-link fences,
hiding from infra-red eyes,
dodging 30-30 bullets.   5
They leave familiar smells,
warmth and sounds
as ancient
as the trampled stones.

Running to America.   10

There is a woman
in her finest
border-crossing wear:
A purple blouse from
an older sister, a pair of worn   15
shoes from church bazaar.
A tattered coat
from a former lover.

There is a child
dressed in black.   20
Fear sparkling from
dark Indian eyes;
clinging to
a beheaded Barbie doll.

And the men,   25
some hardened, quiet.
Others young and loud.
You see something like this
in prisons.

Soon they will cross   30
on their bellies; kissing
black earth.

Running to America.

Strange voices
whisper behind garbage cans,   35
beneath freeway passes,
next to broken bottles.
The spatter of words,
textured and multi-colored,
invoke demons.   40

They must run to America.

Their skin,
color of earth,
is a brand
for all the great ranchers,   45
for the killing floors
on Soto Street,
and as slaughter
for the garment row.

Still they come.   50
A hungry people
have no country.

Their tears
are the grease
of the bobbing machines   55
that rip into cloth
that make clothes
that keep you warm.

They have endured
the sun's stranglehold,   60
el cortito,°
foundry heats
and dark caves
of mines
hungry for men.   65

Still they come,
wandering bravely
through the thickness
of this strange land's
maddening ambivalence.   70

Their cries are singed
with fires of hope.
Their babies are born
with a lion
in their hearts.   75
Who can confine them?
Who can tell them
which lines never to cross?

For the green rivers,
for their looted gold,   80
escaping the blood of a land
that threatens to drown them,

they have come,
running to America.

---

61. el cortito: "The short one" — the short-handled hoe, which forces field laborers to
work in a stooped position; prolonged use can result in degeneration of the spine. It was
banned from California fields in 1975.

Mary Jo Salter   b. 1954

Half a Double Sonnet   [1994]

for Ben

Their ordeal over, now the only trouble
was conveying somehow to a boy of three
that for a week or two he'd be seeing double.
Surely he wouldn't recall the surgery
years later, but what about the psychic scars?   5
And so, when the patch came off, they bought the toy
he'd wanted most. He held it high. "Two cars!"
he cried; and drove himself from joy to joy.
Two baby sisters . . . One was enough of Clare,
but who could complain? — considering that another   10
woman had stepped forward to take care
of the girls, which left him all alone with Mother.
Victory! Even when he went to pee,
he was seconded in his virility.

Percy Bysshe Shelley   1792–1822

Ozymandias°   [1818]

I met a traveler from an antique land
Who said: Two vast and trunkless legs of stone
Stand in the desert. . . . Near them, on the sand,
Half sunk, a shattered visage lies, whose frown,
And wrinkled lip, and sneer of cold command,   5
Tell that its sculptor well those passions read
Which yet survive, stamped on these lifeless things,
The hand that mocked them, and the heart that fed:
And on the pedestal these words appear:
"My name is Ozymandias, king of kings: 10
Look on my works, ye Mighty, and despair!"
Nothing beside remains. Round the decay
Of that colossal wreck, boundless and bare
The lone and level sands stretch far away.

Ozymandias: The Greek name for Ramses II of Egypt (thirteenth century B.C.E.), who
erected the largest statue in Egypt as a memorial to himself.

Alfred, Lord Tennyson   1809–1892

Ulysses°   [1833]

It little profits that an idle king,
By this still hearth, among these barren crags,
Matched with an agèd wife, I mete and dole
Unequal laws unto a savage race,°
That hoard, and sleep, and feed, and know not me.   5

I cannot rest from travel; I will drink
Life to the lees. All times I have enjoyed
Greatly, have suffered greatly, both with those
That loved me, and alone; on shore, and when
Through scudding drifts° the rainy Hyades°   10
Vexed the dim sea. I am become a name;
For always roaming with a hungry heart
Much have I seen and known—cities of men
And manners, climates, councils, governments,
Myself not least, but honored of them all—   15
And drunk delight of battle with my peers,
Far on the ringing plains of windy Troy.
I am a part of all that I have met;
Yet all experience is an arch wherethrough
Gleams that untraveled world whose margin fades   20
Forever and forever when I move.
How dull it is to pause, to make an end,
To rust unburnished, not to shine in use!
As though to breathe were life! Life piled on life
Were all too little, and of one to me   25
Little remains; but every hour is saved
From that eternal silence, something more,

Ulysses (the Roman form of Odysseus): The hero of Homer's epic *The Odyssey*, which tells the story of Odysseus's adventures on his voyage back to his home, the little island of Ithaca, after he and the other Greek heroes had defeated Troy. It took Odysseus ten years to reach Ithaca, the small, rocky island of which he was king, where his wife (Penelope) and son (Telemachus) had been waiting for him. Upon his return he defeated the suitors who had been trying to marry the faithful Penelope, and he resumed the kingship and his old ways of life. Here Homer's story ends, but in Canto 26 of the *Inferno* Dante extended the story: Odysseus eventually became restless and dissatisfied with his settled life and decided to return to the sea and sail west, into the unknown sea, and seek whatever adventures he might find there. Tennyson's poem amplifies the speech delivered in Dante's poem as Ulysses challenges his men to accompany him on this new voyage. **3–4. mete . . . race:** Administer inadequate (unequal to what is needed) laws to a still somewhat lawless race. **10. scudding drifts:** Wind-driven spray; **Hyades:** Five stars in the constellation Taurus whose rising, it was assumed, would be followed by rain.

A bringer of new things; and vile it were
For some three suns° to store and hoard myself,   *years*
And this gray spirit yearning in desire   30
To follow knowledge like a sinking star,
Beyond the utmost bound of human thought.

    This is my son, mine own Telemachus,
To whom I leave the scepter and the isle—
Well-loved of me, discerning to fulfill   35
This labor, by slow prudence to make mild
A rugged people, and through soft degrees
Subdue them to the useful and the good.
Most blameless is he, centered in the sphere
Of common duties, decent not to fail   40
In offices of tenderness, and pay
Meet adoration to my household gods,
When I am gone. He works his work, I mine.

    There lies the port; the vessel puffs her sail;
There gloom the dark, broad seas. My mariners,   45
Souls that have toiled, and wrought, and thought with me—
That ever with a frolic welcome took
The thunder and the sunshine, and opposed
Free hearts, free foreheads—you and I are old;
Old age hath yet his honor and his toil.   50
Death closes all; but something ere the end,
Some work of noble note, may yet be done,
Not unbecoming men that strove with Gods.
The lights begin to twinkle from the rocks;
The long day wanes; the slow moon climbs; the deep   55
Moans round with many voices. Come, my friends,
'Tis not too late to seek a newer world.
Push off, and sitting well in order smite
The sounding furrows; for my purpose holds
To sail beyond the sunset, and the baths°   60
Of all the western stars, until I die.
It may be that the gulfs will wash us down;
It may be we shall touch the Happy Isles,°
And see the great Achilles,° whom we knew.
Though much is taken, much abides; and though   65
We are not now that strength which in old days

---

60. **baths:** The outer river or ocean surrounding the flat earth, in Greek cosmology, into which the stars descended upon setting. **63. Happy Isles:** The Islands of the Blessed, or Elysian Fields, in Greek myth, which lay in the western seas beyond the Strait of Gibraltar and were the abode of heroes after death. **64. Achilles:** The hero of the Greeks, and Odysseus's comrade, in Homer's *Iliad*.

Moved earth and heaven, that which we are, we are—
One equal temper of heroic hearts,
Made weak by time and fate, but strong in will
To strive, to seek, to find, and not to yield.   70

APPROACHING THE AUTHOR

In the third grade, **Natasha Trethewey** wrote a series of poems about
Martin Luther King Jr. that her librarian bound and placed in the school
library.
    For more about her, see page 1082.

Natasha Trethewey   b. 1966

Domestic Work, 1937   [2000]

All week she's cleaned
someone else's house,
stared down her own face
in the shine of copper-
bottomed pots, polished   5
wood, toilets she'd pull
the lid to—that look saying

Let's make a change, girl.

But Sunday mornings are hers—
church clothes starched   10
and hanging, a record spinning
on the console, the whole house
dancing. She raises the shades,
washes the rooms in light,
buckets of water, Octagon soap.   15

Cleanliness is next to godliness . . .

Windows and doors flung wide,
curtains two-stepping
forward and back, neck bones
bumping in the pot, a choir   20
of clothes clapping on the line.

Nearer my God to Thee . . .

She beats time on the rugs,
blows dust from the broom
like dandelion spores, each one   25
a wish for something better.

Quincy Troupe   b. 1939

A Poem for "Magic"°   [1991; rev. 1996]

for Earvin "Magic" Johnson, Donnell Reid & Richard Franklin

take it to the hoop, "magic" johnson,
take the ball dazzling down the open lane
herk & jerk & raise your six-feet, nine-inch frame
into air sweating screams of your neon name
"magic" johnson, nicknamed "windex" way back   5
in high school
                    cause you wiped glass backboards
so clean, where you first juked & shook
wiled your way to glory
                    a new-style fusion of shake-&-bake   10
energy, using everything possible, you created your own
space to fly through — any moment now
we expect your wings to spread feathers for that spooky takeoff
of yours — then, shake & glide & ride up in space
till you hammer home a clothes-lining deuce off glass   15
now, come back down with a reverse hoodoo gem
off the spin & stick in sweet, popping nets clean
from twenty feet, right side
put the ball on the floor again, "magic"
slide the dribble behind your back, ease it deftly   20
between your bony stork legs, head bobbing everwhichaway
up & down, you see everything on the court
off the high yoyo patter
                    stop & go dribble
you thread a needle-rope pass sweet home   25
to kareem cutting through the lane
                                        his skyhook pops the cords
now, lead the fastbreak, hit worthy on the fly
now, blindside a pinpoint behind-the-back pass for two more
off the fake, looking the other way, you raise off-balance   30
into electric space
sweating chants of your name
turn, 180 degrees off the move, your legs scissoring space
like a swimmer's yoyoing motion in deep water

"**Magic**": Earvin "Magic" Johnson Jr. (b. 1959), star basketball player at Lansing
(Michigan) Everett High School (1973–1977) and Michigan State University (1977–1979)
and for the Los Angeles Lakers (1979–1991 and 1996). He was honored in 1996 as one of
the Fifty Greatest Players in National Basketball Association History.

stretching out now toward free flight   35
you double-pump through human trees
                               hang in place
slip the ball into your left hand
then deal it like a las vegas card dealer off squared glass
into nets, living up to your singular nickname   40
so "bad" you cartwheel the crowd toward frenzy
wearing now your electric smile, neon as your name

in victory, we suddenly sense your glorious uplift
your urgent need to be champion
& so we cheer with you, rejoice with you   45
                            for this quicksilver, quicksilver,
quicksilver moment of fame
so put the ball on the floor again, "magic"
juke & dazzle, shake & bake down the lane
take the sucker to the hoop, "magic" johnson,   50
recreate reverse hoodoo gems off the spin
deal alley-oop dunkathon magician passes
now, double-pump, scissor, vamp through space
hang in place
                        & put it all up in the sucker's face, "magic" johnson,   55
& deal the roundball like the juju man that you am
like the sho-nuff shaman that you am, "magic,"
like the sho-nuff spaceman you am

Walt Whitman   1819–1892

From Song of Myself   [*1855*; 1891–1892]°

1

I celebrate myself, and sing myself,
And what I assume you shall assume,
For every atom belonging to me as good belongs to you.

I loafe and invite my soul,
I lean and loafe at my ease observing a spear of summer grass.   5

[*1855*; 1891–1892]: The poem was first published in 1855 as an untitled section of *Leaves of Grass*. It was a rough, rude, and vigorous example of antebellum American cultural politics and free-verse experimentation. The version excerpted here, from the sixth edition (1891–1892), is much longer, more carefully crafted, and more conventionally punctuated.

My tongue, every atom of my blood, form'd from this soil, this air,
Born here of parents born here from parents the same, and their parents
    the same,
I, now thirty-seven years old in perfect health begin,
Hoping to cease not till death.

Creeds and schools in abeyance,   10
Retiring back a while suffic'd at what they are, but never forgotten,
I harbor for good or bad, I permit to speak at every hazard,
Nature without check with original energy.

. . . .

21

I am the poet of the Body and I am the poet of the Soul,
The pleasures of heaven are with me and the pains of hell are with me,
The first I graft and increase upon myself, the latter I translate into a
    new tongue.

I am the poet of the woman the same as the man,   425
And I say it is as great to be a woman as to be a man,
And I say there is nothing greater than the mother of men.

I chant the chant of dilation or pride,
We have had ducking and deprecating about enough,
I show that size is only development.   430

Have you outstript the rest? are you the President?
It is a trifle, they will more than arrive there every one, and still pass on.

I am he that walks with the tender and growing night,
I call to the earth and sea half-held by the night.

Press close bare-bosom'd night—press close magnetic nourishing night!   435
Night of south winds—night of the large few stars!
Still nodding night—mad naked summer night.

Smile O voluptuous cool-breath'd earth!
Earth of the slumbering and liquid trees!
Earth of departed sunset—earth of the mountains misty-topt!   440
Earth of the vitreous pour of the full moon just tinged with blue!
Earth of shine and dark mottling the tide of the river!
Earth of the limpid gray of clouds brighter and clearer for my sake!
Far-swooping elbow'd earth—rich apple-blossom'd earth!
Smile, for your lover comes.   445

Prodigal, you have given me love—therefore I to you give love!
O unspeakable passionate love.

. . . .

24

Walt Whitman, a kosmos, of Manhattan the son,
Turbulent, fleshy, sensual, eating, drinking and breeding,
No sentimentalist, no stander above men and women or apart from them,
No more modest than immodest.   500

Unscrew the locks from the doors!
Unscrew the doors themselves from their jambs!

Whoever degrades another degrades me,
And whatever is done or said returns at last to me.

Through me the afflatus° surging and surging, through me the
      current and index.   505

I speak the pass-word primeval, I give the sign of democracy,
By God! I will accept nothing which all cannot have their
      counterpart of on the same terms.

Through me many long dumb voices,
Voices of the interminable generations of prisoners and slaves,
Voices of the diseas'd and despairing and of thieves and dwarfs,   510
Voices of cycles of preparation and accretion,
And of the threads that connect the stars, and of wombs and of the father-stuff,
And of the rights of them the others are down upon.

. . . .

52

The spotted hawk swoops by and accuses me, he complains of my
      gab and my loitering.

I too am not a bit tamed, I too am untranslatable,
I sound my barbaric yawp over the roofs of the world.

The last scud of day holds back for me,
It flings my likeness after the rest and true as any on the shadow'd
      wilds,   1335
It coaxes me to the vapor and the dusk.

I depart as air, I shake my white locks at the runaway sun,
I effuse my flesh in eddies, and drift it in lacy jags.

I bequeath myself to the dirt to grow from the grass I love,
If you want me again look for me under your boot-soles.   1340

_____

505. **afflatus:** Inspiration, from Latin meaning "to blow on."

You will hardly know who I am or what I mean,
But I shall be good health to you nevertheless,
And filter and fibre your blood.

Failing to fetch me at first keep encouraged,
Missing me one place search another,   1345
I stop somewhere waiting for you.

Kevin Young   b. 1970

Blues   [2003]

Gimme some fruit
Gimme some fruit
Fresh salted melon
maybe some mango too

You had me eating pork ribs   5
You had me eatin ham
You had me so I was feedin
straight out your hand

Gimme some fruit, baby
Gimme some fru-uit   10
Something red
& juicy I can sink
these teeths into

You had me eating peas Lord
You had me eatin spam   15
(You had me so turned round)
I never dreamt all you said
came straight out a can

Gimme some fruit
Gimme some fru-uit
Gimme something strong girl   20
to clear my system a you

You served me up
like chicken
You deviled me like ham
Alls the while I never knew   25
you had you another man

Gimme some fruit, girl
Gimme some tomato too
What else is a poor   30
carnivore like me
without you supposed to do

Approaching
DRAMA

Photo: John D. Kisch/Separate Cinema/Archive/Getty Images.

Playwright August Wilson in front of the Huntington Theatre in Boston, Massachusetts for a performance of his 1995 Pulitzer Prize–winning play, Seven Guitars. The play is part of Wilson's Pittsburgh Cycle, a decade-by-decade chronicle of African American life in twentieth-century Pittsburgh, Pennsylvania. (See pp. 729–30 for a short biography.)

Live performance is still the most organic of all the media. Because it's not done with machines or editing, it's got all the imperfections, all the mistakes, and all the magic of real talent.

John Leguizamo

(American Actor, Comedian, and Playwright)

Reading Drama
Participating in Serious Play

"The play's the thing," said Hamlet. Drama has captured minds, hearts, and imaginations since the times of the ancient Greeks. Then and now, people and actions "come to life." As we laugh, cry, fear, hope, and despair with the characters of a drama, our own hopes, dreams, and fears are touched and our own lives are enriched and enlarged. That happens when we attend a production, but it can also occur when we read a play. Duplicating the complex, interactive experience that live theater creates may be impossible when reading a play, but you can approximate it by bringing the characters and actions to life in the theater of your mind.

WHAT IS DRAMA?

Drama is one of the oldest forms of verbal art. From earliest times, people have enjoyed pretending, or "acting something out." This "let's pretend" became more highly developed as people planned and organized their playacting for the benefit and entertainment of an audience, composing words to say and instructions on how to move.

Drama has deep connections to religion: Greek tragedy grew out of the worship of Dionysus, Passover reenacts the flight of the Israelites from Egypt, and the Catholic Mass is a dramatic representation of the sacrificial death of Christ. Drama enables an audience to participate, vicariously, in some of the deeply meaningful archetypal or mythic events in cultural history. Before the printing press made wide dissemination of texts possible, drama was a basic form of verbal art, and performance was a viable way to

663

present one's work. Thus a study of literature is not complete without including plays.

Drama as Performance   The word *drama* derives from the Greek word meaning "to do, act, or perform." From the time of the Greeks, *drama* was used to describe literary works that could be acted out or performed.

Watching a Performance   Watching "live action" on the stage differs from watching a performance on film, on DVD, on television, or online — it demands a different use of imagination and intellect. At a play, the viewer constantly makes decisions about who or what to pay particular attention to, whether to focus in on one character's expressions or "pan out" to take in the entire stage. Trying to notice everything important and not to miss key words, glances, or gestures, in addition to responding emotionally to characters and situations, can be exhausting as well as exhilarating. For performances on screen, you watch what the camera shows you; the decisions you would make if you were watching a stage production are made by the camera's eye instead.

Risks in Performance   Live theater also has a kind of "suspense of production" that film lacks. An actor risks missing a line or tripping during an entrance. Mistakes lead to another "take" in filming or are cut out, but in live theater they're evident for all to see. Actors live with the anxiety of potential embarrassment and enjoy the challenge of either coming through flawlessly or recovering beautifully from a slip. But audience members feel some anxiety too. They don't want to see actors embarrassed or the effect of the performance damaged, so in the back of their minds is the hope everything will go well (and a twinge of fear that it won't). There is no such anxiety in watching a film — we know all the slips, at least those that were caught, have been edited away.

Audience Interaction   Also, the audience at a live theater, by responding emotionally and imaginatively to the action on stage, makes a contribution to performance. Actors in live theater are aware of and energized by an involved, appreciative audience. A mutual synergy develops between actors and audience that leads to a deeper experience for both.

Reading a Play   There is no question about it: All that a performance involves cannot be duplicated in reading a play. But awareness of what happens in a real theater enhances one's reading of a play. Reading a play well takes a lot of imaginative participation. Does it require more than fiction or poetry? Such comparisons aren't helpful, in the end. An active reader pours herself or himself into whatever reading is at hand. Drama, like all literature, demands a lot of a reader, but the rewards are well worth it.

WHY READ DRAMA?

When we read a play, we assume that there is value in treating a play as a literary work. In reading a play, we concentrate on the words, not on the performance. Those words embody the pure play, the play as written rather than as cut and rearranged and interpreted for a particular performance; the words last and remain the same. Reading allows us to pause and reflect, to go back and look at earlier lines, to do the kind of close analysis of structure, characters, and style we've been doing for stories and poems.

One of the most exciting types of theaters is the theater of your mind and imagination. Here you can stage, direct, and perform whatever play you are reading. Reading the texts of plays has long been regarded as an enjoyable and valuable thing to do. But we need to recognize from the start that this kind of reading differs from reading stories and poems. Imagining a play requires particular reading skills and approaches.

ACTIVE READING: Drama

A **play** is a "dramatic work": That is, it doesn't *tell* a story and doesn't have a narrator the way narrative does. A play *acts out* a story, bringing the people and events to life, imaginatively, on a stage. The text of a play looks different from the way a story or a poem looks on the page.

- *Consider the cast.* The first thing you see in most cases is the cast of characters, the **dramatis personae** (the "persons of the drama"), a list of the people who appear in the drama. The same list is included in the program when you attend a theater performance, with the names of the actors who play the roles.

    A good starting point for reading (or watching) a play is to go through the list carefully, trying to remember the names of the characters and their relationships with each other. When reading a play with a large cast of characters, such as a play by Shakespeare, some people jot down names and diagram their relationships on a slip of paper for easy reference.

- *Pay attention to stage directions.* After listing the cast of characters, the printed play may offer **stage directions**, a description of what the playwright visualizes for the scenery on the stage and perhaps the age and appearance of the characters and the way they are dressed, sometimes even a personality characteristic. These are intended, of course, as guidelines for the director, set designer, and costume designer in planning how to produce the work on the stage. When reading a play, it's fun to fill these roles yourself and imagine the actors, their stage movements, the set design, and the costumes.

You are likely to find more extensive stage directions in a modern play than in one by Sophocles or Shakespeare. A dramatist always writes to fit the facilities available at the time (the kind of theater, scenery, and stage machinery). The scenery Sophocles or Shakespeare could count on was less elaborate than what came later, so they often used imagery in the text to indicate the scene. For example, many Elizabethan plays were acted in open-air theaters during the afternoon, so to indicate darkness Shakespeare has a character say that it's dark and may have someone carry a lantern. The directions included in modern plays vary widely. Some playwrights go into extensive detail illustrating everything from the color of the walls to the type of table sitting in a corner of a room, to the lighting and atmosphere they think is appropriate. Others may offer the sparest generalizations: "a room, some furniture."

- *Use your imagination.* Your imagination functions differently for a play than for a story or poem. The texts of stories, because they are meant to be read, include descriptions to help along your imagination ("the man with stringy brown hair plodded up the dimly lighted staircase"). A play assumes you are seeing the character on the stage, so it doesn't provide the same description. In watching a play, the role of the imagination is to accept the pretense that the actor really is the character and that what you see on the stage really is a kitchen or a forest. One of the challenges in reading a play is picturing the scene and characters in your mind. Stage directions help you to visualize the characters and action in your imagination.

- *Read the lines.* After the stage directions come the lines of the play itself, the script the actors memorize as they prepare to perform the play on stage, together with further stage directions for particular actions (including entrances and exits). What you see on the page is the name of the character, followed by words indicating what the character says or does. In reading the text of a play, first look at the name of the speaker — notice who and what the character is; then go on to what the character says. As you keep reading, use your intellect and imagination to connect the speeches to each other. Watch for interactions between characters and for the ways the diction varies among characters. Just as when you read a story, you will come to experience the characters developing as they reply to what other characters say.

- *Imagine the action.* The characters will also expand and develop as you imagine the movements that would take place on stage: people arriving and leaving, meeting each other, moving at various paces and with particular styles of movement and gestures, reacting to each other, using props, and interacting with the set. Remember always that this is a drama: You are observing the characters on the stage of your imagination as they act out a scene of considerable importance in the life of at least one of them.

REREADING: Drama

To experience a play fully, you need to read it more than once. As with a story or poem, during the first reading, you'll concentrate primarily on what's going on. Only on the second or third time through do you begin to appreciate fully what the work offers. Many of the suggestions for rereading fiction and poetry (pp. 108–09 and 462–63) apply to rereading drama as well. We comment here on how they apply particularly to rereading a play.

- *The second time you read a play, slow down.* The first time through you usually read quickly because you want to find out what happens to the characters as they deal with a dramatic situation. You probably don't pay close attention to the way characters are expressing themselves or to the subtleties embedded in their speeches. Like poets and story writers, dramatists write carefully—each phrase is thoughtfully shaped and every word counts. On second reading, linger on speeches to enjoy the style, to catch the nuances that reveal subtleties in character, and to notice details that foreshadow later events that you now realize are significant.

- *Pay attention to little things.* The second time through, you can be more alert for easily overlooked details, things most readers do not notice the first time, and to the subtlety of techniques that the author uses. (The same thing is true of watching a play. Seeing it a second time—like watching a movie a second or third or tenth time—helps you to appreciate it more fully.) You notice new things during subsequent readings—especially little things, like a gesture or an item on a table in act 1 that turns out to be significant in act 3. What may appear at first reading to be merely a set or stage direction is recognized on rereading to be of wider significance and thus is experienced more meaningfully.

- *Be selective about parts to reread, if you have to.* Because of the length of a three- or five-act play, it may be difficult to find the time to reread the whole work. In some cases (if you need to write a long paper studying the play thoroughly, for example), you'll need to find the time for a complete rereading. In other cases, if you can't reread the entire play, at least reread scenes and passages that are crucial to revealing character traits or plot development.

- *Remember the reading strategies we gave you for fiction and poetry.* Pay attention to the title; look up things that aren't familiar; research people, times, and places that relate to the plot; notice the opening and closing lines; reflect on what the characters are like and what motivates them, on the organization of the plot, and on the significance of the actions and events.

- *Read some parts aloud.* Dramatic dialogue is meant to be heard. Reading sections of the play aloud, working to interpret the expression, rhythms, and tone effectively, will help you hear other parts more clearly and meaningfully in your mind's ear as you read silently. And it can be fun. Divide the parts among a few of your friends and see what happens.

Action is eloquence.

William Shakespeare

(English Poet and Playwright; see pp. 569, 881, and 1079)

Character, Conflict, and Dramatic Action

CHAPTER **23**

Thinking about Who Does What to Whom and Why

Almost everyone enjoys watching stories acted out. Even if you don't attend live theater all that often, you probably watch television or movies. Television producers certainly recognize this appeal and place enormous importance on garnering huge audiences. Advertisers know it and tap into those shows that have the highest ratings, all because we love to watch everything from soaps to sitcoms to serious drama. There's something compelling about watching a skilled actor entering a role and bringing a character to life, making us laugh at comic characters and empathize with tragic ones.

Reading scripts can never substitute for watching an excellent performance: The script was meant for performance, after all. But reading plays, as we say in Chapter 22, has its own rewards, and learning to do it well is worth some effort. Whether you're watching or reading a play, the essential core is the same: character, conflict, and dramatic action. Drama usually focuses on characters, the created persons who appear or are referred to in a play. Those characters come to life primarily through conflict. And the conflict is presented through dramatic action on a stage, whether in a theater or in the imagination. You have already worked with conflict and character earlier in this book (see pp. 115–16 and 178–81). This chapter deals

669

with how development of characters and conflicts is achieved through dialogue and dramatic action, the distinctive methods used by drama.

APPROACHING THE READING

Plays and their productions are not always two hours (or more) in length and constructed in three or five acts. **One-act plays**—sometimes only ten or fifteen minutes in length—are an important theatrical form and work with the same elements as longer plays (see p. 816). The guidelines for reading a play laid out in Chapter 22, especially the section "Active Reading: Drama" (pp. 665–67), apply just as well to one-act plays as to three- or five-act plays. Practice applying the guidelines to the following very short play, *The New New*.

This script does not start with a list of characters: They are instead identified in the stage directions. If you attended a performance of the play, the program would most likely list the names of the five characters (and of the actor playing each role), in order of appearance: Jenny, Marcy, Bradley, Craig, and Naomi. Because the text gives no details about their ages or appearance, you will need to make decisions about these as you imagine the play, just as a director would in planning a performance.

The text says nothing about where or when the action takes place. It presumably could take place in any large city and at any time (the program at a performance might well state, after the list of characters, "Time: the present"). The stage directions (in italics) supply guidance about staging the action: In *The New New*, the action alternates between two offices on opposite sides of the stage. Your imagination can furnish the offices in any way you like, though a performance could get by with simply a table, a couple of chairs, and a telephone on each side.

It is a dramatic convention that, when a stage is divided this way, the audience will assume that characters on the one side cannot hear characters talking on the other side. You will need to use your imagination to move back and forth between the two offices. In a performance, such movement might be signaled by lighting the side of the stage in which characters are talking, while darkening the other side. However, for a simple performance without special lighting equipment, the characters' voices will draw the audience's attention from side to side without it.

As you read the play itself, pay attention to who is speaking and thus, in this case, which side of the stage is active at the moment. Also be sure to notice the stage directions. As an active reader, you'll need to know what is happening in the present, especially any conflicts that emerge. You will also need to piece together what has happened in the past, what has led up to the present situation, and to figure out what the characters are like from what they say and do and what is said about them (including two important characters who do not appear on the stage). And you will want to reflect on the choices that the characters are making and the values that their words and actions reveal.

Kelly Stuart b. 1961

The New New [2002]

*Jenny and Marcy in one "office" area—they are stapling brochures or doing some
other type of repetitive office work. Bradley and Craig in another office—they are
actually separated by a long corridor, but should be represented as being in isolated
areas of the stage.*

JENNY: I'm going to have an affair with him.

MARCY: But Jenny, you're failing his class.

JENNY: He says I can take an incomplete if I want, and he'll help me make it up
over the summer.

BRADLEY: I need a new word for new.

CRAIG: Fresh.

BRADLEY: Too hip hop. This is more white.

CRAIG (*opening a thesaurus*): Thesaurus check.

*(Naomi, a nervous, down-at-the-heels woman appears and stands, hoping to engage
Marcy and Jenny's attention.)*

MARCY: Isn't he what, like, uh, married?

JENNY: Yeah, but we have this INTENSE
CONNECTION. It's like, ECONOMICS
is not my forte. I find the whole subject abysmal. But he's got this precision of mind and I want that. I think
that's what's missing in me, and I'm
so, like, attracted to that.

NAOMI: I'm here to see Bradley Zuckerman?

*(Jenny and Marcy look at her, deciding she's
a nonentity.)*

APPROACHING THE AUTHOR

Kelly Stuart frequently travels to Turkey to
study the plight of the Kurds, an ethnic
group whose oppression receives little media
coverage. Though once attacked by Turkish
embassy officials while filming a peaceful
protest of Kurds, she continues her work,
transforming her experiences into both a
play and a documentary in progress.

For more about her, see page 1080.

CRAIG (*reading*): Fresh, modern. Modernistic. Neoteric.

BRADLEY: Neoteric?

(They shrug in unison. Craig continues.)

CRAIG: Novel. Newfangled. Newsprung. Revived. Reinvigorating.

BRADLEY: " . . . Reinvigorated the genre of prison memoir."

CRAIG: That's stale.

BRADLEY: It's become stale to say something is NEW. What's the new new? We
need the new NEW.

MARCY: Did you ask me a question?

NAOMI: Bradley Zuckerman?

MARCY: Do you have an appointment?

NAOMI: When is he back?

MARCY: Do you have an appointment?

NAOMI: When is he back?

JENNY: Do you have an appointment?

NAOMI: I'll wait.

MARCY: We discourage that.

JENNY: He's not coming in. He's with marketing. So you would simply be wasting your time.

NAOMI: Where's marketing?

(*Marcy turns back to Jenny, leaving Naomi standing awkwardly. They whisper to each other, occasionally looking Naomi's way. Naomi watches. They giggle.*)

BRADLEY: A laser-sharp vision. The voice. The, something, vision and voice. His. New. The . . . What. There's no more words.

CRAIG: I liked Neoteric.

BRADLEY: Nobody will know what that means.

CRAIG: A powerful neoteric account, of the agony behind prison walls.

BRADLEY: I'm sorry, that sounds like gobbledygook. Um . . . deadpan, self-deprecating and, witty. But it's also new and it's important we say that.

CRAIG: It's a first novel.

BRADLEY: It's a memoir.

CRAIG: Actually, we can't call it a memoir. It's a kind of memoiristic novel.

BRADLEY: Why can't we call it a memoir?

CRAIG: Legal affairs said—

BRADLEY: OK it's a novel in the form of a memoir, based on real-life authentic experience.

(*Naomi continues to stand looking at the women. They ignore her. Their conversation has become audible again:*)

JENNY: There is like, so much electricity there. When he's looking at me, it's like I get zapped.

MARCY: Well I really want you to meet this guy.

JENNY: The writer?

MARCY: Yeah. Jimmy.

BRADLEY: The absurdity and the agony of life as a convict.

CRAIG: Agony isn't a word that sells.

BRADLEY: Agonizing, and yet entertaining.

CRAIG: That sounds so *People* magazine.

(*They scan a thesaurus.*)

JENNY: What does he write about?

MARCY: Um, prison. Jail. The Penal system.

JENNY: Oh.

MARCY: He had like, an MBA from Yale but I think he was like, convicted of manslaughter.

JENNY: Oh. A murderer.

MARCY: Manslaughter. I think. It was accidental. Self Defense. Some kind of fight, with this guy named Monster. This six foot two, three hundred pound monster. An accidental death that he was convicted of — I guess, I guess, he pled guilty.

JENNY: Oh.

MARCY: To spare something, more like, the death penalty. I mean, I guess he cut a deal.

(Jenny notices Naomi staring at her.)

JENNY: Can we help you with something else?

NAOMI: Who are you talking about?

MARCY: I'm going to have to ask you to leave, OK?

NAOMI: I need to see Bradley Zuckerman.

MARCY: Leave a number and go or I'll have to call security.

NAOMI: I'd like to know who you're talking about.

JENNY: Did you not hear us? Do we HAVE to call security?

(Naomi abruptly leaves. The two women shake their heads in disgust.)

MARCY: These people will do anything to make you take a manuscript. Anyway he's — he's just really charismatic and charming and smart. I mean, it is so odd, when you meet him, you'll see, what an odd juxtaposition to think of this guy in prison. I mean, I'm really FOND of him. And his writing is really super evocative of the, you know, of the Kafkaesque° nature of life in prison. He's sexy too.

JENNY: So why don't you sleep with him?

MARCY: I'm trying to be monogamous now. And Bradley is like, editing his book. I can't do that. Sleep with the guy Bradley edits.

(Naomi makes a cross past the stage. Disappears.)

BRADLEY: I used to get these calls from prison, collect calls every Tuesday. I thought of these calls as my "Tuesdays with Jimmy."° He was just this witty, sardonic ethnographer of prison life. Of the ingenuity. And the angle, the engagement I found with the theme of this — civilized business executive locked up with all these illiterate thugs, and how he survived.

CRAIG: I love that he used like, sales techniques.

BRADLEY: Yes.

CRAIG: Stuff he learned from corporate sales seminars: Body language mirroring.

BRADLEY: I guess it all works.

(For a beat, they mirror each other's body language. Naomi enters and stares at them. They ignore her.)

Kafkaesque: A feeling of senseless, sometimes menacing disorientation, as conveyed in the works of Austrian author Franz Kafka (1883–1924). **"Tuesdays with Jimmy":** Alluding to Mitch Albom's best-selling book *Tuesdays with Morrie* (1997).

CRAIG: In a way it doesn't matter how we market this thing because film rights
have already gone to Ben Stiller.°

BRADLEY: Really?

CRAIG: Mike Medavoy° loved it. The release will coincide with the movie.

BRADLEY: But that's . . . I mean, there's a literary value.

CRAIG: It's great. Ben Stiller.

BRADLEY: Ben Stiller. That's great.

NAOMI: Excuse me—

CRAIG: It's a comedy. That's how they see it. It's going to sell like a motherfucker.

NAOMI: Is this marketing?

CRAIG: Yes.

NAOMI: I'm looking for Bradley Zuckerman.

CRAIG: Bradley—

BRADLEY: He doesn't work here. You have the wrong department.

NAOMI: I was told he's in marketing.

MARCY: I just think you'd have more in common with him than with your
economics professor.

JENNY: Why? Because he's a criminal?

MARCY: But he's not really.

BRADLEY: No, uh, he works in creative development.

NAOMI: But they said in his office that he was in here.

BRADLEY: No. He's not here. Have you seen him Craig?

CRAIG: Haven't seen him.

BRADLEY: Would you like to leave a message for him?

CRAIG: I'm sorry. You really can't wait here. Would you like to leave him a message? (*He hands her a notepad. She stands looking at it. She begins to write,
furiously.*)

MARCY: Being convicted of manslaughter had nothing to do with the arc of his
life. It was just, this aberration.

JENNY: Who did he kill again?

MARCY: This drug dealer guy. You're going to like him. I told him about you, he's
interested in meeting you.

JENNY: So he's like,—out?

MARCY: On Parole.

(*Naomi has finished writing.*)

NAOMI: Will you make sure Bradley Zuckerman gets this?

BRADLEY: Certainly.

(*Naomi gives them the pad of paper and exits. The men giggle.*)

BRADLEY: Oh my God that was close.

CRAIG: "No I'm not Bradley."

Ben Stiller: Benjamin Edward Stiller (b. 1965), American actor, film director, and producer.
Mike Medavoy: Morris Mike Medavoy (b. 1941), American film producer and film studio executive.

BRADLEY: "BRADLEY? NO. I HAVEN'T SEEN HIM." Anyway, Jesus. What does she want? (*Craig is reading the pad of paper. He hands it to Bradley.*) My brother's name was Jeremy. Not Monster. He was five foot three, one hundred thirty pounds. Not six foot two, three hundred fifty. My brother was tortured and strangled over the course of a two-hour, period. The shape of a turtle and a steer were imprinted on my brother's neck, from the cowboy belt your so-called "author" used. My brother's face was badly beaten, bones protruded from his bloody face. My brother was a medical assistant. He was a human being, not a monster. To see this man profit, it's killing me and I wonder if you ever gave that a thought?

CRAIG: I still think, um. The SPIRIT of the—I mean, he was true to the SPIRIT of, the book's not about the crime in any case and uh, legally, there's no . . .

BRADLEY: You knew this?

CRAIG: It's not really an issue.

BRADLEY: I mean, the thing of it is, I—I really like Jimmy.

CRAIG: Yeah, and who is she? Who is she really? Like what do you know?

BRADLEY: And the thing of it is, it's about Jimmy's writing. I think his writing redeems him.

CRAIG: Yeah. That's why we never, like bothered to check.

MARCY: You know it's already been optioned as a movie? For Ben Stiller.

JENNY: I love Ben Stiller.

MARCY: Then I think, really, you're going to love Jimmy.

BRADLEY: I'm fixing him up with my girlfriend's sister. I wouldn't do that if I didn't like him, if I thought he wasn't, a good person. Yeah. It's fine. It's.

CRAIG: I mean,—this . . . —like, she's the victim's sister. That's all. What do you expect?

JENNY: So, what are we going to do, like, go out to dinner together? Are we—

MARCY: Yeah.

JENNY: I'm up for that.

(*Bradley looks seriously confused. Lights fade.*)

END OF PLAY

REFLECTING ON WHAT YOU'VE READ

1. Describe the characters—Jenny, Marcy, Bradley, Craig, and Naomi. What are you given that helps you get to know them? Which characters (if any) are you drawn to? Which ones are you put off by? Why?

2. There are two characters important to the play that we don't see, Jeremy and Jimmy. Describe what they are like. What are the advantages of not having Jimmy appear on stage? What is revealing about Naomi being the only one who knows Jeremy's name?

3. Identify different kinds of conflicts that appear within the play and ones that exist behind what occurs on stage. Do any of these conflicts raise issues that are meaningful or important to you? If so, explain.

4. Even though there isn't much action in this play, particular movements are important. Pick out those that we should notice and explain their significance.

READING FOR CHARACTER

Just as with fiction, some of the first questions to ask about a play likely involve the characters. Who are they? What are they like? Why do they act, speak, and feel the way they do? In drama, characters are developed in some of the same ways described earlier for fiction: showing, saying, telling, entering a character's mind, and naming (pp. 178–79). Saying and telling in particular are central in drama because of the significance of dialogue.

Showing   What a character is like comes out in part from the character's actions. We get to know about a character from what she or he does, often in a more reliable way than from what the character says or what is said about her or him: Actions in this case do speak louder than words. For Marcy and Jenny to turn their backs on Naomi and giggle at her, for example, especially when combined with the way they talk to her, reveals a good deal about them.

Saying   Conversation between two or more characters, or **dialogue**, is the fundamental method of writing used in drama. Much of what occurs in a play starts from and relies on characters talking to each other. From what the characters say to each other, the audience or reader pieces the story together, including details about relevant events in the past and foreshadowings of what may occur in the future. And dialogue provides the primary means for becoming familiar with the characters: What they say and to whom, and especially how they say it, reveal things about them and about others and help us understand the conflicts and motivations that give rise to the action.

Thus, in *The New New*, what Jenny and Marcy talk about (using sex to pass an economics course, meeting a charming ex-con) and what Bradley and Craig talk about (finding ways to market a "memoiristic novel" about surviving in prison without verifying facts about the writer) evince the shallowness of their characters. For all of them, life centers in words, not realities, in words that, instead of clarifying and revealing, avoid, cover up, and distort.

Telling   We also learn about characters through dialogue as one character tells what another is like. When one character (whether in drama or fiction) tells us about another, the description may be accurate and reliable, or it may be inaccurate and misleading. In *The New New* we know what Naomi's brother is like from the note she writes, and we accept what she says as true because the other characters can't dispute it. And we learn about Jimmy first from what Marcy and Bradley say about him ("he's just really charismatic and charming and smart" and "He was just this witty, sardonic ethnographer of prison life") and then from what Naomi writes about him: "My brother was tortured and strangled over the course of a two-hour, period." What Marcy and Bradley say reveals more about them than about the person they are discussing. Not only do they not actually know what Jimmy is like but they also don't seem to care. "And the thing of it is," Bradley says, "it's about Jimmy's writing. I think his writing redeems him." In other words, how one successfully manipulates words is more important than what one does.

Entering   Entering a character's thoughts is less frequent in drama than in fiction, but it does occur in some instances (not, however, in *The New New*). In a **soliloquy**, a speaker alone onstage, or off to the side of the stage away from other characters, reveals to the audience what is going through her or his mind. Shakespeare uses soliloquies frequently, especially in his tragedies. Hamlet's "To be or not to be" speech (p. 928) is a famous example.

> Review the discussion "Categories of Characterization," on pages 179–80. Most of the terminology introduced for fiction there—**protagonist**, **antagonist**; **major character**, **minor character**; **round character**, **flat character**—can be applied to drama as well.

READING FOR DIALOGUE

Dialogue is Central   Although all of the above methods are important, dialogue remains most significant. When we watch a play, we need to listen closely to the words of the dialogue; reading a play requires the same attentiveness and a great deal of imaginative involvement as well.

Aspects of style that we discussed earlier in the book apply here as well, and appropriateness remains the key factor: Word choice and sentence structure need to fit the character using the words and expressing the sentences. A good playwright is able to create stylistic differences in the dialogue of various characters as an aspect of characterization. And determining the tone is important in individual speeches as well as in a play as a whole.

One of the pleasures in reading a play is imagining how the dialogue would sound on stage—what pace, sound, inflections, and tones of voice fit each character. Should the actor shout or whisper "Shut up!"? How does she or he express anger or grief or bewilderment, or all three at once? What words should be emphasized? In reading a play, we get to be the actors, experimenting with each line to decide how to express it most effectively and get across its meaning most completely, including what it reveals about the speaker.

READING FOR CONFLICT

In drama, characters are most often found in a situation involving **conflict**, a struggle or confrontation between opposing characters or a character and opposing forces. Conflict is important to drama first because it usually creates action on the stage — whether external and physical or internal and psychological — and thus creates the kind of excitement, suspense, and tension we associate with the word *drama*. Even outside the theater, we hear the word *drama* used that way, for example, in describing a news story about a dramatic standoff. Second, conflict is important because the nature of the conflict, the issues involved, and the way it is handled generally bring out aspects of character: The essence and the depths of a person come out as she or he confronts a challenging situation.

The kinds of conflict in drama range as widely as those in fiction, but the same three broad categories discussed in Chapter 5 (pp. 110–43) — physical conflict, social conflict, and internal or psychological conflict — are useful here as well.

No physical conflict occurs in *The New New*, though the plot grows out of the brutal killing of Naomi's brother that occurred several years before. Social conflict appears in the contempt with which Marcy and Jenny treat the "nonentity" Naomi, a "nervous, down-at-the-heels" woman from a lower social stratum than theirs, who clearly lacks their education and sophistication (this is shown partly in the style in which her note to Bradley is written, especially the odd comma after "two-hour," which is apparent to a reader though perhaps not to someone watching the play). Internal conflict emerges when Bradley is confronted with the fact that he never did give a thought to the victim of Jimmy's crime, never investigated the truth of what Jimmy told him. Taken in by Jimmy's charm and charisma and by the opportunity to publish a best-selling book, he is converting a callous murderer into a wealthy celebrity.

Chapter 5 points out that watching for conflicts is a good way to get to the crucial issues in a work of fiction. That is even more true for a play. Identifying areas of conflict as you watch or read a play, or as you watch a movie or television show, usually takes you directly to the heart of its action and significance.

READING FOR DRAMATIC ACTION

Some dramatic productions do not use action on a stage. In reader's theater, for example, actors typically perch on stools and read their parts to each other and the audience. In most theater productions, however, actors move about onstage "acting out" what is going on.

Movement on Stage   Dramatic action is almost always a fundamental aspect of drama, and conflict often becomes part of the play's dramatic action: Characters differ, argue, quarrel, challenge each other, and find solutions to their problems or difficulties. Therefore, another challenge for you as the reader of a play is using your imagination to visualize the action while reading the text. For the play to be complete, the dramatic action needs to be seen, on stage or in the mind's theater.

Actions on Stage   In some cases, the script of the play supplies guidelines for what actions should accompany the words, either in stage directions or in the lines themselves. Thus, stage directions in *The New New* state that Craig "hands [Naomi] a notepad" She writes on it furiously, gives it back to Craig, and leaves. Craig hands it to Bradley, and the first person pronouns ("My brother") indicate that Bradley reads it aloud, so the audience can know what Naomi wrote. For the most part, however, actors and directors are left to decide how characters should move on stage (called "blocking" in theater parlance) and what gestures they should use. As a reader, you are both director and actor, so you get to use your imagination to picture on the stage of your mind the actions, gestures, and expressions of all the characters.

Timing   A key part of any action is timing: When the text is acted out on stage, the pace depends on variations in the intensity of different moments. Words almost always take more time to say aloud than to read silently. Some lines need to be spoken more slowly or quickly than others. Action on the stage occurs during lines, between lines, or while no one is speaking. Actions can be large—a sword fight—or smaller, perhaps a character walking across the stage, looking out a window, or searching in a desk drawer. Both large and small actions can be significant. Sometimes characters come on stage, do something, and leave without saying any words at all. Sometimes pauses occur between sentences or between words in a speech, as one character looks angrily at another or ponders what another character has just said. In a play, as in life, pauses or silences often say as much as or even more than words do. For such reasons, a scene that takes five minutes to read might take ten minutes to act out. Here too it is important for you the reader to imagine the pace at which things are taking place, especially where the script does not include specific indications.

CHECKLIST on Reading for Character, Conflict, and Dramatic Action

❏ Be aware of what the characters are like, what is important to them, what values they hold, what motivates them.

❏ Be attentive to the methods of characterization important in drama, especially the use of *dialogue* and *dramatic action*: what a character *says*, what the character *does*, and what other characters *say about* her or him.

❏ Consider how fully characters are *developed* — whether they are round or flat, whether they change in the course of the play or stay pretty much the same.

❏ Look for conflicts — physical, social, internal — and use them as a way to "get into" the drama and to explore its complexity.

FURTHER READING

APPROACHING THE READING

This intriguing play is one that likely will connect to your own experience. Almost every kid has wanted to be or pretended to be a superhero, the way the compelling main character in *I Am Not Batman* does. He needs desperately to be Batman, and yet he realizes why he is not and why he never will be. His home life and the neighborhood he lives in are revealed mostly through experiences that would never happen to Batman and through the kid's deep concern for JanitorMan. Because there is only one character who tells the story in a monologue, physical conflict doesn't occur on stage, but it is going on off stage; and intense inner conflict goes on within the boy. Giving the play at least two readings will enable you to appreciate the character development and internal dramatic action. Your second reading will differ from your first because you will see how early parts of the play carefully set up the ending as a moving dramatic revelation.

APPROACHING THE AUTHOR

When **Marco Ramirez** was in high school, he wrote a one-act play about his grandfathers playing dominoes and discussing their experiences as Cuban refugees. He said of the composition process, "To get my first draft written, it took three or four days of working from six in the afternoon to about three in the morning, with Mom coming by and hitting me in the head and saying, 'Go to bed already'. . . . I thought, 'When she reads it she'll understand.'" The play was such a hit at his high school that the Coconut Grove Playhouse in Miami invited the troupe to perform it at a professional theater

For more about
Charley Gallay/Getty.   him, see page 1077.

Marco Ramirez　b. 1983

I Am Not Batman　　[2007]

Sudden drumming, then quiet. Lights up on a BOY, *maybe 7, maybe 27, wearing a hooded sweatshirt. He looks out directly before him, breathing nervously. A* DRUMMER *sits behind a drum set placed in the middle of the stage, in some kind of silhouette. The* BOY *is excited, but never gets ahead of himself.*

BOY: It's the middle of the night and the sky is glowing like mad radioactive red. And if you squint you could maybe see the moon through a thick layer of cigarette smoke and airplane exhaust that covers the whole city, like a mosquito net that won't let the angels in.

(*LIGHT SNARE DRUMMING.*)

And if you look up high enough you could see me. Standing on the edge of a eighty-seven story building, —

(*Thick steam shoots out of some pipes behind him —*)

— And up there, a place for gargoyles and broken clock towers that have stayed still and dead for maybe like a hundred years — up there is *me*.

(*DRUMS.*)

And I'm freakin' *Batman*.

(*CYMBAL.*)

And I gots Bat-mobiles and Bat-a-rangs and freakin' Bat-caves like for real, and all it takes is a broom closet or a back room or a fire escape, and Danny's hand-me-down jeans are gone.

(*BOOM.*)

And my navy blue polo shirt? —

(*—BOOM—*)

— The-one-that-looks-kinda-good-on-me-but-has-that-hole-on-it-near-the-butt-from-when-it-got-snagged-on-the-chain-link-fence-behind-Arturo's-but-it-isn't-even-a-big-deal-'cause-I-tuck-that-part-in-and-it's-like-all-good? —

(*—BOOM—*)

— *that* blue polo shirt? —

(*—BOOM—*)

— It's gone too. And I get like, like transformation-al.

(BOOM. SNARE.)

And nobody pulls out a belt and whips Batman for talking back—

(—SNARE—)

—Or for *not* talking back,—

(—SNARE, CRASH—)

And nobody calls Batman simple—

(—SNARE—)

—Or stupid—

(—SNARE—)

—Or skinny—

(—CYMBAL—)

—And *nobody* fires Batman's brother from the Eastern Taxi Company 'cause they was making cutbacks, neither, 'cause they got nothing but respect, and not like *afraid*-respect. Just like *respect*-respect. 'Cause nobody's afraid of you.

'Cause Batman doesn't mean nobody no harm.

(BOOM.)

Ever.

(SNARE, SNARE.)

'Cause all Batman really wants to do is save people and maybe pay Abuela's bills one day and die happy and maybe get like mad famous. For real.

. . . And kill the Joker.

(DRUMS.)

Tonight, like most nights, I'm all alone. And I'm watching . . . And I'm waiting . . .

Like a eagle. Or like a—no, yea, like a eagle.

(The DRUMS start low but constant, almost tribal.)

And my cape is flappin' in the wind ('cause it's freakin' long), and my pointy ears are on, and that mask that covers like half my face is on too, and I got like bulletproof stuff all in my chest so no one could hurt me and nobody—*nobody*—is gonna come between Batman,

(CYMBAL.)

and Justice.

(*The SLOW KICKS continue, now there are SHORT hits randomly placed on the drum set. They somehow resemble city noise.*)

From where I am I could hear everything.

(*The DRUMS build, then STOP.*)

Somewhere in the city there's a old lady picking Styrofoam leftovers up outta a trash can and she's putting a piece of sesame chicken someone spit out into her own mouth.

(*SNARE.*)

And somewhere there's a doctor with a whack haircut in a black lab coat trying to find a cure for the diseases that are gonna make us all extinct for real one day.

(*SNARE. SNARE.*)

And somewhere there's a man, a man in a janitor's uniform, stumbling home drunk and dizzy after spending half his paycheck on forty-ounce bottles of twist-off beer and the other half on a four-hour visit to some lady's house on a street where the lights have all been shot out by people who'd rather do what they do, in *this* city, in the dark.

And half a block away from JanitorMan there's a group of good-for-nothings who don't know no better waiting to beat JanitorMan with rusted bicycle chains and imitation Louisville Sluggers, and if they don't find a cent on him—which they won't—they'll just pound at him till the muscles in their arms start burning, till there's no more teeth to crack out.

But they don't count on me.

(*The BOY becomes proud, stands up straight.*)

They don't count on no dark knight (with a stomach full of grocery store brand macaroni-and-cheese and cut up Vienna sausages),

'Cause they'd rather believe I don't exist,

(*CYMBAL. The DRUMS start to build slowly again. The steam comes out thicker and thicker.*)

And from eighty-seven stories up I could hear one of the good-for-nothings say "Gimmethecash" real fast (like that) just "Gimmethefuckingcash" and I see JanitorMan mumble something in drunk language and turn pale and from eighty-seven stories up I could hear his stomach trying to hurl its way out of his Dickies.

So I swoop down like mad fast and I'm like darkness. I'm like SWOOSH—

(*—A LIGHT DRUMROLL—*)

—And I throw a Bat-a-rang at the one naked lightbulb—

(—Light CYMBAL—)

And they're all like "whoa-motherfucker-who-just-turned-out-the-lights?" —

(Silence. The BOY breathes, re-enacting their fear, the largest and lowest CYMBAL builds slowly throughout this.)

"What's that over there?" —
— "What?" —
— "Gimme whatchou got old man" —
— "Did anybody hear that?!" —
— "Hear what? There ain't nothing" —
— "No, really" —
— "There ain't. No. Bat."

(The CYMBAL reaches its height.)

But then —

(—A KICK on the drums as the BOY suddenly springs into action—)

—One out of three good-for-nothings gets it to the head!

And number Two swings blindly into the dark cape before him but before his fist hits anything I grab a trash can lid and —

(—A CRASH on a CYMBAL—)

—right in the gut, and number One comes back with a jump-kick but I know judo-karate too so I'm like—

(—CRASH, happy from the response, he adds this part.)

—Twice—

(—CRASH—)

—but before I can do any more damage suddenly we all hear a CLIC—CLIC—

(—The DRUMMER's TOMS finish, BOOM. The steam stops.)

And suddenly everything gets quiet.

(The steam clears.)

And the one good-for-nothing left standing grips a handgun and aims straight up, like he's holding Jesus hostage, like he's threatening maybe to blow a hole in the moon.

And the good-for-nothing who got it to the head who tried to jump-kick me and the other good-for-nothing who got it in the gut is both scrambling back away from the dark figure before him.

And the drunk man the JanitorMan is huddled in a corner, praying to Saint Anthony 'cause that's the only one he could remember.

(*HIT. HIT.*)

And there's me,

(*CYMBAL. HIT HIT.*)

Eyes glowing white, cape blowing softly in the wind.

(*HIT. HIT.*)

Bulletproof chest heaving. My heart beating right through it in a Morse code for "fuck with me, just once, come on, just try."

(*HIT. HIT. HIT.*)

And the one good-for-nothing left standing, the one with the handgun, he laughs, he lowers his arm, and he points it at me and gives the moon a break, and he aims it right between my pointy ears, like goalposts and he's special teams.

(*The BOY stands, frozen, afraid.*)

And JanitorMan is still calling Saint Anthony but he ain't pickin' up,

(*Silence.*)

And for a second it seems like . . . *maybe I'm gonna lose.*

(*The BOY takes a breath. Sudden courage.*)

Naw.

(*—SNARE. The BOY mimes the fight.*)

SHOO—SHOO! FUACATA! —

(*—SNARE—*)

—"Don't kill me mannn!!" —

(*—CYMBAL—*)

—SNAP! —

(*—SNARE—*)

—Wrist CRACK—

(*—SNARE—*)

—Neck—

(*—SNARE—*)

—SLASH! —

(*—CYMBAL—*)

—Skin—meets—acid—

(− SNARE −)

− "AHH!!" −

(− SNARE.)

And he's on the floor. And I'm standing over him. And I got the gun in MY hands now. And I hate guns, I hate holding 'em cause I'm Batman, and −

ASTERICKS: Batman don't like guns 'cause his parents got iced by guns a long time ago − but for just a second, my eyes glow white, and I hold this thing, for I could speak to the good-for-nothing in a language he maybe understands,

(*He aims the gun up at the sky.*)

. . . CLIC − CLIC . . .

(*The BASS DRUM.*)

And the good-for-nothings become good-for-disappearing into whatever toxic-waste-chemical-sludge-shit-hole they crawled out of.

(*A pause.*)

And it's just me and JanitorMan.

And I pick him up.

And I wipe sweat and cheap perfume off his forehead.

And he begs me not to hurt him and I grab him tight by his JanitorMan shirt collar and I pull him to my face, and he's taller than me, but the cape helps, so he listens when I look him straight in the eyes and I say two words to him:

"Go home."

And he does, checking behind his shoulder every ten feet.

And I SWOOSH from building to building on his way there, 'cause I know where he lives. And I watch his hands tremble as he pulls out his keychain and opens the door to his building.

And I'm back in bed before he even walks in through the front door.

(*SNARE.*)

And I hear him turn on the faucet and pour himself a glass of warm tap water.

And he puts the glass back in the sink.

(*SNARE.*)

And I hear his footsteps,

(*BOOM. BOOM.*)

And they get slower as they get to my room.

(*BOOM.*)

And he creaks my door open like mad slow.

(*Silence.*)

And he takes a step in, which he never does.

(*BOOM.*)

And he's staring off into nowhere, his face the color of sidewalks in summer, and I act like I'm just waking up, and I say,

"What's up, Pop?"

And JanitorMan says nothing to me.

But I see, in the dark, I see his arms go limp and his head turns back, like towards me, and he lifts it for I could see his face,

For I could see his eyes,

And his cheeks is dripping but not with sweat.

And he just stands there, breathing, like he remembers my eyes glowing white.

Like he remembers my bulletproof chest.

Like he remembers he's my pop.

(*Silence.*)

And for a long time I don't say nothing.

(*SILENCE.*)

And he turns around, hand on the doorknob, and he ain't looking my way but I hear him mumble two words to me.

(*A pause.*)

"I'm sorry."

(*A pause, the BOY is suddenly strong again.*)

And I lean over and open my window just a crack.

. . . If you look up high enough you could see me.

(*A couple SLOW KICKS, and some more, quiet, echoing SHORT hits.*)

And from where I am? . . . I could hear everything.

(*A slow blackout.*)

END OF PLAY

REFLECTING ON WHAT YOU READ

1. A good way to start is to summarize the story—what has happened in the past and what is happening now. Watch how dramatic intensity increases through the monologue and builds toward a climax. At what point did you begin to realize what's going on? How much of what the boy describes really happens, and how much does he imagine? How were you able to tell real and imaginary events apart?

2. How would you describe the boy? How old do you think he is, considering that the stage directions say "maybe 7, maybe 27"? What do you think that implies? What did you discover about the boy's relationship with his father? About their family life and social status? What are the ways the boy attempts to deal with all that he faces?

3. Consider the choice of Batman as the boy's hero. Would the effect be different if the play used "Superman" or "Iron Man" or "Spiderman" instead?

4. The play challenges a reader to imagine the drums in the background. Why do you think the drummer is included in the play? Why drums? What do they add? What would be lost if they were not present?

RESPONDING THROUGH Writing

WRITING ABOUT CHARACTER, CONFLICT, AND DRAMATIC ACTION

Journal Entries

1. Record two or more dialogues you have overheard or been involved in. Write a journal entry that discusses why real-life dialogue seems artificial on the page and why the artful dialogue from a play seems real.

2. Write a journal entry in which you discuss what makes the dialogue of Jenny and Marcy distinct from that of Bradley and Craig in Kelly Stuart's *The New New* (p. 671).

3. Watch a television sitcom or drama, paying attention to techniques used in developing characters. Write a journal entry explaining and evaluating them.

Literary Analysis Papers

4. Write a paper examining the use of style in Kelly Stuart's *The New New* (p. 671). You might focus on how the way that characters express themselves is used to characterize them, individually and as a group.

5. Write an analysis of the two characters in Kelly Stuart's *The New New* (p. 671) whom we do not see, Jeremy and Jimmy. Touch on aspects such as

what each is like, how we learn about them, why each is important to the play, and how the effect would be different if they did appear in the play.

6. Write a paper on Suzanne Bradbeer's use of various types of conflict and their significance in *Okoboji* (p. 822).

Comparison-Contrast Papers

7. Write out the first page of Ernest Hemingway's dialogue-filled story "Hills Like White Elephants" (p. 197) the way it would look if it were a play instead of a short story, using Deanna Alisa Ableser's *Black Coffee* (p. 817) as a model. Then compare and contrast the two versions and write a paper discussing how it would be different, or not much different, to read "Hills Like White Elephants" if it were written as a play rather than as a short story.

8. Write a paper comparing and contrasting the methods of characterization in Kelly Stuart's *The New New* (p. 671) and Suzanne Bradbeer's *Okoboji* (p. 822).

TIPS for Writing about Character, Conflict, and Dramatic Action

- **Start with conflict.** Exploring and analyzing the conflicts in a play can lead to an effective paper topic, especially because conflict reveals many aspects of a play, such as themes, character, problems and their resolution or lack of resolution, ambiguities, and even setting. Watch for different kinds of conflict—physical, social, and internal/psychological. (The latter, when central to a play, can work especially well as a paper topic.)

- **Consider character.** If you decide to write a paper in which you discuss a single character or several characters, you should not only describe what that character or those characters are like but also explain how various character traits are revealed (pay attention especially to what the characters do, say, and tell about others) and how the characters change or grow or are confronted with a need to change.

- **Watch for juxtapositions.** Always look for juxtapositions—parallel or contrasting characters, scenes, actions, images, and similar elements—in any play that you decide to write about. Juxtaposition can be especially important in revealing character development and in the development of themes.

- **Focus on style or structure.** Some plays lend themselves to a useful analysis of style or dramatic strategies. A paper could examine how style is used for characterization by showing how elements such as diction, sentence structure and length, and choice of images and figures of speech are suited to the character and differ from those of other characters. A paper also could examine dramatic strategies: the way or ways the action is structured, in the play as a whole or in a key scene or two, perhaps the way it builds to a climax and is resolved, or the way an easily overlooked small action or incident is used as a pivotal point for the entire play.

- **Use specific details and illustrations.** It is very important when writing about drama to decide whether to deal with the whole play or to select a scene or two to examine thoroughly. In either case, you must support your points and explanations with specific details and illustrations from the text.

WRITING ABOUT CONNECTIONS

Making internal connections is standard dramatic technique, as the playwright establishes relationships (juxtapositions, comparisons, contrasts) between words, characters, dramatic actions, symbols, or ideas. For a reader, looking at two works and making external connections can also be a valuable way of understanding themes in a play as these are brought out through character, conflict, and dramatic action. Here are some examples:

1. "Houses of Unhappiness": Marital Struggles in Henrik Ibsen's *A Doll's House* (p. 996) and August Wilson's *Fences* (p. 733)

2. "I Gotta Be Me": Contrasts in Men's Attitudes toward Women and Women's Attitudes toward Themselves and Other Women in Susan Gaspell's *Trifles* (p. 693) and Henrik Ibsen's *A Doll's House* (p. 996)

3. "Fathers and Sons": Family Tensions in Marco Ramirez's *I Am Not Batman* (p. 681) and Suzanne Bradbeer's *Okoboji* (p. 822)

WRITING RESEARCH PAPERS

1. Dr. Rank in Henrik Ibsen's *A Doll's House* (p. 996) is dying from a sexually transmitted disease (STD) passed on from his father. Research nineteenth-century knowledge of and social attitudes toward STDs, and write a paper using what you find to discuss the importance of that motif in the play (and perhaps how it was regarded by readers then and how it might be regarded today).

2. In the past few years, there has been much controversy over a number of "memoirs" that included material that was not factual. This issue is the background for Kelly Stuart's *The New New* (p. 671). Research this controversy and its ethical implications. Write a paper in which you take a stand on the issue and incorporate *The New New* in your discussion.

The color, the grace and levitation, the structural pattern in motion, the quick interplay of live beings, suspended like fitful lightning in a cloud, these things are the play, not words on paper, nor thoughts and ideas of an author. **Tennessee Williams**

(Pulitzer Prize–Winning American Playwright)

Setting and Structure

CHAPTER 24

Examining Where, When, and How It Happens

Think of the place shown each week in your favorite TV show. If it's an ongoing series, some or much of the action likely takes place in the same building, street, or room every week. You come to know those made-up places, those "sets" (the backdrops and properties constructed for staging a scene in a play or film), almost as well as the kitchen in your own house. For years one of the most popular shows on television, *Cheers*, took place almost completely in a Boston pub. The set of that imaginary neighborhood pub became so familiar that tourists visiting Boston expect to find and walk into the real Cheers.

Dramatic actions by characters occur in a location that is almost always significant and that is represented by a stage set. Reading as well as watching a play must include thoughtful consideration of sets and setting and of the way the dramatic action occurring in them is structured and connected in a meaningful way. Setting and structure in fiction were discussed earlier in this book. This chapter examines their significance for drama and the distinctive ways they are handled in a play.

READING FOR SETTING

Setting—where, when, and in what circumstances actions occur—is just as important in drama as it is in fiction. Significant aspects of setting include the *place* of the action (in broad terms such as region, country, or city and in narrow terms such as neighborhood, street, or building), the *time* at which the action occurs (the century, year, season, day, hour), and the *cultural context* of the action (social and historical circumstances that characterize the time and place). Each of these is discussed at length in Chapter 8.

The Set on Stage   Sets are an important aspect of setting in plays, movies, and TV, an aspect not present in fiction and poetry because they lack the performance dimension of drama. The **set** is the physical setup on the stage, including the background (backdrop), structures, **properties** (or "props," all movable articles, such as furniture and objects handled by the actors), and lighting. Set is often the first thing you encounter when watching a play in a theater, but imagining how the play might be set is also an important part of staging the play in the theater of your mind.

Playwrights and Sets   Plays written before the mid-1800s may indicate their setting but offer little guidance on how specific sets are to be designed. Modern playwrights, on the other hand, in addition to indicating the setting of a play, often give detailed instructions on how to construct the set and even how characters should look and be dressed. In *Trifles*, the play beginning on the next page, for example, such instructions offer guidance not only to set and costume designers but also to readers, who are given a host of detailed images to help them as they attempt to picture the set, characters, and action in their minds.

APPROACHING THE READING

The following play falls into the popular genre of the mystery story as law officers attempt to solve a murder case. It also explores matters of human interest and of moral and legal importance. As you read, pay attention to the handling of dialogue and action, to the ways characters are revealed and developed, and to the conflicts presented. Notice also the way Susan Glaspell spells out how to construct the set and how characters should appear. Concentrate on visualizing the play in your mind as fully and sharply as you can. Also consider the importance of its rural, isolated setting—how it contributes to what has happened, and does happen, and to our reaction to it all.

Susan Glaspell   1882–1948

Trifles   [1916]

CHARACTERS

GEORGE HENDERSON (County Attorney)
HENRY PETERS (Sheriff)
LEWIS HALE (a neighboring farmer)
MRS. PETERS
MRS. HALE

SCENE: *The kitchen in the now abandoned farmhouse of John Wright, a gloomy kitchen, and left without having been put in order — unwashed pans under the sink,*

a loaf of bread outside the bread-box, a dish-towel on the table — other signs of incompleted work. At the rear the outer door opens and the Sheriff comes in followed by the County Attorney and Hale. The Sheriff and Hale are men in middle life, the County Attorney is a young man; all are much bundled up and go at once to the stove. They are followed by the two women — the Sheriff's wife first; she is a slight wiry woman, a thin nervous face. Mrs. Hale is larger and would ordinarily be called more comfortable looking, but she is disturbed now and looks fearfully about as she enters. The women have come in slowly, and stand close together near the door.

APPROACHING THE AUTHOR

Needing a break in 1922 from the theater group they founded in Provincetown, Massachusetts, **Susan Glaspell** and her husband decided to act on a long-held dream of his and move to Greece. They settled in Delphi, on the slopes of Mt. Parnassus, where they adopted an archaic lifestyle, attempting to live as shepherds.

© The Granger Collection.

For more about her, see page 1064.

COUNTY ATTORNEY (*rubbing his hands*): This feels good. Come up to the fire, ladies.

MRS. PETERS (*after taking a step forward*): I'm not — cold.

SHERIFF (*unbuttoning his overcoat and stepping away from the stove as if to mark the beginning of official business*): Now, Mr. Hale, before we move things about, you explain to Mr. Henderson just what you saw when you came here yesterday morning.

COUNTY ATTORNEY: By the way, has anything been moved? Are things just as you left them yesterday?

SHERIFF (*looking about*): It's just the same. When it dropped below zero last night I thought I'd better send Frank out this morning to make a fire for us — no use getting pneumonia with a big case on, but I told him not to touch anything except the stove — and you know Frank.

COUNTY ATTORNEY: Somebody should have been left here yesterday.

SHERIFF: Oh—yesterday. When I had to send Frank to Morris Center for that man who went crazy—I want you to know I had my hands full yesterday. I knew you could get back from Omaha by today and as long as I went over everything here myself—

COUNTY ATTORNEY: Well, Mr. Hale, tell just what happened when you came here yesterday morning.

HALE: Harry and I had started to town with a load of potatoes. We came along the road from my place and as I got here I said, "I'm going to see if I can't get John Wright to go in with me on a party telephone." I spoke to Wright about it once before and he put me off, saying folks talked too much anyway, and all he asked was peace and quiet—I guess you know about how much he talked himself; but I thought maybe if I went to the house and talked about it before his wife, though I said to Harry that I didn't know as what his wife wanted made much difference to John—

COUNTY ATTORNEY: Let's talk about that later, Mr. Hale. I do want to talk about that, but tell now just what happened when you got to the house.

HALE: I didn't hear or see anything; I knocked at the door, and still it was all quiet inside. I knew they must be up, it was past eight o'clock. So I knocked again, and I thought I heard somebody say, "Come in." I wasn't sure, I'm not sure yet, but I opened the door—this door (*indicating the door by which the two women are still standing*) and there in that rocker—(*pointing to it*) sat Mrs. Wright.

(*They all look at the rocker.*)

COUNTY ATTORNEY: What—was she doing?

HALE: She was rockin' back and forth. She had her apron in her hand and was kind of—pleating it.

COUNTY ATTORNEY: And how did she—look?

HALE: Well, she looked queer.

COUNTY ATTORNEY: How do you mean—queer?

HALE: Well, as if she didn't know what she was going to do next. And kind of done up.

COUNTY ATTORNEY: How did she seem to feel about your coming?

HALE: Why, I don't think she minded—one way or other. She didn't pay much attention. I said, "How do, Mrs. Wright it's cold, ain't it?" And she said, "Is it?"—and went on kind of pleating at her apron. Well, I was surprised; she didn't ask me to come up to the stove, or to set down, but just sat there, not even looking at me, so I said, "I want to see John." And then she—laughed. I guess you would call it a laugh. I thought of Harry and the team outside, so I said a little sharp: "Can't I see John?" "No," she says, kind o' dull like. "Ain't he home?" says I. "Yes," says she, "he's home." "Then why can't I see him?" I asked her, out of patience. "'Cause he's dead," says she. *Dead?* says I. She just nodded her head, not getting a bit excited, but rockin' back and forth. "Why—where is he?" says I, not knowing what to say. She just pointed upstairs—like that (*himself pointing to the room above*). I got up, with the idea of going up there. I walked from there to here—then I says, "Why, what did he die of?" "He died of a rope round his neck," says she, and just went on pleatin' at her apron. Well, I went out and called Harry. I thought I might—need help. We went upstairs and there he was lyin'—

COUNTY ATTORNEY: I think I'd rather have you go into that upstairs, where you can point it all out. Just go on now with the rest of the story.

HALE: Well, my first thought was to get that rope off. It looked . . . (*stops, his face twitches*) . . . but Harry, he went up to him, and he said, "No, he's dead all right, and we'd better not touch anything." So we went back down stairs. She was still sitting that same way. "Has anybody been notified?" I asked. "No," says she unconcerned. "Who did this, Mrs. Wright?" said Harry. He said it business-like—and she stopped pleatin' of her apron. "I don't know," she says. "You don't *know*?" says Harry. "No," says she. "Weren't you sleepin' in the bed with him?" says Harry. "Yes," says she, "but I was on the inside." "Somebody slipped a rope round his neck and strangled him and you didn't wake up?" says Harry. "I didn't wake up," she said after him. We must 'a looked as if we didn't see how that could be, for after a minute she said, "I sleep sound." Harry was going to ask her more questions but I said maybe we ought to let her tell her story first to the coroner, or the sheriff, so Harry went fast as he could to Rivers' place, where there's a telephone.

COUNTY ATTORNEY: And what did Mrs. Wright do when she knew that you had gone for the coroner?

HALE: She moved from that chair to this one over here (*pointing to a small chair in the corner*) and just sat there with her hands held together and looking down. I got a feeling that I ought to make some conversation, so I said I had come in to see if John wanted to put in a telephone, and at that she started to laugh, and then she stopped and looked at me—scared. (*The County Attorney, who has had his notebook out, makes a note.*) I dunno, maybe it wasn't scared. I wouldn't like to say it was. Soon Harry got back, and then Dr. Lloyd came, and you, Mr. Peters, and so I guess that's all I know that you don't.

COUNTY ATTORNEY (*looking around*): I guess we'll go upstairs first—and then out to the barn and around there. (*to the Sheriff*) You're convinced that there was nothing important here—nothing that would point to any motive?

SHERIFF: Nothing here but kitchen things.

(*The County Attorney, after again looking around the kitchen, opens the door of a cupboard closet. He gets up on a chair and looks on a shelf. Pulls his hand away, sticky.*)

COUNTY ATTORNEY: Here's a nice mess.

(*The women draw nearer.*)

MRS. PETERS (*to the other woman*): Oh, her fruit; it did freeze. (*to the Lawyer*) She worried about that when it turned so cold. She said the fire'd go out and her jars would break.

SHERIFF: Well, can you beat the women! Held for murder and worryin' about her preserves.

COUNTY ATTORNEY: I guess before we're through she may have something more serious than preserves to worry about.

HALE: Well, women are used to worrying over trifles.

(*The two women move a little closer together.*)

COUNTY ATTORNEY (*with the gallantry of a young politician*): And yet, for all their worries, what would we do without the ladies? (*The women do not unbend. He goes to the sink, takes a dipperful of water from the pail and pouring it into a basin, washes his hands. Starts to wipe them on the roller-towel, turns it for a cleaner place.*) Dirty towels! (*kicks his foot against the pans under the sink*) Not much of a housekeeper, would you say, ladies?

MRS. HALE (*stiffly*): There's a great deal of work to be done on a farm.

COUNTY ATTORNEY: To be sure. And yet (*with a little bow to her*) I know there are some Dickson county farmhouses which do not have such roller towels.

(*He gives it a pull to expose its length again.*)

MRS. HALE: Those towels get dirty awful quick. Men's hands aren't always as clean as they might be.

COUNTY ATTORNEY: Ah, loyal to your sex, I see. But you and Mrs. Wright were neighbors. I suppose you were friends, too.

MRS. HALE (*shaking her head*): I've not seen much of her of late years. I've not been in this house — it's more than a year.

COUNTY ATTORNEY: And why was that? You didn't like her?

MRS. HALE: I liked her all well enough. Farmers' wives have their hands full, Mr. Henderson. And then —

COUNTY ATTORNEY: Yes —?

MRS. HALE (*looking about*): It never seemed a very cheerful place.

COUNTY ATTORNEY: No — it's not cheerful. I shouldn't say she had the homemaking instinct.

MRS. HALE: Well, I don't know as Wright had, either.

COUNTY ATTORNEY: You mean that they didn't get on very well?

MRS. HALE: No, I don't mean anything. But I don't think a place'd be any cheerfuller for John Wright's being in it.

COUNTY ATTORNEY: I'd like to talk more of that a little later. I want to get the lay of things upstairs now.

(*He goes to the left, where three steps lead to a stair door.*)

SHERIFF: I suppose anything Mrs. Peters does'll be all right. She was to take in some clothes for her, you know, and a few little things. We left in such a hurry yesterday.

COUNTY ATTORNEY: Yes, but I would like to see what you take, Mrs. Peters, and keep an eye out for anything that might be of use to us.

MRS. PETERS: Yes, Mr. Henderson.

(*The women listen to the men's steps on the stairs, then look about the kitchen.*)

MRS. HALE: I'd hate to have men coming into my kitchen, snooping around and criticizing.

(*She arranges the pans under sink which the Lawyer had shoved out of place.*)

MRS. PETERS: Of course it's no more than their duty.

MRS. HALE: Duty's all right, but I guess that deputy sheriff that came out to make the fire might have got a little of this on. (*gives the roller towel a pull*) Wish I'd thought of that sooner. Seems mean to talk about her for not having things slicked up when she had to come away in such a hurry.

MRS. PETERS (*who has gone to a small table in the left rear corner of the room, and lifted one end of a towel that covers a pan*): She had bread set.

(*Stands still.*)

MRS. HALE (*eyes fixed on a loaf of bread beside the breadbox, which is on a low shelf at the other side of the room. Moves slowly toward it*): She was going to put this in there. (*picks up loaf, then abruptly drops it. In manner of returning to familiar things*) It's a shame about her fruit. I wonder if it's all gone. (*gets up on the chair and looks*) I think there's some here that's all right, Mrs. Peters. Yes—here; (*holding it toward the window*) this is cherries, too. (*looking again*) I declare I believe that's the only one. (*Gets down, bottle in her hand. Goes to the sink and wipes it off on the outside.*) She'll feel awful bad after all her hard work in the hot weather. I remember the afternoon I put up my cherries last summer.

(*She puts the bottle on the big kitchen table, center of the room. With a sigh, is about to sit down in the rocking-chair. Before she is seated realizes what chair it is; with a slow look at it, steps back. The chair which she has touched rocks back and forth.*)

MRS. PETERS: Well, I must get those things from the front room closet. (*She goes to the door at the right, but after looking into the other room, steps back.*) You coming with me, Mrs. Hale? You could help me carry them.

(*They go in the other room; reappear, Mrs. Peters carrying a dress and skirt, Mrs. Hale following with a pair of shoes.*)

MRS. PETERS: My, it's cold in there.

(*She puts the clothes on the big table, and hurries to the stove.*)

MRS. HALE (*examining the skirt*): Wright was close. I think maybe that's why she kept so much to herself. She didn't even belong to the Ladies Aid. I suppose she felt she couldn't do her part, and then you don't enjoy things when you feel shabby. She used to wear pretty clothes and be lively, when she was Minnie Foster, one of the town girls singing in the choir. But that—oh, that was thirty years ago. This all you was to take in?

MRS. PETERS: She said she wanted an apron. Funny thing to want, for there isn't much to get you dirty in jail, goodness knows. But I suppose just to make her feel more natural. She said they was in the top drawer in this cupboard.

Yes, here. And then her little shawl that always hung behind the door. (*opens stair door and looks*) Yes, here it is.

(*Quickly shuts door leading upstairs.*)

MRS. HALE (*abruptly moving toward her*): Mrs. Peters?

MRS. PETERS: Yes, Mrs. Hale?

MRS. HALE: Do you think she did it?

MRS. PETERS (*in a frightened voice*): Oh, I don't know.

MRS. HALE: Well, I don't think she did. Asking for an apron and her little shawl. Worrying about her fruit.

MRS. PETERS (*starts to speak, glances up, where footsteps are heard in the room above. In a low voice*): Mr. Peters says it looks bad for her. Mr. Henderson is awful sarcastic in a speech and he'll make fun of her sayin' she didn't wake up.

MRS. HALE: Well, I guess John Wright didn't wake when they was slipping that rope under his neck.

MRS. PETERS: No, it's strange. It must have been done awful crafty and still. They say it was such a — funny way to kill a man, rigging it all up like that.

MRS. HALE: That's just what Mr. Hale said. There was a gun in the house. He says that's what he can't understand.

MRS. PETERS: Mr. Henderson said coming out that what was needed for the case was a motive; something to show anger, or — sudden feeling.

MRS. HALE (*who is standing by the table*): Well, I don't see any signs of anger around here. (*She puts her hand on the dish towel which lies on the table, stands looking down at table, one half of which is clean, the other half messy.*) It's wiped to here. (*Makes a move as if to finish work, then turns and looks at loaf of bread outside the breadbox. Drops towel. In that voice of coming back to familiar things.*) Wonder how they are finding things upstairs. I hope she had it a little more red-up° there. You know, it seems kind of *sneaking.* Locking her up in town and then coming out here and trying to get her own house to turn against her!

MRS. PETERS: But Mrs. Hale, the law is the law.

MRS. HALE: I s'pose 'tis. (*unbuttoning her coat*) Better loosen up your things, Mrs. Peters. You won't feel them when you go out.

(*Mrs. Peters takes off her fur tippet,° goes to hang it on hook at back of room, stands looking at the under part of the small corner table.*)

MRS. PETERS: She was piecing a quilt.

(*She brings the large sewing basket and they look at the bright pieces.*)

MRS. HALE: It's log cabin pattern. Pretty, isn't it? I wonder if she was goin' to quilt it or just knot it?

(*Footsteps have been heard coming down the stairs. The Sheriff enters followed by Hale and the County Attorney.*)

---

red-up: Tidy; picked up. **tippet:** A shoulder cape.

SHERIFF: They wonder if she was going to quilt it or just knot it!

(*The men laugh, the women look abashed.*)

COUNTY ATTORNEY (*rubbing his hands over the stove*): Frank's fire didn't do much up there, did it? Well, let's go out to the barn and get that cleared up.

(*The men go outside.*)

MRS. HALE (*resentfully*): I don't know as there's anything so strange, our takin' up our time with little things while we're waiting for them to get the evidence. (*She sits down at the big table smoothing out a block with decision.*) I don't see as it's anything to laugh about.

MRS. PETERS (*apologetically*): Of course they've got awful important things on their minds.

(*Pulls up a chair and joins Mrs. Hale at the table.*)

MRS. HALE (*examining another block*): Mrs. Peters, look at this one. Here, this is the one she was working on, and look at the sewing! All the rest of it has been so nice and even. And look at this! It's all over the place! Why, it looks as if she didn't know what she was about!

(*After she has said this they look at each other, then start to glance back at the door. After an instant Mrs. Hale has pulled at a knot and ripped the sewing.*)

MRS. PETERS: Oh, what are you doing, Mrs. Hale?

MRS. HALE (*mildly*): Just pulling out a stitch or two that's not sewed very good. (*threading a needle*) Bad sewing always made me fidgety.

MRS. PETERS (*nervously*): I don't think we ought to touch things.

MRS. HALE: I'll just finish up this end. (*suddenly stopping and leaning forward*) Mrs. Peters?

MRS. PETERS: Yes, Mrs. Hale?

MRS. HALE: What do you suppose she was so nervous about?

MRS. PETERS: Oh—I don't know. I don't know as she was nervous. I sometimes sew awful queer when I'm just tired. (*Mrs. Hale starts to say something, looks at Mrs. Peters, then goes on sewing.*) Well I must get these things wrapped up. They may be through sooner than we think. (*putting apron and other things together*) I wonder where I can find a piece of paper, and string.

MRS. HALE: In that cupboard, maybe.

MRS. PETERS (*looking in cupboard*): Why, here's a bird-cage. (*holds it up*) Did she have a bird, Mrs. Hale?

MRS. HALE: Why, I don't know whether she did or not—I've not been here for so long. There was a man around last year selling canaries cheap, but I don't know as she took one; maybe she did. She used to sing real pretty herself.

MRS. PETERS (*glancing around*): Seems funny to think of a bird here. But she must have had one, or why would she have a cage? I wonder what happened to it.

MRS. HALE: I s'pose maybe the cat got it.

MRS. PETERS: No, she didn't have a cat. She's got that feeling some people have about cats — being afraid of them. My cat got in her room and she was real upset and asked me to take it out.

MRS. HALE: My sister Bessie was like that. Queer, ain't it?

MRS. PETERS (*examining the cage*): Why, look at this door. It's broke. One hinge is pulled apart.

MRS. HALE (*looking too*): Looks as if someone must have been rough with it.

MRS. PETERS: Why, yes.

(*She brings the cage forward and puts it on the table.*)

MRS. HALE: I wish if they're going to find any evidence they'd be about it. I don't like this place.

MRS. PETERS: But I'm awful glad you came with me, Mrs. Hale. It would be lonesome for me sitting here alone.

MRS. HALE: It would, wouldn't it? (*dropping her sewing*) But I tell you what I do wish, Mrs. Peters. I wish I had come over sometimes when *she* was here. I — (*looking around the room*) — wish I had.

MRS. PETERS: But of course you were awful busy, Mrs. Hale — your house and your children.

MRS. HALE: I could've come. I stayed away because it weren't cheerful — and that's why I ought to have come. I — I've never liked this place. Maybe because it's down in a hollow and you don't see the road. I dunno what it is, but it's a lonesome place and always was. I wish I had come over to see Minnie Foster sometimes. I can see now — (*shakes her head*)

MRS. PETERS: Well, you mustn't reproach yourself, Mrs. Hale. Somehow we just don't see how it is with other folks until — something comes up.

MRS. HALE: Not having children makes less work — but it makes a quiet house, and Wright out to work all day, and no company when he did come in. Did you know John Wright, Mrs. Peters?

MRS. PETERS: Not to know him; I've seen him in town. They say he was a good man.

MRS. HALE: Yes — good; he didn't drink, and kept his word as well as most, I guess, and paid his debts. But he was a hard man, Mrs. Peters. Just to pass the time of day with him — (*shivers*) Like a raw wind that gets to the bone. (*pauses, her eye falling on the cage*) I should think she would 'a wanted a bird. But what do you suppose went with it?

MRS. PETERS: I don't know, unless it got sick and died.

(*She reaches over and swings the broken door, swings it again, both women watch it.*)

MRS. HALE: You weren't raised round here, were you? (*Mrs. Peters shakes her head*) You didn't know — her?

MRS. PETERS: Not till they brought her yesterday.

MRS. HALE: She — come to think of it, she was kind of like a bird herself — real sweet and pretty, but kind of timid and — fluttery. How — she — did — change. (*silence; then as if struck by a happy thought and relieved to get back to everyday*) *things*) Tell you what, Mrs. Peters, why don't you take the quilt in with you? It might take up her mind.

MRS. PETERS: Why, I think that's a real nice idea, Mrs. Hale. There couldn't possibly be any objection to it, could there? Now, just what would I take? I wonder if her patches are in here — and her things.

(They look in the sewing basket.)

MRS. HALE: Here's some red. I expect this has got sewing things in it. (*brings out a fancy box*) What a pretty box. Looks like something somebody would give you. Maybe her scissors are in here. (*Opens box. Suddenly puts her hand to her nose.*) Why — (*Mrs. Peters bends nearer, then turns her face away.*) There's something wrapped up in this piece of silk.

MRS. PETERS: Why, this isn't her scissors.

MRS. HALE (*lifting the silk*): Oh, Mrs. Peters — it's —

(Mrs. Peters bends closer.)

MRS. PETERS: It's the bird.

MRS. HALE (*jumping up*): But, Mrs. Peters — look at it! It's neck! Look at its neck! It's all — other side *to*.

MRS. PETERS: Somebody — wrung — its — neck.

(Their eyes meet. A look of growing comprehension, of horror. Steps are heard outside. Mrs. Hale slips box under quilt pieces, and sinks into her chair. Enter Sheriff and County Attorney. Mrs. Peters rises.)

COUNTY ATTORNEY (*as one turning from serious things to little pleasantries*): Well ladies, have you decided whether she was going to quilt it or knot it?

MRS. PETERS: We think she was going to — knot it.

COUNTY ATTORNEY: Well, that's interesting, I'm sure. (*seeing the birdcage*) Has the bird flown?

MRS. HALE (*putting more quilt pieces over the box*): We think the — cat got it.

COUNTY ATTORNEY (*preoccupied*): Is there a cat?

(Mrs. Hale glances in quick covert way at Mrs. Peters.)

MRS. PETERS: Well, not *now*. They're superstitious, you know. They leave.

COUNTY ATTORNEY (*to Sheriff Peters, continuing an interrupted conversation*): No sign at all of anyone having come from the outside. Their own rope. Now let's go up again and go over it piece by piece. (*They start upstairs.*) It would have to have been someone who knew just the —

(Mrs. Peters sits down. The two women sit there not looking at one another, but as if peering into something and at the same time holding back. When they talk now it is in the manner of feeling their way over strange ground, as if afraid of what they are saying, but as if they cannot help saying it.)

MRS. HALE: She liked the bird. She was going to bury it in that pretty box.

MRS. PETERS (*in a whisper*): When I was a girl—my kitten—there was a boy took a hatchet, and before my eyes—and before I could get there—(*covers her face an instant*) If they hadn't held me back I would have—(*catches herself, looks upstairs where steps are heard, falters weakly*)—hurt him.

MRS. HALE (*with a slow look around her*): I wonder how it would seem never to have had any children around. (*pause*) No, Wright wouldn't like the bird—a thing that sang. She used to sing. He killed that, too.

MRS. PETERS (*moving uneasily*): We don't know who killed the bird.

MRS. HALE: I knew John Wright.

MRS. PETERS: It was an awful thing was done in this house that night, Mrs. Hale. Killing a man while he slept, slipping a rope around his neck that choked the life out of him.

MRS. HALE: His neck. Choked the life out of him.

(*Her hand goes out and rests on the birdcage.*)

MRS. PETERS (*with rising voice*): We don't know who killed him. We don't *know*.

MRS. HALE (*her own feeling not interrupted*): If there'd been years and years of nothing, then a bird to sing to you, it would be awful—still, after the bird was still.

MRS. PETERS (*something within her speaking*): I know what stillness is. When we homesteaded in Dakota, and my first baby died—after he was two years old, and me with no other then—

MRS. HALE (*moving*): How soon do you suppose they'll be through, looking for the evidence?

MRS. PETERS: I know what stillness is. (*pulling herself back*) The law has got to punish crime, Mrs. Hale.

MRS. HALE (*not as if answering that*): I wish you'd seen Minnie Foster when she wore a white dress with blue ribbons and stood up there in the choir and sang. (*a look around the room*) Oh, I *wish* I'd come over here once in a while! That was a crime! That was a crime! Who's going to punish that?

MRS. PETERS (*looking upstairs*): We mustn't—take on.

MRS. HALE: I might have known she needed help! I know how things can be—for women. I tell you, it's queer, Mrs. Peters. We live close together and we live far apart. We all go through the same things—it's all just a different kind of the same thing. (*brushes her eyes, noticing the bottle of fruit, reaches out for it*) If I was you, I wouldn't tell her her fruit was gone. Tell her it *ain't*. Tell her it's all right. Take this in to prove it to her. She—she may never know whether it was broke or not.

MRS. PETERS (*takes the bottle, looks about for something to wrap it in; takes petticoat from the clothes brought from the other room, very nervously begins winding this around the bottle. In a false voice*): My, it's a good thing the men couldn't hear us. Wouldn't they just laugh! Getting all stirred up over a little thing like a—dead canary. As if that could have anything to do with—with—wouldn't they *laugh*!

(*The men are heard coming down stairs.*)

MRS. HALE (*under her breath*): Maybe they would—maybe they wouldn't.

COUNTY ATTORNEY: No, Peters, it's all perfectly clear except a reason for doing it. But you know juries when it comes to women. If there was some definite thing. Something to show—something to make a story about—a thing that would connect up with this strange way of doing it—

(*The women's eyes meet for an instant. Enter Hale from outer door.*)

HALE: Well, I've got the team around. Pretty cold out there.

COUNTY ATTORNEY: I'm going to stay here a while by myself. (*to the Sheriff*) You can send Frank out for me, can't you? I want to go over everything. I'm not satisfied that we can't do better.

SHERIFF: Do you want to see what Mrs. Peters is going to take in?

(*The Lawyer goes to the table, picks up the apron, laughs.*)

COUNTY ATTORNEY: Oh, I guess they're not very dangerous things the ladies have picked out. (*Moves a few things about, disturbing the quilt pieces which cover the box. Steps back*) No, Mrs. Peters doesn't need supervising. For that matter, a sheriff's wife is married to the law. Ever think of it that way, Mrs. Peters?

MRS. PETERS: Not—just that way.

SHERIFF (*chuckling*): Married to the law. (*moves toward the other room*) I just want you to come in here a minute, George. We ought to take a look at these windows.

COUNTY ATTORNEY (*scoffingly*): Oh, windows!

SHERIFF: We'll be right out, Mr. Hale.

(*Hale goes outside. The Sheriff follows the County Attorney into the other room. Then Mrs. Hale rises, hands tight together, looking intensely at Mrs. Peters, whose eyes make a slow turn, finally meeting Mrs. Hale's. A moment Mrs. Hale holds her, then her own eyes point the way to where the box is concealed. Suddenly Mrs. Peters throws back quilt pieces and tries to put the box in the bag she is wearing. It is too big. She opens box, starts to take bird out, cannot touch it, goes to pieces, stands there helpless. Sound of a knob turning in the other room. Mrs. Hale snatches the box and puts it in the pocket of her big coat. Enter County Attorney and Sheriff.*)

COUNTY ATTORNEY (*facetiously*): Well, Henry, at least we found out that she was not going to quilt it. She was going to—what is it you call it, ladies?

MRS. HALE (*her hand against her pocket*): We call it—knot it, Mr. Henderson.

CURTAIN

REFLECTING ON WHAT YOU'VE READ

1. Summarize the action and explain the significance of details in the plot and setting (the mess in the kitchen, the jam and jam jars, the quilting and Mrs. Wright's way of working, the bird and birdcage, the choice of a rope as weapon, and so on).

2. Examine the way the story is presented as a mystery play. Do you notice situations or lines that are conventional in detective stories you've read or seen in movies or on television? Find uses of foreshadowing in the play and explain what makes them effective.

3. List several conflicts and several types of conflict in the play. Which conflicts focus your attention on issues that seem important in the play? List several such issues.

4. Reflect on the characters: Who are the major characters, what is important to them, what motivates them, how do they change (if they do), and why? How does your impression of them change? Who are the minor characters, and what are their roles and significance?

5. This play was written in 1916. If you were directing a production of the play, would you give it a setting in the past (perhaps "Time: the early 1900s") or in the present? Why? How would that decision affect costuming, set design, props, and so on? What difference, if any, would that decision have on the central issues explored in the play?

The General Setting   The stage directions locate the play in a farmhouse, apparently in western Iowa or eastern Nebraska, since Sheriff Peters mentions that the county attorney, George Henderson, has just returned from Omaha (p. 694). But the geographic region has little effect on this play. Glaspell was born and raised in Iowa and worked for a short time as a journalist in Des Moines. She moved to the Northeast more than a decade before she wrote *Trifles*, and its setting could just as easily be rural New England.

The Specific Setting   More significant for setting is that the farmhouse is isolated and depressing. As Mrs. Hale says, "I—I've never liked this place. Maybe because it's down in a hollow and you don't see the road. I dunno what it is, but it's a lonesome place and always was" (p. 700). Such isolation is important to the play: Mrs. Wright lacks contact with other people, sees neither neighbors nor friends. Her only source of companionship is a husband who rarely talks to or interacts with others.

The Overall Set   In her headnote, Glaspell was more specific about set than setting. The set is the kitchen of the Wrights' home, and the detailed stage directions give a reader lots of help in imagining how the room appears (gloomy, probably sparsely furnished, in a state of considerable disorder, with a door to outside in the rear wall) and what the room contains (a breadbox, a sink with dirty pots under it, a stove, and a table). Glaspell also scatters stage directions throughout the text. We learn later, among other details, that the room contains a cupboard, a rocking chair, a small table in the left rear corner with a large sewing basket under it, a small chair in another corner, and a roller towel on the wall near the sink, and that there is at least one window, a door at the right into another room, and steps at the left leading to a door, behind which are the stairs to the second floor.

Reading a Set   The way each stage designer envisions Glaspell's directions is individual and unique — just as the way you visualize it will be. Some stage designers attempt to recreate authentic, early twentieth-century details, while others give it a more timeless feel and do not try for historical "correctness." Reading a set, and reading a play, is like all other kinds of reading. There is no single set design, or a single interpretation of a text, that all readers must seek to attain. Instead, we should decide what is appropriate for the drama itself and relish the diversity and enrichment that results when others see things differently from the way we do.

READING FOR STRUCTURE

External Form   The structuring of a play, like that of a poem, involves external form as well as internal form. The external form starts with features such as the list of characters; the stage directions; the division of the text into speeches headed by tags identifying the characters; and the stage directions guiding the actors on details such as action, tone, or expression.

Division into Acts   External form includes the division of longer plays into acts and scenes. An **act** is a major division of a drama, a significant section of the action. In performance, the end of an act is signaled by an intermission or by the lowering of the stage curtain. In reading, the text is usually marked as act 1, act 2, and so forth.

Division into Scenes   Scenes are minor divisions in a drama — a single act may be divided into scenes, or a one-act play might consist of several scenes. Often a new scene jumps ahead to a different time or moves to a different location. Scene changes are signaled in different ways: The stage may empty while the curtain remains raised, or the lights may go out, or the scenery may be reconfigured. Sometimes locations are identified for the audience in the printed program. But it is left to the imagination of the reader or viewer to bridge such gaps by making the needed connections or by realizing what is only hinted at.

Internal Form   The internal structure of a play centers on **plot**, the structural pattern by which it is organized and developed. The plot in drama involves many of the same issues as plot in fiction.

- *Beginnings*: starting **in medias res**, for example, making use of **exposition** to explain things that occurred before the initial action of

the play, and making use of **flashbacks** to clarify events prior to the beginning of the play.
- *Middles*: using conflicts, suspense, gaps, foreshadowings, and repetitions to increase plot "complications" and build to a climax.
- *Endings*: resolving (or in some cases not resolving) the mysteries, problems, or tensions that have developed in the beginning and middle.

Terms and techniques dealing with structure are discussed thoroughly in Chapter 5. Reviewing pages 113–18 will prepare you for studying plot in drama.

The Five-Act Play   Some theorists hold that the internal structure of a play involves a natural dramatic rhythm that develops in five divisions or steps, which they believe correspond with the traditional five-act structure of a play.

- *Introduction or exposition*: The introduction, or **exposition**, occurs early in the play, usually as one or more characters deliver speeches providing information required for following the action of the play: introducing characters, filling in prior action and the background from which the central conflict will develop, and establishing setting and tone.
- *Complication*: **Complication** is the rising action of the play; entanglements caused by the central conflict are set in motion.
- *Crisis or climax*: The **crisis** is the turning point in the action, the point at which the protagonist's situation turns for the better or worse. **Climax** is the point at which a significant emotional response is elicited. It does not always coincide with the moment of crisis.
- *Reversal*: Reversal is the falling action of a play, the depiction of the change in fortune experienced by the protagonist.
- *Catastrophe and resolution, or dénouement*: The term **catastrophe**, used mostly for tragedy, depicts the action, the unhappy ending, that results from crisis/climax and reversal. **Resolution**, or restoration of order, usually follows the catastrophe. **Dénouement** (French for "unknotting") is often used for the final unraveling of the plot complications in a comedy, though the unknotting at the end turns into a tying up of loose ends.

COMPRESSION AND CONTRAST

Compression   Dramatic works are shaped also by use of two key structural principles: compression and contrast. The first, *compression*, is necessary because a playwright usually works under fairly strict time constraints (a work of fiction can extend to any length to tell its story). Audiences generally expect a play to last no more than three hours. There are plays that run four or five hours and some even for days, but those are the exceptions. Therefore, playwrights are usually aware of time and use techniques that enable them to compress their material economically. Being aware of such techniques can help you understand how a play and a play's structure work and why some details have to be handled to fit the constraints of time.

To compress their material, playwrights tend to start close to the most exciting or significant scene (see "Beginnings," p. 705). *Trifles*, for example, opens the morning after Mr. Wright dies because the play is most concerned with the motivation for the murder and the way Mrs. Hale and Mrs. Peters come to regard that motivation. In reading or watching plays, you need to get used to arriving in the middle of a conversation and to use what is said to figure out what happened earlier. Often it is said that dramatic action occurs only in the present: What occurs on the stage is always "now." Even when a flashback is acted out, we see the past events occurring as we watch. Events that are not acted out are narrated through exposition, the way Mr. Hale fills in his experiences of the previous day. Playwrights also compress by using exposition to clarify information that the audience needs to know about earlier events and by using foreshadowing to alert us about things to watch for in what follows (see "Middles," p. 706). And they compress material by organizing events into moments, or scenes (p. 705).

Symbols   Playwrights can achieve compression through the use of **symbols**, images or actions or characters that are first and fundamentally themselves in the play but also embody an abstract idea. What is said on pages 252–54 about symbols in fiction applies equally to drama. The same types of symbols are used in drama, and the same formal devices convey to a reader or viewer that an image, action, or character may be symbolic: repetition, description, placement in noticeable positions (title, beginning, ending, climactic scene), or a sense of weightiness or significance beyond the literal function in the work. The birdcage in *Trifles*, for example, is a literal object in the story, but it also suggests qualities of the relationship between Mr. and Mrs. Wright. Mrs. Wright used to enjoy singing and her song, like the bird's, was stifled by Mr. Wright. She, like the bird, lived in a cage, trapped and broken figuratively in spirit, the way the bird's neck was broken literally. Symbols help achieve compression because the symbols — objects, character types, or actions — are seen on stage by the audience and require few words and little time to convey their meaning. The viewer, or the reader watching the play imaginatively, has the opportunity to recognize the symbol and to take part in discerning its appropriateness and meaning.

Contrast   *Contrast* is important to playwrights both as a means of compression and as a way to establish relationships in a play. Dramatists regularly establish parallels or contrasts between two or more situations, characters, actions, or symbols to get us to notice things about each that we might miss without the pairing. Often parallel items reinforce a point or theme or serve as a means of repetition, a valuable technique for creating emphasis, while contrasts direct our attention to differences and distinctions more clearly and forcefully. In *Trifles*, the stillness in the house Mrs. Peters experienced after losing a child enabled her to empathize with the similar still-ness Mrs. Wright must have felt after the death of the canary. The principal contrast of the play is between the women and the men, with their different approaches, outlooks, and attitudes. The term **foil** is used for a character who stands in contrast to another character and thus calls attention to distinctive features of the second character or to significant differences between the two. Naomi can be taken as a foil to Bradley in *The New New* (p. 671).

☑ CHECKLIST on Reading for Setting and Structure

❑ Be attentive to setting in terms of place; time; and historical, social, and cultural context, and to the effects of setting in a play.

❑ Be attentive to stage directions provided by the playwright, and use descriptions of sets, props, costumes, stage movements, and character descriptions to sharpen your images as you visualize the plays.

❑ Be alert for symbols of different kinds (literary, conventional, traditional, and archetypal) and the various ways they can contribute to a play.

❑ Notice the structuring of plot in a play: its handling of beginning, mid-dle, and ending; its use of gaps, flashbacks, suspense, foreshadowing, and repetition; and its use of compression and contrasts.

❑ Know the traditional five-part dramatic pattern (introduction, compli-cation, climax, reversal, and resolution) and test to see if it applies to a particular play.

FURTHER READING

APPROACHING THE READING

The mysterious events in the following play take place in a big, old, eerie house in Quebec, on a proverbial dark and stormy night. These events in the present were set up some time ago in another old house, this one in Providence, Rhode Island. As you read, note when the action switches settings—from one side of the set to the other—as it did in *The New New*. You'll also need to piece together what happened in the past, making connections between things characters say and noticing subtle hints that lead to a surprising ending, one that will probably make you want to read the play again.

Don Nigro   b. 1949

Letters from Quebec to Providence in the Rain   [2008]

CHARACTERS

PETRUS: Late twenties.
VANESSA: Late twenties.
JONATHAN: Early twenties.
MARIANNE: Early twenties.

SETTING

An old house in Quebec, and another old house in Providence. Both are present onstage at once. Some furniture, which is part of both houses. Time and space interpenetrate. There's a desk and chair down right, a bed right, an old-fashioned clawfoot bathtub up center, a sofa left, and a chair and small round table down left.

TIME

The present, and the not too distant past.

Sound of whippoorwills in the darkness. Lights up on Petrus at the desk down right and, in dimmer light for the moment, Jonathan sitting in his chair down left and Marianne in the bathtub up—center.

APPROACHING THE AUTHOR

Don Nigro says of his beginnings as a writer: "I started writing when I was a young child, and I started lying, and lying turned me into a writer." Aside from lying, he has said that an ability to empathize with people has helped him develop as a playwright.

For more about him, see page 1073.

PETRUS (*taking some letters out of an old book*): This is very odd.

VANESSA (*coming into the light, in bathrobe, barefoot*): This is Quebec. Everything is odd here. Not very odd. Just a little bit odd. Just a bit off center, as if one were living in two places at the same time. Everything has two reflections here.

PETRUS: I've found some letters in this old book.

VANESSA: Whose book is it? Yours or mine?

PETRUS: I don't know whose book it is. Well, it's mine now. I bought it this morning, on impulse, from a girl selling books by the river. When I got home, I opened it up, and these letters fell out.

VANESSA: You didn't open the book before you bought it?

PETRUS: It was raining. I was rushing to get home.

VANESSA: You were rushing to get home, so you stopped to buy an old book?

PETRUS: I had a sudden impulse. She looked so lonely, there in the rain.

VANESSA: She was selling books in the rain?

PETRUS: It's Drago's *Occult Notebooks*. I've been looking for this book for many, many years. I thought I'd never find a copy.

VANESSA: Who is Drago?

PETRUS: N. J. Drago. A Romanian writer. Rather obscure and difficult, but brilliant. It's quite a rare book. I got it for practically nothing.

VANESSA: So you stole from the poor girl?

PETRUS: I didn't steal from her. I paid what she asked for it.

VANESSA: But you knew it was worth more. The creature is half mad, selling books in the rain, and you're drawn to her on impulse, no doubt because of her melancholy beauty, and then you cheat her out of a rare book.

PETRUS: You're missing the point here.

VANESSA: No I'm not. I have always very much appreciated the romance of found objects. At least, I seem to remember that I have. Everything is still a little blurry in my head. Found objects can seem to radiate a powerful numinosity. Now there's a word I didn't know I knew. Numinosity. Is that a word? A sense that objects or events or even certain persons or places possess tremendous significance, that one has stumbled upon them for some purpose unknown to one, that one is suddenly able to perceive the vague outline of a pattern in what would appear to be entirely random events. It appears I may be more intelligent than I'd realized. Or possibly just demented.

PETRUS: What's really interesting here is the letters.

VANESSA: You found some letters in an old book. One's likely to stumble upon anything in the pages of an old book. Flowers. Note cards. Fragments of human skin.

PETRUS: They're written to someone named Vanessa.

VANESSA: And that is interesting because—?

PETRUS: Because your name is Vanessa.

VANESSA: And?

PETRUS: Doesn't that seem an odd coincidence to you?

VANESSA: I have no doubt there are a number of persons in Quebec named Vanessa. This is still Quebec, isn't it? Sometimes I wake up from a dream and I seem to be in an entirely different place. I suppose it's the medication.

PETRUS: I'm sure there are other persons named Vanessa in Quebec. But they're not living in my house, are they?

VANESSA: Not that I know of. Who are the letters from?

PETRUS: They're from somebody named Jonathan. And they were mailed from Quebec to Providence.

VANESSA: So this is Providence?

PETRUS: No. This is Quebec.

VANESSA: If they were mailed to Providence, then how did they get back to Quebec?

PETRUS: Clearly, in this book.

(*Lights up on Jonathan, sitting at the table down left, speaking as a letter but not writing.*)

JONATHAN: Dearest Vanessa. I got the key to Rum House from a horrible old woman with a face like a salamander and moved in three days ago. The plaster is flaking off the walls, and there's something scuttling in the cupboards, but I feel surprisingly at home in Quebec, as if I'd lived here in a previous life.

VANESSA: I had a brother named Jonathan.

PETRUS: A brother? Did you?

JONATHAN: It rains here every evening, and in the morning there is fog, and always the song of the whippoorwills in the cherry trees by the river.

PETRUS: You've never mentioned having a brother.

JONATHAN: I've been exploring the overgrown garden, which is a miasma of tangled vines.

VANESSA: I don't any more. He's dead now.

JONATHAN: I have on more than one occasion had the overwhelming sensation that I am not alone in this house. Last night I could have sworn I heard a young girl talking to herself upstairs in the bath.

(Lights up on Marianne in the tub.)

MARIANNE: Once upon a time, she said, Vanessa and Jonathan lived in Quebec.

PETRUS: What did your brother die of?

MARIANNE: Then Vanessa went to college, to Brown University, in Providence, Rhode Island, to study creative writing, and there she met her roommate, Marianne.

JONATHAN: When I made my way up the creaking steps to the lavatory, I saw that I had apparently left the light on.

VANESSA: He fell down a staircase and broke his neck.

JONATHAN: I opened the creaking door. The water was running. The tub was about to overflow. But nobody was there.

MARIANNE: Marianne was an apothecary's daughter who loved telling herself stories in the bath.

PETRUS: Did your brother write you letters?

MARIANNE: Petrus, you wicked boy, will you close that door? You're letting in goblins.

VANESSA: Yes. As a matter of fact, I believe he did. When I lived in Providence. I went to school there. At Brown. I went to Brown.

MARIANNE: At Christmas break, Vanessa brought her roommate Marianne home to Quebec to meet her brother. Marianne was a very beautiful creative writing major, and when Jonathan met her, he fell hopelessly in love with her, as nearly everybody did.

JONATHAN: The bathroom smelled like the freshly shampooed hair of Marianne.

VANESSA: I might have gone to Princeton or to Harvard, but I was fascinated by Lovecraft.° The writer. H. P. Lovecraft. Dark creatures lurking in basements. Unspeakable impossibly ancient gelatinous beings from outer space. Lovecraft lived in Providence. He prowled the streets at night, looking for God knows what. He was terribly lonely. I used to walk the streets at night and think of him.

PETRUS: He mentions a girl named Marianne in these letters.

Lovecraft: H. P. Lovecraft (1890–1937), American writer of horror, fantasy, and science fiction.

VANESSA: I knew a girl named Marianne. I brought her home for Christmas break, and my brother fell hopelessly in love with her. But she was used to it. Many people fell in love with her. She had a certain melancholy beauty. It was very annoying. The surest way to make someone not want you is to love them. Don't you find that?

MARIANNE: I used to walk by Lovecraft's house at night, in Providence. (*Sound of whippoorwills.*) He was haunted by the sound of whippoorwills.

JONATHAN: How is Marianne? I haven't seen her in so long. Does she ever speak of me? You never mention her any more in your letters.

MARIANNE: Petrus? Is that you out there on the staircase?

VANESSA: Idea for a story. A man stops at a girl's book stall by the river one morning in the rain, drawn there perhaps by the melancholy beauty of the girl. He opens one of the books and some old letters fall out. He's always been fond of the little mysterious things found in old books. He has always appreciated the romance of found objects. Query to self: What is the book? Lovecraft's *Color Out of Space*? The *Occult Notebooks* of N. J. Drago? How old are the letters? Do they smell like perfume? Sweet or citrus? His name is Petrus Van Hoek. He's an artist.

MARIANNE: After her return to Providence, Jonathan wrote Marianne hundreds of love letters, passionate, desperately tender, beautiful letters. But Marianne never wrote back.

VANESSA: Is there perhaps a photograph in among the letters? A photograph of a girl?

JONATHAN: Dearest Marianne. I am writing to tell you that I've fallen desperately and hopelessly in love with you. It would perhaps be more prudent to pretend this was not the case, but I feel so strongly that all deception in my relations to you are repugnant to me.

MARIANNE: I love a strange city where I do not speak the language. I prefer it that way.

PETRUS: There is a photograph in this letter. Of a very pretty girl.

VANESSA: Does she have a melancholy beauty?

PETRUS: She looks rather familiar.

VANESSA: Yes. That's good. A girl who looks oddly familiar. He's overcome by the eerie sensation that he's known her before, in another life, perhaps. On the back of the photograph it says "From Marianne, With Love."

PETRUS: It does say that, actually.

VANESSA: Of course it does. Does the man who buys the book fall in love with the girl in the photograph?

PETRUS: I don't know. Does he?

MARIANNE: Everybody falls in love with me.

JONATHAN: I wonder if somehow my letters to you have gone astray.

VANESSA: The man is convinced he knows the girl. But he can't quite remember. Perhaps he doesn't want to remember.

MARIANNE: Petrus, is that you?

VANESSA: Perhaps it involves the memory of something terrible that happened. Something he wants to forget. Is the girl in some danger? Is there something about the letter that terrifies him? Is there a lock of hair, perhaps?

PETRUS: Vanessa, look at the photograph. Do you know this girl?

VANESSA: (*Examining the photograph.*) I'm not certain. It's so difficult to tell what's real. You know I've just got out of that place. Between the drugs I took before I went there, and all the drugs they gave me, and the shock treatments, my memory is like scrambled eggs.

MARIANNE: Oh, Vanessa, I have met the most wonderful young man. His name is Petrus Van Hoek, and he is an artist who studies the anatomy of young women. He has been studying my anatomy in great detail, and he reports that it is magnificent. He says I have a marvelous, melancholy beauty. He is presently taking photographs of me in the bath.

VANESSA: I remember a basement full of embalming bottles. And the cries of the whippoorwills.

JONATHAN: Dearest Vanessa. I have seen her. I have seen her naked in her bath.

VANESSA: There are some things I don't exactly remember, but I seem to remember having once been able to remember. Unless of course I've made them up. But are they my stories, or Marianne's stories? And are they fiction, or are they reminiscence? Madness must be like this.

MARIANNE: Petrus? Would you like to come up and wash my back?

VANESSA: I remember that she had a lover.

PETRUS: Why wouldn't she have a lover? A beautiful girl like that.

VANESSA: Yes, but up until then, you see, it had been just us two. Just Marianne and me. Many were in love with me, and everybody was in love with her, but mostly we two laughed at them. We were very happy, in our little world in Providence. We didn't want to spoil it by letting men in. Men exist to defile beauty. But then she found this artist. Or he found her. Perhaps she was modeling to put herself through school. It's very expensive, you know. But this one, for some reason, she wanted. And I was jealous.

MARIANNE: I've just met a wonderful man. His name is Petrus Van Hoek.

VANESSA: So the roommate finds her in the tub. She is forever taking long baths.

MARIANNE: Is somebody out there?

VANESSA: And the roommate confronts her.

MARIANNE: Petrus? Is that you?

VANESSA: Why do you give yourself to such a person? she says. He doesn't care about you. Not like I do. Why would you want to spoil everything by allowing this person to violate you?

JONATHAN: I don't understand why she won't answer my letters. It's driving me insane.

VANESSA: He's just a man, she says. He doesn't know how to care about you. But I love you.

MARIANNE: And I love you too, dear.

VANESSA: Says Marianne.

MARIANNE: Would you hand me the towel? I have a date with Petrus.

JONATHAN: I can't stand it any more. I must go to Providence to see her, confront her, tell her how much I love her.

VANESSA: Idea for the ending: jealous girl strangles her beloved in the bathtub.

JONATHAN: I knock and knock at the door but nobody answers. The door is unlocked. I walk into the old house. Vanessa? I say. Marianne? There is no answer. I can hear water dripping upstairs. I walk up the creaking staircase. I open the door to the bathroom. I find her lying dead in the tub. Then suddenly there is only darkness.

VANESSA: The murderess is hiding behind the door. She strikes him violently on the head with the bulldog door stop, and only later realizes that it's her brother. He is never quite right in the head after. But then, he was a man, after all. He'd never been all that bright.

JONATHAN: Lying naked there in the water. So beautiful.

VANESSA: Then she begins receiving mysterious letters from Quebec. She knows her brother must be sending them. Sometimes there are three or four letters a day, all about Marianne. She can't take it any more. Finally she goes back to Quebec to convince him to stop writing her these letters. She confronts him on the staircase.

PETRUS: What does she do?

(Sound of whippoorwills.)

VANESSA: She can hear the sound of whippoorwills.

PETRUS: What did you do?

VANESSA: They find her wandering in the streets of Quebec in the rain. Only she insists that it's not Quebec. It's Providence, she says. You may think it's Quebec, but just look in the mirror. My image in the mirror does not speak this language.

PETRUS: Vanessa, what did you do?

VANESSA: She woke up in another place. A quiet place. And every day a man came to see her. He sat with her every day and read to her. Spoke with her. He read to her from a very odd book.

JONATHAN: I go all about the house, calling her name. But nobody is there. The library is full of old books and papers. I wonder if they're my books and papers. I open an old book on the desk. It's the *Occult Notebooks* of N. J. Drago. The name written on the inside front cover is Petrus Van Hoek.

MARIANNE: Petrus? Is that you?

JONATHAN: I open the book to a random page and read: On my antiquarian trip from Oswego and Ticonderoga to Quebec, I was often confused by the cries of whippoorwills.

VANESSA: You're Petrus. You're the one who loved her.

PETRUS: Yes.

VANESSA: But why did you come to see me every day? Why have you brought me here?

PETRUS: I think you know.

VANESSA: I didn't mean to hurt her.

PETRUS: It's time for your bath now.

VANESSA: Yes. My bath.

MARIANNE: A beautiful girl, drowned in her bath.

VANESSA: I must take my bath now.

MARIANNE: Petrus? Is that you? Is somebody on the stairs?

PETRUS: I'll be up soon.

(*The light fades on them and goes out. Sound of whippoorwills in the darkness.*)

END OF PLAY

REFLECTING ON WHAT YOU'VE READ

1. In this play, the flashbacks make it challenging to follow exactly what has happened, what is happening, and why. It will help if you outline the important events in chronological order. Be ready to explain what happened to whom and why, and how the play's structure achieves the playwright's desired effects.

2. What characteristics usually associated with horror stories (starting with setting) do you find in the play?

3. It is important to pay especially close attention to Petrus and Vanessa, to the way their character traits are revealed through the whole play. Does your view of them change as the play progresses? By the conclusion, what is each like? How does the way they are characterized fit the horror-story genre?

4. Don Nigro seems to have made up N. J. Drago, but H. P. Lovecraft was an actual person — a writer of horror stories — who lived in Providence for much of his life. Stephen King called him "the twentieth century's greatest practitioner of the classic horror tale." Check the Internet for information about him. Then think about how Nigro makes Lovecraft part of the story and what impact his presence has. Consider, too, what particular ways Lovecraft's works may have influenced the play.

RESPONDING THROUGH WRITING

WRITING ABOUT SETTING AND STRUCTURE

Journal Entries

1. Write a journal entry listing how the structuring of Susan Glaspell's *Trifles* (p. 693) both corresponds to and doesn't correspond to a popular TV detective drama.

2. In your journal, write a list of stage movements in Susan Glaspell's *Trifles* (p. 693), both those noted in the stage directions and those suggested by the text, and comment on their significance. Note especially what is indicated by the way that characters are positioned in relation to one another.

3. Write a journal entry listing various uses of irony in Susan Glaspell's *Trifles* (p. 693) and commenting on their importance to the effect and meaning of the play.

Literary Analysis Papers

4. Write a paper analyzing the means of characterization in Susan Glaspell's *Trifles* (p. 693) and the relation of characters to the play's theme. Include the two key characters who do not appear on the stage, Mr. and Mrs. Wright.

5. Write a paper analyzing the unity of structure and theme in Susan Glaspell's *Trifles* (p. 693) or Suzanne Bradbeer's *Okoboji* (p. 822).

6. Write a paper examining the dramatic structure of Don Nigro's *Letters from Quebec to Providence in the Rain* (p. 709) and its contribution to the effect of the play.

Comparison-Contrast Papers

7. Compare and contrast the birdcage in Susan Glaspell's *Trifles* (p. 693) and the doll house in Henrik Ibsen's *A Doll's House* (p. 996) as feminist metaphors.

8. Compare and contrast Susan Glaspell's *Trifles* (p. 693) to a contemporary TV detective program, focusing on generic conventions they have in common and conventions they do not share.

WRITING ABOUT CONNECTIONS

Setting and structure invariably offer opportunities for you to work with connections within a play. When you attend to the setting, pay special attention to how any action connects to its location in a meaningful way and notice how the structure arranges the various parts of a play, interconnecting them in an orderly and illuminating fashion. Equally interesting is the examination of thematic connections between different plays that have implications regarding setting and structure. Here are a few examples:

1. "By a Higher Standard": The Conflict of Law and Justice in Susan Glaspell's *Trifles* (p. 693) and William Shakespeare's *Hamlet* (p. 881)

TIPS for Writing about Setting and Structure

- **Specific settings.** Even though the importance of setting in drama varies depending on the play, it often has a key role. For the location of the action to be described in specific detail usually indicates that it will be influential, affecting characterization, tone, assumptions about social and cultural attitudes, and themes. In such cases, it should at least be referred to, even in a paper on a different topic. It might also be suitable in itself as the main focus of a paper.

- **General settings.** When setting is general or unspecified (when the action could occur anywhere at any time), it could mean that it is less significant than a specific setting. However, there are plays, such as some by Samuel Beckett, in which the abstract setting and time hold important meaning. It will be helpful and valuable to mention and explain how an unspecified setting affects or does not affect the impact of the play.

- **Arrangement.** The way a play's action is organized structurally often contributes significantly to its impact. When this is the case, analyzing that arrangement can be an insightful topic for a paper. Pay attention especially to the opening, to the means by which background information is supplied, to the way the action builds to a climax, and to how things are brought to a conclusion.

- **Crucial scenes.** Because full-length plays are difficult to cover completely in a short paper, it may be necessary to focus on key scenes in a paper on structure. Often it works best to choose scenes that are the most dramatic, in which characters and ideas are involved in crucial conflicts. In some plays, however, the crucial conflict may occur in a very subtle manner, so don't overlook what may appear at first to be a less important scene. Revealing the impact of a seemingly minor or insignificant scene can be an interesting and effective paper topic.

- **Contrast.** Analyzing contrast — the structural juxtaposition of scenes, images, and ideas, and the use of one character as a foil to another — can be one of the most interesting and effective ways to find a topic and focus a paper on drama.

2. "I'd Do It Again": Murder and Its Motivations in Susan Glaspell's *Trifles* (p. 693) and Don Nigro's *Letters from Quebec to Providence in the Rain* (p. 709)

3. "Serving Time in Invisible Prisons": Social Entrapments in Susan Glaspell's *Trifles* (p. 693) and Marco Ramirez's *I Am Not Batman* (p. 681)

WRITING RESEARCH PAPERS

1. Read the description of feminist criticism on pages 1120–22 and do additional research into feminist approaches to literature. Apply what you find in a paper analyzing Susan Glaspell's *Trifles* (p. 693) and/or Henrik Ibsen's *A Doll's House* (p. 996).

2. Do research on the appeal of detective stories (in books, on TV, in movies and plays), including Susan Glaspell's *Trifles* (p. 693), as a cultural phenomenon. What is it about our culture that makes such stories popular? Try to find out if that popularity extends to other cultures and include that in your consideration. Write a research paper on what you find.

Writing has been to me like a bath from which I have risen feeling cleaner, healthier, and freer.

Henrik Ibsen

(Norwegian Playwright; see pp. 996 and 1068)

Writing about Drama

CHAPTER **25**

Applying What You've Learned

Drama enters the ongoing conversation about literature most often through performances of plays. People attend a play and then talk about what they experienced, especially with others who saw the same production. Writing extends the conversation in the form of drama reviews in newspapers and periodicals and on the Web. This chapter, however, does not focus on writing (or talking) about drama on the stage—about the director's interpretation; how the actors played their roles; and the effect of the sets, lighting, other technical devices, and costumes. Instead it discusses how to write effectively about plays when you read them as literature (the same as our emphasis in Chapters 22–24). We concentrate not on the way a particular production handled the play but rather on the way a reader interacts with a text's presentation of action, characters, and setting. The suggestions offered in "Writing Short Papers" in Chapter 2 (pp. 37–57) apply to writing about drama, as they do to any literary paper. And much that is covered in Chapters 9 and 18 on writing about fiction and poetry carries over to writing about drama as well. This chapter adds to those chapters by offering suggestions particularly applicable if you are asked to write about plays.

We gave one of our introduction to literature classes the assignment to write a paper on an aspect of theme or dramatic technique in one of the short plays in Chapters 23 or 24. This chapter will follow one of the students, Julian Hinson, as he wrote about Kelly Stuart's *The New New* (p. 671). If you haven't read the play or don't remember it well, reading or rereading it now will make this chapter easier to follow and apply to your own work.

STEP 1. PREWRITING: FINDING A TOPIC

Looking for a topic on drama has a lot in common with looking for a topic on fiction. In both cases you usually have a story involving conflict and theme and characters whose personalities and/or actions are explored and developed. Focusing on one or more of these elements could lead you to a topic. Plays often deal with issues of general human interest, moral significance, or social or relational problems. Looking at the way the play handles these and explores the ideas connected to them could lead you to a paper topic. In a play, dialogue and dramatic action take the place of narrative. You might be able to find a topic by focusing on dramatic techniques — on how the playwright individualizes characters through differences in dialogue, for example, or how the playwright uses foreshadowing, symbolism, contrasting scenes, or juxtaposition of characters (foils) to affect an audience's response.

Here's how Julian settled on his topic:

When we were given the assignment, I decided almost at once to work on the play I liked best when we read it for class earlier, Kelly Stuart's *The New New*. I sat down right after class to reread the play. The first time I read it, a week or so ago, it was confusing, partly because of its odd title and partly because of the way it jumps back and forth between the two men and the two women. This time as I read it, I drew lines in the text each time the focus shifted from the one group to the other, and that made it easier to follow. Then I read the play aloud with another student, dividing the roles between us. That helped clarify what the lines mean because we had to concentrate on their tone and expression. After doing this, I realized that what interested me most were the moral issues brought up by the play. I decided that would be my topic.

Courtesy of Julian Hinson.

Playing Director   A topic possibility unique to drama is a paper in which you assume the role of director. In this sort of paper, you would explain how you as director interpret the play, how you want your cast to present the characters, and why. You might describe how you would stage the play — what kind of set, props, costumes, lighting, sound, and music you would use and what kind of stage movement (called blocking) and action you would want. The decisions you make and descriptions you give will clarify your reading and interpretation of the play.

If you're still searching for a topic, you might look again at the suggestions given at the end of Chapters 23 and 24 (pp. 688 and 715).

STEP 2. PREWRITING: NARROWING THE TOPIC

Just as with a short story or novel, you can't write about everything in a play. You need to narrow your focus to what is especially pertinent to or valuable for your topic. Marking "key passages" (see p. 47) works very well for plays. As you go over the passages you've marked and the notes you've written, check if they connect with each other. That could point you toward a way of limiting or narrowing the topic from the entire work to selected parts.

This is the way Julian narrowed and focused his topic:

> When I returned to the assignment the next evening, the open-endedness of the assignment led me to explore as many aspects of morality in the play as I could. After some false starts I jotted down a tentative title, "The Degeneration of Morals in *The New New*," and drafted a working thesis: "The use and abuse of language in *The New New* reflects a breakdown in contemporary moral values."

STEP 3. PREWRITING: DECIDING ON AN APPROACH

Development of your topic will proceed more easily if you identify what general approach you will take in the paper: literary analysis, comparison-contrast, social and cultural analysis, or a combination of these (see pp. 40–43).

Here's the way Julian proceeded with this step:

> After reflecting a bit on the topic and preliminary thesis I had drafted, it seemed clear to me that I was undertaking a thematic analysis of the play. So I proceeded to take further analytical steps. I returned to the play and began searching for examples of major distortions of ethics and minor misdemeanors, hoping to show that in their essence, both "little white lies" and multimillion-dollar cover-ups differ very little from each other. To write properly an analysis involving a new *new*, I figured it would be wise to struggle through the same problem Bradley and Craig did. I looked up the word *new* in a dictionary and found the following definitions: "something of recent origin" or "recently brought into being."

STEP 4. PREWRITING: FRAMING A THESIS AND PREPARING AN OUTLINE

In previous chapters on writing, we said that an effective literary paper needs to have a thesis, to argue for and suppport a central idea or claim about the play and convince readers that your position is sound or worthy of serious consideration (see pages 43–45). In writing about drama (just as with fiction), it's never enough to provide only a plot summary.

Here's how it worked out for Julian:

> I was fortunate that the preliminary thesis I wrote while narrowing my topic was idea-based and continued to be what I wanted to examine in the paper. It doesn't always work out this way for me. So I concentrated on coming up with an outline to organize the ideas I was interested in:

(continued)

The Values of Society as Seen in *The New New*
Introduction: implications of "new"

1. Connections between distortions of words and distortions in morals
2. Decline in media values during the lifetimes of generation Y
3. Music on MTV and BET are evidence of a decline in morals
4. Spin doctors make decline seem like improvement
5. Society allows success to transcend ethical concerns
6. The problem is apathy, that people no longer really care

STEP 5. WRITING: DEVELOPING AND SUPPORTING THE THESIS

After outlining the central ideas in your argument, you need to develop and support those ideas by explaining and illustrating, including quotations, and using the literary present (see pp. 46–50). This is a crucial step: Even great ideas aren't convincing unless they are well supported.

Julian returned to his paper a day or two later and here's how he worked on development and support:

I reread the play, looking for phrases that I could use in developing each of the points in my outline or that needed clarifying. Here's what I came up with:

1. redeems; neoteric; witty sardonic ethnographer; thesaurus check (searching for *synonyms*, not *meanings*)
2. Jenny's affair with a teacher; INTENSE CONNECTION
3. (I decided to drop this point [that music on MTV and BET are evidence of a decline in morals] because there isn't support for it in the play.)
4. we can't *call it* a memoir; Monster; marketing department
5. failing his class; his writing redeems him; witty sardonic ethnographer
6. the way they proceed despite what Naomi told them; never bother to check

I then began working on a rough draft, incorporating those phrases and using them to develop my ideas.

STEP 6. REVISING, PROOFREADING, AND FORMATTING

In Chapter 2 we explained the importance of careful revision and editing (proofreading) and offered suggestions for how to do them (see pp. 50–51). Here's what Julian did:

When I read my rough draft the next day, I felt the paper didn't flow in logical sequence. So I read the play again and reread what I had written and decided my points would be better integrated if I rearranged paragraphs to follow the structure of Kelly Stuart's ideas as they develop in the beginning, middle, and end of her play. I also revised the title to something that would be catchier and convey the point of the paper more clearly.

Here's my final outline:

Title: Out with the Old, in with the New: The Spin on Contemporary Values in *The New New*
Introduction: implications of "new"

1. In contemporary society, success transcends ethics
2. That's particularly evident in the entertainment industry
3. Distortions of words connect to decline in morals
4. Spin doctors make decline seem like improvement
5. The problem is apathy, that people no longer really care
   Conclusion

What initially seemed a simple play turned out to be a fairly complex and nuanced consideration of modern attitudes toward social and personal ethics. That led me to do a lot of thinking in the shower long after I had finished the paper.

 TIPS for Quoting Drama

For general advice on fitting quotations into your paragraphs and sentences, review the sections on handling quotations (p. 48) and "A Closer Look at Punctuating and Formatting Quotations" (p. 59). Much of what is said on those pages applies to quoting from a play. But quoting from a play poses some special challenges. Here are some tips on how to handle drama quotations:

- **Quote economically.** Whenever possible, make the quotations you use short and pointed. Focus on key lines, phrases, or words instead of typing out extended passages. Often a careful lead-in phrase or introductory sentence or two can clarify the context and your point, and thus reduce the need for a long quotation.

- **Quoting one speech, prose.** Handle prose passages from one speech in a play as you do quotations from any other prose. Merge quotations of four or fewer lines into your sentence; format longer passages as block quotations (see p. 59).

- **Quoting one speech, verse.** Handle passages from one speech in a play written in verse (many of Shakespeare's plays, for example) as you do quotations from poetry. Merge quotations of one to three lines into your sentence, using slashes to indicate line divisions; format passages of four lines or more as block quotations (see p. 59).

- **Quoting more than one speech.** Format passages quoting from more than one speech as block quotations. For each character, indent the first line a half inch; type the character's name in capitals, followed by a colon, and then the text of the speech; indent additional lines in the same speech another half inch (using hanging indents). For an example, see Julian's paper, page 724.

- **Citing passages from plays in verse.** For plays written in verse and divided into acts and scenes, identify passages by giving the act, scene,

(continued)

and line numbers in parentheses after the quotation. Use arabic numbers, separated by periods, even if the original uses roman numerals. This is especially helpful for older plays that have been reprinted many times. A page number isn't much help if you have a different edition from the one used in someone's paper. Thus, a citation of the famous "To be or not to be" speech in the first scene of the third act of *Hamlet* (pp. 928–29) would appear as (3.1.56–88). Include the title of the play if other plays are cited in the paper. Give the edition from which you are quoting on the Works Cited page.

- **Citing passages from plays in prose.** For plays written in prose, cite passages by page number in parentheses after the quotation. Give the edition from which you are quoting on the Works Cited page.

SAMPLE STUDENT SHORT PAPER

Hinson 1

Julian Hinson
Professor Schakel
English 105-04
1 December 2016

Out with the Old, in with the New:
The Spin on Contemporary Values in *The New New*

Authors often think of their titles last. The title, however, is the first thing that the reader sees, and it has a significant impact as the reader considers it before, during, and after finishing the work. *The New New* may seem at first a confusing title, yet it is intriguing as well. *New*, when used as an adjective, describes something unfamiliar, previously unseen, and recently brought into being. Yet when used as a noun, *New* can be seen as a socially acceptable norm, as in the phrases "Ring in the new" or "What's new?" Kelly Stuart combines both forms of the word into *Thesis sentence.*   a title and uses her short play *The New New* to show that new attitudes toward language reflect unfavorable changes in society's attitude toward morals.

Hinson 2

The play opens with lines that indicate "new" grounds for making decisions that have moral implications. Stuart opens her play with lines that once, at least, would have shocked readers:

> JENNY: I'm going to have an affair with him.
>
> MARCY: But Jenny, you're failing his class.
>
> JENNY: He says I can take an incomplete if I want, and he'll help me make it up over the summer. (899)

Marcy's reply establishes that there is something fundamentally wrong with Jenny's statement, but her reply does not follow along ethical lines. It is, instead, based on Jenny's poor performance in the class. Marcy's response assumes that were Jenny acing the class, her actions would be acceptable, a reflection on the immunity of the successful in our society. Since Jimmy, the man convicted of manslaughter and the author of the new book, is an excellent writer — "his writing redeems him" (903) — neither Craig nor Bradley nor anyone else in their company ever bothered to check the validity of his story. In the play and often in modern society, morals take a backseat to pleasure. Bradley's diction as he describes talking to Jimmy shows how immune a successful, entertaining man can be:

> I used to get these calls from prison, collect calls every Tuesday. I thought of these calls as my "Tuesdays with Jimmy." He was just this witty, sardonic ethnographer of prison life. . . . [This] civilized business executive locked up with all these illiterate thugs. . . . (901)

If Bradley had not found it "engaging" to hear about a businessman spending time in jail with petty thieves, he might have paid more attention to the fact that Jimmy survived prison, and probably managed to get his conviction reduced to manslaughter, through his ability to use "sales techniques."

The tendency to allow success to trump ethics is evident in much of the contemporary entertainment industry. One can, for

Quotation introduced formally with colon.

Builds argument with assertions and illustrations.

Quotation blended into sentence.

Block quotation with speaker identified in the text.

Transition and topic sentence.

example, attend a movie rated PG and find that previews contain distinctly R images, yet each of those previews contains the disclaimer: "The following preview is suitable for all ages." Selling a new movie is more important than being sensitive to what ratings guidelines are supposed to achieve. An evening in front of the TV offers ample evidence of a significant decline in media values, despite claims to the contrary by corporate executives. Stuart reveals the current susceptibility to "spin doctors" through Bradley and Craig's manipulation of the story of Naomi's murdered brother, Jeremy. Bradley and Craig are in the marketing department: Their job is to use words to sell a product. As Craig puts it, "Agony isn't a word that sells" (900). By changing Jeremy's name to "Monster" and placing the emphasis on Jimmy's writing, they are able to promote this "memoiristic novel" as good literature.

Transition and topic sentence.

The New New shows how the meanings of words can be severely distorted. Before the advent of this new "norm," an "INTENSE CONNECTION" (899) did not warrant sleeping with one's professor. In the same manner that the word "New" is replaced by "neoteric," Bradley views "agonizing" in the same light as "entertaining." Marcy's attachment to Jimmy grows to "fondness" without her knowledge of the truth of why this seemingly "juxtaposed" man is actually in prison. Throughout the play, Stuart attempts to show the reader that, both for characters in her play and for much of society, words as a whole have lost their significance. Craig consults a thesaurus, looking for synonyms, not a dictionary, looking for meanings. Words carry no consequence and, without consequence, there can be no accountability, much less responsibility. This explains how something as small as a "thesaurus check" can acquit a killer of his crime. Had Bradley used the word "bitter" instead of "witty [and] sardonic," the book would have been viewed in a distinctly different light.

Transition and topic sentence.

The end of the play shows the result of neglecting what words actually mean. Naomi's note provides a benchmark for how far the wordsmiths Bradley and Craig have traveled in arriving at their distorted tale:

Hinson 4

> My brother's name was Jeremy. Not Monster. He was five
> foot three, one hundred thirty pounds. Not six foot two,
> three hundred fifty. My brother was tortured and strangled
> over the course of a two-hour, period. The shape of a
> turtle and a steer were imprinted on my brother's neck,
> from the cowboy belt your so-called "author" used. My
> brother's face was badly beaten, bones protruded from his
> bloody face. My brother was a medical assistant. He was a
> human being, not a monster. (903)

Despite this evidence to the contrary of everything Bradley and
Craig have sought to prove about Jimmy, they continue to justify
their choice of author and remove his crime from the "real" story
in their book. As Craig puts it, "I still think, um. The SPIRIT of
the — I mean, he was true to the SPIRIT of, the book's not about
the crime in any case . . ." (903).

Society is often willing to overlook an egregious fault in *Transition.*
something as long as it works toward a desired end. When confronted, people are willing to justify the perpetrator on the basis
of another "good" trait that works in her or his favor: "Being
convicted of manslaughter had nothing to do with the arc of
his life. It was just, this aberration" (902). The story has
traveled so far from its original truth that a movie has been
optioned for Ben Stiller, a comedy actor, and Marcy assumes
that a "love" of Ben Stiller provides a basis for Jenny to love
Jimmy.

Stuart is not trying to depict the two men as evil or say
that they are selfish enough to deliberately seek profit from an- *Topic sentence.*
other man's death. Instead, she shows that the problem in society
is apathy: People don't care about words being emptied of meaning or about the results of doing so. Despite Naomi's plea — "To
see this man profit, it's killing me and I wonder if you ever gave
that a thought?" (903) — the two men are content to ignore the
truth of the story because they "really like Jimmy" (903). Bradley
continues to play matchmaker, placing his "girlfriend's sister" at
risk because he thinks Jimmy is a good man, and Craig attributes
Naomi's emotions to mere blood relation: " . . . [S]he's the victim's
sister. That's all. What do you expect?" (903).

Conclusion.   At the end of the play, one can assume that Stuart gets the words of her title from Bradley and Craig's dilemma, but in spirit, her choice of a title slowly reveals and labels a problem embedded in contemporary society, the acceptance of a new new and a wrong norm.

The plays ultimately are about love, honor, duty, betrayal—what I call the Big Themes.

August Wilson

August Wilson's Fences — A Casebook

Wrestling with One Writer's Work

August Wilson was born Frederick August Kittel on April 27, 1945, the son of Daisy Wilson, an African American cleaning woman, and Frederick August Kittel, a German immigrant baker who lived with the family only intermittently. His early years were spent in the Hill district, a black neighborhood of Pittsburgh. When his mother married David Bedford, a black ex-convict and former high school football star, the family moved to the largely white community of Hazelwood, Pennsylvania, and later back to the Hill. Wilson's brothers kept their father's name, but Wilson decided, in 1965, to adopt his mother's maiden name, thus signaling his loyalty to his African American heritage.

He dropped out of Gladstone High School in 1960, after a ninth-grade teacher, believing Wilson could not have written or done the research for a twenty-page paper on Napoleon Bonaparte, accused him of plagiarism. From that point, he educated himself by reading his way through the section of black authors in the local library, discovering writers such as James Baldwin, Richard Wright, Langston Hughes, and Ralph Ellison. Reading works by black authors convinced him to be a writer himself, and he prepared by reading voraciously in fiction, poetry, and drama. He wrote and published some poetry but soon found himself drawn to the theater. In 1968, he cofounded a theater company in Pittsburgh, Black Horizons on the Hill, through which he hoped to raise consciousness and politicize the community, and began writing one-act plays.

August Wilson performing his solo show How I Learned What I Learned *at the U.S. Comedy Arts Festival in March 2004 in Aspen, Colorado.*
AP Photo/E. Pablo Kosmicki

He moved to St. Paul, Minnesota, in 1978, taking with him a satirical play, *Black Bart and the Sacred Hills*, adapted from his poems. He found a job writing for the Science Museum of Minnesota and in 1980 became involved with the Minneapolis Playwrights Center. He regarded *Jitney*, written in 1979, as his first real play. He submitted it and three other early plays, unsuccessfully, to the Eugene O'Neill Theater Center's National Playwrights Conference in Waterford, Connecticut. Finally, in 1982, *Ma Rainey's Black Bottom* was accepted. At the O'Neill, Wilson impressed Lloyd Richards, director of the O'Neill Workshop and artistic director of the Yale Drama School. Richards taught Wilson stagecraft and helped him learn to revise his work and went on to direct Wilson's first six plays from workshops through Broadway productions.

Ma Rainey (premiered in 1984) was followed by *Fences* (1985) and *Joe Turner's Come and Gone* (1986). All three won the prestigious New York Drama Critics Circle Award (he eventually won a total of seven). In addition he won a Tony award, three American Theatre Critics awards, and two Pulitzer Prizes for Drama, first for *Fences* and later for *The Piano Lesson* (1989). These works became part of a cycle of ten plays Wilson undertook, chronicling the experience of African Americans in the United States, one play for each decade of the twentieth century:

1900s — *Gem of the Ocean* (2003)

1910s — *Joe Turner's Come and Gone* (1984)

1920s — *Ma Rainey's Black Bottom* (1982)

1930s — *The Piano Lesson* (1989)

1940s — *Seven Guitars* (1995)

1950s — *Fences* (1985)

1960s — *Two Trains Running* (1990)

James Earl Jones as Troy
Maxson in the 1987
Broadway production
of Fences.
Photofest, Inc.

1970s — *Jitney* (1982)
1980s — *King Hedley II* (2001)
1990s — *Radio Golf* (2005)

The series is designed to inform later generations about the hardships and indignities earlier generations experienced but did not talk about to their children. All the plays are set in Pittsburgh except *Ma Rainey's Black Bottom*, which is set in Chicago.

The final play in the cycle, *Radio Golf*, premiered in March 2005 at the Yale Repertory Theatre. Two months later Wilson was diagnosed with inoperable liver cancer. He died on 2 October 2005. Soon after his death, the Virginia Theatre in New York was renamed the August Wilson Theatre. This is the first Broadway theater to be named for an African American and is a tribute to his stature as one of the seminal figures in twentieth-century American drama.

The material in this chapter can be used in three ways for writing assignments. The first is to write a paper on *Fences* without reading the

Lynn Thigpen and James Earl Jones in the 1987 Broadway production of Fences.
Photofest, Inc.

secondary materials (the reviews, interviews, and critical essays) in the chapter. You would treat the play as if it were included in the "Collection of Plays," and your paper would not draw on outside sources. If you choose this option, remember that, if you do read any secondary materials, even parts of them, you must acknowledge it by including them in a bibliography, even if you don't quote from or refer to them.

In a second way of using this chapter, your instructor might ask you to write a paper on *Fences* using only sources included in the chapter. That gives you practice working with and incorporating ideas from secondary sources, selecting passages to quote and blending quotations into your writing, and constructing a Works Cited page. But it isn't a full research paper because you aren't responsible for finding material to use in the paper. Reasons an instructor might select this way of working are that it doesn't require as much time to complete as a full-blown research project does, and you and your instructor will be working with material you are both familiar with. For such a paper, you should review the guidelines for handling quotations on pages 59–60, and you should read "Appendix on Reading Critical Essays" (pp. 1095–1107) and the sections on punctuating quotations (pp. 59-60), writing a research paper (pp. 73-75), incorporating sources (pp. 75-77), avoiding plagiarism (pp. 86-88), and documenting sources (pp. 78-79 and 89-102). We have included original publication information and pages numbers for the works in this chapter; these can be used as if you had access to the actual books and periodicals.

A third way to use this chapter is as a starting point for an actual research paper. That is, after reading *Fences* and the secondary materials in this chapter, you would begin searching additional sources, such as more interviews with Wilson and additional plays or essays written by him, and use additional biographical or critical works about his thoughts and works. For such a project, in addition to reviewing the guidelines for handling quotations on pages 59-60 and reading the "Appendix on Reading Critical Essays" (pp. 1095-1107), you should read or review all of Chapter 3, "Writing a Literary Research Paper" (pp. 61-102).

August Wilson   1945–2005

Fences°   [1985]

When the sins of our fathers visit us
We do not have to play host.
We can banish them with forgiveness
As God, in His Largeness and Laws.
                          — *August Wilson* [p. x]°

CHARACTERS

TROY MAXSON   GABRIEL, Troy's brother
JIM BONO, Troy's friend   CORY, Troy and Rose's son
ROSE, Troy's wife   RAYNELL, Troy's daughter [p. xiii]
LYONS, Troy's oldest son by
   previous marriage

SETTING

The setting is the yard which fronts the only entrance to the Maxson household, an ancient two-story brick house set back off a small alley in a big-city neighborhood. The entrance to the house is gained by two or three steps leading to a wooden porch badly in need of paint.

A relatively recent addition to the house and running its full width, the porch lacks congruence. It is a sturdy porch with a flat roof. One or two chairs of dubious value sit at one end where the kitchen window opens onto the porch. An old-fashioned icebox stands silent guard at the opposite end.

Wilson, August. *Fences: A Play.* New American Library, 1986. (Page citations in square brackets refer to the original publication.)

The yard is a small dirt yard, partially fenced, except for the last scene, with a wooden sawhorse, a pile of lumber, and other fence-building equipment set off to the side. Opposite is a tree from which hangs a ball made of rags. A base-ball bat leans against the tree. Two oil drums serve as garbage receptacles and sit near the house at right to complete the setting. [p. xv]

THE PLAY

Near the turn of the century, the destitute of Europe sprang on the city with tenacious claws and an honest and solid dream. The city devoured them. They swelled its belly until it burst into a thousand furnaces and sewing machines, a thousand butcher shops and bakers' ovens, a thousand churches and hospitals and funeral parlors and money-lenders. The city grew. It nourished itself and offered each man a partnership limited only by his talent, his guile, and his willingness and capacity for hard work. For the immigrants of Europe, a dream dared and won true.

The descendants of African slaves were offered no such welcome or participation. They came from places called the Carolinas and the Virginias, Georgia, Alabama, Mississippi, and Tennessee. They came strong, eager, searching. The city rejected them and they fled and settled along the riverbanks and under bridges in shallow, ramshackle houses made of sticks and tar-paper. They collected rags and wood. They sold the use of their muscles and their bodies. They cleaned houses and washed clothes, they shined shoes, and in quiet desperation and vengeful pride, they stole, and lived in pursuit of their own dream. That they could breathe free, finally, and stand to meet life with the force of dignity and whatever eloquence the heart could call upon.

By 1957, the hard-won victories of the European immigrants had solidified the industrial might of America. War had been confronted and won with new energies that used loyalty and patriotism as its fuel. Life was rich, full, and flourishing. The Milwaukee Braves won the World Series, and the hot winds of change that would make the sixties a turbulent, racing, dangerous, and provocative decade had not yet begun to blow full. [p. xvii]

ACT ONE / Scene One

It is 1957. Troy and Bono enter the yard, engaged in conversation. Troy is fifty-three years old, a large man with thick, heavy hands; it is this largeness that he strives to fill out and make an accommodation with. Together with his blackness, his largeness informs his sensibilities and the choices he has made in his life.

Of the two men, Bono is obviously the follower. His commitment to their friendship of thirty-odd years is rooted in his admiration of Troy's honesty, capacity for hard work, and his strength, which Bono seeks to emulate.

It is Friday night, payday, and the one night of the week the two men engage in a ritual of talk and drink. Troy is usually the most talkative and at times he can be crude and almost vulgar, though he is capable of rising to profound heights of expression. The men carry lunch buckets and wear or carry burlap aprons and are dressed in clothes suitable to their jobs as garbage collectors.

BONO: Troy, you ought to stop that lying!

TROY: I ain't lying! The nigger had a watermelon this big.

(*He indicates with his hands.*)

Talking about . . . "What watermelon, Mr. Rand?" I liked to fell out! "What watermelon, Mr. Rand?" . . . And it sitting there big as life.

BONO: What did Mr. Rand say? [p. 3]

TROY: Ain't said nothing. Figure if the nigger too dumb to know he carrying a watermelon, he wasn't gonna get much sense out of him. Trying to hide that great big old watermelon under his coat. Afraid to let the white man see him carry it home.

BONO: I'm like you . . . I ain't got no time for them kind of people.

TROY: Now what he look like getting mad cause he see the man from the union talking to Mr. Rand?

BONO: He come to me talking about . . . "Maxson gonna get us fired." I told him to get away from me with that. He walked away from me calling you a troublemaker. What Mr. Rand say?

TROY: Ain't said nothing. He told me to go down the Commissioner's office next Friday. They called me down there to see them.

BONO: Well, as long as you got your complaint filed, they can't fire you. That's what one of them white fellows tell me.

TROY: I ain't worried about them firing me. They gonna fire me cause I asked a question? That's all I did. I went to Mr. Rand and asked him, "Why? Why you got the white mens driving and the colored lifting?" Told him, "what's the matter, don't I count? You think only white fellows got sense enough to drive a truck. That ain't no paper job! Hell, anybody can drive a truck. How come you got all whites driving and the colored lifting?" He told me "take it to the union." Well, hell, that's what I done! Now they wanna come up with this pack of lies.

BONO: I told Brownie if the man come and ask him any questions . . . just tell the truth! It ain't nothing but [p. 4] something they done trumped up on you cause you filed a complaint on them.

TROY: Brownie don't understand nothing. All I want them to do is change the job description. Give everybody a chance to drive the truck. Brownie can't see that. He ain't got that much sense.

BONO: How you figure he be making out with that gal be up at Taylors' all the time . . . that Alberta gal?

TROY: Same as you and me. Getting just as much as we is. Which is to say nothing.

BONO: It is, huh? I figure you doing a little better than me . . . and I ain't saying what I'm doing.

TROY: Aw, nigger, look here . . . I know you. If you had got anywhere near that gal, twenty minutes later you be looking to tell somebody. And the first one you gonna tell . . . that you gonna want to brag to . . . is gonna be me.

BONO: I ain't saying that. I see where you be eyeing her.

TROY: I eye all the women. I don't miss nothing. Don't never let nobody tell you Troy Maxson don't eye the women.

BONO: You been doing more than eyeing her. You done bought her a drink or two.

TROY: Hell yeah, I bought her a drink! What that mean? I bought you one, too. What that mean cause I buy her a drink? I'm just being polite.

BONO: It's alright to buy her one drink. That's what you call being polite. But when you wanna be buying two or three . . . that's what you call eyeing her [p. 5].

TROY: Look here, as long as you known me . . . you ever known me to chase after women?

BONO: Hell yeah! Long as I done known you. You forgetting I knew you when.

TROY: Naw, I'm talking about since I been married to Rose?

BONO: Oh, not since you been married to Rose. Now, that's the truth, there. I can say that.

TROY: Alright then! Case closed.

BONO: I see you be walking up around Alberta's house. You supposed to be at Taylors' and you be walking up around there.

TROY: What you watching where I'm walking for? I ain't watching after you.

BONO: I seen you walking around there more than once.

TROY: Hell, you liable to see me walking anywhere! That don't mean nothing cause you see me walking around there.

BONO: Where she come from anyway? She just kinda showed up one day.

TROY: Tallahassee. You can look at her and tell she one of them Florida gals. They got some big healthy women down there. Grow them right up out the ground. Got a little bit of Indian in her. Most of them niggers down in Florida got some Indian in them.

BONO: I don't know about that Indian part. But she damn sure big and healthy. Woman wear some big stockings. [p. 6] Got them great big old legs and hips as wide as the Mississippi River.

TROY: Legs don't mean nothing. You don't do nothing but push them out of the way. But them hips cushion the ride!

BONO: Troy, you ain't got no sense.

TROY: It's the truth! Like you riding on Goodyears!

(*Rose enters from the house. She is ten years younger than Troy, her devotion to him stems from her recognition of the possibilities of her life without him: a succession of abusive men and their babies, a life of partying and running the streets, the Church, or aloneness with its attendant pain and frustration. She recognizes Troy's spirit as a fine and illuminating one and she either ignores or forgives his faults, only some of which she recognizes. Though she doesn't drink, her presence is an integral part of the Friday night rituals. She alternates between the porch and the kitchen, where supper preparations are under way.)*

ROSE: What you all out here getting into?

TROY: What you worried about what we getting into for? This is men talk, woman.

ROSE: What I care what you all talking about? Bono, you gonna stay for supper?

BONO: No, I thank you, Rose. But Lucille say she cooking up a pot of pigfeet.

TROY: Pigfeet! Hell, I'm going home with you! Might even stay the night if you got some pigfeet. You got something in there to top them pigfeet, Rose? [p. 7]

ROSE: I'm cooking up some chicken. I got some chicken and collard greens.

TROY: Well, go on back in the house and let me and Bono finish what we was talking about. This is men talk. I got some talk for you later. You know what kind of talk I mean. You go on and powder it up.

ROSE: Troy Maxson, don't you start that now!

TROY (*puts his arm around her*): Aw, woman . . . come here. Look here, Bono . . . when I met this woman . . . I got out that place, say, "Hitch up my pony, saddle up my mare . . . there's a woman out there for me somewhere. I looked here. Looked there. Saw Rose and latched on to her." I latched on to her and told her—I'm gonna tell you the truth—I told her, "Baby, I don't wanna marry, I just wanna be your man." Rose told me . . . tell him what you told me, Rose.

ROSE: I told him if he wasn't the marrying kind, then move out the way so the marrying kind could find me.

TROY: That's what she told me. "Nigger, you in my way. You blocking the view! Move out the way so I can find me a husband." I thought it over two or three days. Come back —

ROSE: Ain't no two or three days nothing. You was back the same night.

TROY: Come back, told her . . . "Okay, baby . . . but I'm gonna buy me a banty rooster and put him out there in the backyard . . . and when he see a stranger come, he'll flap his wings and crow . . ." Look here, Bono, I could watch the front door by myself . . . it was that back door I was worried about. [p. 8]

ROSE: Troy, you ought not talk like that. Troy ain't doing nothing but telling a lie.

TROY: Only thing is . . . when we first got married . . . forget the rooster . . . we ain't had no yard!

BONO: I hear you tell it. Me and Lucille was staying down there on Logan Street. Had two rooms with the outhouse in the back. I ain't mind the outhouse none. But when that goddamn wind blow through there in the winter . . . that's what I'm talking about! To this day I wonder why in the hell I ever stayed down there for six long years. But see, I didn't know I could do no better. I thought only white folks had inside toilets and things.

ROSE: There's a lot of people don't know they can do no better than they doing now. That's just something you got to learn. A lot of folks still shop at Bella's.

TROY: Ain't nothing wrong with shopping at Bella's. She got fresh food.

ROSE: I ain't said nothing about if she got fresh food. I'm talking about what she charge. She charge ten cents more than the A&P.°

TROY: The A&P ain't never done nothing for me. I spends my money where I'm treated right. I go down to Bella, say, "I need a loaf of bread, I'll pay you Friday." She give it to me. What sense that make when I got money to go and spend it somewhere else and ignore the person who done right by me? That ain't in the Bible.

ROSE: We ain't talking about what's in the Bible. What sense it make to shop there when she overcharge?

TROY: You shop where you want to. I'll do my shopping where the people been good to me. [p. 9]

ROSE: Well, I don't think it's right for her to overcharge. That's all I was saying.

BONO: Look here . . . I got to get on. Lucille going be raising all kind of hell.

TROY: Where you going, nigger? We ain't finished this pint. Come here, finish this pint.

BONO: Well, hell, I am . . . if you ever turn the bottle loose.

TROY (*hands him the bottle*): The only thing I say about the A&P is I'm glad Cory got that job down there. Help him take care of his school clothes and things. Gabe done moved out and things getting tight around here. He got that job. . . . He can start to look out for himself.

ROSE: Cory done went and got recruited by a college football team.

TROY: I told that boy about that football stuff. The white man ain't gonna let him get nowhere with that football. I told him when he first come to me with it. Now you come telling me he done went and got more tied up in it. He ought to go and get recruited in how to fix cars or something where he can make a living.

ROSE: He ain't talking about making no living playing football. It's just something the boys in school do. They gonna send a recruiter by to talk to you. He'll tell you he ain't talking about making no living playing football. It's a honor to be recruited.

TROY: It ain't gonna get him nowhere. Bono'll tell you that.

BONO: If he be like you in the sports . . . he's gonna be alright. Ain't but two men ever played baseball as good as [p. 10] you. That's Babe Ruth and Josh Gibson.° Them's the only two men ever hit more home runs than you.

A&P: Chain of grocery stores operated by the Great Atlantic and Pacific Tea Company. **Babe Ruth and Josh Gibson:** George Herman Ruth (1895–1948) was a pitcher and then an outfielder for the Boston Red Sox (1914–1919), New York Yankees (1920–1934), and Boston Braves (1935). His sixty home runs in the 1927 season set a major league record that stood until 1961. Joshua Gibson (1911–1947), the greatest power hitter in the Negro Leagues and often referred to as the black Babe Ruth, was credited with having hit eighty-four home runs in a single season. In 1972 he was elected to the Baseball Hall of Fame, the second Negro League player (after Satchel Paige) to be so honored.

TROY: What it ever get me? Ain't got a pot to piss in or a window to throw it out of.

ROSE: Times have changed since you was playing baseball, Troy. That was before the war. Times have changed a lot since then.

TROY: How in hell they done changed?

ROSE: They got lots of colored boys playing ball now. Baseball and football.

BONO: You right about that, Rose. Times have changed, Troy. You just come along too early.

TROY: There ought not never have been no time called too early! Now you take that fellow . . . what's that fellow they had playing right field for the Yankees back then? You know who I'm talking about, Bono. Used to play right field for the Yankees.

ROSE: Selkirk?°

TROY: Selkirk! That's it! Man batting .269, understand? .269. What kind of sense that make? I was hitting .432 with thirty-seven home runs! Man batting .269 and playing right field for the Yankees! I saw Josh Gibson's daughter yesterday. She walking around with raggedy shoes on her feet. Now I bet you Selkirk's daughter ain't walking around with raggedy shoes on her feet! I bet you that!

ROSE: They got a lot of colored baseball players now. Jackie Robinson° was the first. Folks had to wait for Jackie Robinson. [p. 11]

TROY: I done seen a hundred niggers play baseball better than Jackie Robinson. Hell, I know some teams Jackie Robinson couldn't even make! What you talking about Jackie Robinson. Jackie Robinson wasn't nobody. I'm talking about if you could play ball then they ought to have let you play. Don't care what color you were. Come telling me I come along too early. If you could play . . . then they ought to have let you play.

(*Troy takes a long drink from the bottle.*)

ROSE: You gonna drink yourself to death. You don't need to be drinking like that.

TROY: Death ain't nothing. I done seen him. Done wrassled with him. You can't tell me nothing about death. Death ain't nothing but a fastball on the outside corner. And you know what I'll do to that! Lookee here, Bono . . . am I lying? You get one of them fastballs, about waist high, over the outside corner of the plate where you can get the meat of the bat on it . . . and good god! You can kiss it goodbye. Now, am I lying?

Selkirk: George Selkirk (1934–1987), successor to Babe Ruth in right field for the Yankees. In nine seasons (1934–1942) he had a cumulative batting average of .290 with 108 home runs. In 1940 his average was .269 with 19 home runs. **Jackie Robinson:** Jack Roosevelt Robinson (1919–1972), first and second baseman for the Brooklyn Dodgers from 1947 to 1956, was the first African American to play in the major leagues.

BONO: Naw, you telling the truth there. I seen you do it.

TROY: If I'm lying . . . that 450 feet worth of lying!

(*Pause.*)

That's all death is to me. A fastball on the outside corner.

ROSE: I don't know why you want to get on talking about death.

TROY: Ain't nothing wrong with talking about death. That's part of life. Everybody gonna die. You gonna die, I'm gonna die. Bono's gonna die. Hell, we all gonna die.

ROSE: But you ain't got to talk about it. I don't like to talk about it. [p. 12]

TROY: You the one brought it up. Me and Bono was talking about baseball . . . you tell me I'm gonna drink myself to death. Ain't that right, Bono? You know I don't drink this but one night out of the week. That's Friday night. I'm gonna drink just enough to where I can handle it. Then I cuts it loose. I leave it alone. So don't you worry about me drinking myself to death. 'Cause I ain't worried about Death. I done seen him. I done wrestled with him.

　　Look here, Bono . . . I looked up one day and Death was marching straight at me. Like Soldiers on Parade! The Army of Death was marching straight at me. The middle of July, 1941. It got real cold just like it be winter. It seem like Death himself reached out and touched me on the shoulder. He touch me just like I touch you. I got cold as ice and Death standing there grinning at me.

ROSE: Troy, why don't you hush that talk.

TROY: I say . . . What you want, Mr. Death? You be wanting me? You done brought your army to be getting me? I looked him dead in the eye. I wasn't fearing nothing. I was ready to tangle. Just like I'm ready to tangle now. The Bible say be ever vigilant. That's why I don't get but so drunk. I got to keep watch.

ROSE: Troy was right down there in Mercy Hospital. You remember he had pneumonia? Laying there with a fever talking plumb out of his head.

TROY: Death standing there staring at me . . . carrying that sickle in his hand. Finally he say, "You want bound over for another year?" See, just like that . . . "You want bound over for another year?" I told him, "Bound over hell! Let's settle this now!"

　　It seem like he kinda fell back when I said that, and all the cold went out of me. I reached down and grabbed that sickle and threw it just as far as I could throw it . . . and me and him commenced to wrestling. [p. 13]

　　We wrestled for three days and three nights. I can't say where I found the strength from. Every time it seemed like he was gonna get the best of me, I'd reach way down deep inside myself and find the strength to do him one better.

ROSE: Every time Troy tell that story he find different ways to tell it. Different things to make up about it.

TROY: I ain't making up nothing. I'm telling you the facts of what happened. I wrestled with Death for three days and three nights and I'm standing here to tell you about it.

(*Pause.*)

Alright. At the end of the third night we done weakened each other to where we can't hardly move. Death stood up, throwed on his robe . . . had him a white robe with a hood on it. He threwed on that robe and went off to look for his sickle. Say, "I'll be back." Just like that. "I'll be back." I told him, say, "Yeah, but . . . you gonna have to find me!" I wasn't no fool. I wasn't going looking for him. Death ain't nothing to play with. And I know he's gonna get me. I know I got to join his army . . . his camp followers. But as long as I keep my strength and see him coming . . . as long as I keep up my vigilance . . . he's gonna have to fight to get me. I ain't going easy.

BONO: Well, look here, since you got to keep up your vigilance . . . let me have the bottle.

TROY: Aw hell, I shouldn't have told you that part. I should have left out that part.

ROSE: Troy be talking that stuff and half the time don't even know what he be talking about.

TROY: Bono know me better than that. [p. 14]

BONO: That's right. I know you. I know you got some Uncle Remus° in your blood. You got more stories than the devil got sinners.

TROY: Aw hell, I done seen him too! Done talked with the devil.

ROSE: Troy, don't nobody wanna be hearing all that stuff.

(*Lyons enters the yard from the street. Thirty-four years old, Troy's son by a previous marriage, he sports a neatly trimmed goatee, sport coat, white shirt, tieless and buttoned at the collar. Though he fancies himself a musician, he is more caught up in the rituals and "idea" of being a musician than in the actual practice of the music. He has come to borrow money from Troy, and while he knows he will be successful, he is uncertain as to what extent his lifestyle will be held up to scrutiny and ridicule.*)

LYONS: Hey, Pop.

TROY: What you come "Hey, Popping" me for?

LYONS: How you doing, Rose?

(*He kisses her.*)

Mr. Bono. How you doing?

BONO: Hey, Lyons . . . how you been?

TROY: He must have been doing alright. I ain't seen him around here last week.

Uncle Remus: The fictional title character and narrator of a collection of African American folktales compiled by author Joel Chandler Harris and first published in 1881.

ROSE: Troy, leave your boy alone. He come by to see you and you wanna start all that nonsense.

TROY: I ain't bothering Lyons.

(*Offers him the bottle.*)

Here . . . get you a drink. We got an understanding. I know why he come by to see me and he know I know. [p. 15]

LYONS: Come on, Pop . . . I just stopped by to say hi . . . see how you was doing.

TROY: You ain't stopped by yesterday.

ROSE: You gonna stay for supper, Lyons? I got some chicken cooking in the oven.

LYONS: No, Rose . . . thanks. I was just in the neighborhood and thought I'd stop by for a minute.

TROY: You was in the neighborhood alright, nigger. You telling the truth there. You was in the neighborhood cause it's my payday.

LYONS: Well, hell, since you mentioned it . . . let me have ten dollars.

TROY: I'll be damned! I'll die and go to hell and play blackjack with the devil before I give you ten dollars.

BONO: That's what I wanna know about . . . that devil you done seen.

LYONS: What . . . Pop done seen the devil? You too much, Pops.

TROY: Yeah, I done seen him. Talked to him too!

ROSE: You ain't seen no devil. I done told you that man ain't had nothing to do with the devil. Anything you can't understand, you want to call it the devil.

TROY: Look here, Bono . . . I went down to see Hertzberger about some furniture. Got three rooms for two-ninety-eight. That what it say on the radio. "Three rooms . . . two-ninety-eight." Even made up a little song about it. Go down there . . . man tell me I can't get no [p. 16] credit. I'm working every day and can't get no credit. What to do? I got an empty house with some raggedy furniture in it. Cory ain't got no bed. He's sleeping on a pile of rags on the floor. Working every day and can't get no credit. Come back here—Rose'll tell you—madder than hell. Sit down . . . try to figure what I'm gonna do. Come a knock on the door. Ain't been living here but three days. Who know I'm here? Open the door . . . devil standing there bigger than life. White fellow . . . got on good clothes and everything. Standing there with a clipboard in his hand. I ain't had to say nothing. First words come out of his mouth was . . . "I understand you need some furniture and can't get no credit." I liked to fell over. He say, "I'll give you all the credit you want, but you got to pay the interest on it." I told him, "Give me three rooms worth and charge whatever you want." Next day a truck pulled up here and two men unloaded them three rooms. Man what drove the truck give me a book. Say send ten dollars, first of every month to the address in the book and everything will be alright. Say if I miss a payment the devil was coming back and it'll be hell to pay. That was fifteen years ago. To this day . . . the first of the month I send my ten dollars, Rose'll tell you.

ROSE: Troy lying.

TROY: I ain't never seen that man since. Now you tell me who else that could have been but the devil? I ain't sold my soul or nothing like that, you understand. Naw, I wouldn't have truck with the devil about nothing like that. I got my furniture and pays my ten dollars the first of the month just like clockwork.

BONO: How long you say you been paying this ten dollars a month?

TROY: Fifteen years! [p. 17]

BONO: Hell, ain't you finished paying for it yet? How much the man done charged you?

TROY: Aw hell, I done paid for it. I done paid for it ten times over! The fact is I'm scared to stop paying it.

ROSE: Troy lying. We got that furniture from Mr. Glickman. He ain't paying no ten dollars a month to nobody.

TROY: Aw hell, woman. Bono know I ain't that big a fool.

LYONS: I was just getting ready to say . . . I know where there's a bridge for sale.

TROY: Look here, I'll tell you this . . . it don't matter to me if he was the devil. It don't matter if the devil give credit. Somebody has got to give it.

ROSE: It ought to matter. You going around talking about having truck with the devil . . . God's the one you gonna have to answer to. He's the one gonna be at the Judgment.

LYONS: Yeah, well, look here, Pop . . . let me have that ten dollars. I'll give it back to you. Bonnie got a job working at the hospital.

TROY: What I tell you, Bono? The only time I see this nigger is when he wants something. That's the only time I see him.

LYONS: Come on, Pop, Mr. Bono don't want to hear all that. Let me have the ten dollars. I told you Bonnie working.

TROY: What that mean to me? "Bonnie working." I don't care if she working. Go ask her for the ten dollars if she working. Talking about "Bonnie working." Why ain't you working? [p. 18]

LYONS: Aw, Pop, you know I can't find no decent job. Where am I gonna get a job at? You know I can't get no job.

TROY: I told you I know some people down there. I can get you on the rubbish if you want to work. I told you that the last time you came by here asking me for something.

LYONS: Naw, Pop . . . thanks. That ain't for me. I don't wanna be carrying nobody's rubbish. I don't wanna be punching nobody's time clock.

TROY: What's the matter, you too good to carry people's rubbish? Where you think that ten dollars you talking about come from? I'm just supposed to haul people's rubbish and give my money to you cause you too lazy to work. You too lazy to work and wanna know why you ain't got what I got.

ROSE: What hospital Bonnie working at? Mercy?

LYONS: She's down at Passavant working in the laundry.

TROY: I ain't got nothing as it is. I give you that ten dollars and I got to eat beans the rest of the week. Naw . . . you ain't getting no ten dollars here.

LYONS: You ain't got to be eating no beans. I don't know why you wanna say that.

TROY: I ain't got no extra money. Gabe done moved over to Miss Pearl's paying her the rent and things done got tight around here. I can't afford to be giving you every payday.

LYONS: I ain't asked you to give me nothing. I asked you to loan me ten dollars. I know you got ten dollars. [p. 19]

TROY: Yeah, I got it. You know why I got it? Cause I don't throw my money away out there in the streets. You living the fast life . . . wanna be a musician . . . running around in them clubs and things . . . then, you learn to take care of yourself. You ain't gonna find me going and asking nobody for nothing. I done spent too many years without.

LYONS: You and me is two different people, Pop.

TROY: I done learned my mistake and learned to do what's right by it. You still trying to get something for nothing. Life don't owe you nothing. You owe it to yourself. Ask Bono. He'll tell you I'm right.

LYONS: You got your way of dealing with the world . . . I got mine. The only thing that matters to me is the music.

TROY: Yeah, I can see that! It don't matter how you gonna eat . . . where your next dollar is coming from. You telling the truth there.

LYONS: I know I got to eat. But I got to live too. I need something that gonna help me to get out of the bed in the morning. Make me feel like I belong in the world. I don't bother nobody. I just stay with the music cause that's the only way I can find to live in the world. Otherwise there ain't no telling what I might do. Now I don't come criticizing you and how you live. I just come by to ask you for ten dollars. I don't wanna hear all that about how I live.

TROY: Boy, your mamma did a hell of a job raising you.

LYONS: You can't change me, Pop. I'm thirty-four years old. If you wanted to change me, you should have been there when I was growing up. I come by to see you . . . ask for ten dollars and you want to talk about how I was raised. You don't know nothing about how I was raised. [p. 20]

ROSE: Let the boy have ten dollars, Troy.

TROY (*to Lyons*): What the hell you looking at me for? I ain't got no ten dollars. You know what I do with my money.

(*To Rose.*)

Give him ten dollars if you want him to have it.

ROSE: I will. Just as soon as you turn it loose.

TROY (*handing Rose the money*): There it is. Seventy-six dollars and forty-two cents. You see this, Bono? Now, I ain't gonna get but six of that back.

ROSE: You ought to stop telling that lie. Here, Lyons.

(*She hands him the money.*)

LYONS: Thanks, Rose. Look . . . I got to run . . . I'll see you later.

TROY: Wait a minute. You gonna say, "thanks, Rose" and ain't gonna look to see where she got that ten dollars from? See how they do me, Bono?

LYONS: I know she got it from you, Pop. Thanks. I'll give it back to you.

TROY: There he go telling another lie. Time I see that ten dollars . . . he'll be owing me thirty more.

LYONS: See you, Mr. Bono.

BONO: Take care, Lyons!

LYONS: Thanks, Pop. I'll see you again.

(*Lyons exits the yard.*) [p. 21]

TROY: I don't know why he don't go and get him a decent job and take care of that woman he got.

BONO: He'll be alright, Troy. The boy is still young.

TROY: The *boy* is thirty-four years old.

ROSE: Let's not get off into all that.

BONO: Look here . . . I got to be going. I got to be getting on. Lucille gonna be waiting.

TROY (*puts his arm around Rose*): See this woman, Bono? I love this woman. I love this woman so much it hurts. I love her so much . . . I done run out of ways of loving her. So I got to go back to basics. Don't you come by my house Monday morning talking about time to go to work . . .'cause I'm still gonna be stroking!

ROSE: Troy! Stop it now!

BONO: I ain't paying him no mind, Rose. That ain't nothing but gin-talk. Go on, Troy. I'll see you Monday.

TROY: Don't you come by my house, nigger! I done told you what I'm gonna be doing.

(*The lights go down to black.*) [p. 22]

Scene Two

The lights come up on Rose hanging up clothes. She hums and sings softly to herself. It is the following morning.

ROSE (*sings*): Jesus, be a fence all around me every day
     Jesus, I want you to protect me as I travel on my way.
     Jesus, be a fence all around me every day.

(*Troy enters from the house.*)

ROSE (*continued*): Jesus, I want you to protect me
     As I travel on my way.

(*To Troy.*)

'Morning. You ready for breakfast? I can fix it soon as I finish hanging up these clothes.

TROY: I got the coffee on. That'll be alright. I'll just drink some of that this morning.

ROSE: That 651 hit yesterday. That's the second time this month. Miss Pearl hit for a dollar . . . seem like those that need the least always get lucky. Poor folks can't get nothing.

TROY: Them numbers don't know nobody. I don't know why you fool with them. You and Lyons both.

ROSE: It's something to do. [p. 23]

TROY: You ain't doing nothing but throwing your money away.

ROSE: Troy, you know I don't play foolishly. I just play a nickel here and a nickel there.

TROY: That's two nickels you done thrown away.

ROSE: Now I hit sometimes . . . that makes up for it. It always comes in handy when I do hit. I don't hear you complaining then.

TROY: I ain't complaining now. I just say it's foolish. Trying to guess out of six hundred ways which way the number gonna come. If I had all the money niggers, these Negroes, throw away on numbers for one week — just one week — I'd be a rich man.

ROSE: Well, you wishing and calling it foolish ain't gonna stop folks from playing numbers. That's one thing for sure. Besides . . . some good things come from playing numbers. Look where Pope done bought him that restaurant off of numbers.

TROY: I can't stand niggers like that. Man ain't had two dimes to rub together. He walking around with his shoes all run over bumming money for cigarettes. Alright. Got lucky there and hit the numbers . . .

ROSE: Troy, I know all about it.

TROY: Had good sense, I'll say that for him. He ain't throwed his money away. I seen niggers hit the numbers and go through two thousand dollars in four days. Man bought him that restaurant down there . . . fixed it up real nice . . . and then didn't want nobody to come in it! A Negro go in there and can't get no kind of service. I seen a white fellow come in there and order a bowl of stew. [p. 24] Pope picked all the meat out the pot for him. Man ain't had nothing but a bowl of meat! Negro come behind him and ain't got nothing but the potatoes and carrots. Talking about what numbers do for people, you picked a wrong example. Ain't done nothing but make a worser fool out of him than he was before.

ROSE: Troy, you ought to stop worrying about what happened at work yesterday.

TROY: I ain't worried. Just told me to be down there at the Commissioner's office on Friday. Everybody think they gonna fire me. I ain't worried about them firing me. You ain't got to worry about that.

(*Pause.*)

Where's Cory? Cory in the house? (*Calls.*) Cory?

ROSE: He gone out.

TROY: Out, huh? He gone out 'cause he know I want him to help me with this fence. I know how he is. That boy scared of work.

(*Gabriel enters. He comes halfway down the alley and, hearing Troy's voice, stops.*)

TROY (*continues*): He ain't done a lick of work in his life.

ROSE: He had to go to football practice. Coach wanted them to get in a little extra practice before the season start.

TROY: I got his practice . . . running out of here before he get his chores done.

ROSE: Troy, what is wrong with you this morning? Don't nothing set right with you. Go on back in there and go to bed . . . get up on the other side. [p. 25]

TROY: Why something got to be wrong with me? I ain't said nothing wrong with me.

ROSE: You got something to say about everything. First it's the numbers . . . then it's the way the man runs his restaurant . . . then you done got on Cory. What's it gonna be next? Take a look up there and see if the weather suits you . . . or is it gonna be how you gonna put up the fence with the clothes hanging in the yard.

TROY: You hit the nail on the head then.

ROSE: I know you like I know the back of my hand. Go on in there and get you some coffee . . . see if that straighten you up. 'Cause you ain't right this morning.

(*Troy starts into the house and sees Gabriel. Gabriel starts singing. Troy's brother, he is seven years younger than Troy. Injured in World War II, he has a metal plate in his head. He carries an old trumpet tied around his waist and believes with every fiber of his being that he is the Archangel Gabriel. He carries a chipped basket with an assortment of discarded fruits and vegetables he has picked up in the strip district and which he attempts to sell.*)

GABRIEL (*singing*): Yes, ma'am, I got plums
You ask me how I sell them
Oh ten cents apiece
Three for a quarter
Come and buy now
'Cause I'm here today
And tomorrow I'll be gone

(*Gabriel enters.*)

Hey, Rose! [p. 26]

ROSE: How you doing, Gabe?

GABRIEL: There's Troy . . . Hey, Troy!

TROY: Hey, Gabe.

(*Exit into kitchen.*)

ROSE (*to Gabriel*): What you got there?

GABRIEL: You know what I got, Rose. I got fruits and vegetables.

ROSE (*looking in basket*): Where's all these plums you talking about?

GABRIEL: I ain't got no plums today, Rose. I was just singing that. Have some tomorrow. Put me in a big order for plums. Have enough plums tomorrow for St. Peter and everybody.

(*Troy re-enters from kitchen, crosses to steps.*)

(*To Rose.*)

Troy's mad at me.

TROY: I ain't mad at you. What I got to be mad at you about? You ain't done nothing to me.

GABRIEL: I just moved over to Miss Pearl's to keep out from in your way. I ain't mean no harm by it.

TROY: Who said anything about that? I ain't said anything about that.

GABRIEL: You ain't mad at me, is you?

TROY: Naw . . . I ain't mad at you, Gabe. If I was mad at you I'd tell you about it. [p. 27]

GABRIEL: Got me two rooms. In the basement. Got my own door too. Wanna see my key?

(*He holds up a key.*)

That's my own key! Ain't nobody else got a key like that. That's my key! My two rooms!

TROY: Well, that's good, Gabe. You got your own key . . . that's good.

ROSE: You hungry, Gabe? I was just fixing to cook Troy his breakfast.

GABRIEL: I'll take some biscuits. You got some biscuits? Did you know when I was in heaven . . . every morning me and St. Peter would sit down by the gate and eat some big fat biscuits? Oh, yeah! We had us a good time. We'd sit there and eat us them biscuits and then St. Peter would go off to sleep and tell me to wake him up when it's time to open the gates for the judgment.

ROSE: Well, come on . . . I'll make up a batch of biscuits.

(*Rose exits into the house.*)

GABRIEL: Troy . . . St. Peter got your name in the book. I seen it. It say . . . Troy Maxson. I say . . . I know him! He got the same name like what I got. That's my brother!

TROY: How many times you gonna tell me that, Gabe?

GABRIEL: Ain't got my name in the book. Don't have to have my name. I done died and went to heaven. He got your name though. One morning St. Peter was looking at his book . . . marking it up for the judgment . . . and he let me see your name. Got it in there under M. Got Rose's name . . . I ain't seen it like I seen yours . . . but I know it's in there. He got a great big book. Got everybody's [p. 28] name what was ever been born. That's what he told me. But I seen your name. Seen it with my own eyes.

TROY: Go on in the house there. Rose going to fix you something to eat.

GABRIEL: Oh, I ain't hungry. I done had breakfast with Aunt Jemimah. She come by and cooked me up a whole mess of flapjacks. Remember how we used to eat them flapjacks?

TROY: Go on in the house and get you something to eat now.

GABRIEL: I got to sell my plums. I done sold some tomatoes. Got me two quarters. Wanna see?

(*He shows Troy his quarters.*)

I'm gonna save them and buy me a new horn so St. Peter can hear me when it's time to open the gates.

(*Gabriel stops suddenly. Listens.*)

Hear that? That's the hellhounds. I got to chase them out of here. Go on get out of here! Get out!

(*Gabriel exits singing.*)

Better get ready for the judgment
Better get ready for the judgment
My Lord is coming down

(*Rose enters from the house.*)

TROY: He gone off somewhere.
GABRIEL (*offstage*): Better get ready for the judgment
Better get ready for the judgment morning
Better get ready for the judgment
My God is coming down [p. 29]
ROSE: He ain't eating right. Miss Pearl say she can't get him to eat nothing.
TROY: What you want me to do about it, Rose? I done did everything I can for the man. I can't make him get well. Man got half his head blown away . . . what you expect?
ROSE: Seem like something ought to be done to help him.
TROY: Man don't bother nobody. He just mixed up from that metal plate he got in his head. Ain't no sense for him to go back into the hospital.
ROSE: Least he be eating right. They can help him take care of himself.
TROY: Don't nobody wanna be locked up, Rose. What you wanna lock him up for? Man go over there and fight the war . . . messin' around with them Japs, get half his head blown off . . . and they give him a lousy three thousand dollars. And I had to swoop down on that.
ROSE: Is you fixing to go into that again?
TROY: That's the only way I got a roof over my head . . . cause of that metal plate.
ROSE: Ain't no sense you blaming yourself for nothing. Gabe wasn't in no condition to manage that money. You done what was right by him. Can't nobody say you ain't done what was right by him. Look how long you took care of him . . . till he wanted to have his own place and moved over there with Miss Pearl.
TROY: That ain't what I'm saying, woman! I'm just stating the facts. If my brother didn't have that metal plate in his head . . . I wouldn't have a pot to piss in or a window to [p. 30] throw it out of. And I'm fifty-three years old. Now see if you can understand that!

(*Troy gets up from the porch and starts to exit the yard.*)

ROSE: Where you going off to? You been running out of here every Saturday for weeks. I thought you was gonna work on this fence?

TROY: I'm gonna walk down to Taylors'. Listen to the ball game. I'll be back in a bit. I'll work on it when I get back.

(*He exits the yard. The lights go to black.*) [p. 31]

Scene Three

The lights come up on the yard. It is four hours later. Rose is taking down the clothes from the line. Cory enters carrying his football equipment.

ROSE: Your daddy like to had a fit with you running out of here this morning without doing your chores.

CORY: I told you I had to go to practice.

ROSE: He say you were supposed to help him with this fence.

CORY: He been saying that the last four or five Saturdays, and then he don't never do nothing, but go down to Taylors'. Did you tell him about the recruiter?

ROSE: Yeah, I told him.

CORY: What he say?

ROSE: He ain't said nothing too much. You get in there and get started on your chores before he gets back. Go on and scrub down them steps before he gets back here hollering and carrying on.

CORY: I'm hungry. What you got to eat, Mama? [p. 33]

ROSE: Go on and get started on your chores. I got some meat loaf in there. Go on and make you a sandwich . . . and don't leave no mess in there.

(*Cory exits into the house. Rose continues to take down the clothes. Troy enters the yard and sneaks up and grabs her from behind.*)

Troy! Go on, now. You liked to scared me to death. What was the score of the game? Lucille had me on the phone and I couldn't keep up with it.

TROY: What I care about the game? Come here, woman. (*He tries to kiss her.*)

ROSE: I thought you went down Taylors' to listen to the game. Go on, Troy! You supposed to be putting up this fence.

TROY (*attempting to kiss her again*): I'll put it up when I finish with what is at hand.

ROSE: Go on, Troy. I ain't studying you.

TROY (*chasing after her*): I'm studying you . . . fixing to do my homework!

ROSE: Troy, you better leave me alone.

TROY: Where's Cory? That boy brought his butt home yet?

ROSE: He's in the house doing his chores.

TROY (*calling*): Cory! Get your butt out here, boy!

(*Rose exits into the house with the laundry. Troy goes over to the pile of wood, picks up a board, and starts sawing. Cory enters from the house.*) [p. 34]

TROY: You just now coming in here from leaving this morning?

CORY: Yeah, I had to go to football practice.

TROY: Yeah, what?

CORY: Yessir.

TROY: I ain't but two seconds off you noway. The garbage sitting in there over-flowing . . . you ain't done none of your chores . . . and you come in here talking about "Yeah."

CORY: I was just getting ready to do my chores now, Pop . . .

TROY: Your first chore is to help me with this fence on Saturday. Everything else come after that. Now get that saw and cut them boards.

(*Cory takes the saw and begins cutting the boards. Troy continues working. There is a long pause.*)

CORY: Hey, Pop . . . why don't you buy a TV?

TROY: What I want with a TV? What I want one of them for?

CORY: Everybody got one. Earl, Ba Bra . . . Jesse!

TROY: I ain't asked you who had one. I say what I want with one?

CORY: So you can watch it. They got lots of things on TV. Baseball games and everything. We could watch the World Series. [p. 35]

TROY: Yeah . . . and how much this TV cost?

CORY: I don't know. They got them on sale for around two hundred dollars.

TROY: Two hundred dollars, huh?

CORY: That ain't that much, Pop.

TROY: Naw, it's just two hundred dollars. See that roof you got over your head at night? Let me tell you something about that roof. It's been over ten years since that roof was last tarred. See now . . . the snow come this winter and sit up there on that roof like it is . . . and it's gonna seep inside. It's just gonna be a little bit . . . ain't gonna hardly notice it. Then the next thing you know, it's gonna be leaking all over the house. Then the wood rot from all that water and you gonna need a whole new roof. Now, how much you think it cost to get that roof tarred?

CORY: I don't know.

TROY: Two hundred and sixty-four dollars . . . cash money. While you thinking about a TV, I got to be thinking about the roof . . . and whatever else go wrong here. Now if you had two hundred dollars, what would you do . . . fix the roof or buy a TV?

CORY: I'd buy a TV. Then when the roof started to leak . . . when it needed fixing . . . I'd fix it.

TROY: Where you gonna get the money from? You done spent it for a TV. You gonna sit up and watch the water run all over your brand new TV.

CORY: Aw, Pop. You got money. I know you do.

TROY: Where I got it at, huh? [p. 36]

CORY: You got it in the bank.

TROY: You wanna see my bankbook? You wanna see that seventy-three dollars and twenty-two cents I got sitting up in there.

CORY: You ain't got to pay for it all at one time. You can put a down payment on it and carry it on home with you.

TROY: Not me. I ain't gonna owe nobody nothing if I can help it. Miss a payment and they come and snatch it right out your house. Then what you got? Now, soon as I get two hundred dollars clear, then I'll buy a TV. Right now, as soon as I get two hundred and sixty-four dollars, I'm gonna have this roof tarred.

CORY: Aw . . . Pop!

TROY: You go on and get you two hundred dollars and buy one if ya want it. I got better things to do with my money.

CORY: I can't get no two hundred dollars. I ain't never seen two hundred dollars.

TROY: I'll tell you what . . . you get you a hundred dollars and I'll put the other hundred with it.

CORY: Alright, I'm gonna show you.

TROY: You gonna show me how you can cut them boards right now.

(Cory begins to cut the boards. There is a long pause.)

CORY: The Pirates won today. That makes five in a row.

TROY: I ain't thinking about the Pirates. Got an all-white team. Got that boy . . . that Puerto Rican boy . . . Clemente.° [p. 37] Don't even half-play him. That boy could be something if they give him a chance. Play him one day and sit him on the bench the next.

CORY: He gets a lot of chances to play.

TROY: I'm talking about playing regular. Playing every day so you can get your timing. That's what I'm talking about.

CORY: They got some white guys on the team that don't play every day. You can't play everybody at the same time.

TROY: If they got a white fellow sitting on the bench . . . you can bet your last dollar he can't play! The colored guy got to be twice as good before he get on the team. That's why I don't want you to get all tied up in them sports. Man on the team and what it get him? They got colored on the team and don't use them. Same as not having them. All them teams the same.

CORY: The Braves got Hank Aaron and Wes Covington.° Hank Aaron hit two home runs today. That makes forty-three.

TROY: Hank Aaron ain't nobody. That's what you supposed to do. That's how you supposed to play the game. Ain't nothing to it. It's just a matter of timing . . . getting the right follow-through. Hell, I can hit forty-three home runs right now!

Clemente: Roberto Clemente (1934–1972), right fielder for the Pittsburgh Pirates from 1955 to 1971, was the first player of Latin American descent to be elected into the Baseball Hall of Fame. In 1956, he played in 147 games and had a .311 batting average; in 1957, he played in 111 games and his average dropped to .253. **Hank Aaron and Wes Covington:** Henry Louis Aaron (b. 1934), African American outfielder, hit 44 home runs for the Milwaukee Braves in 1957 and went on to break Babe Ruth's career home run record. John Wesley Covington (b. 1932), African American outfielder, hit 21 homers for the Milwaukee Braves in 1957.

CORY: Not off no major-league pitching, you couldn't.

TROY: We had better pitching in the Negro leagues. I hit seven home runs off of Satchel Paige.° You can't get no better than that!

CORY: Sandy Koufax.° He's leading the league in strike-outs. [p. 38]

TROY: I ain't thinking of no Sandy Koufax.

CORY: You got Warren Spahn and Lew Burdette.° I bet you couldn't hit no home runs off of Warren Spahn.

TROY: I'm through with it now. You go on and cut them boards.

(*Pause.*)

Your mama tell me you done got recruited by a college football team? Is that right?

CORY: Yeah. Coach Zellman say the recruiter gonna be coming by to talk to you. Get you to sign the permission papers.

TROY: I thought you supposed to be working down there at the A&P. Ain't you suppose to be working down there after school?

CORY: Mr. Stawicki say he gonna hold my job for me until after the football season. Say starting next week I can work weekends.

TROY: I thought we had an understanding about this football stuff? You suppose to keep up with your chores and hold that job down at the A&P. Ain't been around here all day on a Saturday. Ain't none of your chores done . . . and now you telling me you done quit your job.

CORY: I'm gonna to be working weekends.

TROY: You damn right you are! And ain't no need for nobody coming around here to talk to me about signing nothing.

CORY: Hey, Pop . . . you can't do that. He's coming all the way from North Carolina. [p. 39]

TROY: I don't care where he coming from. The white man ain't gonna let you get nowhere with that football noway. You go on and get your book-learning so you can work yourself up in that A&P or learn how to fix cars or build houses or something, get you a trade. That way you have something can't

---

Satchel Paige: Leroy "Satchel" Paige (1906–1982), star pitcher in the Negro Leagues from 1926 to 1947, played in the major leagues for the Cleveland Indians (1948–1949), the St. Louis Browns (1951–1953), and the Kansas City Athletics (1965). He was the first African American elected to the Baseball Hall of Fame. **Sandy Koufax:** Sanford Koufax (b. 1935), pitcher for the Brooklyn and Los Angeles Dodgers from 1955 to 1966. He recorded 122 strikeouts in 1957. Jack Sanford ended up leading the league that year with 188 strikeouts for the Philadelphia Phillies. **Warren Spahn and Lew Burdette:** Warren Edward Spahn (1921–2003) is the winningest left-handed pitcher in major league history with 363 victories, all but seven of those wins coming with the Boston-Milwaukee Braves, 1942–1964. He had a 21–11 record in 1957 when he won the Cy Young Award and won the fourth game of the 1958 World Series. Selva Lewis Burdette (b. 1926), pitcher for six major league teams from 1950 to 1967, had a 17–9 record for Milwaukee in 1957, won three games in the 1957 World Series, and was named that series' Most Valuable Player.

nobody take away from you. You go on and learn how to put your hands to some good use. Besides hauling people's garbage.

CORY: I get good grades, Pop. That's why the recruiter wants to talk with you. You got to keep up your grades to get recruited. This way I'll be going to college. I'll get a chance . . .

TROY: First you gonna get your butt down there to the A&P and get your job back.

CORY: Mr. Stawicki done already hired somebody else 'cause I told him I was playing football.

TROY: You a bigger fool than I thought . . . to let somebody take away your job so you can play some football. Where you gonna get your money to take out your girlfriend and whatnot? What kind of foolishness is that to let somebody take away your job?

CORY: I'm still gonna be working weekends.

TROY: Naw . . . naw. You getting your butt out of here and finding you another job.

CORY: Come on, Pop! I got to practice. I can't work after school and play football too. The team needs me. That's what Coach Zellman say . . .

TROY: I don't care what nobody else say. I'm the boss . . . you understand? I'm the boss around here. I do the only saying what counts. [p. 40]

CORY: Come on, Pop!

TROY: I asked you . . . did you understand?

CORY: Yeah . . .

TROY: What?!

CORY: Yessir.

TROY: You go on down there to that A&P and see if you can get your job back. If you can't do both . . . then you quit the football team. You've got to take the crookeds with the straights.

CORY: Yessir.

(Pause.)

Can I ask you a question?

TROY: What the hell you wanna ask me? Mr. Stawicki the one you got the questions for.

CORY: How come you ain't never liked me?

TROY: Liked you? Who the hell say I got to like you? What law is there say I got to like you? Wanna stand up in my face and ask a damn fool-ass question like that. Talking about liking somebody. Come here, boy, when I talk to you.

(Cory comes over to where Troy is working. He stands slouched over and Troy shoves him on his shoulder.)

Straighten up, goddammit! I asked you a question . . . what law is there say I got to like you?

CORY: None.

TROY: Well, alright then! Don't you eat every day?

(*Pause.*)

Answer me when I talk to you! Don't you eat every day? [p. 41]

CORY: Yeah.

TROY: Nigger, as long as you in my house, you put that sir on the end of it when you talk to me!

CORY: Yes . . . sir.

TROY: You eat every day.

CORY: Yessir!

TROY: Got a roof over your head.

CORY: Yessir!

TROY: Got clothes on your back.

CORY: Yessir.

TROY: Why you think that is?

CORY: Cause of you.

TROY: Aw, hell I know it's 'cause of me . . . but why do you think that is?

CORY (*hesitant*): Cause you like me.

TROY: Like you? I go out of here every morning . . . bust my butt . . . putting up with them crackers every day . . . cause I like you? You about the biggest fool I ever saw.

(*Pause.*)

It's my job. It's my responsibility! You understand that? A man got to take care of his family. You live in my house . . . sleep you behind on my bedclothes . . . fill you belly up with my food . . . cause you my son. You my flesh and blood. Not 'cause I like you! Cause it's my duty to [p. 42] take care of you. I owe a responsibility to you! Let's get this straight right here . . . before it go along any further . . . I ain't got to like you. Mr. Rand don't give me my money come payday cause he likes me. He gives me cause he owe me. I done give you everything I had to give you. I gave you your life! Me and your mama worked that out between us. And liking your black ass wasn't part of the bargain. Don't you try and go through life worrying about if somebody like you or not. You best be making sure they doing right by you. You understand what I'm saying, boy?

CORY: Yessir.

TROY: Then get the hell out of my face, and get on down to that A&P.

(*Rose has been standing behind the screen door for much of the scene. She enters as Cory exits.*)

ROSE: Why don't you let the boy go ahead and play football, Troy? Ain't no harm in that. He's just trying to be like you with the sports.

TROY: I don't want him to be like me! I want him to move as far away from my life as he can get. You the only decent thing that ever happened to me.

I wish him that. But I don't wish him a thing else from my life. I decided seventeen years ago that boy wasn't getting involved in no sports. Not after what they did to me in the sports.

ROSE: Troy, why don't you admit you was too old to play in the major leagues? For once . . . why don't you admit that?

TROY: What do you mean too old? Don't come telling me I was too old. I just wasn't the right color. Hell, I'm fifty-three years old and can do better than Selkirk's .269 right now! [p. 43]

ROSE: How's was you gonna play ball when you were over forty? Sometimes I can't get no sense out of you.

TROY: I got good sense, woman. I got sense enough not to let my boy get hurt over playing no sports. You been mothering that boy too much. Worried about if people like him.

ROSE: Everything that boy do . . . he do for you. He wants you to say "Good job, son." That's all.

TROY: Rose, I ain't got time for that. He's alive. He's healthy. He's got to make his own way. I made mine. Ain't nobody gonna hold his hand when he get out there in that world.

ROSE: Times have changed from when you was young, Troy. People change. The world's changing around you and you can't even see it.

TROY (*slow, methodical*): Woman . . . I do the best I can do. I come in here every Friday. I carry a sack of potatoes and a bucket of lard. You all line up at the door with your hands out. I give you the lint from my pockets. I give you my sweat and my blood. I ain't got no tears. I done spent them. We go upstairs in that room at night . . . and I fall down on you and try to blast a hole into forever. I get up Monday morning . . . find my lunch on the table. I go out. Make my way. Find my strength to carry me through to the next Friday.

(*Pause.*)

That's all I got, Rose. That's all I got to give. I can't give nothing else.

(*Troy exits into the house. The lights go down to black.*) [p. 44]

Scene Four

It is Friday. Two weeks later. Cory starts out of the house with his football equipment. The phone rings.

CORY (*calling*): I got it!

(*He answers the phone and stands in the screen door talking.*)

Hello? Hey, Jesse. Naw . . . I was just getting ready to leave now.

ROSE (*calling*): Cory!

CORY: I told you, man, them spikes is all tore up. You can use them if you want, but they ain't no good. Earl got some spikes.

ROSE (*calling*): Cory!

CORY (*calling to Rose*): Mam? I'm talking to Jesse.

(Into phone.)

When she say that? *(Pause.)* Aw, you lying, man. I'm gonna tell her you said that.

ROSE *(calling)*: Cory, don't you go nowhere!

CORY: I got to go to the game, Ma!

(Into the phone.)

Yeah, hey, look, I'll talk to you later. Yeah, I'll meet you over Earl's house. Later. Bye, Ma. [p. 45]

(Cory exits the house and starts out the yard.)

ROSE: Cory, where you going off to? You got that stuff all pulled out and thrown all over your room.

CORY *(in the yard)*: I was looking for my spikes. Jesse wanted to borrow my spikes.

ROSE: Get up there and get that cleaned up before your daddy get back in here.

CORY: I got to go to the game! I'll clean it up *when I get back.*

(Cory exits.)

ROSE: That's all he need to do is see that room all messed up.

(Rose exits into the house. Troy and Bono enter the yard. Troy is dressed in clothes other than his work clothes.)

BONO: He told him the same thing he told you. Take it to the union.

TROY: Brownie ain't got that much sense. Man wasn't thinking about nothing. He wait until I confront them on it . . . then he wanna come crying seniority.

(Calls.)

Hey, Rose!

BONO: I wish I could have seen Mr. Rand's face when he told you.

TROY: He couldn't get it out of his mouth! Liked to bit his tongue! When they called me down there to the Commissioner's office . . . he thought they was gonna fire me. Like everybody else. [p. 46]

BONO: I didn't think they was gonna fire you. I thought they was gonna put you on the warning paper.

TROY: Hey, Rose!

(To Bono.)

Yeah, Mr. Rand like to bit his tongue.

(Troy breaks the seal on the bottle, takes a drink, and hands it to Bono.)

BONO: I see you run right down to Taylors' and told that Alberta gal.

TROY *(calling)*: Hey Rose! *(To Bono.)* I told everybody. Hey, Rose! I went down there to cash my check.

ROSE (*entering from the house*): Hush all that hollering, man! I know you out here. What they say down there at the Commissioner's office?

TROY: You supposed to come when I call you, woman. Bono'll tell you that.

(*To Bono.*)

Don't Lucille come when you call her?

ROSE: Man, hush your mouth. I ain't no dog . . . talk about "come when you call me."

TROY (*puts his arm around Rose*): You hear this, Bono? I had me an old dog used to get uppity like that. You say, "C'mere, Blue!" . . . and he just lay there and look at you. End up getting a stick and chasing him away trying to make him come.

ROSE: I ain't studying you and your dog. I remember you used to sing that old song.

TROY (*he sings*): Hear it ring! Hear it ring!

I had a dog his name was Blue. [p. 47]

ROSE: Don't nobody wanna hear you sing that old song.

TROY (*sings*): You know Blue was mighty true.

ROSE: Used to have Cory running around here singing that song.

BONO: Hell, I remember that song myself.

TROY (*sings*): You know Blue was a good old dog.

Blue treed a possum in a hollow log.

That was my daddy's song. My daddy made up that song.

ROSE: I don't care who made it up. Don't nobody wanna hear you sing it.

TROY (*makes a song like calling a dog*): Come here, woman.

ROSE: You come in here carrying on, I reckon they ain't fired you. What they say down there at the Commissioner's office?

TROY: Look here, Rose . . . Mr. Rand called me into his office today when I got back from talking to them people down there . . . it come from up top . . . he called me in and told me they was making me a driver.

ROSE: Troy, you kidding!

TROY: No I ain't. Ask Bono.

ROSE: Well, that's great, Troy. Now you don't have to hassle them people no more.

(*Lyons enters from the street.*) [p. 48]

TROY: Aw hell, I wasn't looking to see you today. I thought you was in jail. Got it all over the front page of the *Courier* about them raiding Sefus's place . . . where you be hanging out with all them thugs.

LYONS: Hey, Pop . . . that ain't got nothing to do with me. I don't go down there gambling. I go down there to sit in with the band. I ain't got nothing to do with the gambling part. They got some good music down there.

TROY: They got some rogues . . . is what they got.

LYONS: How you been, Mr. Bono? Hi, Rose.

BONO: I see where you playing down at the Crawford Grill tonight.

ROSE: How come you ain't brought Bonnie like I told you. You should have brought Bonnie with you, she ain't been over in a month of Sundays.

LYONS: I was just in the neighborhood . . . thought I'd stop by.

TROY: Here he come . . .

BONO: Your daddy got a promotion on the rubbish. He's gonna be the first colored driver. Ain't got to do nothing but sit up there and read the paper like them white fellows.

LYONS: Hey, Pop . . . if you knew how to read you'd be alright.

BONO: Naw . . . naw . . . you mean if the nigger knew how to *drive* he'd be all right. Been fighting with them people about driving and ain't even got a license. Mr. Rand know you ain't got no driver's license? [p. 49]

TROY: Driving ain't nothing. All you do is point the truck where you want it to go. Driving ain't nothing.

BONO: Do Mr. Rand know you ain't got no driver's license? That's what I'm talking about. I ain't asked if driving was easy. I asked if Mr. Rand know you ain't got no driver's license.

TROY: He ain't got to know. The man ain't got to know my business. Time he find out, I have two or three driver's licenses.

LYONS (*going into his pocket*): Say, look here, Pop . . .

TROY: I knew it was coming. Didn't I tell you, Bono? I know what kind of "Look here, Pop" that was. The nigger fixing to ask me for some money. It's Friday night. It's my payday. All them rogues down there on the avenue . . . the ones that ain't in jail . . . and Lyons is hopping in his shoes to get down there with them.

LYONS: See, Pop . . . if you give somebody else a chance to talk sometime, you'd see that I was fixing to pay you back your ten dollars like I told you. Here . . . I told you I'd pay you when Bonnie got paid.

TROY: Naw . . . you go ahead and keep that ten dollars. Put it in the bank. The next time you feel like you wanna come by here and ask me for something . . . you go on down there and get that.

LYONS: Here's your ten dollars, Pop. I told you I don't want you to give me nothing. I just wanted to borrow ten dollars.

TROY: Naw . . . you go on and keep that for the next time you want to ask me. [p. 50]

LYONS: Come on, Pop . . . here go your ten dollars.

ROSE: Why don't you go on and let the boy pay you back, Troy?

LYONS: Here you go, Rose. If you don't take it I'm gonna have to hear about it for the next six months. (*He hands her the money.*)

ROSE: You can hand yours over here too, Troy.

TROY: You see this, Bono. You see how they do me.

BONO: Yeah, Lucille do me the same way.

(*Gabriel is heard singing onstage. He enters.*)

GABRIEL: Better get ready for the Judgment! Better get ready for . . . Hey! . . . Hey! . . . There's Troy's boy!

LYONS: How you doing, Uncle Gabe?

GABRIEL: Lyons . . . The King of the Jungle! Rose . . . hey, Rose. Got a flower for you.

(*He takes a rose from his pocket.*)

Picked it myself. That's the same rose like you is!

ROSE: That's right nice of you, Gabe.

LYONS: What you been doing, Uncle Gabe?

GABRIEL: Oh, I been chasing hellhounds and waiting on the time to tell St. Peter to open the gates.

LYONS: You been chasing hellhounds, huh? Well . . . you doing the right thing, Uncle Gabe. Somebody got to chase them. [p. 51]

GABRIEL: Oh, yeah . . . I know it. The devil's strong. The devil ain't no pushover. Hellhounds snipping at everybody's heels. But I got my trumpet waiting on the judgment time.

LYONS: Waiting on the Battle of Armageddon, huh?

GABRIEL: Ain't gonna be too much of a battle when God get to waving that Judgment sword. But the people's gonna have a hell of a time trying to get into heaven if them gates ain't open.

LYONS (*putting his arm around Gabriel*): You hear this, Pop. Uncle Gabe, you alright!

GABRIEL (*laughing with Lyons*): Lyons! King of the Jungle.

ROSE: You gonna stay for supper, Gabe? Want me to fix you a plate?

GABRIEL: I'll take a sandwich, Rose. Don't want no plate. Just wanna eat with my hands. I'll take a sandwich.

ROSE: How about you, Lyons? You staying? Got some short ribs cooking.

LYONS: Naw, I won't eat nothing till after we finished playing.

(*Pause.*)

You ought to come down and listen to me play, Pop.

TROY: I don't like that Chinese music. All that noise.

ROSE: Go on in the house and wash up, Gabe . . . I'll fix you a sandwich.

GABRIEL (*to Lyons, as he exits*): Troy's mad at me. [p. 52]

LYONS: What you mad at Uncle Gabe for, Pop.

ROSE: He thinks Troy's mad at him cause he moved over to Miss Pearl's.

TROY: I ain't mad at the man. He can live where he want to live at.

LYONS: What he move over there for? Miss Pearl don't like nobody.

ROSE: She don't mind him none. She treats him real nice. She just don't allow all that singing.

TROY: She don't mind that rent he be paying . . . that's what she don't mind.

ROSE: Troy, I ain't going through that with you no more. He's over there cause he want to have his own place. He can come and go as he please.

TROY: Hell, he could come and go as he please here. I wasn't stopping him. I ain't put no rules on him.

ROSE: It ain't the same thing, Troy. And you know it.

(Gabriel comes to the door.)

Now, that's the last I wanna hear about that. I don't wanna hear nothing else about Gabe and Miss Pearl. And next week . . .

GABRIEL: I'm ready for my sandwich, Rose.

ROSE: And next week . . . when that recruiter come from that school . . . I want you to sign that paper and go on and let Cory play football. Then that'll be the last I have to hear about that. [p. 53]

TROY *(to Rose as she exits into the house)*: I ain't thinking about Cory nothing.

LYONS: What . . . Cory got recruited? What school he going to?

TROY: That boy walking around here smelling his piss . . . thinking he's grown. Thinking he's gonna do what he want, irrespective of what I say. Look here, Bono . . . I left the Commissioner's office and went down to the A&P . . . that boy ain't working down there. He lying to me. Telling me he got his job back . . . telling me he working weekends . . . telling me he working after school . . . Mr. Stawicki tell me he ain't working down there at all!

LYONS: Cory just growing up. He's just busting at the seams trying to fill out your shoes.

TROY: I don't care what he's doing. When he get to the point where he wanna disobey me . . . then it's time for him to move on. Bono'll tell you that. I bet he ain't never disobeyed his daddy without paying the consequences.

BONO: I ain't never had a chance. My daddy came on through . . . but I ain't never knew him to see him . . . or what he had on his mind or where he went. Just moving on through. Searching out the New Land. That's what the old folks used to call it. See a fellow moving around from place to place . . . woman to woman . . . called it searching out the New Land. I can't say if he ever found it. I come along, didn't want no kids. Didn't know if I was gonna be in one place long enough to fix on them right as their daddy. I figured I was going searching too. As it turned out I been hooked up with Lucille near about as long as your daddy been with Rose. Going on sixteen years. [p. 54]

TROY: Sometimes I wish I hadn't known my daddy. He ain't cared nothing about no kids. A kid to him wasn't nothing. All he wanted was for you to learn how to walk so he could start you to working. When it come time for eating . . . he ate first. If there was anything left over, that's what you got. Man would sit down and eat two chickens and give you the wing.

LYONS: You ought to stop that, Pop. Everybody feed their kids. No matter how hard times is . . . everybody care about their kids. Make sure they have something to eat.

TROY: The only thing my daddy cared about was getting them bales of cotton in to Mr. Lubin. That's the only thing that mattered to him. Sometimes I used to wonder why he was living. Wonder why the devil hadn't come and got him. "Get them bales of cotton in to Mr. Lubin" and find out he owe him money . . .

LYONS: He should have just went on and left when he saw he couldn't get nowhere. That's what I would have done.

TROY: How he gonna leave with eleven kids? And where he gonna go? He ain't knew how to do nothing but farm. No, he was trapped and I think he knew it. But I'll say this for him . . . he felt a responsibility toward us. Maybe he ain't treated us the way I felt he should have . . . but without that responsibility he could have walked off and left us . . . made his own way.

BONO: A lot of them did. Back in those days what you talking about . . . they walk out their front door and just take on down one road or another and keep on walking.

LYONS: There you go! That's what I'm talking about.

BONO: Just keep on walking till you come to something else. Ain't you never heard of nobody having the walking [p. 55] blues? Well, that's what you call it when you just take off like that.

TROY: My daddy ain't had them walking blues! What you talking about? He stayed right there with his family. But he was just as evil as he could be. My mama couldn't stand him. Couldn't stand that evilness. She run off when I was about eight. She sneaked off one night after he had gone to sleep. Told me she was coming back for me. I ain't never seen her no more. All his women run off and left him. He wasn't good for nobody.

When my turn come to head out, I was fourteen and got to sniffing around Joe Canewell's daughter. Had us an old mule we called Greyboy. My daddy sent me out to do some plowing and I tied up Greyboy and went to fooling around with Joe Canewell's daughter. We done found us a nice little spot, got real cozy with each other. She about thirteen and we done figured we was grown anyway . . . so we down there enjoying ourselves . . . ain't thinking about nothing. We didn't know Greyboy had got loose and wandered back to the house and my daddy was looking for me. We down there by the creek enjoying ourselves when my daddy come up on us. Surprised us. He had them leather straps off the mule and commenced to whupping me like there was no tomorrow. I jumped up, mad and embarrassed. I was scared of my daddy. When he commenced to whupping on me . . . quite naturally I run to get out of the way.

(Pause.)

Now I thought he was mad cause I ain't done my work. But I see where he was chasing me off so he could have the gal for himself. When I see what the matter of it was, I lost all fear of my daddy. Right there is where I become a man . . . at fourteen years of age.

(Pause.)

Now it was my turn to run him off. I picked up them same reins that he had used on me. I picked up them reins and commenced to whupping on him. The gal jumped up [p. 56] and run off . . . and when my daddy turned to face me, I could see why the devil had never come to get him . . . cause he was the devil himself. I don't know what happened. When I woke up, I was laying right there by the creek, and Blue . . . this old dog we had . . . was licking my face. I thought I was blind. I couldn't see nothing. Both my eyes were swollen shut. I layed there and cried. I didn't know what I was gonna do. The only thing I knew was the time had come for me to leave my daddy's house. And right there the world suddenly got big. And it was a long time before I could cut it down to where I could handle it.

Part of that cutting down was when I got to the place where I could feel him kicking in my blood and knew that the only thing that separated us was the matter of a few years.

(*Gabriel enters from the house with a sandwich.*)

LYONS: What you got there, Uncle Gabe?

GABRIEL: Got me a ham sandwich. Rose gave me a ham sandwich.

TROY: I don't know what happened to him. I done lost touch with everybody except Gabriel. But I hope he's dead. I hope he found some peace.

LYONS: That's a heavy story, Pop. I didn't know you left home when you was fourteen.

TROY: And didn't know nothing. The only part of the world I knew was the forty-two acres of Mr. Lubin's land. That's all I knew about life.

LYONS: Fourteen's kinda young to be out on your own. (*Phone rings.*) I don't even think I was ready to be out on my own at fourteen. I don't know what I would have done. [p. 57]

TROY: I got up from the creek and walked on down to Mobile. I was through with farming. Figured I could do better in the city. So I walked the two hundred miles to Mobile.

LYONS: Wait a minute . . . you ain't walked no two hundred miles, Pop. Ain't nobody gonna walk no two hundred miles. You talking about some walking there.

BONO: That's the only way you got anywhere back in them days.

LYONS: Shhh. Damn if I wouldn't have hitched a ride with somebody!

TROY: Who you gonna hitch it with? They ain't had no cars and things like they got now. We talking about 1918.

ROSE (*entering*): What you all out here getting into?

TROY (*to Rose*): I'm telling Lyons how good he got it. He don't know nothing about this I'm talking.

ROSE: Lyons, that was Bonnie on the phone. She say you supposed to pick her up.

LYONS: Yeah, okay, Rose.

TROY: I walked on down to Mobile and hitched up with some of them fellows that was heading this way. Got up here and found out . . . not only couldn't you get a job . . . you couldn't find no place to live. I thought I was in freedom. Shhh. Colored folks living down there on the riverbanks in whatever kind of shelter they could find for themselves. Right down there under the Brady Street Bridge. Living in shacks made of sticks and tarpaper. Messed around there and went from bad to worse. Started stealing. First it was food. Then I figured, hell, if I steal [p. 58] money I can buy me some food. Buy me some shoes too! One thing led to another. Met your mama. I was young and anxious to be a man. Met your mama and had you. What I do that for? Now I got to worry about feeding you and her. Got to steal three times as much. Went out one day looking for somebody to rob . . . that's what I was, a robber. I'll tell you the truth. I'm ashamed of it today. But it's the truth. Went to rob this fellow . . . pulled out my knife . . . and he pulled out a gun. Shot me in the chest. I felt just like somebody had taken a hot branding iron and laid it on me. When he shot me I jumped at him with my knife. They told me I killed him and they put me in the penitentiary and locked me up for fifteen years. That's where I met Bono. That's where I learned how to play baseball. Got out that place and your mama had taken you and went on to make life without me. Fifteen years was a long time for her to wait. But that fifteen years cured me of that robbing stuff. Rose'll tell you. She asked me when I met her if I had gotten all that foolishness out of my system. And I told her, "Baby, it's you and baseball all what count with me." You hear me, Bono? I meant it too. She say, "Which one comes first?" I told her, "Baby, ain't no doubt it's baseball . . . but you stick and get old with me and we'll both outlive this baseball." Am I right, Rose? And it's true.

ROSE: Man, hush your mouth. You ain't said no such thing. Talking about, "Baby, you know you'll always be number one with me." That's what you was talking.

TROY: You hear that, Bono. That's why I love her.

BONO: Rose'll keep you straight. You get off the track, she'll straighten you up.

ROSE: Lyons, you better get on up and get Bonnie. She waiting on you. [p. 59]

LYONS (*gets up to go*): Hey, Pop, why don't you come on down to the Grill and hear me play?

TROY: I ain't going down there. I'm too old to be sitting around in them clubs.

BONO: You got to be good to play down at the Grill.

LYONS: Come on, Pop . . .

TROY: I got to get up in the morning.

LYONS: You ain't got to stay long.

TROY: Naw, I'm gonna get my supper and go on to bed.

LYONS: Well, I got to go. I'll see you again.

TROY: Don't you come around my house on my payday.

ROSE: Pick up the phone and let somebody know you coming. And bring Bonnie with you. You know I'm always glad to see her.

LYONS: Yeah, I'll do that, Rose. You take care now. See you, Pop. See you, Mr. Bono. See you, Uncle Gabe.

GABRIEL: Lyons! King of the Jungle!

(*Lyons exits.*)

TROY: Is supper ready, woman? Me and you got some business to take care of. I'm gonna tear it up too.

ROSE: Troy, I done told you now! [p. 60]

TROY (*puts his arm around Bono*): Aw hell, woman . . . this is Bono. Bono like family. I done known this nigger since . . . how long I done know you?

BONO: It's been a long time.

TROY: I done known this nigger since Skippy was a pup. Me and him done been through some times.

BONO: You sure right about that.

TROY: Hell, I done know him longer than I known you. And we still standing shoulder to shoulder. Hey, look here, Bono . . . a man can't ask for no more than that.

(Drinks to him.)

I love you, nigger.

BONO: Hell, I love you too . . . but I got to get home see my woman. You got yours in hand. I got to go get mine.

(Bono starts to exit as Cory enters the yard, dressed in his football uniform. He gives Troy a hard, uncompromising look.)

CORY: What you do that for, Pop?

(He throws his helmet down in the direction of Troy.)

ROSE: What's the matter? Cory . . . what's the matter?

CORY: Papa done went up to the school and told Coach Zellman I can't play football no more. Wouldn't even let me play the game. Told him to tell the recruiter not to come.

ROSE: Troy . . .

TROY: What you Troying me for. Yeah, I did it. And the boy know why I did it. [p. 61]

CORY: Why you wanna do that to me? That was the one chance I had.

ROSE: Ain't nothing wrong with Cory playing football, Troy.

TROY: The boy lied to me. I told the nigger if he wanna play football . . . to keep up his chores and hold down that job at the A&P. That was the conditions. Stopped down there to see Mr. Stawicki . . .

CORY: I can't work after school during the football season, Pop! I tried to tell you that Mr. Stawicki's holding my job for me. You don't never want to listen to nobody. And then you wanna go and do this to me!

TROY: I ain't done nothing to you. You done it to yourself.

CORY: Just cause you didn't have a chance! You just scared I'm gonna be better than you, that's all.

TROY: Come here.

ROSE: Troy . . .

(Cory reluctantly crosses over to Troy.)

TROY: Alright! See. You done made a mistake.

CORY: I didn't even do nothing!

TROY: I'm gonna tell you what your mistake was. See . . . you swung at the ball and didn't hit it. That's strike one. See, you in the batter's box now. You swung and you missed. That's strike one. Don't you strike out!

(Lights fade to black.) [p. 62]

ACT TWO / Scene One

The following morning. Cory is at the tree hitting the ball with the bat. He tries to mimic Troy, but his swing is awkward, less sure. Rose enters from the house.

ROSE: Cory, I want you to help me with this cupboard.

CORY: I ain't quitting the team. I don't care what Poppa say.

ROSE: I'll talk to him when he gets back. He had to go see about your Uncle Gabe. The police done arrested him. Say he was disturbing the peace. He'll be back directly. Come on in here and help me clean out the top of this cupboard.

(Cory exits into the house. Rose sees Troy and Bono coming down the alley.)

Troy . . . what they say down there?

TROY: Ain't said nothing. I give them fifty dollars and they let him go. I'll talk to you about it. Where's Cory?

ROSE: He's in there helping me clean out these cupboards.

TROY: Tell him to get his butt out here.

(Troy and Bono go over to the pile of wood. Bono picks up the saw and begins sawing.) [p. 65]

TROY (*to Bono*): All they want is the money. That makes six or seven times I done went down there and got him. See me coming they stick out their hands.

BONO: Yeah. I know what you mean. That's all they care about . . . that money. They don't care about what's right.

(Pause.)

Nigger, why you got to go and get some hard wood? You ain't doing nothing but building a little old fence. Get you some soft pine wood. That's all you need.

TROY: I know what I'm doing. This is outside wood. You put pine wood inside the house. Pine wood is inside wood. This here is outside wood. Now you tell me where the fence is gonna be?

BONO: You don't need this wood. You can put it up with pine wood and it'll stand as long as you gonna be here looking at it.

TROY: How you know how long I'm gonna be here, nigger? Hell, I might just live forever. Live longer than old man Horsely.

BONO: That's what Magee used to say.

TROY: Magee's a damn fool. Now you tell me who you ever heard of gonna pull their own teeth with a pair of rusty pliers.

BONO: The old folks . . . my granddaddy used to pull his teeth with pliers. They ain't had no dentists for the colored folks back then.

TROY: Get clean pliers! You understand? Clean pliers! Sterilize them! Besides we ain't living back then. All Magee had to do was walk over to Doc Goldblum's. [p. 66]

BONO: I see where you and that Tallahassee gal . . . that Alberta . . . I see where you all done got tight.

TROY: What you mean "got tight"?

BONO: I see where you be laughing and joking with her all the time.

TROY: I laughs and jokes with all of them, Bono. You know me.

BONO: That ain't the kind of laughing and joking I'm talking about.

(Cory enters from the house.)

CORY: How you doing, Mr. Bono?

TROY: Cory? Get that saw from Bono and cut some wood. He talking about the wood's too hard to cut. Stand back there, Jim, and let that young boy show you how it's done.

BONO: He's sure welcome to it.

(Cory takes the saw and begins to cut the wood.)

Whew-e-e! Look at that. Big old strong boy. Look like Joe Louis.° Hell, must be getting old the way I'm watching that boy whip through that wood.

CORY: I don't see why Mama want a fence around the yard noways.

TROY: Damn if I know either. What the hell she keeping out with it? She ain't got nothing nobody want.

BONO: Some people build fences to keep people out . . . and other people build fences to keep people in. Rose wants to hold on to you all. She loves you. [p. 67]

TROY: Hell, nigger, I don't need nobody to tell me my wife loves me. Cory . . . go on in the house and see if you can find that other saw.

CORY: Where's it at?

TROY: I said find it! Look for it till you find it!

(Cory exits into the house.)

What's that supposed to mean? Wanna keep us in?

BONO: Troy . . . I done known you seem like damn near my whole life. You and Rose both. I done know both of you all for a long time. I remember when you met Rose. When you was hitting them baseball out the park. A lot of them old gals was after you then. You had the pick of the litter. When you picked Rose, I was happy for you. That was the first time I knew you had any sense. I said . . . My man Troy knows what he's doing . . . I'm gonna follow this nigger . . . he might take me somewhere. I been following you too. I done learned a whole heap of things about life watching you. I done learned how to tell where the shit lies. How to tell it from the alfalfa. You done learned me a lot of things. You showed me how to not make the same mistakes . . . to take life as it comes along and keep putting one foot in front of the other.

Joe Louis: Joseph Louis Barrow (1914–1981), African American boxer, was known as the "Brown Bomber" and held the world heavyweight title from 1937 to 1949, longer than any other man in history.

(*Pause.*)

    Rose a good woman, Troy.

TROY: Hell, nigger, I know she a good woman. I been married to her for eighteen years. What you got on your mind, Bono?

BONO: I just say she a good woman. Just like I say anything. I ain't got to have nothing on my mind.

TROY: You just gonna say she a good woman and leave it hanging out there like that? Why you telling me she a good woman? [p. 68]

BONO: She loves you, Troy. Rose loves you.

TROY: You saying I don't measure up. That's what you trying to say. I don't measure up cause I'm seeing this other gal. I know what you trying to say.

BONO: I know what Rose means to you, Troy. I'm just trying to say I don't want to see you mess up.

TROY: Yeah, I appreciate that, Bono. If you was messing around on Lucille I'd be telling you the same thing.

BONO: Well, that's all I got to say. I just say that because I love you both.

TROY: Hell, you know me . . . I wasn't out there looking for nothing. You can't find a better woman than Rose. I know that. But seems like this woman just stuck onto me where I can't shake her loose. I done wrestled with it, tried to throw her off me . . . but she just stuck on tighter. Now she's stuck on for good.

BONO: You's in control . . . that's what you tell me all the time. You responsible for what you do.

TROY: I ain't ducking the responsibility of it. As long as it sets right in my heart . . . then I'm okay. Cause that's all I listen to. It'll tell me right from wrong every time. And I ain't talking about doing Rose no bad turn. I love Rose. She done carried me a long ways and I love and respect her for that.

BONO: I know you do. That's why I don't want to see you hurt her. But what you gonna do when she find out? What you got then? If you try and juggle both of them . . . sooner or later you gonna drop one of them. That's common sense. [p. 69]

TROY: Yeah, I hear what you saying, Bono. I been trying to figure a way to work it out.

BONO: Work it out right, Troy. I don't want to be getting all up between you and Rose's business . . . but work it so it come out right.

TROY: Aw hell, I get all up between you and Lucille's business. When you gonna get that woman that refrigerator she been wanting? Don't tell me you ain't got no money now. I know who your banker is. Mellon don't need that money bad as Lucille want that refrigerator. I'll tell you that.

BONO: Tell you what I'll do . . . when you finish building this fence for Rose . . . I'll buy Lucille that refrigerator.

TROY: You done stuck your foot in your mouth now!

(*Troy grabs up a board and begins to saw. Bono starts to walk out the yard.*)

Hey, nigger . . . where you going?

BONO: I'm going home. I know you don't expect me to help you now. I'm protecting my money. I wanna see you put that fence up by yourself. That's what I want to see. You'll be here another six months without me.

TROY: Nigger, you ain't right.

BONO: When it comes to my money . . . I'm right as fireworks on the Fourth of July.

TROY: Alright, we gonna see now. You better get out your bankbook.

(Bono exits, and Troy continues to work. Rose enters from the house.) [p. 70]

ROSE: What they say down there? What's happening with Gabe?

TROY: I went down there and got him out. Cost me fifty dollars. Say he was disturbing the peace. Judge set up a hearing for him in three weeks. Say to show cause why he shouldn't be recommitted.

ROSE: What was he doing that cause them to arrest him?

TROY: Some kids was teasing him and he run them off home. Say he was howling and carrying on. Some folks seen him and called the police. That's all it was.

ROSE: Well, what's you say? What'd you tell the judge?

TROY: Told him I'd look after him. It didn't make no sense to recommit the man. He stuck out his big greasy palm and told me to give him fifty dollars and take him on home.

ROSE: Where's he at now? Where'd he go off to?

TROY: He's gone about his business. He don't need nobody to hold his hand.

ROSE: Well, I don't know. Seem like that would be the best place for him if they did put him into the hospital. I know what you're gonna say. But that's what I think would be best.

TROY: The man done had his life ruined fighting for what? And they wanna take and lock him up. Let him be free. He don't bother nobody.

ROSE: Well, everybody got their own way of looking at it I guess. Come on and get your lunch. I got a bowl of lima [p. 71] beans and some cornbread in the oven. Come and get something to eat. Ain't no sense you fretting over Gabe.

(Rose turns to go into the house.)

TROY: Rose . . . got something to tell you.

ROSE: Well, come on . . . wait till I get this food on the table.

TROY: Rose!

(She stops and turns around.)

I don't know how to say this.

(Pause.)

I can't explain it none. It just sort of grows on you till it gets out of hand. It starts out like a little bush . . . and the next thing you know it's a whole forest.

ROSE: Troy . . . what is you talking about?

TROY: I'm talking, woman, let me talk. I'm trying to find a way to tell you . . . I'm gonna be a daddy. I'm gonna be somebody's daddy.

ROSE: Troy . . . you're not telling me this? You're gonna be . . . what?

TROY: Rose . . . now . . . see . . .

ROSE: You telling me you gonna be somebody's daddy? You telling your *wife* this?

(Gabriel enters from the street. He carries a rose in his hand.)

GABRIEL: Hey, Troy! Hey, Rose!

ROSE: I have to wait eighteen years to hear something like this. [p. 72]

GABRIEL: Hey, Rose . . . I got a flower for you.

(He hands it to her.)

That's a rose. Same rose like you is.

ROSE: Thanks, Gabe.

GABRIEL: Troy, you ain't mad at me is you? Them bad mens come and put me away. You ain't mad at me is you?

TROY: Naw, Gabe, I ain't mad at you.

ROSE: Eighteen years and you wanna come with this.

GABRIEL *(takes a quarter out of his pocket)*: See what I got? Got a brand new quarter.

TROY: Rose . . . it's just . . .

ROSE: Ain't nothing you can say, Troy. Ain't no way of explaining that.

GABRIEL: Fellow that give me this quarter had a whole mess of them. I'm gonna keep this quarter till it stop shining.

ROSE: Gabe, go on in the house there. I got some watermelon in the frigidaire. Go on and get you a piece.

GABRIEL: Say, Rose . . . you know I was chasing hellhounds and them bad mens come and get me and take me away. Troy helped me. He come down there and told them they better let me go before he beat them up. Yeah, he did!

ROSE: You go on and get you a piece of watermelon, Gabe. Them bad mens is gone now. [p. 73]

GABRIEL: Okay, Rose . . . gonna get me some watermelon. The kind with the stripes on it.

(Gabriel exits into the house.)

ROSE: Why, Troy? Why? After all these years to come dragging this in to me now. It don't make no sense at your age. I could have expected this ten or fifteen years ago, but not now.

TROY: Age ain't got nothing to do with it, Rose.

ROSE: I done tried to be everything a wife should be. Everything a wife could be. Been married eighteen years and I got to live to see the day you tell me you been seeing another woman and done fathered a child by her. And you know I ain't never wanted no half nothing in my family. My whole family is half. Everybody got different fathers and mothers . . . my two sisters and my brother. Can't hardly tell who's who. Can't never sit down and talk about Papa and Mama. It's your papa and your mama and my papa and my mama . . .

TROY: Rose . . . stop it now.

ROSE: I ain't never wanted that for none of my children. And now you wanna drag your behind in here and tell me something like this.

TROY: You ought to know. It's time for you to know.

ROSE: Well, I don't want to know, goddamn it!

TROY: I can't just make it go away. It's done now. I can't wish the circumstance of the thing away.

ROSE: And you don't want to either. Maybe you want to wish me and my boy away. Maybe that's what you want? Well, you can't wish us away. I've got eighteen years of my life [p. 74] invested in you. You ought to have stayed upstairs in my bed where you belong.

TROY: Rose . . . now listen to me . . . we can get a handle on this thing. We can talk this out . . . come to an understanding.

ROSE: All of a sudden it's "we." Where was "we" at when you was down there rolling around with some god-forsaken woman? "We" should have come to an understanding before you started making a damn fool of yourself. You're a day late and a dollar short when it comes to an understanding with me.

TROY: It's just . . . She gives me a different idea . . . a different understanding about myself. I can step out of this house and get away from the pressures and problems . . . be a different man. I ain't got to wonder how I'm gonna pay the bills or get the roof fixed. I can just be a part of myself that I ain't never been.

ROSE: What I want to know . . . is do you plan to continue seeing her. That's all you can say to me.

TROY: I can sit up in her house and laugh. Do you understand what I'm saying. I can laugh out loud . . . and it feels good. It reaches all the way down to the bottom of my shoes.

(*Pause.*)

Rose, I can't give that up.

ROSE: Maybe you ought to go on and stay down there with her . . . if she a better woman than me.

TROY: It ain't about nobody being a better woman or nothing. Rose, you ain't the blame. A man couldn't ask for no woman to be a better wife than you've been. I'm responsible [p. 75] for it. I done locked myself into a pattern trying to take care of you all that I forgot about myself.

ROSE: What the hell was I there for? That was my job, not somebody else's.

TROY: Rose, I done tried all my life to live decent . . . to live a clean . . . hard . . . useful life. I tried to be a good husband to you. In every way I knew how. Maybe I come into the world backwards, I don't know. But . . . you born with two strikes on you before you come to the plate. You got to guard it closely . . . always looking for the curve ball on the inside corner. You can't afford to let none get past you. You can't afford a call strike. If you going down . . . you going down swinging. Everything lined up against you. What you gonna do. I fooled them, Rose. I bunted. When I found you and Cory and a halfway decent job . . . I was safe. Couldn't nothing touch me. I wasn't gonna strike out no more. I wasn't going back to the penitentiary. I wasn't gonna lay in the streets with a bottle of wine. I was safe. I had me a family. A job. I wasn't gonna get that last strike. I was on first looking for one of them boys to knock me in. To get me home.

ROSE: You should have stayed in my bed, Troy.

TROY: Then when I saw that gal . . . she firmed up my backbone. And I got to thinking that if I tried . . . I just might be able to steal second. Do you understand after eighteen years I wanted to steal second.

ROSE: You should have held me tight. You should have grabbed me and held on.

TROY: I stood on first base for eighteen years and I thought . . . well, goddamn it . . . go on for it! [p. 76]

ROSE: We're not talking about baseball! We're talking about you going off to lay in bed with another woman . . . and then bring it home to me. That's what we're talking about. We ain't talking about no baseball.

TROY: Rose, you're not listening to me. I'm trying the best I can to explain it to you. It's not easy for me to admit that I been standing in the same place for eighteen years.

ROSE: I been standing with you! I been right here with you, Troy. I got a life too. I gave eighteen years of my life to stand in the same spot with you. Don't you think I ever wanted other things? Don't you think I had dreams and hopes? What about my life? What about me? Don't you think it ever crossed my mind to want to know other men? That I wanted to lay up somewhere and forget about my responsibilities? That I wanted someone to make me laugh so I could feel good? You not the only one who's got wants and needs. But I held on to you, Troy. I took all my feelings, my wants and needs, my dreams . . . and I buried them inside you. I planted a seed and watched and prayed over it. I planted myself inside you and waited to bloom. And it didn't take me no eighteen years to find out the soil was hard and rocky and it wasn't never gonna bloom.

But I held on to you, Troy. I held you tighter. You was my husband. I owed you everything I had. Every part of me I could find to give you. And upstairs in that room . . . with the darkness falling in on me . . . I gave everything I had to try and erase the doubt that you wasn't the finest man in the world. And wherever you was going . . . I wanted to be there with you. Cause you was my husband. Cause that's the only way I was gonna survive as your wife. You always talking about what you give . . . and what you don't have to give. But you take too. You take . . . and don't even know nobody's giving!

(Rose turns to exit into the house; Troy grabs her arm.) [p. 77]

TROY: You say I take and don't give!

ROSE: Troy! You're hurting me!

TROY: You say I take and don't give.

ROSE: Troy . . . you're hurting my arm! Let go!

TROY: I done give you everything I got. Don't you tell that lie on me.

ROSE: Troy!

TROY: Don't you tell that lie on me!

(Cory enters from the house.)

CORY: Mama!

ROSE: Troy. You're hurting me.

TROY: Don't you tell me about no taking and giving.

(Cory comes up behind Troy and grabs him. Troy, surprised, is thrown off balance just as Cory throws a glancing blow that catches him on the chest and knocks him down. Troy is stunned, as is Cory.)

ROSE: Troy. Troy. No!

(Troy gets to his feet and starts at Cory.)

Troy . . . no. Please! Troy!

(Rose pulls on Troy to hold him back. Troy stops himself.)

TROY *(to Cory):* Alright. That's strike two. You stay away from around me, boy. Don't you strike out. You living with a full count. Don't you strike out.

(Troy exits out the yard as the lights go down.) [p. 78]

Scene Two

It is six months later, early afternoon. Troy enters from the house and starts to exit the yard. Rose enters from the house.

ROSE: Troy, I want to talk to you.

TROY: All of a sudden, after all this time, you want to talk to me, huh? You ain't wanted to talk to me for months. You ain't wanted to talk to me last night. You ain't wanted no part of me then. What you wanna talk to me about now?

ROSE: Tomorrow's Friday.

TROY: I know what day tomorrow is. You think I don't know tomorrow's Friday? My whole life I ain't done nothing but look to see Friday coming and you got to tell me it's Friday.

ROSE: I want to know if you're coming home.

TROY: I always come home, Rose. You know that. There ain't never been a night I ain't come home.

ROSE: That ain't what I mean . . . and you know it. I want to know if you're coming straight home after work.

TROY: I figure I'd cash my check . . . hang out at Taylors' with the boys . . . maybe play a game of checkers . . . [p. 79]

ROSE: Troy, I can't live like this. I won't live like this. You livin' on borrowed time with me. It's been going on six months now you ain't been coming home.

TROY: I be here every night. Every night of the year. That's 365 days.

ROSE: I want you to come home tomorrow after work.

TROY: Rose . . . I don't mess up my pay. You know that now. I take my pay and I give it to you. I don't have no money but what you give me back. I just want to have a little time to myself . . . a little time to enjoy life.

ROSE: What about me? When's my time to enjoy life?

TROY: I don't know what to tell you, Rose. I'm doing the best I can.

ROSE: You ain't been home from work but time enough to change your clothes and run out . . . and you wanna call that the best you can do?

TROY: I'm going over to the hospital to see Alberta. She went into the hospital this afternoon. Look like she might have the baby early. I won't be gone long.

ROSE: Well, you ought to know. They went over to Miss Pearl's and got Gabe today. She said you told them to go ahead and lock him up.

TROY: I ain't said no such thing. Whoever told you that is telling a lie. Pearl ain't doing nothing but telling a big fat lie.

ROSE: She ain't had to tell me. I read it on the papers.

TROY: I ain't told them nothing of the kind. [p. 80]

ROSE: I saw it right there on the papers.

TROY: What it say, huh?

ROSE: It said you told them to take him.

TROY: Then they screwed that up, just the way they screw up everything. I ain't worried about what they got on the paper.

ROSE: Say the government send part of his check to the hospital and the other part to you.

TROY: I ain't got nothing to do with that if that's the way it works. I ain't made up the rules about how it work.

ROSE: You did Gabe just like you did Cory. You wouldn't sign the paper for Cory . . . but you signed for Gabe. You signed that paper.

(*The telephone is heard ringing inside the house.*)

TROY: I told you I ain't signed nothing, woman! The only thing I signed was the release form. Hell, I can't read, I don't know what they had on that paper! I ain't signed nothing about sending Gabe away.

ROSE: I said send him to the hospital . . . you said let him be free . . . now you done went down there and signed him to the hospital for half his money. You went back on yourself, Troy. You gonna have to answer for that.

TROY: See now . . . you been over there talking to Miss Pearl. She done got mad cause she ain't getting Gabe's rent money. That's all it is. She's liable to say anything.

ROSE: Troy, I seen where you signed the paper. [p. 81]
TROY: You ain't seen nothing I signed. What she doing got papers on my brother anyway? Miss Pearl telling a big fat lie. And I'm gonna tell her about it too! You ain't seen nothing I signed. Say . . . you ain't seen nothing I signed.

(*Rose exits into the house to answer the telephone. Presently she returns.*)

ROSE: Troy . . . that was the hospital. Alberta had the baby.
TROY: What she have? What is it?
ROSE: It's a girl.
TROY: I better get on down to the hospital to see her.
ROSE: Troy . . .
TROY: Rose . . . I got to go see her now. That's only right . . . what's the matter . . . the baby's all right, ain't it?
ROSE: Alberta died having the baby.
TROY: Died . . . you say she's dead? Alberta's dead?
ROSE: They said they done all they could. They couldn't do nothing for her.
TROY: The baby? How's the baby?
ROSE: They say it's healthy. I wonder who's gonna bury her.
TROY: She had family, Rose. She wasn't living in the world by herself.
ROSE: I know she wasn't living in the world by herself. [p. 82]
TROY: Next thing you gonna want to know if she had any insurance.
ROSE: Troy, you ain't got to talk like that.
TROY: That's the first thing that jumped out your mouth. "Who's gonna bury her?" Like I'm fixing to take on that task for myself.
ROSE: I am your wife. Don't push me away.
TROY: I ain't pushing nobody away. Just give me some space. That's all. Just give me some room to breathe.

(*Rose exits into the house. Troy walks about the yard.*)

TROY (*with a quiet rage that threatens to consume him*): Alright . . . Mr. Death. See now . . . I'm gonna tell you what I'm gonna do. I'm gonna take and build me a fence around this yard. See? I'm gonna build me a fence around what belongs to me. And then I want you to stay on the other side. See? You stay over there until you're ready for me. Then you come on. Bring your army. Bring your sickle. Bring your wrestling clothes. I ain't gonna fall down on my vigilance this time. You ain't gonna sneak up on me no more. When you ready for me . . . when the top of your list say Troy Maxson . . . that's when you come around here. You come up and knock on the front door. Ain't nobody else got nothing to do with this. This is between you and me. Man to man. You stay on the other side of that fence until you ready for me. Then you come up and knock on the front door. Anytime you want. I'll be ready for you.

(*The lights go down to black.*) [p. 83]

Scene Three

The lights come up on the porch. It is late evening three days later. Rose sits listening to the ball game waiting for Troy. The final out of the game is made and Rose switches off the radio. Troy enters the yard carrying an infant wrapped in blankets. He stands back from the house and calls.

(Rose enters and stands on the porch. There is a long, awkward silence, the weight of which grows heavier with each passing second.)

TROY: Rose . . . I'm standing here with my daughter in my arms. She ain't but a wee bittie little old thing. She don't know nothing about grownups' business. She innocent . . . and she ain't got no mama.

ROSE: What you telling me for, Troy?

(She turns and exits into the house.)

TROY: Well . . . I guess we'll just sit out here on the porch.

(He sits down on the porch. There is an awkward indelicateness about the way he handles the baby. His largeness engulfs and seems to swallow it. He speaks loud enough for Rose to hear.)

A man's got to do what's right for him. I ain't sorry for nothing I done. It felt right in my heart.

(To the baby.)

What you smiling at? Your daddy's a big man. Got these great big old hands. But sometimes he's scared. And right [p. 85] now your daddy's scared cause we sitting out here and ain't got no home. Oh, I been homeless before. I ain't had no little baby with me. But I been homeless. You just be out on the road by your lonesome and you see one of them trains coming and you just kinda go like this . . .

(He sings as a lullaby.)

Please, Mr. Engineer let a man ride the line
Please, Mr. Engineer let a man ride the line
I ain't got no ticket please let me ride the blinds

(Rose enters from the house. Troy, hearing her steps behind him, stands and faces her.)

She's my daughter, Rose. My own flesh and blood. I can't deny her no more than I can deny them boys.

(Pause.)

You and them boys is my family. You and them and this child is all I got in the world. So I guess what I'm saying is . . . I'd appreciate it if you'd help me take care of her.

ROSE: Okay, Troy . . . you're right. I'll take care of your baby for you . . . cause . . . like you say . . . she's innocent . . . and you can't visit the sins of the father upon the child. A motherless child has got a hard time.

(*She takes the baby from him.*)

From right now . . . this child got a mother. But you a womanless man.

(*Rose turns and exits into the house with the baby. Lights go down to black.*) [p. 86]

Scene Four

It is two months later. Lyons enters from the street. He knocks on the door and calls.

LYONS: Hey, Rose! (*Pause.*) Rose!

ROSE (*from inside the house*): Stop that yelling. You gonna wake up Raynell. I just got her to sleep.

LYONS: I just stopped by to pay Papa this twenty dollars I owe him. Where's Papa at?

ROSE: He should be here in a minute. I'm getting ready to go down to the church. Sit down and wait on him.

LYONS: I got to go pick up Bonnie over her mother's house.

ROSE: Well, sit it down there on the table. He'll get it.

LYONS (*enters the house and sets the money on the table*): Tell Papa I said thanks. I'll see you again.

ROSE: Alright, Lyons. We'll see you.

(*Lyons starts to exit as Cory enters.*)

CORY: Hey, Lyons. [p. 87]

LYONS: What's happening, Cory? Say man, I'm sorry I missed your graduation. You know I had a gig and couldn't get away. Otherwise, I would have been there, man. So what you doing?

CORY: I'm trying to find a job.

LYONS: Yeah I know how that go, man. It's rough out here. Jobs are scarce.

CORY: Yeah, I know.

LYONS: Look here, I got to run. Talk to Papa . . . he know some people. He'll be able to help get you a job. Talk to him . . . see what he say.

CORY: Yeah . . . alright, Lyons.

LYONS: You take care. I'll talk to you soon. We'll find some time to talk.

(*Lyons exits the yard. Cory wanders over to the tree, picks up the bat, and assumes a batting stance. He studies an imaginary pitcher and swings. Dissatisfied with the result, he tries again. Troy enters. They eye each other for a beat. Cory puts the bat down and exits the yard. Troy starts into the house as Rose exits with Raynell. She is carrying a cake.*)

TROY: I'm coming in and everybody's going out.

ROSE: I'm taking this cake down to the church for the bakesale. Lyons was by to see you. He stopped by to pay you your twenty dollars. It's laying in there on the table.

TROY (*going into his pocket*): Well . . . here go this money. [p. 88]

ROSE: Put it in there on the table, Troy. I'll get it.

TROY: What time you coming back?

ROSE: Ain't no use in you studying me. It don't matter what time I come back.

TROY: I just asked you a question, woman. What's the matter . . . can't I ask you a question?

ROSE: Troy, I don't want to go into it. Your dinner's in there on the stove. All you got to do is heat it up. And don't you be eating the rest of them cakes in there. I'm coming back for them. We having a bakesale at the church tomorrow.

(*Rose exits the yard. Troy sits down on the steps, takes a pint bottle from his pocket, opens it, and drinks. He begins to sing.*)

TROY: Hear it ring! Hear it ring!
Had an old dog his name was Blue
You know Blue was mighty true
You know Blue was a good old dog
Blue trees a possum in a hollow log
You know from that he was a good old dog

(*Bono enters the yard.*)

BONO: Hey, Troy.

TROY: Hey, what's happening, Bono?

BONO: I just thought I'd stop by to see you.

TROY: What you stop by and see me for? You ain't stopped by in a month of Sundays. Hell, I must owe you money or something. [p. 89]

BONO: Since you got your promotion I can't keep up with you. Used to see you every day. Now I don't even know what route you working.

TROY: They keep switching me around. Got me out in Greentree now . . . hauling white folks' garbage.

BONO: Greentree, huh? You lucky, at least you ain't got to be lifting them barrels. Damn if they ain't getting heavier. I'm gonna put in my two years and call it quits.

TROY: I'm thinking about retiring myself.

BONO: You got it easy. You can *drive* for another five years.

TROY: It ain't the same, Bono. It ain't like working the back of the truck. Ain't got nobody to talk to . . . feel like you working by yourself. Naw, I'm thinking about retiring. How's Lucille?

BONO: She alright. Her arthritis get to acting up on her sometime. Saw Rose on my way in. She going down to the church, huh?

TROY: Yeah, she took up going down there. All them preachers looking for somebody to fatten their pockets.

(*Pause.*)

    Got some gin here.

BONO: Naw, thanks. I just stopped by to say hello.

TROY: Hell, nigger . . . you can take a drink. I ain't never known you to say no to a drink. You ain't got to work tomorrow.

BONO: I just stopped by. I'm fixing to go over to Skinner's. We got us a domino game going over his house every Friday. [p. 90]

TROY: Nigger, you can't play no dominoes. I used to whup you four games out of five.

BONO: Well, that learned me. I'm getting better.

TROY: Yeah? Well, that's alright.

BONO: Look here . . . I got to be getting on. Stop by sometime, huh?

TROY: Yeah, I'll do that, Bono. Lucille told Rose you bought her a new refrigerator.

BONO: Yeah, Rose told Lucille you had finally built your fence . . . so I figured we'd call it even.

TROY: I knew you would.

BONO: Yeah . . . okay. I'll be talking to you.

TROY: Yeah, take care, Bono. Good to see you. I'm gonna stop over.

BONO: Yeah. Okay, Troy.

(*Bono exits. Troy drinks from the bottle.*)

TROY: Old Blue died and I dig his grave
    Let him down with a golden chain
    Every night when I hear old Blue bark
    I know Blue treed a possum in Noah's Ark.
    Hear it ring! Hear it ring!

(*Cory enters the yard. They eye each other for a beat. Troy is sitting in the middle of the steps. Cory walks over.*)

CORY: I got to get by. [p. 91]

TROY: Say what? What's you say?

CORY: You in my way. I got to get by.

TROY: You got to get by where? This is my house. Bought and paid for. In full. Took me fifteen years. And if you wanna go in my house and I'm sitting on the steps . . . you say excuse me. Like your mama taught you.

CORY: Come on, Pop . . . I got to get by.

(*Cory starts to maneuver his way past Troy. Troy grabs his leg and shoves him back.*)

TROY: You just gonna walk over top of me?

CORY: I live here too!

TROY (*advancing toward him*): You just gonna walk over top of me in my own house?

CORY: I ain't scared of you.

TROY: I ain't asked if you was scared of me. I asked you if you was fixing to walk over top of me in my own house? That's the question. You ain't gonna say excuse me? You just gonna walk over top of me?

CORY: If you wanna put it like that.

TROY: How else am I gonna put it?

CORY: I was walking by you to go into the house cause you sitting on the steps drunk, singing to yourself. You can put it like that.

TROY: Without saying excuse me???

(*Cory doesn't respond.*)

I asked you a question. Without saying excuse me??? [p. 92]

CORY: I ain't got to say excuse me to you. You don't count around here no more.

TROY: Oh, I see . . . I don't count around here no more. You ain't got to say excuse me to your daddy. All of a sudden you done got so grown that your daddy don't count around here no more . . . Around here in his own house and yard that he done paid for with the sweat of his brow. You done got so grown to where you gonna take over. You gonna take over my house. Is that right? You gonna wear my pants. You gonna go in there and stretch out on my bed. You ain't got to say excuse me cause I don't count around here no more. Is that right?

CORY: That's right. You always talking this dumb stuff. Now, why don't you just get out my way.

TROY: I guess you got someplace to sleep and something to put in your belly. You got that, huh? You got that? That's what you need. You got that, huh?

CORY: You don't know what I got. You ain't got to worry about what I got.

TROY: You right! You one hundred percent right! I done spent the last seventeen years worrying about what you got. Now it's your turn, see? I'll tell you what to do. You grown . . . we done established that. You a man. Now, let's see you act like one. Turn your behind around and walk out this yard. And when you get out there in the alley . . . you can forget about this house. See? Cause this is my house. You go on and be a man and get your own house. You can forget about this. Cause this is mine. You go on and get yours cause I'm through with doing for you.

CORY: You talking about what you did for me . . . what'd you ever give me? [p. 93]

TROY: Them feet and bones! That pumping heart, nigger! I give you more than anybody else is ever gonna give you.

CORY: You ain't never gave me nothing! You ain't never done nothing but hold me back. Afraid I was gonna be better than you. All you ever did was try and make me scared of you. I used to tremble every time you called my name. Every time I heard your footsteps in the house. Wondering all the time . . . what's Papa gonna say if I do this? . . . What's he gonna say if I do that? . . . What's Papa gonna say if I turn on the radio? And Mama, too . . . she tries . . . but she's scared of you.

TROY: You leave your mama out of this. She ain't got nothing to do with this.

CORY: I don't know how she stand you . . . after what you did to her.

TROY: I told you to leave your mama out of this!

(*He advances toward Cory.*)

CORY: What you gonna do . . . give me a whupping? You can't whup me no more. You're too old. You just an old man.

TROY (*shoves him on his shoulder*): Nigger! That's what you are. You just another nigger on the street to me!

CORY: You crazy! You know that?

TROY: Go on now! You got the devil in you. Get on away from me!

CORY: You just a crazy old man . . . talking about I got the devil in me.

TROY: Yeah, I'm crazy! If you don't get on the other side of that yard . . . I'm gonna show you how crazy I am! Go on . . . get the hell out of my yard. [p. 94]

CORY: It ain't your yard. You took Uncle Gabe's money he got from the army to buy this house and then you put him out.

TROY (*advances on Cory*): Get your black ass out of my yard!

(*Troy's advance backs Cory up against the tree. Cory grabs up the bat.*)

CORY: I ain't going nowhere! Come on . . . put me out! I ain't scared of you.

TROY: That's my bat!

CORY: Come on!

TROY: Put my bat down!

CORY: Come on, put me out.

(*Cory swings at Troy, who backs across the yard.*)

What's the matter? You so bad . . . put me out!

(*Troy advances toward Cory.*)

CORY (*backing up*): Come on! Come on!

TROY: You're gonna have to use it! You wanna draw that bat back on me . . . you're gonna have to use it.

CORY: Come on! . . . Come on!

(*Cory swings the bat at Troy a second time. He misses. Troy continues to advance toward him.*)

TROY: You're gonna have to kill me! You wanna draw that bat back on me. You're gonna have to kill me. [p. 95]

(*Cory, backed up against the tree, can go no farther. Troy taunts him. He sticks out his head and offers him a target.*)

Come on! Come on!

(*Cory is unable to swing the bat. Troy grabs it.*)

TROY: Then I'll show you.

(*Cory and Troy struggle over the bat. The struggle is fierce and fully engaged. Troy ultimately is the stronger and takes the bat from Cory and stands over him ready to swing. He stops himself.*)

Go on and get away from around my house.

(*Cory, stung by his defeat, picks himself up, walks slowly out of the yard and up the alley.*)

CORY: Tell Mama I'll be back for my things.

TROY: They'll be on the other side of that fence.

(*Cory exits.*)

TROY: I can't taste nothing. Helluljah! I can't taste nothing no more. (*Troy assumes a batting posture and begins to taunt Death, the fastball on the outside corner.*) Come on! It's between you and me now! Come on! Anytime you want! Come on! I be ready for you . . . but I ain't gonna be easy.

(*The lights go down on the scene.*) [p. 96]

Scene Five

The time is 1965. The lights come up in the yard. It is the morning of Troy's funeral. A funeral plaque with a light hangs beside the door. There is a small garden plot off to the side. There is noise and activity in the house as Rose, Lyons, and Bono have gathered. The door opens and Raynell, seven years old, enters dressed in a flannel nightgown. She crosses to the garden and pokes around with a stick. Rose calls from the house.

ROSE: Raynell!

RAYNELL: Mam?

ROSE: What you doing out there?

RAYNELL: Nothing.

(*Rose comes to the door.*)

ROSE: Girl, get in here and get dressed. What you doing?

RAYNELL: Seeing if my garden growed.

ROSE: I told you it ain't gonna grow overnight. You got to wait.

RAYNELL: It don't look like it never gonna grow. Dag! [p. 97]

ROSE: I told you a watched pot never boils. Get in here and get dressed.

RAYNELL: This ain't even no pot, Mama.

ROSE: You just have to give it a chance. It'll grow. Now you come on and do what I told you. We got to be getting ready. This ain't no morning to be playing around. You hear me?

RAYNELL: Yes, mam.

(*Rose exits into the house. Raynell continues to poke at her garden with a stick. Cory enters. He is dressed in a Marine corporal's uniform, and carries a duffel bag. His posture is that of a military man, and his speech has a clipped sternness.*)

CORY (*to Raynell*): Hi.

(*Pause.*)

I bet your name is Raynell.

RAYNELL: Uh huh.

CORY: Is your mama home?

(*Raynell runs up on the porch and calls through the screen door.*)

RAYNELL: Mama . . . there's some man out here. Mama?

(*Rose comes to the door.*)

ROSE: Cory? Lord have mercy! Look here, you all!

(*Rose and Cory embrace in a tearful reunion as Bono and Lyons enter from the house dressed in funeral clothes.*)

BONO: Aw, looka here . . . [p. 98]

ROSE: Done got all grown up!

CORY: Don't cry, Mama. What you crying about?

ROSE: I'm just so glad you made it.

CORY: Hey Lyons. How you doing, Mr. Bono.

(*Lyons goes to embrace Cory.*)

LYONS: Look at you, man. Look at you. Don't he look good, Rose. Got them Corporal stripes.

ROSE: What took you so long.

CORY: You know how the Marines are, Mama. They got to get all their paperwork straight before they let you do anything.

ROSE: Well, I'm sure glad you made it. They let Lyons come. Your Uncle Gabe's still in the hospital. They don't know if they gonna let him out or not. I just talked to them a little while ago.

LYONS: A Corporal in the United States Marines.

BONO: Your daddy knew you had it in you. He used to tell me all the time.

LYONS: Don't he look good, Mr. Bono?

BONO: Yeah, he remind me of Troy when I first met him.

(*Pause.*)

Say, Rose, Lucille's down at the church with the choir. I'm gonna go down and get the pallbearers lined up. I'll be back to get you all.

ROSE: Thanks, Jim. [p. 99]

CORY: See you, Mr. Bono.

LYONS (*with his arm around Raynell*): Cory . . . look at Raynell. Ain't she precious? She gonna break a whole lot of hearts.

ROSE: Raynell, come and say hello to your brother. This is your brother, Cory. You remember Cory.

RAYNELL: No, Mam.

CORY: She don't remember me, Mama.

ROSE: Well, we talk about you. She heard us talk about you. (*To Raynell.*) This is your brother, Cory. Come on and say hello.

RAYNELL: Hi.

CORY: Hi. So you're Raynell. Mama told me a lot about you.

ROSE: You all come on into the house and let me fix you some breakfast. Keep up your strength.

CORY: I ain't hungry, Mama.

LYONS: You can fix me something, Rose. I'll be in there in a minute.

ROSE: Cory, you sure you don't want nothing? I know they ain't feeding you right.

CORY: No, Mama . . . thanks. I don't feel like eating. I'll get something later.

ROSE: Raynell . . . get on upstairs and get that dress on like I told you. [p. 100]

(*Rose and Raynell exit into the house.*)

LYONS: So . . . I hear you thinking about getting married.

CORY: Yeah, I done found the right one, Lyons. It's about time.

LYONS: Me and Bonnie been split up about four years now. About the time Papa retired. I guess she just got tired of all them changes I was putting her through.

(*Pause.*)

I always knew you was gonna make something out yourself. Your head was always in the right direction. So . . . you gonna stay in . . . make it a career . . . put in your twenty years?

CORY: I don't know. I got six already, I think that's enough.

LYONS: Stick with Uncle Sam and retire early. Ain't nothing out here. I guess Rose told you what happened with me. They got me down the workhouse. I thought I was being slick cashing other people's checks.

CORY: How much time you doing?

LYONS: They give me three years. I got that beat now. I ain't got but nine more months. It ain't so bad. You learn to deal with it like anything else. You got to take the crookeds with the straights. That's what Papa used to say. He used to say that when he struck out. I seen him strike out three times in a row . . . and the next time up he hit the ball over the grandstand. Right out there in Homestead Field. He wasn't satisfied hitting in the seats . . . he want to hit it over everything! After the game he had two hundred people standing around waiting to shake his hand. You got to take the crookeds with the straights. Yeah, Papa was something else. [p. 101]

CORY: You still playing?

LYONS: Cory . . . you know I'm gonna do that. There's some fellows down there we got us a band . . . we gonna try and stay together when we get out . . . but yeah, I'm still playing. It still helps me to get out of bed in the morning. As long as it do that I'm gonna be right there playing and trying to make some sense out of it.

ROSE (*calling*): Lyons, I got these eggs in the pan.

LYONS: Let me go on and get these eggs, man. Get ready to go bury Papa.

(*Pause.*)

How you doing? You doing alright?

(*Cory nods. Lyons touches him on the shoulder and they share a moment of silent grief. Lyons exits into the house. Cory wanders about the yard. Raynell enters.*)

RAYNELL: Hi.

CORY: Hi.

RAYNELL: Did you used to sleep in my room?

CORY: Yeah . . . that used to be my room.

RAYNELL: That's what Papa call it. "Cory's room." It got your football in the closet.

(*Rose comes to the door.*)

ROSE: Raynell, get in there and get them good shoes on.

RAYNELL: Mama, can't I wear these? Them other one hurt my feet. [p. 102]

ROSE: Well, they just gonna have to hurt your feet for a while. You ain't said they hurt your feet when you went down to the store and got them.

RAYNELL: They didn't hurt then. My feet done got bigger.

ROSE: Don't you give me no backtalk now. You get in there and get them shoes on.

(*Raynell exits into the house.*)

Ain't too much changed. He still got that piece of rag tied to that tree. He was out here swinging that bat. I was just ready to go back in the house. He swung that bat and then he just fell over. Seem like he swung it and stood there with this grin on his face . . . and then he just fell over. They carried him on down to the hospital, but I knew there wasn't no need . . . why don't you come on in the house?

CORY: Mama . . . I got something to tell you. I don't know how to tell you this . . . but I've got to tell you . . . I'm not going to Papa's funeral.

ROSE: Boy, hush your mouth. That's your daddy you talking about. I don't want hear that kind of talk this morning. I done raised you to come to this? You standing there all healthy and grown talking about you ain't going to your daddy's funeral?

CORY: Mama . . . listen . . .

ROSE: I don't want to hear it, Cory. You just get that thought out of your head.

CORY: I can't drag Papa with me everywhere I go. I've got to say no to him. One time in my life I've got to say no.

ROSE: Don't nobody have to listen to nothing like that. I know you and your daddy ain't seen eye to eye, but I ain't [p. 103] got to listen to that kind of talk this morning. Whatever was between you and your daddy . . . the time has come to put it aside. Just take it and set it over there on the shelf and forget about it. Disrespecting your daddy ain't gonna make you a man, Cory. You got to find a way to come to that on your own. Not going to your daddy's funeral ain't gonna make you a man.

CORY: The whole time I was growing up . . . living in his house . . . Papa was like a shadow that followed you everywhere. It weighed on you and sunk into your flesh. It would wrap around you and lay there until you couldn't tell which one was you anymore. That shadow digging in your flesh. Trying to crawl in. Trying to live through you. Everywhere I looked, Troy Maxson was staring back at me . . . hiding under the bed . . . in the closet. I'm just saying I've got to find a way to get rid of that shadow, Mama.

ROSE: You just like him. You got him in you good.

CORY: Don't tell me that, Mama.

ROSE: You Troy Maxson all over again.

CORY: I don't want to be Troy Maxson. I want to be me.

ROSE: You can't be nobody but who you are, Cory. That shadow wasn't nothing but you growing into yourself. You either got to grow into it or cut it down to fit you. But that's all you got to make life with. That's all you got to measure yourself against that world out there. Your daddy wanted you to be everything he wasn't . . . and at the same time he tried to make you into everything he was. I don't know if he was right or wrong . . . but I do know he meant to do more good than he meant to do harm. He wasn't always right. Sometimes when he touched he bruised. And sometimes when he took me in his arms he cut. [p. 104]

When I first met your daddy I thought . . . Here is a man I can lay down with and make a baby. That's the first thing I thought when I seen him. I was thirty years old and had done seen my share of men. But when he walked up to me and said, "I can dance a waltz that'll make you dizzy," I thought, Rose Lee, here is a man that you can open yourself up to and be filled to bursting. Here is a man that can fill all them empty spaces you been tipping around the edges of. One of them empty spaces was being somebody's mother.

I married your daddy and settled down to cooking his supper and keeping clean sheets on the bed. When your daddy walked through the house he was so big he filled it up. That was my first mistake. Not to make him leave some room for me. For my part in the matter. But at that time I wanted that. I wanted a house that I could sing in. And that's what your daddy gave me. I didn't know to keep up his strength I had to give up little pieces of mine. I did that. I took on his life as mine and mixed up the pieces so that you couldn't hardly tell which was which anymore. It was my choice. It was my life and I didn't have to live it like that. But that's what life offered me in the way of being a woman and I took it. I grabbed hold of it with both hands.

By the time Raynell came into the house, me and your daddy had done lost touch with one another. I didn't want to make my blessing off of nobody's misfortune . . . but I took on to Raynell like she was all them babies I had wanted and never had.

(*The phone rings.*)

Like I'd been blessed to relive a part of my life. And if the Lord see fit to keep up my strength . . . I'm gonna do her just like your daddy did you . . . I'm gonna give her the best of what's in me.

RAYNELL (*entering, still with her old shoes*): Mama . . . Reverend Tollivier on the phone. [p. 105]

(*Rose exits into the house.*)

RAYNELL: Hi.

CORY: Hi.

RAYNELL: You in the Army or the Marines?

CORY: Marines.

RAYNELL: Papa said it was the Army. Did you know Blue?

CORY: Blue? Who's Blue?

RAYNELL: Papa's dog what he sing about all the time.

CORY (*singing*): Hear it ring! Hear it ring!
I had a dog his name was Blue
You know Blue was mighty true
You know Blue was a good old dog
Blue treed a possum in a hollow log
You know from that he was a good old dog.
Hear it ring! Hear it ring!

(*Raynell joins in singing.*)

CORY AND RAYNELL: Blue treed a possum out on a limb
Blue looked at me and I looked at him
Grabbed that possum and put him in a sack
Blue stayed there till I came back
Old Blue's feets was big and round
Never allowed a possum to touch the ground.

Old Blue died and I dug his grave
I dug his grave with a silver spade
Let him down with a golden chain
And every night I call his name [p. 106]
Go on Blue, you good dog you
Go on Blue, you good dog you

RAYNELL: Blue laid down and died like a man
Blue laid down and died . . .
BOTH: Blue laid down and died like a man
Now he's treeing possums in the Promised Land
I'm gonna tell you this to let you know
Blue's gone where the good dogs go
When I hear old Blue bark
When I hear old Blue bark
Blue treed a possum in Noah's Ark
Blue treed a possum in Noah's Ark.

(Rose comes to the screen door.)

ROSE: Cory, we gonna be ready to go in a minute.
CORY *(to Raynell)*: You go on in the house and change them shoes like Mama
told you so we can go to Papa's funeral.
RAYNELL: Okay, I'll be back.

*(Raynell exits into the house. Cory gets up and crosses over to the tree. Rose stands
in the screen door watching him. Gabriel enters from the alley.)*

GABRIEL *(calling)*: Hey, Rose!
ROSE: Gabe?
GABRIEL: I'm here, Rose. Hey Rose, I'm here!

(Rose enters from the house.)

ROSE: Lord . . . Look here, Lyons! [p. 107]
LYONS: See, I told you, Rose . . . I told you they'd let him come.
CORY: How you doing, Uncle Gabe?
LYONS: How you doing, Uncle Gabe?
GABRIEL: Hey, Rose. It's time. It's time to tell St. Peter to open the gates. Troy,
you ready? You ready, Troy. I'm gonna tell St. Peter to open the gates. You
get ready now.

*(Gabriel, with great fanfare, braces himself to blow. The trumpet is without a
mouthpiece. He puts the end of it into his mouth and blows with great force, like a
man who has been waiting some twenty-odd years for this single moment. No sound
comes out of the trumpet. He braces himself and blows again with the same result.
A third time he blows. There is a weight of impossible description that falls away and
leaves him bare and exposed to a frightful realization. It is a trauma that a sane and
normal mind would be unable to withstand. He begins to dance. A slow, strange
dance, eerie and life-giving. A dance of atavistic signature and ritual. Lyons attempts
to embrace him. Gabriel pushes Lyons away. He begins to howl in what is an attempt
at song, or perhaps a song turning back into itself in an attempt at speech. He
finishes his dance and the gates of heaven stand open as wide as God's closet.)*

That's the way that go!
(BLACKOUT.) [p. 108]

Lloyd Richards

Director's Introduction°   [1986]

Fences is the second major play of a poet turned playwright, August Wilson. One of the most compelling storytellers to begin writing for the theater in many years, he has taken the responsibility of telling the tale of the encounter of the released black slaves with a vigorous and ruthless growing America decade by decade. *Fences* encompasses the 1950s and a black family trying to put down roots in the slag-slippery hills of a middle American urban industrial city that one might correctly mistake for Pittsburgh, Pennsylvania.

To call August Wilson a storyteller is to align him at one and the same time with the ancient aristocrats of dramatic writing who stood before the tribes and made compelling oral history into legend, as well as with the modern playwrights who bring an audience to their feet at the end of an evening of their work because that audience knows that they have encountered themselves, their concerns, and their passions, and have been moved and enriched by the experience. In *Fences*, August Wilson tells the story of four generations of black Americans and of how they have passed on a legacy of morals, mores, attitudes, and patterns through stories with and without music.

He tells the story of Troy Maxson, born to a sharecropper father who was frustrated by the fact that every crop took him further into debt. The father knew himself as a failure and took it out on everyone at hand, including his young son, Troy, and his wives, all of whom "leave him." Troy learns violence from him, but he also learns the value of work and the fact that a man takes responsibility for his family no matter how difficult circumstances may be. He learns respect [p. vii]° for a home, the importance of owning land, and the value of an education because he doesn't have one.

An excellent baseball player, Troy learns that in the land of equal opportunity, chances for a black man are not always equal, and that the same country that deprived him asked sacrifice of his brother in World War II and got it. Half his brother's head was blown away, and he is now a disoriented and confused beautiful man. He learns that he must fight and win the little victories that — given his life — must assume the proportion of major triumphs. He learns that day to day and moment to moment he lives close to death and must wrestle with death to survive. He learns that to take a chance and grab a moment of beauty can crumble the delicate fabric of an intricate value system and leave one desolate and alone. Strength of body and strength of purpose are not enough. Chance and the color of one's skin, chance again, can tip the balance. "You've got to take the crooked with the straight."

Troy Maxson spins yarns, raps, tells stories to his family and friends in that wonderful environment of the pretelevision, pre-airconditioned era when the

Richards, Lloyd. **Director's Introduction.** *Fences: A Play,* by August Wilson, New American Library, 1986, pp. vii–viii.
(Page citations in square brackets refer to the original publication.)

back porch and the backyard were the platform for some of the most exciting tales of that time. From this platform and through his behavior he passes on to his extended family principles for living, which members of his family accept or refute through the manner in which they choose to live their own lives.

How is this reformed criminal perceived? What should be learned from him? What accepted? What passed on? Is his life to be discarded or honored? That is the story of *Fences*, which we build to keep things and people out or in.

New Haven, Connecticut
March 6, 1986 [p. viii]

Clive Barnes

Fiery *Fences*: A Review°　　　　　　　　　　　　　　　　[1987]

Once in a rare while, you come across a play — or a movie or a novel — that seems to break away from the confines of art into a dense, complex realization of reality. A veil has been torn aside, the artist has disappeared into a transparency. We look with our own eyes, feel with our own hearts.

That was my reaction to August Wilson's pulsing play *Fences*, which opened last night at the Forty-sixth Street Theater, with James Earl Jones in full magnificent cry heading a cast of actors as good as you could find anywhere.

I wasn't just moved. I was transfixed — by intimations of a life, impressions of a man, images of a society.

Wilson, who a couple of seasons back gave us the arresting but fascinatingly flawed *Ma Rainey's Black Bottom*, always insists in interviews that he is writing from the wellspring of black experience in America.

This is undoubtedly true. Had Wilson been white, his plays would have been different — they would have had a different fire in a different belly.

But calling Wilson a "black" playwright is irrelevant. What makes *Fences* so engrossing, so embracing, so simply powerful, is his startling ability to tell a story, reveal feeling, paint emotion.

In many respects, *Fences* falls into the classic pattern of the American realistic drama — a family play, with a tragically doomed American father locked in conflict with his son. Greek tragedy with a Yankee accent.

The timing of the play — the late '50s — is carefully pinpointed in the history of black America as that turning point in the civil rights movement when a dream unfulfilled became a promise deferred.

The hero is Troy Maxson — and I suggest that he will be remembered as one of the great characters in American drama, and Jones always recalled as the first actor to play him.

Troy is as complex and as tormented as black America itself. He started life as a refugee from the South, and as a thief and, eventually, a killer.

Life in a penitentiary gave him the iron determination to reshape his life — as did, later, a feverish brush with death.

Barnes, Clive. "Fiery Fences: A Review." *New York Post*, 27 Mar. 1987, p. C23.

Prison also taught him baseball; when he came out, he became a tempera-mental star of the Negro Leagues. And now — in 1957 — he can look at the likes of Jackie Robinson and Hank Aaron, making it in the Major Leagues of big-time whiteball, with a mixture of anger, envy, and contempt.

A garbage collector, Troy has typically had to fight through his union to become the first black driver of a garbage truck. Equally typically, he hasn't even got a driver's license.

He sees himself as a man fenced in with responsibilities, but he has created some of those fences himself — some intended to keep people out, some to keep people in.

He is a family man — with a second wife, Rose, and their son Cory, as well as Gabriel, his brother, half-crazed by a war injury, and Lyons, Troy's older son by a previous marriage.

His life is secure — but limited. His son wants to go to college on a foot-ball scholarship, but Troy, wary of professional sports, refuses to let him try his luck.

Troy — although fully aware of his wife's qualities and warned by his best friend, Jim — falls in love with a younger woman, who becomes pregnant.

What is particularly pungent about Wilson's play is how the story and the characters are plugged into their particular historic relevance, ranging from the lessons of prison to the metaphors of baseball. It is this that makes the play resonate with all its subtle vibrations of truth and actuality.

This is in no sense a political play — but quite dispassionately it says: This is what it was like to be a black man of pride and ambition from the South, trying to live and work in the industrial North in the years just before and just after World War II.

The writing is perfectly geared to its people and its place. It jumps from the author's mind onto the stage, its language catching fire in the rarefied atmo-sphere of drama.

However fine the play is — and it is the strongest, most passionate American dramatic writing since Tennessee Williams — no praise can be too high for the staging by Lloyd Richards.

Helped by the cinematic accuracy of James D. Sandefur's setting, Richards has made the play into a microcosm in which we can see the tiny reflections of parts of ourselves, parts of America, and parts of history.

He gives every actor a sense of purpose and belonging — and makes the play their nightly story. Wonderful acting, but also marvelous direction.

James Earl Jones remakes himself in Troy's image. It is a performance of such astonishing credibility that it offers the audience a guilty sense of actually spying on the character, unobserved and unwanted.

But this is only one performance of note; in her way, Mary Alice, as Troy's wife, is just as powerful, her pain and reality just as painfully real. And then there is Courtney B. Vance as Troy's alienated son, another performance of bewildering truth and honesty.

Add to these Ray Aranha, Charles Brown, Frankie F. Faison, and Karima Miller, and you have an ensemble cast as good as you will ever find.

Fences gave me one of the richest experiences I have ever had in the theater.

Frank Rich

Family Ties in Wilson's *Fences*: A Review°   [1987]

To hear his wife tell it, Troy Maxson, the middle-aged Pittsburgh sanitation worker at the center of *Fences*, is "so big" that he fills up his tenement house just by walking through it. Needless to say, that description could also apply to James Earl Jones, the actor who has found what may be the best role of his career in August Wilson's new play, at the Forty-sixth Street Theater. But the remarkable stature of the character — and of the performance — is not a matter of sheer size. If Mr. Jones's Troy is a mountainous man prone to tyrannical eruptions of rage, he is also a dignified, delicate figure capable of cradling a tiny baby, of pleading gravely to his wife for understanding, of standing still to stare death unflinchingly in the eye. A black man, a free man, a descendant of slaves, a menial laborer, a father, a husband, a lover — Mr. Jones's Troy embraces all the contradictions of being black and male and American in his time.

That time is 1957 — three decades after the period of Mr. Wilson's previous and extraordinary *Ma Rainey's Black Bottom*. For blacks like Troy in the industrial North of *Fences*, social and economic equality is more a legal principle than a reality: The Maxsons' slum neighborhood, a panorama of grimy brick and smokestack-blighted sky in James D. Sandefur's eloquent design, is a cauldron of busted promises, waiting to boil over. The conflagration is still a decade away — the streetlights burn like the first sparks of distant insurrection — so Mr. Wilson writes about the pain of an extended family lost in the wilderness of de facto segregation and barren hope.

It speaks of the power of the play — and of the cast assembled by the director, Lloyd Richards — that Mr. Jones's patriarch doesn't devour the rest of *Fences* so much as become the life force that at once nurtures and stunts the characters who share his blood. The strongest countervailing player is his wife, Rose, luminously acted by Mary Alice. Rose is a quiet woman who, as she says "planted herself" in the "hard and rocky" soil of her husband. But she never bloomed: Marriage brought frustration and betrayal in equal measure with affection.

Even so, Ms. Alice's performance emphasizes strength over self-pity, open anger over festering bitterness. The actress finds the spiritual quotient in the acceptance that accompanies Rose's love for a scarred, profoundly complicated man. It's rare to find a marriage of any sort presented on stage with such balance — let alone one in which the husband has fathered children by three different women. Mr. Wilson grants both partners the right to want to escape the responsibilities of their domestic drudgery while affirming their respective claims to forgiveness.

The other primary relationship of *Fences* is that of Troy to his son Cory (Courtney B. Vance) — a promising 17-year-old football player being courted by a college recruiter. Troy himself was once a baseball player in the Negro

Rich, Frank. "Family Ties in Wilson's *Fences*: A Review." *New York Times*, 27 Mar. 1987, p. C3.

Leagues — early enough to hit homers off Satchel Paige, too early to benefit from Jackie Robinson's breakthrough — and his bitter, long-ago disappointment leads him to decree a different future for his son. But while Troy wants Cory to settle for a workhorse trade guaranteeing a weekly paycheck, the boy resists. The younger Maxson is somehow convinced that the dreams of his black generation need not end in the city's mean alleys with the carting of white men's garbage.

The struggle between father and son over conflicting visions of black identity, aspirations, and values is the play's narrative fulcrum, and a paradigm of violent divisions that would later tear apart a society. As written, the conflict is also a didactic one, reminiscent of old-fashioned plays, black and white, about disputes between first-generation American parents and their rebellious children.

In *Ma Rainey* — set at a blues recording session — Mr. Wilson's characters were firecrackers exploding in a bottle, pursuing jagged theatrical riffs reflective of their music and of their intimacy with the Afro-American experience that gave birth to that music. The relative tameness of *Fences* — with its laboriously worked-out titular metaphor, its slow-fused act 1 exposition — is as much an expression of its period as its predecessor was of the hotter '20s. Intentionally or not — and perhaps to the satisfaction of those who found the more esthetically daring *Ma Rainey* too "plotless" — Mr. Wilson invokes the clunkier dramaturgy of Odets, Miller, and Hansberry on this occasion.

Such formulaic theatrical tidiness, while exasperating at times, proves a minor price for the gripping second act (strengthened since the play's Yale debut in 1985) and for the scattered virtuoso passages throughout. Like *Ma Rainey* and the latest Wilson work seen at Yale (*Joe Turner's Come and Gone*, also promised for New York), *Fences* leaves no doubt that Mr. Wilson is a major writer, combining a poet's ear for vernacular with a robust sense of humor (political and sexual), a sure instinct for crackling dramatic incident, and a passionate commitment to a great subject.

Mr. Wilson continues to see history as fully as he sees his characters. In one scene, Troy and his oldest friend (played with brimming warmth by Ray Aranha) weave an autobiographical "talking blues" — a front-porch storytelling jaunt from the antebellum plantation through the preindustrial urban South, jail, and northward migration. *Fences* is pointedly bracketed by two disparate wars that swallowed up black manhood, and, as always with Mr. Wilson, is as keenly cognizant of its characters' bonds to Africa, however muted here, as their bondage to white America. One hears the cadences of a centuries-old heritage in Mr. Jones's efforts to shout down the devil. It is a frayed scrap of timeless blues singing, unpretty but unquenchable, that proves the overpowering cathartic link among the disparate branches of the Maxson family tree.

Under the exemplary guidance of Mr. Richards — whose staging falters only in the awkward scene transitions — the entire cast is impressive, including Frankie R. Faison in the problematic (but finally devastating) role of a brain-damaged, horn-playing uncle named Gabriel, and Charles Brown, as a Maxson son who falls into the sociological crack separating the play's two principal generations. As Cory, Courtney B. Vance is not only formidable in challenging Mr. Jones to a psychological (and sometimes physical) kill-or-be-killed battle for supremacy but also seems to grow into Troy's vocal timbre and visage by the final scene. Like most sons, Mr. Vance just can't elude "the shadow" of his father, no matter how hard he tries. Such is the long shadow Mr. Jones's father casts in *Fences* that theatergoers from all kinds of families may find him impossible to escape.

Bonnie Lyons

An Interview with August Wilson°   [1999]

Q: Elsewhere you've talked about writing as a way of effecting social change and said that all your plays are political, but that you try not to make them didactic or polemical. Can you talk a little about how plays can effect social change without being polemical or didactic?

A: I don't write primarily to effect social change. I believe writing can do that, but that's not why I write. I work as an artist. However, all art is political in the sense that it serves the politics of someone. Here in America whites have a particular view of blacks, and I think my plays offer them a different and new way to look at black Americans. For instance, in *Fences* they see a garbageman, a person they really don't look at, although they may see a garbageman every day. By looking at Troy's life, white people find out that the content of this black garbageman's life is very similar to their own, that he is affected by the same things — love, honor, beauty, betrayal, duty. Recognizing that these things are as much a part of his life as of theirs can [p. 2]° be revolutionary and can affect how they think about and deal with black people in their lives.

Q: How would that same play, *Fences*, affect a black audience?

A: Blacks see the content of their lives being elevated into art. They don't always know that is possible, and it's important to know that.

Q: You've talked about how important black music was for your development. Was there any black literature that showed you that black lives can be the subject of great art?

A: *Invisible Man*. When I was fourteen I discovered the Negro section of the library. I read *Invisible Man*, Langston Hughes, and all the thirty or forty books in the section, including the sociology. I remember reading a book that talked about the "Negro's power of hard work" and how much that phrase affected me. At the time I used to cut the lawn for a blind man named Mr. Douglas, who was the father of the Olympic track star. After I read that, I didn't so much cut his lawn as plow it, to show the Negro power of hard work. Looking back, I see that I had never seen those words together: "Negro power." Later of course in

Lyons, Bonnie. "An Interview with August Wilson." *Contemporary Literature*, vol. 40, no. 1, Spring 1999, pp. 1–21.
(Page citations in square brackets refer to the original publication.)

the sixties that became "black power." Forty years ago we had few black writers compared to today. There have been forty years of education and many more college graduates. And it's important to remember that blacks don't have a long history of writing. We come from an oral tradition. At one point in America it was a crime to teach blacks to read and write. So it's only in the past 150 years that we've been writing in this country.

Q: Elsewhere you've said that the primary opposition in your plays is between blacks who deny their African roots and those who don't. Would you still describe your work that way?

A: Today I would say that the conflict in black America is between the middle class and the so-called underclass, and that conflict goes back to those who deny themselves and those who aren't willing to. America offers blacks a contract that says, "If you leave all that African stuff over there and adopt the values of the dominant culture, you can participate." For the most part, black Americans have [p. 3] rejected that sort of con job. Many blacks in the ghettos say, "If I got to give up who I am, if I can't be like me, then I don't want it." The ones who accept go on to become part of the growing black middle class and in some areas even acquire some power and participation in society, but when they finally arrive where they arrive, they are no longer the same people. They are clothed in different manners and ways of life, different thoughts and ideas. They've acculturated and adopted white values. . . . [p. 4]

Q: Elsewhere you've said you want your audience to see your characters as Africans, not just black folks in America. Can you talk about that?

A: I'm talking about black Americans having uniquely African ways of participating in the world, of doing things, different ways of socializing. I have no fascination with Africa itself. I've never been to Africa and have no desire to go. I've been invited several times and turned down the invitations because I don't like to travel. When my daughter went to college, she called me all excited that she was studying about Timbuktu. I told her, "You study your grandma and her grandmother before you go back to Timbuktu." People don't want to do that because soon you wind up with slavery, and that's a [p. 7] condition people want to run away from. It's much easier to go back to the glory days of Timbuktu, but to do that is falsely romantic. It doesn't get you anywhere. I remember when I first went with a friend to a Passover seder and heard them say, "When we were slaves in the land of Egypt." I met a kid in 1987 in New York who thought slavery ended in 1960. This is God's honest truth. He was seventeen years old and he thought slavery ended in 1960. That's our fault. Like the Jews, we need to celebrate our emancipation; it would give us a way of identifying and expressing a sense of unity.

Q: Do you see anything anomalous about your wanting blacks to see themselves as Africans but your not having any desire even to visit Africa?

A: I'm simply saying blacks should hold on to what they are. You don't have to go to Africa to be an African. I live and breathe that. Even in the sixties, with all the romantic involvement with Africa, I never wore a dashiki to participate in the black power movement. Africa is right here in the southern part of the United States, which is our ancestral homeland. I don't need to make that leap across the ocean. When the first African died on the continent of North America, that was the beginning of my history.

Q: Speaking of your history, I remember reading that you said the first word you typed was your own name. Do you have any interest in autobiography?

A: Not about me as an individual. I don't like to read biographies or autobiographies myself. And if your material is autobiographical, sooner or later you're going to run out of material. I take the entire black experience in America, from the first black in 1619 until now, and claim that as my material. That's my story, my life story, and that's a lot to write about. But in truth, whatever subject you take, you as a writer are going to come up with something that is based on who you are, so even in choosing the black experience I am writing it from my own perspective. . . . [p. 8]

Q: Do you think you define plot the same way Aristotle did?

A: For me plot grows out of characterization, so there are no plot points. The play doesn't flow from plot point to plot point. I guess it's easy to plot that way, since every TV drama moves along those lines. It becomes very mechanical. Some people call my plays plotless; that's simply because they haven't been able to recognize the plot in [p. 11] them. In my plays you don't say, "Here is a point here, hold on to this because we're going to need it." I think you need to hold on to everything. In my plays things happen gradually, and you come to see why things are in the play. For example, in *Seven Guitars* you hear four men talking, and you may think the play is not going anywhere. But it is. All that stuff, every single thing they talk about, connects and is important to your understanding of the drama.

Q: It may seem a strange connection, but are your plays more like Chekhov's° than most playwrights', both in their being ensemble plays and in their seeming plotlessness?

A: I think you're right. I didn't know Chekhov's work, so there is no question of influence, but when I saw *Uncle Vanya*, I thought, "He's cool. I like this play. Yes, it's just people sitting around talking, and the drama is made out of the talk, but there are things going on, a lot of stuff is happening." . . . [p. 12]

Q: In the past you've mentioned the importance of listening to your characters and trusting them. Can you talk about that a bit?

A: You listen to them, but you never lose consciousness that they are your creations. When I first started writing plays I couldn't write good dialogue because I didn't respect how black people talked. I thought that in order to make art out of it I had to change it, make it into something different. Once I learned to value and respect my characters, I could really hear them. How you talk is how you think; the language describes the one who speaks it. When I have characters, I just let them start talking. The important thing is not to censor them, to trust them to just talk. What they are talking about may not seem to

---

Chekhov: Anton Chekhov (1860–1904), Russian playwright and short-story writer.

have anything to do with what you as a writer were writing about, but it does. Just let them talk and it will connect, because you as the artist will make it connect. . . . [p. 13] The more my characters talk, the more I find out about them. And the more I find out about them, the more material I have. So I encourage them, I tell them, "Tell me some more." I just write it down, and it starts to make connections. . . . [p. 14]

Q: In your cycle of plays, you'll have one play per decade of this century, but in your introductory note to *Seven Guitars* you say, "Despite my interest in history, I've always been more concerned with culture." Could you talk a little about history versus culture?

A: I'm more interested in the historical context than in actual history, so, for example, I changed the actual historical date of a Joe Louis boxing match because it suited my dramatic purposes. I always come back to the quote from James Baldwin about the black tradition, which he defined as "That field of manners and rituals of intercourse that will sustain a man once he's left his father's house." [p. 16] The primary focus of my work is looking at black culture as it changes and grows in evolving historical contexts . . .

Q: In addition to plays, you've written poetry, and now you're also writing a novel. Can you talk about the differences between those forms, and whether material comes to you in one form or another?

A: For me, poetry is distilled language. Somewhere I read poetry defined as enlarging the sayable. I like that definition, and I think poetry is the highest form of literature. Writing a novel is like setting [p. 17] out on this vast, uncharted ocean. I never knew how anyone could do it. But now I see that like any kind of writing, you start with the first word and finish the first page. Then you've got a page and you go on to the next. I realized that writing a novel is like writing a play in that you don't have to know where you're going. You just go and you find out as you go along . . .

Q: Playwrights have taken quite varying positions about the importance of production. Edward Albee° has taken an extreme position, saying, "A first-rate play exists completely on the page and is never improved by production; it is only proved by production." Do you agree?

A: I agree with that, because the play is there on the page; it provides a road map or a blueprint. I don't write for a production; I write for the page, just like a poem. A play, like a poem, exists on the page even if no one ever reads it aloud. But I don't want to underestimate what a good production with actors embodying the characters offers. But depending on the imagination of the reader, he may get more by reading the play than by seeing a weak production. . . . [p. 18]

Q: One playwright has said that drama is made up of sound and silence. Do you see drama that way?

A: No doubt drama is made up of sound and silence, but I see conflict at the center. What you do is set up a character who has certain beliefs and you

---

Edward Albee: U.S. playwright, b. 1928. For the position expressed, see *Conversations with Edward Albee*, edited by Philip C. Kolin (UP of Mississippi, 1988), p. 137.

establish a situation where those beliefs are challenged and that character is forced to examine those beliefs and perhaps change them. That's the kind of dramatic situation which engages an audience.

Q: Then is the conflict primarily internal rather than external, between characters?

A: Internal, right, where the character has to reexamine his whole body of beliefs. The play has to shake the very foundation of his whole system of beliefs and force him to make a choice. Then I think [p. 19] you as a playwright have accomplished something, because that process also forces the audience to go through the same inner struggle. When I teach my workshops I tell my students that if a guy announces, "I'm going to kill Joe," and there's a knock on the door, the audience is going to want to know if that's Joe and why this guy wants to kill him and whether we would also want to kill him if we were in the same situation. The audience is engaged in the questions. [p. 20]

Miles Marshall Lewis

Miles Marshall Lewis Talks with August Wilson°   [2005]

Miles Marshall Lewis: Despite the similarities between *Fences* and *Death of a Salesman*, and the art of playwriting as a predominantly white discipline, you've cited your greatest literary influence as poet-playwright Amiri Baraka.° How would you say he influenced you?

August Wilson: I'm not sure what they say about *Fences* as it relates to *Death of a Salesman*. At the time I wrote *Fences*, I had not read *Death of a Salesman*, had not seen *Death of a Salesman*, did not know anything about *Death of a Salesman*.

My greatest influence has been the blues. And that's a literary influence, because I think the blues is the best literature that we as [p. 410]° black Americans have. My interest in Baraka comes from the '60s and the Black Power movement. So it's more for Baraka's political ideas, which I loved and still am an exponent of. Through all those years I was a follower, if you will, of Baraka. He had an influence on my thinking.

MML: Were you exposed first to his poetry or his plays?

AW: The poetry in particular. The book called *Black Magic*, which is sort of a collection of several books. That's '69 — I wore that book out, the cover got

---

Lewis, Miles Marshall. "Miles Marshall Lewis Talks with August Wilson." *The Believer Book of Writers Talking to Writers*, edited by Vendela Vida, Believer Books, 2005, pp. 409–27.
Amiri Baraka: U.S. poet, playwright, essayist, and music critic; born Everett LeRoy Jones in 1934, he changed his name to LeRoi Jones in 1952, to Imamu Ameer Baraka in 1967, and later to Amiri Baraka.
(Page citations in square brackets refer to the original publication.)

taped up with Scotch tape, the pages falling out. That was my bible, I carried it wherever I went. So that in particular. I wasn't writing plays back then, so I wasn't influenced by his playwriting—although, to me, his best plays are collected in a book called *Four Black Revolutionary Plays*, with *Madheart*, *Great Goodness of Life*, *A Black Mass*, and *Experimental Death Unit 1*. They contributed a lot to my thinking just in terms of getting stuff on the page.

MML: How specifically was the blues an influence on your work?

AW: Blues is the bedrock of everything I do. All the characters in my plays, their ideas and their attitudes, the stance that they adopt in the world, are all ideas and attitudes that are expressed in the blues. If all this were to disappear off the face of the earth and some people two million unique years from now would dig out this civilization and come across some blues records, working as anthropologists, they would be able to piece together who these people were, what they thought about, what their ideas and attitudes toward pleasure and pain were, all of that. All the components of culture. Just like they do with the Egyptians, they piece together all that stuff. And all you need is the blues. So to me the blues is the book, it's the bible, it's everything. . . . [p. 411]

MML: Your characters also often riff off of each other like jazz musicians, particularly in *Seven Guitars*. Your work in general is like improvising on a theme: the life of southern blacks who migrated to the North in the twentieth century. How has jazz impacted your creative process?

AW: I think that's the core of black aesthetics: the ability to improvise. That is what has enabled our survival. . . . [p. 412]

AW: People say, "Well, you writin a play in 1911 and you weren't alive in 1911. Did you do any research?" I say, I don't do research. They say, "Well, how do you know?" Because the plays ultimately are about love, honor, duty, betrayal—what I call the Big Themes. So you could set it in the '80s and make use of various things, but you're telling a story that is using the Big Themes. . . . [p. 417]

MML: Essayist Sandra Shannon has criticized the women in your plays, saying, "His feminine portrayals tend to slip into comfort zones of what seem to be male-fantasized roles." Feminist critic bell hooks said of *Fences* that "patriarchy is not critiqued" and "sexist values are reinscribed." I was wondering if you've given thought to this in relation to approaching the final play in your cycle, which takes place in the 1990s, a time when women are arguably their most liberated and independent.

AW: I can't approach them any different than I have, man, cause all my women are independent. People can say anything they want, that's valid, they're liable to say anything they want. I don't agree with that. You gotta write women like . . . they can't express ideas and attitudes that women of the feminist movement in the '60s made. Even though I'm aware of all that, you gotta be very careful if you're trying to create a character like that, that they don't come up with any greater understanding of themselves and their relationship to the world than women had at that time.

As a matter of fact, all my characters are at the edge of that, they pushing them boundaries, they have more understanding. I had to cut back and say,

"These are feminist ideas." My mother was a feminist, though she wouldn't express it that way. She don't know nothing about no feminist women and whatnot but she didn't accept her place. She raised three daughters, and my sisters are the same way. So that's where I get my women from. I grew up in a household with four women. [p. 422]

Missy Dehn Kubitschek

August Wilson's Gender Lesson°   [1994]

Like much African American literature of the last two decades, August Wilson's cycle of plays takes its readers/viewers on an extended historical examination of gendered interactions in the black community. Although his earliest play, *Ma Rainey's Black Bottom* (1984), does not focus on gender to the same extent as his later works, it sets the premises under which they develop their statements: the presence of a powerful African American spirituality and the difficulty of preserving it in an economic system controlled by white racists. *Fences* (1985) forcefully demonstrates the spiritual alienation of men and women from one another, and of men from their children. The play shows men and women speaking different languages, reflecting different understandings of the spiritual cosmos. . . . [p. 183]°

Centered on the economic disruption of black men's and women's relationships, *Fences* shows men and women speaking the different languages imposed/derived from their unconscious acceptance of an implicitly Eurocentric view of separate male and female spheres. The development of a situation in which men and women are speaking different languages that no longer refer to the same spiritual realities can be approached through a juxtaposition of two models of gender relations. Nineteenth-century European models divide sex roles into separate spheres in a hierarchical schema. A second set of models derives from the experiences of women in traditional nonindustrial societies or in minority communities in the United States.

Delineated by Paula Gunn Allen's *The Sacred Hoop* and Trinh Minh-ha's *Woman, Native, Other*, and implied by other works such as Gloria Anzaldua's *Borderlands/La Frontera* and bell hooks's *Feminist Theory: From Margin to Center*, this second paradigm represents men and women as possessing somewhat different spiritual gifts and hence different social responsibilities, but sharing some areas of influence. Men's and women's spheres of activity are fundamentally connected, mutually contributive parts of community. . . . [p. 184]

Separate spheres were for black Americans unachievable in the nineteenth century and available only to a small middle class in the twentieth. Historically, the separate-spheres ideology has combined with white male economic control

Kubitschek, Missy Dehn. "August Wilson's Gender Lesson." *May All Your Fences Have Gates: Essays on the Drama of August Wilson*, edited by Alan Nadel, Iowa UP, 1994, pp. 183–99. (Page citations in square brackets refer to the original publication.)

to erode African American families and communities by preventing black men from achieving the only culturally endorsed definition of manhood and by subordinating the activities of black women, sometimes making them competitive in formerly common arenas of endeavor. *Fences* explores the damage that results when European constructions of sex roles separate, hierarchically order, and then alienate men and women; at the same time, the play suggests a palimpsest of a more empowering traditional model.

Troy Maxson's definition of his manhood centers on his ability to support his family economically, though he intermittently glimpses the inadequacy of this conception. He describes, for example, his own father's economically pressured definition of his children as workers, and only workers, with considerable pain. He also recognizes his father's lack of joy, his selfishness, his demeaning treatment of his children, his abuse of his wife. Simultaneously [p. 185] Troy says, "He wasn't good for nobody" (762) but affirms that he strove to accomplish the one thing necessary, securing the necessities for his family.

Under this superimposed definition of manhood, another, broader, definition struggles to reemerge, the sense that economic relations ought not to be the whole of a father's relationship to his children. Troy cannot express such an idea directly. Though he suffered for lack of his father's love (and was further deprived when his mother left), he tries to force Cory to be satisfied with the same father/son relationship:

> It's my job. It's my responsibility! You understand that? A man got to take care of his family. You live in my house . . . sleep you behind on my bedclothes . . . fill you belly up with my food . . . cause you my son. You my flesh and blood. Not 'cause I like you! Cause it's my duty to take care of you. I owe a responsibility to you! (755)

His intermittent recognition of his father's inadequacy does not lead to any other conception of fatherhood.

Trying not to fail Cory as he failed Lyons (imprisonment prevented him from supporting his first family), Troy virtually recreates the destructive relationship between his father and himself. Not only does he insist on Cory's working for salary, he identifies the family's resources—the house and its furnishings, food—as his own property, his son as a dependent rather than a contributor. Troy expresses disgust at Lyons's easy acceptance of such a relationship; only a boy accepts such a position, and only because he has no choice.

Troy's bitterness at whites' power to exclude him from prestigious and well-paid labor (major league baseball) makes the likenesses between himself and Cory into threats. Unable to recognize changes in social conditions, he sees Cory's talents as a temptation to irresponsibility. He insists on conditions that make it impossible for Cory to satisfy his work requirement and also to attend necessary athletic practices. Although he claims to be protecting Cory from inevitable disappointment, he is deforming another generation with Procrustean° gender definitions.

Procrustean: Creating uniformity or conformity forcefully, without allowing for variety or individuality.

Following his only model, he plays his father's role with a slightly different script. Troy breaks from his father at fourteen, but the separation is temporary, geographic rather than temperamental or psychic; he understands his father later, when "I could feel him kicking in my blood and knew that the only thing that separated us was the matter of a few years" (763). Given the [p. 186] economic conditions and his understanding of his role, Troy can only recreate in another generation the economic exploitation and competition between father and son.

Fences demonstrates that, as the European/Victorian doctrine of separate spheres combines with very limited economic opportunities, relationships between black men and women deteriorate. The very list of characters for *Fences* testifies to patriarchal hegemony, with its implications of subordination for women — all but one of the characters are identified solely by their relationship to Troy, as "Troy's oldest son" or "Troy's wife"; significantly, Cory is identified as "Troy and Rose's son," an assertion of women's ongoing presence and importance for heritage.

Men's and women's languages in *Fences* reflect the separation of their spheres of activity. In their most intensely emotional scene (act 2, scene 1), Troy and Rose attempt to communicate with metaphors that diverge sharply. Troy repeatedly uses baseball metaphors that Rose implicitly rejects by returning always to the concrete level of action:

ROSE: You should have held me tight. You should have grabbed me and held on.
TROY: I stood on first base for eighteen years and I thought . . . well, goddamn it . . . go on for it!
ROSE: We're not talking about baseball! We're talking about you going off to lay in bed with another woman. (772)

Troy's account doesn't lose track of the concrete level, but his metaphorical expression is confined to — and confines — the experience to an arena that he has only limited access to and that excludes Rose entirely. Troy chooses baseball, the game whose racial segregation has prevented his enjoying the economic or status benefits of his athletic prowess, as his vehicle. But baseball is, of course, also sex-segregated. Troy hopes for "one of them boys to knock me in" because metaphorically and literally, it has become impossible for any woman to play on his team, to advance him in his competitive quest. Instead, Rose disappears entirely from the metaphor, and Alberta is objectified, a base to steal. Inevitably Rose refuses the metaphor that excludes her and includes women only as objects.

Whereas Troy's metaphor comes from the social (and therefore hierarchical) world, Rose's metaphor in this scene derives from the natural world. Her expression emphasizes her expectation that her experience will partake of the [p. 187] cycle of living things, and her frustration that it does not come to fulfillment: "I took all my feelings, my wants and needs, my dreams . . . and I buried them inside you. I planted a seed and watched and prayed over it. I planted myself inside you and waited to bloom. And it didn't take me no eighteen years to find out the soil was hard and rocky and it wasn't never gonna bloom" (772). In his role as divine fool, Gabriel underlines Rose's connections to nature by giving her flowers and commenting that she shares their essence. Rose's imagery, moreover, leaves open the possibility of shared ground as Troy's does not, for Troy at least appears in Rose's imagery, even though he is represented as an environment of dubious hospitality. Rose's natural imagery suggests continuity, as Troy's game imagery suggests a discrete series, and although women's experience provides the source of this natural imagery, the experience is itself not socially limited to one gender.

Fences does not, of course, present black men as failed human beings and women as the preservers of undamaged original spiritualities (a conception that would result from the separate-spheres doctrine's idealization of women's purity). The division into separate spheres affects Rose as well as Troy. Her impassioned denunciation of his affair and its results reveals the conflict between European and African ideals of kinship: "And you know I ain't never wanted no half nothing in my family. My whole family is half. Everybody got different fathers and mothers . . . my two sisters and my brother. Can't hardly tell who's who. Can't never sit down and talk about Papa and Mama. It's your papa and your mama and my papa and my mama" (771). On the one hand, Rose is angry about a kind of confused ancestral heritage, the lack of archetypal Mama and Papa, and their replacement by lowercase, less powerful specifics. On the other, her idea of a proper family reflects the European, nuclear ideal rather than the traditional African or African American conception of extended family.

The last scene shows the simultaneous influence of both paradigms. On the one hand, Raynell, like Rose, is associated with the natural world of the garden while Cory appears in military uniform, a clear suggestion of continued separation of sex roles. On the other hand, a shared spirituality persists. Troy's father's song, "Old Blue," for instance, survives because both Raynell and Cory have heard Troy's version. Singing it together, they ritually evoke the ancestors.

More important, both Rose and Gabriel reclaim spiritual powers by refusing European systems and returning to traditional understandings and roles. Rose, however equivocally, finally refuses the role offered to her by separate [p. 188] spheres — female victim of a superior male power — to embrace her own responsibility for constructing a shared space with Troy:

> When I first met your daddy I thought . . . Here is a man I can lay down with and make a baby. [. . .] I thought, Rose Lee, here is a man that you can open yourself up to and be filled to bursting. [. . .]
> When your daddy walked through the house he was so big he filled it up. That was my first mistake. Not to make him leave some room for me. For my part in the matter. But at that time I wanted that. I wanted a house that I could sing in. And that's what your daddy gave me. I didn't know to

keep up his strength I had to give up little pieces of mine. I did that.
[. . .] It was my choice. It was my life and I didn't have to live it like that.
But that's what life offered me in the way of being a woman and I took it.
(786, first ellipsis Wilson's)

Troy controlled what should have been their shared space because Rose did not
claim and exercise her power. Rose does not blame Troy, however, indicating
that a different outcome would have been possible if she had understood the
implications of ceding power. At the same time, she implies that her choice was
not entirely determined by personality: "That's what life offered me in the way
of being a woman."

Fences shows mutual autonomy with shared responsibilities as a more fulfilling paradigm than that of separate spheres. Rose tells Cory directly that reclaiming her power and independence made her happier. Although she had initially
rejected traditional ideas of kinship, referring to Raynell as "your baby," Rose
went on to agree to Troy's request to care for her with "this child got a mother.
But you a womanless man" (777). Thus, she no longer accepted Troy's presence
throughout the shared house; instead, as the price of having shared responsibilities for Raynell, she insisted on redefining the whole relationship. The timing of
Rose's communication of joint responsibility—Cory is engaged—makes an alternative available to her son that he did not witness in their home. Troy's mother
had left by the time he rejected his father, and with no other model to emulate,
Troy inevitably recreates his father's role and vision. Rose's presence—more
important, her communication—opens other possibilities for Cory.

In a more direct and absolute critique of Western models, Gabriel replaces
a failed Christianity with an empowering African spirituality. Convinced that
it's time for him to perform the role that Christianity assigns to the Archangel
Gabriel, Gabriel decides to end the world by blowing his trumpet. When the
[p. 189] damaged instrument makes no noise, "a weight of impossible description [. . .] falls away" (788). His consequent "frightful realization" makes him
begin to dance, then to howl. This "atavistic signature and ritual" (788) of
dance and sound then opens the gate of heaven, and the last words of the play
are Gabriel's triumphant "That's the way that go!" [p. 190]

WORKS CITED

Allen, Paula Gunn. *The Sacred Hoop: Recovering the Feminine in American Indian
    Traditions*. Boston: Beacon, 1986.
Anzaldua, Gloria. *Borderlands/La Frontera*. San Francisco: Spinsters/Aunt Lute,
    1987.
hooks, bell. *Feminist Theory: From Margin to Center*. Boston: South End Press,
    1984.
Trinh, Minh-ha. *Woman, Native, Other*. Bloomington: Indiana UP, 1989.
Wilson, August. *Fences*. New York: New American Library/Signet, 1986.
——. *Ma Rainey's Black Bottom*. New York: New American Library, Plume, 1985.

Harry J. Elam, Jr.

August Wilson°   [2005]

With two Pulitzer Prizes, two Tony awards, and numerous other accolades, August Wilson stands out as one of if not the most preeminent playwrights in the contemporary American theater. Wilson's self-imposed dramatic project is to review African American history in the twentieth century by writing a play for each decade. With each work, he recreates and reevaluates the choices that blacks have made in the past by refracting them through the lens of the present. Wilson focuses on the experiences and daily lives of ordinary black people within particular historical circumstances. Carefully situating each play at critical junctures in African American history, Wilson explores the pain and perseverance, the determination and dignity in these black lives. . . . [p. 318]°

Critical to each play in Wilson's historical cycle is the concept that one must go backwards in order to move forward. Repeatedly, Wilson creates black characters who are displaced and disconnected from their history and from their individual identity, and are in search of spiritual resurrection and cultural reconnection. For these characters, past events have a commanding influence on their present dreams and aspirations. Their personal stories are inextricably linked to the history of African American struggle and survival in this country. Wilson's dramatic cycle demonstrates the impact of the past on the present. Ethics and aesthetics conjoin as the personal dynamics of his characters' lives have profound political consequences. He terms his project "a four hundred-year-old autobiography, which is the black experience" (qtd. in Shannon 179–80). As an African American "autobiography," Wilson's work links African American collective memory with Wilson's own memories and with his activist racial agenda. His family background and own life experiences are evident in this project. [p. 319]

Wilson . . . found his own true voice as a dramatist as the decade of the 1960s drew to a close. Affected by the urgencies around black cultural nationalism of the late 1960s, Wilson, along with his friend Rob Penny, cofounded Pittsburgh's Black Horizon's Theatre, a revolutionary-inclined African American theater. With his work at Black Horizon's, Wilson encountered one of the influences that continue to shape his dramas, the fiery playwright and poet Amiri Baraka (LeRoi Jones), the leading theater practitioner of the black revolutionary theater movement of the late 1960s and early 1970s. . . . Wilson maintains that Baraka's words and cultural politics inspired his own desire to use drama as a means to social ends.

In and around the same time, Wilson discovered three more influences: Jorge Luis Borges, Romare Bearden, and the blues. Argentinean short-story writer Borges became significant to Wilson because of his ability to blend the metaphysical and the mystical within his complex plot lines. With his skillful

Elam, Harry J., Jr. "August Wilson." *A Companion to Twentieth-Century American Drama*, edited by David Krasner, Blackwell Publishing, 2005, pp. 318–33.
(Page citations in square brackets refer to the original publication.)

use of narration, Borges mixes the fantastical and the spiritual as his characters follow difficult and convoluted pathways. Within plays such as *Fences*, *Joe Turner's Come and Gone*, *The Piano Lesson*, and *Gem of the Ocean*, Wilson's incorporation of the supernatural and metaphysical has been influenced by the writing of Borges.

Wilson discovered the work of fellow Pittsburgh native Romare Bearden in 1977, when his friend Charles Purdy purchased a copy of his collage *The Prevalence of Ritual* (1964). Viewing this artwork had a profound effect on Wilson: "My response was visceral. I was looking at myself in ways I hadn't thought of before and have never ceased to think of since. In Bearden I found my artistic mentor and sought, and still aspire, to make my plays the equal of his canvases" (qtd. in Fishman 134). Bearden's collages *Millhands Lunch Bucket* (1978) and *The Piano Lesson* (1984) directly inspired Wilson's plays *Joe Turner* and *Piano Lesson*, respectively. Bearden's formula for [p. 320] collage, his use of found objects, and his blending of past and present are examples reflected in Wilson's pastiche style of playwriting and his interest in the impact of history upon present conditions. Within the artistry of both men, the metaphorical and ritualistic coexist with everyday experiences of African Americans. Unfortunately, the two men never met in Bearden's lifetime.

Despite the impact of Bearden, Borges, and Baraka on Wilson and his work, the most significant and most transformative of the four influences (referred to as the "4Bs" because all begin with the letter "B") is the blues. Twelve years prior to encountering Bearden in 1965, Wilson discovered the blues while listening to an old recording of Bessie Smith's "Nobody in Town Can Bake a Sweet Jellyroll Like Mine." This recording transformed his life and his cultural ideology. The blues become not only a guiding force in his writing, but also the foundation he discovers for African American expressive culture and for what Wilson believes is a distinctly African American way of "being" (*Three Plays* ix–x). According to Wilson, the cultural, social, political, and spiritual all interact within the blues. Forged in and from the economics of slavery as a method of mediating the pains and dehumanization of that experience, the blues are purposefully duplicitous, containing a matrix of meanings. The blues for Wilson continue to offer a methodology for negotiating the difficult spaces of African American existence and achieving African American survival.

Structurally, Wilson's "bluesology" acts as an aesthetic and cultural intervention disrupting the conventional frame of realism. Rather than plot or action, character and the lyrical music of the dialogue drive the plays. Wilson, a poet before he became a playwright, celebrates the poetic power contained in the speech of poor and uneducated peoples. Wilson allows his characters to voice their history in the verbal equivalent of musical solos. For instance, Troy Maxson—an illiterate garbage man and central figure in *Fences*—fashions his identity and self-awareness through bold expressive tales. Like the ancient city of Troy, he is an epic force, impregnable and larger than life. Troy's stories, which serve to describe the African American experiences as well as his individual life, expand the realistic canvas of the play, reaching beyond the conventional temporal and spatial limits to reveal the inner presence of history impacting on an individual.

Ralph Ellison calls the blues a unique combination of "the tragic and the comic," of poetry and ritual (256). Wilson's plays embody this blues formula on a multitude of occasions. In each of the plays, Wilson's characters engage in a series of vernacular games, the dozens, and signifyin'. All these cultural activities are extensions of the blues or variations on a blues theme. Wilson sets his works in sites that enable such communal engagement, verbal jousting, and oral transmission of culture. . . . [p. 321]

In Wilson's plays, music and song act as metaphors for African American identity, spirit, and soul. Through the invisible presence and symbolic activities of offstage white characters, Wilson suggests that the dominant culture has continually sought to subjugate African American humanity and suppress the power and ability of African Americans to sing their song without looking over their shoulder.

Wilson's blues theology privileges the blues musician. He posits the blues musician as a potentially powerful site of black resistive agency. Too often, however, the [p. 323] musicians fail to realize the power they possess. As with any gift or power, the power of the blues musician exacts certain costs and expectations from the ones to whom it is given. Lyons in *Fences*, Jeremy in *Joe Turner's Come and Gone*, and Winning Boy in *The Piano Lesson*, for instance, all represent blues musicians who have misunderstood the spiritual force of the blues song and the cultural responsibility inherent in their ability to play the blues. As a result, they are exploited for their music and fall victim to those who wish to control their spirit and song. . . . Still, it is on and through these musicians that Wilson positions himself as blues musician improvising on a theme. Toledo's° declarations of the need for African Americans to recognize their connections to Africa represent an important element of Wilson's blues theology. Wilson believes that in order for African Americans to be able to sing their own song, to feel truly liberated in the American context, they must rediscover their "African-ness." Wilson puts it this way: "One of the things I'm trying to say in my writing is that we can never begin to make a contribution to the society except as Africans" (qtd. in Savran 296). Toledo, accordingly, reprimands the band and himself for not being African and for being imitation white men. . . .

The ending of *Ma Rainey*, in which one of the band members murders another, is a complex and confounding blues moment. It stands in stark contrast to endings of Wilson's later dramas such as *Fences*, *Joe Turner*, and *Piano Lesson*, in which characters reach moments of spiritual fulfillment, acknowledge their relationships to the African American past, and perform actions of self-actualization, self-determination, and collective communion. . . . [p. 324]

Toledo: Philosophical pianist in *Ma Rainey's Black Bottom*.

Wilson claims that he started *Fences* (1986), his first Pulitzer Prize–winning play, with "the image of a man standing in his yard with a baby in his arms" (qtd. in DeVries 25). Beginning with this image, Wilson sought to subvert the dominant culture's representations of African American men as irresponsible, absentee fathers. Wilson creates Troy Maxson, a larger-than-life figure, who feels an overwhelming sense of duty and responsibility to his family. With an impenetrable resolve, he perceives familial values only from his perspective. Troy's self-involved concept of familial duty and responsibility prevents him from seeing the harm he causes, the pain his decisions inflict on other family members.

Through a series of retrospective stories performed by Troy, Wilson reveals Troy's victimization by and resentment of the forces of social and economic oppression. Wilson also uses these moments to disclose the influence that Troy's prior relationship with his father now exacts on his relationship with his own son Cory. Physically beaten by his father, Troy was forced to strike out on his own. During the course of the play, Cory must undergo a similar rite of passage. Repeating the family history, Cory physically confronts his father, is beaten by Troy, and is forced to leave his father's house. The repetition of behavior patterns by father and son underscores Wilson's conviction that history plays an important role in determining contemporary identity. Only by literally confronting the embodiment of the past, one's father or "forefathers," can one gain entrance into the future or ascendancy into adulthood.

In the play's second act, Troy's adultery provides the catalyst that propels his wife, Rose, to reassess her position, to gain a greater self-awareness, and to change. Rose blooms. Although Rose spiritually distances herself from Troy, she does not leave the marriage. Her final assessment of their marriage, delivered to her son Cory in the last scene, functions to reconcile father and son and emphasizes Rose's own resignation to "what life offered me in terms of being a woman" (1016). At the close of *Fences*, Cory is able to accept the continued "presence" of his father in his life. This acceptance comes after Cory has returned home from the Marines and announces to Rose his intent to boycott his father's funeral. Wilson juxtaposes Cory's return with the entrance of a new character, Troy's seven-year-old daughter from his affair, Raynell (Cory's half-sister). Wilson uses Raynell as a critical element in his redemptive strategy. Raynell visually represents the inextricable connection between past and present. Not only is she the manifestation of Troy's past infidelities but the signifier of his redemption. Her appearance enables both the audience and Cory to understand better the importance of inheritance, the perpetuation and veneration of history. In addition, here as in other Wilson works the child, Raynell, symbolizes the hope for [p. 325] the family's future. Significantly, her entrance into the action occurs not just on the day of Troy's funeral, but in the year 1965, in the midst of the civil rights era, a period of intense struggle and new opportunity for African Americans. [p. 326]

WORKS CITED

DeVries, Hilary. "A Song in Search of Itself." *American Theatre* 3.10 (January 1987): 22–25.

Ellison, Ralph. "Blues People." *Shadow and Act*. New York: Random House, 1964. 247–58.

Fishman, Joan. "Romare Bearden, August Wilson, and the Traditions of African Performance." *May All Your Fences Have Gates: Essays on the Drama of August Wilson*. Ed. Alan Nadel. Iowa City: U Iowa P, 1994. 133–49.

Savran, David. *In Their Own Words: Contemporary American Playwrights*. New York: Theatre Communications Group, 1988.

Shannon, Sandra G. "The Role of Memory in August Wilson's Four-Hundred-Year Autobiography." *Memory and Cultural Politics: New Approaches to American Ethnic Literature*. Ed. Amritjit Singh, Commas Skerrett, and Robert E. Hogan. Boston: Northeastern UP, 1996. 175–93.

Wilson, August. *Fences*. New York: New American Library, 1986.

——. *Joe Turner's Come and Gone*. New York: New American Library, 1988.

——. *Ma Rainey's Black Bottom*. New York: New American Library, 1985.

——. *The Piano Lesson*. New York: Plume, 1990.

——. *Three Plays*. Pittsburgh: University of Pittsburgh Press, 1991.

Susan Koprince

Baseball as History and Myth in August Wilson's *Fences*°   [2006]

The game of baseball has long been regarded as a metaphor for the American dream—an expression of hope, democratic values, and the drive for individual success. According to John Thorn, baseball has become "the great repository of national ideals, the symbol of all that [is] good in American life: fair play (sportsmanship); the rule of law (objective arbitration of disputes); equal opportunity (each side has its innings); the brotherhood of man (bleacher harmony); and more" (qtd. in Elias 3). Baseball's playing field itself has been viewed as archetypal—a walled garden, an American Eden marked by youth and timelessness. (There are no clocks in the game, and the runners move counter-clockwise around the bases.) As former Yale University president and former baseball commissioner Bart Giamatti once wrote, baseball is "the last pure place where Americans can dream" (qtd. in Elias 9).

In his Pulitzer Prize–winning drama *Fences*..., however, August Wilson uses...[p. 349]° the mythology of baseball to reveal the failed promise of the American dream. As Deeanne Westbrook observes in *Ground Rules: Baseball and*

Koprince, Susan. "Baseball as History and Myth in August Wilson's *Fences*." *African American Review*, vol. 40, no. 2, Summer 2006, pp. 349–58.
(Page citations in square brackets refer to the original publication.)

Myth (1996), baseball's playing field can be understood as an archetypal garden—an image of innocence and timeless space—an American Eden. In W. P. Kinsella's novel *Shoeless Joe* (1982), for example, the protagonist Ray Kinsella rediscovers Eden by building a baseball park in his Iowa cornfield, creating "a walled garden of eternal youth." Players from baseball's past enter this magical garden, "not middle-aged or elderly, as they were at their deaths, but young, as they were at their moments of peak performance. They occupy the mythic present" (Westbrook 102).

In *Fences* the closest that Troy comes to participating in the American dream—and hence inhabiting such a paradise—is during his life in the Negro Leagues. Wilson associates the American dream with Troy's younger days as a ballplayer: with self-affirmation, limitless possibilities, and the chance for heroic success. The very act of hitting a home run—especially when the ball is hit over the fence—suggests extraordinary strength and the ability to transcend limits. Troy's son Lyons recalls seeing his father hit a home run over the grandstand: "Right out there in Homestead Field. He wasn't satisfied hitting in the seats . . . he want to hit it over everything! After the game he had two hundred people standing around waiting to shake his hand" (784). Troy himself claims that he hit seven home runs off of Satchel Paige. "You can't get no better than that," he boasts (753).

For Troy, however, the American dream has turned into a prolonged nightmare. Instead of limitless opportunity, he has come to know racial discrimination and poverty. At age fifty-three, this former Negro League hero is a garbage collector who ekes out a meager existence, working arduously to support his family and living from hand to mouth. "I do the best I can do," he tells Rose. "I come in here every Friday. I carry a sack of potatoes and a bucket of lard. You all line up at the door with your hands out. I give you the lint from my pockets. I give you my sweat and my blood. I ain't got no tears. I done spent them" (756). Troy claims that he would not even have a roof over his head if it were not for the $3,000 that the government gave to his mentally disabled brother, Gabriel, following a serious head injury in World War II.

Wilson accentuates Troy's exclusion from the American Eden by converting baseball's mythical garden into an ironic version of paradise. In the stage directions to *Fences*, Wilson indicates that the legendary "field of dreams" has been reduced to the "small dirt yard" (734) in front of Troy's home—his current playing field. Incompletely fenced, the yard contains lumber and other fence-building materials, as well as two oil drums used as garbage containers. A baseball bat—"the most visible symbol of [Troy's] [p. 353] deferred dreams" (Shannon, *Fences* 46)—is propped up against a tree, from which there hangs "a ball made of rags" (734). As the setting reveals, Troy does not inhabit a walled garden of timeless youth. At fifty-three, he cannot reclaim his past glory as a power hitter; nor can he participate in the American dream. His playing field in 1957 has deteriorated into one of dirt, garbage, and rags. Indeed, only after Troy's death at the end of the play, when his fence is completed and when his daughter Raynell plants a small garden in front of the house, is there even a suggestion of a walled paradise.

According to Westbrook, baseball's archetypal playing field can also become a battleground—a scene of violent confrontation—much like the heroic fights at Valhalla, the "home of the slain" in Norse mythology. Each morning the warriors arm themselves for combat and battle one another fiercely in the great courtyard, returning to the banquet hall in the evening to feast and boast of their exploits. As Westbrook notes, "The ritualized aggression of both Valhalla and baseball field is rule governed . . . and endlessly repeatable" (811). The baseball players are modern-day warriors, the bat and ball are weapons, and the game itself a substitute for combat.

In *Fences* Wilson converts Troy's playing field into a battleground—an image reinforced by references to World War II (during which Gabriel got "half his head blown off" [749]), to the "Army of Death" (740), and to the Battle of Armageddon (when, according to Gabriel, "God get to waving that Judgment sword" [760]). Throughout the play Troy is pictured as a batter/warrior, fighting to earn a living and to stay alive in a world that repeatedly discriminates against him. As Shannon has noted, Troy sees life as a baseball contest; he sees himself as perpetually in the batter's box (*Dramatic Vision* 110). He tells Rose: "You got to guard [the plate] closely . . . always looking for the curve ball on the inside corner. You can't afford to let none get past you. You can't afford a call strike. If you going down . . . you going down swinging" (772).

Troy's front yard is literally turned into a battleground during his confrontations with his younger son, Cory. Bitter about his own exclusion from major-league baseball, Troy is resistant when Cory wants to attend college on a football scholarship, telling his son that black athletes have to be twice as talented to make the team and that "the white man ain't gonna let you get nowhere with that football noway" (753). But Cory, who seems to believe in the promise of the American dream—particularly for black athletes in the 1950s—insists that Troy is selfishly holding him back from success: "You just scared I'm gonna be better than you, that's all" (765). The intergenerational conflict reaches a climax in act 2, when Troy and Cory engage in an ironic version of the all-American father-and-son game of catch (Birdwell 91). "Get your black ass out of my yard!" (781), Troy warns Cory, after which the two combatants fight furiously over Troy's bat/weapon until Cory is expelled from his father's playing field.

Troy's efforts to prevent his son from playing football can be viewed as a form of what Harry J. Elam Jr. calls "racial madness"—a term that suggests that social and political forces can impact the black psyche and that decades of oppression can induce a collective psychosis.[1] In *Fences* this racial madness is illustrated most vividly in the character of Troy's mentally handicapped brother, Gabriel, but it is also revealed in Troy himself, who is so overwhelmed by bitterness that he destroys his son's dream of a college education—a dream that most fathers would happily support. Instead, Troy instructs Cory to stick with his job at the A&P or learn a trade like carpentry or auto mechanics: "That way you have something can't nobody take away from you" (753). There is a certain method, however, to Troy's madness; for why should he expect college football (another white power structure) to [p. 354] treat his son any better than major-league baseball treated him? Why should he believe, in 1957, that times have really changed for black men? Anxious for Cory to find economic security, and, more importantly, self-respect, Troy exclaims to Rose, "I don't want him to be like me! I want him to move as far away from my life as he can get" (755).

In Amiri Baraka's play *Dutchman* (1964), the African American protagonist Clay advocates a violent solution to the problem of racial madness, telling his white adversary, Lula, that "the only thing that would cure the neurosis would be your murder. Simple as that. . . . Crazy niggers turning their backs on sanity. When all it need is that simple act. Murder. Just Murder!" (qtd. in Elam 63). In *Fences* Troy's response to the racial madness that infects him is much less revolutionary than Clay's, but it is combative nonetheless. Troy chooses to challenge the white man, literally, by engaging in a form of social activism, that is, by taking a job complaint to his boss, Mr. Rand, and then to the commissioner's office. Moreover, he teaches his son how to fight. During their climactic struggle in act 2, Troy deliberately confronts Cory, taunting him, grabbing the bat from him, and insisting that he teach Cory how to swing. Determined to prepare his son for combat in a racist society, Troy uses the weapons and language of baseball as his teaching tools. "Don't you strike out," he tells Cory after an earlier altercation. "You living with a full count. Don't you strike out" (733).

Troy's playing field is the scene not only of father-son conflict, but of marital strife as well. In act 2 Rose learns that Troy has been unfaithful to her and has fathered a child with his mistress, Alberta. When Troy tries to explain (and even justify) his infidelity by using baseball analogies, Rose is not impressed. "We're not talking about baseball!" she says. "We're talking about you going off to lay in bed with another woman . . . and then bring it home to me. That's what we're talking about. We ain't talking about no baseball" (772). After the conflict between Rose and Troy escalates into a cold war — the two of them rarely speaking to one another — it is the wounded Rose, rather than Troy, who eventually dominates the battle, taking in his motherless daughter and telling Troy: "From right now . . . this child got a mother. But you a womanless man" (777) . . . [p. 355]

Although Wilson's dramas are typically grounded in elements of African and African American cultures — including ritual, superstition, the blues, and jazz — *Fences* is unique in that it appropriates a traditionally white cultural form — baseball — in order to portray an African American experience in the twentieth century. By adopting this white cultural form, Wilson artfully expresses Troy Maxson's double consciousness — his complicated experience as a black man in a white-dominated world. At the same time, Wilson creates a "subversive narrative" that competes with the American Dream itself (Shannon, *Fences* 20). Thus, he demonstrates that the national pastime has been stained by racism, that the Edenic promise of America is illusory, and that the traditional mythology of baseball must ultimately make room for a new and revolutionary mythos: that of the defiant African American warrior.

NOTE

[1]Invoking the theories of psychiatrist-philosopher Frentz Fanon as well as the perspectives of Du Bois, Ellison, and others, Elam emphasizes that "racial madness" does not imply a pathology in blackness itself. Rather it is "a trope that became operative in clinical practice, literary creation, and cultural theory in the modern period as artists, critics, and practitioners identified social and cultural roots for black psychological impairment" (59). During his discussion of racial madness in *Fences*, Elam focuses on Troy's brain-damaged brother, Gabriel, whom he describes as a force for redemption.

WORKS CITED

Birdwell, Christine. "Death as a Fastball on the Outside Corner: *Fences*' Troy Maxson and the American Dream." *Aethlon: The Journal of Sport Literature* 8.1 (Fall 1990): 87–96.

Elam, Harry J. Jr. *The Past as Present in the Drama of August Wilson*. Ann Arbor: U Michigan P, 2004.

Elias, Robert. "A Fit for a Fractured Society." *Baseball and the American Dream: Race, Class, Gender, and the National Pastime*. Ed. Robert Elias. Armonk, N.Y.: M. E. Sharpe, 2001. 3–33.

Kinsella, W. P. *Shoeless Joe*. 1982. New York: Ballantine, 1990.

Shannon, Sandra G. *August Wilson's* Fences: *A Reference Guide*. Westport, Conn.: Greenwood, 2003.

——. *The Dramatic Vision of August Wilson*. Washington, D.C.: Howard UP, 1995.

Westbrook, Deeanne. *Ground Rules: Baseball and Myth*. Urbana: U Illinois P, 1996.

Wilson, August. *Fences*. New York: New American Library, 1986.

RESPONDING THROUGH Writing

Here are some suggestions for writing on August Wilson, but for a chapter like this one, you should not limit yourself to these topics. An important purpose behind the chapter is to help you learn how to find good topics on your own. You may make changes in the topics (with your instructor's permission) and make changes in how they are categorized (using a topic from the first six as a research topic, for example, instead of one using no outside sources.)

PAPERS USING NO OUTSIDE SOURCES

Literary Analysis Papers

1. Write a paper analyzing the use of baseball as a plot element and as a metaphor for life in *Fences*.

2. Write a paper exploring different kinds of fences, literal ones and figurative ones suggesting enclosures, in *Fences*.

Comparison-Contrast Papers

3. Write a paper comparing and contrasting the attitudes toward change evinced by Troy and by other characters in *Fences*.

4. Write a comparison-contrast paper showing how Bono serves as a foil for Troy or how Lyons serves as a foil for Cory in *Fences*.

Cultural Studies Papers

5. The church has traditionally been an important part of African American culture. Write a paper examining the use and effect of the language of and the practice of Christianity in *Fences*.

6. Write a paper on the attitudes toward and meaning of work in *Fences*.

PAPERS USING LIMITED OUTSIDE SOURCES

Literary Analysis Papers

1. In his interview with Bonnie Lyons, August Wilson says that inner conflict is at the center of drama (p. 794). Using what he says there and what reviewers and critics included in this chapter say, write a paper discussing the inner conflicts that drive the action in *Fences*.

2. In his interview with Miles Marshall Lewis, August Wilson says his plays are about the "Big Themes" — "love, honor, duty, betrayal" (p. 797). Drawing on that interview and other secondary writings in this chapter, write a paper discussing the extent to which those themes are present and influential in *Fences*.

Comparison-Contrast Papers

3. Frank Rich's reference to the "conflicting visions" of Troy and Cory (p. 793) is echoed by other secondary works included in this chapter. Building on their comments, write a paper comparing and contrasting the visions of the two men and discussing the reasons for and effects of the tensions between them.

4. Lloyd Richards, the original director of *Fences*, writes that the play tells the story of four generations of black Americans (p. 789). Write a paper examining differences and similarities in what happens to them, especially changes — or lack of change — in their relationships with white Americans. Use secondary materials in this chapter, as well as the play, for support.

Cultural Studies Papers

5. Write a paper examining the roles of and attitudes toward women in *Fences*, using the secondary materials in this chapter as well as the play itself for illustrations and supporting details.

6. Harry J. Elam, Jr. says that at the heart of Wilson's plays is "the concept that one must go backwards in order to move forward" (p. 805). Write a paper in which you explore the applicability of that claim in *Fences*, using the secondary materials in this chapter as well as the play for support.

PAPERS INVOLVING FURTHER RESEARCH

Literary Analysis Papers

1. Wilson once said that listening to a recording of Bessie Smith's "Nobody in Town Can Bake a Jelly Roll Like Mine" awakened his interest in the blues. Write a research paper on the use and influence of the blues on his play *Fences* (consider the rhythms, outlook, and sensibility that characterize the blues).

2. Harry J. Elam, Jr. says that Wilson, who wrote poetry before turning to drama, "allows his characters to voice their history in the verbal equivalent of musical solos" (p. 806). Write a paper analyzing the "poetic" or "musical" style Wilson gives to characters in *Fences*, especially in major speeches. Focus on the text of the play, but bring in the secondary materials in this chapter and other critical materials you find elsewhere for additional support.

Comparison-Contrast Papers

3. Susan Koprince (p. 809) is one of several critics who write about the mythic implications of baseball as a metaphor for the American dream in *Fences*. Write a paper comparing and contrasting her insights with those of two or three other critics and explain which you find most helpful or convincing and why.

4. Do research on August Wilson's life, using the material in this chapter and going beyond it. Write a paper in which you compare and contrast what happens in Troy Maxson's life to events in or associated with Wilson's life or the lives of people he knew, focusing on how Wilson transforms biographical material to make the play "work."

Cultural Studies Papers

5. Write a research paper examining August Wilson's incorporation and adaptation of African American folklore traditions in *Fences*.

6. In August Wilson's master plan of writing ten plays, one embodying the spirit of each of the decades of the twentieth century, *Fences* was the play for the 1950s. Write a research paper on how *Fences* is representative of — or epitomizes — events and changes taking place in that decade.

CHAPTER 27 A Collection of Plays

Viewing from Various Vantage Points

TWO TEN-MINUTE PLAYS

Unlike the idiosyncratic nature of flash fiction and short-short poems, which defy easy categorization, the short play doesn't differ all that much from a play of standard length. Its primary distinction from longer plays is that it is more constrained by performance time and therefore is, more often than not, only one act long.

The dramatic elements of a short play do not differ from those of a longer play either. However, the climax, instead of happening after a developed buildup, is more like that of a conventional short story, in which a particular moment has a sudden, profound effect on a character. The dramatic intensity of such a moment is crafted into the structures of both short plays and plays with several acts. Again, the difference lies in the length of time leading to and following the climax. Think about it in terms of a crucial moment in a long-term relationship and one on a first date: Both can be dramatic. The difference is in the length of time the drama develops.

As you read the following ten-minute plays, bring to them all the resources you would bring to a play of two, three, four, or five acts.

Deanna Alisa Ableser   b. 1970

Black Coffee   [2012]

CHARACTERS:

MAN: Mid thirties to Mid forties. Attractive, yet very unassuming. Has a
     kind hearted nature overall, but loves to enjoy the humor in life.
WOMAN: Mid thirties to Mid forties. Also attractive, but has a "Plain Jane"
     sense about her. Eccentric, yet aware of her own eccentricities.

SETTING AND TIME:

Coffee Shop in the City. Later afternoon/Early evening

*A MAN and a WOMAN are sitting at a table at a coffee shop. The WOMAN
is reading a book while the MAN is doing some work. WOMAN is showing a
deep internal struggle . . . trying to get up the courage to say something. Finally,
she turns to the MAN.*

WOMAN: (*softly*) It's killing me not to be kissing you right now.
MAN: (*obviously taken aback*) Excuse me?
WOMAN: (*embarrassed*) Dammit. I knew I shouldn't have said it . . . I knew I
     shouldn't have said it . . . I knew . . .
MAN: It's okay.
WOMAN: No, it's not. I'm sorry. I mean, I shouldn't have said it . . . it was just
     so . . . and you were looking so . . . and it's just killing me . . .
MAN: It's really okay. It's been a long day anyway.
WOMAN: (*rambling*) That's so nice of you to say. I mean, really really nice. I
     mean, usually, I usually don't say these things and I'm usually very level
     headed and I just don't know what got into me. I was just minding my
     business and you were just sitting there and looking so . . . well, looking so
     gorgeous . . . and I just figured . . . well, what the hell, what have I got to
     lose? I mean, he's not going to hit me in a public place and I can always
     run quickly and hide in the bathroom if it gets really bad so I just figured
     I'd open my mouth and . . .
MAN: You talk a lot, don't you?
WOMAN: (*slightly embarrassed*) I've been accused of that before. Being silent
     has never been what you would call a strength of mine. So, again I
     apologize . . . please go back to your coffee or tea or caffè latte or mocha
     or iced . . . .
MAN: It's a coffee . . . black, no sugar, no cream, no ice blended, no frappé
     whatcha.
WOMAN: It does get kinda complicated, doesn't it?
MAN: Following the trend, I suppose. Name's Matt.
WOMAN: Alice.
MAN: Well, Alice, you did make my day more interesting.
WOMAN: Better than boring, right?

MAN: Better than boring, right.

WOMAN: Well, thanks for not hitting me or running off screaming into the night or something like that . . .

MAN: I'm not usually a wild and crazy type of guy.

WOMAN: (slightly intrigued) Not usually?

MAN: Not usually . . . but if the situation warrants it, I just might see what way the wind blows . . . you know, go with the flow.

WOMAN: (pausing and then clearing her throat) So, then, could it possibly be a possibility?

MAN: You weren't actually serious, were you?

WOMAN: It's okay . . . you're right . . . it's been a long day.

WOMAN picks up her drink and starts adding tons of sugar . . . obviously not looking. SHE drinks and gags.

MAN looks at her with curiosity.

MAN: Maybe we could start again. (Pause) Matt.

MAN holds out his hand for WOMAN to shake.

WOMAN: Alice.

WOMAN shakes MAN's hand.

MAN: That's a nice name. What's that you're drinking?

WOMAN: (realizing as she speaks what she is saying) It's just a double frappé with soy and an extra shot of espresso with a dollop of . . .

WOMAN stops what she is saying and looks at the cup.

WOMAN: You're right . . . it's complicated.

MAN: You ever done this before?

WOMAN: Done this?

MAN: How we started out . . . I mean, it's quite unusual to go up to a man and proposition him totally out of the blue . . . well, not quite a full proposition, but quite forward nonetheless.

WOMAN: I know . . . I know . . . I should have just minded my own business, drank my overly labeled drink and gone on my merry way. I think something's in the air.

MAN: Well . . . I've never been one to stand in the way of someone's karmic path, so, please, go ahead . . . whenever you're ready . . .

MAN puts down his cup and seems ready to kiss WOMAN.

WOMAN puts down her cup and stares at MAN for a bit. It is now SHE who is taken aback and confused.

WOMAN: It's really okay with you?

MAN: It's only a kiss.

WOMAN: You really do have delicious lips.

MAN: It's not my weakest point.

WOMAN: Are you sure it's okay with you? I mean, it's quite a tender thing . . . a kiss . . . a gentle intimacy.

MAN: I'm fine with it. I mean, there's not a contract attached to it, is there? It's just a kiss . . . simple.

WOMAN: You're sure you're sure? I don't want to cross any boundaries.

MAN: You really do talk a lot, don't you?

WOMAN: It's not my strongest point.

> *WOMAN glances nervously at MAN's lips.*

WOMAN: This starts something, doesn't it?

MAN: It can.

WOMAN: If I want it to, right?

MAN: It can.

WOMAN: I'm not completely sure I'm ready for that.

> *WOMAN leans slightly closer to MAN.*

WOMAN: (*taking a deep breath*) You smell amazing.

MAN: You're not signing any contract, remember? You always have a choice. It's really quite simple.

WOMAN: That's easy enough for you to say. I'd like to classify it as extremely complicated, if that's okay with you.

MAN: Fine . . . it's your kiss. Call it extremely complicated.

WOMAN: But are you completely sure? I mean, I don't want to cross any boundaries and you were just sitting there minding your own business. I should have just shut my big mouth and kept on drinking, but no, I just blabber and blabber until . . .

MAN: (*interrupting her*) It's just a kiss.

> *WOMAN starts blushing and tries to hide it*

MAN: (*trying to make her feel more comfortable by changing the subject*) Can I treat you to a muffin? Pastry? Cookie?

WOMAN: Does that excuse it?

MAN: It's just a kiss.

WOMAN: That's okay, right?

MAN: It's okay . . . a simple kiss . . . I told you, no contract.

WOMAN: You're a lot more intriguing than I thought.

MAN: I'll take that as a backhanded compliment.

WOMAN: So, how do we do this?

MAN: It should be simple enough. I mean, people have been doing it for years. It's not like we're reinventing the wheel.

WOMAN: Would you like to be seated?

MAN: This is a comfortable chair.

WOMAN: And you'd like me how? I mean, if we're going to do this . . . we should do it right.

MAN: Are you seriously always like this?

WOMAN: I told you . . . it's never been a strength of mine . . . not blabbering on like some moronic fool . . . and here I am again . . . yapping and yapping and . . .

> *MAN gives her the "enough" look and SHE stops talking.*

MAN: You know you really are quite beautiful.

> *WOMAN blushes and turns her face.*

WOMAN: I'm really not sure what this starts.

MAN: Does that really matter?

WOMAN: In some ways.

MAN: Are you really sure?

WOMAN: It has to start something. I mean, we can't just kiss and go our merry ways.

MAN: I'm sure it's happened before.

WOMAN: But now you're really starting to intrigue me. I've already gone through so many possible scenarios in my head.

MAN: We've only been sitting here talking for about 10 minutes.

WOMAN: Actually it's been closer to 6.

> *MAN smirks and lets out a short laugh.*

WOMAN: (*self-deprecating*) It took me a while to get up the courage to speak to you.

MAN: I'm not really that remarkable.

WOMAN: In how this plays out in my mind, you are.

MAN: How could you possibly have played this out in your mind in 6 minutes?

WOMAN: It's one of my stronger points.

MAN: (*raising his eyebrows and moving closer to WOMAN*) So, then how does it play out?

WOMAN: I win.

MAN: You win? That's pretty vague, don't you think?

WOMAN: I can see how it appears that way.

MAN: So, let's stop playing around. You've played it all out in that funky little brain of yours. How do we end up?

WOMAN: I'm not quite sure sharing that is the most strategic move to play at this point.

MAN: (*smelling something wafting in the air*) You smell like something sweet from my childhood . . . I can't quite place it.

WOMAN: (*not responding to MAN*) Can I touch your cheeks first? They look so soft.

> *MAN leans forward and WOMAN gently caresses one cheek and then another. MAN is obviously very intrigued by this action but is off in thought elsewhere.*

WOMAN: There's such a draw to you . . . I can't quite explain it.

MAN: Cinnamon rolls.

WOMAN: What?

MAN: You smell like the sweet cinnamon rolls from my childhood.

WOMAN: Was my touch that unremarkable?

MAN: Not at all . . . it's just that cinnamon was so strong. Your touch was . . . I can't quite place it. Are you sure I can't get you a muffin? The cookies are quite delicious here.

WOMAN: I'd actually like a plain coffee. No sugar. No cream.

MAN: You're willing to take that risk?

WOMAN: I've become more and more intrigued. In the past 2 minutes, I've decided that plain coffee is a rewarding risk.

MAN: I'm glad I've had a good influence on you.

WOMAN: It does save calories that way.

MAN: I'll be right back.

> *MAN goes up to order coffee.*
> *WOMAN starts frantically going through purse.*
> *She pulls out mirror and is trying to fix her hair and pulls out a small*
> *perfume and spritzes herself. MAN comes back with coffee.*

MAN: Here it is. Plain. No sugar. No cream. Zero calories.

> *WOMAN takes coffee, but doesn't drink it yet.*

MAN: Is there something wrong?

WOMAN: I just like to let it cool off a bit. You know, they have that warning: Caution: Hot beverages are hot.

MAN: You don't really read those warnings, do you?

WOMAN: I like to be careful.

MAN: And yet you approach complete strangers in coffee shops and proposition them?

WOMAN: I take calculated risks.

MAN: You really are quite beautiful.

WOMAN: Thanks for the coffee.

MAN: Plain coffee is much cheaper than your fancy drinks.

WOMAN: I'd like to think it's not all about the money.

MAN: It's not all about the money.

WOMAN: You're not as boring as I first thought.

MAN: Would you like to try the coffee?

WOMAN: I'm not quite ready.

MAN: It's only a warning that they put to protect themselves . . . you know, save their asses . . . all that liability stuff. It's not really that hot.

WOMAN: You really do have delicious lips.

MAN: It's just a warning.

WOMAN: I know.

MAN: I remember when my mom would make cinnamon rolls. The house smelled so full of life.

> *WOMAN reaches out to MAN and they share a tender kiss.*

WOMAN: Cinnamon is one of my favorite smells.

MAN: You really are quite intriguing.

> *WOMAN picks up coffee and drinks it.*

MAN: Well?

WOMAN: You really do have delicious lips.

MAN: And the coffee?

WOMAN: It's simple. No contract.

MAN: Can I help you with your jacket? It's cold outside.

WOMAN: It's nice to have company.

MAN: I'm glad you took a risk with the coffee. It will save you a lot of money in the long run.

> *MAN helps WOMAN put on jacket and THEY start walking. HE kisses*
> *her cheek.*

MAN: I love the smell of cinnamon.

> *Lights fade.*

THE END

Suzanne Bradbeer b. 1961

Okoboji   [2011]

For Karen

CHARACTERS:

ALAN HARPER: late 40s to 60s. An artist from Boston.
ANNIE HANSGEN: early 20s. A girl from Iowa.

SETTING:

West Okoboji Lake, Iowa.

TIME:

The present.

(Alan and Annie, looking at West Okoboji Lake. It is an early morning in Iowa)

ALAN: So this is it.
ANNIE: Yes.
ALAN: The famous blue lake . . .
ANNIE: Yeah.
ALAN: Cobalt. Cobalt blue. It's almost a Prussian blue, but not quite. No, it's
    definitely cobalt. My favorite color. Have you ever been to Boston?
ANNIE: No. I'd like to someday.
ALAN: There's a painting at the Museum of Fine Arts, it's by William Merritt
    Chase, have you heard of William Merritt Chase?
ANNIE: No.
ALAN: I don't much care for him, I find him a little prissy in his subject matter,
    but I like this particular painting, and he uses this exact shade of blue.
ANNIE: I'd love to see it.
ALAN: This exact shade of blue. . . .

    (UNCOMFORTABLE, he looks behind them)

LOOK at all those *trees.*
ANNIE: I know, aren't they beautiful? Oak trees are my favorite.
ALAN: I hate nature.
ANNIE: *(Picking up a feather from the ground)* Look, a hawk's feather! Look!
ALAN: Are you Indian?
ANNIE: No.
ALAN: I mean, sorry, Native American?
ANNIE: No.
ALAN: How do you know so much about the fauna and the flora?
ANNIE: You mean, the hawk's feather?
ALAN: Hawk's feather, oak trees, yes, how do you know all that?
ANNIE: Um, the oak is a pretty common tree? And the red-tailed hawk,

they've made their homes all over this country — in meadows, mountains — the desert. They even have them in cities, like where you're from, Boston; I even heard there were these red-tailed hawks on Fifth Avenue in New York, a hawk couple named Pale Male and Lola.

ALAN: Fascinating. (*He looks back at the lake, considering*) They say this is one of only three true blue water lakes on the planet. 'Course you probably already know that, what with your obsessive cataloguing of the natural world.

ANNIE: _____

ALAN: One of three on the planet and yet I had never heard of West Okoboji Lake until a year ago. Do you know where the other two blue water lakes are?

ANNIE: Lake Geneva in Switzerland, and Lake Louise in Alberta, Canada.

ALAN: Correct. I wonder how many people in the world have seen all three? Maybe there's a group, a society you can join, I could probably go online and find the Blue Water Lake Club.

ANNIE: Sounds neat.

ALAN: Sounds hideous. I hate clubs. Turns out though, I could be a founding member.

ANNIE: You've seen all three? Really?

ALAN: Lake Geneva, beautiful of course. Lake Louise, Brian was conceived in the Hotel Banff on the shores of Lake Louise. At least that's what we always liked to say. Brian's mother and I were very . . . at any rate, let's just say it's hard to pinpoint the exact moment. But I like to think it was in the Hotel Banff. (*Beat*) I'M always quite moved by rarity. One of only three blue water lakes. Biggest diamond in the world. Only son.

ANNIE: (*Beat*) Brian's eyes were this color.

ALAN: Yes.

ANNIE: That was one of the first things I noticed about him. I've never met anyone else with eyes that were/ so blue.

ALAN: Brian's great-great-great grandfather was a Colonel in the Revolutionary Army. A Colonel is a very high rank, during the Revolution it was second only to General and, and I, I don't know what made me think of that except that he, the Colonel, he seemed to be quite fond of nature too. Very fond. Very, very fond. We have a few of his letters; he survived the war and wrote constantly, *incessantly* about his travels up and down the Massachusetts Shore, up and down, up and down he went. They're quite valuable these letters — boring! But valuable. Why are you smiling?

ANNIE: We used to call Brian "the Colonel." Even in the short time we knew him here. It was very important to him that people respect the lake and the woods. The, flora and the fauna. He always spoke to everyone in a nice way, but he was very firm about it, if they were littering, or being careless, he was very firm.

ALAN: Were they mean to him?

ANNIE: Who?

ALAN: Anyone, was anyone mean to him?

ANNIE: No. *No*.

ALAN: He was bullied quite a lot, when he was in school.

ANNIE: He told me.

ALAN: So, calling him the Colonel, they weren't being, mocking/ or, or—?

ANNIE: No, not at all—

ALAN: Because a boy less like a colonel you could hardly hope to find.

ANNIE: We called him the Colonel because he/ had very—

ALAN: Yes, I remember that he advised people not to litter.

ANNIE: It wasn't just that, he, he had standards of behavior, very high standards of behavior—for himself especially. And he was very, responsible
and, and—oh!—and he always identified time in that military way, like
nine o'clock at night wasn't nine o'clock, it was 2100 hours.

ALAN: 2100 hours, yes. He started doing that when he was about seven, for
some reason.

ANNIE: And he valued loyalty. And, and doing the right thing. And niceness,
I think he valued niceness most of all.

ALAN: Brian was much more like his mother. I had a good night's sleep that night.

ANNIE: Sir?

ALAN: I don't usually sleep well, but that night I was sleeping very well. Until
the call. I don't understand how I slept through . . . that moment. I don't
understand that. They say he died immediately.

ANNIE: Yes.

ALAN: I thought maybe they lied. To spare me, I thought maybe they lied.

ANNIE: No.

ALAN: (*This is what he's been waiting to say*) See, I would prefer to think that
you fired the gun—accidentally, accidentally of course—but I would prefer
to think that you fired it, rather than . . . rather than what you want me to
think.

ANNIE: I don't want you to think anything.

ALAN: But can you understand that? Can you understand how a father would
prefer to think that?

ANNIE: . . . I guess.

ALAN: So this, this *Inquiry*, or inquest, or—

ANNIE: Autopsy, it was just/ an autopsy—

ALAN: Whatever it was, it doesn't have a workable result for me.

ANNIE: But why—I mean, that was a month ago—why/ are you—

ALAN: And I've been giving it a great deal of thought in the last month, a great
deal. As you can imagine. And I just think that maybe you should admit
what *really* happened.

ANNIE: I'm sorry, but didn't you read the report, the forensics were very clear.

ALAN: I don't care about God-damn forensics! I care about my boy. You were
there; you could have shot him, you'd/ both been—

ANNIE: No.

ALAN: Yes! A bunch of you had been drinking earlier that night, you admitted
as much. And maybe, maybe you'd never held a gun before/ and maybe
you—

ANNIE: How can you say that to me?

ALAN: Where did he get the gun?

ANNIE: It's not hard to get a gun.

ALAN: Maybe you were curious and wanted to see what it felt like and maybe Brian was trying to show you but neither of you realized that the gun was loaded/ and maybe—

ANNIE: Is this why you came all the way back here?

ALAN: No one would blame you, I would make sure/ of that.

ANNIE: He shot himself in front of me, Mr. Harper.

ALAN: No he didn't. It was an accident.

ANNIE: He shot himself in front of me.

ALAN: If you ever have children you might understand how cruel you're being right now.

ANNIE: (*Beat*) I'm sorry.

ALAN: My *son* was not cruel.

ANNIE: No, he wasn't.

ALAN: That's a very cruel thing, if it's true. To do what he did in front of you.

ANNIE: I don't think he meant to.

ALAN: See! It was an accident!

ANNIE: I just meant that he didn't mean for me to see; he didn't expect/ me to—

ALAN: Why can't you say it was an accident—just tell me it was a god-damn accident—what the hell is wrong with you?!

ANNIE: . . . It was an accident. (*Silence*)

ALAN: I could wish you were a better liar.

ANNIE: . . . Me too. (*Beat*) I knew he was depressed, I think he was depressed for a long time. We talked about it sometimes. He said he considered it part of his life. But it wasn't the only part. And it doesn't take away from the things that made him happy. This lake made him happy, especially this time of day, especially right here. Remembering his Mom made him happy. And you, your paintings, your paintings made him happy.

ALAN: _____

ANNIE: You don't hate nature.

ALAN: What?!

ANNIE: You said you hated nature. You're a painter, I don't think you hate nature.

ALAN: You don't know me. You don't know me and you barely knew my son—you knew him, what, ten months? You can't know someone in ten months.

ANNIE: He talked about showing you this lake. He said the first thing you'd do would be to identify the exact color.

ALAN: Anyone would do that.

ANNIE: And say it was your favorite color, and then mention some obscure painter who has three names.

ALAN: William Merritt Chase is hardly obscure. (*Beat*) It's true Brian was often amused by what he called my, predictability. Did he tell you that? (*Annie nods*)

ALAN: What else did he say about me?

ANNIE: I know that he loved you, Mr. Harper. (*Silence*)

ALAN: I'm not a warm person, I am aware of that you know. Did you just roll your eyes?

ANNIE: Did I? Sorry. I thought I just rolled them in my mind. Sorry.

ALAN: It's all right. (*Looking around*) This is a nice spot. And it was nice of you to bring me here. You seem like a nice kid. I'm ready to go back now. (*He walks off, then looks back at Annie who hasn't moved*) Are you coming?

ANNIE: . . . I'm not a nice kid. . . .

ALAN: What?

ANNIE: (*Distraught*) I let him down, he needed me and I let him down.

ALAN: How?

ANNIE: He reached out to me, that last week he left me a couple messages but I was preoccupied, I don't even know with what, with nothing, with my own boring problems, which were nothing, they were nothing! ! I didn't get back to him until the party. I knew he was depressed and I didn't get back to him until that party, what is wrong with me?!

ALAN: (*Carefully*) I shouldn't have said those things to you. I'm sorry.

ANNIE: I'm not a nice kid!

ALAN: You didn't let him down.

ANNIE: You don't know!

ALAN: I do know. I know a few things. I've lived a long time and in spite of all evidence to the contrary, I know a few things. You didn't let him down. (*Looking at her*) You don't believe me? (*Annie shakes her head*)

ALAN: I'm your elder. I think that means you have to believe whatever I say.

ANNIE: I'm sorry, but I don't.

ALAN: Well. Then . . . then we'll just have to stay in touch till I figure out how to convince you. Can we do that? (*Annie shrugs, helpless*)

ALAN: (*Gently*) Let's do that, let's stay in touch. Now tell me something. Why are you still carrying around that dirty feather?

ANNIE: (*Looking at the feather, surprised she still has it*) Birds are believed to carry messages of the spirit. Did you know that? A bird feather represents strength and, protection. And a hawk feather, a hawk feather is extra special. If you find a feather like this, you're supposed to let it go back into the wind with a prayer, or, or a message.

ALAN: I thought you weren't an Indian.

ANNIE: I'm not, I'm just, from Iowa.

ALAN: (*Of the feather*) You're supposed to send it back into the wind?

ANNIE: (*Annie nods*) With a prayer, or a message.

ALAN: Then, let's do it.

ANNIE: Do what?

ALAN: Let's send a message. (*Annie hesitates. Then she holds the feather aloft. Alan stands next to her, but not touching her. Beat. Annie lets go of the feather and they watch it fly off over the lake. Lights out*)

END OF PLAY

THREE CLASSIC PLAYS

THE IMPACT OF GENRE AND THEATER

Chapters 23 and 24 focus on the elements of drama that need attention as you read a play—the handling of character, dialogue, dramatic action, setting, and structure. To appreciate drama fully, however, you also need some familiarity with the traditional dramatic genres and how they changed—for example, what *comedy* and *tragedy* meant at the time a playwright was writing. And you need to be aware of the kind of theaters in which plays were and are acted. Playwrights nearly always write with specific stage structures in mind, usually reflecting the theater designs and practices of their day. For the three plays that follow, from very different time periods, we provide introductions giving information regarding the assumptions about genre and the theater designs in use when the playwright was writing.

In looking at theaters we consider not just the shape and size of the buildings and stages, but also the conventions used on those stages. **Conventions**, in this case, are assumptions shared by playwrights and audiences about how an action on the stage can be accepted as believable, even real. Conventions rely on what nineteenth-century poet and critic Samuel Taylor Coleridge called a "willing suspension of disbelief"—that is, a willingness not to question the truth, accuracy, or probability of what occurs in a work so that one can enter and enjoy it as if it were real. For example, lighting could not be controlled on an outdoor Elizabethan stage; so, if in a drama from that time period an actor says it is so dark he can't even see his hand in front of his face, the playwright and audience accept it as true, even though they can see the actor clearly.

THE GREEK THEATER

The first of the three plays, *Oedipus the King*, was originally performed in Athens in a large, open-air stadium designed for the annual festival of Dionysus, the Greek god of fertility. At the center of the structure was the circular "orchestra," or "dancing place," where the chorus moved from side to side and chanted their lines. At its center was an altar used for religious ceremonies, of which the drama was a part. Circling two-thirds of the orchestra was the *theatron* or "seeing place": tiers of wooden or stone seats for the audience, which rose up a hillside and created a bowl large enough to hold 15,000 people. Comparing that to today, when a 1,500–2,000-seat capacity is considered a large theater, gives some indication of how important these ceremonies were in Athenian culture.

Closing off the circle was the *skene* (literally, the "hut"), a wooden building where actors changed masks or costumes. Three doors opened onto the *proskenion*, a long, narrow section that served as the main acting area. (The term **proscenium**, for the apron or forestage of a modern theater, came from the Greek word.) The actors moved back and forth between the

Classical Greek Theater. This engraving of the Theater of Dionysus in Athens, Greece represents the features typical of a classical theater.
Getty Images

proskenion and the orchestra. The roof of the *skene* was also used as an acting area; it could, for example, suggest a cliff or the place of the gods.

Acting Style Performing in such a huge theater made it impossible to rely on subtle voice inflections, slight gestures, or facial expressions. Actors wore large masks to identify their characters, with megaphonic mouthpieces to project their voices; they used exaggerated gestures so even those seated at the top of the *theatron* could see them. In reading a Greek play, therefore, think of a stately style of acting, with the flowing movements of a formal dance company and the dignity of a traditional religious celebration. Visualizing it as a kind of ballet or pageant without music comes closer to its spirit than imagining it as a realistic drama.

The Chorus The earliest Dionysian religious celebrations used only a **chorus** of ten to twelve men dressed in goat skins who chanted in unison, with no individual speakers. (*Tragedy* derives from the Greek word for "goat song.") Their material was not dialogue but a long, formal poem (an **ode**) written in sections called **strophe**, **antistrophe**, and **epode**. The chorus chanted the strophe on one side of the orchestra, moved across to the other side in a choreographed pattern to deliver the antistrophe, and then moved again for the epode, if the play included epodes. The choral lyric continued to be a convention of later Greek drama as well, and the chorus grew in size to as many as fifty people: When you read speeches by the chorus in *Oedipus the King,* as on page 836, imagine hearing numerous voices reciting together and moving about the orchestra in a stately rhythm—the entire chorus chanting and moving at times, or half of the group addressing the other half, or the members of the chorus conversing with the leader of the chorus.

The Actors   The earliest Dionysian celebrations had no individual actors. A single actor (the Greek word is *hypocrites*) was added in the mid-sixth century B.C.E., reputedly by Thespis of Athens. The actor spoke between the choral odes, acting out parts in the story and conversing with the leader of the chorus. A second actor was added by the dramatist Aeschylus, thus making possible conflict between protagonist and antagonist, and a third actor was introduced by Sophocles, in the next century, allowing greater interaction between individuals as well as between individuals and the chorus. Actors could play more than one role by changing masks and costumes, which they would have done in performing *Oedipus*.

The Role of the Chorus   Although the focus shifted increasingly to the actors, the chorus continued to be an important part of Greek drama. Actors entered and exited, but the chorus was present for most of the performance. In *Oedipus*, they are onstage from the time they enter after line 168. The chorus—or the leader speaking for the rest—at times stands outside the action to provide background information. They listen in on what characters say and comment on it or react to what is done or point out the moral. Sometimes the chorus interacts with characters and gives characters advice or warnings. Sometimes the chorus does not "get" what is going on and requires more explanation from the characters—which enlightens the audience as well. The chorus provides a continuous point of reference for the audience and serves as an intermediary, often addressing the audience directly.

Action Offstage   A convention of Greek drama is that little action occurs on the stage. What conflict does happen onstage is not a physical clash but rather verbal and emotional sparring. Violence was never shown on the Greek stage; when it was part of the plot, it was reported to the audience. You will find that to be the case in *Oedipus*.

Greek Tragedy as Genre   As stated earlier, *tragedy* comes from the Greek word *tragōidía*, for "goat-song," and was likely connected to the sacrifice of goats as part of an annual festival honoring Dionysus. The festival included an ode, or *dithyramb*, chanted by a chorus, lamenting the death of Dionysus. Thespis is usually given credit for transforming the content of the *dithyramb* from a hymn honoring the god to tragic stories about famous heroes. A **tragedy** in literary usage is a play or work characterized by serious and significant actions that often lead to a disastrous result for the protagonist. Until the 1700s, tragedies were usually written in poetry and mostly in an elevated and dignified literary style. Their tone is correspondingly sober and weighty. Although the central character comes to a tragic end, Greek tragedies usually conclude with a restoration of order and an expectation of a brighter future for those who survive.

Familiar Plots, Dramatic Irony   Greek tragic plots were generally drawn from old, familiar myths, so the audience already knew the story when they attended a play. The audience's interest was in the way the story was handled. Perhaps the play would change the primary emphasis, present the theme from an alternative angle, or change the way the characters express themselves. Knowing that the plots would be familiar to the audience permitted playwrights to use **dramatic irony** liberally, for the viewers knew what lay ahead for the characters, though the characters themselves did not.

Effects of Tragedy   Aristotle, discussing literature in his *Poetics* (c. 330 B.C.E.), described tragedy as raising fear and pity in its audience and as having the effect of a **catharsis**, which has usually been translated as "purgation" or "purification." What he meant by this is widely disputed, but a common summation is as follows. The play first raises emotions: Members of the audience pity the hero and feel fear lest they encounter a fate similar to the hero's. But the artistic handling of the conclusion releases and quiets those emotions, as order is restored and the hero faces her or his destiny with fortitude, thus affirming the courage and dignity of humankind. In Aristotle's view, such raising and releasing of emotion has a healthy effect, psychologically and physically: The audience goes away feeling not dejected but relieved and strengthened.

Tragic Heroes   Because the central figures in myths are heroes and gods, the protagonists of Greek tragedies are persons of high rank or great importance. However, it is interesting that Aristotle, in his analysis of tragedy, said the hero should *not* be superhumanly good, for any calamity falling on such a person would be too hard to accept, nor should any character be thoroughly evil, for the downfall of such a person is deserved and therefore would not elicit pity. As you read *Oedipus*, look for the traits Aristotle described, those that make Oedipus good but not perfect. The important issue for Aristotle is the reason why such a change from prosperity to adversity in fortune occurs.

Hamartia   The Greek tragic hero goes from prosperity to adversity as a result of a mistake, an error in judgment, a frailty. Aristotle's word for this is **hamartia**. It's important to keep in mind that *hamartia* is not the same as a character flaw. Some critics explain all tragedies in terms of a "**tragic flaw**" in the hero and cite Aristotle as their source; some fix on Oedipus's quick temper as a character flaw that leads to his downfall. But the cause of a character's downfall is not always a defect or flaw. As you read or view a Greek play, looking for what leads to the tragic downfall, it is preferable to watch for missteps, or errors in judgment the hero makes (*hamartia*), rather than for flaws in him.

Pity and Fear   If Aristotle is right, you should feel a sense of pity for Oedipus because of what happens as a result of his mistakes and a sense of fear that, if this basically good and decent character could experience such a tragic series of events, it could happen to anyone. You should also experience a sense of relief ("purgation")—relief that Oedipus accepts the outcome with piety and humility and that order is restored in Thebes.

APPROACHING THE READING

As the following play begins, the city of Thebes is afflicted with a plague and the citizens have come to their king, Oedipus, asking him to rescue them from it, as earlier he had rescued them from a Sphinx who held the city in thrall. As a reward for that feat, he had been made king and had married the widow of the previous king, who had been killed in an early instance of road rage. Oedipus receives a report from the oracle at Delphi, declaring that the city is afflicted because of its failure to identify and punish the man responsible for the previous king's death. Oedipus vows to find and evict the killer, not realizing that he himself is the guilty party. As the story unfolds, scene by scene, Oedipus learns the awful truth, that in attempting to escape his fate, he—ironically—had fulfilled it. The play makes effective use of dramatic irony (see p. 830): Readers or those viewing a performance realize the truth before Oedipus does, and thus watch with horror as he moves step-by-step toward the awful realization that will destroy his life.

> ### APPROACHING THE AUTHOR
>
> In the years after **Sophocles** died, several legends cropped up about the cause of his death: The most famous is that he died while trying to recite a long line from his play *Antigone* without taking a breath. Another holds that he choked on grapes at a festival. Still another says he died of happiness after hearing of *Antigone*'s success at a theater competition.
>
> For more about him, see page 1080.

Sophocles   496?–406 B.C.

Oedipus the King   [ca. 430 B.C.]
Translated by David Grene

CHARACTERS

OEDIPUS, *king of Thebes*
JOCASTA, *his wife*
CREON, *his brother-in-law*
TEIRESIAS, *an old blind prophet*
A PRIEST
FIRST MESSENGER
SECOND MESSENGER
A HERDSMAN
A CHORUS OF OLD MEN OF THEBES

SCENE: *In front of the palace of Oedipus at Thebes. To the right of the stage near the altar stands the Priest with a crowd of children. Oedipus emerges from the central door.*

OEDIPUS: Children, young sons and daughters of old Cadmus,°
    why do you sit here with your suppliant crowns?
    The town is heavy with a mingled burden
    of sounds and smells, of groans and hymns and incense;
    I did not think it fit that I should hear   5
    of this from messengers but came myself,—
    I Oedipus whom all men call the Great.

(He turns to the Priest.)

    You're old and they are young; come, speak for them.
    What do you fear or want, that you sit here
    suppliant? Indeed I'm willing to give all   10
    that you may need; I would be very hard
    should I not pity suppliants like these.
PRIEST: O ruler of my country, Oedipus,
    you see our company around the altar;
    you see our ages; some of us, like these,   15
    who cannot yet fly far, and some of us
    heavy with age; these children are the chosen
    among the young, and I the priest of Zeus.°
    Within the market place sit others crowned
    with suppliant garlands, at the double shrine   20
    of Pallas° and the temple where Ismenus°
    gives oracles by fire. King, you yourself
    have seen our city reeling like a wreck
    already; it can scarcely lift its prow
    out of the depths, out of the bloody surf.   25
    A blight is on the fruitful plants of the earth,
    A blight is on the cattle in the fields,
    a blight is on our women that no children
    are born to them; a God that carries fire,
    a deadly pestilence, is on our town,   30
    strikes us and spares not, and the house of Cadmus
    is emptied of its people while black Death
    grows rich in groaning and in lamentation.
    We have not come as suppliants to this altar
    because we thought of you as of a God,   35

---

1. Cadmus: According to tradition, the founder and first king of Thebes.   **18. Zeus:** The god of the sky and ruler of the Olympian gods.   **21. Pallas:** Pallas Athena, goddess of wisdom and guardian of cities. Daughter of Zeus. **Ismenus:** A river-god of central Greece.

but rather judging you the first of men
in all the chances of this life and when
we mortals have to do with more than man.
You came and by your coming saved our city,
freed us from tribute which we paid of old   40
to the Sphinx,° cruel singer. This you did
in virtue of no knowledge we could give you,
in virtue of no teaching; it was God
that aided you, men say, and you are held
with God's assistance to have saved our lives.   45
Now Oedipus, greatest in all men's eyes,
here falling at your feet we all entreat you,
find us some strength for rescue.
Perhaps you'll hear a wise word from some God,
perhaps you will learn something from a man   50
(for I have seen that for the skilled of practice
the outcome of their counsels live the most).
Noblest of men, go, and raise up our city,
go, — and give heed. For now this land of ours
calls you its savior since you saved it once.   55
So, let us never speak about your reign
as of a time when first our feet were set
secure on high, but later fell to ruin.
Raise up our city, save it and raise it up.
Once you have brought us luck with happy omen;   60
be no less now in fortune.
If you will rule this land, as now you rule it,
better to rule it full of men than empty.
For neither tower nor ship is anything
when empty, and none live in it together.   65
OEDIPUS: I pity you, children. You have come full of longing,
but I have known the story before you told it
only too well. I know you are all sick,
yet there is not one of you, sick though you are,
that is as sick as I myself.   70
Your several sorrows each have single scope
and touch but one of you. My spirit groans
for city and myself and you at once.

---

41. **Sphinx:** In Greek mythology, a winged monster with the head and breasts of a woman and the body of a lion. The Sphinx terrorized Thebes, confronting those who came near her with a riddle — "What walks on four feet in the morning, two at noon, and three in the evening?" — and killing them when they did not answer correctly. When Oedipus gave the correct answer, "Man" (as a baby crawling on all fours, as an adult walking erect, and in old age using a cane), the Sphinx killed herself and the city was freed.

You have not roused me like a man from sleep;
know that I have given many tears to this,   75
gone many ways wandering in thought,
but as I thought I found only one remedy
and that I took. I sent Menoeceus' son
Creon, Jocasta's brother, to Apollo,°
to his Pythian temple,°   80
that he might learn there by what act or word
I could save this city. As I count the days,
it vexes me what ails him; he is gone
far longer than he needed for the journey.
But when he comes, then, may I prove a villain,   85
if I shall not do all the God commands.

PRIEST: Thanks for your gracious words. Your servants here
    signal that Creon is this moment coming.

OEDIPUS: His face is bright. O holy Lord Apollo,
    grant that his news too may be bright for us   90
    and bring us safety.

PRIEST: It is happy news,
    I think, for else his head would not be crowned
    with sprigs of fruitful laurel.

OEDIPUS: We will know soon,
    he's within hail. Lord Creon, my good brother,   95
    what is the word you bring us from the God?

(Creon enters.)

CREON: A good word, — for things hard to bear themselves
    if in the final issue all is well
    I count complete good fortune.

OEDIPUS: What do you mean?
    What you have said so far   100
    leaves me uncertain whether to trust or fear.

CREON: If you will hear my news before these others
    I am ready to speak, or else to go within.

OEDIPUS: Speak it to all;
    the grief I bear, I bear it more for these   105
    than for my own heart.

CREON: I will tell you, then,
    what I heard from the God.
    King Phoebus° in plain words commanded us

---

79. Apollo: Phoebus Apollo, god of prophesy as well as of healing, learning, and the arts.
80. Pythian temple: The temple of Apollo at Delphi, on the slopes of Mount Parnassus, that housed the most prestigious and authoritative oracle (priestess uttering a message from the gods) of ancient Greece.   **108. King Phoebus:** Apollo.

to drive out a pollution from our land,
pollution grown ingrained within the land;   110
drive it out, said the God, not cherish it,
till it's past cure.
OEDIPUS: What is the rite
of purification? How shall it be done?
CREON: By banishing a man, or expiation
of blood by blood, since it is murder guilt   115
which holds our city in this destroying storm.
OEDIPUS: Who is this man whose fate the God pronounces?
CREON: My Lord, before you piloted the state
we had a king called Laius.
OEDIPUS: I know of him by hearsay. I have not seen him.   120
CREON: The God commanded clearly: let some one
punish with force this dead man's murderers.
OEDIPUS: Where are they in the world? Where would a trace
of this old crime be found? It would be hard
to guess where.
CREON: The clue is in this land;   125
that which is sought is found;
the unheeded thing escapes:
so said the God.
OEDIPUS: Was it at home,
or in the country that death came upon him,
or in another country travelling?   130
CREON: He went, he said himself, upon an embassy,
but never returned when he set out from home.
OEDIPUS: Was there no messenger, no fellow traveller
who knew what happened? Such a one might tell
something of use.   135
CREON: They were all killed save one. He fled in terror
and he could tell us nothing in clear terms
of what he knew, nothing, but one thing only.
OEDIPUS: What was it?
If we could even find a slim beginning   140
in which to hope, we might discover much.
CREON: This man said that the robbers they encountered
were many and the hands that did the murder
were many; it was no man's single power.
OEDIPUS: How could a robber dare a deed like this   145
were he not helped with money from the city,
money and treachery?
CREON: That indeed was thought.
But Laius was dead and in our trouble
there was none to help.

OEDIPUS: What trouble was so great to hinder you   150
    inquiring out the murder of your king?
CREON: The riddling Sphinx induced us to neglect
    mysterious crimes and rather seek solution
    of troubles at our feet.
OEDIPUS: I will bring this to light again. King Phoebus   155
    fittingly took this care about the dead,
    and you too fittingly.
    And justly you will see in me an ally,
    a champion of my country and the God.
    For when I drive pollution from the land   160
    I will not serve a distant friend's advantage,
    but act in my own interest. Whoever
    he was that killed the king may readily
    wish to dispatch me with his murderous hand;
    so helping the dead king I help myself.   165

    Come, children, take your suppliant boughs and go;
    up from the altars now. Call the assembly
    and let it meet upon the understanding
    that I'll do everything. God will decide
    whether we prosper or remain in sorrow.   170
PRIEST: Rise, children — it was this we came to seek,
    which of himself the king now offers us.
    May Phoebus who gave us the oracle
    come to our rescue and stay the plague.

(Exeunt° all but the Chorus.)

CHORUS: Strophe°
    What is the sweet spoken word of God from the shrine of Pytho° rich
        in gold   175
    that has come to glorious Thebes?
    I am stretched on the rack of doubt, and terror and trembling hold
    my heart, O Delian Healer,° and I worship full of fears
    for what doom you will bring to pass, new or renewed in the revolving
        years.
    Speak to me, immortal voice,   180
    child of golden Hope.
        Antistrophe°
    First I call on you, Athene,° deathless daughter of Zeus,

---

s. d. **Exeunt:** (Latin) "they go out," or leave the stage. **Strophe:** Choral ode sung by the Chorus as they move from stage right to stage left. **175. shrine of Pytho:** See note to line 80. **178. Delian Healer:** Apollo, who was born on the island Delos. **Antistrophe:** Choral ode sung by the Chorus as they move back from stage left to stage right. **183. Athene:** Pallas Athena. See note to line 21.

and Artemis,° Earth Upholder,
who sits in the midst of the market place in the throne which men
    call Fame,
and Phoebus, the Far Shooter, three averters of Fate,   185
come to us now, if ever before, when ruin rushed upon the state,
you drove destruction's flame away
out of our land.

   Strophe
Our sorrows defy number;
all the ship's timbers are rotten;   190
taking of thought is no spear for the driving away of the plague.
There are no growing children in this famous land;
there are no women bearing the pangs of childbirth.
You may see them one with another, like birds swift on the wing,
quicker than fire unmastered,   195
speeding away to the coast of the Western God.°

   Antistrophe
In the unnumbered deaths
of its people the city dies;
those children that are born lie dead on the naked earth
unpitied, spreading contagion of death; and grey-haired mothers and wives 200
everywhere stand at the altar's edge, suppliant, moaning;
the hymn to the healing God rings out but with it the wailing voices are
    blended.
From these our sufferings grant us, O golden Daughter of Zeus,
glad-faced deliverance.

   Strophe
There is no clash of brazen shields but our fight is with the War God,   205
a War God ringed with the cries of men, a savage God who burns us;
grant that he turn in racing course backwards out of our country'sbounds
to the great palace of Amphitrite° or where the waves of the Thracian sea
deny the stranger safe anchorage.
Whatsoever escapes the night   210
at last the light of day revisits;
so smite the War God, Father Zeus,
beneath your thunderbolt,
for you are the Lord of the lightning, the lightning that
    carries fire.

   Antistrophe
And your unconquered arrow shafts, winged by the golden
    corded bow,   215

---

184. Artemis: Twin sister of Apollo, goddess of the moon, hunting, and female chastity.   196. Western God: Evening.   208. Amphitrite: Sea-goddess and wife of Poseidon.

Lycean King,° I beg to be at our side for help;
and the gleaming torches of Artemis with which she scours the
    Lycean hills,
and I call on the God with the turban of gold, who gave his name
    to this country of ours,
the Bacchic God° with the wind flushed face,
Evian One, who travel   220
with the Maenad company,°
combat the God that burns us
with your torch of pine;
for the God that is our enemy is a God unhonored among the
    Gods.

                                (Oedipus returns.)

OEDIPUS: For what you ask me—if you will hear my words,   225
and hearing welcome them and fight the plague,
you will find strength and lightening of your load.
Hark to me; what I say to you, I say
as one that is a stranger to the story
as stranger to the deed. For I would not   230
be far upon the track if I alone
were tracing it without a clue. But now,
since after all was finished, I became
a citizen among you, citizens—
now I proclaim to all the men of Thebes: 235
who so among you knows the murderer
by whose hand Laius, son of Labdacus,
died—I command him to tell everything
to me,—yes, though he fears himself to take the blame
on his own head; for bitter punishment   240
he shall have none, but leave this land unharmed.
Or if he knows the murderer, another,
a foreigner, still let him speak the truth.
For I will pay him and be grateful, too.
But if you shall keep silence, if perhaps   245
some one of you, to shield a guilty friend,
or for his own sake shall reject my words—
hear what I shall do then:
I forbid that man, whoever he be, my land,

---

216. **Lycean King:** Apollo. 219. **Bacchic God . . . Evian One:** Dionysus (Bacchus), god of
the grape harvest, wine, and wild celebrations, whose followers addressed him with the ritual
cry "evoi." 221. **Maenad company:** Female celebrants who accompany Dionysus.

my land where I hold sovereignty and throne;   250
and I forbid any to welcome him
or cry him greeting or make him a sharer
in sacrifice or offering to the Gods,
or give him water for his hands to wash.
I command all to drive him from their homes,   255
since he is our pollution, as the oracle
of Pytho's God° proclaimed him now to me.
So I stand forth a champion of the God
and of the man who died.
Upon the murderer I invoke this curse—   260
whether he is one man and all unknown,
or one of many—may he wear out his life
in misery to miserable doom!
If with my knowledge he lives at my hearth
I pray that I myself may feel my curse.   265
On you I lay my charge to fulfill all this
for me, for the God, and for this land of ours
destroyed and blighted, by the God forsaken.

Even were this no matter of God's ordinance
it would not fit you so to leave it lie,   270
unpurified, since a good man is dead
and one that was a king. Search it out.
Since I am now the holder of his office,
and have his bed and wife that once was his,
and had his line not been unfortunate   275
we would have common children—(fortune leaped
upon his head)—because of all these things,
I fight in his defense as for my father,
and I shall try all means to take the murderer
of Laius the son of Labdacus   280
the son of Polydorus and before him
of Cadmus and before him of Agenor.°
Those who do not obey me, may the Gods
grant no crops springing from the ground they plough
nor children to their women! May a fate   285
like this, or one still worse than this consume them!
For you whom these words please, the other Thebans,
may Justice as your ally and all the Gods
live with you, blessing you now and for ever!

---

257. **Pytho's God:** Pytho was a name for the location of the Delphic oracle.   280–82. **Labdacus, Polydorus, Cadmus, and Agenor:** Laius's father, grandfather, great-grandfather, and great-great-grandfather.

CHORUS: As you have held me to my oath, I speak: 290
    I neither killed the king nor can declare
    the killer; but since Phoebus set the quest
    it is his part to tell who the man is.
OEDIPUS: Right; but to put compulsion on the Gods
    against their will—no man can do that.   295
CHORUS: May I then say what I think second best?
OEDIPUS: If there's a third best, too, spare not to tell it.
CHORUS: I know that what the Lord Teiresias
    sees, is most often what the Lord Apollo
    sees.° If you should inquire of this from him   300
    you might find out most clearly.
OEDIPUS: Even in this my actions have not been sluggard.
    On Creon's word I have sent two messengers
    and why the prophet is not here already
    I have been wondering.
CHORUS: His skill apart   305
    there is besides only an old faint story.
OEDIPUS: What is it?
    I look at every story.
CHORUS: It was said
    that he was killed by certain wayfarers.
OEDIPUS: I heard that, too, but no one saw the killer.   310
CHORUS: Yet if he has a share of fear at all,
    his courage will not stand firm, hearing your curse.
OEDIPUS: The man who in the doing did not shrink
    will fear no word.
CHORUS: Here comes his prosecutor:
    led by your men the godly prophet comes   315
    in whom alone of mankind truth is native.

                              (Enter Teiresias, led by a little boy.)

OEDIPUS: Teiresias, you are versed in everything,
    things teachable and things not to be spoken,
    things of the heaven and earth-creeping things.
    You have no eyes but in your mind you know   320
    with what a plague our city is afflicted.
    My lord, in you alone we find a champion,
    in you alone one that can rescue us.
    Perhaps you have not heard the messengers,
    but Phoebus sent in answer to our sending   325
    an oracle declaring that our freedom

---

300. **sees:** Play on words, since Teiresias was blind.

from this disease would only come when we
should learn the names of those who killed King Laius,
and kill them or expel from our country.
Do not begrudge us oracles from birds,°   330
or any other way of prophecy
within your skill; save yourself and the city,
save me; redeem the debt of our pollution
that lies on us because of this dead man.
We are in your hands; pains are most nobly taken   335
to help another when you have means and power.

TEIRESIAS: Alas, how terrible is wisdom when
it brings no profit to the man that's wise!
This I knew well, but had forgotten it,
else I would not have come here.

OEDIPUS: What is this?   340
How sad you are now you have come!

TEIRESIAS: Let me
go home. It will be easiest for us both
to bear our several destinies to the end
if you will follow my advice.

OEDIPUS: You'd rob us
of this your gift of prophecy? You talk   345
as one who had no care for law nor love
for Thebes who reared you.

TEIRESIAS: Yes, but I see that even your own words
miss the mark; therefore I must fear for mine.

OEDIPUS: For God's sake if you know of anything,   350
do not turn from us; all of us kneel to you,
all of us here, your suppliants.

TEIRESIAS: All of you here know nothing. I will not
bring to the light of day my troubles, mine—
rather than call them yours.

OEDIPUS: What do you mean?   355
You know of something but refuse to speak.
Would you betray us and destroy the city?

TEIRESIAS: I will not bring this pain upon us both,
neither on you nor on myself. Why is it
you question me and waste your labor? I   360
will tell you nothing.

OEDIPUS: You would provoke a stone! Tell us, you villain,
tell us, and do not stand there quietly
unmoved and balking at the issue.

---

330. **oracles from birds:** Prophesy of future events based on the flight of birds.

TEIRESIAS: You blame my temper but you do not see   365
    your own that lives within you; it is me
    you chide.

OEDIPUS: Who would not feel his temper rise
    at words like these with which you shame our city?

TEIRESIAS: Of themselves things will come, although I hide them   370
    and breathe no word of them.

OEDIPUS: Since they will come
    tell them to me.

TEIRESIAS: I will say nothing further.
    Against this answer let your temper rage
    as wildly as you will.

OEDIPUS: Indeed I am
    so angry I shall not hold back a jot   375
    of what I think. For I would have you know
    I think you were complotter° of the deed
    and doer of the deed save insofar
    as for the actual killing. Had you had eyes
    I would have said alone you murdered him.   380

TEIRESIAS: Yes? Then I warn you faithfully to keep
    the letter of your proclamation and
    from this day forth to speak no word of greeting
    to these nor me; you are the land's pollution.

OEDIPUS: How shamelessly you started up this taunt!   385
    How do you think you will escape?

TEIRESIAS: I have.
    I have escaped; the truth is what I cherish
    and that's my strength.

OEDIPUS: And who has taught you truth?
    Not your profession surely!

TEIRESIAS: You have taught me,
    for you have made me speak against my will.   390

OEDIPUS: Speak what? Tell me again that I may learn it better.

TEIRESIAS: Did you not understand before or would you
    provoke me into speaking?

OEDIPUS: I did not grasp it,
    not so to call it known. Say it again.

TEIRESIAS: I say you are the murderer of the king   395
    whose murderer you seek.

OEDIPUS: Not twice you shall
    say calumnies like this and stay unpunished.

TEIRESIAS: Shall I say more to tempt your anger more?

---

377. **complotter:** A participant in a plot or conspiracy.

OEDIPUS: As much as you desire; it will be said
    in vain.
TEIRESIAS: I say that with those you love best   400
    you live in foulest shame unconsciously
    and do not see where you are in calamity.
OEDIPUS: Do you imagine you can always talk
    like this, and live to laugh at it hereafter?
TEIRESIAS: Yes, if the truth has anything of strength.   405
OEDIPUS: It has, but not for you; it has no strength
    for you because you are blind in mind and ears
    as well as in your eyes.
TEIRESIAS: You are a poor wretch
    to taunt me with the very insults which
    every one soon will heap upon yourself.   410
OEDIPUS: Your life is one long night so that you cannot
    hurt me or any other who sees the light.
TEIRESIAS: It is not fate that I should be your ruin,
    Apollo is enough; it is his care
    to work this out.
OEDIPUS: Was this your own design   415
    or Creon's?
TEIRESIAS: Creon is no hurt to you,
    but you are to yourself.
OEDIPUS: Wealth, sovereignty and skill outmatching skill
    for the contrivance of an envied life!
    Great store of jealousy fill your treasury chests,   420
    if my friend Creon, friend from the first and loyal,
    thus secretly attacks me, secretly
    desires to drive me out and secretly
    suborns this juggling, trick-devising quack,
    this wily beggar who has only eyes   425
    for his own gains, but blindness in his skill.
    For, tell me, where have you seen clear, Teiresias,
    with your prophetic eyes? When the dark singer,
    the sphinx, was in your country, did you speak
    word of deliverance to its citizens?   430
    And yet the riddle's answer was not the province
    of a chance comer. It was a prophet's task
    and plainly you had no such gift of prophecy
    from birds nor otherwise from any God
    to glean a word of knowledge. But I came,   435
    Oedipus, who knew nothing, and I stopped her.
    I solved the riddle by my wit alone.
    Mine was no knowledge got from birds. And now
    you would expel me,

because you think that you will find a place   440
by Creon's throne. I think you will be sorry,
both you and your accomplice, for your plot
to drive me out. And did I not regard you
as an old man, some suffering would have taught you
that what was in your heart was treason.   445

CHORUS: We look at this man's words and yours, my king,
and we find both have spoken them in anger.
We need no angry words but only thought
how we may best hit the God's meaning for us.

TEIRESIAS: If you are king, at least I have the right   450
no less to speak in my defense against you.
Of that much I am master. I am no slave
of yours, but Loxias',° and so I shall not
enroll myself with Creon for my patron.
Since you have taunted me with being blind,   455
here is my word for you.
You have your eyes but see not where you are
in sin, nor where you live, nor whom you live with.
Do you know who your parents are? Unknowing
you are an enemy to kith and kin   460
in death, beneath the earth, and in this life.
A deadly footed, double striking curse,
from father and mother both, shall drive you forth
out of this land, with darkness on your eyes,
that now have such straight vision. Shall there be   465
a place will not be harbor to your cries,
a corner of Cithaeron° will not ring
in echo to your cries, soon, soon, —
when you shall learn the secret of your marriage,
which steered you to a haven in this house, —   470
haven no haven, after lucky voyage?
And of the multitude of other evils
establishing a grim equality
between you and your children, you know nothing.
So, muddy with contempt my words and Creon's!   475
Misery shall grind no man as it will you.

OEDIPUS: Is it endurable that I should hear
such words from him? Go and a curse go with you!
Quick, home with you! Out of my house at once!

TEIRESIAS: I would not have come either had you not called me.   480

---

453. **Loxias:** A name for Apollo as the god of incomprehensible oracular sayings.
467. **Cithaeron:** Mountain in Greece where Oedipus was abandoned as an infant.

OEDIPUS: I did not know then you would talk like a fool—
   or it would have been long before I called you.
TEIRESIAS: I am a fool then, as it seems to you—
   but to the parents who have bred you, wise.
OEDIPUS: What parents? Stop! Who are they of all the world?   485
TEIRESIAS: This day will show your birth and will destroy you.
OEDIPUS: How needlessly your riddles darken everything.
TEIRESIAS But it's in riddle answering you are strongest.
OEDIPUS: Yes. Taunt me where you will find me great.
TEIRESIAS: It is this very luck that has destroyed you.   490
OEDIPUS: I do not care, if it has saved this city.
TEIRESIAS: Well, I will go. Come, boy, lead me away.
OEDIPUS: Yes, lead him off. So long as you are here,
   you'll be a stumbling block and a vexation;
   once gone, you will not trouble me again.
TEIRESIAS: I have said   495
   what I came here to say not fearing your
   countenance: there is no way you can hurt me.
   I tell you, king, this man, this murderer
   (whom you have long declared you are in search of,
   indicting him in threatening proclamation   500
   as murderer of Laius)—he is here.
   In name he is a stranger among citizens
   but soon he will be shown to be a citizen
   true native Theban, and he'll have no joy
   of the discovery: blindness for sight   505
   and beggary for riches his exchange,
   he shall go journeying to a foreign country
   tapping his way before him with a stick.
   He shall be proved father and brother both
   to his own children in his house; to her   510
   that gave him birth, a son and husband both;
   a fellow sower in his father's bed
   with that same father that he murdered.
   Go within, reckon that out, and if you find me
   mistaken, say I have no skill in prophecy.   515

                    (*Exeunt separately Teiresias and Oedipus.*)

CHORUS: *Strophe*
   Who is the man proclaimed
   by Delphi's prophetic rock
   as the bloody handed murderer,
   the doer of deeds that none dare name?
   Now is the time for him to run   520
   with a stronger foot

than Pegasus°
for the child of Zeus° leaps in arms upon him
with fire and the lightning bolt,
and terribly close on his heels   525
are the Fates° that never miss.

Antistrophe
Lately from snowy Parnassus°
clearly the voice flashed forth,
bidding each Theban track him down,
the unknown murderer.   530
In the savage forests he lurks and in
the caverns like
the mountain bull.
He is sad and lonely, and lonely his feet
that carry him far from the navel of earth;   535
but its prophecies, ever living,
flutter around his head.

Strophe
The augur has spread confusion,
terrible confusion;
I do not approve what was said   540
nor can I deny it.
I do not know what to say;
I am in a flutter of foreboding;
I never heard in the present
nor past of a quarrel between   545
the sons of Labdacus and Polybus°,
that I might bring as proof
in attacking the popular fame
of Oedipus, seeking
to take vengeance for undiscovered   550
death in the line of Labdacus.

Antistrophe
Truly Zeus and Apollo are wise
and in human things all knowing;
but amongst men there is no
distinct judgment, between the prophet   555
and me—which of us is right.

---

522. **Pegasus:** Divine winged stallion sired by Poseidon in his role as horse-god.   523. **child of Zeus:** Apollo.   526. **the Fates:** The Furies, three female spirits who sought out and punished evildoers.   527. **Parnassus:** Mountain in Greece sacred to Apollo.   546. **sons of Labdacus and Polybus:** Laius and Oedipus (Polybus is the Corinthian king who had adopted Oedipus and was thought to be his father).

One man may pass another in wisdom
but I would never agree
with those that find fault with the king
till I should see the word   560
proved right beyond doubt. For once
in visible form the Sphinx
came on him and all of us
saw his wisdom and in that test
he saved the city. So he will not be condemned by my mind.   565

(*Enter Creon.*)

CREON: Citizens, I have come because I heard
deadly words spread about me, that the king
accuses me. I cannot take that from him.
If he believes that in these present troubles
he has been wronged by me in word or deed   570
I do not want to live on with the burden
of such a scandal on me. The report
injures me doubly and most vitally—
for I'll be called a traitor to my city
and traitor also to my friends and you.   575
CHORUS: Perhaps it was a sudden gust of anger
that forced that insult from him, and no judgment.
CREON: But did he say that it was in compliance
with schemes of mine that the seer told him lies?
CHORUS: Yes, he said that, but why, I do not know.   580
CREON: Were his eyes straight in his head? Was his mind right
when he accused me in this fashion?
CHORUS: I do not know; I have no eyes to see
what princes do. Here comes the king himself.

(*Enter Oedipus.*)

OEDIPUS: You, sir, how is it you come here? Have you so much   585
brazen-faced daring that you venture in
my house although you are proved manifestly
the murderer of that man, and though you tried,
openly, highway robbery of my crown?
For God's sake, tell me what you saw in me,   590
what cowardice or what stupidity,
that made you lay a plot like this against me?
Did you imagine I should not observe
the crafty scheme that stole upon me or
seeing it, take no means to counter it?   595
Was it not stupid of you to make the attempt,
to try to hunt down royal power without

the people at your back or friends? For only
with the people at your back or money can
the hunt end in the capture of a crown.   600
CREON: Do you know what you're doing? Will you listen
    to words to answer yours, and then pass judgment?
OEDIPUS: You're quick to speak, but I am slow to grasp you,
    for I have found you dangerous,—and my foe.
CREON: First of all hear what I shall say to that.   605
OEDIPUS: At least don't tell me that you are not guilty.
CREON: If you think obstinacy without wisdom
    a valuable possession, you are wrong.
OEDIPUS: And you are wrong if you believe that one,
    a criminal, will not be punished only   610
    because he is my kinsman.
CREON: This is but just—
    but tell me, then, of what offense I'm guilty?
OEDIPUS: Did you or did you not urge me to send
    to this prophetic mumbler?
CREON: I did indeed,
    and I shall stand by what I told you.   615
OEDIPUS: How long ago is it since Laius. . . .
CREON: What about Laius? I don't understand.
OEDIPUS: Vanished—died—was murdered?
CREON: It is long,
    a long, long time to reckon.
OEDIPUS: Was this prophet
    in the profession then?
CREON: He was, and honored   620
    as highly as he is today.
OEDIPUS: At that time did he say a word about me?
CREON: Never, at least when I was near him.
OEDIPUS: You never made a search for the dead man?
CREON: We searched, indeed, but never learned of anything.   625
OEDIPUS: Why did our wise old friend not say this then?
CREON: I don't know; and when I know nothing, I
    usually hold my tongue.
OEDIPUS: You know this much,
    and can declare this much if you are loyal.
CREON: What is it? If I know, I'll not deny it.   630
OEDIPUS: That he would not have said that I killed Laius
    had he not met you first.
CREON: You know yourself
    whether he said this, but I demand that I
    should hear as much from you as you from me.
OEDIPUS: Then hear,—I'll not be proved a murderer.   635

CREON: Well, then. You're married to my sister.
OEDIPUS: Yes,
    that I am not disposed to deny.
CREON: You rule
    this country giving her an equal share
    in the government?
OEDIPUS: Yes, everything she wants
    she has from me.
CREON: And I, as thirdsman to you,   640
    am rated as the equal of you two?
OEDIPUS: Yes, and it's there you've proved yourself false friend.
CREON: Not if you will reflect on it as I do.
    Consider, first, if you think any one
    would choose to rule and fear rather than rule   645
    and sleep untroubled by a fear if power
    were equal in both cases. I, at least,
    I was not born with such a frantic yearning
    to be a king—but to do what kings do.
    And so it is with every one who has learned   650
    wisdom and self-control. As it stands now,
    the prizes are all mine—and without fear.
    But if I were the king myself, I must
    do much that went against the grain.
    How should despotic rule seem sweeter to me   655
    than painless power and an assured authority?
    I am not so besotted yet that I
    want other honors than those that come with profit.
    Now every man's my pleasure; every man greets me;
    now those who are your suitors fawn on me,—   660
    success for them depends upon my favor.
    Why should I let all this go to win that?
    My mind would not be traitor if it's wise;
    I am no treason lover, of my nature,
    nor would I ever dare to join a plot.   665
    Prove what I say. Go to the oracle
    at Pytho and inquire about the answers,
    if they are as I told you. For the rest,
    if you discover I laid any plot
    together with the seer, kill me, I say,   670
    not only by your vote but by my own.
    But do not charge me on obscure opinion
    without some proof to back it. It's not just
    lightly to count your knaves as honest men,
    nor honest men as knaves. To throw away   675
    an honest friend is, as it were, to throw

your life away, which a man loves the best.
In time you will know all with certainty;
time is the only test of honest men,
one day is space enough to know a rogue.   680
CHORUS: His words are wise, king, if one fears to fall.
    Those who are quick of temper are not safe.
OEDIPUS: When he that plots against me secretly
    moves quickly, I must quickly counterplot.
    If I wait taking no decisive measure   685
    his business will be done, and mine be spoiled.
CREON: What do you want to do then? Banish me?
OEDIPUS: No, certainly; kill you, not banish you.[1]
CREON: I do not think that you've your wits about you.
OEDIPUS: For my own interests, yes.
CREON: But for mine, too,   690
    you should think equally.
OEDIPUS: You are a rogue.
CREON: Suppose you do not understand?
OEDIPUS: But yet
    I must be ruler.
CREON: Not if you rule badly.
OEDIPUS: O, city, city!
CREON: I too have some share
    in the city; it is not yours alone.   695
CHORUS: Stop, my lords! Here—and in the nick of time
    I see Jocasta coming from the house;
    with her help lay the quarrel that now stirs you.

                                                    (*Enter Jocasta.*)

JOCASTA: For shame! Why have you raised this foolish squabbling
    brawl? Are you not ashamed to air your private   700
    griefs when the country's sick? Go in, you, Oedipus,
    and you, too, Creon, into the house. Don't magnify
    your nothing troubles.
CREON: Sister, Oedipus,
    your husband, thinks he has the right to do
    terrible wrongs—he has but to choose between   705
    two terrors: banishing or killing me.

———————————

[1]Two lines omitted here owing to the confusion in the dialogue consequent on the loss of a
third line. The lines as they stand in Jebb's edition (1902) are:
Oed.: That you may show what manner of thing is envy.
Creon: You speak as one that will not yield or trust.
[*Oed.* lost line.]

OEDIPUS: He's right, Jocasta; for I find him plotting
   with knavish tricks against my person.

CREON: That God may never bless me! May I die
   accursed, if I have been guilty of   710
   one tittle of the charge you bring against me!

JOCASTA: I beg you, Oedipus, trust him in this,
   spare him for the sake of this his oath to God,
   for my sake, and the sake of those who stand here.

CHORUS: Be gracious, be merciful,   715
   we beg of you.

OEDIPUS: In what would you have me yield?

CHORUS: He has been no silly child in the past.
   He is strong in his oath now.
   Spare him.   720

OEDIPUS: Do you know what you ask?

CHORUS: Yes.

OEDIPUS: Tell me then.

CHORUS: He has been your friend before all men's eyes; do not cast him
   away dishonored on an obscure conjecture.   725

OEDIPUS: I would have you know that this request of yours
   really requests my death or banishment.

CHORUS: May the Sun God,° king of Gods, forbid! May I die without God's
   blessing, without friends' help, if I had any such thought. But my
   spirit is broken by my unhappiness for my wasting country; and   730
   this would but add troubles amongst ourselves to the other
   troubles.

OEDIPUS: Well, let him go then—if I must die ten times for it,
   or be sent out dishonored into exile.
   It is your lips that prayed for him I pitied,
   not his; wherever he is, I shall hate him.   735

CREON: I see you sulk in yielding and you're dangerous
   when you are out of temper; natures like yours
   are justly heaviest for themselves to bear.

OEDIPUS: Leave me alone! Take yourself off, I tell you.

CREON: I'll go, you have not known me, but they have,   740
   and they have known my innocence.

                                         (Exit.)

CHORUS: Won't you take him inside, lady?

JOCASTA: Yes, when I've found out what was the matter.

CHORUS: There was some misconceived suspicion of a story, and on the
   other side the sting of injustice.   745

---

728. Sun God: Apollo.

JOCASTA: So, on both sides?

CHORUS: Yes.

JOCASTA: What was the story?

CHORUS: I think it best, in the interests of the country, to leave it where
it ended.   750

OEDIPUS: You see where you have ended, straight of judgment
although you are, by softening my anger.

CHORUS: Sir, I have said before and I say again—be sure that I would have
been proved a madman, bankrupt in sane council, if I should put
you away, you who steered the country I love safely when she   755
was crazed with troubles. God grant that now, too, you may
prove a fortunate guide for us.

JOCASTA: Tell me, my lord, I beg of you, what was it
that roused your anger so?

OEDIPUS: Yes, I will tell you.
I honor you more than I honor them.   760
It was Creon and the plots he laid against me.

JOCASTA: Tell me—if you can clearly tell the quarrel—

OEDIPUS: Creon says
that I'm the murderer of Laius.

JOCASTA: Of his own knowledge or on information?

OEDIPUS: He sent this rascal prophet to me, since   765
he keeps his own mouth clean of any guilt.

JOCASTA: Do not concern yourself about this matter;
listen to me and learn that human beings
have no part in the craft of prophecy.
Of that I'll show you a short proof.   770
There was an oracle once that came to Laius,—
I will not say that it was Phoebus' own,
but it was from his servants—and it told him
that it was fate that he should die a victim
at the hands of his own son, a son to be born   775
of Laius and me. But, see now, he,
the king, was killed by foreign highway robbers
at a place where three roads meet—so goes the story;
and for the son—before three days were out
after his birth King Laius pierced his ankles   780
and by the hands of others cast him forth
upon a pathless hillside. So Apollo
failed to fulfill his oracle to the son,
that he should kill his father, and to Laius
also proved false in that the thing he feared,   785
death at his son's hands, never came to pass.
So clear in this case were the oracles,
so clear and false. Give them no heed, I say;

what God discovers need of, easily
   he shows to us himself.

OEDIPUS: O dear Jocasta,   790
   as I hear this from you, there comes upon me
   a wandering of the soul—I could run mad.

JOCASTA: What trouble is it, that you turn again
   and speak like this?

OEDIPUS: I thought I heard you say
   that Laius was killed at a crossroads.   795

JOCASTA: Yes, that was how the story went and still
   that word goes round.

OEDIPUS: Where is this place, Jocasta,
   where he was murdered?

JOCASTA: Phocis is the country
   and the road splits there, one of two roads from Delphi,
   another comes from Daulia.

OEDIPUS: How long ago is this?   800

JOCASTA: The news came to the city just before
   you became king and all men's eyes looked to you.
   What is it, Oedipus, that's in your mind?

OEDIPUS: What have you designed, O Zeus, to do with me?

JOCASTA: What is the thought that troubles your heart?   805

OEDIPUS: Don't ask me yet—tell me of Laius—
   How did he look? How old or young was he?

JOCASTA: He was a tall man and his hair was grizzled
   already—nearly white—and in his form
   not unlike you.

OEDIPUS: O God, I think I have   810
   called curses on myself in ignorance.

JOCASTA: What do you mean? I am terrified
   when I look at you.

OEDIPUS: I have a deadly fear
   that the old seer had eyes. You'll show me more
   if you can tell me one more thing.

JOCASTA: I will.   815
   I'm frightened,—but if I can understand,
   I'll tell you all you ask.

OEDIPUS: How was his company?
   Had he few with him when he went this journey,
   or many servants, as would suit a prince?

JOCASTA: In all there were but five, and among them   820
   a herald; and one carriage for the king.

OEDIPUS: It's plain—its plain—who was it told you this?

JOCASTA: The only servant that escaped safe home.

OEDIPUS: Is he at home now?

JOCASTA: No, when he came home again
      and saw you king and Laius was dead,   825
      he came to me and touched my hand and begged
      that I should send him to the fields to be
      my shepherd and so he might see the city
      as far off as he might. So I
      sent him away. He was an honest man,   830
      as slaves go, and was worthy of far more
      than what he asked of me.
OEDIPUS: O, how I wish that he could come back quickly!
JOCASTA: He can. Why is your heart so set on this?
OEDIPUS: O dear Jocasta, I am full of fears   835
      that I have spoken far too much; and therefore
      I wish to see this shepherd.
JOCASTA: He will come;
      but, Oedipus, I think I'm worthy too
      to know what it is that disquiets you.
OEDIPUS: It shall not be kept from you, since my mind   840
      has gone so far with its forebodings. Whom
      should I confide in rather than you, who is there
      of more importance to me who have passed
      through such a fortune?
      Polybus was my father, king of Corinth,   845
      and Merope,° the Dorian, my mother.
      I was held greatest of the citizens
      in Corinth till a curious chance befell me
      as I shall tell you—curious, indeed,
      but hardly worth the store I set upon it.   850
      There was a dinner and at it a man,
      a drunken man, accused me in his drink
      of being bastard. I was furious
      but held my temper under for that day.
      Next day I went and taxed my parents with it;   855
      they took the insult very ill from him,
      the drunken fellow who had uttered it.
      So I was comforted for their part, but
      still this thing rankled always, for the story
      crept about widely. And I went at last   860
      to Pytho,° though my parents did not know.
      But Phoebus sent me home again unhonored
      in what I came to learn, but he foretold
      other and desperate horrors to befall me,
      that I was fated to lie with my mother,   865

---

861. Pytho: See note to line 257.

and show to daylight an accursed breed
which men would not endure, and I was doomed
to be murderer of the father that begot me.
When I heard this I fled, and in the days
that followed I would measure from the stars   870
the whereabouts of Corinth—yes, I fled
to somewhere where I should not see fulfilled
the infamies told in that dreadful oracle.
And as I journeyed I came to the place
where, as you say, this king met with his death.   875
Jocasta, I will tell you the whole truth.
When I was near the branching of the crossroads,
going on foot, I was encountered by
a herald and a carriage with a man in it,
just as you tell me. He that led the way   880
and the old man himself wanted to thrust me
out of the road by force. I became angry
and struck the coachman who was pushing me.
When the old man saw this he watched his moment,
and as I passed he struck me from his carriage,   885
full on the head with his two pointed goad.°
But he was paid in full and presently
my stick had struck him backwards from the car
and he rolled out of it. And then I killed them
all. If it happened there was any tie   890
of kinship twixt this man and Laius,
who is then now more miserable than I,
what man on earth so hated by the Gods,
since neither citizen nor foreigner
may welcome me at home or even greet me,   895
but drive me out of doors? And it is I,
I and no other have so cursed myself.
And I pollute the bed of him I killed
by the hands that killed him. Was I not born evil?
Am I not utterly unclean? I had to fly   900
and in my banishment not even see
my kindred nor set foot in my own country,
or otherwise my fate was to be yoked
in marriage with my mother and kill my father,
Polybus who begot me and had reared me.   905
Would not one rightly judge and say that on me
these things were sent by some malignant God?
O no, no, no—O holy majesty

---

886. **goad:** a pointed rod used for prodding animals.

of God on high, may I not see that day!
May I be gone out of men's sight before   910
I see the deadly taint of this disaster
come upon me.

CHORUS: Sir, we too fear these things. But until you see this man face to
face and hear his story, hope.

OEDIPUS: Yes, I have just this much of hope—to wait until the herdsman
comes.   915

JOCASTA: And when he comes, what do you want with him?

OEDIPUS: I'll tell you; if I find that his story is the same as yours, I at least
will be clear of this guilt.

JOCASTA: Why? What so particularly did you learn from my story?

OEDIPUS: You said that he spoke of highway *robbers* who killed Laius. Now   920
if he uses the same number, it was not I who killed him. One man
cannot be the same as many. But if he speaks of a man travelling
alone, then clearly the burden of the guilt inclines towards me.

JOCASTA: Be sure, at least, that this was how he told the story. He cannot
unsay it now, for every one in the city heard it—not I alone. But,   925
Oedipus, even if he diverges from what he said then, he shall
never prove that the murder of Laius squares rightly with the
prophecy—for Loxias declared that the king should be killed by
his own son. And that poor creature did not kill him surely,—
for he died himself first. So as far as prophecy goes, henceforward
I shall not look to the right hand or the left.   930

OEDIPUS: Right. But yet, send some one for the peasant to bring him here;
do not neglect it.

JOCASTA: I will send quickly. Now let me go indoors. I will do nothing
except what pleases you.

                                                           (*Exeunt.*)

CHORUS: *Strophe*
        May destiny ever find me   935
        pious in word and deed
        prescribed by the laws that live on high:
        laws begotten in the clear air of heaven,
        whose only father is Olympus;
        no mortal nature brought them to birth,   940
        no forgetfulness shall lull them to sleep;
        for God is great in them and grows not old.

        Antistrophe
        Insolence breeds the tyrant, insolence
        if it is glutted with a surfeit, unseasonable, unprofitable,
        climbs to the roof-top and plunges   945
        sheer down to the ruin that must be,
        and there its feet are no service.

But I pray that the God may never
abolish the eager ambition that profits the state.
For I shall never cease to hold the God as our protector.   950

> *Strophe*
If a man walks with haughtiness
of hand or word and gives no heed
to Justice and the shrines of Gods
despises — may an evil doom
smite him for his ill-starred pride of heart! —   955
if he reaps gains without justice
and will not hold from impiety
and his fingers itch for untouchable things.
When such things are done, what man shall contrive
to shield his soul from the shafts of the God?   960
When such deeds are held in honor,
why should I honor the Gods in the dance?

> *Antistrophe*
No longer to the holy place,
to the navel of earth I'll go
to worship, nor to Abae°   965
nor to Olympia,
unless the oracles are proved to fit,
for all men's hands to point at.
O Zeus, if you are rightly called
the sovereign lord, all-mastering,   970
let this not escape you nor your ever-living power!
The oracles concerning Laius
are old and dim and men regard them not.
Apollo is nowhere clear in honor; God's service perishes.

(Enter Jocasta, carrying garlands.)

JOCASTA: Princes of the land, I have had the thought to go   975
to the Gods' temples, bringing in my hand
garlands and gifts of incense, as you see.
For Oedipus excites himself too much
at every sort of trouble, not conjecturing,
like a man of sense, what will be from what was,   980
but he is always at the speaker's mercy,
when he speaks terrors. I can do no good
by my advice, and so I came as suppliant
to you, Lycaean Apollo, who are nearest.
These are the symbols of my prayer and this   985

---

965. **Abae:** ancient town in northeastern Greece famous for its Apollonian oracle.

my prayer: grant us escape free of the curse.
Now when we look to him we are all afraid;
he's pilot of our ship and he is frightened.

(*Enter Messenger.*)

MESSENGER: Might I learn from you, sirs, where is the house of Oedipus? Or
    best of all, if you know, where is the king himself?   990
CHORUS: This is his house and he is within doors. This lady is his wife and
    mother of his children.
MESSENGER: God bless you, lady, and God bless your household! God bless
    Oedipus' noble wife!
JOCASTA: God bless you, sir, for your kind greeting! What do you want   995
    of us that you have come here? What have you to tell us?
MESSENGER: Good news, lady. Good for your house and for your husband.
JOCASTA: What is your news? Who sent you to us?
MESSENGER: I come from Corinth and the news I bring will give you pleasure.
    Perhaps a little pain too.   1000
JOCASTA: What is this news of double meaning?
MESSENGER: The people of the Isthmus will choose Oedipus to be their king.
    That is the rumor there.
JOCASTA: But isn't their king still old Polybus?
MESSENGER: No. He is in his grave. Death has got him.   1005
JOCASTA: Is that the truth? Is Oedipus' father dead?
MESSENGER: May I die myself if it be otherwise!
JOCASTA (*to a servant*): Be quick and run to the King with the news! O oracles
    of the Gods, where are you now? It was from this man Oedipus fled, lest
    he should be his murderer! And now he is dead, in the course of   1010
    nature, and not killed by Oedipus.

(*Enter Oedipus.*)

OEDIPUS: Dearest Jocasta, why have you sent for me?
JOCASTA: Listen to this man and when you hear reflect what is the outcome
    of the holy oracles of the Gods.
OEDIPUS: Who is he? What is his message for me?   1015
JOCASTA: He is from Corinth and he tells us that your father Polybus is
    dead and gone.
OEDIPUS: What's this you say, sir? Tell me yourself.
MESSENGER: Since this is the first matter you want clearly told: Polybus has
    gone down to death. You may be sure of it.   1020
OEDIPUS: By treachery or sickness?
MESSENGER: A small thing will put old bodies asleep.
OEDIPUS: So he died of sickness, it seems, — poor old man!
MESSENGER: Yes, and of age — the long years he had measured.
OEDIPUS: Ha! Ha! O dear Jocasta, why should one   1025

look to the Pythian hearth°? Why should one look
to the birds screaming overhead? They prophesied
that I should kill my father! But he's dead,
and hidden deep in earth, and I stand here
who never laid a hand on spear against him, —   1030
unless perhaps he died of longing for me,
and thus I am his murderer. But they,
the oracles, as they stand—he's taken them
away with him, they're dead as he himself is,
and worthless.

JOCASTA: That I told you before now.   1035
OEDIPUS: You did, but I was misled by my fear.
JOCASTA: Then lay no more of them to heart, not one.
OEDIPUS: But surely I must fear my mother's bed?
JOCASTA: Why should man fear since chance is all in all
      for him, and he can clearly foreknow nothing?   1040
      Best to live lightly, as one can, unthinkingly.
      As to your mother's marriage bed,—don't fear it.
      Before this, in dreams too, as well as oracles,
      many a man has lain with his own mother.
      But he to whom such things are nothing bears   1045
      his life most easily.
OEDIPUS: All that you say would be said perfectly
      if she were dead; but since she lives I must
      still fear, although you talk so well, Jocasta.
JOCASTA: Still in your father's death there's light of comfort?   1050
OEDIPUS: Great light of comfort; but I fear the living.
MESSENGER: Who is the woman that makes you afraid?
OEDIPUS: Merope, old man, Polybus' wife.
MESSENGER: What about her frightens the queen and you?
OEDIPUS: A terrible oracle, stranger, from the Gods.   1055
MESSENGER: Can it be told? Or does the sacred law
      forbid another to have knowledge of it?
OEDIPUS: O no! Once on a time Loxias said
      that I should lie with my own mother and
      take on my hands the blood of my own father.   1060
      And so for these long years I've lived away
      from Corinth; it has been to my great happiness;
      but yet it's sweet to see the face of parents.
MESSENGER: This was the fear which drove you out of Corinth?
OEDIPUS: Old man, I did not wish to kill my father.   1065

1026. Pythian hearth: Altar in the temple at Delphi, where offerings to Apollo were made by
the priestess.

MESSENGER: Why should I not free you from this fear, sir,
    since I have come to you in all goodwill?
OEDIPUS: You would not find me thankless if you did.
MESSENGER: Why, it was just for this I brought the news, —
    to earn your thanks when you had come safe home.   1070
OEDIPUS: No, I will never come near my parents.
MESSENGER: Son,
    it's very plain you don't know what you're doing.
OEDIPUS: What do you mean, old man? For God's sake, tell me.
MESSENGER: If your homecoming is checked by fears like these.
OEDIPUS: Yes, I'm afraid that Phoebus may prove right.   1075
MESSENGER: The murder and the incest?
OEDIPUS: Yes, old man;
    that is my constant terror.
MESSENGER: Do you know
    that all your fears are empty?
OEDIPUS: How is that,
    if they are father and mother and I their son?
MESSENGER: Because Polybus was no kin to you in blood.   1080
OEDIPUS: What, was not Polybus my father?
MESSENGER: No more than I but just so much.
OEDIPUS: How can
    my father be my father as much as one
    that's nothing to me?
MESSENGER: Neither he nor I
    begat you.
OEDIPUS: Why then did he call me son?   1085
MESSENGER: A gift he took you from these hands of mine.
OEDIPUS: Did he love so much what he took from another's hand?
MESSENGER: His childlessness before persuaded him.
OEDIPUS: Was I a child you bought or found when I
    was given to him?
MESSENGER: On Cithaeron's slopes   1090
    in the twisting thickets you were found.
OEDIPUS: And why
    were you a traveler in those parts?
MESSENGER: I was
    in charge of mountain flocks.
OEDIPUS: You were a shepherd?
    A hireling vagrant?
MESSENGER: Yes, but at least at that time
    the man that saved your life, son.   1095
OEDIPUS: What ailed me when you took me in your arms?
MESSENGER: In that your ankles should be witnesses.
OEDIPUS: Why do you speak of that old pain?

MESSENGER: I loosed you;
    the tendons of your feet were pierced and fettered, —
OEDIPUS: My swaddling clothes brought me a rare disgrace.   1100
MESSENGER: So that from this you're called your present name.°
OEDIPUS: Was this my father's doing or my mother's?
    For God's sake, tell me.
MESSENGER: I don't know, but he
    who gave you to me has more knowledge than I.
OEDIPUS: You yourself did not find me then? You took me   1105
    from someone else?
MESSENGER: Yes, from another shepherd.
OEDIPUS: Who was he? Do you know him well enough
    to tell?
MESSENGER: He was called Laius' man.
OEDIPUS: You mean the king who reigned here in the old days?
MESSENGER: Yes, he was that man's shepherd.
OEDIPUS: Is he alive   1110
    still, so that I could see him?
MESSENGER: You who live here
    would know that best.
OEDIPUS: Do any of you here
    know of this shepherd whom he speaks about
    in town or in the fields? Tell me. It's time
    that this was found out once for all.   1115
CHORUS: I think he is none other than the peasant
    whom you have sought to see already; but
    Jocasta here can tell us best of that.
OEDIPUS: Jocasta, do you know about this man
    whom we have sent for? Is he the man he mentions?   1120
JOCASTA: Why ask of whom he spoke? Don't give it heed;
    nor try to keep in mind what has been said.
    It will be wasted labor.
OEDIPUS: With such clues
    I could not fail to bring my birth to light.
JOCASTA: I beg you — do not hunt this out — I beg you,   1125
    if you have any care for your own life.
    What I am suffering is enough.
OEDIPUS: Keep up
    your heart, Jocasta. Though I'm proved a slave,
    thrice slave, and though my mother is thrice slave,
    you'll not be shown to be of lowly lineage.   1130
JOCASTA: O be persuaded by me, I entreat you;
    do not do this.

1101. name: *Oedipus* means "swollen foot" or "clubfoot."

OEDIPUS: I will not be persuaded to let be
  the chance of finding out the whole thing clearly.
JOCASTA: It is because I wish you well that I   1135
  give you this counsel—and it's the best counsel.
OEDIPUS: Then the best counsel vexes me, and has
  for some while since.
JOCASTA: O Oedipus, God help you!
  God keep you from the knowledge of who you are!
OEDIPUS: Here, some one, go and fetch the shepherd for me;   1140
  and let her find her joy in her rich family!
JOCASTA: O Oedipus, unhappy Oedipus!
  that is all I can call you, and the last thing
  that I shall ever call you.

                                                      (*Exit.*)

CHORUS: Why has the queen gone, Oedipus, in wild   1145
  grief rushing from us? I am afraid that trouble
  will break out of this silence.
OEDIPUS: Break out what will! I at least shall be
  willing to see my ancestry, though humble.
  Perhaps she is ashamed of my low birth,   1150
  for she has all a woman's high-flown pride.
  But I account myself a child of Fortune,
  beneficent Fortune, and I shall not be
  dishonored. She's the mother from whom I spring;
  the months, my brothers, marked me, now as small,   1155
  and now again as mighty. Such is my breeding,
  and I shall never prove so false to it,
  as not to find the secret of my birth.
CHORUS: *Strophe*
  If I am a prophet and wise of heart
  you shall not fail, Cithaeron,   1160
  by the limitless sky, you shall not!—
  to know at tomorrow's full moon
  that Oedipus honors you,
  as native to him and mother and nurse at once;
  and that you are honored in dancing by us, as finding favor in sight of   1165
  our king.
  Apollo, to whom we cry, find these things pleasing!

      Antistrophe
  Who was it bore you, child? One of
  the long-lived nymphs who lay with Pan°—

1169. Pan: Pastoral god of fertility, patron of shepherds, associated with the wilderness.

the father who treads the hills?   1170
Or was she a bride of Loxias, your mother?° The grassy slopes
are all of them dear to him. Or perhaps Cyllene's king°
or the Bacchants' God° that lives on the tops
of the hills received you a gift from some
one of the Helicon Nymphs,° with whom he mostly plays?   1175

(Enter an old man, led by Oedipus' servants.)

OEDIPUS: If some one like myself who never met him
may make a guess, — I think this is the herdsman,
whom we were seeking. His old age is consonant
with the other. And besides, the men who bring him
I recognize as my own servants. You   1180
perhaps may better me in knowledge since
you've seen the man before.
CHORUS: You can be sure
I recognize him. For if Laius
had ever an honest shepherd, this was he.
OEDIPUS: You, sir, from Corinth, I must ask you first,   1185
is this the man you spoke of?
MESSENGER: This is he
before your eyes.
OEDIPUS: Old man, look here at me
and tell me what I ask you. Were you ever
a servant of King Laius?
HERDSMAN: I was, —
no slave he bought but reared in his own house.   1190
OEDIPUS: What did you do as work? How did you live?
HERDSMAN: Most of my life was spent among the flocks.
OEDIPUS: In what part of the country did you live?
HERDSMAN: Cithaeron and the places near to it.
OEDIPUS: And somewhere there perhaps you knew this man?   1195
HERDSMAN: What was his occupation? Who?
OEDIPUS: This man here,
have you had any dealings with him?
HERDSMAN: No —
not such that I can quickly call to mind.

1171. Or . . . mother: That is, "Or was she, your mother, a bride of Loxias?" 1172.
Cyllebe's king: Hermes, the messenger of the gods, was born on the rural mountain
Cellebe. 1173. Bacchants' God: Dionysus (Bacchus), who was accompanied by the Bacchants,
his priests or votaries. 1175. Helicon Nymphs: The Muses — water nymphs, patron goddesses of
the arts, who were associated with the springs of Mount Helicon.

MESSENGER: That is no wonder, master. But I'll make him remember what he
does not know. For I know, that he well knows the country of   1200
Cithaeron, how he with two flocks, I with one kept company for
three years—each year half a year—from spring till autumn time
and then when winter came I drove my flocks to our fold home
again and he to Laius' steadings. Well—am I right or not in what
I said we did?   1205
HERDSMAN: You're right—although it's a long time ago.
MESSENGER: Do you remember giving me a child
to bring up as my foster child?
HERDSMAN: What's this?
Why do you ask this question?
MESSENGER: Look old man,
here he is—here's the man who was that child!   1210
HERDSMAN: Death take you! Won't you hold your tongue?
OEDIPUS: No, no,
do not find fault with him, old man. Your words
are more at fault than his.
HERDSMAN: O best of masters,
how do I give offense?
OEDIPUS: When you refuse
to speak about the child of whom he asks you.   1215
HERDSMAN: He speaks out of his ignorance, without meaning.
OEDIPUS: If you'll not talk to gratify me, you
will talk with pain to urge you.
HERDSMAN: O please, sir,
don't hurt an old man, sir.
OEDIPUS (*to the servants*):   Here, one of you,
twist his hands behind him.
HERDSMAN: Why, God help me, why?   1220
What do you want to know?
OEDIPUS: You gave a child
to him,—the child he asked you of?
HERDSMAN: I did.
I wish I'd died the day I did.
OEDIPUS: You will
unless you tell me truly.
HERDSMAN: And I'll die
far worse if I should tell you.
OEDIPUS: This fellow   1225
is bent on more delays, as it would seem.
HERDSMAN: O no, no! I have told you that I gave it.
OEDIPUS: Where did you get this child from? Was it your own or did you
get it from another?

HERDSMAN: Not
   my own at all; I had it from some one.   1230
OEDIPUS: One of these citizens? or from what house?
HERDSMAN: O master, please—I beg you, master, please
   don't ask me more.
OEDIPUS: You're a dead man if I
   ask you again.
HERDSMAN: It was one of the children
   of Laius.
OEDIPUS: A slave? Or born in wedlock?   1235
HERDSMAN: O God, I am on the brink of frightful speech.
OEDIPUS: And I of frightful hearing. But I must hear.
HERDSMAN: The child was called his child; but she within,
   your wife would tell you best how all this was.
OEDIPUS: *She* gave it to you?
HERDSMAN: Yes, she did, my lord.   1240
OEDIPUS: To do what with it?
HERDSMAN: Make away with it.
OEDIPUS: She was so hard—its mother?
HERDSMAN: Aye, through fear
   of evil oracles.
OEDIPUS: Which?
HERDSMAN: They said that he
   should kill his parents.
OEDIPUS: How was it that you
   gave it away to this old man?
HERDSMAN: O master,   1245
   I pitied it, and thought that I could send it
   off to another country and this man
   was from another country. But he saved it
   for the most terrible troubles. If you are
   the man he says you are, you're bred to misery.   1250
OEDIPUS: O, O, O, they will all come,
   all come out clearly! Light of the sun, let me
   look upon you no more after today!
   I who first saw the light bred of a match
   accursed, and accursed in my living   1255
   with them I lived with, cursed in my killing.

                   (*Exeunt all but the Chorus.*)

CHORUS: *Strophe*
   O generations of men, how I
   count you as equal with those who live
   not at all!

What man, what man on earth wins more   1260
of happiness than a seeming
and after that turning away?
Oedipus, you are my pattern of this,
Oedipus, you and your fate!
Luckless Oedipus, whom of all men   1265
I envy not at all.

    Antistrophe
Inasmuch as he shot his bolt
beyond the others and won the prize
of happiness complete—
O Zeus—and killed and reduced to nought   1270
the hooked taloned maid° of the riddling speech,
standing a tower against death for my land: hence he was called my king
and hence
was honored the highest of all
honors; and hence he ruled   1275
in the great city of Thebes.

    Strophe
But now whose tale is more miserable?
Who is there lives with a savager fate?
Whose troubles so reverse his life as his?
O Oedipus, the famous prince   1280
for whom a great haven
the same both as father and son
sufficed for generation,
how, O how, have the furrows ploughed
by your father endured to bear you, poor wretch,   1285
and hold their peace so long?

    Antistrophe
Time who sees all has found you out
against your will; judges your marriage accursed,
begetter and begot at one in it.
O child of Laius,   1290
would I had never seen you.
I weep for you and cry
a dirge of lamentation.
To speak directly, I drew my breath
from you at the first and so now I lull   1295
my mouth to sleep with your name.

                                 (*Enter a second messenger.*)

1271. hooked taloned maid: The Sphinx.

SECOND MESSENGER: O Princes always honored by our country,
 what deeds you'll hear of and what horrors see,
 what grief you'll feel, if you as true born Thebans
 care for the house of Labdacus's sons.   1300
 Phasis° nor Ister° cannot purge this house,
 I think, with all their streams, such things
 it hides, such evils shortly will bring forth
 into the light, whether they will or not;
 and troubles hurt the most   1305
 when they prove self-inflicted.
CHORUS: What we had known before did not fall short
 of bitter groaning's worth; what's more to tell?
SECOND MESSENGER: Shortest to hear and tell—our glorious queen
 Jocasta's dead.
CHORUS: Unhappy woman! How?   1310
SECOND MESSENGER: By her own hand. The worst of what was done
 you cannot know. You did not see the sight.
 Yet insofar as I remember it
 you'll hear the end of our unlucky queen.
 When she came raging into the house she went 1315
 straight to her marriage bed, tearing her hair
 with both her hands, and crying upon Laius
 long dead—Do you remember, Laius,
 that night long past which bred a child for us
 to send you to your death and leave   1320
 a mother making children with her son?
 And then she groaned and cursed the bed in which
 she brought forth husband by her husband, children
 by her own child, an infamous double bond.
 How after that she died I do not know,—   1325
 for Oedipus distracted us from seeing.
 He burst upon us shouting and we looked
 to him as he paced frantically around,
 begging us always: Give me a sword, I say,
 to find this wife no wife, this mother's womb, 1330
 this field of double sowing whence I sprang
 and where I sowed my children! As he raved
 some god showed him the way—none of us there.
 Bellowing terribly and led by some
 invisible guide he rushed on the two doors,— 1335
 wrenching the hollow bolts out of their sockets,

1301. Phasis: The Rioni or Rion river, the main river of western Georgia. **1301. Ister:** The Danube river.

he charged inside. There, there, we saw his wife
hanging, the twisted rope around her neck.
When he saw her, he cried out fearfully
and cut the dangling noose. Then, as she lay,   1340
poor woman, on the ground, what happened after,
was terrible to see. He tore the brooches—
the gold chased brooches fastening her robe—
away from her and lifting them up high
dashed them on his own eyeballs, shrieking out   1345
such things as: they will never see the crime
I have committed or had done upon me!
Dark eyes, now in the days to come look on
forbidden faces, do not recognize
those whom you long for—with such imprecations   1350
he struck his eyes again and yet again
with the brooches. And the bleeding eyeballs gushed
and stained his beard—no sluggish oozing drops
but a black rain and bloody hail poured down.
So it has broken—and not on one head   1355
but troubles mixed for husband and for wife.
The fortune of the days gone by was true
good fortune—but today groans and destruction
and death and shame—of all ills can be named
not one is missing.   1360
CHORUS: Is he now in any ease from pain?
SECOND MESSENGER: He shouts
    for some one to unbar the doors and show him
    to all the men of Thebes, his father's killer,
    his mother's—no I cannot say the word,
    it is unholy—for he'll cast himself,   1365
    out of the land, he says, and not remain
    to bring a curse upon his house, the curse
    he called upon it in his proclamation. But
    he wants for strength, aye, and some one to guide him;
    his sickness is too great to bear. You, too,   1370
    will be shown that. The bolts are opening.
    Soon you will see a sight to waken pity
    even in the horror of it.

                            (*Enter the blinded Oedipus.*)

CHORUS: This is a terrible sight for men to see!
    I never found a worse!   1375
    Poor wretch, what madness came upon you!
    What evil spirit leaped upon your life
    to your ill-luck—a leap beyond man's strength!

Indeed I pity you, but I cannot
look at you, though there's much I want to ask   1380
and much to learn and much to see.
I shudder at the sight of you.

OEDIPUS: O, O,
where am I going? Where is my voice
borne on the wind to and fro?   1385
Spirit, how far have you sprung?

CHORUS: To a terrible place whereof men's ears
may not hear, nor their eyes behold it.

OEDIPUS: Darkness!
Horror of darkness enfolding, resistless, unspeakable visitant sped by an ill
wind in haste!   1390
madness and stabbing pain and memory
of evil deeds I have done!

CHORUS: In such misfortunes it's no wonder
if double weighs the burden of your grief.

OEDIPUS: My friend,   1395
you are the only one steadfast, the only one that attends on me;
you still stay nursing the blind man.
Your care is not unnoticed. I can know
your voice, although this darkness is my world.

CHORUS: Doer of dreadful deeds, how did you dare   1400
so far to do despite to your own eyes?
what spirit urged you to it?

OEDIPUS: It was Apollo, friends, Apollo,
that brought this bitter bitterness, my sorrows to completion.
But the hand that struck me   1405
was none but my own.
Why should I see
whose vision showed me nothing sweet to see?

CHORUS: These things are as you say.

OEDIPUS: What can I see to love?   1410
What greeting can touch my ears with joy?
Take me away, and haste—to a place out of the way!
Take me away, my friends, the greatly miserable,
the most accursed, whom God too hates
above all men on earth!   1415

CHORUS: Unhappy in your mind and your misfortune,
would I had never known you!

OEDIPUS: Curse on the man who took
the cruel bonds from off my legs, as I lay in the field.
He stole me from death and saved me,   1420
no kindly service.
Had I died then

I would not be so burdensome to friends.
CHORUS: I, too, could have wished it had been so.
OEDIPUS: Then I would not have come   1425
    to kill my father and marry my mother infamously.
    Now I am godless and child of impurity,
    begetter in the same seed that created my wretched self.
    If there is any ill worse than ill,
    that is the lot of Oedipus.   1430
CHORUS: I cannot say your remedy was good;
    you would be better dead than blind and living.
OEDIPUS: What I have done here was best done—don't tell me
    otherwise, do not give me further counsel.
    I do not know with what eyes I could look   1435
    upon my father when I die and go
    under the earth, nor yet my wretched mother—
    those two to whom I have done things deserving
    worse punishment than hanging. Would the sight
    of children, bred as mine are, gladden me?   1440
    No, not these eyes, never. And my city,
    its towers and sacred places of the Gods,
    of these I robbed my miserable self
    when I commanded all to drive *him* out,
    the criminal since proved by God impure   1445
    and of the race of Laius.
    To this guilt I bore witness against myself—
    with what eyes shall I look upon my people?
    No. If there were a means to choke the fountain
    of hearing I would not have stayed my hand   1450
    from locking up my miserable carcass,
    seeing and hearing nothing; it is sweet
    to keep our thoughts out of the range of hurt.

    Cithaeron, why did you receive me? why
    having received me did you not kill me straight?   1455
    And so I had not shown to men my birth.

    O Polybus and Corinth and the house,
    the old house that I used to call my father's—
    what fairness you were nurse to, and what foulness
    festered beneath! Now I am found to be   1460
    a sinner and a son of sinners. Crossroads,
    and hidden glade, oak and the narrow way
    at the crossroads, that drank my father's blood
    offered you by my hands, do you remember
    still what I did as you looked on, and what   1465
    I did when I came here? O marriage, marriage!

you bred me and again when you had bred
bred children of your child and showed to men
brides, wives and mothers and the foulest deeds
that can be in this world of ours.   1470

Come — it's unfit to say what is unfit
to do. — I beg of you in God's name hide me
somewhere outside your country, yes, or kill me,
or throw me into the sea, to be forever
out of your sight. Approach and deign to touch me   1475
for all my wretchedness, and do not fear.
No man but I can bear my evil doom.
CHORUS: Here Creon comes in fit time to perform
or give advice in what you ask of us.
Creon is left sole ruler in your stead.   1480
OEDIPUS: Creon! Creon! What shall I say to him?
How can I justly hope that he will trust me?
In what is past I have been proved towards him
an utter liar.

                                               (Enter Creon.)

CREON: Oedipus, I've come
not so that I might laugh at you nor taunt you   1485
with evil of the past. But if you still
are without shame before the face of men
reverence at least the flame that gives all life,
our Lord the Sun, and do not show unveiled
to him pollution such that neither land   1490
nor holy rain nor light of day can welcome.

                                               (To a servant.)

Be quick and take him in. It is most decent
that only kin should see and hear the troubles
of kin.
OEDIPUS: I beg you, since you've torn me from   1495
my dreadful expectations and have come
in a most noble spirit to a man
that has used you vilely — do a thing for me.
I shall speak for your own good, not for my own.
CREON: What do you need that you would ask of me?   1500
OEDIPUS: Drive me from here with all the speed you can
to where I may not hear a human voice.
CREON: Be sure, I would have done this had not I
wished first of all to learn from the God the course
of action I should follow.

OEDIPUS: But his word   1505
has been quite clear to let the parricide,°
the sinner, die.
CREON: Yes, that indeed was said.
But in the present need we had best discover
what we should do.
OEDIPUS: And will you ask about
a man so wretched?
CREON: Now even you will trust   1510
the God.
OEDIPUS: So. I command you—and will beseech you—
to her that lies inside that house give burial
as you would have it; she is yours and rightly
you will perform the rites for her. For me—
never let this my father's city have me   1515
living a dweller in it. Leave me live
in the mountains where Cithaeron is, that's called
my mountain, which my mother and my father
while they were living would have made my tomb.
So I may die by their decree who sought   1520
indeed to kill me. Yet I know this much:
no sickness and no other thing will kill me.
I would not have been saved from death if not
for some strange evil fate. Well, let my fate
go where it will.
    Creon, you need not care   1525
about my sons; they're men and so wherever
they are, they will not lack a livelihood.
But my two girls—so sad and pitiful—
whose table never stood apart from mine,
and everything I touched they always shared—   1530
O Creon, have a thought for them! And most
I wish that you might suffer me to touch them
and sorrow with them.

    (*Enter Antigone and Ismene, Oedipus' two daughters.*)

O my lord! O true noble Creon! Can I
really be touching them, as when I saw?   1535
What shall I say?
Yes, I can hear them sobbing—my two darlings!
and Creon has had pity and has sent me
what I loved most?
Am I right?   1540

1506. **parricide:** one who kills a parent or another close relation.

CREON: You're right: it was I gave you this
    because I knew from old days how you loved them
    as I see now.
OEDIPUS: God bless you for it, Creon,
    and may God guard you better on your road
    than he did me!
            O children,   1545
    where are you? Come here, come to my hands,
    a brother's hands which turned your father's eyes,
    those bright eyes you knew once, to what you see,
    a father seeing nothing, knowing nothing,
    begetting you from his own source of life.   1550
    I weep for you—I cannot see your faces—
    I weep when I think of the bitterness
    there will be in your lives, how you must live
    before the world. At what assemblages
    of citizens will you make one? to what   1555
    gay company will you go and not come home
    in tears instead of sharing in the holiday?
    And when you're ripe for marriage, who will he be,
    the man who'll risk to take such infamy
    as shall cling to my children, to bring hurt   1560
    on them and those that marry with them? What
    curse is not there? "Your father killed his father
    and sowed the seed where he had sprung himself
    and begot you out of the womb that held him."
    These insults you will hear. Then who will marry you?   1565
    No one, my children; clearly you are doomed
    to waste away in barrenness unmarried.
    Son of Menoeceus,° since you are all the father
    left these two girls, and we, their parents, both
    are dead to them—do not allow them to wander   1570
    like beggars, poor and husbandless.
    They are of your own blood.
    And do not make them equal with myself
    in wretchedness; for you can see them now
    so young, so utterly alone, save for you only.   1575
    Touch my hand, noble Creon, and say yes.
    If you were older, children, and were wiser,
    there's much advice I'd give you. But as it is,
    let this be what you pray: give me a life

1568. Son of Menoeceus: Creon.

wherever there is opportunity   1580
to live, and better life than was my father's.

CREON: Your tears have had enough of scope; now go within the house.

OEDIPUS: I must obey, though bitter of heart.

CREON: In season, all is good.

OEDIPUS: Do you know on what conditions I obey?

CREON: You tell me them,   1585
and I shall know them when I hear.

OEDIPUS: That you shall send me out
to live away from Thebes.

CREON: That gift you must ask of the Gods.

OEDIPUS: But I'm now hated by the Gods.

CREON: So quickly you'll obtain your prayer.

OEDIPUS: You consent then?

CREON: What I do not mean, I do not use to say.

OEDIPUS: Now lead me away from here.

CREON: Let go the children, then, and come.   1590

OEDIPUS: Do not take them from me.

CREON: Do not seek to be master in everything,
for the things you mastered did not follow you throughout your life.

(As Creon and Oedipus go out.)

CHORUS: You that live in my ancestral Thebes, behold this Oedipus, —
him who knew the famous riddles and was a man most masterful;
not a citizen who did not look with envy on his lot —   1595
see him now and see the breakers of misfortune swallow him!
Look upon that last day always. Count no mortal happy till
he has passed the final limit of his life secure from pain.

ELIZABETHAN DRAMA

England during the reigns of Elizabeth I (1558–1603) and James I (1603–1625) witnessed an outpouring of splendidly written drama and an increase in theatrical activity: It was one of the greatest periods for drama in history. Dramatists such as Thomas Kyd, Christopher Marlowe, Ben Jonson, Francis Beaumont, John Fletcher, John Webster, and, of course, William Shakespeare wrote during this time, and theaters such as the Curtain, the Rose, the Globe, and the Fortune drew large audiences from across the social classes. To get a feel for the life of the theater during that time, watch the film *Shakespeare in Love* (1998), directed by John Madden and starring Gwyneth Paltrow and Joseph Fiennes. It offers a wonderfully lively, imaginative reenactment of the era's theater scene.

The Globe   In 1599, the Lord Chamberlain's Company, to which Shakespeare belonged — he was acting as well as writing plays for them — opened a new theater, the Globe. It was a typical theater of the time (see the sketch on page 876): All were circular or octagonal structures with the center open to the sky. The audience was seated in several balconies on three sides, nearly surrounding the actors, who performed mostly on a "thrust stage" that extended out into the audience. The stage was covered to protect the actors from rain. These theaters could hold up to three thousand patrons, but the closeness of audience to stage, coupled with patrons standing in the "pit" around—and even leaning on—the edge of the stage, created an intimacy impossible in the large Greek theaters.

The Acting Areas   At the back of the thrust stage was a wall with two curtained doors used for entrances and exits and sometimes as places where characters hid and overheard what was said onstage. An upper gallery, normally used to seat wealthy patrons, was sometimes employed as an additional acting area. Most of the action, however, took place toward the front of the thrust stage, with audience members in the pit crowded around all three sides. This close proximity of the audience to the actors added to the effectiveness of Shakespeare's famous **soliloquies**. Imagine standing in the pit as a character comes to the front of the stage and expresses her or his most private thoughts and feelings, speaking directly to the audience (as is the case in Hamlet's famous soliloquies). Often the character is alone, but if other characters are onstage, the convention is that they do not hear or pay attention to the soliloquy.

Poetic Drama   As you read *Hamlet*, you will find fairly long speeches, with most of the play written in blank verse (unrhymed iambic pentameter). Poetry was used because most serious literature at the time was written in verse: epics, ballads, and elegies as well as lyric poetry. Poetic drama is a convention of Elizabethan theater: It's certainly not realistic that a soldier on a battlefield would talk in iambic pentameter, but the audience accepted it by suspending their disbelief. And Shakespeare could count on members of the audience to be attentive listeners, on the whole able to follow speeches packed with meaning and to catch intricate wordplay. He was also fortunate to have excellent actors in his company, such as Richard Burbage and Will Kempe, who could deliver such speeches powerfully.

Props and Scenery   The Elizabethan theater used very little scenery. It relied on the convention that the actors' words would supply spectators with as much as was needed to imagine where the action was occurring and the details of the scene. Thus, the location of *Hamlet* is signaled to the audience by the play's full title, *Hamlet, Prince of Denmark,* and most of the action takes place in various parts of Elsinore Castle. In act 4, scene 4, for example, Fortinbras's lines supply the information the audience needs. They identify who the speaker is and indicate that the location has shifted to the border or coast of Denmark: "Go, captain, from me greet the Danish king. / Tell him that, by his license, Fortinbras / Craves the conveyance of a promis'd march / Over his kingdom."

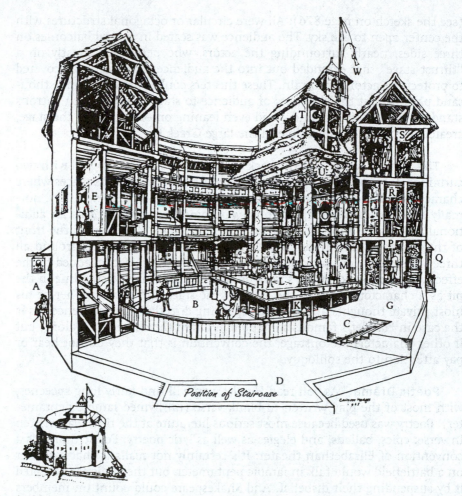

Position of Staircase

A Main entrance
B The yard
C Entrances to lowest gallery
D Position of entrances to staircase and upper galleries
E Corridor serving the different sections of the middle gallery
F Middle gallery ("Twopenny Rooms")
G Position of "Gentlemen's Rooms" or "Lords' Rooms"
H The stage
J The hanging being put up round the stage
K The "hell" under the stage
L The stage trap leading down to the hell

M Stage doors
N Curtained "place behind the stage"
O Gallery above the stage, used as required sometimes by musicians, sometimes by spectators, and often as part of the play
P Backstage area (the tiring-house)
Q Tiring-house door
R Dressing rooms
S Wardrobe and storage
T The hut housing the machine for lowering enthroned gods, etc., to the stage
U The "heavens"
W Hoisting the playhouse flag

A Conjectural Reconstruction of the Globe Theatre, 1599–1613.

Drawing by C. Walter Hodges from his *Globe Restored*, 1968. Image reprinted with permission of the Folger Shakespeare Library.

Lighting   Because performances were held midafternoon in an open-air structure, little could be done to indicate darkness in a scene. The playwright relied mostly on words. Thus, in the opening scene of *Hamlet*, Bernardo's words "'Tis now struck twelve" inform the audience that it is midnight and thus dark (he might come in carrying a torch as well, though in this case the stage directions do not specify that). Near the end of the scene, words convey that darkness is decreasing as dawn approaches, though spectators watching in the Globe wouldn't have been able to see the difference: "But, look, the morn, in russet mantle clad, / Walks o'er the dew of yon high eastward hill" (1.1.166–67).

Indoor Performances   Performances in Shakespeare's day were not limited, however, to public theaters like the Globe. Acting companies also performed indoors, sometimes at court for the monarch and courtiers, sometimes in the banqueting halls of noble families, sometimes at private theaters such as the Blackfriars and the Whitefriars. These acting places replicated the open-air theaters as much as possible, with a thrust stage and tiring-house backdrop with doors. Indoors, more could be done with scenery and props; in fact, costumes and scenery became quite spectacular for *masques*, pageantlike entertainments with some elements similar to present-day opera and musical comedy.

The Plots   Like the Greeks before them, Elizabethan playwrights generally used stories already familiar to the audience. Originality was achieved through the alteration of familiar details, the development of character, and the freshness of expression, not in the creation of new stories. The audience concentrated on the way things were changed and how ideas were expressed rather than on following an unfamiliar plot. Reading a plot summary of a Shakespeare play can give a present-day reader the same informed view of the drama that Shakespeare's contemporaries held. Unlike Greek plays, Elizabethan dramas showed a great deal of action on the stage, including violent action. For example, Hamlet and Laertes fight and die onstage in the fifth act of *Hamlet*, and the play ends with four dead bodies strewn across the set. Murders and suicides, which occurred offstage and were only reported in Greek plays, are shown onstage in Elizabethan drama.

Effects of Evil   Tragedies from this era tend to deal with the results of evil in the world. Often they show how a misstep or an association with an antagonist harboring evil intentions results in a consequence that far exceeds what the protagonist seems to deserve. Or they show the destruction of an innocent victim caught in an evil web not of her or his own making. The protagonists continue to be persons of high status and importance (whose actions affect many people), or at least they are from the upper ranks of society.

Kinds of Tragedy

Elizabethan tragedy appears in several subtypes:

- One popular variety, influenced by drama of the Roman era, is *revenge tragedy*, in which an avenger who seeks to exact revenge for the death of a relative or comrade dies achieving that aim. The best-known tragedy of this type is Shakespeare's *Hamlet*.
- Another popular subtype, *tragedy of passion*, occurs when characters die as a result of excessively passionate reactions or relationships. Unrestrained passion that leads to an unbalanced life was believed to be a recipe for disaster; one was to use reason to restrain emotions and actions. Shakespeare's *Romeo and Juliet* illustrates this subtype: Love at first sight, a hasty marriage of young lovers, and other rash behavior are propelled by intense emotions, which lead the pair to their unfortunate and untimely deaths.
- A third subtype, *tragedy of fate*, depicts characters who cannot escape the doom that fortune has in store for them. *Romeo and Juliet* fits this category as well. From the opening lines, in which Romeo and Juliet are referred to as "star-crossed lovers," their doom seems inescapable. This fate is not the same as the divine inevitability of the Greeks; rather, it is an inexplicable, unavoidable destiny, with chance, accident, and coincidence playing major roles.
- In still another subtype, *tragedy of character*, disastrous results stem from an individual's character traits—not necessarily weaknesses or flaws but often strengths and virtues that are carried too far or applied unwisely. Shakespeare's great tragedies—*Hamlet*, *Othello*, *King Lear*, *Macbeth*—are tragedies of character, with protagonists of great depth and complexity. To understand such characters well, it's important to read and reflect carefully.

A FEW NOTES ON COMEDY

Comedy, like tragedy, emerged from Greek religious ceremonies, particularly from Dionysian fertility rites. The word *comedy* derives from the Greek *kômos*, meaning "revel" or "merry-making." At its most basic, comedy is a narrative or drama with a happy ending. No matter what the characters go through, if the ending is happy, the play is a comedy. All's well that ends well.

THE PHYSICAL AND THE FOOLISH

In early Greek comedies, the revelry involved explicit sexuality. Although later comedies became less blatantly sexual, they retained the earthy, physical qualities of their Dionysian origins. Comedy continues to emphasize the physical or sensuous nature of humans; their ridiculousness, weaknesses, and foibles; their physical relationships; and their outrageous behaviors and foolish misunderstandings.

CELEBRATION OF LIFE

The tone of comedy is lighter than that of tragedy and its style less elevated; it is usually written in prose. It uses humor to evoke smiles and laughter from its readers and audience. Comedy generally has a realistic strain, dealing with ordinary people in everyday activities, but the events often include exaggeration and unrealistic circumstances, with characters turning things upside down, breaking rules, reversing normal relationships, and falling into incongruous situations. Comedies celebrate life, with all the disorder, misunderstandings, and confusion that often accompany it. Comedies tend to begin in disorder and end with the restoration of order, and they often conclude with a dance, a marriage, or a celebration symbolizing harmony and happiness.

OLD COMEDY AND NEW COMEDY

Greek drama initiated two major strains of comedy that have remained influential through the centuries. The earlier strain was **Old Comedy**, represented by the satiric works of Aristophanes (c. 450–385 B.C.E.), predecessor of later satiric comedy playwrights. Old Comedy was replaced by **New Comedy**, originated by the Greek playwright Menander (c. 342–292 B.C.E.) and developed further by the Roman dramatists Plautus (c. 254–184 B.C.E.) and Terence (c. 190–159 B.C.E.). New Comedy concerns the obstacles faced by young lovers and the unpredictable changes of fortune they encounter; it pokes fun at the foibles and attitudes of the lovers as well as those around them. New Comedy developed later into the *comedy of manners*, which laughs at people's behavior and attitudes, at their follies and vanities.

ELIZABETHAN COMEDY

In the Elizabethan era, two playwrights were successful in comedy: Ben Jonson and William Shakespeare. Jonson was known for satiric comedy, influenced by and adapting Old Comedy. Shakespeare was best known for *romantic comedy*, in which he adapted New Comedy but also was influenced by Greek prose romances. Romantic comedy typically involves young lovers who face obstacles to fulfilling their relationship (perhaps parental opposition, a competing lover, their own differences, poverty, separation because of war or travel, or coincidences that prevent them from being together). After facing numerous complications and encountering several near disasters, all of which make a favorable outcome seem impossible, the lovers at last are united and their union accepted. Hollywood movies and TV shows continue the romantic comedy tradition today.

APPROACHING THE AUTHOR

Almost no evidence of any kind, let alone writings, exist for **William Shakespeare** in the years between 1585 and 1592.

© Corbis

Numerous theories abound about these "lost years," including one that contends he was caught poaching near Strafford and escaped to London to avoid persecution. More probable is that he worked as a schoolmaster during those years.

For more about him, see page 1079.

APPROACHING THE READING

We initially glimpse Hamlet as a troubled young man, moping by himself at the side of the stage, dressed entirely in black. Why? There are lots of reasons. Away at college, he had received a message telling him that his father died suddenly and unexpectedly. He headed home, shocked and grieving and probably expecting to be chosen as the next king by the board of electors. When he got home, he discovered his uncle had manipulated matters so that he was elected king, hastily, perhaps secretly, instead of Hamlet. Then his uncle began courting Hamlet's mother. Shortly after, they got married, before the proper grieving period for a husband, much less for a king, had expired. Small wonder Hamlet feels gloomy. Then he sees, or thinks he sees, the ghost of his father.

Hamlet has been called an uncertain play about uncertainties. In one sense it is a play about the difficulty of *knowing*—difficult for Hamlet and for readers and viewers of the play. A ghost appears (or seems to appear) to him, tells him his father was murdered by his uncle, and tells him to avenge the death. How is one to know how to take all that? There are no such things as ghosts, are there? If there are, what are they and where do they come from? From God? Or from the devil, urging one to do evil deeds so one's soul will be damned to hell? How is Hamlet to know? How are we to know? Was his father murdered? It appeared to be a natural death. And if he was murdered, is it actually Hamlet's duty to seek revenge? Hamlet's father was a Catholic who complains that he was killed without having an opportunity to confess, be absolved, and receive the last rites of the church (1.5.76–79). Hamlet presumably would have been taught that Christians are not to seek revenge: "Vengeance is mine, I will repay, saith the Lord" (Romans 12:19). How is Hamlet to know how to respond to all of this? How are we to know how to respond to it? As you read the play, you will come to understand why people have been fascinated by Hamlet for over four hundred years.

William Shakespeare   1564–1616

Hamlet, Prince of Denmark   [c. 1600]

DRAMATIS PERSONAE

CLAUDIUS, *king of Denmark*
HAMLET, *son to the late King Hamlet, and nephew to the present king*
POLONIUS, *Lord Chamberlain*
HORATIO, *friend to Hamlet*
LAERTES, *son to Polonius*
VOLTIMAND ⎤
CORNELIUS   ⎟
ROSENCRANTZ ⎬ *courtiers*
GUILDENSTERN ⎟
OSRIC   ⎟
GENTLEMAN   ⎦
PRIEST, OR DOCTOR OF DIVINITY
MARCELLUS ⎤ *officers*
BERNARDO ⎦
FRANCISCO, *a solider*
REYNALDO, *servant to Polonius*
PLAYERS
TWO CLOWNS, *gravediggers*
FORTINBRAS, *prince of Norway*
CAPTAIN
ENGLISH AMBASSADORS

GERTRUDE, *Queen of Denmark, mother to Hamlet*
OPHELIA, *daughter to Polonius*

LORDS, LADIES, OFFICERS, SOLDIERS, SAILORS, MESSENGERS, AND OTHER ATTENDANTS
GHOST *of Hamlet's father*
Scene: Denmark.

Note: *Hamlet* was first published in 1603, in a slender book called a "quarto" (made up from sheets of printer's paper folded twice, creating four leaves — eight pages — approximately 9½ by 12 inches in size). This was an unauthorized version, of unknown origin and very different in length and in details from subsequent versions. The following year a much longer version was published (now referred to as the Second Quarto), which seems to have drawn upon Shakespeare's own copy of the play as well as some parts of the First Quarto. Two other quartos were published subsequently, with corrections to the Second Quarto. In 1623, the first collected edition of Shakespeare's plays was published, now called the First Folio (made up from sheets of printer's paper folded once, creating pages twice as large as a quarto). The First Folio text of *Hamlet* omits more than two hundred lines found in the Second Quarto, but it also introduces some new lines that clarify passages and seem to be from a transcript of a draft written by Shakespeare. The play as printed here mainly follows the Second Quarto text, but passages unique to the Folio have been inserted (enclosed in square brackets) and some corrections from it and the First Quarto have been adopted. The *Dramatis Personae* list, the act and scene divisions, the stage directions enclosed in square brackets, and the indications of scene location in the notes are later editorial additions.

[ACT 1 / Scene 1]°

(*Enter Bernardo and Francisco, two sentinels, [meeting].*)

BERNARDO: Who's there?
FRANCISCO: Nay, answer me.° Stand and unfold yourself.
BERNARDO: Long live the King!
FRANCISCO: Bernardo?
BERNARDO: He.   5
FRANCISCO: You come most carefully upon your hour.
BERNARDO: 'Tis now struck twelve. Get thee to bed, Francisco.
FRANCISCO: For this relief much thanks. 'Tis bitter cold,
    And I am sick at heart.
BERNARDO: Have you had quiet guard?
FRANCISCO: Not a mouse stirring.   10
BERNARDO: Well, good night.
    If you do meet Horatio and Marcellus,
    The rivals° of my watch, bid them make haste.

(*Enter Horatio and Marcellus.*)

FRANCISCO: I think I hear them. Stand, ho! Who is there?
HORATIO: Friends to this ground.
MARCELLUS: And liegemen to the Dane.°   15
FRANCISCO: Give you° good night.
MARCELLUS: O, farewell, honest soldier.
    Who hath relieved you?
FRANCISCO: Bernardo hath my place.
    Give you good night.   (*Exit Francisco.*)
MARCELLUS: Holla, Bernardo!
BERNARDO: Say,
    What, is Horatio there?
HORATIO: A piece of him.
BERNARDO: Welcome, Horatio. Welcome, good Marcellus.   20
HORATIO: What, has this thing appear'd again tonight?
BERNARDO: I have seen nothing.
MARCELLUS: Horatio says 'tis but our fantasy,
    And will not let belief take hold of him
    Touching this dreaded sight, twice seen of us.   25
    Therefore I have entreated him along
    With us to watch the minutes of this night,
    That if again this apparition come
    He may approve° our eyes and speak to it.

ACT 1, SCENE 1. **Location:** Elsinore castle. A guard platform. **2. me:** Francisco emphasizes that
he is the sentry currently on watch. **13. rivals:** Partners. **15. liegemen to the Dane:**
Men sworn to serve the Danish king. **16. Give you:** God give you. **29. approve:** Corroborate.

HORATIO: Tush, tush, 'twill not appear.
BERNARDO:　　　　　Sit down awhile,　　　　　　　　　　　　　　30
　　And let us once again assail your ears,
　　That are so fortified against our story,
　　What we have two nights seen.
HORATIO:　　　　　　　Well, sit we down,
　　And let us hear Bernardo speak of this.
BERNARDO: Last night of all,　　　　　　　　　　　　　　　　35
　　When yond same star that's westward from the pole°
　　Had made his° course t' illume that part of heaven
　　Where now it burns, Marcellus and myself,
　　The bell then beating one—

(Enter Ghost.)

MARCELLUS: Peace, break thee off! Look where it comes again!　40
BERNARDO: In the same figure, like the King that's dead.
MARCELLUS: Thou art a scholar.° Speak to it, Horatio.
BERNARDO: Looks 'a° not like the King? Mark it, Horatio.
HORATIO: Most like. It harrows me with fear and wonder.
BERNARDO: It would be spoke to.
MARCELLUS:　　　　Speak to it,° Horatio.　　　　　　　　45
HORATIO: What art thou that usurp'st this time of night,
　　Together with that fair and warlike form
　　In which the majesty of buried Denmark°
　　Did sometimes° march? By heaven I charge thee speak!
MARCELLUS: It is offended.
BERNARDO:　　　　See, it stalks away.　　　　　　　　　　50
HORATIO: Stay! Speak, speak. I charge thee, speak.

　　　　　　　　　　　　　　　　　　　(Exit Ghost.)

MARCELLUS: 'Tis gone, and will not answer.
BERNARDO: How now, Horatio? You tremble and look pale.
　　Is not this something more than fantasy?
　　What think you on 't?　　　　　　　　　　　　　　　　55
HORATIO: Before my God, I might not this believe
　　Without the sensible° and true avouch
　　Of mine own eyes.
MARCELLUS: Is it not like the King?
HORATIO: As thou art to thyself.
　　Such was the very armor he had on　　　　　　　　　60
　　When he the ambitious Norway° combated.

---

36. pole: Polestar.　**37. his:** Its.　**42. scholar:** One learned in Latin and able to address spirits.
43. 'a: He.　**45. It . . . it:** A ghost could not speak until spoken to.　**48. buried Denmark:** The
buried king of Denmark.　**49. sometimes:** Formerly.　**57. sensible:** Confirmed by the senses.
61. Norway: King of Norway.

So frown'd he once when, in an angry parle,°
He smote the sledded° Polacks° on the ice.
'Tis strange.
MARCELLUS: Thus twice before, and jump° at this dead hour,   65
    With martial stalk hath he gone by our watch.
HORATIO: In what particular thought to work I know not,
    But, in the gross and scope° of mine opinion,
    This bodes some strange eruption to our state.
MARCELLUS: Good now,° sit down, and tell me, he that knows,   70
    Why this same strict and most observant watch
    So nightly toils° the subject° of the land,
    And why such daily cast° of brazen cannon,
    And foreign mart° for implements of war,
    Why such impress° of shipwrights, whose sore task   75
    Does not divide the Sunday from the week.
    What might be toward,° that this sweaty haste
    Doth make the night joint-laborer with the day?
    Who is 't that can inform me?
HORATIO: That can I,
    At least, the whisper goes so. Our last king,   80
    Whose image even but now appear'd to us,
    Was, as you know, by Fortinbras of Norway,
    Thereto prick'd on° by a most emulate° pride,
    Dar'd to the combat; in which our valiant Hamlet—
    For so this side of our known world esteem'd him—   85
    Did slay this Fortinbras; who, by a seal'd compact,
    Well ratified by law and heraldry,
    Did forfeit, with his life, all those his lands
    Which he stood seiz'd° of, to the conqueror;
    Against the° which a moi'ty competent°   90
    Was gaged° by our king, which had return'd
    To the inheritance of Fortinbras
    Had he been vanquisher, as, by the same comart°
    And carriage° of the article design'd,
    His fell to Hamlet. Now, sir, young Fortinbras,   95
    Of unimproved mettle° hot and full,

---

62. parle: Parley. 63. sledded: Traveling on sleds. Polacks: Poles. 65. jump: Exactly. 68. gross
and scope: General view. 70. Good now: An expression denoting entreaty or expostulation.
72. toils: Causes to toil. subject: Subjects. 73. cast: Casting. 74. mart: Buying and selling.
75. impress: Impressment, conscription. 77. toward: In preparation. 83. prick'd on: Incited.
emulate: Ambitious. 89. seiz'd: Possessed. 90. Against the: In return for. moi'ty competent:
Sufficient portion. 91. gaged: Engaged, pledged. 93. comart: Joint bargain (?). 94. carriage:
Import, bearing. 96. unimproved mettle: Undisciplined spirits.

Hath in the skirts° of Norway here and there
Shark'd up° a list of lawless resolutes°
For food and diet° to some enterprise
That hath a stomach° in 't, which is no other —　　　　100
As it doth well appear unto our state —
But to recover of us, by strong hand
And terms compulsatory, those foresaid lands
So by his father lost. And this, I take it,
Is the main motive of our preparations,　　　　105
The source of this our watch, and the chief head°
Of this post-haste and romage° in the land.

BERNARDO: I think it be no other but e'en so.
　　Well may it sort° that this portentous figure
　　Comes armed through our watch so like the King　　　110
　　That was and is the question of these wars.

HORATIO: A mote° it is to trouble the mind's eye.
　　In the most high and palmy° state of Rome,
　　A little ere the mightiest Julius fell,
　　The graves stood tenantless and the sheeted° dead　　115
　　Did squeak and gibber in the Roman streets;
　　As° stars with trains of fire and dews of blood,
　　Disasters° in the sun; and the moist star°
　　Upon whose influence Neptune's° empire stands°
　　Was sick almost to doomsday° with eclipse.　　　　120
　　And even the like precurse° of fear'd events,
　　As harbingers° preceding still° the fates
　　And prologue to the omen° coming on,
　　Have heaven and earth together demonstrated
　　Unto our climatures° and countrymen.　　　　125

(*Enter Ghost.*)

　　But soft, behold! Lo where it comes again!
　　I'll cross° it, though it blast me. Stay, illusion!
　　If thou hast any sound, or use of voice,
　　Speak to me!　　　　　　　　　　(*It spreads his arms.*)

---

97. skirts: Outlying regions, outskirts. **98. Shark'd up:** Got together in haphazard fashion. **resolutes:** Desperadoes. **99. food and diet:** No pay but their keep. **100. stomach:** Relish of danger. **106. head:** Source. **107. romage:** Bustle, commotion. **109. sort:** Suit. **112. mote:** Speck of dust. **113. palmy:** Flourishing. **115. sheeted:** Shrouded. **117. As:** This abrupt transition suggests that matter is possibly omitted between lines 116 and 117. **118. Disasters:** Unfavorable signs of aspects. **moist star:** Moon, governing tides. **119. Neptune:** God of the sea. **stands:** Depends. **120. sick...doomsday:** See Matthew 24:29 and Revelation 6:12. **121. precurse:** Heralding, foreshadowing. **122. harbingers:** Forerunners. **still:** Continually. **123. omen:** Calamitous event. **125. climatures:** Regions. **127. cross:** Meet, face directly.

If there be any good thing to be done   130
That may to thee do ease and grace to me,
Speak to me!
If thou art privy to thy country's fate,
Which, happily,° foreknowing may avoid,
O, speak!   135
Or if thou hast uphoarded in thy life
Extorted treasure in the womb of earth,
For which, they say, you spirits oft walk in death,

(*The cock crows.*)

    Speak of it. Stay, and speak! Stop it, Marcellus.
MARCELLUS: Shall I strike at it with my partisan?°   140
HORATIO: Do, if it will not stand.   [*They strike at it.*]
BERNARDO: 'Tis here!
HORATIO: 'Tis here!
MARCELLUS: 'Tis gone.   [*Exit Ghost.*]
    We do it wrong, being so majestical,
    To offer it the show of violence;
    For it is, as the air, invulnerable,   145
    And our vain blows malicious mockery.
BERNARDO: It was about to speak when the cock crew.
HORATIO: And then it started like a guilty thing
    Upon a fearful summons. I have heard,
    The cock, that is the trumpet to the morn,   150
    Doth with his lofty and shrill-sounding throat
    Awake the god of day, and, at his warning,
    Whether in sea or fire, in earth or air,
    Th' extravagant and erring° spirit hies
    To his confine; and of the truth herein   155
    This present object made probation.°
MARCELLUS: It faded on the crowing of the cock.
    Some say that ever 'gainst° that season comes
    Wherein our Savior's birth is celebrated,
    The bird of dawning singeth all night long,   160
    And then, they say, no spirit dare stir abroad;
    The nights are wholesome, then no planets strike,°
    No fairy takes,° nor witch hath power to charm,
    So hallowed and so gracious° is that time.
HORATIO: So have I heard and do in part believe it.   165
    But, look, the morn, in russet mantle clad,

---

134. happily: Haply, perchance. 140. partisan: Long-handled spear. 154. extravagant and
erring: Wandering. (The words have similar meaning.) 156. probation: Proof. 158. 'gainst:
Just before. 162. strike: Exert evil influence. 163. takes: Bewitches. 164. gracious: Full of
goodness.

Walks o'er the dew of yon high eastward hill.
Break we our watch up, and by my advice
Let us impart what we have seen tonight
Unto young Hamlet; for, upon my life,   170
This spirit, dumb to us, will speak to him.
Do you consent we shall acquaint him with it,
As needful in our loves, fitting our duty?
MARCELLUS: Let's do 't, I pray, and I this morning know
Where we shall find him most conveniently.   175

                                                             (*Exeunt.*)°

[Scene 2]°

(*Flourish. Enter Claudius, King of Denmark, Gertrude the Queen, Councilors, Polonius
and his son Laertes, Hamlet, cum aliis*° [*including Voltimand and Cornelius*].)

KING: Though yet of Hamlet our dear brother's death
The memory be green, and that it us befitted
To bear our hearts in grief and our whole kingdom
To be contracted in one brow of woe,
Yet so far hath discretion fought with nature   5
That we with wisest sorrow think on him,
Together with remembrance of ourselves.
Therefore our sometime sister, now our queen,
Th' imperial jointress° to this warlike state,
Have we, as 'twere with a defeated joy—   10
With an auspicious and a dropping eye,
With mirth in funeral and with dirge in marriage,
In equal scale weighing delight and dole—
Taken to wife. Nor have we herein barr'd
Your better wisdoms, which have freely gone   15
With this affair along. For all, our thanks.
Now follows that you know° young Fortinbras,
Holding a weak supposal° of our worth,
Or thinking by our late dear brother's death
Our state to be disjoint and out of frame,   20
Colleagued with° this dream of his advantage,°
He hath not fail'd to pester us with message
Importing° the surrender of those lands
Lost by his father, with all bands° of law,
To our most valiant brother. So much for him.   25

[S.D.] *Exeunt:* Latin for "they go out." ACT 1, SCENE 2. Location: The castle. [S.D.] *cum aliis:*
With others. **9. jointress:** Woman possessed of a joint tenancy of an estate. **17. know:**
Be informed (that). **18. weak supposal:** Low estimate. **21. Colleagued with:** Joined to,
allied with. **dream . . . advantage:** Illusory hope of success. **23. Importing:** Pertaining to.
24. bands: Contracts.

Now for ourself and for this time of meeting.
Thus much the business is: we have here writ
To Norway, uncle of young Fortinbras —
Who, impotent and bed-rid, scarcely hears
Of this his nephew's purpose — to suppress   30
His° further gait° herein, in that the levies,
The lists, and full proportions are all made
Out of his subject;° and we here dispatch
You, good Cornelius, and you, Voltimand,
For bearers of this greeting to old Norway,   35
Giving to you no further personal power
To business with the King, more than the scope
Of these delated° articles allow.   [*Gives a paper.*]
Farewell, and let your haste commend your duty.
CORNELIUS, VOLTIMAND: In that, and all things, will we show our duty. 40
KING: We doubt it nothing. Heartily farewell.

                                  [*Exit Voltimand and Cornelius*]

And now, Laertes, what's the news with you?
You told us of some suit; what is 't, Laertes?
You cannot speak of reason to the Dane°
And lose your voice.° What wouldst thou beg, Laertes,   45
That shall not be my offer, not thy asking?
The head is not more native° to the heart,
The hand more instrumental° to the mouth,
Than is the throne of Denmark to thy father.
What wouldst thou have, Laertes?
LAERTES: My dread lord,   50
Your leave and favor to return to France,
From whence though willingly I came to Denmark
To show my duty in your coronation,
Yet now I must confess, that duty done,
My thoughts and wishes bend again toward France   55
And bow them to your gracious leave and pardon.°
KING: Have you your father's leave? What says Polonius?
POLONIUS: H'ath, my lord, wrung from me my slow leave
By laborsome petition, and at last
Upon his will I seal'd my hard° consent.   60
I do beseech you, give him leave to go.

---

31. His: Fortinbras's. **gait:** Proceeding.   **31–33. in that . . . subject:** Since the levying of troops
and supplies is drawn entirely from the King of Norway's own subjects.   **38. delated:** Detailed.
(Variant of *dilated.*)   **44. the Dane:** The Danish king.   **45. lose your voice:** Waste your
speech.   **47. native:** Closely connected, related.   **48. instrumental:** Serviceable.   **56. leave
and pardon:** Permission to depart.   **60. hard:** Reluctant.

KING: Take thy fair hour, Laertes. Time be thine,
    And thy best graces spend it at thy will!
    But now, my cousin° Hamlet, and my son—
HAMLET: A little more than kin, and less than kind.°   65
KING: How is it that the clouds still hang on you?
HAMLET: Not so, my lord. I am too much in the sun.°
QUEEN: Good Hamlet, cast thy nighted color off,
    And let thine eye look like a friend on Denmark.
    Do not forever with thy veiled° lids   70
    Seek for thy noble father in the dust.
    Thou know'st 'tis common,° all that lives must die,
    Passing through nature to eternity.
HAMLET: Ay, madam, it is common.
QUEEN: If it be,
    Why seems it so particular with thee?   75
HAMLET: Seems, madam! Nay, it is. I know not "seems."
    'Tis not alone my inky cloak, good mother,
    Nor customary suits of solemn black,
    Nor windy suspiration of forc'd breath,
    No, nor the fruitful° river in the eye,   80
    Nor the dejected havior° of the visage,°
    Together with all forms, moods, shapes of grief,
    That can denote me truly. These indeed seem,
    For they are actions that a man might play.
    But I have that within which passes show;   85
    These but the trappings and the suits of woe.
KING: 'Tis sweet and commendable in your nature, Hamlet,
    To give these mourning duties to your father.
    But you must know your father lost a father,
    That father lost, lost his, and the survivor bound   90
    In filial obligation for some term
    To do obsequious° sorrow. But to persever°
    In obstinate condolement° is a course
    Of impious stubbornness. 'Tis unmanly grief.
    It shows a will most incorrect to heaven,   95
    A heart unfortified, a mind impatient,
    An understanding simple and unschool'd.
    For what we know must be and is as common

---

64. **cousin:** Any kin not of the immediate family. 65. **A little . . . kind:** Closer than an ordinary nephew (since I am stepson), and yet more separated in natural feeling (with pun on *kind*, meaning affectionate and natural, lawful). This line is often read as an aside, but it need not be. 67. **sun:** The sunshine of the King's royal favor (with pun on *son*). 70. **veiled:** Downcast. 72. **common:** Of universal occurrence. (But Hamlet plays on the sense of *vulgar* in line 74.) 80. **fruitful:** Abundant. 81. **havior:** Appearance. **visage:** Face. 92. **obsequious:** Suited to obsequies or funerals. **persever:** Persevere. 93. **condolement:** Sorrowing.

As any the most vulgar thing to sense,°
Why should we in our peevish opposition   100
Take it to heart? Fie, 'tis a fault to heaven,
A fault against the dead, a fault to nature,
To reason most absurd, whose common theme
Is death of fathers, and who still hath cried,
From the first corse° till he that died today,   105
"This must be so." We pray you, throw to earth
This unprevailing° woe, and think of us
As of a father; for let the world take note,
You are the most immediate° to our throne,
And with no less nobility of love   110
Than that which dearest father bears his son
Do I impart toward you. For your intent
In going back to school in Wittenberg,°
It is most retrograde° to our desire,
And we beseech you, bend you° to remain   115
Here in the cheer and comfort of our eye,
Our chiefest courtier, cousin, and our son.
QUEEN: Let not thy mother lose her prayers, Hamlet.
I pray thee stay with us, go not to Wittenberg.
HAMLET: I shall in all my best obey you, madam.   120
KING: Why, 'tis a loving and a fair reply.
Be as ourself in Denmark, Madam, come.
This gentle and unforc'd accord of Hamlet
Sits smiling to my heart, in grace whereof
No jocund° health that Denmark drinks today   125
But the great cannon to the clouds shall tell,
And the King's rouse° the heaven shall bruit again,°
Respeaking earthly thunder.° Come away.

(*Flourish. Exeunt all but Hamlet.*)

HAMLET: O, that this too too sullied° flesh would melt,
Thaw, and resolve itself into a dew!   130
Or that the Everlasting had not fix'd
His canon° 'gainst self-slaughter! O God, God,
How weary, stale, flat, and unprofitable
Seem to me all the uses of this world!
Fie on 't, ah, fie! 'Tis an unweeded garden   135

---

99. **As . . . sense:** As the most ordinary experience. **105. corse:** Corpse. **107. unprevail-
ing:** Unavailing. **109. most immediate:** Next in succession. **113. Wittenberg:** Famous
German university founded in 1502. **114. retrograde:** Contrary. **115. bend you:** Incline
yourself. **125. jocund:** Merry. **127. rouse:** Draft of liquor. **bruit again:** Loudly echo.
128. thunder: Of trumpet and kettledrum sounded when the King drinks, see 1.4.8–12.
129. sullied: Defiled. (The early quartos read *sallied*, the Folio *solid*.) **132. canon:** Law.

That grows to seed. Things rank and gross in nature
Possess it merely.° That it should come to this!
But two months dead—nay, not so much, not two.
So excellent a king, that was to° this
Hyperion° to a satyr; so loving to my mother   140
That he might not beteem° the winds of heaven
Visit her face too roughly. Heaven and earth,
Must I remember? Why, she would hang on him
As if increase of appetite had grown
By what it fed on, and yet, within a month—   145
Let me not think on 't. Frailty, thy name is woman!—
A little month, or ere those shoes were old
With which she followed my poor father's body,
Like Niobe,° all tears, why she, even she—
O God, a beast, that wants discourse of reason,°   150
Would have mourn'd longer—married with my uncle,
My father's brother, but no more like my father
Than I to Hercules. Within a month,
Ere yet the salt of most unrighteous tears
Had left the flushing in her galled° eyes,   155
She married. O, most wicked speed, to post
With such dexterity to incestuous° sheets!
It is not nor it cannot come to good.
But break, my heart, for I must hold my tongue.

(*Enter Horatio, Marcellus, and Bernardo.*)

HORATIO: Hail to your lordship!
HAMLET: I am glad to see you well.   160
    Horatio!—or I do forget myself.
HORATIO: The same, my lord, and your poor servant ever.
HAMLET: Sir, my good friend; I'll change° that name with you.
    And what make° you from Wittenberg, Horatio?
    Marcellus?   165
MARCELLUS: My good lord.
HAMLET: I am very glad to see you. [*To Bernardo.*] Good even, sir.—
    But what, in faith, make you from Wittenberg?
HORATIO: A truant disposition, good my lord.

---

137. **merely:** Completely.   139. **to:** In comparison to.   140. **Hyperion:** Titan sun-god, father
of Helios.   141. **beteem:** Allow.   149. **Niobe:** Tantalus's daughter, queen of Thebes, who
boasted that she had more sons and daughters than Leto; for this, Apollo and Artemis, children
of Leto, slew her fourteen children. She was turned by Zeus into a stone that continually
dropped tears.   150. **wants . . . reason:** Lacks the faculty of reason.   155. **galled:** Irritated,
inflamed.   157. **incestuous:** In Shakespeare's day, the marriage of a man like Claudius to his
deceased brother's wife was considered incestuous.   163. **change:** Exchange (i.e., the name of
friend).   164. **make:** Do.

HAMLET: I would not hear your enemy say so,   170
    Nor shall you do my ear that violence
    To make it truster of your own report
    Against yourself. I know you are no truant.
    But what is your affair in Elsinore?
    We'll teach you to drink deep ere you depart.   175

HORATIO: My lord, I came to see your father's funeral.

HAMLET: I prithee do not mock me, fellow student;
    I think it was to see my mother's wedding.

HORATIO: Indeed, my lord, it followed hard° upon.

HAMLET: Thrift, thrift, Horatio! The funeral bak'd meats   180
    Did coldly furnish forth the marriage tables.
    Would I had met my dearest° foe in heaven
    Or° ever I had seen that day, Horatio!
    My father! — Methinks I see my father.

HORATIO: Where, my lord?

HAMLET: In my mind's eye, Horatio.   185

HORATIO: I saw him once. 'A° was a goodly king.

HAMLET: 'A was a man, take him for all in all,
    I shall not look upon his like again.

HORATIO: My lord, I think I saw him yesternight.

HAMLET: Saw? Who?   190

HORATIO: My lord, the King your father.

HAMLET: The King my father?

HORATIO: Season your admiration° for a while
    With an attent° ear, till I may deliver,
    Upon the witness of these gentlemen,
    This marvel to you.

HAMLET: For God's love, let me hear!   195

HORATIO: Two nights together had these gentlemen,
    Marcellus and Bernardo, on their watch,
    In the dead waste and middle of the night,
    Been thus encount'red. A figure like your father,
    Armed at point° exactly, cap-a-pe,°   200
    Appears before them, and with solemn march
    Goes slow and stately by them. Thrice he walk'd
    By their oppress'd and fear-surprised eyes
    Within his truncheon's° length, whilst they, distill'd
    Almost to jelly with the act° of fear,   205
    Stand dumb and speak not to him. This to me

---

179. hard: Close. **182. dearest:** Direst. **183. Or:** Ere, before. **186. 'A:** He. **192. Season your admiration:** Restrain your astonishment. **193. attent:** Attentive. **200. at point:** Completely. **cap-a-pe:** From head to foot. **204. truncheon:** Officer's staff. **205. act:** Action, operation.

In dreadful secrecy impart they did,
And I with them the third night kept the watch,
Where, as they had delivered, both in time,
Form of the thing, each word made true and good,   210
The apparition comes. I knew your father;
These hands are not more like.
HAMLET: But where was this?
MARCELLUS: My lord, upon the platform where we watch.
HAMLET: Did you not speak to it?
HORATIO: My lord, I did,
But answer made it none. Yet once methought   215
It lifted up it° head and did address
Itself to motion, like as it would speak;
But even then the morning cock crew loud,
And at the sound it shrunk in haste away,
And vanish'd from our sight.
HAMLET: 'Tis very strange.   220
HORATIO: As I do live, my honor'd lord, 'tis true,
And we did think it writ down in our duty
To let you know of it.
HAMLET: Indeed, indeed, sirs. But this troubles me.
Hold you the watch tonight?
ALL: We do, my lord.   225
HAMLET: Arm'd, say you?
ALL: Arm'd, my lord.
HAMLET: From top to toe?
ALL: My lord, from head to foot.
HAMLET: Then saw you not his face?
HORATIO: O, yes, my lord. He wore his beaver° up.   230
HAMLET: What, looked he frowningly?
HORATIO: A countenance more
In sorrow than in anger.
HAMLET: Pale or red?
HORATIO: Nay, very pale.
HAMLET: And fix'd his eyes upon you?
HORATIO: Most constantly.
HAMLET: I would I had been there.
HORATIO: It would have much amaz'd you.   235
HAMLET: Very like, very like. Stay'd it long?
HORATIO: While one with moderate haste might tell° a hundred.
MARCELLUS, BERNARDO: Longer, longer.
HORATIO: Not when I saw 't.
HAMLET: His beard was grizzl'd—no?   240

---

216. it: Its.   **230. beaver:** Visor on the helmet.   **237. tell:** Count.

HORATIO: It was, as I have seen it in his life,
  A sable silver'd.°
HAMLET: I will watch tonight.
  Perchance 'twill walk again.
HORATIO: I warr'nt it will.
HAMLET: If it assume my noble father's person,
  I'll speak to it, though hell itself should gape
  And bid me hold my peace. I pray you all,   245
  If you have hitherto conceal'd this sight,
  Let it be tenable° in your silence still,
  And whatsomever else shall hap tonight,
  Give it an understanding, but no tongue.
  I will requite your loves. So, fare you well.   250
  Upon the platform, 'twixt eleven and twelve,
  I'll visit you.
ALL: Our duty to your honor.
HAMLET: Your loves, as mine to you. Farewell.

                          (*Exeunt [all but Hamlet].*)

  My father's spirit in arms! All is not well.
  I doubt° some foul play. Would the night were come!   255
  Till then sit still, my soul. Foul deeds will rise,
  Though all the earth o'erwhelm them, to men's eyes.

(*Exit.*)

[Scene 3]°

(*Enter Laertes and Ophelia, his sister.*)

LAERTES: My necessaries are embark'd. Farewell.
  And, sister, as the winds give benefit
  And convoy is assistant,° do not sleep
  But let me hear from you.
OPHELIA: Do you doubt that?
LAERTES: For Hamlet, and the trifling of his favor,   5
  Hold it a fashion and a toy in blood,°
  A violet in the youth of primy° nature,
  Forward,° not permanent, sweet, not lasting,
  The perfume and suppliance° of a minute—
  No more.
OPHELIA: No more but so?

---

240. sable silver'd: Black mixed with white. **247. tenable:** Held tightly. **255. doubt:** Suspect.
ACT 1, SCENE 3. **Location:** Polonius's chambers. **3. convoy is assistant:** Means of conveyance
are available. **6. toy in blood:** Passing amorous fancy. **7. primy:** In its prime, springtime.
8. Forward: Precocious. **9. suppliance:** Supply, filler.

LAERTES: Think it no more.   10
    For nature crescent° does not grow alone
    In thews° and bulk, but, as this temple° waxes,
    The inward service of the mind and soul
    Grows wide withal.° Perhaps he loves you now,
    And now no soil° nor cautel° doth besmirch   15
    The virtue of his will;° but you must fear,
    His greatness weigh'd,° his will is not his own.
    [For he himself is subject to his birth.]
    He may not, as unvalued persons do,
    Carve° for himself; for on his choice depends   20
    The safety and health of this whole state,
    And therefore must his choice be circumscrib'd
    Unto the voice and yielding° of that body
    Whereof he is the head. Then if he says he loves you,
    It fits your wisdom so far to believe it   25
    As he in his particular act and place
    May give his saying deed,° which is no further
    Than the main voice of Denmark goes withal.
    Then weigh what loss your honor may sustain
    If with too credent° ear you list° his songs,   30
    Or lose your heart, or your chaste treasure open
    To his unmaster'd importunity.
    Fear it, Ophelia, fear it, my dear sister,
    And keep you in the rear of your affection,
    Out of the shot° and danger of desire.   35
    The chariest° maid is prodigal enough
    If she unmask her beauty to the moon.
    Virtue itself scapes not calumnious strokes.
    The canker galls° the infants of the spring
    Too oft before their buttons° be disclos'd,°   40
    And in the morn and liquid dew° of youth
    Contagious blastments° are most imminent.
    Be wary then; best safety lies in fear.
    Youth to itself rebels, though none else near.
OPHELIA: I shall the effect of this good lesson keep   45
    As watchman to my heart. But, good my brother,
    Do not, as some ungracious pastors do,

---

11. **crescent**: Growing, waxing. 12. **thews**: Bodily strength. **temple**: Body. 14. **Grows
wide withal**: Grows along with it. 15. **soil**: Blemish. **cautel**: Deceit. 16. **will**: Desire.
17. **greatness weigh'd**: High position considered. 20. **Carve**: Choose pleasure. 23. **voice
and yielding**: Assent, approval. 27. **deed**: Effect. 30. **credent**: Credulous. **list**: Listen to.
35. **shot**: Range. 36. **chariest**: Most scrupulously modest. 39. **canker galls**: Cankerworm
destroys. 40. **buttons**: Buds. **disclos'd**: Opened. 41. **liquid dew**: Time when dew is fresh.
42. **blastments**: Blights.

Show me the steep and thorny way to heaven,
Whiles, like a puff'd° and reckless libertine,
Himself the primrose path of dalliance treads,   50
And recks° not his own rede.°

(Enter Polonius.)

LAERTES: O, fear me not.
I stay too long. But here my father comes.
A double blessing is a double° grace;
Occasion° smiles upon a second leave.

POLONIUS: Yet here, Laertes? Aboard, aboard, for shame!   55
The wind sits in the shoulder of your sail,
And you are stay'd for. There — my blessing with thee!
And these few precepts in thy memory
Look thou character.° Give thy thoughts no tongue
Nor any unproportion'd thought his° act.   60
Be thou familiar,° but by no means vulgar.°
Those friends thou hast, and their adoption tried,°
Grapple them to thy soul with hoops of steel,
But do not dull thy palm with entertainment
Of each new-hatch'd, unfledg'd courage.° Beware   65
Of entrance to a quarrel, but, being in,
Bear't that° th' opposed may beware of thee.
Give every man thy ear, but few thy voice;
Take each man's censure,° but reserve thy judgment.
Costly thy habit as thy purse can buy,   70
But not express'd in fancy; rich, not gaudy,
For the apparel oft proclaims the man,
And they in France of the best rank and station
Are of a most select and generous chief° in that.
Neither a borrower nor a lender be,   75
For loan oft loses both itself and friend,
And borrowing dulleth edge of husbandry.°
This above all: to thine own self be true,
And it must follow, as the night the day,
Thou canst not then be false to any man.   80
Farewell. My blessing season° this in thee!
LAERTES: Most humbly do I take my leave, my lord.
POLONIUS: The time invests° you. Go, your servants tend.°

---

49. **puff'd:** Bloated. 51. **recks:** Heeds. **rede:** Counsel. 53. **double:** I.e., Laertes has already
bidden his father goodbye. 54. **Occasion:** Opportunity. 59. **character:** Inscribe. 60. **his:** Its.
61. **familiar:** Sociable. **vulgar:** Common. 62. **tried:** Tested. 65. **courage:** Young man of spirit.
67. **Bear't that:** Manage it so that. 69. **censure:** Opinion, judgment. 74. **generous chief:** Refined preeminence (in choosing what clothes to wear). 77. **husbandry:** Thrift. 81. **season:**
Mature. 83. **invests:** Besieges, **tend:** Attend, wait.

LAERTES: Farewell, Ophelia, and remember well
    What I have said to you.
OPHELIA: 'Tis in my memory lock'd,   85
    And you yourself shall keep the key of it.
LAERTES: Farewell.   (*Exit Laertes.*)
POLONIUS: What is 't, Ophelia, he hath said to you?
OPHELIA: So please you, something touching the Lord Hamlet.
POLONIUS: Marry,° well bethought.   90
    'Tis told me he hath very oft of late
    Given private time to you, and you yourself
    Have of your audience been most free and bounteous.
    If it be so—as so 'tis put on° me,
    And that in way of caution—I must tell you   95
    You do not understand yourself so clearly
    As it behooves my daughter and your honor.
    What is between you? Give me up the truth.
OPHELIA: He hath, my lord, of late made many tenders°
    Of his affection to me.   100
POLONIUS: Affection? Pooh! You speak like a green girl,
    Unsifted° in such perilous circumstance.
    Do you believe his tenders, as you call them?
OPHELIA: I do not know, my lord, what I should think.
POLONIUS: Marry, I will teach you. Think yourself a baby   105
    That you have ta'en these tenders° for true pay,
    Which are not sterling.° Tender° yourself more dearly,
    Or—not to crack the wind° of the poor phrase,
    Running it thus—you'll tender me a fool.°
OPHELIA: My lord, he hath importun'd me with love   110
    In honorable fashion.
POLONIUS: Ay, fashion° you may call it. Go to, go to.
OPHELIA: And hath given countenance° to his speech, my lord,
    With almost all the holy vows of heaven.
POLONIUS: Ay, springes° to catch woodcocks.° I do know,   115
    When the blood burns, how prodigal the soul
    Lends the tongue vows. These blazes, daughter,
    Giving more light than heat, extinct in both
    Even in their promise, as it is a-making,
    You must not take for fire. From this time   120

---

90. Marry: By the Virgin Mary (a mild oath).   **94. put on:** Impressed on, told to.   **99. tenders:** Offers.   **102. Unsifted:** Untried.   **106. tenders:** With added meaning here of *promises to pay.*   **107. sterling:** Legal currency. **Tender:** Hold,   **108. crack the wind:** Run it until it is broken, winded.   **109. tender me a fool:** (1) Show yourself to me as a fool, (2) show me up as a fool, (3) present me with a grandchild (*fool* was a term of endearment for a child). **112. fashion:** Mere form, pretense.   **113. countenance:** Credit, support.   **115. springes:** Snares. **woodcocks:** Birds easily caught; here used to connote gullibility.

Be something scanter of your maiden presence.
Set your entreatments° at a higher rate
Than a command to parle.° For Lord Hamlet,
Believe so much in him° that he is young,
And with a larger tether may he walk   125
Than may be given you. In few,° Ophelia,
Do not believe his vows, for they are brokers,°
Not of that dye° which their investments° show,
But mere implorators° of unholy suits,
Breathing° like sanctified and pious bawds,   130
The better to beguile. This is for all:
I would not, in plain terms, from this time forth
Have you so slander° any moment leisure
As to give words or talk with the Lord Hamlet.
Look to 't, I charge you. Come your ways.   135
OPHELIA: I shall obey, my lord.   (*Exeunt.*)

[Scene 4]°

(*Enter Hamlet, Horatio, and Marcellus.*)

HAMLET: The air bites shrewdly; it is very cold.
HORATIO: It is a nipping and an eager air.
HAMLET: What hour now?
HORATIO: I think it lacks of twelve.
MARCELLUS: No, it is struck.
HORATIO: Indeed? I heard it not.
It then draws near the season   5
Wherein the spirit held his wont to walk.

(*A flourish of trumpets, and two pieces° go off [within].*)

What does this mean, my lord?
HAMLET: The King doth wake° tonight and takes his rouse,°
Keeps wassail,° and the swagg'ring up-spring° reels;
And as he drains his draughts of Rhenish° down,   10
The kettle-drum and trumpet thus bray out
The triumph of his pledge.°

---

122. **entreatments:** Negotiations for surrender (a military term).   123. **parle:** Discuss terms
with the enemy. (Polonius urges his daughter, in the metaphor of military language, not to meet
with Hamlet and consider giving in to him merely because he requests an interview.)
124. **so . . . him:** This much concerning him.   126. **In few:** Briefly.   127. **brokers:** Go-betweens,
procurers.   128. **dye:** Color or sort. **investments:** Clothes (i.e., they are not what they seem).
129. **mere implorators:** Out-and-out solicitors.   130. **Breathing:** Speaking.   133. **slander:**
Bring disgrace or reproach upon. ACT 1, SCENE 4. **Location:** The guard platform. [S.D.] ***pieces:*** I.e.,
of ordnance, cannon.   8. **wake:** Stay awake and hold revel. **rouse:** Carouse, drinking bout.
9. **wassail:** Carousal. **up-spring:** Wild German dance.   10. **Rhenish:** Rhine wine.   12. **triumph . . .**
pledge: His feat in draining the wine in a single draft.

HORATIO: Is it a custom?
HAMLET: Ay, marry, is 't,
  But to my mind, though I am native here
  And to the manner° born, it is a custom   15
  More honor'd in the breach than the observance.°
  This heavy-headed revel east and west°
  Makes us traduc'd and tax'd of° other nations.
  They clepe° us drunkards, and with swinish phrase°
  Soil our addition;° and indeed it takes   20
  From our achievements, though perform'd at height,°
  The pith and marrow of our attribute.
  So, oft it chances in particular men,
  That for some vicious mole of nature° in them,
  As in their birth—wherein they are not guilty,   25
  Since nature cannot choose his° origin—
  By the o'ergrowth of some complexion,°
  Oft breaking down the pales° and forts of reason,
  Or by some habit that too much o'er-leavens°
  The form of plausive° manners, that these men,   30
  Carrying, I say, the stamp of one defect,
  Being nature's livery,° or fortune's star,°
  Their virtues else, be they as pure as grace,
  As infinite as man may undergo,
  Shall in the general censure take corruption   35
  From that particular fault. The dram of eale°
  Doth all the noble substance of a doubt
  To his own scandal.

(*Enter Ghost.*)

HORATIO: Look, my lord, it comes!
HAMLET: Angels and ministers of grace defend us!
  Be thou a spirit of health° or goblin damn'd,   40
  Bring with thee airs from heaven or blasts from hell,
  Be thy intents wicked or charitable,
  Thou com'st in such a questionable° shape

---

15. **manner:** Custom (of drinking).   16. **More . . . observance:** Better neglected than followed.
17. **east and west:** I.e., everywhere.   18. **tax'd of:** Censured by.   19. **clepe:** Call. **with swinish phrase:** By calling us swine.   20. **addition:** Reputation.   21. **at height:** Outstandingly.   24. **mole of nature:** Natural blemish in one's constitution.   26. **his:** Its.   27. **complexion:** Humor (i.e., one of the four humors or fluids thought to determine temperament).   28. **pales:** Palings, fences (as of a fortification).   29. **o'er-leavens:** Induces a change throughout (as yeast works in dough).   30. **plausive:** Pleasing.   32. **nature's livery:** Endowment from nature. **fortune's star:** Mark placed by fortune.   36–38. **The dram . . . scandal:** Small drop of evil blots out the noble substance of the whole and brings it into disrepute.   38. **To . . . scandal:** To the disgrace of the whole enterprise.   40. **of health:** Of spiritual good.   43. **questionable:** Inviting question or conversation.

That I will speak to thee. I'll call thee Hamlet,
King, father, royal Dane. O, answer me!   45
Let me not burst in ignorance, but tell
Why thy canoniz'd° bones, hearsed° in death,
Have burst their cerements;° why the sepulcher
Wherein we saw thee quietly interr'd
Hath op'd his ponderous and marble jaws   50
To cast thee up again. What may this mean,
That thou, dead corse, again in complete steel
Revisits thus the glimpses of the moon,°
Making night hideous, and we fools of nature°
So horridly to shake our disposition   55
With thoughts beyond the reaches of our souls?
Say, why is this? Wherefore? What should we do?

                                            ([*Ghost*] *beckons* [*Hamlet*].)

HORATIO: It beckons you to go away with it,
     As if it some impartment° did desire
     To you alone.
MARCELLUS: Look with what courteous action   60
     It waves you to a more removed ground.
     But do not go with it.
HORATIO: No, by no means.
HAMLET: It will not speak. Then I will follow it.
HORATIO: Do not, my lord.
HAMLET: Why, what should be the fear?
     I do not set my life at a pin's fee,°   65
     And for my soul, what can it do to that,
     Being a thing immortal as itself?
     It waves me forth again. I'll follow it.
HORATIO: What if it tempt you toward the flood, my lord
     Or to the dreadful summit of the cliff   70
     That beetles o'er° his° base into the sea,
     And there assume some other horrible form
     Which might deprive your sovereignty of reason,°
     And draw you into madness? Think of it.
     The very place puts toys of desperation,°   75
     Without more motive, into every brain
     That looks so many fathoms to the sea
     And hears it roar beneath.

---

47. **canoniz'd:** Buried according to the canons of the church. **hearsed:** Coffined. **48. cerements:** Grave-clothes. **53. glimpses of the moon:** Earth by night. **54. fools of nature:** Mere men, limited to natural knowledge. **59. impartment:** Communication. **65. fee:** Value. **71. beetles o'er:** Overhangs threateningly. **his:** Its. **73. deprive . . . reason:** Take away the rule of reason over your mind. **75. toys of desperation:** Fancies of desperate acts, i.e., suicide.

HAMLET: It waves me still.
   Go on, I'll follow thee.
MARCELLUS: You shall not go, my lord.

                                                        [They try to stop him.]

HAMLET: Hold off your hands!   80
HORATIO: Be rul'd, you shall not go.
HAMLET: My fate cries out,
   And makes each petty artery° in this body
   As hardy as the Nemean lion's° nerve.°
   Still am I call'd. Unhand me, gentlemen.
   By heaven, I'll make a ghost of him that lets° me!   85
   I say, away! Go on. I'll follow thee.

                                  (Exeunt Ghost and Hamlet.)

HORATIO: He waxes desperate with imagination.
MARCELLUS: Let's follow. 'Tis not fit thus to obey him.
HORATIO: Have after. To what issue° will this come?
MARCELLUS: Something is rotten in the state of Denmark.   90
HORATIO: Heaven will direct it.°
MARCELLUS: Nay, let's follow him.   *(Exeunt.)*

   [Scene 5]°

(Enter Ghost and Hamlet.)

HAMLET: Whither wilt thou lead me? Speak. I'll go no further.
GHOST: Mark me.
HAMLET: I will.
GHOST: My hour is almost come,
   When I to sulph'rous and tormenting flames
   Must render up myself.
HAMLET: Alas, poor ghost!
GHOST: Pity me not, but lend thy serious hearing   5
   To what I shall unfold.
HAMLET: Speak. I am bound to hear.
GHOST: So art thou to revenge, when thou shalt hear.
HAMLET: What?
GHOST: I am thy father's spirit,
   Doom'd for a certain term to walk the night,   10
   And for the day confin'd to fast° in fires,
   Till the foul crimes° done in my days of nature
   Are burnt and purg'd away. But that° I am forbid

---

82. artery: Sinew. **83. Nemean lion:** One of the monsters slain by Hercules in his twelve labors.
nerve: Sinew **85. lets:** Hinders. **89. issue:** Outcome. **91. it:** The outcome. ACT 1, SCENE 5.
Location: The battlements of the castle. **11. fast:** Do penance. **12. crimes:** Sins. **13. But that:**
Were it not that.

To tell the secrets of my prison-house,
I could a tale unfold whose lightest word   15
Would harrow up thy soul, freeze thy young blood,
Make thy two eyes, like stars, start from their spheres,°
Thy knotted and combined locks° to part,
And each particular hair to stand an end,°
Like quills upon the fearful porpentine.°   20
But this eternal blazon° must not be
To ears of flesh and blood. List, list, O, list!
If thou didst ever thy dear father love—

HAMLET: O God!

GHOST: Revenge his foul and most unnatural murder.   25

HAMLET: Murder?

GHOST: Murder most foul, as in the best it is,
But this most foul, strange, and unnatural.

HAMLET: Haste me to know 't, that I, with wings as swift
As meditation or the thoughts of love,   30
May sweep to my revenge.

GHOST: I find thee apt;
And duller shouldst thou be than the fat weed
That roots itself in ease on Lethe° wharf,°
Wouldst thou not stir in this. Now, Hamlet, hear.
'Tis given out that, sleeping in my orchard,   35
A serpent stung me. So the whole ear of Denmark
Is by a forged process° of my death
Rankly abus'd.° But know, thou noble youth,
The serpent that did sting thy father's life
Now wears his crown.

HAMLET: O my prophetic soul!   40
My uncle!

GHOST: Ay, that incestuous, that adulterate° beast,
With witchcraft of his wits, with traitorous gifts—
O wicked wit and gifts, that have the power
So to seduce!—won to his shameful lust   45
The will of my most seeming-virtuous queen.
O Hamlet, what a falling off was there!
From me, whose love was of that dignity
That it went hand in hand even with the vow

---

17. spheres: Eye sockets, here compared to the orbits or transparent revolving spheres in
which, according to Ptolemaic astronomy, the heavenly bodies were fixed. **18. knotted . . .
locks:** Hair neatly arranged and confined. **19. an end:** On end. **20. fearful porpentine:**
Frightened porcupine. **21. eternal blazon:** Revelation of the secrets of eternity. **33. Lethe:**
The river of forgetfulness in Hades. **wharf:** Bank. **37. forged process:** Falsified account.
38. abus'd: Deceived. **42. adulterate:** Adulterous.

I made to her in marriage, and to decline　　　　　　　　　50
Upon a wretch whose natural gifts were poor
To those of mine!
But virtue, as it never will be moved,
Though lewdness court it in a shape of heaven,°
So lust, though to a radiant angel link'd,　　　　　　　　　55
Will sate itself in a celestial bed,
And prey on garbage.
But, soft, methinks I scent the morning air.
Brief let me be. Sleeping within my orchard,
My custom always of the afternoon,　　　　　　　　　　　60
Upon my secure° hour thy uncle stole,
With juice of cursed hebona° in a vial,
And in the porches of my ears did pour
The leprous° distillment, whose effect
Holds such an enmity with blood of man　　　　　　　　　65
That swift as quicksilver it courses through
The natural gates and alleys of the body,
And with a sudden vigor it doth posset°
And curd, like eager° droppings into milk,
The thin and wholesome blood. So did it mine,　　　　　70
And a most instant tetter° bark'd° about,
Most lazar-like,° with vile and loathsome crust,
All my smooth body.
Thus was I, sleeping, by a brother's hand
Of life, of crown, of queen, at once dispatch'd,°　　　　　75
Cut off even in the blossoms of my sin,
Unhous'led,° disappointed,° unanel'd,°
No reck'ning made, but sent to my account
With all my imperfections on my head.
O, horrible! O, horrible, most horrible!　　　　　　　　　80
If thou hast nature° in thee, bear it not.
Let not the royal bed of Denmark be
A couch for luxury° and damned incest.
But, howsomever thou pursues this act,
Taint not thy mind, nor let thy soul contrive　　　　　　85
Against thy mother aught. Leave her to heaven

---

54. shape of heaven: Heavenly form. **61. secure:** Confident, unsuspicious. **62. hebona:** Poison. (The word seems to be a form of *ebony*, though it is thought perhaps to be related to *henbane*, a poison, or to *ebenus*, yew.) **64. leprous:** Causing leprosy-like disfigurement. **68. posset:** Coagulate, curdle. **69. eager:** Sour, acid. **71. tetter:** Eruption of scabs. **bark'd:** Covered with a rough covering, like bark on a tree. **72. lazar-like:** Leper-like. **75. dispatch'd:** Suddenly deprived. **77. Unhous'led:** Without having received the sacrament [of Holy Communion]. **disappointed:** Unready (spiritually) for the last journey. **unanel'd:** Without having received extreme unction. **81. nature:** The promptings of a son. **83. luxury:** Lechery.

And to those thorns that in her bosom lodge,
To prick and sting her. Fare thee well at once.
The glow-worm shows the matin° to be near,
And 'gins to pale his uneffectual fire.°   90
Adieu, adieu, adieu! Remember me.   [*Exit.*]
HAMLET: O all you host of heaven! O earth! What else?
And shall I couple° hell? O fie! Hold, hold, my heart,
And you, my sinews, grow not instant old,
But bear me stiffly up. Remember thee!   95
Ay, thou poor ghost, whiles memory holds a seat
In this distracted globe.° Remember thee!
Yea, from the table° of my memory
I'll wipe away all trivial fond° records,
All saws° of books, all forms,° all pressures° past   100
That youth and observation copied there,
And thy commandment all alone shall live
Within the book and volume of my brain,
Unmix'd with baser matter. Yes, by heaven!
O most pernicious woman!   105
O villain, villain, smiling, damned villain!
My tables—meet it is I set it down,
That one may smile, and smile, and be a villain.
At least I am sure it may be so in Denmark.

                                             [*Writing.*]

So, uncle, there you are. Now to my word;   110
It is "Adieu, adieu! Remember me."
I have sworn 't.

(*Enter Horatio and Marcellus.*)

HORATIO: My lord, my lord!
MARCELLUS: Lord Hamlet!
HORATIO: Heavens secure him!
HAMLET: So be it!
MARCELLUS: Illo, ho, ho,° my lord!   115
HAMLET: Hillo, ho, ho,° boy! Come, bird, come.
MARCELLUS: How is 't, my noble lord?
HORATIO: What news, my lord?
HAMLET: O, wonderful!
HORATIO: Good my lord, tell it.
HAMLET: No, you will reveal it.

---

89. matin: Morning. **90. uneffectual fire:** Cold light. **93. couple:** Add. **97. globe:** Head.
98. table: Writing tablet. **99. fond:** Foolish. **100. saws:** Wise sayings. **forms:** Images. **pressures:** Impressions stamped. **115. Illo, ho, ho:** Halloo. **116. Hillo, ho, ho:** A falconer's call to a hawk in air. Hamlet is playing upon Marcellus's *Illo.*

HORATIO: Not I, my lord, by heaven.

MARCELLUS: Nor I, my lord.   120

HAMLET: How say you, then, would heart of man once think it?
    But you'll be secret?

HORATIO, MARCELLUS: Ay, by heaven, my lord.

HAMLET: There's never a villain dwelling in all Denmark
    But he's an arrant° knave.

HORATIO: There needs no ghost, my lord, come from the grave   125
    To tell us this.

HAMLET: Why, right, you are in the right.
    And so, without more circumstance° at all,
    I hold it fit that we shake hands and part,
    You as your business and desire shall point you—
    For every man hath business and desire,   130
    Such as it is—and for my own poor part,
    Look you, I'll go pray.

HORATIO: These are but wild and whirling words, my lord.

HAMLET: I am sorry they offend you, heartily;
    Yes, faith, heartily.

HORATIO: There's no offense, my lord.   135

HAMLET: Yes, by Saint Patrick,° but there is, Horatio,
    And much offense too. Touching this vision here,
    It is an honest° ghost, that let me tell you.
    For your desire to know what is between us,
    O'ermaster 't as you may. And now, good friends   140
    As you are friends, scholars, and soldiers,
    Give me one poor request.

HORATIO: What is 't, my lord? We will.

HAMLET: Never make known what you have seen tonight.

HORATIO, MARCELLUS: My lord, we will not.

HAMLET: Nay, but swear't.

HORATIO: In faith,   145
    my lord, not I.

MARCELLUS: Nor I, my lord, in faith.

HAMLET: Upon my sword.°   [*Holds out his sword.*]

MARCELLUS: We have sworn, my lord, already.

HAMLET: Indeed, upon my sword, indeed.

                           (*Ghost cries under the stage.*)

GHOST: Swear.

HAMLET: Ha, ha, boy, say'st thou so? Art thou there, truepenny?°   150

---

124. **arrant:** Thoroughgoing.   127. **circumstance:** Ceremony.   136. **Saint Patrick:** The keeper of purgatory and patron saint of all blunders and confusion.   138. **honest:** I.e., a real ghost and not an evil spirit.   147. **sword:** The hilt in the form of a cross.   150. **truepenny:** Honest old fellow.

Come on, you hear this fellow in the cellarage.
Consent to swear.
HORATIO: Propose the oath, my lord.
HAMLET: Never to speak of this that you have seen,
Swear by my sword.
GHOST [*beneath*]: Swear.   155
HAMLET: Hic et ubique?° Then we'll shift our ground.

[*He moves to another spot.*]

Come hither, gentlemen,
And lay your hands again upon my sword.
Swear by my sword.
Never to speak of this that you have heard.   160
GHOST [*beneath*]: Swear by his sword.
HAMLET: Well said, old mole! Canst work i' th' earth so fast?
A worthy pioner!° Once more remove, good friends.

[*Moves again.*]

HORATIO: O day and night, but this is wondrous strange!
HAMLET: And therefore as a stranger give it welcome.   165
There are more things in heaven and earth, Horatio,
Than are dreamt of in your philosophy.°
But come;
Here, as before, never, so help you mercy,
How strange or odd soe'er I bear myself—   170
As I perchance hereafter shall think meet
To put an antic° disposition on—
That you, at such times seeing me, never shall,
With arms encumb'red° thus, or this headshake,
Or by pronouncing of some doubtful phrase,   175
As "Well, well, we know," or "We could, an if° we would,"
Or "If we list° to speak," or "There be, an if they might,"
Or such ambiguous giving out,° to note°
That you know aught of me—this do swear,
So grace and mercy at your most need help you.   180
GHOST [*beneath*]: Swear.   [*They swear.*]
HAMLET: Rest, rest, perturbed spirit! So, gentlemen,
With all my love I do commend me to you;
And what so poor a man as Hamlet is

---

156. Hic et ubique: Here and everywhere (Latin).   163. pioner: Pioneer, digger, miner.
167. your philosophy: This subject called "natural philosophy" or "science" that people
talk about.   172. antic: Fantastic.   174. encumb'red: Folded or entwined.   176. an if: If.
177. list: Were inclined.   178. giving out: Profession of knowledge. note: Give a sign,
indicate.

May do, t' express his love and friending to you,   185
God willing, shall not lack. Let us go in together,
And still° your fingers on your lips, I pray.
The time is out of joint. O cursed spite,
That ever I was born to set it right!

[They wait for him to leave first.]

Nay, come, let's go together.   (*Exeunt.*)

[ACT 2 / Scene 1]°

(*Enter old Polonius, with his man [Reynaldo].*)

POLONIUS: Give him this money and these notes, Reynaldo.
REYNALDO: I will, my lord.
POLONIUS: You shall do marvel's° wisely, good Reynaldo,
    Before you visit him, to make inquire
    Of his behavior.
REYNALDO: My lord, I did intend it.   5
POLONIUS: Marry, well said, very well said. Look you, sir,
    Inquire me first what Danskers° are in Paris,
    And how, and who, what means,° and where they keep,°
    What company, at what expense; and finding
    By this encompassment° and drift° of question   10
    That they do know my son, come you more nearer
    Than your particular demands will touch it.°
    Take° you, as 'twere, some distant knowledge of him,
    As thus, "I know his father and his friends,
    And in part him." Do you mark this, Reynaldo?   15
REYNALDO: Ay, very well, my lord.
POLONIUS: "And in part him, but," you may say, "not well.
    But, if't be he I mean, he's very wild,
    Addicted so and so," and there put on° him
    What forgeries° you please — marry, none so rank   20
    As may dishonor him, take heed of that,
    But, sir, such wanton,° wild, and usual slips,
    As are companions noted and most known
    To youth and liberty.
REYNALDO: As gaming, my lord.

---

187. **still:** Always. Act 2, Scene 1. **Location:** Polonius's chambers.   3. **marvel's:** Marvelous(ly).
7. **Danskers:** Danes.   8. **what means:** What wealth (they have). **keep:** Dwell.   10. **encompass-
ment:** Roundabout talking. **drift:** Gradual approach or course.   **11–12. come . . . it:** You will find
out more this way than by asking pointed questions (particular demands).   13. **Take:** Assume,
pretend.   19. **put on:** Impute to.   20. **forgeries:** Invented tales.   22. **wanton:** Sportive, unrestrained.

POLONIUS: Ay, or drinking, fencing, swearing,   25
    Quarreling, drabbing°—you may go so far.
REYNALDO: My lord, that would dishonor him.
POLONIUS: Faith, no, as you may season° it in the charge.
    You must not put another scandal on him
    That he is open to incontinency;°   30
    That's not my meaning. But breathe his faults so quaintly°
    That they may seem the taints of liberty,°
    The flash and outbreak of a fiery mind,
    A savageness in unreclaimed° blood,
    Of general assault.°
REYNALDO: But, my good lord—   35
POLONIUS: Wherefore should you do this?
REYNALDO: Ay, my lord,
    I would know that.
POLONIUS: Marry, sir, here's my drift,
    And, I believe, it is a fetch of wit.°
    You laying these slight sullies on my son,
    As 'twere a thing a little soil'd i' th' working,°   40
    Mark you,
    Your party in converse,° him you would sound,°
    Having ever° seen in the prenominate crimes°
    The youth you breathe° of guilty, be assur'd
    He closes with you in this consequence:°   45
    "Good sir," or so, or "friend," or "gentleman,"
    According to the phrase or the addition°
    Of man and country.
REYNALDO: Very good, my lord.
POLONIUS: And then, sir, does 'a this—'a does—what was I about to say?
    By the mass, I was about to say something.   50
    Where did I leave?
REYNALDO: At "closes in the consequence."
POLONIUS: At "closes in the consequence," ay, marry.
    He closes thus: "I know the gentleman;
    I saw him yesterday, or th' other day,   55
    Or then, or then, with such, or such, and, as you say,
    There was 'a gaming, there o' ertook in 's rouse,°
    There falling out° at tennis," or perchance,

---

26. **drabbing:** Whoring. 28. **season:** Temper, soften. 30. **incontinency:** Habitual loose
behavior. 31. **quaintly:** Delicately, ingeniously. 32. **taints of liberty:** Faults resulting from
freedom. 34. **unreclaimed:** Untamed. 35. **general assault:** Tendency that assails all unrestrained youth. 38. **fetch of wit:** Clever trick. 40. **soil'd i' th' working:** Shopworn.
42. **converse:** Conversation. **sound:** Sound out. 43. **Having ever:** If he has ever. **prenominate
crimes:** Before-mentioned offenses. 44. **breathe:** Speak. 45. **closes . . . consequence:** Follows
your lead in some fashion as follows. 47. **addition:** Title. 57. **o'ertook in 's rouse:** Overcome
by drink. 58. **falling out:** Quarreling.

"I saw him enter such a house of sale,"
Videlicet,° a brothel, or so forth.   60
See you now,
Your bait of falsehood takes this carp° of truth;
And thus do we of wisdom and of reach,°
With windlasses° and with assays of bias,°
By indirections find directions° out.   65
So by my former lecture and advice
Shall you my son. You have me, have you not?
REYNALDO: My lord, I have.
POLONIUS: God buy ye; fare ye well.
REYNALDO: Good my lord.
POLONIUS: Observe his inclination in yourself.°   70
REYNALDO: I shall, my lord.
POLONIUS: And let him ply° his music.
REYNALDO: Well, my lord.
POLONIUS: Farewell.   (*Exit Reynaldo.*)

(*Enter Ophelia.*)

                    How now, Ophelia, what's the matter?
OPHELIA: O, my lord, my lord, I have been so affrighted!
POLONIUS: With what, i' th' name of God?   75
OPHELIA: My lord, as I was sewing in my closet,°
    Lord Hamlet, with his doublet° all unbrac'd,°
    No hat upon his head, his stockings fouled,
    Ungart'red, and down-gyved to his ankle,°
    Pale as his shirt, his knees knocking each other,   80
    And with a look so piteous in purport
    As if he had been loosed out of hell
    To speak of horrors—he comes before me.
POLONIUS: Mad for thy love?
OPHELIA: My lord, I do not know,
    But truly I do fear it.
POLONIUS: What said he?   85
OPHELIA: He took me by the wrist and held me hard.
    Then goes he to the length of all his arm,
    And, with his other hand thus o'er his brow
    He falls to such perusal of my face
    As 'a would draw it. Long stay'd he so.   90

---

60. **Videlicet:** Namely. 61. **carp:** A fish. 63. **reach:** Capacity, ability. 64. **windlasses:**
Circuitous paths (literally, circuits made to head off the game in hunting). **assays of bias:**
Attempts through indirection (like the curving path of the bowling ball, which is biased
or weighted to one side). 65. **directions:** The way things really are. 70. **in yourself:** In
your own person (as well as by asking questions). 72. **let him ply:** See that he continues to
study. 76. **closet:** Private chamber. 77. **doublet:** Close-fitting jacket. **unbrac'd:** Unfastened.
79. **down-gyved to his ankle:** Fallen to the ankles (like gyves or fetters).

At last, a little shaking of mine arm
And thrice his head thus waving up and down,
He rais'd a sigh so piteous and profound
As it did seem to shatter all his bulk°
And end his being. That done, he lets me go, 95
And, with his head over his shoulder turn'd,
He seem'd to find his way without his eyes,
For out o' doors he went without their helps,
And, to the last, bended their light on me.

POLONIUS: Come, go with me. I will go seek the King. 100
This is the very ecstasy° of love
Whose violent property° fordoes° itself
And leads the will to desperate undertakings
As oft as any passion under heaven
That does afflict our natures. I am sorry. 105
What, have you given him any hard words of late?

OPHELIA: No, my good lord, but, as you did command,
I did repel his letters and denied
His access to me.

POLONIUS: That hath made him mad.
I am sorry that with better heed and judgment 110
I had not quoted° him. I fear'd he did but trifle
And meant to wrack thee; but, beshrew my jealousy!°
By heaven, it is as proper to our age°
To cast beyond° ourselves in our opinions
As it is common for the younger sort 115
To lack discretion. Come, go we to the King.
This must be known, which, being kept close,° might move
More grief to hide than hate to utter love.°
Come.   (*Exeunt.*)

[Scene 2]°

(*Flourish. Enter King and Queen, Rosencrantz, and Guildenstern [with others].*)

KING: Welcome, dear Rosencrantz and Guildenstern.
Moreover that° we much did long to see you,
The need we have to use you did provoke
Our hasty sending. Something have you heard

---

94. **bulk:** Body. 101. **ecstasy:** Madness. 102. **property:** Nature. **fordoes:** Destroys.
111. **quoted:** Observed. 112. **beshrew my jealousy:** A plague upon my suspicious nature. 113. **proper . . . age:** Characteristic of us (old) men. 114. **cast beyond:** Overshoot,
miscalculate. 117. **close:** Secret. 117–118. **might . . . love:** Might cause more grief (to others) by hiding the knowledge of Hamlet's strange behavior to Ophelia than hatred by telling it.
ACT 2, SCENE 2. **Location:** The castle. 2. **Moreover that:** Besides the fact that.

Of Hamlet's transformation—so call it,   5
Sith° nor th' exterior nor° the inward man
Resembles that° it was. What it should be,
More than his father's death, that thus hath put him
So much from th' understanding of himself,
I cannot dream of. I entreat you both   10
That, being of so young days° brought up with him,
And sith so neighbor'd to his youth and havior,
That you vouchsafe your rest° here in our court
Some little time, so by your companies
To draw him on to pleasures, and to gather   15
So much as from occasion you may glean,
Whether aught to us unknown afflicts him thus,
That, open'd,° lies within our remedy.
QUEEN: Good gentlemen, he hath much talk'd of you
And sure I am two men there is not living   20
To whom he more adheres. If it will please you
To show us so much gentry° and good will
As to expend your time with us awhile
For the supply and profit° of our hope,
Your visitation shall receive such thanks   25
As fits a king's remembrance.
ROSENCRANTZ: Both your Majesties
Might, by the sovereign power you have of us,
Put your dread pleasures more into command
Than to entreaty.
GUILDENSTERN: But we both obey,
And here give up ourselves in the full bent°   30
To lay our service freely at your feet,
To be commanded.
KING: Thanks, Rosencrantz and gentle Guildenstern.
QUEEN: Thanks, Guildenstern and gentle Rosencrantz.
And I beseech you instantly to visit.   35
My too much changed son. Go, some of you,
And bring these gentlemen where Hamlet is.
GUILDENSTERN: Heavens make our presence and our practices
Pleasant and helpful to him!
QUEEN: Ay, amen!

    (*Exeunt Rosencrantz and Guildenstern* [*with some Attendants*].)

(*Enter Polonius.*)

---

6. **Sith:** Since. **nor . . . nor:** Neither . . . nor.   7. **that:** What.   11. **of . . . days:** From such early
youth.   13. **vouchsafe your rest:** Please to stay.   18. **open'd:** Revealed.   22. **gentry:** Courtesy.
24. **supply and profit:** Aid and successful outcome.   30. **in . . . bent:** To the utmost degree of
our capacity.

POLONIUS: Th' ambassadors from Norway, my good lord,   40
    Are joyfully return'd.
KING: Thou still° hast been the father of good news.
POLONIUS: Have I, my lord? I assure my good liege
    I hold my duty, as I hold my soul,
    Both to my God and to my gracious king;   45
    And I do think, or else this brain of mine
    Hunts not the trail of policy so sure
    As it hath us'd to do, that I have found
    The very cause of Hamlet's lunacy.
KING: O, speak of that! That do I long to hear.   50
POLONIUS: Give first admittance to th' ambassadors.
    My news shall be the fruit° to that great feast.
KING: Thyself do grace to them, and bring them in.

                             (*Exit Polonius.*)

    He tells me, my dear Gertrude, he hath found
    The head and source of all your son's distemper.   55
QUEEN: I doubt° it is no other but the main,°
    His father's death, and our o'erhasty marriage.

(*Enter Ambassadors [Voltimand and Cornelius, with Polonius].*)

KING: Well, we shall sift° him. — Welcome, my good friends!
    Say, Voltimand, what from our brother Norway?
VOLTIMAND: Most fair return of greetings and desires.   60
    Upon our first,° he sent out to suppress
    His nephew's levies, which to him appear'd
    To be a preparation 'gainst the Polack,
    But, better look'd into, he truly found
    It was against your Highness. Whereat griev'd   65
    That so his sickness, age, and impotence
    Was falsely borne in hand,° sends out arrests
    On Fortinbras, which he, in brief, obeys,
    Receives rebuke from Norway, and in fine°
    Makes vow before his uncle never more   70
    To give th' assay° of arms against your Majesty.
    Whereon old Norway, overcome with joy,
    Gives him three score thousand crowns in annual fee,
    And his commission to employ those soldiers,
    So levied as before, against the Polack,   75
    With an entreaty, herein further shown,

---

42. still: Always.   52. fruit: Dessert.   56. doubt: Fear, suspect. main: Chief point, principal concern.   58. sift: Question.   61. Upon our first: At our first words on the business.   67. borne in hand: Deluded, taken advantage of.   69. in fine: In the end.   71. assay: Trial.

[*Giving a paper.*]

That it might please you to give quiet pass
Through your dominions for this enterprise,
On such regards of safety and allowance°
As therein are set down.
KING: It likes° us well;   80
And at our more consider'd° time we'll read,
Answer, and think upon this business.
Meantime we thank you for your well-took labor.
Go to your rest; at night we'll feast together.
Most welcome home!   (*Exeunt Ambassadors.*)
POLONIUS: This business is well ended.   85
My liege, and madam, to expostulate°
What majesty should be, what duty is,
Why day is day, night night, and time is time,
Were nothing but to waste night, day, and time.
Therefore, since brevity is the soul of wit,°   90
And tediousness the limbs and outward flourishes,
I will be brief. Your noble son is mad.
Mad call I it, for, to define true madness,
What is 't but to be nothing else but mad?
But let that go.
QUEEN: More matter, with less art.   95
POLONIUS: Madam, I swear I use no art at all.
That he is mad, 'tis true; 'tis true 'tis pity,
And pity 'tis 'tis true—a foolish figure,°
But farewell it, for I will use no art.
Mad let us grant him, then, and now remains   100
That we find out the cause of this effect,
Or rather say, the cause of this defect,
For this effect defective comes by cause.°
Thus it remains, and the remainder thus.
Perpend.°   105
I have a daughter—have while she is mine—
Who, in her duty and obedience, mark,
Hath given me this. Now gather, and surmise.
[*Reads the letter.*] "To the celestial and my soul's idol,
the most beautified Ophelia"—   110
That's an ill phrase, a vile phrase; "beautified" is a vile
phrase. But you shall hear. Thus: [*Reads.*]

---

79. On . . . allowance: With such pledges of safety and provisos. **80. likes:** Pleases.
81. consider'd: Suitable for deliberation. **86. expostulate:** Expound. **90. wit:** Sound sense
or judgment. **98. figure:** Figure of speech. **103. For . . . cause:** I.e., for this defective behavior, this madness has a cause. **105. Perpend:** Consider.

"In her excellent white bosom, these, etc."

QUEEN: Came this from Hamlet to her?

POLONIUS: Good madam, stay awhile; I will be faithful.   [*Reads.*] 115

> "Doubt° thou the stars are fire,
>> Doubt that the sun doth move,
> Doubt truth to be a liar,
>> But never doubt I love.

O dear Ophelia, I am ill at these numbers.° I have   120
not art to reckon° my groans. But that I love thee
best, O most best, believe it. Adieu.

>> Thine evermore, most dear lady, whilst this
>>> machine° is to him, Hamlet."

This in obedience hath my daughter shown me,
And, more above,° hath his solicitings,   125
As they fell out° by time, by means, and place,
All given to mine ear.

KING: But how hath she
Receiv'd his love?

POLONIUS: What do you think of me?

KING: As of a man faithful and honorable.

POLONIUS: I would fain prove so. But what might you think,   130
When I had seen this hot love on the wing—
As I perceiv'd it, I must tell you that,
Before my daughter told me—what might you,
Or my dear Majesty your Queen here, think,
If I had play'd the desk or table-book,°   135
Or given my heart a winking,° mute and dumb,
Or look'd upon this love with idle sight?°
What might you think? No, I went round° to work,
And my young mistress thus I did bespeak:°
"Lord Hamlet is a prince, out of thy star;°   140
This must not be." And then I prescripts gave her,
That she should lock herself from his resort,
Admit no messengers, receive no tokens.
Which done, she took the fruits of my advice;
And he, repelled—a short tale to make—   145
Fell into a sadness, then into a fast,
Thence to a watch,° thence into a weakness,
Thence to a lightness,° and, by this declension,°

---

116. **Doubt:** Suspect, question.   120. **ill ... numbers:** Unskilled at writing verses.   121. **reckon:** (1) Count, (2) number metrically, scan.   123. **machine:** Body.   125. **more above:** Moreover.   126. **fell out:** Occurred.   135. **play'd ... table-book:** Remained shut up, concealing the information.   136. **winking:** Closing of the eyes.   137. **with idle sight:** Complacently or uncomprehendingly.   138. **round:** Roundly, plainly.   139. **bespeak:** Address.   140. **out of thy star:** Above your sphere, position.   147. **watch:** State of sleeplessness.   148. **lightness:** Light-headedness. **declension:** Decline, deterioration.

Into the madness wherein now he raves,
And all we mourn for.
KING: Do you think this?   150
QUEEN: It may be, very like.
POLONIUS: Hath there been such a time—I would fain know that—
That I have positively said "'Tis so,"
When it prov'd otherwise?
KING: Not that I know.
POLONIUS: [*pointing to his head and shoulder*]: Take this from this, if this be
otherwise.   155
If circumstances lead me, I will find
Where truth is hid, though it were hid indeed
Within the center.°
KING: How may we try it further?
POLONIUS: You know, sometimes he walks four hours together
Here in the lobby.
QUEEN: So he does indeed.   160
POLONIUS: At such a time I'll loose my daughter to him.
Be you and I behind and arras° then.
Mark the encounter. If he love her not
And be not from his reason fall'n thereon,°
Let me be no assistant for a state,   165
But keep a farm and carters.
KING: We will try it.

(*Enter Hamlet [reading on a book].*)

QUEEN: But look where sadly the poor wretch comes reading.
POLONIUS: Away, I do beseech you both, away.
I'll board° him presently.

                    (*Exeunt King and Queen [with Attendants].*)

               O, give me leave.
How does my good Lord Hamlet?   170
HAMLET: Well, God-a-mercy.°
POLONIUS: Do you know me, my lord?
HAMLET: Excellent well. You are a fishmonger.°
POLONIUS: Not I, my lord.
HAMLET: Then I would you were so honest a man.   175
POLONIUS: Honest, my lord?
HAMLET: Ay, sir. To be honest, as this world goes, is to be one man pick'd out of
ten thousand.

---

158. center: Middle point of the earth (which is also the center of the Ptolemaic universe). **162. arras:** Hanging, tapestry. **164. thereon:** On that account. **169. board:** Accost.
171. God-a-mercy: Thank you. **173. fishmonger:** Fish merchant.

POLONIUS: That's very true, my lord.

HAMLET: For if the sun breed maggots in a dead dog, being a good kissing 180 carrion° — Have you a daughter?

POLONIUS: I have, my lord.

HAMLET: Let her not walk i' th' sun.° Conception° is a blessing, but as your daughter may conceive, friend, look to 't.

POLONIUS [aside]: How say you by that? Still harping on my daughter. Yet he 185 knew me not at first; 'a said I was a fishmonger. 'A is far gone. And truly in my youth I suff'red much extremity for love, very near this. I'll speak to him again. — What do you read, my lord?

HAMLET: Words, words, words.

POLONIUS: What is the matter,° my lord?   190

HAMLET: Between who?

POLONIUS: I mean, the matter that you read, my lord.

HAMLET: Slanders, sir, for the satirical rogue says here that old men have gray beards, that their faces are wrinkled, their eyes purging° thick amber and plum-tree gum, and that they have a plentiful lack of wit, 195 together with most weak hams. All which, sir, though I most power- fully and potently believe, yet I hold it not honesty° to have it thus set down, for you yourself, sir, shall grow old as I am, if like a crab you could go backward.

POLONIUS [*aside*]: Though this be madness, yet there is method in 't. — Will you 200 walk out of the air, my lord?

HAMLET: Into my grave.

POLONIUS: Indeed, that's out of the air. [*Aside.*] How pregnant° sometimes his replies are! A happiness° that often madness hits on, which reason and sanity could not so prosperously° be deliver'd of. I will leave 205 him, [and suddenly contrive the means of meeting between him] and my daughter. — My honorable lord, I will most humbly take my leave of you.

HAMLET: You cannot, sir, take from me any thing that I will more willingly part withal — except my life, except my life, except my life.   210

(*Enter Guildenstern and Rosencrantz.*)

POLONIUS: Fare you well, my lord.

HAMLET: These tedious old fools!°

POLONIUS: You go to seek the Lord Hamlet; there he is.

ROSENCRANTZ [*to Polonius*]: God save you, sir!

[*Exit Polonius.*]

180–182. **good kissing carrion:** A good piece of flesh for kissing, or for the sun to kiss. 183. **i' th' sun:** With additional implication of the sunshine of princely favors. **Concep- tion:** (1) Understanding, (2) pregnancy. 190. **matter:** Substance (but Hamlet plays on the sense of basis for a dispute). 194. **purging:** Discharging. 197. **honesty:** Decency. 203. **pregnant:** Full of meaning. 204. **happiness:** Felicity of expression. 205. **prosperously:** Successfully. 212. **old fools:** I.e., old men like Polonius.

GUILDENSTERN: My honor'd lord!   215

ROSENCRANTZ: My most dear lord!

HAMLET: My excellent good friends! How dost thou, Guildenstern? Ah, Rosencrantz! Good lads, how do you both?

ROSENCRANTZ: As the indifferent° children of the earth.

GUILDENSTERN: Happy in that we are not over-happy. On Fortune's cap we are 220 not the very button.

HAMLET: Nor the soles of her shoe?

ROSENCRANTZ: Neither, my lord.

HAMLET: Then you live about her waist, or in the middle of her favors?

GUILDENSTERN: Faith, her privates° we.   225

HAMLET: In the secret parts of Fortune? O, most true; she is a strumpet.° What news?

ROSENCRANTZ: None, my lord, but the world's grown honest.

HAMLET: Then is doomsday near. But your news is not true. [Let me question more in particular. What have you, my good friends, deserv'd at the hands 230 of Fortune that she sends you to prison hither?

GUILDENSTERN: Prison, my lord?

HAMLET: Denmark's a prison.

ROSENCRANTZ: Then is the world one.

HAMLET: A goodly one, in which there are many confines,° wards,° and dun- 235 geons, Denmark being one o' th' worst.

ROSENCRANTZ: We think not so, my lord.

HAMLET: Why then 'tis none to you, for there is nothing either good or bad but thinking makes it so. To me it is a prison.

ROSENCRANTZ: Why then, your ambition makes it one. 'Tis too narrow for your 240 mind.

HAMLET: O God, I could be bounded in a nutshell and count myself a king of infinite space, were it not that I have bad dreams.

GUILDENSTERN: Which dreams indeed are ambition, for the very substance of the ambitious° is merely the shadow of a dream.   245

HAMLET: A dream itself is but a shadow.

ROSENCRANTZ: Truly, and I hold ambition of so airy and light a quality that it is but a shadow's shadow.

HAMLET: Then are our beggars bodies,° and our monarchs and outstretch'd° heroes the beggars' shadows. Shall we to th' court? For, by my fay,° I cannot 250 reason.

ROSENCRANTZ, GUILDENSTERN: We'll wait upon° you.

---

219. indifferent: Ordinary.   **225. privates:** Close acquaintances (with sexual pun on *private parts*).   **226. strumpet:** Prostitute (a common epithet for indiscriminate Fortune, see line 449 p. 923).   **235. confines:** Places of confinement. **wards:** Cells.   **244–245. the very . . . ambitious:** That seemingly very substantial thing which the ambitious pursue. **249. bodies:** Solid substances rather than shadows (since beggars are not ambitious). **out-stretch'd:** (1) Far-reaching in their ambition, (2) elongated as shadows.   **250. fay:** Faith. **252. wait upon:** Accompany, attend.

HAMLET: No such matter. I will not sort° you with the rest of my servants, for, to speak to you like an honest man, I am most dreadfully
attended.°] But, in the beaten way° of friendship, what make° you at 255
Elsinore?

ROSENCRANTZ: To visit you, my lord, no other occasion.

HAMLET: Beggar that I am, I am even poor in thanks; but I thank you, and sure,
dear friends, my thanks are too dear a halfpenny.° Were you not sent for?
Is it your own inclining? Is it a free visitation? Come, come, deal justly with 260
me. Come, come; nay, speak.

GUILDENSTERN: What should we say, my lord?

HAMLET: Why, anything, but to th' purpose. You were sent for; and there
is a kind of confession in your looks which your modesties have not
craft enough to color. I know the good King and Queen have sent for 265
you.

ROSENCRANTZ: To what end, my lord?

HAMLET: That you must teach me. But let me conjure° you, by the rights of
our fellowship, by the consonancy of our youth,° by the obligation of
our ever-preserv'd love, and by what more dear a better proposer° 270
could charge° you withal, be even° and direct with me, whether you
were sent for, or no?

ROSENCRANTZ [aside to Guildenstern]: What say you?

HAMLET [aside]: Nay then, I have an eye of° you.—If you love me, hold not
off. 275

GUILDENSTERN: My lord, we were sent for.

HAMLET: I will tell you why; so shall my anticipation prevent your discovery,° and your secrecy to the King and Queen molt no feather.° I have
of late—but wherefore I know not—lost all my mirth, forgone all
custom of exercises; and indeed it goes so heavily with my disposition 280
that this goodly frame, the earth, seems to me a sterile promontory;
this most excellent canopy, the air, look you, this brave° o'erhanging
firmament, this majestical roof fretted° with golden fire, why, it ap-
peareth nothing to me but a foul and pestilent congregation of va-
pors. What a piece of work is a man! How noble in reason, how 285
infinite in faculties, in form and moving how express° and admirable, in action how like an angel, in apprehension how like a god!
The beauty of the world, the paragon of animals! And yet, to me,

---

253. **sort:** Class, associate. 254–255. **dreadfully attended:** Waited upon in slovenly fashion.
255. **beaten way:** Familiar path. **make:** Do. 259. **dear a halfpenny:** Expensive at the price of a
halfpenny, i.e., of little worth. 268. **conjure:** Adjure, entreat. 269. **consonancy of our youth:** The
fact that we are of the same age. 270. **better proposer:** More skillful propounder.
271. **charge:** Urge. **even:** Straight, honest. 274. **of:** On. 277–278. **prevent your discovery:**
Forestall your disclosure. 278. **molt no feather:** Not diminish in the least. 282. **brave:** Splendid.
283. **fretted:** Adorned (with fret-work, as in a vaulted ceiling). 286. **express:** Well-framed, exact,
expressive.

what is this quintessence° of dust? Man delights not me—no, nor
woman neither, though by your smiling you seem to say so.   290
ROSENCRANTZ: My lord, there was no such stuff in my thoughts.
HAMLET: Why did you laugh then, when I said "man delights not me"?
ROSENCRANTZ: To think, my lord, if you delight not in man, what lenten enter-
tainment° the players shall receive from you. We coted° them on the way,
and hither are they coming, to offer you service.   295
HAMLET: He that plays the king shall be welcome; his Majesty shall have tribute
of me. The adventurous knight shall use his foil and target,° the lover shall
not sigh gratis, the humorous man° shall end his part in peace, [the clown
shall make those laugh whose lungs are tickle o' th' sere°], and the lady
shall say her mind freely, or the blank verse shall halt° for 't. What players   300
are they?
ROSENCRANTZ: Even those you were wont to take such delight in, the tragedians
of the city.
HAMLET: How chances it they travel? Their residence,° both in reputation and
profit, was better both ways.   305
ROSENCRANTZ: I think their inhibition° comes by the means of the innovation.°
HAMLET: Do they hold the same estimation they did when I was in the city? Are
they so follow'd?
ROSENCRANTZ: No, indeed, are they not.   310
[HAMLET: How comes it? Do they grow rusty?
ROSENCRANTZ: Nay, their endeavor keeps in the wonted° pace. But there is,
sir, an aery° of children, little eyases,° that cry out on the top of question,° and are most tyrannically° clapp'd for 't. These are now the fashion, and so berattle° the common stages°—so they call them—that   315
many wearing rapiers° are afraid of goose-quills° and dare scarce come
thither.
HAMLET: What, are they children? Who maintains 'em? How are they escoted?° Will they pursue the quality° no longer than they can sing?°

---

289. **quintessence:** The fifth essence of ancient philosophy, beyond earth, water, air, and fire, supposed to be the substance of the heavenly bodies and to be latent in all things. 293–294. **lenten
entertainment:** Meager reception (appropriate to Lent). 294. **coted:** Over-took and passed beyond. 297. **foil and target:** Sword and shield. 298. **humorous man:** Eccentric character, dominated by one trait or "humor." 299. **tickle o' th' sere:** Easy on the trigger, ready to laugh easily.
(*Sere* is part of a gunlock.) 300. **halt:** Limp. 304. **residence:** Remaining in one place, i.e., in
the city. 306. **inhibition:** Formal prohibition (from acting plays in the city). 306. **innovation:** I.e., the new fashion in satirical plays performed by boy actors in the "private" theaters; or
possibly a political uprising; or the strict limitations set on the theater in London in 1600.
312. **wonted:** Usual. 313. **aery:** Nest. **eyases:** Young hawks. 313–314. **cry . . . question:**
Speak shrilly, dominating the controversy (in decrying the public theaters). 314. **tyranni-
cally:** Outrageously. 315. **berattle:** Berate. **common stages:** Public theaters. 316. **many
wearing rapiers:** Many men of fashion, who were afraid to patronize the common players for fear
of being satirized by the poets who wrote for the children. **goose-quills:** Pens of satirists. 318–19.
escoted: Maintained. 319. **quality:** (Acting) profession. **no longer . . . sing:** Only until their
voices change.

Will they not say afterwards, if they should grow themselves to com- 320
mon° players—as it is most like, if their means are no better—their
writers do them wrong, to make them exclaim against their own
succession?°

ROSENCRANTZ: Faith, there has been much to do° on both sides, and the nation
holds it no sin to tarre° them to controversy. There was, for a while, no 325
money bid for argument° unless the poet and the player went to cuffs in
the question.°

HAMLET: Is 't possible?

GUILDENSTERN: O, there has been much throwing about of brains.

HAMLET: Do the boys carry it away?°   330

ROSENCRANTZ: Ay, that they do, my lord—Hercules and his load° too.°]

HAMLET: It is not very strange, for my uncle is King of Denmark, and those
that would make mouths° at him while my father liv'd, give twenty,
forty, fifty, a hundred ducats° apiece for his picture in little.° 'Sblood,°
there is something in this more than natural, if philosophy could find 335
it out.

(*A flourish [of trumpets within].*)

GUILDENSTERN: There are the players.

HAMLET: Gentlemen, you are welcome to Elsinore. Your hands, come then.
Th' appurtenance of welcome is fashion and ceremony. Let me com-
ply° with you in this garb,° lest my extent° to the players, which, I tell 340
you, must show fairly outwards,° should more appear like entertain-
ment° than yours. You are welcome. But my uncle-father and aunt-
mother are deceiv'd.

GUILDENSTERN: In what, my dear lord?

HAMLET: I am but mad north-north-west.° When the wind is southerly I know 345
a hawk from a handsaw.°

(*Enter Polonius.*)

POLONIUS: Well be with you, gentlemen!

320–321. common: Regular, adult.   **323. succession:** Future careers.   **324. to do:** Ado.
325. tarre: Set on (as dogs).   **326. argument:** Plot for a play.   **327. went . . . question:** Came to blows in the play itself.   **330. carry it away:** Win the day.   **331. Hercules . . .
load:** Thought to be an allusion to the sign of the Globe Theatre, which was Hercules bearing
the world on his shoulder.   **311–331. How . . . load too:** The passage, omitted from the early
quartos, alludes to the so-called War of the Theatres, 1599–1602, the rivalry between the children companies and the adult actors.   **333. mouths:** Faces.   **334. ducats:** Gold coins. **in
little:** In miniature. **'Sblood:** By His (God's, Christ's) blood.   **339–340. comply:** Observe the
formalities of courtesy.   **340. garb:** Manner. **my extent:** The extent of my showing courtesy.
show fairly outwards: Look cordial to outward appearances. **entertainment:** A (warm) reception.   **345. north-north-west:** Only partly, at times.   **346. hawk, handsaw:** Mattock (*or hack*)
and a carpenter's cutting tool respectively; also birds, with a play on *hernshaw* or heron.

HAMLET: Hark you, Guildenstern, and you too; at each ear a hearer. That great
  baby you see there is not yet out of his swaddling-clouts.°
ROSENCRANTZ: Happily° he is the second time come to them; for they say an old 350
  man is twice a child.
HAMLET: I will prophesy he comes to tell me of the players; mark it.—You say
  right, sir, o' Monday morning, 'twas then indeed.
POLONIUS: My lord, I have news to tell you.
HAMLET: My lord, I have news to tell you. When Roscius° was an actor in Rome— 355
POLONIUS: The actors are come hither, my lord.
HAMLET: Buzz,° buzz!
POLONIUS: Upon my honor—
HAMLET: Then came each actor on his ass—   360
POLONIUS: The best actors in the world, either for tragedy, comedy, history, pas-
  toral, pastoral-comical, historical-pastoral, tragical-historical, tragical-
  comical-historical-pastoral, scene individable,° or poem unlimited.°
  Seneca° cannot be too heavy, nor Plautus° too light. For the law of writ and
  the liberty,° these are the only men.   365
HAMLET: O Jephthah, judge of Israel,° what a treasure hadst thou!
POLONIUS: What a treasure had he, my lord?
HAMLET: Why,
  "One fair daughter, and no more,
  The which he loved passing° well."   370
POLONIUS [aside]: Still on my daughter.
HAMLET: Am I not i' th' right, old Jephthah?
POLONIUS: If you call me Jephthah, my lord, I have a daughter that I love passing well.
HAMLET: Nay, that follows not.   375
POLONIUS: What follows, then, my lord?
HAMLET: Why,
  "As by lot, God wot,"°
and then, you know,
  "It came to pass, as most like° it was."   380
The first row° of the pious chanson° will show you more, for look where
my abridgement° comes.

(Enter the Players.)

---

349. **swaddling-clouts:** Cloths in which to wrap a newborn baby.   350. **Happily:** Haply, perhaps.   355. **Roscius:** A famous Roman actor who died in 62 B.C.E.   358. **Buzz:** An interjection
used to denote stale news.   363. **scene individable:** A play observing the unity of place. **poem unlimited:** A play disregarding the unities of time and place.   364. **Seneca:** Writer of Latin tragedies.
Plautus: Writer of Latin comedy.   364–365. **law . . . liberty:** Dramatic composition both according
to rules and without rules, i.e., "classical" and "romantic" dramas.   366. **Jephthah . . . Israel:**
Jephthah had to sacrifice his daughter; see Judges 11. Hamlet goes on to quote from a ballad on the
theme.   370. **passing:** Surpassingly.   378. **wot:** Knows.   380. **like:** Likely, probable.   381.
row: Stanza. **chanson:** Ballad, song.   382. **my abridgement:** Something that cuts short my conversation; also, a diversion.

You are welcome, masters; welcome, all. I am glad to see thee well. Welcome, good friends. O, old friend! Why, thy face is valanc'd° since I saw
thee last. Com'st thou to beard° me in Denmark? What, my young lady° 385
and mistress? By 'r lady, your ladyship is nearer to heaven than when I saw
you last, by the altitude of a chopine.° Pray God your voice, like a piece
of uncurrent° gold, be not crack'd within the ring.° Masters, you are all
welcome. We'll e'en to 't like French falconers, fly at anything we see. We'll
have a speech straight.° Come, give us a taste of your quality; come, a pas- 390
sionate speech.

FIRST PLAYER: What speech, my good lord?

HAMLET: I heard thee speak me a speech once, but it was never acted, or, if
it was, not above once, for the play, I remember, pleas'd not the million; 'twas caviary to the general.° But it was—as I receiv'd it, and 395
others, whose judgments in such matters cried in the top of°
mine—an excellent play, well digested in the scenes, set down with
as much modesty as cunning.° I remember one said there were no
sallets° in the lines to make the matter savory, nor no matter in the
phrase that might indict° the author of affectation, but call'd it an 400
honest method, as wholesome as sweet, and by very much more handsome than fine.° One speech in 't I chiefly lov'd: 'twas Aeneas' tale to
Dido, and thereabout of it especially when he speaks of Priam's
slaughter.° If it live in your memory, begin at this line: let me see,
let me see— 405
"The rugged Pyrrhus,° like th' Hyrcanian beast"° —
'Tis not so. It begins with Pyrrhus:
"The rugged Pyrrhus, he whose sable° arms,
Black as his purpose, did the night resemble
When he lay couched in the ominous horse,° 410
Hath now this dread and black complexion smear'd
With heraldry more dismal.° Head to foot
Now is he total gules,° horridly trick'd°
With blood of fathers, mothers, daughters, sons,

---

384. valanc'd: Fringed (with a beard).   385. beard: Confront (with obvious pun). young lady: Boy
playing women's parts.   387. chopine: Thick-soled shoe of Italian fashion.   388. uncurrent: Not
passable as lawful coinage. crack'd . . . ring: Changed from adolescent to male voice, no longer
suitable for women's roles. (Coins featured rings enclosing the sovereign's head; if the coin was
cracked within this ring, it was unfit for currency.)   390. straight: At once.   395. caviary to the
general: Caviar to the multitude, i.e., a choice dish too elegant for coarse tastes.   396. cried in
the top of: Spoke with greater authority than.   398. cunning: Skill.   399. sallets: Salad, i.e.,
spicy improprieties.   400. indict: Convict.   402. fine: Elaborately ornamented, showy.
403–404. Priam's slaughter: The slaying of the ruler of Troy, when the Greeks finally took the
city.   406. Pyrrhus: A Greek hero in the Trojan War, also known as Neoptolemus, son of
Achilles. Hyrcanian beast: I.e., the tiger. (See Virgil, Aeneid, 4.266; compare the whole speech
with Marlowe's Dido Queen of Carthage, 2.1.214 ff.)   408. sable: Black (for reasons of camouflage during the episode of the Trojan horse).   410. ominous horse: Trojan horse, by which
the Greeks gained access to Troy.   412. dismal: Ill-omened.   413. gules: Red (a heraldic
term). trick'd: Adorned, decorated.

Bak'd and impasted° with the parching streets,°   415
That lend a tyrannous and a damned light
To their lord's° murder. Roasted in wrath and fire,
And thus o'er-sized° with coagulate gore,
With eyes like carbuncles, the hellish Pyrrhus
Old grandsire Priam seeks."   420
So proceed you.
POLONIUS: 'Fore God, my lord, well spoken, with good accent and good discretion.
FIRST PLAYER: "Anon he finds him
Striking too short at Greeks. His antique sword,   425
Rebellious to his arm, lies where it falls,
Repugnant° to command. Unequal match'd,
Pyrrhus at Priam drives, in rage strikes wide,
But with the whiff and wind of his fell° sword
Th' unnerved father falls. [Then senseless Ilium,°]   430
Seeming to feel this blow, with flaming top
Stoops to his° base, and with a hideous crash
Takes prisoner Pyrrhus' ear. For, lo! His sword,
Which was declining on the milky head
Of reverend Priam, seem'd i' th' air to stick.   435
So as a painted° tyrant Pyrrhus stood,
And, like a neutral to his will and matter,°
Did nothing.
But, as we often see, against° some storm,
A silence in the heavens, the rack° stand still,   440
The bold winds speechless, and the orb below
As hush as death, anon the dreadful thunder
Doth rend the region,° so, after Pyrrhus' pause,
Aroused vengeance sets him new a-work,
And never did the Cyclops'° hammers fall   445
On Mars's armor forg'd for proof eterne°
With less remorse than Pyrrhus' bleeding sword
Now falls on Priam.
Out, out, thou strumpet Fortune! All you gods,
In general synod,° take away her power!   450
Break all the spokes and fellies° from her wheel,
And bowl the round nave° down the hill of heaven,
As low as to the fiends!"

---

415. **impasted:** Crusted, like a thick paste. **with . . . streets:** By the parching heat of the streets (because of the fires everywhere).   417. **their lord's:** Priam's   418. **o'er-sized:** Covered as with size or glue.   427. **Repugnant:** Disobedient, resistant.   429. **fell:** Cruel.   430. **senseless Ilium:** Insensate Troy.   432. **his:** Its.   436. **painted:** Painted in a picture.   437. **like . . . matter:** As though poised indecisively between his intention and its fulfillment.   439. **against:** Just before.   440. **rack:** Mass of clouds.   443. **region:** Sky.   445. **Cyclops:** Giant armor makers in the smithy of Vulcan.   446. **proof eterne:** Eternal resistance to assault.   450. **synod:** Assembly.   451. **fellies:** Pieces of wood forming the rim of a wheel.   452. **nave:** Hub.

POLONIUS: This is too long.

HAMLET: It shall to the barber's with your beard.—Prithee say on. He's for a   455
jig° or a tale of bawdry, or he sleeps. Say on, come to Hecuba.°

FIRST PLAYER: "But who, ah woe! had seen the mobled° queen"—

HAMLET: "The mobled queen?"

POLONIUS: That's good. "Mobled queen" is good.

FIRST PLAYER: "Run barefoot up and down, threat'ning the flames   460
With bisson rheum,° a clout° upon that head
Where late the diadem stood, and for a robe,
About her lank and all o'er-teemed° loins,
A blanket, in the alarm of fear caught up—
Who this had seen, with tongue in venom steep'd,   465
'Gainst Fortune's state° would treason have pronounc'd.°
But if the gods themselves did see her then
When she saw Pyrrhus make malicious sport
In mincing with his sword her husband's limbs,
The instant burst of clamor that she made,   470
Unless things mortal move them not at all,
Would have made milch° the burning eyes of heaven,
And passion in the gods."

POLONIUS: Look whe'er° he has not turn'd his color and has tears. in 's eyes.
Prithee, no more.   475

HAMLET: 'Tis well; I'll have thee speak out the rest of this soon. Good my lord,
will you see the players well bestow'd?° Do you hear, let them be well
us'd, for they are the abstract° and brief chronicles of the time. After your
death you were better have a bad epitaph than their ill report while you
live.   480

POLONIUS: My lord, I will use them according to their desert.

HAMLET: God's bodkin,° man, much better! Use every man after his desert,
and who shall scape whipping? Use them after your own honor and
dignity. The less they deserve, the more merit is in your bounty. Take
them in.   485

POLONIUS: Come, sirs.

HAMLET: Follow him, friends. We'll hear a play tomorrow. [As they start to leave,
Hamlet detains the First Player.] Dost thou hear me, old friend?
Can you play the Murder of Gonzago?

FIRST PLAYER: Ay, my lord.   490

HAMLET: We'll ha't tomorrow night. You could, for need, study a speech of some
dozen or sixteen lines, which I would set down and insert in 't, could you
not?

---

456. **jig:** Comic song and dance often given at the end of a play. **Hecuba:** Wife of Priam.   457.
mobled: Muffled.   461. **bisson rheum:** Blinding tears. **clout:** Cloth.   463. **o'erteemed:** Worn
out with bearing children.   466. **state:** Rule, managing. **pronounc'd:** Proclaimed.   472.
milch: Milky moist with tears.   474. **whe'er:** Whether.   477. **bestow'd:** Lodged.   478. **abstract:** Summary account.   482. **God's bodkin:** By God's (Christ's) little body, *bodykin* (not
to be confused with *bodkin*, dagger).

FIRST PLAYER: Ay, my lord.

HAMLET: Very well. Follow that lord, and look you mock him not. — My good 495
    friends, I'll leave you till night. You are welcome to Elsinore.

(Exeunt Polonius and Players.)

ROSENCRANTZ: Good my lord!

(Exeunt [Rosencrantz and Guildenstern].)

HAMLET: Ay, so, God buy you. — Now I am alone.
    O, what a rogue and peasant slave am I!
    Is it not monstrous that this player here,   500
    But in a fiction, in a dream of passion,
    Could force his soul so to his own conceit°
    That from her working all his visage wann'd,°
    Tears in his eyes, distraction in his aspect,
    A broken voice, and his whole function suiting   505
    With forms to his conceit?° And all for nothing!
    For Hecuba!
    What's Hecuba to him, or he to Hecuba,
    That he should weep for her? What would he do,
    Had he the motive and the cue for passion   510
    That I have? He would drown the stage with tears
    And cleave the general ear with horrid speech,
    Make mad the guilty and appall the free,°
    Confound the ignorant, and amaze indeed
    The very faculties of eyes and ears. Yet I,   515
    A dull and muddy-mettled° rascal, peak,°
    Like John-a-dreams,° unpregnant of° my cause,
    And can say nothing — no, not for a king
    Upon whose property° and most dear life
    A damn'd defeat was made. Am I a coward?   520
    Who calls me villain? Breaks my pate across?
    Plucks off my beard, and blows it in my face?
    Tweaks me by the nose? Gives me the lie° i' th' throat,
    As deep as to the lungs? Who does me this?
    Ha,'swounds,° I should take it; for it cannot be   525
    But I am pigeon-liver'd,° and lack gall

---

502. conceit: Conception.   **503. wann'd:** Grew pale.   **505–506. his whole . . . conceit:** His whole being responded with actions to suit his thought.   **513. free:** Innocent.   **517. muddy-mettled:** Dull-spirited. **peak:** Mope, pine.   **518. John-a-dreams:** Sleepy dreaming idler. **unpregnant of:** Not quickened by.   **520. property:** The crown; perhaps also character, quality.   **524. Gives me the lie:** Calls me a liar.   **525. 'swounds:** By His (Christ's) wounds.   **526. pigeon-liver'd:** The pigeon or dove was popularly supposed to be mild because it secreted no gall.

To make oppression bitter, or ere this
I should have fatted all the region kites°
With this slave's offal. Bloody, bawdy villain!
Remorseless, treacherous, lecherous, kindless° villain!   530
[O, vengeance!]
Why, what an ass am I! This is most brave,
That I, the son of a dear father murder'd,
Prompted to my revenge by heaven and hell,
Must, like a whore, unpack my heart with words,   535
And fall a-cursing, like a very drab,°
A stallion!° Fie upon't, foh! About,° my brains!
Hum, I have heard
That guilty creatures sitting at a play
Have by the very cunning of the scene   540
Been struck so to the soul that presently°
They have proclaim'd their malefactions;
For murder, though it have no tongue, will speak
With most miraculous organ. I'll have these players
Play something like the murder of my father   545
Before mine uncle. I'll observe his looks;
I'll tent° him to the quick. If'a do blench,°
I know my course. The spirit that I have seen
May be the devil, and the devil hath power
T' assume a pleasing shape; yea, and perhaps   550
Out of my weakness and my melancholy,
As he is very potent with such spirits,°
Abuses° me to damn me. I'll have grounds
More relative° than this. The play's the thing
Wherein I'll catch the conscience of the King.   555

(*Exit.*)

[ACT 3 / Scene 1]°

(*Enter King, Queen, Polonius, Ophelia, Rosencrantz, Guildenstern, Lords.*)

KING: And can you, by no drift of conference,°
Get from him why he puts on this confusion,
Grating so harshly all his days of quiet

---

528. **region kites:** Kites (birds of prey) of the air, from the vicinity. 530. **kindless:** Unnatural. 536. **drab:** Prostitute. 537. **stallion:** Prostitute (male or female). (Many editors follow the Folio reading of *scullion.*) **About:** About it, to work. 541. **presently:** At once. 547. **tent:** Probe. **blench:** Quail, flinch. 552. **spirits:** Humors (of melancholy). 553. **Abuses:** Deludes. 554. **relative:** Closely related, pertinent. ACT 3, SCENE 1. **Location:** The castle. 1. **drift of conference:** Direction of conversation.

With turbulent and dangerous lunacy?

ROSENCRANTZ: He does confess he feels himself distracted,   5
But from what cause'a will by no means speak.

GUILDENSTERN: Nor do we find him forward° to be sounded,°
But with a crafty madness keeps aloof
When we would bring him on to some confession
Of his true state.

QUEEN: Did he receive you well?   10

ROSENCRANTZ: Most like a gentleman.

GUILDENSTERN: But with much forcing of his disposition.°

ROSENCRANTZ: Niggard of question,° but of our demands
Most free in his reply.

QUEEN: Did you assay° him
To any pastime?   15

ROSENCRANTZ: Madam, it so fell out that certain players
We o'er-raught° on the way. Of these we told him,
And there did seem in him a kind of joy
To hear of it. They are here about the court,
And, as I think, they have already order   20
This night to play before him.

POLONIUS: 'Tis most true,
And he beseech'd me to entreat your Majesties
To hear and see the matter.

KING: With all my heart, and it doth much content me
To hear him so inclin'd.   25
Good gentlemen, give him a further edge,°
And drive his purpose into these delights.

ROSENCRANTZ: We shall, my lord.

          (*Exeunt Rosencrantz and Guildenstern.*)

KING: Sweet Gertrude, leave us too,
For we have closely° sent for Hamlet hither,
That he, as 'twere by accident, may here   30
Affront° Ophelia.
Her father and myself, [lawful espials,°]
Will so bestow ourselves that seeing, unseen,
We may of their encounter frankly judge,
And gather by him, as he is behav'd,   35
If 't be th' affliction of his love or no
That thus he suffers for.

---

7. **forward**: Willing. **sounded**: Tested deeply. **12. disposition**: Inclination. **13. question**: Conversation. **14. assay**: Try to win. **17. o'er-raught**: Overtook and passed. **26. edge**: Incitement. **29. closely**: Privately. **31. Affront**: Confront, meet. **32. espials**: Spies.

QUEEN: I shall obey you.
And for your part, Ophelia, I do wish
That your good beauties be the happy cause
Of Hamlet's wildness. So shall I hope your virtues   40
Will bring him to his wonted way again,
To both your honors.
OPHELIA: Madam, I wish it may.

[Exit Queen.]

POLONIUS: Ophelia, walk you here. — Gracious,° so please you,
We will bestow ourselves. *[To Ophelia.]* Read on this book,

[Gives her a book.]

That show of such an exercise° may color°   45
    Your loneliness. We are oft to blame in this —
'Tis too much prov'd° — that with devotion's visage
And pious action we do sugar o'er
The devil himself.
KING *[aside]*: O, 'tis too true!
How smart a lash that speech doth give my conscience!   50
The harlot's cheek, beautied with plast'ring art,
Is not more ugly to° the thing° that helps it
Than is my deed to my most painted word.
O heavy burden!
POLONIUS: I hear him coming. Let's withdraw, my lord.   55

[King and Polonius withdraw.°]

(Enter Hamlet. [Ophelia pretends to read a book.])

HAMLET: To be, or not to be, that is the question:
Whether 'tis nobler in the mind to suffer
The slings and arrows of outrageous fortune,
Or to take arms against a sea of troubles,
And by opposing end them. To die, to sleep —   60
No more — and by a sleep to say we end
The heart-ache and the thousand natural shocks
That flesh is heir to. 'Tis a consummation
Devoutly to be wish'd. To die, to sleep;

---

43. Gracious: Your Grace (i.e., the King).   **45. exercise:** Act of devotion. (The book she reads is one of devotion.) **color:** Give a plausible appearance to.   **47. too much prov'd:** Too often shown to be true, too often practiced.   **52. to:** Compared to. **thing:** I.e., the cosmetic. [S.D.] **withdraw:** The king and Polonius may retire behind an arras. The stage directions specify that they "enter" again near the end of the scene.

To sleep, perchance to dream. Ay, there's the rub,°   65
For in that sleep of death what dreams may come
When we have shuffled° off this mortal coil,°
Must give us pause. There's the respect°
That makes calamity of so long life.°
For who would bear the whips and scorns of time,   70
Th' oppressor's wrong, the proud man's contumely,°
The pangs of despis'd° love, the law's delay,
The insolence of office,° and the spurns°
That patient merit of th' unworthy takes,
When he himself might his quietus° make   75
With a bare bodkin?° Who would fardels° bear,
To grunt and sweat under a weary life,
But that the dread of something after death,
The undiscover'd country from whose bourn°
No traveler returns, puzzles the will,   80
And makes us rather bear those ills we have
Than fly to others that we know not of?
Thus conscience does make cowards of us all
And thus the native hue° of resolution
Is sicklied o'er with the pale cast° of thought,   85
And enterprises of great pitch° and moment°
With this regard° their currents° turn awry,
And lose the name of action. — Soft you now,
The fair Ophelia. Nymph, in thy orisons°
Be all my sins rememb'red.
OPHELIA: Good my lord,   90
How does your honor for this many a day?
HAMLET: I humbly thank you; well, well, well.
OPHELIA: My lord, I have remembrances of yours,
That I have longed long to re-deliver.
I pray you, now receive them.   [*Offers tokens.*] 95
HAMLET: No, not I, I never gave you aught.
OPHELIA: My honor'd lord, you know right well you did,
And with them words of so sweet breath compos'd
As made these things more rich. Their perfume lost,
Take these again, for to the noble mind   100

---

65. **rub:** Literally, an obstacle in the game of bowls. 67. **shuffled:** Sloughed, cast. **coil:** Turmoil. 68. **respect:** Consideration. 69. **of . . . life:** So long-lived. 71. **contumely:** Insolent abuse. 72. **despis'd:** Rejected. 73. **office:** Officialdom. **spurns:** Insults. 75. **quietus:** Acquittance; here, death. 76. **bodkin:** Dagger. **fardels:** Burdens. 79. **bourn:** Boundary. 84. **native hue:** Natural color, complexion. 85. **cast:** Shade of color. 86. **pitch:** Height (as of a falcon's flight). **moment:** Importance. 87. **regard:** Respect, consideration. **currents:** Courses. 89. **orisons:** Prayers.

Rich gifts wax poor when givers prove unkind.
There, my lord.   [*Gives tokens.*]

HAMLET: Ha, ha! Are you honest?°

OPHELIA: My lord?

HAMLET: Are you fair?°   105

OPHELIA: What means your lordship?

HAMLET: That if you be honest and fair, your honesty° should admit no discourse° to your beauty.

OPHELIA: Could beauty, my lord, have better commerce° than with honesty?

HAMLET: Ay, truly, for the power of beauty will sooner transform honesty from 110
what it is to a bawd than the force of honesty can translate beauty into his
likeness. This was sometime° a paradox,° but now the time° gives it proof.
I did love you once.

OPHELIA: Indeed, my lord, you made me believe so.

HAMLET: You should not have believ'd me, for virtue cannot so inoculate° our 115
old stock but we shall relish of it.° I lov'd you not.

OPHELIA: I was the more deceiv'd.

HAMLET: Get thee to a nunn'ry.° Why wouldst thou be a breeder of sinners? I am myself indifferent honest;° but yet I could accuse me of
such things that it were better my mother had not borne me: I am very 120
proud, revengeful, ambitious, with more offenses at my beck° than I
have thoughts to put them in, imagination to give them shape, or time
to act them in. What should such fellows as I do crawling between earth and heaven? We are arrant knaves, all; believe none of us.
Go thy ways to a nunn'ry. Where's your father?   125

OPHELIA: At home, my lord.

HAMLET: Let the doors be shut upon him, that he may play the fool nowhere but
in 's own house.
Farewell.

OPHELIA: O, help him, you sweet heavens!

HAMLET: If thou dost marry, I'll give thee this plague for thy dowry: be thou as 130
chaste as ice, as pure as snow, thou shalt not escape calumny. Get thee to
a nunn'ry, farewell. Or, if thou wilt needs marry, marry a fool, for wise men
know well enough what monsters° you° make of them. To a nunn'ry, go,
and quickly too. Farewell.

OPHELIA: Heavenly powers, restore him!   135

---

103. **honest:** (1) Truthful; (2) chaste. **105. fair:** (1) Beautiful; (2) just, honorable. **107.
your honesty:** Your chastity. **107–108. discourse:** Familiar dealings. **109. commerce:**
Dealings. **113. sometime:** Formerly. **paradox:** A view opposite to commonly held opinion.
the time: The present age. **115. inoculate:** Graft, be engrafted to. **116. but . . . it:** That we
do not still have about us a taste of the old stock; i.e., retain our sinfulness. **118. nunn'ry:** (1)
Convent; (2) brothel. **119. indifferent honest:** Resonably virtuous. **121. beck:** Command.
133. monsters: An allusion to the horns of a cuckold. **you:** You women.

HAMLET: I have heard of your paintings too, well enough. God hath given you
one face, and you make yourselves another. You jig,° and amble, and you
lisp, you nickname God's creatures, and make your wantonness your ignorance.° Go to, I'll no more on 't; it hath made me mad. I say, we will have
no more marriage. Those that are married already — all but one — shall live. 140
The rest shall keep as they are. To a nunn'ry, go.   (*Exit.*)

OPHELIA: O, what a noble mind is here o'erthrown!
The courtier's, soldier's, scholar's, eye, tongue, sword,
Th' expectancy and rose of the fair state,°
The glass of fashion and the mold of form,°   145
Th' observ'd of all observers,° quite, quite down!
And I, of ladies most deject and wretched,
That suck'd the honey of his music vows,
Now see that noble and most sovereign reason,
Like sweet bells jangled, out of time and harsh,   150
That unmatch'd form and feature of blown° youth
Blasted with ecstasy.° O, woe is me,
T' have seen what I have seen, see what I see!

(*Enter King and Polonius.*)

KING: Love? His affections do not that way tend;
Nor what he spake, though it lack'd form a little,   155
Was not like madness. There's something in his soul,
O'er which his melancholy sits on brood,
And I do doubt° the hatch and the disclose°
Will be some danger; which for to prevent,
I have in quick determination   160
Thus set it down: he shall with speed to England,
For the demand of° our neglected tribute.
Haply the seas and countries different
With variable° objects shall expel
This something-settled° matter in his heart,   165
Whereon his brains still beating puts him thus
From fashion of himself.° What think you on't?

POLONIUS: It shall do well. But yet do I believe
The origin and commencement of his grief

---

137. **jig:** Dance and sing affectedly and wantonly. **138–139. make . . . ignorance:** Excuse
your affection on the grounds of your ignorance. **144. Th' expectancy . . . state:** The hope
and ornament of the kingdom made fair (by him). **145. The glass . . . form:** The mirror of
fashion and the pattern of courtly behavior. **146. observ'd . . . observers:** The center of
attention and honor in the court. **151. blown:** Blooming. **152. ecstasy:** Madness. **158. doubt:**
Fear. **disclose:** Disclosure. **162. For . . . of:** To demand. **164. variable:** Various. **165. something-
settled:** Somewhat settled. **167. From . . . himself:** Out of his natural manner.

Sprung from neglected love. — How now, Ophelia?   170
You need not tell us what Lord Hamlet said;
We heard it all. — My lord, do as you please,
But, if you hold it fit, after the play
Let his queen mother all alone entreat him
To show his grief. Let her be round° with him;   175
And I'll be plac'd, so please you, in the ear
Of all their conference. If she find him not,
To England send him, or confine him where
Your wisdom best shall think.
KING: It shall be so.   180
Madness in great ones must not unwatch'd go.

                                                        (*Exeunt.*)

[Scene 2]°

(*Enter Hamlet and three of the Players.*)

HAMLET: Speak the speech, I pray you, as I pronounc'd it to you, trip-
pingly on the tongue. But if you mouth it, as many of our players°
do, I had as lief the town-crier spoke my lines. Nor do not saw the
air too much with your hand, thus, but use all gently; for in the very
torrent, tempest, and, as I may say, whirlwind of your passion, you   5
must acquire and beget a temperance that may give it smoothness.
O, it offends me to the soul to hear a robustious° periwig-pated°
fellow tear a passion to tatters, to very rags, to split the ears of the
groundlings,° who for the most part are capable of° nothing but
inexplicable dumb-shows and noise. I would have such a fellow   10
whipp'd for o'er-doing Termagant.° It out-herods Herod.° Pray you,
avoid it.
FIRST PLAYER: I warrant your honor.
HAMLET: Be not too tame neither, but let your own discretion be your
tutor. Suit the action to the word, the word to the action, with this spe-   15
cial observance, that you o'erstep not the modesty of nature. For anything so o'erdone is from° the purpose of playing, whose end, both
at the first and now, was and is, to hold, as 't were, the mirror up to

---

175. round: Blunt.   ACT 3, SCENE 2. **Location:** The castle.   **2. our players:** Indefinite use; i.e.,
players nowadays.   **7. robustious:** Violent, boisterous.   **periwig-pated:** Wearing a wig.   **9.
groundlings:** Spectators who paid least and stood in the yard of the theater.   **capable of:** Suscep-
tible of being influenced by.   **11. Termagant:** A god of the Saracens; a character in the St. Nicho-
las play, where one of his worshipers, leaving him in charge of goods, returns to find them stolen;
whereupon he beats the god or idol, which howls vociferously.   **Herod:** Herod of Jewry. (A character in *The Slaughter of the Innocents* and other cycle plays. The part was played with great noise
and fury.)   **17. from:** Contrary to.

nature, to show virtue her feature, scorn her own image, and
the very age and body of the time his° form and pressure.° Now this 20
overdone, or come tardy off,° though it makes the unskillful laugh,
cannot but make the judicious grieve, the censure of which one°
must in your allowance o'erweigh a whole theater of others. O, there
be players that I have seen play, and heard others praise, and that
highly, not to speak it profanely, that, neither having th' accent of 25
Christians nor the gait of Christian, pagan, nor man, have so strutted and bellow'd that I have thought some of nature's journeymen°
had made men and not made them well, they imitated humanity
so abominably.

FIRST PLAYER: I hope we have reform'd that indifferently° with us, sir.   30

HAMLET: O, reform it altogether. And let those that play your clowns speak no
more than is set down for them; for there be of them° that will themselves
laugh, to set on some quantity of barren° spectators to laugh too, though
in the mean time some necessary question of the play be then to be
consider'd. That's villainous, and shows a most pitiful ambition in the fool 35
that uses it. Go, make you ready.

                                                    [*Exeunt Players.*]

(*Enter Polonius, Guildenstern, and Rosencrantz.*)

How now, my lord? Will the King hear this piece of work?

POLONIUS: And the Queen too, and that presently.°

HAMLET: Bid the players make haste.

                                                    [*Exit Polonius.*]

Will you two help to hasten them?   40

ROSENCRANTZ: Ay, my lord.   (*Exeunt they two.*)

HAMLET: What ho, Horatio!

(*Enter Horatio.*)

HORATIO: Here, sweet lord, at your service.

HAMLET: Horatio, thou art e'en as just a man
As e'er my conversation cop'd withal.°

HORATIO: O, my dear lord—

HAMLET: Nay, do not think I flatter;   45
For what advancement may I hope from thee
That no revenue hast but thy good spirits,

---

20. his: Its. **pressure:** Stamp, impressed character. **21. come tardy off:** Inadequately done.
22. the censure . . . one: The judgement of even one of whom. **27. journeymen:** Laborers not
yet masters in their trade. **30. indifferently:** Tolerably. **32. of them:** Some among them.
33. barren: I.e., of wit. **38. presently:** At once. **44. my . . . withal:** My contact with people
provided opportunity for encounter with.

To feed and clothe thee? Why should the poor be flatter'd?
No, let the candied° tongue lick absurd pomp,
And crook the pregnant° hinges of the knee   50
Where thrift° may follow fawning. Dost thou hear?
Since my dear soul was mistress of her choice
And could of men distinguish her election,
Sh' hath seal'd thee for herself, for thou hast been
As one, in suff'ring all, that suffers nothing,   55
A man that Fortune's buffets and rewards
Hast ta'en with equal thanks; and blest are those
Whose blood° and judgment are so well commeddled°
That they are not a pipe for Fortune's finger
To sound what stop° she please. Give me that man   60
That is not passion's slave, and I will wear him
In my heart's core, ay, in my heart of heart,
As I do thee. — Something too much of this. —
There is a play tonight before the King.
One scene of it comes near the circumstance   65
Which I have told thee of my father's death.
I prithee, when thou seest that act afoot,
Even with the very comment of thy soul°
Observe my uncle. If his occulted° guilt
Do not itself unkennel in one speech,   70
It is a damned° ghost that we have seen,
And my imaginations are as foul
As Vulcan's stithy.° Give him heedful note,
For I mine eyes will rivet to his face,
And after we will both our judgments join   75
In censure of his seeming.°
HORATIO: Well, my lord.
If 'a steal aught the whilst this play is playing,
And scape detecting, I will pay the theft.

([*Flourish.*] *Enter trumpets and kettledrums, King, Queen, Polonius, Ophelia*
[*Rosencrantz, Guildenstern, and other Lords, with Guards carrying torches*].)

HAMLET: They are coming to the play. I must be idle. Get you a place.

[*The King, Queen, and courtiers sit.*]

---

49. candied: Sugared, flattering. **50. pregnant:** Compliant. **51. thrift:** Profit. **58. blood:**
Passion. **commeddled:** Commingled. **60. stop:** Hole in a wind instrument for controlling
the sound. **68. very . . . soul:** Inward and sagacious criticism. **69. occulted:** Hidden.
71. damned: In league with Satan. **73. stithy:** Smithy, place of stiths (anvils). **76. censure
of his seeming:** Judgment of his appearance or behavior.

KING: How fares our cousin Hamlet?   80

HAMLET: Excellent, i' faith, of the chameleon's dish:° I eat the air, promise-
cramm'd. You cannot feed capons so.

KING: I have nothing with° this answer, Hamlet. These words are not
mine.°

HAMLET: No, nor mine now. [*To Polonius.*] My lord, you played once i' th'   85
university, you say?

POLONIUS: That did I, my lord; and was accounted a good actor.

HAMLET: What did you enact?

POLONIUS: I did enact Julius Caesar. I was killed i' th' Capitol; Brutus kill'd
me.   90

HAMLET: It was a brute part of him to kill so capital a calf there. Be the players
ready?

ROSENCRANTZ: Ay, my lord; they stay upon your patience.

QUEEN: Come hither, my dear Hamlet, sit by me.

HAMLET: No, good mother, here's metal more attractive.   95

POLONIUS [*to the King*]: O, ho, do you mark that?

HAMLET: Lady, shall I lie in your lap?

                                               [*Lying down at Ophelia's feet.*]

OPHELIA: No, my lord.

[HAMLET: I mean, my head upon your lap?

OPHELIA: Ay, my lord.]   100

HAMLET: Do you think I meant country° matters?

OPHELIA: I think nothing, my lord.

HAMLET: That's a fair thought to lie between maids' legs.

OPHELIA: What is, my lord?

HAMLET: Nothing.   105

OPHELIA: You are merry, my lord.

HAMLET: Who, I?

OPHELIA: Ay, my lord.

HAMLET: O God, your only jig-maker.° What should a man do but be merry? For
look you how cheerfully my mother looks, and my father died within 's°   110
two hours.

OPHELIA: Nay, 'tis twice two months, my lord.

HAMLET: So long? Nay then, let the devil wear black for I'll have a suit of
sables.° O heavens! Die two months ago, and not forgotten yet? Then

---

81. chameleon's dish: Chameleons were supposed to feed on air. Hamlet deliberately misin-
terprets the King's *fares* as *feeds.* By his phrase *eat the air* he also plays on the idea of feeding
himself with the promise of succession, of being the *heir.*   **83. have . . . with:** Make nothing of.
83–84. are not mine: Do not respond to what I asked.   **101. country:** With a bawdy pun.
109. only jig-maker: Very best composer of jigs (song and dance).   **110. within's:** Within
this.   **113–114. suit of sables:** Garments trimmed with the fur of the sable and hence suited
for a wealthy person, not a mourner (with a pun on *sable* black).

there's hope a great man's memory may outlive his life half a year. But, 115
by 'r lady, 'a must build churches, then, or else shall 'a suffer not thinking
on,° with the hobby-horse, whose epitaph is "For, O, for, O, the hobby-
horse is forgot."°

(*The trumpets sound. Dumb show follows.*)

(*Enter a King and a Queen [very lovingly]; the Queen embracing him, and he her.
[She kneels and makes show of protestation unto him.] He takes her up, and declines
his head upon her neck. He lies him down upon a bank of flowers. She, seeing him
asleep, leaves him. Anon comes in another man, takes off his crown, kisses it, pours
poison in the sleeper's ears, and leaves him. The Queen returns; finds the King dead,
makes passionate action. The Poisoner, with some three or four, come in again, seem
to condole with her. The dead body is carried away. The Poisoner woos the Queen
with gifts; she seems harsh awhile but in the end accepts love.*)

                                                                    [*Exeunt.*]

OPHELIA: What means this, my lord?
HAMLET: Marry, this' miching mallecho;° it means mischief.   120
OPHELIA: Belike° this show imports the argument° of the play.
(*Enter Prologue.*)
HAMLET: We shall know by this fellow. The players cannot keep counsel;° they'll
    tell all.
OPHELIA: Will 'a tell us what this show meant?
HAMLET: Ay, or any show that you will show him. Be not you° asham'd to show, 125
    he'll not shame to tell you what it means.
OPHELIA: You are naught, you are naught.° I'll mark the play.
PROLOGUE: For us, and for our tragedy,
    Here stooping° to your clemency,
    We beg your hearing patiently.   [*Exit.*] 130
HAMLET: Is this a prologue, or the posy of a ring?°
OPHELIA: 'Tis brief, my lord.
HAMLET: As woman's love.

(*Enter [two players as] King and Queen.*)

PLAYER KING: Full thirty times hath Phoebus' cart° gone round
    Neptune's salt wash° and Tellus'° orbed ground,   135

116–117. **suffer ... on:** Undergo oblivion. 117–118. **"For ... forgot":** Verse of a song
occurring also in *Love's Labor's Lost*, 3.1.30. The hobby-horse was a character made up to
resemble a horse, appearing in the Morris dance and such May-game sports. This song laments
the disappearance of such customs under pressure from the Puritans. 120. **this' miching
mallecho:** This is sneaking mischief. 121. **Belike:** Probably. **argument:** Plot. 122. **counsel:**
Secret. 125. **Be not you:** If you are not. 127. **naught:** Indecent. 129. **stooping:** Bowing.
131. **posy ... ring:** Brief motto in verse inscribed in a ring. 134. **Phoebus' cart:** The sun
god's chariot. 135. **salt wash:** The sea. **Tellus:** Goddess of the earth, of the *orbed ground*.

And thirty dozen moons with borrowed° sheen
About the world have times twelve thirties been,
Since love our hearts and Hymen° did our hands
Unite commutual° in most sacred bands.

PLAYER QUEEN: So many journeys may the sun and moon   140
    Make us again count o'er ere love be done!
    But, woe is me, you are so sick of late,
    So far from cheer and from your former state,
    That I distrust you. Yet, though I distrust,°
    Discomfort you, my lord, it nothing° must.   145
    For women's fear and love hold quantity;°
    In neither aught, or in extremity.
    Now, what my love is, proof° hath made you know,
    And as my love is siz'd, my fear is so.
    Where love is great, the littlest doubts are fear;   150
    Where little fears grow great, great love grows there.

PLAYER KING: Faith, I must leave thee, love, and shortly too;
    My operant° powers their functions leave to do.°
    And thou shalt live in this fair world behind,
    Honor'd, belov'd; and haply one as kind   155
    For husband shalt thou—

PLAYER QUEEN: O, confound the rest!
    Such love must needs be treason in my breast.
    In second husband let me be accurst!
    None wed the second but who kill'd the first.

HAMLET: Wormwood, wormwood.°   160

PLAYER QUEEN: The instances° that second marriage move°
    Are base respects of thrift,° but none of love.
    A second time I kill my husband dead,
    When second husband kisses me in bed.

PLAYER KING: I do believe you think what now you speak,   165
    But what we do determine oft we break.
    Purpose is but the slave to memory,°
    Of violent birth, but poor validity,°
    Which now, like fruit unripe, sticks on the tree,
    But fall unshaken when they mellow be.   170

---

136. **borrowed:** Reflected.   138. **Hymen:** God of matrimony.   139. **commutual:** Mutually.
144. **distrust:** Am anxious about.   145. **nothing:** Not at all.   146. **hold quantity:** Keep
proportion with one another.   148. **proof:** Experience.   153. **operant:** Active. **leave to
do:** Cease to perform.   160. **wormwood:** A bitter-tasting plant.   161. **instances:** Motives.
move: Motivate.   162. **base . . . thrift:** Ignoble considerations of material prosperity.
167. **Purpose . . . memory:** Our good intentions are subject to forgetfulness.   168. **validity:**
Strength, durability.

Most necessary 'tis that we forget
To pay ourselves what to ourselves is debt.°
What to ourselves in passion we propose,
The passion ending, doth the purpose lose.
The violence of either grief or joy   175
Their own enactures° with themselves destroy.
Where joy most revels, grief doth most lament;
Grief joys, joy grieves, on slender accident.
This world is not for aye,° nor 'tis not strange
That even our loves should with our fortunes change;   180
For 'tis a question left us yet to prove,
Whether love lead fortune, or else fortune love.
The great man down, you mark his favorite flies;
The poor advanc'd makes friends of enemies.
And hitherto doth love on fortune tend;   185
For who not needs° shall never lack a friend,
And who in want° a hollow friend doth try,°
Directly seasons him° his enemy.
But, orderly to end where I begun,
Our wills and fates do so contrary run   190
That our devices still° are overthrown;
Our thoughts are ours, their ends° none of our own.
So think thou wilt no second husband wed,
But die thy thoughts when thy first lord is dead.
PLAYER QUEEN: Nor earth to me give food, nor heaven light,   195
Sport and repose lock from me day and night,
To desperation turn my trust and hope,
An anchor's cheer° in prison be my scope!°
Each opposite° that blanks° the face of joy
Meet what I would have well and it destroy!   200
Both here and hence° pursue me lasting strife,
If, once a widow, ever I be wife!
HAMLET: If she should break it now!
PLAYER KING: 'Tis deeply sworn. Sweet, leave me here awhile;
My spirits grow dull, and fain I would beguile   205
The tedious day with sleep.   [Sleeps.]
PLAYER QUEEN: Sleep rock thy brain,
And never come mischance between us twain!

                                                       [Exit.]

171–172. Most . . . debt: It's inevitable that in time we forget the obligations we have imposed
on ourselves.   176. enactures: Fulfillments.   179. aye: Ever.   186. who not needs: He who is
not in need (of wealth).   187. who in want: He who is in need. try: Test (his generosity).   188. seasons him: Ripens him into.   191. devices still: Intentions continually.   192. ends: Results. 198. anchor's cheer: Anchorite's or hermit's fare. my scope: The extent of my happiness.   199.
opposite: Adverse thing. blanks: Causes to blanch or grow pale.   201. hence: In the life hereafter.

HAMLET: Madam, how like you this play?

QUEEN: The lady doth protest too much, methinks.

HAMLET: O, but she'll keep her word.   210

KING: Have you heard the argument?° Is there no offense in 't?

HAMLET: No, no, they do but jest, poison in jest; no offense i' th' world.

KING: What do you call the play?

HAMLET: "The Mouse-trap." Marry, how? Tropically.° This play is the image of a
    murder done in Vienna. Gonzago is the Duke's name; his wife, Baptista. 215
    You shall see anon. 'Tis a knavish piece of work, but what of that? Your
    Majesty, and we that have free° souls, it touches us not. Let the gall'd jade°
    winch,° our withers° are unwrung.°

(*Enter Lucianus.*)

    This is one Lucianus, nephew to the King.

OPHELIA: You are as good as a chorus,° my lord.   220

HAMLET: I could interpret between you and your love, if I could see the puppets
    dallying.°

OPHELIA: You are keen, my lord, you are keen.

HAMLET: It would cost you a groaning to take off mine edge.

OPHELIA: Still better, and worse.°   225

HAMLET: So° you mistake° your husbands. Begin, murderer, leave thy damnable
    faces, and begin. Come, the croaking raven doth bellow for revenge.

LUCIANUS: Thoughts black, hands apt, drugs fit, and time agreeing,
    Confederate season,° else no creature seeing,   230
    Thou mixture rank, of midnight weeds collected,
    With Hecate's ban° thrice blasted, thrice infected,
    Thy natural magic and dire property
    On wholesome life usurp immediately.

> [*Pours the poison into the sleeper's ears.*]

HAMLET: 'A poisons him i' th' garden for his estate. His name's Gonzago. The 235
    story is extant, and written in very choice Italian. You shall see anon how
    the murderer gets the love of Gonzago's wife.

> [*Claudius rises.*]

---

211. argument: Plot.   **214. Tropically:** Figuratively. (The first quarto reading, *trapically*, suggests
a pun on *trap* in *Mouse-trap.*)   **217. free:** Guiltless.   **gall'd jade:** Horse whose hide is rubbed by
saddle or harness.   **218. winch:** Wince.   **withers:** The part between the horse's shoulder blades.
un-wrung: Not rubbed sore.   **220. chorus:** In many Elizabethan plays the forthcoming action
was explained by an actor known as the "chorus"; at a puppet show the actor who spoke the
dialogue was known as an "interpreter," as indicated by the lines following.   **222. dally-
ing:** With sexual suggestion, continued in *keen*, i.e., sexually aroused, *groaning*, i.e., moaning in
pregnancy, and *edge*, i.e., sexual desire or impetuosity.   **225. Still . . . worse:** More keen-witted
and less decorous.   **226. So:** Even thus (in marriage). **mistake:** Mistake, take erringly, false-
heartedly.   **230. Confederate season:** The time and occasion conspiring (to assist the murderer).   **232. Hecate's ban:** The curse of Hecate, the goddess of witchcraft.

OPHELIA: The King rises.
[HAMLET: What, frighted with false fire?°]
QUEEN: How fares my lord?   240
POLONIUS: Give o'er the play.
KING: Give me some light. Away!
POLONIUS: Lights, lights, lights!

(*Exeunt all but Hamlet and Horatio.*)

HAMLET:
    "Why, let the strucken deer go weep,
        The hart ungalled° play.
    For some must watch,° while some must sleep;   245
        Thus runs the world away."°
Would not this,° sir, and a forest of feathers°—if the rest of my fortunes
turn Turk with° me—with two Provincial roses° on my raz'd° shoes, get me
a fellowship in a cry of players?°   250
HORATIO: Half a share.
HAMLET: A whole one, I.
    "For thou dost know, O Damon dear,
        This realm dismantled° was
    Of Jove himself, and now reigns here   255
        A very, very—pajock."°
HORATIO: You might have rhym'd.
HAMLET: O good Horatio, I'll take the ghost's word for
a thousand pound. Didst perceive?
HORATIO: Very well, my lord.   260
HAMLET: Upon the talk of pois'ning?
HORATIO: I did very well note him.

(*Enter Rosencrantz and Guildenstern.*)

HAMLET: Ah, ha! Come, some music! Come, the recorders!°
    "For if the King like not the comedy,
        Why then, belike, he likes it not, perdy"°   265
Come, some music!
GUILDENSTERN: Good my lord, vouchsafe me a word with you.
HAMLET: Sir, a whole history.

---

239. false fire: The blank discharge of a gun loaded with powder but not shot.   **245. ungalled:**
Unafflicted.   **246. watch:** Remain awake.   **244–47. Why . . . away:** Probably from an old
ballad, with allusion to the popular belief that a wounded deer retires to weep and die; cf. *As
You Like It*, 2.1.66.   **248. this:** The play. **feathers:** Allusion to the plumes that Elizabethan
actors were fond of wearing.   **249. turn Turk with:** Turn renegade against, go back on.
Provincial roses: Rosettes of ribbon, named for roses grown in a part of France. **raz'd:** With
ornamental slashing.   **250. fellowship . . . players:** Partnership in a theatrical company.
254. dismantled: Stripped, divested.   **256. pajock:** Peacock, a bird with a bad reputation
(here substituted for the obvious rhyme-word *ass*).   **263. recorders:** Wind instruments like
the flute.   **265. perdy:** A corruption of the French *par dieu*, by God.

GUILDENSTERN: The King, sir—

HAMLET: Ay, sir, what of him?   270

GUILDENSTERN: Is in his retirement marvelous distemp'red.

HAMLET: With drink, sir?

GUILDENSTERN: No, my lord, with choler.°

HAMLET: Your wisdom should show itself more richer to signify this to the doctor, for for me to put him to his purgation would perhaps plunge him into 275
more choler.

GUILDENSTERN: Good my lord, put your discourse into some frame° and start not
so wildly from my affair.

HAMLET: I am tame, sir. Pronounce.

GUILDENSTERN: The Queen, your mother, in most great affliction of spirit, hath 280
sent me to you.

HAMLET: You are welcome.

GUILDENSTERN: Nay, good my lord, this courtesy is not of the right breed. If it
shall please you to make me a wholesome answer, I will do your mother's
commandment; if not, your pardon° and my return shall be the end of my 285
business.

HAMLET: Sir, I cannot.

ROSENCRANTZ: What, my lord?

HAMLET: Make you a wholesome answer; my wit's diseas'd. But, sir, such answer
as I can make, you shall command, or rather, as you say, my mother. 290
Therefore no more, but to the matter. My mother, you say—

ROSENCRANTZ: Then thus she says: your behavior hath struck her into amazement and admiration.°

HAMLET: O wonderful son, that can so stonish a mother! But is there no sequel
at the heels of this mother's admiration? Impart.   295

ROSENCRANTZ: She desires to speak with you in her closet,° ere you go to bed.

HAMLET: We shall obey, were she ten times our mother. Have you any further
trade with us?

ROSENCRANTZ: My lord, you once did love me.

HAMLET: And do still, by these pickers and stealers.°   300

ROSENCRANTZ: Good my lord, what is your cause of distemper? You do surely bar
the door upon your own liberty, if you deny your griefs to your friend.

HAMLET: Sir, I lack advancement.

ROSENCRANTZ: How can that be, when you have the voice of the King himself for 305
your succession in Denmark?

HAMLET: Ay, sir, but "While the grass grows"°—the proverb is something°
musty.

---

273. **choler:** Anger. (But Hamlet takes the word in its more basic humors sense of *bilious
disorder*.)   277. **frame:** Order.   285. **pardon:** Permission to depart.   293. **admiration:**
Wonder.   296. **closet:** Private chamber.   300. **pickers and stealers:** Hands (so called from
the catechism, "to keep my hands from picking and stealing").   307. **"While . . . grows":** The
rest of the proverb is "the silly horse starves"; Hamlet may not live long enough to succeed to
the kingdom.   **something:** Somewhat.

(*Enter the Players with recorders.*)

O, the recorders! Let me see one. [*He takes a recorder.*] To withdraw° with
you: why do you go about to recover the wind° of me, as if you would drive 310
me into a toil?°
GUILDENSTERN: O, my lord, if my duty be too bold, my love is too unmannerly.°
HAMLET: I do not well understand that. Will you play upon this pipe?
GUILDENSTERN: My lord, I cannot.   315
HAMLET: I pray you.
GUILDENSTERN: Believe me, I cannot.
HAMLET: I do beseech you.
GUILDENSTERN: I know no touch of it, my lord.
HAMLET: It is as easy as lying. Govern these ventages° with your fingers and 320
thumb, give it breath with your mouth, and it will discourse most eloquent
music. Look you, these are the stops.
GUILDENSTERN: But these cannot I command to any utt'rance of harmony; I have
not the skill.
HAMLET: Why, look you now, how unworthy a thing you make of me! You 325
would play upon me, you would seem to know my stops, you would
pluck out the heart of my mystery, you would sound me from my
lowest note to the top of my compass,° and there is much music,
excellent voice, in this little organ,° yet cannot you make it speak.
'Sblood, do you think I am easier to be play'd on than a pipe? Call 330
me what instrument you will, though you can fret° me, you cannot
play upon me.

(*Enter Polonius.*)

God bless you, sir!
POLONIUS: My lord, the Queen would speak with you, and presently.°
HAMLET: Do you see yonder cloud that's almost in shape of a camel?   335
POLONIUS: By th' mass, and 'tis like a camel, indeed.
HAMLET: Methinks it is like a weasel.
POLONIUS: It is back'd like a weasel.
HAMLET: Or like a whale?
POLONIUS: Very like a whale.   340
HAMLET: Then I will come to my mother by and by.° [*Aside.*] They fool me°
to the top of my bent.° — I will come by and by.
POLONIUS: I will say so.   [*Exit.*]

---

309. **withdraw:** Speak privately.   310. **recover the wind:** Get the windward side.   311. **toil:**
Snare.   312. **if . . . unmannerly:** If I am using an unmannerly boldness, it is my love that
occasions it.   320. **ventages:** Stops of the recorder.   328. **compass:** Range (of voice).
329. **organ:** Musical instrument.   331. **fret:** Irritate (with a quibble on *fret* meaning the
piece of wood, gut, or metal that regulates the fingering on an instrument).   334. **presently:**
At once.   341. **by and by:** Immediately. **fool me:** Make me play the fool.   342. **top of my
bent:** Limit of my ability or endurance (literally, the extent to which a bow may be bent).

HAMLET: "By and by" is easily said.
  Leave me, friends.   345

                              [*Exeunt all but Hamlet.*]

'Tis now the very witching time° of night,
When churchyards yawn and hell itself breathes out
Contagion to this world. Now could I drink hot blood,
And do such bitter business as the day
Would quake to look on. Soft, now to my mother.   350
O heart, lose not thy nature! Let not ever
The soul of Nero° enter this firm bosom.
Let me be cruel, not unnatural;
I will speak daggers to her, but use none.
My tongue and soul in this be hypocrites: 355
How in my words somever° she be shent,°
To give them seals° never, my soul, consent!

                                                         (*Exit.*)

[Scene 3]°

(*Enter King, Rosencrantz, and Guildenstern.*)

KING: I like him not, nor stands it safe with us
  To let his madness range. Therefore prepare you.
  I your commission will forthwith dispatch,°
  And he to England shall along with you.
  The terms° of our estate° may not endure   5
  Hazard so near 's as doth hourly grow
  Out of his brows.°
GUILDENSTERN: We will ourselves provide.
  Most holy and religious fear it is
  To keep those many many bodies safe
  That live and feed upon your Majesty.   10
ROSENCRANTZ: The single and peculiar° life is bound
  With all the strength and armor of the mind
  To keep itself from noyance,° but much more
  That spirit upon whose weal depends and rests
  The lives of many. The cess° of majesty   15

---

346. **witching time:** Time when spells are cast and evil is abroad. 352. **Nero:** Murderer
of his mother, Agrippina. 356. **How . . . somever:** However much by my words. **shent:**
Rebuked. 357. **give them seals:** Confirm them with deeds. ACT 3, SCENE 3. **Location:** The
castle. 3. **dispatch:** Prepare, cause to be drawn up. 5. **terms:** Condition, circumstances.
our estate: My royal position. 7. **brows:** Threatening frowns. 11. **single and peculiar:**
Individual and private. 13. **noyance:** Harm. 15. **cess:** Decease.

Dies not alone, but like a gulf° doth draw
What's near it with it; or it is a messy wheel
Fix'd on the summit of the highest mount,
To whose huge spokes ten thousand lesser things
Are mortis'd and adjoin'd, which, when it falls,   20
Each small annexment, petty consequence,
Attends° the boist'rous ruin. Never alone
Did the King sigh, but with a general groan.
KING: Arm° you, I pray you, to this speedy voyage,
For we will fetters put about this fear,   25
Which now goes too free-footed.
ROSENCRANTZ: We will haste us.

(Exeunt Gentlemen [Rosencrantz and Guildenstern].)

(Enter Polonius.)

POLONIUS: My lord, he's going to his mother's closet.
Behind the arras° I'll convey myself
To hear the process.° I'll warrant she'll tax him home,°
And, as you said, and wisely was it said,   30
'Tis meet that some more audience than a mother,
Since nature makes them partial, should o'erhear
The speech, of vantage.° Fare you well, my liege.
I'll call upon you ere you go to bed,
And tell you what I know.
KING: Thanks, dear my lord.   35

(Exit [Polonius].)

O, my offense is rank, it smells to heaven;
It hath the primal eldest curse° upon 't,
A brother's murder. Pray can I not,
Though inclination be as sharp as will.°
My stronger guilt defeats my strong intent,   40
And, like a man to double business bound,
I stand in pause where I shall first begin,
And both neglect. What if this cursed hand
Were thicker than itself with brother's blood,
Is there not rain enough in the sweet heavens   45

---

16. gulf: Whirlpool. 22. Attends: Participates in. 24. Arm: Prepare. 28. arras: Screen of
tapestry placed around the walls of household apartments. (On the Elizabethan stage, the arras
was presumably over a door or discovery space in the tiring-house facade.) 29. process:
Proceedings. tax him home: Reprove him severely. 33. of vantage: From an advantageous
place. 37. primal eldest curse: The curse of Cain, the first murderer; he killed his brother
Abel. 39. Though . . . will: Though my desire is as strong as my determination.

To wash it white as snow? Whereto serves mercy
But to confront the visage of offense?°
And what's in prayer but this twofold force,
To be forestalled° ere we come to fall,
Or pardon'd being down? Then I'll look up;   50
My fault is past. But, O, what form of prayer
Can serve my turn? "Forgive me my foul murder"?
That cannot be, since I am still possess'd
Of those effects for which I did the murder,
My crown, mine own ambition, and my queen.   55
May one be pardon'd and retain th' offense?
In the corrupted currents° of this world
Offense's gilded hand° may shove by justice,
And oft 'tis seen the wicked prize° itself
Buys out the law. But 'tis not so above.   60
There is no shuffling,° there the action lies°
In his° true nature, and we ourselves compell'd,
Even to the teeth and forehead° of our faults,
To give in evidence. What then? What rests?°
Try what repentance can. What can it not?   65
Yet what can it, when one cannot repent?
O wretched state! O bosom black as death!
O limed° soul, that, struggling to be free,
Art more engag'd!° Help, angels! Make assay.°
Bow, stubborn knees, and heart with strings of steel,   70
Be soft as sinews of the new-born babe!
All may be well.

                                              [*He kneels.*]

(*Enter Hamlet [with sword drawn].*)

HAMLET: Now might I do it pat,° now 'a is a-praying;
And now I'll do't. And so 'a goes to heaven;
And so am I reveng'd. That would be scann'd:°   75
A villain kills my father, and for that,
I, his sole son, do this same villain send

46–47. Whereto . . . offense: For what function does mercy serve other than to undo the effects
of sin? **49. forestalled:** Prevented (from sinning). **57. currents:** Courses. **58. gilded
hand:** Hand offering gold as a bribe. **59. wicked prize:** Prize won by wickedness. **61. shuffling:** Escape by trickery. **the action lies:** The accusation is made manifest, comes up for consideration (a legal metaphor). **62. his:** Its. **63. teeth and forehead:** Face to face, concealing
nothing. **64. rests:** Remains. **68. limed:** Caught as with birdlime, a sticky substance used to
ensnare birds. **69. engag'd:** Embedded. **assay:** Trial. **73. pat:** Opportunely. **75. would be
scann'd:** Needs to be looked into.

To heaven.
Why, this is hire and salary, not revenge.
'A took my father grossly,° full of bread,°   80
With all his crimes broad blown,° as flush° as May;
And how his audit° stands who knows save heaven?
But in our circumstance and course° of thought,
'Tis heavy with him. And am I then reveng'd,
To take him in the purging of his soul,   85
When he is fit and season'd for his passage?
No!
Up, sword, and know thou a more horrid hent.°

                                                        [*Puts up his sword.*]

When he is drunk asleep, or in his rage,
Or in th' incestuous pleasure of his bed,   90
At game a-swearing, or about some act
That has no relish of salvation in 't—
Then trip him, that his heels may kick at heaven,
And that his soul may be as damn'd and black
As hell, whereto it goes. My mother stays.   95
This physic° but prolongs thy sickly days.   (*Exit.*)
KING: My words fly up, my thoughts remain below.
Words without thoughts never to heaven go.

                                                                     (*Exit.*)

[Scene 4]°

(*Enter [Queen] Gertrude and Polonius.*)

POLONIUS: 'A will come straight. Look you lay° home to him.
Tell him his pranks have been too broad° to bear with,
And that your Grace hath screen'd and stood between
Much heat° and him. I'll sconce° me even here.
Pray you, be round° [with him.   5
HAMLET (*within*): Mother, mother, mother!]
QUEEN: I'll warrant you, fear me not.
Withdraw, I hear him coming.

                                                [*Polonius hides behind the arras.*]

---

80. grossly: Not spiritually prepared. **full of bread:** Enjoying his worldly pleasures. (See Ezekiel 16:49) **81. crimes broad blown:** Sins in full bloom. **flush:** Lusty.   **82. audit:** Account.   **83. in . . . course:** As we see it in our mortal situation.   **88. know . . . hent:** Await to be grasped by me on a more horrid occasion.   **96. physic:** Purging (by prayer). ACT 3, SCENE 4. **Location:** The queen's private chamber.   **1. lay:** Thrust (i.e., reprove him soundly).   **2. broad:** Unrestrained.   **4. Much heat:** The king's anger. **sconce:** Ensconce, hide.   **5. round:** Blunt.

(*Enter Hamlet.*)

HAMLET: Now, mother, what's the matter?
QUEEN: Hamlet, thou hast thy father° much offended.   10
HAMLET: Mother, you have my father much offended.
QUEEN: Come, come, you answer with an idle° tongue.
HAMLET: Go, go, you question with a wicked tongue.
QUEEN: Why, how now, Hamlet?
HAMLET: What's the matter now?
QUEEN: Have you forgot me?
HAMLET: No, by the rood,° not so:
    You are the Queen, your husband's brother's wife   15
    And — would it were not so! — you are my mother.
QUEEN: Nay, then, I'll set those to you that can speak.
HAMLET: Come, come, and sit you down; you shall not budge.
    You go not till I set you up a glass
    Where you may see the inmost part of you.   20
QUEEN: What wilt thou do? Thou wilt not murder me?
    Help, ho!
POLONIUS [*behind*]: What, ho! Help!
HAMLET [*drawing*]: How now? A rat? Dead, for a ducat, dead!

          [*Makes a pass through the arras.*]

POLONIUS [*behind*]: O, I am slain! [*Falls and dies.*]   25
QUEEN: O me, what hast thou done?
HAMLET: Nay, I know not. Is it the King?
QUEEN: O, what a rash and bloody deed is this!
HAMLET: A bloody deed — almost as bad, good mother,
    As kill a king, and marry with his brother.   30
QUEEN: As kill a king!
HAMLET: Ay, lady, it was my word.

          [*Parts the arras and discovers Polonius.*]

    Thou wretched, rash, intruding fool, farewell!
    I took thee for thy better. Take thy fortune.
    Thou find'st to be too busy is some danger. —
    Leave wringing of your hands. Peace, sit you down,   35
    And let me wring your heart, for so I shall,
    If it be made of penetrable stuff,
    If damned custom° have not braz'd° it so
    That it be proof° and bulwark against sense.°
QUEEN: What have I done, that thou dar'st wag thy tongue   40
    In noise so rude against me?

---

10. thy father: Your stepfather, Claudius. **12. idle:** Foolish. **14. rood:** Cross. **38. damned custom:** Habitual wickedness. **braz'd:** Brazened, hardened. **39. proof:** Armor. **sense:** Feeling.

HAMLET: Such an art
    That blurs the grace and blush of modesty,
    Calls virtue hypocrite, takes off the rose
    From the fair forehead of an innocent love
    And sets a blister° there, makes marriage-vows   45
    As false as dicers' oaths. O, such a deed
    As from the body of contraction° plucks
    The very soul, and sweet religion° makes
    A rhapsody° of words. Heaven's face does glow
    O'er this solidity and compound mass   50
    With heated visage, as against the doom,
    Is thought-sick at the act.°
QUEEN: Ay me, what act,
    That roars so loud and thunders in the index?°
HAMLET: Look here, upon this picture, and on this,
    The counterfeit presentment° of two brothers.   55

                                                [*Shows her two likenesses.*]

    See, what a grace was seated on this brow:
    Hyperion's° curls, the front° of Jove himself,
    An eye like Mars, to threaten and command,
    A station° like the herald Mercury
    New-lighted on a heaven-kissing hill—   60
    A combination and a form indeed,
    Where every god did seem to set his seal,
    To give the world assurance of a man.
    This was your husband. Look you now, what follows:
    Here is your husband, like a mildew'd ear,°   65
    Blasting his wholesome brother. Have you eyes?
    Could you on this fair mountain leave to feed,
    And batten° on this moor?° Ha, have you eyes?
    You cannot call it love, for at your age
    The heyday° in the blood is tame, it's humble,   70
    And waits upon the judgment, and what judgment
    Would step from this to this? Sense,° sure, you have,
    Else could you not have motion, but sure that sense

---

45. sets a blister: Brands as a harlot. **47. contraction:** The marriage contract. **48. religion:**
Religious vows. **49. rhapsody:** Senseless string. **49–52. Heaven's . . . act:** Heaven's face
flushes with anger to look down upon this solid world, this compound mass, with hot face as
though the day of doom were near, and is thought-sick at the deed (i.e., Gertrude's marriage).
53. index: Table of contents, prelude, or preface. **55. counterfeit presentment:** Portrayed
representation. **57. Hyperion:** The sun god. **front:** Brow. **59. station:** Manner of standing.
65. ear: I.e., of grain. **68. batten:** Gorge. **moor:** Barren upland. **70. heyday:** State of
excitement. **72. Sense:** Perception through the five senses (the functions of the middle or
sensible soul).

Is apoplex'd,° for madness would not err,
Nor sense to ecstasy was ne'er so thrall'd   75
But it reserv'd some quantity of choice
To serve in such a difference. What devil was't
That thus hath cozen'd° you at hoodman-blind?°
Eyes without feeling, feeling without sight,
Ears without hands or eyes, smelling sans° all,   80
Or but a sickly part of one true sense
Could not so mope.°
O shame, where is thy blush? Rebellious hell,
If thou canst mutine° in a matron's bones,
To flaming youth let virtue be as wax,   85
And melt in her own fire. Proclaim no shame
When the compulsive ardor gives the charge,
Since frost itself as actively doth burn,
And reason panders will.°
QUEEN: O Hamlet, speak no more!
    Thou turn'st mine eyes into my very soul,   90
    And there I see such black and grained° spots
    As will not leave their tinct.°
HAMLET: Nay, but to live
    In the rank sweat of an enseamed° bed,
    Stew'd in corruption, honeying and making love
    Over the nasty sty—
QUEEN: O, speak to me no more.   95
    These words, like daggers, enter in my ears.
    No more, sweet Hamlet!
HAMLET: A murderer and a villain,
    A slave that is not twentieth part the tithe°
    Of your precedent° lord, a vice° of kings,
    A cutpurse of the empire and the rule,   100
    That from a shelf the precious diadem stole,
    And put it in his pocket!
QUEEN: No more!

---

74. **apoplex'd:** Paralyzed. (Hamlet goes on to explain that without such a paralysis of will, mere madness would not so err, nor would the five senses so enthrall themselves to *ecstasy* or lunacy; even such deranged states of mind would be able to make the obvious choice between Hamlet Senior and Claudius.)   78. **cozen'd:** Cheated. **hoodman-blind:** Blindman's bluff. 80. **sans:** Without.   82. **mope:** Be dazed, act aimlessly.   84. **mutine:** Mutiny.   86–89. **Proclaim . . . will:** Call it no shameful business when the compelling ardor of youth delivers the attack, i.e., commits lechery, since the frost of advanced age burns with as active a fire of lust and reason perverts itself by fomenting lust rather than restraining it.   91. **grained:** Dyed in grain, indelible.   92. **tinct:** Color.   93. **enseamed:** Laden with grease.   98. **tithe:** Tenth part.   99. **precedent:** Former (i.e., the elder Hamlet). **vice:** Buffon (a reference to the vice of the morality plays).

(*Enter Ghost [in his nightgown].*)

HAMLET: A king of shreds and patches° —
  Save me, and hover o'er me with your wings,
  You heavenly guards! What would your gracious figure?   105
QUEEN: Alas, he's mad!
HAMLET: Do you not come your tardy son to chide,
  That, laps'd in time and passion,° lets go by
  Th' important° acting of your dread command?
  O, say!   110
GHOST: Do not forget. This visitation
  Is but to whet thy almost blunted purpose.
  But, look, amazement° on thy mother sits.
  O, step between her and her fighting soul!
  Conceit° in weakest bodies strongest works.   115
  Speak to her, Hamlet.
HAMLET: How is it with you, lady?
QUEEN: Alas, how is't with you,
  That you do bend your eye on vacancy,
  And with th' incorporal° air do hold discourse?
  Forth at your eyes your spirits wildly peep,   120
  And, as the sleeping soldiers in th' alarm,
  Your bedded° hair, like life in excrements,°
  Start up and stand an° end. O gentle son,
  Upon the heat and flame of thy distemper
  Sprinkle cool patience. Whereon do you look?   125
HAMLET: On him, on him! Look you how pale he glares!
  His form and cause conjoin'd,° preaching to stones,
  Would make them capable.° — Do not look upon me,
  Lest with this piteous action you convert
  My stern effects.° Then what I have to do   130
  Will want true color° — tears perchance for blood.
QUEEN: To whom do you speak this?
HAMLET: Do you see nothing there?
QUEEN: Nothing at all, yet all that is I see.
HAMLET: Nor did you nothing hear?
QUEEN: No, nothing but ourselves.

---

103. shreds and patches: Motley, the traditional costume of the clown or fool.
108. laps'd . . . passion: Having allowed time to lapse and passion to cool.   **109. important:**
Importunate, urgent.   **113. amazement:** Distraction.   **115. Conceit:** Imagination.   **119. incorporal:** Immaterial.   **122. bedded:** Laid in smooth layers. **excrements:** Outgrowths. **123. an:** On.
127. His . . . conjoin'd: His appearance joined to his cause for speaking.   **128. capable:**
Receptive.   **129–130. convert . . . effects:** Divert me from my stern duty.   **131. want true
color:** Lack plausibility so that (with a play on the normal sense of *color*) I shall shed tears
instead of blood.

HAMLET: Why, look you there, look how it steals away!   135
    My father, in his habit° as he lived!
    Look, where he goes, even now, out at the portal!

                                   (Exit Ghost.)

QUEEN: This is the very coinage of your brain.
    This bodiless creation ecstasy°
    Is very cunning in.
HAMLET: Ecstasy?   140
    My pulse, as yours, doth temperately keep time,
    And makes as healthful music. It is not madness
    That I have utter'd. Bring me to the test,
    And I the matter will reword, which madness
    Would gambol° from. Mother, for love of grace,   145
    Lay not that flattering unction° to your soul
    That not your trespass but my madness speaks.
    It will but skin and film the ulcerous place,
    Whiles rank corruption, mining° all within,
    Infects unseen. Confess yourself to heaven,   150
    Repent what's past, avoid what is to come,
    And do not spread the compost° on the weeds
    To make them ranker. Forgive me this my virtue;°
    For in the fatness° of these pursy° times
    Virtue itself of vice must pardon beg,   155
    Yea, curb° and woo for leave° to do him good.
QUEEN: O Hamlet, thou hast cleft my heart in twain.
HAMLET: O, throw away the worser part of it,
    And live the purer with the other half.
    Good night. But go not to my uncle's bed;   160
    Assume a virtue, if you have it not.
    That monster, custom, who all sense doth eat,°
    Of habits devil,° is angel yet in this,
    That to the use of actions fair and good
    He likewise gives a frock or livery°   165
    That aptly is put on. Refrain tonight,
    And that shall lend a kind of easiness
    To the next abstinence; the next more easy;

---

136. habit: Dress. **138. ecstasy:** Madness. **145. gambol:** Skip away. **146. unction:** Ointment. **149. mining:** Working under the surface. **152. compost:** Manure. **153. this my virtue:** My virtuous talk in reproving you. **154. fatness:** Grossness. **pursy:** Short-winded, corpulent. **156. curb:** Bow, bend the knee. **leave:** Permission. **162. who . . . eat:** Who consumes all proper or natural feeling. **163. Of habits devil:** Devil-like in prompting evil habits. **165. livery:** An outer appearance, a customary garb (and hence a predisposition easily assumed in time of stress).

For use° almost can change the stamp of nature,
And either° . . . the devil, or throw him out   170
With wondrous potency. Once more, good night;
And when you are desirous to be bless'd,°
I'll blessing beg of you. For this same lord,

[*Pointing to Polonius.*]

I do repent; but heaven hath pleas'd it so
To punish me with this, and this with me,   175
That I must be their scourge and minister.°
I will bestow° him, and will answer well
The death I gave him. So, again, good night.
I must be cruel only to be kind.
Thus bad begins and worse remains behind.°   180
One word more, good lady.
QUEEN: What shall I do?
HAMLET: Not this, by no means, that I bid you do:
Let the bloat° king tempt you again to bed,
Pinch wanton on your cheek, call you his mouse,
And let him, for a pair of reechy° kisses,   185
Or paddling in your neck with his damn'd fingers,
Make you to ravel all this matter out,
That I essentially am not in madness,
But mad in craft. 'Twere good° you let him know,
For who that's but a queen, fair, sober, wise,   190
Would from a paddock,° from a bat, a gib,°
Such dear concernings° hide? Who would do so?
No, in despite of sense and secrecy,
Unpeg the basket° on the house's top,
Let the birds fly, and, like the famous ape,°   195
To try conclusions,° in the basket creep
And break your own neck down.

---

169. use: Habit.   **170. And either:** A defective line usually emended by inserting the word
master after *either*, following the fourth quarto and early editors.   **172. be bless'd:** Become
blessed, i.e., repentant.   **176. their scourge and minister:** Agent of heavenly retribution. (By
scourge, Hamlet also suggests that he himself will eventually suffer punishment in the process
of fulfilling heaven's will.)   **177. bestow:** Stow, dispose of.   **180. behind:** To come.
183. bloat: Bloated.   **185. reechy:** Dirty, filthy.   **189. good:** Said ironically; also the following eight lines.   **191. paddock:** Toad.   **gib:** Tomcat.   **192. dear concernings:** Important
affairs.   **194. Unpeg the basket:** Open the cage, i.e., let out the secret.   **195. famous ape:** In a
story now lost.   **196. conclusions:** Experiments (in which the ape apparently enters a cage
from which birds have been released and then tries to fly out of the cage as they have done,
falling to his death).

QUEEN: Be thou assur'd, if words be made of breath,
    And breath of life, I have no life to breathe
    What thou hast said to me.   200
HAMLET: I must to England; you know that?
QUEEN: Alack,
    I had forgot. 'Tis so concluded on.
HAMLET: There's letters seal'd, and my two school-fellows,
    Whom I will trust as I will adders fang'd,
    They bear the mandate; they must sweep my way,°   205
    And marshal me to knavery. Let it work.
    For 'tis the sport to have the enginer°
    Hoist with° his own petar,° and 't shall go hard
    But I will delve one yard below their mines,°
    And blow them at the moon. O, 'tis most sweet,   210
    When in one line two crafts° directly meet.
    This man shall set me packing.°
    I'll lug the guts into the neighbor room.
    Mother, good night indeed. This counselor
    Is now most still, most secret, and most grave,   215
    Who was in life a foolish prating knave.
    Come, sir, to draw toward an end° with you.
    Good night, mother.

                      (*Exeunt [severally, Hamlet dragging in Polonius].*)

[ACT 4 / Scene 1]°

(*Enter King and Queen, with Rosencrantz and Guildenstern.*)

KING: There's matter in these sighs, these profound heaves
    You must translate; 'tis fit we understand them.
    Where is your son?
QUEEN: Bestow this place on us a little while.

                      [*Exeunt Rosencrantz and Guildenstern.*]

    Ah, mine own lord, what have I seen tonight!   5
KING: What, Gertrude? How does Hamlet?

---

205. sweep my way: Go before me. **207. enginer:** Constructor of military contrivances. **208. Hoist with:** Blown up by. **petar:** Petard, an explosive used to blow in a door or make a breach. **209. mines:** Tunnels used in warfare to undermine the enemy's emplacements; Hamlet will countermine by going under their mines. **211. crafts:** Acts of guile, plots, **212. set me packing:** Set me to making schemes, and set me to lugging (him) and, also, send me off in a hurry. **217. draw . . . end:** Finish up (with a pun on *draw*, pull). Act 4, Scene 1. **Location:** The castle.

QUEEN: Mad as the sea and wind when both contend
  Which is the mightier. In his lawless fit,
  Behind the arras hearing something stir,
  Whips out his rapier, cries, "A rat, a rat!"   10
  And, in this brainish apprehension,° kills
  The unseen good old man.
KING: O heavy deed!
  It had been so with us, had we been there.
  His liberty is full of threats to all—
  To you yourself, to us, to everyone.   15
  Alas, how shall this bloody deed be answer'd?
  It will be laid to us, whose providence°
  Should have kept short,° restrain'd, and out of haunt°
  This mad young man. But so much was our love
  We would not understand what was most fit,   20
  But, like the owner of a foul disease,
  To keep it from divulging,° let it feed
  Even on the pith of life. Where is he gone?
QUEEN: To draw apart the body he hath kill'd,
  O'er whom his very madness, like some ore°   25
  Among a mineral° of metals base,
  Shows itself pure: 'a weeps for what is done.
KING: O Gertrude, come away!
  The sun no sooner shall the mountains touch
  But we will ship him hence, and this vile deed 30
  We must, with all our majesty and skill,
  Both countenance and excuse. Ho, Guildenstern!

(Enter Rosencrantz and Guildenstern.)

  Friends both, go join you with some further aid.
  Hamlet in madness hath Polonius slain,
  And from his mother's closet hath he dragg'd him. 35
  Go seek him out; speak fair, and bring the body
  Into the chapel. I pray you, haste in this.

        [Exeunt Rosencrantz and Guildenstern.]

  Come, Gertrude, we'll call up our wisest friends
  And let them know both what we mean to do
  And what's untimely done°   40

---

11. **brainish** **apprehension:** Headstrong conception. **17.** **providence:** Foresight.
18. short: On a short tether. **out of haunt:** Secluded. **22. divulging:** Becoming evident.
25. ore: Vein of gold. **26. mineral:** Mine. **40. And . . . done:** A defective line; conjectures
as to the missing words include *so, haply, slander* (Capell and others); *for, haply, slander* (Theobald and others).

Whose whisper o'er the world's diameter,°
As level° as the cannon to his blank,°
Transports his pois'ned shot, may miss our name,
And hit the woundless° air. O, come away!
My soul is full of discord and dismay.   (*Exeunt.*) 45

[Scene 2]°

(*Enter Hamlet.*)

HAMLET: Safely stow'd.
[ROSENCRANTZ, GUILDENSTERN (*within*): Hamlet! Lord Hamlet!]
HAMLET: But soft, what noise? Who calls on Hamlet? O, here they come.

(*Enter Rosencrantz and Guildenstern.*)

ROSENCRANTZ: What have you done, my lord, with the dead body?
HAMLET: Compounded it with dust, whereto 'tis kin.   5
ROSENCRANTZ: Tell us where 'tis, that we may take it thence
     And bear it to the chapel.
HAMLET: Do not believe it.
ROSENCRANTZ: Believe what?
HAMLET: That I can keep your counsel and not mine own. Besides, to be
     demanded of° a sponge, what replication° should be made by the son of a 10
     king?
ROSENCRANTZ: Take you me for a sponge, my lord?
HAMLET: Ay, sir, that soaks up the King's countenance,° his rewards, his au-
     thorities. But such officers do the King best service in the end. He keeps
     them, like an ape an apple, in the corner of his jaw, first mouth'd, to be last 15
     swallow'd. When he needs what you have glean'd, it is but squeezing you,
     and, sponge, you shall be dry again.
ROSENCRANTZ: I understand you not, my lord.
HAMLET: I am glad of it. A knavish speech sleeps in° a foolish ear.
ROSENCRANTZ: My lord, you must tell us where the body is, and go with us to 20
     the King.
HAMLET: The body is with the King, but the King is not with the body.° The King
     is a thing—
GUILDENSTERN: A thing, my lord?
HAMLET: Of nothing.° Bring me to him. [Hide fox, and all after.°]   25

(*Exeunt.*)

---

41. diameter: Extent from side to side.   **42. As level:** With as direct aim. **blank:** White spot in
the center of a target.   **44. woundless:** Invulnerable. ACT 4, SCENE 2. **Location:** The castle.
10. demanded of: Questioned by. **replication:** Reply.   **13. countenance:** Favor.   **19. sleeps
in:** Has no meaning to.   **22. The . . . body:** Perhaps alludes to the legal commonplace of "the
king's two bodies," which drew a distinction between the sacred office of kingship and the particular mortal who possessed it at any given time.   **25. Of nothing:** Of no account. **Hide . . . after:** An
old signal cry in the game of hide-and-seek, suggesting that Hamlet now runs away from them.

[Scene 3]°

(*Enter King, and two or three.*)

KING: I have sent to seek him, and to find the body.
How dangerous is it that this man goes loose!
Yet must not we put the strong law on him.
He's lov'd of the distracted° multitude,
Who like not in their judgment, but their eyes,   5
And where 'tis so, th' offender's scourge° is weigh'd,°
But never the offense. To bear° all smooth and even,
This sudden sending him away must seem
Deliberate pause.° Diseases desperate grown
By desperate appliance are reliev'd,   10
Or not at all.

(*Enter Rosencrantz, [Guildenstern,] and all the rest.*)

           How now? What hath befall'n?
ROSENCRANTZ: Where the dead body is bestow'd, my lord,
We cannot get from him.
KING: But where is he?
ROSENCRANTZ: Without, my lord; guarded, to know your pleasure.
KING: Bring him before us.   15
ROSENCRANTZ: Ho! Bring in the lord.

(*They enter [with Hamlet].*)

KING: Now, Hamlet, where's Polonius?
HAMLET: At supper.
KING: At supper? Where?
HAMLET: Not where he eats, but where 'a is eaten. A certain convocation of   20
politic worms° are e'en at him. Your worm is your only emperor for diet.°
We fat all creatures else to fat us, and we fat ourselves for maggots. Your fat
king and your lean beggar is but variable service,° two dishes, but to one
table — that's the end.
KING: Alas, alas!   25
HAMLET: A man may fish with the worm that hath eat° of a king, and eat of the
fish that hath fed of that worm.
KING: What dost thou mean by this?

ACT 4, SCENE 3. **Location:** The castle. **4. distracted:** Fickle, unstable. **6. scourge:** Punishment.
weigh'd: Taken into consideration. **7. bear:** Manage. **9. Deliberate pause:** Carefully considered action. **21. politic worms:** Crafty worms (suited to a master spy like Polonius). **diet:** Food,
eating (with perhaps a punning reference to the Diet of Worms, a famous convocation held in
1521). **23. variable service:** Different courses of a single meal. **26. eat:** Eaten (pro-
nounced "et").

HAMLET: Nothing but to show you how a king may go a progress° through the
    guts of a beggar.   30
KING: Where is Polonius?
HAMLET: In heaven. Send thither to see. If your messenger find him not
    there, seek him i' th' other place yourself. But if indeed you find him
    not within this month, you shall nose him as you go up the stairs
    into the lobby.   35
KING: [*to some Attendants*]: Go seek him there.
HAMLET: 'A will stay till you come.

                                                    [*Exit Attendants.*]

KING: Hamlet, this deed, for thine especial safety.—
    Which we do tender,° as we dearly° grieve
    For that which thou hast done—must send thee hence   40
    [With fiery quickness.] Therefore prepare thyself.
    The bark° is ready, and the wind at help,
    Th' associates tend,° and everything is bent°
    For England.
HAMLET: For England!
KING: Ay, Hamlet.
HAMLET: Good.
KING: So is it, if thou knew'st our purposes.   45
HAMLET: I see a cherub° that sees them. But, come, for England! Farewell, dear
    mother.
KING: Thy loving father, Hamlet.
HAMLET: My mother. Father and mother is man and wife, man and wife is one
    flesh, and so, my mother. Come, for England!   (*Exit.*) 50
KING: Follow him at foot;° tempt him with speed aboard.
    Delay it not; I'll have him hence tonight.
    Away! For everything is seal'd and done
    That else leans on° th' affair. Pray you, make haste.

                                                    [*Exeunt all but the King.*]

    And, England,° if my love thou hold'st at aught—   55
    As my great power thereof may give thee sense,
    Since yet thy cicatrice° looks raw and red
    After the Danish sword, and thy free awe°
    Pays homage to us—thou mayst not coldly set°

---

29. progress: Royal journey of state. **39. tender:** Regard, hold dear. **dearly:** Intensely.
42. bark: Sailing vessel. **43. tend:** Wait. **bent:** In readiness. **46. cherub:** Cherubim are angels of knowledge. **51. at foot:** Close behind, at heel. **54. leans on:** Bears upon, is related to.
55. England: King of England. **57. cicatrice:** Scar. **58. free awe:** Voluntary show of
respect. **59. set:** Esteem.

Our sovereign process,° which imports at full,   60
By letters congruing° to that effect,
The present° death of Hamlet. Do it, England,
For like the hectic° in my blood he rages,
And thou must cure me. Till I know 'tis done,
Howe'er my haps,° my joys were ne'er begun.   65

                                                    (*Exit.*)

[Scene 4]°

(*Enter Fortinbras with his Army over the stage.*)

FORTINBRAS: Go, captain, from me greet the Danish king.
    Tell him that, by his license,° Fortinbras
    Craves the conveyance° of a promis'd march
    Over his kingdom. You know the rendezvous.
    If that his Majesty would aught with us,   5
    We shall express our duty in his eye;°
    And let him know so.
CAPTAIN: I will do 't, my lord.
FORTINBRAS: Go softly° on.   [*Exeunt all but the Captain.*]

(*Enter Hamlet, Rosencrantz, [Guildenstern,] etc.*)

HAMLET: Good sir, whose powers° are these?
CAPTAIN: They are of Norway, sir.   10
HAMLET: How purposed, sir, I pray you?
CAPTAIN: Against some part of Poland.
HAMLET: Who commands them, sir?
CAPTAIN: The nephew to old Norway, Fortinbras.
HAMLET: Goes it against the main° of Poland, sir,   15
    Or for some frontier?
CAPTAIN: Truly to speak, and with no addition,°
    We go to gain a little patch of ground
    That hath in it no profit but the name.
    To pay° five ducats, five, I would not farm it;°   20
    Nor will it yield to Norway or the Pole
    A ranker° rate, should it be sold in fee.°

---

60. **process:** Command. 61. **congruing:** Agreeing. 62. **present:** Immediate. 63. **hectic:**
Persistent fever. 65. **haps:** Fortunes. ACT 4, SCENE 4. **Location:** The coast of Denmark.
2. **license:** Permission. 3. **conveyance:** Escort, convoy. 6. **eye:** Presence. 8. **softly:**
Slowly. 9. **powers:** Forces. 15. **main:** Main part. 17. **addition:** Exaggeration. 20. **To pay:**
I.e., for a yearly rental of. **farm it:** Take a lease of it. 22. **ranker:** Higher. **in fee:** Fee simple,
outright.

HAMLET: Why, then the Polack never will defend it.
CAPTAIN: Yes, it is already garrison'd.
HAMLET: Two thousand souls and twenty thousand ducats   25
    Will not debate the question of this straw.°
    This is th' imposthume° of much wealth and peace,
    That inward breaks, and shows no cause without
    Why the man dies. I humbly thank you, sir.
CAPTAIN: God buy you, sir.   [*Exit.*]
ROSENCRANTZ: Will 't please you go, my lord?   30
HAMLET: I'll be with you straight. Go a little before.

                  [*Exit all except Hamlet.*]

    How all occasions do inform against° me,
    And spur my dull revenge! What is a man,
    If his chief good and market of° his time
    Be but to sleep and feed? A beast, no more.   35
    Sure he that made us with such large discourse,°
    Looking before and after, gave us not
    That capability and god-like reason
    To fust° in us unus'd. Now, whether it be
    Bestial oblivion,° or some craven scruple   40
    Of thinking too precisely on th' event° —
    A thought which, quarter'd, hath but one part wisdom
    And ever three parts coward — I do not know
    Why yet I live to say "This thing's to do,"
    Sith° I have cause and will and strength and means   45
    To do 't. Examples gross° as earth exhort me:
    Witness this army of such mass and charge°
    Led by a delicate and tender prince,
    Whose spirit, with divine ambition puff'd
    Makes mouths° at the invisible event,   50
    Exposing what is mortal and unsure
    To all that fortune, death, and danger dare,
    Even for an egg-shell. Rightly to be great
    Is not to stir without great argument,
    But greatly to find quarrel in a straw   55
    When honor's at the stake. How stand I then,
    That have a father kill'd, a mother stain'd,
    Excitements of° my reason and my blood,

---

26. debate . . . straw: Settle this trifling matter. **27. imposthume:** Abscess. **32. inform against:** Denounce, betray; take shape against. **34. market of:** Profit of compensation for. **36. discourse:** Power of reasoning. **39. fust:** Grow moldy. **40. oblivion:** Forgetfulness. **41. event:** Outcome. **45. Sith:** Since. **46. gross:** Obvious. **47. charge:** Expense. **50. Makes mouths:** Makes scornful faces. **58. Excitements of:** Promptings by.

And let all sleep, while, to my shame, I see
The imminent death of twenty thousand men,   60
That, for a fantasy° and trick° of fame,
Go to their graves like beds, fight for a plot°
Whereon the numbers cannot try the cause,°
Which is not tomb enough and continent°
To hide the slain? O, from this time forth,   65
My thoughts be bloody, or be nothing worth!

(*Exit.*)

[Scene 5]°

(*Enter Horatio, [Queen] Gertrude, and a Gentleman.*)

QUEEN: I will not speak with her.
GENTLEMAN: She is importunate, indeed distract.
   Her mood will needs be pitied.
QUEEN: What would she have?
GENTLEMAN: She speaks much of her father, says she hears
   There's tricks° i' th' world, and hems, and beats her heart,°   5
   Spurns enviously at straws,° speaks things in doubt°
   That carry but half sense. Her speech is nothing,
   Yet the unshaped use° of it doth move
   The hearers to collection;° they yawn° at it,
   And botch° the words up fit to their own thoughts,   10
   Which, as her winks and nods and gestures yield° them,
   Indeed would make one think there might be thought,°
   Though nothing sure, yet much unhappily.
HORATIO: 'Twere good she were spoken with, for she may strew
   Dangerous conjectures in ill-breeding° minds.   15
QUEEN: Let her come in.   [*Exit Gentlemen.*]
   [*Aside.*] To my sick soul, as sin's true nature is,
   Each toy° seems prologue to some great amiss.°

---

61. **fantasy:** Fanciful caprice. **trick:** Trifle.   62. **plot:** I.e., of ground.   63. **Whereon . . .**
cause: On which there is insufficient room for the soldiers needed to engage in a military
contest.   64. **continent:** Receptacle, container. ACT 4, SCENE 5. **Location:** The castle.
5. **tricks:** Deceptions. **heart:** Breast.   6. **Spurns . . . straws:** Kicks spitefully, takes offense at
trifles. **in doubt:** Obscurely.   8. **unshaped use:** Distracted manner.   9. **collection:** Inference,
a guess at some sort of meaning. **yawn:** Wonder, grasp.   10. **botch:** Patch.   11. **yield:** Delivery, bring forth (her words).   12. **thought:** Conjectured.   15. **ill-breeding:** Prone to suspect
the worst.   18. **toy:** Trifle. **amiss:** Calamity.

So full of artless jealousy is guilt,
It spills itself in fearing to be spilt.°   20

(*Enter Ophelia [distracted].*)

OPHELIA:
    Where is the beauteous majesty of Denmark?
QUEEN: How now, Ophelia?
OPHELIA: (*she sings*):
        "How should I your true love know
            From another one?
        By his cockle hat° and staff,   25
            And his sandal shoon."°
QUEEN: Alas, sweet lady, what imports this song?
OPHELIA: Say you? Nay, pray you, mark.
        "He is dead and gone, lady,   (*Song.*)
            He is dead and gone;   30
        At his head a grass-green turf,
            At his heels a stone."
    O, ho!
QUEEN: Nay, but Ophelia —
OPHELIA: Pray you mark.   35
    [*Sings.*] "White his shroud as the mountain snow" —

    (*Enter King.*)

QUEEN: Alas, look here, my lord.
OPHELIA:
        "Larded° all with flowers   (*Song.*)
        Which bewept to the ground did not go
            With true-love showers."   40
KING: How do you, pretty lady?
OPHELIA: Well, God 'ild° you! They say the owl° was a baker's daughter.
    Lord, we know what we are, but know not what we may be. God be at
    your table!
KING: Conceit° upon her father.   45
OPHELIA: Pray let's have no words of this; but when they ask you what it means,
    say you this:
        "Tomorrow is Saint Valentine's° day.   (*Song.*)
            All in the morning betime,

19–20. So . . . spilt: Guilt is so full of suspicion that it unskillfully betrays itself in fearing betrayal. **25. cockle hat:** Hat with cockleshell stuck in it as a sign that the wearer had been a pilgrim to the shrine of St. James of Compostella in Spain. **26. shoon:** Shoes.
38. Larded: Decorated. **42. God 'ild:** God yield or reward. **owl:** Refers to a legend about a baker's daughter who was turned into an owl for refusing Jesus bread. **45. Conceit:** Brooding.
48. Valentine's: This song alludes to the belief that the first girl seen by a man on the morning of this day was his valentine or true love.

And I a maid at your window,   50
    To be your Valentine.
Then up he rose, and donn'd his clo'es,
    And dupp'd° the chamber-door,
Let in the maid, that out a maid
    Never departed more."   55

KING: Pretty Ophelia!

OPHELIA: Indeed, la, without an oath, I'll make an end on 't:
[*Sings.*] "By Gis° and by Saint Charity,
    Alack, and fie for shame!
Young men will do 't, if they come to 't;   60
    By Cock,° they are to blame.
Quoth she, 'Before you tumbled me,
    You promised me to wed.'"
He answers:
"'So would I ha' done, by yonder sun,   65
    An thou hadst not come to my bed.'"

KING: How long hath she been thus?

OPHELIA: I hope all will be well. We must be patient, but I cannot choose but
weep, to think they would lay him i' th' cold ground. My brother shall
know of it; and so I thank you for your good counsel. Come, my coach!
Good night, ladies; good night, sweet ladies; good night, good night.   70

                                        [*Exit.*]

KING: Follow her close; give her good watch, I pray you.

                                    [*Exit Horatio.*]

O, this is the poison of deep grief; it springs
All from her father's death—and now behold!
O Gertrude, Gertrude,
When sorrows come, they come not single spies,°   75
But in battalions. First, her father slain;
Next, your son gone, and he most violent author
Of his own just remove; the people muddied,°
Thick and unwholesome in their thoughts and whispers,
For good Polonius' death; and we have done but greenly,°   80
In hugger-mugger° to inter him; poor Ophelia
Divided from herself and her fair judgment,
Without the which we are pictures, or mere beasts;
Last, and as much containing as all these,
Her brother is in secret come from France,   85

---

53. **dupp'd:** Opened.   58. **Gis:** Jesus.   61. **Cock:** A perversion of *God* in oaths.   75. **spies:**
Scouts sent in advance of the main force.   78. **muddied:** Stirred up, confused.   80. **greenly:**
Imprudently, foolishly.   81. **hugger-mugger:** Secret haste.

Feeds on his wonder, keeps himself in clouds,°
And wants° not buzzers° to infect his ear
With pestilent speeches of his father's death,
Wherein necessity, of matter beggar'd,°
Will nothing stick our person to arraign   90
In ear and ear.° O my dear Gertrude, this,
Like to a murd'ring-piece,° in many places
Gives me superfluous death.   (*A noise within.*)

[QUEEN: Alack, what noise is this?]

KING: Attend!
Where are my Switzers?° Let them guard the door.

(*Enter a Messenger.*)

What is the matter?
MESSENGER: Save yourself, my lord!   95
The ocean, overpeering of his list,°
Eats not the flats° with more impiteous° haste
Than young Laertes, in a riotous head,°
O'erbears your officers. The rabble call him lord,
And, as° the world were now but to begin,   100
Antiquity forgot, custom not known,
The ratifiers and props° of every word,°
They cry, "Choose we! Laertes shall be king!"
Caps, hands, and tongues applaud it to the clouds,
"Laertes shall be king, Laertes king!"   105

(*A noise within.*)

QUEEN: How cheerfully on the false trail they cry!
O, this is counter,° you false Danish dogs!

(*Enter Laertes with others.*)

KING: The doors are broke.
LAERTES: Where is this King? Sirs, stand you all without.
ALL: No, let's come in.

---

86. **in clouds:** I.e., of suspicion and rumor.   87. **wants:** Lacks. **buzzers:** Gossipers, informers. 89. **of matter beggar'd:** Unprovided with facts.   90–91. **Will . . . and ear:** Will not hesitate to accuse my (royal) person in everybody's ears.   92. **murd'ring-piece:** Cannon loaded so as to scatter its shot.   94. **Switzers:** Swiss guards, mercenaries.   96. **overpeering of his list:** Overflowing its shore.   97. **flats:** Flatlands near shore. **impiteous:** Pitiless.   98. **head:** Armed force.   100. **as:** As if.   102. **ratifiers . . . word:** All ancient traditions and customs that underprop our every promise. **word:** Promise.   107. **counter:** A hunting term meaning to follow the trail in a direction opposite to that which the game has taken.

LAERTES: I pray you, give me leave.   110
ALL: We will, we will.

> *[They retire without the door.]*

LAERTES: I thank you. Keep the door. O thou vile king,
  Give me my father!
QUEEN: Calmly, good Laertes.

> *[She tries to hold him back.]*

LAERTES: That drop of blood that's calm proclaims me bastard,
  Cries cuckold to my father, brands the harlot   115
  Even here, between the chaste unsmirched brow
  Of my true mother.
KING: What is the cause, Laertes,
  That thy rebellion looks so giant-like?
  Let him go, Gertrude. Do not fear our° person.
  There's such divinity doth hedge a king   120
  That treason can but peep to what it would,°
  Acts little of his will.° Tell me, Laertes,
  Why thou art thus incens'd. Let him go, Gertrude.
  Speak, man.
LAERTES: Where is my father?
KING: Dead.
QUEEN: But not by him.   125
KING: Let him demand his fill.
LAERTES: How came he dead? I'll not be juggled with.
  To hell, allegiance! Vows, to the blackest devil!
  Conscience and grace, to the profoundest pit!
  I dare damnation. To this point I stand,   130
  That both the worlds I give to negligence,°
  Let come what comes, only I'll be reveng'd
  Most throughly° for my father.
KING: Who shall stay you?
LAERTES: My will, not all the world's.°
  And for my means, I'll husband them so well,   135
  They shall go far with little.
KING: Good Laertes,
  If you desire to know the certainty

---

119. **fear our:** Fear for my.   121. **can . . . would:** Can only glance; as from far off or through a barrier, at what it would intend.   122. **Acts . . . will:** (But) performs little of what it intends. 131. **both . . . negligence:** Both this world and the next are of no consequence to me. 133. **throughly:** Thoroughly.   134. **My will . . . world's:** I'll stop (stay) when my will is accomplished, not for anyone else's.

Of your dear father, is 't writ in your revenge
That, swoopstake,° you will draw both friend and foe,
Winner and loser?   140
LAERTES: None but his enemies.
KING: Will you know them then?
LAERTES: To his good friends thus wide I'll ope my arms,
    And, like the kind life-rend'ring pelican,°
    Repast° them with my blood.
KING: Why, now you speak
Like a good child and a true gentleman.   145
That I am guiltless of your father's death,
And am most sensibly° in grief for it,
It shall as level° to your judgment 'pear
As day does to your eye.
                    (*A noise within:*) "Let her come in."
LAERTES: How now? What noise is that?   150

(*Enter Ophelia.*)

    O heat, dry up my brains! Tears seven times salt
    Burn out the sense and virtue° of mine eye!
    By heaven, thy madness shall be paid with weight°
    Till our scale turn the beam.° O rose of May!
    Dear maid, kind sister, sweet Ophelia!   155
    O heavens, is 't possible a young maid's wits
    Should be as mortal as an old man's life?
    [Nature is fine in° love, and where 'tis fine,
    It sends some precious instance° of itself
    After the thing it loves.°]   160
OPHELIA: "They bore him barefac'd on the bier;   (*Song.*)
            [Hey non nonny, nonny, hey nonny,]
        And in his grave rain'd many a tear"—
    Fare you well, my dove!
LAERTES: Hadst thou thy wits, and didst persuade° revenge,   165
    It could not move thus.
OPHELIA: You must sing "A-down a-down,
    And you "call him a-down-a.""

---

139. swoopstake: Literally, taking all stakes on the gambling table at once, i.e., indiscriminately; *draw* is also a gambling term.   **143. pelican:** Refers to the belief that the female pelican fed its young with its own blood.   **144. Repast:** Feed.   **147. sensibly:** Feelingly.   **148. level:** Plain.   **152. virtue:** Faculty, power.   **153. paid with weight:** Repaid, avenged equally or more.   **154. beam:** Crossbar of a balance.   **158. fine in:** Refined by.   **159. instance:** Token.   **160. After . . . loves:** Into the grave, along with Polonius.   **165. persuade:** Argue cogently for.   **167–68.** Ophelia is assigning to others present—"you, and you"—the refrains they are to sing in response to her traditional song.

O, how the wheel° becomes it! It is the false steward° that stole his master's
daughter.   170

LAERTES: This nothing's more than matter.°

OPHELIA: There's rosemary,° that's for remembrance; pray you, love, remember.
And there is pansies,° that's for thoughts.

LAERTES: A document° in madness, thoughts and remembrance fitted.

OPHELIA: There's fennel° for you, and columbines.° There's rue° for you, and   175
here's some for me; we may call it herb of grace o' Sundays. You may
wear your rue with a difference.° There's a daisy.° I would give you some
violets,° but they wither'd all when my father died. They say 'a made a
good end—

[Sings.] "For bonny sweet Robin is all my joy."   180

LAERTES: Thought° and affliction, passion, hell itself,
She turns to favor° and to prettiness.

OPHELIA:
> "And will 'a not come again?   (Song.)
> And will 'a not come again?
>   No, no, he is dead,   185
>   Go to thy death-bed,
> He never will come again.
>
> "His beard was as white as snow,
> All flaxen was his poll.°
>   He is gone, he is gone,   190
>   And we cast away moan.
> God 'a' mercy on his soul!"
> And of all Christians' souls, I pray God. God b' wi' you.

                                                                                   [Exit.]

LAERTES: Do you see this, O God?

KING: Laertes, I must commune with your grief,   195
Or you deny me right. Go but apart,
Make choice of whom your wisest friends you will,
And they shall hear and judge 'twixt you and me.
If by direct or by collateral° hand
They find us touch'd,° we will our kingdom give,   200

---

169. **wheel:** Spinning wheel as accompaniment to the song, or refrain. **false steward:** The
story is unknown.   171. **This . . . matter:** This seeming nonsense is more meaningful than
sane utterance.   172. **rosemary:** Used as a symbol of remembrance both at weddings and
at funerals.   173. **pansies:** Emblems of love and courtship; perhaps from French *pensées*,
thoughts.   174. **document:** Instruction, lesson.   175. **fennel:** Emblem of flattery. **columbines:** Emblems of unchastity or ingratitude. **rue:** Emblem of repentance; when mingled
with holy water, it was known as *herb of grace*.   177. **with a difference:** Suggests that
Ophelia and the queen have different causes of sorrow and repentance; perhaps with a play
on *rue* in the sense of ruth, pity. **daisy:** Emblem of dissembling, faithlessness.   178. **violets:**
Emblems of faithfulness.   181. **Thought:** Melancholy.   182. **favor:** Grace.   189. **poll:**
Head.   199. **collateral:** Indirect.   200. **us touch'd:** Me implicated.

Our crown, our life, and all that we call ours,
To you in satisfaction; but if not,
Be you content to lend your patience to us,
And we shall jointly labor with your soul
To give it due content.

LAERTES: Let this be so.   205
His means of death, his obscure funeral —
No trophy,° sword, nor hatchment° o'er his bones,
No noble rite nor formal ostentation° —
Cry to be heard, as 'twere from heaven to earth,
That I must call't in question.

KING: So you shall;   210
And where th' offense is, let the great ax fall.
I pray you go with me.   (*Exeunt.*) 215

[Scene 6]°

(*Enter Horatio and others.*)

HORATIO: What are they that would speak with me?
GENTLEMAN: Seafaring men, sir. They say they have letters for you.
HORATIO: Let them come in.   [*Exit Gentleman.*]
    I do not know from what part of the world
    I should be greeted, if not from lord Hamlet.   5

(*Enter Sailors.*)

FIRST SAILOR: God bless you sir.
HORATIO: Let him bless thee too.
FIRST SAILOR: 'A shall, sir, an 't please him. There's a letter for you, sir — it came
    from th' ambassador that was bound for England — if your name be
    Horatio, as I am let to know it is.   [*Gives letter.*] 10
HORATIO [*reads*]: "Horatio, when thou shalt have over-look'd this, give
    these fellows some means° to the King; they have letters for him. Ere
    we were two days old at sea, a pirate of very warlike appointment° gave
    us chase. Finding ourselves too slow of sail, we put on a compell'd
    valor, and in the grapple I boarded them. On the instant they got 15
    clear of our ship, so I alone became their prisoner. They have dealt
    with me like thieves of mercy,° but they knew what they did: I am to
    do a good turn for them. Let the King have the letters I have sent, and
    repair thou to me with as much speed as thou wouldest fly death. I
    have words to speak in thine ear will make thee dumb; yet are they 20

---

207. **trophy:** Memorial, **hatchment:** Tablet displaying the armorial bearings of a deceased
person. 208. **ostentation:** Ceremony. ACT 4, SCENE 6. Location: The castle. 12. **means:**
Means of access. 13. **appointment:** Equipage. 17. **thieves of mercy:** Merciful thieves.

much too light for the bore° of the matter. These good fellows will
bring thee where I am. Rosencrantz and Guildenstern hold their
course for England. Of them I have much to tell thee. Farewell.

        He that thou knowest thine, Hamlet."
Come, I will give you way for these your letters,   25
And do 't the speedier that you may direct me
To him from whom you brought them.   (*Exeunt.*)

[Scene 7]°

(*Enter King and Laertes.*)

KING: Now must your conscience my acquittance seal,°
    And you must put me in your heart for friend,
    Sith you have heard, and with a knowing ear,
    That he which hath your noble father slain
    Pursued my life.
LAERTES: It well appears. But tell me   5
    Why you proceeded not against these feats°
    So criminal and so capital° in nature,
    As by your safety, greatness, wisdom, all things else,
    You mainly° were stirr'd up.
KING: O, for two special reasons,
    Which may to you, perhaps, seem much unsinew'd,°   10
    But yet to me th' are strong. The Queen his mother
    Lives almost by his looks, and for myself—
    My virtue or my plague, be it either which—
    She's so conjunctive° to my life and soul
    That, as the star moves not but in his sphere,°   15
    I could not but by her. The other motive,
    Why to a public count° I might not go,
    Is the great love the general gender° bear him,
    Who, dipping all his faults in their affection,
    Would, like the spring° that turneth wood to stone,   20
    Convert his gyves° to graces, so that my arrows,
    Too slightly timber'd° for so loud° a wind,
    Would have reverted to my bow again
    And not where I had aim'd them.

---

21. **bore:** Caliber, i.e., importance. ACT 4, SCENE 7. **Location:** The castle. 1. **my acquittance seal:** Confirm or acknowledge my innocence. 6. **feats:** Acts. 7. **capital:** Punishable by death. 9. **mainly:** Greatly. 10. **unsinew'd:** Weak. 14. **conjunctive:** Closely united. 15. **sphere:** The hollow sphere in which, according to Ptolemaic astronomy, the planets moved. 17. **count:** Account, reckoning. 18. **general gender:** Common people. 20. **spring:** A spring with such a concentration of lime that it coats a piece of wood with limestone, in effect gilding it. 21. **gyves:** Fetters (which, gilded by the people's praise, would look like badges of honor). 22. **slightly timber'd:** Light. **loud:** Strong.

LAERTES: And so have I a noble father lost,   25
    A sister driven into desp'rate terms,°
    Whose worth, if praises may go back° again,
    Stood challenger on mount° of all the age
    For her perfections. But my revenge will come.

KING: Break not your sleeps for that. You must not think   30
    That we are made of stuff so flat and dull
    That we can let our beard be shook with danger
    And think it pastime. You shortly shall hear more.
    I lov'd your father, and we love ourself;
    And that, I hope, will teach you to imagine —   35

(*Enter a Messenger with letters.*)

    [How now? What news?]
MESSENGER: [Letters, my lord, from Hamlet:]
    These to your Majesty, this to the Queen.

                                                    [*Gives letters.*]

KING: From Hamlet? Who brought them?
MESSENGER: Sailors, my lord, they say; I saw them not.
    They were given me by Claudio. He receiv'd them   40
    Of him that brought them.
KING: Laertes, you shall hear them.
    Leave us.   [*Exit Messenger.*]
    [*Reads.*] "High and mighty, you shall know I am set naked° on your king-
    dom. Tomorrow shall I beg leave to see your kingly eyes, when I shall, first
    asking your pardon° thereunto, recount the occasion of my sudden and   45
    more strange return.   Hamlet."
    What should this mean? Are all the rest come back?
    Or is it some abuse,° and no such thing?
LAERTES: Know you the hand?
KING: 'Tis Hamlet's character.° "Naked!"
    And in a postscript here, he says "alone."   50
    Can you devise° me?
LAERTES: I am lost in it, my lord. But let him come.
    It warms the very sickness in my heart
    That I shall live and tell him to his teeth,
    "Thus didst thou."
KING: If it be so, Laertes —   55
    As how should it be so? How otherwise?° —

---

26. terms: State, condition. **27. go back:** Recall Ophelia's former virtues. **28. on mount:** On high. **43. naked:** Destitute, unarmed, without following. **45. pardon:** Permission. **48. abuse:** Deceit. **49. character:** Handwriting. **51. devise:** Explain to. **56. As . . . otherwise:** How can this (Hamlet's return) be true? Yet how otherwise than true (since we have the evidence of his letter).

Will you be ruled by me?

LAERTES: Ay, my lord,
So° you will not o'errule me to a peace.

KING: To thine own peace. If he be now returned,
As checking at° his voyage, and that he means   60
No more to undertake it, I will work him
To an exploit, now ripe in my device,
Under the which he shall not choose but fall;
And for his death no wind of blame shall breathe,
But even his mother shall uncharge the practice°   65
And call it accident.

LAERTES: My lord, I will be rul'd,
The rather if you could devise it so
That I might be the organ.°

KING: It falls right.
You have been talk'd of since your travel much,
And that in Hamlet's hearing, for a quality   70
Wherein, they say, you shine. Your sum of parts°
Did not together pluck such envy from him
As did that one, and that, in my regard,
Of the unworthiest siege.°

LAERTES: What part is that, my lord?

KING: A very riband in the cap of youth,   75
Yet needful too, for youth no less becomes
The light and careless livery that it wears
Than settled age his sables° and his weeds,°
Importing health° and graveness. Two months since
Here was a gentleman of Normandy.   80
I have seen myself, and serv'd against, the French,
And they can well° on horseback, but this gallant
Had witchcraft in 't; he grew unto his seat,
And to such wondrous doing brought his horse
As had he been incorps'd and demi-natured°   85
With the brave beast. So far he topp'd° my thought
That I, in forgery° of shapes and tricks,
Come short of what he did.

LAERTES: A Norman was 't?

KING: A Norman.

LAERTES: Upon my life, Lamord.

---

58. So: Provided that.   **60. checking at:** Turning aside from (like a falcon leaving the quarry
to fly at a chance bird).   **65. uncharge the practice:** Acquit the stratagem of being a plot.
68. organ: Agent, instrument.   **71. Your . . . parts:** All your other virtues.   **74. unworthiest
siege:** Least important rank.   **78. sables:** Rich robes furred with sable. **weeds:** Garments.
79. Importing health: Indicating prosperity.   **82. can well:** Are skilled.   **85. incorps'd and
demi-natured:** Of one body and nearly of one nature (like the centaur).   **86. topp'd:**
Surpassed.   **87. forgery:** Invention.

KING: The very same.   90
LAERTES: I know him well. He is the brooch° indeed
    And gem of all the nation.
KING: He made confession° of you,
    And gave you such a masterly report
    For art and exercise in your defense,   95
    And for your rapier most especial,
    That he cried out, 'twould be a sight indeed,
    If one could match you. The scrimers° of their nation,
    He swore, had neither motion, guard, nor eye,
    If you oppos'd them. Sir, this report of his   100
    Did Hamlet so envenom with his envy
    That he could nothing do but wish and beg
    Your sudden coming o'er to play° with you.
    Now, out of this—
LAERTES: What out of this, my lord?
KING: Laertes, was your father dear to you?   105
    Or are you like the painting of a sorrow,
    A face without a heart?
LAERTES: Why ask you this?
KING: Not that I think you did not love your father,
    But that I know love is begun by time,°
    And that I see, in passages of proof,°   110
    Time qualifies° the spark and fire of it.
    There lives within the very flame of love
    A kind of wick or snuff° that will abate it,
    And nothing is at a like goodness still,°
    For goodness, growing to a plurisy,°   115
    Dies in his own too much.° That° we would do,
    We should do when we would; for this "would" changes
    And hath abatements° and delays as many
    As there are tongues, are hands, are accidents,°
    And then this "should" is like a spendthrift's sigh,°   120
    That hurts by easing.° But, to the quick o' th' ulcer;
    Hamlet comes back. What would you undertake
    To show yourself your father's son in deed
    More than in words?

---

91. **brooch:** Ornament.   93. **confession:** Admission of superiority.   98. **scrimers:** Fencers.
103. **play:** Fence.   109. **begun by time:** Subject to change.   110. **passages of proof:** Actual
instances.   111. **qualifies:** Weakens.   113. **snuff:** The charred part of a candlewick.   114. **nothing . . . still:** Nothing remains at a constant level of perfection.   115. **plurisy:** Excess, pleth-
ora.   116. **in . . . much:** Of its own excess.   **That:** That which.   118. **abatements:**
Diminutions.   119. **accidents:** Occurrences, incidents.   120. **spendthrift's sigh:** An allusion
to the belief that each sigh cost the heart a drop of blood.   121. **hurts by easing:** Costs the
heart blood even while it affords emotional relief.

LAERTES: To cut his throat i' th' church!
KING: No place, indeed, should murder sanctuarize;°   125
　　 Revenge should have no bounds. But, good Laertes,
　　 Will you do this,° keep close within your chamber.
　　 Hamlet return'd shall know you are come home.
　　 We'll put on those° shall praise your excellence
　　 And set a double varnish on the fame   130
　　 The Frenchman gave you, bring you in fine° together,
　　 And wager on your heads. He, being remiss,°
　　 Most generous,° and free from all contriving,
　　 Will not peruse the foils, so that, with ease,
　　 Or with a little shuffling, you may choose   135
　　 A sword unbated,° and in a pass of practice°
　　 Requite him for your father.
LAERTES: I will do 't.
　　 And for that purpose I'll anoint my sword.
　　 I bought an unction° of a mountebank°
　　 So mortal that, but dip a knife in it,   140
　　 Where it draws blood no cataplasm° so rare,
　　 Collected from all simples° that have virtue
　　 Under the moon, can save the thing from death
　　 That is but scratch'd withal. I'll touch my point
　　 With this contagion, that, if I gall° him slightly,   145
　　 It may be death.
KING: Let's further think of this,
　　 Weigh what convenience both of time and means
　　 May fit us to our shape.° If this should fail,
　　 And that our drift look through our bad performance,°
　　 'Twere better not assay'd. Therefore this project   150
　　 Should have a back or second, that might hold
　　 If this did blast in proof,° Soft, let me see.
　　 We'll make a solemn wager on your cunnings—
　　 I ha 't!
　　 When in your motion you are hot and dry—   155
　　 As° make your bouts more violent to that end—
　　 And that he calls for drink, I'll have prepar'd him
　　 A chalice for the nonce,° whereon but sipping,

---

125. **sanctuarize:** Protect from punishment (alludes to the right of sanctuary with which certain religious places were invested).   127. **Will you do this:** If you wish to do this.   129. **put on those:** Instigate those who.   131. **in fine:** Finally.   132. **remiss:** Negligently unsuspicious.   133. **generous:** Noble-minded.   136. **unbated:** Not blunted, having no button. **pass of practice:** Treacherous thrust.   139. **unction:** Ointment. **mountebank:** Quack doctor.   141. **cataplasm:** Plaster or poultice.   142. **simples:** Herbs.   145. **gall:** Graze, wound.   148. **shape:** Part that we propose to act.   149. **drift . . . performance:** I.e., intention be disclosed by our bungling.   152. **blast in proof:** Burst in the test (like a cannon).   156. **As:** And you should.   158. **nonce:** Occasion.

If he by chance escape your venom'd stuck,°
Our purpose may hold there. [*A cry within.*] But stay, what noise?   160

(*Enter Queen.*)

QUEEN: One woe doth tread upon another's heel,
    So fast they follow. Your sister's drowned, Laertes.
LAERTES: Drown'd! O, where?
QUEEN: There is a willow grows askant° the brook
    That shows his hoar° leaves in the glassy stream;   165
    Therewith fantastic garlands did she make
    Of crow-flowers, nettles, daisies, and long purples°
    That liberal° shepherds give a grosser name,
    But our cold° maids do dead men's fingers call them.
    There on the pendent boughs her crownet° weeds   170
    Clamb'ring to hang, an envious sliver° broke,
    When down her weedy° trophies and herself
    Fell in the weeping brook. Her clothes spread wide,
    And mermaid-like awhile they bore her up,
    Which time she chanted snatches of old lauds,°   175
    As one incapable° of her own distress,
    Or like a creature native and indued°
    Unto that element. But long it could not be
    Till that her garments, heavy with their drink,
    Pull'd the poor wretch from her melodious lay   180
    To muddy death.
LAERTES: Alas, then she is drown'd?
QUEEN: Drown'd, drown'd.
LAERTES: Too much of water hast thou, poor Ophelia,
    And therefore I forbid my tears. But yet
    It is our trick;° nature her custom holds,   185
    Let shame say what it will. [*He weeps.*] When these are gone,
    The woman will be out.° Adieu, my lord.
    I have a speech of fire, that fain would blaze,
    But that this folly drowns it.   (*Exit.*)
KING: Let's follow, Gertrude.
    How much I had to do to calm his rage!   190
    Now fear I this will give it start again;
    Therefore let's follow.   (*Exeunt.*)

---

159. **stuck:** Thrust (from *stoccado*, a fencing term).   164. **askant:** Aslant.   165. **hoar:** White
or gray.   167. **long purples:** Early purple orchids.   168. **liberal:** Free-spoken.   170. **cold:**
Chaste.   170. **crownet:** Made into a chaplet or coronet.   171. **envious sliver:** Malicious
branch.   172. **weedy:** I.e., of plants.   175. **lauds:** Hymns.   176. **incapable:** Lacking capacity
to apprehend.   177. **indued:** Adapted by nature.   185. **It is our trick:** Weeping is our natural
way (when sad).   186–187. **When . . . out:** When my tears are all shed, the woman in me
will be expended, satisfied.

[ACT 5 / Scene 1]°

(*Enter two Clowns*° [*with spades, etc.*])

FIRST CLOWN: Is she to be buried in Christian burial when she willfully seeks her own salvation?

SECOND CLOWN: I tell thee she is; therefore make her grave straight.° The crowner° hath sat on her, and finds it Christian burial.

FIRST CLOWN: How can that be, unless she drown'd herself in her own   5
defense?

SECOND CLOWN: Why, 'tis found so.

FIRST CLOWN: It must be "se offendendo";° it cannot be else. For here lies the point: if I drown myself wittingly, it argues an act, and an act hath three branches—it is to act, to do, and to perform. Argal,° she drown'd herself   10
wittingly.

SECOND CLOWN: Nay, but hear you, goodman delver—

FIRST CLOWN: Give me leave. Here lies the water; good. Here stands the man; good. If the man go to this water, and drown himself, it is, will he,° nill he, he goes, mark you that. But if the water come to him and drown him, he   15
drowns not himself. Argal, he that is not guilty of his own death shortens not his own life.

SECOND CLOWN: But is this law?

FIRST CLOWN: Ay, marry, is 't—crowner's quest° law.

SECOND CLOWN: Will you ha' the truth on 't? If this had not been a gentle-   20
woman, she should have been buried out o' Christian burial.

FIRST CLOWN: Why, there thou say'st.° And the more pity that great folk should have count'nance° in this world to drown or hang themselves, more than their even-Christen.° Come, my spade. There is no ancient gentlemen but gard'ners, ditchers, and grave-makers. They hold up   25
Adam's profession.

SECOND CLOWN: Was he a gentleman?

FIRST CLOWN: 'A was the first that ever bore arms.

[SECOND CLOWN: Why, he had none.

FIRST CLOWN: What, art a heathen? How dost thou understand the Scripture?   30
The Scripture says "Adam digg'd." Could he dig without arms?] I'll put another question to thee. If thou answerest me not to the purpose, confess thyself° —

SECOND CLOWN: Go to.

ACT 5, SCENE 1. **Location:** A churchyard. [S.D.] *Clowns:* Rustics.   **3. straight:** Straightway, immediately.   **4. crowner:** Coroner.   **8. "se offendendo":** A comic mistake for *se defendendo*, term used in verdicts of justifiable homicide.   **10. Argal:** Corruption of *ergo*, therefore. **14. will he:** Will he not.   **19. quest:** Inquest.   **22. there thou say'st:** That's right. **23. count'nance:** Privilege.   **24. even-Christen:** Fellow Christian.   **33. confess thyself:** The saying continues, "and be hanged."

FIRST CLOWN: What is he that builds stronger than either the mason, the ship- 35
    wright, or the carpenter?

SECOND CLOWN: The gallows-maker, for that frame outlives a thousand
    tenants.

FIRST CLOWN: I like thy wit well, in good faith. The gallows does well, but how
    does it well? It does well to those that do ill. Now thou dost ill to say the 40
    gallows is built stronger than the church. Argal, the gallows may do well to
    thee. To 't again, come.

SECOND CLOWN: "Who builds stronger than a mason, a shipwright, or a
    carpenter?"

FIRST CLOWN: Ay, tell me that, and unyoke.° 45

SECOND CLOWN: Marry, now I can tell.

FIRST CLOWN: To 't.

SECOND CLOWN: Mass,° I cannot tell.

(Enter Hamlet and Horatio [at a distance].)

FIRST CLOWN: Cudgel thy brains no more about it, for your dull ass will not mend
    his pace with beating; and, when you are ask'd this question next, say "a 50
    grave-maker." The houses he makes lasts till doomsday. Go, get thee in, and
    fetch me a stoup° of liquor.

[Exit Second Clown. First Clown digs.]

    "In youth, when I did love, did love,°   *(Song.)*
        Methought it was very sweet,
    To contract—O—the time for—a—my behove,° 55
        O, methought there—a—was nothing—a—meet."°

HAMLET: Has this fellow no feeling of his business, that 'a sings at grave-
    making?

HORATIO: Custom hath made it in him a property of easiness.°

HAMLET: 'Tis e'en so. The hand of little employment hath the daintier 60
    sense.°

FIRST CLOWN: *(Song.)*
    "But age, with his stealing steps,
        Hath claw'd me in his clutch,

---

45. unyoke: After this great effort you may unharness the team of your wits.   **48. Mass:** By
the Mass.   **52. stoup:** Two-quart measure.   **53. In . . . love:** This and the two following stanzas, with nonsensical variations, are from a poem attributed to Lord Vaux and printed in *Tottel's
Miscellany* (1557). The O and a (for "ah") seemingly are the grunts of the digger.   **55. To
contract . . . behove:** To shorten the time for my own benefit (perhaps he means to *prolong* it).
56. meet: Suitable, i.e., more suitable.   **59. property of easiness:** Something he can do easily
and without thinking.   **60–61. daintier sense:** More delicate sense of feeling.

And ha th shipped me into the land,°
As if I had never been such."   65

[*Throws up a skull.*]

HAMLET: That skull had a tongue in it, and could sing once. How the knave
jowls° it to the ground, as if 'twere Cain's jaw-bone, that did the first murder! This might be the pate of a politician,° which this ass now o'erreaches,°
one that would circumvent God, might it not?

HORATIO: It might, my lord.   70

HAMLET: Or of a courtier, which could say "Good morrow, sweet lord!
How dost thou, sweet lord?" This might be my Lord Such-a-one, that
prais'd my Lord Such-a-one's horse when 'a meant to beg it, might
it not?

HORATIO: Ay, my lord.   75

HAMLET: Why, e'en so, and now my Lady Worm's, chapless,° and knock'd about
the mazzard° with a sexton's spade. Here's fine revolution,° an° we had the
trick to see 't. Did these bones cost no more the breeding,° but to play at
loggats° with them? Mine ache to think on 't.

FIRST CLOWN: (*Song.*)
"A pick-axe, and a spade, a spade,   80
      For and° a shrouding sheet;
   O, a pit of clay for to be made
      For such a guest is meet."

[*Throws up another skull.*]

HAMLET: There's another. Why may not that be the skull of a lawyer?
Where be his quiddities° now, his quillities,° his cases, his tenures,° 85
and his tricks? Why does he suffer this mad knave now to knock him
about the sconce° with a dirty shovel, and will not tell him of his
action of battery? Hum! This fellow might be in 's time a great buyer
of land, with his statutes, his recognizances,° his fines, his double°
vouchers,° his recoveries.° [Is this the fine of his fines, and the 90
recovery of his recoveries,] to have his fine pate full of fine dirt?° Will

---

64. into the land: Probably "Toward my grave" (but note the lack of rhyme in *steps, land*).
67. jowls: Dashes. **68. politician:** Schemer, plotter. **69. o'erreaches:** Circumvents, gets the
better of (with a quibble on the literal sense). **76. chapless:** Having no lower jaw. **77. maz-
zard:** Head (literally, a drinking vessel). **revolution:** Change. **an:** If. **78. the breeding:** In the
breeding, raising. **79. loggats:** A game in which pieces of hardwood are thrown to lie as near as
possible to a stake. **81. For and:** And moreover. **85. quiddities:** Subtleties, quibbles (from
Latin *quid*, a thing), **quillities:** Verbal niceties, subtle distinctions (variation of *quiddities*). **tenures:** The holding of a piece of property or office, or the conditions or period of such holding. **87. sconce:** Head. **89. statutes, recognizances:** Legal documents guaranteeing a debt by
attaching land and property. **89–90. fines, recoveries:** Ways of converting entailed estates into
"fee simple" or freehold. **89. double:** Signed by two signatories. **90. vouchers:** Guarantees of
the legality of a title to real estate. **90–91. fine of his fines . . . fine pate . . . fine dirt:** End of his
legal maneuvers . . . elegant head . . . minutely sifted dirt.

his vouchers vouch him no more of his purchases, and double [ones
too], than the length and breadth of a pair of indentures?° The very
conveyances° of his lands will scarcely lie in this box,° and must th'
inheritor° himself have no more, ha?   95

HORATIO: Not a jot more, my lord.

HAMLET: Is not parchment made of sheep-skins?

HORATIO: Ay, my lord, and of calf-skins too.

HAMLET: They are sheep and calves which seek out assurance in that.° I will
speak to this fellow.—Whose grave's this, sirrah?°   100

FIRST CLOWN: Mine, sir.

  [Sings.] "O, a pit of clay for to be made
        [For such a guest is meet]."

HAMLET: I think it be thine, indeed, for thou liest in 't.

FIRST CLOWN: You lie out on 't, sir, and therefore 'tis not yours. For my part, I do   105
not lie in 't, yet it is mine.

HAMLET: Thou dost lie in 't, to be in 't and say it is thine. 'Tis for the dead, not
for the quick;° therefore thou liest.

FIRST CLOWN: 'Tis a quick lie, sir; 'twill away again from me to you.

HAMLET: What man dost thou dig it for?   110

FIRST CLOWN: For no man, sir.

HAMLET: What woman, then?

FIRST CLOWN: For none, neither.

HAMLET: Who is to be buried in 't?

FIRST CLOWN: One that was a woman, sir, but, rest her soul, she's dead.   115

HAMLET: How absolute° the knave is! We must speak by the card,° or equivoca-
tion° will undo us. By the Lord, Horatio, this three years I have taken note
of it: the age is grown so pick'd° that the toe of the peasant comes so near
the heel of the courtier, he galls his kibe.° How long hast thou been a grave-
maker?   120

FIRST CLOWN: Of all the days i' th' year, I came to 't that day that our last king
Hamlet overcame Fortinbras.

HAMLET: How long is that since?

FIRST CLOWN: Cannot you tell that? Every fool can tell that. It was that
very day that young Hamlet was born—he that is mad, and sent into   125
England.

---

93. **pair of indentures:** Legal document drawn up in duplicate on a single sheet and then cut
apart on a zigzag line so that each pair was uniquely matched. (Hamlet may refer to two rows of
teeth, or dentures.)   94. **conveyances:** Deeds. **this box:** The skull.   95. **inheritor:** Possessor,
owner.   99. **assurance in that:** Safety in legal parchments.   100. **sirrah:** Term of address to
inferiors.   108. **quick:** Living.   116. **absolute:** Positive, decided. **by the card:** By the mariner's
card on which the points of the compass were marked, i.e., with precision. 116–17. **equivocation:**
Ambiguity in the use of terms. 118. **pick'd:** Refined, fastidious. 119. **galls his kibe:**
Chafes the courtier's chilblain (a swelling or sore caused by cold).

HAMLET: Ay, marry, why was he sent into England?

FIRST CLOWN: Why, because 'a was mad. 'A shall recover his wits there, or, if 'a do not, 'tis no great matter there.

HAMLET: Why?   130

FIRST CLOWN: 'Twill not be seen in him there. There the men are as mad as he.

HAMLET: How came he mad?

FIRST CLOWN: Very strangely, they say.

HAMLET: How strangely?   135

FIRST CLOWN: Faith, e'en with losing his wits.

HAMLET: Upon what ground?

FIRST CLOWN: Why, here in Denmark. I have been sexton here, man and boy, thirty years.

HAMLET: How long will a man lie i' th' earth ere he rot?   140

FIRST CLOWN: Faith, if 'a be not rotten before 'a die — as we have many pocky° corses [now-a-days], that will scarce hold the laying in — 'a will last you some eight year or nine year. A tanner will last you nine year.

HAMLET: Why he more than another?

FIRST CLOWN: Why, sir, his hide is so tann'd with his trade that 'a will keep out 145 water a great while, and your water is a sore decayer of your whore-son dead body. [*Picks up a skull.*] Here's a skull now hath lain you° i' th' earth three and twenty years.

HAMLET: Whose was it?

FIRST CLOWN: A whoreson mad fellow's it was. Whose do you think it was?   150

HAMLET: Nay, I know not.

FIRST CLOWN: A pestilence on him for a mad rogue! 'A pour'd a flagon of Rhenish° on my head once. This same skull, sir, was Yorick's skull, the King's jester.

HAMLET: This?   155

FIRST CLOWN: E'en that.

HAMLET: [Let me see.] [*Takes the skull.*] Alas, poor Yorick! I knew him, Hora-tio, a fellow of infinite jest, of most excellent fancy. He hath borne me on his back a thousand times; and now, how abhorr'd in my imagi-160 nation it is! My gorge rises at it. Here hung those lips that I have kiss'd I know not how oft. Where be your gibes now? Your gam-bols, your songs, your flashes of merriment that were wont to set the table on a roar? Not one now, to mock your own grinning? Quite chap-fall'n?° Now get you to my lady's chamber, and tell her, let her paint an inch thick, to this favor° she must come; make her laugh at 165 that. Prithee, Horatio, tell me one thing.

HORATIO: What's that, my lord?

HAMLET: Dost thou think Alexander look'd o' this fashion i' th' earth?

HORATIO: E'en so.

---

141. pocky: Rotten, diseased (literally, with the pox, or syphilis). **147. lain you:** Lain. **153. Rhen-ish:** Rhine wine. **164. chap-fall'n:** (1) Lacking the lower jaw; (2) dejected. **165. favor:** Aspect, appearance.

HAMLET: And smelt so? Pah! [*Puts down the skull.*]   170
HORATIO: E'en so, my lord.
HAMLET: To what base uses we may return, Horatio! Why may not imagi-
    nation trace the noble dust of Alexander, till 'a find it stopping a bung-
    hole?
HORATIO: 'Twere to consider too curiously,° to consider so.   175
HAMLET: No, faith, not a jot, but to follow him thither with modesty°
    enough, and likelihood to lead it. [As thus]: Alexander died, Alexander
    was buried, Alexander returneth to dust; the dust is earth; of earth
    we make loam;° and why of that loam, whereto he was converted,
    might they not stop a beer-barrel?   180
    Imperious° Caesar, dead and turn'd to clay,
    Might stop a hole to keep the wind away.
    O, that that earth which kept the world in awe
    Should patch a wall t' expel the winter's flaw!°
    But soft, but soft awhile! Here comes the King.   185

(*Enter King, Queen, Laertes, and the Corse* [*of Ophelia, in procession, with Priest, Lords etc.*].)

    The Queen, the courtiers. Who is this they follow?
    And with such maimed rites? This doth betoken
    The corse they follow did with desp'rate hand
    Fordo it° own life. 'Twas of some estate.°
    Couch° we awhile, and mark.   190
             [*He and Horatio conceal themselves.*
             Ophelia's body is taken to the grave.]
LAERTES: What ceremony else?
HAMLET: [*to Horatio*]: That is Laertes, a very noble youth. Mark.
LAERTES: What ceremony else?
PRIEST: Her obsequies° have been as far enlarg'd
    As we have warranty. Her death was doubtful,   195
    And, but that great command o'ersways the order,
    She should in ground unsanctified been lodg'd
    Till the last trumpet. For° charitable prayers,
    Shards,° flints, and pebbles should be thrown on her.
    Yet here she is allow'd her virgin crants,°   200
    Her maiden strewments,° and the bringing home
    Of bell and burial.°

---

175. **curiously:** Minutely. 176. **modesty:** Moderation. 179. **loam:** Clay mixture for brick-making or other clay use. 181. **Imperious:** Imperial. 184. **flaw:** Gust of wind. 189. **Fordo it:** Destroy its. **estate:** Rank. 190. **Couch:** Hide, lurk. 194. **obsequies:** Funeral rites. 198. **For:** In place of. 199. **Shards:** Broken bits of pottery. 200. **crants:** Garland. 201. **strewments:** Traditional strewing of flowers. 201–202. **bringing . . . burial:** Laying to rest of the body in consecrated ground, to the sound of the bell.

LAERTES: Must there no more be done?

PRIEST: No more be done.
    We should profane the service of the dead
    To sing a requiem and such rest to her   205
    As to peace-parted souls.

LAERTES: Lay her i' th' earth,
    And from her fair and unpolluted flesh
    May violets° spring! I tell thee, churlish priest,
    A minist'ring angel shall my sister be
    When thou liest howling!

HAMLET [*to Horatio*]:   What, the fair Ophelia!   210

QUEEN [*scattering flowers*]: Sweets to the sweet! Farewell.
    I hoped thou shouldst have been my Hamlet's wife.
    I thought thy bride-bed to have deck'd, sweet maid,
    And not have strew'd thy grave.

LAERTES: O, treble woe
    Fall ten times treble on that cursed head   215
    Whose wicked deed thy most ingenious sense°
    Depriv'd thee of! Hold off the earth awhile,
    Till I have caught her once more in mine arms.

                      [*Leaps into the grave and embraces Ophelia.*]

    Now pile your dust upon the quick and dead,
    Till of this flat a mountain you have made   220
    T' o'ertop old Pelion,° or the skyish head
    Of blue Olympus.°

HAMLET [*coming forward*]: What is he whose grief
    Bears such an emphasis, whose phrase of sorrow
    Conjures the wand'ring stars,° and makes them stand
    Like wonder-wounded hearers? This is I,   225
    Hamlet the Dane.°

LAERTES: The devil take thy soul!

                            [*Grappling with him.*]

HAMLET: Thou pray'st not well.
    I prithee, take thy fingers from my throat;
    For, though I am not splenitive° and rash,
    Yet have I in me something dangerous,   230
    Which let thy wisdom fear. Hold off thy hand.

---

207. **violets:** See 4.5.181 and note.   216. **ingenious sense:** Mind endowed with finest qualities.   220, 221. **Pelion, Olympus:** Mountains in the north of Thessaly; see also *Ossa* at line
251.   224. **wand'ring stars:** Planets.   226. **the Dane:** This title normally signifies the king,
see 1.1.15 and note.   229. **splenitive:** Quick-tempered.

KING: Pluck them asunder.
QUEEN: Hamlet, Hamlet!
ALL: Gentlemen!
HORATIO: Good my lord, be quiet.

[*Hamlet and Laertes are parted.*]

HAMLET: Why, I will fight with him upon this theme
    Until my eyelids will no longer wag.°   235
QUEEN: O my son, what theme?
HAMLET: I lov'd Ophelia. Forty thousand brothers
    Could not with all their quantity of love
    Make up my sum. What wilt thou do for her?
KING: O, he is mad, Laertes.   240
QUEEN: For love of God, forbear him.
HAMLET: 'Swounds, show me what thou' do.
    Woo 't° weep? Woo 't fight? Woo 't fast? Woo 't tear thyself?
    Woo 't drink up eisel?° Eat a crocodile?
    I'll do 't. Dost thou come here to whine?   245
    To outface me with leaping in her grave?
    Be buried quick° with her, and so will I.
    And, if thou prate of mountains, let them throw
    Millions of acres on us, till our ground,
    Singeing his pate° against the burning zone,°   250
    Make Ossa° like a wart! Nay, an thou 'It mouth,°
    I'll rant as well as thou.
QUEEN: This is mere° madness,
    And thus a while the fit will work on him;
    Anon, as patient as the female dove
    When that her golden couplets° are disclos'd,°   255
    His silence will sit drooping.
HAMLET: Hear you, sir.
    What is the reason that you use me thus?
    I lov'd you ever. But it is no matter.
    Let Hercules himself do what he may,
    The cat will mew, and dog will have his day.°   260
KING: I pray thee, good Horatio, wait upon him.

(*Exit Hamlet and Horatio.*)

---

235. **wag:** Move. 243. **Woo 't:** Wilt thou. 244. **eisel:** Vinegar. 247. **quick:** Alive. 250. **his pate:** Its head, i.e., top. **burning zone:** Sun's orbit. 251. **Ossa:** Another mountain in Thessaly. (In their war against the Olympian gods, the giants attempted to heap Ossa, Pelion, and Olympus on one another to scale heaven.) **mouth:** Rant. 252. **mere:** Utter. 255. **golden couplets:** Two baby pigeons, covered with yellow down. **disclos'd:** Hatched. 259–60. **Let . . . day:** Despite any blustering attempts at interference, every person will sooner or later do what he must do.

[*To Laertes.*] Strengthen your patience in° our last night's speech;
We'll put the matter to the present push.° —
Good Gertrude, set some watch over your son. —
This grave shall have a living° monument.   265
An hour of quiet shortly shall we see;
Till then, in patience our proceeding be.   (*Exeunt.*)

[Scene 2]°

(*Enter Hamlet and Horatio.*)

HAMLET: So much for this, sir; now shall you see the other.°
    You do remember all the circumstance?
HORATIO: Remember it, my lord!
HAMLET: Sir, in my heart there was a kind of fighting
    That would not let me sleep. Methought I lay   5
    Worse than the mutines° in the bilboes.° Rashly,°
    And prais'd be rashness for it—let us know,°
    Our indiscretion sometime serves us well
    When our deep plots do pall,° and that should learn° us
    There's a divinity that shapes our ends,   10
    Rough-hew° them how we will—
HORATIO: That is most certain.
HAMLET: Up from my cabin,
    My sea-gown scarf'd about me, in the dark
    Grop'd I to find out them, had my desire,
    Finger'd° their packet, and in fine° withdrew   15
    To mine own room again, making so bold,
    My fears forgetting manners, to unseal
    Their grand commission; where I found, Horatio—
    Ah, royal knavery!—an exact command,
    Larded° with many several sorts of reasons   20
    Importing° Denmark's health and England's too,
    With, ho, such bugs° and goblins in my life,°
    That, on the supervise,° no leisure bated,°
    No, not to stay the grinding of the axe,
    My head should be struck off.

---

262. in: By recalling. **263. present push:** Immediate test. **265. living:** Lasting; also refers
(for Laertes' benefit) to the plot against Hamlet. ACT 5, SCENE 2. **Location:** The castle. **1. see
the other:** Hear the other news. **6. mutines:** Mutineers. **bilboes:** Shackles. **Rashly:** On
impulse (this adverb goes with lines 12ff.). **7. know:** Acknowledge. **9. pall:** Fail. **learn:**
Teach. **11. Rough-hew:** Shape roughly. **15. Finger'd:** Pilfered, pinched. **in fine:** Finally, in
conclusion. **20. Larded:** Enriched. **21. Importing:** Relating to. **22. bugs:** Bugbears, hob-
goblins. **in my life:** To be feared if I were allowed to live. **23. supervise:** Reading. **leisure
bated:** Delay allowed.

HORATIO: Is 't possible?   25
HAMLET: Here's the commission; read it at more leisure.

                                                    [*Gives document.*]

    But wilt thou hear now how I did proceed?
HORATIO: I beseech you.
HAMLET: Being thus benetted round with villainies,
    Or I could make a prologue to my brains,   30
    They had begun the play.° I sat me down,
    Devis'd a new commission, wrote it fair.°
    I once did hold it, as our statists° do,
    A baseness° to write fair, and labor'd much
    How to forget that learning, but, sir, now   35
    It did me yeoman's° service. Wilt thou know
    Th' effect° of what I wrote?
HORATIO: Ay, good my lord.
HAMLET: An earnest conjuration from the King,
    As England was his faithful tributary,
    As love between them like the palm might flourish,
    As peace should still her wheaten garland° wear   40
    And stand a comma° 'tween their amities,
    And many such-like as's° of great charge,°
    That, on the view and knowing of these contents,
    Without debasement further, more or less,   45
    He should those bearers put to sudden death,
    Not shriving time° allow'd.
HORATIO: How was this seal'd?
HAMLET: Why, even in that was heaven ordinant.°
    I had my father's signet° in my purse,
    Which was the model of that Danish seal;   50
    Folded the writ up in the form of th' other,
    Subscrib'd° it, gave 't th' impression,° plac'd it safely,
    The changeling° never known. Now, the next day
    Was our sea-fight, and what to this was sequent
    Thou knowest already.   55

───────────────

30–31. Or . . . play: Before I could consciously turn my brain to the matter, it had started
working on a plan. (*Or* means *ere.*)   **32. fair:** In a clear hand.   **33. statists:** Statesmen.
34. baseness: Lower-class trait.   **36. yeoman's:** Substantial, workmanlike.   **37. effect:** Purport.
41. wheaten garland: Symbolic of fruitful agriculture, of peace.   **42. comma:** Indicating continuity, link.   **43. as's:** (1) The "whereases" of formal document, (2) asses. **charge:** (1) Import,
(2) burden.   **47. shriving time:** Time for confession and absolution.   **48. ordinant:** Directing.
49. signet: Small seal.   **52. Subscrib'd:** Signed. **impression:** With a wax seal.   **53. changeling:**
The substituted letter (literally, a fairy child substituted for a human one).

HORATIO: So Guildenstern and Rosencrantz go to 't.
HAMLET: [Why, man, they did make love to this employment.]
    They are not near my conscience. Their defeat
    Does by their own insinuation° grow.
    'Tis dangerous when the baser nature comes   60
    Between the pass° and fell° incensed points
    Of mighty opposites.
HORATIO: Why, what a king is this!
HAMLET: Does it not, think thee, stand° me now upon—
    He that hath killed my king and whor'd my mother,
    Popp'd in between th' election° and my hopes,   65
    Thrown out his angle° for my proper° life,
    And with such coz'nage°—is 't not perfect conscience
    [To quit° him with this arm? And is 't not to be damn'd
    To let this canker° of our nature come
    In further evil?   70
HORATIO: It must be shortly known to him from England
    What is the issue of the business there.
HAMLET: It will be short. The interim is mine,
    And a man's life 's no more than to say "One."°
    But I am very sorry, good Horatio,   75
    That to Laertes I forgot myself,
    For by the image of my cause I see
    The portraiture of his. I'll court his favors.
    But, sure, the bravery° of his grief did put me
    Into a tow'ring passion.
HORATIO: Peace, who comes here?]   80

(*Enter a Courtier [Osric].*)

OSRIC: Your lordship is right welcome back to Denmark.
HAMLET: I humbly thank you, sir. [*To Horatio.*] Dost know this water-fly?
HORATIO: No, my good lord.
HAMLET: Thy state is the more gracious, for 'tis a vice to know him. He hath
    much land, and fertile. Let a beast be lord of beasts, and his crib shall stand 85
    at the King's mess.° 'Tis a chough,° but, as I say, spacious in the possession
    of dirt.
OSRIC: Sweet lord, if your lordship were at leisure, I should impart a thing to you
    from his Majesty.
HAMLET: I will receive it, sir, with all diligence of spirit. Put your bonnet to his 90
    right use; 'tis for the head.

---

59. insinuation: Interference. **61. pass:** Thrust. **fell:** Fierce. **63. stand:** Become incumbent. **65. election:** The Danish monarch was "elected" by a small number of high-ranking electors. **66. angle:** Fishing line. **proper:** Very. **67. coz'nage:** Trickery. **68. quit:** Repay. **69. canker:** Ulcer. **74. a man's . . . "One":** To take a man's life requires no more than to count to one as one duels. **79. bravery:** Bravado. **85–86. Let . . . mess:** If a man, no matter how beastlike, is as rich in possessions as Osric, he may eat at the king's table. **86. chough:** Chattering jackdaw.

OSRIC: I thank your lordship, it is very hot.

HAMLET: No, believe me, 'tis very cold; the wind is northerly.

OSRIC: It is indifferent° cold, my lord, indeed.

HAMLET: But yet methinks it is very sultry and hot for my complexion.°   95

OSRIC: Exceedingly, my lord; it is very sultry, as 'twere — I cannot tell how.
My lord, his Majesty bade me signify to you that 'a has laid a great wager
on your head. Sir, this is the matter —

HAMLET: I beseech you, remember —

[Hamlet moves him to put on his hat.]

OSRIC: Nay, good my lord; for my ease,° in good faith. Sir, here is newly 100
come to court Laertes — believe me, an absolute gentleman, full of
most excellent differences,° of very soft society° and great showing.°
Indeed, to speak feelingly° of him, he is the card° or calendar° of gentry,° for you shall find in him the continent of what part° a gentleman
would see.   105

HAMLET: Sir, his definement° suffers no perdition° in you, though, I know,
to divide him inventorially° would dozy° th' arithmetic of memory,
and yet but yaw° neither° in respect of° his quick sail. But, in the ver-
ity of extolment,° I take him to be a soul of great article,° and his infu-
sion° of such dearth and rareness,° as, to make true diction° of him, 110
his semblable° is his mirror, and who else would trace° him, his um-
brage,° nothing more.

OSRIC: Your lordship speaks most infallibly of him.

HAMLET: The concernancy,° sir? Why do we wrap the gentleman in our more
rawer breath?°   115

OSRIC: Sir?

HORATIO: Is 't not possible to understand in another tongue?° You will do 't,°
sir, really.

HAMLET: What imports the nomination° of this gentleman?

OSRIC: Of Laertes?   120

---

94. **indifferent:** Somewhat.   95. **complexion:** Temperament.   100. **for my ease:** A conventional reply declining the invitation to put his hat back on.   102. **differences:** Special qualities.
soft society: Agreeable manners. **great showing:** Distinguished appearance.   103. **feelingly:** With just perception. **card:** Chart, map. **calendar:** Guide. **gentry:** Good breeding.   104. **the continent ... part:** One who contains in him all the qualities (a *continent* is
that which contains).   106. **definement:** Definition. (Hamlet proceeds to mock Osric by using
his lofty diction back at him.) **perdition:** Loss, diminution.   107. **divide him inventori-
ally:** Enumerate his graces. **dozy:** Dizzy.   108. **yaw:** To move unsteadily (said of a ship), **neither:** For all that. **in respect of:** In comparison with.   108–109. **in ... extolment:** In true
praise (of him).   109. **article:** Moment or importance. **infusion:** Essence, character imparted
by nature.   110. **dearth and rareness:** Rarity. **make true diction:** Speak truly.   111. **sem-
blable:** Only true likeness. **who ... trace:** Any other person who would wish to follow. **um-
brage:** Shadow.   114. **concernancy:** Import, relevance.   115. **breath:** Speech.   117. **to
understand ... tongue:** For Osric to understand when someone else speaks in his manner.
(Horatio twits Osric for not being able to understand the kind of flowery speech he himself uses
when Hamlet speaks in such a vein.) **You will do 't:** You can if you try.   119. **nomination:**
Naming.

HORATIO [*to Hamlet*]: His purse is empty already; all 's golden words are spent.

HAMLET: Of him, sir.

OSRIC: I know you are not ignorant—

HAMLET: I would you did, sir; yet, in faith, if you did, it would not much ap- 125
prove° me. Well, sir?

OSRIC: You are not ignorant of what excellence Laertes is—

HAMLET: I dare not confess that, lest I should compare° with him in excellence;
but to know a man well were to know himself.°

OSRIC: I mean, sir, for his weapon; but in the imputation laid on him by them,° 130
in his meed° he's unfellow'd.°

HAMLET: What's his weapon?

OSRIC: Rapier and dagger.

OSRIC: That's two of his weapons—but well.

OSRIC: The King, sir, hath wager'd with him six Barbary horses, against the 135
which he has impawn'd,° as I take it, six French rapiers and poniards, with
their assigns,° as girdle, hangers,° and so. Three of the carriages,° in faith,
are very dear to fancy,° very responsive° to the hilts, most delicate° carriages, and of very liberal conceit.°

HAMLET: What call you the carriages?   140

HORATIO [*to Hamlet*]: I knew you must be edified by the margent° ere you had
done.

OSRIC: The carriages, sir, are the hangers.

HAMLET: The phrase would be more germane to the matter if we could carry a
cannon by our sides; I would it might be hangers till then. But, on: six 145
Barb'ry horses against six French swords, their assigns, and three liberal-
conceited carriages; that's the French bet against the Danish. Why is this
impawn'd, as you call it?

OSRIC: The King, sir, hath laid,° sir, that in a dozen passes° between yourself and
him, he shall not exceed you three hits. He hath laid on twelve for nine, 150
and it would come to immediate trial, if your lordship would vouchsafe the
answer.

HAMLET: How if I answer no?

OSRIC: I mean, my lord, the opposition of your person in trial.

---

126. approve: Commend.   128. compare: Seem to compete.   129. but...himself: To recognize excellence in another man, one must know oneself.   130. imputation...them: Reputation given him by others.   131. meed: Merit. unfellow'd: Unmatched.   136. impawn'd: Staked,
wagered.   137. assigns: Appurtenances. hangers: Straps on the sword belt (*girdle*) from which
the sword hung. carriages: An affected way of saying *hangers*; literally, gun-carriages.   138.
dear to fancy: Fancifully designed, tasteful. responsive: Corresponding closely, matching.   139. delicate: I.e., in workmanship.   139. liberal conceit: Elaborate design.   141.
margent: Margin of a book, place for explanatory notes.   149. laid: Wagered. passes: Bouts.
(The odds of the betting are hard to explain. Possibly the king bets that Hamlet will win at least
five out of twelve, at which point Laertes raises the odds against himself by betting he will
win nine.)

HAMLET: Sir, I will walk here in the hall. If it please his Majesty, it is the 155
   breathing time° of day with me. Let the foils be brought, the gentleman
   willing, and the King hold his purpose, I will win for him an I can; if not,
   I will gain nothing but my shame and the odd hits.

OSRIC: Shall I deliver you so?

HAMLET: To this effect, sir—after what flourish your nature will.   160

OSRIC: I commend my duty to your lordship.

HAMLET: Yours, yours. [*Exit Osric.*] He does well to commend it himself; there
   are no tongues else for 's turn.

HORATIO: This lapwing° runs away with the shell on his head.

HAMLET: 'A did comply, sir, with his dug,° before 'a suck'd it. Thus has he—and 165
   many more of the same breed that I know the drossy° age dotes on—only
   got the tune° of the time and, out of an habit of encounter,° a kind of
   yesty° collection,° which carries them through and through the most
   fann'd and winnow'd° opinions; and do but blow them to their trial, the
   bubbles are out.°   170

(*Enter a Lord.*)

LORD: My lord, his Majesty commended him to you by young Osric, who
   brings back to him that you attend him in the hall. He sends to know
   if your pleasure hold to play with Laertes, or that you will take longer
   time.

HAMLET: I am constant to my purposes; they follow the King's pleasure. If his 175
   fitness speaks,° mine is ready; now or whensoever, provided I be so able as
   now.

LORD: The King and Queen and all are coming down.

HAMLET: In happy time.°

LORD: The Queen desires you to use some gentle entertainment° to Laertes be- 180
   fore you fall to play.

HAMLET: She well instructs me.   [*Exit Lord.*]

HORATIO: You will lose, my lord.

HAMLET: I do not think so. Since he went into France, I have been in continual
   practice; I shall win at the odds. But thou wouldst not think how ill all's 185
   here about my heart; but it is no matter.

HORATIO: Nay, good my lord—

---

156. **breathing time:** Exercise period.   164. **lapwing:** A bird that draws intruders away from its
nest and was thought to run about when newly hatched with its head in the shell; a seeming reference to Osric's hat.   165. **comply . . . dug:** Observe ceremonious formality toward his mother's teat.   166. **drossy:** Frivolous.   167. **tune:** Temper, mood, manner of speech.   167. **habit
of encounter:** Demeanor of social intercourse.   168. **yesty:** Yeasty, frothy. **collection:** I.e., of
current phrases.   169. **fann'd and winnow'd:** Select and refined.   169–170. **blow . . . out:** Put
them to the test, and their ignorance is exposed.   175–176. **If . . . speaks:** If his readiness answers to the time.   179. **In happy time:** A phrase of courtesy indicating acceptance.   180. **entertainment:** Greeting.

HAMLET: It is but foolery, but it is such a kind of gain-giving,° as would perhaps
    trouble a woman.

HORATIO: If your mind dislike anything, obey it. I will forestall their repair   190
    hither, and say you are not fit.

HAMLET: Not a whit, we defy augury. There is special providence in the
    fall of a sparrow. If it be now, 'tis not to come; if it be not to come,
    it will be now, if it be not now, yet it will come. The readiness is all.
    Since no man of aught he leaves knows what is 't to leave betimes,° 195
    let be.

*(A table prepar'd. [Enter] trumpets, drums, and Officers with cushions; King,
Queen, [Osric,] and all the State; foils, daggers, [and wine borne in;] and Laertes.)*

KING: Come, Hamlet, come, and take this hand from me.

[The King puts Laertes' hand into Hamlet's.]

HAMLET: Give me your pardon, sir. I have done you wrong,
    But pardon 't, as you are a gentleman.
    This presence° knows,   200
    And you must needs have heard, how I am punish'd
    With a sore distraction. What I have done
    That might your nature, honor, and exception°
    Roughly awake, I here proclaim was madness.
    Was 't Hamlet wrong'd Laertes? Never Hamlet.   205
    If Hamlet from himself be ta'en away,
    And when he's not himself does wrong Laertes,
    Then Hamlet does it not, Hamlet denies it.
    Who does it, then? His madness. If 't be so,
    Hamlet is of the faction that is wrong'd;   210
    His madness is poor Hamlet's enemy.
    [Sir, in this audience,]
    Let my disclaiming from a purpos'd evil
    Free me so far in your most generous thoughts
    That I have shot my arrow o'er the house   215
    And hurt my brother.

LAERTES: I am satisfied in nature,°
    Whose motive in this case should stir me most
    To my revenge. But in my terms of honor
    I stand aloof, and will no reconcilement
    Till by some elder masters of known honor   220
    I have a voice° and precedent of peace
    To keep my name ungor'd. But till that time,

---

188. gain-giving: Misgiving.   **195. what . . . betimes:** What is the best time to leave it.   **200. presence:** Royal assembly.   **203. exception:** Disapproval.   **216. in nature:** As to my personal feelings.   **221. voice:** Authoritative pronouncement.

　　I do receive your offer'd love like love,
　　And will not wrong it.
HAMLET: 　　　　　　　　I embrace it freely,
　　And will this brothers' wager frankly play.　　　　　　　225
　　Give us the foils. Come on.
LAERTES: 　　　　　　　　　　　Come, one for me.
HAMLET: I'll be your foil,° Laertes. In mine ignorance
　　Your skill shall, like a star i' th' darkest night,
　　Stick fiery off° indeed.
LAERTES: 　　　　　　　　You mock me, sir.
HAMLET: No, by this hand.　　　　　　　　　　　　　　230
KING: Give them the foils, young Osric. Cousin Hamlet,
　　You know the wager?
HAMLET: 　　　　　　　　Very well, my lord.
　　Your Grace has laid the odds o' th' weaker side.
KING: I do not fear it; I have seen you both.
　　But since he is better'd,° we have therefore odds.　　　235
LAERTES: This is too heavy, let me see another.

　　　　　　　　　　　　　[*Exchanges his foil for another.*]

HAMLET: This likes me well. These foils have all a length?

　　　　　　　　　　　　　　[*They prepare to play.*]

OSRIC: Ay, my good lord.
KING: Set me the stoups of wine upon that table.
　　If Hamlet give the first or second hit,　　　　　　　　240
　　Or quit° in answer of the third exchange,
　　Let all the battlements their ordnance fire.
　　The King shall drink to Hamlet's better breath,
　　And in the cup an union° shall he throw,
　　Richer than that which four successive kings　　　　　245
　　In Denmark's crown have worn. Give me the cups,
　　And let the kettle° to the trumpet speak,
　　The trumpet to the cannoneer without,
　　The cannons to the heavens, the heaven to earth,
　　"Now the King drinks to Hamlet." Come, begin.　　　250

　　　　　　　　　　　　　　(*Trumpets the while.*)

　　And you, the judges, bear a wary eye.

---

227. foil: Thin metal background which sets a jewel off (with pun on the blunted rapier for fencing).　**229. Stick fiery off:** Stand out brilliantly.　**235. is better'd:** Has improved; is the odds-on favorite.　**241. quit:** Repay (with a hit).　**244. union:** Pearl (so called, according to Pliny's *Natural History*, 9, because pearls are *unique*, never identical).　**247. kettle:** Kettledrum.

HAMLET: Come on sir.
LAERTES: Come, my lord.   [*They play. Hamlet scores a hit.*]
HAMLET: One.
LAERTES: No.
HAMLET: Judgment.
OSRIC: A hit, a very palpable hit.

(*Drum, trumpets, and shot. Flourish. A piece goes off.*)

LAERTES: Well, again.
KING: Stay, give me drink. Hamlet, this pearl is thine.

[*He throws a pearl in Hamlet's cup and drinks.*]

Here's to thy health. Give him the cup.   255
HAMLET: I'll play this bout first, set it by awhile.
    Come. [*They play.*] Another hit; what say you?
LAERTES: A touch, a touch. I do confess 't.
KING: Our son shall win.
QUEEN: He's fat,° and scant of breath.
    Here, Hamlet, take my napkin,° rub thy brows.   260
    The Queen carouses° to thy fortune, Hamlet.
HAMLET: Good madam!
KING: Gertrude, do not drink.
QUEEN: I will, my lord; I pray you pardon me.

[*Drinks.*]

KING [*aside*]: It is the pois'ned cup. It is too late.
HAMLET: I dare not drink yet, madam; by and by.   265
QUEEN: Come, let me wipe thy face.
LAERTES [*to King*]: My lord, I'll hit him now.
KING: I do not think 't
LAERTES [*aside*]: And yet it is almost against my conscience.
HAMLET: Come, for the third, Laertes. You do but dally.
    I pray you, pass with your best violence;   270
    I am afeard you make a wanton of me.°
LAERTES: Say you so? Come on.   [*They play.*]
OSRIC: Nothing, neither way.
LAERTES: Have at you now!

[*Laertes wounds Hamlet; then, in scuffling,
they change rapiers,° and Hamlet wounds Laertes.*]

---

259. fat: Not physically fit, out of training.   **260. napkin:** Handkerchief.   **261. carouses:**
Drinks a toast.   **271. make . . . me:** Treat me like a spoiled child, holding back to give me an
advantage.   [s.D.] ***in scuffling, they change rapiers:*** This stage direction occurs in the Folio. According to a widespread stage tradition, Hamlet receives a scratch, realizes that Laertes' sword is
unbated, and accordingly forces an exchange.

KING: Part them! They are incens'd.
HAMLET: Nay, come, again.   [*The Queen falls.*]
OSRIC: Look to the Queen there, ho!   275
HORATIO: They bleed on both sides. How is it, my lord?
OSRIC: How is 't, Laertes?
LAERTES: Why, as a woodcock° to mine own springe,° Osric;
    I am justly kill'd with mine own treachery.
HAMLET: How does the Queen?
KING: She swoons to see them bleed.   280
QUEEN: No, no, the drink, the drink — O my dear Hamlet —
    The drink, the drink! I am pois'ned.   [*Dies.*]
HAMLET: O villainy! Ho, let the door be lock'd!
    Treachery! Seek it out.   [*Laertes falls.*]
LAERTES: It is here, Hamlet. Hamlet, thou art slain.   285
    No med'cine in the world can do thee good;
    In thee there is not half an hour's life.
    The treacherous instrument is in thy hand,
    Unbated° and envenom'd. The foul practice
    Hath turn'd itself on me. Lo, here I lie,   290
    Never to rise again. Thy mother's pois'ned.
    I can no more. The King, the King's to blame.
HAMLET: The point envenom'd too? Then, venom, to thy work.

                                            [*Stabs the King.*]

ALL: Treason! Treason!   295
KING: O, yet defend me, friends; I am but hurt.
HAMLET: Here, thou incestuous, murd'rous, damned Dane,
              [*He forces the King to drink the poisoned cup.*]
    Drink off this potion. Is thy union° here?
    Follow my mother.   [*King dies.*]
LAERTES: He is justly serv'd.
    It is a poison temper'd° by himself.   300
    Exchange forgiveness with me, noble Hamlet.
    Mine and my father's death come not upon thee,
    Nor thine on me!   [*Dies.*]
HAMLET: Heaven make thee free of it! I follow thee.
    I am dead, Horatio. Wretched Queen, adieu!   305
    You that look pale and tremble at this chance,
    That are but mutes° or audience to this act,
    Had I but time — as this fell° sergeant,° Death,
    Is strict in his arrest — O, I could tell you —

---

278. woodcock: A bird, a type of stupidity or as a decoy. **springe:** Trap, snare.   **289. Unbated:** Not blunted with a button.   **298. union:** Pearl (see line 244; with grim puns on the word's other meanings: marriage, shared death).   **300. temper'd:** Mixed.   **307. mutes:** Silent observers. **308. fell:** Cruel. **sergeant:** Sheriff's officer.

But let it be. Horatio, I am dead;   310
Thou livest. Report me and my cause aright
To the unsatisfied.
HORATIO: Never believe it.
I am more an antique Roman° than a Dane.
Here's yet some liquor left.

        [He attempts to drink from the poisoned cup. Hamlet prevents him.]

HAMLET: As th' art a man,
Give me the cup! Let go! By heaven, I'll ha 't.   315
O God, Horatio, what a wounded name,
Things standing thus unknown, shall I leave behind me!
If thou didst ever hold me in thy heart,
Absent thee from felicity awhile,
And in this harsh world draw thy breath in pain   320
To tell my story.

        (A march afar off [*and a volley within*].)

       What warlike noise is this?
OSRIC: Young Fortinbras, with conquest come from Poland,
To the ambassadors of England gives
This warlike volley.
HAMLET: O, I die, Horatio!
The potent poison quite o'ercrows° my spirit.   325
I cannot live to hear the news from England,
But I do prophesy th' election lights
On Fortinbras. He has my dying voice.°
So tell him, with th' occurrents° more and less
Which have solicited°—the rest is silence.   [*Dies.*] 330
HORATIO: Now cracks a noble heart. Good night, sweet prince;
And flights of angels sing thee to thy rest!

                      [*March within.*]

Why does the drum come hither?

(Enter Fortinbras, with the [*English*] *Ambasvsadors* [*with drum, colors, and attendants*].)

FORTINBRAS: Where is this sight?
HORATIO: What is it you would see?
If aught of woe or wonder, cease your search.   335
FORTINBRAS: This quarry° cries on havoc.° O proud Death.

---

313. Roman: It was the Roman custom to follow masters in death.   **325. o'ercrows:** Triumphs
over.   **328. voice:** Vote.   **329. occurrents:** Events, incidents.   **330. solicited:** Moved, urged.
336. quarry: Heap of dead. **cries on havoc:** Proclaims a general slaughter.

What feast is toward° in thine eternal cell,
That thou so many princes at a shot
So bloodily hast struck?
FIRST AMBASSADOR: The sight is dismal;
And our affairs from England come too late.   340
The ears are senseless that should give us hearing,
To tell him his commandment is fulfill'd,
That Rosencrantz and Guildenstern are dead.
Where should we have our thanks?
HORATIO: Not from his° mouth,
Had it th' ability of life to thank you.   345
He never gave commandment for their death.
But since, so jump° upon this bloody question,°
You from the Polack wars, and you from England,
Are here arriv'd, give order that these bodies
High on a stage° be placed to the view,   350
And let me speak to th' yet unknowing world
How these things came about. So shall you hear
Of carnal, bloody, and unnatural acts,
Of accidental judgments,° casual° slaughters,
Of deaths put on° by cunning and forc'd cause,   355
And, in this upshot, purposes mistook
Fall'n on th' inventors' heads. All this can I
Truly deliver.
FORTINBRAS: Let us haste to hear it,
And call the noblest to the audience.
For me, with sorrow I embrace my fortune.   360
I have some rights of memory° in this kingdom,
Which now to claim my vantage° doth invite me.
HORATIO: Of that I shall have also cause to speak,
And from his mouth whose voice will draw on more.°
But let this same be presently° perform'd,   365
Even while men's minds are wild, lest more mischance
On° plots and errors happen.
FORTINBRAS: Let four captains
Bear Hamlet, like a soldier, to the stage,
For he was likely, had he been put on,°
To have prov'd most royal; and, for his passage,°   370

---

337. toward: In preparation.   344. his: Claudius's.   347. jump: Precisely.   question: Dispute.   350. stage: Platform.   354. judgments: Retributions.   casual: Occurring by chance.
355. put on: Instigated.   361. of memory: Traditional, remembered.   362. vantage: Presence at this opportune moment.   364. voice . . . more: Vote will influence still others.   365. presently: Immediately.   367. On: On the basis of.   369. put on: Invested in royal office and so put to the test.   370. passage: Death.

The soldiers' music and the rite of war
Speak loudly for him.
Take up the bodies. Such a sight as this
Becomes the field,° but here shows much amiss.
Go, bid the soldiers shoot.   375

(*Exeunt [marching, bearing off the dead bodies; a peal of ordnance is shot off].*)

POST-ELIZABETHAN THEATERS

Theaters in England were closed for almost twenty years (1641–1660) when
the monarchy was replaced by a Puritan-led republic. When the monarchy
was restored in 1660, theaters were allowed to reopen. Outdoor theatres
were replaced with indoor ones, a trend influenced by theaters in France,
where many members of the English aristocracy had lived in exile during
Puritan rule. Like the Elizabethan indoor theaters (see p. 877), the new theaters had boxes on three sides (the expensive seats), a gallery above (the
cheap seats), and a seating area in front of the stage (the "pit," the fashionable place to be). A major innovation was the addition of a proscenium arch,
with a curtain that opened at the beginning of the play. The acting was done
in front of the arch, on the forestage. Behind the arch were a series of painted
flats that could slide together and provide scenic backdrops for the action
(as, for example, an indoor flat, a city street flat, a forest flat). Another major
change was that, for the first time in England, women were allowed to act on
stage. No longer were women's roles played by boys dressed as women.

Modern Theaters   Growing increasingly larger in size, such theaters
were the model in England from the late 1600s until the mid-1800s, when
the "modern stage" developed. The modern era saw the action of a play
moved behind the proscenium arch and the forestage pretty much eliminated. Thus, what had been called the rear stage (now referred to just as the
"stage") became the main acting area.

Box Set   The result of the evolution of the stage area was the emer-
gence of the "box set." Playwrights began writing for a stage that they
thought of as a box behind the arch. They visualized the box as an actual
room and instructed stage designers to build it with real windows and doors
that could open and close and realistic carpets and furniture. Instead of the
action taking place in front of artificial, painted flats, it took place within
what looked like a room in an actual house. Three walls of the room were
visible to the audience; the fourth wall, of course, was not. The major convention of the modern theater is the "invisible fourth wall" through which
the audience can see into the room, though the actors behave as if the wall
were present and couldn't be crossed.

---

374. **field:** I.e., of battle.

The Quest for Realism   The modern stage was what Henrik Ibsen had in mind as he wrote *A Doll's House*. His stage directions (p. 997) are detailed and specific. The room described may seem old-fashioned and quaint to us, but for Ibsen's contemporaries it would have been typical of the upper-class society portrayed in the play. Ibsen wanted it to seem genuine, as he aimed for a realistic, totally believable story—in setting, plot, characters, and subject matter.

Lighting   Creating a realistic effect was aided by improvements in lighting: Candles were replaced with gas lamps, which later were replaced with electric lights. The bare Elizabethan stage and the painted flats of its successor required a great deal of imaginative involvement by the audience. Realistic drama lessened how much the audience needed to imagine. Ideally audience members would forget they were watching a play and instead feel like they were observing real life.

Unity of Place   One effect of the box set is a restriction on setting. Shakespeare's bare stage allowed him to change locations easily, just by having characters say the right words. The box set filled the stage and was difficult to move, so *A Doll's House* takes place entirely in the Helmers' living room. Nora is onstage much of the time. Mrs. Linde, Dr. Rank, and Krogstad visit her in that room; her scenes with her husband are there as well. A key event—Nora dancing her tarantella—occurs in the Stenborgs' apartment directly above the room shown onstage, so the audience doesn't see it; it is reported by Torvald. In the twentieth century, large theaters developed revolving platforms onstage that, by rotating between scenes, presented two or three realistic box-set stages. But nineteenth-century theaters preceded such technology, so playwrights had to accept unity of place, writing to fit the entire play into one location.

Late Eighteenth- and Nineteenth-Century Plays   Drama was at a low ebb from the mid-eighteenth century through the mid-nineteenth century. In general, audiences did not like tragedy; some of Shakespeare's tragedies were even revised to give them happy endings. The preference among theatergoers was sentimental plays and melodramas, so that's what playwrights needed to write. There was also a reaction against plots that focused on only the upper classes. One result was the rise of the domestic tragedy, whose protagonists were ordinary members of the middle or lower classes. What audiences did love were spectacular productions, with lavish costumes and scenery and special effects, even if the texts needed to be cut back severely to accommodate such extravaganzas. Henrik Ibsen's *A Doll's House* was part of a reaction against such sentimentalism and spectacle. Influenced by the realistic, or naturalistic, movement in fiction, Ibsen and several contemporary playwrights portrayed ordinary people and everyday life in as real and believable a way as they could. Their plays challenged audiences to respond to more important social issues and deeper psychological concerns than had the drama of the previous century.

The Problem Play   Out of the realism movement arose a particular dramatic subtype: the **problem play**, a serious work that dramatizes and psychologically explores a real-life—usually contemporary—social, political, or ethical problem faced by ordinary people, all in an effort to confront the audience with relevant moral dilemmas. Although in a broad sense the term covers all drama dealing with problems of human life, it is used more narrowly for the "drama of ideas" that emerged in the late 1800s in the work of, for example, Ibsen, Irish playwright George Bernard Shaw (1856–1950), and English playwright John Galsworthy (1867–1933). Ibsen became famous (or, at the time, notorious) for a series of plays in which he dealt with marriage (*A Doll's House*, 1879), syphilis and social and religious values (*Ghosts*, 1881), and communities faced with unpleasant truths exposed by outsiders (*An Enemy of the People*, 1882). In his later plays he moved on to psychological examinations of characters entangled in self-destructive relationships. The best-known of these is *Hedda Gabler* (1890).

APPROACHING THE READING

A Doll's House opens in the Christmas season, with the characters expecting a happy, carefree, family-centered celebration. They end up, however, facing a crisis created by thwarted expectations: Torvald Helmer and his wife, Nora, discover idealism is an unstable marriage foundation. Pay attention especially to the way characters (major ones and minor ones) are developed and to the dilemmas the characters (especially Nora) face. Think about what makes the conflicts realistic. Notice how complex the causes of the conflicts are, how you can't simply say "She/he is good/bad." Consider all the things that influence the characters and their reactions.

The ending was very controversial when the play was first produced. Consider whether what Nora does is the best thing to do. (And if so, best for whom?) Think about whether the play should be regarded as affirming women's rights or affirming human rights, or both. Consider also what performing the play with its original staging, in a box set, added to its impact.

Henrik Ibsen   1828–1906

A Doll's House   [1879]

Translated by B. Farquharson Sharp

DRAMATIS PERSONAE

TORVALD HELMER
NORA, his wife
DOCTOR RANK
MRS. LINDE

NILS KROGSTAD
Helmer's three young children
ANNE, their nurse
A Housemaid
A Porter

APPROACHING THE AUTHOR

Henrik Ibsen was born into a highly afflu-
ent family, but shortly after his birth, his
father's business collapsed, leaving the
family in poverty. Financial difficulty is a
theme throughout his plays, as it was
throughout his life.
    For more about him, see page 1068.

SCENE: *The action takes place in Helmer's house.*

ACT I

SCENE: *A room furnished comfortably and tastefully, but not extravagantly. At the back, a door to the right leads to the entrance-hall, another to the left leads to Helmer's study. Between the doors stands a piano. In the middle of the left-hand wall is a door, and beyond it a window. Near the window are a round table, armchairs and a small sofa. In the right-hand wall, at the farther end, another door; and on the same side, nearer the footlights, a stove, two easy chairs and a rocking-chair; between the stove and the door, a small table. Engravings on the walls; a cabinet with china and other small objects; a small book-case with well-bound books. The floors are carpeted, and a fire burns in the stove. It is winter.*

    A bell rings in the hall; shortly afterward the door is heard to open. Enter Nora, humming a tune and in high spirits. She is in outdoor dress and carries a number of parcels; these she lays on the table to the right. She leaves the outer door open after her, and through it is seen a Porter who is carrying a Christmas Tree and a basket, which he gives to the Maid who has opened the door.

NORA: Hide the Christmas Tree carefully, Helen. Be sure the children do not see it until this evening, when it is dressed. (*To the Porter, taking out her purse.*) How much?

PORTER: Sixpence.

NORA: There is a shilling. No, keep the change. (*The Porter thanks her, and goes out. Nora shuts the door. She is laughing to herself, as she takes off her hat and coat. She takes a packet of macaroons from her pocket and eats one or two; then goes cautiously to her husband's door and listens.*) Yes, he is in. (*Still humming, she goes to the table on the right.*)

HELMER (*calls out from his room*): Is that my little lark twittering out there?

NORA (*busy opening some of the parcels*): Yes, it is!

HELMER: Is it my little squirrel bustling about?

NORA: Yes!

HELMER: When did my squirrel come home?

NORA: Just now. (*Puts the bag of macaroons into her pocket and wipes her mouth.*) Come in here, Torvald, and see what I have bought.

HELMER: Don't disturb me. (*A little later, he opens the door and looks into the room, pen in hand.*) Bought, did you say? All these things? Has my little spendthrift been wasting money again?

NORA: Yes but, Torvald, this year we really can let ourselves go a little. This is the first Christmas that we have not needed to economize.

HELMER: Still, you know, we can't spend money recklessly.

NORA: Yes, Torvald, we may be a wee bit more reckless now, mayn't we? Just a tiny wee bit! You are going to have a big salary and earn lots and lots of money.

HELMER: Yes, after the New Year; but then it will be a whole quarter before the salary is due.

NORA: Pooh! we can borrow until then.

HELMER: Nora! (*Goes up to her and takes her playfully by the ear.*) The same little featherhead! Suppose, now that I borrowed fifty pounds today, and you spent it all in the Christmas week, and then on New Year's Eve a slate fell on my head and killed me, and—

NORA (*putting her hands over his mouth*): Oh! don't say such horrid things.

HELMER: Still, suppose that happened,—what then?

NORA: If that were to happen, I don't suppose I should care whether I owed money or not.

HELMER: Yes, but what about the people who had lent it?

NORA: They? Who would bother about them? I should not know who they were.

HELMER: That is like a woman! But seriously, Nora, you know what I think about that. No debt, no borrowing. There can be no freedom or beauty about a home life that depends on borrowing and debt. We two have kept bravely on the straight road so far, and we will go on the same way for the short time longer that there need be any struggle.

NORA (*moving toward the stove*): As you please, Torvald.

HELMER (*following her*): Come, come, my little skylark must not droop her wings. What is this! Is my little squirrel out of temper? (*Taking out his purse.*) Nora, what do you think I have got here?

NORA (*turning round quickly*): Money!

HELMER: There you are. (*Gives her some money.*) Do you think I don't know what a lot is wanted for housekeeping at Christmas-time?

NORA (*counting*): Ten shillings—a pound—two pounds! Thank you, thank you, Torvald; that will keep me going for a long time.

HELMER: Indeed it must.

NORA: Yes, yes, it will. But come here and let me show you what I have bought. And all so cheap! Look, here is a new suit for Ivar, and a sword; and a horse and a trumpet for Bob; and a doll and dolly's bedstead for Emmy,—they are very plain, but anyway she will soon break them in pieces. And here are dress-lengths and handkerchiefs for the maids; old Anne ought really to have something better.

HELMER: And what is in this parcel?

NORA (*crying out*): No, no! you mustn't see that until this evening.

HELMER: Very well. But now tell me, you extravagant little person, what would you like for yourself?

NORA: For myself? Oh, I am sure I don't want anything.

HELMER: Yes, but you must. Tell me something reasonable that you would particularly like to have.

NORA: No, I really can't think of anything—unless, Torvald—

HELMER: Well?

NORA (*playing with his coat buttons, and without raising her eyes to his*): If you really want to give me something, you might—you might—

HELMER: Well, out with it!

NORA (*speaking quickly*): You might give me money, Torvald. Only just as much as you can afford; and then one of these days I will buy something with it.

HELMER: But, Nora—

NORA: Oh, do! dear Torvald; please, please do! Then I will wrap it up in beautiful gilt paper and hang it on the Christmas Tree. Wouldn't that be fun?

HELMER: What are little people called that are always wasting money?

NORA: Spendthrifts—I know. Let us do as you suggest, Torvald, and then I shall have time to think what I am most in want of. That is a very sensible plan, isn't it?

HELMER (*smiling*): Indeed it is—that is to say, if you were really to save out of the money I give you, and then really buy something for yourself. But if you spend it all on the housekeeping and any number of unnecessary things, then I merely have to pay up again.

NORA: Oh but, Torvald—

HELMER: You can't deny it, my dear little Nora. (*Puts his arm round her waist.*) It's a sweet little spendthrift, but she uses up a deal of money. One would hardly believe how expensive such little persons are!

NORA: It's a shame to say that. I do really save all I can.

HELMER (*laughing*): That's very true,—all you can. But you can't save anything!

NORA (*smiling quietly and happily*): You haven't any idea how many expenses we skylarks and squirrels have, Torvald.

HELMER: You are an odd little soul. Very like your father. You always find some new way of wheedling money out of me, and, as soon as you have got it, it seems to melt in your hands. You never know where it has gone. Still, one must take you as you are. It is in the blood; for indeed it is true that you can inherit these things, Nora.

NORA: Ah, I wish I had inherited many of papa's qualities.

HELMER: And I would not wish you to be anything but just what you are, my sweet little skylark. But, do you know, it strikes me that you are looking rather—what shall I say—rather uneasy today?

NORA: Do I?

HELMER: You do, really. Look straight at me.

NORA (*looks at him*): Well?

HELMER (*wagging his finger at her*): Hasn't Miss Sweet Tooth been breaking rules in town today?

NORA: No; what makes you think that?

HELMER: Hasn't she paid a visit to the confectioner's?

NORA: No, I assure you, Torvald—

HELMER: Not been nibbling sweets?

NORA: No, certainly not.

HELMER: Not even taken a bite at a macaroon or two?

NORA: No, Torvald, I assure you really—

HELMER: There, there, of course I was only joking.

NORA (*going to the table on the right*): I should not think of going against your wishes.

HELMER: No, I am sure of that; besides, you gave me your word—(*Going up to her.*) Keep your little Christmas secrets to yourself, my darling. They will all be revealed tonight when the Christmas Tree is lit, no doubt.

NORA: Did you remember to invite Doctor Rank?

HELMER: No. But there is no need; as a matter of course he will come to dinner with us. However, I will ask him when he comes in this morning. I have ordered some good wine. Nora, you can't think how I am looking forward to this evening.

NORA: So am I! And how the children will enjoy themselves, Torvald!

HELMER: It is splendid to feel that one has a perfectly safe appointment, and a big enough income. It's delightful to think of, isn't it?

NORA: It's wonderful!

HELMER: Do you remember last Christmas? For a full three weeks beforehand you shut yourself up every evening until long after midnight, making ornaments for the Christmas Tree, and all the other fine things that were to be a surprise to us. It was the dullest three weeks I ever spent!

NORA: I didn't find it dull.

HELMER (*smiling*): But there was precious little result, Nora.

NORA: Oh, you shouldn't tease me about that again. How could I help the cat's going in and tearing everything to pieces?

HELMER: Of course you couldn't, poor little girl. You had the best of intentions to please us all, and that's the main thing. But it is a good thing that our hard times are over.

NORA: Yes, it is really wonderful.

HELMER: This time I needn't sit here and be dull all alone, and you needn't ruin your dear eyes and your pretty little hands—

NORA (*clapping her hands*): No, Torvald, I needn't any longer, need I! It's wonderfully lovely to hear you say so! (*Taking his arm.*) Now I will tell you how I have been thinking we ought to arrange things, Torvald. As soon as Christmas is over—(*A bell rings in the hall.*) There's the bell. (*She tidies the room a little.*) There's some one at the door. What a nuisance!

HELMER: If it is a caller, remember I am not at home.

MAID (*in the doorway*): A lady to see you, ma'am,—a stranger.

NORA: Ask her to come in.

MAID (*to Helmer*): The doctor came at the same time, sir.

HELMER: Did he go straight into my room?

MAID: Yes, sir.

Helmer goes into his room. The Maid ushers in Mrs. Linde, who is in travelling dress, and shuts the door.

MRS. LINDE (*in a dejected and timid voice*): How do you do, Nora?

NORA (*doubtfully*): How do you do—

MRS. LINDE: You don't recognise me, I suppose.

NORA: No, I don't know—yes, to be sure, I seem to—(*Suddenly.*) Yes! Christine!
Is it really you?

MRS. LINDE: Yes, it is I.

NORA: Christine! To think of my not recognising you! And yet how could I—(*In
a gentle voice.*) How you have altered, Christine!

MRS. LINDE: Yes, I have indeed. In nine, ten long years—

NORA: Is it so long since we met? I suppose it is. The last eight years have been
a happy time for me, I can tell you. And so now you have come into the
town, and have taken this long journey in winter—that was plucky of you.

MRS. LINDE: I arrived by steamer this morning.

NORA: To have some fun at Christmas-time, of course. How delightful! We will
have such fun together! But take off your things. You are not cold, I hope.
(*Helps her.*) Now we will sit down by the stove, and be cosy. No, take this
armchair; I will sit here in the rocking-chair. (*Takes her hands.*) Now you
look like your old self again; it was only the first moment—You are a little
paler, Christine, and perhaps a little thinner.

MRS. LINDE: And much, much older, Nora.

NORA: Perhaps a little older; very, very little; certainly not much. (*Stops suddenly and speaks seriously.*) What a thoughtless creature I am, chattering
away like this. My poor, dear Christine, do forgive me.

MRS. LINDE: What do you mean, Nora?

NORA (*gently*): Poor Christine, you are a widow.

MRS. LINDE: Yes; it is three years ago now.

NORA: Yes, I knew; I saw it in the papers. I assure you, Christine, I meant ever
so often to write to you at the time, but I always put it off and something
always prevented me.

MRS. LINDE: I quite understand, dear.

NORA: It was very bad of me, Christine. Poor thing, how you must have suffered.
And he left you nothing?

MRS. LINDE: No.

NORA: And no children?

MRS. LINDE: No.

NORA: Nothing at all, then.

MRS. LINDE: Not even any sorrow or grief to live upon.

NORA (*looking incredulously at her*): But, Christine, is that possible?

MRS. LINDE (*smiles sadly and strokes her hair*): It sometimes happens, Nora.

NORA: So you are quite alone. How dreadfully sad that must be. I have three
lovely children. You can't see them just now, for they are out with their
nurse. But now you must tell me all about it.

MRS. LINDE: No, no; I want to hear about you.

NORA: No, you must begin. I mustn't be selfish today; today I must only think
of your affairs. But there is one thing I must tell you. Do you know we have
just had a great piece of good luck?

MRS. LINDE: No, what is it?

NORA: Just fancy, my husband has been made manager of the Bank!

MRS. LINDE: Your husband? What good luck!

NORA: Yes, tremendous! A barrister's profession is such an uncertain thing, especially if he won't undertake unsavoury cases; and naturally Torvald has never been willing to do that, and I quite agree with him. You may imagine how pleased we are! He is to take up his work in the Bank at the New Year, and then he will have a big salary and lots of commissions. For the future we can live quite differently—we can do just as we like. I feel so relieved and so happy, Christine! It will be splendid to have heaps of money and not need to have any anxiety, won't it?

MRS. LINDE: Yes, anyhow I think it would be delightful to have what one needs.

NORA: No, not only what one needs, but heaps and heaps of money.

MRS. LINDE (*smiling*): Nora, Nora, haven't you learned sense yet? In our school-days you were a great spendthrift.

NORA (*laughing*): Yes, that is what Torvald says now. (*Wags her finger at her.*) But "Nora, Nora" is not so silly as you think. We have not been in a position for me to waste money. We have both had to work.

MRS. LINDE: You too?

NORA: Yes; odds and ends, needlework, crotchet-work, embroidery, and that kind of thing. (*Dropping her voice.*) And other things as well. You know Torvald left his office when we were married? There was no prospect of promotion there, and he had to try and earn more than before. But during the first year he overworked himself dreadfully. You see, he had to make money every way he could, and he worked early and late; but he couldn't stand it, and fell dreadfully ill, and the doctors said it was necessary for him to go south.

MRS. LINDE: You spent a whole year in Italy, didn't you?

NORA: Yes. It was no easy matter to get away, I can tell you. It was just after Ivar was born; but naturally we had to go. It was a wonderfully beautiful journey, and it saved Torvald's life. But it cost a tremendous lot of money, Christine.

MRS. LINDE: So I should think.

NORA: It cost about two hundred and fifty pounds. That's a lot, isn't it?

MRS. LINDE: Yes, and in emergencies like that it is lucky to have the money.

NORA: I ought to tell you that we had it from papa.

MRS. LINDE: Oh, I see. It was just about that time that he died, wasn't it?

NORA: Yes; and, just think of it, I couldn't go and nurse him. I was expecting little Ivar's birth every day and I had my poor sick Torvald to look after. My dear, kind father—I never saw him again, Christine. That was the saddest time I have known since our marriage.

MRS. LINDE: I know how fond you were of him. And then you went off to Italy?

NORA: Yes; you see we had money then, and the doctors insisted on our going, so we started a month later.

MRS. LINDE: And your husband came back quite well?

NORA: As sound as a bell!

MRS. LINDE: But—the doctor?

NORA: What doctor?

MRS. LINDE: I thought your maid said the gentleman who arrived here just as I did, was the doctor?

NORA: Yes, that was Doctor Rank, but he doesn't come here professionally. He is our greatest friend, and comes in at least once every day. No, Torvald has not had an hour's illness since then, and our children are strong and healthy and so am I. (*Jumps up and claps her hands.*) Christine! Christine! It's good to be alive and happy! — But how horrid of me; I am talking of nothing but my own affairs. (*Sits on a stool near her, and rests her arms on her knees.*) You mustn't be angry with me. Tell me, is it really true that you did not love your husband? Why did you marry him?

MRS. LINDE: My mother was alive then, and was bedridden and helpless, and I had to provide for my two younger brothers; so I did not think I was justified in refusing his offer.

NORA: No, perhaps you were quite right. He was rich at that time, then?

MRS. LINDE: I believe he was quite well off. But his business was a precarious one; and, when he died, it all went to pieces and there was nothing left.

NORA: And then? —

MRS. LINDE: Well, I had to turn my hand to anything I could find — first a small shop, then a small school, and so on. The last three years have seemed like one long working-day, with no rest. Now it is at an end, Nora. My poor mother needs me no more, for she is gone; and the boys do not need me either; they have got situations and can shift for themselves.

NORA: What a relief you must feel it —

MRS. LINDE: No, indeed; I only feel my life unspeakably empty. No one to live for anymore. (*Gets up restlessly.*) That was why I could not stand the life in my little backwater any longer. I hope it may be easier here to find something which will busy me and occupy my thoughts. If only I could have the good luck to get some regular work — office work of some kind —

NORA: But, Christine, that is so frightfully tiring, and you look tired out now. You had far better go away to some watering-place.

MRS. LINDE (*walking to the window*): I have no father to give me money for a journey, Nora.

NORA (*rising*): Oh, don't be angry with me!

MRS. LINDE (*going up to her*): It is you that must not be angry with me, dear. The worst of a position like mine is that it makes one so bitter. No one to work for, and yet obliged to be always on the lookout for chances. One must live, and so one becomes selfish. When you told me of the happy turn your fortunes have taken — you will hardly believe it — I was delighted not so much on your account as on my own.

NORA: How do you mean? — Oh, I understand. You mean that perhaps Torvald could get you something to do.

MRS. LINDE: Yes, that was what I was thinking of.

NORA: He must, Christine. Just leave it to me; I will broach the subject very cleverly — I will think of something that will please him very much. It will make me so happy to be of some use to you.

MRS. LINDE: How kind you are, Nora, to be so anxious to help me! It is doubly
   kind in you, for you know so little of the burdens and troubles of life.

NORA: I—? I know so little of them?

MRS. LINDE (*smiling*): My dear! Small household cares and that sort of
   thing!—You are a child, Nora.

NORA (*tosses her head and crosses the stage*): You ought not to be so superior.

MRS. LINDE: No?

NORA: You are just like the others. They all think that I am incapable of anything really serious—

MRS. LINDE: Come, come—

NORA: —that I have gone through nothing in this world of cares.

MRS. LINDE: But, my dear Nora, you have just told me all your troubles.

NORA: Pooh!—those were trifles. (*Lowering her voice.*) I have not told you the
   important thing.

MRS. LINDE: The important thing? What do you mean?

NORA: You look down upon me altogether, Christine—but you ought not to. You
   are proud, aren't you, of having worked so hard and so long for your mother?

MRS. LINDE: Indeed, I don't look down on anyone. But it is true that I am both
   proud and glad to think that I was privileged to make the end of my
   mother's life almost free from care.

NORA: And you are proud to think of what you have done for your brothers?

MRS. LINDE: I think I have the right to be.

NORA: I think so, too. But now, listen to this; I too have something to be proud
   and glad of.

MRS. LINDE: I have no doubt you have. But what do you refer to?

NORA: Speak low. Suppose Torvald were to hear! He mustn't on any account—no
   one in the world must know, Christine, except you.

MRS. LINDE: But what is it?

NORA: Come here. (*Pulls her down on the sofa beside her.*) Now I will show you
   that I too have something to be proud and glad of. It was I who saved
   Torvald's life.

MRS. LINDE: "Saved"? How?

NORA: I told you about our trip to Italy. Torvald would never have recovered if
   he had not gone there—

MRS. LINDE: Yes, but your father gave you the necessary funds.

NORA (*smiling*): Yes, that is what Torvald and all the others think, but—

MRS. LINDE: But—

NORA: Papa didn't give us a shilling. It was I who procured the money.

MRS. LINDE: You? All that large sum?

NORA: Two hundred and fifty pounds. What do you think of that?

MRS. LINDE: But, Nora, how could you possibly do it? Did you win a prize in the
   Lottery?

NORA (*contemptuously*): In the Lottery? There would have been no credit in that.

MRS. LINDE: But where did you get it from, then?

NORA (*humming and smiling with an air of mystery*): Hm, hm! Aha!

MRS. LINDE: Because you couldn't have borrowed it.

NORA: Couldn't I? Why not?

MRS. LINDE: No, a wife cannot borrow without her husband's consent.

NORA (*tossing her head*): Oh, if it is a wife who has any head for business — a wife who has the wit to be a little bit clever —

MRS. LINDE: I don't understand it at all, Nora.

NORA: There is no need you should. I never said I had borrowed the money. I may have got it some other way. (*Lies back on the sofa.*) Perhaps I got it from some other admirer. When anyone is as attractive as I am —

MRS. LINDE: You are a mad creature.

NORA: Now, you know you're full of curiosity, Christine.

MRS. LINDE: Listen to me, Nora dear. Haven't you been a little bit imprudent?

NORA (*sits up straight*): Is it imprudent to save your husband's life?

MRS. LINDE: It seems to me imprudent, without his knowledge, to —

NORA: But it was absolutely necessary that he should not know! My goodness, can't you understand that? It was necessary he should have no idea what a dangerous condition he was in. It was to me that the doctors came and said that his life was in danger, and that the only thing to save him was to live in the south. Do you suppose I didn't try, first of all, to get what I wanted as if it were for myself? I told him how much I should love to travel abroad like other young wives; I tried tears and entreaties with him; I told him that he ought to remember the condition I was in, and that he ought to be kind and indulgent to me; I even hinted that he might raise a loan. That nearly made him angry, Christine. He said I was thoughtless, and that it was his duty as my husband not to indulge me in my whims and caprices — as I believe he called them. Very well, I thought, you must be saved — and that was how I came to devise a way out of the difficulty —

MRS. LINDE: And did your husband never get to know from your father that the money had not come from him?

NORA: No, never. Papa died just at that time. I had meant to let him into the secret and beg him never to reveal it. But he was so ill then — alas, there never was any need to tell him.

MRS. LINDE: And since then have you never told your secret to your husband?

NORA: Good Heavens, no! How could you think so? A man who has such strong opinions about these things! And besides, how painful and humiliating it would be for Torvald, with his manly independence, to know that he owed me anything! It would upset our mutual relations altogether; our beautiful happy home would no longer be what it is now.

MRS. LINDE: Do you mean never to tell him about it?

NORA (*meditatively, and with a half smile*): Yes — someday, perhaps, after many years, when I am no longer as nice-looking as I am now. Don't laugh at me! I mean, of course, when Torvald is no longer as devoted to me as he is now; when my dancing and dressing-up and reciting have palled on him; then it may be a good thing to have something in reserve — (*Breaking off.*) What nonsense! That time will never come. Now; what do you think of my great secret, Christine? Do you still think I am of no use? I can tell you, too, that this affair has caused me a lot of worry. It has been by no means easy for me to meet my engagements punctually. I may tell you that there is something that is called, in business, quarterly interest, and another thing called payment in installments, and it is always so dreadfully difficult to manage them. I have had to save a little here and there, where I could, you understand. I have not been able to put aside much from my housekeeping money, for Torvald must have a good table. I couldn't let my children be shabbily dressed; I have felt obliged to use up all he gave me for them, the sweet little darlings!

MRS. LINDE: So it has all had to come out of your own necessaries of life, poor Nora?

NORA: Of course. Besides, I was the one responsible for it. Whenever Torvald has given me money for new dresses and such things, I have never spent more than half of it; I have always bought the simplest and cheapest things. Thank Heaven, any clothes look well on me, and so Torvald has never noticed it. But it was often very hard on me, Christine — because it is delightful to be really well dressed, isn't it?

MRS. LINDE: Quite so.

NORA: Well, then I have found other ways of earning money. Last winter I was lucky enough to get a lot of copying to do; so I locked myself up and sat writing every evening until quite late at night. Many a time I was desperately tired; but all the same it was a tremendous pleasure to sit there working and earning money. It was like being a man.

MRS. LINDE: How much have you been able to pay off in that way?

NORA: I can't tell you exactly. You see, it is very difficult to keep an account of a business matter of that kind. I only know that I have paid every penny that I could scrape together. Many a time I was at my wits' end. (*Smiles.*) Then I used to sit here and imagine that a rich old gentleman had fallen in love with me —

MRS. LINDE: What! Who was it?

NORA: Be quiet! — that he had died; and that when his will was opened it contained, written in big letters, the instruction: "The lovely Mrs. Nora Helmer is to have all I possess paid over to her at once in cash."

MRS. LINDE: But, my dear Nora — who could the man be?

NORA: Good gracious, can't you understand? There was no old gentleman at all; it was only something that I used to sit here and imagine, when I couldn't think of any way of procuring money. But it's all the same now; the tiresome old person can stay where he is, as far as I am concerned; I don't care about him or his will either, for I am free from care now. (*Jumps up.*) My goodness, it's delightful to think of, Christine! Free from care! To be able to be free from care, quite free from care; to be able to play and romp with the children; to be able to keep the house beautifully and have everything just as Torvald likes it! And, think of it, soon the spring will come and the big blue sky! Perhaps we shall be able to take a little trip — perhaps I shall see the sea again! Oh, it's a wonderful thing to be alive and be happy. (*A bell is heard in the hall.*)

MRS. LINDE (*rising*): There is the bell; perhaps I had better go.

NORA: No, don't go; no one will come in here; it is sure to be for Torvald.

SERVANT (*at the hall door*): Excuse me, ma'am—there is a gentleman to see the master, and as the doctor is with him—

NORA: Who is it?

KROGSTAD (*at the door*): It is I, Mrs. Helmer (*Mrs. Linde starts, trembles, and turns to the window.*)

NORA (*takes a step towards him, and speaks in a strained, low voice*): You? What is it? What do you want to see my husband about?

KROGSTAD: Bank business—in a way. I have a small post in the Bank, and I hear your husband is to be our chief now—

NORA: Then it is—

KROGSTAD: Nothing but dry business matters, Mrs. Helmer; absolutely nothing else.

NORA: Be so good as to go into the study, then. (*She bows indifferently to him and shuts the door into the hall; then comes back and makes up the fire in the stove.*)

MRS. LINDE: Nora—who was that man?

NORA: A lawyer, of the name of Krogstad.

MRS. LINDE: Then it really was he.

NORA: Do you know the man?

MRS. LINDE: I used to—many years ago. At one time he was a solicitor's clerk in our town.

NORA: Yes, he was.

MRS. LINDE: He is greatly altered.

NORA: He made a very unhappy marriage.

MRS. LINDE: He is a widower now, isn't he?

NORA: With several children. There now, it is burning up. (*Shuts the door of the stove and moves the rocking-chair aside.*)

MRS. LINDE: They say he carries on various kinds of business.

NORA: Really! Perhaps he does; I don't know anything about it. But don't let us think of business; it is so tiresome.

DOCTOR RANK (*comes out of Helmer's study. Before he shuts the door he calls to him*): No, my dear fellow, I won't disturb you; I would rather go in to your wife for a little while. (*Shuts the door and sees Mrs. Linde.*) I beg your pardon; I am afraid I am disturbing you too.

NORA: No, not at all. (*Introducing him.*) Doctor Rank, Mrs. Linde.

RANK: I have often heard Mrs. Linde's name mentioned here. I think I passed you on the stairs when I arrived, Mrs. Linde?

MRS. LINDE: Yes, I go up very slowly; I can't manage stairs well.

RANK: Ah! some slight internal weakness?

MRS. LINDE: No, the fact is I have been overworking myself.

RANK: Nothing more than that? Then I suppose you have come to town to amuse yourself with our entertainments?

MRS. LINDE: I have come to look for work.

RANK: Is that a good cure for overwork?

MRS. LINDE: One must live, Doctor Rank.

RANK: Yes, the general opinion seems to be that it is necessary.

NORA: Look here, Doctor Rank—you know you want to live.

RANK: Certainly. However wretched I may feel, I want to prolong the agony as long as possible. All my patients are like that. And so are those who are morally diseased; one of them, and a bad case too, is at this very moment with Helmer—

MRS. LINDE: (*sadly*): Ah!

NORA: Whom do you mean?

RANK: A lawyer of the name of Krogstad, a fellow you don't know at all. He suffers from a diseased moral character, Mrs. Helmer; but even he began talking of its being highly important that he should live.

NORA: Did he? What did he want to speak to Torvald about?

RANK: I have no idea; I only heard that it was something about the Bank.

NORA: I didn't know this—what's his name—Krogstad had anything to do with the Bank.

RANK: Yes, he has some sort of appointment there. (*To Mrs. Linde.*) I don't know whether you find also in your part of the world that there are certain people who go zealously snuffing about to smell out moral corruption, and, as soon as they have found some, put the person concerned into some lucrative position where they can keep their eye on him. Healthy natures are left out in the cold.

MRS. LINDE: Still I think the sick are those who most need taking care of.

RANK (*shrugging his shoulders*): Yes, there you are. That is the sentiment that is turning Society into a sick-house.

Nora, who has been absorbed in her thoughts, breaks out into smothered laughter and claps her hands.

RANK: Why do you laugh at that? Have you any notion what Society really is?

NORA: What do I care about tiresome Society? I am laughing at something quite different, something extremely amusing. Tell me, Doctor Rank, are all the people who are employed in the Bank dependent on Torvald now?

RANK: Is that what you find so extremely amusing?

NORA (*smiling and humming*): That's my affair! (*Walking about the room.*) It's perfectly glorious to think that we have—that Torvald has so much power over so many people. (*Takes the packet from her pocket.*) Doctor Rank, what do you say to a macaroon?

RANK: What, macaroons? I thought they were forbidden here.

NORA: Yes, but these are some Christine gave me.

MRS. LINDE: What! I?—

NORA: Oh, well, don't be alarmed! You couldn't know that Torvald had forbidden them. I must tell you that he is afraid they will spoil my teeth. But, bah!—once in a way—That's so, isn't it, Doctor Rank? By your leave! (*Puts a macaroon into his mouth.*) You must have one too, Christine. And I shall have one, just a little one—or at most two. (*Walking about.*) I am tremendously happy. There is just one thing in the world now that I should dearly love to do.

RANK: Well, what is that?

NORA: It's something I should dearly love to say, if Torvald could hear me.

RANK: Well, why can't you say it?

NORA: No, I daren't; it's so shocking.

MRS. LINDE: Shocking?

RANK: Well, I should not advise you to say it. Still, with us you might. What is it you would so much like to say if Torvald could hear you?

NORA: I should just love to say—Well, I'm damned!

RANK: Are you mad?

MRS. LINDE: Nora, dear—!

RANK: Say it, here he is!

NORA (*hiding the packet*): Hush! Hush! Hush! (*Helmer comes out of his room, with his coat over his arm and his hat in his hand.*)

NORA: Well, Torvald dear, have you got rid of him?

HELMER: Yes, he has just gone.

NORA: Let me introduce you—this is Christine, who has come to town.

HELMER: Christine—? Excuse me, but I don't know—

NORA: Mrs. Linde, dear; Christine Linde.

HELMER: Of course. A school friend of my wife's, I presume?

MRS. LINDE: Yes, we have known each other since then.

NORA: And just think, she has taken a long journey in order to see you.

HELMER: What do you mean?

MRS. LINDE: No, really, I—

NORA: Christine is tremendously clever at bookkeeping, and she is frightfully anxious to work under some clever man, so as to perfect herself—

HELMER: Very sensible, Mrs. Linde.

NORA: And when she heard you had been appointed manager of the Bank—the news was telegraphed, you know—she travelled here as quick as she could. Torvald, I am sure you will be able to do something for Christine, for my sake, won't you?

HELMER: Well, it is not altogether impossible. I presume you are a widow, Mrs. Linde?

MRS. LINDE: Yes.

HELMER: And have had some experience of bookkeeping?

MRS. LINDE: Yes, a fair amount.

HELMER: Ah! well, it's very likely I may be able to find something for you—

NORA (*clapping her hands*): What did I tell you? What did I tell you?

HELMER: You have just come at a fortunate moment, Mrs. Linde.

MRS. LINDE: How am I to thank you?

HELMER: There is no need. (*Puts on his coat.*) But today you must excuse me—

RANK: Wait a minute; I will come with you. (*Brings his fur coat from the hall and warms it at the fire.*)

NORA: Don't be long away, Torvald dear.

HELMER: About an hour, not more.

NORA: Are you going too, Christine?

MRS. LINDE (*putting on her cloak*): Yes, I must go and look for a room.

HELMER: Oh, well then, we can walk down the street together.

NORA (*helping her*): What a pity it is we are so short of space here; I am afraid it is impossible for us—

MRS. LINDE: Please don't think of it! Goodbye, Nora dear, and many thanks.

NORA: Goodbye for the present. Of course you will come back this evening. And you too, Dr. Rank. What do you say? If you are well enough? Oh, you must be! Wrap yourself up well. (*They go to the door all talking together. Children's voices are heard on the staircase.*)

NORA: There they are! There they are! (*She runs to open the door. The Nurse comes in with the children.*) Come in! Come in! (*Stoops and kisses them.*) Oh, you sweet blessings! Look at them, Christine! Aren't they darlings?

RANK: Don't let us stand here in the draught.

HELMER: Come along, Mrs. Linde; the place will only be bearable for a mother now!

Rank, Helmer, and Mrs. Linde go downstairs. The Nurse comes forward with the children; Nora shuts the hall door.

NORA: How fresh and well you look! Such red cheeks like apples and roses. (*The children all talk at once while she speaks to them.*) Have you had great fun? That's splendid! What, you pulled both Emmy and Bob along on the sledge?—both at once?—that was good. You are a clever boy, Ivar. Let me take her for a little, Anne. My sweet little baby doll! (*Takes the baby from the Maid and dances it up and down.*) Yes, yes, mother will dance with Bob too. What! Have you been snowballing? I wish I had been there too! No, no, I will take their things off, Anne; please let me do it, it is such fun. Go in now, you look half frozen. There is some hot coffee for you on the stove.

The Nurse goes into the room on the left. Nora takes off the children's things and throws them about, while they all talk to her at once.

NORA: Really! Did a big dog run after you? But it didn't bite you? No, dogs don't bite nice little dolly children. You mustn't look at the parcels, Ivar. What are they? Ah, I daresay you would like to know. No, no—it's something nasty! Come, let us have a game! What shall we play at? Hide and Seek? Yes, we'll play Hide and Seek. Bob shall hide first. Must I hide? Very well, I'll hide first. (*She and the children laugh and shout, and romp in and out of the room; at last Nora hides under the table, the children rush in and out for her, but do not see her; they hear her smothered laughter, run to the table, lift up the cloth and find her. Shouts of laughter. She crawls forward and pretends to frighten them. Fresh laughter. Meanwhile there has been a knock at the hall door, but none of them has noticed it. The door is half opened, and Krogstad appears. He waits a little; the game goes on.*)

KROGSTAD: Excuse me, Mrs. Helmer.

NORA (*with a stifled cry, turns round and gets up on to her knees*): Ah! what do you want?

KROGSTAD: Excuse me, the outer door was ajar; I suppose someone forgot to shut it.

NORA (*rising*): My husband is out, Mr Krogstad.

KROGSTAD: I know that.

NORA: What do you want here, then?

KROGSTAD: A word with you.

NORA: With me? — (*To the children, gently.*) Go in to nurse. What? No, the strange man won't do mother any harm. When he has gone we will have another game. (*She takes the children into the room on the left, and shuts the door after them.*) You want to speak to me?

KROGSTAD: Yes, I do.

NORA: Today? It is not the first of the month yet.

KROGSTAD: No, it is Christmas Eve, and it will depend on yourself what sort of a Christmas you will spend.

NORA: What do you mean? Today it is absolutely impossible for me—

KROGSTAD: We won't talk about that until later on. This is something different. I presume you can give me a moment?

NORA: Yes — yes, I can — although —

KROGSTAD: Good. I was in Olsen's Restaurant and saw your husband going down the street—

NORA: Yes?

KROGSTAD: With a lady.

NORA: What then?

KROGSTAD: May I make so bold as to ask if it was a Mrs. Linde?

NORA: It was.

KROGSTAD: Just arrived in town?

NORA: Yes, today.

KROGSTAD: She is a great friend of yours, isn't she?

NORA: She is. But I don't see—

KROGSTAD: I knew her too, once upon a time.

NORA: I am aware of that.

KROGSTAD: Are you? So you know all about it; I thought as much. Then I can ask you, without beating about the bush—is Mrs. Linde to have an appointment in the Bank?

NORA: What right have you to question me, Mr. Krogstad? — You, one of my husband's subordinates! But since you ask, you shall know. Yes, Mrs. Linde is to have an appointment. And it was I who pleaded her cause, Mr. Krogstad, let me tell you that.

KROGSTAD: I was right in what I thought, then.

NORA (*walking up and down the stage*): Sometimes one has a tiny little bit of influence, I should hope. Because one is a woman, it does not necessarily follow that—. When anyone is in a subordinate position, Mr. Krogstad, they should really be careful to avoid offending anyone who—who—

KROGSTAD: Who has influence?

NORA: Exactly.

KROGSTAD (*changing his tone*): Mrs. Helmer, you will be so good as to use your influence on my behalf.

NORA: What? What do you mean?

KROGSTAD: You will be so kind as to see that I am allowed to keep my subordinate position in the Bank.

NORA: What do you mean by that? Who proposes to take your post away from you?

KROGSTAD: Oh, there is no necessity to keep up the pretence of ignorance. I can quite understand that your friend is not very anxious to expose herself to the chance of rubbing shoulders with me; and I quite understand, too, whom I have to thank for being turned off.

NORA: But I assure you—

KROGSTAD: Very likely; but, to come to the point, the time has come when I should advise you to use your influence to prevent that.

NORA: But, Mr. Krogstad, I *have* no influence.

KROGSTAD: Haven't you? I thought you said yourself just now—

NORA: Naturally I did not mean you to put that construction on it. What should make you think I have any influence of that kind with my husband?

KROGSTAD: Oh, I have known your husband from our student days. I don't suppose he is any more unassailable than other husbands.

NORA: If you speak slightingly of my husband, I shall turn you out of the house.

KROGSTAD: You are bold, Mrs. Helmer.

NORA: I am not afraid of you any longer. As soon as the New Year comes, I shall in a very short time be free of the whole thing.

KROGSTAD (*controlling himself*): Listen to me, Mrs. Helmer. If necessary, I am prepared to fight for my small post in the Bank as if I were fighting for my life.

NORA: So it seems.

KROGSTAD: It is not only for the sake of the money; indeed, that weighs least with me in the matter. There is another reason—well, I may as well tell you. My position is this. I daresay you know, like everybody else, that once, many years ago, I was guilty of an indiscretion.

NORA: I think I have heard something of the kind.

KROGSTAD: The matter never came into court; but every way seemed to be closed to me after that. So I took to the business that you know of. I had to do something; and, honestly, I don't think I've been one of the worst. But now I must cut myself free from all that. My sons are growing up; for their sake I must try and win back as much respect as I can in the town. This post in the Bank was like the first step up for me—and now your husband is going to kick me downstairs again into the mud.

NORA: But you must believe me, Mr. Krogstad; it is not in my power to help you at all.

KROGSTAD: Then it is because you haven't the will; but I have means to compel you.

NORA: You don't mean that you will tell my husband that I owe you money?

KROGSTAD: Hm!—suppose I were to tell him?

NORA: It would be perfectly infamous of you. (*Sobbing.*) To think of his learning my secret, which has been my joy and pride, in such an ugly, clumsy way—that he should learn it from you! And it would put me in a horribly disagreeable position—

KROGSTAD: Only disagreeable?

NORA (*impetuously*): Well, do it, then!—and it will be the worse for you. My husband will see for himself what a blackguard you are, and you certainly won't keep your post then.

KROGSTAD: I asked you if it was only a disagreeable scene at home that you were afraid of?

NORA: If my husband does get to know of it, of course he will at once pay you what is still owing, and we shall have nothing more to do with you.

KROGSTAD (*coming a step nearer*): Listen to me, Mrs. Helmer. Either you have a very bad memory or you know very little of business. I shall be obliged to remind you of a few details.

NORA: What do you mean?

KROGSTAD: When your husband was ill, you came to me to borrow two hundred and fifty pounds.

NORA: I didn't know anyone else to go to.

KROGSTAD: I promised to get you that amount—

NORA: Yes, and you did so.

KROGSTAD: I promised to get you that amount, on certain conditions. Your mind was so taken up with your husband's illness, and you were so anxious to get the money for your journey, that you seem to have paid no attention to the conditions of our bargain. Therefore it will not be amiss if I remind you of them. Now, I promised to get the money on the security of a bond which I drew up.

NORA: Yes, and which I signed.

KROGSTAD: Good. But below your signature there were a few lines constituting your father a surety for the money; those lines your father should have signed.

NORA: Should? He did sign them.

KROGSTAD: I had left the date blank; that is to say, your father should himself have inserted the date on which he signed the paper. Do you remember that?

NORA: Yes, I think I remember—

KROGSTAD: Then I gave you the bond to send by post to your father. Is that not so?

NORA: Yes.

KROGSTAD: And you naturally did so at once, because five or six days afterward you brought me the bond with your father's signature. And then I gave you the money.

NORA: Well, haven't I been paying it off regularly?

KROGSTAD: Fairly so, yes. But—to come back to the matter in hand—that must have been a very trying time for you, Mrs. Helmer.

NORA: It was, indeed.

KROGSTAD: Your father was very ill, wasn't he?

NORA: He was very near his end.

KROGSTAD: And he died soon afterwards?

NORA: Yes.

KROGSTAD: Tell me, Mrs. Helmer, can you by any chance remember what day your father died? — on what day of the month, I mean.

NORA: Papa died on the 29th of September.

KROGSTAD: That is correct; I have ascertained it for myself. And, as that is so, there is a discrepancy (*taking a paper from his pocket*) which I cannot account for.

NORA: What discrepancy? I don't know —

KROGSTAD: The discrepancy consists, Mrs. Helmer, in the fact that your father signed this bond three days after his death.

NORA: What do you mean? I don't understand —

KROGSTAD: Your father died on the 29th of September. But, look here; your father has dated his signature the 2nd of October. It is a discrepancy, isn't it? (*Nora is silent.*) Can you explain it to me? (*Nora is still silent.*) It is a remarkable thing, too, that the words "2nd of October," as well as the year, are not written in your father's handwriting but in one that I think I know. Well, of course it can be explained; your father may have forgotten to date his signature, and someone else may have dated it haphazard before they knew of his death. There is no harm in that. It all depends on the signature of the name; and *that* is genuine, I suppose, Mrs. Helmer? It was your father himself who signed his name here?

NORA (*after a short pause, throws her head up and looks defiantly at him*): No, it was not. It was I that wrote papa's name.

KROGSTAD: Are you aware that is a dangerous confession?

NORA: In what way? You shall have your money soon.

KROGSTAD: Let me ask you a question; why did you not send the paper to your father?

NORA: It was impossible; papa was so ill. If I had asked him for his signature, I should have had to tell him what the money was to be used for; and when he was so ill himself I couldn't tell him that my husband's life was in danger — it was impossible.

KROGSTAD: It would have been better for you if you had given up your trip abroad.

NORA: No, that was impossible. That trip was to save my husband's life; I couldn't give that up.

KROGSTAD: But did it never occur to you that you were committing a fraud on me?

NORA: I couldn't take that into account; I didn't trouble myself about you at all. I couldn't bear you, because you put so many heartless difficulties in my way, although you knew what a dangerous condition my husband was in.

KROGSTAD: Mrs. Helmer, you evidently do not realise clearly what it is that you have been guilty of. But I can assure you that my one false step, which lost

me all my reputation, was nothing more or nothing worse than what you
have done.

NORA: You? Do you ask me to believe that you were brave enough to run a risk
to save your wife's life?

KROGSTAD: The law cares nothing about motives.

NORA: Then it must be a very foolish law.

KROGSTAD: Foolish or not, it is the law by which you will be judged, if I produce
this paper in court.

NORA: I don't believe it. Is a daughter not to be allowed to spare her dying father
anxiety and care? Is a wife not to be allowed to save her husband's life? I
don't know much about law; but I am certain that there must be laws per-
mitting such things as that. Have you no knowledge of such laws—you who
are a lawyer? You must be a very poor lawyer, Mr. Krogstad.

KROGSTAD: Maybe. But matters of business—such business as you and I have
had together—do you think I don't understand that? Very well. Do as you
please. But let me tell you this—if I lose my position a second time, you
shall lose yours with me. (*He bows, and goes out through the hall.*)

NORA (*appears buried in thought for a short time, then tosses her head*): Nonsense!
Trying to frighten me like that!—I am not so silly as he thinks. (*Begins to
busy herself putting the children's things in order.*) And yet—? No, it's impossible! I did it for love's sake.

CHILDREN (*in the doorway on the left*): Mother, the stranger man has gone out
through the gate.

NORA: Yes, dears, I know. But, don't tell anyone about the stranger man. Do you
hear? Not even papa.

CHILDREN: No, mother; but will you come and play again?

NORA: No, no,—not now.

CHILDREN: But, mother, you promised us.

NORA: Yes, but I can't now. Run away in; I have such a lot to do. Run away in,
my sweet little darlings. (*She gets them into the room by degrees and shuts the
door on them; then sits down on the sofa, takes up a piece of needlework and
sews a few stitches, but soon stops.*) No! (*Throws down the work, gets up, goes
to the hall door and calls out.*) Helen! bring the Tree in. (*Goes to the table on
the left, opens a drawer, and stops again.*) No, no! it is quite impossible!

MAID (*coming in with the Tree*): Where shall I put it, ma'am?

NORA: Here, in the middle of the floor.

MAID: Shall I get you anything else?

NORA: No, thank you. I have all I want.   (*Exit Maid.*)

NORA (*begins dressing the tree*): A candle here—and flowers here—. The horrible
man! It's all nonsense—there's nothing wrong. The Tree shall be splendid!
I will do everything I can think of to please you, Torvald!—I will sing for
you, dance for you—(*Helmer comes in with some papers under his arm.*) Oh!
are you back already?

HELMER: Yes. Has anyone been here?

NORA: Here? No.

HELMER: That is strange. I saw Krogstad going out of the gate.

NORA: Did you? Oh yes, I forgot, Krogstad was here for a moment.

HELMER: Nora, I can see from your manner that he has been here begging you to say a good word for him.

NORA: Yes.

HELMER: And you were to appear to do it of your own accord; you were to conceal from me the fact of his having been here; didn't he beg that of you too?

NORA: Yes, Torvald, but—

HELMER: Nora, Nora, and you would be a party to that sort of thing? To have any talk with a man like that, and give him any sort of promise? And to tell me a lie into the bargain?

NORA: A lie—?

HELMER: Didn't you tell me no one had been here? (*Shakes his finger at her.*) My little songbird must never do that again. A songbird must have a clean beak to chirp with—no false notes! (*Puts his arm around her waist.*) That is so, isn't it? Yes, I am sure it is. (*Lets her go.*) We will say no more about it. (*Sits down by the stove.*) How warm and snug it is here! (*Turns over his papers.*)

NORA (*after a short pause, during which she busies herself with the Christmas Tree*): Torvald!

HELMER: Yes.

NORA: I am looking forward tremendously to the fancy-dress ball at the Stenborgs' the day after tomorrow.

HELMER: And I am tremendously curious to see what you are going to surprise me with.

NORA: It was very silly of me to want to do that.

HELMER: What do you mean?

NORA: I can't hit upon anything that will do; everything I think of seems so silly and insignificant.

HELMER: Does my little Nora acknowledge that at last?

NORA (*standing behind his chair with her arms on the back of it*): Are you very busy, Torvald?

HELMER: Well—

NORA: What are all those papers?

HELMER: Bank business.

NORA: Already?

HELMER: I have got authority from the retiring manager to undertake the necessary changes in the staff and in the rearrangement of the work; and I must make use of the Christmas week for that, so as to have everything in order for the new year.

NORA: Then that was why this poor Krogstad—

HELMER: Hm!

NORA (*leans against the back of his chair and strokes his hair*): If you hadn't been so busy I should have asked you a tremendously big favor, Torvald.

HELMER: What is that? Tell me.

NORA: There is no one has such good taste as you. And I do so want to look nice at the fancy-dress ball. Torvald, couldn't you take me in hand and decide what I shall go as, and what sort of a dress I shall wear?

HELMER: Aha! so my obstinate little woman is obliged to get someone to come to her rescue?

NORA: Yes, Torvald, I can't get along a bit without your help.

HELMER: Very well, I will think it over, we shall manage to hit upon something.

NORA: That is nice of you. (*Goes to the Christmas Tree. A short pause.*) How pretty the red flowers look—. But, tell me, was it really something very bad that this Krogstad was guilty of?

HELMER: He forged someone's name. Have you any idea what that means?

NORA: Isn't it possible that he was driven to do it by necessity?

HELMER: Yes; or, as in so many cases, by imprudence. I am not so heartless as to condemn a man altogether because of a single false step of that kind.

NORA: No, you wouldn't, would you, Torvald?

HELMER: Many a man has been able to retrieve his character, if he has openly confessed his fault and taken his punishment.

NORA: Punishment—?

HELMER: But Krogstad did nothing of that sort; he got himself out of it by a cunning trick, and that is why he has gone under altogether.

NORA: But do you think it would—?

HELMER: Just think how a guilty man like that has to lie and play the hypocrite with every one, how he has to wear a mask in the presence of those near and dear to him, even before his own wife and children. And about the children—that is the most terrible part of it all, Nora.

NORA: How?

HELMER: Because such an atmosphere of lies infects and poisons the whole life of a home. Each breath the children take in such a house is full of the germs of evil.

NORA (*coming nearer him*): Are you sure of that?

HELMER: My dear, I have often seen it in the course of my life as a lawyer. Almost everyone who has gone to the bad early in life has had a deceitful mother.

NORA: Why do you only say—mother?

HELMER: It seems most commonly to be the mother's influence, though naturally a bad father's would have the same result. Every lawyer is familiar with the fact. This Krogstad, now, has been persistently poisoning his own children with lies and dissimulation; that is why I say he has lost all moral character. (*Holds out his hands to her.*) That is why my sweet little Nora must promise me not to plead his cause. Give me your hand on it. Come, come, what is this? Give me your hand. There now, that's settled. I assure you it would be quite impossible for me to work with him; I literally feel physically ill when I am in the company of such people.

NORA (*takes her hand out of his and goes to the opposite side of the Christmas Tree*): How hot it is in here; and I have such a lot to do.

HELMER (*getting up and putting his papers in order*): Yes, and I must try and read through some of these before dinner; and I must think about your costume, too. And it is just possible I may have something ready in gold paper to hang up on the Tree. (*Puts his hand on her head.*) My precious little singing-bird! (*He goes into his room and shuts the door after him.*)

NORA (*after a pause, whispers*): No, no—it isn't true. It's impossible; it must be impossible.

The Nurse opens the door on the left.

NURSE: The little ones are begging so hard to be allowed to come in to mamma.

NORA: No, no, no! Don't let them come in to me! You stay with them, Anne.

NURSE: Very well, ma'am. (*Shuts the door.*)

NORA (*pale with terror*): Deprave my little children? Poison my home? (*A short pause. Then she tosses her head.*) It's not true. It can't possibly be true.

ACT II

THE SAME SCENE: *The Christmas Tree is in the corner by the piano, stripped of its ornaments and with burnt-down candle-ends on its dishevelled branches. Nora's cloak and hat are lying on the sofa. She is alone in the room, walking about uneasily. She stops by the sofa and takes up her cloak.*

NORA (*drops her cloak*): Someone is coming now! (*Goes to the door and listens.*) No—it is no one. Of course, no one will come today, Christmas Day—nor tomorrow either. But, perhaps—(*opens the door and looks out*). No, nothing in the letter box; it is quite empty. (*Comes forward.*) What rubbish! Of course he can't be in earnest about it. Such a thing couldn't happen; it is impossible—I have three little children.

Enter the Nurse from the room on the left, carrying a big cardboard box.

NURSE: At last I have found the box with the fancy dress.

NORA: Thanks; put it on the table.

NURSE (*doing so*): But it is very much in want of mending.

NORA: I should like to tear it into a hundred thousand pieces.

NURSE: What an idea! It can easily be put in order—just a little patience.

NORA: Yes, I will go and get Mrs. Linde to come and help me with it.

NURSE: What, out again? In this horrible weather? You will catch cold, ma'am, and make yourself ill.

NORA: Well, worse than that might happen. How are the children?

NURSE: The poor little souls are playing with their Christmas presents, but—

NORA: Do they ask much for me?

NURSE: You see, they are so accustomed to have their mamma with them.

NORA: Yes, but, nurse, I shall not be able to be so much with them now as I was before.

NURSE: Oh well, young children easily get accustomed to anything.

NORA: Do you think so? Do you think they would forget their mother if she went away altogether?

NURSE: Good heavens! — went away altogether?

NORA: Nurse, I want you to tell me something I have often wondered about — how could you have the heart to put your own child out among strangers?

NURSE: I was obliged to, if I wanted to be little Nora's nurse.

NORA: Yes, but how could you be willing to do it?

NURSE: What, when I was going to get such a good place by it? A poor girl who has got into trouble should be glad to. Besides, that wicked man didn't do a single thing for me.

NORA: But I suppose your daughter has quite forgotten you.

NURSE: No, indeed she hasn't. She wrote to me when she was confirmed, and when she was married.

NORA (*putting her arms round her neck*): Dear old Anne, you were a good mother to me when I was little.

NURSE: Little Nora, poor dear, had no other mother but me.

NORA: And if my little ones had no other mother, I am sure you would — What nonsense I am talking! (*Opens the box.*) Go in to them. Now I must —. You will see tomorrow how charming I shall look.

NURSE: I am sure there will be no one at the ball so charming as you, ma'am. (*Goes into the room on the left.*)

NORA (*begins to unpack the box, but soon pushes it away from her*): If only I dared go out. If only no one would come. If only I could be sure nothing would happen here in the meantime. Stuff and nonsense! No one will come. Only I mustn't think about it. I will brush my muff. What lovely, lovely gloves! Out of my thoughts, out of my thoughts! One, two, three, four, five, six — (*Screams.*) Ah! there is someone coming —. (*Makes a movement towards the door, but stands irresolute.*)

Enter Mrs. Linde from the hall, where she has taken off her cloak and hat.

NORA: Oh, it's you, Christine. There is no one else out there, is there? How good of you to come!

MRS. LINDE: I heard you were up asking for me.

NORA: Yes, I was passing by. As a matter of fact, it is something you could help me with. Let us sit down here on the sofa. Look here. Tomorrow evening there is to be a fancy-dress ball at the Stenborgs', who live above us; and Torvald wants me to go as a Neapolitan fisher-girl, and dance the Tarantella that I learned at Capri.

MRS. LINDE: I see; you are going to keep up the character.

NORA: Yes, Torvald wants me to. Look, here is the dress; Torvald had it made for me there, but now it is all so torn, and I haven't any idea —

MRS. LINDE: We will easily put that right. It is only some of the trimming come unsewn here and there. Needle and thread? Now then, that's all we want.

NORA: It *is* nice of you.

MRS. LINDE (*sewing*): So you are going to be dressed up tomorrow, Nora. I will tell you what—I shall come in for a moment and see you in your fine feathers. But I have completely forgotten to thank you for a delightful evening yesterday.

NORA (*gets up, and crosses the stage*): Well, I don't think yesterday was as pleasant as usual. You ought to have come to town a little earlier, Christine. Certainly Torvald does understand how to make a house dainty and attractive.

MRS. LINDE: And so do you, it seems to me; you are not your father's daughter for nothing. But tell me, is Doctor Rank always as depressed as he was yesterday?

NORA: No; yesterday it was very noticeable. I must tell you that he suffers from a very dangerous disease. He has consumption of the spine, poor creature. His father was a horrible man who committed all sorts of excesses; and that is why his son was sickly from childhood, do you understand?

MRS. LINDE (*dropping her sewing*): But, my dearest Nora, how do you know anything about such things?

NORA (*walking about*): Pooh! When you have three children, you get visits now and then from—from married women, who know something of medical matters, and they talk about one thing and another.

MRS. LINDE: (*goes on sewing. A short silence*) Does Doctor Rank come here every day?

NORA: Every day regularly. He is Torvald's most intimate friend, and a great friend of mine too. He is just like one of the family.

MRS. LINDE: But tell me this—is he perfectly sincere? I mean, isn't he the kind of man that is very anxious to make himself agreeable?

NORA: Not in the least. What makes you think that?

MRS. LINDE: When you introduced him to me yesterday, he declared he had often heard my name mentioned in this house; but afterwards I noticed that your husband hadn't the slightest idea who I was. So how could Doctor Rank—?

NORA: That is quite right, Christine. Torvald is so absurdly fond of me that he wants me absolutely to himself, as he says. At first he used to seem almost jealous if I mentioned any of the dear folk at home, so naturally I gave up doing so. But I often talk about such things with Doctor Rank, because he likes hearing about them.

MRS. LINDE: Listen to me, Nora. You are still very like a child in many things, and I am older than you in many ways and have a little more experience. Let me tell you this—you ought to make an end of it with Doctor Rank.

NORA: What ought I to make an end of?

MRS. LINDE: Of two things, I think. Yesterday you talked some nonsense about a rich admirer who was to leave you money—

NORA: An admirer who doesn't exist, unfortunately! But what then?

MRS. LINDE: Is Doctor Rank a man of means?

NORA: Yes, he is.

MRS. LINDE: And has no one to provide for?

NORA: No, no one; but—

MRS. LINDE: And comes here every day?

NORA: Yes, I told you so.

MRS. LINDE: But how can this well-bred man be so tactless?

NORA: I don't understand you at all.

MRS. LINDE: Don't prevaricate, Nora. Do you suppose I don't guess who lent you the two hundred and fifty pounds?

NORA: Are you out of your senses? How can you think of such a thing! A friend of ours, who comes here every day! Do you realise what a horribly painful position that would be?

MRS. LINDE: Then it really isn't he?

NORA: No, certainly not. It would never have entered into my head for a moment. Besides, he had no money to lend then; he came into his money afterwards.

MRS. LINDE: Well, I think that was lucky for you, my dear Nora.

NORA: No, it would never have come into my head to ask Doctor Rank. Although I am quite sure that if I had asked him —

MRS. LINDE: But of course you won't.

NORA: Of course not. I have no reason to think it could possibly be necessary. But I am quite sure that if I told Doctor Rank —

MRS. LINDE: Behind your husband's back?

NORA: I must make an end of it with the other one, and that will be behind his back too. I *must* make an end of it with him.

MRS. LINDE: Yes, that is what I told you yesterday, but —

NORA (*walking up and down*): A man can put a thing like that straight much easier than a woman —

MRS. LINDE: One's husband, yes.

NORA: Nonsense! (*Standing still.*) When you pay off a debt you get your bond back, don't you?

MRS. LINDE: Yes, as a matter of course.

NORA: And can tear it into a hundred thousand pieces, and burn it up — the nasty dirty paper!

MRS. LINDE (*looks hard at her, lays down her sewing and gets up slowly*): Nora, you are concealing something from me.

NORA: Do I look as if I were?

MRS. LINDE: Something has happened to you since yesterday morning. Nora, what is it?

NORA (*going nearer to her*): Christine! (*Listens.*) Hush! There's Torvald come home. Do you mind going in to the children for the present? Torvald can't bear to see dressmaking going on. Let Anne help you.

MRS. LINDE (*gathering some of the things together*): Certainly — but I am not going away from here until we have had it out with one another. (*She goes into the room on the left, as Helmer comes in from the hall.*)

NORA (*going up to Helmer*): I have wanted you so much, Torvald dear.

HELMER: Was that the dressmaker?

NORA: No, it was Christine; she is helping me to put my dress in order. You will see I shall look quite smart.

HELMER: Wasn't that a happy thought of mine, now?

NORA: Splendid! But don't you think it is nice of me, too, to do as you wish?

HELMER: Nice?—because you do as your husband wishes? Well, well, you little rogue, I am sure you did not mean it in that way. But I am not going to disturb you; you will want to be trying on your dress, I expect.

NORA: I suppose you are going to work.

HELMER: Yes. (*Shows her a bundle of papers.*) Look at that. I have just been into the bank. (*Turns to go into his room.*)

NORA: Torvald.

HELMER: Yes.

NORA: If your little squirrel were to ask you for something very, very prettily—?

HELMER: What then?

NORA: Would you do it?

HELMER: I should like to hear what it is, first.

NORA: Your squirrel would run about and do all her tricks if you would be nice, and do what she wants.

HELMER: Speak plainly.

NORA: Your skylark would chirp about in every room, with her song rising and falling—

HELMER: Well, my skylark does that anyhow.

NORA: I would play the fairy and dance for you in the moonlight, Torvald.

HELMER: Nora—you surely don't mean that request you made to me this morning?

NORA (*going near him*): Yes, Torvald, I beg you so earnestly—

HELMER: Have you really the courage to open up that question again?

NORA: Yes, dear, you *must* do as I ask; you *must* let Krogstad keep his post in the bank.

HELMER: My dear Nora, it is his post that I have arranged Mrs. Linde shall have.

NORA: Yes, you have been awfully kind about that; but you could just as well dismiss some other clerk instead of Krogstad.

HELMER: This is simply incredible obstinacy! Because you chose to give him a thoughtless promise that you would speak for him, I am expected to—

NORA: That isn't the reason, Torvald. It is for your own sake. This fellow writes in the most scurrilous newspapers; you have told me so yourself. He can do you an unspeakable amount of harm. I am frightened to death of him—

HELMER: Ah, I understand; it is recollections of the past that scare you.

NORA: What do you mean?

HELMER: Naturally you are thinking of your father.

NORA: Yes—yes, of course. Just recall to your mind what these malicious creatures wrote in the papers about papa, and how horribly they slandered him. I believe they would have procured his dismissal if the Department had not sent you over to inquire into it, and if you had not been so kindly disposed and helpful to him.

HELMER: My little Nora, there is an important difference between your father and me. Your father's reputation as a public official was not above suspicion. Mine is, and I hope it will continue to be so, as long as I hold my office.

NORA: You never can tell what mischief these men may contrive. We ought to be so well off, so snug and happy here in our peaceful home, and have no cares—you and I and the children, Torvald! That is why I beg you so earnestly—

HELMER: And it is just by interceding for him that you make it impossible for me to keep him. It is already known at the Bank that I mean to dismiss Krogstad. Is it to get about now that the new manager has changed his mind at his wife's bidding—

NORA: And what if it did?

HELMER: Of course!—if only this obstinate little person can get her way! Do you suppose I am going to make myself ridiculous before my whole staff, to let people think that I am a man to be swayed by all sorts of outside influence? I should very soon feel the consequences of it, I can tell you! And besides, there is one thing that makes it quite impossible for me to have Krogstad in the Bank as long as I am manager.

NORA: Whatever is that?

HELMER: His moral failings I might perhaps have overlooked, if necessary—

NORA: Yes, you could—couldn't you?

HELMER: And I hear he is a good worker, too. But I knew him when we were boys. It was one of those rash friendships that so often prove an incubus in afterlife. I may as well tell you plainly, we were once on very intimate terms with one another. But this tactless fellow lays no restraint on himself when other people are present. On the contrary, he thinks it gives him the right to adopt a familiar tone with me, and every minute it is "I say, Helmer, old fellow!" and that sort of thing. I assure you it is extremely painful for me. He would make my position in the Bank intolerable.

NORA: Torvald, I don't believe you mean that.

HELMER: Don't you? Why not?

NORA: Because it is such a narrow-minded way of looking at things.

HELMER: What are you saying? Narrow-minded? Do you think I am narrow-minded?

NORA: No, just the opposite, dear—and it is exactly for that reason.

HELMER: It's the same thing. You say my point of view is narrow-minded, so I must be so too. Narrow-minded! Very well—I must put an end to this. (*Goes to the hall door and calls.*) Helen!

NORA: What are you going to do?

HELMER (*looking among his papers*): Settle it. (*Enter Maid.*) Look here; take this letter and go downstairs with it at once. Find a messenger and tell him to deliver it, and be quick. The address is on it, and here is the money.

MAID: Very well, sir. (*Exit with the letter.*)

HELMER (*putting his papers together*): Now then, little Miss Obstinate.

NORA (*breathlessly*): Torvald—what was that letter?

HELMER: Krogstad's dismissal.

NORA: Call her back, Torvald! There is still time. Oh Torvald, call her back! Do it for my sake — for your own sake — for the children's sake! Do you hear me, Torvald? Call her back! You don't know what that letter can bring upon us.

HELMER: It's too late.

NORA: Yes, it's too late.

HELMER: My dear Nora, I can forgive the anxiety you are in, although really it is an insult to me. It is, indeed. Isn't it an insult to think that I should be afraid of a starving quill-driver's vengeance? But I forgive you nevertheless, because it is such eloquent witness to your great love for me. (*Takes her in his arms.*) And that is as it should be, my own darling Nora. Come what will, you may be sure I shall have both courage and strength if they be needed. You will see I am man enough to take everything upon myself.

NORA (*in a horror-stricken voice*): What do you mean by that?

HELMER: Everything, I say —

NORA (*recovering herself*): You will never have to do that.

HELMER: That's right. Well, we will share it, Nora, as man and wife should. That is how it shall be. (*Caressing her.*) Are you content now? There! there! — Not these frightened dove's eyes! The whole thing is only the wildest fancy! — Now, you must go and play through the Tarantella and practise with your tambourine. I shall go into the inner office and shut the door, and I shall hear nothing; you can make as much noise as you please. (*Turns back at the door.*) And when Rank comes, tell him where he will find me. (*Nods to her, takes his papers and goes into his room, and shuts the door after him.*)

NORA (*bewildered with anxiety, stands as if rooted to the spot, and whispers*): He was capable of doing it. He will do it. He will do it in spite of everything. — No, not that! Never, never! Anything rather than that! Oh, for some help, some way out of it! (*The door-bell rings.*) Doctor Rank! Anything rather than that — anything, whatever it is! (*She puts her hands over her face, pulls herself together, goes to the door and opens it. Rank is standing without, hanging up his coat. During the following dialogue it begins to grow dark.*)

NORA: Good day, Doctor Rank. I knew your ring. But you mustn't go in to Torvald now; I think he is busy with something.

RANK: And you?

NORA (*brings him in and shuts the door after him*): Oh, you know very well I always have time for you.

RANK: Thank you. I shall make use of as much of it as I can.

NORA: What do you mean by that? As much of it as you can?

RANK: Well, does that alarm you?

NORA: It was such a strange way of putting it. Is anything likely to happen?

RANK: Nothing but what I have long been prepared for. But I certainly didn't expect it to happen so soon.

NORA (*gripping him by the arm*): What have you found out? Doctor Rank, you must tell me.

RANK (*sitting down by the stove*): It is all up with me. And it can't be helped.

NORA (*with a sigh of relief*): Is it about yourself?

RANK: Who else? It is no use lying to one's self. I am the most wretched of all my patients, Mrs. Helmer. Lately I have been taking stock of my internal economy. Bankrupt! Probably within a month I shall lie rotting in the churchyard.

NORA: What an ugly thing to say!

RANK: The thing itself is cursedly ugly, and the worst of it is that I shall have to face so much more that is ugly before that. I shall only make one more examination of myself; when I have done that, I shall know pretty certainly when it will be that the horrors of dissolution will begin. There is something I want to tell you. Helmer's refined nature gives him an unconquerable disgust at everything that is ugly; I won't have him in my sickroom.

NORA: Oh, but, Doctor Rank—

RANK: I won't have him there. Not on any account. I bar my door to him. As soon as I am quite certain that the worst has come, I shall send you my card with a black cross on it, and then you will know that the loathsome end has begun.

NORA: You are quite absurd today. And I wanted you so much to be in a really good humour.

RANK: With death stalking beside me?—To have to pay this penalty for another man's sin? Is there any justice in that? And in every single family, in one way or another, some such inexorable retribution is being exacted—

NORA (*putting her hands over her ears*): Rubbish! Do talk of something cheerful.

RANK: Oh, it's a mere laughing matter, the whole thing. My poor innocent spine has to suffer for my father's youthful amusements.

NORA (*sitting at the table on the left*): I suppose you mean that he was too partial to asparagus and pâté de foie gras, don't you?

RANK: Yes, and to truffles.

NORA: Truffles, yes. And oysters too, I suppose?

RANK: Oysters, of course, that goes without saying.

NORA: And heaps of port and champagne. It is sad that all these nice things should take their revenge on our bones.

RANK: Especially that they should revenge themselves on the unlucky bones of those who have not had the satisfaction of enjoying them.

NORA: Yes, that's the saddest part of it all.

RANK (*with a searching look at her*): Hm!—

NORA (*after a short pause*): Why did you smile?

RANK: No, it was you that laughed.

NORA: No, it was you that smiled, Doctor Rank!

RANK (*rising*): You are a greater rascal than I thought.

NORA: I am in a silly mood today.

RANK: So it seems.

NORA (*putting her hands on his shoulders*): Dear, dear Doctor Rank, death mustn't take you away from Torvald and me.

RANK: It is a loss you would easily recover from. Those who are gone are soon forgotten.

NORA (*looking at him anxiously*): Do you believe that?

RANK: People form new ties, and then—

NORA: Who will form new ties?

RANK: Both you and Helmer, when I am gone. You yourself are already on the high road to it, I think. What did that Mrs. Linde want here last night?

NORA: Oho!—you don't mean to say you are jealous of poor Christine?

RANK: Yes, I am. She will be my successor in this house. When I am done for, this woman will—

NORA: Hush! don't speak so loud. She is in that room.

RANK: Today again. There, you see.

NORA: She has only come to sew my dress for me. Bless my soul, how unreasonable you are! (*Sits down on the sofa.*) Be nice now, Doctor Rank, and tomorrow you will see how beautifully I shall dance, and you can imagine I am doing it all for you—and for Torvald too, of course. (*Takes various things out of the box.*) Doctor Rank, come and sit down here, and I will show you something.

RANK (*sitting down*): What is it?

NORA: Just look at those!

RANK: Silk stockings.

NORA: Flesh-coloured. Aren't they lovely? It is so dark here now, but tomorrow—. No, no, no! you must only look at the feet. Oh well, you may have leave to look at the legs too.

RANK: Hm!—

NORA: Why are you looking so critical? Don't you think they will fit me?

RANK: I have no means of forming an opinion about that.

NORA (*looks at him for a moment*): For shame! (*Hits him lightly on the ear with the stockings.*) That's to punish you. (*Folds them up again.*)

RANK: And what other nice things am I to be allowed to see?

NORA: Not a single thing more, for being so naughty. (*She looks among the things, humming to herself.*)

RANK (*after a short silence*): When I am sitting here, talking to you as intimately as this, I cannot imagine for a moment what would have become of me if I had never come into this house.

NORA (*smiling*): I believe you do feel thoroughly at home with us.

RANK (*in a lower voice, looking straight in front of him*): And to be obliged to leave it all—

NORA: Nonsense, you are not going to leave it.

RANK (*as before*): And not be able to leave behind one the slightest token of one's gratitude, scarcely even a fleeting regret—nothing but an empty place which the first comer can fill as well as any other.

NORA: And if I asked you now for a—? No!

RANK: For what?

NORA: For a big proof of your friendship—

RANK: Yes, yes!

NORA: I mean a tremendously big favour.

RANK: Would you really make me so happy for once?

NORA: Ah, but you don't know what it is yet.

RANK: No—but tell me.

NORA: I really can't, Doctor Rank. It is something out of all reason; it means advice, and help, and a favour—

RANK: The bigger a thing it is the better. I can't conceive what it is you mean. Do tell me. Haven't I your confidence?

NORA: More than anyone else. I know you are my truest and best friend, and so I will tell you what it is. Well, Doctor Rank, it is something you must help me to prevent. You know how devotedly, how inexpressibly deeply Torvald loves me; he would never for a moment hesitate to give his life for me.

RANK (*leaning towards her*): Nora—do you think he is the only one—?

NORA (*with a slight start*): The only one—?

RANK: The only one who would gladly give his life for your sake.

NORA (*sadly*): Is that it?

RANK: I was determined you should know it before I went away, and there will never be a better opportunity than this. Now you know it, Nora. And now you know, too, that you can trust me as you would trust no one else.

NORA (*rises, deliberately and quietly*): Let me pass.

RANK (*makes room for her to pass him, but sits still*): Nora!

NORA (*at the hall door*): Helen, bring in the lamp. (*Goes over to the stove.*) Dear Doctor Rank, that was really horrid of you.

RANK: To have loved you as much as anyone else does? Was that horrid?

NORA: No, but to go and tell me so. There was really no need—

RANK: What do you mean? Did you know—? (*Maid enters with lamp, puts it down on the table, and goes out.*) Nora—Mrs. Helmer—tell me, had you any idea of this?

NORA: Oh, how do I know whether I had or whether I hadn't? I really can't tell you—To think you could be so clumsy, Doctor Rank! We were getting on so nicely.

RANK: Well, at all events you know now that you can command me, body and soul. So won't you speak out?

NORA (*looking at him*): After what happened?

RANK: I beg you to let me know what it is.

NORA: I can't tell you anything now.

RANK: Yes, yes. You mustn't punish me in that way. Let me have permission to do for you whatever a man may do.

NORA: You can do nothing for me now. Besides, I really don't need any help at all. You will find that the whole thing is merely fancy on my part. It really is so—of course it is! (*Sits down in the rocking-chair, and looks at him with a smile.*) You are a nice sort of man, Doctor Rank!—Don't you feel ashamed of yourself, now the lamp has come?

RANK: Not a bit. But perhaps I had better go—forever?

NORA: No, indeed, you shall not. Of course you must come here just as before. You know very well Torvald can't do without you.

RANK: Yes, but you?

NORA: Oh, I am always tremendously pleased when you come.

RANK: It is just that, that put me on the wrong track. You are a riddle to me. I have often thought that you would almost as soon be in my company as in Helmer's.

NORA: Yes — you see there are some people one loves best, and others whom one would almost always rather have as companions.

RANK: Yes, there is something in that.

NORA: When I was at home, of course I loved papa best. But I always thought it tremendous fun if I could steal down into the maids' room, because they never moralised at all, and talked to each other about such entertaining things.

RANK: I see — it is *their* place I have taken.

NORA (*jumping up and going to him*): Oh, dear, nice Doctor Rank, I never meant that at all. But surely you can understand that being with Torvald is a little like being with papa —

Enter Maid from the hall.

MAID: If you please, ma'am. (*Whispers and hands her a card.*)

NORA (*glancing at the card*): Oh! (*Puts it in her pocket.*)

RANK: Is there anything wrong?

NORA: No, no, not in the least. It is only something — it is my new dress —

RANK: What? Your dress is lying there.

NORA: Oh, yes, that one; but this is another. I ordered it. Torvald mustn't know about it —

RANK: Oho! Then that was the great secret.

NORA: Of course. Just go in to him; he is sitting in the inner room. Keep him as long as —

RANK: Make your mind easy; I won't let him escape. (*Goes into Helmer's room.*)

NORA (*to the Maid*): And he is standing waiting in the kitchen?

MAID: Yes; he came up the back stairs.

NORA: But didn't you tell him no one was in?

MAID: Yes, but it was no good.

NORA: He won't go away?

MAID: No; he says he won't until he has seen you, ma'am.

NORA: Well, let him come in — but quietly. Helen, you mustn't say anything about it to anyone. It is a surprise for my husband.

MAID: Yes, ma'am, I quite understand. (*Exit.*)

NORA: This dreadful thing is going to happen! It will happen in spite of me! No, no, no, it can't happen — it shan't happen! (*She bolts the door of Helmer's room. The Maid opens the hall door for Krogstad and shuts it after him. He is wearing a fur coat, high boots and a fur cap.*)

NORA (*advancing towards him*): Speak low — my husband is at home.

KROGSTAD: No matter about that.

NORA: What do you want of me?

KROGSTAD: An explanation of something.

NORA: Make haste then. What is it?

KROGSTAD: You know, I suppose, that I have got my dismissal.

NORA: I couldn't prevent it, Mr. Krogstad. I fought as hard as I could on your side, but it was no good.

KROGSTAD: Does your husband love you so little, then? He knows what I can expose you to, and yet he ventures—

NORA: How can you suppose that he has any knowledge of the sort?

KROGSTAD: I didn't suppose so at all. It would not be the least like our dear Torvald Helmer to show so much courage—

NORA: Mr. Krogstad, a little respect for my husband, please.

KROGSTAD: Certainly—all the respect he deserves. But since you have kept the matter so carefully to yourself, I make bold to suppose that you have a little clearer idea, than you had yesterday, of what it actually is that you have done?

NORA: More than you could ever teach me.

KROGSTAD: Yes, such a bad lawyer as I am.

NORA: What is it you want of me?

KROGSTAD: Only to see how you were, Mrs. Helmer. I have been thinking about you all day long. A mere cashier, a quill-driver, a—well, a man like me—even he has a little of what is called feeling, you know.

NORA: Show it, then; think of my little children.

KROGSTAD: Have you and your husband thought of mine? But never mind about that. I only wanted to tell you that you need not take this matter too seriously. In the first place there will be no accusation made on my part.

NORA: No, of course not; I was sure of that.

KROGSTAD: The whole thing can be arranged amicably; there is no reason why anyone should know anything about it. It will remain a secret between us three.

NORA: My husband must never get to know anything about it.

KROGSTAD: How will you be able to prevent it? Am I to understand that you can pay the balance that is owing?

NORA: No, not just at present.

KROGSTAD: Or perhaps that you have some expedient for raising the money soon?

NORA: No expedient that I mean to make use of.

KROGSTAD: Well, in any case, it would have been of no use to you now. If you stood there with ever so much money in your hand, I would never part with your bond.

NORA: Tell me what purpose you mean to put it to.

KROGSTAD: I shall only preserve it—keep it in my possession. No one who is not concerned in the matter shall have the slightest hint of it. So that if the thought of it has driven you to any desperate resolution—

NORA: It has.

KROGSTAD: If you had it in your mind to run away from your home—

NORA: I had.

KROGSTAD: Or even something worse—

NORA: How could you know that?

KROGSTAD: Give up the idea.

NORA: How did you know I had thought of *that*?

KROGSTAD: Most of us think of that at first. I did, too—but I hadn't the courage.

NORA (*faintly*): No more had I.

KROGSTAD (*in a tone of relief*): No, that's it, isn't it—you hadn't the courage either?

NORA: No, I haven't—I haven't.

KROGSTAD: Besides, it would have been a great piece of folly. Once the first storm at home is over—. I have a letter for your husband in my pocket.

NORA: Telling him everything?

KROGSTAD: In as lenient a manner as I possibly could.

NORA (*quickly*): He mustn't get the letter. Tear it up. I will find some means of getting money.

KROGSTAD: Excuse me, Mrs. Helmer, but I think I told you just now—

NORA: I am not speaking of what I owe you. Tell me what sum you are asking my husband for, and I will get the money.

KROGSTAD: I am not asking your husband for a penny.

NORA: What do you want, then?

KROGSTAD: I will tell you. I want to rehabilitate myself, Mrs. Helmer; I want to get on; and in that your husband must help me. For the last year and a half I have not had a hand in anything dishonourable, and all that time I have been struggling in most restricted circumstances. I was content to work my way up step by step. Now I am turned out, and I am not going to be satisfied with merely being taken into favour again. I want to get on, I tell you. I want to get into the Bank again, in a higher position. Your husband must make a place for me—

NORA: That he will never do!

KROGSTAD: He will; I know him; he dare not protest. And as soon as I am in there again with him, then you will see! Within a year I shall be the manager's right hand. It will be Nils Krogstad and not Torvald Helmer who manages the Bank.

NORA: That's a thing you will never see!

KROGSTAD: Do you mean that you will—?

NORA: I have courage enough for it now.

KROGSTAD: Oh, you can't frighten me. A fine, spoilt lady like you—

NORA: You will see, you will see.

KROGSTAD: Under the ice, perhaps? Down into the cold, coal-black water? And then, in the spring, to float up to the surface, all horrible and unrecognisable, with your hair fallen out—

NORA: You can't frighten me.

KROGSTAD: Nor you me. People don't do such things, Mrs. Helmer. Besides, what use would it be? I should have him completely in my power all the same.

NORA: Afterwards? When I am no longer —

KROGSTAD: Have you forgotten that it is I who have the keeping of your reputation? (*Nora stands speechlessly looking at him.*) Well, now, I have warned you. Do not do anything foolish. When Helmer has had my letter, I shall expect a message from him. And be sure you remember that it is your husband himself who has forced me into such ways as this again. I will never forgive him for that. Goodbye, Mrs. Helmer. (*Exit through the hall.*)

NORA (*goes to the hall door, opens it slightly and listens*): He is going. He is not putting the letter in the box. Oh no, no! That's impossible! (*Opens the door by degrees.*) What is that? He is standing outside. He is not going downstairs. Is he hesitating? Can he —? (*A letter drops into the box; then Krogstad's footsteps are heard, till they die away as he goes downstairs. Nora utters a stifled cry, and runs across the room to the table by the sofa. A short pause.*)

NORA: In the letter box. (*Steals across to the hall door.*) There it lies — Torvald, Torvald, there is no hope for us now!

Mrs. Linde comes in from the room on the left, carrying the dress.

MRS. LINDE: There, I can't see anything more to mend now. Would you like to try it on —?

NORA (*in a hoarse whisper*): Christine, come here.

MRS. LINDE (*throwing the dress down on the sofa*): What is the matter with you? You look so agitated!

NORA: Come here. Do you see that letter? There, look — you can see it through the glass in the letter box.

MRS. LINDE: Yes, I see it.

NORA: That letter is from Krogstad.

MRS. LINDE: Nora — it was Krogstad who lent you the money!

NORA: Yes, and now Torvald will know all about it.

MRS. LINDE: Believe me, Nora, that's the best thing for both of you.

NORA: You don't know all. I forged a name.

MRS. LINDE: Good heavens —!

NORA: I only want to say this to you, Christine — you must be my witness.

MRS. LINDE: Your witness? What do you mean? What am I to —?

NORA: If I should go out of my mind — and it might easily happen —

MRS. LINDE: Nora!

NORA: Or if anything else should happen to me — anything, for instance, that might prevent my being here —

MRS. LINDE: Nora! Nora! You are quite out of your mind.

NORA: And if it should happen that there were some one who wanted to take all the responsibility, all the blame, you understand —

MRS. LINDE: Yes, yes — but how can you suppose —?

NORA: Then you must be my witness, that it is not true, Christine. I am not out of my mind at all! I am in my right senses now, and I tell you no one else

has known anything about it; I, and I alone, did the whole thing. Remember
that.

MRS. LINDE: I will, indeed. But I don't understand all this.

NORA: How should you understand it? A wonderful thing is going to happen!

MRS. LINDE: A wonderful thing?

NORA: Yes, a wonderful thing!—But it is so terrible, Christine; it *mustn't* happen, not for all the world.

MRS. LINDE: I will go at once and see Krogstad.

NORA: Don't go to him; he will do you some harm.

MRS. LINDE: There was a time when he would gladly do anything for my sake.

NORA: He?

MRS. LINDE: Where does he live?

NORA: How should I know—? Yes (*feeling in her pocket*), here is his card. But the
letter, the letter—!

HELMER (*calls from his room, knocking at the door*): Nora!

NORA (*cries out anxiously*): Oh, what's that? What do you want?

HELMER: Don't be so frightened. We are not coming in; you have locked the
door. Are you trying on your dress?

NORA: Yes, that's it. I look so nice, Torvald.

MRS. LINDE (*who has read the card*): I see he lives at the corner here.

NORA: Yes, but it's no use. It is hopeless. The letter is lying there in the box.

MRS. LINDE: And your husband keeps the key?

NORA: Yes, always.

MRS. LINDE: Krogstad must ask for his letter back unread, he must find some
pretence—

NORA: But it is just at this time that Torvald generally—

MRS. LINDE: You must delay him. Go in to him in the meantime. I will come
back as soon as I can. (*She goes out hurriedly through the hall door.*)

NORA (*goes to Helmer's door, opens it and peeps in*): Torvald!

HELMER (*from the inner room*): Well? May I venture at last to come into my own
room again? Come along, Rank, now you will see—(*Halting in the doorway.*) But what is this?

NORA: What is what, dear?

HELMER: Rank led me to expect a splendid transformation.

RANK (*in the doorway*): I understood so, but evidently I was mistaken.

NORA: Yes, nobody is to have the chance of admiring me in my dress until tomorrow.

HELMER: But, my dear Nora, you look so worn out. Have you been practising too
much?

NORA: No, I have not practised at all.

HELMER: But you will need to—

NORA: Yes, indeed I shall, Torvald. But I can't get on a bit without you to help
me; I have absolutely forgotten the whole thing.

HELMER: Oh, we will soon work it up again.

NORA: Yes, help me, Torvald. Promise that you will! I am so nervous about
it—all the people—. You must give yourself up to me entirely this evening.

Not the tiniest bit of business—you mustn't even take a pen in your hand.
Will you promise, Torvald dear?

HELMER: I promise. This evening I will be wholly and absolutely at your service,
you helpless little mortal. Ah, by the way, first of all I will just—(*Goes
towards the hall door.*)

NORA: What are you going to do there?

HELMER: Only see if any letters have come.

NORA: No, no! Don't do that, Torvald!

HELMER: Why not?

NORA: Torvald, please don't. There is nothing there.

HELMER: Well, let me look. (*Turns to go to the letter box. Nora, at the piano, plays
the first bars of the Tarantella. Helmer stops in the doorway.*) Aha!

NORA: I can't dance tomorrow if I don't practise with you.

HELMER (*going up to her*): Are you really so afraid of it, dear?

NORA: Yes, so dreadfully afraid of it. Let me practise at once; there is time now,
before we go to dinner. Sit down and play for me, Torvald dear; criticise me,
and correct me as you play.

HELMER: With great pleasure, if you wish me to. (*Sits down at the piano.*)

NORA (*takes out of the box a tambourine and a long variegated shawl. She hastily
drapes the shawl round her. Then she springs to the front of the stage and calls
out*): Now play for me! I am going to dance!

*Helmer plays and Nora dances. Rank stands by the piano behind Helmer, and looks
on.*

HELMER (*as he plays*): Slower, slower!

NORA: I can't do it any other way.

HELMER: Not so violently, Nora!

NORA: This is the way.

HELMER (*stops playing*): No, no—that is not a bit right.

NORA (*laughing and swinging the tambourine*): Didn't I tell you so?

RANK: Let me play for her.

HELMER (*getting up*): Yes, do. I can correct her better then.

*Rank sits down at the piano and plays. Nora dances more and more wildly. Helmer
has taken up a position beside the stove, and during her dance gives her frequent
instructions. She does not seem to hear him; her hair comes down and falls over her
shoulders; she pays no attention to it, but goes on dancing. Enter Mrs. Linde.*

MRS. LINDE (*standing as if spellbound in the doorway*): Oh!—

NORA (*as she dances*): Such fun, Christine!

HELMER: My dear darling Nora, you are dancing as if your life depended on it.

NORA: So it does.

HELMER: Stop, Rank; this is sheer madness. Stop, I tell you! (*Rank stops playing,
and Nora suddenly stands still. Helmer goes up to her.*) I could never have
believed it. You have forgotten everything I taught you.

NORA (*throwing away the tambourine*): There, you see.

HELMER: You will want a lot of coaching.

NORA: Yes, you see how much I need it. You must coach me up to the last minute. Promise me that, Torvald!

HELMER: You can depend on me.

NORA: You must not think of anything but me, either today or tomorrow; you mustn't open a single letter—not even open the letter box—

HELMER: Ah, you are still afraid of that fellow—

NORA: Yes, indeed I am.

HELMER: Nora, I can tell from your looks that there is a letter from him lying there.

NORA: I don't know; I think there is; but you must not read anything of that kind now. Nothing horrid must come between us until this is all over.

RANK (*whispers to Helmer*): You mustn't contradict her.

HELMER (*taking her in his arms*): The child shall have her way. But tomorrow night, after you have danced—

NORA: Then you will be free. (*The Maid appears in the doorway to the right.*)

MAID: Dinner is served, ma'am.

NORA: We will have champagne, Helen.

MAID: Very good, ma'am.   [*Exit.*]

HELMER: Hullo!—are we going to have a banquet?

NORA: Yes, a champagne banquet until the small hours. (*Calls out.*) And a few macaroons, Helen—lots, just for once!

HELMER: Come, come, don't be so wild and nervous. Be my own little skylark, as you used.

NORA: Yes, dear, I will. But go in now and you too, Doctor Rank. Christine, you must help me to do up my hair.

RANK (*whispers to Helmer as they go out*): I suppose there is nothing—she is not expecting anything?

HELMER: Far from it, my dear fellow; it is simply nothing more than this childish nervousness I was telling you of. (*They go into the right-hand room.*)

NORA: Well!

MRS. LINDE: Gone out of town.

NORA: I could tell from your face.

MRS. LINDE: He is coming home tomorrow evening. I wrote a note for him.

NORA: You should have let it alone; you must prevent nothing. After all, it is splendid to be waiting for a wonderful thing to happen.

MRS. LINDE: What is it that you are waiting for?

NORA: Oh, you wouldn't understand. Go in to them, I will come in a moment. (*Mrs. Linde goes into the dining room. Nora stands still for a little while, as if to compose herself. Then she looks at her watch.*) Five o'clock. Seven hours until midnight; and then four-and-twenty hours until the next midnight. Then the Tarantella will be over. Twenty-four and seven? Thirty-one hours to live.

HELMER (*from the doorway on the right*): Where's my little skylark?

NORA (*going to him with her arms outstretched*): Here she is!

ACT III

THE SAME SCENE: *The table has been placed in the middle of the stage, with chairs round it. A lamp is burning on the table. The door into the hall stands open. Dance music is heard in the room above. Mrs. Linde is sitting at the table idly turning over the leaves of a book; she tries to read, but does not seem able to collect her thoughts. Every now and then she listens intently for a sound at the outer door.*

MRS. LINDE (*looking at her watch*): Not yet — and the time is nearly up. If only he does not —. (*Listens again.*) Ah, there he is. (*Goes into the hall and opens the outer door carefully. Light footsteps are heard on the stairs. She whispers.*) Come in. There is no one here.

KROGSTAD (*in the doorway*): I found a note from you at home. What does this mean?

MRS. LINDE: It is absolutely necessary that I should have a talk with you.

KROGSTAD: Really? And is it absolutely necessary that it should be here?

MRS. LINDE: It is impossible where I live; there is no private entrance to my rooms. Come in; we are quite alone. The maid is asleep, and the Helmers are at the dance upstairs.

KROGSTAD (*coming into the room*): Are the Helmers really at a dance tonight?

MRS. LINDE: Yes, why not?

KROGSTAD: Certainly — why not?

MRS. LINDE: Now, Nils, let us have a talk.

KROGSTAD: Can we two have anything to talk about?

MRS. LINDE: We have a great deal to talk about.

KROGSTAD: I shouldn't have thought so.

MRS. LINDE: No, you have never properly understood me.

KROGSTAD: Was there anything else to understand except what was obvious to all the world — a heartless woman jilts a man when a more lucrative chance turns up?

MRS. LINDE: Do you believe I am as absolutely heartless as all that? And do you believe that I did it with a light heart?

KROGSTAD: Didn't you?

MRS. LINDE: Nils, did you really think that?

KROGSTAD: If it were as you say, why did you write to me as you did at the time?

MRS. LINDE: I could do nothing else. As I had to break with you, it was my duty also to put an end to all that you felt for me.

KROGSTAD (*wringing his hands*): So that was it. And all this — only for the sake of money!

MRS. LINDE: You must not forget that I had a helpless mother and two little brothers. We couldn't wait for you, Nils; your prospects seemed hopeless then.

KROGSTAD: That may be so, but you had no right to throw me over for anyone else's sake.

MRS. LINDE: Indeed I don't know. Many a time did I ask myself if I had the right to do it.

KROGSTAD (*more gently*): When I lost you, it was as if all the solid ground went
  from under my feet. Look at me now—I am a shipwrecked man clinging to
  a bit of wreckage.

MRS. LINDE: But help may be near.

KROGSTAD: It *was* near; but then you came and stood in my way.

MRS. LINDE: Unintentionally, Nils. It was only today that I learned it was your
  place I was going to take in the Bank.

KROGSTAD: I believe you, if you say so. But now that you know it, are you not
  going to give it up to me?

MRS. LINDE: No, because that would not benefit you in the least.

KROGSTAD: Oh, benefit, benefit—I would have done it whether or no.

MRS. LINDE: I have learned to act prudently. Life, and hard, bitter necessity have
  taught me that.

KROGSTAD: And life has taught me not to believe in fine speeches.

MRS. LINDE: Then life has taught you something very reasonable. But deeds you
  must believe in?

KROGSTAD: What do you mean by that?

MRS. LINDE: You said you were like a shipwrecked man clinging to some wreckage.

KROGSTAD: I had good reason to say so.

MRS. LINDE: Well, I am like a shipwrecked woman clinging to some wreckage—no
  one to mourn for, no one to care for.

KROGSTAD: It was your own choice.

MRS. LINDE: There was no other choice—then.

KROGSTAD: Well, what now?

MRS. LINDE: Nils, how would it be if we two shipwrecked people could join
  forces?

KROGSTAD: What are you saying?

MRS. LINDE: Two on the same piece of wreckage would stand a better chance
  than each on their own.

KROGSTAD: Christine!

MRS. LINDE: What do you suppose brought me to town?

KROGSTAD: Do you mean that you gave me a thought?

MRS. LINDE: I could not endure life without work. All my life, as long as I can
  remember, I have worked, and it has been my greatest and only pleasure.
  But now I am quite alone in the world—my life is so dreadfully empty and
  I feel so forsaken. There is not the least pleasure in working for one's self.
  Nils, give me someone and something to work for.

KROGSTAD I don't trust that. It is nothing but a woman's overstrained sense of
  generosity that prompts you to make such an offer of yourself.

MRS. LINDE: Have you ever noticed anything of the sort in me?

KROGSTAD: Could you really do it? Tell me—do you know all about my past life?

MRS. LINDE: Yes.

KROGSTAD: And do you know what they think of me here?

MRS. LINDE: You seemed to me to imply that with me you might have been quite
  another man.

KROGSTAD: I am certain of it.

MRS. LINDE: Is it too late now?

KROGSTAD: Christine, are you saying this deliberately? Yes, I am sure you are. I see it in your face. Have you really the courage, then—?

MRS. LINDE: I want to be a mother to someone, and your children need a mother. We two need each other. Nils, I have faith in your real character—I can dare anything together with you.

KROGSTAD (*grasps her hands*): Thanks, thanks, Christine! Now I shall find a way to clear myself in the eyes of the world. Ah, but I forgot—

MRS. LINDE (*listening*): Hush! The Tarantella! Go, go!

KROGSTAD: Why? What is it?

MRS. LINDE: Do you hear them up there? When that is over, we may expect them back.

KROGSTAD: Yes, yes—I will go. But it is all no use. Of course you are not aware what steps I have taken in the matter of the Helmers.

MRS. LINDE: Yes, I know all about that.

KROGSTAD: And in spite of that have you the courage to—?

MRS. LINDE: I understand very well to what lengths a man like you might be driven by despair.

KROGSTAD: If I could only undo what I have done!

MRS. LINDE: You cannot. Your letter is lying in the letter box now.

KROGSTAD: Are you sure of that?

MRS. LINDE: Quite sure, but—

KROGSTAD (*with a searching look at her*): Is that what it all means?—That you want to save your friend at any cost? Tell me frankly. Is that it?

MRS. LINDE: Nils, a woman who has once sold herself for another's sake, doesn't do it a second time.

KROGSTAD: I will ask for my letter back.

MRS. LINDE: No, no.

KROGSTAD: Yes, of course I will. I will wait here until Helmer comes; I will tell him he must give me my letter back—that it only concerns my dismissal—that he is not to read it—

MRS. LINDE: No, Nils, you must not recall your letter.

KROGSTAD: But, tell me, wasn't it for that very purpose that you asked me to meet you here?

MRS. LINDE: In my first moment of fright, it was. But twenty-four hours have elapsed since then, and in that time I have witnessed incredible things in this house. Helmer must know all about it. This unhappy secret must be disclosed; they must have a complete understanding between them, which is impossible with all this concealment and falsehood going on.

KROGSTAD: Very well, if you will take the responsibility. But there is one thing I can do in any case, and I shall do it at once.

MRS. LINDE (*listening*): You must be quick and go! The dance is over; we are not safe a moment longer.

KROGSTAD: I will wait for you below.

MRS. LINDE: Yes, do. You must see me back to my door.

KROGSTAD: I have never had such an amazing piece of good fortune in my life!
(*Goes out through the outer door. The door between the room and the hall remains open.*)

MRS. LINDE (*tidying up the room and laying her hat and cloak ready*): What a difference! what a difference! Someone to work for and live for—a home to bring comfort into. That I will do, indeed. I wish they would be quick and come—(*Listens.*) Ah, there they are now. I must put on my things. (*Takes up her hat and cloak. Helmer's and Nora's voices are heard outside; a key is turned, and Helmer brings Nora almost by force into the hall. She is in an Italian costume with a large black shawl around her; he is in evening dress, and a black domino° [loose cloak] which is flying open.*)

NORA (*hanging back in the doorway, and struggling with him*): No, no, no!—don't take me in. I want to go upstairs again; I don't want to leave so early.

HELMER: But, my dearest Nora—

NORA: Please, Torvald dear—please, *please*—only an hour more.

HELMER: Not a single minute, my sweet Nora. You know that was our agreement. Come along into the room; you are catching cold standing there. (*He brings her gently into the room, in spite of her resistance.*)

MRS. LINDE: Good evening.

NORA: Christine!

HELMER: You here, so late, Mrs. Linde?

MRS. LINDE: Yes, you must excuse me; I was so anxious to see Nora in her dress.

NORA: Have you been sitting here waiting for me?

MRS. LINDE: Yes, unfortunately I came too late, you had already gone upstairs; and I thought I couldn't go away again without having seen you.

HELMER (*taking off Nora's shawl*): Yes, take a good look at her. I think she is worth looking at. Isn't she charming, Mrs. Linde?

MRS. LINDE: Yes, indeed she is.

HELMER: Doesn't she look remarkably pretty? Everyone thought so at the dance. But she is terribly self-willed, this sweet little person. What are we to do with her? You will hardly believe that I had almost to bring her away by force.

NORA: Torvald, you will repent not having let me stay, even if it were only for half an hour.

HELMER: Listen to her, Mrs. Linde! She had danced her Tarantella, and it had been a tremendous success, as it deserved—although possibly the performance was a trifle too realistic—a little more so, I mean, than was strictly compatible with the limitations of art. But never mind about that! The chief thing is, she had made a success—she had made a tremendous success. Do you think I was going to let her remain there after that, and spoil the effect? No, indeed! I took my charming little Capri maiden—my capricious little Capri maiden, I should say—on my arm; took one quick turn round the room; a curtsey on either side, and, as they say in novels, the beautiful apparition disappeared. An exit ought always to be effective, Mrs. Linde; but that is what I cannot make Nora understand. Pooh! This room is hot. (*Throws his domino on a chair, and opens the door of his room.*) Hullo! It's all dark in here. Oh, of course — excuse me —. (*He goes in, and lights some candles.*)

NORA (*in a hurried and breathless whisper*): Well?

MRS. LINDE (*in a low voice*): I have had a talk with him.

NORA: Yes, and —

MRS. LINDE: Nora, you must tell your husband all about it.

NORA (*in an expressionless voice*): I knew it.

MRS. LINDE: You have nothing to be afraid of as far as Krogstad is concerned; but you must tell him.

NORA: I won't tell him.

MRS. LINDE: Then the letter will.

NORA: Thank you, Christine. Now I know what I must do. Hush —!

HELMER (*coming in again*): Well, Mrs. Linde, have you admired her?

MRS. LINDE: Yes, and now I will say good night.

HELMER: What, already? Is this yours, this knitting?

MRS. LINDE (*taking it*): Yes, thank you, I had very nearly forgotten it.

HELMER: So you knit?

MRS. LINDE: Of course.

HELMER: Do you know, you ought to embroider.

MRS. LINDE: Really? Why?

HELMER: Yes, it's far more becoming. Let me show you. You hold the embroidery thus in your left hand, and use the needle with the right — like this — with a long, easy sweep. Do you see?

MRS. LINDE: Yes, perhaps —

HELMER: But in the case of knitting — that can never be anything but ungraceful; look here — the arms close together, the knitting-needles going up and down — it has a sort of Chinese effect —. That was really excellent champagne they gave us.

MRS. LINDE: Well, — good night, Nora, and don't be self-willed any more.

HELMER: That's right, Mrs. Linde.

MRS. LINDE: Good night, Mr. Helmer.

HELMER (*accompanying her to the door*): Good night, good night. I hope you will get home all right. I should be very happy to — but you haven't any great distance to go. Good night, good night. (*She goes out; he shuts the door after her, and comes in again.*) Ah! — at last we have got rid of her. She is a frightful bore, that woman.

NORA: Aren't you very tired, Torvald?

HELMER: No, not in the least.

NORA: Nor sleepy?

HELMER: Not a bit. On the contrary, I feel extraordinarily lively. And you? — you really look both tired and sleepy.

NORA: Yes, I am very tired. I want to go to sleep at once.

HELMER: There, you see it was quite right of me not to let you stay there any longer.

NORA: Everything you do is quite right, Torvald.

HELMER (*kissing her on the forehead*): Now my little skylark is speaking reasonably. Did you notice what good spirits Rank was in this evening?

NORA: Really? Was he? I didn't speak to him at all.

HELMER: And I very little, but I have not for a long time seen him in such good form. (*Looks for a while at her and then goes nearer to her.*) It is delightful to be at home by ourselves again, to be all alone with you—you fascinating, charming little darling!

NORA: Don't look at me like that, Torvald.

HELMER: Why shouldn't I look at my dearest treasure?—at all the beauty that is mine, all my very own?

NORA (*going to the other side of the table*): You mustn't say things like that to me tonight.

HELMER (*following her*): You have still got the Tarantella in your blood, I see. And it makes you more captivating than ever. Listen—the guests are beginning to go now. (*In a lower voice.*) Nora—soon the whole house will be quiet.

NORA: Yes, I hope so.

HELMER: Yes, my own darling Nora. Do you know, when I am out at a party with you like this, why I speak so little to you, keep away from you, and only send a stolen glance in your direction now and then?—do you know why I do that? It is because I make believe to myself that we are secretly in love, and you are my secretly promised bride, and that no one suspects there is anything between us.

NORA: Yes, yes—I know very well your thoughts are with me all the time.

HELMER: And when we are leaving, and I am putting the shawl over your beautiful young shoulders—on your lovely neck—then I imagine that you are my young bride and that we have just come from the wedding, and I am bringing you for the first time into our home—to be alone with you for the first time—quite alone with my shy little darling! All this evening I have longed for nothing but you. When I watched the seductive figures of the Tarantella, my blood was on fire; I could endure it no longer, and that was why I brought you down so early—

NORA: Go away, Torvald! You must let me go. I won't—

HELMER: What's that? You're joking, my little Nora! You won't—you won't? Am I not your husband—? (*A knock is heard at the outer door.*)

NORA (*starting*): Did you hear—?

HELMER (*going into the hall*): Who is it?

RANK (*outside*): It is I. May I come in for a moment?

HELMER (*in a fretful whisper*): Oh, what does he want now? (*Aloud.*) Wait a minute! (*Unlocks the door.*) Come, that's kind of you not to pass by our door.

RANK: I thought I heard your voice, and felt as if I should like to look in. (*With a swift glance round.*) Ah, yes!—These dear familiar rooms. You are very happy and cosy in here, you two.

HELMER: It seems to me that you looked after yourself pretty well upstairs too.

RANK: Excellently. Why shouldn't I? Why shouldn't one enjoy everything in this
   world? — At any rate as much as one can, and as long as one can. The wine
   was capital —

HELMER: Especially the champagne.

RANK: So you noticed that too? It is almost incredible how much I managed to
   put away!

NORA: Torvald drank a great deal of champagne tonight too.

RANK: Did he?

NORA: Yes, and he is always in such good spirits afterwards.

RANK: Well, why should one not enjoy a merry evening after a well-spent day?

HELMER: Well spent? I am afraid I can't take credit for that.

RANK (*clapping him on the back*): But I can, you know!

NORA: Doctor Rank, you must have been occupied with some scientific
   investigation today.

RANK: Exactly.

HELMER: Just listen! — Little Nora talking about scientific investigations!

NORA: And may I congratulate you on the result?

RANK: Indeed you may.

NORA: Was it favourable, then?

RANK: The best possible, for both doctor and patient — certainty.

NORA (*quickly and searchingly*): Certainty?

RANK: Absolute certainty. So wasn't I entitled to make a merry evening of it after
   that?

NORA: Yes, you certainly were, Doctor Rank.

HELMER: I think so too, so long as you don't have to pay for it in the morning.

RANK: Oh well, one can't have anything in this life without paying for it.

NORA: Doctor Rank — are you fond of fancy-dress balls?

RANK: Yes, if there is a fine lot of pretty costumes.

NORA: Tell me — what shall we two wear at the next?

HELMER: Little featherbrain! — are you thinking of the next already?

RANK: We two? Yes, I can tell you. You shall go as a good fairy —

HELMER: Yes, but what do you suggest as an appropriate costume for that?

RANK: Let your wife go dressed just as she is in every day life.

HELMER: That was really very prettily turned. But can't you tell us what you will
   be?

RANK: Yes, my dear friend, I have quite made up my mind about that.

HELMER: Well?

RANK: At the next fancy-dress ball I shall be invisible.

HELMER: That's a good joke!

RANK: There is a big black hat — have you never heard of hats that make you
   invisible? If you put one on, no one can see you.

HELMER (*suppressing a smile*): Yes, you are quite right.

RANK: But I am clean forgetting what I came for. Helmer, give me a cigar — one
   of the dark Havanas.

HELMER: With the greatest pleasure. (*Offers him his case.*)

RANK (*takes a cigar and cuts off the end*): Thanks.

NORA (*striking a match*): Let me give you a light.

RANK: Thank you. (*She holds the match for him to light his cigar.*) And now goodbye!

HELMER: Goodbye, goodbye, dear old man!

NORA: Sleep well, Doctor Rank.

RANK: Thank you for that wish.

NORA: Wish me the same.

RANK: You? Well, if you want me to—Sleep well! And thanks for the light. (*He nods to them both and goes out.*)

HELMER (*in a subdued voice*): He has drunk more than he ought.

NORA (*absently*): Maybe. (*Helmer takes a bunch of keys out of his pocket and goes into the hall.*) Torvald! what are you going to do there?

HELMER: Empty the letter box; it is quite full; there will be no room to put the newspaper in tomorrow morning.

NORA: Are you going to work tonight?

HELMER: You know quite well I'm not. What is this? Someone has been at the lock.

NORA: At the lock—?

HELMER: Yes, someone has. What can it mean? I should never have thought the maid—. Here is a broken hairpin. Nora, it is one of yours.

NORA (*quickly*): Then it must have been the children—

HELMER: Then you must get them out of those ways. There, at last I have got it open. (*Takes out the contents of the letter box, and calls to the kitchen.*) Helen!—Helen, put out the light over the front door. (*Goes back into the room and shuts the door into the hall. He holds out his hand full of letters.*) Look at that—look what a heap of them there are. (*Turning them over.*) What on earth is that?

NORA (*at the window*): The letter—No! Torvald, no!

HELMER: Two cards—of Rank's.

NORA: Of Doctor Rank's?

HELMER (*looking at them*): Doctor Rank. They were on the top. He must have put them in when he went out.

NORA: Is there anything written on them?

HELMER: There is a black cross over the name. Look there—what an uncomfortable idea! It looks as if he were announcing his own death.

NORA: It is just what he is doing.

HELMER: What? Do you know anything about it? Has he said anything to you?

NORA: Yes. He told me that when the cards came it would be his leave-taking from us. He means to shut himself up and die.

HELMER: My poor old friend! Certainly I knew we should not have him very long with us. But so soon! And so he hides himself away like a wounded animal.

NORA: If it has to happen, it is best it should be without a word—don't you think so, Torvald?

HELMER (*walking up and down*): He had so grown into our lives. I can't think of him as having gone out of them. He, with his sufferings and his loneliness, was like a cloudy background to our sunlit happiness. Well, perhaps it is best so. For him, anyway. (*Standing still.*) And perhaps for us too, Nora. We two are thrown quite upon each other now. (*Puts his arms round her.*) My darling wife, I don't feel as if I could hold you tight enough. Do you know, Nora, I have often wished that you might be threatened by some great danger, so that I might risk my life's blood, and everything, for your sake.

NORA (*disengages herself, and says firmly and decidedly*): Now you must read your letters, Torvald.

HELMER: No, no; not tonight. I want to be with you, my darling wife.

NORA: With the thought of your friend's death—

HELMER: You are right, it has affected us both. Something ugly has come be-tween us—the thought of the horrors of death. We must try and rid our minds of that. Until then—we will each go to our own room.

NORA (*hanging on his neck*): Good night, Torvald—Good night!

HELMER (*kissing her on the forehead*): Good night, my little singing-bird: Sleep sound, Nora. Now I will read my letters through. (*He takes his letters and goes into his room, shutting the door after him.*)

NORA (*gropes distractedly about, seizes Helmer's domino, throws it round her, while she says in quick, hoarse, spasmodic whispers*): Never to see him again. Never! Never! (*Puts her shawl over her head.*) Never to see my children again either—never again. Never! Never!—Ah! the icy, black water—the unfathomable depths—If only it were over! He has got it now—now he is reading it. Goodbye, Torvald and my children! (*She is about to rush out through the hall, when Helmer opens his door hurriedly and stands with an open letter in his hand.*)

HELMER: Nora!

NORA: Ah!—

HELMER: What is this? Do you know what is in this letter?

NORA: Yes, I know. Let me go! Let me get out!

HELMER (*holding her back*): Where are you going?

NORA (*trying to get free*): You shan't save me, Torvald!

HELMER (*reeling*): True? Is this true, that I read here? Horrible! No, no—it is impossible that it can be true.

NORA: It is true. I have loved you above everything else in the world.

HELMER: Oh, don't let us have any silly excuses.

NORA (*taking a step towards him*): Torvald—!

HELMER: Miserable creature—what have you done?

NORA: Let me go. You shall not suffer for my sake. You shall not take it upon yourself.

HELMER: No tragedy airs, please. (*Locks the hall door.*) Here you shall stay and give me an explanation. Do you understand what you have done? Answer me! Do you understand what you have done?

NORA (*looks steadily at him and says with a growing look of coldness in her face*): Yes, now I am beginning to understand thoroughly.

HELMER (*walking about the room*): What a horrible awakening! All these eight years—she who was my joy and pride—a hypocrite, a liar—worse, worse—a criminal! The unutterable ugliness of it all!—For shame! For shame! (*Nora is silent and looks steadily at him. He stops in front of her.*) I ought to have suspected that something of the sort would happen. I ought to have foreseen it. All your father's want of principle—be silent!—all your father's want of principle has come out in you. No religion, no morality, no sense of duty—, How I am punished for having winked at what he did! I did it for your sake, and this is how you repay me.

NORA: Yes, that's just it.

HELMER: Now you have destroyed all my happiness. You have ruined all my future. It is horrible to think of! I am in the power of an unscrupulous man; he can do what he likes with me, ask anything he likes of me, give me any orders he pleases—I dare not refuse. And I must sink to such miserable depths because of a thoughtless woman!

NORA: When I am out of the way, you will be free.

HELMER: No fine speeches, please. Your father had always plenty of those ready, too. What good would it be to me if you were out of the way, as you say? Not the slightest. He can make the affair known everywhere; and if he does, I may be falsely suspected of having been a party to your criminal action. Very likely people will think I was behind it all—that it was I who prompted you! And I have to thank you for all this—you whom I have cherished during the whole of our married life. Do you understand now what it is you have done for me?

NORA (*coldly and quietly*): Yes.

HELMER: It is so incredible that I can't take it in. But we must come to some understanding. Take off that shawl. Take it off, I tell you. I must try and appease him some way or another. The matter must be hushed up at any cost. And as for you and me, it must appear as if everything between us were just as before—but naturally only in the eyes of the world. You will still remain in my house, that is a matter of course. But I shall not allow you to bring up the children; I dare not trust them to you. To think that I should be obliged to say so to one whom I have loved so dearly, and whom I still—. No, that is all over. From this moment happiness is not the question; all that concerns us is to save the remains, the fragments, the appearance—

A ring is heard at the front-door bell.

HELMER (*with a start*): What is that? So late! Can the worst—? Can he—? Hide yourself, Nora. Say you are ill.

Nora stands motionless. Helmer goes and unlocks the hall door.

MAID (*half-dressed, comes to the door*): A letter for the mistress.

HELMER: Give it to me. (*Takes the letter, and shuts the door.*) Yes, it is from him. You shall not have it; I will read it myself.

NORA: Yes, read it.

HELMER (*standing by the lamp*): I scarcely have the courage to do it. It may mean
    ruin for both of us. No, I must know. (*Tears open the letter, runs his eye over
    a few lines, looks at a paper enclosed, and gives a shout of joy.*) Nora! (*She looks
    at him questioningly.*) Nora!—No, I must read it once again—. Yes, it is
    true! I am saved! Nora, I am saved!

NORA: And I?

HELMER: You too, of course; we are both saved, both you and I. Look, he sends
    you your bond back. He says he regrets and repents—that a happy change
    in his life—never mind what he says! We are saved, Nora! No one can do
    anything to you. Oh, Nora, Nora!—no, first I must destroy these hateful
    things. Let me see—. (*Takes a look at the bond.*) No, no, I won't look at it.
    The whole thing shall be nothing but a bad dream to me. (*Tears up the bond
    and both letters, throws them all into the stove, and watches them burn.*)
    There—now it doesn't exist any longer. He says that since Christmas Eve
    you—. These must have been three dreadful days for you, Nora.

NORA: I have fought a hard fight these three days.

HELMER: And suffered agonies, and seen no way out but—. No, we won't call
    any of the horrors to mind. We will only shout with joy, and keep saying,
    "It's all over! It's all over!" Listen to me, Nora. You don't seem to realise
    that it is all over. What is this?—such a cold, set face! My poor little Nora,
    I quite understand; you don't feel as if you could believe that I have for-
    given you. But it is true, Nora, I swear it; I have forgiven you everything. I
    know that what you did, you did out of love for me.

NORA: That is true.

HELMER: You have loved me as a wife ought to love her husband. Only you had
    not sufficient knowledge to judge of the means you used. But do you sup-
    pose you are any the less dear to me, because you don't understand how to
    act on your own responsibility? No, no; only lean on me; I will advise you
    and direct you. I should not be a man if this womanly helplessness did not
    just give you a double attractiveness in my eyes. You must not think any-
    more about the hard things I said in my first moment of consternation,
    when I thought everything was going to overwhelm me. I have forgiven you,
    Nora; I swear to you I have forgiven you.

NORA: Thank you for your forgiveness. (*She goes out through the door to the right.*)

HELMER: No, don't go—. (*Looks in.*) What are you doing in there?

NORA (*from within*): Taking off my fancy dress.

HELMER (*standing at the open door*): Yes, do. Try and calm yourself, and make
    your mind easy again, my frightened little singing-bird. Be at rest, and feel
    secure; I have broad wings to shelter you under. (*Walks up and down by the
    door.*) How warm and cosy our home is, Nora. Here is shelter for you; here
    I will protect you like a hunted dove that I have saved from a hawk's claws;
    I will bring peace to your poor beating heart. It will come, little by little,
    Nora, believe me. Tomorrow morning you will look upon it all quite differ-
    ently; soon everything will be just as it was before. Very soon you won't
    need me to assure you that I have forgiven you; you will yourself feel the

certainty that I have done so. Can you suppose I should ever think of such a thing as repudiating you, or even reproaching you? You have no idea what a true man's heart is like, Nora. There is something so indescribably sweet and satisfying, to a man, in the knowledge that he has forgiven his wife—forgiven her freely, and with all his heart. It seems as if that had made her, as it were, doubly his own; he has given her a new life, so to speak; and she has in a way become both wife and child to him. So you shall be for me after this, my little scared, helpless darling. Have no anxiety about anything, Nora; only be frank and open with me, and I will serve as will and conscience both to you—. What is this? Not gone to bed? Have you changed your things?

NORA (*in every day dress*): Yes, Torvald, I have changed my things now.

HELMER: But what for?—so late as this.

NORA: I shall not sleep tonight.

HELMER: But, my dear Nora—

NORA (*looking at her watch*): It is not so very late. Sit down here, Torvald. You and I have much to say to one another. (*She sits down at one side of the table.*)

HELMER: Nora—what is this?—this cold, set face?

NORA: Sit down. It will take some time; I have a lot to talk over with you.

HELMER (*sits down at the opposite side of the table*): You alarm me, Nora!—And I don't understand you.

NORA: No, that is just it. You don't understand me, and I have never understood you either—before tonight. No, you mustn't interrupt me. You must simply listen to what I say. Torvald, this is a settling of accounts.

HELMER: What do you mean by that?

NORA (*after a short silence*): Isn't there one thing that strikes you as strange in our sitting here like this?

HELMER: What is that?

NORA: We have been married now eight years. Does it not occur to you that this is the first time we two, you and I, husband and wife, have had a serious conversation?

HELMER: What do you mean by serious?

NORA: In all these eight years—longer than that—from the very beginning of our acquaintance, we have never exchanged a word on any serious subject.

HELMER: Was it likely that I would be continually and forever telling you about worries that you could not help me to bear?

NORA: I am not speaking about business matters. I say that we have never sat down in earnest together to try and get at the bottom of anything.

HELMER: But, dearest Nora, would it have been any good to you?

NORA: That is just it; you have never understood me. I have been greatly wronged, Torvald—first by papa and then by you.

HELMER: What! By us two—by us two, who have loved you better than anyone else in the world?

NORA (*shaking her head*): You have never loved me. You have only thought it pleasant to be in love with me.

HELMER: Nora, what do I hear you saying?

NORA: It is perfectly true, Torvald. When I was at home with papa, he told me his opinion about everything, and so I had the same opinions; and if I differed from him I concealed the fact, because he would not have liked it. He called me his doll-child, and he played with me just as I used to play with my dolls. And when I came to live with you—

HELMER: What sort of an expression is that to use about our marriage?

NORA (*undisturbed*): I mean that I was simply transferred from papa's hands into yours. You arranged everything according to your own taste, and so I got the same tastes as you—or else I pretended to, I am really not quite sure which—I think sometimes the one and sometimes the other. When I look back on it, it seems to me as if I had been living here like a poor woman—just from hand to mouth. I have existed merely to perform tricks for you, Torvald. But you would have it so. You and papa have committed a great sin against me. It is your fault that I have made nothing of my life.

HELMER: How unreasonable and how ungrateful you are, Nora! Have you not been happy here?

NORA: No, I have never been happy. I thought I was, but it has never really been so.

HELMER: Not—not happy!

NORA: No, only merry. And you have always been so kind to me. But our home has been nothing but a playroom. I have been your doll-wife, just as at home I was papa's doll-child; and here the children have been my dolls. I thought it great fun when you played with me, just as they thought it great fun when I played with them. That is what our marriage has been, Torvald.

HELMER: There is some truth in what you say—exaggerated and strained as your view of it is. But for the future it shall be different. Playtime shall be over, and lesson-time shall begin.

NORA: Whose lessons? Mine, or the children's?

HELMER: Both yours and the children's, my darling Nora.

NORA: Alas, Torvald, you are not the man to educate me into being a proper wife for you.

HELMER: And you can say that!

NORA: And I—how am I fitted to bring up the children?

HELMER: Nora!

NORA: Didn't you say so yourself a little while ago—that you dare not trust me to bring them up?

HELMER: In a moment of anger! Why do you pay any heed to that?

NORA: Indeed, you were perfectly right. I am not fit for the task. There is another task I must undertake first. I must try and educate myself—you are not the man to help me in that. I must do that for myself. And that is why I am going to leave you now.

HELMER (*springing up*): What do you say?

NORA: I must stand quite alone, if I am to understand myself and everything about me. It is for that reason that I cannot remain with you any longer.

HELMER: Nora, Nora!

NORA: I am going away from here now, at once. I am sure Christine will take me in for the night—

HELMER: You are out of your mind! I won't allow it! I forbid you!

NORA: It is no use forbidding me anything any longer. I will take with me what belongs to myself. I will take nothing from you, either now or later.

HELMER: What sort of madness is this!

NORA: Tomorrow I shall go home—I mean, to my old home. It will be easiest for me to find something to do there.

HELMER: You blind, foolish woman!

NORA: I must try and get some sense, Torvald.

HELMER: To desert your home, your husband and your children! And you don't consider what people will say!

NORA: I cannot consider that at all. I only know that it is necessary for me.

HELMER: It's shocking. This is how you would neglect your most sacred duties.

NORA: What do you consider my most sacred duties?

HELMER: Do I need to tell you that? Are they not your duties to your husband and your children?

NORA: I have other duties just as sacred.

HELMER: That you have not. What duties could those be?

NORA: Duties to myself.

HELMER: Before all else, you are a wife and a mother.

NORA: I don't believe that any longer. I believe that before all else I am a reasonable human being, just as you are—or, at all events, that I must try and become one. I know quite well, Torvald, that most people would think you right, and that views of that kind are to be found in books; but I can no longer content myself with what most people say, or with what is found in books. I must think over things for myself and get to understand them.

HELMER: Can you not understand your place in your own home? Have you not a reliable guide in such matters as that?—Have you no religion?

NORA: I am afraid, Torvald, I do not exactly know what religion is.

HELMER: What are you saying?

NORA: I know nothing but what the clergyman said, when I went to be confirmed. He told us that religion was this, and that, and the other. When I am away from all this, and am alone, I will look into that matter too. I will see if what the clergyman said is true, or at all events if it is true for me.

HELMER: This is unheard of in a girl of your age! But if religion cannot lead you aright, let me try and awaken your conscience. I suppose you have some moral sense? Or—answer me—am I to think you have none?

NORA: I assure you, Torvald, that is not an easy question to answer. I really don't know. The thing perplexes me altogether. I only know that you and I look at it in quite a different light. I am learning, too, that the law is quite another thing from what I supposed; but I find it impossible to convince myself that the law is right. According to it a woman has no right to spare her old dying father, or to save her husband's life. I can't believe that.

HELMER: You talk like a child. You don't understand the conditions of the world in which you live.

NORA: No, I don't. But now I am going to try. I am going to see if I can make
    out who is right, the world or I.

HELMER: You are ill, Nora; you are delirious; I almost think you are out of your
    mind.

NORA: I have never felt my mind so clear and certain as tonight.

HELMER: And is it with a clear and certain mind that you forsake your husband
    and your children?

NORA: Yes, it is.

HELMER: Then there is only one possible explanation.

NORA: What is that?

HELMER: You do not love me anymore.

NORA: No, that is just it.

HELMER: Nora!—And you can say that?

NORA: It gives me great pain, Torvald, for you have always been so kind to me,
    but I cannot help it. I do not love you any more.

HELMER (*regaining his composure*): Is that a clear and certain conviction too?

NORA: Yes, absolutely clear and certain. That is the reason why I will not stay
    here any longer.

HELMER: And can you tell me what I have done to forfeit your love?

NORA: Yes, indeed I can. It was tonight, when the wonderful thing did not hap-
    pen; then I saw you were not the man I had thought you.

HELMER: Explain yourself better. I don't understand you.

NORA: I have waited so patiently for eight years; for, goodness knows, I knew
    very well that wonderful things don't happen every day. Then this horrible
    misfortune came upon me; and then I felt quite certain that the wonderful
    thing was going to happen at last. When Krogstad's letter was lying out
    there, never for a moment did I imagine that you would consent to accept
    this man's conditions. I was so absolutely certain that you would say to
    him: Publish the thing to the whole world. And when that was done—

HELMER: Yes, what then?—When I had exposed my wife to shame and disgrace?

NORA: When that was done, I was so absolutely certain, you would come for-
    ward and take everything upon yourself, and say: I am the guilty one.

HELMER: Nora—!

NORA: You mean that I would never have accepted such a sacrifice on your part?
    No, of course not. But what would my assurances have been worth against
    yours? That was the wonderful thing which I hoped for and feared; and it
    was to prevent that, that I wanted to kill myself.

HELMER: I would gladly work night and day for you, Nora—bear sorrow and want
    for your sake. But no man would sacrifice his honour for the one he loves.

NORA: It is a thing hundreds of thousands of women have done.

HELMER: Oh, you think and talk like a heedless child.

NORA: Maybe. But you neither think nor talk like the man I could bind myself
    to. As soon as your fear was over—and it was not fear for what threatened
    me, but for what might happen to you—when the whole thing was past, as
    far as you were concerned it was exactly as if nothing at all had happened.

Exactly as before, I was your little skylark, your doll, which you would in future treat with doubly gentle care, because it was so brittle and fragile. (*Getting up.*) Torvald—it was then it dawned upon me that for eight years I had been living here with a strange man, and had borne him three children—. Oh, I can't bear to think of it! I could tear myself into little bits!

HELMER (*sadly*): I see, I see. An abyss has opened between us—there is no denying it. But, Nora, would it not be possible to fill it up?

NORA: As I am now, I am no wife for you.

HELMER: I have it in me to become a different man.

NORA: Perhaps—if your doll is taken away from you.

HELMER: But to part!—To part from you! No, no, Nora, I can't understand that idea.

NORA (*going out to the right*): That makes it all the more certain that it must be done. (*She comes back with her cloak and hat and a small bag which she puts on a chair by the table.*)

HELMER: Nora, Nora, not now! Wait until tomorrow.

NORA (*putting on her cloak*): I cannot spend the night in a strange man's room.

HELMER: But can't we live here like brother and sister—?

NORA (*putting on her hat*): You know very well that would not last long. (*Puts the shawl round her.*) Goodbye, Torvald. I won't see the little ones. I know they are in better hands than mine. As I am now, I can be of no use to them.

HELMER: But some day, Nora—some day?

NORA: How can I tell? I have no idea what is going to become of me.

HELMER: But you are my wife, whatever becomes of you.

NORA: Listen, Torvald. I have heard that when a wife deserts her husband's house, as I am doing now, he is legally freed from all obligations towards her. In any case, I set you free from all your obligations. You are not to feel yourself bound in the slightest way, any more than I shall. There must be perfect freedom on both sides. See, here is your ring back. Give me mine.

HELMER: That too?

NORA: That too.

HELMER: Here it is.

NORA: That's right. Now it is all over. I have put the keys here. The maids know all about everything in the house—better than I do. Tomorrow, after I have left her, Christine will come here and pack up my own things that I brought with me from home. I will have them sent after me.

HELMER: All over! All over!—Nora, shall you never think of me again?

NORA: I know I shall often think of you, the children, and this house.

HELMER: May I write to you, Nora?

NORA: No—never. You must not do that.

HELMER: But at least let me send you—

NORA: Nothing—nothing—

HELMER: Let me help you if you are in want.

NORA: No. I can receive nothing from a stranger.

HELMER: Nora—can I never be anything more than a stranger to you?

NORA (*taking her bag*): Ah, Torvald, the most wonderful thing of all would have to happen.

HELMER: Tell me what that would be!

NORA: Both you and I would have to be so changed that—. Oh, Torvald, I don't believe any longer in wonderful things happening.

HELMER: But I will believe in it. Tell me! So changed that—?

NORA: That our life together would be a real wedlock. Goodbye. (*She goes out through the hall.*)

HELMER (*sinks down on a chair at the door and buries his face in his hands*): Nora! Nora! (*Looks round, and rises.*) Empty. She is gone. (*A hope flashes across his mind.*) The most wonderful thing of all—?

The sound of a door shutting is heard from below.

MODERN AND CONTEMPORARY THEATERS

Most theaters of the early and mid-twentieth century continued to have a proscenium arch. But dramatists and the theater as a whole have moved away from the realism of the late 1800s and early 1900s. In late modern and contemporary theater—both in the plays written now and productions of earlier plays—it is assumed that the audience knows the set is an artistic construction that requires imaginative participation. Playwrights as they write and producers as they plan productions no longer confine themselves to a realistic room in a box set, with all action occurring within that one space. They break through the "glass wall" and allow action to take place on the forestage as well as behind the arch. Thus the actors and audience are no longer always separated by the proscenium arch, as they are in Ibsen's theater. The action reaches out toward or into the audience. In some plays, characters even address the audience.

Nonrealistic Set   Such changes are evident in the postmodern, nonrealistic set that Arthur Miller conceived of for his well-known play *Death of a Salesman* (1949). While the proscenium stage and curtain are still there, what the audience sees on stage is not one room from the inside but several rooms from the outside. The outer and inner walls of the house are invisible (perhaps with only the bottom couple of feet of the walls, outlining the rooms), which allows spectators to see into several rooms. As Miller conceived it, "The kitchen at center seems actual enough, for there is a kitchen table with three chairs, and a refrigerator. But no other fixtures are seen. . . . To the right of the kitchen, on a level raised two feet, is a bedroom furnished only with a brass bedstead and a straight chair. . . . Behind the kitchen, on a level raised six and a half feet, is the boys' bedroom, at present barely visible. Two beds are dimly seen." August Wilson's 1985 play *Fences* (p. 733) also could be staged in such a nonrealistic way. The set is not a room in a house but an outside view of a house and the yard around it: "The setting is the yard which fronts the only entrance to the Maxson household, an ancient two-story brick house set back off a small alley in a big city neighborhood" (p. 733). The point is that contemporary drama does not require realistic box sets the way that modern drama did.

Contemporary Theaters   Theater in the mid- to late 1900s moved still further away from realism in text and stagecraft. Many contemporary theaters reach out to the audience not just through the imagination but also physically, by thrusting the stage out into the audience (returning to the Elizabethan methods) or by placing the stage in the center of the theater, with the audience surrounding it on all sides. Directors today take full advantage of a theater. Scenes might take place on the catwalks, in the audience, or in the aisles. Actors sometimes enter and exit through the audience, using the same aisles. Some plays even have a character initially seated in the audience who later rises and joins the action. Sets are changed between scenes while the audience watches, with the actors often moving furniture and props themselves.

Sets, Props, and Lighting   A thrust stage or theater-in-the-round cannot, of course, have rooms with real walls. Sets and props usually are simple and minimal or impressionistic and symbolic rather than realistically detailed. Playwrights and stage designers often think in terms of platforms connected by ramps and stairways to allow multiple locations. Modern equipment produces lighting effects undreamed of even a few decades ago. All of this means that playwrights today are free to imagine a far greater variety of spaces.

Nonconventional Presentations of Drama   Not all contemporary drama is produced in conventional theaters. Experimental or avant-garde drama uses the stage differently, often challenging the audience's ideas of theater itself. Ten-minute plays also, in many cases, make do with minimal settings and props. Some playwrights move outside traditional theaters, writing plays to be performed in bare halls or even on the streets, sometimes with workers and ordinary people instead of trained actors playing the roles. Others utilize a single actor on an empty stage to deliver a monologue—as in, for example, Marco Ramirez's *I Am Not Batman* (p. 681). Today's productions of drama from earlier times often use such nonconventional staging methods. Imagine how watching *A Doll's House* or *Hamlet* would be different if set in one of these experimental ways.

Serious Drama   The word *drama*, in addition to meaning a literary work intended for performance or the whole body of such works, also means any particularly striking or interesting event or series of events that involve conflict and tension. In literature or theater today, the word *drama* is often used to describe a play that is not a comedy and does not have a tragic ending but deals with serious events involving conflict and tension. August Wilson's *Fences* (p. 733) is such a play. So, too, are many of the works by late twentieth-century and early twenty-first-century playwrights. You may have noticed film genres such as *comedy*, *action*, and *drama*—not *tragedy*.

Biographical Sketches

This section offers brief biographical sketches of most of the authors included in this book. For fuller biographical information, the most convenient print sources are the *Dictionary of Literary Biography* and *Contemporary Authors*, both published by Gale and running into hundreds of volumes. Each is available online in many libraries.

Biographical information for many authors is also found on the Internet. The Web sites of the Academy of American Poets and of The Poetry Foundation are valuable and convenient for information about poets. *Voices from the Gaps: Women Writers of Color* also is very helpful, though it is no longer being updated. Sites for many individual authors are available as well, as are personal home pages for some contemporary poets and sites maintained by scholars or fans of writers old and new.

To emphasize how writers work with each other and are influenced by other writers, when the names of authors represented in this anthology appear within a biographical entry, they are in small capital letters, as a reminder that those biographical notes might shed further light on the author at hand.

DEANNA ABLESER (b. 1970) is a theatre teacher at Dana Middle School in Hawthorne, California. Deanna was the recipient of the 2006 VSA Playwright Discovery Teacher Award and was honored at the John F. Kennedy Center for the Performing Arts. She has a Master's of Fine Arts in Theatre and a Master's in Education from the University of Southern California. She has been teaching and directing award-winning youth theatre for the past twenty years. Brooklyn Publishers, Smith and Kraus, Lazy Bee Scripts, Applause Theatre and Cinema Books, and Youth Plays currently publish her monologues, scenes, and plays.

CHIMAMANDA NGOZI ADICHIE (b. 1977) was born and grew up in Nigeria, where her father was a professor of statistics at the University of Nigeria and her mother was registrar. She studied medicine and pharmacy for a year and a half, then moved to the United States to study communications and political science at Drexel University. She earned her B.A. degree at Eastern Connecticut State University and received master's degrees in creative writing from Johns Hopkins University and in African studies from Yale University. In 2008 she was awarded a MacArthur Fellowship. She was a Hodder Fellow at Princeton University and a fellow at the Radcliffe Institute for Advanced Study. She has published a collection of poetry (*Decisions* [1997]), a play (*For Love of Biafra* [1998]), a collection of short stories (*The Thing Around Your Neck* [2009]), and three novels (*Purple Hibiscus* [2003], *Half of a Yellow Sun* [2007], and *Americanah* [2013]), as well as many other short stories. She has received numerous awards for her work. She divides her time between Nigeria, where she teaches writing workshops, and the United States.

SHERMAN ALEXIE (b. 1966), was born in Wellpinit, a tiny town on the 150,000-acre Spokane Indian Reservation in eastern Washington, about fifty miles northeast of Spokane. His father is Coeur d'Alene Indian and his mother is Spokane Indian. Alexie learned to read by age three, and his love of reading as he grew up created barriers between him and his peers: He describes himself as a geek during his school years. He was the only Native American in Reardan High School, where he was an excellent student and a star basketball player. He attended Gonzaga University in Spokane for two years, then Washington State University in Pullman, from which he graduated in 1991. He started out as a premed student, but a human anatomy class on the one hand and a poetry workshop on the other changed his direction. He discovered he loved writing and was good at it, and that he didn't love human anatomy. Writing soon became the center of his life. He has published ten books of poetry, five novels (among them a best-selling young adult book, *The Absolutely True Diary of a Part-Time Indian* [2007]), and several collections of short fiction, including *The Lone Ranger and Tonto Fistfight in Heaven* (1993) and most recently *Blasphemy: New and Selected Stories* (2013). He has also been successful in film, as writer, director, and producer — most notably *Smoke Signals* (1998). He is also successful as a stand-up comedian. He has won numerous awards, including a PEN/Faulkner award for *War Dances* (2010) and the Native Writers' Circle of the Americas Lifetime Achievement Award in 2010.

MAYA ANGELOU (1928–2014) was born in St. Louis, Missouri, and named Marguerite Annie Johnson (her older brother gave her the nickname "Maya"). She worked as a dancer, singer, actor, civil rights organizer, editor, university administrator, and journalist before turning to writing full-time in 1968, at the urging of her friend, JAMES BALDWIN. She is best known for a series of seven autobiographies, beginning with *I Know Why the Caged Bird Sings* (1969 — the first nonfiction best seller by an African American woman), which brought her international fame. A prolific poet, her collection *Just Give Me a Cool Drink of Water 'fore I Die* (1971) was nominated for the Pulitzer Prize. She recited her poem "On the Pulse of Morning" at President Bill Clinton's inauguration in 1993. In addition to the works mentioned above, she published three books of essays; several more books of poetry; and a long list of plays, movies, and

television shows. She was awarded the Spingarn Medal in 1994, the National Medal of Arts in 2000, the Presidential Medal of Freedom in 2011, and over fifty honorary degrees by colleges and universities.

SUSAN ATEFAT-PECKHAM (1970–2004) was a first-generation American born to Iranian parents. She spent most of her life in France, Switzerland, and the United States. She received her undergraduate degree at Baylor University, where she planned on a career as a physician. However, partway through her college years, she discovered poetry and was encouraged to write by her future husband. She earned a Ph.D. in English and creative writing from the University of Nebraska and taught at Hope College and at Georgia State College and University. In addition to her poetry, she was a noted writer of creative nonfiction, having been cited in Best American Essays; an accomplished pianist; and an excellent painter, something that influenced the vibrancy and color-filled quality of her poems. Her poems lead the reader into the usually hidden lives of Iranian women living in the dual worlds of tradition and the contemporary.

MARGARET ATWOOD (b. 1939) was born in Ottawa and grew up in northern Ontario, in Quebec, and in Toronto. She began writing while attending high school in Toronto. She received her undergraduate degree from Victoria College at the University of Toronto and her master's degree from Radcliffe College. She won the E. J. Pratt Medal for a privately printed book of poems, *Double Persephone* (1961), and has published nineteen more collections of poetry. She was perhaps best known for her thirteen novels, which include *The Handmaid's Tale* (1983), *The Robber Bride* (1994), and *The Blind Assassin* (2000 — winner of the Booker Prize). She has also published ten collections of short stories, seven children's books, and ten books of nonfiction, and she has edited several anthologies. Her work has been translated into more than thirty languages, including Farsi, Japanese, Turkish, Finnish, Korean, Icelandic, and Estonian.

W.[YSTAN] H.[UGH] AUDEN (1907–1973) was born in York, England. He went to private school and then to Oxford University, where he began to write poetry. He supported himself by teaching and publishing, and wrote books based on his travels to Iceland, Spain, and China. He also wrote (with Chester Kallman) several librettos, including one for Igor Stravinsky's *The Rake's Progress* (1951). He lived in the United States from 1939 until his death and became a U.S. citizen in 1946. His work combines lively intelligence, quick wit, and immense craftsmanship, and often focuses on social concerns.

JIMMY SANTIAGO BACA (b. 1952) was born in Sante Fe, New Mexico, and is of Chicano and Apache heritage. Abandoned by his parents at the age of two, he lived with one of his grandparents for several years before being placed in an orphanage. He lived on the streets as a youth and was imprisoned for six years for drug possession. In prison, he taught himself to read and write, and began to compose poetry. A fellow inmate convinced him to submit some of his poems for publication. He has since published a dozen books of poetry, a memoir, a collection of stories and essays, a play, a screenplay, and a novel (*A Glass of Water* [2009]). He lives outside Albuquerque in a one-hundred-year-old adobe house.

JAMES BALDWIN (1924–1987) was born in Harlem to an unmarried domestic worker. When Baldwin was three, his mother married a factory worker and storefront preacher who was a hard, cruel man. At age fourteen, Baldwin began preaching at the small Fireside Pentecostal Church in Harlem, and the cadences of black preaching continued to influence his writing style later in his life. His first story appeared in a church newspaper when he was about twelve. He left home at seventeen and lived in Greenwich Village, where he met Richard Wright, who encouraged him to continue his writing and helped him win a Eugene Saxton Fellowship. Strained relations with his stepfather, problems over sexual identity, the suicide of a friend, and racial oppression in the United States led Baldwin to move to France when he was nineteen, though he returned to the United States frequently to lecture and teach; from 1957 onward, he spent half of each year in New York City. His first novel, the partially autobiographical *Go Tell It on the Mountain*, was published in 1953. His second novel, *Giovanni's Room* (1956), dealt with a white

American expatriate who must come to terms with his homosexuality, and *Another Country* (1962) explored racial and gay sexual tensions among New York intellectuals. He published several more novels, plays, and essay collections, including *Nobody Knows My Name* (1961) and *The Fire Next Time* (1963).

TONI CADE BAMBARA (1939–1995) was born in New York City and grew up in Harlem and Bedford-Stuyvesant. She began writing stories when she was a child and continued writing and taking writing courses in high school and at Queens College, where she majored in theater arts and English. Bambara completed her master's degree in American literature while serving as program director at Colony Settlement House in Brooklyn; she then began teaching at City College of New York. She first became known for editing a groundbreaking collection of African American women's writing, *The Black Woman: An Anthology* (1970). She went on to publish four collections of stories, two novels, many screenplays, and a book for children. In addition to being an important figure among the group of African American writers who emerged in the 1960s, Bambara was an activist in the civil rights and women's movements.

JIM BARNES (b. 1933), born in Oklahoma of Choctaw and Welsh heritage, worked for ten years as a lumberjack. He studied at Southeastern Oklahoma State University and received his M.A. and Ph.D. from the University of Arkansas. He has published many books of poetry, most recently *Visiting Picasso* (2007); several books of translations and criticism; and over 500 poems in more than 100 journals, including *Chicago Review, American Scholar, Prairie Schooner,* and *Georgia Review.* He is the founding editor of the Chariton Review Press and editor of *Chariton Review.* He taught at Truman State University from 1970 to 2003 and then at Brigham Young University. He presently lives in Santa Fe.

WENDELL BERRY (b. 1934) was born in Henry County, Kentucky, the first of four children of Virginia and John Berry, a lawyer and tobacco farmer. He attended Millersburg Military Institute, earned his B.A. and M.A. from the University of Kentucky, and was a Wallace Stegner Fellow at Stanford University.

A prolific author of poetry, essays, short stories, and novels, he is also recognized for his academic, cultural, environmental, and economic criticism. His ancestors have farmed in Henry County for five generations, and since 1965 he has farmed a 125-acre homestead, Lane's Landing. His literary works focus on the life that he deeply values, one that includes sustainable agriculture, community, a connection to place, local economics, good work, and the interconnectedness of all life. He is a fellow at Britain's Temenos Academy, which is devoted to studying all faiths and spiritual paths.

ELIZABETH BISHOP (1911–1979), born in Worcester, Massachusetts, was raised in Nova Scotia by her grandparents after her father died and her mother was committed to an asylum. She attended Vassar College, intending to study medicine, but was encouraged by MARIANNE MOORE to be a poet. From 1935 to 1937, she traveled in France, Spain, northern Africa, Ireland, and Italy and then settled in Key West, Florida, for four years, after which she lived in Rio de Janeiro for almost twenty years. She wrote slowly and carefully and produced a small body of poetry (totaling only around one hundred poems). Technically sophisticated, formally varied, witty and thoughtful, her poetry reveals in precise, true-to-life images her impressions of the physical world. She served as Consultant in Poetry at the Library of Congress from 1949 to 1950.*

PETER BLUE CLOUD (1935–2011), born in Quebec, was a Turtle Mohawk and former ironworker. In addition to editing publications such as the *Alcatraz Newsletter, Akwesasne Notes,* and *Coyote's Journal,* he published several volumes of poetry, including *White Corn Sister* (1979) and *Clans of Many Nations: Selected Poems, 1969–1994* (1995). His visionary poems often drew on native storytelling traditions, native dance structures, and native chant and drumming. One can experience in his poems the influence of these as well as the impact of industrial values on native ways of life.

SUZANNE BRADBEER (b. 1961) is a playwright, librettist, and children's story writer. She grew up in the South, attended college in the Midwest, and currently lives in New York City. She earned her B.A. degree at Augustana College in Illinois, with a major in French. After college (and working at Thomas Jefferson's Monticello for almost a year), she started studying acting, then went on to take workshops and classes in playwriting. After she began writing, she went to plays five nights a week for two years: uptown, downtown, from readings to Broadway. She has written many award-winning full-length and one-act plays, most recently *The God Game* (2014). She is the librettist for the musicals *Cocus and Doot* (Vital Theatre Company) and *Max and the Truffle Pig* (New York Music Festival). She has written a series of children's books used to facilitate a Head Start teaching program through Penn State University, and she contributed to the books *Playwrights in Rehearsal* (Susan Letzler Cole) and *Writing the 10-Minute Play* (Glenn Alterman).

RAY BRADBURY (1920–2012), short story writer, essayist, playwright, screenwriter and poet, was born in Waukegan, Illinois. He graduated from a Los Angeles high school in 1938. Although his formal education ended there, he became a "student of life," selling newspapers on L.A. street corners from 1938 to 1942 and spending his nights in the public library and his days at the typewriter. He became a full-time writer in 1943 and contributed numerous short stories to periodicals before publishing a collection of them, *Dark Carnival,* in 1947. His reputation was established with the publication of *The Martian Chronicles* in 1950 and *Fahrenheit 451* in 1953, which many consider to be his masterpiece. Bradbury published twenty-seven novels; close to 600 short stories; and numerous poems, essays, and plays. His short stories have appeared in more than 1,000 school curriculum "recommended reading" anthologies. He was awarded the O. Henry Memorial Award, the Benjamin Franklin Award, the World Fantasy Award for

---

*The first appointment of a Consultant in Poetry at the Library of Congress was made in 1937. The title was changed to Poet Laureate Consultant in Poetry in 1986. Appointments are made for one year, beginning in September, and sometimes have been renewed for a second year.

Lifetime Achievement, the Grand Master Award from the Science Fiction Writers of America, the PEN Center USA West Lifetime Achievement Award, among others. In November 2000, he received the National Book Foundation Medal for Distinguished Contribution to American Letters, and in 2004 he received the National Medal of Arts, presented by President George W. Bush and Laura Bush. On his death in 2012, the *New York Times* called Bradbury "the writer most responsible for bringing modern science fiction into the literary mainstream."

GWENDOLYN BROOKS (1917–2000), born in Topeka, Kansas, was raised in Chicago and wrote her first poems at age seven. She began studying poetry at the Southside Community Art Center. Her second collection of poems, *Annie Allen* (1949), earned the first Pulitzer Prize given to an African American poet. She served as Consultant in Poetry at the Library of Congress from 1985 to 1986 and worked in community programs and poetry workshops in Chicago to encourage young African American writers.

ELIZABETH BARRETT BROWNING (1806–1861) was born in Durham, England, and studied with her brother's tutor. Her first book of poetry was published when she was thirteen, and she soon became the most famous female poet to that point in English history. A riding accident at the age of sixteen left her a semi-invalid in the house of her possessive father, who had forbidden any of his eleven children to marry. She and ROBERT BROWNING were forced to elope (she was thirty-nine at the time); they lived in Florence, Italy, where she died fifteen years later. Her best-known book of poems was *Sonnets from the Portuguese* (1850), a sequence of forty-four sonnets recording the growth of her love for Robert.

ROBERT BROWNING (1812–1889) was the son of a bank clerk in Camberwell, then a suburb of London. As an aspiring poet in 1844, he admired ELIZABETH BARRETT's poetry and began a correspondence with her that led to one of the world's most famous romances. Their courtship lasted until 1846 when they were secretly wed and ran off to Italy, where they lived until Elizabeth's death in 1861. The years in Florence were among the happiest for both of

them. To her he dedicated *Men and Women* (1855), which contains his best poetry. Although she was the more popular poet during her lifetime, his reputation grew upon his return to London after her death, assisted somewhat by public sympathy for him. The late 1860s were the peak of his career: He and ALFRED, LORD TENNYSON were mentioned together as the foremost poets of the age. His fame and influence continued to grow through the remainder of his life until his death in 1889.

DENNIS BRUTUS (1924–2009) was born in Zimbabwe of South African parents. He attended the University of Witwaterstand and taught for fourteen years in South African high schools but was banned from teaching (and his university law studies) because of his leadership in the campaign to exclude South Africa from the Olympic Games as long as the country practiced apartheid in sports. He was arrested and sentenced to eighteen months of hard labor. His *Letters to Martha* (1968) are poems about his experiences as a prisoner on Robben Island. After leaving South Africa in 1966 with a Rhodesian passport, Brutus made his home in England, then moved to the United States, where he taught at the University of Denver, Northwestern University, and the University of Pittsburgh and published twelve books of poetry. In 1983, after engaging in a protracted legal struggle and appearing on ABC's *Nightline* with Ted Koppel, he won the right to stay in the United States as a political refugee. He returned to South Africa in 2007 and died at his home in Cape Town.

RAFAEL CAMPO (b. 1964) is a graduate of Amherst College and Harvard Medical School. He teaches and practices general internal medicine at Harvard Medical School and Beth Israel Deaconess Medical Center in Boston, where his medical practice serves mostly Latinos, gay/lesbian/bisexual/transgendered people, and people with HIV infection. He is also on the faculty of the Lesley University Creative Writing MFA program. He is the author of six award-winning collections of poetry, most recently *Alternative Medicine* (2013), as well as two collections of essays (*The Poetry of Healing: A Doctor's Education in Empathy, Identity, and Desire* [1997] and

The Healing Art: A Doctor's Black Bag of Poetry [2003]). He is a recipient of a John Simon Guggenheim Foundation fellowship, the Annual Achievement Award from the National Hispanic Academy of Arts and Sciences, and a Pushcart Prize. He has served as Visiting Writer at Amherst College; artist in residence at Stanford University; George A. Miller Endowment Visiting Scholar at the University of Illinois, Champagne-Urbana; and Fanny Hurst Visiting Poet at Brandeis University.

LORNA DEE CERVANTES (b. 1954) was born in San Francisco and grew up in San Jose. There she studied at San Jose City College and San Jose State University. She is the author of four volumes of poetry: *Emplumada* (1981), which won an American Book Award; *From the Cables of Genocide: Poems on Love and Hunger* (1991); *Drive: The First Quartet: New Poems, 1980-2005* (2006); and *Ciento: 100 100-Word Love Poems* (2011). She has been coeditor of *Red Dirt*, a cross-cultural poetry journal, and her work has been included in many anthologies. Cervantes, who considers herself "a Chicana writer, a feminist writer, a political writer," lives in Boulder, Colorado, where she was a professor at the University of Colorado.

MAY-LEE CHAI (b. 1967) was born in Redlands, California, the eldest daughter of an artistically gifted Irish American mother and Shanghai-born political scientist father. She has lived in fourteen states and four countries. She majored in French and Chinese studies at Grinnell College in Iowa, and earned M.A. degrees in East Asian studies from Yale University and in creative writing from the University of Colorado in Boulder. She has studied at universities in France, China, and Taiwan, and has worked as a reporter with the Associated Press. She was awarded a National Endowment for the Arts fellowship. She is author of seven books in a variety of genres: three novels (*My Lucky Face* [2003]; *Dragon Chica* [2010]; and *Tiger Girl* [2013]); a short story collection (*Glamorous Asians* [2004]); a personal memoir (*Hapa Girl* [2008]); a family memoir (*The Girl from Purple Mountain* [2002]); and a nonfiction book (*China A to Z*, with Winberg Chai [2007; 2nd edition 2015]), in addition to short stories and essays in many journals. She has taught at various universities, including San Francisco State

University, the University of Wyoming, Amherst College, and currently the University of North Carolina Wilmington.

MARILYN CHIN (b. 1955) is a first-generation Chinese American, born in Hong Kong and raised in Portland, Oregon. She is the author of three volumes of poetry — *Dwarf Bamboo* (1987); *The Phoenix Gone, The Terrace Empty* (1994); and *Rhapsody in Plain Yellow* (2002) — and a novel, *Revenge of the Mooncake Vixen* (2009). She also is a coeditor of *Dissident Song: A Contemporary Asian American Anthology* (1991) and has translated poems by the modern Chinese poet Ai Qing and cotranslated poems by the Japanese poet Gozo Yoshimasu. She has received numerous awards for her poetry, including a Stegner Fellowship, the PEN/Josephine Miles Award, and four Pushcart Prizes. She is codirector of the M.F.A. program at San Diego State University.

KATE CHOPIN (1851–1904) was born Katherine O'Flaherty in St. Louis. Her father, an Irish immigrant and a very successful businessman, died when she was four. Her mother was of a prominent French Creole family. Chopin received an excellent education at the Academy of the Sacred Heart and from her mother and grandmother, and on graduation was known as a brilliant storyteller, a youthful cynic, and an accomplished pianist. At age nineteen she married Oscar Chopin and had six children. They lived in the Creole community of Natchitoches Parish, Louisiana, until his death in 1882, when she moved back to St. Louis. After her mother died a year later, friends encouraged her to write as a way to deal with her grief and anger, and in doing so she turned to Creole country for her subjects and themes. She became both a nationally acclaimed and popular author. Her masterpiece, *The Awakening* (1899), a lyrical study of a young woman whose deep personal discontents lead to adultery and suicide, was praised for its craft but criticized for its content and created a scandal. Chopin, always sensitive to her critics and declining in health, wrote little after it.

CHRYSTOS (b. 1946) is a Menominee writer and activist whose works explore themes of feminism, social justice, and native rights. She was born in San Francisco and now lives on

Bainbridge Island, Washington. She has published five collections of poetry: *Not Vanishing* (1988), *Dream On* (1991), *In Her I Am* (1993), *Fugitive Colors* (1995), and *Fire Power* (1995). She has won numerous awards, including a National Endowment for the Arts fellowship, the Sappho Award of Distinction from the Astrea Lesbian Foundation for Justice, and the Aude Lorde International Poetry Award.

SANDRA CISNEROS (b. 1954) was born in Chicago to a Mexican father and Chicana mother. She grew up in ghetto neighborhoods of Chicago, moving frequently and thus never feeling settled. She spoke English at school and Spanish at home and on many trips to Mexico to visit her grandmother. She wrote poetry in high school and was editor of the school literary magazine, and she went on to earn a B.A. from Loyola University and an M.F.A. from the University of Iowa Writers' Workshop. She discovered her literary voice in a graduate seminar, when she experimented with writing about growing up as a poor Latina in Chicago. She has published two novels, three books of poetry, two books of stories, and a children's book in both Spanish and English. She was awarded a MacArthur Foundation Fellowship in 1995. Cisneros has taught at various colleges and universities, including the University of California, University of Michigan, and the University of New Mexico. She now lives in San Antonio, Texas.

LUCILLE CLIFTON (1936–2010) was born in Depew, New York, and studied at Howard University. She published many books of poetry, including *Blessing the Boats: New and Selected Poems 1988-2000* (2000), which won the National Book Award. Her last book was *Voices* (2008). She also published a memoir and more than twenty books for children. She taught at several colleges and worked in the Office of Education in Washington, D.C. She served as poet laureate for the state of Maryland. Her poems typically reflect her ethnic pride, womanist principles, and race and gender consciousness.

JUDITH ORTIZ COFER (b. 1952) was born in Hormigueros, Puerto Rico. Her family moved to Paterson, New Jersey, in 1955. For the next decade, she grew up moving between those two very different worlds. She graduated from Augusta College in Georgia, married and had a daughter, completed a graduate degree, and began teaching English. But, she says, something was missing from her life: She realized that she needed to write. Her first book of poetry, *Reaching for the Mainland* (1987), was followed by several others, including, most recently, *A Love Story Beginning in Spanish: Poems* (2006). She has also published novels for adults and a memoir, *Silent Dancing: A Partial Remembrance of a Puerto Rican Childhood* (1990), and a book about writing, *Woman in Front of the Sun: On Becoming a Writer* (2000). She has written several award-winning books for young adults, including *An Island Like You: Stories of the Barrio* (1996) and *If I Could Fly* (2011), and several books for children, including *The Poet Upstairs* (2012). She is Regents' and Franklin Professor of English and Creative Writing, Emerita, at the University of Georgia and lives with her husband on the family farm near Louisville, Georgia.

BILLY COLLINS (b. 1941), was born and raised in New York City. Perhaps no poet since ROBERT FROST has managed to combine high critical acclaim with broad popular appeal the way Collins has. The typical Collins poem opens on a clear and hospitable note but soon takes an unexpected turn; poems that begin in irony may end in a moment of lyric surprise. Collins sees his poetry as "a form of travel writing" and considers humor "a door into the serious." He is the author of at least fifteen books of poetry, most recently, *Horoscopes for the Dead: Poems* (2011); *Aimless Love: New and Selected Poems* (2013); and *Voyage* (2014), a book-length poem for children illustrated by Karen Romagna. In 2009, he edited, with illustrator David Sibley, *Bright Wings: An Illustrated Anthology of Poems about Birds*. He served as Poet Laureate Consultant in Poetry at the Library of Congress from 2001 to 2003 and as New York State Poet Laureate from 2004 to 2006. He has taught at Columbia University; Sarah Lawrence College; and Lehman College, City University of New York.

VICTOR HERNÁNDEZ CRUZ (b. 1949) was born in Aguas Buenas, Puerto Rico, and moved to New York City with his family at the age of five. His first book of poetry, *Papa Got His Gun, and Other Poems* (1966), was published when he was seventeen. Since then he has published numerous other collections, most recently *The Mountain in the Sea* (2006). In 1971, Cruz visited Puerto Rico and reconnected with his ancestral heritage; eighteen years later, he returned to Puerto Rico to live. He now divides his time between Puerto Rico and New York. Much of his work explores the relation between the English language and his native Spanish, playing with grammatical and syntactical conventions within both languages to create his own bilingual idiom.

COUNTEE CULLEN (1903–1946) was born in either Louisville, Kentucky; Baltimore, Maryland; or (as he himself claimed) New York City. He was adopted by the Reverend Frederick A. Cullen and his wife and grew up, as he put it, "in the conservative atmosphere of a Methodist parsonage." He studied at New York University and Harvard University. A forerunner of the Harlem Renaissance movement, he was, in the 1920s, the most popular black literary figure in America. From the 1930s until his death, he wrote less and worked as a junior high French teacher. For many years after his death, his reputation was eclipsed by that of other Harlem Renaissance writers, particularly LANGSTON HUGHES and ZORA NEALE HURSTON; recently, however, there has been a resurgence of interest in his life and work.

E. E. CUMMINGS (1894–1962) was born in Cambridge, Massachusetts, where his father was a Unitarian minister and a sociology lecturer at Harvard University. He graduated from Harvard and then served as an ambulance driver during World War I. *The Enormous Room* (1922) is an account of his confinement in a French prison camp during the war. After the war, he lived in rural Connecticut and Greenwich Village, with frequent visits to Paris. In his work, Cummings experimented with form, punctuation, spelling, and syntax, abandoning traditional techniques and structures to create a new, highly idiosyncratic means of poetic expression. At the time of his death, he was the second most widely read poet in the United States, after ROBERT FROST.

EDWIDGE DANTICAT (b. 1969), was born and spent her childhood in Haiti, where she began writing at nine years old. She moved to New York when she was twelve, living with her parents in a heavily Haitian American neighborhood. Two years later she published her first writing in English, "A Haitian-American Christmas: Cremace and Creole Theatre," in a citywide magazine written by teenagers. She entered Barnard College in New York City intending to become a nurse but changed directions and graduated with a major in French literature, then went on to earn an MFA in creative writing from Brown University. She has written or edited at least sixteen books in a variety of genres: adult novels, young adult novels, memoirs, travel books, and social criticism. Her most recent works are the novel *Claire of the Sea Light* (2013), the children's picture book *Mama's Nightingale* (2015), and the young adult novel *Untwine* (2015). She has received many awards and honors, including a MacArthur Fellowship in 2009.

LYDIA DAVIS (b. 1947) was born into a literary family: her father was a critic and professor of English, her mother a fiction writer and teacher. In first grade, she learned to read English; in second grade, which she spent in Austria, she learned to read German. She has published many books of short stories, including *The Collected Stories of Lydia Davis* (2009) and *Can't and Won't: Stories* (2014). Her stories are known for their humor and brevity, many only one or two sentences long. She is also a translator of the works of Proust, Foucault, and other French writers, including a new version of *Madame Bovary* (2010). In 2003, she received a MacArthur Fellowship. She was nominated for the National Book Award in 2007 and was a PEN/Hemingway finalist for her collection *Break It Down* (1986).

TOI DERRICOTTE (b. 1941) was born and raised in Detroit, where she earned a B.A. in special education from Wayne State University. She is the author of five collections of poetry, including *The Undertaker's Daughter* (2011), as well as an award-winning memoir, *The Black Notebooks* (1997). With poet Cornelius Eady, she cofounded Cave Canem, which offers workshops and retreats for African American poets. Among many honors she has received is the Distinguished Pioneering of the Arts Award from United Black Artists. She is Professor Emerita at the University of Pittsburgh.

JOANNE DIAZ (b. 1972) earned an M.F.A in creative writing from New York University and a Ph.D. in English literature from Northwestern University. She is the author of *The Lessons* (2011), winner of the Gerald Cable First Book Award; *My Favorite Tyrants* (2014), winner of the Brittingham Prize: and, with Ian Morris, coeditor of *The Little Magazine in America* (2015). Her poems have appeared in many magazines and journals, including *The American Poetry Review*, *The Missouri Review*, *Poetry*, *The Southern Review*, and *Third Coast*. She is the recipient of fellowships from the Illinois Arts Council, the National Endowment for the Arts, the Bread Loaf Writers Conference, and the Sustainable Arts Foundation. She is an associate professor in the English department at Illinois Wesleyan University.

EMILY DICKINSON (1830–1886) was born in Amherst, Massachusetts, and lived there her entire life, rarely leaving. She briefly attended a women's seminary but became homesick and left before a year was out. Dickinson never married and became reclusive later in life, forgoing even the village routines and revelries she enjoyed. She published very few of the more than seventeen hundred poems she wrote; most were written for herself or for inclusion in her many letters. Not until 1955 was there a complete edition of her poems that attempted to present them as originally written.

JOHN DONNE (1572–1631) was born in London to a prosperous Catholic family (he was related to Sir Thomas More and the playwright John Heywood). Donne studied at Oxford University for several years but did not take a degree. He fought with Sir Walter Raleigh in two naval strikes against Spain. In 1601, Donne's promising political career was permanently derailed by his precipitous marriage to Anne More without her father's consent. He was briefly imprisoned, lost a very promising position with Sir Thomas Egerton, and spent years seeking further political employment before finally being convinced by King James in 1615 to take holy orders as priest of the Church of England. His life was described by Isaac Walton later in the century as being divided into two parts. In Phase I he was "Jack Donne" of Lincoln's Inn: When young, Donne employed a sophisticated urban wit in his earlier love poetry, like that of "A Valediction: Forbidding Mourning." In Phase II he was John Donne, dean of St. Paul's: After Donne took his vows in 1615, his poetry became markedly less amorous and more religious in tone. His *Holy Sonnets* are as dense and complex as his earlier work, with his talent now directed toward exploration of his relationship with God.

MARK DOTY (b. 1953) was born in Maryville, Tennessee. He earned a B.A. from Drake University in Des Moines, Iowa, and an M.F.A. in creative writing from Goddard College in Plainfield, Vermont. He is the author of twelve collections of poetry, most recently *Deep Lane* (2015), and three memoirs: *Heaven's Coast* (1996), about the loss of his partner, Wally Roberts; *Firebird* (1999), a gay coming-of-age story and a chronicle of a gradual process of finding in art a place of personal belonging; and *Dog Years* (2007), about the relationships between humans and the dogs they love. He has taught at Brandeis University, Sarah Lawrence College, Vermont College, and the University of Iowa Writers' Workshop. He is currently Distinguished Professor and Writer-in-Residence in the Department of English at Rutgers University.

RITA DOVE (b. 1952) was born in Akron, Ohio. Her father was the first research chemist to break the race barrier in the tire industry. She graduated from Miami University in Oxford, Ohio, with a degree in English. After a year at Tübingen University in Germany on a Fulbright fellowship, she joined the University of Iowa Writers' Workshop, where she earned her M.F.A. in 1977. She has taught at Tuskegee Institute and Arizona State University and is now Commonwealth Professor of English at the University of Virginia. She was appointed Poet Laureate Consultant in Poetry at the Library of Congress in 1993, making her the youngest person to receive the highest official honor in American letters. She is the author of numerous collections of poetry, including *Thomas and Beulah* (1986), a book-length sequence, loosely based on the lives of her grandparents, that was awarded the Pulitzer Prize in 1987. She received the 1996 National Humanities Medal and the 2011 National Medal of Arts, and is the only poet to have received both.

DENISE DUHAMEL (b. 1961) was born in Woonsocket, Rhode Island. She received her B.F.A. from Emerson College and her M.F.A. from Sarah Lawrence College. She has published numerous collections of poetry, most recently *Blowout* (2013). She was winner of the Crab Orchard Poetry Prize for her collection *The Star-Spangled Banner* (1999). Duhamel has also collaborated with Maureen Seaton on several books of poetry, most recently *Caprice: Collected, Uncollected, & New Collaborations* (2015). She has been anthologized widely and has been included in four volumes of *The Best American Poetry*. She teaches creative writing at Florida International University.

PAUL LAURENCE DUNBAR (1872–1906) was the first African American to gain national eminence as a poet. Born and raised in Dayton, Ohio, he was the son of ex-slaves. He was an outstanding student: The only African American in his class, he was both class president and class poet. Although he lived to be only thirty-three years old, Dunbar was prolific, writing short stories, novels, librettos, plays, songs, and essays as well as the poetry for which he became well known. He was popular with both black and white readers of his day. His style encompasses two distinct voices — the standard English of the classical poet and the evocative dialect of the turn-of-the-twentieth-century black community in America.

T.[HOMAS] S.[TEARNS] ELIOT (1888–1965) was born and raised in St. Louis. He went to prep school in Massachusetts and then to Harvard University, where he earned an M.A. in philosophy in 1910 and started his doctoral dissertation. He studied at the Sorbonne in Paris, and then at Marburg in Germany in 1914. The war forced him to Oxford, where he got married and abandoned philosophy for poetry. After teaching and working in a bank, he became an editor at Faber and Faber and editor of the journal *Criterion*. He was the dominant force in English poetry for several decades. He became a British citizen and a member of the Church of England in 1927. He won the Nobel Prize for Literature in 1948. He also wrote plays, essays, and a series of poems on cats that became the basis of a musical by Andrew Lloyd Weber.

RALPH ELLISON (1914–1994) was born in Oklahoma City, where his mother worked as a servant after the death of her husband when Ellison was three. She brought home discarded books and phonograph records from houses where she worked, and from them Ellison developed an interest in literature and music. He studied music at Tuskegee Institute in Alabama and then went to New York, where he met LANGSTON HUGHES and Richard Wright, who encouraged him in his writing. Ellison's literary reputation rests on one novel, *Invisible Man* (1952), which received the National Book Award for fiction and was listed in a Book Week poll in 1965 as the most distinguished American novel of the preceding twenty years. It deals with a young black man moving from the South to the North and learning about how racial prejudice leads to discrimination on the one hand and to being unnoticed and inconsequential on the other. "Battle Royal" (p. 271) is the first chapter of that novel. Ellison also published a scattering of short stories (collected posthumously in *Flying Home and Other Stories* [1996]) and two books of essays. A second novel was incomplete when he died (excerpts from the manuscript were published as *Juneteenth* in 1999).

ANITA ENDREZZE (b. 1952), of Yaqui and European ancestry, was born in Long Beach, California, and earned her M.A. from Eastern Washington University. She is a poet, writer, and painter (in watercolor and acrylics) who also works in fiber and creates handmade books. She is a member of Atlatl, a Native American arts service organization. In addition to four volumes of poetry, she has published a children's novel, short stories, and nonfiction. She lives in Everett, Washington, where she is a storyteller, teacher, and writer.

LOUISE ERDRICH (b. 1954) was born in Minnesota to a French-Ojibwe mother and a German-born father. She grew up near the Turtle Mountain Reservation in North Dakota and is a member of the Turtle Mountain Band of Chippewa. Her grandfather was tribal chief of the reservation. She was among the first women admitted to Dartmouth College, where she began writing; she also studied at Johns Hopkins University. She has published fourteen novels, six children's books, three collections of poetry, three books of nonfiction, and a collection of short stories. In 2009, her novel *The Plague of Doves* was named a finalist for the Pulitzer Prize in fiction. She was awarded the Library of Congress Prize for American Fiction at the National Book Festival in 2015. She lives in Minneapolis and is the owner of Birchbark Books, a small independent bookstore.

MARTÍN ESPADA (b. 1957) was born in Brooklyn and has an eclectic résumé: radio journalist in Nicaragua; welfare rights paralegal; advocate for mental health patients; night desk clerk in a transient hotel; attendant in a primate nursery; groundskeeper at a minor league ballpark; bindery worker in a printing plant; bouncer in a bar; and practicing lawyer in Chelsea, Massachusetts. Author of twelve books of poetry, his latest collection is *Vivas to Those Who Have Failed* (2016). His earlier book *Alabanza: New and Selected Poems, 1982-2002* (2003) received the Paterson Award for Sustained Literary Achievement and was named an American Library Association Notable Book of the Year. He is an essayist, editor, and translator as well as a poet. He lives in Amherst, Massachusetts, where he is professor of English at the University of Massachusetts at Amherst.

WILLIAM FAULKNER (1897-1962) was born into an old southern family in New Albany, Mississippi. When he was five, his family moved to Oxford, a small city in northern Mississippi that was his home for most of the rest of his life. He attended the University of Mississippi for three semesters, having been admitted as a war veteran, although he had not finished high school, and published poems and short stories in the campus newspaper. He continued writing while working at odd jobs for several years in New York and New Orleans and published his first novel, *Soldier's Pay*, in 1926. Success as a novelist came when he began writing about the northern Mississippi area he knew best and created the mythical Yoknapatawpha County. His discovery that this "little postage stamp of native soil was worth writing about" enabled him to write a series of acclaimed experimental novels, including *The Sound and the Fury* (1920),

As I Lay Dying (1930), *Light in August* (1932), and *Absalom, Absalom!* (1936), in which he traces the disintegration of the South through several generations. Until the publication of the anthology *The Portable Faulkner* brought him wide recognition in 1946, he supported himself by publishing short stories (nearly a hundred) in magazines and by writing screenplays in Hollywood. In 1949, he received the Nobel Prize for Literature and delivered one of the most influential acceptance speeches ever given at a Nobel ceremony (available online).

ROBERT FROST (1874-1963) was born in San Francisco and lived there until he was eleven. When his father died, the family moved to Massachusetts, where Robert did well in school, especially in the classics, but he dropped out of both Dartmouth College and Harvard University. He went unrecognized as a poet until 1913, when he was first published in England, where he had moved with his wife and four children. Upon returning to the United States, he quickly achieved success with more publications and became the most celebrated poet in mid-twentieth-century America. He held a teaching position at Amherst College and received many honorary degrees, as well as an invitation to recite a poem at John F. Kennedy's inauguration. Although his work is principally associated with the life and landscape of New England, and though he is a poet of traditional verse forms and metrics, he is also a quintessentially modern poet in his adherence to language as it is actually spoken, in the psychological complexity of his portraits, and in the degree to which his work is infused with layers of ambiguity and irony.

DAGOBERTO GILB (b. 1950) was born and grew up in Los Angeles, raised by a Chicana mother who divorced his German father soon after Dagoberto was born. He attended the University of California, Santa Barbara, where he majored in philosophy and religion, after which he moved to El Paso and spent sixteen years making a living as a construction worker, twelve of them as a journeyman, high-rise carpenter. During this time, he began writing stories, several of which were published in a variety of journals. His collection of stories *The Magic of Blood* (1993) won the 1994 PEN/Hemingway Award, and his novel *The Last Known Residence of Mickey Acuña* (1994) was named a Notable Book of the Year by the *New York Times Book Review*. His most recent books are a collection of essays, *Gritos* (2003); a novel, *The Flowers* (2008); and a collection of stories, *Before the End, After the Beginning*, (2011). He is writer-in-residence and executive director of Centro Victoria: Center for Mexican American Literature and Culture, at the University of Houston–Victoria.

Susan Glaspell (1882–1948) was born and raised in Davenport, Iowa. She worked as a journalist before enrolling at Drake University in Des Moines; after graduating in 1899, she worked for two years as a reporter for the Des Moines *Daily News* and then returned to Davenport to write. Her short stories began to be accepted by magazines such as *Harper's* and the *American*. Her first novel, *The Glory of the Conquered*, was published in 1909. She married George Cram Cook, a novelist and utopian socialist, in 1916; they moved to New York and, at Cook's urging, she began to write plays. They founded the Provincetown Players in Provincetown, Massachusetts, in the summer of 1916 and moved the theater to New York that fall, where it served as a venue for producing innovative plays by American playwrights. Glaspell wrote *Trifles* (p. 693) for the Players' first season. Glaspell and Cook lived in Greece from 1922 until Cook's death in 1924, after which she settled in Provincetown for the rest of her life and continued writing. She published over fifty short stories, nine novels, eleven plays, and one biography. She was awarded a Pulitzer Prize for Drama for *Alison's House* (1931), based on the life of poet Emily Dickinson.

Ray González (b. 1952) received his M.F.A. in creative writing from Southwest Texas State University. He has published ten books of poetry, including *The Heat of Arrivals* (1997), which won the 1997 Josephine Miles Book Award, and *The Hawk Temple at Tierra Grande* (2003), winner of a 2003 Minnesota Book Award in Poetry. He is the author of three books of nonfiction (*Memory Fever* [1999]; *The Underground Heart* [2002], which received the 2003 Carr P. Collins/Texas Institute of

Letters Award for Best Book of Nonfiction; and *Renaming the Earth* [2008]) and two collections of short stories (*The Ghost of John Wayne* [2001] and *Circling the Tortilla Dragon* [2002]), and he is the editor of numerous anthologies. He has served as poetry editor for the *Bloomsbury Review* since 1980. He teaches creative writing at the University of Minnesota.

Angelina Weld Grimké (1880–1958) was born in Boston to a mixed racial background: Her mother was from a prominent white family; her father was the son of a white man and a black slave. Grimké's father was able to earn a law degree from Harvard University (and become executive director of the National Association for the Advancement of Colored People [NAACP]) through the support of two white aunts in South Carolina who acknowledged their ties to their brother's mixed-race children. Her parents named her after her great aunt Angelina Grimké Weld, a famous white abolitionist and women's rights advocate. When Grimké was three years old, her mother left her father, taking her daughter with her. After four years, she returned Angelina to her father and the child never saw her mother again. Grimké attended one of the finest schools in Massachusetts, the Carleton Academy in Ashburnham, graduated from the Boston Normal School with a degree in physical education, taught until 1907, and then moved to Washington, D.C., and taught English until she retired in 1926. While in Washington, she wrote poetry, fiction, reviews, and biographical sketches. Her best-known work, the only one published as a book, was the play *Rachel* (1916).

Joy Harjo (b. 1951) was born in Tulsa, Oklahoma. Her mother was of Cherokee-French descent and her father was Creek. She moved to the Southwest and began writing poetry in her early twenties. She then earned her B.A. at the University of New Mexico and her M.F.A. from the University of Iowa Writers' Workshop. Harjo has published many collections of poetry, including *In Mad Love and War* (1990), which received an American Book Award and the Delmore Schwartz Memorial Award; *How We Became Human: New and Selected Poems* (2002); and most recently *Conflict Resolution for Holy Beings* (2015). She also performs her poetry and plays saxophone with her band, Poetic Justice. Of "She Had Some Horses" (p. 579) Harjo has said, "This is the poem I'm asked most about and the one I have the least to say about. I don't know where it came from."

NATHANIEL HAWTHORNE (1804–1864) was born in Salem, Massachusetts, into a family that had been prominent in the area since colonial times. His father died when Nathaniel was four. Later, relatives recognized his literary talent and financed his education at Bowdoin College. After graduation, he lived at home writing short "tales" and a novel *Fanshawe*, which he self-published in 1828 and later dismissed as immature. He wrote prolifically in the 1830s, producing a number of successful short stories including "Young Goodman Brown" (p. 359). He published two collections of stories that were well received — *Twice-Told Tales* (1837; expanded edition 1842) and *Mosses from an Old Manse* (1846) — but had difficulty supporting himself by his writings. In 1845, he was appointed surveyor of the Boston Custom House by President James Polk but was dismissed from this post when Zachary Taylor became president. He then worked intensely on his most famous novel, *The Scarlet Letter*, published in 1850. In addition to five novels and romances, Hawthorne published nearly 120 stories and sketches and several books for children, and he left behind numerous notebooks with sketches from his travels and ideas for additional stories and novels. He was one of the first American writers to explore the hidden motivations of his characters and often used allegorical approaches to explore the complexities of moral choices and his characters' struggles with sin and guilt.

ROBERT HAYDEN (1913–1980) was raised in a poor neighborhood in Detroit and had an emotionally tumultuous childhood. Because of impaired vision, he was unable to participate in sports and spent his time reading instead. He graduated from high school in 1932 and attended Detroit City College (later Wayne State University). His first book of poems, *Heart-Shape in the Dust*, was published in 1940. After working for newspapers and on other projects, he studied under W. H. AUDEN in the graduate creative writing program at the University of Michigan. He taught at Fisk University and at the University of Michigan. His poetry gained international recognition in the 1960s, and he was awarded the grand prize for poetry at the First World Festival of Negro Arts in Dakar, Senegal, in 1966 for his book *Ballad of Remembrance*. In 1976, he became the first African American to be appointed as Consultant in Poetry at the Library of Congress.

TERRANCE HAYES (b. 1971) was born in Columbia, South Carolina. In addition to being a writer, he is an accomplished artist and athlete. After receiving a B.A. from Coker College, where he was named an Academic All-American for his athletic and academic accomplishments, he earned an M.F.A. from the University of Pittsburgh. His first book of poetry, *Muscular Music* (1999), won both the Whiting Writers Award and the Kate Tufts Discovery Award. *Hip Logic* (2002) won the National Poetry Series Award, and *Lighthead* (2010) won the National Book Award for Poetry. His most recent poetry collection is *How to Be Drawn* (2015). He was a 2014 MacArthur Fellow and was awarded a Guggenheim Fellowship. After teaching at Xavier University, he returned to Pittsburgh, where he taught for twelve years at Carnegie Mellon University. He is now a professor of English at the University of Pittsburgh.

ERNEST HEMINGWAY (1899–1961) was born in Oak Park, a conservative, upper-middle-class suburb of Chicago, but he spent his summers at Walloon Lake in northern Michigan, where he learned to love the outdoors and fishing and hunting. He decided to become a journalist instead of going to college and worked as a reporter for the *Kansas City Star*, where he was taught to write with short sentences, short paragraphs, active verbs, compression, clarity, and immediacy, qualities apparent in his fiction writing. He tried to enlist for service in World War I but was turned down because of poor eyesight. Instead, he volunteered as a Red Cross ambulance driver. Shortly after arriving in Italy, he was seriously wounded, with over two hundred pieces of shrapnel in his legs. After the war he lived in Paris, worked as a newspaper correspondent for the *Toronto Daily Star*, and mingled with prominent writers and artists. Between 1925 and 1929, he published four major works of fiction, including two novels — *The Sun Also Rises* (1926) and *A Farewell to Arms* (1929) — and went from being unknown to being one of the most important writers of his generation. He moved first to Key West, Florida, where he grew to love big-game fishing, and later to Havana, Cuba. He continued writing, continued his interests in fishing and big-game hunting, and served as a war correspondent during the Spanish civil war and the Chinese-Japanese war, thus fostering further the macho persona he built throughout his life. His last major novels were *For Whom the Bell Tolls* (1940) and *The Old Man and the Sea* (1953), which was awarded the Pulitzer Prize for Fiction. He was awarded the Nobel Prize for Literature in 1954. Seven years later, in poor health and afflicted with severe depression, he committed suicide, as his father had some three decades earlier.

BOB HICOK (b. 1960), was born in Grand Ledge, Michigan, and worked for many years as an automotive die designer and computer system administrator in Ann Arbor, Michigan. He earned an M.F.A. (without having an undergraduate degree) from Vermont College of Fine Arts, having already published four books of poems. His first collection of poetry, *The Legend of Light* (1995), won the Felix Pollack Prize for Poetry and was named an American Library Association Booklist Notable Book of the Year. He has published six more books: *Plus Shipping* (1998); *Animal Soul* (2001), a finalist for the National Book Critics Circle Award; *Insomnia Diary* (2004); *This Clumsy Living* (2007); *Words for Empty and Words for Full* (2010); and *Elegy Owed* (2013), also a finalist for the National Book Critics Circle Award. He has taught creative writing at Western Michigan University and Virginia Tech University, and he currently teaches at Purdue University.

LINDA HOGAN (b. 1947) is a poet, novelist, essayist, playwright, and activist widely considered to be one of the most influential and provocative Native American figures in the contemporary American literary landscape. She was born in Denver. Because her father, who was from the Chickasaw Nation, was in the army and was transferred frequently during Hogan's childhood, she lived in various locations while she was growing up, but she considers Oklahoma to be her true home. In her late twenties, while working with children with orthopedic disabilities, she began writing during her lunch hours, though she had no previous experience as a writer and little experience reading literature. She pursued her writing by commuting to the University of Colorado, Colorado Springs, for her undergraduate degree and earning an M.A. in English and creative writing at the University of Colorado, Boulder, in 1978. She has written and edited many books — poetry, novels, and nonfiction — and received numerous awards for her work, including a Lifetime Achievement Award from the Native Writers Circle of the Americas. She is professor emerita in the University of Colorado English department and the writer in residence for the Chickasaw Nation.

ANNA MARIA HONG recently completed a two-collection series of sonnets titled *The Glass Age*. Embracing traditional English and Italian forms as well as more experimental hybrids and departures, her poems sometimes shun the sonnet's formal rhyme schemes and other constraints, bending and torqueing the sonnet's shape to stretch the limits of the form. The 2010–2011 Bunting Fellow in Poetry at Harvard University's Radcliffe Institute for Advanced Study, she earned a B.A. in philosophy at Yale University and an M.F.A. in creative writing from the University of Texas Michener Center for Writers. Her poems have been published in venues including *Boston Review*, *Exquisite Corpse*, *jubilat*, *Fence*, *Green Mountains Review*, *Verse Daily*, *Fairy Tale Review*, *Mandorla*, and *POOL*. She is the editor of *Growing Up Asian American*, an anthology of fiction and memoir. A three-time Pushcart Fellowship nominee, she has received residencies from Yaddo, Djerassi, Valparaiso, and AIR West Norway and has taught at Eastern Michigan University, the University of Washington Bothell, the UCLA Extension Writers' Program, and Ursinus College.

GARRETT KAORU HONGO (b. 1951) was born in Volcano, Hawaii; grew up on Oahu and in Los

Angeles; and did graduate work in Japanese language and literature at the University of Michigan. Hongo has published six books of poetry, including *The River of Heaven* (1988), which was the Lamont Poetry Selection of the Academy of American Poets and a finalist for the Pulitzer Prize. His most recent collection is *Coral Road: Poems* (2011). He has also written *Volcano: A Memoir of Hawai'i* (1995) and edited collections of Asian American verse. He teaches at the University of Oregon, Eugene, where he directed the creative writing program from 1989 to 1993. His work often uses rich textures and sensuous details to comment on conditions endured by Japanese Americans during World War II and thereafter.

GERARD MANLEY HOPKINS (1844–1889) was born in London, the eldest of eight children. His father was a ship insurer who also wrote a book of poetry. Hopkins studied at Balliol College, Oxford, and, after converting to Catholicism, taught in a school in Birmingham. In 1868, he became a Jesuit and burned all of his early poetry, considering it "secular" and worthless. He then worked as a priest and teacher in working-class London, Glasgow, and Merseyside, and later as professor of classics at University College, Dublin. Hopkins went on to write many poems on spiritual themes, but he published little during his lifetime; his poems were not known until they were published by his friend Robert Bridges in 1918. They convey a spiritual sensuality, celebrating the wonder of nature both in their language and their rhythms.

A. E. HOUSMAN (1859–1936) was born in Fockbury, Worcestershire. A promising student at Oxford University, he failed his final exams because of emotional turmoil caused by his suppressed homosexual love for a fellow student. He spent the next ten years feverishly studying and writing scholarly articles while working as a clerk at the patent office. Housman was rewarded with the chair of Latin at University College, London, and later at Cambridge. His poetry, like his scholarship, was meticulous, impersonal in tone, and limited in output: two slender volumes — *A Shropshire Lad* (1896) and *Last Poems* (1922) — during his lifetime and a small book of *More Poems* (1936) after his death. His poems often take up the theme of doomed

youths acting out their brief lives in the context of the human histories implicit in agricultural communities and activities, especially the English countryside and traditions he loved.

LANGSTON HUGHES (1902–1967) was born in Joplin, Missouri, and grew up in Lincoln, Illinois, and Cleveland, Ohio. During his high school years, he began writing poetry. He attended Columbia University for a year; held odd jobs as an assistant cook, a launderer, and a busboy; and traveled to Africa and Europe working as a seaman. In 1924, he moved to Harlem. Hughes's first book of poetry, *The Weary Blues*, was published in 1926. He finished his college education at Lincoln University in Pennsylvania three years later. He wrote novels, short stories, plays, songs, children's books, essays, and memoirs as well as poetry and is also known for his engagement with the world of jazz and the influence it had on his writing. His life and work were enormously important in shaping the artistic contributions of the Harlem Renaissance of the 1920s.

ZORA NEALE HURSTON (1891–1960) was born to a family of sharecroppers in Notasula, Alabama, but grew up in Eatonville, Florida, a town founded by African Americans. After her mother's death in 1904, Hurston lived with various relatives. She never finished grade school. At sixteen she joined a traveling theater group and later did domestic work for a white household. The woman for whom she worked arranged for her to attend high school at Morgan Academy (now known as Morgan State University) in Baltimore. In her twenties, she attended Howard University, where she published her first stories in student publications and later in newspapers and magazines. In 1925, she moved to New York City and became active in the Harlem Renaissance. She collaborated with LANGSTON HUGHES in a folk comedy, *Mule Bone* (1931). Her first book, *The Eatonville Anthology* (1927), gained her national attention. At Barnard College, she took courses in anthropology and studied traditional folklore in Alabama and native culture in the Caribbean. During the 1930s and early 1940s, she completed graduate work at Columbia University and published four novels and an autobiography. Hurston published more books than any other African American woman writer of her time — novels, collections of stories, nonfiction, an autobiography — but she earned very little from her writing and spent her final years in near poverty. In the mid-1970s, her work was rediscovered, and she is now recognized as an important American author.

HENRIK IBSEN (1828–1906) was born in Skien, a tiny coastal town in southeast Norway. Although his father was successful and wealthy at the time of Ibsen's birth, his business failed soon after, and Ibsen grew up in poverty. He was familiar with the economic hardships he later depicted often in his plays. He worked for six years as apprentice to a druggist in the seaport town of Grimstad to help support his family, and he intended to study medicine but failed the university entrance examinations. By his early twenties, he was deeply involved in a small local theater in Bergen. In 1857, he was appointed artistic director for the new National Theatre and held that post until it went bankrupt in 1862. He received a travel grant from the government and moved with his wife and son to Rome, living for the next twenty-seven years in various European cities. In 1875, he began to experiment with realistic plays exploring social issues related to middle-class life. He is best known for a series of "problem plays" that shocked but also fascinated audiences, among them *A Doll's House* (1879; see p. 996) and *Hedda Gabler* (1890). In 1891, he returned to Norway for the rest of his life and continued to write until suffering a stroke in 1900. He received worldwide recognition on his seventieth birthday as the greatest dramatist of the nineteenth century.

HONORÉE FANONNE JEFFERS (b. 1967) grew up in Durham, North Carolina, and Atlanta, Georgia, and earned an M.F.A. in Creative Writing at the University of Alabama. She has published four books of poetry: *The Gospel of Barbecue* (2000), which won the 1999 Stan and Tom Wick Prize for Poetry and was the finalist for the 2001 Paterson Poetry Prize; *Outlandish Blues* (2003); *Red Clay Suite* (2007); and most recently *The Glory Gets* (2015). She won the 2002 Julia Peterkin

Award for Poetry and awards from the Barbara Deming Memorial Fund and the Rona Jaffe Foundation. Her poetry has been published in the anthologies *At Our Core: Women Writing about Power*, *Dark Eros*, and *Identity Lessons* and in many journals, including *Callaloo*, *Kenyon Review*, and *Prairie Schooner*. She has been teaching at the University of Oklahoma since 2002.

HA JIN (b. 1956) was born in Liaoning, China. At thirteen, he joined the People's Liberation Army during the Cultural Revolution. At sixteen, he began to educate himself in Chinese literature, and at nineteen he left the army and began teaching himself English while working the night shift as a railroad telegrapher. He then entered Heilongjiang University, earning a bachelor's degree in English studies. He received a master's degree in Anglo-American literature at Shandong University. He came to the United States to study at Brandeis University, and while he was there, the Tiananmen Square massacre occurred. The government's repression of dissent led him to stay in the United States, complete his Ph.D., and write about China in English, "to preserve the integrity of his work." He went on to teach, first at Emory University and currently at Boston University. His first novel, *Waiting*, won the 1999 National Book Award for Fiction. He has published six volumes of poetry, seven novels, six collections of short stories, and a book of essays.

GEORGIA DOUGLAS JOHNSON (1880–1966) was born in Atlanta and attended Atlanta University. She went on to study music at the Oberlin Conservatory (Ohio) and the Cleveland College of Music. Her ambition was to be a composer, but to earn a living she taught high school in Alabama and Washington, D.C., and later worked for the federal government. She was prolific as a poet, fiction writer, playwright, songwriter, and journalist; in addition to writing a syndicated newspaper column from 1926 to 1932, she wrote twenty-eight plays, thirty-one short stories, and over two hundred poems. She was the most widely published of all the women poets of the Harlem Renaissance period. Beyond her importance as a writer, she played an influential role in Washington circles by providing a salon in her home as a meeting place for artists and writers.

ALLISON JOSEPH (b. 1967) was born in London to Caribbean parents and grew up in Toronto and the Bronx. She earned her B.A. from Kenyon College and her M.F.A. from Indiana University. She is the author of seven collections of poetry: *What Keeps Us Here* (1992), winner of Ampersand Press's 1992 Women Poets Series Competition and the John C. Zacharis First Book Award); *Soul Train* (1997); *In Every Seam* (1997); *Imitation of Life* (2003); *Worldly Pleasures* (2004); *Voice* (2009); and *My Father's Kites* (2010). Her poems are often attuned to the experiences of women and minorities. She is editor of the *Crab Orchard Review* and holds the Judge Williams Holmes Cook Endowed Professorship and directs the M.F.A. program in creative writing at Southern Illinois University, Carbondale.

JAMES JOYCE (1882–1941) was born in Rathgar, a suburb of Dublin. His father, descended from an old, wealthy Cork family, drank his family into poverty. However, Joyce received an excellent classical education at a Jesuit school and University College, Dublin, where he studied modern languages and began writing. He became alienated from the Catholic religion and from Ireland, and in 1902 he left Dublin for Paris; he returned in 1903 to be with his mother, who was dying of cancer. From 1905 he lived in Trieste and Zurich, and from 1920 to 1939 as part of the vibrant colony of expatriate authors in Paris. Although he was not able to live in Ireland, all of his writings concern Ireland and his memories of it. His first book was a collection of poems, *Chamber Music*, published in 1907. His major collection of stories, *Dubliners*, appeared in 1914, followed in 1916 by the autobiographical novel that established his reputation as a major writer, *A Portrait of the Artist as a Young Man*. The novel regarded generally as his masterpiece, *Ulysses*, was published in 1922 in Paris. (*Ulysses* was not published in the United States until 1933 and not in England until 1937 because legal difficulties prohibited uncensored publication in those countries prior to that.) His final novel, *Finnegans Wake*, appeared in 1939. To escape

the German occupation of France, he returned that year to Zurich, where he had lived while writing *Ulysses*, and died there slightly more than a year later.

JOHN KEATS (1795–1821) was born in London. His father, a worker at a livery stable who married his employer's daughter and inherited the business, was killed by a fall from a horse when Keats was eight. When his mother died of tuberculosis six years later, Keats and his siblings were entrusted to the care of a guardian, a practical-minded man who took Keats out of school at fifteen and apprenticed him to a doctor. As soon as he qualified for medical practice in 1815, he abandoned medicine for poetry, which he had begun writing two years earlier. In 1818, the year he contracted tuberculosis, he also fell madly in love with a pretty, vivacious young woman named Fanny Brawne, whom he could not marry because of his poverty, illness, and devotion to poetry. In the midst of such stress and emotional turmoil, his masterpieces poured out between January and September 1819: the great odes, a number of sonnets, and several longer lyric poems. In February 1820, his health failed rapidly; he went to Italy in the autumn, in hopes that the warmer climate would improve his health, but he died there on February 23, 1821. His poems are rich with sensuous, lyrical beauty and emotional resonance, reflecting his delight in life as well as his awareness of life's brevity and difficulty.

JANE KENYON (1947–1995) was born in Ann Arbor, Michigan, and grew up in the Midwest. She earned her B.A. and M.A. from the University of Michigan. She was married to poet Donald Hall from 1972 until her death from leukemia in 1995. During her lifetime, she published four books of poetry — *From Room to Room* (1978), *The Boat of Quiet Hours* (1986), *Let Evening Come* (1990), and *Constance* (1993) — and a book of translation, *Twenty Poems of Anna Akhmatova* (1985). Two additional volumes were published after her death: *Otherwise: New and Selected Poems* (1996) and *A Hundred White Daffodils: Essays, Interviews, the Akhmatova Translations, Newspaper Columns, and One*

Poem (1999). At the time of her death, she was New Hampshire's poet laureate.

ETGAR KERET (b. 1967) was born in Ramat Gan, Israel, to parents who survived the Holocaust. He became a writer at nineteen while doing military service with the Israeli army. His first book, *Pipelines* (1992), a collection of short stories, was largely ignored but his second book, *Missing Kissinger* (1994), a collection of fifty very short stories, was a success. One of the stories in it, "Siren," is included in the curriculum for the Israeli matriculation exam in literature. He has become one of the best known writers in Israel, writing in both Hebrew and English. In addition to seven collections of short stories, he has published graphic fiction; a children's book; and a memoir, *Seven Good Years* (2015). He is also a scriptwriter and is actively involved in Israeli television and film. He lives in Tel Aviv and is a lecturer at Ben-Gurion University of the Negev and at Tel Aviv University.

JAMAICA KINCAID (b. 1949) was born Elaine Potter Richardson in St. Johns, Antigua, the West Indies, and completed her British-style secondary education there. She lived with her stepfather, a carpenter, and her mother until 1965, when she was sent to Westchester, New York, to work as an au pair. After working for three years and taking night classes at a community college, she attended Franconia College in New Hampshire for a year. Because her family disapproved of her writing, she changed her name to Jamaica Kincaid when she began publishing stories in magazines. Her work drew the attention of William Shawn, editor of the *New Yorker*, who hired her as a staff writer in 1976. For the next nine years, she wrote columns for the "Talk of the Town" section. In 1978, she first published a story in the *New Yorker*; it later became part of her first book, a collection entitled *At the Bottom of the River* (1984), which won the Morton Dauwen Zabel Award of the American Academy and Institute of Arts and Letters. She has also published five novels; several nonfiction books, including *A Small Place* (1988), about Antigua; and a memoir, *My Brother* (1997). She taught creative writing for many years at Bennington College and now teaches at Claremont McKenna College in Claremont, California, and at Harvard University.

YUSEF KOMUNYAKAA (b. 1947) was born and grew up in Bogalusa, Louisiana. He earned degrees at the University of Colorado; Colorado State University; and the University of California, Irvine. His numerous books of poems include *Neon Vernacular: New and Selected Poems, 1977–1989* (1994), for which he received the Pulitzer Prize and the Kingsley Tufts Poetry Award, and *Thieves of Paradise* (1998), which was a finalist for the National Book Critics Circle Award. Other publications include *Blues Notes: Essays, Interviews & Commentaries* (2000); *The Jazz Poetry Anthology* (coedited with J. A. Sascha Feinstein [1991]); and *The Insomnia of Fire* by Nguyen Quang Thieu (cotranslated with Martha Collins [1995]). He has taught at the University of New Orleans, Indiana University, and Princeton University, and currently is a professor in the creative writing program at New York University.

TED KOOSER (b. 1939) was born in Ames, Iowa. He received his B.A. from Iowa State University and his M.A. in English from the University of Nebraska–Lincoln. He is the author of twelve collections of poetry, including *Sure Signs* (1980); *One World at a Time* (1985); *Weather Central* (1994); *Winter Morning Walks: One Hundred Postcards to Jim Harrison* (2000), winner of the 2001 Nebraska Book Award for poetry; and *Delights & Shadows* (2004), winner of the 2005 Pulitzer Prize for Poetry. His most recent collection is *Splitting an Order* (2014). His fiction and nonfiction books include *Local Wonders: Seasons in the Bohemian Alps* (2002; winner of the Nebraska Book Award for Nonfiction in 2003), and *Braided Creek: A Conversation in Poetry* (2003), written with fellow poet and longtime friend Jim Harrison. His honors include two National Endowment for the Arts fellowships in poetry, a Pushcart Prize, the Stanley Kunitz Prize, and a merit award from the Nebraska Arts Council. He served as the United States Poet Laureate Consultant in Poetry to the Library of Congress from 2004 to 2006. He lives on acreage near the village of Garland, Nebraska and is a visiting professor in the English department of the University of Nebraska–Lincoln.

MAXINE KUMIN (1925–2014) was born in Philadelphia and received her B.A. and M.A.

at Radcliffe College. She published eighteen books of poetry, including *Up Country: Poems of New England* (1972), for which she received the Pulitzer Prize. Her most recent collections were *Where I Live: New and Selected Poems 1990–2010* (2010) and *And Short the Season* (2014). She also published two memoirs, *Inside the Halo and Beyond: The Anatomy of a Recovery* (2000) and *The Pawnbroker's Daughter* (2015); six novels; a collection of short stories; twenty-five children's books; and six books of essays. She served as Consultant in Poetry to the Library of Congress from 1981 to 1982 and as poet laureate of New Hampshire.

LI-YOUNG LEE (b. 1957) was born in Jakarta, Indonesia, to Chinese parents. His father, who had been personal physician to Mao Tse-tung, relocated his family to Indonesia, where he helped found Gamaliel University. In 1959, the Lee family fled the country to escape anti-Chinese sentiment, and they settled in the United States in 1964. Lee studied at the University of Pittsburgh, the University of Arizona, and the Brockport campus of the State University of New York. He has taught at several universities, including Northwestern University and the University of Iowa. He is the author of four collections of poetry — *Rose* (1986), which won the Delmore Schwartz Memorial Poetry Award; *The City in Which I Love You* (1991), which was the 1990 Lamont Poetry Selection; *Book of My Nights* (2001); and *Behind My Eyes* (2008) — and a memoir, *The Winged Seed: A Remembrance* (1995), which received an American Book Award from the Before Columbus Foundation. In his poems, one often senses a profound sense of exile, the influence of his father's presence, and a rich spiritual sensuousness.

DENISE LEVERTOV (1923–1997) was born in Ilford, Essex. Her mother was Welsh and her father was a Russian Jew who became an Anglican priest. She was educated at home and claimed to have decided to become a writer at the age of five. Her first book, *The Double Image* (1946), brought her recognition as one of a group of poets dubbed the "New Romantics." Her poems often blend the sense of an objective observer with the sensibility of a spiritual searcher. She moved to the United States after marrying the American writer

Mitchell Goodman. There she turned to free-verse poetry and, with her first American book, *Here and Now* (1956), she became an important voice in the American avant-garde. In the 1960s, she became involved in the movement protesting the Vietnam War. She went on to publish more than twenty collections of poetry, four books of prose, and three volumes of poetry in translation. From 1982 to 1993, she taught at Stanford University. She spent the last decade of her life in Seattle.

PHILIP LEVINE (1928–2015) was born in Detroit and received his degrees from Wayne State University and the University of Iowa. He is the author of twenty books of poetry, including *The Simple Truth* (1994), which won the Pulitzer Prize. He also published a collection of essays, *The Bread of Time: Toward an Autobiography* (1994); edited *The Essential Keats* (1987); and coedited and translated books of poetry by Spanish poet Gloria Fuertes and Mexican poet Jamie Sabines. He taught at many universities, including California State in Fresno; New York University; Columbia; Princeton; Brown; Tufts; and the University of California, Berkeley.

CLAUDE MCKAY (1890–1948), the son of poor farmworkers, was born in Sunny Ville, Jamaica. He was educated by his older brother, who possessed a library of English novels, poetry, and scientific texts. At age twenty, McKay published a book of verse in dialect called *Songs of Jamaica*, recording his impressions of black life in Jamaica. In 1912, he traveled to the United States to attend Tuskegee Institute. He soon left to study agriculture at Kansas State University. In 1914, he moved to Harlem and became an influential member of the Harlem Renaissance. After committing to communism and traveling to Moscow in 1922, he lived for some time in Europe and Morocco, writing fiction. McKay later repudiated communism, converted to Roman Catholicism, and returned to the United States. He published several books of poetry as well as an autobiography, *A Long Way from Home* (1937).

ANDREW MARVELL (1621–1678) was born in Hull, Yorkshire, and educated at Trinity College, Cambridge. After traveling in Europe, he worked as a tutor and in a government office (as assistant to John Milton) and later became a member of Parliament for Hull. Marvell was known in his lifetime as a writer of rough satires in verse and prose. His "serious" poetry, like "To His Coy Mistress" (p. 640), was not published until after his death. It is a famous exploration of the *carpe diem* theme (see the Glossary of Literary Terms, p. 1133).

ORLANDO RICARDO MENES (b. 1958) was born in Lima, Peru, to Cuban parents who immigrated to Miami when he was ten. He also spent two years in Spain in the early 1970s. He holds a B.A. and M.A. in English from the University of Florida and a Ph.D. from the University of Illinois at Chicago. His first collection of poetry, *Borderlands with Angels,* was winner of the 1994 Bacchae Press Chapbook Competition. He has also published *Rumba atop the Stones* (2001); *Furia* (2005); *Fetish* (2013, winner of the Prairie Schooner Book Prize); and *Heresies* (2015). He has also edited the volume *Renaming Ecstasy: Latino Writings on the Sacred* (2002). For years, photography was one of his passions, and in 1992, he had an exhibition of photographs at Books and Books in Miami Beach. He teaches in the creative writing program at the University of Notre Dame.

KATHERINE MIN (b. 1959) was born in Champaign-Urbana, Illinois, and grew up in Charlottesville, Virginia, and Clifton Park, New York. She graduated from Amherst College and the Columbia School of Journalism. Her short stories have appeared in numerous literary journals and anthologies. "Courting a Monk" (p. 394) won a Pushcart Prize in 1998. Her novel *Secondhand World* was selected as one of the best books of 2006 by *School Library Journal* and as one of the best debut novels of the year by the *Rocky Mountain News*, and was a winter guide pick on *MSNBC.com*. She has taught at Plymouth State University and in the Iowa Summer Writing Festival and currently teaches at the University of North Carolina Asheville.

GARY MIRANDA (b. 1938) was born in Bremerton, Washington, and grew up in the Pacific Northwest. After spending six years in a Jesuit seminary, he went on to do graduate work at San Jose State College and the University of California, Irvine. He is the author of three collections of poetry, *Listeners at the Breathing Place* (1978), *Grace Period* (1983), and *Turning Sixty* (2001), and has published a translation of Rainer Maria Rilke's *Duino Elegies* (1980). He lives in Portland, Oregon.

JANICE MIRIKITANI (b. 1941) was born in California, a Sansei or third-generation Japanese American. As an infant, she was interned with her family in Rohwer, Arkansas, during World War II. She has published five volumes of poetry (most recently *Out of the Dust* [2014]), and edited several anthologies of poetry, prose, and essays, among them *Ayumi: Japanese American Anthology* (1980) and *Watch Out, We're Talking: Speaking out about Incest and Abuse* (1993). She is the recipient of many awards and honors, including the American Book Lifetime Achievement Award for Literature, the Woman Warrior in Arts and Culture Award from the Pacific Asian-American Bay Area Women's Coalition, and the first Woman of Words Award from the Women's Foundation. Executive director of Glide Church and president of the Glide Foundation, she has lived in San Francisco since 1963 and was poet laureate of San Francisco from 2000 to 2002.

MARIANNE MOORE (1887–1972) was born near St. Louis and grew up in Carlisle, Pennsylvania. After studying at Bryn Mawr College and Carlisle Commercial College, she taught at a government Indian school in Carlisle. She moved to Brooklyn, where she became an assistant at the New York Public Library. She loved baseball and spent a good deal of time watching her beloved Brooklyn Dodgers. She began to write imagist poetry and to contribute to the *Dial*, a prestigious literary magazine. She served as acting editor of the *Dial* from 1925 to 1929 and later as editor for four years. Moore was widely recognized for her work, receiving among other honors the Bollingen Prize for Poetry, the National Book Award, and the Pulitzer Prize.

PAT MORA (b. 1942) was born and grew up in El Paso, Texas. She is a descendant of four Mexican grandparents who came to Texas during the Mexican Revolution of 1910 and during the early twentieth century. She earned degrees at Texas Western College and the University of Texas at El Paso. She has published more than thirty volumes of poetry, nonfiction, and children's picture books and received many awards for her work, including the Kellogg National Leadership Fellowship, four Southwest Book Awards, and the Premio Aztlan Literature Award. She has been a distinguished visiting professor at the University of New Mexico, a museum director, and a consultant for U.S.–Mexico youth exchanges. She has spent much of her teaching time working with young writers. Now retired but still teaching on her own, she lives in Santa Fe, New Mexico, and Cincinnati, Ohio.

DAVID MURA (b. 1952), a third-generation Japanese American, was born in Great Lakes, Illinois, and graduated from Grinnell College in Iowa; he did graduate work at the University of Minnesota and Vermont College. Mura is a poet, creative nonfiction writer, critic, playwright, and performance artist. He is author of numerous books of poetry, including *After We Lost Our Way* (1989), which was selected as a National Poetry Series winner; two novels; and two memoirs, *Turning Japanese: Memoirs of a Sansei* (1991), which was a *New York Times* Notable Book of the Year, and *Where the Body Meets Memory: An Odyssey of Race, Sexuality & Identity* (1996). His most recent poetry collection is *The Last Incantations: Poems* (2014).

MARILYN NELSON (b. 1946) was born in Cleveland, Ohio, and grew up on numerous military bases. Her father was a U.S. serviceman in the air force, one of the last Tuskegee Airmen, and her mother was a teacher. While still in elementary school, Nelson started writing. She earned her B.A. from the University of California, Davis; her M.A. from the University of Pennsylvania; and her Ph.D. from the University of Minnesota. *The Homeplace* (1990), *The Fields of Praise: New and Selected Poems* (1997), and *Carver: A Life in Poems* (2001) were all finalists for the National Book Award. Her most recent collection is *Faster Than Light: New and Selected Poems, 1996–2011* (2012). In addition to her many poetry collections for adults and children, she has translated from the Danish Halfdan Rasmussen's *Hundreds of*

Hens and Other Poems. She is founder and director of Soul Mountain Retreat, a writer's colony that encourages and supports poets who belong to underrepresented racial or cultural groups. She is professor emerita of English at the University of Connecticut and was poet laureate of Connecticut from 2001 to 2006.

DON NIGRO (b. 1949) was born in Malvern, Ohio. He received his B.A. in English from the Ohio State University and his M.F.A. in playwriting from the University of Iowa. He has written more than four hundred plays, twenty-eight of them produced off Broadway. Two of them, *The Dark Sonnets of the Lady* (1992) and *Anima Mundi* (1994), were nominated for the National Repertory Theatre Foundation's National Play Award. The film *The Manor* (1999) was adapted from his play *Ravenscroft* (1991). His works have been performed throughout the United States and Canada as well as in London and Budapest. He has been the James Thurber Writer in Residence at Thurber House and has taught at the Playwrights Workshop at the University of Iowa, as well as at Ohio State, Kent State, Indiana State, and the University of Massachusetts at Amherst.

NAOMI SHIHAB NYE (b. 1952) was born in St. Louis of a Palestinian father and an American mother and grew up in both the United States and Jerusalem. She received her B.A. from Trinity University in San Antonio, Texas, where she still resides with her family. She is the author of many books of poems, including *You and Yours* (2005), which received the Isabella Gardner Poetry Award. Nye has won many other awards and fellowships, among them four Pushcart Prizes, the Jane Addams Children's Book Award, and the Paterson Poetry Prize. She has also written short stories and books for children and has edited anthologies, several of which focus on the lives of children and represent work from around the world. She is a singer-songwriter and on several occasions has traveled to the Middle East and Asia for the U.S. Information Agency to promote international goodwill through the arts. Nye's work often attests to a universal sense of exile, from place, home, love, and one's self, and the way the human spirit confronts it.

JOYCE CAROL OATES (b. 1938) was born in Lockport, New York. She began storytelling in early childhood, composing picture stories even before she could write. Only after earning a B.A. from Syracuse University and an M.A. from the University of Wisconsin did she focus on writing as a career. Her first book was a collection of stories, *By the North Gate* (1963). Since then she has gone on to become one of the most versatile, prolific, and important American writers of her time, publishing more than a hundred books — novels, story collections, poetry, plays, children's books, and literary criticism. She has been nominated for the Nobel Prize for Literature three times. She is the Roger S. Berlind Distinguished Professor of Humanities, Professor of Creative Writing, emerita, at Princeton University.

TIM O'BRIEN (b. 1946) was born in Austin, Minnesota, and grew up in Worthington, Minnesota. He attended Macalester College in Minneapolis and, on graduation, was drafted for military service in Vietnam. He served from 1969 to 1970 as an infantry foot soldier in the Americal division, which was involved in the My Lai massacre in 1968, an event that figures prominently in O'Brien's novel *In the Lake of the Woods* (1994). While in Vietnam, he rose to the rank of sergeant and received the Purple Heart. After Vietnam, he entered graduate school at Harvard University but left to become a newspaper reporter, a career he pursued until the publication of his first book, *If I Die in a Combat Zone, Box Me Up and Ship Me Home* (1973). He has gone on to write several other novels, including *Going after Cacciato* (1978), which won the National Book Award. His collection of stories *The Things They Carried* (1990) was a finalist for the National Book Critics Circle Award and for the Pulitzer Prize, and winner of the Heartland Award from the *Chicago Tribune* and of the French prize for the best foreign book of the year; it was chosen by the *New York Times Book Review* as one of the nine best books of the year in all categories. He lives in Texas and teaches alternate years in the creative writing program at Texas State University.

FLANNERY O'CONNOR (1925–1964) was born in Savannah, Georgia. She earned her B.A. from Georgia State College for Women in Milledgeville, Georgia, and an M.F.A. from the University of Iowa Writers' Workshop. When she was twenty-five, she was found to have disseminated lupus, an incurable disease from which her father had died when she was thirteen. She returned to Milledgeville for treatments that slowed the progress of the disease. Living with her mother on the family dairy farm, she wrote in the mornings and rested, read, and carried on correspondence in the afternoons, and she traveled to give occasional lectures as health permitted. She published two novels, *Wise Blood* (1952) and *The Violent Bear It Away* (1960), and two collections of stories, *A Good Man Is Hard to Find* (1955) and *Everything That Rises Must Converge* (1965). A collection of lectures and essays, *Mystery and Manners* (1969) and a volume of correspondence, *The Habit of Being* (1979), were published posthumously. Despite her career being cut short, O'Connor is widely recognized as a major southern writer. Her short stories are generally considered to be her finest work; they are carefully crafted, often focusing on grotesque characters redeemed by grace; have a crisp humor; and reflect the influence of her Catholic faith. *Complete Stories*, a collection of the thirty-one stories she wrote, won the National Book Award for fiction in 1972.

SHARON OLDS (b. 1942) was born in San Francisco and educated at Stanford and Columbia universities. She has written twelve books of poetry and received numerous important prizes and awards, among them the 2013 Pulitzer Prize in Poetry for *Stag's Leap: Poems* (2012), the 1984 National Book Critics Circle Award, and the first San Francisco Poetry Center Award in 1980. She is known for writing intensely personal, emotional poetry that graphically depicts family life as well as global political events. "Sharon Olds is enormously self-aware," says critic David Leavitt. "Her poetry is remarkable for its candor, its eroticism, and its power to move." She lives in New York City and was New York State Poet from 1998 to 2000. She teaches in the graduate writing program at New York University.

MARY OLIVER (b. 1935) was born in Cleveland and educated at Ohio State University and

Vassar College. She is the author of some thirty volumes of poetry, including *American Primitive* (1983), which won the Pulitzer Prize, and four books of prose. Her most recent book is *Dog Songs: Poems* (2013). She held the Catharine Osgood Foster Chair for Distinguished Teaching at Bennington College until 2001 and now lives in Provincetown, Massachusetts. Oliver is one of the most respected among poets concerned for the natural world.

TILLIE OLSEN (1912?–2007) was born either near Mead, Nebraska, or in Omaha, Nebraska. Her parents were Jewish immigrants who fled from the Russian czarist repression after the revolution of 1905. In the 1920s, her father became a leader in the Nebraska Socialist Party. After the eleventh grade, she had to leave school to help support her family during the Great Depression. She joined the Young Communist League (YCL) and throughout her life was active politically, especially in causes rooted to her attachment to poor and oppressed workers. Early in 1932, she wrote four chapters of her first novel, *Yonnondio*. Part of one chapter was published as "The Iron Throat" in the *Partisan Review* in 1934 and was acclaimed critically. She wrote very little for the next two decades, during which she married, had a child, and had to care for the child alone, much as described in her story "I Stand Here Ironing" (p. 405). She then had three more children with Jack Olsen, a YCL comrade whom she moved in with in 1936 and married in 1944. When her youngest child entered school in 1953, she was able to take creative writing classes at San Francisco State College and Stanford University. "Tell Me a Riddle" won the O. Henry Award for Best Short Story of the Year (1961). It and three other stories were published in *Tell Me a Riddle* (1961), selected by *Time* magazine for its "best-ten-books" list in 1962. Olsen then went on to complete *Yonnondio* (1974) and a nonfiction work, *Silences* (1978). She played an important role in reclaiming the works of neglected women authors. Despite her limited literary output, she received wide recognition for the quality of her fiction and for the importance of her contributions to the feminist movement.

MICHAEL OPPENHEIMER (b. 1943) was born in Berkeley, California, and grew up on a cattle ranch in Colorado. He earned his undergraduate degree at Antioch College and his master's degree at University of San Francisco, Lone Mountain College. In addition to writing fiction, Oppenheimer has worked as a reporter, teacher, and publisher. He currently lives in Bellingham, Washington.

DANIEL OROZCO (b. 1958) grew up in San Francisco and received his B.A. from Stanford University and his M.F.A. from the University of Washington. He is best known for his short stories, which have appeared in anthologies such as the *Best American Essays*, *Best American Short Stories*, and *Best American Mystery Stories*, and in *Harper's*, *McSweeney's*, *Zoetrope*, and others. "Orientation" originally appeared in the *Seattle Review* and was included in *The Best American Short Stories 1995*. His first collection, *Orientation: And Other Stories*, was published in 2011. He is the recipient of a National Endowment for the Arts fellowship and a Whiting Writers' Award. He teaches in the creative writing program at the University of Idaho.

WILFRED OWEN (1893–1918) was born in Oswestry, Shropshire, and went to school at Birkenhead Institute and Shrewsbury Technical School. He studied at London University but was forced to withdraw for financial reasons. After that he went to Dunsden, Oxfordshire, as a vicar's assistant. At Dunsden, Owen grew disaffected with the church and left to teach in France. He enlisted in 1915 and six months later was hospitalized in Edinburgh, where he met Siegfried Sassoon, whose war poems had just been published. Owen was sent back to the front and was killed one week before the armistice. He is the most widely recognized of the "war poets," a group of World War I writers who brought the realism of war into poetry.

ZZ PACKER (b. 1973) was born in Chicago and grew up in Atlanta and Louisville. Her given name is *Zuwena*, Swahili for "good." After teachers kept mispronouncing her name, she began introducing herself as "ZZ" and, she says, "It just kind of stuck." She was nineteen when she published her first significant work in *Seventeen* magazine. She had planned to become an electrical engineer but decided to attend Yale University instead of Massachusetts Institute of Technology. She went on to earn an M.A. at Johns Hopkins and an M.F.A. from the University of Iowa Writers' Workshop. She was named a Stegner Fellow in Fiction at Stanford. Her first collection, *Drinking Coffee Elsewhere* (2003), was a finalist for the PEN/Faulkner Award. In 2010 she was selected for the *New Yorker*'s "20 under 40" fiction issue. She has served on the creative writing faculty or served as writer-in-residence at California College of the Arts, Tulane University, San Jose State University, the University of Texas at Austin, Vassar College, Texas State University, and Princeton University. Since 2013 she has taught creative writing at San Francisco State University.

SUSAN ATEFAT PECKHAM — See ATEFAT-PECKHAM.

SYLVIA PLATH (1932–1963) grew up in a middle-class family in Boston and showed early promise as a writer, having stories and poems published in magazines such as *Seventeen* while she was in high school. As a student at Smith College, she was selected for an internship at *Mademoiselle* magazine and spent a month working in New York in the summer of 1953. Upon her return home, she suffered a serious breakdown, attempted suicide, was institutionalized, and then returned to Smith College for her senior year in 1954. She received a Fulbright fellowship to study at Cambridge University in England, where she met poet Ted Hughes. They were married in 1956. They lived in the United States as well as England, and Plath studied under Robert Lowell at Boston University. Her marriage to Hughes broke up in 1962, and from her letters and poems, it appears that she was approaching another breakdown. On February 11, 1963, she committed suicide. Four books of poetry appeared during her lifetime, and her *Selected Poems* was published in 1985. The powerful, psychologically intense poetry for which she is best known was written after 1960, influenced by the "confessional" style of Lowell.

EDGAR ALLAN POE (1809–1849) was born in Boston. His parents were touring actors; both died before he was three years old, and he was taken into the home of John Allan, a prosperous merchant in Richmond, Virginia, and baptized Edgar Allan Poe. His childhood was uneventful, although he studied in England for five years (1815–1820). In 1826, he entered the University of Virginia but stayed for only a year because of gambling debts. He began to write and published a book of poems in 1827. He joined the army and gained an appointment to West Point but was dismissed after six months for disobeying orders. He turned to fiction writing and journalism to support himself. He began publishing stories and was appointed editor of the *Southern Literary Messenger* in Richmond, but his job was terminated after two years because of his drinking. He achieved success as an artist and editor in New York City (1837), then in Philadelphia (1838–1844), and again in New York (1844–1849) but failed to satisfy his employers and to secure a livelihood, and thus lived in or close to poverty his entire adulthood. He is famous for his horror tales and is credited with inventing the detective story, as well as for writing poetry with prominent use of rhythms, alliteration, and assonance that gives it a strongly musical quality.

KATHERINE ANNE PORTER (1890–1980), a descendant of Daniel Boone, was born in Indian Creek, Texas. When she was two, her mother died; she was raised by her grandmother and attended convent schools. At sixteen, she ran away to get married, but left her husband a few years later to be an actress. She worked briefly as a reporter in Chicago and Denver. Between 1918 and 1921, she became involved in revolutionary politics and worked as a journalist and teacher in Mexico, the setting for several of her stories. She traveled in the late 1920s to Europe, settling in Paris during the early 1930s, and began publishing stories in magazines. Her first book, *Flowering Judas and Other Stories* (1930), won high praise. It was followed by *Noon Wine* (1937), *Pale Horse, Pale Rider: Three Short Novels* (1939), and numerous other books of essays, stories, and nonfiction. Her only novel, *Ship of Fools* (1962), on which she worked for twenty years, was published when she was seventy-two. Her *Collected Stories* (1965) won the

Pulitzer Prize for Fiction and the National Book Award.

EZRA POUND (1885–1972) was born in Idaho but grew up outside Philadelphia and began studying at the University of Pennsylvania at the age of sixteen. He was fired from a teaching job at Wabash College and left for Europe, where he lived for the next few decades in Venice and London. There, Pound founded several literary movements — including imagism and Vorticism — and began his major work, the *Cantos*. During World War II he did radio broadcasts from Italy in support of Mussolini, for which he was indicted for treason in the United States. Judged mentally unfit for trial, he remained in an asylum in Washington, D.C., until 1958, when the charges were dropped. Pound spent his last years in Italy.

MARCO RAMIREZ (b. 1983) is a native of Miami, Florida. He was only eighteen, a high school senior, when his one-act play *Domino* was performed at Miami's Coconut Grove Playhouse in 2001. He twice won the Heideman Award given by the Humana Festival for New Plays at the Actors Theater of Louisville, once for *I Am Not Batman* (2007) and once for *3:59 A.M.* (2009). He is a graduate of the Juilliard School, where he studied under the instruction of playwrights Christopher Durang and Marsha Norman. He has had plays produced at the Kennedy Center, Julliard, the Arsht Center, Louisville's Humana Festival, and other venues.

DUDLEY RANDALL (1914–2002) was born in Washington, D.C., but lived most of his life in Detroit. His first published poem appeared in the *Detroit Free Press* when he was thirteen. He worked for Ford Motor Company and then for the U.S. Postal Service and served in the South Pacific during World War II. He graduated from Wayne State University in 1949 and then from the library school at the University of Michigan. In 1965, Randall established the Broadside Press, one of the most important publishers of modern black poetry. "Ballad of Birmingham" (p. 646), written in response to the 1963 bombing of a church in which four African American girls were killed, has been set to music and recorded. It became an "anthem" for many in the civil rights movement.

JACK RIDL (b. 1944) was born and grew up in New Wilmington, Pennsylvania. His father was a basketball coach and his mother had family connections with circuses throughout the United States. He has said that he spent his life watching the big shows from behind the scenes. He has published six collections of poetry — *The Same Ghost* (1984), *Be tween* (1988), *Poems from* The Same Ghost *and* Be tween (1993), *Broken Symmetry* (2006), *Losing Season* (2009), and *Practicing to Walk Like a Heron* (2013) — and three chapbooks: *After School* (1988); *Against Elegies* (0000), selected by BILLY COLLINS as winner of the Center for Book Arts 2001 Poetry Chapbook Competition; and *Outside the Center Ring* (2006). His poems have appeared in numerous anthologies and poetry journals. He taught at Hope College for thirty-four years before retiring in 2006; in 1996, he was named Michigan Professor of the Year by the Council for the Advancement and Support of Education.

ATSURO RILEY (b. 1960) grew up in South Carolina. His first book, *Romey's Order* (2010), received the Kate Tufts Discovery Award, *The Believer* Poetry Award, and a Witter Bynner Award from the Library of Congress. Riley's poetry has been called "percussive" because of a heavily stressed texture that is rich in consonants. The poems often focus on elemental images connected to the lives of those living in a particular landscape, whether Vietnam during the war or rural life in the South. His works have been compared to those of GERARD MANLEY HOPKINS in their range of intensities and rich attention to often overlooked detail. Riley has received a Pushcart Prize and the J. Howard and M. J. Wood Prize from *Poetry* magazine.

ALBERTO RÍOS (b. 1952) was born to a Guatemalan father and an English mother in Nogales, Arizona, on the Mexican border. He earned a B.A. in English and one in psychology and an M.F.A. at the University of Arizona. In addition to twelve books of poetry, the most recent being *A Small Story About the Sky* (2015), he has published three collections of short stories, and a memoir, *Capirotada: A Nogales Memoir* (1999). His work often fuses realism, surrealism, and magical realism, as exemplified by "Nani" (p. 648). Since 1994, he has been Regents Professor of English at Arizona State University, where he has taught since 1982 and holds the Katharine C. Turner Endowed Chair in English. In 2013, he was named Arizona's first poet laureate.

EDWIN ARLINGTON ROBINSON (1869–1935) was born in Head Tide, Maine, and grew up in the equally provincial Maine town of Gardiner, the setting for much of his poetry. He was forced to leave Harvard University after two years because of his family's financial difficulties. He published his first two books of poetry in 1896 and 1897 ("Richard Cory" [p. 532] appeared in the latter). For the next quarter-century, Robinson chose to live in poverty and write his poetry, supporting himself through temporary jobs and charity from friends. President Theodore Roosevelt, at the urging of his son Kermit, used his influence to get Robinson a sinecure in the New York Custom House in 1905, giving him time to write. He published numerous books of mediocre poetry in the next decade. The tide turned for him with *The Man against the Sky* (1916); the numerous volumes that followed received high praise and sold well. He was awarded three Pulitzer Prizes: for *Collected Poems* (1921), *The Man Who Died Twice* (1924), and *Tristram* (1927). Robinson was the first major American poet of the twentieth century, unique in that he devoted his life to poetry and willingly paid the price in poverty and obscurity.

LUIS J. RODRIGUEZ (b. 1954) was born in El Paso, Texas, but grew up in Watts and East Los Angeles, California. By eleven, he was already involved in gangs, and by the time he was eighteen, he had lost twenty-five friends to gang fights and killings. From this life came his best-selling memoir, *Always Running: La Vida Loca, Gang Days in L.A.* (1993), winner of the Carl Sandburg Award from the Friends of the Chicago Library Association. Rodriguez now lives in Chicago, where he is also a journalist and critic, his work appearing in a wide variety of national magazines. He is regarded as one of the leading Chicano writers in the country, with fourteen published books in memoir, fiction, nonfiction, children's literature, and poetry. He is also known for helping start community organizations, like Chicago's Guild Complex, one of the largest literary arts organizations in the Midwest; Humboldt Park Teen Reach in Chicago; and Tia Chucha Press, one of this country's premier small presses. He is a founder of Youth Struggling for Survival, a Chicago-based nonprofit working with gang and non–gang youth. He works as a gang intervention specialist in Los Angeles, Chicago, and other cities as well as in Mexico and Central America.

THEODORE ROETHKE (1908–1963) was the son of a commercial greenhouse operator in Saginaw, Michigan. As a child, he spent much time in the greenhouse, and the impressions of nature he formed there later influenced the subjects and imagery of his verse. Roethke graduated from the University of Michigan and studied at Harvard University. Although he published only eight books of poetry, they were held in high regard by critics, some of whom considered him among the best poets of his generation. *The Waking* was awarded the Pulitzer Prize in 1954; *Words for the Wind* (1958) received the Bollingen Prize and the National Book Award. He taught at many colleges and universities and gained a reputation as an exceptional teacher of poetry writing, though his career was interrupted several times by serious mental breakdowns.

MARY JO SALTER (b. 1954) was born in Grand Rapids, Michigan, and was raised in Detroit, Michigan, and Baltimore, Maryland. She earned her B.A. from Harvard, where she studied under ELIZABETH BISHOP, and her M.A. from Cambridge University. She is the author of six collections of poetry, most recently *Nothing by Design* (2013). She is often aligned with The New Formalists but has said that she is only interested in finding the appropriate way of saying something in a poem and that rhyme and meter please her and help her say what she wants to say. Salter often connects domestic concerns to locales both in this country and in Iceland, Italy, England, and France to reveal her confrontation with the ineffable. In addition to being a poet, Salter is an essayist, a playwright, and a lyricist. She worked as an editor at the *Atlantic Monthly* and *The New Republic*, and is a coeditor of *The Norton Anthology of Poetry*.

She taught at Mount Holyoke College from 1985 to 2007 and currently is a professor in the writing seminars program at Johns Hopkins University. She served as vice president of the Poetry Society of America from 1995 to 2007.

CARL SANDBURG (1878–1967) was born in Galesburg, Illinois, to Swedish immigrant working-class parents. He left school after the eighth grade; he entered college later and did well as a writer but did not take a degree. He traveled and worked at a variety of jobs, mostly in journalism, until he was able to support himself from his writing and lecturing (on Abraham Lincoln and Mary Todd Lincoln, as well as on poetry). He published more than fifty books in many genres — poetry, fiction, prose, biography, children's stories, autobiography — and won two Pulitzer Prizes: in 1940 for the second volume of his Lincoln biography, *Abraham Lincoln: The War Years* (1939), and in 1951 for *The Complete Poems of Carl Sandburg* (1950). Sandburg gave American poetry a needed direction and intensity through his hard-hitting, energetic, often politicized verse, which was more notable for its content than for its craft.

MARJANE SATRAPI (b. 1969) was born in Rasht, Iran, and grew up in Tehran in a family that was involved with communist and socialist movements prior to the Iranian Revolution. She attended the Lycée Français and witnessed the growing suppression of civil liberties, the fall of the shah, the rise of the Khomeini regime, and the first years of the Iran-Iraq War. She was sent to Vienna when she was fourteen to escape the dictatorial government. Her career began when she met the French comics artist David B. (pen name of Pierre-François Beauchard). She has become known worldwide through her autobiographical graphic novels. She also is a writer and illustrator of children's books. The animated film adaptation of *Persepolis* was nominated for an Academy Award for Best Animated Feature. Satrapi lives in Paris.

GEORGE SAUNDERS (b. 1958) was born in Amarillo, Texas, and grew up on the south side of Chicago. In 1981, he received a B.S. in geophysical engineering from Colorado School of Mines in Golden, Colorado, and an M.A. in creative writing from Syracuse University in 1989. His stories and essays have appeared in numerous magazines, particularly the *New Yorker*. He has published four collections of short fiction — *CivilWarLand in Bad Decline: Stories and a Novella* (1996), *Pastoralia* (2000), *In Persuasion Nation* (2006), and *Tenth of December* (2013); a novel, *The Brief and Frightening Reign of Phil* (2005); and a children's book, *The Very Persistent Gappers of Frip* (2000). He was chosen as one of the Top Twenty Writers Under Forty by the *New Yorker* in its Summer Fiction Issue for 1999. Among awards he has received are a MacArthur Fellowship and a Guggenhein Fellowship.

WILLIAM SHAKESPEARE (1564–1616) was born in Stratford-upon-Avon, England, where his father was a glovemaker and bailiff, and presumably went to grammar school there. He married Anne Hathaway in 1582, and sometime before 1592 he left for London to work as a playwright and an actor. Shakespeare joined the Lord Chamberlain's Men (later the King's Men), an acting company for which he wrote thirty-five plays, before retiring to Stratford around 1612. In addition to being a skillful dramatist, he was perhaps the finest lyric poet of his day, as exemplified by songs scattered through his plays, two early nondramatic poems (*Venus and Adonis* and *The Rape of Lucrece*), and the sonnet sequence expected of all noteworthy writers in the Elizabethan age. Shakespeare's sonnets were probably written in the 1590s, though they were not published until 1609.

PERCY BYSSHE SHELLEY (1792–1822) was born into a wealthy aristocratic family in Sussex County, England. He was educated at Eton and then went on to Oxford University but was expelled after six months for writing a defense of atheism, the first price he would pay for his nonconformity and radical (for his time) commitment to social justice. The following year he eloped with Harriet Westbrook, daughter of a tavern keeper, despite his belief that marriage was a tyrannical and degrading social institution (she was sixteen, he eighteen). He became a disciple of the radical social philosopher William Godwin; fell in love with

Godwin's daughter, Mary Wollstonecraft Godwin (later the author of *Frankenstein*); and went to live with her in France. Two years later, after Harriet committed suicide, Shelley and Godwin married and moved to Italy, where they shifted about restlessly and Shelley was generally short on money and in poor health. Under such trying circumstances, he wrote his greatest works. He died at age thirty, when the boat he was in was overturned by a sudden storm.

LESLIE MARMON SILKO (b. 1948) was born in Albuquerque of mixed Pueblo, Mexican, and white ancestry and grew up on the Laguna Pueblo Reservation in New Mexico. She earned her B.A. with honors from the University of New Mexico. In a long and productive writing career (she was already writing stories in elementary school), she has published poetry, novels, short stories, essays, letters, and film scripts. The best known of her works is her 1977 novel, *Ceremony*. She taught creative writing first at the University of New Mexico and later at the University of Arizona. She has been named a Living Cultural Treasure by the New Mexico Humanities Council and has received the Native Writers' Circle of the Americas Lifetime Achievement Award. She was awarded a MacArthur Foundation grant in 1981.

SOPHOCLES (496?–406 B.C.E.), born the son of a wealthy merchant in Athens, enjoyed the advantages of the thriving Greek Empire. He studied all of the arts. By the age of sixteen, he was known for his beauty and grace and was chosen to lead a choir of boys at a celebration of the victory of Salamis. He served as a statesman, general, treasurer, and priest as well as, with Aeschylus and Euripides, one of the three major authors of Greek tragedy. He was an accomplished actor and performed in many of his own plays. Fragments indicate that he wrote over 120 plays, of which only seven are extant. His plays introduced several innovations to Greek theater, particularly adding a third actor, which allowed for more dialogue and greater complexity of action and reduced the role of the chorus. He also changed the form of drama. Aeschylus had used three tragedies to tell a single story; Sophocles made

each play a complete and independent work, which required greater compression of action and resulted in greater dramatic intensity.

ART SPIEGELMAN (b. 1948) was born in Stockholm, Sweden, to Polish-Jewish refugees. He immigrated with his parents to the United States in his early childhood, grew up in Rego Park in Queens, New York, and graduated from the High School of Art and Design in Manhattan. His parents wanted him to be a dentist. He attended what is now Binghamton University and, although he did not graduate, thirty years later they awarded him an honorary doctorate. He credits Harvey Kurtzman, the creator of *Mad Magazine*, as his inspiration for creating comics. In the 1960s and 1970s, he was a major figure in the underground comics movement. He and his wife, Francoise Mouly, started the hugely influential magazine *Raw*, which first serialized *Maus*. *Maus* received unprecedented attention and critical acclaim, including an exhibition of it at the Museum of Modern Art and a special Pulitzer Prize in 1992. In 2005, *Time* magazine named Spiegelman one of their "Top 100 Most Influential People." He is an advocate for comics and has taught courses on the history and aesthetics of comics at schools such as the University of California, Santa Cruz, and the School of Visual Arts in New York City.

WILLIAM STAFFORD (1914–1995) was born in Hutchinson, Kansas, and studied at the University of Kansas and then at the University of Iowa Writers' Workshop. In between, he was a conscientious objector during World War II and worked in labor camps. In 1948, Stafford moved to Oregon, where he taught at Lewis and Clark College until he retired in 1980. His first major collection of poems, *Traveling through the Dark* (1962), was published when Stafford was forty-eight. It won the National Book Award in 1963. He went on to publish more than sixty-five volumes of poetry and prose and came to be known as a very influential teacher of poetry. From 1970 to 1971, he was Consultant in Poetry at the Library of Congress.

KELLY STUART (b. 1961) is a playwright and video artist originally from Los Angeles. She is the author of many highly successful plays, among them *Demonology* (1996), *Mayhem* (2004), *The Life of Spiders* (2005), and *The Disappearing World* (2007). She received a Guthrie New Play grant and commission, which enabled her to spend extensive time in eastern Turkey to research and write *Shadow Language* (2007), which deals with the Kurdish "problem," American idealism, and political asylum issues in the United States. She was the recipient of a Whiting Fellowship in 2000 (for *The Life of Spiders*), a 2004 artists' fellowship from the New York Foundation of the Arts, and the Armenian Dramatic Arts Alliance' Third Biennial William Saroyan Prize for Playwriting for *Belonging to the Sky* (2013). Stuart lives in New York and teaches playwriting at Columbia University.

SEKOU SUNDIATA (1948–2007) was born and raised in Harlem. His work was deeply influenced by the music, poetry, and oral traditions of African American culture. A self-proclaimed radical in the 1970s, for the past several decades he used poetry to comment on the life and times of our culture. His work, which encompasses print, performance, music, and theater, received praise for its fusion of soul, jazz, and hip-hop grooves with political insight, humor, and rhythmic speech. He regularly recorded and performed on tour with artists such as Craig Harris and Vernon Reid.

AMY TAN (b. 1952) was born in Oakland, California. Her father had been educated as an engineer in Beijing; her mother left China in 1949, just before the Communist revolution. After her father's death, Tan and her mother lived in Switzerland, where Tan attended high school. She received her B.A. and M.A. in English and linguistics from San Jose State University, took a job as a language development consultant to the Alameda County Association for Retarded Citizens, and later directed a training project for developmentally disabled children. She became a highly successful freelance business writer specializing in corporate communications for companies such as AT&T, IBM, and Pacific Bell, but she found the work unsatisfying and began writing fiction. A visit to China with her mother in 1987, and meeting relatives there, gave her the realization, as she put it, that "I belonged to my family and my family belonged to China." Inspired by LOUISE ERDRICH's *Love Medicine* (1986), she began to write stories about her own minority culture. A literary agent read one of them and secured her an advance that allowed her to write full-time, resulting in her very successful first book, *The Joy Luck Club* (1989). She has gone on to write six more novels; two children's books; and a collection of essays, *The Opposite of Fate: A Book of Musings* (2003). She is also the lead singer for the Rock Bottom Remainders, a rock band made up of fellow writers who make select appearances at charities and benefits that support free-speech issues.

ALFRED, LORD TENNYSON (1809–1892) was born in Somersby, Lincolnshire, and grew up there in the tense atmosphere of his unhappy father's rectory. He went to Trinity College, Cambridge, but was forced to leave because of family and financial problems, so he returned home to study and practice the craft of poetry. His early volumes, published in 1830 and 1832, received bad reviews, but his *In Memoriam* (1850), an elegy for his close friend Arthur Hallam, who died of a brain seizure, won acclaim. He was unquestionably the most popular poet of his time (the "poet of the people") and arguably the greatest of the Victorian poets. He succeeded WILLIAM WORDSWORTH as poet laureate, a position he held from 1850 until his death.

DYLAN THOMAS (1914–1953) was born in Swansea, Wales, and after grammar school became a journalist. He worked as a writer for the rest of his life. His first book of poetry, *Eighteen Poems*, appeared in 1934 and was followed by *Twenty-five Poems* (1936), *Deaths and Entrances* (1946), and *Collected Poems* (1952). His poems are often rich in textured rhythms and images. He also wrote prose, chiefly short stories collectively appearing as *Portrait of the Artist as a Young Dog* (1940), and a number of film scripts and radio plays. His most famous work, *Under Milk Wood*, written as a play for voices, was first performed in New York on May 14, 1953. Thomas's radio broadcasts and his lecture tours and poetry readings in the United States brought him fame and popularity. Alcoholism contributed to his early death in 1953.

JAMES THURBER (1894–1961), born in Columbus, Ohio, was an American cartoonist, author, journalist, and playwright, best known for cartoons and stories published in the *New Yorker* magazine. He attended the Ohio State University, although he did not graduate because partial blindness prevented him from completing a required ROTC course. After living in France for several years, he moved to New York and worked for the *New Yorker* from 1926 until 1935. His cartoons were featured regularly and made the cover art six times. Thurber published nearly forty books, including five children's books. His first book, *Is Sex Necessary? or, Why You Feel The Way You Do* (1929), was written with fellow *New Yorker* staff member E. B. White. He won a Tony Award for the Broadway play *A Thurber Carnival* (1960), in which he starred as himself.

ALISON TOWNSEND (b. 1953) was born in Pennsburg, Pennsylvania, and grew up there and in rural New York State. She earned her B.A. at Marlboro College, and her M.F.A. at Vermont College of Fine Arts. She has published four collections of poetry: *What the Body Knows (2002), The Blue Dress (2003), And Still the Music (2007),* and *Persephone in America* (2009), which won the Crab Orchard Open Competition Poetry Prize. Her poetry and essays appear widely, in journals such as *Chautauqua, Feminist Studies, Parabola, Quarter After Eight, The Southern Review,* and *Zone Three,* and she had "Notable Essays" mentioned in *Best American Essays 2014* and *2015.* She has received many awards, including a Pushcart Prize, publication in *Best American Poetry,* a Wisconsin Arts Board literary fellowship, and the University of Wisconsin–Whitewater's 2013 Chancellor's Regional Literary Award. She is Emerita Professor of English at the University of Wisconsin–Whitewater, and lives on four acres of prairie and oak savanna in the farm country outside Madison, Wisconsin. She is completing a collection of personal essays, *The Name for Woman is River: Body. Memory, and the Landscapes of Home.*

NATASHA TRETHEWEY (b. 1966) was born in Gulfport, Mississippi. She has degrees from the University of Georgia, Hollins University, and the University of Massachusetts at Amherst. She has won many awards for her poetry, including the inaugural Cave Canem Poetry Prize for her first collection, *Domestic Work* (2000). Her second collection, *Bellocq's Ophelia* (2002), received the 2003 Mississippi Institute of Arts and Letters Book Prize and was a finalist for both the Academy of American Poets' James Laughlin and Lenore Marshall prizes. In 2007, her collection *Native Guard* received the Pulitzer Prize. *Beyond Katrina: A Meditation on the Mississippi Gulf,* a book of poetry, essays, and letters, was published in 2010. Her most recent poetry collection is *Thrall* (2012). She has taught at Auburn University, the University of North Carolina, and Duke University. In 2009–2010, she was the James Weldon Johnson Fellow in African American Studies at Yale University's Beinecke Rare Books and Manuscript Library. She currently is the Robert W. Woodruff Professor of English and Creative Writing at Emory University, where she also directs the creative writing program. She served as United States Poet Laureate Consultant in Poetry to the Library of Congress from 2012 to 2014.

QUINCY TROUPE (b. 1939) was born in New York City and grew up in St. Louis, Missouri. He is the author of nineteen books, including eight volumes of poetry, most recently *The Architecture of Language* (2006). He is recipient of two American Book Awards, for his collection of poetry *Snake-Back Solos* (1980) and his nonfiction book *Miles the Autobiography* (1989). In 1991, he received the prestigious Peabody Award for writing and coproducing the seven-part Miles Davis Radio Project that aired on National Public Radio in 1990. *Transcircularities: New and Selected Poems* (2002) received the Milt Kessler Award for 2003 and was a finalist for the Paterson Poetry Prize. Troupe has taught at the University of California, Los Angeles; Ohio University; the College of Staten Island (CUNY); Columbia University (in the graduate writing program); and the University of California, San Diego. He is now professor emeritus of creative writing and American and Caribbean literature at the University of California, San Diego. He is the founding editorial director of *Code* magazine and former artistic director of "Arts on the Cutting Edge," a reading and performance series at the Museum of Contemporary Art, San Diego. He was the first official poet laureate of the state of California, appointed to the post in 2002 by Governor Gray Davis.

JOHN UPDIKE (1932–2009) was born in Reading, Pennsylvania, but grew up in the small nearby city of Shillington. He earned his B.A. at Harvard University, where he contributed to and later edited the *Harvard Lampoon*. He spent 1954–1955 at the Ruskin School of Drawing and Fine Arts in Oxford, England, then worked at the *New Yorker* until 1957, when he left to become a full-time writer. In 1959, he published his first book of stories, *The Same Door*, and his first novel, *The Poorhouse Fair*, and he moved from New York City to Massachusetts, where he lived most of the time until his death. A prolific writer, Updike published over sixty books — novels, collections of poems, short stories, essays, criticism, and a memoir. He received numerous awards, including the National Medal of Art and the National Medal for the Humanities. Two of his novels, *Rabbit Is Rich* (1981) and *Rabbit at Rest* (1990), won Pulitzer Prizes.

ALICE WALKER (b. 1944) was born in Eatonton, Georgia. Her parents were sharecropper farmers. When she was eight, she lost sight in one eye when one of her older brothers accidentally shot her with a BB gun. She was valedictorian of her high school class. Encouraged by her teachers and her mother to continue her education, she attended Spelman College in Atlanta, a school for black women, for two years, and graduated from Sarah Lawrence College. From the mid-1960s to the mid-1970s, she lived in Tougaloo, Mississippi. She was active in the civil rights movement of the 1960s and remains an involved activist today. Her first book was a collection of poetry, *Once* (1968). She is a prolific writer, having gone on to publish over thirty books of poetry, novels, short stories, and nonfiction. Her best-known novel, *The Color Purple* (1982), won the American Book Award and the Pulitzer Prize for Fiction and was made into a motion picture directed by Steven Spielberg.

WALT WHITMAN (1819–1892) was born in rural Long Island, the son of a farmer and carpenter. He attended grammar school in Brooklyn and took his first job as a printer's errand boy for the *Long Island Patriot*. Attending the opera; dabbling in politics; participating in street life; and gaining experience as student, printer, reporter, writer, carpenter, farmer, seashore observer, and teacher provided the bedrock for his future poetic vision of an ideal society based on the realization of self. Although Whitman liked to portray himself as uncultured, he read widely in the King James Bible, WILLIAM SHAKESPEARE, Homer, Dante, Aeschylus, and SOPHOCLES. He worked for many years in the newspaper business and began writing poetry only in 1847. In 1855, at his own expense, Whitman published the first edition of *Leaves of Grass*, a thin volume of twelve long untitled poems. Written in a highly original and innovative free verse, influenced significantly by music and with a wide-ranging subject matter, the work seemed strange to most of the poet's contemporaries, but they did recognize its value: Ralph Waldo Emerson wrote to him, less than three weeks after Whitman sent him a copy, "I greet you at the beginning of a great career." He spent much of the remainder of his life revising and expanding this book. *Leaves of Grass* today is considered a masterpiece of world literature, marking the beginning of modern American poetry. Whitman is widely regarded as America's national poet.

WILLIAM CARLOS WILLIAMS (1883–1963) was born in Rutherford, New Jersey; his father was an English emigrant and his mother was of mixed Basque descent from Puerto Rico. He decided to be both a writer and a doctor while in high school in New York City. He graduated from the medical school at the University of Pennsylvania, where he was a friend of EZRA POUND and Hilda Doolittle. After an internship in New York, Williams practiced general medicine in Rutherford, writing poems between seeing patients. His first book of poems was published in 1909, and he subsequently published poems, novels, short stories, plays, criticism, and essays. Initially one of the principal poets of the imagist movement, Williams sought later to invent an entirely fresh — and distinctly American — poetic sensibility, whose subject matter was centered on the everyday circumstances of life and the lives of common people. Williams, like Wallace

Stevens, became one of the major poets of the twentieth century and exerted great influence on poets of his own and later generations.

AUGUST WILSON (1945–2005) — See page 729.

WILLIAM WORDSWORTH (1770–1850) was born and raised in the Lake District of England. Both of his parents died by the time he was thirteen. He studied at Cambridge University, toured Europe on foot, and lived in France for a year during the first part of the French Revolution. He returned to England, leaving behind a lover, Annette Vallon, and their daughter, Caroline, from whom he was soon cut off by war between England and France. He met Samuel Taylor Coleridge, and in 1798, they together published *Lyrical Ballads*, the first great work of the English Romantic movement. He changed poetry forever by his decision to use common language in his poetry instead of artificial poetic diction (see the Glossary of Literary Terms, p. 1144). In 1799, he and his sister Dorothy moved to Grasmere, in the Lake District, where he married Mary Hutchinson, a childhood friend. His greatest works were produced between 1797 and 1808. He continued to write for the next forty years but never regained the heights of his early verse. In 1843, he was named poet laureate, a position he held until his death in 1850.

XU XI (b. 1954) was born in Hong Kong and lived there until her mid-twenties. She started writing stories in English when she was a child. She earned a B.A. in English from the State University of New York at Plattsburgh and an M.F.A. in fiction from the University of Massachusetts at Amherst. She pursued a career in international marketing for eighteen years, working for several major multinationals, while also writing and publishing fiction. She is the author of nine books of fiction and essays, and editor or coeditor of three anthologies of Hong Kong writing in English. Her most recent novel, *Habit of a Foreign Sky* (2010), was short-listed for the inaugural Man Asian Literary Prize. Other awards include an O. Henry Prize, a New York State Foundation of the Arts fiction fellowship, a *Ploughshares* Cohen award for best story, first place in a short story contest by *South China*

Morning Post, among others. She has taught creative writing and lectured on global culture at universities in Asia, the United States, and Europe. She is faculty chair at Vermont College of Fine Arts M.F.A. in Writing and has been a member of the prose faculty since 2002.

WILLIAM BUTLER YEATS (1865–1939) was born in Sandymount, Dublin, to an Anglo-Irish family. On leaving high school in 1883, he decided to be an artist, like his father, and attended art school, but he soon gave it up to concentrate on poetry. His first poems were published in 1885 in the *Dublin University Review*. Religious by temperament but unable to accept orthodox Christianity, Yeats explored throughout his life esoteric philosophies in search of a tradition that would substitute for a lost religion. He became a member of the Theosophical Society and the Order of the Golden Dawn, two groups interested in Eastern occultism, and later developed a private system of symbols and mystical ideas. Through the influence of Lady Gregory, a writer and promoter of literature, he became interested in Irish nationalist art, helping to found the Irish National Theatre and the famous Abbey Theatre. He was actively involved in Irish politics, especially after the Easter Rising of 1916. He continued to write and to revise earlier poems, leaving behind, at his death, a body of verse that, in its variety and power, placed him among the greatest twentieth-century poets of the English language. He was awarded the Nobel Prize for Literature in 1923.

KEVIN YOUNG (b. 1970) was born and raised in Lincoln, Nebraska. He received his B.A. from Harvard, where he took poetry workshops from Seamus Heaney. After holding a Stegner Fellowship in Poetry at Stanford University, he earned an M.F.A. in creative writing from Brown University. Young has published eight books of poetry, among them *Jelly Roll* (2003), a finalist for the National Book Award, and *Ardency: A Chronicle of the Amistad Rebels* (2011). His most recent books are a collection of essays, *The Grey Album: On the Blackness of Blackness* (2012), and a book of poems, *Book of Hours* (2014). He is also an editor of several anthologies, including *The Hungry Ear: Poems of Food and Drink* (2012). He has taught at the University of Georgia;

Indiana University; and Emory University, where he is Atticus Haygood Professor of Creative Writing and English and Curator of Literary Collections at the Raymond Danowski Poetry Library. His poetry is often celebrated for his way of working with the story and music inherent in the oral tradition.

RAY A. YOUNG BEAR (b. 1950) was born and grew up in the Mesquakie Tribal Settlement near Tama, Iowa. His poetry has been influenced by his maternal grandmother, Ada Kapayou Old Bear, and his wife, Stella L. Young Bear. He attended Pomona College in California as well as Grinnell College, the University of Iowa, Iowa State University, and Northern Iowa University. He has taught creative writing and Native American literature at the Institute of American Indian Art, Eastern Washington University, the University of Iowa, and Iowa State University. Young Bear and his wife cofounded the Woodland Song and Dance Troupe of Arts Midwest in 1983. Young Bear's group has performed traditional Mesquakie music in this country and the Netherlands. Author of five books of poetry, a collection of short stories, and a novel, he has contributed to contemporary Native American poetry and to the study of it for nearly five decades.

Appendix on Scansion

This appendix returns to the use of meter in poetry, extending the discussion begun in Chapter 18. We say in that chapter that meter forms an important component of rhythm for poems using it, especially ones having a regular beat created by a repeating pattern of stressed and unstressed syllables. In Chapter 18, we indicate the beat in metrical lines by using capital letters for stressed syllables (i AM bic ME ter GOES like THIS) to show that you can hear meter by listening for the stressed (louder) syllables, those that get more emphasis than the unstressed syllables. That's the important thing for readers beginning to read poetry attentively: hearing a steady beat when it's present and being able to distinguish poetry that has such a beat from poetry that does not. As you read more poetry, however, you may want to deal with meter in a more sophisticated way. This appendix introduces the traditional system of scansion and shows how metrical analysis contributes to a fuller understanding and appreciation of a poem written in meter.

Here is a brief review of some basic concepts and terminology introduced in Chapter 18. Go back to pages 544–62 to review them if you need to.

FOOT   A two- or three-syllable metrical unit made up (usually) of one stressed and one or two unstressed syllables. The most important metrical feet are these:

> *Iamb:* unstressed, stressed: da DA (for example, "awake")
> *Trochee:* stressed, unstressed: DA da ("wakeful")
> *Anapest:* unstressed, unstressed, stressed: da da DA ("in a dream")
> *Dactyl:* stressed, unstressed, unstressed: DA da da ("sleepily")
> *Spondee:* stressed, stressed: DA DA ("dream house")

LINE LENGTH   Line lengths are measured by the number of feet in the line and are labeled with names derived from Greek roots:

> *Trimeter:* a line with three metrical feet
> *Tetrameter:* a line with four metrical feet
> *Pentameter:* a line with five metrical feet
> *Hexameter:* a line with six metrical feet

These are the most common line lengths; more rare are monometer (one foot) and heptameter (seven).

The meter in a poem is highlighted and clarified through a process called **scansion**. To scan a poem involves marking its stressed syllables—whether the stress is heavy or light—with an accent mark (´) and marking its unstressed syllables with a curved line (˘). A vertical line indicates the way the lines divide into feet. You don't need to distinguish stronger from weaker stresses—only syllables that receive at least *some* stress from those that receive *none*.

Ĭám | bĭc mé | tĕr góes | líke thís.[1]

You then describe (or label) the type of foot used most often in the line and the line length—in this case, iambic tetrameter.

The ideal way to scan a poem is to listen for where you stress syllables, when reading with a natural emphasis, not a singsong regularity. Where *you* stress syllables is important: Scansion is not a mechanical process; it involves your interpretation. Scansion reflects the way a poem actually is read and so will differ slightly from one reader to another. Practice hearing the stresses as a recurring background beat, somewhat like the bass guitar or drums. But do not emphasize the beat; instead, concentrate on the words as you feel the beat underneath them.

You can use logic to do a rough but generally adequate scansion. First, start with multisyllabic words, using a dictionary if necessary to put ´ on the accented syllables and ˘ on the unaccented ones. Then put stress marks on important shorter words (most nouns and verbs, for example). Rhyming syllables almost always are stressed. Helping words (such as *a, an, to*) are rarely stressed and can safely be given ˘ marks. Just examining a poem thoughtfully will show where at least three-fourths of the stressed or unstressed syllables fall. The remainder can be sounded or figured out: For example, in ˘˘ ? ˘˘, the ? will almost surely be stressed; five unstressed syllables in a row would be very unusual. After such an analysis, read the poem aloud to test how well the stress patterns you identified match what you hear.

To begin practicing scansion, read the following stanza, which describes the setting of the island of Shalott in the days of King Arthur.

---

[1]In dividing lines into feet, begin by looking for the way that yields the greatest number of identical groupings of twos or threes because most feet in a poem will be the same; then figure out the exceptions.

Notice that dividing lines into feet may involve breaking up words. Feet work primarily with syllables, not words. However, in a line like "Evening traffic homeward burns" (from Yvor Winters's "Before Disaster"), which could be scanned as either iambic or trochaic, trochaic seems preferable because it keeps the words together ("Évenĭng | tráffĭc | hómewărd | búrns" rather than "Éve | nĭng tráf | fĭc hóme | wărd búrns").

Alfred, Lord Tennyson 1809–1892

From The Lady of Shalott   [1832]

On either side the river lie
Long fields of barley and of rye,
That clothe the wold° and meet the sky;   *plain*
And through the field the road runs by
To many-tower'd Camelot;   5
And up and down the people go,
Gazing where the lilies blow
Round an island there below,
The island of Shalott.

Now read it again, the way we have scanned the lines:

On éi | ther síde | the rí | ver líe
Long fields | of bár | ley and² | of rýe,
That clóthe | the wóld | and méet | the ský;
And thróugh | the fíeld | the róad | runs bý
To ma | ny-tów | er'd Cá | melot;
And úp | and dówn | the péo | ple gó,
Gáz | ing whére | the líl | ies blów
Róund | an ís | land thére | belów,
The ís | land óf | Shalott.

Notice how several metrical substitutions control emphasis and make
the sound natural, not artificially "poetic." Lines 1, 3, 5, and 6 are in regular iambic feet and have the important role of establishing the prevailing
"beat," but line 2 begins with a spondee ("Long fields"), and lines 7 and 8
lack the opening, unstressed syllable; unlike the opening six lines, they
begin with a stressed syllable and have only seven syllables, instead of eight.

For practice, try scanning the following lines. Mark the stressed sylla-
bles with ´ and unstressed syllables with ˘, and use | to divide lines into
feet. Try first to do it by hearing the beat; if that doesn't work, figure it out
logically, following the steps we suggest above. To compare your result with
the way we scanned it, see page 1094.

---

²A reversed accent [`] can be used for a very lightly stressed syllable, such as the slight
stress a normally unstressed word (like *and*) receives when its position in a line calls for it.

Samuel Taylor Coleridge 1772–1834

Metrical Feet [1806]

Lesson for a Boy

Trochee trips from long to short.
From long to long in solemn sort
Slow Spondee stalks; strong foot! yet ill able
Ever to come up with Dactyl trisyllable.
Iambics march from short to long; — 5
With a leap and a bound the swift Anapests throng.

To illustrate further, we will consider what scansion might add to our understanding and enjoyment of the following poem. Read it twice, once silently, once aloud, listening for the beat. Then, without looking ahead to our scansion on page 1090, scan the poem, marking the stressed and unstressed syllables and dividing the lines into feet.

Richard Lovelace 1618–1657

To Lucasta, Going to the Wars [1649]

Tell me not, Sweet, I am unkind,
   That from the nunnery
Of thy chaste breast and quiet mind
   To war and arms I fly.

True, a new mistress now I chase, 5
   The first foe in the field;
And with a stronger faith embrace
   A sword, a horse, a shield.

Yet this inconstancy is such
   As you too shall adore; 10
I could not love thee, dear, so much,
   Loved I not honor more.

On page 1090 is the way we scanned it. Compare your scansion with ours. Ours isn't the "right" way — it's our way; it's what we hear when we read the poem aloud. If your scansion is different from ours, test yours by listening to yourself read the line aloud and make sure you have marked the syllables the way you actually read them. Then decide which way of reading you prefer.

Tèll me | nót, Swéet, | Í am | ŭnkínd,
　That frŏm | thĕ nún |nĕrý
Ŏf thy̆ | cháste bréast | ănd qúi | ĕt mínd
　Tŏ wár | ănd árms | Ĭ flý.
Trúe, ă | néw mĭs | trèss nŏw | Ĭ cháse,   5
　The fírst | fŏe ín | thĕ fíeld;
Ănd wíth | ă stróng | ĕr faíth | ĕm brăce
　Ă swórd, | ă hórse, | ă shíeld.
Yĕt thís | ĭncón | stăncý | ĭs súch
　Ăs yóu | tŏo shăll | ădóre;   10
Ĭ cóuld | nŏt lóve | thĕe, déar, | sŏ múch,
　Lóved Í | nŏt hón | ŏr móre.

Often it's difficult to tell from the first line of a poem what its prevailing meter is. The metrical pattern emerges later. That's the case with "To Lucasta." It opens with a trochee, a spondee, a trochee, and an iamb. The effect is to start the poem off in a conversational tone as the speaker, about to leave for military service, explains his departure to the woman he loves. The stressed syllables put emphasis on the important words: "Tell," "not," "I," and "un-kind." The speaker begs to be heard but above all to be understood.

The next three lines establish that the prevailing meter is iambic, in alternating tetrameter and trimester lines. Lines 2 and 4 are regular iambic trimeter lines, and line 3 would be regular iambic tetrameter except for the substituted spondee in the second foot, which puts added emphasis on his lover's "chaste breast." The first stanza flows easily, conversationally, without a full stop until the end of line 4. The regular meter and smooth rhythm reinforce the contrast between the regular life of faith, peace, chastity, and quiet, and the sudden introduction in line 4 of "war" and "arms," to which he, unaccountably, is about to fly.

The irregular metrics of lines 5 and 6 coincide with the irregularity of the situation. Our ears by now have become accustomed to iambs, and we begin to expect them, so we are jolted by two irregular lines: trochee, spondee, iamb, iamb, then iamb, trochee, iamb. But the metrics fit the meaning, irregular meter expressing an irregular thought: that he is pursuing a new mistress and expects his lover to find that acceptable in spite of her "chaste breast" and "quiet mind." The speaker feels sufficiently confident of her agreement that he returns to regular iambics to describe his new faithfulness in lines 7 and 8, to reinforce the thought that his embracing of "A sword, a horse, a shield" is a "regular" idea. The rhythm of this stanza is slower than the first stanza, with lots of brief pauses signaled by commas and a semicolon (caesuras). Also, the alliterating "f" sounds make line 6 slower because they are hard to say together, and the list in line 8, with its two commas, contributes to making the stanza sound thoughtful and a bit hesitant.

Accepting inconstancy as constant is a paradox, set up by the spondee opening the third stanza, "Yet this," and the rhythm of lines 9 and 10 is unbroken and assertive. The truth and urgency of both sides of the paradox are reinforced by spondees in three successive lines: In line 10, the speaker asserts that she "too shall" not just accept his decision but, like him, will "adore" it once she understands it. In line 11 the speaker uses a spondee to affirm his unchanged devotion to her: He continues to "love thee, dear," as the three successive stressed syllables convey. And the last line uses a spondee ("Loved I") to set up the decisive point that the honor that requires him to fight is the same honor that enables her to trust in the faithfulness of his devotion to her. The eight monosyllabic words in line 11 march slowly, forcefully, into the final line, which the speaker believes (rightly? wrongly?) will be totally persuasive to his lover.

Let's try this now on a more complex passage, a famous speech from Shakespeare's tragedy *Macbeth* (5.5.19–28). It occurs when Macbeth nears the end of his life. His evil deeds have been found out, his opponents are closing in on his castle, and he is told that his wife has just committed suicide. Full of grief and despair, Macbeth utters a bleak assessment of human existence. Read the passage and then scan it yourself before looking at the way we did it:

Tomorrow, and tomorrow, and tomorrow
Creeps in this petty pace from day to day
To the last syllable of recorded time,
And all our yesterdays have lighted fools
The way to dusty death. Out, out, brief candle!   5
Life's but a walking shadow, a poor player
That struts and frets his hour upon the stage
And then is heard no more. It is a tale
Told by an idiot, full of sound and fury,
Signifying nothing.   10

Here is the way we scan the lines, but it is important to realize that this is not *the one correct* way to scan it. Differences in pronunciation and interpretation can lead to entirely acceptable differences in scansion of a poem. (Acceptable differences do not include mispronunciations. You may need to look up pronunciations, as well as definitions, of unfamiliar words to be fair both to the sound and to the meaning of a poem.)

Tomor | row, and | tomor | row, and | tomorrow
Creeps in | this pet | ty pace | from day | to day
To the last | sylla | ble of | record | ed time,
And all | our yes | terdays | have light | ed fools
The way | to dust | y death. | Out, out, | brief can | dle!   5

Life's but| a walk| ing shad| ow, a poor| player
That struts| and frets| his hour| upon| the stage
And then| is heard| no more.| It is| a tale
Told by an| idiot,| full of| sound and| fury,
Signi| fying| nothing.   10

The passage, like much of the poetry in Shakespeare's plays, is written in **blank verse** (unrhymed iambic pentameter). The first line is regular, except for the extra unstressed syllable on the final iamb. That syllable, together with the two caesuras and the time it takes to say each "tomorrow," lengthens the line and slows it down so that rhythmically it creeps, the way Macbeth says life does. Stressing "and" twice adds to the sense of circularity and monotony that Macbeth finds in life.

The second line begins with one of the most common metric substitutions, an initial trochee instead of an iamb, which puts extra emphasis on the key word *creeps*. That the rest of the line is regular echoes the steady, plodding pace by which life proceeds, and it sets up the irregular, unexpected anapest and trochee of the first half of line 3 — to think of the very end, the final millisecond, of history ("recorded time") is jolting, and the meter jolts us as well. After two irregular lines, the expected, regular iambics return for the rest of line 3, all of line 4, and half of line 5, again suiting the steady, plodding pace by which Macbeth says that people follow one another through life toward death, the past like a lantern lighting the way as people foolishly imitate what those before them have done.

The rest of line 5 is irregular: two spondees and an extra unstressed syllable: "Out, out, | brief candle!" Although life may seem to plod, it is short; Macbeth expresses the wish that his would end. The double stresses of the spondees, emphasized by the caesuras that make one linger, give strength to the words "Out, out," and another spondee with an extra syllable and a definite end stop make us dwell on "brief candle!" The rhythm, which had been slow but steady, becomes broken and forceful here and in the following line. Line 6 also is irregular and unusual — a trochee, two iambs, an anapest, and a trochee. This is an unusual metrical combination, difficult to enunciate, just as its thought (that there is no reality, that life is empty and meaningless) is difficult for most people to accept. That slow, contorted line rhythmically leads into a line and a half that are metrically regular, reestablishing the expected meter. The mostly monosyllabic words, full of stops and fricatives, seem almost drumlike, booming their assertions about the brevity and unreality of people's stage-play lives: "That STRUTS and FRETS his HOUR upON the STAGE / And THEN is HEARD no MORE."

After the full-stop caesura, the iambs continue for two feet, but the drum disappears with the lightly stressed "is." But these quieter, softer lines ("It is | a tale / Told by an | idiot, | full of | sound and | fury, / Signi | fying | nothing") are perhaps even more intense than those before them because they describe life as having no more shape and significance than the babblings of an insane person. The meter in lines 9 and 10—two dactyls and six trochees—is madly unusual and amazingly effective. Emphasis on "tale | Told" is heightened by stressing both and linking them by alliteration. The two dactyls, "Told by an idiot," can only be read slowly, with difficulty, which places unmissable emphasis on "idiot." The dactyls and the six trochees following illustrate the anticlimactic potential of "falling meter," as with each foot we seem to sink lower than the one before.

The length of the ninth line, with its two extra syllables, makes an idiot's tale seem not only chaotic but also almost endless. The unifying sounds of the last six feet (alliteration linking "full" and "fury" and also "sound" and "signifying") makes them forceful; the rhythm, steady in line 9, becomes less steady in line 10 (the stress on "fy" is so light that one may hear "signifying") and almost fades away (to "nothing").

When you are watching *Macbeth*, you probably do not think about the fact that much of it is poetry and can be discussed for its figures, sounds, meter, and rhythm like the short poems we examine throughout this book. Even though you are not thinking about or realizing the presence of the poetry, however, it contributes in an important way to the intensity and emotional power of the play.

For additional practice, scan the following lines and label the prevailing metrical foot and line length without looking at the next page.

Woman much missed, how you call to me, call to me,
Saying that now you are not as you were
When you had changed from the one who was all to me,
But as at first, when our day was fair.
                                        —Thomas Hardy

That time of year thou mayst in me behold
When yellow leaves, or none, or few, do hang
Upon those boughs which shake against the cold,
Bare ruined choirs, where late the sweet birds sang.
                                        —William Shakespeare

"Good speed!" cried the watch, as the gate-bolts undrew;
"Speed!" echoed the wall to us galloping through;
Behind shut the postern, the lights sank to rest,
And into the midnight we galloped abreast.
                                        —Robert Browning

Piping down the valleys wild,
Piping songs of pleasant glee,
On a cloud I saw a child,
And he laughing said to me:
      —William Blake

Now look at page 1094 and compare your results with ours.

trochaic tetrameter	Trochee | trips from | long to | short.
iambic tetrameter	From long | to long | in sol | emn sort
spondaic tetrameter	Slow Spon | dee stalks; | strong foot! |yet
plus two weak syllables	ill able
dactylic tetrameter	Ever to | come up with | Dactyl tri | syllable.
iambic tetrameter	Iam | bics march | from short | to long;—
anapestic tetrameter	With a leap | and a bound | the swift An |
	apests throng.

      —Samuel Taylor Coleridge, "Metrical Feet"

	Woman much | missed, how you | call to me, | call to me,
dactylic	Saying that | now you are | not as you | were
tetrameter	When you had | changed from the | one who was | all to me,
	But as at | first, when our | day was | fair.

          —Thomas Hardy

	That time | of year | thou mayst | in me | behold
iambic	When yel | low leaves, | or none, | or few, | do hang
pentameter	Upon | those boughs | which shake | against | the cold,
	Bare ru | ined choirs, | where late | the sweet | birds sang.

          —William Shakespeare

	"Good speed!" | cried the watch, | as the gate | -bolts undrew;
anapestic	"Speed!" ech | oed the wall | to us gal | loping through;
tetrameter	Behind | shut the pos | tern, the lights | sank to rest,
	And in | to the mid | night we gal | loped abreast.

          —Robert Browning

	Piping | down the | valleys | wild,
trochaic	Piping | songs of | pleasant | glee,
tetrameter	On a | cloud I | saw a | child,
	And he | laughing | said to | me:

          —William Blake

Appendix on Reading Critical Essays

When you see a movie you really like, you not only may want to see it again but you may also want to find out more about it — what other films an actor has appeared in (and perhaps some details about her or his life), some background on the director and information on the screenwriter, what changes were made from the work on which it was based (if adapted from another source), and what well-informed film critics said about it. As you look for information about these topics in newspapers, in magazines, or on the Internet, you are engaging in research. You can do the same for literary works. You can learn a lot about a work by reading it several times, reflecting on it and taking notes about it, listening to what is said about it in class, and discussing it with your classmates. For rich, complex works, there is always more to learn, beyond the classroom.

The Ongoing Conversation   Learning more in this case can be interesting and even exciting because it brings you deeper into the great ongoing conversation about literature that we've referred to several times in this book. That conversation starts with people talking about works they like and sharing their enthusiasms, dislikes, and questions. It continues as they move that exchange to paper (or computer screens). It extends further through the efforts of literary scholars who publish their critical insights about a particular work or era or theme.

Participating In That Conversation   Obviously, you can participate in early stages of that conversation. But it's important for you, as a student of literature, to enter the later stages as well by reading, reflecting on, and responding to the critical writings of literary scholars, thus incorporating them into your own literary experience. This appendix offers suggestions on how to read and assess critical essays about literary works, something that can be an important step toward an even more interesting and provocative involvement in the wider world of literary study.

WHAT ARE CRITICAL ESSAYS?

The word *critical* in its literary use (and in its use for the arts in general) does not mean "inclined to find fault or judge severely," as in "My uncle is such a critical person—always ripping somebody apart." Rather, it means exercising skillful and well-informed judgment about the techniques, ideas, or merits in, for example, a work of literature or a play, a concert, a dance performance, or an art exhibit.

Literary critics are scholars who have learned a great deal about literature, usually through work toward academic degrees but sometimes through extensive reading on their own. When they prepare to write a critical essay on a work, they read the work many times, they read everything else the author has written, and they read critical essays and books written about the work and author by other critics. Through previous study, they probably have learned a good deal already about the time and places in which the author lived, and about writers and works that influenced the author, but they may do additional study as preparation for a particular essay.

For us to read what such expert authorities write about a work can yield insights—which we otherwise might miss—and a fuller understanding of the work itself, its context, and how it came into being.

WHY READ CRITICAL ESSAYS?

Reading critical essays helps in a number of ways. However, you will find them most useful if you read them at the right point. We recommend strongly that you not read critical essays about a story, poem, or play before you have read the work itself several times and formulated your own thoughts about it. If you start reading criticism before you know the text well and form your own ideas about it, the ideas in the essays may overwhelm your thoughts and lead you merely to accept or adapt what you read. With your own conclusions already in mind, you'll be better able to evaluate the criticism, to disagree with the critic as well as to agree, and to accept refinements of your own insights.

Once you know a work well and have begun shaping your ideas about it, there are five good reasons for reading critical studies of the work:

1. To see how your own ideas are like and unlike those of other readers
2. To have your attention drawn to parts or aspects of the work whose significance you haven't recognized and to begin to imagine new ways of reading a text—new interpretations of or perspectives on it
3. To learn where the literary conversation about an author or a work stands and what scholars regard as strengths and weaknesses in what other critics have written

4. To discover new ways of constructing a literary argument; refuting earlier positions; offering counterarguments; and using explanation, elaboration, and evidence effectively
5. To gain a better understanding of the background or culture or literary tradition of a work by reading the results of a scholar's primary research (because you don't have time to do research on everything yourself, you often learn through reading the results of other people's research)

Each of these reasons has a practical benefit when you are working on a paper. Reading critical essays can give you a more informed and balanced stance as you explore a work. You can be more confident about your ability to find support for a position you want to uphold and for entering the ongoing discussion as you write your paper. If need be, you may be able to refine your tentative thesis into a more effective idea-based thesis by connecting it with points about which critics disagree or about which one modifies what another has said—the way Susan Farrell challenges prevailing views about "Everyday Use" in the sample essay later in this appendix.

ACTIVE READING: Critical Essays

In Chapters 2, 3, 11, 20, and 25, we describe a number of conventions you should follow in writing a literary paper—being sure that you state a thesis in the introduction, starting each paragraph with a topic sentence, and so on. There is a strategic reason for following those conventions: They enable your reader to grasp your paper easily, and they establish confidence in you as a writer worth attending to. The importance of what we say in those chapters may become more evident as you read critical essays and find yourself using those conventions to trace the steps in the argument and to understand what is being said.

Here are some guidelines for reading critical essays. (For reading critical books, begin by looking at the table of contents, noticing the overall outline of the book; read the preface to find out the aims, approach, and outlook of the book; and then apply the guidelines to each chapter.)

• *Pick out the thesis and identify the central idea that the paper or chapter will explore.* The thesis is likely found near the end of the introductory paragraph or section. Look also for references to previous studies and notice how the essay you are reading differs from or disagrees with them. Use such references to identify what is new about the central idea and about the essay.

- *Look for the topic sentence in each paragraph.* The first sentence usually states the central idea to be discussed in the paragraph. (The second sentence may do this instead if the first is mainly a transitional sentence.)

- *Watch for the way the ideas are advanced and supported.* Outline the steps in the argument (the thesis sentence and topic sentences may provide an outline). Consider the reasoning used in laying out ideas and connecting points to each other. Consider the nature and adequacy of the evidence provided in support of the reasoning.

- *Identify and take into account the theoretical approach being taken in the essay.* The appendix on Approaching Critical Theory (p. 1108) summarizes a number of ways that scholars approach literature, such as doing literary analysis; literary interpretation; historical background research; or analysis from a Marxist, psychoanalytic, or feminist perspective. Knowing where a critical work is coming from—what its assumptions and intentions are—helps you to follow its arguments and to do justice to its ideas.

- *Look at the footnotes and/or Works Cited list to see if there are other studies you might want to read yourself.*

SAMPLE ESSAY

Try these strategies in reading the following essay. If you did not read Alice Walker's story "Everyday Use" in Chapter 6 (p. 152) or if you do not remember it well, read it before reading the essay. For the convenience of readers, we have changed the page numbers for quotations of "Everyday Use" originally given in the essay to the pages on which they are found in this book.

Notice as you read the essay that the first paragraph situates the study in the ongoing discussion of "Everyday Use." It sketches out the positions held by other critics, summarizing and quoting from a few representative analyses of the story and listing many other studies in a footnote. Then it states the thesis to be explored in this essay, one that clearly is argumentative because it asserts a position almost directly opposite to the one most critics hold. The rest of the essay elaborates on that argument and explains why the author adheres to it. As you read, it is important to differentiate between sentences that *advance* the argument and sentences that *support* and *illustrate* the argument. To make that easier, we have put the former in boldface and added some marginal notes.

Susan Farrell

Fight vs. Flight: A Re-evaluation of Dee in Alice Walker's "Everyday Use"   [1998]

Most readers of Alice Walker's short story "Everyday Use," published in her 1973 collection *In Love and Trouble*, agree that the point of the story is to show, as Nancy Tuten argues, a mother's "awakening to one daughter's superficiality and to the other's deep-seated understanding of heritage" (125).[1] These readers praise the "simplicity" of Maggie and her mother, along with their allegiance to their specific family identity and folk heritage as well as their refusal to change at the whim of an outside world that doesn't really have much to do with them. Such a reading condemns the older, more worldly sister, Dee, as "shallow," "condescending," and "manipulative," as overly concerned with style, fashion, and aesthetics, and thus as lacking a "true" understanding of her heritage. **In this essay, conversely, I will argue that this popular view is far too simple a reading of the story. While Dee is certainly insensitive and selfish to a certain degree, she nevertheless offers a view of heritage and a strategy for contemporary African Americans to cope with an oppressive society that are, in some ways, more valid than those offered by Mama and Maggie.**

We must remember from the beginning that the story is told by Mama; the perceptions are filtered through her mind and her views of her two daughters are not to be accepted uncritically. Several readers have pointed out that Mama's view of Maggie is not quite accurate—that Maggie is not as passive or as "hangdog" as she appears.[2] **Might Mama's view of her older daughter, Dee, not be especially accurate as well? Dee obviously holds a central place in Mama's world.** The story opens with the line: "I will wait for her in the yard that Maggie and I made so clean and wavy yesterday afternoon" (152). As Houston Baker and Charlotte Pierce-Baker point out, "The mood at the story's beginning is one of ritualistic waiting," of preparation "for the arrival of a goddess" (715). Thus, Dee seems to attain almost mythic stature in Mama's imagination as she and Maggie wait for the as-yet unnamed "her" to appear. Such an opening may lead readers to suspect that Mama has a rather troubled relationship with her older daughter. Dee inspires in Mama a type of awe and fear more suitable to the advent of a goddess than the love one might expect a mother to feel for a returning daughter.

Mama, in fact, **displaces what seem to be her own fears onto Maggie** when she speculates that Maggie will be cowed by Dee's arrival. Mama conjectures that

Method: summary of views held by other critics.

Thesis.

Method: building on earlier critics.

Central idea for Section I.

> Maggie will be nervous until after her sister goes: she will stand hopelessly in corners, homely and ashamed of the burn scars down her arms and legs, eyeing her sister with a mixture of envy and awe. She thinks her sister has held life always in the palm of one hand, that "no" is a word the world never learned to say to her. (152)

Method: close reading of text.

But Mama here emphasizes the perceptual nature of this observation — she says that Maggie *thinks* these things, encouraging readers to wonder whether or not this first perception of Dee is true. We also find out in the next section, when Mama relates her Johnny Carson television fantasy, that she herself is the one who will be "nervous" until after Dee goes, that she is ashamed of her own appearance and very much seeks her daughter's approval. Mama confesses that, in "real life," she is "a large, big-boned woman with rough, man-working hands" (152). However, in her television fantasy, as Mama tells us,

Evidence: summary and quotation.

> all this does not show. . . . I am the way my daughter would want me to be: a hundred pounds lighter, my skin like an uncooked barley pancake. My hair glistens in the hot bright lights. Johnny Carson has much to do to keep up with my quick and witty tongue. (153)

It is important to remember, though, that **this Johnny Carson daydream is Mama's fantasy of a mother–child reunion,** *not* **Dee's.** In fact, Mama even acknowledges that this particular scenario might not be to Dee's taste — she imagines Dee pinning an orchid on her even though Dee had previously told Mama she thinks orchids are "tacky flowers" (152). Thus, although Tuten equates Dee's values with those of "the white Johnny Carson society" (126), it seems to me that we have to question whether Mama's vision of her light-skinned, slender, witty self is actually Dee's wish or only Mama's perception of what she imagines Dee would like her to be.

Elsewhere, as well, we see **that Mama is often wrong about her expectations of Dee and her readings of Dee's emotions.** She writes that she "used to think" Dee hated Maggie as much as she hated the previous house that burned down (153). Mama implies, though, that she has since changed her mind about this. Further, as Mama and Maggie continue to wait for Dee's arrival, Mama "deliberately" turns her back on the house, expecting Dee to hate this house as much as Mama believes she hated the earlier one: "No doubt when Dee sees it she will want to tear it down" (154). When Dee does arrive, however, she has a camera with her and "never takes a shot without making sure the house is included" (155). Of course, most readers see this as evidence of Dee's fickle changing with whatever

Method: contrast with other critics.

fad happens to be current. Once it becomes fashionable to have rural, poverty-stricken roots, Dee wants a record of her own humble beginnings. This might very well be true. Yet **I would argue that we have only Mama's word for Dee's earlier haughtiness, and this could have been exaggerated,** much as Mama hints that her earlier suspicion of Dee's hatred for Maggie was inaccurate. The more subtle point here is that **Mama's expectations of Dee tell us more about Mama herself than they do about Dee.** Again, Mama seems to view Dee with a mixture of awe, envy, and fear. Although she resents Dee because she expects Dee will want "to tear the house down," Mama still takes her cue from her older daughter, herself turning her back on the house, perhaps in an effort to appease this daughter, who looms so large in Mama's imagination.

In contrast to her own fearfulness, **Mama, with grudging admiration, remembers Dee as a fearless girl.** While Mama imagines herself unable to look white people in the eye, talking to them only "with one foot raised in flight," Dee "would always look anyone in the eye. Hesitation was no part of her nature" (153). Mama remembers Dee as self-centered and demanding, yes, but she also remembers this daughter as **a determined fighter.** Dee is concerned with style, but she'll do whatever is necessary to improve her circumstances. For instance, when Dee wants a new dress, she "makes over" an old green suit someone had given her mother. Rather than passively accept her lot, as Mama seems trained to do, Dee "was determined to stare down any disaster in her efforts" (153). **Mama's fearful nature is also apparent in her reaction to knowledge.** Words for Mama are associated with "lies" and "other folks' habits" (153). She remembers feeling "trapped and ignorant" as Dee reads to her and Maggie "without pity" (153). This is partly because Mama never had an education herself. When her school was closed down in 1927, after she had completed only the second grade, Mama, like the other African Americans in her community, didn't fight: "colored asked fewer questions than they do now," she tells us (154). Again, Mama is trained in acquiescence while Dee refuses to meekly accept the status quo.

Most critics see Dee's education and her insistence on reading to Mama and Maggie as further evidence of her separation from and lack of understanding for her family identity and heritage. Tuten, for instance, argues that, in this story, "Walker stresses not only the importance of language but also the destructive effects of its misuse. . . . Rather than providing a medium for newfound awareness and for community, . . . verbal skill equips Dee to oppress and manipulate others and to isolate herself" (125). Similarly, Donna Winchell writes that "Dee tries to force on" Maggie and her mother "knowledge they probably do not need." She continues,

Central idea for Section II.

Method: accumulation of details.

Method: contrast with other critics.

Mrs. Johnson can take an objective look at who and what she is and find not disillusionment but an easy satisfaction. Simple pleasures — a dip of snuff, a cooling breeze across a clean swept yard, church songs, the soothing movements of milk cows — are enough. (82)

Method: showing other critics may be mistaken.

But are these "simple pleasures" really enough for Mama in the story? When she imagines her future she seems vaguely unhappy and apprehensive about it: "[Maggie] will marry John Thomas (who has mossy teeth in an earnest face) and then I'll be free to sit here and I guess just sing church songs to myself. Although I never was a good singer. Never could carry a tune" (154). Not quite sure what she will do with herself when Maggie marries, Mama can only imagine herself alone, engaging in an activity which she feels she is not even very good at. Although she perhaps goes about it in the wrong way — Mama says that Dee "pressed us to her with the serious way she read," only to "shove us away at just the moment, like dimwits, we seemed about to understand" (153) — Dee at least tries to change what she foresees as Mama's fairly dismal future, a vision of her future Mama herself seems to reinforce rather than dispute. **Thus, I'd suggest the possibility that Dee's attempt to educate Mama and Maggie may be read much more positively than other critics have suggested.** Again, we must remember that Mama's perspective is the only one we see throughout the story. Told from Dee's point of view, we might expect a very different rendering of this incident. Rather than simply abandon her mother and sister in their ignorance and poverty, in their acquiescence to an oppressive system, Dee tries her best to extend her own education to them, which is surely not such a bad thing.

When Dee does finally arrive, **both Maggie and her mother react again with fear of the unknown, of something strange and different.** But as Dee approaches, Mama notices that the brightly colored African dress that Dee wears "throw[s] back the light of the sun" (154). Mama feels her "whole face warming from the heat waves it throws out" (154). She also admires the way that the "dress is loose and flows," and, despite her initial reaction, even decides that she likes it as Dee moves closer to her. In her admiration of the

Central idea for Section III.

dress, **Mama illustrates Walker's point that everything new is not to be feared, that change can be positive, not only negative.** Maggie, however, remains fearful, even in the face of the friendliness of Dee's companion, who grins and greets Mrs. Johnson and Maggie warmly: "Asalamalakim, my mother and sister!" (155). When he tries to hug Maggie, though, she falls back against a chair and trembles. And later, when he tries to teach Maggie a new handshake, her hand remains limp and she quickly withdraws it from his.

Shortly after this, Dee announces that she is no longer Dee but "Wangero Leewanika Kemanjo." She has newly adopted an African name since, as she explains: "I couldn't bear it any longer, being named after the people who oppress me" (155). Many readers point to Dee's proclamation of her new name as the turning point in the story, the point at which Dee pushes her mother too far. They point out that Dee is rejecting her family heritage and identity in this scene. **Yet it seems to me that Dee and Mama are *both* right here.** Mama's recounting of the family history of the name is surely accurate, but what the critics fail to point out is that Dee's assertion that the name comes from "the people who oppress" her is also accurate. While most readers see Mama and Maggie as having a "true" sense of heritage as opposed to Dee's false or shallow understanding of the past, both Mama and Dee are blind to particular aspects of heritage. Dee has much to learn about honoring her particular and individual family history, but Mama has much to learn about the history of African Americans in general, and about fighting oppression. Although each is stubborn, both Dee and Mama do make a concession to the other here. Dee tells Mama that she needn't use the new name if she doesn't want to, while Mama shows her willingness to learn and to use the name.

Method: contrast with other critics.

Mama's secret admiration for Dee's fighting spirit leaks out again when she explicitly connects the "beef-cattle peoples down the road" to Dee and her boyfriend, "Hakim-a-barber." We see that the neighbors down the road, like Dee's boyfriend, are most likely black Muslims: they also say "Asalamalakim" when they meet, and Hakim explains that he accepts "some of their doctrines," although farming is not his style. Like Dee, these neighbors are also fighters. When "white folks" poison some of their cattle, they "stayed up all night with rifles in their hands" (156). Tellingly, Mama, who can't look white people in the eye and who never asked questions when her school closed down, is intrigued by this younger generation's refusal to acquiesce. She "walked a mile and a half" down the road "just to see the sight" of blacks armed for resistance (156). **Mixed with her resentment against her older daughter's worldliness and self-centered attitude, Mama also grudgingly respects and even envies the willingness to fight evinced both by Dee and the black Muslim neighbors.**

Method: new way of reading the text.

Maggie's forbearance in the story contrasts with Dee's boldness. When Dee haughtily insists that Maggie would ruin Grandma's quilts by using them every day, and that hanging the quilts would be the only way to preserve them, Maggie, "like somebody used to never winning anything, or having anything reserved for her," meekly replies: "She can have them, Mama, . . . I can 'member Grandma Dee without the quilts" (158). Mama, though, does not react so meekly. She sees Maggie standing with her scarred hands hidden in her skirt and says: "When I looked at her like that something hit me in the top of my head and ran down to the soles of my feet. Just like when I'm in church and the spirit of God touches me and I get happy and shout" (158). This powerful feeling causes Mama to do something she "never had done before": she "snatched the quilts out of Miss Wangero's hands and dumped them into Maggie's lap" (158). Ironically, in acting against Dee's wishes here, Mama is truly behaving more like Dee, with her refusal to back down, her willingness to stand up for herself, than she is like the patient and long-suffering Maggie. So perhaps, along with the younger, changing generation coming of age in the early 1970s that she is associated with, Dee, despite her outward obnoxiousness, has taught Mama something about fighting back. Or perhaps Dee has inherited more of her stubbornness and self-determination from her Mama than previously suspected. But, in any case, it seems too easy and neat a reading to simply praise Mama and Maggie for understanding their heritage while dismissing Dee as shallow and self-serving, when Mama's final courageous act ties her more closely to this older daughter than to the younger one she is trying to protect.

Central idea for Section IV.

Method: parallel situation in another work by Walker.

Walker raised similar problems concerning the willingness to fight for a cause versus the desire to remain passive in her novel *Meridian*, published in 1976, three years after *In Love and Trouble*. In this novel, Walker's main character, Meridian Hill, is at first passive and dreamy. She drifts into an early marriage and pregnancy, since these things seem to be expected of her, but she doesn't truly find direction in her life until she becomes involved with the early Civil Rights movement. As a movement worker, though, Meridian is tempted toward becoming a martyr for her cause. When asked if she would "kill for the revolution," Meridian remains unable to answer. Although readers see the complexities of Meridian's ambivalence here, other activists call her a coward and a masochist for her lack of commitment. In her forbearance and initial willingness to sacrifice her own needs if necessary, Meridian shares much in common with Maggie of "Everyday Use." Meridian's college roommate, Anne-Marion Coles, on the other hand, is similar to Dee. Aggressive and determined to change her life, Anne-Marion, unlike Meridian, easily asserts her willingness to kill if necessary. But, also like Dee in the way she treats Mama and Maggie, Anne-Marion is self-centered and at times unthinkingly cruel to the weaker, more fragile Meridian.

Summary to bring out similarities between the two works.

While Meridian is certainly a more sympathetic character than Anne-Marion throughout the novel, just as Maggie and Mama are more appealing than Dee in many ways, by the end Walker shows us that Meridian has something to learn from Anne-Marion and her other militant colleagues in the movement. . . .

Readers of these two works may at first be seduced into affirming the passive acquiescence of characters such as Mama, Maggie, and Meridian because they are, in many ways, more palatable, more likeable, than such aggressive fighters as Dee and Anne-Marion. These determined, fierce women, however, have much to teach the more forbearing, self-sacrificing characters in both works. Yet, at the same time, we see that a spirit of rebellion, without a corresponding spirituality and respect for such traditional black institutions as the church or the folk arts of "Everyday Use," can be empty as well. Though defiant and aggressive, both Dee and Anne-Marion are selfish and capricious in their social activism. Finally, then, in "Everyday Use," **Walker shows that Mama's moment of triumph is achieved because she is able to attain a balance between the two types of her heritage represented by her very different daughters**—at the end Mama combines Maggie's respect for tradition with Dee's pride and refusal to back down, the combination Walker seems to feel is necessary if true social change is to come about.

Completion of thesis idea.

NOTES

Informative endnotes.

1. See especially, along with Tuten's *Explicator* article, Houston Baker and Charlotte Pierce-Baker's "Patches: Quilts and Community in Alice Walker's 'Everyday Use,'" Margaret D. Bauer's "Alice Walker: Another Southern Writer Criticizing Codes Not Put to 'Everyday Use,'" and Donna Haisty Winchell's Twayne Series book on Alice Walker (80–84).

Note listing related critical studies.

2. Tuten, for instance, argues that the "action of the story . . . in no way supports Mama's reading of her younger daughter," that Maggie "conveys disgust with her sister rather than envy and awe" as Mama believes (127). Similarly, Baker and Pierce-Baker point out that, "in her epiphanic moment of recognition," Mama must perceive "the fire-scarred Maggie—the stay-at-home victim of southern scarifications—in a revised light," that she must reassess "what she wrongly interprets as Maggie's hang-dog resignation before Dee" (717).

Note providing further supporting evidence.

WORKS CITED

Baker, Houston, and Charlotte Pierce-Baker. "Patches: Quilts and Community in Alice Walker's 'Everyday Use.'" *The Southern Review*, vol. 21, no. 4, Autumn 1985, pp. 706–20.

Bauer, Margaret D. "Alice Walker: Another Southern Writer Criticizing Codes Not Put to 'Everyday Use.'" *Studies in Short Fiction*, vol. 29, no. 2, Spring 1992, pp. 143–51.

Tuten, Nancy. "Alice Walker's 'Everyday Use.'" *The Explicator*, vol. 51, no. 2, Winter 1993, pp. 125–28.

Walker, Alice. "Everyday Use." *In Love and Trouble*, Harcourt, 1973, pp. 47–59. Reprinted in *Approaching Literature: Reading, Thinking, Writing*, edited by Peter Schakel and Jack Ridl, Bedford/St. Martin's, 2017, pp. 152–58.
——. *Meridian.* Harcourt, 1976.
Winchell, Donna Haisty. *Alice Walker.* Twayne, 1992.

Outline   Most scholars, when they read such an essay, pick out the central idea in each paragraph and jot down an outline of the main steps in the argument. Here is an example of the sort of outline a reader might sketch out:

> Thesis: Dee offers a view of heritage and way of coping with society more valid than those of Mama and Maggie
>   I. Mama's view of Dee may not be reliable
>   A. She displaces her fears of Dee onto Maggie
>   B. The Johnny Carson daydream is Mama's fantasy, not Dee's
>   C. Mama is often wrong about Dee
>   II. Contrast between Dee's fearlessness and Mama's fearfulness
>   A. Dee as a determined fighter
>   B. Mama's fear of knowledge
>   C. Mama's fear of the future
>   III. Mama's attitude changes as she interacts with Dee
>   A. Mama seems more open to new things than Maggie
>   B. Both Mama and Dee need to gain a more adequate understanding of heritage
>   C. Mama admires Dee's fighting spirit
>   D. Mama behaves like Dee (not like Maggie) by fighting back against Dee's demands
>   IV. The same pattern (passivity vs. fighting back) is evident in *Meridian*
> Restatement of thesis: Mama triumphs as she achieves a balance between the approaches and attitudes of Dee and Maggie.

Such an outline enables you to view the argument as a whole—what the individual points are and how they relate to each other. That's valuable in understanding the essay and in assessing the strength of what it says.

Kinds of Evidence   It's also important to notice the kinds of evidence that an author uses to support her or his argument. In Farrell's essay, most of the evidence comes through close reading of the text, with supporting details and quotations from it. But the author also uses the authoritative opinions of other scholars in support of her own positions when she regards them as sound, and she argues against them when she believes their interpretations are not accurate or adequate. And the author uses an additional kind of supporting evidence: a parallel situation in another work by Walker, the novel *Meridian*. (We include only the first paragraph of that section, to show how the author introduces the comparison, and omit the following three paragraphs because they discuss a work that is not included in this book and will be unfamiliar to many of you.)

REREADING: Critical Essays

An important step in reading critical essays is evaluation: After all, the essay is trying to persuade you, so it is crucial that you not simply accept automatically what has been written, that you have the skills necessary to decide how good the points and arguments in the essay are. Making that decision usually requires rereading all, or the key parts of, the essay. To evaluate the essay well, start by comparing the critic's ideas with your own. This is why it is important that you know the work itself well and that you formulate your own interpretation of it before reading any critical essay. Here are some suggestions for evaluating critical essays.

- *Compare the critic's interpretation with your own interpretation.* The first step in evaluation is to formulate your own judgment as clearly and substantially as you can. Then compare the critic's interpretations to your own—how convincing do they seem to you? Does the critic use the text accurately and fairly and draw sensible conclusions about details in it? Does the critic take everything into account or pass over details that don't support her or his conclusions? Do the steps in the critic's argument proceed logically, and is the case that is presented sound and convincing?

- *Compare what one critic says with what other critics say.* Perhaps comparison is the best method of evaluation. To assess fully what one critic says, read the interpretations of several or many other critics. By comparing what one says with what another says, you will begin to get a sense of what ideas need to be explored in a work, what sections or details need to be taken into consideration, what approaches prove to be most productive and illuminating. In some cases, you will find some critics agreeing with or replying to or refuting the interpretations of others (as you found in Farrell's essay above). What the critics say about each other will be very helpful in testing and shaping your own conclusions about a critical essay—though, of course, you will need to evaluate the soundness of each as you make your comparisons.

Approaching
Critical Theory

This book is about approaching literature. It's valuable to realize that you always approach something from somewhere. We have tried to connect reading literature to your everyday life: You come to this course with prior interests and experiences, and the way you approach what you read, even your ability to relate to it at all, depends on where you're "coming from."

ALL READING IS THEORY BASED In addition to this personal way to approach a work, there is another sense of approaching literature from somewhere. All readers approach their reading from a critical or theoretical perspective, even though they may not be aware of it. There are many such perspectives—some practical, others more abstract and philosophical. This appendix, though it cannot cover all approaches, does indicate the range of past and present approaches used by readers.

BENEFITS OF BEING AWARE OF THEORY Having an awareness of critical and theoretical perspectives helps as you read literary works themselves—helps you sharpen and refine your own approaches to reading, helps you become a more flexible reader, and helps you vary your approaches for different works and in different situations. And being familiar with critical theories is beneficial as you read scholarly books and essays about literature. As we said in "Appendix on Reading Critical Essays" (p. 1095), knowing where a critical work is coming from, what its assumptions and intentions are, can help in following its arguments and in understanding why two readers of the same text can arrive at quite different readings. (Note, however, that scholars usually do not limit themselves to only one approach; they often combine approaches, or elements from different approaches, to fit a particular work or problem.)

CHRONOLOGICAL APPROACH TO THEORY The following survey of approaches is arranged in roughly chronological order to provide a brief history of literary criticism and to indicate how some theories developed out of, or as a reaction to, other theories—though theories have often overlapped, or run simultaneously, with others.

BIOGRAPHICAL CRITICISM

BEGINNING WITH THE BEGINNINGS English literature didn't become a subject of academic study until the late 1800s. At that point the emphasis was on its beginnings, on the study of Old English and Middle English language and writings. The assumption was that students didn't need much help with literature from Shakespeare onward: Those works were considered part of their reading for pleasure, not part of the academic curriculum.

FOCUSING ON AUTHORS By the 1930s, academic study of English literature had begun to include later authors, though still not contemporary literature, the attention focusing particularly on the historical backgrounds of works and on the lives of authors. Scholars used literary works as a source of information about authors (not always being careful to keep a first-person narrator or speaker separate from the author) and used details from an author's life to gain a better understanding of a work (not always being careful to remember that a writer can make things up).

INSIGHTS FROM BIOGRAPHY Biographical criticism today involves research into the details of an author's life to shed light on the author's works, an important and basic form of literary study. Publishers have recognized its value by publishing biographical encyclopedias for literary figures and by including biographical sketches of the authors in anthologies such as this textbook (see p. 1053). Knowledge about an author can enable us in many cases to notice details or ideas in a work we might otherwise miss. If you decide to attempt biographical criticism, be sure it actually *is* criticism and not just a *report* on the author's life. The paper must involve analysis, and it must use biographical data to illuminate meaning and build its interpretations on what is in the text, not on extraneous material from outside the text.

HISTORICAL CRITICISM

FOCUSING ON CONTEXT As biographical knowledge enhances your understanding of a work, so does awareness of the social, political, cultural, and intellectual context in which it was conceived and written. Literary historians research such backgrounds and bring what they find to bear on a work, explaining details used in the work and clarifying the meaning of the work as its original readers would have understood it. They research sources that the author drew on and influences that shaped the form and content of the work. They connect the work to other works written at the time, to describe the literary environment that surrounds it and compare it to works written earlier, to understand how it relates to the traditional handling of similar forms and ideas.

HEMINGWAY AND HISTORY   To see how historical criticism is used, look again at the discussion of "Hills Like White Elephants" in Chapter 8 (p. 197). There we describe the historical context and social milieu in which Hemingway wrote and in which the story was set. We show how awareness of events and attitudes of the time clarifies details in plot, characterization, and setting and proves helpful in understanding the story.

USING HISTORICAL APPROACHES   You can try using such an approach for a paper assignment, if you'd like — probably a research paper. Learning about history almost invariably involves doing research into the era you're interested in. As with biographical criticism, be sure what you write is actually criticism, not just a report on the time period. A historical study also must involve analysis and must use data to illuminate meaning and build its interpretations on what is in the text, not on extraneous material from outside the text.

PSYCHOLOGICAL CRITICISM

FOCUSING ON FREUD   Biographical criticism — or a good deal of it, at least — began to turn in a psychological direction during the 1940s and 1950s. This was a result of the growing interest in the parent of psychoanalysis, Sigmund Freud, who sought a scientific understanding of the mind and mental illness. His methods and conclusions were revolutionary and controversial, and have been — and continue to be — both applied and challenged on many grounds. The field of psychoanalysis has now moved far beyond Freud — so far, in fact, that he is given slight attention in psychology courses today. However, his work had a great impact on twentieth-century literature and twentieth- and twenty-first-century literary criticism.

THE CONSCIOUS AND THE UNCONSCIOUS   A brief summary of Freud's thought is needed before we can consider its effect on literature. Crucial to its early phase is Freud's realization of a dynamic tension between the conscious and the unconscious in mental activity. This was a radical shift. Pre-Freudian belief held that one could *know* and *control* oneself. The idea that there are parts of the self knowable only through analysis is almost universally accepted now, but it was strikingly new when Freud advanced it. He described three areas of consciousness, each of which can contain causes for human behavior. First is the *conscious* level, the things we are aware of. Second is the *preconscious* level, feelings and sensations we are not presently aware of but that can be brought to the surface if we reflect on them. Third is the *unconscious* level, the realm of things we are not aware of, though they influence us greatly.

ID, EGO, SUPEREGO In his second phase, Freud replaced the conscious and unconscious with the very different and now familiar concepts of the id, ego, and superego. The *id*, a reservoir of biological impulses and drives, demands instant gratification of its needs and desires—for food, relieving ourselves, sexual gratification. But instant satisfaction is not always possible, and when satisfaction must be postponed, tensions build up that cause inner conflict. We are often unaware that such tensions and conflicts exert an influence on our lives and actions. The *ego* (rational, controlled, partially conscious) is concerned first with pleasure, through the elimination of inner tensions and conflicts, but also with self-preservation, which requires that urges and needs be dealt with in a practical, realistic way. The id, for example, tells us we need to eat, and the ego *wants* to concur, but the ego, balancing the id's desire with the restraint imposed by the *superego* (the rules and taboos internalized through parental and societal influences), tells us to wait until lunchtime.

OEDIPUS COMPLEX, ELECTRA COMPLEX In a third phase of his work, Freud focused on the development of the ego in children. Freud held that part of the normal emotional development of a child includes an unconscious wish to replace the parent of the child's sex in the affection of the parent of the opposite sex: A little boy wants to eliminate his father and marry his mother (Oedipus complex) and a little girl wants to eliminate her mother and marry her father (Electra complex). Although many aspects of his approach to the stages of early childhood development have been challenged or discredited, evidence of them is found in literary criticism, to clarify what lies behind a character's attitudes or actions, and in literary works, as authors influenced by Freudian theories apply them as they develop characters and plots.

REPRESSION Another controversial Freudian theory important for literary study is that of *repression*. This theory holds that memories (that is, bundles of psychic energy) of situations with painful or threatening or guilt-laden associations are unconsciously pushed out of consciousness and sealed off so we will not have to deal with them consciously. When such matters are repressed, the pent-up energy has an effect on the personality—a repressed memory of childhood abuse, for example, may interfere with a person's adult relationships. It may take something of great force to break through the barrier, but only when it has been broken through is the person freed from the pain and its effects.

CHARACTER ANALYSIS Psychological criticism is most commonly used to analyze characters in a work. The psychological critic attempts to clarify a character's actions, motivations, and attitudes by bringing modern psychoanalytical insights to bear on them. The critic does with characters what a psychoanalyst does with a patient: probes beneath the surface, exploring what unconscious conflicts and tensions, or repressed memories, may underlie the character's behavior.

"YOUNG GOODMAN BROWN"   This approach isn't profitable with every story, poem, or play: Some works don't give us enough in-depth information about their characters to undertake a psychological analysis. Such an analysis would be possible for the title character in "Young Goodman Brown" (p. 359). It's a fairly long story and we are told a good deal about Young Goodman Brown's background and behavior, enough to show in a convincing way that many of his actions and attitudes come not from his conscious thought but from unconscious and repressed guilt, fears, and conflicts.

PURSUING A PSYCHOLOGICAL APPROACH   A psychological analysis is what you will probably want to use if you decide to write a paper taking a psychological approach. Your approach does not need to be Freudian — other psychological theories also can be used to amplify literature. But to work responsibly, you will need to know a good deal about whichever one you use. If you haven't taken at least one psychology course, trying this approach might not be advisable.

MYTHOLOGICAL CRITICISM

FOCUSING ON MYTH   What Freud attempted for the individual consciousness, another group of theorists in the late 1940s began to do for cultures, or the human race as a whole. Theorists who came to be known as *mythological critics* (or *archetypal critics*) focused their attention on the myths that underlie many literary works. *Myth* here must be understood not in its popular sense of a "fictitious story, or unscientific account, theory, belief," but in its literary sense of an anonymous story arising from a culture's oral traditions that involves gods or heroic figures and explores matters beyond and above everyday life, concerning origins, endings, aspirations, purpose, and meaning. Myths often appear in the earliest and seemingly simplest stories told in a culture — folktales, fairy tales, or religious writings, for example.

THE ROLE OF ARCHETYPES   Myths usually build on literary archetypes — symbols, character types, and plot lines that have been used again and again in a culture until they come to carry a wide, nearly universal significance and thus move most readers at a very deep emotional level. Throughout the centuries, writer after writer has drawn on motifs such as the quest, the journey into experience, and the Cinderella pattern in developing the plot of a story. Such writers use a typical or recurring symbol, character type, or plot motif that, in the words of archetypal theorist Northrop Frye, "connects one poem with another and thereby helps to unify and integrate our literary experience."[1]

SEASONAL CYCLES   Among the most used and most important of such archetypal images are the seasonal cycle of spring, summer, autumn, and winter; the daily cycle of dawn, zenith, sunset, and night; and the life cycle of youth, adulthood, old age, and death. Throughout history, poets have seen analogies among these natural cycles. Each time we speak of the "sunset" and "golden" years of life in referring to old age or describe death as being "sleep," we are, consciously or unconsciously, invoking those archetypes.

THE MONOMYTH   Beyond the meaning of the individual cycles is the significance of the patterns as a whole. "In the solar cycle of the day," Frye explains, "the seasonal cycle of the year, and the organic cycle of human life, there is a single pattern of significance"; elsewhere he calls that pattern the "story of the loss and regaining of identity," which is "the framework of all literature," the single story or "monomyth" underlying it all.[2] Other theorists hold that the "single story" focuses on the earth mother[3] or on the hero.[4] All of the theories, however, share a belief in the close relationship between literature and life. "Putting works of literature in such a context gives them an immense reverberating dimension of significance . . . , in which every literary work catches the echoes of all other works of its type in literature, and so ripples out into the rest of literature and thence into life."[5]

For an example of an essay that uses a mythological approach, see Susan Koprince's "Baseball as History and Myth in August Wilson's *Fences*" (p. 733), which explores baseball, together with its archetypal implications, as a metaphor for the American dream. Before trying this approach in a paper, you should review the sections on symbols in Chapter 10 (pp. 252–54) and perhaps do some additional reading on myths and archetypes. You could work with a story like Nathaniel Hawthorne's "Young Goodman Brown" (p. 359), a poem like William Shakespeare's "That time of year thou mayst in me behold" (available online) or A. E. Housman's "To an Athlete Dying Young" (p. 633), or a play like Shakespeare's *Hamlet* (p. 881), or look for a work in which the mythical and archetypal aspects are less obvious or more subtle.

---

[1]Northrop Frye. *Anatomy of Criticism, Four Essays*. Princeton UP, 1957, p. 99.

[2]Northrop Frye. *Fables of Identity: Studies in Poetic Mythology*. Harcourt, 1963, p. 15; Frye, *The Educated Imagination*. Indiana UP, 1964, p. 55.

[3]Robert Graves. *The White Goddess: A Historical Grammar of Poetic Myth*. Faber, 1948.

[4]Joseph Campbell. *The Hero with a Thousand Faces*. Princeton UP, 1949. Bollingen Series 17.

[5]Frye, *Fables of Identity*, 37.

NEW CRITICISM (FORMALISM)

FOCUSING ON THE TEXT The literary approach most influential in the twentieth century, and still important today, is called New Criticism, or Formalism (from its concentration on the *formal* elements of a work). It originated in the 1930s and for over forty years it dominated the study of literature. New Criticism was in part a reaction against an approach that makes biography or history primary and treats the literary text as secondary, either regarding it merely as a source of information or as material to the interpretation of which biographical and historical knowledge provides all the clues we need. New Criticism insists on the primacy of the text, appreciated as worthwhile for its own sake, for its aesthetic beauty, for its way of considering and helping understand the human condition generally. New Criticism takes texts themselves very seriously, looks at them closely as self-contained works of art, and affirms that literature has its own epistemology, or theory of knowledge.

EXPLICATION AS METHOD New Criticism borrowed from France a method of teaching literature called *explication de texte*. The word *explicate* comes from Latin roots meaning "to unfold, to give an account of" and means to explain in detail. A key method of New Criticism is to explain the interconnections and ambiguities (multiple meanings) within a work, or within an important passage from a work, through a detailed, close analysis of its language—the meanings, relationships, and complexities of its words, images, figures, and symbols. In all this, what the author *intended* to do is not relevant—what matters is what the work *actually* says and does. New Critics, therefore, read works repeatedly. The first reading is less important than the later ones because one does not yet know where the work is headed and cannot see how early parts connect to parts further along.

UNITY OF FORM AND MEANING As one rereads, again and again, one begins to see connections and to grasp the way large and small features relate to each other. Central to New Criticism are unity and universality. In the words of Cleanth Brooks, one of the developers of the approach, "The primary concern of criticism is with the problem of unity—the kind of whole which the literary work forms or fails to form, and the relation of the various parts to each other in building up this whole."[6] The unity sought is unity of meaning; but meaning, for New Critics, cannot be separated from form. Thus, a New Critic focuses on the speaker (or persona), conflicts and tensions, the arrangement of parts and details, and the relationships between them. A New Critic pays particular attention to metaphors as ways of unifying dissimilar things and to irony and paradox as ways that apparent contradictions can be resolved (and thus unified).

---

[6]Cleanth Brooks. "The Formalist Critics." *Kenyon Review*, vol. 13, no. 1, Winter 1951, p. 72.

THEORY OF KNOWLEDGE   New Criticism tends to look especially for issues of significance to all people, in all times — issues of life and relationship, worth and purpose, love, aging, death, faith, and doubt. The foundation of New Critical theory is its claim that literature has its own kind of knowledge — experiential knowledge conveyed imaginatively — and that this knowledge is superior to the abstract, impersonal knowledge of science. An overreliance on scientific approaches, New Critics believe, has led to fragmentation and "dissociation" within society and even within individuals. In the face of such disintegration, New Criticism emphasizes wholeness and unity. Literature offers a hope of wholeness, of a "unified sensibility" combining intellect and feeling, of redemption from the disintegration — the division, specialization, and alienation — that science has sometimes inflicted on the modern world.

CRITICAL METHOD   Today New Criticism is viewed more as a critical method than as a way of knowing. Anyone who engages in detailed close reading of a text is a descendant of New Criticism, even if she or he doesn't look for universal meanings or think in terms of being a New Critic. The method we have used in this book borrows from New Criticism in the way it teaches close attention to details in literary works, though we are more concerned with readers and the reading process than New Criticism itself is.

EXAMPLES IN THIS BOOK   Two of the student papers in this book offer good examples of New Critical readings. Sunkyo Hong's paper on "First Snow" (p. 594) is New Critical in the way it focuses on imagery, figures of speech, and rhetorical strategies to clarify how the poem enables the reader to participate imaginatively in the experience that Mary Oliver is describing. And Julian Hinson's paper on *The New New* (p. 724) looks closely at the handling of language in a play about the use and misuse of words and the moral distortions that language can cover up. If you want to try doing a paper with a New Critical approach, look at the Literary Analysis sections in the lists of writing prompts found in Chapters 5–10, 14–19, and 23–24 for suggestions of selections and topics you might use to explore them.

READER-RESPONSE CRITICISM

FOCUSING ON THE READER   Reader-response criticism (or reader-oriented criticism) contrasts sharply with New Criticism by focusing primarily on the reader instead of the text and on individual effect instead of universal meaning. The roots of reader-response criticism go back to the 1930s and were laid down as a reaction against historical and biographical approaches, which gave little consideration to the role of the reader. Louise Rosenblatt began developing a reader-response theory just about the time New Criticism was emerging. New Criticism caught on and became widely accepted, while for several decades Rosenblatt's work was mostly neglected. Interest in the reader reemerged in the 1960s as a reaction against New Criticism's text-centered neglect of the reader. Reader-response criticism has become increasingly popular and influential, especially as a classroom approach.

READING AS TRANSACTION   Reader-response criticism, as we say in Chapter 1, is based on the assumption that reading is a transaction between an author, a reader, and a text in a cultural context. Reader-response criticism studies the steps through which the reader, by interacting with a text, completes the work in her or his mind. It does not just *describe* the response a work elicits from a reader ("here's what the work makes me feel") but examines the *activity* involved in reading—*how* the work produces the effects and feelings it does as a reader interacts with it. Reader-response criticism focuses on the sequential apprehension of a work—on the experience of grasping each line or each paragraph without knowing what comes later and on the process of putting the pieces together. Rereading is just as important for reader-response criticism as for New Criticism, but unlike for New Criticism, the first reading is regarded as crucially significant.

READERS AND TEXTS   Most reader-response theories have a more subjective view of a text than New Criticism does, thinking of a text as more like a musical score that is meant to be "performed," brought to life by a reader, than as a permanent artistic object. The degrees of subjectivity vary. Some versions see the reader's interaction with the text as controlled to some extent by formal structures included in the text. For these, the text is a stable and "objective" entity that sets limits on the reader. A work cannot mean just anything the reader says it does: The reader must pay close attention to the text to notice and follow the cues it supplies and must be able to provide evidence from within the text to support the way she or he interprets it.

INTERPRETIVE COMMUNITIES   Other, more subjective reader-response approaches de-emphasize the words on the page and place more emphasis on a text created in the reader's mind. This raises the question of whether there are any limits on the reader. Does a text then mean anything the reader says it does? Perhaps not. One way to consider that limits do exist, without giving up subjectivity of the text, is to recognize that reading occurs within "interpretive communities." In their broadest sense, interpretive communities are groups of readers who share a common situation, similar assumptions about how literary works are actualized, or an agreement about how literary conventions are used in approaching a text. The community provides a context within which individual experiencing of a work can be assessed. A class, for example, is an interpretive community. So are the readers of a professional journal and a group of scholars who specialize in a given area of literature.

COLLECTIVE JUDGMENTS   The role of such a group is not to arrive at a single "best" reading or to judge which among several readings is the "right" one or is "better" than others. Rather, by its endorsements and discouragements, each interpretive community indicates which readings go too far for that community, which ones it regards as *unacceptable*. This too will vary. What is unacceptable to one group of readers may not be to another. It is the collective judgments of interpretive communities, in this view, not texts or readers, that create stability. Even within the same community, readings will vary because texts are not objective, and different readers enact them in individual ways. Constraints do exist: A text can "mean" many things, but not just anything. The constraints, however, are not *in* the text but grow out of the strategies, assumptions, and conventions of the community.

For an example of reader interaction with a text, bringing it to life as a meaningful work, see Annie Otto's brief essay on the title of Alice Walker's "The Flowers" (p. 35).

MARXIST CRITICISM

FOCUSING ON MARX'S IDEAS   Although acceptance of Marxism has waned over the past few decades, Karl Marx's social and economic theories had a major impact around the world through much of the twentieth century. That was true for literature as well: While Marxist ideas influenced authors and literary critics from the 1920s on, they emerged more prominently in the 1960s. They remain an important strand in literary study, one with which students of literature should be conversant. A brief introduction to the basic tenets of Marxist thought is helpful in understanding the foundations of and procedures used in Marxist criticism.

CLASS CONFLICT   Marx's main interest was in economic power and the ways in which it is disguised and manipulated. His analysis of society starts with the exploitation of workers by owners and capitalists, which creates class conflict between the bourgeoisie (the middle and upper classes—the owners and capitalists) and the proletariat (the workers, those who must sell their labor to the owners and capitalists). The subjugation of the workers, Marx held, is maintained by *ideology*, that is, the beliefs, values, and ways of thinking through which human beings perceive what they believe to be reality and carry out their roles in society. The ideology of an era (Marx called it the "superstructure") is determined by the contemporary socioeconomic system (the "base") and reflects the beliefs, values, and interests of the dominant class in it.

THE EFFECT OF IDEOLOGY   Ideology includes everything that shapes the individual's mental picture of life experience — not what life really is, but the way it is perceived. This ideology may seem to people at the time just the natural, inevitable way of seeing and explaining things. But Marxists claim that it seems that way only because ideology quietly, subtly works to legitimize and maintain the position, power, and economic interests of the ruling class and, for the working classes, to cover up the reality of their exploitation. Ideology helps preserve the status quo by making what is artificial and oppressive seem natural and inevitable. According to Marxists, such ideology must be exposed and overcome if people are to gain relief from their oppressors.

BRINGING IDEOLOGY INTO CONSCIOUSNESS   Early Marxist criticism concentrated on exposing the presence of bourgeois attitudes, values, and orientation in literary works. Later Marxist criticism became more sophisticated in analyzing the ideology underlying literature and societies: bringing out the beliefs, values, and ways of thinking through which people perceive what they believe to be reality and on which they carry out their roles in society. In the latter part of the twentieth century, Fredric Jameson used insights from psychoanalysis to reenergize Marxist criticism. The function of ideology, Jameson held, is to "repress" revolutionary ideas or tendencies, to push them into the "political unconscious."[7] As ideology works itself into a text, things must be omitted: "In order to say anything, there are other things *which must not be said*."[8] As a result, gaps and contradictions occur and generally go unnoticed. Like psychoanalysts, Marxist critics focus on the text's "unconscious," on what is unspoken and repressed, and bring it into "consciousness."

READING AGAINST THE GRAIN   To expose the ideology in literary works, the main approach of Marxist criticism is to read "against the grain." The metaphor comes from carpentry: It is easiest to plane a board by pushing "with the grain": The plane moves easily; can glide over irregularities and inconsistencies in the wood; and produces smooth, pleasing results. Pushing "against the grain" is harder and usually causes rough edges. To apply the metaphor to reading, it is easiest and most natural to read a work "with the grain" — that is, to accept and follow the conventions and signals that correspond with the ideology behind it. Reading with the grain allows a reader to glide over problems and leads to smooth, reassuring results, compatible with what the dominant culture values and approves. It is harder to read "against the grain," to resist the conventions of the dominant culture's ideology, to challenge and question them instead of

---

[7]Frederic Jameson. *The Political Unconscious: Narrative as a Socially Symbolic Act.* Cornell UP, 1981.

[8]Pierre Machery. Quoted in Raman Selden, *A Reader's Guide to Contemporary Literary Theory.* UP of Kentucky, 1985, p. 41.

accepting and following them. The role of a Marxist approach to literature is to bring what is hidden into the open, to expose underlying ideology, and to make readers see its effect.

COMMITMENT TO THE CAUSE   Marxist criticism is committed criticism: It aims not only to illuminate readers but also to arouse them to involvement and action; it seeks to have an impact on the lives and values of readers and to effect changes in society. As with psychological criticism, you should not attempt writing a paper from a Marxist perspective unless you have read and understood a good deal from Marx's works and from works studying his positions. Attempting to do so without being well informed is likely to lead to superficial and even erroneous results. And it seems fair to point out that if you write a Marxist critique without sharing Marx's beliefs about class conflict and the need for rising up against the injustices of the capitalist system, you might fulfill an academic assignment, but your work will not be authentic Marxist criticism, which requires passionate commitment to a set of ideas designed to initiate significant societal change.

APPLYING THE APPROACH   The value of a Marxist approach can be illustrated by using it to consider "The Homes of England," a poem written around 1825 by Felicia Hemans (1793–1835)—and available online. The poem celebrates a variety of English homes, starting with the magnificent country houses of the rich: "The stately Homes of England, / How beautiful they stand! / Amidst their tall ancestral trees, / O'er all the pleasant land." Following stanzas go on to discuss "merry" and "blessed" homes in idyllic terms, moving down to "The Cottage Homes of England! / By thousands on her plains, / They are smiling o'er the silvery brooks / And round the hamlet fanes [churches]." A Marxist critic would expose the underlying ideology and point out what goes unsaid, and unseen, in the poem. Hemans, though not wealthy herself, saw her country through the lens of patriotic, upper-class landowners and capitalists. England was a land of "free, fair Homes" where all citizens lived with the "glad spirit" of children and loved their "country and its God."

But that is not how all of England was. It is how the upper classes perceived it. Hemans's setting is rural England; she makes no mention of the wretched homes in city slums where exploited factory workers and their families lived at the time. The lower classes are invisible to the upper classes, who profit from the lower classes but are oblivious to their lives and welfare. Rural areas had their poor as well, living not in romantic cottages but in huts and hovels. These homes, too, don't appear in the poem (the poem does refer to "hut and hall," but the very phrase seems to equate them, as equally pleasant, happy dwellings). A Marxist critic would bring out how acceptance of this ideology—this sense that all are free, happy, and content—is a way to keep the lower classes from realizing the inequity of their situation and from wanting to rebel against it.

FEMINIST CRITICISM AND EXPANSION OF THE CANON

MALE DOMINANCE OF LITERARY STUDIES   Prior to 1970, especially during the period in which New Criticism was in vogue, literary standards and agendas were dominated by white male academics. A large majority of college and university teachers and scholars were male; all of the founders of New Criticism were male; most of the writers studied and approved of by New Criticism were male. Cleanth Brooks and Robert Penn Warren's landmark New Critical textbook *Understanding Poetry* (1938) included poems by 89 men and 5 women (11 poems are anonymous). Of the poems included, 220 were by men, 8 by women (one an example of a "bad" poem). In the original edition of a very influential formalist textbook on poetry, Laurence Perrine's *Sound and Sense* (1956), 107 male, but only 10 female, poets were represented (169 poems by men, 18 by women).

MALE ORIENTATION IN NEW CRITICISM   The tendency of male critics to favor works by men was reinforced by the theoretical position of New Criticism. New Criticism looked in literature for universal themes—themes it assumed would apply equally to women and men of all classes, cultures, and times. The shapers of New Criticism, however, did not seem aware of the extent to which their own backgrounds and presuppositions—their ideologies—defined those "universal" issues: The issues were ones raised by well-educated, upper-class, conservative men. Just as their method of reading sought to unify and integrate aspects of literary works, so too the themes they found in the works involved social unity and integration. Issues of importance to marginal groups—women, people of color, lower classes—did not fit the mold and were overlooked (only one poem by an ethnic American author—Countee Cullen's "Incident"—appears in the original *Sound and Sense*; none is included in *Understanding Poetry*).

THE FEMINIST MOVEMENT   Against this background arose a feminist protest movement, which initiated a radical rethinking of the canon. Pivotal in its development was Kate Millett's *Sexual Politics* (1970), which began to raise the consciousness of women to the fact that, generally speaking, all avenues of power in Western culture were under male control. That was true of the production and study of literature. White males set the criteria for what was good literature and decided whose books would be published and whose works would be anthologized. They had the power, therefore, to determine who would be read, who would receive attention, who would achieve fame.

BECOMING A RESISTING READER   Feminist criticism reacted against this power initially by asking what happens to a work written by a male when it is read from a consciously feminine perspective instead of an assumed male perspective. The first act of a feminist reader, according to critic Judith Fetterley, is to become a "resisting reader" instead of an assenting reader[9] — that is, to question and challenge the assumptions of a work about roles, power, and values. A resisting reader exposes the masculine biases (the patriarchal ideology) in a work. This requires paying attention not only to what is said but also to what is not said. Even works in which no women are present may convey an attitude toward women: What does their absence say? How does the fact that no women are present shape and color the situation? Are there details that (perhaps unintentionally or unconsciously) demean women or treat subjects in a way that is potentially insulting to women?

ENLARGING THE CANON   From a reappraisal of works by men, feminist criticism moved on to the study of literature written by women — what Elaine Showalter has termed *gynocriticism*. This involves, on the one hand, the reexamination of women authors who have long been accepted in the canon, and on the other hand, even more significantly, the discovery or rediscovery of many neglected or forgotten women writers, past and present. The result has been to open up the literary canon to include works by women that earlier criticism had excluded.

INCLUDING THE "SOMETHING ELSE"   One criticism of early varieties of feminist criticism is that much of it treats *woman* as a universal category without recognizing differences among women — differences of race, economic and social class, and national origin — that contribute to their identity. Contemporary feminists such as Gayatri Spivak say that, while all women are female, they are something else as well (such as working class or upper class, heterosexual or lesbian, African American or living in a postcolonial nation), and the "something else" is important to consider. Such an approach has led feminists to feel affinities with all those who are considered "the Other" or are marginalized on the basis of race, ethnicity, class, sexual orientation, or social background.

REACHING OUT TO OTHER MARGINALIZED GROUPS   Thus, feminist critics took the lead in raising for ethnic minorities the same questions and concerns raised about women — particularly for African

---

[9]Judith Fetterley. *The Resisting Reader: A Feminist Approach to American Fiction.* Indiana UP, 1978.

Americans at first, and then for Latinos, Native Americans, and other ethnic minorities: How are they treated in works by white authors? Are they stereotyped in insensitive and demeaning ways? Are there details that (perhaps unintentionally or unconsciously) demean minorities or treat subjects in a way that is potentially insulting to the minority group? Are ethnic characters rendered invisible? Are they not included at all? If so, what does their absence say? Ethnic critics began to point out the dearth of writers of color in anthologies and literature courses; to call attention to ethnic authors who had been accepted in the canon or were on its fringes; and to discover or rediscover many neglected or forgotten writers of color, past and present. As the canon expanded to include woman writers, so it expanded to include ethnic authors. *Approaching Literature's* table of contents is evidence of the result.

AN ORIENTATION, NOT A METHOD   Feminist criticism, like Marxist criticism, does not focus on a *method* (the way New Criticism and reader-response criticism do). Instead, it is an orientation, a set of principles that can be fused with a variety of critical approaches. Thus, there can be feminist-reader-response criticism, feminist-deconstructive criticism, and so on. Feminist criticism, in addition to indicating some things to *do* with a work of literature, points out issues to be aware of in a work. It is a committed criticism that aims to heighten awareness, to effect changes in attitudes and behavior, to correct injustices, and to improve society and individual situations. You can use a feminist approach yourself by experimenting with being a resisting reader, by being open to the writings and concerns of women authors, and by focusing papers and discussions on issues of the sort raised in this section.

FEMINISM IN "EVERYDAY USE"   Susan Farrell's essay "Fight vs. Flight: A Re-evaluation of Dee in Alice Walker's 'Everyday Use'" (p. 1099) illustrates how awareness of theoretical approaches can help in understanding the premises on which a scholarly essay is based. Nowhere does the essay say that it is taking a feminist approach to the story, but that is its effect. The essay undertakes a reassessment of Dee, a character with modern feminist inclinations — she went to college to prepare herself for a career, she is fearless and a fighter, she stands up for herself and refuses to back down from what she believes in.

Most critics see the story as putting Dee down because she fails to recognize the difference between her own attitude toward her heritage (fashionable, though separate from her past experience) and that of her mother and sister, who continue to live in that heritage, with its values permeating their daily experiences. Farrell's essay, however, defends Dee, showing that she offers — through her feminist ways — a strategy for contemporary African Americans to cope with an oppressive society, a strategy, Farrell argues, that Dee's mother admires, envies, and eventually emulates.

GENDER STUDIES

FOCUSING ON SOCIALLY CONSTRUCTED DISTINCTIONS   The protest movement that began as feminist criticism has moved on in large part
to the more inclusive area of gender studies. Gender studies focus on the
idea that gender is socially constructed on attitudes toward masculinity and
femininity that are rooted in deeply but uncritically held beliefs of a society.
Most varieties of gender studies assume a difference between the terms *sex*
and *gender*. *Sex* refers to the physical characteristics of women and men
biologically; *gender* refers to traits designated as "feminine" and "masculine." A person is born biologically female or male, but one *acquires* a "gender" (society's conceptions of "woman" and "man"). In Simone de
Beauvoir's words, "One is not born a woman, one becomes one."[10]

BINARY OPPOSITIONS   Gender studies show that such distinctions in
the West traditionally have been shaped through the use of binary oppositions:

masculine / feminine

father / mother

son / daughter

brother / sister

active / passive

reason / emotion

intelligent / sensitive

Through the centuries, the items on the left side of these pairings generally
have been favored (or *privileged*) over those on the right side. Gender criticism exposes the pairings as false oppositions, contending that all these
traits can be part of one's identity.

ALL TYPES OF OPPRESSION   Gender criticism covers *all* "the critical
ramifications of sexual oppression,"[11] including gay, lesbian, and queer
studies. Just as early feminist critics brought attention to the way women
traditionally have been forced to approach literature from a masculine perspective, so gay, lesbian, and queer studies have called attention to the way
texts traditionally are read from a heterosexual viewpoint. Many readers
assume that a relationship described in a work is heterosexual even when
that is not indicated directly. It is not a valid assumption. Lesbian and gay
critics have produced revisionist rereadings — often provocative and illuminating — of many texts that previously were read as straight.

For an example of gender criticism, see Missy Dehn Kubitschek's essay
"August Wilson's Gender Lesson" (p. 800).

---

[10]Simone de Beauvoir. *The Second Sex.* 1949. Translated by H. M. Parshley, Vintage, 1974, p. 301.
[11]Jonathan Culler. *On Deconstruction: Theory and Criticism after Structuralism.* Cornell
UP, 1982, p. 56.

DECONSTRUCTION

One of the best known contemporary literary theories, deconstruction, is also one of the most controversial and difficult. You may have heard of deconstruction, and maybe even used the verb *deconstruct* without realizing its use in literary studies.

FOCUSING ON OPPOSITIONAL THINKING   Deconstruction challenges the logical principles on which the thinking of the Western world since Socrates has been based. Fundamental to Western logic, for example, is the law of noncontradiction (that is, "A" is not the same as "not A") and the use of binary oppositions that have become deeply embedded in our thought: We try to understand things by considering them in pairs that differentiate them. Remember some of the binaries in the section on gender studies:

masculine / feminine

active / passive

reason / emotion

intelligent / sensitive

Here's another list similar to that one:

conscious / unconscious

being / nonbeing

reality / image

right / wrong

thing / sign

speech / writing

Western thinking, from the Greeks on, has privileged the left side of this list over the right side. Such privileging reflects the classical, or Hellenic (Greek), influence on Western philosophy, with its love of reason, logic, order, clarity, coherence, and unity. A key aspect of deconstruction is to challenge that impulse to divide and stratify. Things are not always separate and opposed. They can be different without being opposed; they can also be interdependent and interactive.

QUESTIONING PHILOSOPHICAL ASSUMPTIONS   Deconstruction — like Marxist and feminist criticism — is not a critical *method* the way New Criticism is. Rather, it is a philosophical approach, a way of thinking, a critique of the assumptions that underlie systems such as New Criticism, which emphasize order, coherence, and unity. Deconstructionists posit that a text has no stable reference, and they therefore question assumptions about the ability of language to represent reality. Language is not fixed and limited: It always conveys meanings different from or beyond what we intend.

LOOKING FOR CRACKS Deconstruction focuses on gaps and ambiguities that expose a text's instability and indeterminacy, the "crack" in the seeming unity or coherence of its argument. "Meaning" is not present in the work but is filled in by the reader in the act of reading. According to deconstruction, meaning is totally contextual. A literary work does not *reflect* reality; rather, works *create* their own reality. One cannot go outside a text — to the author's intentions or to references to the outside world — to determine its signification. The text is "self-referential": Only as we look closely at a work and consider its full range of interplay and implication can its signification emerge.

CLOSE ANALYSIS OF LANGUAGE A deconstructive reading, therefore, looks very closely at language, perhaps even more attentively than New Criticism does. It treats language "playfully," showing how the multiple meanings in words (the doubleness of language) contribute to the instability of texts. It picks out key binary oppositions, identifying which term in those oppositions is being privileged (given preference) and showing how such privileging imposes an interpretive template on the subject being examined. It watches for inconsistencies in the apparent unity and stability of a work, as exposed by gaps (comparing what is privileged and what is passed over, or "marginalized").

BINARY OPPOSITIONS IN "SONNY'S BLUES" The values of a deconstructive reading can be illustrated through analyzing James Baldwin's "Sonny's Blues" (p. 324). The story is grounded in a binary opposition, between words and music. The narrator is strongly oriented toward words, while Sonny is oriented toward music. The story opens with the narrator reading about Sonny in a newspaper (that, ironically, is their only means of communication at that point). Also, the story shows the narrator reading, or attempting to read, not just words but people and situations.

VERBALIZING THE NONVERBAL Keith E. Byerman has said of the narrator in "Sonny's Blues" that "the story, in part, is about his misreadings" or his "inability to read properly."[12] As Byerman explains, the narrator is constantly turning nonverbal experiences into words. For example, when the narrator listens in the nightclub, he declares that both the terribleness and triumph of music is that "it has no words." Yet, immediately afterward, he begins reading language into the music, describing it as a conversation: "The dry, low, black man *said* something awful on the drums, Creole *answered*, and the drums *talked back*. Then the horn insisted, sweet and high, slightly detached perhaps, and Creole listened, *commenting* now and then" (p. 346; italics added).

---

[12]Keith E. Byerman. "Words and Music: Narrative Ambiguity in 'Sonny's Blues.'" *Studies in Short Fiction*, vol. 19, no. 4, Fall 1982, p. 367.

Byerman suggests that Baldwin uses the verbalizing of the nonverbal early in the story as a way to undercut the narrator and to show his need for deeper understanding. However, something more complex than that is going on near the end. Byerman notes the lack of preparation for the narrator's sophisticated analysis of music in the final scene. The narrator throughout has expressed his antipathy to music and an inability to comprehend its appeal. Yet suddenly he expresses profound understanding of how music affects a listener. But Byerman does not deal fully with the contradictory nature of the narrator's sudden grasp of music, or with the "crack" this creates in the text.

DECONSTRUCTING THE STORY   A deconstructionist would recognize that what we are hearing, actually, is the author's voice breaking through the narrator's voice, conveying the meaning he finds in music. That, in turn, undermines the author's own undercutting of the narrator: The author himself cannot resist verbalizing the meaning of music. Or he cannot avoid it because the final section of the story rests on a binary opposition it attempts to deconstruct: Words and music are similar as well as different. Music, like objects and like words, must be "interpreted"—there is no escape from "reading." But the reading that music invites is open and indirect. Baldwin, however, gives a direct and closed reading in an attempt to convey openness and indirection. The story thus has a level of complexity, through its contradictions, which Byerman's New Critical reading does not pick up but which a deconstructive approach can bring out.

CULTURAL CRITICISM

FOCUSING ON CULTURES   From the 1980s onward, much of literary study has been focused on culture, but not the promotion of "high culture" advocated by Matthew Arnold in the mid- to late 1800s. Cultural criticism explores the relationship between an author and her or his work and the cultural context in which they exist. An author, writing at a specific time in a specific place, inevitably is influenced by contemporary events and attitudes, whether she or he accepts and reflects prevailing attitudes or ignores, rejects, or challenges them.

CULTURAL INCLUSIVENESS   The work of anthropologists has changed the primary meaning of *culture* from a single, static, universal, elitist "high culture" to a set of dynamic, interactive, always changing *cultures*. Contemporary cultural criticism (sometimes referred to as cultural studies) is inclusive ethnically, with a strong multicultural emphasis. It emphasizes that cultural achievements of worth are produced by people from a variety of social, economic, and ethnic backgrounds, past as well as present, and that criticism should enable us to appreciate this diversity of accomplishment. And it is inclusive regarding subject matter — it does not limit itself to the literature of "high culture" but also draws on popular culture as a valuable indicator of cultural values. It studies comic books as well as novels, hit movies as well as theater, MTV as well as public television, pop songs as well as jazz, graffiti as well as gallery art. The emphasis in cultural studies is on how people *relate to* all levels of art rather than on their aesthetic standards and on getting them to recognize and work with "the best" literature, music, or art.

INFLUENCED AND INFLUENCING   Cultural criticism focuses on what a work conveys about social attitudes and social relations, focusing especially on the impact of details such as social background, sex, class, ethnicity, power, and privilege. Cultural critics concentrate on the way a work embodies a cultural context, how the events, ideas, or attitudes in a work were influenced by the economic conditions, political situation, or social conventions existing when it was written, but they also explore the way a work exists as *part of* a culture and how it can influence, and perhaps change, the economic conditions, political situation, or social conventions of its time or later times.

INTERDISCIPLINARY   Thus the theory tends to work with interdisciplinary approaches. Cultural criticism often views works in relation to other works (literary works, especially ones outside the traditional canon, but also journals, memoirs, and diaries of ordinary people; church records; medical reports; architectural drawings; and so on); to social and economic conditions that affected them; to the way they were shaped by those who held power (including editors, publishers, and reviewers, for example); and to the way they reinforced conditions of power, intentionally or not.

For an example of a paper engaging in cultural criticism, see Harry J. Elam, Jr.'s "August Wilson" (p. 805), which explores a variety of cultural influences on Wilson and discusses how his works have critiqued and influenced U.S. culture of the late twentieth and early twenty-first centuries.

NEW HISTORICISM

FOCUSING AGAIN ON HISTORY   An influential variety of cultural studies, New Historicism, grew out of a sense that New Criticism and deconstruction, through their neglect of the social and cultural milieu in which a work had been written, were leaving out something important and valuable. New Historicists would say that, by focusing almost wholly on what occurs within a text, New Critics and deconstructionists cut themselves off from the ways historical context can clarify and illuminate a work. They lose referentiality. Despite many differences, the varieties of historicist critics have in common a belief in referentiality — that works of literature are influenced by, and influence, reality.

THE UNDERLYING THEORY   New Historicism starts from a theory of history different from that which underlies "old historicism," with its emphasis on facts and events, its selective focus on the kinds of events that get recorded in official documents, and its explanations of causes and effects and of development toward an end. New Historicists assume that it is nearly impossible to reconstruct the past. We have only stories about the past, not objective facts and events existing independently; the stories are constructed by historians, reflecting the historians' assumptions and purposes and the choices they inevitably make about what to include, what to emphasize, what to omit. French philosophical historian Michel Foucault says that all historians are "situated." It is difficult for historians to recognize their own cultural practices and assumptions and even more difficult to get outside them and enter those of another age.

AN INTERDISCIPLINARY APPROACH   The work of New Historicists is influenced by deconstruction and reader-response criticism, with their emphasis on subjectivity, and by cultural studies generally, with its attention to the myriad forces that shape events and motivations. New Historicists do not concentrate on economic and political forces or on the better-documented activities of the rich and famous, as the old historicism did. Like other types of cultural studies, New Historicism is open to other disciplines in its attempts to elucidate how art is shaped by, and shapes, social, historical, and economic conditions, and how art is affected by politics and has political effects itself.

NEW HISTORICISM AND "ODE ON A GRECIAN URN"   Consider, for example, John Keats's 1819 poem "Ode on a Grecian Urn" (p. 636). The poem was a central text discussed in Cleanth Brooks's famous book of New Critical essays, *The Well Wrought Urn*.[13] In his close examination of the poem, Brooks suggests that it is proper for the personified urn to ignore names, dates, and special circumstances and to concentrate instead on universal truths. Brooks ignores historical context and influences as a whole; instead, he takes a few details and orders them so that we better appreciate the beauty of the poem and its own impact as myth.

SITUATING THE POEM   New Historicists, in contrast, would hold that it is important to situate the poem in its historical context and to ask, in this case, how economic and political conditions of early nineteenth-century

---

[13]Cleanth Brooks. *The Well Wrought Urn: Studies in the Structure of Poetry*. Reynal, 1947.

England shaped Keats's image of ancient Greece. New Historicists tend to start their analysis by discussing a particular object or event and then proceed to connect that object or event to the poem so that readers come to see "the event as a social text and the literary text as a social event."[14]

THE URN AND MUSEUMS   Brook Thomas, for example, asks where Keats would have seen such an urn. The answer—in a museum—leads into a discussion of the rise of art museums in eighteenth- and nineteenth-century Europe, as cultural artifacts from the past were placed in collections to be contemplated as art, isolated from their social setting. "In Keats's poem an urn that once had a practical social function now sparks aesthetic contemplation about the nature of truth, beauty, and the past." Thomas then says that reflecting on how the urn assumes a purely aesthetic function in a society that was becoming increasingly practical helps clarify "how our modern notion of art has been defined in response to the social order."[15]

SOCIAL IMPLICATIONS OF THE TEXT   To the New Historicist, even the urn's position in a museum raises political issues. The presence of a Grecian urn in an English museum can lead to reflections on the political implications of a cultural heritage. Englishmen in the nineteenth century, although they sympathized with the struggle for liberation in Greece, nevertheless took cultural treasures out of the country and put them on display in London. Thomas concludes that Keats's poem is "a social text, one that in telling us about the society that produced it also tells us about the society we inhabit today"[16] and should lead to reflection not just on present attitudes toward museums in the United States but also on the implications of the way Keats's English poem has become a museum-type artifact in U.S. culture today.

POSTCOLONIAL CRITICISM

FOCUSING ON COLONIZATION   Postcolonial theory deals with cultural expression and behavior relating to the formerly or currently colonized parts of the world. Postcolonial criticism involves the analysis of literature by native writers who are living in colonized countries or who emigrated

---

[14]Brook Thomas. "The New Literary Historicism." *A Companion to American Thought*, edited by Richard Wightman Fox and James T. Kloppenberg, Blackwell, 1995, p. 490.

[15]Brook Thomas. "The Historical Necessity for — and Difficulties with — New Historical Analysis in Introductory Literature Courses." *College English*, vol. 49, no. 5, September 1987, p. 518.

[16]Ibid., p. 519.

from such countries. We limit the discussion here to literature written in English in parts of the world that were colonized by Great Britain or the United States: primarily, then, Australia, New Zealand, parts of the Caribbean, South America, Africa, and Asia. Postcolonial criticism focuses particularly on how colonized peoples attempt to assert their identity and to claim their heritage separate from, or other than, the colonizing culture. It also involves analysis of works written about colonized countries by writers from the colonizing countries, particularly as such writers misrepresent the cultures they describe, imposing on them their own cultural values and sense of cultural superiority.

THE STRUGGLES OF COLONIZED PEOPLES   Postcolonial criticism deals with all aspects of the struggle that occurs when one culture is subjugated by another, with what happens when one culture, because of the political power behind it, is able to dominate the other and to establish the impression of being superior to the other. It deals with the creation of Otherness, especially through the use of dialectical thinking to create pairs such as us/them, same/other, white/colored, rational/irrational, ordered/chaotic. Postcolonial criticism also addresses the way colonized peoples lose their past, are removed from history, and are forced to give up many of their cultural beliefs and practices. It confronts the way colonized peoples must forsake their language and cooperate with the conquerors if they want to get ahead economically. It reveals how the colonized peoples must cope with the memories and continuing legacy of being an occupied nation.

Glossary of Literary Terms

Abstract language Language that names general or intangible concepts, such as *love, truth,* and *beauty.* See also CONCRETE LANGUAGE.

Accent The emphasis, or stress, given a syllable in articulation. Metrical accent is the placement of stress as determined by the metrical and rhythmic pattern of a poetic line. See also STRESS.

Act One of the major divisions of a dramatic work. See also SCENE.

Alexandrine A poetic line with six iambic feet. Also called a *hexameter.*

Allegory A literary form or approach in which objects, persons, and actions make coherent sense on a literal level but also are equated in a sustained and obvious way with (usually) abstract meanings that lie outside the story. A classic example in prose is John Bunyan's *The Pilgrim's Progress;* in narrative poetry, Edmund Spenser's *The Faerie Queene;* in drama, the medieval English play *Everyman.* Nathaniel Hawthorne's "Young Goodman Brown" (p. 359) is a moral allegory in which the names convey the abstract qualities developed in a second level of meaning beyond that of the literal events and characters in the story.

Alliteration The repetition of identical initial consonant sounds in the stressed syllables of words relatively near to each other. See also CONSONANCE.

Allusion Echoes or brief references to a literary or artistic work or a historical figure, event, or object, as, for example, the references to Lazarus and Hamlet in T. S. Eliot's "The Love Song of J. Alfred Prufrock" (see p. 624). It is usually a way of placing one's poem within, or alongside, a whole other context that is thus evoked in a very economical fashion.

Ambiguity (1) In expository prose, an undesirable doubtfulness or uncertainty of meaning or intention, resulting from imprecision in use of words or construction of sentences. (2) In poetry, the desirable condition of admitting more than one possible meaning, resulting from the capacity of language to function on levels other than the literal. Related terms sometimes employed are *ambivalence* and *polysemy.* See also PUN.

Anapest   A metrical foot consisting of three syllables, with two unaccented syllables followed by an accented one (*da da DA*— "in a dream"). In anapestic meter, anapests are the predominant foot in a line or poem.

Antagonist   The character who opposes the protagonist in a narrative or dramatic work. See also PROTAGONIST.

Antihero   A protagonist in a narrative or dramatic work who lacks the attributes of a traditional hero.

Antistrophe   (1) The second stanza in a three-stanza segment of a choral ode in Greek drama. It is preceded by (and identical in form to) the strophe, which is sung while the chorus moves from stage right to stage left. During the antistrophe, the chorus moves back to stage right before singing the epode. (2) The second stanza in a three-stanza segment of an ode (thus, stanzas two, five, eight, and so on). See also CHORUS; EPODE; ODE; STROPHE.

Antithesis   A figure of speech in which contrasting words, sentences, or ideas are expressed in balanced, parallel grammatical structures; for example, "She had some horses she loved. / She had some horses she hated" (Joy Harjo, "She Had Some Horses," p. 579).

Apostrophe   A figure of speech in which an absent person is addressed as though present or an abstract quality or a nonhuman entity is addressed. In the latter case, it is a particular type of PERSONIFICATION.

Approximate rhyme   See SLANT RHYME.

Archetype   An image, symbol, character type, or plot line that occurs frequently enough in literature, religion, myths, folktales, and fairy tales to be recognizable as an element of universal literary experience and thus to evoke a deep emotional response. See page 1112.

Aside   A convention in drama in which a character utters thoughts intended for the audience to hear that supposedly cannot be heard by the other characters onstage.

Assonance   The repetition of identical or similar vowel sounds in words relatively near to each other whose consonant sounds differ. See also SLANT RHYME.

Atmosphere   The feeling, or emotional aura, created in a reader or audience by a literary work, especially as such feeling is evoked by the setting or landscape.

Ballad   A poem that tells a story and is meant to be recited or sung; originally a folk art, transmitted orally from person to person and generation to generation. Many of the popular ballads were not written down and published until the eighteenth century, though their origins may have been centuries earlier.

Ballad stanza   A quatrain in iambic meter rhyming *abcb* with (usually) four feet in the first and third lines, three in the second and fourth.

Biographical criticism   See page 1109.

Blank verse   Lines of unrhymed iambic pentameter.

Cacophony   A harsh or unpleasant combination of sounds, as, for example, "But when loud surges lash the sounding shore, / The hoarse, rough verse should like the torrent roar" (Alexander Pope, "An Essay on Criticism," ll. 368–69 — available online). See also EUPHONY.

Caesura   A pause or break within a line of verse, usually signaled by a mark of punctuation.

Canon   In the Christian tradition, the books accepted by the church as divinely inspired and approved for inclusion in the Bible. In literary studies, it means (1) the list of works generally accepted as the authentic work of a particular author (e.g., the Shakespearean canon) or (2) literary works that are given special status by the literary establishment within a society as works most worthy of study and emulation.

Carpe diem   "Seize the day," a Latin phrase from an ode by Horace. It is the label for a theme common in literature, especially sixteenth- and seventeenth-century English love poetry, that life is short and fleeting and that therefore one must make the most of present pleasures. See, for example, Robert Herrick's "To the Virgins, to Make Much of Time" (available online) and Andrew Marvell's "To His Coy Mistress" (p. 640).

Catastrophe   The concluding section of a play, particularly of a tragedy, describing the fall or death of the protagonist that results from the climax. The term *dénouement* is more commonly used for comedy. See also DÉNOUEMENT.

Catharsis   Term used by Aristotle in the *Poetics* to describe the outcome of viewing a tragedy. The term has usually been translated as "purgation" or "purification," though what Aristotle meant by it is widely disputed. A tragedy, it seems to say, engenders pity and fear in its audience, then releases and quiets those emotions, a process that has a healthy effect, psychologically and physically: The audience goes away feeling not dejected but relieved.

Center of consciousness technique   A third-person limited point of view in which a narrator relates a story through what is thought, felt, seen, and experienced by one of the characters, showing only what that character is conscious of.

Character   (1) A figure, human or personified, in a literary work; characters may be animals or some other beings. (2) A literary genre that offers a brief sketch of a personality type or an example of a virtue or vice, such as a country bumpkin or a braggart soldier.

Characterization   The process or use of techniques by which an author describes and develops the characters in a literary work.

Chaucerian stanza   A seven-line iambic stanza rhyming *ababbcc*, sometimes having an alexandrine (hexameter) closing line. It was first used in English by Geoffrey Chaucer (c. 1343–1400) in *Troilus and Criseyde*, as well as in many of his later poems (thus the name *Chaucerian stanza*), and was widely used in English poetry of the fifteenth and sixteenth centuries. It is also referred to as RHYME ROYAL.

Chorus   In its literary sense, the group of performers in Greek theater whose dancing and singing provided exposition and comment on the action of a play. In later theater, a single character identified as "chorus" who has a function similar to that of the Greek chorus.

Chronological order   The arrangement of events (real or fictional) in the order in which they happened. See page 114.

Climax   The moment of greatest tension or emotional intensity in a plot.

Closed form   A poetic organization that evinces any repetition of meter, rhyme, or stanza. See also OPEN FORM.

Closet drama   A play that is intended to be read rather than performed.

Colloquial language   The diction, syntax, and idioms characteristic of informal speech.

Comedy   In medieval times, a literary work that has a happy ending and is written in a style less exalted than that of tragedy (e.g., Dante's *Divine Comedy*). More broadly, a humorous and entertaining work, particularly such a work in drama. See also TRAGEDY.

Comic relief   A humorous scene, passage, or character in an otherwise serious play; sometimes described as providing an audience with a momentary relief from the emotional intensity of a tragedy but at the same time heightening the seriousness of the work.

Complication   One of the traditional elements of plot, describing the protagonist's entanglements resulting from plot conflicts.

Concrete language   Language that names material things. See also ABSTRACT LANGUAGE.

Concrete poem   A poem arranged in a shape suggestive of the poem's subject matter.

Conflict   A confrontation or struggle between opposing characters or forces in a literary work, which gives rise to and is a focal point for the action of the plot.

Connotation   The shared or communal range of associations and emotional implications a word may carry in addition to its dictionary definitions. See also DENOTATION.

Consonance   The repetition of consonant sounds in the same or nearby lines. See also SLANT RHYME.

Convention   A rule, method, practice, or characteristic established by usage; a customary feature.

Couplet   A unit consisting of two consecutive lines of poetry with the same end rhyme. See also HEROIC COUPLET.

Crisis   The turning point in a plot, the moment at which a situation changes decisively for better or for worse. See also CLIMAX.

Cultural criticism   See page 1126.

Dactyl   A metrical foot consisting of three syllables, an accented one followed by two unaccented ones (*DA da da*—"sleepily"). In dactylic meter, dactyls are the predominant foot of a line or poem.

Deconstruction   See page 1124.

Denotation   The basic meaning of a word; a word's dictionary definition. See also CONNOTATION.

Dénouement   From the French for "unknotting," the untangling of events at the end of a play that resolves the conflicts (or leaves them satisfyingly unresolved), clarifies what is needed for understanding the outcome, and ties up the loose ends. It can be used in tragedy but is generally used in comedy. See also CATASTROPHE.

Deus ex machina   From the Latin for "god out of the machine," refers to the mechanical device by which the actor playing a god was lowered to the stage in Greek drama to rescue characters from a seemingly impossible situation. It now denotes the use of any unexpected or artificial means to resolve an irresolvable conflict.

Dialect   One of several varieties of a language, differing in vocabulary, grammar, and/or pronunciation, and identified with a certain region; community; or social, ethnic, or occupational group. Often one dialect comes to be considered the "standard."

Dialogue   A conversation between two or more characters in a literary work.

Diction   Choice of words; the kind of words, phrases, and figurative language that make up a work of literature. See also POETIC DICTION.

Dimeter   A line of verse consisting of two metrical feet.

Double rhyme   A rhyme in which the accented, rhyming syllable is followed by one or more identical, unstressed syllables: *thrilling* and *killing*, *marry* and *tarry*. An older label, *feminine rhyme*, is generally no longer used. See also SINGLE RHYME.

Downstage   The part of the stage closest to the audience.

Drama   (1) A literary composition that tells a story, usually involving human conflict, by means of dialogue and action rather than narration. (2) In modern and contemporary theater, any play that is not a comedy or a musical. (3) The dramas of a particular writer or culture, considered as a whole (e.g., Shakespearean drama, medieval drama). See also CLOSET DRAMA; PLAY.

Dramatic irony   A situation in which a reader or audience knows more than the speakers or characters, either about future events or about the discrepancy between a meaning intended by a speaker or character and that recognized by a reader or an audience. See also IRONY; SITUATIONAL IRONY; VERBAL IRONY.

Dramatic monologue   A poem consisting of speech by one speaker, overheard in a dramatic moment and usually addressing a character or characters who do not speak. The speaker's words reveal what is going on in the scene and expose significant depths of the speaker's temperament, attitudes, and values. See also SOLILOQUY.

Dramatis personae   The characters in a play, or a list of such characters.

Dynamic character   A character shown as changing and growing because of what happens to her or him. See also STATIC CHARACTER.

Elegy   In Greek and Roman literature, a serious, meditative poem written in elegiac meter (alternating hexameter and pentameter lines); since the 1600s, a sustained and formal poem lamenting the death of a particular person, usually ending with a consolation, or setting forth meditations on death or another solemn theme. The adjective *elegiac* is also used to describe a general tone of sadness or a worldview that emphasizes suffering and loss. It is most often applied to Anglo-Saxon poems such as *Beowulf* or *The Seafarer* but also can be used for modern poems, as, for example, A. E. Housman's poems in *A Shropshire Lad*.

End rhyme   Rhyme at the ends of lines in a poem. See also INTERNAL RHYME.

End-stopped line   A line in which a grammatical pause (punctuation mark) and the completion of the meaning coincide at the end. See also RUN-ON LINE.

English sonnet   A sonnet consisting of three quatrains (four-line units, typically rhyming *abab cdcd efef*) and a couplet (two rhyming lines). Usually the subject is introduced in the first quatrain, expanded in the second, and expanded still further in the third; the couplet adds a logical, pithy conclusion or gives a surprising twist. Also called the *Shakespearean sonnet*. See also ITALIAN SONNET.

Enjambment   See RUN-ON LINE.

Epic   A long narrative poem that celebrates the achievements of great heroes and heroines, often determining the fate of a tribe or nation, in formal language and an elevated style. Examples include Homer's *Iliad* and *Odyssey,* Virgil's *Aeneid,* and John Milton's *Paradise Lost*.

Epic simile   An extended or elaborate simile in which the image used to describe the subject is developed in considerable detail.

Epigram   Originally, an inscription on a building, tomb, or gravestone; in modern usage, a short poem, usually polished and witty with a surprising twist at the end. (Its other dictionary definition, "any terse, witty, pointed statement," is a characteristic of some dramatic writing, for example, the comedies of Oscar Wilde.)

Epigraph   In literature, a quotation at the beginning of a poem, story, chapter, play, or book. See, for example, the epigraph from Dante at the beginning of T. S. Eliot's "The Love Song of J. Alfred Prufrock" (p. 624).

Epilogue   Final remarks by an actor after the main action of a play has ended, usually summing up or commenting on the play, or asking for critics and the audience to receive it favorably. In novels, an epilogue may be added to reveal what happens to the characters in future years, after the plot proper concludes.

Epiphany   An appearance or manifestation, especially of a divine being; in literature, since James Joyce adapted the term to secular use, a sudden sense of radiance and revelation one may feel while perceiving a commonplace object; a moment or event in which the essential nature of a person, a situation, or an object is suddenly perceived. The term is more common in the criticism of fiction, narrative poetry, and drama than in lyric poetry.

Epode   (1) The third stanza in a three-stanza segment of an ode in Greek drama, sung while the chorus is standing still. (2) The third stanza in a three-stanza segment of an ode. See also ANTISTROPHE; CHORUS; ODE; STROPHE.

Essay   A relatively brief discussion, usually in prose, of a limited, nonfictional topic or idea.

Euphony   Sounds that strike the ear as smooth, musical, and agreeable, as, for example, "Soft is the strain when Zephyr gently blows, / And the smooth stream in smoother numbers flows" (Alexander Pope, "An Essay on Criticism," ll. 366–67 — available online). See also CACOPHONY.

Exact rhyme   Rhyme in which the vowel sound and all sounds following it are the same: *spite* and *night* or *ache* and *fake*.

Exaggeration   See HYPERBOLE.

Explication   A method entailing close analysis of a text, opening it up line by line, clarifying how diction, images, figurative language, symbols, sounds, rhythm, form, and allusions contribute toward shaping the work's meaning and effect. See page 1114.

Exposition   A nondramatized explanation, often a speech by a character or the narrator, that describes things that occurred before the initial action of a narrative or drama, filling in background information that the audience needs to make sense of the story.

Extended metaphor   A metaphoric comparison that is sustained and expanded over a number of lines.

Falling action   The action following the climax of a traditionally structured play as the tension lessens and the play moves toward the catastrophe or dénouement. See also RISING ACTION.

Falling meter   A foot (usually trochee or dactyl) in which the first syllable is stressed, followed by unstressed syllables that give a sense of stepping down. See also RISING METER.

Farce   A dramatic work intended to excite laughter and that depends less on plot and character than on improbable situations, gross incongruities, coarse wit, and horseplay.

Feminine rhyme   See DOUBLE RHYME.

Feminist criticism   See page 1120.

Fiction   From the Latin verb "to make." (1) Narrated stories in prose — usually short stories, novellas, or novels — that are drawn from the imagination or are an imaginative reworking of actual experiences. Incidents and details in a work of fiction can originate in fact, history, or everyday life, but the characters and events as a whole are primarily invented, or altered, in the author's imagination. (2) The made-up situation underlying any literary work; the feigned or imagined situation underlying it. See also NOVEL; NOVELLA; SHORT STORY.

Figurative language   See FIGURE OF SPEECH.

Figure of speech   Use of language that departs from customary construction, order, or significance in order to achieve a special effect or meaning. It occurs in two forms: (1) trope (from a word for "turn"), or "figure of thought," in which a word or phrase is turned or twisted to make it mean something different from its usual significance; and (2) "rhetorical figure," which creates a surprising effect by using words in unexpected ways without altering what the words mean. See also METAPHOR; METONYMY; PERSONIFICATION; SIMILE; SYNECDOCHE.

First-person point of view   The *I* who tells a story from a first-person point of view, either as an outside observer or as someone directly or indirectly involved in the action of the story.

Fixed form   In poetry, definite, repeating patterns of line, rhyme scheme, or stanza.

Flashback   A literary device that interrupts a narrative to present earlier material, often something that occurred before the opening of the work, through a character's memories or dreams or through juxtaposition of earlier and later events.

Flash fiction   Fiction that is extremely brief, typically only a few hundred words or fewer in its entirety. See page 296.

Flat character   A character represented through only one or two main features or aspects that can often be summed up in a sentence or two. See also ROUND CHARACTER.

Foil   A character used as a contrast with another character, thus highlighting the latter's distinctive attributes or character traits.

Foot   The basic unit in metrical verse, comprised of (usually) one stressed and one or more unstressed syllables. See also ANAPEST; DACTYL; IAMB; SPONDEE; TROCHEE.

Foreshadowing   Words, gestures, or other actions that hint at future events or outcomes in a literary work.

Form   (1) Genre or literary type (e.g., the lyric form); (2) patterns of meter, lines, and rhymes (stanzaic form); or (3) the organization of the parts of a literary work in relation to its total effect (e.g., "The form [structure] of this poem is very effective"). See also STRUCTURE.

Formalist criticism   See page 1114.

Found poem   A passage from a nonpoetic source such as a newspaper, a magazine, an advertisement, a textbook, or elsewhere in everyday life that contains some element of poetry: meter (sometimes), effective rhythm, phrasings that can be divided into lines, imaginative uses of language and sound, and so on.

Fourth wall   The theatrical convention, dating from the nineteenth century and realistic drama, whereby an audience seems to be looking through an invisible fourth wall into the room of an actual house created by the other three walls of a box set.

Free verse   See OPEN FORM.

Gay and lesbian criticism   See page 1123.

Gender criticism   See page 1123.

Genre   A recurring type of literature; a literary form as defined by rules or conventions followed in it (e.g., tragedy, comedy, epic, lyric, pastoral, novel, short story, essay).

Gothic story   Fiction in which magic, mystery, and effects creating a sense of horror, or an atmosphere of brooding and unknown terror, play a major role.

Graphic fiction   Fictional stories related in comic book-style images and words, usually published as books, not magazines or in newspapers. See page 301.

Haiku   A lyric form, originating in Japan, of seventeen syllables in three lines, the first and third having five syllables, and the second seven presenting an image of a natural object or scene that expresses a distinct emotion or spiritual insight.

Hamartia   An error in judgment, a mistake, a frailty that, according to Aristotle's *Poetics,* results in a tragic hero's change in fortune from prosperity to adversity. *Hamartia* is sometimes mistakenly equated with tragic flaw. It does not, however, refer to a character flaw but rather to a central or defining aspect of the character. In reading plays critically, watching for an error or misstep (*hamartia*) is more advisable than looking for a defect in character (tragic flaw). See also TRAGIC FLAW.

Heptameter   A poetic line with seven metrical feet.

Hero, heroine   The protagonist, or central character, in a literary work.

Heroic couplet   Couplet in iambic pentameter with a full stop, usually, at the end. Also called *closed couplet.*

Hexameter   See ALEXANDRINE.

Historical criticism   See page 1109.

Hubris (hybris)   Greek for "insolence"; excessive pride that can lead to the downfall of the protagonist in a tragedy.

Hyperbole   Exaggeration; a figure of speech in which something is stated more strongly than is logically warranted. See also UNDERSTATEMENT.

Iamb   A metrical foot consisting of two syllables, an unaccented one followed by an accented one (*da DA*—"awake"). In iambic meter, iambs are the predominant foot in a line or poem.

Image   (1) A word or group of words that refers to a sensory experience or to an object that can be known by one or more of the senses. *Imagery* signifies all such language in a poem or other literary work collectively and can include any of the senses (visual imagery, auditory imagery, tactile imagery, kinetic imagery, imagery of smell or taste). (2) A metaphor or other comparison. *Imagery* in this sense refers to the characteristic that several images in a poem have in common, for example, the winter imagery in Judith Ortiz Cofer's "Cold as Heaven" (p. 539).

Imagery   See IMAGE.

Implied metaphor   Metaphor in which the verb *to be* is omitted and one aspect of the comparison is implied rather than stated directly, as, for example, "Police cars cockroach through the tunnel streets" in Dennis Brutus's "Nightsong: City" (p. 527).

In medias res   Latin for "into the middle things"; used to describe the technique of starting a narrative at an engaging point well into the story and filling in the background events later as needed.

Interior monologue   The representation of unspoken mental activity—thoughts, impressions, and memories—as if directly overheard by the reader, without being selected and organized by a narrator, either in an associative, disjointed, nonlogical, nongrammatical way (stream of consciousness) or in a logical, grammatical flow of thoughts and memories moving through a person's mind, as if being spoken to an external listener. It is sometimes set off typographically, for example, by using italics rather than quotation marks.

Internal rhyme   Rhyme that occurs between words within a line, between words within lines near each other, or between a word within a line and one at the end of the same or a nearby line.

Irony   A feeling, tone, mood, or attitude arising from the awareness that what is (reality) is opposite from, and usually worse than, what seems (appearance). Irony is not the same as mere coincidence. Irony has different forms: What a person *says* may be ironic (see VERBAL IRONY); a discrepancy between what a character knows or means and what a reader or audience knows can be ironic (see DRAMATIC IRONY); a general situation can be ironic (see SITUATIONAL IRONY).

Italian sonnet   A sonnet composed of an octave (an eight-line unit), rhyming *abbaabba,* and a sestet (a six-line unit), often rhyming *cdecde* or *cdcdcd,* although variations are frequent. The octave usually develops an idea or a question or a problem; then the poem pauses, or "turns," and the sestet completes the idea, answers the question, or resolves the difficulty. Sometimes called a *Petrarchan sonnet.* See also ENGLISH SONNET.

Juxtaposition   Placement of things side by side or close together for comparison or contrast or to create something new from the union, without necessarily making them grammatically parallel.

Limited omniscient point of view   Use of a narrator who is omniscient in some areas or to some extent but is not completely all-knowing.

Line   A sequence of words printed as a separate entity on a page; the basic structural unit in poetry (except prose poems).

Literal   In accordance with the primary or strict meaning of a word or words; not figurative or metaphorical.

Literary present   Use of present tense verbs when discussing fictional events. See page 49.

Litotes   See UNDERSTATEMENT.

Lyric   Originally, a poem sung to the accompaniment of a lyre; now a poem, usually short, expressing the personal emotion and ideas of a single speaker.

Major character   A character who is prominent in the plot and theme of a short story, novel, or play, filling a central role in advancing the action and determining the outcome of the work. See also ROUND CHARACTER.

Marxist criticism   See page 1117.

Masculine rhyme   See SINGLE RHYME.

Melodrama   Originally, a drama with musical accompaniment that enhanced its emotional impact; in the nineteenth century, it became a type of play relying on broadly drawn heroes and villains, suspenseful plots, improbable escapes, the triumph of good over evil, and an excessive appeal to the emotions of the audience.

Metaphor A figure of speech in which two things usually thought to be dissimilar are treated as if they were alike and have characteristics in common, as, for example, "numbers were fractious beasts," in Anita Endrezze's "The Girl Who Loved the Sky" (p. 474). See also IMPLIED METAPHOR.

Metaphysical poetry The work of a number of seventeenth-century English poets characterized by philosophical subtlety and intellectual rigor; subtle, often outrageous logic; imitation of actual speech, sometimes resulting in "rough" meter and style; and far-fetched analogies. Sometimes applied to modern verse sharing some of these characteristics.

Meter A steady beat, or measured pulse, created by a repeating pattern of accents, syllables, or both.

Metonymy A figure of speech in which the name of one thing is substituted for that of something closely associated with it, as in commonly used phrases such as "The *White House* announced today . . ." See also SYNECDOCHE.

Metrics The study of the patterns of rhythm in poetry.

Minor character A character who fills a supportive role in the plot and theme of a short story, novel, or play, and is not central to the action or outcome of the work. See also FLAT CHARACTER.

Monometer A poetic line with one metrical foot.

Morality play A form of drama that originated in the Middle Ages and presents a dramatized allegory in which abstractions (such as mercy, conscience, perseverance, and shame) are personified and engage in a struggle for a human soul.

Motif A recurring element — image, idea, feature, action, or theme — that is elaborated or developed throughout a work.

Motivation The combination of personality traits and circumstances that impel a character to act in a particular way.

Mystery play A medieval play based on biblical history; a scriptural play.

Myth Anonymous stories arising from a culture's oral traditions that involve gods or heroic figures; explore matters beyond everyday life; and concern origins, endings, aspirations, purpose, and meaning.

Mythological criticism See page 1112.

Naïve narrator A narrator too young or too inexperienced to understand fully the implications of what she or he is talking about. See also NARRATOR; RELIABLE NARRATOR; UNRELIABLE NARRATOR.

Narrative A narrated story, in prose or verse; an account of events involving characters and what they do and say, told by a storyteller (narrator).

Narrator The storyteller through whom an author relates a narrative. See also FIRST-PERSON POINT OF VIEW; NAÏVE NARRATOR; POINT OF VIEW; RELIABLE NARRATOR; UNRELIABLE NARRATOR.

Naturalism   A literary movement of the late nineteenth and early twentieth centuries that applies the principles of scientific determinism to literature and views humans as animals in a natural world who respond to environmental forces — physical or socioeconomic — and internal stresses and drives, none of which they can control or understand.

Near rhyme   See SLANT RHYME.

New Comedy   Greek comedy of the fourth and third centuries B.C.E. that depicts the obstacles faced by young lovers and the unpredictable changes of fortune they encounter, and pokes fun at the foibles and attitudes of the lovers as well as those around them.

New Criticism   See page 1114.

New Historicism   See page 1127.

Novel   Although the term can refer to any extended fictional narrative in prose, it is generally used for narratives that emphasize complexity of character and development of a unifying theme. See also FICTION; NOVELLA; SHORT STORY.

Novella   A fictional prose narrative longer than a short story but shorter than a novel; commonly fifty to one hundred pages in length. See also FICTION; NOVEL; SHORT STORY.

Objective point of view   A narrative approach in which a narrator describes events only from the outside, without looking into the mind of any of the characters or explaining why any of the characters do what they do.

Octameter   A poetic line with eight metrical feet.

Octave   The first, eight-line segment of an Italian sonnet.

Ode   (1) In Greek drama, a speech delivered by the chorus. (2) A long lyric poem, serious (often intellectual) in tone, elevated and dignified in style, dealing with a single theme. The ode is generally more complicated in form than other lyric poems. Some odes retain a formal division into strophe, antistrophe, and epode, which reflects the ode's origins in Greek drama. See also ANTISTROPHE; CHORUS; EPODE; STROPHE.

Off rhyme   See SLANT RHYME.

Old Comedy   Comedy, such as that of Aristophanes in the fifth century B.C.E., employing raucous (sometimes coarse) humor, elements of satire and farce, and often a critique of contemporary persons or political and social norms.

Omniscient point of view   The point of view in a work of fiction in which the narrator is capable of knowing everything about a story's events and characters, including their inner feelings.

One-act play   A short play that is complete in one act.

Onomatopoeia   The use of words whose sounds supposedly resemble the sounds they denote, such as *hiss* or *buzz*, or a group of words whose sounds help to convey what is being described.

Open form   A poetic form free of any predetermined metrical and stanzaic patterns. See also CLOSED FORM.

Orchestra   From the Greek word for "dance." In Greek theater, the area in front of the skene where the chorus performed its songs and dances. Later, a pit for musicians in front of the stage; still later, the group of musicians working there.

Ottava rima   An eight-line stanza in iambic pentameter rhyming *abababcc*.

Overstatement   See HYPERBOLE.

Oxymoron   A figure of speech combining in one phrase (usually adjective-noun) two seemingly contradictory elements, such as "loving hate" or "feather of lead, bright smoke, cold fire, sick health" (Shakespeare, *Romeo and Juliet* 1.1.176–80). Oxymoron is a type of PARADOX.

Pantoum   A poem consisting of four-line stanzas rhyming *abab*. The second and fourth lines of one stanza serve as the first and third lines of the next stanza, and the first and third lines of the first stanza reappear as the fourth and second lines of the last stanza, so that the poem begins and ends with the same line.

Paradox   A figure of speech in which a statement initially seeming self-contradictory or absurd turns out, when seen in another light, to make good sense. See also OXYMORON.

Parallelism   (1) A verbal arrangement in which elements of equal weight within phrases, sentences, or paragraphs are expressed in a similar grammatical order and structure. (2) A principle of poetic structure in which consecutive lines in open form are related by a line's repeating, expanding on, or contrasting with the idea of the line or lines before it, as in the biblical psalms or the poems of Walt Whitman (see p. 657).

Parody   In modern usage, a humorous or satirical imitation of a serious piece of literature or writing. In the sixteenth and seventeenth centuries, poets such as George Herbert practiced "sacred parody" by adapting secular lyrics to devotional themes.

Partial rhyme   See SLANT RHYME.

Pastoral   (1) As an adjective, that which deals with a rural setting and affirms a rustic way of life. (2) As a noun, a literary type associated with shepherds and country living.

Pause   See CAESURA.

Pentameter   A poetic line with five metrical feet.

Persona   (1) Literally, the mask through which actors spoke in Greek plays. (2) In some critical approaches of recent decades, the "character" projected by the author, the *I* of a narrative poem or novel, or the speaker whose voice is heard in a lyric poem. In this view, the poem is an artificial construct distanced from the poet's autobiographical self. See also VOICE.

Personification   A figure of speech in which something nonhuman (an abstraction or a natural object) is treated as if it had human (not just living) characteristics or actions. See also APOSTROPHE.

Petrarchan sonnet   See ITALIAN SONNET.

Play   A drama intended for performance before a theatrical audience. See also CLOSET DRAMA.

Plot   (1) The selection and arrangement of events in a narrative to present them most effectively to the reader and bring out their causal connections. (2) The action that takes place within a play, considered by Aristotle in the *Poetics* to be the most important of the six elements of drama. See also SUBPLOT.

Poem   A term whose meaning exceeds all attempts at definition. Here is a slightly modified version of an attempt at definition by William Harmon and C. Hugh Holman in *A Handbook to Literature* (1996): A poem is a literary composition, written or oral, typically characterized by imagination, emotion, sense impressions, and concrete language that invites attention to its own physical features, such as sound or appearance on the page.

Poetic diction   In general, a specialized language used in or considered appropriate to poetry. In the late seventeenth and the eighteenth centuries, a refined use of language that excluded "common" speech from poetry as indecorous and substituted elevated circumlocutions or archaic synonyms, or such forms as *ope* and *e'er*.

Point of view   The vantage point from which an author presents a story, combining person (first, second, or third, named or anonymous) and perspective (objective, omniscient, limited). See also CENTER OF CONSCIOUSNESS TECHNIQUE; STREAM OF CONSCIOUSNESS TECHNIQUE.

Problem play   A serious work that dramatizes a real-life, usually contemporary, social, political, or ethical problem. Although in a broad sense it covers all drama dealing with problems of human life, it is used more narrowly for the "drama of ideas" that emerged in the late nineteenth century in the work, for example, of Norwegian playwright Henrik Ibsen (see p. 996).

Prologue   (1) The opening section of a Greek tragedy. (2) Words spoken before the beginning of a play, usually a monologue by one of the actors providing background information.

Property (prop)   A movable object used on stage, especially one handled by an actor while performing.

Proscenium   The part of the stage in a modern theater between the orchestra and the curtain. The proscenium arch is the arch over the front of the stage from which the curtain hangs and which separates the stage from the audience.

Prose poem   A poem printed as prose, with lines wrapping at the right margin rather than being divided through predetermined line breaks.

Prosody   The principles of versification, especially of meter, rhythm, rhyme, and stanza forms.

Protagonist   The most important or leading character in a literary work. See also ANTAGONIST.

Psychological criticism   See page 1110.

Pun   A "play on words" based on similarity in sound between two words having very different meanings, as when *fractious* in Anita Endrezze's line "numbers were fractious beasts" ("The Girl Who Loved the Sky," p. 474) suggests *fractions* in addition to its dictionary meanings of "unruly, readily angered, quarrelsome." Also called *paronomasia*. Often used to produce AMBIGUITY in sense 2 of that word's definition.

Quatrain   A stanza of four lines or other four-line unit within a larger form, such as a sonnet.

Reader-response criticism   See page 1115.

Realism   (1) An approach to literature that attempts to depict accurately the everyday life of a time and place. (2) A literary movement that developed in the latter half of the nineteenth century characterized by an objective presentation of material and realistic depiction of setting, characters, and details.

Recognition   A significant realization or discovery by a character, usually the protagonist, that moves the plot forward by changing the circumstances of a play.

Refrain   One or more identical or deliberately similar lines repeated throughout a poem, sometimes with meaningful variation, such as the final line of a stanza or as a block of lines between stanzas or sections.

Reliable narrator   A narrator who tells her or his story accurately and honestly. See also NAÏVE NARRATOR; NARRATOR; UNRELIABLE NARRATOR.

Resolution   The culmination of a fictional plot that resolves the conflicts or leaves them satisfyingly unresolved.

Rhyme   The repetition of the accented vowel sound of a word and all succeeding consonant sounds. See also EXACT RHYME; SLANT RHYME.

Rhyme royal   An alternative term for CHAUCERIAN STANZA because it was used by King James I of Scotland in his poem *The Kingis Quair* ("The King's Book"), written about 1424.

Rhyme scheme   The pattern of end rhymes in a poem or stanza; the recurring sequence is usually described by assigning a letter to each word sound, the same word sounds having the same letter (e.g., *abbaabba*).

Rhythm   The patterned "movement" of language created by the choice of words and their arrangement, usually described through metaphors such as fast or slow, smooth or halting, graceful or rough, deliberate or frenzied, syncopated or disjointed. Rhythm in poetry is affected, in addition to meter, by factors such as line length; line endings; pauses (or lack of them) within lines; spaces within, at the beginning or end of, or between lines; word choice; and combinations of sounds.

Rising action   The part of a plot leading up to the climax and marked by increasingly tense and complicated conflict. See also FALLING ACTION.

Rising meter   A foot (usually an iamb or an anapest) in which the final, stressed syllable is preceded by one or two unstressed syllables, thus giving a sense of stepping up. See also FALLING METER.

Romance   (1) In medieval narrative poetry or prose, a tale involving knights and kings, adventures, ladies in distress, courtly love, and chivalric ideals. (2) In modern fiction, a work characterized by remote and exotic settings, exciting and heroic action, passionate love, and mysterious or supernatural experiences. (3) In drama, a play neither wholly comic nor wholly tragic, often containing elements of the supernatural.

Round character   A complex, fully developed character either shown as changing and growing because of what happens to her or him or described in such rich detail that we have a clear sense of how she or he would, or will, change even though we don't see it happening. See also FLAT CHARACTER.

Run-on line   A line whose sense and grammatical structure continue to the next. The technique is called *enjambment*. See also END-STOPPED LINE.

Sarcasm   A harsh and cutting form of VERBAL IRONY, often involving apparent praise that is obviously not meant seriously.

Satire   A work, or manner within a work, that combines a critical attitude with humor and wit with the intent of improving human institutions or humanity.

Scansion   The division of metrical verse into feet in order to determine and label the meter of a poem. See also FOOT; METER; page 1086.

Scene   (1) A subdivision of an ACT in drama, or—in modern drama—a section of a play that is not divided into acts. (2) See SETTING. (3) A variant spelling of *skene*.

Script   The written text of a play, which includes the stage directions, dramatic monologues, and the dialogue between characters.

Sentimentality   A term used to describe a work seeking to elicit an emotional response in a reader or spectator that exceeds what the situation warrants.

Sestet   The last six lines of an ITALIAN SONNET.

Sestina   A lyric poem consisting of six six-line stanzas and a three-line concluding stanza (or "envoy"). The six end-words of the first stanza must be used as the end-words of the other five stanzas, in a specified pattern (the first line ends with the end-word from the last line of the previous stanza, the second line with that of the first line of the previous stanza, the third line with that of the previous fifth line, the fourth line with that of the previous second line, the fifth line with that of the previous fourth line, the sixth line with that of the previous third line). The three lines of the envoy must use the end-words of lines 5, 3, and 1 from the first stanza, in that order, and must include the other three end-words within the lines.

Set   The physical equipment of a stage, including backdrops, furniture, properties, and lighting.

Setting   The overall context—where, when, in what circumstances—in which the action in a fictional or dramatic work takes place.

Shakespearean sonnet   See ENGLISH SONNET.

Shaped poem   See CONCRETE POEM.

Short story   A brief prose work of narrative fiction characterized by a carefully crafted plot and style, complexity in characterization and point of view, and unity of effect. See also FICTION; NOVEL; NOVELLA.

Simile   Expression of a direct similarity, using words such as *like*, *as*, or *than*, between two things usually regarded as dissimilar (e.g., "His face was as white as a sheet."). It is important to distinguish *simile* from *comparison*, where the two things joined by *like* or *as* are not dissimilar.

Single rhyme   A rhyme in which the stressed, rhyming syllable is the final syllable in the rhyme: *west* and *stressed*, *away* and *today*. Formerly called *masculine rhyme*. See also DOUBLE RHYME.

Situational irony   A kind of irony in which a result turns out very different from, and usually more sinister than, what a character expected or hoped for. Unlike dramatic irony, in situational irony the reader does not necessarily know more than the characters and may be as surprised by what happens as the characters are. See also DRAMATIC IRONY; IRONY; VERBAL IRONY.

Slant rhyme   A form of rhyme in which words contain similar sounds but do not rhyme perfectly (usually involving assonance or — more frequently — consonance). See also ASSONANCE; CONSONANCE.

Soliloquy   A monologue delivered by a character in a play while alone on stage or otherwise out of hearing of the other characters, often revealing the character's inner thoughts or feelings. Sometimes applied to a poem imitating this feature. See also DRAMATIC MONOLOGUE.

Sonnet   A fourteen-line poem usually written in iambic pentameter. Originally lyrical love poems, sonnets came to be used also for meditations on religious themes, death, and nature and are now open to all subjects. Some sonnets have varied from the traditional form — using hexameter lines, fewer or more than fourteen lines, or an appended coda. Sometimes sonnets are grouped in a "sonnet sequence," with implied narrative progression in the situations imagined as underlying the successive utterances. See also ENGLISH SONNET; ITALIAN SONNET; SPENSERIAN SONNET.

Speaker   The imagined voice in a nonnarrative poem of someone uttering the words of the poem, either that of the poet quite directly or of a character expressing views or feelings the poet may or may not share.

Spenserian sonnet   A variation of the English sonnet that employs the structure of three quatrains plus a couplet, but joins the quatrains by linking rhymes: *abab bcbc cdcd ee*.

Spenserian stanza   A stanza of nine iambic lines, the first eight pentameter and the ninth hexameter, rhyming *ababbcbcc*. It was created by Edmund Spenser (1552–1599) for his allegorical epic *The Faerie Queene* (1590, 1596) and was used frequently by English poets in the nineteenth century.

Spondee   A metrical foot made up of two stressed syllables (*DA DA* — "dream house"), with no unstressed syllables. Spondees cannot be the predominant foot in a poem; they are usually substituted for iambs or trochees as a way of increasing emphasis.

Stage directions   Written instructions in the script of a play, typically placed in parentheses and set in italics, telling actors how to move on the stage or how to deliver a particular word or speech.

Stage left, stage right   Areas of the stage seen from the point of view of an actor facing the audience. Stage left, therefore, is on the audience's right-hand side, and vice versa.

Stanza   A grouping of poetic lines into a section, either according to form — each section having the same number of lines and the same prosody — or according to thought, creating irregular units comparable to paragraphs in prose. Irregular stanzas are sometimes called STROPHES.

Static character   A character in a narrative or dramatic work who is not shown as changing. See also DYNAMIC CHARACTER.

Stichomythia   A form of repartee in dialogue originating in ancient Greek drama — brief, alternating lines that reply sharply to each other in wordings that echo and vary what the preceding character expressed.

Stock character   A traditional character defined by a single, stereotypical characteristic, such as an innocent young woman, a rakish young man, or a clever servant.

Story   Any account of a related series of events in sequential order, usually chronological order (the order in which they happened).

Stream of consciousness technique   An attempt to convey the unstructured, even at times chaotic, flow of random sense perceptions, mental pictures, memories, sounds, thoughts, and feelings — prerational mental activity, before the mind orders it into a coherent form or shape — through an associative rather than a logical style, usually without ordinary punctuation or complete sentences.

Stress   In metrics, the greater emphasis given to some words and syllables relative to that received by adjacent words and syllables. See also ACCENT.

Strophe   (1) The first part in a three-stanza segment of a choral ODE in Greek drama, sung while the chorus moves from stage right to stage left. (2) The first stanza in a three-stanza segment of an ode. (3) See STANZA. See also ANTISTROPHE; CHORUS; EPODE; ODE.

Structure   (1) The planned framework — the general plan or outline — of a literary work. (2) Narrower patterns within the overall framework. See also FORM.

Style   In writing, the distinctive, individual manner in which a writer uses words; constructs sentences; incorporates nonliteral expressions; and handles rhythm, timing, and tone. Also, the manner characteristic of a group of writers (as in "period style").

Subplot   A subordinate or minor story in a dramatic or narrative work, often related thematically or structurally to the main plot. See also PLOT.

Substitution   The use of a different kind of foot in place of the one normally demanded by the predominant meter of a poem, as a way of calling attention to an idea, emphasizing the dominant foot by variation from it, speeding up or slowing down the pace, or signaling a switch in meaning.

Suspense   A sense of uncertainty and concern about how things in a literary work will turn out, when disaster will fall or rescue will occur, who did what, or what the effects on the characters or events will be.

Symbol   Something that represents both itself and something else. A literary symbol is a prominent or repeated image or action that is present in the poem, story, or play and is seen, touched, smelled, heard, tasted, or experienced imaginatively but also conveys a cluster of abstract meanings beyond itself.

Synecdoche   A special kind of METONYMY in which part of a thing is substituted for the whole of which it is a part, as in the commonly used phrases "give me a hand," "lend me your ears," or "many mouths to feed."

Syntax   The arrangement of words in a sentence to show their relationship to one another.

Tercet   A stanza of three lines, each usually ending with the same rhyme. See also TERZA RIMA; TRIPLET.

Terza rima   A poetic form consisting of three-line stanzas (TERCETS) with interlinked rhymes, *aba bcb cdc ded efe*, and so on, made famous by Dante's use of it in *The Divine Comedy.*

Tetrameter   A poetic line with four metrical feet.

Text   Traditionally, a piece of writing. In recent READER-RESPONSE CRITICISM (see page 1115), *text* has come to mean the words with which the reader interacts; in this view, a literary work is not an object, not a shape on the page or a spoken performance, but what is completed in the reader's mind.

Theme   The central idea embodied or explored in a literary work, what it all adds up to; the general concept, explicit or implied, that the work incorporates and makes persuasive to the reader.

Thesis   A succinct statement of the central idea or proposition to be explored in an expository essay.

Third-person narrator   The type of narration with a storyteller who is not identified; uses the pronouns *he, she, it,* or *they* — but not *I* — in speaking of her- or himself; asserts no connection between the narrator and the characters in the story; and tells the story with some objectivity and distance.

Title   The name attached to a work of literature. Usually a title, when assigned by the author, is an integral part of a work and needs to be considered in interpreting it. In some cases, a title for a poem has been added as a means of identifying it and is not integral to its interpretation. Sometimes a poem is untitled and the first line is used as a convenient way of referring to the poem (e.g., in Emily Dickinson's poems), but it should not be thought of as a title and does not follow the capitalization rules for titles.

Tone   The attitude, or "stance," toward the subject and toward the reader or audience implied in a literary work; the "tone of voice" it seems to project.

Tragedy   A story recounting a causally related series of serious and important events that culminate in an unhappy ending for the protagonist. See also COMEDY.

Tragic flaw   The theory, attributed to Aristotle's *Poetics,* that the downfall of the hero in a tragedy is caused by a defect, or flaw, in her or his character. See also *HAMARTIA* and page 830.

Tragicomedy   A play whose plot could be appropriate to tragedy until the final act, when it turns out unexpectedly to have the happy ending of a comedy. The tone and style of tragicomedy are serious and the outcome could well be disaster or death, but somehow the disaster is averted, and at the end order and harmony prevail. See also COMEDY; TRAGEDY.

Trimeter   A poetic line with three metrical feet.

Triplet   A group of three consecutive lines with the same rhyme, often used for variation in a long sequence of couplets. See also TERCET.

Trochee   A metrical foot consisting of two syllables, an accented one followed by an unaccented one (*DA da* — "wakeful"). In trochaic meter, trochees are the predominant foot in a line or poem.

Type   (1) See GENRE. (2) A character who represents a class or kind of person, either atypical and individualized, or stereotypical (see STOCK CHARACTER). (3) A variety of symbol, especially as used in religion for something that is to come, such as "a type of Christ."

Understatement   A figure of speech expressing something in an unexpectedly restrained way, which often has the effect of increasing rather than reducing emphasis. See also HYPERBOLE.

Unity   A sense of wholeness and cohesion in a literary work, as all of its parts work together according to some organizing principle to achieve common effect.

Unreliable narrator   A narrator who may be in error in her or his reporting or understanding of things, or who distorts things, deliberately or unintentionally. See also NAÏVE NARRATOR; NARRATOR; RELIABLE NARRATOR.

Upstage   The part of the stage farthest from the audience.

Verbal irony   A figure of speech in which what is said is nearly the opposite of what is meant. See also DRAMATIC IRONY; IRONY; SARCASM; SITUATIONAL IRONY.

Verisimilitude   The semblance of truth; the use of abundant detail to create the appearance of reality in a literary work.

Verse   (1) A unit of poetry, the same thing as a stanza or line. (2) A rhythmic composition, often in meter and rhyme, regardless of merit (the term *poetry* is often reserved for verse of high merit).

Viewpoint   See POINT OF VIEW.

Villanelle   A nineteen-line lyric poem divided into five tercets and a final four-line stanza, rhyming *aba aba aba aba aba abaa*. Line 1 is repeated to form lines 6, 12, and 18; line 3 is repeated to form lines 9, 15, and 19. See, for example, Dylan Thomas's "Do not go gentle into that good night" (p. 584) and Rafael Campo's "The Enemy" (p. 609).

Voice   The supposed authorial presence in poems that do not obviously employ persona as a distancing device.

Acknowledgments (*continued from p. iv*)

Deanna Alisa Ableser, *Black Coffee*. Copyright © 2012 by Deanna Alisa Ableser. Reprinted by permission of the author. For performance rights, contact Deanna Alisa Ableser (abbywriter123@gmail.com).

Chimamanda Ngozi Adichie, "The Thing around Your Neck" from *The Thing around Your Neck* by Chimamanda Ngozi Adichie. Copyright © 2009 by Chimamanda Ngozi Adichie. Reprinted by permission of the Wylie Agency LLC and by permission of Alfred A. Knopf Canada, a division of Penguin Random House Canada Limited.

Sherman Alexie, "The Lone Ranger and Tonto Fistfight in Heaven" from *The Lone Ranger and Tonto Fistfight in Heaven* by Sherman Alexie. Copyright © 1993, 2005 by Sherman Alexie. Used by permission of Grove/Atlantic, Inc. Any third-party use of this material, outside this publication, is prohibited. "Superman and Me" is reprinted by permission of Nancy Stauffer Associates. Copyright © 1998 by Sherman Alexie. All rights reserved.

Maya Angelou, "Africa" from *Oh Pray My Wings Are Gonna Fit Me Well* by Maya Angelou. Copyright © 1975 by Maya Angelou. Used by permission of Random House, an imprint and division of Penguin Random House LLC. All rights reserved. Any third-party use of this material, outside this publication, is prohibited. Interested parties must apply directly to Penguin Random House LLC for permission.

Susan Atefat-Peckham, "Dates" from *That Kind of Sleep*. Copyright © 2001 by Susan Atefat-Peckham. Reprinted with the permission of The Permissions Company, Inc., on behalf of Coffee House Press, Minneapolis, Minnesota, www.coffeehousepress.org.

Margaret Atwood, "Happy Endings" from *Good Bones and Simple Murders* by Margaret Atwood, copyright © 1983, 1992, 1994 by O. W. Toad Ltd. Used by permission of McClelland & Stewart, a division of Penguin Random House Canada Limited, and by permission of Nan A. Talese, an imprint of the Knopf Doubleday Publishing Group, a division of Penguin Random House LLC. All rights reserved. Any third-party use of this material, outside this publication, is prohibited. Interested parties must apply directly to Penguin Random House LLC for permission.

W. H. Auden, "Musée des Beaux Arts" from *W. H. Auden: Collected Poems* by W. H. Auden. Copyright © 1940 and renewed 1968 by W. H. Auden. Used by permission of Random House, an imprint and division of Penguin Random House LLC. All rights reserved. Any third-party use of this material, outside this publication, is prohibited. Interested parties must apply directly to Penguin Random House LLC for permission.

Jimmy Santiago Baca, "Family Ties" from *Black Mesa Poems*. Copyright © 1989 by Jimmy Santiago Baca. Reprinted by permission of New Directions Publishing Corp.

James Baldwin, "Sonny's Blues" was originally published in *Partisan Review*. Collected in *Going to Meet the Man*, published by Vintage Books. Copyright © 1957 by James Baldwin. Copyright renewed. Used by arrangement with the James Baldwin Estate.

Toni Cade Bambara, "The Lesson" from *Gorilla, My Love* by Toni Cade Bambara. Copyright © 1972 by Toni Cade Bambara. Used by permission of Random House, an imprint and division of Penguin Random House LLC. All rights reserved. Any third-party use of this material, outside this publication, is prohibited. Interested parties must apply directly to Penguin Random House LLC for permission.

Clive Barnes, "Fiery Fences: A Review," *New York Post*, March 27, 1987. Copyright © 1987 by Clive Barnes. Reprinted by permission.

Jim Barnes, "Return to La Plata, Missouri" from *The American Book of the Dead: Poems*. Copyright © 1982 by Jim Barnes. Used with permission of the University of Illinois Press.

Wendell Berry, "The Peace of Wild Things" from *New Collected Poems*. Copyright © 2012 by Wendell Berry. Reprinted by permission of Counterpoint.

David Bevington, notes to accompany *Hamlet, Prince of Denmark*, from David Bevington, *The Complete Works of Shakespeare*, 4th edition. Copyright © 1992. Reprinted by permission of Pearson Education, Inc., New York, New York.

Elizabeth Bishop, "Sestina" from *Poems* by Elizabeth Bishop. Copyright © 2011 by the Alice H. Methfessel Trust; publisher's note and compilation copyright © 2011 by Farrar, Straus & Giroux, LCC. Reprinted by permission of Farrar, Straus and Giroux, LLC.

Peter Blue Cloud, "Crazy Horse Monument" from *Clans of Many Nations: Selected Poems 1969–1994*. Copyright © 1995 by Peter Blue Cloud/Aroniawenrate. Reprinted with the permission of The Permissions Company, Inc., on behalf of White Pine Press, www.whitepine.org.

Suzanne Bradbeer, *Okoboji*. Copyright © 2011 by Suzanne Bradbeer. Reprinted by permission of Abrams Artists Agency on behalf of the author.

Ray Bradbury, "The Smile," published in *Fantastic* (Summer 1952). Copyright © 1952 by Ziff Davis, renewed 1980 by Ray Bradbury. Reprinted by permission of Don Congdon Associates, Inc.

Gwendolyn Brooks, "The Bean Eaters" from *Blacks* by Gwendolyn Brooks. Copyright © 1991 by Gwendolyn Brooks. Reprinted by consent of Brooks Permissions. "We Real Cool" from *Blacks* by Gwendolyn Brooks. Copyright © 1991 by Gwendolyn Brooks. Reprinted by consent of Brooks Permissions.

Dennis Brutus, "Nightsong: City" from *A Simple Lust: Selected Poems*. Copyright © 1973 by Dennis Brutus. Reprinted by permission.

Rafael Campo, "The Enemy" from *The Enemy* by Rafael Campo. Copyright © 2007 by Rafael Campo. Reprinted by permission of Georges Borchardt, Inc., on behalf of the author.

Lorna Dee Cervantes, "Freeway 280" in *Emplumada* by Lorna Dee Cervantes. Copyright © 1981. Reprinted by permission of the author.

May-lee Chai, "Your Grandmother, the War Criminal," from *Glamorous Asians* by May-lee Chai (University of Indianapolis Press). Copyright © 2004 by May-lee Chai. First published in *The North American Review*. Reprinted by permission of the author.

Marilyn Chin, "How I Got That Name" from *The Phoenix Gone, the Terrace Empty* (Minneapolis: Milkweed Editions). Copyright © 1994 by Marilyn Chin. Reprinted with permission from Milkweed Editions, www .milkweed.org. "The True Story of Mr. and Mrs. Wong," from *Rhapsody in Plain Yellow* by Marilyn Chin. Copyright © 2002 by Marilyn Chin. Used by permission of the author and W. W. Norton & Company, Inc.

Chrystos, "Traditional Style Indian Garage." First appeared in *ZYZZYVA*, Fall 2003. Copyright © 2003. Used by permission of the author, Chrystos.

Sandra Cisneros, "The House on Mango Street" from *The House on Mango Street*. Copyright © 1984 by Sandra Cisneros. Published by Vintage Books, a division of Random House, Inc., and in hardcover by Alfred A. Knopf in 1994. Reprinted by permission of Susan Bergholz Literary Services, New York, NY, and Lamy, NM. All rights reserved.

Lucille Clifton, "at the cemetery, walnut grove plantation, south carolina, 1989" from *The Collected Poems of Lucille Clifton*. Copyright © 1991 by Lucille Clifton. Reprinted with the permission of The Permissions Company, Inc., on behalf of BOA Editions Ltd., www.boaeditions.org. "homage to my hips" from *Two-Headed Woman*. Copyright © 1980 by Lucille Clifton. Now appears in *The Collected Poems of Lucille Clifton, 1965–2010* by Lucille Clifton, published by BOA Editions. Reprinted by permission of Curtis Brown, Ltd.

Judith Ortiz Cofer, "Cold as Heaven" from *Reaching for the Mainland and Selected New Poems* by Judith Ortiz Cofer. Copyright © 1987. Reprinted by permission of Bilingual Press/Editorial Bilingüe, Arizona State University, Tempe, AZ.

Billy Collins, "Nostalgia" from *Questions about Angels* by Billy Collins. Copyright © 1991. Reprinted by permission of the University of Pittsburgh Press.

Victor Hernández Cruz, "Problems with Hurricanes" from *Maraca: New and Selected Poems, 1965–2000*. Copyright © 2001 by Victor Hernández Cruz. Reprinted with the permission of The Permissions Company, Inc., on behalf of Coffee House Press, www.coffeehousepress.org.

Countee Cullen, "Incident" from *Color* by Countee Cullen. Copyright © 1925 by Harper & Brothers; copyright renewed 1952 by Ida M. Cullen. Copyrights held by the Amistad Research Center, Tulane University, administered by Thompson and Thompson, Brooklyn, NY.

E. E. Cummings, "Buffalo Bill's," copyright 1923, 1951, © 1991 by The Trustees for the E. E. Cummings Trust. Copyright © 1976 by George James Firmage. "next to of course god america i,'" copyright © 1926, 1954, © 1991 by the Trustees for the E. E. Cummings Trust. Copyright © 1985 by George James Firmage. From *Complete Poems: 1904–1962* by E. E. Cummings, edited by George J. Firmage. Used by permission of Liveright Publishing Corporation.

Edwidge Danticat, "New York Day Women" from *Krik? Krak!* by Edwidge Danticat. Copyright © 1991, 1995 by Edwidge Danticat. Reprinted by permission of Soho Press, Inc. All rights reserved.

Lydia Davis, "Blind Date" from *The Collected Stories of Lydia Davis*. Copyright © 2009 by Lydia Davis. Reprinted by permission of Farrar, Straus & Giroux, LLC.

Toi Derricotte, "A Note on My Son's Face" from *Captivity* by Toi Derricotte. Copyright © 1989. Reprinted by permission of the University of Pittsburgh Press.

Joanne Diaz, "Pride and Prejudice" from *My Favorite Tyrants* by Joanne Diaz. Copyright © 2014 by the Board of Regents of the University of Wisconsin System. Reprinted by permission of the University of Wisconsin Press.

Emily Dickinson, "Because I could not stop for Death—" and "I'm Nobody! Who are you?" Reprinted by permission of the publishers and the Trustees of Amherst College from *The Poems of Emily Dickinson*, edited by Thomas H. Johnson, Cambridge, Mass.: The Belknap Press of Harvard University Press. Copyright © 1951, 1955, 1979, 1983 by the President and Fellows of Harvard College.

Mark Doty, "Tiara" from *Bethlehem in Broad Daylight* by Mark Doty. Copyright © 1991 by Mark Doty. Reprinted by permission of David R. Godine, Publisher, Inc.

Rita Dove, "Horse and Tree" from *Grace Notes* by Rita Dove. Copyright © 1989 by Rita Dove. Used by permission of the author and W. W. Norton & Company, Inc.

Denise Duhamel, "One Afternoon When Barbie Wanted to Join the Military" from *Queen for a Day: Selected and New Poems* by Denise Duhamel. Copyright © 2001. Reprinted by permission of the University of Pittsburgh Press.

Harry J. Elam Jr., excerpts from "August Wilson" in *A Companion to Twentieth-Century American Drama*, edited by David Krasner. Reprinted by permission of Harry J. Elam Jr.

Ralph Ellison, "Chapter 1 [Battle Royal]" from *Invisible Man* by Ralph Ellison. Copyright © 1948 and renewed 1976 by Ralph Ellison. Used by permission of Random House, an imprint and division of Penguin Random House LLC. All rights reserved. Any third-party use of this material, outside this publication, is prohibited. Interested parties must apply directly to Penguin Random House LLC for permission.

Anita Endrezze, "The Girl Who Loved the Sky" from *At the Helm of Twilight* (Broken Moon Press). Copyright © 1992. Reprinted by permission of the author.

Louise Erdrich, "The Red Convertible" from *Love Medicine: New and Expanded Edition* by Louise Erdrich. Copyright © 1984, 1993 by Louise Erdrich. Reprinted by permission of Henry Holt and Company, LLC. All rights reserved.

Martín Espada, "Latin Night at the Pawnshop," copyright © 1990 by Martín Espada, from *Alabanza* by Martín Espada. Used by permission of the author and W. W. Norton & Company, Inc.

Susan Farrell, "Fight vs. Flight: A Re-evaluation of Dee in Alice Walker's 'Everyday Use'" from *Studies in Short Fiction* 35.2 (Spring 1998): 179–86. Reprinted by permission of the author.

William Faulkner, "A Rose for Emily" from *Collected Stories of William Faulkner* by William Faulkner. Copyright © 1930 and renewed 1958 by William Faulkner. Used by permission of Random House, an imprint and division of Penguin Random House LLC. All rights reserved. Any third-party use of this material, outside of this publication, is prohibited. Interested parties must apply directly to Penguin Random House LLC for permission.

Megan Foss, "Love Letters," *Creative Nonfiction* 9 (1998): 13–33. Copyright © 1998. Reprinted by permission of the Creative Nonfiction Foundation.

Dagoberto Gilb, "Love in L.A." from *The Magic of Blood* by Dagoberto Gilb (University of New Mexico Press, 1993). Copyright © 1993. Story originally published in *Buffalo*. Reprinted by permission of the author.

Ray González, "The Jalapeño Contest" from *The Ghost of John Wayne and Other Stories* by Ray González. Copyright © 2001 by Ray González. Reprinted by permission of the University of Arizona Press.

Angelina Weld Grimké, "A Winter Twilight" from the Angelina Weld Grimké papers. Reprinted by permission of the Moorland-Spingarn Research Center, Howard University.

Joy Harjo, "She Had Some Horses" from *She Had Some Horses* by Joy Harjo. Copyright © 1983 by Joy Harjo. Used by permission of the author and W. W. Norton & Company, Inc.

Robert Hayden, "Those Winter Sundays," copyright © 1966 by Robert Hayden, from *Collected Poems of Robert Hayden* by Robert Hayden, edited by Frederick Glaysher. Used by permission of Liveright Publishing Corporation.

Terrance Hayes, "Talk" from *Wind in a Box* by Terrance Hayes. Copyright © 2006 by Terrance Hayes. Used by permission of Penguin Books, an imprint of Penguin Publishing Group, a division of Penguin Random House LLC.

Ernest Hemingway, "Hills Like White Elephants" from *The Short Stories of Ernest Hemingway* by Ernest Hemingway. Copyright © 1927 by Charles Scribner's Sons. Copyright © renewed 1955 by Ernest Hemingway. Reprinted with the permission of Scribner, a division of Simon & Schuster, Inc. All rights reserved.

Bob Hicok, "In the Loop" from *Words for Empty and Words for Full* by Bob Hicok. Copyright © 2010. Reprinted by permission of the University of Pittsburgh Press.

Linda Hogan, "Crow Law" from *The Book of Medicines*. Copyright © 1993 by Linda Hogan. Reprinted with the permission of The Permissions Company, Inc., on behalf of Coffee House Press, Minneapolis, Minnesota, www.coffeehousepress.org.

Anna Maria Hong, "The Frog-Prince" was first published in the *Harvard Gazette*. Copyright © 2015. Reprinted by permission of Anna Maria Hong.

Garrett Kaoru Hongo, "Yellow Light" from *Yellow Light* by Garrett Kaoru Hongo. Copyright © 1982 by Garrett Kaoru Hongo. Reprinted with permission of Wesleyan University Press.

Langston Hughes, "Harlem (2)" from *The Collected Poems of Langston Hughes* by Langston Hughes, edited by Arnold Rampersad with David Roessel, Associate Editor. Copyright © 1994 by the Estate of Langston Hughes. Used by permission of Alfred A. Knopf, an imprint of the Knopf Doubleday Publishing Group, a division of Penguin Random House LLC. All rights reserved. Any third-party use of this material, outside of this publication, is prohibited. Interested parties must apply directly to Penguin Random House LLC for permission. "Thank You, M'am" from *Short Stories* by Langston Hughes. Copyright © 1996 by Ramona Bass and Arnold Rampersad. Reprinted by permission of Hill and Wang, a division of Farrar, Straus and Giroux, LLC.

Honorée Fanonne Jeffers, "Cotton Field Sestina" from *Red Clay Suite* by Honorée Fanonne Jeffers. Copyright © 2007 by Honorée Fanonne Jeffers. Reprinted with permission from Southern Illinois University Press.

Ha Jin, "Saboteur" from *The Bridegroom: Stories* by Ha Jin. Copyright © 2000 by Ha Jin. Used by permission of Pantheon Books, an imprint of the Knopf Doubleday Publishing Group, a division of Penguin Random House LLC. All rights reserved. Any third-party use of this material, outside of this publication, is prohibited. Interested parties must apply directly to Penguin Random House LLC for permission.

Georgia Douglas Johnson, "Wishes" from *Crisis* magazine, April 1927. Copyright © 1927. Reprinted by permission of Crisis Publishing Company, Inc. Bedford/St. Martin's/Macmillan Learning wishes to thank the Crisis Publishing Co., Inc., the publisher of the magazine of the National Association for the Advancement of Colored People, for the use of this material.

Allison Joseph, "On Being Told I Don't Speak Like a Black Person" from *Imitation of Life*. Copyright © 2003 by Allison Joseph. Reprinted with the permission of The Permissions Company, Inc., on behalf of Carnegie Mellon University Press, www.cmu.edu/universitypress.

Jane Kenyon, "Let Evening Come" from *Collected Poems*. Copyright © 2005 by The Estate of Jane Kenyon. Reprinted with the permission of The Permissions Company, Inc., on behalf of Graywolf Press, Minneapolis, Minnesota, www.graywolfpress.org.

Etgar Keret, "Crazy Glue" from *The Girl on the Fridge* by Etgar Keret, translated by Miriam Shlesinger and Sondra Silverston. Copyright © 1992, 1994 by Etgar Keret. English translation © copyright by Etgar Keret. Reprinted by permission of Farrar, Straus and Giroux, LLC.

Jamaica Kincaid, "Girl" from *At the Bottom of the River* by Jamaica Kincaid. Copyright © 1983 by Jamaica Kincaid. Reprinted by permission of Farrar, Straus & Giroux, LLC.

Yusef Komunyakaa, "Facing It" from *Dien Cai Dau*. Copyright © 1988 by Yusef Komunyakaa. Reprinted with permission of Wesleyan University Press.

Ted Kooser, "Abandoned Farmhouse" from *Sure Signs: New and Selected Poems*. Copyright © 1980. Reprinted by permission of the University of Pittsburgh Press.

Susan Koprince, "Baseball as History and Myth in August Wilson's *Fences*." Copyright © 2006 by Susan Koprince. Reprinted by permission of the author.

Missy Dehn Kubitschek, "August Wilson's Gender Lesson" from *May All Your Fences Have Gates: Essays on the Drama of August Wilson*, ed. by Alan Nadel, pp. 183–99. Copyright © 1994 by Missy Dehn Kubitschek. Reprinted by permission of the author.

Maxine Kumin, "The Sound of Night" from *Halfway* by Maxine Kumin. Reprinted by permission of The Anderson Literary Agency Inc.

Li-Young Lee, "Eating Alone" from *Rose*. Copyright © 1986 by Li-Young Lee. Reprinted with the permission of The Permissions Company, Inc., on behalf of BOA Editions Ltd., www.boaeditions.org.

Denise Levertov, "Leaving Forever" from *Poems 1960-1967*. Copyright © 1964 by Denise Levertov. Reprinted by permission of New Directions Publishing Corp.

Philip Levine, "What Work Is" from *What Work Is* by Philip Levine. Copyright © 1991 by Philip Levine. Used by permission of Alfred A. Knopf, an imprint of the Knopf Doubleday Publishing Group, a division of Penguin Random House LLC. All rights reserved. Any third-party use of this material, outside this publication, is prohibited. Interested parties must apply directly to Penguin Random House LLC for permission.

Miles Marshall Lewis, "Talks with August Wilson" from *The Believer Book of Writers Talking to Writers*, ed. by Vendela Vida. Copyright © 2005 by Vendela Vida. Reprinted by permission.

Bonnie Lyons, "An Interview with August Wilson," *Contemporary Literature* 40.1 (Spring 1999): 1–21. Copyright © 1999 by the Board of Regents of the University of Wisconsin System. Reproduced by the permission of the University of Wisconsin Press.

Orlando Ricardo Menes, "Courtyard of Clotheslines, Angel Hill" from *Fetish: Poems* by Orlando Ricardo Menes. Copyright © 2013 by the Board of Regents of the University of Nebraska. Reprinted by permission of the University of Nebraska Press.

Katherine Min, "Courting a Monk" was first published in *Triquarterly Review* 95 (Winter 1995/1996), pp. 101–13. Copyright © 1995 by Katherine Min. Reprinted by permission of the author.

Gary Miranda, "Love Poem" from *Grace Period*. Copyright © 1983 Princeton University Press. Reprinted by permission of the author.

Janice Mirikitani, "For a Daughter Who Leaves" from *Love Works*. Copyright © 2001 by Janice Mirikitani. Reprinted by permission of City Light Books.

Marianne Moore, "Poetry" (1967 version) from *The Collected Poems of Marianne Moore* by Marianne Moore. Copyright © 1935 by Marianne Moore; renewed 1963, 1967 by Marianne Moore and T. S. Eliot. Reprinted with the permission of Scribner, a division of Simon & Schuster, Inc. All rights reserved.

Pat Mora, "Elena" is reprinted with permission from the publisher of *My Own True Name* by Pat Mora (© 2000 Arte Público Press–University of Houston).

David Mura, "Grandfather-in-Law" from *After We Lost Our Way* by David Mura. Copyright © 1989 by David Mura. Reprinted by permission of the author.

Marilyn Nelson, "Minor Miracle" from *The Fields of Praise: New and Selected Poems* by Marilyn Nelson. Copyright © 1997 by Marilyn Nelson. Reprinted by permission of the author and Louisiana State University Press.

Don Nigro, *Letters from Quebec to Providence in the Rain*. Copyright © 2008 by Don Nigro. CAUTION: Professionals and amateurs are hereby warned that *Letters from Quebec to Providence in the Rain*, being fully protected under the copyright laws of the United States of America, the British Commonwealth countries, including Canada, and the other countries of the Copyright Union, is subject to a royalty. All rights, including professional, amateur, motion picture, recitation, public reading, radio, television and cable broadcasting, and the rights of translation into foreign languages, are strictly reserved. Any inquiry regarding the availability of performance rights, or the purchase of individual copies of the authorized acting edition, must be directed to Samuel French Inc., 235 Park Avenue South, Fifth Floor, New York, NY 10003, with other locations in Hollywood and London.

Naomi Shihab Nye, "Kindness" from *Words under the Words: Selected Poems* by Naomi Shihab Nye. Copyright © 1995 by Naomi Shihab Nye. Reprinted with the permission of the author.

Joyce Carol Oates, "Where Are You Going, Where Have You Been?" from *The Wheel of Love and Other Stories* by Joyce Carol Oates. Copyright © 1970 by the *Ontario Review*. Reprinted by permission of John Hawkins & Associates, Inc.

Tim O'Brien, "The Things They Carried" from *The Things They Carried* by Tim O'Brien. Copyright © 1990 by Tim O'Brien. Reprinted by permission of Houghton Mifflin Harcourt Publishing Company. All rights reserved.

Flannery O'Connor, "A Good Man Is Hard to Find" from *A Good Man Is Hard to Find and Other Stories* by Flannery O'Connor. Copyright © 1953 by Flannery O'Connor and renewed 1981 by Regina O'Connor. Reprinted by permission of Houghton Mifflin Harcourt Publishing Company. All rights reserved.

Sharon Olds, "Parents' Day" from *The Wellspring: Poems* by Sharon Olds. Copyright © 1996 by Sharon Olds. Used by permission of Alfred A. Knopf, an imprint of the Knopf Doubleday Publishing Group, a division of Penguin Random House LLC. All rights reserved. Any third-party use of this material, outside this publication, is prohibited. Interested parties must apply directly to Penguin Random House LLC for permission.

Mary Oliver, "First Snow" from *American Primitive* by Mary Oliver. Copyright © 1983 by Mary Oliver. Used by permission of Little, Brown & Company.

Tillie Olsen, "I Stand Here Ironing" from *Tell Me a Riddle, Requa I, and Other Works* by Tillie Olsen. Copyright © 1961 by Tillie Olsen. Reprinted by permission of the University of Nebraska Press.

Michael Oppenheimer, "The Paring Knife." First published in *Sundog* vol. 4, no. 1 (1982). Copyright © Michael Oppenheimer. Reprinted by permission of the author.

Daniel Orozco, "Orientation," from *Orientation and Other Stories* by Daniel Orozco. Copyright © 2011 by Daniel Orozco. Reprinted by permission of Farrar, Straus & Giroux, LLC.

ZZ Packer, "Brownies" from *Drinking Coffee Elsewhere* by ZZ Packer. Copyright © 2003 by ZZ Packer. Used by permission of Riverhead Books, an imprint of Penguin Publishing Group, a division of Penguin Random House LLC.

Sylvia Plath, "Metaphors" from *Crossing the Water* by Sylvia Plath. Copyright © 1960 by Ted Hughes. Reprinted by permission of HarperCollins Publishers and Faber and Faber, Ltd.

Katherine Anne Porter, "The Jilting of Granny Weatherall" from *Flowering Judas and Other Stories* by Katherine Anne Porter. Copyright © 1930 and renewed 1958 by Katherine Anne Porter. Reprinted by permission of Houghton Mifflin Harcourt Publishing Company. All rights reserved.

Ezra Pound, "In a Station of the Metro" from *Personae*. Copyright © 1926 by Ezra Pound. Reprinted by permission of New Directions Publishing Corp.

Marco Ramirez, *I Am Not Batman*. Copyright © 2007 Marco Ramirez. All rights reserved. Reprinted by permission of Playscripts, Inc. To purchase acting editions of this play, or to obtain stock and amateur performance rights, you must contact Playscripts, Inc.: Web site: http://www.playscripts.com; email: info@playscripts.com; phone: 1-866-NEW-PLAY (639-7529).

Dudley Randall, "Ballad of Birmingham" from *Roses and Revolutions: The Selected Writings of Dudley Randall*. Reprinted by permission of the Dudley Randall Literary Estate.

Frank Rich, "Family Ties in Wilson's *Fences*," *New York Times*, March 27, 1987. Copyright © 1987 by The New York Times. All rights reserved. Used by permission and protected by the Copyright Laws of the United States. The printing, copying, redistribution, or retransmission of this Content without express written permission is prohibited.

Jack Ridl, "My Brother—A Star" from *be tween* by Jack Ridl (New Wilmington, PA: Dawn Valley Press, 1988). Copyright © 1988 by Jack Ridl. Reprinted by permission of the author.

Atsuro Riley, "Drill" from *Romey's Order*. Copyright © 2010 by the University of Chicago. Reprinted by permission of the University of Chicago Press.

Alberto Ríos, "Nani" from *Whispering to Fool the Wind*. Copyright © 1982 by Alberto Ríos. Reprinted by permission of the author.

Luis J. Rodriguez, "Running to America" from *Poems across the Pavement*. Copyright © 1998 by Luis J. Rodriguez. Published by Tía Chucha Press. Reprinted by permission of Susan Bergholz Literary Services, New York, NY, and Lamy, NM. All rights reserved.

Theodore Roethke, "My Papa's Waltz," copyright 1942 by Hearst Magazines, Inc., from *Collected Poems* by Theodore Roethke. Used by permission of Doubleday, an imprint of the Knopf Doubleday Publishing Group, a division of Penguin Random House LLC. All rights reserved. Any third-party use of this material, outside this publication, is prohibited. Interested parties must apply directly to Penguin Random House LLC for permission.

Mary Jo Salter, "Half a Double Sonnet" from *Sunday Skaters* by Mary Jo Salter. Copyright © 1994 by Mary Jo Salter. Used by permission of Alfred A. Knopf, an imprint of the Knopf Doubleday Publishing Group, a division of Penguin Random House LLC. All rights reserved. Any third-party use of this material, outside this publication, is prohibited. Interested parties must apply directly to Penguin Random House LLC for permission.

Carl Sandburg, "Fog" from *Chicago Poems* by Carl Sandburg. Copyright © 1916 by Holt, Rinehart and Winston and renewed 1944 by Carl Sandburg. Reprinted by permission of Houghton Mifflin Harcourt Publishing Company. All rights reserved.

Marjane Satrapi, "The Veil" from *Persepolis: The Story of a Childhood* by Marjane Satrapi, translation copyright © 2003 by L'Association, Paris, France. Used by permission of Pantheon Books, an imprint of the Knopf Doubleday Publishing Group, a division of Penguin Random House LLC. All rights reserved. Any third-party use of this material, outside this publication, is prohibited. Interested parties must apply directly to Penguin Random House LLC for permission.

George Saunders, "Sticks" from *Tenth of December: Stories* by George Saunders. Copyright © 2013 by George Saunders. Used by permission of Random House, an imprint and division of Penguin Random House LLC. All rights reserved. Any third-party use of this material, outside this publication, is prohibited. Interested parties must apply directly to Penguin Random House LLC for permission.

Leslie Marmon Silko, "Prayer to the Pacific" from *Storyteller* by Leslie Marmon Silko. Copyright © 1981, 2012 by Leslie Marmon Silko. Used by permission of Viking Books, an imprint of Penguin Publishing Group, a division of Penguin Random House LLC.

Sophocles, *Oedipus the King,* translated by David Grene, from *Sophocles I.* Copyright © 1942 by the University of Chicago. Reprinted by permission of the University of Chicago Press.

Art Spiegelman, from *The Complete Maus: A Survivor's Tale* by Art Spiegelman. *Maus,* Volume I copyright © 1973, 1980, 1981, 1982, 1983, 1984, 1985, 1986 by Art Spiegelman; *Maus,* Volume II copyright © 1986, 1989, 1990, 1991 by Art Spiegelman. Used by permission of Pantheon Books, an imprint of the Knopf Doubleday Publishing Group, a division of Penguin Random House LLC. All rights reserved. Any third-party use of this material, outside this publication, is prohibited. Interested parties must apply directly to Penguin Random House LLC for permission.

William Stafford, "Traveling through the Dark" from *The Way It Is: New & Selected Poems.* Copyright © 1998 by the Estate of William Stafford. Reprinted with the permission of The Permissions Company, Inc., on behalf of Graywolf Press, Minneapolis, Minnesota, www.graywolfpress.org.

Kelly Stuart, *The New New,* first published in *The Best Ten-Minute Plays for 3 or More Actors* (2004), eds. Michael Bigelow Dixon and Liz Engelman, is reprinted by permission of the author. Copyright © 2003 by Kelly Stuart.

Sekou Sundiata, "Blink Your Eyes" by Sekou Sundiata is reprinted by permission of the Estate of Robert Feaster.

Amy Tan, "Two Kinds" from *The Joy Luck Club* by Amy Tan. Copyright © 1989 by Amy Tan. Used by permission of G. P. Putnam's Sons, an imprint of Penguin Publishing Group, a division of Penguin Random House LLC.

Dylan Thomas, "Do not go gentle into that good night" from *The Poems of Dylan Thomas.* Copyright © 1952 by Dylan Thomas. Reprinted by permission of New Directions Publishing Corp.

James Thurber, "The Catbird Seat" from *The Thurber Carnival* by James Thurber. Copyright © 1945 by Rosemary A. Thurber. Reprinted by arrangement with Rosemary A. Thurber and the Barbara Hogenson Agency, Inc. All rights reserved. To read more about James Thurber, go to www.ThurberHouse.org.

Alison Townsend, "The Barbie Birthday" from *The Blue Dress.* Copyright © 2003, 2008 by Alison Townsend. Reprinted with the permission of The Permissions Company, Inc., on behalf of White Pine Press, www.whitepine.org.

Natasha Trethewey, "Domestic Work 1937" from *Domestic Work.* Copyright © 1998, 2000 by Natasha Trethewey. Reprinted with the permission of The Permissions Company, Inc., on behalf of Graywolf Press, www.graywolfpress.org.

Quincy Troupe, "A Poem for 'Magic'" from *Avalanche.* Copyright © 1996 by Quincy Troupe. Reprinted with the permission of The Permissions Company, Inc., on behalf of Coffee House Press, Minneapolis, Minnesota, www.coffeehousepress.org.

John Updike, "A & P" from *Pigeon Feathers and Other Stories* by John Updike. Copyright © 1962, copyright renewed 1990 by John Updike. Used by permission of Alfred A. Knopf, an imprint of the Knopf Doubleday Publishing Group, a division of Penguin Random House LLC. All rights reserved. Any third-party use of this material, outside this publication, is prohibited. Interested parties must apply directly to Penguin Random House LLC for permission.

Alice Walker, "Everyday Use" and "The Flowers," from *In Love & Trouble: Stories of Black Women* by Alice Walker. Copyright © 1973 by Alice Walker. Reprinted by permission of Houghton Mifflin Harcourt Publishing Company. All rights reserved.

William Carlos Williams, "The Red Wheelbarrow" from *The Collected Poems: Volume 1, 1909–1939.* Copyright © 1938 by New Directions Publishing Corp. Reprinted by permission of New Directions Publishing Corp.

August Wilson, *Fences.* Copyright © 1986 by August Wilson. "Introduction" by Lloyd Richards, copyright © 1985 by Lloyd Richards. Used by permission of New American Library, an imprint of Penguin Publishing Group, a division of Penguin Random House LLC.

Xu Xi, "Famine." Copyright © 2004, 2005 by Xu Xi. Reprinted by permission of the Harold Matson Co., Inc. All rights reserved.

Kevin Young, "Blues" from *Jelly Roll: A Blues* by Kevin Young. Copyright © 2003 by Kevin Young. Used by permission of Alfred A. Knopf, an imprint of the Knopf Doubleday Publishing Group, a division of Penguin Random House LLC. All rights reserved. Any third-party use of this material, outside this publication, is prohibited. Interested parties must apply directly to Penguin Random House LLC for permission.

Ray A. Young Bear, "grandmother" from *Manifestation Wolverine: The Collected Poetry of Ray Young Bear* (2015). Originally published in *Winter of the Salamander* by Ray A. Young Bear. Copyright © 1980, 2015 by Ray A. Young Bear. Reprinted with the permission of Fletcher & Company, LLC.

Index of Authors and Titles